A
HANDBOOK TO LITERATURE

A HANDBOOK TO LITERATURE

Tenth Edition

WILLIAM HARMON
University of North Carolina, Chapel Hill

Based on Earlier Editions by

William Flint Thrall, Addison Hibbard, and C. Hugh Holman

Upper Saddle River, New Jersey 07458

Library of Congress Cataloging-in-Publication Data
Harmon, William, 1938–
A handbook to literature / William Harmon.—10th ed.
p. cm.
"Based on earlier editions by William Flint Thrall, Addison Hibbard, and C. Hugh Holman."
Appendices list the winners of the Nobel Prize for literature and the Pulizer Prizes for fiction, poetry, and drama; a table of monetary terms and values.
Includes index.
ISBN 0-13-134442-0
1. Literature—Dictionaries. I. Thrall, William Flint, b. 1880. Handbook to literature. II. Title.
PN41.H355 2005
803—dc22
2005049285

Editorial Director: Leah Jewell
Acquisitions Editor: Vivian Garcia
Editorial Assistant: Melissa Casciano
Production Liaison: Joanne Hakim
Marketing Manager: Emily Cleary
Marketing Assistant: Kara Pottle
Manufacturing Buyer: Brian Mackey
Cover Art Director: Jayne Conte
Cover Design: Bruce Kenselaar
Cover Image: Sally Harmon
Director, Image Resource Center: Melinda Reo
Manager, Rights and Permissions: Zina Arabia
Manager, Visual Research: Beth Brenzel
Manager, Cover Visual Research & Permissions: Karen Sanatar
Photo Researcher: Elaine Soares
Photo Coordinator: Richard Rodrigues
Composition/Full-Service Project Management: GGS Book Services, Atlantic Highlands
Printer/Binder: The Courier Companies

Credits borrowed from other sources and reproduced, with permission, in this textbook appear on appropriate page within text.

Acknowledgments: E. E. Cummings, "Complete Poems: 1904–1962." Reprinted by permission of Liveright Publishing Corporation, New York, NY. Robert Creeley, "Collected Poems of Robert Creeley, 1945–1975." Reprinted by permission of University of California Press, Berkeley, CA.

Pearson Education LTD., London
Pearson Education Singapore, Pte. Ltd
Pearson Education, Canada, Ltd
Pearson Education–Japan
Pearson Education Australia PTY, Limited
Pearson Education North Asia Ltd
Pearson Educación de Mexico, S.A. de C.V.
Pearson Education Malaysia, Pte. Ltd
Pearson Education, Upper Saddle River, New Jersey

10 9 8 7 6 5 4 3 2 1

ISBN 0-13-134442-0

Contents

Preface to the Tenth Edition

Clive James has said of Wayne Booth's *The Rhetoric of Fiction*, "A prodigious range of learning is expressed in hearteningly straightforward prose, but the effect is to leave you wondering what special use there is in presenting the student with yet another codified list of rhetorical devices. Separated from the works of fiction in which Professor Booth has so ably detected them, these devices are lifeless except as things to be memorized for the passing of examinations. There is also a strong chance that any student who spends much time studying rhetorical devices will not read the works of fiction, or will read them with his attention unnaturally focused on technical concerns." James's own rhetoric works so skillfully that a reader will probably agree with the main point for a few minutes; but someone who read James's opinion when it first appeared twenty-five years ago ought to have known that Booth's book is nothing like a codified list of devices and that what Booth signifies as "rhetoric" is nothing like what is usually meant by "rhetorical devices."

Even so, James makes sense, as he almost always does. But now, old enough to entertain literary memories going back more than fifty years, I know that James is wrong when he pictures the student "who spends much time studying rhetorical devices" as one who will not read works of fiction. Nothing could be further from the truth. The more I read as a student—and I read a good deal—the more I wanted to know about the devices, rhetorical, grammatical, prosodic, graphic. I first read *Ulysses* less than fifteen years after Joyce's death, and it was still possible to enjoy it as a novel without footnotes and so forth. There were a few studies, and, poor as I was, I bought a copy of Stuart Gilbert's *James Joyce's Ulysses;* I know I was not alone in getting a kick out of the material on the "Aeolus" chapter—the Cave of the Winds transformed into a newspaper office where devices of rhetoric were daily staples. With relish and fascination, I studied the long list of Greek and Latin terms that Joyce provided. I do not know that my devotion to such lists kept me from literature (I do know that when I wrote a paper on Shakespeare's sonnet 66 and dropped the name "asyndeton," the teacher, a most distinguished scholar, penciled a little question mark in the margin).

Having worked on six editions of this handbook over twenty years, I have to admit there is little for me to add in the way of groundbreaking or pioneering discoveries. I have enjoyed finding out about certain things—Manga and "Jumping the Shark" and Coffee Table Book, suggested by my three children, born in three different decades between 1966 and 1989. All have made many more contributions, as though sharing my sentiment that the project has long been a family enterprise. The new appendix on monetary terms and values was a challenge and a pleasure to prepare. I am grateful to my wife for carrying out most of the calculations, based on a website maintained by

Economic History Services. I am delighted to record debts and thanks to Joseph M. Flora, Albrecht B. Strauss, Cynthia Clay Adams, Paul Mellencamp, Mark Sigmon, and Zac Barker, who furnished information of various sorts, and to Vivian Garcia and Melissa Casciano of Prentice-Hall who have joined a succession of those who represent the publisher in providing support and assistance and whose influence continues in the current edition (Jennifer Crewe, Barbara Heinssen, and Carrie Brandon). I also wish to thank the following reviewers of this edition: Matthew Allen Fike, Winthrop University; Whitney D. Smith, College of Southern Idaho; Carol A. Galbus, Winona State University; Fidel Fajardo-Acosto, Creighton University; Craig White, University of Houston–Clear Lake; and Julie Yen, California State University–Sacramento.

I wish I had the space to add an essay on the invaluable contributions made by Robert Kirkpatrick, a great reader and inspired teacher as well as a cherished colleague and friend for thirty-five years, who died in early 2004. With his office two doors away from mine, our running discussion of prosody and literature in general covered decades. He was an acknowledged expert on the Romantics, to be sure, but he was also master of many other realms, including classical antiquity, religion, Byzantium, cookery, psychiatry, and much else.

It is time that I confessed my debt to two redoubtable institutions, *The Oxford English Dictionary* and *The Times Literary Supplement*. I cannot imagine doing without them even for a day. In fact, some items in the Handbook (and at least one scholarly note and one poem) have been inspired just by the *TLS* crossword. With the *OED* I have carried on a conversation that began even before I bought my own copy in 1964 (thirteen volumes for £65, which then amounted to $182, almost a month's pay for a young Naval officer). With the *OED* now in CD-ROM form and as an online site available through a university library, one can stay up-to-date and even submit e-mails with suggestions for corrections and additions.

I prepared the fifth edition in 1984–1985 with nothing in the way of information technology except an electric typewriter. Then, cutting and pasting literally involved scissors and paste. Now we have four computers at home and two more in our offices, and we move data back and forth at the speed of light. All that has had little effect on literature as such, and novels and plays and poems are still pretty much what they always were: texts you can buy and performances you can attend. But film studies have changed completely in the past twenty years, since works that were unavailable or very difficult and expensive to obtain are now as easy to access as books in shops and libraries. Watching a film in your living room may be inferior to watching in a theater, true, but it is superior to not being able to watch at all. And the detailed work of scholarship is much enhanced by computers, especially the search and storage functions. Alas, very few autograph-letters-signed and typed-letters-signed come in the mail any more, and I send very few myself, but e-mail is much more efficient. And signed paper materials are all the more valuable, even though I can no longer contribute boxes of letters, postcards, manuscripts, and such materials to my university library. Bookshops still exercise a powerful charm, but the location and collection of rare texts is much easier now. A dealer in far Saskatoon can sell rare material to a reader in Cancun or Rangoon with a few clicks of the mouse, and everybody's a winner. Of course, that makes a basic Handbook all the more necessary. Now I shall get back to the eleventh edition.

William Harmon

To the User

The *Handbook* proper is a listing of terms variously defined, discussed, explained, and illustrated, with no attempt at exhaustiveness, completeness, or novelty. As with certain earlier editions, this tenth edition provides selected references for some of the more important, difficult, or controversial entries. As in earlier editions, the initial capitals heading the chapters have been chosen from twenty-six different typefaces significant in the history of writing and printing.

• Terms being defined are given in **boldface** type.

• Within the body of the definition, the term in question, along with variants and derivatives, is in *italics*.

• A term used in a sense defined elsewhere may be printed in SMALL CAPITALS to indicate a cross-reference.

• If other articles in the Handbook seem helpful, the statement "See an appropriate article" is included. For example, the entry on **Complication** includes the terms PLOT, RESOLUTION, DRAMATIC STRUCTURE, RISING ACTION, ACT, and TRAGEDY, all of which are listed in the *Handbook*: Each appears in SMALL CAPITALS to indicate that entries thereon may be consulted. The word complication itself is italicized in the body of the entry.

Immediately following the alphabetical listing, the Outline of Literary History tabulates the most important events in the literary history of English-speaking people, along with a few undeniably significant non-English items. Since the fifth edition, the *Handbook* has included an Index of Proper Names, which lists the names and pseudonyms of all actual persons mentioned in the *Handbook* proper. The Index gives the title or short title of articles in which the person is mentioned.

The following abbreviations and symbols are used in the main body of this *Handbook:*

b. = born
c. = circa (around, about)
d. = died
ed. = editor, edition, edited by
edd. = editions
eds. = editors
˘ = breve (marks the first vowel in short syllables of quantitative scansion and weak syllables of qualitative scansion)
¯ = macron (marks the first vowel in long syllables of quantitative scansion)
ˊ = acute accent (marks the first vowel in syllables with primary stress in qualitative scansion)
ˋ = grave accent (marks the first vowel in syllables with secondary stress in qualitative scansion as in séc˘ondár˘y)

A HANDBOOK TO LITERATURE

Poliphilus 1928. Typeface cut by Monotype Corp., Ltd., in England. Based on typeface cut by Francesco Griffo in 1499.

Abbey Theatre Associated with the IRISH LITERARY REVIVAL, the *Abbey Theatre* was an outgrowth of an earlier group, the Irish Literary Theatre, founded by W. B. Yeats and Lady Gregory in 1899, which later became the Irish National Theatre Society and still later moved to the Abbey Theatre in Dublin. It endured, producing plays with a markedly national emphasis, until the theater burned in 1951. W. B. Yeats was director of the Abbey Theatre until his death in 1939. Among the major playwrights of the company were Yeats, Lady Gregory, J. M. Synge, Sean O'Casey, James Stephens, and Lord Dunsany. See CELTIC RENAISSANCE.

Abecedarian, Abecedarius, Abecedary An acrostic so arranged that the initial letters of successive lines (or other units) form an alphabet. Strictly speaking, each word in a line should begin with the same letter, although this difficult task is seldom attempted. Such a poem by Alaric Alexander Watts, published in 1817, begins, "An Austrian army, awfully arrayed, / Boldly by battery besieged Belgrade" and ends "Yield, yield, ye youths! ye yeomen, yield your yell! / Zeus', Zarpater's, Zoroaster's zeal, / Attracting all, arms against acts appeal!" Many Psalms (e.g., 9, 10, 34, 37, 111, 112, 119, and 145) adhere to some principle of following successive letters of the Hebrew alphabet.

ABC, A B C, A.B.C. (1) An alphabetical acrostic; a poem in which stanzas or lines begin with the letters of the alphabet, such as Geoffrey Chaucer's poem sometimes called "Chaucer's A B C," a prayer that is a translation of a French poem. (2) A primer teaching the alphabet or other elementary parts of a field of study, such as Ezra Pound's *A B C of Reading* and *A B C of Economics*.

ABC-Book, Abcee-Book, Absey-Book A PRIMER or HORN-BOOK that introduces a subject; sometimes in the form of a CATECHISM or DIALOGUE.

Abjuration The act or the expression of solemn renunciation.

Above the Fold The area of the front page that shows when a newspaper is in a news rack. The most conspicuous part of the most important page of a paper.

Abridgment A shortened version of a work, but one that attempts to preserve essential elements. See ABSTRACT, EPITOME, SYNOPSIS, PRÉCIS.

Absolute A term applied to anything totally independent of conditions, limitations, controls, or modifiers. In vocabulary, *absolute* refers to a word, such as "unique," that cannot be compared or qualified. In grammatical structure, *absolute* refers to a phrase that is free of the customary syntactical relationships to other parts of the sentence. W. B. Yeats favored *absolutes*, as in "How can I, *that girl standing there*" and "what rough beast, *its hour come round at last*." Certain comparative and superlative forms are called *absolute* if there is no indication of a specific context: "higher education" and "last resort" give no explicit details that justify the implied ranking. In CRITICISM, *absolute* implies inviolable standards by which a work should be measured. An *absolutist* critic holds that immutable values determine moral and aesthetic worth.

Abstract (noun) A severe ABRIDGMENT that summarizes the principal ideas or arguments advanced in a much longer work. *Abstracts* of articles and dissertations are widely produced today.

Abstract (adjective) In reference to meaning, the term *abstract* is opposed to CONCRETE. With graphic art, the *abstract* usually means nonrepresentational or nonobjective.

Absurd In contemporary literature and criticism, a term applied to the sense that human beings, cut off from their roots, live in meaningless isolation in an alien universe. Although the literature of the *absurd* employs many of the devices of EXPRESSIONISM and SURREALISM, its philosophical base is a form of EXISTENTIALISM, which views human beings as moving from the nothingness from which they came to the nothingness in which they will end through an existence marked by anguish and absurdity. Albert Camus' *The Myth of Sisyphus* is one central expression of this philosophy. Extreme forms of illogic, inconsistency, and nightmarish FANTASY mark the literature expressing this concept. The idea of the *absurd* has been powerfully expressed in drama (see ABSURD, THEATER OF THE) and in the NOVEL, where Joseph Heller, Thomas Pynchon, Günter Grass, and Kurt Vonnegut, Jr., have practiced it with distinction. See ANTIHERO; ANTINOVEL.

[References: Arnold P. Hinchcliffe, *The Absurd* (1969); Wolodymyr T. Zyla, ed., *From Surrealism to the Absurd* (1970).]

Absurd, Theater of the A term invented by Martin Esslin for the kind of drama that presents a view of the absurdity of the human condition by the abandoning of usual or rational devices and by the use of nonrealistic form. Conceived in perplexity and spiritual anguish, the *theater of the absurd* portrays not a series of connected incidents telling a story but a pattern of images presenting people as bewildered creatures in an incomprehensible universe. The first true example of the *theater of the absurd* was Eugène Ionesco's *The Bald Soprano* (1950). The most widely acclaimed play of the school is Samuel Beckett's *Waiting for Godot* (1953). Other playwrights in the school, which flourished in Europe and America in the 1950s and 1960s, include Jean Genêt, Arthur Adamov, Edward Albee, Arthur Kopit, and Harold Pinter. See ABSURD; BLACK HUMOR.

[Reference: Martin Esslin, *The Theatre of the Absurd*, 3rd ed. (1980).]

Academic As a neutral term, *academic* refers to schools and academies in general. As a negative term, however, it means aridly theoretical in ideas or pedantic, conventional, and formalistic in style.

Academic Drama Plays written and performed in schools and colleges in the Elizabethan age. See SCHOOL PLAYS.

Academies Associations devoted to the advancement of special fields of interest. The term is derived from "the olive grove of Academe" where Plato taught at Athens. (Evidently the land had belonged to a man named Academus.) One general purpose of literary *academies* has been, to quote the charter of l'Académie française (originated c. 1629), "to labor with all care and diligence to give certain rules to our language and to render it pure, eloquent, and capable of treating the arts and sciences." In addition to the French Academy and the Royal Society of London for Improving Natural Knowledge, the following are important: The Royal Academy of Arts founded in 1768 (England); the Real Academia Española founded in 1713 (Spain); and the American Academy of Arts and Letters founded in 1904. More like the original academy of Plato was the famous "Platonic Academy" led by Marsilio Ficino at Florence in the late fifteenth century, which disseminated the doctrines of NEOPLATONISM.

Acatalectic Metrically complete; applied to lines that carry out the basic metrical and rhythmic pattern of a poem. See CATALEXIS.

Accent In PROSODY, the EMPHASIS given to a SYLLABLE in articulation. *Accent* is considered a complex matter of force, timbre, duration, loudness, pitch, and various combinations of these. Customarily, however, it is used to describe some aspect of relative emphasis (strong or weak), as opposed to duration or quantity (long or short). A distinction is sometimes made between *accent* as the normal emphasis and STRESS as the emphasis required by a rhythmic pattern.

In VERSIFICATION, *accent* usually implies contrast; that is, a patterned succession of opposites, in this case, accented and unaccented syllables. In traditional terminology ICTUS is the name applied to the stress itself, ARSIS the name applied to the stressed syllable, and THESIS the name applied to the unstressed syllable. (The Greek usage, however, predating this Latin usage, applied THESIS to the stressed and ARSIS to the unstressed syllables.)

There are three basic types of *accent* in English: word *accent* or the normal stress on syllables; rhetorical *accent*, in which the placement of stress is determined by the meaning of the words; and metrical *accent*, in which the placement of stress is determined by the rhythmic pattern of the line. If the metrical *accent* does violence to the word accent, the resulting alteration in pronunciation is called WRENCHED ACCENT, a phenomenon common in the folk ballad.

In linguistics, *accent* refers to the pronunciation of words and phrases according to regional or social patterns. See QUANTITY, METRICS, SCANSION, STRESS.

[References: Derek Attridge, *The Rhythms of English Poetry* (1982); John Hollander, *Vision and Resonance: Two Senses of Poetic Form*, 2nd ed. (1985; orig. 1975).]

Accentualism Paul Fussell's term for "the theory of the line which considers the number of stresses to be its fundamental prosodic skeleton." Unlike SYLLABISM, which regards English as a language like French, with consistently uniform syllables, this theory recognizes that English is like German in having syllables of widely varying length and strength. The exponents of *accentualism* include Joshua Steele (*Prosodia Rationalis*,

1779), William Blake, and most of the significant writers of verse of the nineteenth century.

[Reference: Paul Fussell, *Theory of Prosody in Eighteenth-Century England* (1954).]

Accentual-Syllabic Verse Verse that depends for its RHYTHM both on the number of syllables per line and on the pattern of accented and unaccented syllables. The basic measures in English poetry are *accentual-syllabic*. See METER, FOOT.

Accidental (noun) In TEXTUAL CRITICISM, an *accidental* is any element of a text not essential to the meaning of the words; most commonly, *accidentals* include capitalization, spelling, and punctuation. See SUBSTANTIVE.

[Reference: Philip Gaskell, *A New Introduction to Bibliography* (1995).]

Accismus A form of IRONY, a pretended refusal that is insincere or hypocritical. Caesar's refusal of the crown, as reported by Casca in Shakespeare's *Julius Caesar* (1, 2) and Richard's disavowal of his kingly qualities in Shakespeare's *Richard III* (3, 7) are examples.

Acephalous "Headless"; see HEADLESS LINE.

Acknowledgments A conventional component of the FRONT MATTER of some printed documents—particularly nonfiction—wherein authors acknowledge help received from individuals and institutions.

Acmeism A movement in Russian poetry, begun around 1912 by members of the Poets' Guild to promote precise treatment of realistic subjects. The movement's emphasis on exactness of word and clarity of image invites comparison with its Anglo-American contemporary, Imagism. The founders of *Acmeism* were Nikolai Gumilev and Sergei Gorodetski. The organized group lasted only a few years, but the influence of its greatest adherents—such as Anna Akhmatova (who was married to Gumilev) and Osip Mandelstam—continues through the present day.

Acronym A word formed by combining the initial letters or syllables of a series of words to form a name, as "radar," from "*ra*dio *d*etecting *a*nd *r*anging." An *acronym* is akin to ACROSTIC.

Acrophony Calling a written symbol by the name of something that has that symbol at its beginning. Phoenician "Aleph" (Greek "alpha"), which means "ox," became the name of the first letter in the word. In Old English, the symbols *æ* and *þ*, which come at the beginning of the tree names "ash" and "thorn," are called "ash" and "thorn."

Acrostic A composition, usually VERSE, arranged in such a way that it spells words, phrases, or sentences when certain letters are selected according to an orderly sequence. The device was used by early Greek and Latin writers as well as by the monks of the Middle Ages. Though creditable verse has appeared in this form, *acrostics* are likely to be tricks of versifying. An *acrostic* in which the initial letters form a word is called a true *acrostic*. In the poem at the end of Lewis Carroll's *Through the Looking*

Glass, the first letters of the lines spell out "Alice Pleasance Liddell." The poem begins:

> **A** boat, beneath a sunny sky,
> **L**ingering onward dreamily
> **I**n an evening of July—
> **C**hildren three that nestle near,
> **E**ager eye and willing ear. . . .

An *acrostic* in which the final letters form the word is called a TELESTICH. Here is an example of a true *acrostic*-telestich presented through a riddle: 1. By Apollo was my first made. 2. A shoemaker's tool. 3. An Italian patriot. 4. A tropical fruit. The components "lyre," "awl," "Mazzini," and "banana" yield the *acrostic* "Lamb" and the telestich "Elia" (Charles Lamb's pen name):

1.	L	yr	E
2.	A	w	L
3.	M	azzin	I
4.	B	anan	A

An *acrostic* in which the middle letters form the word is called a MESOSTICH; one in which the first letter of the first line, the second letter of the second line, the third letter of the third line, etc., form the word is called a *cross acrostic*, of which Poe's "A Valentine" is an example. An *acrostic* in which the initial letters form the alphabet is called an ABECEDARIUS. In some ingenious varieties of word puzzles (sometimes called *double-crostics*), the first letters of the names of an author and a work come at the beginnings of words composed of letters from a quotation from that work.

Act A major division of a DRAMA. The major parts of ancient Greek plays, distinguished by the appearance of the CHORUS, generally fell, as Aristotle implies, into five parts. The Latin tragedies of Seneca were divided into five *acts*; and, when English dramatists in the ELIZABETHAN AGE began using *act* divisions, they followed their Roman models, as did other modern European dramatists. In varying degrees the five-act structure corresponded to the five main divisions of dramatic action: EXPOSITION, COMPLICATION, CLIMAX, FALLING ACTION, and CATASTROPHE. The five-*act* structure was followed until the late nineteenth century, when under the influence of Ibsen, the fourth and fifth *acts* were combined. Since the end of the nineteenth century, the standard form for serious drama has been three *acts*, for musical comedy and comic opera usually two; but great variation is used, with serious plays frequently divided into EPISODES or SCENES, without act-division. Late in the nineteenth century a shorter form, the ONE-ACT PLAY, developed. See DRAMATIC STRUCTURE, FREYTAG'S PYRAMID.

Action The series of events that constitute a PLOT, what the characters say, do, think, or in some cases fail to do. Orderly *action* differs from aimless or episodic activity; an *action* customarily has a beginning, middle, and end. The *action* of a work is the answer to the question "What happens?"

Action-Adventure A style of entertainment popular in film and television productions after about 1950. In such MELODRAMA, the plot is little more than an elementary pattern of revenge or good-defeating-evil, characters are two-dimensional, and language conventional and undistinguished, with all the emphasis on action (often violent) and SPECIAL EFFECTS.

Actoid One of the robotic SOAP actors in Alan Ayckbourn's comedy *Comic Potential*, emotionally managed by remote control from the future. Employed metaphorically for a person or character without will or personality.

Actor A person who performs in a drama in any form; the term has replaced the earlier PLAYER. The word has been applied to male and female performers alike.

Actor-Manager A theater manager who also acts; a familiar type during the century after 1825. David Garrick had functioned as an *actor-manager* during the eighteenth century; later *actor-managers* include Charles Hawtrey and Herbert Beerbohm-Tree.

Actress A female ACTOR.

Adage A PROVERB or SAYING made familiar by long use. Examples: "No bees, no honey" (Erasmus, *Adagia*); "A stitch in time saves nine."

Adaptation The rewriting of a work from its original form to fit it for another MEDIUM; also the new form of such a rewritten work. A NOVEL may be *adapted* for the STAGE, MOTION PICTURES, or TELEVISION; a PLAY may be rewritten as a NOVEL. The term normally implies an attempt to retain the chief CHARACTERS, ACTIONS, and as much as possible of the language and tone of the original.

Addenda (plural of **Addendum**) Matter to be added to a piece of writing. *Addenda* may be appended in late stages of production or, after production, on a separate slip attached to the original document. *Addenda* are usually items inadvertently omitted or received too late for inclusion.

Adonic Verse In Greek and Latin PROSODY, the measure that consists of a DACTYL and a SPONDEE, as ¯ ˘ ˘ | ¯ ¯ or a dactyl and a TROCHEE, as ¯ ˘ ˘ | ¯ ˘, probably so called after the Adonia, the festival of Adonis.

Adventure Story (or **Film**) A story in which ACTION—often exterior, usually physical, and frequently violent—is the predominant material, stressed above CHARACTERIZATION, MOTIVATION, or THEME. SUSPENSE is engendered by the question "What will happen next?" rather than "Why?" or "To whom?" In a broader sense, as Henry James insisted in "The Art of Fiction," everything in fiction can be thought of as an *adventure*; he said, "It is an adventure—an immense one—for me to write this little article." A recognizable subgenre is the outdoor-adventure film, of which the WESTERN remains the most popular form.

Adversarius The character in a FORMAL SATIRE who is addressed by the PERSONA and who functions to elicit and shape that speaker's remarks. Arbuthnot is *adversarius* to Pope in "The Epistle to Dr. Arbuthnot." Such a character serves to create a situation within which he or she may speak or play a role similar to that of a STRAIGHT MAN.

A. e. g. Bookseller's abbreviation of "all edges gilt," referring to the paper on which a book is printed.

Aesthetic Distance A term used to describe the effect produced when an emotion or an experience, whether autobiographical or not, is so objectified that it can be understood as being independent of the immediate experience of its maker. This objectification involves whatever can displace immediacy and VERISIMILITUDE. The term also applies to the reader's or audience's awareness that art and reality are separate. In this sense it is sometimes called "psychic distance." It is related to T. S. Eliot's OBJECTIVE CORRELATIVE. See OBJECTIVITY, *VERFREMDUNGSEFFEKT*.

Aestheticism A nineteenth-century literary movement that rested on the credo of "ART FOR ART'S SAKE." Its roots reached back to Théophile Gautier's preface to *Mademoiselle de Maupin* (1835), which claimed that art has no utility, Poe's theory of "the poem per se" and his rejection of the "heresy of the didactic," Baudelaire's *Les Fleurs du Mal*, and Mallarmé. Its origins had a close kinship to the reverence for beauty of the PRE-RAPHAELITES. Its dominant figures were Oscar Wilde, who insisted on the separation of art and morality, and Wilde's master, Walter Pater. The English PARNASSIANS— Ernest Dowson, Lionel Johnson, Andrew Lang, and Edmund Gosse—were a part of the movement but were primarily concerned with questions of form rather than sharp separations of art from moral issues. Tennyson angrily paraphrased "art for art's sake" as meaning:

> The filthiest of all paintings painted well
> Is mightier than the purest painted ill!

Aesthetics The study or philosophy of the beautiful in nature and art. It has both a philosophical dimension—What is art? What is beauty? What is the relationship of the beautiful to other values?—and a psychological dimension—What is the source of aesthetic enjoyment? How is beauty perceived and recognized? From what impulse do art and beauty arise? The aesthetic study of literature concentrates on the sense of the beautiful rather than on moral, social, or practical considerations. When pursued rigorously, it leads to "ART FOR ART'S SAKE" and AESTHETICISM.

The Kantian tradition takes the *aesthetic* as the name of the attempt to bridge the gap between material and spiritual, a world of forces and magnitudes. Aesthetic objects, with their union or fusion of sensuous form and spiritual content, would serve as guarantors of the possibility of articulating the material with the spiritual. This sense of the aesthetic is not only Kant's: It is the one at issue in more recent debates, such as those involving Terry Eagleton (*The Ideology of the Aesthetic*) and Paul de Man (*The Aesthetic Ideology*).

Aet., Aetat. Abbreviations for the Latin *aetatis suae*, "of his or her age." The term is used to designate the year of a person's life at which an event occurred. A picture of Henry David Thoreau bearing the legend "*aet. 35*" would be one made during Thoreau's thirty-fifth year, that is, when he was thirty-four years old.

Affective Fallacy The judging of a work of art in terms of its results, especially its emotional effect. The term was introduced by W. K. Wimsatt, Jr., and M. C. Beardsley to describe the "confusion between the poem and its result (what it is and what it does)." It complements the INTENTIONAL FALLACY. Notable versions of the affective fallacy are Aristotle's CATHARSIS and Longinus's "transport."

[Reference: W. K. Wimsatt, *The Verbal Icon: Studies in the Meaning of Poetry* (1954).]

Affix A verbal element added before (PREFIX), inside (INFIX), or after (SUFFIX) a base to change the meaning.

African American Literature Frequently called Afro-American or Black literature. The formal study of such writing, at one time a neglected area of American literary scholarship, is increasingly important. This heightened interest in the work of African Americans has come about for two primary reasons: the growing recognition of African Americans as a significant part of American culture and the recovery or development of a body of writing of impressive scope and quality.

For all practical purposes, African American literature began in the eighteenth century with the poetry of two slaves, Jupiter Hammon and Phillis Wheatley. The first half of the nineteenth century saw further efforts by slave poets, among them George Moses Horton, but it was particularly marked by a flood of autobiographical records of the slaves' terrible experiences, known as SLAVE NARRATIVES, of which the most famous is that by Frederick Douglass. There were also polemical pamphlets and fiery sermons, and in 1853 William Wells Brown, an escaped slave, published the first novel by an African American, *Clotel, or, the President's Daughter*. As the century closed, Charles W. Chesnutt began publishing the novels that established him as an important literary figure.

In the modern age, a host of skillful African American writers have produced distinguished work in every field. There have been poets such as Paul Laurence Dunbar, James Weldon Johnson, Langston Hughes, Arna Bontemps, Countee Cullen, Gwendolyn Brooks (who was in 1949 the first African American to receive the PULITZER PRIZE), Michael Harper, Nikki Giovanni, Don L. Lee, Ethridge Knight, Clarence Major, and Rita Dove. The period since 1900 has been as particularly rich in African American novelists, including such writers as W. E. B. Du Bois, Walter White, Jean Toomer, Claude McKay, Zora Neale Hurston, Ann Petry, Richard Wright, Ralph Ellison, James Baldwin, Toni Morrison, Alice Walker, and Ishmael Reed. There have been a number of African American playwrights, among them Hall Johnson, Wallace Thurman, Langston Hughes, Lorraine Hansberry, Ossie Davis, and Imamu Baraka.

These African Americans, by writing with passion and conviction of the place they and their race have occupied and endured in a predominantly white society, have broadened the range, enriched the sympathy, and deepened the quality of American literary expression. Their contributions, notable most obviously for their power, are major forces changing the earlier American literary monolith of the white middle class.

[References: Houston A. Baker, Jr., *Black Literature in America* (1971); Joanne M. Braxton and Andrée Nicola McLaughlin, eds., *Wild Women in the Whirlwind: Afro-American Culture and the Contemporary Literary Renaissance* (1990); Henry Louis Gates, Jr., ed., *Black Literature and Literary Theory* (1984); Marjorie Pryse and Hortense J. Spillers, eds., *Conjuring: Black Women, Fiction, and Literary Tradition* (1985);

Darwin Turner, ed., *Black Literature: Essays* (1969); William D. Washington Edward C. Gruber, ed., *Black Literature: An Anthology of Outstanding Black Writers* (1972).]

"After" Some titles, especially of poems, suggest that a work was written *after* the manner of a certain writer, work, or body of literature, or *after* the reading of a work. These titles are typical: "After a Passage in Baudelaire" (Robert Duncan), "After Anacreon" (Lew Welch), "After Lorca" (both Robert Creeley and Ted Hughes), "After Plotinus" (William Stafford), and "After the Persian" (Louise Bogan). Frank O'Hara wrote "After Wyatt" and "An Airplane Whistle (after Heine)." G. K. Chesterton's "Variations of an Air" consists of three parodic versions of "Old King Cole" subtitled "after Lord Tennyson," "after W. B. Yeats," and "after Walt Whitman." Allen Ginberg's "After Yeats" is joined by Margaret McCann's "After Bob (After Yeats)." A. C. Swinburne wrote a poem called "After Looking into Carlyle's Reminiscences" (calling Carlyle "this dead snake").

Age of Johnson in English Literature The interval between 1750 and 1798 was a markedly transitional age in English literature. The NEOCLASSICISM that dominated the first half of the century was yielding in many ways to the impulse toward ROMANTICISM, although the period was still predominantly neoclassical. The NOVEL, which had come into being in the decades before 1750, continued to flourish, with sentimental attitudes and GOTHIC horrors becoming a significant part of its content. Little was accomplished in drama, except for the creation of "laughing" comedy by Sheridan and Goldsmith in reaction against SENTIMENTAL COMEDY. The chief poets were Burns, Gray, Cowper, Johnson, and Crabbe—a list that indicates how thoroughly the pendulum was swinging away from Pope and Dryden. Yet it was Samuel Johnson—poet, lexicographer, essayist, novelist, journalist, and neoclassic critic—who was the major literary figure, and his friend Boswell's biography of him (1791) was the greatest work of the age, challenged for such honor only by Gibbon's monumental history, *The Decline and Fall of the Roman Empire* (1776). An interest in the past (particularly the Middle Ages), in the PRIMITIVE, and in the literature of the folk was developing and was contributing with increasing strength to the growing tide of ROMANTICISM. It is sometimes called the AGE OF SENSIBILITY, emphasizing the emergence of new attitudes and the development of sensibility as a major literary expression. See NEOCLASSIC PERIOD, AGE OF SENSIBILITY, SENSIBILITY.

Age of Reason A term often applied to the NEOCLASSIC PERIOD IN ENGLISH LITERATURE and sometimes to the REVOLUTIONARY AND EARLY NATIONAL PERIOD IN AMERICAN LITERATURE, because these periods emphasized self-knowledge, self-control, RATIONALISM, discipline, and the rule of law, order, and DECORUM in public and private life and in art.

Age of the Romantic Movement in England, 1798–1832 Although a major romantic poet, Robert Burns, had died in 1796, William Blake's *Songs of Innocence* had appeared in 1789, and adumbrations of romanticism had been apparent in English writing throughout much of the eighteenth century, the publication of *Lyrical Ballads* by Wordsworth and Coleridge in 1798 is often regarded as marking the beginning of a period of more than three decades in which romanticism triumphed in British letters, a period that is often said to have ended in 1832, with the death of Scott. During these thirty-four years, the careers of Wordsworth, Coleridge, Byron, Mary and P. B. Shelley,

Felicia Hemans, and Keats flowered; Scott created the HISTORICAL NOVEL and made it a force in international literature; Wordsworth and Coleridge articulated a revolutionary theory of romantic poetry; Jane Austen wrote her NOVELS OF MANNERS; Mary Shelley uncannily combined the GOTHIC novel and SCIENCE FICTION, along with philosophic vision; and Lamb, DeQuincey, and Hazlitt raised the PERSONAL ESSAY to a high level of accomplishment. Romanticism did not die with Scott, but the decade of the thirties saw it begin a process of accommodation. See ROMANTICISM, ROMANTIC PERIOD IN ENGLISH LITERATURE, *Outline of Literary History*.

Age of Sensibility A name frequently applied by literary historians, such as W. J. Bate, Harold Bloom, and Northrop Frye, to the last half of the eighteenth century in England, the time earlier called the AGE OF JOHNSON. The term *Age of Sensibility* results from seeing the interval between 1750 and 1798 as a seedfield for emerging romantic qualities in literature, such as PRIMITIVISM, SENSIBILITY, and the originality of the individual talent. The older term, AGE OF JOHNSON, tends to emphasize the strong continuing neoclassic qualities in the literature of the time. See AGE OF JOHNSON, NEOCLASSIC PERIOD, AGE OF THE ROMANTIC MOVEMENT, ROMANTIC PERIOD IN ENGLISH LITERATURE.

Agent An amateur or professional representative acting as an artist's go-between in dealings with publishers, editors, producers, and other executives, chiefly in legal and financial matters but also occasionally including personal and artistic advice and assistance. The profession of literary *agent* dates back to the late nineteenth century, when A. P. Watt, sometimes considered the first professional *agent*, counted Thomas Hardy and Rudyard Kipling among his clients. Before the close of the nineteenth century, Watt was joined by J. B. Pinker and Curtis Brown.

Agitprop "Agitational PROPAGANDA," originally in behalf of the Soviet Union and communist ideology (the word is a Russian combination dating from the 1930s); later applied to any propagandistic effort.

Agnomination (also **Adnomination, Annomination**) A term used between 1600 and 1800 to mean, variously, any PLAY ON WORDS, especially such as involved names of persons, as in Robert Greene's distortion of Shakespeare's name to "Shake-scene"; also applied to ALLITERATION in general.

Agon Literally, a contest of any kind. In Greek tragedy it was a prolonged dispute, often a formal debate in which the CHORUS divided and took sides with the disputants. In the OLD COMEDY in Greece this debate, called EPIRRHEMATIC AGON, involved elaborate exchanges between the chorus and the debaters, and addresses to the audience. In discussions of PLOT, *agon* it has come to mean any conflict. Leading CHARACTERS are classified according to their relationship to this conflict, displayed by the element *agon* inside their designations: PROTAGONIST, ANTAGONIST, DEUTERAGONIST, and so on. As its title suggests, Milton's *Samson Agonistes* belongs in the category of the *agon*; T. S. Eliot's fragmentary *Sweeney Agonistes* seems to be a burlesque or caricature of the tradition. In the 1950s Igor Stravinsky composed a ballet called *Agon*.

Agrarians Literally, people living in an agricultural society, or espousing the merits of such a society, as the PHYSIOCRATS did. In this sense most espousers of PASTORAL traditions are *agrarians*. Thomas Jefferson was a noted early American *agrarian*. In literary history and criticism, however, the term is usually applied to a group of Southern American writers in Nashville, Tennessee, who published *The Fugitive* (1922–1925), a little magazine of poetry and some criticism championing agrarian REGIONALISM but attacking "the old high-caste Brahmins of the Old South." Most of its contributors were associated with Vanderbilt University; among them were John Crowe Ransom, Allen Tate, Donald Davidson, Robert Penn Warren, and Merrill Moore. In the 1930s, championing an agrarian economy as opposed to that of industrial capitalism, they issued a collective manifesto, *I'll Take My Stand*. Between 1933 and 1937 they were active in the publication of *The American Review*, a socioeconomic magazine that also analyzed contemporary literature. They found an effective literary organ in *The Southern Review* (1935–1942) under the editorship of Cleanth Brooks and Robert Penn Warren. In addition to their poetry and novels, the *Agrarians* were among the founders of the NEW CRITICISM.

Agroikos A character added by Northrop Frye to the traditional three STOCK CHARACTERS of Greek OLD COMEDY. The usual *agroikos* is a rustic who is easily deceived, a form of the country bumpkin.

[Reference: Northrop Frye, *Anatomy of Criticism* (1957).]

Alazon The braggart or impostor in Greek comedy. He takes many forms: the quack, the religious fanatic, the swaggering soldier, the pedant—anyone pretentious who is held up to ridicule. From Plautus's *Miles Gloriosus* he enters English literature, where he is a STOCK CHARACTER in Elizabethan drama. He has been widely used in other literary forms, particularly the novel. James Fenimore Cooper's Dr. Obed Battius, in *The Prairie*, is a good example of a later mutation of this character. A modern comic strip featured a character named Will Bragg. See MILES GLORIOSUS.

Alba A Provençal lament over the parting of lovers at the break of day, the name coming from the Provençal for "dawn." It has no fixed metrical form, but each stanza usually ends with "alba." The first *alba* is "Reis glorios" (c. 1200) by Giraut de Bornelh. With the next generation of troubadours the *alba* grew to a distinct literary form. On occasion they were religious, being addressed to the Virgin. See AUBADE.

Alcaics Verses written according to the manner of the odes of Alcaeus, usually a four-stanza poem, each stanza composed of four lines, the first two being HENDECASYLLABIC, the third being nine syllables, and the fourth DECASYLLABIC. Because the classical pattern is based on quantitative DACTYLS and TROCHEES, exact English *Alcaics* are practically impossible. The most notable English attempt is in Tennyson's "Milton," which begins:

Ō| mīghtў- | mōuth'd ĭn-|vēntŏr ŏf | hārmŏnīes . . . .

Alexandrianism The spirit prevailing in the literary and scientific work of Hellenistic writers flourishing in Alexandria for about three centuries after 325 B.C. The literature is distinguished by originality, novelty, learning, and devotion to ancestral models. The academic studies are distinguished by BIBLIOPHILIA, attention to detail, the establishment and collection of CANONS, and thoroughgoing editing and annotating. The greatest names associated with *Alexandrianism* are Callimachus, Philetas, Theocritus, and Lycophron.

Alexandrine A verse with six IAMBIC feet (iambic HEXAMETER). The form, that of HEROIC VERSE in France, received its name possibly from its use in Old French romances of the twelfth and thirteenth centuries describing the adventures of Alexander the Great, or possibly from the name of Alexandre Paris, a French poet who used this meter. Its appearance in English has been credited to Wyatt and Surrey. Perhaps the most conspicuous instance of its successful use in English is by Spenser, who, in his SPENSERIAN STANZA, after eight PENTAMETER lines employed a HEXAMETER line (*Alexandrine*) in the ninth. Both the line and its occasional bad effect are described in Pope's couplet:

> A needless Alexandrine ends the song,
> That, like a wounded snake, drags its slow length along.

Some *Alexandrines*, far from needless, are used to avoid the monotony and patness of pentameter in certain stanzas, such as RHYME ROYAL (see Wordsworth's "Resolution and Independence") and the SONNET (see Keats's "On Sitting Down to Read King Lear Once Again" and Longfellow's "Mezzo Cammin").

Alienation Effect This term—translating the German *VERFREMDUNGSEFFEKT*—was put forward by the playwright Bertolt Brecht as a desirable quality of theater, by means of which the audience is kept at such a distance that unthinking emotional and personal involvement is inhibited while political messages are delivered. The *alienation effect* can be achieved by any device that departs from representational realism and fidelity to everyday experience: masks, alien setting, disturbances of time sequence, rupturing of the FOURTH WALL. The alienation effect in some ways resembles the DEFAMILIARIZATION of the Russian FORMALISTS and the general notion of AESTHETIC DISTANCE.

Alienisparsison In the terminology of Welsh prosody, *alienisparsison* is the effect produced by a foreign DIPHTHONG followed by certain consonant clusters (for example, *rs* in GRAVISPARSISON and *dr* in FORTISPARSISON).

Allegory A form of extended METAPHOR in which objects, persons, and actions in a NARRATIVE are equated with meanings that lie outside the narrative itself. Thus, it represents one thing in the guise of another—an abstraction in that of a concrete image. By a process of double signification, the order of words represents actions and characters, and they, in turn, represent ideas. *Allegory* often clarifies this process by giving patently meaningful names to persons and places. The characters are usually personifications of abstract qualities, the action and the setting representative of the relationships among these abstractions. *Allegory* attempts to evoke a dual interest, one in the events, characters, and setting presented, and the other in the ideas they are intended to convey or the significance they bear. The characters, events, and setting may be historical, fictitious, or fabulous; the test is that these materials be so employed that they represent meanings independent of the action in the surface story. Such meanings may be religious, moral, political, personal, or satiric. Thus, Spenser's *The Faerie Queene* is on one level a chivalric ROMANCE, but it embodies ideological meanings. Bunyan's *Pilgrim's Progress* describes the efforts of a Christian to achieve a godly life by triumphing over inner obstacles to his faith, these obstacles being represented by outward objects such as the Slough of Despond and Vanity Fair.

It is important but by no means always easy to distinguish between *allegory* and SYMBOLISM, which attempts to suggest other levels of meaning without making a structure of ideas the controlling influence in the work, as it is in *allegory*. The traditional distinction between "symbol" and *allegory* is put forth by Coleridge, whose *Statesman's Manual* argues that "an allegory is but a translation of abstract notions into picture-language," whereas "a Symbol always partakes of the Reality which it makes intelligible." Coleridge's position has been attacked by modern theorists of *allegory*, from Walter Benjamin to Paul de Man. Recent theory has seen in *allegory* and allegorical representations a recognition of the contingent, arbitrary nature of symbolization in literature—a foregrounding of the process of symbolization or representation itself. de Man argues that "the symbol postulates the possibility of an identity or identification, allegory designates primarily a distance. . . ." Among the kinds of *allegory*, in addition to those suggested above, are PARABLE, FABLE, EXEMPLUM, and BEAST EPIC. See also ANAGOGE, FOUR SENSES OF INTERPRETATION.

[References: H. Berger, Jr., *The Allegorical Temper: Vision and Reality in Book II of Spenser's Faerie Queene* (1957); Paul de Man, *Allegories of Reading* (1979), *Blindness and Insight* (1983), *The Rhetoric of Romanticism* (1984); Angus Fletcher, *Allegory: The Theory of a Symbolic Mode* (1964); Edwin Honig, *Dark Conceit: The Making of Allegory* (1959); C. S. Lewis, *The Allegory of Love* (1936, 1958); Rosemuond Tuve, *Allegorical Imagery* (1966).]

Allelograph A variant form of a word used in the vicinity of the basic form itself, as in Wordsworth's line "Ne'er saw I, never felt, a calm so deep" ("ne'er" and "never") and Pound's "What thou lovest well. . . . What thou lov'st well" ("lovest" and "lov'st").

Alliteration The repetition of initial identical CONSONANT sounds or any vowel sounds in successive or closely associated syllables, especially stressed syllables. In rare cases—such as "No*w* is the *w*inter"—the effect joins the end of a syllable with the beginning of the next. A good example of consonantal *alliteration* is Coleridge's lines:

> The fair breeze blew, the white foam flew,
> The furrow followed free.

Vowel *alliteration* is shown in the sentence: "Apt alliteration's artful aid is often an occasional ornament in prose." Possible *alliteration* of sounds within words appears in Tennyson's lines:

> The *m*oan of doves in i*mm*e*m*orial el*m*s,
> And *m*ur*m*uring of innu*m*erable bees.

Several different patterns of *alliteration* can be seen in one of Housman's stanzas:

These, in the day when heaven was falling,
The hour when earth's foundations fled,
Followed their mercenary calling
And took their wages and are dead.

One pattern connects the initial consonants of "day," "dead," and the stressed middle syllable of "foundations." Another connects "falling," "fled," "followed," and "foundations," in the last of which the *alliterated* syllable is relatively unstressed. Yet another pattern, somewhat harder to hear and see, connects the initial vowels in "hour" and "earth's." *Alliteration*, limited to ONSETS, which are mostly consonants, seems to dwell in the ear for a much shorter time than RHYME, which involves both vowels and consonants and seems to stay in the memory over a period of thirty or more syllables. As though to compensate for such relative poverty of effect, *alliteration* sometimes complicates its patterns with CYNGHANEDD and COLITERATION.

OLD ENGLISH VERSIFICATION rested in large measure on *alliteration*, as did much Middle English poetry. In modern verse, *alliteration* has usually been a secondary ornament, although poets as unlike as Whitman, Swinburne, Hardy, Pound, Eliot, Auden, and Larkin have made extensive and skillful use of it.

Alliterative Prose A medieval tradition of giving dignity to prose by adding prosodic devices from ALLITERATIVE VERSE. The SERMONS of Aelfric and Wulfstan, who flourished early in the eleventh century, are marked by pronounced PROSE-RHYTHMS and ALLITERATION.

Alliterative Romance A METRICAL ROMANCE written in ALLITERATIVE VERSE, especially produced during the revival of interest in alliterative poetry in the fourteenth century, e.g., *William of Palerne* (unrhymed long lines similar to the alliterative verse of the Old English Period), *Sir Gawain and the Green Knight* (in stanzas of varying numbers of long lines followed by five short rhymed lines), and the "alliterative" *Le Morte Darthur*. See MEDIEVAL ROMANCE.

Alliterative Verse A term applied to verse forms, usually Germanic or Celtic in origin, in which the metrical structure is based on patterned repetition of initial sounds within the lines. The most common form in all Old English poetry and in Middle English poetry between the twelfth and fourteenth centuries. See OLD ENGLISH VERSIFICATION, MIDDLE ENGLISH PERIOD.

Alloeostropha (also spelled *alloeostrophe*) Milton's term for the variable division of the choric ODES in *Samson Agonistes* into what he called irregular "stanzas or pauses."

Allohistory Another name for ALTERNATIVE HISTORY.

Allonym The name of an actual person other than the author that is signed by the author to a work. The term is also applied to the work so signed. A recent writer on economics, George J. W. Goodman, has adopted "Adam Smith" as his *allonym*, presumably in homage to the eighteenth-century Scottish economist of that name (1723–1790). Compare with PSEUDONYM.

Allusion A figure of speech that makes brief reference to a historical or literary figure, event, or object. Biblical *allusions* are frequent in English literature, such as Shakespeare's "A Daniel come to judgment" in *The Merchant of Venice*. Strictly speaking, *allusion* is always indirect. It seeks, by tapping the knowledge and memory of the reader, to secure a resonant emotional effect from the associations already existing in the reader's mind. When, for example, Melville names a ship the *Pequod* in *Moby-Dick*, the reader knowing the Pequod tribe to be extinct will suspect the vessel to be fated for extinction. The effectiveness of allusion depends on a body of knowledge shared by writer and reader. Complex literary allusion is characteristic of much modern writing, and discovering the meaning and value of the allusions is frequently essential to understanding the work. A good example is T. S. Eliot's *The Waste Land* and the author's notes to that poem. James Joyce employed allusions of all kinds, many obscure and very complex. Donald Davie's title *Essex Poems* alludes to Thomas Hardy's title *Wessex Poems*. Although usage has never been precise, *allusion* ought to be distinguished carefully from outright QUOTATION, obvious ECHO, and direct or annotated REFERENCE.

[Reference: John Hollander, *The Figure of Echo: A Mode of Allusion in Milton and After* (1981).]

Allusion Book A collection of allusions to a writer or a writer's works, sometimes for a specific period. A "Spenser Allusion Book, 1599–1750," for example, would catalgue allusions to Spenser found in works from the period indicated.

Almanac In medieval times an almanac was a permanent table showing the movements of the heavenly bodies, from which calculations for any year could be made. Later, *almanacs* or calendars for short spans of years and, finally, for single years were prepared. A further step came with the inclusion of useful information, especially for farmers. This use of the *almanac* as a storehouse of general information led ultimately to such modern works as the annual *World Almanac*, a compendium of historical and statistical data not limited to the single year. As early as the sixteenth century, forecasts, first of the weather and later of such events as plagues and wars, were important features of *almanacs*.

The *almanac* figures marginally in literature. Spenser's *Shepheardes Calender* (1579) takes its title from a French "Kalendar of Shepards" and consists of twelve poems, under the titles of the twelve months, with some attention paid to the seasonal implications. By the latter part of the seventeenth century, *almanacs* contained efforts at humor, consisting usually of coarse jokes. This feature was elaborated somewhat later, with some refinement such as maxims and pithy sayings, as in Franklin's *Poor Richard's Almanac* (1732–1758), itself partly inspired by the English comic *almanac*, *Poor Robin*. In Germany in the eighteenth and nineteenth centuries, *almanacs* included printed poetry of a high order. The Davy Crockett *almanacs*, issued in America between 1835 and 1856, recorded many frontier TALL TALES based mainly on oral tradition and helped to preserve a significant aspect of American culture.

Altar Poem Another term for a CARMEN FIGURATUM, a poem in which the lines are so arranged that they form a design on the page, taking the shape of the subject, frequently an altar or a cross. See CARMEN FIGURATUM.

Εἰμάρσενός με στήτας
πόσις, μέροψ δίσαβος,
τεῦξ', οὐ σποδεύνας, ἶνις,ἐμπούσας, μόρος
Τεύκροιο βούτα καί κυνὸς τεκνώματος,
Χρύσας δ' ἀίτας, ἆμος ἑψάνδρα
τὸα γυιόχαλκον οὖρον ἔρραισεν,
δν ωπάτωρ δίσευνος,
μόρησε ματρόρριπτος,
ἐμὸν δὲ τεῦγμ' ἀθρήσας
Θεοκρίτοιο κτύντας,
Τριεσπέροιο καύτας,
θώϋξεν †ἀνιύξας
χάλεψε γάρ νιν ἰῷ
σύργαστρος ἐκδὺς γῆρας,
τὸν δ' †άεί λινεῦντ' ἐν ἀμφικλύστῳ
Πανός τε ματρὸς εὐνέτας, φὼρ
δίζωος ἰνίς τ' ἀνδροβρῶτος ἰλιοραιστᾶν
ἦρ' ἀρδίων ἐς Τευκρίδ' ἄγαγον τρίπορθον.

"The Altar" by Dosidias (*Greek Anthology*)

THE ALTAR

A broken ALTAR, Lord, thy servant reares,
Made of a heart, and cemented with teares:
Whose parts are as thy hand did frame;
No workmans tool hath touch'd the fame.
A HEART alone
Is such a stone,
As nothing but
Thy pow'r doth cut.
Wherefore each part
Of my hard heart
Meets in this frame,
To praise thy name.
That, if I chance to hold my peace,
These stones to praise thee may not cease.
O let thy blessed SACRIFICE be mine,
And sanctifie this ALTAR to be thine.

"The Altar" by George Herbert (1633)

Alterity The general idea of otherness, expressed most influentially in the philosophy of G. W. F. Hegel, who argued that much Western thought defined itself by reference to opposition to something alien or other. Although the word appears as early as

Coleridge's *Notes on Shakespeare, alterity* has been much explored in postmodern literary and cultural theory.

[References: Emmanuel Levinas, *Alterity and Transcendence*, tr. Michael B. Smith (1999); Stefan Herbrechter, *Lawrence Durrell, Postmodernism, and the Ethics of Alterity* (1999).]

Alternative History A species of fiction—also called ALLOHISTORY—in which much depends on some major reversal of known geography or history. Vassily Aksyonov's *The Island of Crimea*, for example, postulates that the Crimea is an island instead of a peninsula, with far-reaching geopolitical effects. Among the better-known exercises in the mode are Vladimir Nabokov's *Ada* and William Gibson and Bruce Sterling's *The Difference Engine*. In Robert Harris's *Fatherland* (also a made-for-cable movie) World War II has ended with America defeating Japan but not Germany, which now controls most of Europe. Philip K. Dick's *The Man in the High Castle* has the Axis powers winning War World II. Inside the novel, which is set in America in 1962, a character named Hawthorne Abendsen writes an *alternative history* called *The Grasshopper Lies Heavy*, in which the Axis powers lose World War II. Philip Roth's *The Plot Against America* (2004) is a recent example.

Ambages A form of circumlocution in which the truth is spoken in a way that tends to deceive or mislead. The RIDDLE

Brothers and sisters have I none,
But this man's father is my father's son—

is an example in which the relationship of "this man" to the speaker (i.e., son to father) is concealed in an accurate statement.

Ambiguity The state of having more than one meaning, with resultant uncertainty as to the intended significance of the statement. The chief causes of unintentional *ambiguity* are undue brevity and compression, "cloudy" reference of pronoun, faulty or inverted sequence, and the use of a word with two or more meanings. A writer who aims to be clear should avoid ambiguous wording such as "the days before us" or "He helped the lady across the street." Attempts to combine causation and negation often produce unwanted *ambiguity*, as in "He was not in the hospital because he was sick." However, in literature of the highest order may be found another aspect of *ambiguity*, which results from the capacity of language to function on levels other than that of denotation. In literature, words demonstrate an astounding capacity for suggesting two or more equally suitable senses in a given context, for conveying a core meaning and accompanying it with overtones of great richness and complexity, and for operating with two or more meanings at the same time. One attribute of the finest poets is their ability to tap what I. A. Richards has called the "resourcefulness of language" and to supercharge words with great pressure of meaning. The kind of *ambiguity* that results from this capacity of words to stimulate simultaneously several different streams of thought, all of which make sense, is a characteristic of the richness and concentration that make great poetry.

Because modern English lacks the inflections that distinguish nominative nouns from those in oblique cases, syntactic *ambiguity* arises in clauses that depart from the usual subject-verb-object arrangement. The line "And all the air a solemn stillness holds" (Gray's "Elegy Written in a Country Churchyard") is wonderfully ambiguous: all the air holds a stillness, and a stillness holds all the air. In a grammatically animated passage in Tennyson's "Lucretius," two figures follow each other in hallucinatory *ambiguity*: "And here an Oread . . . a satyr, a satyr, see, / Follows" in a show of "Twynatured" syntactic doubleness. A handful of English words—"still," "fast," "certain," "primate," "phenomenon," "let," "doubt"—can have meanings that are not only different but virtually antithetical. In "The Windhover," Gerard Manley Hopkins uses "buckle" to mean both "come together" and "fall apart." *Ambiguity* at this extreme pitch has been exploited in poems by T. S. Eliot and Robert Frost. Early in this century, Sigmund Freud, inspired by the now-discredited speculations of the linguist Karl Abel, suggested that the language of dreams made use of what he and Abel called "the antithetical sense of primal words." Even such a simple matter as the versatility of the *s* suffix in modern English (plural noun, singular possessive noun, third-person singular present-tense verb) can furnish a species of *ambiguity*, as in such titles as Joyce's *Finnegans Wake* and Richard Wilbur's *The Beautiful Changes*.

William Empson, in *Seven Types of Ambiguity* (orig. publ. 1930), extended the meaning of the term. Although some feel that another word besides *ambiguity* should be used for language functioning with artistic complexity (among those suggested have been multiple meanings and PLURISIGNATION), Empson's "seven types" of linguistic complexity "which adds some nuance to the direct statement of prose" are effective tools for the examination of literature. These "types of *ambiguity*" are (1) details of language that are effective in several ways at once; (2) alternative meanings that are ultimately resolved into the one meaning intended by the author; (3) two seemingly unconnected meanings that are given in one word; (4) alternative meanings that act together to clarify a complicated state of mind in the author; (5) a SIMILE that refers imperfectly to two incompatible things and by this "fortunate confusion" shows the author discovering the idea as he or she writes; (6) a statement that is so contradictory or irrelevant that readers are made to invent their own interpretations; and (7) a statement so fundamentally contradictory that it reveals a basic division in the author's mind.

[References: Paul de Man, *Allegories of Reading* (1979); William Empson, *Seven Types of Ambiguity*, 3rd ed. (1977; earlier editions 1930, 1947); Stanley Fish, *Is There a Text in This Class? The Authority of Interpretive Communities* (1980).]

Ambivalence The existence of mutually conflicting feelings or attitudes. The term is often used to describe the contradictory attitudes an author takes toward characters or societies and also to describe a confusion of attitude or response called forth by a work. The opening of Keats's "On Sitting Down to Read King Lear Once Again"—"O golden-tongued Romance, with serene lute! / Fair-plumèd Syren, Queen of far-away!"—furnishes a number of examples of *ambivalence*, especially in the complicated mixture of feelings as the poet bids "Adieu" to the dangerously attractive muse. "Golden-tongued" suggests "wonderfully melodious" but also "deceptive"; "serene" suggests "peaceful" but also "falsely placid"; "fair-plumèd" suggests both "attractive" and "showy and shallow"; "Syren" embraces both "attractive" and "dangerously seductive"; "far-away" suggests "enchanted realms" but also "escapist imaginations"—and all of these ambivalences are underscored by the way the accent shifts within a single consonantal frame in "serene" and "Syren."

Ambo A stage direction meaning "both." Shakespeare's *Much Ado About Nothing* (5,1) includes "Exeunt ambo," "both go out."

American Academy of Arts and Letters An organization created in 1904 to recognize accomplishment in literature, art, or music. The American Social Science Association in 1898, realizing the need for a society devoted entirely to the interests of letters and the fine arts, organized the National Institute of Arts and Letters, with membership limited to 250. Six years later a smaller society composed of the fifty most distiguished members of the Institute was organized as the *American Academy of Arts and Letters*. Only members of the Institute could be elected to the Academy. The seven first elected to membership were: William Dean Howells, Augustus Saint-Gaudens, Edmund Clarence Stedman, John La Farge, Samuel Langhorne Clemens, John Hay, and Edward MacDowell. The Academy received a Congressional Charter in 1916. In 1976 the American Academy and Institute of Arts and Letters was formed by a merger of the two bodies, and in 1993 the members voted to abolish the Institute, leaving only a unicameral *American Academy of Arts and Letters*. Annually the organization awards its gold medal for distinguished work in literature and the arts; every five years it confers the William Dean Howells medal for the best American fiction.

American Dream, The A fixture of American life and thought for many decades, "*the American Dream*," positively or ironically, has to do with a grand ideal of the sort of success made possible by the charters and habits of the United States of America since its establishment in 1776. The dream includes freedom, success, wealth, and fulfillment. An early expression is Benjamin Franklin's life, as recorded in his autobiographical writings; by the modern age, the dream was routinely given a tragic or satiric twist, as in Fitzgerald's *The Great Gatsby*. George O'Neil wrote *American Dream: A Play in Three Acts* (1933); Edward Albee wrote a play called *The American Dream* (1961), followed soon after by Norman Mailer's novel *An American Dream* (1965).

[References: Elizabeth Long, *The American Dream and the Popular Novel* (1985); Stanley A Werner, ed., *The American Dream in Literature* (1970).]

American Language A term used to designate certain idioms, pronunciations, and forms peculiar to the English language in America. These differences arise in several ways: Some forms originate in America independently of English speech ("gerrymander" is an example); some expressions that were once native to England have been brought here and have lived after they had died out in England ("fall" for "autumn"); and certain English forms have taken on modified meanings in America (as we use "store" for "shop"). Besides these matters of VOCABULARY, H. L. Mencken points out six respects in which American expression differs from English: syntax, intonation, slang, idiom, grammar, and pronunciation.

[References: Sir William Craigie and J. R. Hulbert, eds., *A Dictionary of American English on Historical Principles* (1938–44); Hans Kurath and Raven I. McDavid, eds., *Linguistic Atlas of the United States and Canada* (1939–continuing); Albert H. Marckwardt, *American English* (1958 rev. by J. L. Dillard 1980; orig. 1958); M. M. Mathews, ed., *Americanisms; A Dictionary of Americanisms on Historical Principles* (1951, 1966); H. L. Mencken, *The American Language, with Supplements* (1919–48).]

American Literature, Periods of Any division of literary history is an arbitrary oversimplification. In the case of America, where the national record long predates the development of a self-sufficient literature, the problem is complicated further by the fact that most divisions into early periods are based on political and social history and most divisions into later periods on the dominance of literary types or movements. Almost all historians of *American literature* have made their own systems of period division. In this handbook *American literature* is treated in a chronological pattern set against the dominant English movements in the *Outline of Literary History*, and the characteristics of its own periods are treated in the following articles:

- COLONIAL PERIOD, 1607–1765
- REVOLUTIONARY AND EARLY NATIONAL PERIOD, 1765–1830
- ROMANTIC PERIOD, 1830–1865
- REALISTIC PERIOD, 1865–1900
- NATURALISTIC AND SYMBOLISTIC PERIOD, 1900–1930
- PERIOD OF CONFORMITY AND CRITICISM, 1930–1960
- PERIOD OF THE CONFESSIONAL SELF, 1960–1989
- POSTMODERN PERIOD, 1990–

If read in sequence, these articles will give a brief history of American writing by periods.

Amoebean Verses PASTORAL verses in matched STROPHES or STANZAS spoken by two speakers alternately. Classical examples are found in Theocritus and Virgil; Sidney's "Ye Goatherd Gods" (*Arcadia*) is an *amoebean* double SESTINA. "Bozzy and Piozzi, or The British Biographers: A Town Eclogue" by John Wolcot ("Peter Pindar") is a satiric example.

Amphibology (Amphibologia or **Amphiboly)** A term applied to statements capable of two different meanings, a kind of AMBIGUITY. In literature, *amphibology* is usually intentional when it occurs. The witches' prophecies in *Macbeth* and Fedallah's deceptive assurances to Captain Ahab in *Moby-Dick* are well-known examples.

Amphibrach A metrical FOOT consisting of three syllables, the first and last unaccented, the second accented. An example is *ărrāngemĕnt.*

Amphigory (or Amphigouri) Verse that sounds good but contains little or no sense or meaning; either NONSENSE verse, such as Edward Lear's, or nonsensical PARODY, such as Swinburne's self-mockery in "Nephelidia," which begins: "From the depth of the dreamy decline of the dawn through a notable nimbus of nebulous noonshine," or more general parody, such as,

> Moon milk and soft curds of milky way
> Mingle in the intricacies of my equation,
> O Calculus in calculable!

Beginning in 1972, the American comic writer Edward Gorey published compilations called *Amphigorey*, *Amphigorey Too*, and *Amphigorey Also*.

Amphimacer A metrical FOOT consisting of three syllables, the first and last accented, the second unaccented: An example is *nēvĕrmōre.*

Amphisbaenic Rhyme Named for the monster in Greek FABLE that has a head at each end and can go in either direction, the term is used to describe backward RHYME—that is, two rhyme words or syllables, the second of which inverts the order of the first, as "step" and "pets." While *amphisbaenic* is an amusingly INKHORN term, it is not really very accurate. A better word may be "BOUSTROPHEDONIC," which means "moving alternately left to right and right to left" and applies to certain ancient methods of writing. Edmund Wilson explored the effects of this sort of rhyme in some of his verse, not all of it light; and Wilson's verse experiments subsequently bore fruit in the work in verse and prose of his sometime friend Vladimir Nabokov.

Amplification A FIGURE OF SPEECH in which bare expressions, likely to be ignored, misunderstood, or underestimated because of bluntness, are emphasized through restatement with additional detail.

Ana Miscellaneous sayings, ANECDOTES, gossip, and scraps of information about a particular person, place, or event; or a book that records such sayings and anecdotes. Englishmen in the seventeenth century were much devoted to this type of writing, *The Table Talk of John Selden* (1689) being typical. The term also exists as a suffix, as in "Goldsmithiana."

Anabasis An account of a military advance or other movement, a general title bestowed in specific homage to Xenophon's account of Cyrus the Younger's expedition into Asia. The best-known modern example is probably *Anabase* (1924) by Saint-John Perse (pseudonym of Alexis Saint-Léger Léger), translated as *Anabasis* by T. S. Eliot in 1930. *The Warriors* (1979) is an imaginative translation to film.

Anachinosis See ANACOENESIS.

Anachronism Assignment of something to a time when it was not in existence. Shakespeare is guilty of sundry *anachronisms* such as Hector's learned reference to Aristotle in *Troilus and Cressida*. The *anachronism*, however, is usually a greater sin to the realist than to the romanticist. Humorists sometimes use *anachronisms* as comic devices. Mark Twain's *A Connecticut Yankee in King Arthur's Court* rests on a sustained, satiric *anachronism*.

Anaclasis (also **Anaklasis**) In IONIC verse: an interchange of the final long syllable of the first METRON (unit of rhythm consisting of one or two feet) with the opening short syllable of the second. A standard application of the lesser Ionic would sound like "Ĭn thĕ drūmrōll ŏf thĕ rāilrōad"; *anaclasis* would produce something like "ĭn thĕ bēatĭng rōllĭng rāilrōad."

Anacoenesis (also **Anachinosis**) Asking a question as though to seek the opinion of one's hearer, reader, opponent, or judge.

Anacoluthon The failure, accidental or deliberate, to complete a sentence according to the structural plan on which it was started. It may be a mistake, as in a sentence that loses its way: "The police arrested the man whom they thought was an escaped convict"—in which "whom" begins as a potential object, as its case-ending requires, but becomes the subject of a subordinate clause. In literary practice, however, the device can work as a powerful index of anxiety or disturbed coherence. Something of this sort occurs in the opening lines of Tennyson's "Ulysses":

> It little profits that an idle king,
> By this still hearth, among these barren crags,
> Match'd with an aged wife, I mete and dole
> Unequal laws unto a savage race. . . .

Here "an idle king" promises to function as the subject of a noun clause but turns out to be merely in apposition with the true subject, "I." The end of Yeats's "The Second Coming" begins as a statement but abruptly turns into a question:

> The darkness drops again; but now I know
> That twenty centuries of stony sleep
> Were vexed to nightmare by a rocking cradle,
> And what rough beast, its hour come round at last,
> Slouches towards Bethlehem to be born?

Anacreontic Poetry Verse in the mood and manner of the lyrics of the Greek poet Anacreon; that is, poems characterized by an erotic, amatory, or Bacchanalian spirit. The characteristic *Anacreontic* line consists of a PYRRHIC FOOT, two TROCHEES, and a SPONDEE, for which the nearest regular English counterpart would be trochaic tetrameter. Whatever the rhythm, *Anacreontic* verses in English tend to be tetrameter, such as the tune called "Anacreon in Heaven," which was appropriated as the setting of Francis Scott Key's "The Star-Spangled Banner." The institution enjoyed popularity in the sixteenth century and again in the eighteenth. Various sorts of *Anacreontic* verses were written by Sidney, Spenser, Prior, Ambrose Philips, and William Oldys. The best-known overtly *Anacreontic* poems in English are by Abraham Cowley and Thomas Moore.

Anacrusis A term denoting one or more extra unaccented syllables at the beginning of a VERSE before the regular rhythm of the line makes its appearance. Literally an upward or back beat. The third line of the following stanza by Shelley is an example:

> What thou art we know not;
> What is most like thee?
> From rainbow clouds there flow not
> Drops so bright to see
> As from thy presence showers a rain of melody.

Anadiplosis A kind of repetition in which a word or phrase coming last or in another important place in one sentence or line is repeated at the beginning of the next, as in these lines from Bartholomew Griffin's *Fidessa*:

> For I have loved long, I crave reward,
> Reward me not unkindly: think of kindness,

Kindness becommeth those of high regard,
Regard with clemency a poor man's blindness.

Anagnorisis In drama, the DISCOVERY or RECOGNITION that leads to the PERIPETY or REVERSAL. Titles from recent American poetry suggest that the figure persists robustly. Jay Wright's *Explications/Interpretations* contains a poem called "Anagnorisis," and Richard Howard's *Like Most Revelations* includes "Centenary Peripeteia and Anagnorisis Beginning with a Line by Henry James."

Anagoge (or **Anagogy**) The mystical or spiritual meaning in biblical and allegorical interpretation. For example, when certain passages in Virgil were interpreted in the Middle Ages as foretelling the coming of Christ, they were being given *anagogical* interpretations. It is the highest of the FOUR SENSES OF INTERPRETATION, the others being the literal, the allegorical, and the moral. Thus, Jerusalem is literally a city, allegorically the Church, morally the believing soul, and *anagogically* the heavenly City of God. These levels of meaning are regularly applied to Dante's *Divine Comedy*.

Anagram A word or phrase made by transposing the letters of another, as "cask" is an *anagram* of "sack." *Anagrams* have usually been employed simply as a trifling exercise of ingenuity, but writers sometimes use them to conceal proper names or to veil messages. It is said, too, that some of the astronomers of the seventeenth century used *anagrams* to conceal certain of their discoveries until it was convenient to announce their findings. *Anagrams* have been used frequently as a means of coining pseudonyms, as "Calvinus" became "Alcuinus," and "Bryan Waller Procter" became "Barry Cornwall, poet"; "Arouet, l.j." (*le jeune*), *u* being a variant of *v* and *j* a variant of *i*, is said to have been the basis of the name "Voltaire." *Erewhon* ("nowhere") is an instance of an *anagram* as a book title. Some *anagrams* that seem frivolous contain hints of deeper seriousness, as in Edmund Wilson's rearrangement of Ezra Pound's name into "azure pond" or Vladimir Nabokov's creation of the sinister "Vivian Darkbloom" from the letters of his own name. The modern American poet A. R. Ammons used a number of serious *anagrams* in his work ("scared sacred" and "cold clod clam calm," for example). Another contemporary, Robert Morgan, has written a serious poem called "Mountain Graveyard" that consists entirely of pairs of significant *anagrams* ("slate tales," "stone notes," and "hated death," for example). Donne's "Elegie: The Anagram" jokes about a human *anagram*:

Though all her parts be not in th'usuall place,
She'hath yet an Anagram of a good face.

And George Herbert so arranges an *anagram* poem that even the title partakes of the wit:

Ana- {MARY / ARMY} *gram*

How well her name an *Army* doth present,
In whom the *Lord of Hosts* did pitch his tent!

A variety of the *anagram*, the PALINDROME, is an arrangement of letters that give the same meaning whether read forward or backward, and is illustrated in the remark by which Adam is alleged to have introduced himself to his wife: "Madam, I'm Adam." It may be noted that the celebrated "Et tu, Brute?" in Shakespeare's *Julius Caesar* is nearly a palindrome.

Analecta (Analects) Literary gleanings, fragments, or passages from the writings of an author or authors; also the title for a collection of choice extracts, for example, *Analects of Confucius*.

Analepsis In the terminology of Robert Graves's *The White Goddess*, a type of vision or trance in which something from the past or the unconscious mind is restored to vivid life in the present or conscious mind. Generally, *analepsis* means any recovery or restoration; a poem by W. H. Auden includes the witty phrase "analeptic swig."

Analogism versus Anomalism A philosophical debate, traceable to classical antiquity and continuing today, that has to do with the question of the genesis and operation of language. Is language analogous to a world or a mind; or is language an anomalous structure with no positive connection to structures outside itself? Certain lineaments of this debate can be seen in the radical difference between NOMINALISM and REALISM.

Analogue Something that is analogous to or like another given thing. An *analogue* may mean a cognate, or a word in one language corresponding with one in another, as the English "mother" is an *analogue* of the Latin *mater*. In literary history two versions of the same story may be called *analogues*, especially if no direct relationship can be established. Thus, the story of the pound of flesh in *Gesta Romanorum* may be called an *analogue* of the similar plot in *The Merchant of Venice*.

Analogy A comparison of two things, alike in certain aspects; particularly a method used in EXPOSITION and DESCRIPTION by which something unfamiliar is explained by being compared to something more familiar. In ARGUMENTATION and logic, *analogy* is frequently employed to justify contentions. *Analogy* is widely used in poetry but also in other forms of writing; a SIMILE is an expressed *analogy*, a METAPHOR an implied one.

Analysis A method by which a thing is separated into parts, and those parts are given rigorous, logical, detailed scrutiny, resulting in a consistent and relatively complete account of the elements of the thing and the principles of their organization. See ANALYTICAL CRITICISM.

Analytical Criticism A term applied to CRITICISM that views the work of art as an autonomous whole and believes that its meaning, nature, and significance can be discovered by applying rigorous and logical systems of analysis to its several parts and their organization. The work of the New Critics has been called analytical criticism. See ANALYSIS; CRITICISM, TYPES OF; NEW CRITICISM.

Analytic Editing A term used in filmmaking and FILM CRITICISM for a special process by which a director and an editor of a film so select the details in a scene that an emphatic meaning is imposed on the viewer; thus, *analytic editing* refers to a director's fundamental approach to cinematic expression. The details selected and the amount of attention given to each become the "language" of the scene. Alfred Hitchcock is often considered the greatest practitioner of *analytic editing*.

Analytic-Prefixal One term for the practices of altering verbal units by means of adding a separate element at the beginning. English, for example, forms the infinitive by placing a separate "to" before a base verb. Many other languages form the infinitive by synthesizing a new unit with suffixes joined to the base. Latin "videre" is the one-word synthetic-suffixal counterpart of English "to see," which is two words in an *analytic-prefixal* configuration. Compare likewise "most high" with "highest."

Analyzed Rhyme A complex form of RHYME that involves breaking down or *analyzing* components. It is an interlocked combination of two or more types of rhyme, usually CONSONANCE and ASSONANCE, although true rhyme sometimes appears. For example, *analyzed rhyme* results from superimposing in a quatrain an *abba* pattern of CONSONANCE RHYME on an *abab* pattern of ASSONANCE RHYME, often with ALLITERATION. Another example would be a quatrain in which the vowel sounds of words in the rhyming position in the first and third lines are the same (ASSONANCE) and the consonant sounds of words in the rhyming position in the second and fourth lines are the same (CONSONANCE). There is no true rhyme in either stanza, since no two words contain both assonance and consonance, both of which are necessary to true rhyme. The rhyme words in the three quatrains of one of W. H. Auden's "Five Songs" demonstrate the procedure: "began / flush / flash / gun // pass / relief / laugh / peace // seen / reproach / reach / own." A rough formula, with "c" and "v" representing consonants and vowels constituting the sounds in rhyming syllables, might look like this: c1v1c2 / c3v2c4 / c3v1c4 / c1v2c2.

[Reference: Edward Lewis Davison, *Some Modern Poets and Other Critical Essays* (1928).]

Ananym A word fabricated by spelling another word backward. On the title page of Martin Geldart's *Sons of Belial*, the author's name appears as "Nitram Tradleg." The place-name "Llareggub" in Dylan Thomas's *Under Milk Wood* qualifies, as, almost, does Samuel Butler's *Erewhon*. Walter de la Mare's "Walter Ramal" comes close.

Anapest Consisting of three syllables, with two unaccented syllables followed by an accented one (˘ ˘ ´). The following lines from Shelley's "The Cloud" are *anapestic*:

> Lĭke ă chīld frŏm thĕ wōmb, lĭke ă ghōst frŏm thĕ tōmb,
> Ĭ ărīse ănd ŭnbūild ĭt ăgāin.

Anaphone (or Anaphony) The acoustic counterpart of the ANAGRAM. In an *anaphone*, the sounds composing one word or phrase are rearranged to make another word or phrase. In Laura (Riding) Jacksons's line "Thus is a universe very soon," it can be heard (though not seen) that the sounds of "very soon" are nearly the same as those of "universe." Some *anaphones* are ANAGRAMS, and vice versa, but such equivalence is not always the case; "ocean" and "canoe" are perfect anagrams but do not sound much alike.

Anaphora One of the devices of REPETITION, in which the same expression (word or words) is repeated at the beginning of two or more lines, clauses, or sentences. It is one of the most obvious of the devices used in the poetry of Walt Whitman, as these opening lines from one of his poems show:

As I ebb'd with the ocean of life,
As I wended the shores I know,
As I walk'd where the ripples continually wash you Paumanok.

The Old Testament is clearly one source and example of this practice. *Anaphora* is the chief device of routine, whether a solemn ritual or a monotonously or menacingly repeated pattern, as in this example from Robert Frost, in which the effect is underscored by END-STOPPED lines:

I have been one acquainted with the night.
I have walked out in rain—and back in rain.
I have outwalked the farthest city light.

I have looked down the saddest city lane.
I have passed by the watchman on his beat
And dropped my eyes, unwilling to explain.

Anaptyxis Insertion of a vowel sound between two consonant sounds, as in pronunciations represented by "athalete," "Henery," "relator," and "nucular" (for "athlete," "Henry," "realtor," and "nuclear").

Anastomosis A scientific term for the interconnection between two entities, such as vessels, channels, or cavities. Also applied to the folding of one word between parts of another, as in Joyce's "underdarkneath" in *Ulysses* or a vernacular phrase such as "my own self." Extended to mean the interrelation, interconnection, intercommunication, or intersubjectivity of persons—used thus in J. Hillis Miller's *Ariadne's Thread* (1992).

Anastrophe Inversion of the usual, normal, or logical order of the parts of a sentence. Anything in language capable of assuming a usual order can be inverted. *Anastrophe* can apply to the usual order of adjectives in English, so that Arnold's "melancholy, long, withdrawing roar," Eliot's "one-night cheap hotels," and Yeats's "terrified vague fingers" all depart from the customary sequence (presumably "long, withdrawing melancholy roar," "cheap one-night hotels," and "vague terrified fingers"). Other common patterns of *anastrophe* affect the adjective-noun succession (inverted in many places in poetry, such as Poe's "midnight dreary") and the standard subject-verb-object order of syntax. For example, the prodigious opening strophe of Whitman's "Out of the Cradle Endlessly Rocking" is a single sentence twenty-two lines long marked by extreme inversion: twenty substantial lines of adverbial and adjectival matter (showing much ANAPHORA), then the main subject, "I," then some protracted adjectival matter, then the object, "a reminiscence," and, finally, after some two hundred preliminary words, the main verb, "sing." See HYPERBATON.

Anathema A formal and solemn denunciation or IMPRECATION, particularly as pronounced by the Greek or Roman Catholic church against an individual, an institution, or a doctrine. The form conventionally reads: *Si quis dixerit, etc., anathema sit*, "If anyone should say (so and so) let him be anathema." One of its most notable appearances in English is in Sterne's *Tristram Shandy* (3, 11).

Anatomy Used as early as Aristotle in the sense of logical dissection or ANALYSIS, this term, which has meant "dissection" in a medical sense, came into common use in England late in the sixteenth century in the meaning explained in Robert Burton's *Anatomy of Melancholy* (1621): "What it is, with all the kinds, causes, symptoms, prognostickes, and severall cures of it." There are several pieces in English literature preceding Burton in which the medical sense of anatomy is still less evident, such as Thomas Nash's *Anatomy of Absurdity* and John Lyly's *Euphues: The Anatomy of Wit*. The *anatomies* anticipated some characteristics of the ESSAY and philosophical and scientific TREATISES of the seventeenth century. The term is also used in Northrop Frye's *Anatomy of Criticism* for that kind of prose work organized around ideas and dealing with intellectual themes and attitudes with prodigious masses of erudition, after the manner of MENIPPEAN SATIRE.

[Reference: Northrop Frye, *Anatomy of Criticism* (1957).]

Anceps (Latin, "two-headed") In classical QUANTITATIVE prosody, a syllable that can be counted as long or short.

Ancients and Moderns, Quarrel of the The controversy that took place in France and England in the late seventeenth and early eighteenth centuries over the relative merits of classical and contemporary cultures. Some of the forces that stimulated the dispute were the RENAISSANCE, which produced a reverence for classical writers; the growth of the new science in the seventeenth century; and the doctrine of progress.

In France the dispute centered on the vigorous advocacy of the moderns by Perrault, Fontenelle, Corneille, and others. They were opposed by Boileau, Racine, La Fontaine, La Bruyère, and others. Perrault in *Parallèles des anciens et des modernes* (1688–1697) and Fontenelle in *Digression sur les anciens et les modernes* (1688) held that the moderns show superior taste and greater polish.

In England the BATTLE OF THE BOOKS began with the publication of Sir William Temple's *An Essay upon the Ancient and Modern Learning* (1690), which rejected the doctrine of progress, criticized the Royal Society, and upheld the claims of the ancients. Temple's work was answered in 1694 by William Wotton's *Reflections upon Ancient and Modern Learning*, which supports the moderns in most branches of learning. The scientific aspects of the quarrel were particularly stressed in England, the English moderns generally being willing to admit the superiority of the ancients in such fields as poetry, oratory, and art.

An episode arose over the *Letters of Phalaris*, which Temple listed as a praiseworthy ancient work. Charles Boyle presently republished these letters and attacked Dr. Richard Bentley for an alleged slight. When Wotton published a second edition of his essay (1697), Bentley included in it an appendix that not only criticized Boyle's edition but presented evidence, later elaborated in his famous *Dissertation* (1699), that the Phalaris letters were spurious. Bentley employed the methods of the new science in the field of classical literature itself, and his study went far toward initiating modern historical scholarship. Jonathan Swift, in the DIGRESSIONS of the *Tale of a Tub* (written c. 1696) and in his famous *Battle of the Books* (written c. 1697, pub. 1704)—the most important literary document produced by the controversy in England—undertook the defense of his patron Temple, though Swift's satire is not altogether one-sided.

Ancilla (literally, "maidservant") An *ancillary* aid in the study of a subject, such as Kathleen Freeman's *Ancilla to the Pre-Socratic Philosophers*.

Anecdote A short NARRATIVE detailing particulars of an interesting episode or event. The term, most frequently referring to the life of an important person, should lay claim to an element of truth. Though *anecdotes* are often used as the basis for SHORT STORIES, an *anecdote* lacks complications of plot and subtleties of character. At one time the term connoted secret and private details of a person's career given forth in the spirit of gossip, though now it is used generally to cover any brief narrative. Anecdotic literature has a long heritage extending from ancient times and comprising books as different as Plutarch's *Parallel Lives*, Athenaeus's *Deipnosophistae*, Procopius's *Anecdota*, and Bishop Percy's *Anecdotes*.

[References: Donald Hall, ed., *The Oxford Book of American Literary Anecdotes* (1981); James Sutherland, ed., *The Oxford Book of Literary Anecdotes* (1975).]

Anglo-Catholic Revival See OXFORD MOVEMENT.

Anglo-French The French language as used in England between 1100 and 1350. See ANGLO-NORMAN (LANGUAGE).

Anglo-Irish Literature Literature produced in English by Irish writers, especially those living in Ireland. It is usually actuated by a conscious effort to use Celtic materials and a style flavored by Irish idioms, called "Hibernian English" or "Anglo-Irish." See CELTIC RENAISSANCE.

Anglo-Italian Sonnet A SONNET combining the rhyme-schemes of the ENGLISH SONNET (*ababcdcdefefgg*) and the ITALIAN SONNET (*abbaabbacdecde*), most often with an OCTAVE from the former and a SESTET from the latter. Examples include Thomas Hardy's "Hap" (*abab cdcd efeffe*), W. B. Yeats's "Leda and the Swan" (*abab cdcd efgefg*), and W. H. Auden's "Who's Who" (*ababcdcd efggfe*).

Anglo-Latin (Literature) A term applied to the learned literature produced in Latin by English writers or others dwelling in England during the Old English and Middle English Periods. Largely in prose, it includes chronicles, serious treatises on theology, philosophy, law, history, and science, though SATIRE (such as Walter Map's *De Nugis Curialium*) and LIGHT VERSE (such as the GOLIARDIC VERSE) were also written, as well as hymns, prayers, and religious plays. See OLD ENGLISH PERIOD, ANGLO-NORMAN PERIOD, MIDDLE ENGLISH PERIOD.

Anglo-Norman (Language) The term *Anglo-Norman* (also ANGLO-FRENCH) is applied to the French language as it was used in England in the period following the Norman Conquest (c. 1100–1350) and also to the literature written in *Anglo-Norman*. The relations of France and England were so close that it is difficult to be certain in all cases whether a given writer or work of the period is *Anglo-Norman* or merely French.

Although "*Anglo-Norman*" and "Anglo-French" are commonly used interchangeably, some writers restrict Anglo-French to French that shows the definite influence of English idioms. *Anglo-Norman*, often limited to the early period of Norman times (1066 and immediately following), sometimes denotes pieces written in England by persons of Norman descent using the Norman dialect of French (sometimes called Franco-Norman). See ANGLO-NORMAN PERIOD.

Anglo-Norman Period The period in English literature between 1100 and 1350, so called because of the dominance of Norman-French culture. The period is also often called the Early Middle English Period and is frequently dated from the Conquest in 1066, although it was early in the twelfth century before the impact of Norman culture was marked on the English or before the Norman conquerors began to think of themselves as inhabitants of the British Isles.

In Europe this was the age of the great crusades and the period of the dominance of French literature. In England, under Henry I, Stephen, and the Plantagenet Kings Henry II, Richard the Lion-Hearted, and John, the conquered Saxon natives and the Norman lords were establishing the working pattern of government that reached its epitomizing statement in the Magna Charta of 1215. Feudalism was established. Parliament came into being, with a movement toward definite limits on the power of the monarchy. Oxford and Cambridge rose as strong universities. The Old English language, the tongue of conquered slaves for a period after the Conquest, not only survived in the period as Middle English but blended with the French dialect of the Norman victors. Gradually it emerged as the language of England, as King John's successor, Henry III, recognized in 1258 when he used English as well as French in a proclamation.

By 1300 English was becoming again the language of the upper classes and was beginning to displace French in schools and legal pleadings. Henry III was succeeded in 1272 by the first of the three Edwards, who ruled England for more than a hundred years (until 1377). Latin was used for learned works, French for courtly literature, and English chiefly for popular works—religious plays, METRICAL ROMANCES, and popular BALLADS. On the continent Dante and Boccaccio flourished. In England and France the body of legend and artful invention that gave England its national hero, Arthur, was coming into being in French, Latin, and English. (See ARTHURIAN LEGEND).

Writings in native English were few. The last entry in the Anglo-Saxon Chronicles was made at Peterborough in 1154. About 1170 a long didactic poem in FOURTEENERS, the *Poema Morale*, appeared. Early in the twelfth century English METRICAL ROMANCES using English themes began to appear, the first being *King Horn*, and flourished throughout the period. The drama made its first major forward leap in this period. The first recorded miracle play in England, *The Play of St. Catherine*, was performed about 1100. By 1300 the mystery plays were moving outside the churches and into the hands of the town guilds. The establishment of the Feast of Corpus Christi in 1311 led to the extension of the cyclic dramas and to the use of movable stages or PAGEANTS. The Chester CYCLE was composed around 1328.

Native English poetry, both in the older alliterative tradition and in the newer French forms, continued to develop. About 1250 came "The Owl and the Nightingale," a *débat* poem; about the same time LYRIC verse was getting under way with poems such as "The Cuckoo Song" ("Summer is i-cumen in"). About 1300 came the heavily didactic *Cursor Mundi*, and around 1340 the popular *The Pricke of Conscience*, describing the misery of earth and glory of heaven. But, significant as these works are in the developing strength of native English writing, the period between 1100 and 1350 is predominantly the age of the Latin CHRONICLE and of the glories of the French and Anglo-Norman writings. Throughout the period, but particularly in the twelfth century, a veritable cultural renaissance took place, which followed the lines of the contemporary literature of France and embraced ROMANCES, TALES, historical works, political poems and SATIRES, LEGENDS, SAINTS' LIVES, didactic works, lyrics and *débats*, as well as religious drama. By 1350 the French qualities of grace, harmony, humor, and chivalric idealism, together with the many characteristic French lyric forms, worldly subjects, and syllabic METERS, had been absorbed into the mainstream of English writing; and, in FOLK BALLAD, in cycle play, in both ALLITERATIVE VERSE and accentual poem, England was ready for a new flowering of native literary art. See *Outline of Literary History*, under "Anglo-Norman Period."

Anglo-Saxon A composite Teutonic tribal group resident in England in post-Roman times. In the fifth and sixth centuries, the Angles and Saxons from the neighborhood of what is now known as Schleswig-Holstein, together with the Jutes, invaded and conquered Britain. From the Angles came the name *England* (Angle-land). After Alfred (ninth century), king of the West Saxons, conquered the Danish-English people of the Anglian territory, the official Latin name for his subjects was *Angli et Saxones* (the English themselves used "*Engle*" and called their language "*Englisc*"). Later, "*Anglo-Saxons*" came to be used to distinguish the residents of England from the Saxons still resident in Europe proper. The term is now broadly used to designate the English peoples whether resident in England or elsewhere; and an even broader and looser usage persists in the mildly calumniatory word "Anglo" and the acronym "WASP" (White Anglo-Saxon Protestant), indifferently applied to persons with no particular claim to being either Anglo-Saxon or Protestant. See OLD ENGLISH PERIOD, ENGLISH LANGUAGE.

Anglo-Saxon Versification See OLD ENGLISH VERSIFICATION.

Angry Young Men A group of British writers in the 1950s and 1960s who demonstrated a particular bitterness in their attacks on outmoded, bourgeois values. The phrase comes from the title of Leslie Paul's autobiography, *The Angry Young Man* (1951). The archetypal example of an Angry Young Man is the protagonist of John Osborne's play *Look Back in Anger* (1957). Other examples are such novels as Kingsley Amis's *Lucky Jim* (1954), John Braine's *Room at the Top* (1957), and Alan Sillitoe's *Loneliness of the Long Distance Runner* (1960). The protagonists of these plays and novels are examples of the ANTIHERO.

Animal Epic See BEAST EPIC.

Anime Japanese adaptation of the French for "animated cartoon," applied to set of styles of films and television productions, frequently tales of FANTASY, SCIENCE FICTION, or HORROR, drawn with extreme stylization and asymmetrical design. Most of the figures have large eyes, unkempt hair, and exaggerated anatomies.

Animism The belief that animals and inanimate objects can possess souls. In certain forms of primitive religion and art and in some literary conventions, objects in nature are invested with human characteristics. Trees, bodies of waters, and such objects are given human personalities and even divine counterparts, such as dryads and nymphs.

Anisobaric A meteorological term having to do with unequal weight or atmospheric pressure; also used in prosody for rhyming syllables that bear significantly different levels of accent, as in the rhyme of "appéar" and "réindèer" in Clement Moore's "A Visit from Saint Nicholas." Other *anisobaric* rhyme-pairs are "séa-chànge" and "stránge" (Shakespeare), "abíde" and "nóontìde" (Hardy), "shów" and "scárecròw" (Yeats), "séem" and "íce-crèam" (Stevens), and "fóotfàll" and "áll" (Ransom).

Annals Narratives of historical events recorded year by year. ANGLO-SAXON monks in the seventh century recorded important events of the year in ecclesiastical calendars after given dates. This practice developed into such records as the *Anglo-Saxon Chronicles*. Both *annals* (as in Ireland) and CHRONICLES (as in England) were frequently written long after the events recorded had taken place, the dating being speculative, especially when efforts were being made to "synchronize" events in secular and in Biblical or ecclesiastical history. The term *annals* in modern times is used rather loosely for historical narrative not necessarily recorded by years and for DIGESTS and records of deliberative bodies and of scientific and artistic organizations, such as *Annals of Congress*, *Annals of Music*, *Annals of Mathematics*. Although *annals* and chronicles are often used interchangeably, *annals* technically implies events of great moment, as in Gray's reference to "The short and simple annals of the poor." See CHRONICLE.

Annotation The addition of explanatory notes to a text by the author or an editor to explain, translate, cite sources, give bibliographical data, comment, gloss, or paraphrase. A VARIORUM EDITION represents the ultimate in *annotation*. An annotated BIBLIOGRAPHY, in addition to the standard bibliographical data, includes comments on the works listed.

Annuals Books appearing in successive numbers at intervals of one year and usually reviewing the events of the year within specified fields of interest, such as college annuals. The term is sometimes applied also to compendiums as the *World Almanac*, embracing historical data and miscellaneous statistics covering a long range of years. In nineteenth-century England and America the term was used to designate yearly compilations of TALES, POEMS, and ESSAYS, illustrated with plates and handsomely bound, issued in the fall of the year for sale around Christmas as GIFT BOOKS. Successful in England between 1822 and 1856, they were equally popular in America. They are significant in American literary history because they were the best market in the first half of the nineteenth century for short fiction, and several works by the likes of Hawthorne, Poe, and Simms first appeared in them. They bore descriptive and sentimental titles, such as *The Gift*, *Friendship's Offering*, *The Odd-Fellow's Offering*, and *The Token*. Scholarly annuals include *American Literary Scholarship*, *Year's Work in English Studies*, and *Studies in Bibliography*.

Anopisthograph A term used for the earliest printed block books, i.e., books printed from engraved blocks of wood. They were printed on only one side of the leaf, and then the leaves were pasted together back to back. An *anopisthograph* may be a MANUSCRIPT or PARCHMENT, as well as a book, and is distinguished by having writing, or print, on only one side of the LEAF. See BLOCK BOOKS.

Antagonist The character directly opposed to the protagonist. A rival, opponent, or enemy of the protagonist. See AGON, PROTAGONIST.

Antanagoge A rhetorical figure variously defined: sometimes as answering a charge with a countercharge, as when one accused of being a thief says to the accuser, "You're another"; sometimes as a compensatory balancing of positive against negative, as when a sports commentator says, "Their offense is lame, but they make up for that by their strong defense."

Anthem In its earlier sense, an *anthem* is an arrangement of words from the Bible, usually from the PSALMS, planned for church worship, with music arranged for responsive singing. In its common and popular use, an *anthem* is any song of praise, rejoicing, or reverence such as national *anthems* and religious *anthems*. See ANTIPHON.

Anthology Literally "a gathering of flowers," the term designates a collection of writing, either prose or poetry, usually by various authors. The *Anthology*, perhaps the most famous of all such collections, is a gathering of some 6000 short Greek poems composed between 490 B.C. and A.D. 1000. Edgar Lee Masters's *Spoon River Anthology* (1915) is a modern Midwestern free-verse counterpart of the collection of epitaphs that make up part of the loose collection known as *The Greek Anthology*. The Bible is sometimes considered an *anthology*, and so is the Koran. A number of *anthologies* have been important in English literary history, among them *Tottel's Miscellany* (1559), which published the chief works of Wyatt and Surrey; *England's Helicon* (1602), which published works of Sidney and Spenser; *Percy's Reliques of Ancient English Poetry* (1756); Palgrave's *Golden Treasury* (1861), a collection of standard works of English poets; and the various Oxford Books, Oxford Anthologies, and Norton Anthologies.

Anthropomorphism The ascription of human characteristics to nonhuman objects. In some mythologies the gods are described as having human form and attributes. Whereas *anthropomorphism* is the conceptual presentation of some nonhuman entity in human form, PERSONIFICATION is the much more limited rhetorical presentation of some nonhuman entity in figuratively human form or with figuratively human qualities. To represent Zeus as an "all-father" with human qualities and features is *anthropomorphism*; to represent time as "Father Time" carrying a scythe and an hourglass is personification.

Antibacchius A metrical foot of three syllables, of which the first two are stressed and the third unstressed (accentual), or the first two are long and the third short (quantitative). An example is: "Clímb down thĕ high móuntăins."

Anticlimax An arrangement of details such that the lesser appears at the point where something greater is expected. The term is customarily used to describe an effect resulting from a decrease in importance in the items of a series. An example, heightened by ANAPHORA, is found in Pope's *Rape of the Lock*:

> Not youthful kings in battle seiz'd alive,
> Not scornful virgins who their charms survive,
> Not ardent lovers robb'd of all their bliss,
> Not ancient ladies when refus'd a kiss,
> Not tyrants fierce that unrepenting die,
> Not Cynthia when her manteau's pinn'd awry,
> E'er felt such rage, resentment, and despair,
> As thou, sad virgin! for thy ravish'd hair.

Antihero A PROTAGONIST of a modern PLAY or NOVEL who has the converse of most of the traditional attributes of the HERO. This hero is graceless, inept, sometimes stupid, sometimes dishonest. The first clear example may be Charles Lumley, in John Wain's *Hurry On Down* (1953), although certainly the concept of a protagonist without heroic qualities is as old as the PICARESQUE NOVEL. Jim Dixon, in Kingsley Amis's novel *Lucky Jim* (1954), Jimmy Porter, in John Osborne's play *Look Back in Anger* (1956), Yossarian, in Joseph Heller's novel *Catch-22* (1961), Tyrone Slothrop, in Thomas Pynchon's *Gravity's Rainbow* (1973), and even "Henry Pussycat" in John Berryman's *Dream Songs* (1969) are all excellent examples.

Anti-Intellectualism A philosophic doctrine that, assigning reason or intellect a subordinate place, questions or denies the ability of the intellect to comprehend the true nature of things. PRAGMATISM, POSITIVISM, and BERGSONISM are all systems that represent a basic *anti-intellectualism*.

Antimasque A grotesque, usually humorous dance interspersed among the beautiful and serious actions and dances of a MASQUE. Often performed by professional actors and dancers, it served as a foil to the masque proper, performed by courtly amateurs. The development and possibly the origin of the *antimasque* are due to Ben Jonson. See MASQUE.

Antimeria (also **Anthemeria, Anthimeria**) A species of ENALLAGE, using one part of speech for another, as in "But me no buts." "But," a conjunction, is used here as first a verb and then a noun. Shakespeare used *antimeria* often, as in "His complexion is perfect gallows" (*The Tempest*, 1, 1) and "The thunder would not peace at my bidding" (*King Lear*, 4, 6). Another practitioner of conspicuous *antimeria*, Gerard Manley Hopkins, used the nouns "self" and "justice" as verbs, and the verb "achieve" as a noun (in the phrase "The achieve of, the mastery of the thing").

Antimetabole The repetition of words in successive clauses in reverse grammatical order. *Antimetabole* is much like CHIASMUS, which reverses grammatical order but not the same words. Molière's sentence, "One should eat to live, not live to eat" and President John F. Kennedy's "Ask not what your country can do for you but what you can do for your country" are examples of *antimetabole*. See CHIASMUS.

Antinovel A form of FICTION produced by writers convinced that the literal phenomenon of experience, not abstracted, internalized, or anthropomorphized through metaphor, is the proper subject matter of the novelist interested in representing reality without imposed interpretations. The *antinovel* experiments with fragmentation and dislocation on the assumption that the reader will be able to reconstruct reality from these disordered and unevaluated pieces of direct experience. The best known of the *antinovelists* is Alain Robbe-Grillet, who believes that the external world is objective and must be described without social or moral superstructures. He eschews metaphor and employs a neutral, flat style. The refusal to allow order into their fictional world leads the *antinovelists* to positions similar to some of those of a modern group to whom they seem opposed, the ANTIREALISTS. The most complete example of the *antinovel* is probably Robbe-Grillet's *Le Voyeur*; other important writers in the school include Nathalie Sarraute, Michel Butor, and Claude Simon.

Antiphon The verse or verses of a PSALM, traditional passage, or portion of the liturgy, changed or sung by alternating choirs during Divine Office in the Roman Catholic church. Drama grew from additions to antiphonal chants in the liturgy. Originally *antiphon* and ANTHEM were synonymous.

Antiphrasis IRONY, the satirical or humorous use of a word or phrase to convey an idea exactly opposite to its real significance. Thus, in Shakespeare's *Julius Caesar*, Antony repeatedly and ironically refers to Caesar's murderers as "honourable men." *Antiphrasis* informs a good deal of casual speech, such as "bad" meaning "good."

Antipophora A rhetorical strategy wherein a question or objection is answered with another question or objection, as in Matthew 21: 23–25: challenged by the priests' and elders' questions, "By what authority doest thou these things? and who gave thee this authority?" Christ answers, "The baptism of John, whence was it? from heaven, or of men?"

Antiquarianism The study of the past through available relics, usually literary or artistic. An organized effort in England, *antiquarianism* is associated with the sixteenth and later centuries. In 1533 King Henry VIII sent John Leland, the "King's Antiquary," throughout England to examine and collect old documents. Leland's notes were used by such later writers as Holinshed and formed the basis for the Society of Antiquaries (1572–1605), of which Sir Walter Ralegh, John Donne, and other literary personages were members. Much Renaissance literature, such as the CHRONICLES, HISTORY PLAYS, topographical poems (like Drayton's *Poly-Olbion*), and patriotic EPICS (like Spenser's *The Faerie Queene*), reflects the antiquarian movement. William Camden was one of the greatest Elizabethan antiquarians. In the seventeenth century Fuller's *Worthies*, John Aubrey's *Lives*, Sir Thomas Browne's *Vulgar Errors*, and the books of Anthony à Wood (historian of Oxford University) were antiquarian in spirit. In the eighteenth century antiquarianism was largely motivated by the interest in primitive peoples. It resulted in Bishop *Percy's Reliques of Ancient English Poetry* (a collection of old BALLADS), Walpole's *Castle of Otranto*, the CELTIC REVIVAL, and the literary FORGERIES of Chatterton and Macpherson and formed an important phase of the ROMANTIC MOVEMENT. The GOTHIC novels and the METRICAL ROMANCES and HISTORICAL NOVELS of Scott reflect it, as, in their way, do the novels of the Brontë sisters.

Antirealistic Novel The contemporary novel of FANTASY, illogicality, and absurdity. The *antirealistic novel* is a fictional counterpart of the THEATER OF THE ABSURD and other modern movements that are extreme manipulations, and often the elimination, of expected and customary forms. Thus, the writer of the *antirealistic novel* abandons many of the expected elements of realistic FICTION, such as coherent PLOT, SETTING, MOTIVATION, CHARACTERIZATION, cause and effect, and even syntax and logic on occasion. The first-generation *antirealists* included James Joyce, Franz Kafka, and the French SURREALISTS. They produced vivid dramatizations of subconscious experience, as in the Nighttown sequence and Molly Bloom's monologue in *Ulysses*, and in Kafka's *The Castle*. The second generation included writers such as Djuna Barnes (*Nightwood*), Malcolm Lowry (*Under the Volcano*), Nathanael West (*The Day of the Locust*), and Henry Miller. Later *antirealists* include Samuel Beckett, Jorge Luis Borges, John Hawkes, Joseph Heller, Toni Morrison, Thomas Pynchon, and Donald Barthelme.

Their works dispense with plot and reduce people to minimal presences in vivid states of anxiety, such as Beckett's Molloy; VIGNETTES presenting a fully imagined new order of reality radically different from ordinary daily life, such as Borges's brief tales; works that distort real experience in the manner of dreams, such as Hawkes's nightmare novels, *The Cannibal* and *The Lime Twig*; and portrayals of an insane kind of order, such as Heller's *Catch-22* and Thomas Pynchon's *The Crying of Lot 49*.

Antispast A prosodic FOOT consisting of four syllables, with the accents falling on the two middle syllables, or a verse pattern in which an IAMBIC foot is followed by a TROCHAIC foot, as in "bĕyónd góĭng."

Antistrophe One of the three stanzaic forms of the Greek choral ODE, the others being STROPHE and EPODE. It is identical in meter with the STROPHE, which precedes it. As the chorus sang the strophe, they moved from right to left; while singing the *antistrophe*, they retraced these steps exactly, moving back to their original positions. (See ODE.) In rhetoric *antistrophe* is the reciprocal conversion of the same words in succeeding phrases or clauses, as T. S. Eliot's "The desert in the garden the garden in the desert" and I. A. Richards's "Harvard Yard in April, April in Harvard Yard."

Antithesis A FIGURE OF SPEECH characterized by strongly contrasting words, clauses, sentences, or ideas, as in "Man proposes, God disposes." Antithesis is a balancing of one term against another. The second line of the following COUPLET by Pope is an example of *antithesis*:

> The hungry judges soon the sentence sign,
> And wretches hang that jury-men may dine.

True antithetical structure demands not only that there be an opposition of idea, but that the opposition in different parts be manifested through similar grammatical structure—the noun "wretches" being opposed by the noun "jury-men" and the verb "hang" by the verb "dine" in the preceding example. In the portrait of "Sporus" in Pope's "Epistle to Dr. Arbuthnot," excessive *antithesis* itself becomes a ground for indictment and an explicit term of acid malediction:

> His wit all seesaw between *that* and *this*,
> Now high, now low, now master up, now miss,
> And he himself one vile antithesis.

Another use of antithesis is found in the so-called Hegelian triad of thesis-antithesis-synthesis that constitutes one type of dialectic.

Antonomasia A FIGURE OF SPEECH in which a proper name is substituted for a general idea that it represents, as in "Some mute inglorious Milton here may rest," where "Milton" is used for "poet." "Watergate" now means a large and complex series of events covering a long period from 1972 on. *Antonomasia* also is used to describe the substitution of an epithet for a proper name, as in using "The Iron Duke" for Wellington or "The Prince of Peace" for Christ. It is a form of PERIPHRASIS.

Aparithmesis Rhetorical enumeration. A passage in T. S. Eliot's "Triumphal March" draws on an inventory from General Ludendorff:

> What comes first? Can you see? Tell us. It is
> 5,800,000 rifles and carbines,
> 102,000 machine guns,
> 28,000 trench mortars,
> 53,000 field and heavy guns. . . .

Aphaeresis (also **Aphairese, Apheresis**) The omission of an initial, unstressed syllable at the beginning of a word, as in "'mid" for "amid," or " 'neath" for "beneath."

Aphorism A concise statement of a principle or precept given in pointed words. The opening sentence of Hippocrates's *Aphorisms* is famous: "Life is short, art is long, opportunity fleeting, experimenting dangerous, reasoning difficult." *Aphorism* usually implies specific authorship and compact, telling expression.

[References: W. H. Auden and Louis Kronenberger, eds., *The Faber Book of Aphorisms* (1964); John Gross, ed., *The Oxford Book of Aphorisms* (1983).]

Apocalyptic A term applied to literature that predicts the ultimate destiny, usually destruction, of the world, often through a kind of symbolism that is obscure, strange, or difficult. *Apocalyptic* writing has also the character of imminent catastrophe, is likely to be grandiose or unrestrained and wild, and often suggests a terrible final judgment. The term is taken from the Apocalypse, the final book of the New Testament, commonly called the Revelation of St. John, a work that describes through complex symbolism the ultimate end of the world. *Apocalyptic* writing, prophesying the end of the world, was common in Jewish and Christian writing between 200 B.C. and A.D. 150. The "prophetic books" of the poet William Blake are considered *apocalyptic*, as is some of the poetry of William Butler Yeats. American fiction is said to have an *apocalyptic* tradition, which includes the work of Charles Brockden Brown, Edgar Allan Poe, Nathaniel Hawthorne, William Faulkner, Nathanael West, and Thomas Pynchon.

Apocalyptics A movement in English poetry flourishing between 1935 and 1950, led by Henry Treece (1912–1966) and J. R. Hendry, editors of the anthologies *The New Apocalypse* (1939) and *The White Horseman* (1941). Resembling SURREALISM in theme and technique, the movement favored extreme IMAGERY, such as that attending Armageddon and APOCALYPSE. Dylan Thomas was sometimes included among the *Apocalyptics*, but he tended to avoid such affiliations; George Barker and David Gascoyne are likewise grouped with the movement.

[References: G. S. Fraser, "Apocalypse in Poetry," in J. F. Hendry and Henry Treece, eds., *The White Horseman: Prose and Verse of the New Apocalypse* (1941); Arthur Edward Salmon, *Poets of the Apocalypse* (1983).]

Apocopated Rhyme Rhyme in which the final stressed syllable of a word is rhymed with the stressed syllable of a word ending in a stressed syllable followed by an unstressed syllable (see MASCULINE RHYME and FEMININE RHYME). A convention sometimes used in modern poetry, it was also a feature of the BALLAD, as in these lines:

Fly around, my pretty little Miss,
Fly around, I say,
Fly around, my pretty little Miss,
You'll drive me almost crazy.

The rhymes here consist of "say" and "cra-." The feminine ending of "crazy" makes this *apocopated rhyme*. The opening lines of W. H. Auden's "Music Is International" end with "speaking," "Greek," "mastered," "last," and so forth. See BROKEN RHYME.

Apocope The omission of one or more sounds from a word, as "even" for "evening" or "bod" for "body." Now and then, it should be noted, an apostrophe at the end of a written word will suggest that *apocope* has taken place when, in fact, something different has occurred. The change from "going" to "goin'" is not, strictly speaking, *apocope* but rather the substitution of one PHONEME for another: /n/ for /ŋ.

Apocrypha *Apocryphal* commonly means "spurious" or "doubtful," because "*apocrypha*," which originally meant "hidden or secret things," came to denote books of the Bible not regarded as inspired and hence excluded from the sacred CANON. Saint Jerome (A.D. 331–402) is said to be the first writer to apply the term to the uncanonical books now known as the *Apocrypha*. Examples of Old Testament *Apocrypha* include: the Book of Enoch (VISION), Life of Adam and Eve (LEGEND), the Wisdom of Solomon (WISDOM LITERATURE), the Testament of Abraham (TESTAMENT), and the Psalter of Solomon (HYMNS). New Testament types include: Acts of Matthew (apostolic "acts"), Third Epistle to the Corinthians, Apocalypse of Peter (VISION), and Gospel of Peter. The influence of *apocryphal* literature, blended with authentic biblical influence, was exerted on such medieval literary types as SAINTS' LEGENDS, VISIONS, SERMONS, and even ROMANCES. Certain books accepted by the medieval church but rejected by Protestants—such as Ecclesiasticus, Baruch, and Maccabees—became *apocryphal* in the sixteenth century, though they were often printed in Protestant Bibles as useful for edification but not authoritative.

In a nonbiblical sense, *apocrypha* is applied to writings that have been attributed to authors but have not been generally accepted into the CANON of their works. Thus, there are Chaucer *apocrypha* and Shakespeare *apocrypha*.

Apocryphon Rare singular of *apocrypha*, meaning a single APOCRYPHAL work, as in "the Genesis Apocryphon."

Apodictic (or **Apodeictic**) A rhetorical term for the sort of argument that is clearly subject to demonstration and proof.

Apo koinou Greek, "in common." Describing a peculiar construction in which two distinct clauses share an unrepeated element in common so that the element serves two grammatical functions. An example occurs in "Sir Patrick Spens":

Our king has written a braid letter,
And seal'd it with his hand,

And sent it to Sir Patrick Spens,
Was walking on the strand.

The two clauses amount to "[he] sent it to Sir Patrick Spens" and "Sir Patrick Spens was walking on the strand." "Sir Patrick Spens" could be called the element *apo koinou*, serving as the object of a preposition in the first clause and the subject in the second. The conclusion of Frank O'Hara's "The Day Lady Died"—"while she whispered a song along the keyboard / to Mal Waldron and everyone and I stopped breathing"—offers the possibility that "everyone" is one of the objects of "to" and also one of the subjects of "stopped."

Apolelymenon Milton's term for the MONOSTROPHIC design of such CHORUSES as those in his *Samson Agonistes*. Milton also used the term, in Greek script, in a note to a jesting Latin ODE ("Ad Ioannem Rousium").

Apollonian (or, earlier, **Apollinian**) A term used, along with DIONYSIAN, by Friedrich Nietzsche, in *The Birth of Tragedy*, to designate contrasting elements in Greek TRAGEDY. Apollo, the god of youth and light, stood for reason, culture, and moral rectitude; Dionysus, the god of wine, for the irrational and undisciplined. These contrasting terms connote much the same opposition as CLASSICISM and ROMANTICISM, and are very similar to Matthew Arnold's HELLENISM AND HEBRAISM, to Schopenhauer's *The World as Will and Idea*, and to Schiller's antinomy of the NAÏVE and the SENTIMENTAL.

Apologia Latin form of APOLOGY, most familiar from John Henry Newman's *Apologia pro Vita Sua*.

Apologue A moral FABLE, such as that in C. Day Lewis's "A Country Comet."

Apology The word often appears in literature, especially in TITLES, in its older sense of DEFENSE, as in Sidney's *Apologie for Poetrie* and Stevenson's *Apology for Idlers*. The Latin form is also used in this sense, as in Cardinal Newman's *Apologia pro Vita Sua*. No admission of wrongdoing or expression of regret is necessarily involved.

Apophasis A rhetorical figure in which one makes an assertion while seeming or pretending to suppress or deny it. "Were I not aware of your high reputation for honesty, I should say that I believe you connived at the fraud yourself."

Apophrades In the ancient Greek calendar, unlucky or unclean days that fell toward the end of a month; the last two days of the Flower Festival in the month of Anthesterion were thought to be a gloomy and forbidden time when the dead visited their old houses. Recently the term has been appropriated in Harold Bloom's criticism as the name of a "revisionary ratio" in which a dead precursor returns.

[Reference: Harold Bloom, *A Map of Misreading* (1975).]

Aporia A difficulty, impasse, or point of doubt and indecision. The unjust steward's meditation in Luke 16:3 is an example: "What shall I do? for my lord taketh away from me the stewardship: I cannot dig; to beg I am ashamed." Used to describe a species of irony in which a speaker expresses uncertainty but really intends none, as in this sentence: "I don't know what scares me more—your stupidity or your dishonesty." *Aporia* has also been used by recent critics to indicate a point of undecidability, which locates the site at which the text most obviously undermines its own rhetorical structure, dismantles, or deconstructs itself.

Aposiopesis The intentional failure to complete a sentence. The form may be used to convey extreme exasperation or to imply a threat, as, "If you do that, why, I'll——." Instances are graphically furnished by a fragmentary passage near the end of Eliot's "The Hollow Men":

> For Thine is
> Life is
> For Thine is the

and in the climactic 28th stanza of Hopkins's "The Wreck of the Deutschland":

> But how shall I . . . make me room there:
> Reach me a . . . Fancy, come faster—
> Strike you the sight of it? look at it loom there.
> Thing that she . . . there then!

A Posteriori A Latin phrase ("from what comes later") for INDUCTIVE reasoning, which proceeds from the specific to the general.

Apostrophe A FIGURE OF SPEECH in which someone (usually but not always absent), some abstract quality, or a nonexistent personage is directly addressed as though present. Characteristic instances of *apostrophe* are found in invocations:

> And chiefly, Thou, O Spirit, that dost prefer
> Before all temples the upright heart and pure,
> Instruct me, for Thou know'st.

Or an address to God, as in Emily Dickinson's:

> Papa Above!
> Regard a Mouse.

Early in Shakespeare's *Julius Caesar*, Cassius, who is actually talking to Brutus, exclaims, "Age, thou art sham'd! / Rome, thou hast lost the breed of noble bloods!" The device is frequently used in patriotic oratory, the speaker addressing some glorious leader of the past and invoking his or her aid in the present, as in Wordsworth's lines:

> Milton! thou should be living at this hour:
> England hath need of thee. . . .

Because it is chiefly associated with deep emotional expression, *apostrophe* form is readily adopted by humorists for purposes of PARODY and SATIRE.

Apothegm An unusually terse, pithy, witty saying, even more concise and pointed than an APHORISM. One of the best known, attributed by Francis Bacon to Queen Elizabeth I, is "Hope is a good breakfast, but it is a bad supper."

Apotropaic "Warding off evil." In some cases, an unattractive *apotropaic* name (such as *Strabo*, "squinter") may be given to a child, so as to avoid the wrath of the gods. Or a word may undergo *apotropaic* deformation to avoid a taboo or delicate subject, as when "cancer" is reduced to its initial letter.

Apparatus (also ***apparatus criticus*, critical apparatus**) The means by which a document is presented for textual study. With a critical edition of a poem, say, an editor will choose one version to serve as the definitive text; the *apparatus* will then provide alternative readings with their sources, along with other information related to the text.

Apposition The placing in immediately succeeding order of two or more coordinate elements, one of which is an explanation, qualification, or modification of the first. Customarily but not always, the element in *apposition* comes second. Compare "My uncle, a man of honor, took no advantage of his opponent's mistake" and "A man of honor, my uncle took no advantage of his opponent's mistake." Walt Whitman's long catalogs, as in section 33 of "Song of Myself," represent extended *apposition*.

Apprenticeship Novel A NOVEL that recounts the youth and young adulthood of a sensitive protagonist who is attempting to learn the nature of the world, discover its meaning and pattern, and acquire a philosophy of life and "the art of living." Goethe's Wilhelm Meister is the archetypal apprenticeship novel; noted examples in English are Samuel Butler's *The Way of All Flesh*, James Joyce's *A Portrait of the Artist as a Young Man*, Somerset Maugham's *Of Human Bondage*, and Thomas Wolfe's *Look Homeward, Angel*. The apprenticeship novel is now usually called a BILDUNGSROMAN. It is also sometimes called an ENTWICKLUNGSROMAN, or "novel of development," or an *ERZIEHUNGSROMAN*, or "novel of education." When an apprenticeship novel deals with the development of an artist or writer, it is called a KÜNSTLERROMAN.

A Priori A Latin phrase ("from what comes before") for DEDUCTIVE reasoning, which proceeds from the general to the specific. In literary criticism, *a priori* is usually pejorative, implying arbitrary judgments based on preconceived postulates. See AXIOM.

Apron Stage The *apron* is the portion of a stage that extends in front of the PROSCENIUM arch. If all or most of the stage is in front of any devices that could give it a frame, the stage is called an *apron stage*. The Elizabethan stage, which was a raised platform with the audience on three sides, is the outstanding example.

Ara A lengthy and formal CURSE, IMPRECATION, ANATHEMA, or MALEDICTION. Psalm 109 is a classic example.

Arabesque A style of decorative design favored by the Moors as a means of giving play to their aesthetic creativity without violating the Islamic prohibition against reproducing natural forms. It employs intricate patterns of interlaced lines from stylized flowers, foliage, fruits, and animal outlines in geometrical or calligraphic designs. The term was used in German ROMANTIC CRITICISM and FICTION to describe a fictional creation that, as defined by Sir Walter Scott in his essay "On the Supernatural in Fictional Composition" (1827), "resembles the arabesque in painting, in which is introduced the most strange and complicated monsters . . . and . . . other creatures of the romantic imagination." Edgar Allan Poe probably got the term from Scott's essay, where it is used as a rough synonym for GROTESQUE. Poe applied the term to his stories in which the material was selected for its strangeness and its appeal to the sense of wonder. He distinguished between the grotesque, which had an element of horror, and the *arabesque*, which had an element of wonder, in his *Tales of the Grotesque and Arabesque* (1840). Something of the arabesque persists in James Joyce's story "Araby."

Arcadian Arcadia, a picturesque plateau region in Greece, the reputed home of PASTORAL poetry, was portrayed by pastoral poets as an ideal land of rural peace and contentment. *Arcadian* thus suggests rural withdrawal and simple happiness and is applied to any person or place that possesses idealized rural simplicity such as that exhibited by the shepherds in conventional pastoral poetry. It is synonymous with bucolic or pastoral. Sir Phillip Sydney, following Italian precedent, uses *Arcadia* as the title of his famous pastoral romance. See ECLOGUE, PASTORAL, IDYLL.

Archaism Obsolete phrasing, idiom, syntax, or spelling. Used intentionally, an archaic style can be useful in recreating the atmosphere of the past, as in Spenser's *The Faerie Queene* and Keats's "The Eve of St. Agnes."

Archetype A term brought into literary criticism from the psychology of Carl Jung, who holds that behind each individual's "unconscious"—the blocked-off residue of the past—lies the "collective unconscious" of the human race—the blocked-off memory of our racial past, even of our prehuman experiences. This unconscious racial memory makes powerfully effective for us a group of "primordial images" shaped by the repeated experience of our ancestors and expressed in myths, religion, dreams, fantasies, and literature. T. S. Eliot says, "The pre-logical mentality persists in civilized man, but becomes available only to or through the poet." The "primordial image" that taps this "prelogical mentality" is called the *archetype*.

The literary critic applies the term to an image, a descriptive detail, a plot pattern, or a character type that occurs frequently in literature, myth, religion, or folklore and is, therefore, believed to evoke profound emotions because it touches the unconscious memory and thus calls into play illogical but strong responses. The archetypal critic studies a work in terms of the images or patterns it has in common with other poems, plays, or novels, and thus by extension as a portion of the total human experience. In this sense the *archetype* is, as Northrop Frye defines it, "a symbol, usually an image, which recurs often enough in literature to be recognizable as an element of one's literary experience as a whole."

[References: Maud Bodkin, *Archetypal Patterns in Poetry; Psychological Studies of Imagination* (1934, 1958); Bettina Knapp, *A Jungian Approach to Literature* (1984).]

Architectonics A critical term that expresses collectively those structural qualities of proportion, unity, emphasis, and scale that make a piece of writing proceed logically and smoothly from beginning to end with no wasted effort, no faulty omissions. The requirements of *architectonics*, a term borrowed from architecture, are felt to have been fulfilled when a piece of literature impresses a reader in the same way as a building, carefully planned and constructed, impresses a spectator. Currently the term is used to describe the successful achieving of organic unity, of "the companionship of the whole," in which the parts are not only perfectly articulated but combined into an integrated whole, so that the work has meaning not through its parts but through its totality.

Archive The repository for historical documents or public records; also the documents and records stored there. Since the eighteenth century, *archive* has been used metaphorically as the title for academic, historical, and scientific PERIODICALS.

Arena Stage A stage on which the actors, surrounded by the audience, make exits and entrances through the aisles. Sometimes, especially in England, the stage is against a wall, with the audience on three sides. The *arena stage* is often called theater in the round. It differs from the traditional APRON STAGE, which extends in front of any framing devices.

Areopagus The "hill of Ares," the seat of the highest judicial court in ancient Athens. By association the name has come to represent any court of final authority. In this sense Milton used the term in his *Areopagitica*, addressed to the British parliament on the question of censorship and the licensing of books.

The "Areopagus" is the name of what some literary historians believe was a literary club in London shortly before 1580, supposedly analogous with the *Pléiade* group in France. Whether there was a formal club or not is doubtful, but certain writers, including Gabriel Harvey, Sir Philip Sidney, Edmund Spenser, and Sir Edward Dyer, engaged in a "movement" to reform English versification on the principles of classical prosody. In their best work, however, Sidney and Spencer abandoned these experiments in classical measures in favor of Italian, French, and native English forms.

Argument A statement summarizing the plot or stating the meaning of a long poem or occasionally of a play. The most familiar English examples are Milton's *Arguments* to each of the books of *Paradise Lost*. One of Herrick's best-known poems is "The Argument of His Book":

> I sing of brooks, of blossoms, birds and bowers,
> Of April, May, of June and Jùly-flowers. . . .

The term is sometimes used by the NEW CRITICS to describe the thesis of a poem. In grammar, *argument* is sometimes used to indicate any of the noun phrases and prepositional phrases in a simple sentence.

Argumentation One of the four chief "forms of discourse," the others being EXPOSITION, NARRATION, and DESCRIPTION. Its purpose is to convince by establishing the truth or falsity of a proposition.

Arianism A Christian heresy expounded by Arius, a priest in Alexandria, in the fourth century. Arius believed that God is ultimately single, unknowable, and alone; that Christ was created by God and is not, therefore, equal to him; and that in the incarnation Christ assumed a body but not a human soul and was, therefore, neither fully human nor divine. *Arianism* was condemned by the First Council of Nicaea (325), but in the confusion of beliefs and allegiances that followed, the Arians for a time triumphed. By 379, however, *Arianism* was outlawed in the Roman Empire. *Arianism* has remained a doctrinal interpretation that has from time to time proved attractive. Milton is accused of tending toward it in his interpretation of the relationship of God and Christ in *Paradise Lost*, although he has also been vigorously—and usually effectively—defended against the charge.

Aristophanic An ancient Greek measure, usually consisting of three quantitative feet: DACTYL, TROCHEE, trochee (or SPONDEE). The measure, considered a variant of the PHERECRATIC—spondee, dactyl, spondee (or trochee)—is mentioned in Sidney's *Arcadia*.

Aristotelian Criticism Literally, criticism by Aristotle, as in the *Poetics*, or criticism that follows the methods used by Aristotle in the *Poetics*, although the exact nature of the Aristotelian method has been a subject of much debate (see CRITICISM). The term *Aristotelian criticism* is sometimes used in contrast to the term Platonic criticism, particularly by NEW CRITICS. In this sense, the term implies a judicial, logical, formal criticism that is centered in the work rather than in its historical, moral, or religious context and that finds its values either within the work itself or inseparably linked to the work; the term is roughly synonymous with intrinsic. Aristotle's chief contribution is a closely reasoned argument in favor of a complex relation—cause and effect, means and end, form and matter—among six qualitative parts or elements of the literary art, particularly as they figure in tragic DRAMA: PLOT (mythos), CHARACTER (ethos), thought and feeling (dianoia), DICTION (lexis), sound (melos), and SPECTACLE (opsis). In an artful arrangement, these elements combine to arouse and release certain emotions, which are said to be "purged" by the experience of poetry. Among Aristotle's other contributions are such terms and concepts as the tragic flaw (HAMARTIA) and purgation (CATHARSIS). See CRITICISM, TYPES OF; PLATONIC CRITICISM; AUTOTELIC; THE CHICAGO CRITICS.

[References: R. S. Crane, *Critics and Criticism* (1952, 1957); Leon Golden, tr., *Aristotle's Poetics*, with commentary by O. B. Hardison, Jr. (1968); Elder Olson, ed., *Aristotle's Poetics and English Literature* (1965).]

Arminianism An anti-Calvinistic theology, founded by Jacobus Arminius in Holland in the early seventeenth century. It opposes the Calvinistic doctrines of election, reprobation, and absolute predestination, asserting that the human will can forfeit divine grace after receiving it and denying that predestination is absolute. It was a strong element in the theological arguments in England and America in the seventeenth and eighteenth centuries. In America Jonathan Edwards was its most powerful attacker. See CALVINISM.

Arsis In METRICS the term is applied today to a stressed syllable. In Greek usage, however, arsis was the name of the unstressed syllable. See ACCENT, THESIS.

Art In general newspaper usage, a photograph. Sometimes in printing, material that is represented by something other than type, such as decorated initial capitals.

Art Ballad A term used to distinguish the literary BALLAD of known authorship from the early BALLADS of unknown authorship. Some successful *art ballads* are "La Belle Dame sans Merci" by Keats, "Rosabelle" by Scott, "Sister Helen" by Dante Gabriel

Rossetti, and "The Ballad of the Despairing Husband" by Robert Creeley. Possibly the most famous poem imitating the ballad manner is "The Rime of the Ancient Mariner" by Coleridge.

Art Brut Another name for OUTSIDER ART. Supposedly, the term *Art Brut* (meaning art that is not necessarily brute or brutal but uncultivated, raw, unadulterated) was coined by Jean Dubuffet with specific reference to visual art.

Art Epic A term employed to distinguish such an EPIC as Milton's *Paradise Lost* or Virgil's *Aeneid* from so-called FOLK EPICS such as *Beowulf*, the *Nibelungenlied*, and the *Iliad* and *Odyssey*. The *art epic* is supposed to be more sophisticated and more consciously moral in purpose than the folk epic. The author takes greater liberties with popular materials and expects less credulity. The events narrated are typically in a more remote past.

"Art for Art's Sake" The doctrine, corresponding to the French *"l'art pour l'art,"* that art is its own excuse for being, that its values are aesthetic and not moral, political, or social. See AESTHETICS, AESTHETICISM.

Arthurian Legend Probably the LEGEND of Arthur grew out of the deeds of some historical person. He was probably not a king, and it is doubtful that his name was Arthur. He was presumably a Welsh or Roman military leader of the Celts in Wales against the Germanic invaders who overran Britain in the fifth century. The deeds of this Welsh hero gradually grew into a vast body of romantic story that provided a glorious past for the Britons to look back on. When Arthur developed into an important king, he yielded his position as a personal hero to a group of great knights who surrounded him. These knights of the Round Table came to represent all that was best in the age of chivalry, and the stories of their deeds make up the most popular group ("Matter of Britain") of the great CYCLES of MEDIEVAL ROMANCE.

There is no mention of Arthur in contemporary accounts of the Germanic invasion, but a Roman citizen named Gildas who lived in Wales mentions in his *De Excidio et Conquestu Britanniae* (written between 500 and 550) the Battle of Mt. Badon, with which later accounts connect Arthur and a valiant Roman leader of a Welsh rally, named Ambrosius Aurelianus. About 800, Nennius, a Welsh chronicler, in his *Historia Britonum* uses the name Arthur in referring to a leader against the Saxons. About a century later an addition to Nennius's history called *Mirabilia* gives further evidences of Arthur's development as a hero, including an allusion to a boar hunt of Arthur's that is detailed in the later Welsh story of Culhwch and Olwen (in the *Mabinogion*). There are other references to Arthur in the annals of the tenth and eleventh centuries, and William of Malmesbury's *Gesta Regum Anglorum* (1125) treats Arthur as a historical figure and identifies him with the Arthur whom the Welsh "rave wildly about" in their "idle tales." A typical British Celt at this time believed that Arthur was not really dead but would return.

About 1135 Geoffrey of Monmouth's *Historia Regum Britanniae*, professedly based on an old Welsh book, added a wealth of matter to the Arthurian legend—how much of it Geoffrey invented cannot now be determined—such as the stories of Arthur's supernatural birth, his weird "passing" to Avalon to be healed of his wounds, and the abduction of Guinevere by Modred. Geoffrey probably was attempting to create for the Norman kings in England a glorious historical background. He traced the history (and even the name) of the Britons from Brut, a descendant of Aeneas, to Arthur. Soon after

Geoffrey, additions to the story were made by the French poet Wace in his *Roman de Brut*, and a little later appear the famous romances of Chrétien de Troyes, in Old French, in which Arthurian themes are given their first highly literary treatment. About 1205 the English poet Layamon added some details in his *Brut*.

The popularity of Arthurian tradition reached its climax in medieval English literature in Malory's *Le Morte Darthur* (printed 1485), a book destined to transmit Arthurian stories to many later English writers, notably Tennyson. Spenser used an Arthurian background for *The Faerie Queene* (1590), and Milton contemplated a national epic on Arthur. Interest in Arthur decreased in the eighteenth century, but Arthurian topics were particularly popular in the nineteenth century, the best-known treatment appearing in Tennyson's *Idylls of the King*. Tennyson's version and E. A. Robinson's *Merlin*, *Lancelot*, and *Tristram* show how different generations have modified the Arthurian stories to suit contemporary modes of thought and individual artistic ends. Arthurian themes received powerful and sympathetic musical treatment in an opera by Dryden with music by Purcell, *King Arthur*, and in some of Richard Wagner's music dramas. The burlesquing treatment of chivalry in Mark Twain's *A Connecticut Yankee in King Arthur's Court* is in contrast to the usual romantic idealization, as is T. H. White's TETRALOGY of novels published under the collective title *The Once and Future King*, which attests to the continuing strength of the *Arthurian legend* and was the basis of an enormously popular musical drama, *Camelot*. See MEDIEVAL ROMANCE, CHRONICLE.

[References: E. K. Chambers, *Arthur of Britain* (1927); Roger Sherman Loomis, ed., *Arthurian Literature in the Middle Ages: A Collaborative History* (1959); Beverly Taylor and Elisabeth Brewer, *The Return of King Arthur: British and American Arthurian Literature since 1900* (1983); Eugène Vinaver, ed., *The Works of Sir Thomas Malory*, 3rd ed. (1954, rev. by P. Field 1990; orig. 1947).]

Article A prose nonfiction composition, usually comparatively brief, that deals with a single topic. Longer than a NOTE but shorter than a MONOGRAPH, an article is customarily a direct, expository, or descriptive factual statement. It usually appears in newspapers, magazines, journals, encyclopedias, handbooks, and textbooks. See ESSAY.

Artificial Comedy A term sometimes used (as by Charles Lamb) for COMEDY reflecting an artificial society, such as the COMEDY OF MANNERS.

Artificiality A term used to characterize a work that is consciously and deliberately mannered, affected, elaborate, conventional, studied, or self-conscious. There is little question that Lyly's style in *Euphues* is artificial and that Burns's is not; about such writers as Donne, Hemingway, and Durrell, however, debate can and does continue.

Asclepiad An ancient Greek measure, normally the following quantitative series: SPONDEE, two or three CHORIAMBS, and an IAMB; mentioned in Sidney's *Arcadia*.

Aside A dramatic convention by which an actor directly addresses the audience but is not supposed to be heard by the other actors on the stage. In RENAISSANCE DRAMA the device was widely used to allow inner feelings to be made known to the audience, as witnessed by the fact that Hamlet's very first line is an *aside*. In the nineteenth century the convention was used for melodramatic and comic effect. Eugene O'Neill's *Strange Interlude* (1928) was an application of the *aside* to the modern theater. By a custom of the theater, an *aside* is assumed to be truthful. See SOLILOQUY.

Assonance Generally, patterning of vowel sounds without regard to consonants. The patterning may be SUCCESSIVE (as in Eliot's "kn*ee*-d*ee*p in the s*a*lt-m*a*rsh"), ALTERNATING (as in Housman's "l*e*ft m*y* n*e*ckt*ie*" or "th*a*t y*ou*ng s*i*nner with the h*a*ndc*u*ffs on h*i*s wr*i*sts"), or CHIASTIC (as in James Joyce's "R*a*in has f*a*llen *a*ll the d*ay*"). *Assonance* sometimes refers to same or similar vowel sounds in stressed syllables that end with different consonant sounds. *Assonance* differs from RHYME in that rhyme typically involves vowel and consonant sounds. "Lake" and "fake" demonstrate full rhyme; "lake" and "fate" *assonance*.

As an enriching ornament within the line, *assonance* is of great use to the poet. Poe and Swinburne used it extensively for musical effect. Gerard Manley Hopkins introduced modern poets to its wide use. The *abab* QUATRAINS of Joyce's "I Hear an Army" use perfect rhyme in the *a*-positions but only *assonance* in the *b*-positions: "knees" and "charioteers," "laughter" and "anvil," and "shore" and "alone"—possibly echoing an Old Irish device. The skill with which Dylan Thomas manipulates *assonance* remains one of his high achievements. Note its complex employment in the first stanza of his "Ballad of the Long-Legged Bait":

The bows glided down, and the coast
Blackened with birds took a last look
At his thrashing hair and whale-blue eye;
The trodden town rang its cobbles for luck.

Assonance is involved in "bows" (pronounced "boughs") and "down"; "blackened," "last," "thrashing," "hair," and "rang"; "took" and "look"; and "trodden" and "cobbles." Note the pattern of ALLITERATION in this stanza and that the rhyming of "look" with "luck" is an example of CONSONANCE RHYME. The definition of *assonance* is an important element in Willy Russell's play *Educating Rita* (1980, made into a movie in 1983). See RHYME.

Assonance Rhyme ASSONANCE is a common substitution for END RHYME in the POPULAR BALLAD, as in these lines from "The Twa Corbies":

—In behint yon auld fail dyke.
I wot there lies a new-slain Knight.

NURSERY RHYMES rely on such rhymes as "top / rock," "dame / lane," and "alone / home," in which the vowel components of the matched syllables are the same but the succeeding consonants are not. Such substitution of assonance for END RHYME is found more frequently in modern poetry than in that of earlier times, but, even so, it has never been a common device. Examples are Yeats's *assonance rhyme* of "love" and "enough" and Pound's of "produced" and "abused."

Asteism Urbane humor, marked by subtle IRONY and polite mockery.

"As-Told-To" Material Writing presented as the work—usually AUTOBIOGRAPHICAL—of a celebrated person, with the understanding that all or much of the actual composition was done by another acting in the role of professional writer or editor.

Asynartete "Not connected": said of a verse measure in which rhythmic members consist of two unrelated patterns, as in CHORIAMBIC verse, which combines TROCHEES and IAMBS.

Asyndeton A condensed form of expression in which elements customarily joined by conjunctions are presented in series without the conjunctions. The most famous example is probably Caesar's "*Veni, vidi, vici*" (I came, I saw, I conquered). Almost equally well known to Americans is Lincoln's ". . . government of the people, by the people, for the people. . . ." Normally, as in both these examples, the omitted conjunction is of the coordinating sort. *Asyndeton* affects subordinating conjunctions in such cases as the substitution of "a man I know" for "a man whom I know."

Atmosphere The prevailing TONE or MOOD of a literary work, particularly—but not exclusively—when that mood is established in part by setting or landscape. It is, however, not simply setting but rather an emotional aura that helps to establish the reader's expectations and attitudes. Examples are the somber mood established by the description of the prison door in the opening chapter of Hawthorne's *The Scarlet Letter*, the brooding sense of fatality engendered by the description of Egdon Heath at the beginning of Hardy's *The Return of the Native*, the sense of "something rotten in the state of Denmark" established by the scene on the battlements at the opening of *Hamlet*, or the opening stanza of Poe's "The Raven."

Attemperation A rhetorical term, revived by Frank Kermode, designating a restriction or softening of something said earlier, as in a passage in the second movement of T. S. Eliot's "East Coker":

> That was a way of putting it—not very satisfactory:
> A periphrastic study in a worn-out poetical fashion,
> Leaving one still with the intolerable wrestle
> With words and meanings. The poetry does not matter.

Attic Writing characterized by a clear, simple, polished, and witty STYLE. Attica, today a province of Greece, was formerly one of the ancient Greek states, with Athens as its capital. Attica rose to such fame for its culture and art that it survives in the adjective *Attic*, which denotes grace and culture and the CLASSIC in art. Joseph Addison, a favorite example of an English author who may be said to have written *Attic* prose, is portrayed as "Atticus" in Pope's "Epistle to Dr. Arbuthnot."

Attic Salt Salt in this sense means "wit." *Attic salt* is writing distinguished by its classic refinement, its intellectual sharpness, and its elegant but stinging wit.

Aubade A LYRIC about dawn or a morning SERENADE, a song of lovers parting at dawn. Originally a French form, it differs from the lamenting Provençal ALBA in usually being joyous. Shakespeare's "Hark! Hark! the Lark!" and Davenant's "The Lark Now Leaves His Watery Nest" are good examples. Such modern instances as John Crowe Ransom's "Parting at Dawn," Marilyn Hacker's "Almost Aubade" and poems called "Aubade" by Dame Edith Sitwell and Philip Larkin show a tinge of IRONY or CYNICISM.

Aube The French word for either ALBA or AUBADE.

Audience Literally, one or more persons who hear something. Specifically, those who experience an artwork through any medium, whether hearing or seeing or some combination. In most uses, an *audience* is gathered deliberately—sometimes even in an auditorium—to experience a work.

Audition A test in which a performer seeking employment appears before judges who may become employers or colleagues.

Augustan Specifically refers to the age of the Emperor Augustus of Rome (ruled 27 B.C. to A.D. 14). But, because the time of Augustus was notable for the perfection of letters and learning, the term has, by analogy, been applied to other epochs in world history when literary culture was high. As Virgil and Horace made the *Augustan* Age of Rome, so Addison and Steele, Swift, and Pope are said to have made the *Augustan* Age of English letters. In a narrow sense the term "English *Augustan* Age" applies only to the reign of Queen Anne (1702–1714); in a broader sense it is sometimes given the dates of Pope—1688–1744. The writers of the age were self-consciously "*Augustan*," aware of the parallels of their writing to Latin literature, given to comparing London to Rome and, in the case of Pope, addressing George II satirically as "Augustus." See NEOCLASSIC PERIOD and the *Outline of Literary History*, in which the period 1700–1750 is designated the "AUGUSTAN AGE."

[References: J. E. Butt, *The Augustan Age*, 2nd ed. (1962); Ian P. Watt, *The Augustan Age: Approaches to Its Literature, Life, and Thought* (1968).]

Augustinianism The doctrines of St. Augustine of Hippo (354–430), author of *Confessions*, the first extended, honest self-analysis, and of the monumental *De Civitate Dei* (The City of God), as well as a vast amount of other writing. He strongly defended the orthodox view of God and human beings against the heresies of Pelagius, who held that there is no original sin, that the human will is absolutely free, and that the grace of God is universal but not indispensable. In opposing PELAGIANISM, St. Augustine exalted the glory of God, stressed original sin, and asserted the necessity of divine grace.

Auteur Theory A term, drawn from the French *politique des auteurs*, used in FILM CRITICISM, where it is applied to a critical method by which a film is viewed as the product of its "*auteur*" or director and is judged by the quality of its expression of the director's personality or worldview. One of the principal film theories, *auteur theory* is more likely to relate a film to others by the same director than it is to consider the particular film as an example of its GENRE or as a reflection of its capacity to record and reveal reality.

Author Earlier, around 1700, *author* was synonymous with editor (as in "editor of a journal"); later it was synonymous with writer. After 1950, conventional assumptions about the definition of *author* have been called into question by Walter Benjamin ("The Author as Producer"), Roland Barthes ("Death of the Author"), and Michel Foucault ("What Is an Author?"). Foucault emphasized that the modern idea of the *author* as creator of the TEXT, which can be explained by investigation of the *author's* life and thought, is a modern invention, maybe even a ROMANTIC invention. To speak of the *author* as a function is to insist that it is not a relation or role that is simply given but is historically and discursively constructed. To question the primacy of the *author* is to suggest (1) that the meaning of a work depends not on its relation to other texts but on its relation to the codes and discursive practices of a culture, and (2) that the reader plays a role in creating meaning.

[References: Walter Benjamin, *Understanding Brecht* (trans. by A. Bostock 1973); Josué V. Harari, ed., *Textual Strategies: Perspectives in Post-Structuralist Criticism* (1979).]

Autobiography The story of a person's life as written by that person. Although a common loose use of the term includes MEMOIRS, DIARIES, JOURNALS, and LETTERS, distinctions among these forms need to be made. Diaries, journals, and letters are not extended, organized narratives prepared for the public eye; autobiographies and memoirs are. But, whereas memoirs deal at least in part with public events and noted personages other than the author, an *autobiography* is a connected narrative of the author's life, with some stress on introspection. Notable great *autobiographies*—and works that tend to clarify the distinction made above—are St. Augustine's *Confessions*, Benvenuto Cellini's *Autobiography*, Franklin's *Autobiography*, and Adams's *The Education of Henry Adams*. Simulated *autobiography* is a device often used in the novel, as in Defoe's *Moll Flanders*, and novels can on occasion be *autobiography* in the guise of fiction, as in those of Thomas Wolfe and in James Joyce's *A Portrait of the Artist as a Young Man*. See BIOGRAPHY.

[References: James Olney, *Metaphors of Self; The Meaning of Autobiography* (1972); ed., *Autobiography: Essays Theoretical and Critical* (1980); *Memory and Narrative: The Weave of Life-Writing* (1998).]

Autotelic A term applied to a nondidactic work; that is, one whose end lies within itself and is not dependent on the achievement of objectives outside the work. See BELIEF, PROBLEM OF.

Auxesis Rhetorical augmentation, either a piling on of detail in no particular order or a climactic arrangement advancing from small to great. John of Gaunt's familiar speech in Shakespeare's *Richard II* (2, 1) is an example of both *auxesis* and ANAPHORA: This royal throne of kings, this scept'red isle,

> This earth of majesty, this seat of Mars,
> This other Eden, demi-paradise,
> This fortress built by Nature for herself
> Against infection and the hand of war,
> This happy breed of men, this little world,
> This precious stone set in the silver sea,
> Which serves it in the office of a wall,
> Or as a moat defensive to a house,
> Against the envy of less happier lands;
> This blessed plot, this earth, this realm, this England. . . .

Avant-Garde A military metaphor drawn from the French "vanguard" and applied to new writing that shows striking (and usually self-conscious) innovations in style, form, and subject matter. The military origin of the term is appropriate, for in every age the *avant-garde* (by whatever name it is known) makes a frontal and often an organized attack on the established forms and literary traditions of its time. A wag remarked, "Everything changes but the *avant-garde*." See ANTINOVEL, ANTIREALISTIC NOVEL, SURREALISM.

Awakening, The Great A phrase applied to a great revival of emotional religion in America, the movement being at its height about 1740–1745 under the leadership of Jonathan Edwards. It arose as an effort to reform religion and morals. Religion, under the "Puritan hierarchy" led by the Mathers, had become rather formal and cold, and the clergy somewhat arrogant. The revival meetings began as early as 1720 in New Jersey. In 1740–42 Edwards conducted a long "revival" at Northampton, Massachusetts, preached in other cities, and published many SERMONS, including "Sinners in the Hands of an Angry God." The conservatives, or "Old Lights," representing the stricter Calvinists, led by the faculties of Harvard and Yale, protested against the excesses of the movement; they were answered by Edwards in his *Treatise on the Religious Affections* (1746). Yet Edwards himself opposed the more extreme exhibitions of emotionalism, and by 1750 a reaction against the movement was underway. See CALVINISM, DEISM, PURITANISM.

Axiom A MAXIM or APHORISM whose truth is held to be self-evident. In logic an *axiom* is a premise accepted as true without the need of demonstration and is used in building an argument. See MAXIM.

B

Scotch Roman 1839. This typeface was probably based on one designed by Richard Austin, c. 1810. Probably ordered from Miller and Richard, Edinburgh, Scotland, and cast by Samuel Nelson Dickinson in the United States.

Bacchius (or **Bacchic**) A three-syllable FOOT usually defined quantitatively as a short followed by two longs or qualitatively as a weak followed by two strongs. Applicable mostly to writing in classical antiquity and to Latin more than to Greek, the Bacchius has not been transferred to verse in English; nor has the reverse, called ANTIBACCHIUS or PALIMBACCHIUS. George Saintsbury (*Historical Manual of English Prosody*) accidentally reversed the usual definitions of "bacchius" and "antibacchius," but neither term matters enough for anyone to have noticed or minded.

Background A term borrowed from painting, where it signifies those parts of the painting against which the principal objects are portrayed. In literature the term is rather loosely used to specify either the SETTING of a piece of writing or the tradition and point of view from which an author presents his or her ideas. Thus, one might speak either (1) of the Russian *background* (setting) of *Anna Karenina* or (2) of the *background* of education, philosophy, and convictions from which Tolstoy wrote the novel.

Baconian Theory This theory—that the plays of William Shakespeare were written by Francis Bacon—grew out of an eighteenth-century English suggestion that Shakespeare, an unschooled countryman, could not have written the plays attributed to him. In the nineteenth century the idea that the plays were by Bacon developed in England and America, with the American Delia Bacon being a particularly influential advocate of *Baconian* authorship. Persons other than Bacon have been suggested as authors of the plays, among them the Earl of Oxford, Sir Walter Ralegh, and Christopher Marlowe (who, according to this theory, was not murdered in 1593). The evidence for any of these theories is fragmentary and inconclusive at best and, at its worst, absurd; and our steadily growing scholarly knowledge of Shakespeare and his world increasingly discredits these theories without silencing their advocates.

Bad Quartos A. W. Pollard's term for certain notably corrupt, garbled, and nearly incoherent early EDITIONS of Shakespeare's plays, in particular the first quartos of *Romeo and Juliet*, *King Henry the Fifth*, *Hamlet*, and *The Merry Wives of Windsor*. There has been a good deal of conjecture as to the source of these *Bad Quartos*, and some scholars have suggested the inclusion of other texts (for example, the "pied bull" 608 edition of *King Lear*) in the category.

[References: Oscar James Campbell, ed., *The Reader's Encyclopedia of Shakespeare* (1966); A. W. Pollard, *Shakespeare Folios and Quartos* (1909).]

Bagatelle In general, a trifle; in art, a work explicitly identified or labeled as a trifle (although some, such as Beethoven's musical *bagatelles*, are hardly trivial).

Balance *Balance* characterizes a structure in which parts of the whole—as words, phrases, or clauses in a sentence—are set off against each other so as to emphasize a contrast. Macaulay's sentence, "The memory of other authors is kept alive by their works; but the memory of Johnson keeps many of his works alive," is an example. *Balance* applies also to the placement of a pause or CAESURA in the syllabic middle of a line of verse. In lines with an even number of feet and of syllables, a balancing caesura has the effect of stability, as in Marvell's "We would sit down, and think which way. . ." and Hardy's "And consummation comes, and jars two hemispheres." Such a caesura after a stressed syllable is called "masculine" and differs markedly from the effect of *balance* that creates a "feminine" caesura in the middle of a ten-syllable line, with a much less stable result, as in Enobarbus's lines in *Antony and Cleopatra*: "The barge she sat in, like a burnish'd throne, / Burnt on the water. The poop was beaten gold. . . ." *Balance* characterizes nicety of proportion among the various elements of a given piece of writing. A story, for example, wherein setting, characterization, and plot are carefully planned, with no element securing undue emphasis, might be said to have fine *balance*.

Ballad A form of VERSE to be sung or recited and characterized by its presentation of a dramatic or exciting EPISODE in simple NARRATIVE form. Though the *ballad* is a form still much written, the so-called popular *ballad* in most literatures belongs to the early periods before written literature was highly developed. In America the folk of the southern Appalachian mountains have maintained a *ballad* tradition. In Australia the "bush" *ballad* is still vigorous and popular. In the West Indies the CALYPSO singers produce something close to the *ballad* with their impromptu songs. Debate continues as to whether the *ballad* originates with an individual composer or as a group or communal activity.

In early *ballads*, the supernatural is likely to play an important part; physical courage and love are frequent themes; the incidents are usually such as happen to common people (as opposed to the nobility) and often have to do with domestic episodes; slight attention is paid to characterization or description; transitions are abrupt; action is largely developed through dialogue; tragic situations are presented with the utmost simplicity, INCREMENTAL REPETITION is common; a single episode of a highly dramatic nature is presented; and often the *ballad* is brought to a close with some sort of summary STANZA. The greatest impetus to the study of *ballad* literature was given by the publication in 1765 of Bishop Percy's *Reliques of Ancient English Poetry*. The standard modern collection still is *The English and Scottish Popular Ballads* (1882–1898) edited by Francis James Child.

The tradition of composing story-songs about current events and personages has been common for a long time. Hardly an event of national interest escapes being made the subject of a so-called *ballad*. Casey Jones, the railroad engineer; Floyd Collins, the cave explorer; the astronauts—all have been the subjects of *ballads*. Popular songs, particularly those engendered by protest movements, have revived the *ballad* form; for example, "Hang Down Your Head, Tom Dooley," or the *ballads* of Bob Dylan or Joan Baez. Strictly speaking, however, these are not *ballads* in the traditional sense; that form probably belongs to a period in the history of Western civilization that is past. See ART BALLAD, BALLAD STANZA, BROADSIDE BALLAD, FOLK BALLAD.

[References: Bertrand H. Bronson, *The Ballad as Song* (1969); D. C. Fowler, *A Literary History of the Popular Ballad* (1968); G. H. Gerould, *The Ballad of Tradition* (1932, 1957).]

Ballad-Opera A sort of BURLESQUE opera that flourished on the English stage for several years following the appearance of John Gay's *The Beggar's Opera* (1728), still the best-known example. Modeled on Italian OPERA, which is burlesqued, it told its story in SONGS set to old tunes and appropriated various elements from FARCE and COMEDY. See OPERA, COMIC OPERA.

Ballad Stanza The stanza of the popular or FOLK BALLAD. Usually it consists of four lines, rhyming *abcb*, with the first and third lines carrying four accented syllables and the second and fourth carrying three. There is variation in the number of unstressed syllables. The RHYME is sometimes approximate, with ASSONANCE and CONSONANCE frequently appearing. A REFRAIN is common. The last stanza of "Sir Patrick Spens" illustrates both the alternation of TETRAMETER and TRIMETER and the substitution of assonance for rhyme:

Half o'er, half o'er to Aberdour
It's fifty fadom deep.
And there lies guid Sir Patrick Spens
Wi' the Scots lords at his feet.

Ballade One of the most popular of the artificial French verse forms. The *ballade* should not, however, be confused with the BALLAD. The *ballade* form has been rather liberally interpreted. Early usage most frequently demanded three STANZAS and an ENVOY, though the number of lines per stanza and of syllables per line varied. Typical earmarks of the *ballade* have been: (1) the REFRAIN (uniform as to wording) recurring regularly at the end of each stanza and of the envoy; (2) the envoy, a peroration of climactic importance and likely to be addressed to a patron; and (3) the use of only three (or at the most four) RHYMES in the entire poem, occurring at the same position in each stanza and with no rhyme-word repeated except in the refrain. Stanzas of varied length have been used in the *ballade*, but the commonest is eight lines rhyming *ababbcbc*, with *bcbc* for the envoy. A good early example of English *ballade* form is Chaucer's "Balade de bon conseyl." One of the best-known modern *ballades* is Dante Gabriel Rossetti's rendering in English of François Villon's "Ballade of Dead Ladies."

Banality A quality of statements that lack effectiveness and seem tasteless or offensive because they express what has been too often thought by too many in METAPHORS and CLICHÉS so conventional that they lose the ability to communicate. *Banal* is perhaps best defined by citing some of its common synonyms: hackneyed, commonplace, stale, STEREOTYPED, trite. See CLICHÉ.

Banner A newspaper headline that goes across the full width of a page.

Barbarism A mistake in the form of a word, or a word that results from such a mistake. Strictly speaking, a *barbarism* results from the violation of an accepted rule of derivation or inflection, as *hern* for *hers*, *goodest* for *best*, *clomb* for *climbed*. Originally it referred to the mixing of foreign words and phrases in Latin or Greek. See SOLECISM.

Bard In modern use, simply a POET. Historically the term refers to poets who recited verses glorifying the deeds of heroes and leaders to the accompaniment of a musical instrument such as the harp. *Bard* technically refers to the early poets of the Celts, as TROUVÈRE refers to those of Normandy, SKALD to those of Scandinavia, and TROUBADOUR to those of Provence. See WELSH LITERATURE.

Baring the Device A concept introduced by Viktor Šklovskij (see FORMALISM [RUSSIAN]) and investigated by him and others among the Russian Formalists. *Baring the device* is the opposite of VERISIMILITUDE: instead of making beholders forget or ignore the fact that they are encountering an artifact, much art *bares its devices* and admits that it is not transparent but opaque, not life or even like life but a willed simulacrum never able to achieve commensurateness with life itself. Once the devices are bared, the work is free to concern itself with its proper business, which is the probing of its own genesis and nature. Laurence Sterne's *Tristram Shandy*, for example—which Sklovskij called "the most typical novel in world literature"—is chiefly about the difficulty of telling a story at all. Poe's "The Philosophy of Composition," now practically an adjunct of "The Raven," proposes to give away all the poet's secrets; Thornton Wilder's *Our Town* dispenses with most settings, costumes, and properties, and a character called the Stage Manager introduces the action. In all these—novel, poem-plus-essay, play—the result of *baring the device* is, paradoxically, often to make the artifice all the more convincing.

Baroque A term of uncertain origin applied first to the architectural style that succeeded the classic style of the RENAISSANCE and flourished, in varied forms in different parts of Europe, from the late sixteenth century until well into the eighteenth century. The *baroque* is a blending of PICTURESQUE elements (the unexpected, the wild, the fantastic, the eccentric) with the more ordered, formal style of the "high RENAISSANCE." The *baroque* stressed movement, energy, and realistic treatment. Although the *baroque* is bold and startling, its "discords and suspensions" are consciously and logically employed. The change to the *baroque* was a radical effort to adapt the traditional modes and forms of expression to the users of a self-conscious modernism. Its efforts to avoid the effects of repose and tranquillity sometimes led to grotesqueness, obscurity, asymmetry, and contortion. The term in its older or popular sense implied the highly fantastic, the whimsical, the bizarre, and the DECADENT. Students of literature may encounter the term (in its older English sense) applied unfavorably to a writer's literary style; or they may read of the *baroque* period or "Age of *Baroque*" (late sixteenth, seventeenth, and early eighteenth centuries); or they may find it applied descriptively and respectfully to certain stylistic features of the *baroque* period. Thus, the broken rhythms of Donne's verse and the verbal subtleties of the English METAPHYSICAL poets have been called *baroque* elements. Richard Crashaw's poetry is said to have expressed the *baroque* spirit. "*Baroque Age*" is often used to designate the period between 1580 and 1680 in the literature of Western Europe, between the decline of the RENAISSANCE and the rise of the ENLIGHTENMENT. See ROCOCO, CONCEIT, METAPHYSICAL POETRY.

[References: Imbrie Buffum, *Studies in the Baroque from Montaigne to Rotrou* (1957); Carl J. Friedrich, *The Age of the Baroque*, 1610–1660 (1952); Lowry Nelson, *Baroque Lyric Poetry* (1961); Murray Roston, *Milton and the Baroque* (1980); Harold B. Segel, *The Baroque Poem: A Comparative Survey* (1974).]

Basic English A simplified English for non-English-speaking peoples, consisting of a vocabulary of 850 words. It was set up by C. K. Ogden, and its strongest advocate in America was I. A. Richards. The New Testament and certain of Plato's works were translated into *Basic English*. At one time, before the Second World War, the movement enjoyed a measure of publicity and popularity, but now the movement seems defunct.

Bathos The effect resulting from the unsuccessful effort to achieve dignity or sublimity of style; an unintentional ANTICLIMAX, dropping from the sublime to the ridiculous. The term gained currency from Pope's use of it in a "Martinus Scriblerus" paper (*Peri Bathous*), which ironically defended the commonplace effects of English POETASTERS on the ground that depth (*bathos*) was a literary virtue of the moderns, as contrasted with the height (*hypsos*) of the ancients. An example of *bathos* given by Pope is:

> Advance the fringed curtains of thy eyes,
> And tell me who comes yonder.

Here the author (Temple) fails because of the (unintentional) ANTICLIMAX resulting from the effort to treat poetically a commonplace idea. (Pope's Scriblerus paper is the earliest recorded use of "anticlimax" in English.)

Battle of the Books, The A quarrel between adherents of classical and of modern writing in the late seventeenth and early eighteenth centuries. See ANCIENTS and MODERNS, QUARREL OF THE.

Battledore (also Battledore-Book) A HORN-BOOK, a printed piece of cardboard for elementary education. It was shaped like a paddle used in badminton or table tennis.

Beast Epic A medieval literary FORM consisting of a series of linked stories grouped around animal characters and often presenting satirical comment on the church or court by means of human qualities attributed to beast characters. The oldest example known seems to be that of Paulus Diaconus, a cleric at the court of Charlemagne, late in the eighth century. In the twelfth and thirteenth centuries the *beast epics* were very popular in northern France, western Germany, and Flanders. The various forms of the *beast epic* have one episode generally treated as the nucleus for the story, such as the healing of the sick lion by the fox's prescription that he wrap himself in the wolf's skin. Some of the other animals common to the form, besides Reynard the Fox, the lion and the wolf, are the cock (Chanticleer), the cat, the hare, the camel, the ant, the bear, the badger, and the stag. The best known of the *beast epics*—and the most influential—is the *Roman de Renart*, a poem of thirty thousand lines comprising twenty-seven sets or "branches" of stories.

Beast Fable A short tale in which the principal actors are animals. See FABLE, BEAST EPIC.

Beat Informally, the idea of RHYTHM in general as well as units of rhythm in particular. *Beat* is customarily thought of in connection with percussive emphasis, but it can be used for any style or pace of rhythm. In a related usage, *beat* is a theatrical term for an informal measure of time, as when a performer is directed not to enter immediately but to "wait two or three *beats*."

Beat Generation A group of American writers of the 1950s and 1960s in rebellion against what they conceived of as the failures of American culture. They expressed their revolt through literary works of loose structure and slang DICTION. To prevailing "establishment" values, they opposed an anti-intellectual freedom, often associated with religious ecstasy, visionary states, or the effect of drugs. The group's ideology included some measure of PRIMITIVISM, orientalism, experimentation, eccentricity, and reliance on inspiration from modern jazz (bebop especially) and from such earlier visionaries as Blake and Whitman. Among the leading members of the loose group were the poets Allen Ginsberg, Gregory Corso, and Lawrence Ferlinghetti, and the novelists Jack Kerouac and William Burroughs.

[Reference: Bruce Cook, *The Beat Generation* (1971).]

Begging the Question A fallacious form of argument in which a conclusion is presented although a premise has not been proved. To say, for example, "Because Senator Goldwater is a right-wing Republican, he can be expected to sympathize with liberal causes" is tantamount to offering this syllogism:

- Major Premise: Right-wing Republicans can be expected to sympathize with liberal causes.
- Minor Premise: Senator Redstate is a right-wing Republican.
- Conclusion: Senator Redstate can be expected to sympathize with liberal causes.

The *question* of whether right-wing Republicans can be expected to sympathize with liberal causes has been *begged*. Also called *PETITIO PRINCIPII*.

Beginning Rhyme RHYME that occurs in the first syllable or syllables of lines. It is so rare that few examples can be found among serious literature, but the beginning of W. S. Merwin's "Noah's Raven" will serve as an illustration:

> Why should I have returned?
> My knowledge would not fit into theirs.
> I found untouched the desert of the unknown. . . .

Belief, Problem of The question of the degree to which the aesthetic value of a literary work is necessarily or properly affected by the acceptability to a reader of its doctrine or philosophic or religious assumptions. Although the question is certainly as old as Plato, it assumed an unusual relevance in the NEW CRITICISM because the traditional answer—that doctrinal acceptability is one of the necessary conditions for aesthetic value—had been brought into serious question. See AUTOTELIC.

Belles-Lettres Literature, more especially that body of writing, comprising DRAMA, POETRY, FICTION, CRITICISM, and ESSAYS, that lives because of inherent imaginative and artistic rather than scientific, philosophical, or intellectual qualities. Lewis Carroll's *Alice in Wonderland*, for example, belongs definitely to the province of *belles-lettres*, whereas the mathematical works of the same man, Charles Lutwidge Dodgson, do not. Now sometimes used to characterize light or artificial writing.

Benthamism The philosophy of Jeremy Bentham. It holds that the ultimate goal of all individuals should be to achieve the greatest happiness for the greatest number. See UTILITARIANISM.

Bergsonism The general ideas and attitudes of Henri Bergson (1859–1941), an influential thinker on such subjects as time, memory, intuition, language, change, evolution, and comedy. One foundation of Bergson's thought is an apprehension of the struggle between the vital and the mechnical. The phrase *élan vital*—life force—comes from one of Bergson's books. Bergson's ideas are important for G. B. Shaw, T. S. Eliot, Marcel Proust, William James, William Faulkner, and many modern French thinkers.

[Reference: Gilles Deleuze, *Bergsonism*, tr. Hugh Tomlinson and Barbara Habberjam (1988); John Mullarkey, *The New Bergson* (1999).]

Bestiary A type of literature, popular during the medieval period, in which the habits of beasts, birds, and reptiles were made the text for allegory. These *bestiaries* often ascribed human attributes to animals and were designed to moralize and to expound church doctrine. The natural history—fabulous rather than scientific—has given popularity to such creatures as the phoenix, siren, and unicorn. Many qualities that literature familiarly attributes to animals come from the *bestiaries*. The development of the type, first attributed to Physiologus, a Greek naturalist of about A.D. 150, was rapidly taken over by Christian preachers throughout Europe. The *bestiary* in one form or another has appeared in various world literatures: Anglo-Saxon, Arabic, Armenian, English, Ethiopian, French, German, Icelandic, Provençal, and Spanish. Kenneth Rexroth's "A Bestiary" is a good modern instance of the form, with its parts arranged according to the alphabet and its lines disposed syllabically, as in the heptasyllabic entry for "Lion":

> The lion is called the king
> Of beasts. Nowadays there are
> Almost as many lions
> In cages as out of them.
> If offered a crown, refuse.

Bibelot An unusually small book, sometimes called a "miniature edition."

Bible From a Greek term meaning "little books," *Bible* is now applied to the collection of writings known as the Holy Scriptures, the sacred writings of the Christian religion. Of the two chief parts, the Old Testament consists of the sacred writings of the ancient Hebrews, and the New Testament of writings of the early Christian period. The Jewish Scriptures include three collections—The Law, The Prophets, and Writings—written in ancient Hebrew at various dates in the pre-Christian era. The New Testament books were written in the Greek DIALECT employed in Mediterranean countries about the time of Christ. An important Greek form of the Hebrew *Bible* is the Septuagint, dating from the Alexandrian period (third century B.C.). Latin versions were made in very early times, of both the Old and New Testament books, including many of the APOCRYPHA.

The most important Latin version, translated by St. Jerome about A.D. 400, is known as the VULGATE. This Latin translation was the *Bible* of the Middle Ages. See next three topics and DEAD SEA SCROLLS.

Bible as Literature The high literary value of many parts of the Judeo-Christian BIBLE has been widely recognized. Many English authors, including Milton, Wordsworth, Scott, and T. S. Eliot, have paid tribute to biblical literature; Coleridge even rated the style of Isaiah and the Epistle to the Hebrews as far superior to that of Homer, Virgil, or Milton. The literary qualities of the BIBLE are accounted for partly by the themes, partly by the character of the Hebrew language, and partly by the literary skill exhibited by biblical writers and translators. The themes are among the greatest that literature can treat: God, humanity, the physical universe, and their interrelations. Such problems as morality, relationship of human beings to the unseen world, and ultimate human destinies are treated with an intensity and vigor seldom matched in world literature. The character of the Hebrew language—abounding in words and phrases of concrete, sensuous appeal and lacking the store of ABSTRACT words characteristic of the Greek—imparted an emotional and imaginative richness to Hebrew writings of a sort that lends itself readily to translation (the idea of pride, for example, is expressed by "puffed up"). The BIBLE is partly in prose and partly in verse, the principles of Hebrew verse being ACCENT and PARALLELISM rather than METER. The literary types found in the BIBLE have been variously classified. A few examples may be given: the SHORT STORY, Ruth, Jonah, Esther; biographical NARRATIVE, the story of Abraham in Genesis; love LYRIC, Song of Solomon; the battle ODE, the SONG of Deborah (Judges 5); EPIGRAM, in Proverbs and elsewhere; devotional LYRIC, PSALMS; dramatic philosophical poem, Job; ELEGY, LAMENT of David for Saul and Jonathan (2 Samuel 1:19-27); LETTERS, the EPISTLES of Paul.

[Reference: Robert Alter and Frank Kermode, eds., *The Literary Guide to the Bible* (1987).]

Bible, English Translations of From Caedmon (seventh century) to Wycliffe (fourteenth century) there were translations and paraphrases in OLD ENGLISH and in MIDDLE ENGLISH of various parts of the BIBLE, all based on the Latin VULGATE. The parts most frequently translated were the Gospels, the Psalms, and the Pentateuch. The Caedmonian poetic paraphrases (seventh century) are extant, but Bede's prose translation of a portion of the Gospel of St. John (seventh century) is not. From the ninth century come GLOSSES of the Book of Psalms and prose translations by King Alfred. The West Saxon Gospels and the GLOSSES in the Lindisfarne Gospels date from the tenth century, and Aelfric's incomplete translations of the Old Testament date from the late tenth and early eleventh centuries. In the fourteenth century there was renewed activity in preparing English versions and commentaries, notably by Richard Rolle of Hampole. In about 1382 came the first edition of the Wycliffe Bible, largely the work of Wycliffe himself. A revision of this work, chiefly the work of John Purvey, 1388, though interdicted by the church from 1408 to 1534, circulated freely in manuscript form for the next 150 years.

Printed English Bibles first appeared in the sixteenth century—products of the new learning of the HUMANISTS and the zeal of the Protestant Reformation—and were mainly based on Greek and Hebrew manuscripts, or recent translations of such manuscripts. Some important English translations are: (1) William Tyndale—the New

Testament (1525–26), the Pentateuch (1530), Jonah (1531). Tyndale is credited with the creation of much of the picturesque phraseology that characterizes later English translations. (2) Miles Coverdale, first complete printed English Bible (1535), based on Tyndale and a Swiss-German translation. (3) "Matthew's" Bible (1537), probably done by John Rogers, based on Tyndale and Coverdale, important as a source for later translations. (4) Taverner's Bible (1539), based on "Matthew's" Bible, but revealing a tendency to greater use of native English words. (5) The Great Bible (1539), sometimes called Cranmer's Bible, because Cranmer sponsored it and wrote a preface for the second edition (1540)—a very large volume designed to be chained to its position in the churches for the use of the public. Coverdale superintended its preparation. It is based largely on "Matthew's" Bible. (6) The Geneva Bible (1560), the joint work of English Protestant exiles in Geneva, including Coverdale and William Whittington, who had published in 1557 in Geneva an English New Testament, which was the first English version divided into CHAPTERS and VERSES. It became the great Bible of the Puritans and ran through sixty editions between 1560 and 1611. (7) Bishops' Bible (1568), prepared by eight bishops and others and issued to combat the Calvinistic, antiepiscopal tendencies of the Geneva Bible. (8) The Rheims-Douai Bible (1582), a Catholic translation based on the VULGATE, issued to counteract the Puritan Geneva Bible and the Episcopal Bishops' Bible. The Old Testament section was not actually printed until 1609. By far the most important and influential of English Bibles is the "Authorized" or King James Version (1611). A revision of the Bishops' Bible, it was sponsored by King James I. The translators, about fifty of the leading Biblical scholars of the time, including Puritans, made use of Greek and Hebrew texts. This version is the most widely read English Bible, and it exerted a profound influence on the literature of the English-speaking peoples through subsequent centuries. The Revised Version (1885) and the standard American edition of the Revised Version (1901), the joint work of English and American scholars, aimed chiefly at scholarly accuracy.

In 1946, a group of American biblical scholars produced an extensive revision of the King James Version of the New Testament, bringing to bear the wealth of modern scholarship, and in 1952 they added the Old Testament. This translation, known as the Revised Standard Version, although generally considered inferior to the King James Version from a literary viewpoint, has been widely accepted because of its accuracy and clarity. A number of renderings into contemporary and idiomatic English have been made in this century of the whole or parts of the Bible. Notable among them are the translations into American idiom by James Moffatt and by Edgar Goodspeed and the translations into British idiom by J. B. Phillips and by Father Ronald Knox. Close PARAPHRASES in the current idiom, often using contemporary slang, such as the *Good News Bible*, are popular today.

The most important recent translation is *The New English Bible*, prepared by a joint committee of the Protestant Churches of the British Isles, who were joined by observers representing the Roman Catholic Church. This version is a totally new translation, utilizing all known manuscripts, including recent discoveries such as the DEAD SEA SCROLLS. It aims at—and generally achieves—accuracy, clarity, and graceful dignity. *The New Testament* appeared in 1961, *The Old Testament* and the APOCRYPHA in 1970. Another new version that seems certain to have wide use and a long life is *The New American Bible*, translated by the Catholic Biblical Association of America. This completely new translation began to be published in parts in 1952, at which time it was known as the Confraternity version. The entire Bible, with the earlier translations revised, was published as *The New American Bible* in 1970. The aim of the translators was to make as exact a version as possible, resting on modern textual scholarship and resisting modification for the sake of literary quality.

[References: Frederick Harrison, *The Bible in Britain* (1949); C. S. Lewis, *The Literary Impact of the Authorised Version* (1950).]

Bible, Influence on Literature The influence of the BIBLE on English literature is so subtly pervasive that it can merely be suggested, not closely traced. Much of its influence has been indirect—through its effect on language and on the mental and moral interests of the English and American people. The English Bibles of the sixteenth century brought the common people a new world by the revival of ancient Hebrew literature. The picturesque imagery and phraseology enriched the lives of the people and profoundly affected not only their conduct but their language and literary tastes.

Great authors commonly show a familiarity with the Bible, and few great English and American writers of recent centuries can be read with satisfaction by one ignorant of biblical literature. The Authorized Version of the Bible has affected subsequent English literature in the use of scriptural themes (Milton's *Paradise Lost*, Bunyan's *Pilgrim's Progress*, Byron's *Cain*); scriptural phraseology, allusions, or modified quotations (as "selling birthright" for a "mess of pottage"); and incorporation, conscious or unconscious, of biblical phraseology into common speech ("highways and hedges," "thorn in the flesh," "a soft answer"). The Bible is thought to have been highly influential in substituting pure English words for Latin words (Tyndale's vocabulary is 97 percent English, that of the Authorized Version, 93 percent). The style of many writers has been directly affected by the study of the Bible, as has Bunyan's, Smart's, Lincoln's, and Hemingway's. Whitman's prosodic methods as well as his vocabulary demonstrate a great debt to the Hebrew poets and prophets. Modern novelists have increasingly turned to the Bible for themes and plots, as in Hemingway's *The Sun Also Rises* and Steinbeck's *East of Eden*; or for what Theodore Ziolkowski has called "fictional transfigurations of Jesus," such as Faulkner's *Light in August* and *A Fable*, Steinbeck's *The Grapes of Wrath*, Fitzgerald's *The Last Tycoon*, and Stephen King's *The Green Mile*.

[Reference: Northrop Frye, *The Great Code: The Bible and Literature* (1982).]

Bibliography Used in several senses. The term may be applied to a SUBJECT BIBLIOGRAPHY; this is a list of books or other printed (or manuscript) material on any chosen topic. A subject *bibliography* may aim at comprehensiveness, even completeness; or it may be a selective list of only such works as are most important, or most easily available, or most closely related to a book or article to which it may be attached. *Bibliographies* following a serious ESSAY, for example, may be merely a list of sources used by the writer of the essay, or they may be meant to point out to the reader sources of additional information on the subject. In a related use, the word designates a list of works of a particular country, author, or printer ("national" and "trade" *bibliography*). *Bibliographies* of these kinds are sometimes called ENUMERATIVE BIBLIOGRAPHIES. The process of making such lists either by students or by professional bibliographers is also referred to as *bibliography.*

In an analytical sense, as it is used by book collectors, bibliophiles, and textual scholars, *bibliography* means the history of writing, printing, binding, illustrating, and publishing—all included in book production. It involves a consideration of all the details of transmitting a text into book form. *Bibliography* in this sense is used by scholars in TEXTUAL CRITICISM—the employing of bibliographical evidence to help settle such questions as the veracity of a text, the order of publication, and the relative value of different editions of a book; whether certain parts of a book were intended to be a part of it originally or were added afterward; whether a later edition was printed from an earlier; and other such problems, which often have an important literary bearing. This sort of bibliographical work has been much stressed since about 1900, especially by members of the London Bibliographical Society, one striking result being the discovery of the forged dates on certain QUARTOS of Shakespeare's PLAYS, actually printed in 1619 but assigned earlier dates on the title pages. (See TEXTUAL CRITICISM.)

Another use of the term *bibliography* is to denote the methods of work of student and author: reading, research, taking of notes, compilation of *bibliography*, preparation of manuscript for the press, publication, etc. These last two uses of the word are of special interest to advanced students who take university courses in *bibliography*. A *bibliography* of *bibliographies* is a list of lists of works dealing with a given subject or subjects. An "annotated *bibliography*" is one in which some or all of the items listed are followed by brief description or critical comment.

[References: Fredson T. Bowers, *Bibliography and Textual Criticism* (1964) and *Principles of Bibliographical Description* (1949); A. Esdaile, *Esdaile's Manual of Bibliography*, 5th ed. (1981, Roy Stokes, ed.); Philip Gaskell, *A New Introduction to Bibliography* (1972, 1995); R. B. McKerrow, *An Introduction to Bibliography for Literary Students* (1927, 1994).]

Bibliophile One who loves books, either as reading matter or as commodities to be collected and traded.

Bildungsroman A NOVEL that deals with the development of a young person, usually from adolescence to maturity; it is frequently autobiographical. Dickens's *Great Expectations* and Samuel Butler's *The Way of All Flesh* are standard examples. Doris Lessing's five-volume *Children of Violence* ranks among the most ambitious and impressive modern instances. *Bildungsroman* and APPRENTICESHIP NOVEL are virtually synonymous, both being derived from Goethe's *Wilhelm Meister's Apprenticeship*, but *Bildungsroman* is currently the more fashionable. See APPRENTICESHIP NOVEL.

[Reference: Randolph P. Shaffner, *The Apprenticeship Novel: A Study of the "Bildungsroman as a Regulative Type in Western Literature* (1984).]

Bill The items making up a theatrical program; also the list of such items. Two short plays, for example, may be performed "on the same *bill*."

Billing The position on a poster or BILL, usually in such a form as "billing above the title" or "*top billing*."

Billingsgate Coarse, foul, vulgar, violent, abusive language. The term is derived from the fact that the fishmongers in *Billingsgate* fish market in London achieved distinction for the scurrility of their language.

Bill-matter Material such as a nickname, *slogan*, or *epithet* used in advertising, especially for performers and athletes. Among the most familiar are "The Swedish Nightingale" (Jenny Lind), "The Man of a Thousand Faces" (Lon Chaney), and "The Forces' Sweetheart" (Vera Lynn).

[Reference: Michael Kilgarriff, *Grace, Beauty and Banjos* (1998).]

Binding The outer part of a book, made of paper or something more substantial, such as cardboard, leather, or other heavy material. Incidental to the book itself, although some *bindings* are more valuable and more artistic than the writing they cover.

Biographical Fallacy The interpretation of a work of art through heavy reliance on aspects of the maker's life as the basis for understanding.

Biography A written account of a person's life, a life history. LETTERS, MEMOIRS, DIARIES, JOURNALS, and AUTOBIOGRAPHIES ought to be distinguished from *biography* proper. Memoirs, diaries, journals, and autobiographies are closely related to each other in that each is recollection written down by the subject of the work. Letters are likely to be colored by various prejudices and purposes. Nearer the *biography* than any of these forms—and yet not an exact parallel—is the "life and times" book, concerned with a life and a period. The writer may do a very fascinating book, interesting as well as instructive, but pure *biography*, in the more modern sense, does not look two ways; it centers its whole attention on its subject.

In England the word *biography* first came into use with Dryden, who, in 1683, called it "the history of particular men's lives." *Biography* today, then, may be defined as the accurate presentation of the life history from birth to death of an individual, along with an effort to interpret the life so as to offer a unified impression of the subject. English *biography* begins perhaps with the ancient runic inscriptions that celebrated the lives of heroes. This desire to commemorate greatness was, later on, united with the encouragement of morality. This purpose accounts for HAGIOGRAPHY—records of saints—which occupied the attention of scholars in the monasteries. One list of early English historical material reports 1,277 writings, almost all of which were devoted to the glorification of one or another Irish or British saint. It was not until Bishop Asser wrote his *Life of Alfred the Great* (893) that anything closely resembling *biography* appears. In the twelfth century, English *biography* reached another milestone when Monk Eadmer, in his *Vita Anselmi*, somehow managed to humanize his subject beyond the capability of former biographers. Introducing LETTERS into his NARRATIVE and reporting ANECDOTES and conversation, he wrote what may be the first pure *biography* in England. The fourteenth- and fifteenth-century *biography* gradually became somewhat less serious, less commemorative, and less didactic. In the middle of the sixteenth century William Roper (1496–1578), More's son-in-law, wrote what is now most often referred to as the first English *biography*, his *Life of Sir Thomas More*, and George Cavendish (1500–1561) wrote his *Life of Wolsey*. With these two books, English *biography* had arrived as a recognized form of literature. Although the didactic purpose and the commemorative spirit were still present, both books made a greater effort to avoid prejudice than previous writers had made. The seventeenth century was, in general, a time of brevities. The character sketch, the ANA, flourished. The CHARACTER was the contemporary enthusiasm. John Aubrey wrote his frank, gossipy *Minutes for Lives* as brief estimates of his contemporaries. Thomas Fuller wrote his *Worthies*. DIARIES, LETTERS, and MEMOIRS were plentiful—for example, the *Memoirs of Lady Fanshawe* and the *Memoirs of Colonel Hutchinson*. The first worthwhile AUTOBIOGRAPHY, perhaps, is that of Lord Herbert. But were it not for Izaak Walton's *Lives* (1640–1678), the century would be largely lacking in *biography*. Walton has been considered the first English professional biographer because he attempted the form deliberately and sustained it over a long period. Opposed to Walton and his biographical manner was Thomas Sprat, whose *Life of Cowley* appeared in 1668. It is to him that the Victorian demand for "decency" in *biography* seems largely due, for Sprat wrote a life that was a cold and dignified thing. "The tradition of 'discreet' biography," writes one critic, "owes its wretched origin to him."

If *biography* almost stood still during the seventeenth century, the eighteenth saw it march forward to the greatest accomplishment it has enjoyed. Boswell's *Life of Johnson* stands, probably for all time, at the head of any list of *biographies*. Two lesser luminaries were Roger North and William Mason—North (*Lives of the Norths*), who insisted that PANEGYRIC be avoided and wrote brightly and colloquially, and Mason (*Life and Writings of Gray*), who carried further the use of letters and largely left his reader to deduce the character of his subject by simply furnishing a wide range of illustrative material.

Johnson himself dignified *biography* by developing a philosophy for the writing of the form and by his insistence that to a real biographer truth was much more important than respect for the dead or their relatives. The writing of the supreme English *biography* was, however, reserved for Johnson's biographer—James Boswell. Boswell gave a new twist to biographic method; he used most of the methods developed by earlier writers, but he wrought of them a new combination. Humor of a sort was here, as well as a great wealth of petty detail from which readers might make their own deductions; here, too, were the ANECDOTE and ANA of the seventeenth century; and here were intimacy and personal comment. To Boswell was given the privilege of making *biography* actual, real, and convincing. In the work of Boswell, *biography* painted a living, breathing human being.

The Boswell tradition was in a fair way of being accepted when Victorianism—with its studiousness, its two-volume "life and letters" *biography*, its "authorized" biographies more or less controlled by relatives of the subject—blurred the picture. True enough, in the nineteenth century, there had been Tom Moore's *Life of Sheridan* and *Letters and Journals of Lord Byron*, as well as Lockhart's *Life of Scott*. But on the whole the freedom that Boswell had brought to this writing was restricted and confined by the Victorians. Religious orthodoxy and pious morality were in the saddle. Tennyson spoke for the epoch: "What business has the public to know about Byron's wildnesses? He has given them fine work and they ought to be satisfied."

By the early years of the twentieth century, the growing scientific attitude had become operative in *biography*, and it brought with it not only a rejection of the polite reticence of the Victorian biographer but also a direct attack on the admiration of famous people. Lytton Strachey, in *Eminent Victorians* (1918) and *Queen Victoria* (1921), wrote lives that were brief, ironic, artistic, and (his critics declare) too often inaccurate. Coupled with Strachey's method have been the assumptions of psychologists, particularly those of Freud, and our century has seen a host of biographical studies that are virtually attempts to read the hidden emotional life and even the unconscious experiences and motives of the subject. Van Wyck Brooks's studies of Mark Twain and Henry James as the products of frustration are particularly significant. Philip Guedalla in England and Richard Ellmann in America have made the modern age not only a period in which *biography* has been popular and widely read and written but also one in which at its best it has achieved high distinction. Literary *biography* has excelled, for some reason, in the portrayal of FICTION writers. To Ellmann's *biographies* of James Joyce and Oscar Wilde on the roll of honor, one could add Carlos Baker's life of Hemingway, Joseph Blotner's of Faulkner, and Matthew J. Bruccoli's of Fitzgerald.

[References: Leon Edel, *Literary Biography* (1957); Mark Longaker, *English Biography in the Eighteenth Century* (1931); Harold Nicolson, *Development of English Biography* (1928); E. H. O'Neill, *A History of American Biography* (1935).]

Bit A very small role in a dramatic piece, most often found in the phrases "*bit* player" and "*bit* part."

Black Humor The use of the morbid and the ABSURD for darkly comic purposes in modern literature. The term refers as much to the tone of anger and bitterness as it does to the grotesque and morbid situations, which often deal with suffering, anxiety, and death. *Black humor* is a substantial element in the ANTINOVEL and the THEATER OF THE ABSURD. Joseph Heller's *Catch-22* is an archetypal example. Other novelists working in the tradition of *black humor* include Günter Grass, Mordecai Richler, Thomas Pynchon, and Kurt Vonnegut. Successful playwrights using *black humor* include Edward Albee, Harold Pinter, and Eugène Ionesco, who called it "tragic farce."

[Reference: Max F. Schulz, *Black Humor Fiction in the Sixties: a Pluralistic Definition of Man and His World* (1973).]

Black Letter A heavy typeface with angular outlines and thick, ornamental serifs. Also called "Gothic," "church text," and "Old English," it was widely used in early printing. The term implies an early work, as in "*black letter* book," where the kind of type indicates the age of the work.

Black Literature See AFRICAN AMERICAN LITERATURE.

Black Mountain School A label applied to certain writers—Charles Olson, Robert Creeley, and Robert Duncan among them—associated with Black Mountain College, an experimental school in North Carolina. They published the *Black Mountain Review*, which was highly influential in the PROJECTIVE VERSE movement. The school itself was a bold experiment in aesthetic education, which included architecture and the graphic arts as well as literature; in its idealism and spirit, the school resembled the BROOK FARM enterprise. Members of the group, including Josef Albers and Jonathan Williams, went on to other and different callings, but the energy of the *Black Mountain School* continued to make itself felt long after the institution as such had gone out of business. The sense of community and adventure persisted in the work of the members and in that of such associated artists as Denise Levertov and Fielding Dawson. See PROJECTIVE VERSE.

[Reference: Martin Duberman, *Black Mountain: An Exploration in Community* (1972).]

Blank Verse Unrhymed but otherwise regular verse, usually iambic pentameter. This form, generally accepted as that best adapted to dramatic verse in English, is commonly used for long poems whether dramatic, philosophic, or narrative. The freedom gained through the lack of RHYME is offset by the demands for variety, which may be obtained by the skillful poet through a number of means: the shifting of the CAESURA, or pause, from place to place within the line; the shifting of the stress among syllables; the use of the RUN-ON LINE, which permits thought-grouping in large or small blocks (VERSE PARAGRAPHS); the variation in tonal qualities by changing the LEVEL of diction from passage to passage; and, finally, the adaptation of the form to reflect differences in the speech of characters and in emotion.

Blank verse appears to have found general favor in England first as a medium for dramatic expression, but with Milton it was turned to epic use and since then has been employed in the writing of idylls and lyrics. The distinction of the first use of *blank verse* in English is customarily given to Surrey, who used it in his translation of parts of the *Aeneid* (before 1547). The earliest dramatic use of *blank verse* in English was in Sackville and Norton's *Gorboduc*, 1561; the earliest use in didactic poetry was in Gascoigne's *Steel Glass*, 1576; but it was only with Marlowe (prior to 1593) that the form first reached the hands of a master capable of using its range of possibilities and passing it on for Shakespeare and Milton to develop. After suffering something of an eclipse during the eighteenth century, *blank verse* enjoyed a new robustness in the work of Wordsworth, Tennyson, and Browning during the nineteenth century. (Some of the SONGS in Tennyson's *The Princess*—"Tears, Idle Tears," "O Swallow, Swallow," and "Now Sleeps the Crimson Petal"—belong to that extremely rare and engaging category, the *blank verse* LYRIC.) In the modern age memorable *blank verse* has been written by Yeats, Robinson, Pound, Eliot, Frost, and—with particular distinction and dignity—Stevens.

Blason Generally, a rationally ordered poem of praise or blame, proceeding detail by detail. Specifically, in the form called *blason du corps feminin*, an ENCOMIUM for one's beloved. Mercutio, in Shakespeare's *Romeo and Juliet*, ridicules the typical *blason*:

> I conjure thee by Rosaline's bright eyes,
> By her high forehead and her scarlet lip,
> By her fine foot, straight leg, and quivering thigh,
> And the demesnes that there adjacent lie.

Shakespeare's Sonnet 106 mentions "the blazon of sweet beauty's best, / Of hand, of foot, of lip, of eye, of brow. . . ."

Many of the love poems by Donne and Herrick partake of the convention, and Marvell's "To His Coy Mistress" includes a *blason*-like inventory of a few of the mistress's praiseworthy features. Sir John Suckling's "A Ballad upon a Wedding" includes a witty inventory of the bride's features. William Carlos Williams's "Portrait of a Lady" qualifies as a *blason* ("Your thighs . . . Your knees . . . your ankles . . ."). Both Gerard Manley Hopkins (in "The Habit of Perfection") and W. H. Auden (in "Precious Five") produced *blasons* addressed to the speaker's own body. A contemporary example has been produced by O. B. Hardison in "Ptolemy's Journal" in the volume *Pro Musica Antiqua* (1977). Wilfred Owen's "Greater Love," a bitterly ironic subversion of the light-hearted conventions of the *blason*, compares the lover's features to those of soldiers killed in action: "Red lips are not so red / As the stained stones kissed by the

English dead. . . . your eyes lose lure / When I behold eyes blinded in my stead!" and on through attitude, voice, heart, and hand. Joyce Kilmer's "Trees" also qualifies.

Bleed A term used in printing to describe the trimmimg of the edges of a sheet or a page in such a way that some of the type or illustration is cut off. If an illustration is so printed that it comes to the very edge of the page, leaving no margin, it is said that the illustration "*bleeds* off." A page so printed or trimmed is called a "*bleed* page."

Blend (or Blend Word) Another name for a PORTMANTEAU WORD.

Block Books Books printed from engraved blocks of wood, as in Flanders and Germany early in the fifteenth century. The printing was on only one side of the sheet, and, in being bound together to make a book, the sheets were often glued together, verso to verso, to form pages printed on both sides.

Blog Originally *weblog*, a technical record of Internet activities, later a site on the Internet maintained by a person or group for diaries, opnions, stories, and other sorts of material, presented in the online equivalent of a *commonplace book.*

Blood and Thunder A class of work specializing in bloodshed and violence. Many of these have to do with crime and high emotion. Sometimes abbreviated to " blood," "blood books," or "penny bloods."

Bloomsbury Group A group of writers and thinkers, many of whom lived in Bloomsbury, a residential district near central London. These writers, with Virginia Woolf as the unofficial leader, began meeting early in the twentieth century and became a powerful force in British literary and intellectual life in the 1920s and 1930s. Their philosophy was derived from G. E. Moore's *Principia Ethica*, which asserts that "the pleasures of human intercourse and the enjoyment of beautiful objects" are the rational ends of social progress. Among the members of the group were John Maynard Keynes, Lytton Strachey, Clive Bell, Roger Fry, E. M. Forster, Duncan Grant, and David Garnett.

[References: Quentin Bell, *Bloomsbury* (1968); Leon Edel, *Bloomsbury: A House of Lions* (1979).]

Blues An African American FOLK SONG developed in the southern United States. A *blues* is characteristically short (three-line STANZA), melancholy, marked by frequent repetition, and sung slowly in a minor mode. Probably each *blues* was originally the composition of one person, but so readily are *blues* appropriated and changed that in practice they are a branch of folk literature. The classic three-line *blues* stanza is much like a HEROIC COUPLET with the first LINE repeated and, frequently, with a conspicuous CAESURA after the second foot of each line:

> Gonna lay my head right on the railroad track,
> Gonna lay my head right on the railroad track,
> 'Cause my baby, she won't take me back.

(Some of Pope's lines can be transformed into admirable *blues* LYRICS:

> A heap of dust alone remains of thee,
> A heap of dust alone remains of thee,
> 'Tis all thou art, and all the proud shall be!)

Having begun in the lively environment of African American song, the *blues* have now grown in scope beyond the orbits implied by both "African American" and "song," so that Jack Kerouac could call a book of poems *Mexico City Blues: 242 Choruses*.

[References: Imamu Amiri Baraka, *Blues People: Negro Music in White America* (1963); S. B. Charters, *The Roots of the Blues* (1981); W. C. Handy, *Blues: An Anthology: Complete Words and Music of 53 Great Songs*, 3rd rev. ed. (1972; orig. 1926).

Bluestockings A term applied to women of pronounced intellectual interests. It gained currency after 1750 as a result of its application (for reasons not now easy to establish beyond dispute) to a London group of women of literary and intellectual tastes who held assemblies or "conversations" to which "literary and ingenious men" were invited. There was no formal organization, and the personnel of the group changed from time to time, so that no exhaustive "membership" list can be given. Among the *bluestockings* were Elizabeth Montagu (the "Queen of the Blues"), Hannah More, Fanny Burney, and Hester Chapone. Horace Walpole was one of the male "members," and Samuel Johnson, Edmund Burke, and David Garrick were at times frequent visitors. The group's activities were directed toward encouraging an interest in literature, fostering the recognition of literary genius, and hence helping to remove the odium that had attached to earlier "learned ladies." It has been used by men as a term of opprobrium to describe pretentiously intellectual and pedantic women.

[Reference: Walter Sidney Scott, *The Bluestocking Ladies* (1947).]

B Movie (sometimes **film** or **feature**) A production, possibly getting its name from "budget," less ambitious and expensive than the highest level of film. Also the second movie in a double feature.

Blurb A term applied in the book trade to the hyperbolically encomiastic matter printed on the jackets of books or elsewhere. The term was invented by Gelett Burgess a century ago.

Boasting Poem A poem in which characters boast of their exploits; frequently found in oral literatures and in works such as ballads and epics. In the BIBLE David is said to have slain his ten thousands; in English perhaps the clearest examples appear in *Beowulf*, in such passages as Unferth's boast and Beowulf's account of his slaying of Grendel. An American folk song called "The Tin Angel Brag" is a more recent example:

> I was born about ten thousand years ago,
> There ain't nothin' in the world that I don't know
> I saw Peter, Paul, and Moses playin' ring around the roses,
> And I'll whup the guy what says it isn't so.
> Queen Elizabeth she fell in love with me,
> We was married in Milwaukee secretly,

But I got tired of sugar and went off with General Hooker
And was fightin' skeeters down in Tennessee.

Bob and Wheel Terms invented during the nineteenth century to describe a phenomenon peculiar to the revival of ALLITERATIVE VERSE in the later MIDDLE ENGLISH PERIOD: after a STROPHE of unrhymed alliterative lines, the poem (most often a MEDIEVAL ROMANCE) shifts into a set of rhymed lines, the first, or "*bob*," very short and the remainder, or "*wheel*," typically a short-lined rhymed QUATRAIN. *Sir Gawain and the Green Knight* consists of 101 such stanzas; the number of alliterative lines is between twelve and thirty-seven. The *bob* has two or three syllables, with the stress on the last; the lines of the *wheel* are usually three-stressed; the rhyme scheme of the *bob and wheel* together is *ababa*. Lines 2382–88 (spoken by Gawain) illustrate two alliterative lines and a *bob and wheel*:

Now am I fawty and falce and ferde haf ben euer
Of trecherye and vntrawþe: boþe bityde sorȝe
and care! — **Bob**
I biknowe yow, knyȝt, here stylle,
Al fawty is my fare;
Letez me ouertake your wylle
And efte I schal be ware. — **Wheel**

(But, though faulty and false, I was still afraid / Of treachery and untruth: may sorrow and care betide them; / I confess to you, knight, here uncomplaining / That my fare is all faulty; / Let me understand your will / And afterwards I shall beware.)

Boldface A heavy typeface, such as that used for the titles of entries in this handbook.

Bombast Originally, any sort of ornamental but unnecessary padding; PLEONASM. Now mostly limited to ranting, insincere, and extravagant language, and outlandish grandiloquence. Elizabethan TRAGEDY, especially early Senecan plays, contains much bombastic style, marked by extravagant IMAGERY. A good example comes from *Hamlet*:

Roasted in wrath and fire,
And thus o'er-sized with coagulate gore,
With eyes like carbuncles, the hellish Pyrrhus
Old grandsire Priam seeks.

Bon Mot A witty REPARTEE or statement. A clever saying. Sometimes abbreviated to "mot."

Book In general, any collection of sheets of paper or a similar material, customarily fastened along one edge and often protected by COVERS. In a more restricted use, *book* means one of the main divisions of a longer work; the Old and New Testaments, for example, are divided into *books*, as are epic poems and long novels. The *book* of a musical show is all the material exclusive of music.

Book Sizes To understand some of the terms used in describing *book sizes*, such as QUARTO and OCTAVO, it is helpful to visualize a sheet of paper, "foolscap" size, 17 inches by 13½ inches.

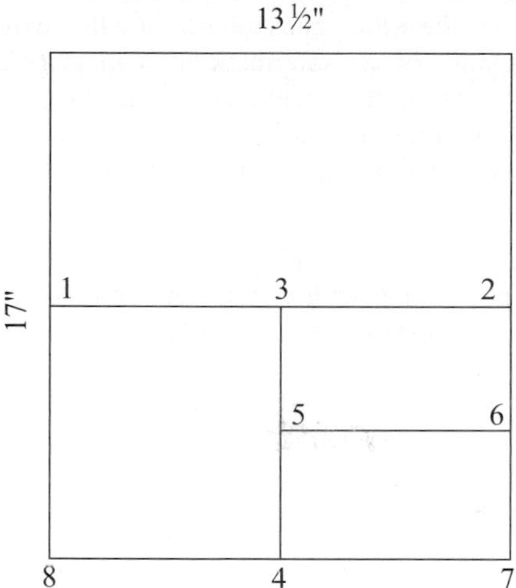

When this sheet is folded along 1–2, 3–4, and 5–6, the resulting folds mark off the sizes of pages. Thus 1–2–7–8 represents one of two leaves cut from the original foolscap and is therefore, a FOLIO (Latin for "leaf ") sheet or page; 2–3–4–7 represents one-fourth of the original sheet and, therefore, gives us a QUARTO page; 2–3–5–6 constitutes one-eighth of the original and gives us an OCTAVO page. A *book size*, then, was originally determined by the number of book leaves cut from a single large sheet. To determine the number of pages cut from the original sheet, count the number of pages to a SIGNATURE; this may often be done by noting the occurrence of the signature marks (themselves sometimes called "signatures") that appear at regular intervals at the foot of a page. These symbols, usually numerals or letters, may be found regularly in early printed books and sometimes in those recently printed. They indicate the beginning of new signatures. The number of leaves (not pages) in a single signature shows the number of leaves cut from the original sheet and is, therefore, the indication of the *book size*. When there are two leaves to the SIGNATURE, the book is a FOLIO; when there are four leaves, it is a QUARTO; and so on. The following table shows the principle as it manifests itself in the more frequently used *book sizes*:

No. of Folds	No. of Leaves	Pages to Signature	Name
1	2	4	FOLIO
2	4	8	QUARTO (4to)
3	8	16	OCTAVO (8vo)
	12	24	DUODECIMO (12mo)
4	16	32	sixteenmo (16mo)
5	32	64	thirty-twomo (32mo)
6	64	128	sixty-fourmo (64mo)

This would be fairly simple, but for the fact that in modern printing there is a variety of sizes of original stock. In addition to the "foolscap 8vo" in the example, we may have Post 8vo, Demy 8vo, Crown 8vo, Royal 8vo, etc., the terms Demy, Crown, and the others referring to varying sizes of original sheets that, in turn, give varying sizes of pages. So complicated has the whole question become that expert bibliographers urge more attention to the position of the watermark on the page (a guide to book measurements too complicated to discuss here) and even then frequently give up the question in despair. Publishers and librarians arbitrarily use 12mo, OCTAVO, etc., for books of certain sizes regardless of the number of pages to the signature.

Boulevard Drama A term applied to sophisticated COMEDY and MELODRAMA popular in the French theater in the nineteenth century. It centered around the Opera House (1861–1874), where the OPERETTAS of Jacques Offenbach, frequently books by Meilhac and Ludovic Halévy, with their extravagance and violent behavior, presented dramatic pictures of the irreverence, prankishness, and material practicality of the French Second Empire. In present-day usage, the term is sometimes applied to brittle, sophisticated COMEDY aimed at a popular audience.

Bourgeois Drama A nearly obsolete term applied to PLAYS that show the life of the common folk and the middle class rather than that of the courtly or the rich. Such widely differing kinds of plays as Heywood's *Interludes*, *Gammer Gurton's Needle*, Dekker's *Shoemaker's Holiday* (REALISTIC COMEDY), and Lillo's *The London Merchant* (DOMESTIC TRAGEDY) are embraced in the term, which in a broad sense refers to the development of middle-class subject matter.

Bourgeois Tragedy See DOMESTIC TRAGEDY.

Boustrophedon Running alternately from left to right and from right to left; a term—literally, "ox plowing"—that describes the direction of writing in certain ancient inscriptions, such as some in Greek before 500 B.C. The term has also been proposed to supersede AMPHISBAENIC as it relates to such a rhyme as "loop" and "pool." A humorous speech in Robert Frost's "From Plane to Plane" gestures in the direction of returning the term to agriculture, from whence it came, applied here to one laborer's style of hoeing:

> You do the way we do
> In reading, don't you, Bill?—at every line end
> Pick up our eyes and carry them back idle
> Across the page to where we started from.
> The other way of reading back and forth,
> Known as boustrophedon, was found too awkward.

Bouts-rimés A kind of literary game in which players are given lists of rhyming words and are expected to write impromptu verses with the rhymes in the order given. The game has been popular in France since the seventeenth century; it was a popular pastime of the BLUESTOCKINGS in England; and clubs devoted to it sprang up in Scotland in the nineteenth century.

Bowdlerize To expurgate a piece of writing by omitting material considered offensive or indecorous especially to female modesty, according to Bowdler's introduction. The word derives from Thomas Bowdler, an English physician, who in 1818 published an expurgated edition of Shakespeare.

Box Set A stage set that realistically represents a room with three walls, the FOURTH WALL being imagined on the side toward the audience.

Brachycatalectic A VERSE that lacks two syllables, normally unstressed. Usually, what is omitted is the unstressed part of an ANAPEST or DACTYL, as in Yeats's line "Hearts with one purpose alone" (in a generally anapestic environment).

Brachylogy Brevity of expression; sometimes used for an instance of brevity or conciseness.

Braggadocio A noisy braggart who is actually a coward. Although the name comes from such a character in Spenser's *The Faerie Queene*, the *braggadocio* is really a STOCK CHARACTER with a long history stretching back to Greek and Roman COMEDY. See MILES GLORIOSUS, ALAZON.

Brahmins Members of the highest caste among the Hindus. The name is applied to certain socially exclusive families of New England, particularly in the nineteenth century. In his novel *Elsie Venner*, Oliver Wendell Holmes so characterizes "the harmless, inoffensive, untitled artistocracy," particularly of Boston and its environs, which became "a caste by the repetition of the same influences generation after generation." The term is customarily used derisively. John P. Marquand portrays *The Late George Apley* as a typical *Brahmin* of rather late vintage.

Breton Lay The term refers both to the relatively brief form of the medieval French ROMANCES, professed to have been sung by Breton minstrels on Celtic themes, and to the English medieval poems written in imitation of such French works. See BRETON ROMANCE, LAY.

Breton Romance A medieval French METRICAL ROMANCE, emphasizing love as the central force in the plot. *Breton romances* drew on the traditions of COURTLY LOVE and frequently dealt with LEGENDS such as the Tristan and Iseult stories or the Arthurian materials. "The Franklin's Tale," in Chaucer's *Canterbury Tales*, is a short form of the *Breton romance* called the BRETON LAY.

Breve The name of the symbol (˘) used to indicate a short syllable in the scansion of QUANTITATIVE VERSE and an unstressed syllable in ACCENTUAL-SYLLABIC VERSE.

Breviary A collection of lessons, calendars, and outlines for services to aid Roman Catholic priests in reciting the Divine Offices for each day and in discharging other churchly responsibilities. The *Breviary* contains the church calendar, Psalter, collects and lessons, collects for the Saint's Days, hours of the Virgin, and burial services, but not the communion service of Mass.

Brief A condensed statement, a RÉSUMÉ, of the main arguments or ideas presented in a speech or piece of writing. In legal practice, a formal summary of laws and authorities bearing on the main points of each case; in church history, a papal letter less formal than a bull.

British Library (earlier, **British Museum**) The British Library is one of the most important in the world. The collection, founded in 1753 through a bequest from Sir Hans Sloane, now embraces more than 6,000,000 printed volumes, 10,000 INCUNABULA, and 75,000 manuscripts. It is located on Great Russell Street, in Bloomsbury, London. The *British Library* is particularly wealthy in its collection of manuscripts including, besides the famous Harleian and Cottonian manuscripts, a series of documents from the third century to the present. Particularly noteworthy are its collections comprising English historical CHRONICLES, ANGLO-SAXON materials, charters, Arthurian romances, the Burney Collection of classical manuscripts, Greek papyri, the genealogical records of English families, and Irish, French, and Italian manuscripts. From time to time it has been given by bequest special libraries such as Archbishop Cranmer's Collection, the Thomas Collection, the C. M. Cracherode Collection, and the Sir Joseph Banks Collection. Other important features are its assortment of items from American, Chinese and Oriental, Hebrew, and Slavonic literatures. According to the British copyright law, the *Library* receives copies of every publication seeking copyright protection. The result is an astonishing grouping together in one place of the learning and literatures of the world.

Broadsheet A single large sheet of paper with printing on one side. At one time, popular verses were peddled in this form, as attested by the beginning of Hardy's "After the Fair":

> The singers are gone from the Cornmarket-place
> With their broadsheets of rhyme. . . .

Broadsheet is sometimes used for a sheet printed on both sides.

Broadside The same as BROADSHEET. While broadsheet has fallen into disuse, *broadside* continues, but the modern examples, far from being cheaply produced, tend to be issued in limited editions, elegantly printed on fine paper and sometimes numbered and signed by the author.

Broadside Ballad Soon after the development of printing in England, BALLADS were prepared for circulation on folio sheets, printed on one side only, two pages to the sheet, and two columns to the page. Because of their manner of publication, these were called *broadsides*. These ballads ranged from reproductions of old favorites of literary distinction to semi-illiterate screeds with little quality. These *broadsides* had great variety of subject matter: accidents, dying speeches of criminals, miraculous events, religious and political harangues. Many were satirical, with unscrupulous personal invective. In the sixteenth century, the heyday of their popularity, they served, as one critic states, as a "people's YELLOW JOURNAL." See also STREET BALLAD.

[References: William Chappell and J. W. Ebsworth, eds., *The Roxburghe Ballads*, 9 v. (1871–99); H. E. Rollins, ed., *The Pack of Autolycus* (1927), and *A Pepysian Garland* (1922).]

Brochure Originally a small work or PAMPHLET with its pages stitched or wired, not bound; now any relatively brief work regardless of type of binding.

Broken Rhyme The breaking of a word at the end of a line for the sake of a rhyme. The novelty and disruption of this rare device have limited its use largely to various sorts of comic verse, including SATIRE and DOGGEREL. Instances of such use turn up in Donne's Satires III and IV:

> Gracchus loves all as one, and thinks that so
> As women do in divers countries go
> In divers habits, yet are still one kind,
> So doth, so is religion; and this blind-
> ness too much light breeds. . . .
>
> [I]t pleased my destiny
> (Guilty of my sin of going), to think me
> As prone to all ill, and of good as forget-
> ful, as proud, as lustful, and as much in debt. . . .

W. S. Gilbert favored *broken rhyme* in some of the lyrics he wrote for operettas, such as this passage from *Iolanthe*:

> 'Neath this blow,
> Worse than stab o' dagger,
> Though we mo-
> mentarily stagger. . . .

One stanza of Lewis Carroll's "Poeta Fit, Non Nascitur" contains a broken rhyme:

> "Last, as to the arrangement:
> Your reader, you should show him,
> Must take what information he
> Can get, and look for no im-
> mature disclosure of the drift
> And purpose of your poem.

E. E. Cummings indulged in a great deal of *broken rhyme* and went so far as to use two broken words to achieve CONSONANCE in a rhyme-slot (the "vac" of "vacuum" and the "democ" of "democracy"). More recently, the songwriter Arlo Guthrie has this *broken rhyme*: "I don't want to die, / I just want to ride my motorcy- / cle." In the nineteenth century Gerard Manley Hopkins boldly explored the use of *broken rhyme* in a wholly serious poem, "The Windhover," the first line of which contains a striking example:

> I caught this morning morning's minion, king-
> dom of daylight's dauphin, dapple-dawn-drawn Falcon, in his
> riding
> Of the rolling level underneath him steady air, and striding
> High there, how he rung upon the rein of a wimpling wing. . . .

See also FUSED RHYME.

Brook Farm A UTOPIAN experiment in communal living, sponsored by the Transcendental Club of Boston. The farm, at West Roxbury, Massachusetts, was taken over in 1841 by a joint stock company, headed by George Ripley. The scheme was supposed to give the residents opportunity for cultural pursuits and leisure at little cost, the farm being supposed, through the rotation of labor, to support the residents who, in most of their time, were to be free to attend lectures, read, write, and converse. The project was influenced by the doctrines of François Fourier and Robert Owen. Although many transcendentalists were interested in the enterprise, it was not the outgrowth of a general activity on their part. Hawthorne was there for a short period (see *The Blithedale Romance*), but such personages as Emerson, Alcott, and Thoreau never actively took part. Dissension among the members, the discovery that the soil was inadequately fertile, and the burning of a new and uninsured central "phalanstery" (the name for a dwelling at such a community) were some of the reasons that in 1846 brought about the end of the project. See TRANSCENDENTALISM.

[References: Edith Roelker Curtis, *A Season in Utopia: The Story of Brook Farm* (1961); Lindsay Swift, *Brook Farm, Its Members, Scholars, and Visitors* (1900).]

Bucolic A term used for PASTORAL writing that deals with rural life in a manner rather formal and fanciful. The plural *bucolics* refers collectively to the pastoral literature of such writers as Theocritus and Virgil. In the present loose usage the expression connotes simply poetry with a rustic background—as in W. H. Auden's mixed sequence called *Bucolics*—and is not necessarily restricted to verse with the conventional pastoral elements. See PASTORAL.

Buffoon A comic character—akin to the CLOWN, fool, and jester—given to raillery, boasting, and indecency.

Bull (also **Irish Bull)** A composition marked by such thoroughgoing incongruity and contradiction that it is at best ridiculous ("I hear footprints") and at worst chaotically nonsensical, as in a letter popularly attributed to Sir Boyle Roche (1743–1807): ". . . Whilst I write this, I hold a pistol in each hand and a sword in the other. I concluded in the beginning that this would be the end of it; and I see I was right, for it is not half over yet. At present there are such goings on, that everything is at a standstill. I should have answered your letter a fortnight ago, but I did not receive it till this morning. . . ."

Bullet In printing, a small solid circle or large period (•) used to supplement punctuation; a feature of the poetry of Robert Duncan. Also used to indicate special items on a list or popular-music chart.

Burden A CHORUS or REFRAIN.

Burlesque A form of COMEDY characterized by ridiculous exaggeration and distortion: the sublime may be made absurd; honest emotions may be turned to SENTIMENTALITY; a serious subject may be treated frivolously or a frivolous subject seriously. The essential quality that makes for *burlesque* is the discrepancy between subject matter and style. That is, a style ordinarily dignified may be used for nonsensical matter, or a style very nonsensical may be used to ridicule a weighty subject. *Burlesque*, as a form of art, manifests itself in sculpture, painting, and even architecture, as well as in literature. It has an ancient lineage in world literature: an author of uncertain identity used it in the *Battle of the Frogs and Mice* to TRAVESTY Homer. Aristophanes made *burlesque* popular, and in France, under Louis XIV, nothing was sacred to the satirist. Chaucer in *Sir Thopas* burlesqued MEDIEVAL ROMANCE as did Cervantes in *Don Quixote*. One of the best-known uses of *burlesque* in drama is Gay's *The Beggar's Opera*. In recent use the term—already broad—has been broadened still further to include stage entertainments consisting of songs, skits, and dances, usually raucous. A distinction between *burlesque* and PARODY is often made, in which *burlesque* is a TRAVESTY of a literary form and parody a travesty of a particular work. It has been suggested that parody works by keeping a targeted style constant while lowering the subject, *burlesque* or travesty by keeping a targeted subject constant while lowering the style. Because "travesty" is connected to "transvestite," the procedure may be expected to change the clothing, so to speak, or the style of a normally dignified subject. See TRAVESTY, PARODY.

[References: Richmond P. Bond, *English Burlesque Poetry, 1700–1750* (1932, 1960); V. C. Clinton-Baddeley, *The Burlesque Tradition in the English Theatre after 1660* (1952); Peter Hobley Davison, *Popular Appeal in English Drama to 1850* (1982); John D. Jump, *Burlesque* (1972).]

Burletta Term used in the late eighteenth century for a variety of musical dramatic forms, somewhat like the BALLAD-OPERA, the EXTRAVAGANZA, and the PANTOMIME. One of its sponsors (George Colman, the younger) asserted that the proper use of the word was for "a drama in rhyme, entirely musical—a short comick piece consisting of recitative and singing, wholly accompanied, more or less, by the orchestra." The form persisted into the nineteenth century, when Henry Mayhew was one of the practitioners.

Burns Stanza A variant form of the TAIL-RHYME STANZA, named for Robert Burns, who used it frequently. It consists of six lines rhyming *aaabab* with TETRAMETER in the *a*-lines and DIMETER or TRIMETER in the *b*-lines, as the following stanza from Burn's "Lines to John Lapraik" illustrates:

Your critic-folk may cock their nose
And say, "How can you e'er propose,
You wha ken hardly verse frae prose,
        To mak a sang?"
But, by your leave, my learned foes,
        Ye're may be wrang.

See HABBIE, STANDARD HABBIE

Business In theatrical usage, physical action (or busy-ness) as distinct from dialogue. Commonly in such phrases as "piece of business" or "bit of business."

Buskin A boot, thick-soled and reaching halfway to the knee, worn by Greek tragedians to increase their stature, even as comedians wore SOCKS for the opposite purpose. By association *buskin* has come to mean tragedy. Milton used "the buskin'd stage" and "Jonson's learned sock" to characterize tragedy and comedy, respectively. The Greek for *buskin*, COTHURNUS, is used both for *buskin* and for the dignified tragic spirit.

Byline In newspapers and other periodicals, the printed line that tells who wrote the piece. Usually the name of a person, but sometimes the name of an agency or wire service.

Byronism Even during his lifetime (1788–1824), Lord Byron provoked the coining of such terms as "Byronic," "Byroniad," and "*Byronism*"—all in recognition of his unique electricity. He was fabulously wealthy as well as fabulously handsome; he possessed extraordinary charm and wit; he was a genuine peer, a genuine patriot, and a great sinner; he was a charismatic hero or villain—and he was a literary genius of the first order. Catching the first full tide of modern journalistic celebrity and publicity, he was capable of shameless self-flattery but also just as capable of touching modesty and self-mockery. He was—or invented—a model of the mysteriously brooding, bitter, vaguely northern loner, sexually polymorphous, reckless and doomed, and always dangerous. For almost two centuries now, a popular image of The Poet has had more in common with Byron than with any other single personage. After Byron's own self-portraits, the greatest manifestations of *Byronism* are the character Heathcliff in Emily Brontë's *Wuthering Heights* and the implicit persona of virtually everything written by E. A. Poe. Byron touched Goethe and Pushkin as well as Tennyson; and the strain was passed along to many a later creator and creature, such as Henry James and his "Jeffrey Aspern" and F. Scott Fitzgerald and his "Jay Gatsby."

Vendome 1952. Designed by François Ganeau.

Cabal An English word derived from the French *cabale* ("cabala") and given added impact by a false or popular etymology construing it as an ACRONYM formed from the first letters of the names of some of Charles II's unpopular ministers, Clifford, Arlington, Buckingham, Ashley, and Lauderdale; hence an ACROSTIC.

Cabaret An establishment, such as a restaurant or night club, with entertainment for customers seated at tables; also the entertainment itself, ordinarily singing, dancing, and comedy routines.

Cacemphaton Foul-sounding or equivocal expression.

Cacophony A harsh, unpleasant combination of sounds; the opposite of EUPHONY. Though most specifically a term used in the criticism of poetry, the word is also employed to indicate any disagreeable sound effect in other forms of writing. *Cacophony* may be an unconscious flaw, or it may be used consciously for effect, as Browning and Hardy often used it.

Cacozelia Bad imitation, especially in the form of affected diction from classical languages.

Cadence In one sense the sound pattern that precedes a marked pause or the end of a sentence, making it interrogatory, hortatory, pleading, or such. In another sense it is the rhythm established in the sequence of stressed and unstressed syllables in a phrasal unit. In a third and broader sense it is the rhythmical movement of writing when it is read aloud, the modulation produced by the rise and fall of the voice, the rhythm that sounds the "inner tune" of a sentence or a line. *Cadence* is customarily used to refer to a larger and looser group of syllables than the formal, metrical movement of regular ACCENTUAL-SYLLABIC VERSE. Modern POETS, such as Ezra Pound and William Carlos Williams, urge the substitution of *cadence* for the conventional prosodic devices, following the groundbreaking example of Whitman. See FREE VERSE.

Caesura (or **Cesura**) A pause or break in a line of verse. Originally, in CLASSICAL literature, the *caesura* characteristically divided a FOOT between two words, usually near the middle of a line. Some poets, however, have sought diversity of rhythmical effect by placing the *caesura* anywhere from near the beginning of a line to near the end. Examples of variously placed *caesurae* are shown in these lines by Marvell:

Had we but world enough, || and time
This coyness, lady, || were no crime.
We would sit down, || and think which way
To walk, || and pass our long love's day.
Thou by the Indian Ganges' side
Shouldst rubies find; || I by the tide
Of Humber would complain. || I would
Love you ten years before the flood,
And you should, if you please, || refuse
Till the conversion of the Jews.

Viewed in another sense, the *caesura* is an instrument of prose rhythm that cuts across and, by varying, modifies the regularity of accentual verse. The interplay of prose sense and verse demand can be observed in the preceding selection. Metricists who follow the classical distinctions use *caesura* to indicate a pause within a foot and DIERESIS to indicate a pause that coincides with the end of the foot. This distinction is seldom made in English METRICS, where *caesura* is employed as the generic term.

Strict constructionists have also insisted that the *caesura* ought to be the single principal pause in a given line; but, just as some lines have no *caesura*, others may have two or more. If the *caesura* comes after an unstressed syllable—as in

To err is human, || to forgive, divine.

it is called a *feminine caesura*.

Calendar The term is occasionally used in literature when some temporal structure is given a work, as in Spenser's *Shepheardes Calender*, which consists of twelve poems entitled for the twelve months. See ALMANAC.

Call (1) Older form of CURTAIN CALL. (2) The gathering persons required for a rehearsal or performance, as in "I have an early *call* tomorrow." (3) In film-making, the series of prompts spoken when a take is beginning, proverbially "Lights . . . camera . . . action," also "Roll sound . . . Roll camera . . . Mark it . . . And action."

Calligraphy The art of beautiful writing. In literature the significance of the term springs from the development of the art during the Middle Ages when the monks gave much attention to copying ancient manuscripts.

Calque A loan-translation. *Kindergarten*, for example, a German word combining "children" and "garden," passes into English as an untranslated *loan-word* "kindergarten" but into modern Hebrew as *gan yeldim*, a *calque* meaning "garden of children."

Calvinism The great religious conflict of medieval times was between AUGUSTINIANISM, which exalted the glory of God at the expense of the dignity of human beings (stressing original sin and the necessity of divine grace), and PELAGIANISM, which asserted the original innocence of human beings and their ability to develop moral and spiritual power through their own efforts. *Calvinism* was a Renaissance representative of the Augustinian point of view.

Some understanding of the teachings of *Calvinism*—the charter of which is John Calvin's famous *Institutes of the Christian Religion* (1536)—is important to the student of literature. The essential doctrines of the system are frequently summed up in the famous Five Points: (1) total depravity, the natural inability of human beings to exercise free will, because they inherited corruption from Adam's fall; (2) unconditional election, which manifests itself through God's election of those to be saved, despite their inability to perform saving works; (3) prevenient and irresistible grace, made available in advance but only to the elect; (4) the perseverance of saints, the predetermined elect inevitably persevering in the path of holiness; and (5) limited atonement, human corruption being partially atoned for by Christ, this atonement being provided the elect through the Holy Spirit, giving them the power to attempt to obey God's will as it is revealed in the Bible.

This system developed both zeal and intolerance on the part of the elect. It fostered education, however, which in early New England was regarded as a religious duty, and thereby profoundly affected the development of American culture. To this attitude of the Calvinistic PURITANS may be traced much of the inspiration for such things as the founding of many colleges and universities, the creation of a system of public schools, and the great activity of early printing presses in America—as well as the development of religious sects. Historically, especially in Europe, it is probable that the political effects of *Calvinism* have encouraged freedom and popular government. According to the theories of certain early modern historians and sociologists (for example, Max Weber), the "Protestant ethic," specifically in the form of *Calvinism*, generated an emphasis on industry and frugality, which in turn generated the conditions that made modern capitalism possible.

In New England the COVENANT THEOLOGY early softened and modified *Calvinism*, but the term Puritan in America usually refers, at least in a philosophical sense, to a belief in the doctrines of *Calvinism*. See AUGUSTINIANISM, COVENANT THEOLOGY, PELAGIANISM.

[References: John Thomas McNeill, *The History and Character of Calvinism* (1954); William Shurr, *Rappaccini's Children: American Writers in a Calvinist World* (1981); Page Smith, *As a City upon a Hill; the Town in American History* (1966); R. H. Tawney, *Religion and the Rise of Capitalism: a Historical Study* (1926); Max Weber, *The Protestant Ethic and the Spirit of Capitalism* (tr. by T. Parsons 1930).]

Calypso A type of music originated in the West Indies, particularly Trinidad. It is a BALLAD-like improvisation in African RHYTHMS. The singers, who compose as they sing, frequently deal satirically with current topics. The pinnacle of *calypso* invention came in a contest in 1937 on the assigned topic of the fate of Edward VIII; the winning improvisation concluded, "You can't abdicate and eat it too." In 1939 W. H. Auden wrote "Calypso," one of a group entitled "Ten Songs"; the poet places accents on certain syllables, with the effect of a Caribbean accent:

> For hé is the óne that I lóve to look ón,
> The ácme of kíndness and pérfectión.
> . . . .
> For lóve's more impórtant and pówerful thán
> Éven a príest or a pólitición.

John Ashbery has written a poem called "Variations, Calypso and Fugue on a Theme of Ella Wheeler Wilcox" in which the *calypso* section is in couplets.

Camera Eye Narration A kind of storytelling, resembling the "Camera Eye" sections of John Dos Passos's *U.S.A.* (1936), in which the writing gives the appearance or impression of being thoroughly objective, realistic, and anatomical.

Campus Novel A work, usually comic, set at a university. Kingsley Amis has written several (including *Lucky Jim*, *One Fat Englishman*, and *Jake's Thing*); Vladimir Nabokov's *Pnin* and *Pale Fire*, Randall Jarrell's *Pictures from an Institution*, Dallas Wiebe's *Skyblue the Badass*, Bernard Malamud's *A New Life*, Weldon Kees's *Fall Quarter*, John Barth's *Giles-Goat Boy*, Joyce Carol Oates's *Nemesis*, Don DeLillo's *White Noise*, and David Lodge's *Changing Places*, *Small World*, and *Nice Work* also belong in this category.

Canon In a figurative sense, a standard of judgment; a criterion. *Canon* is applied to the authorized or accepted list of books belonging in the Christian BIBLE by virtue of having been declared to be divinely inspired. APOCRYPHAL books are uncanonical. A similar use of the term is illustrated in the phrase "the Saints' *Canon*," the list of saints actually authorized or "canonized" by the Church. The term is often extended to mean the accepted list of books of any author, such as Shakespeare. Thus, *Macbeth* belongs without doubt in the *canon* of Shakespeare's work, whereas *Sir John Oldcastle*, though printed as Shakespeare's soon after his death, is not canonical, because the evidence of Shakespeare's authorship is unconvincing.

More recently, the idea of a general literary *canon* has received attention from a critical viewpoint, and the process of *canon*-formation has been interpreted as the work of one part of society to make its own labors central and to reduce the work of others to marginal or trivial status outside the *canon*. For instance, the "traditional" romantic canon (Blake, Coleridge, Wordsworth, Byron, Shelley, Keats) excludes the many publishing women writers of the age. The *canon* controversy has been one of the most formative influences on the study of literature in the second half of the twentieth century.

[References: Leslie Fiedler and Houston Baker, eds., *English Literature: Opening Up the Canon: Selected Papers from the English Institute* (1981); Elaine Showalter, ed., *The New Feminist Criticism: Essays on Women, Literature, and Theory* (1985), Harold Bloom, *The Western Canon: The Books and School of the Ages* (1994).]

Canonical Hours The seven periods of the day set aside for prayers of a specified sort: matins (with lauds), prime, terce, sext, none, vespers, and complin; the structural and thematic basis of W. H. Auden's *Horae Canonicae*.

Canso A Provençal love song, usually in stanzas, sung by the TROUBADOURS. Compare with the variant form CANZO, which is peculiar to northern France.

Cant Insincere, specious language calculated to give the impression of piety or religious fervor. In critical writing the term is used to signify the language and phraseology characteristic of a profession or art, as "the pedagogue's *cant*." In this sense of a special language, the term indicates any technical or special vocabulary or dialect, as "thieves' *cant*," "beggar's *cant*." More loosely still, the word signifies any insincere, superficial display of language, planned to convey an impression of conviction, but devoid of genuine emotion or feeling; that is, language used chiefly for display or effect. See JARGON.

Cantabank Term of contempt for a ballad-singer or other public entertainer on a stage, platform, or—by some accounts—barrel-head.

Canticle Originally, a prose chant or hymn taken verbatim from a Biblical text; later applied to any CHANT, such as St. Francis's "Cantico del Sole," and, in modern usage, to any poem, such as Edith Sitwell's "Canticle of the Rose," with its explicit genesis in the rhythms and symbols of religion, and a song by Paul Simon and Art Garfunkel called "Canticle." *Canticle* is also used to translate the Italian *cantica* (plural *cantiche*), which indicates a grouping of CANTOS, as in Dante's *Divine Comedy* (the *Inferno*, for example, is one of the three *cantiche* or *canticles* of the poem).

Canto A section or division of a long poem. Derived from the Latin *cantus* (SONG), the word originally signified a section of a narrative poem of such length as to be sung by a minstrel in one singing. The books of Spenser's *The Faerie Queene* and Byron's *Childe Harold's Pilgrimage* are divided into *cantos*. Early in this century, Ezra Pound published pieces at first called "cantos of a poem of some length" and eventually called that poem simply *The Cantos*.

Canzo See CANSO.

Canzone A lyrical poem, a song or ballad. The *canzone* is a short poem consisting of equal stanzas and an ENVOY of fewer lines than the stanza. It is impossible to be specific about the verse form because different writers have wrought wide variations in structure. The number of lines per stanza ranges from seven to twenty, and the envoy from three to ten. Petrarch's *canzoni* usually consisted of five or six stanzas and the envoy. In general it may be said that the *canzone* resembles the CHANT ROYAL, though its conventions are less fixed. Others than Petrarch who have written *canzoni* are Dante, Tasso, Leopardi, Chiabrera, and Marchetti. Frequent subjects used were love, nature, and a wide range of emotional reactions to life, particularly if sad. The term and the aspects of the medieval form it designated are used by contemporary poets on occasion for poems of considerable complexity. Recent examples are W. H. Auden's "Canzone: 'When shall we learn, what should be clear as day' " and Marilyn Hacker's "Canzone: 'Consider the three functions of the tongue.' "

Canzonet (also **Canzonetta**) A little song; specifically, a solo with more than one movement. Some of Ben Jonson's poems entitled "Song," such as "Slow, slow, fresh fount, keep time with my salt tears," are set to music found in Henry Youll's *Canzonets to Three Voyces*. *Canzonetta* is chiefly known in the titles of Italian poems translated by D. G. Rossetti.

Caption In the law (and at one time in general usage) a HEADING or TITLE; more recently, material under an illustration; in film, a SUBTITLE.

Caricature Writing that exaggerates certain individual qualities of a person and produces a BURLESQUE, ridiculous effect. *Caricature* more frequently is associated with drawing than with writing, because the related literary terms—SATIRE, BURLESQUE, and PARODY—are more commonly used. *Caricature*, unlike the highest satire, is likely to treat merely personal qualities; although, like satire, it also lends itself to the ridicule of political, religious, and social foibles. A work of fiction, history, or biography that traffics in excessive distortion or exaggeration may be dismissed as a *caricature*.

Carmen Figuratum A FIGURE POEM, a poem so written that the form of the printed words suggests the subject matter. Examples are many of the poems in Richard Willey's *Poematum Liber*, Herbert's "Easter Wings," the humorous "long and sad tail of the Mouse" in *Alice in Wonderland*, Dylan Thomas's "Vision and Prayer," and all of the poems in John Hollander's *Types of Shape*. Because any piece of writing looks like something and has a graphic, visual aspect, any kind of writing may partake of figuration, as when Keats uses capitals to draw attention to the "M" of mountains and the "V" of valleys, when Cummings writes about the "mOon," or (a specimen unearthed by W. K. Wimsatt) a magazine piece points to the answerable style of "bOsOm." Figuration of one sort or another has also been used by A. R. Ammons (particularly in keyboard games included in *The Snow Poems*) and Albert Goldbarth. The term *Calligramme* is also applied to figure poems, after Guillaume Apollinaire's collection entitled *Calligrammes* (1918).

Carnivalesque A term introduced by Mikhail Bakhtin to describe a spirit of carnival in literature, marked by fun, attention to the body, defiance of authority, variety, HETEROGLOSSIA, and play.

[Reference: M. M. Bakhtin, *The Bakhtin Reader: Selected Writings of Bakhtin, Medvedev, and Voloshinov*, ed. Pam Morris (1994).]

Carol (or ***Carole***) In medieval France a *carole* was a dance. The term later was applied to the accompanying song. The leader sang the stanzas, the other dancers singing the REFRAIN. The *carole* became very popular, and in the twelfth and thirteenth centuries, spreading through other European countries, it was instrumental in extending the influence of the French LYRIC. Later, *carol* came to mean any joyous song, then a HYMN of religious joy, and finally a Christmas hymn in particular. Some *carols*, such as "Joseph was an old man," were definitely popular, belonging to the culture of the folk, whereas later ones, such as Charles Wesley's "Hark, the Herald Angels Sing," are the product of a rather more sophisticated literary effort. The Christmas hymn is called a *noël* in France.

Caroline Applied in general to the age of Charles I of England (1625–1642) and in particular to the spirit of the court of Charles. Thus, *Caroline* might cover all the literature of the time, both Cavalier and PURITAN, or it might be used more specifically for writings by the royalist group, such as the CAVALIER LYRICISTS. *Caroline* literature was in some senses a carryover from the ELIZABETHAN and JACOBEAN Periods. Melancholy not only characterized the work of the Metaphysical Poets but permeated the writings of both the conflicting groups, Puritan and Cavalier. Drama was decadent; romanticism was in decline; classicism was advancing; the scientific spirit was growing in spite of the absorption of the people in violent religious controversies. It was in *Caroline* times that the Puritan migration to America was heaviest. The *Caroline* Age was the last segment of the Renaissance in England, if the COMMONWEALTH is considered an interregnum between the RENAISSANCE and the NEOCLASSIC PERIOD. See RENAISSANCE for a sketch of the literature; see BAROQUE, JACOBEAN AGE, CAVALIER LYRICISTS; see also "Caroline Age" in the *Outline of Literary History*.

Carpe Diem "Seize the day." The phrase was used by Horace, among others, and has come to be applied generally to literature, especially to lyric poems, which exemplify the spirit of "Let us eat and drink, for tomorrow we shall die." The theme was very common in sixteenth- and seventeenth-century English love poetry; lover-poets continually were exhorting their mistresses to yield to love while they still had their youth and beauty, as in Robert Herrick's familiar

Gather ye rosebuds while ye may,
Old Time is still a-flying;
And this same flower that smiles today,
Tomorrow will be dying.

The most famous English example is Andrew Marvell's "To His Coy Mistress," which may be a satirical parody of the convention. Persisting into modern times and gaining in depth and subtlety, the theme figures in Henry James's *The Ambassadors* and "The Beast in the Jungle" and—as is almost too obvious to need pointing out—in Robert Frost's "Carpe Diem" and Saul Bellow's *Seize the Day*.

Cartulary (also **Chartulary**) Records of a monastery or other such institution, as well as the book or place in which such records are kept.

Case Book Originally a collection of detailed information about legal and medical cases; now a volume that gathers in one place a body of materials relating to a case or problem of any sort. It is a kind of textbook devoted to a particular problem. In some, texts from books and periodicals are reproduced with their original page numbers, so that a student can prepare documentation without needing to track down original sources.

Catachresis Strictly, any misuse or misapplication of a word. Limited by Quintilian to cases (such as "leg of a table") in which there is a figurative name but no literal expression. Sometimes used for a mixed figure, such as "Blind mouths! that scarce themselves know how to hold / A sheep-hook" in Milton's "Lycidas."

Catalexis Incompleteness of the last foot of a line; truncation by omission of one or two final syllables; the opposite of ANACRUSIS. *Catalexis* secures variety of metrical effects. The term ACATALECTIC is used to designate particular lines where *catalexis* is *not* employed. Poe describes the rhythm and meter of "The Raven" thus: "The former is trochaic—the latter is octameter acatalectic, alternating with heptameter catalectic repeated in the refrain of the fifth verse, and terminating with tetrameter catalectic." (To Poe's credit, the next sentence begins, "Less pedantically. . . .") In the following lines by Thomas Hood, written in DACTYLIC DIMETER, the second and fourth are *catalectic* because the second foot of each lacks the two unaccented syllables that would normally complete the dactyl. The first and third lines, in which the unaccented syllables are *not* cut off and which therefore are metrically complete, are ACATALECTIC.

> One more unfortunate,
> Weary of breath,
> Rashly importunate,
> Gone to her death!

Catalexis is also applied to the truncation of an initial unstressed syllable; the resulting line is called HEADLESS. The first line of the "General Prologue" of Chaucer's *Canterbury Tales* is headless ("Whán thăt Áprĭl wĭth hĭs shówrĕs sóotĕ"), as is the opening of Francis Scott Key's "The Star-Spangled Banner" ("Ŏh, sáy, căn yŏu sée"). *Catalexis* of two syllables, as in the lines by Hood, is sometimes called BRACHYCATALEXIS.

Catalog A list of people, things, or attributes. *Catalogs*, sometimes extended to great length, are characteristic of much primitive literature and of much that is not so primitive as well. The EPIC uses the *catalog* of heroes, of ships, of armor, and such. The Bible has many *catalogs*, the most notable example being the genealogy of Jesus in Matthew, chapter 1. In the Renaissance, one of the conventions of the sonnet and the lyric was the *catalog* of the physical charms of the beloved. (See BLASON.) In modern poetry, the *catalog* has been used by Walt Whitman, William Carlos Williams, Ezra Pound, A. R. Ammons, and Gary Snyder. For an impressively extended *catalog*, see Whitman's *Song of Myself*, section 15.

Catastasis The heightening; the third of the four parts into which the ancients divided a play. See DRAMATIC STRUCTURE. In rhetoric it is the narrative part of the introduction of a speech.

Catastrophe The conclusion of a play, particularly of a TRAGEDY; the last of the four parts into which the ancients divided a play. It is the final stage in the FALLING ACTION, ending the dramatic CONFLICT and consisting of the actions that result from the CLIMAX. Because it is used mostly in connection with a TRAGEDY and involves the death of the hero, it is sometimes used by extension to designate an unhappy ending (or event) in nondramatic fiction and in life as well. In the strict sense, however, every drama has a *catastrophe*; see the line in *King Lear*: "Pat, he comes, like the catastrophe of the old comedy." Today, however, DÉNOUEMENT is more commonly used than *catastrophe* in the case of comedy. See DRAMATIC STRUCTURE.

Catch In music a ROUND for at least three voices, in which each singer begins a line or a phrase behind the preceding one. A popular musical form in the seventeenth and eighteenth centuries, it still occurs predominantly in children's songs; now usually called a ROUND. In METRICS the term *catch*, applied to an extra unstressed syllable at the beginning of a line that would normally begin with a stressed syllable, is a form of ANACRUSIS. *Catch* was also applied in the seventeenth and eighteenth centuries to the intermingling of strong and weak voices in songs wherein the strong voices furnish a bawdy twist. Jonathan Swift wrote such verses.

Catchword A word so often repeated that it is identified with a person or object. In printing, *catchword* has two meanings. The current usage of the term is as the name for a word printed at the top of a column or a page to indicate the first or last word on that page (normally, as in the boldface *catchwords* in this book, the first entry on even-numbered pages and the last on the odd-numbered). At the bottom of each page, under the last word or segment on the last line, early printers customarily printed the first word of the next page. This was called a *catchword.*

Catechism An exercise arranged as questions and answers, especially in use for religious instruction; occasionally adapted for nonreligious purposes, as in the anonymous satirical poem "Mr. J. M. S——e Catechized on His One Epistle to Mr. Pope":

> What makes you write at this odd Rate?
> Why, sir, it is to imitate.
> What makes you steal and trifle so?
> Why 'tis to do, as others do.
> But there's no Meaning to be seen!
> Why, that's the very thing I mean.

Here is an example from two centuries later, by E. E. Cummings:

> Q:dwo
>   we know of anything which can
>   be as dull as one englishman
> A:to

Catena Latin, "chain." A series of quotations—not necessarily linked in the manner of a CHAIN VERSE—used decoratively, such as the group of Old Testament passages preceding the Dedication of the 1655 edition of Henry Vaughan's *Silex Scintillans*.

Catharsis Aristotle's *Poetics* see the objective of TRAGEDY, as being "through pity and fear effecting the proper purgation [*catharsis*] of these emotions," but he does not explain what "proper purgation" means. In his time it had both a medical and a religious signification. In medical terms *catharsis* referred to the discharge from the body of the excess of elements produced by a state of sickness and thus the return to bodily health. Viewed in this sense, *catharsis* is the process by which an unhealthy emotional state produced by an imbalance of feelings is corrected and emotional health restored. An ambiguity in the Greek wording makes it possible that what is purged is not the emotions but the complications of the plot. In religious terms, as expressed in several places by Plato, *catharsis* is the process of purification by which the soul collects its elements, brings itself together from all parts of the body, and can exist "alone by itself, freed from the body as from fetters."

Whatever Aristotle means thereby, *catharsis* remains one of the great unsettled issues. That it implies a beneficial cathartic effect produced by witnessing a tragic action is clear; how it is produced is in question. Some believe that the spectators, by vicarious participation, learn through the fate of the tragic hero, that fear and pity are destructive and thereby learn to avoid them in their own lives (this interpretation is clearly didactic). Others believe that the spectator, being human and thus subject to disturbing emotions of fear and pity, has this imbalance rectified and these internal agitations stilled by having an opportunity vicariously to expend fear and pity on the hero.

Still others see the tragic hero as a scapegoat on which the excessive emotions of the spectator can be placed, leaving the spectator at the end calm, "all passion spent." R. B. Sharpe, in *Irony in the Drama*, suggests that before the conclusion of a tragedy the hero comes to represent to the spectator "what Jung calls a symbol and Frazer a scapegoat—that is, a human figure upon whom we are able to load our emotions, from our loftiest to our lowest, our hopes, and our sins, through such a deep and complete emotional identification that he can carry them away with him into heaven or the wilderness and so free us of the burden and the tension of keeping them for ourselves. This empathic identification is . . . catharsis." Critics have been playing variations on these interpretations ever since Aristotle, and the provocative concept of *catharsis*, although useful and instructive, is certain to remain unclear.

Cauda Another name for the "tail" or short line found in certain verse forms. See TAIL-RHYME ROMANCE, TAIL-RHYME STANZA.

Caudate Sonnet An Italian form, rarely adopted into English, in which a standard fourteen-line SONNET is augmented by the addition of other lines, including "tails." Milton's "On the New Forcers of Conscience under the Long Parliament" is a clear example. The first fourteen lines are in iambic pentameter with the rhyme scheme of an Italian sonnet: *abbaabbacdedec*. There are six additional lines, continuing the rhyme scheme as *cfffgg*; the fifteenth and eighteenth lines are trimeter, and the rest are pentameter. Hopkins's "That Nature Is a Heraclitean Fire and of the Comfort of the Resurrection" probably qualifies also.

Causerie An INFORMAL ESSAY, usually on a literary topic, and frequently in a series. The term is applied to such essays because of their similarity to *Causeries du lundi* by Charles Augustin Sainte-Beuve. In the strictest sense it probably should be limited to the kind of combined biographical and critical treatments for which Sainte-Beuve was noted. Edmund Wilson wrote literary essays that might be called *causeries*.

Cavalier Lyric A poem characteristic of the CAVALIER LYRICISTS; lighthearted in tone; graceful, melodious, and polished in manner; artfully showing Latin classical influences; sometimes licentious and cynical or epigrammatic and witty. At times it breathed the careless BRAGGADOCIO of the military swashbuckler, at times the aristocratic ease of the peaceable courtier. Many of the poems were OCCASIONAL, as Suckling's charming if doggerel-like "Ballad upon a Wedding" or Lovelace's pensive "To Althea from Prison." The themes were love, war, chivalry, and loyalty to the king. The term *Cavalier Lyric* is also applied to a later poem that illustrates the spirit of the times of the CAVALIER LYRICISTS, such as Browning's "Cavalier Tunes" ("Marching Along," "Give a Rouse," and "Boot and Saddle").

Cavalier Lyricists The followers of Charles I (1625–1649) were called Cavaliers, as opposed to the supporters of Parliament, who were called ROUNDHEADS. The *Cavalier Lyricists*, a group of the former who composed lighthearted poems, included Thomas Carew, Richard Lovelace, and Sir John Suckling. These were soldiers and courtiers first and authors of lyrics only incidentally. Robert Herrick, although he was a country parson and not a courtier, is often classed with the *Cavalier Lyricists* because many of his poems included in *Hesperides* are in the vein of the Cavaliers. See CAVALIER LYRIC.

Celtic Literature Literature produced by a people speaking any of the Celtic dialects. Linguistically, the Celts are divided into two main groups. The "Brythonic" Celts include Ancient Britons, Welsh, Cornish (Cornwall), and Bretons (Brittany); and the Goidelic (Gaelic) Celts include the Irish, the Manx (Isle of Man), and the Scottish Gaels. At one time the Celts, an important branch of the Indo-European family, dominated Central and Western Europe. The Continental Celts (including the Bretons) have left no literature. The Celts of Great Britain and Ireland, however, have produced much literature of interest to students of English and American literature. See IRISH LITERATURE, WELSH LITERATURE, SCOTTISH LITERATURE, CELTIC RENAISSANCE.

Celtic Renaissance (or Celtic Revival or Irish Renaissance) A general term for a movement aimed at the preservation of the Gaelic language (the GAELIC MOVEMENT), the reconstruction of early Celtic history and literature, and the stimulation of a new literature authentically Celtic (especially Irish) in spirit. From early in the nineteenth century interest in Celtic antiquities grew, and much work was done in the collection, study, printing, and translation of manuscripts embodying the history and literature of ancient Ireland. There also developed the practice of collecting and printing folktales preserved in oral tradition. In the 1890s came the Gaelic Movement, which stressed the use of the Gaelic language. More fruitful was the contemporaneous Anglo-Irish movement, which stimulated the production of a new literature in English (or "Anglo-Irish") by Irish writers on Irish themes and in the Irish spirit. Standish O'Grady's imaginative treatment of Irish history (1880) provided impetus to the movement, and themes drawn from ancient Irish tradition were exploited in verse and drama. Fortunately, genuinely talented writers were at hand to further the project, such as W. B. Yeats, George W. Russell ("A.E."), George Moore, J. M. Synge, and (later) James Stephens, Lord Dunsany, and Sean O'Casey. From the beginning Lady Gregory was an enthusiastic worker—as collector, popularizer, essayist, and playwright. A striking phase of the *Celtic Renaissance* was its drama. In 1899, under the leadership of Yeats, Moore, Edward Martyn, Lady Gregory, and others, the Irish Literary Theater was founded in Dublin. For it, Yeats and Martyn wrote some plays employing Irish folk materials. Later Yeats joined another group more devoted to the exploitation of native elements, The Irish National Theatre Society, to which he attracted J. M. Synge, the most gifted playwright of the movement, whose *Playboy of the Western World* (1907) and *Deirdre of the Sorrows* (1910) attracted wide recognition. This group worked in the famed Abbey Theatre. Later exemplars of dramatic activity were Lord Dunsany and Sean O'Casey. Still later, Brendan Behan (1923–1964), who could write poems in the Irish Gaelic language, excelled in drama, journalism, travel writing, fiction, and autobiography.

Celtic Revival A term sometimes used for the GAELIC MOVEMENT, the CELTIC RENAISSANCE, or the IRISH LITERARY MOVEMENT, as well as for the eighteenth-century movement described next.

Celtic Revival, The (Eighteenth Century) A literary movement that, in the last half of the eighteenth century, stressed the use of the historical, literary, and mythological traditions of the ancient Celts, particularly the Welsh. Through confusion, Norse mythology was included. *The Celtic Revival* was a part of the romantic movement, in that it stressed the primitive, the remote, the strange, and the mysterious; and it aided the revolt against pseudoclassicism by substituting a new mythology for classical myths and figures. Specifically, it was characterized by an intense interest in the druids and early Welsh bards, numerous translations and imitations of early Celtic poetry appearing in the wake of the discovery of some genuine examples of early Welsh verse. The most influential and gifted poet in the group was Thomas Gray, whose "The Bard" (1757) and "The Progress of Poesy" (1757) reflect early phases of the movement. The most spectacular figure in the group of "Celticists" was James Macpherson, whose long poems, *Fingal* (1762) and *Temora* (1763)—chiefly his own invention but partly English renderings of genuine Gaelic pieces preserved in the Scottish Highlands—were published as translations of the poems of a great Celtic poet of primitive times, Ossian. Both Gray's and Macpherson's work influenced a host of minor poets, who were especially numerous and active in the last two decades of the century. There was also a considerable reflection of the movement in the drama, for example, Home's *The Fatal Discovery* (acted 1769).

[Reference: E. D. Snyder, *The Celtic Revival in English Literature* (1923, reprinted 1965).]

Censorship The policies and practices involved in the testing of an utterance for suitability, often followed by proscription. It can be personal and subjective: The superego exercises *censorship* over one's own words and deeds. It can be casual and unofficial, for any family or group observes rules of what can be said and what cannot be said. *Censorship* can be official, as in military organizations in wartime, or in a prison. Various attempts at the official *censorship* of literary works have eventually failed; nowadays systems of rating and *censorship* apply to exoteric visual media, such as film, television, and photography.

Center for Editions of American Authors (CEAA) A committee of scholars representing the American Literature Section of the Modern Language Association of America for the production of definitive EDITIONS of nineteenth-century American authors. It has now been replaced by the CENTER FOR SCHOLARLY EDITIONS. The *CEAA*, as it was commonly called, established editorial procedures, oversaw the work of editors, and approved texts for publication. It enunciated rigorous and highly sophisticated principles for textual editing; after verification that these principles had been meticulously followed in the preparation of a volume, it awarded the volume the right to display the *Center's* seal of approval. Among the authors having editions sponsored by the *CEAA* are Washington Irving, Charles Brockden Brown, Stephen Crane, Emerson, Howells, William James, Mark Twain, Melville, Simms, Thoreau, Whitman, Frost, and Pound.

Center for Scholarly Editions (CSE) The broad functions of the *Center for Scholarly Editions* are the same as those of the CENTER FOR EDITIONS OF AMERICAN AUTHORS, which it replaced in 1976 on the expiration of the CEAA grants from the National Endowment for the Humanities. Like the CEAA, the *CSE* is administered by a committee of the Modern Language Association. However, it places no restrictions on the content of the editions with which it concerns itself, any kind of work or document from any nation and in any language being eligible for aid by the *Center*. Its goal is to serve as a clearinghouse for information about scholarly editing, to offer advice and consultation to editors of scholarly projects, and to award its emblem to volumes that are found to merit it. See CENTER FOR EDITIONS OF AMERICAN AUTHORS.

Cento A literary patchwork, usually in verse, made up of scraps from one or many authors. An example is a fifth-century life of Christ by the Empress Eudoxia, which is in verse with every line drawn from Homer. Richard Willey compiled a Latin *cento* in the sixteenth century. An anonymous nineteenth-century exercise begins

On Linden when the sun was low,
A frog he would a-wooing go;
He sighed a sigh, and breathed a prayer,
None but the brave deserve the fair.

"Lines Where Beauty Lingers" by Franklin P. Adams ("F.P.A.") approaches pure nonsense:

Tell me not, Sweet, I am unkin
That which her slender waist confined
It fell about the Martinmas
Out of the clover and blue-eyed grass
. . . .
O, my luve's like a red, red rose
Love is a sickness full of woes
Balkis was in her marble town
Ay, tear her tattered ensign down!

Rudyard Kipling's story "Brugglesmith" (1893) features a *cento* sung by a drunkard who seems to foresee *The Waste Land*:

Ye Towers o' Julia, London's lasting wrong,
By mony a foul an' midnight murder fed—
Sweet Thames run softly till I end my song
And yon's the grave as little as my bed.

More recently, R. S. Gwynn has produced "Approaching a Significant Birthday, He Peruses *The Norton Anthology of Poetry*," which ends

Do not go gentle into that good night.
Fame is no plant that grows on mortal soil.
Again he raised the jug up to the light.
Old age hath yet his honor and his toil.
Downward to darkness on extended wings,
Break, break, break, on thy cold gray stones, O sea,
And tell sad stories of the death of kings.
I do not think that they will sing to me.

Chain Rhyme Uncommon in English, this device incorporates elements of ECHO and IDENTICAL RHYME so that the sound of the last syllable of one line recurs as the sound of the first syllable of the next but with a change of meaning. *Chain rhyme* would occur, say, if a line ending "weight" were succeeded by one beginning "wait." Hopkins's "The Leaden Echo and the Golden Echo" furnishes an instance: The Leaden Echo's last word is "despair" and the Golden Echo's first word is "Spare!"

Chain Verse Poetry in which the stanzas are linked through some pattern of repetition. The last line of one stanza may be the first of the next, producing a linked group of stanzas that may be considered a *chain*. The SESTINA may be considered a sort of *chain* with links formed by the repetition of words, phrases, or lines in a predetermined pattern. In Samuel Daniel's *Delia* the last line of the one sonnet may be the first line of the next, but the pattern is inconsistent. The linkage may also be secured by the repetition of rhyme. The VILLANELLE, a nineteen-line poem in tercets followed by a quatrain and having only two rhymes and frequent repetition of lines, is a complex example of *chain verse*.

Chanson A song. Originally composed of two-line stanzas of equal length (couplets), each stanza ending in a refrain, the *chanson* is now more broadly interpreted to include almost any simple poem intended to be sung.

Chanson d'aventure A poem recounting a romantic adventure, often involving a journey on horseback or a sea voyage.

Chanson de geste A "song of great deeds." A term applied to the early French EPIC. The earliest and best existing example, the *Chanson de Roland*, dates from c. 1100. The early *chansons de geste* are written in ten-syllable lines marked by assonance and grouped in strophes of varying length. Cycles developed, such as that of Charlemagne (*gestes du roi*); that of William of Orange, which reflects the efforts of Christian heroes against the invading Saracens; and that dealing with the strife among the rebellious Northern barons. The stories generally reflect chivalric military ideals with little use of love as the theme. The form flourished for several centuries, a total of about eighty examples being extant. These epic tales supplied material ("Matter of France") for MEDIEVAL ROMANCE, including English ROMANCES.

Chant Loosely used to mean a song, but more particularly the term signifies the intoning of words to a monotonous musical measure of few notes. The words of the *chants* in the English Church come from such biblical sources as the PSALMS. CADENCE (in its first sense) is an important element, and usually one note (the "reciting note") is used for a series of successive words or syllables. Dirges are often chanted. Repetition of a few varying musical phrases is a characteristic, and the intonation of the voice plays an important role. *Chants* are generally considered less melodious than songs. In some *chants*, the words come from a prose text.

Chant Royal One of the most complex French verse forms. The tradition demands a dignified, heroic subject such as can best be expressed in rich diction and courtly formalities of speech. The *chant royal* consists of sixty lines arranged in five stanzas of eleven lines each and an ENVOY of five lines, the envoy ordinarily starting with an invocation in the manner of the BALLADE. The usual rhyme scheme is *ababccddedE* for the stanza and *ddedE* (as in the last five lines of the stanza) for the envoy. The capital *E* indicates the recurrence of a complete line as a refrain at the end of each stanza and at the close of the envoy. All stanzas must follow the same pattern, and no rhyme word may appear twice, except in the envoy. Thus, the poet must accomplish the difficult feat of producing sixty lines on only five rhyme sounds. The *chant royal* was popular in France in the fourteenth century, when it was extensively used by Eustace Deschamps, Charles d'Orleans, and Jean Marot. Until the late 1970s, it looked as though the *chant royal* was so difficult that it had to be restricted to a few cases of mannered light verse. That misconception was corrected when the first poem in the first issue of *Poetry* magazine edited by John Frederick Nims was Robert Morgan's "Chant Royal," which nobly satisfies all of the topical and formal requirements. "My Mother's Hard Row to Hoe," in Fred Chappell's *Midquest*, is a variant of the *chant royal* with the rules somewhat relaxed.

Chantey (also **Shanty**) A sailors' song marked by strong rhythm and, in the days of sail, used to accompany certain forms of repetitious hard labor (such as weighing anchor) performed by seamen working in a group. The leader of the singing was referred to as the "chantey man," his responsibility being to sing a line or two introductory to a refrain joined in by the whole group.

Chapbook A small book or pamphlet, usually a single SIGNATURE of sixteen or thirty-two pages, poorly printed and crudely illustrated, sold in England and America through the eighteenth century by peddlers or "chapmen." *Chapbooks* dealt with all sorts of topics and incidents: travel tales, murder cases, prodigies, strange occurrences, witchcraft, fairy tales, biographies, religious legends, and tracts. The term has been revived as the name for miscellaneous small books and pamphlets.

Character A complicated term that includes the idea of the moral constitution of the human personality (Aristotle's sense of *ethos*), the presence of moral uprightness, and the simpler notion of the presence of creatures in art that seem to be human beings of one sort or another; *character* is also a term applied to a literary form that flourished in England and France in the seventeenth and eighteenth centuries. It is a brief descriptive sketch of a personage who typifies some definite quality. The person is described not as an individualized personality but as an example of some vice or virtue or type, such as a busybody, a glutton, a fop, a bumpkin, a garrulous old man, or a happy milkmaid. Similar treatments of institutions and inanimate things, such as "the *character* of a coffee house," also employed the term, and late in the seventeenth century, by a natural extension of the tradition, *character* was applied to longer compositions, sometimes historical, as Lord Halifax's *Character of Charles II*. The vogue of *character*-writing followed the publication in 1592 of a Latin translation of Theophrastus, an ancient Greek writer of similar sketches. Though the *character* may have influenced Ben Jonson in his treatment of humours in comedy, the first English writer to cultivate the form as such was Bishop Joseph Hall in his *Characters of Virtues and Vices* (1608).

Two of his successors were Sir Thomas Overbury (1614) and John Earle (1628). Later, under the influence of the French writer La Bruyère, *characters* became more individualized and were combined with the essay, as in the PERIODICAL ESSAYS of Addison and Steele. Subjects of *characters* were given fanciful proper names, often Latin or Greek, such as "Croesus."

Characterization The creation of imaginary persons so that they seem lifelike. There are three fundamental methods of *characterization*: (1) the explicit presentation by the author of the character through direct EXPOSITION, either in an introductory block or more often piecemeal throughout the work, illustrated by action; (2) the presentation of the character in action, with little or no explicit comment by the author, in the expectation that the reader can deduce the attributes of the actor from the actions; and (3) the representation from within a CHARACTER, without comment by the author, of the impact of actions and emotions on the character's inner self.

Regardless of the method by which a character is presented, the author may concentrate on a dominant trait to the exclusion of other aspects of personality, or the author may attempt to present a fully rounded creation. If the presentation of a single dominant trait is carried to an extreme, not a believable character but a caricature will result. If this method is handled with skill, it can produce striking and interesting two-dimensional characters that lack depth. Mr. Micawber in *David Copperfield* comes close to being such a two-dimensional character through the emphasis that Dickens puts on a very small group of characteristics. Sometimes such characters are given descriptive names, such as Mr. Hammerdown, the auctioneer in *Vanity Fair*. On the other hand, the author may present so convincing a congeries of personality traits that a complex rather than a simple character emerges; such a character is three-dimensional or, in E. M. Forster's term, "round." The fascination of Richardson's Clarissa Harlowe, for example, lies partly in her "divided mind," which involves a dialectical tension between impulses so virtuous as to seem angelic and normal erotic impulses. Shaw's Saint Joan combines nearly irreconcilable components of two antithetical types: the *ingénue* and the MILES GLORIOSUS. Sometimes just a title, such as *Lord Jim*, can reflect such a contradiction or anomaly. (F. Scott Fitzgerald observed that a writer who sets out to create an individual may create a type at the same time, but one who sets out to create a type will create nothing.) Some human creatures portrayed in literature are hardly distinct characters at all but mere properties or furnishings; on the other hand, some nonhuman entities, such as animals, machines, houses, and cities, may function fully as characters. Rome has such a role in Shakespeare's so-called Roman Tragedies, as do the City of London in Eliot's *The Waste Land* and various great rivers in Mark Twain's *Huckleberry Finn* and Conrad's *Heart of Darkness*.

Furthermore, a character may be either STATIC or DYNAMIC. A static character is one who changes little if at all. Things happen *to* such a character without things happening *within*. The pattern of action reveals the character rather than showing the character changing in response to the actions. Sometimes a static character gives the appearance of changing simply because our picture of the character is revealed bit by bit; this is true of Uncle Toby in *Tristram Shandy*, who does not change, although our view of him steadily changes. A dynamic character, on the other hand, is one who is modified by actions and experiences, and one objective of the work in which the character appears is to reveal the consequences of these actions. See POINT OF VIEW, NOVEL, DRAMA, PLOT, CONCRETE UNIVERSAL.

[References: E. M. Forster, *Aspects of the Novel* (1927, 1954); W. J. Harvey, *Character and the Novel* (1965); Edwin Muir, *The Structure of the Novel* (1928, reprinted 1963).]

Charade The silent acting out of the meaning of a syllable or a homonym. You may, for example, point to your hair to suggest "hare." In the game of *charades*, which has been popular for at least two centuries, one player performs a number of syllables that make up a word, to be guessed by other players. The best-known literary example comes in Chapter 51 of Thackeray's *Vanity Fair*, with Becky Sharp and others acting out "night + inn + gale" and "Aga + Memnon."

Charientism, Charientismus Ironic glossing over of a disagreeable subject with more agreeable language, as when Nick Carraway, in Chapter 1 of *The Great Gatsby*, refers to "that delayed Teutonic migration known as the Great War."

Charm A primordial formulaic utterance—related to the SPELL, the CURSE, and the RIDDLE—designed to have magical influence in the conduct of life. It may involve a request for good luck or the "apotropaic" desire to ward off evil; it may be motivated by something as mundane as the need to find lost objects or win a contest. The etymological relation between *charm* and the Latin *carmen* ("song," "poem"), like the relation between "grammar" and "glamor," registers the antiquity and persistence of the connections between speech and magic.

Chartism A nineteenth-century English political movement, the object of which was to win more social recognition and improved material conditions for the lower classes. The Chartists advocated universal suffrage, vote by ballot, annual parliaments, and other reforms. This agenda is given in the *People's Charter* (1838). Carlyle's *Chartism* (1839) is an attack on the movement. The Chartist agitation is favorably reflected in some of Kingsley's novels. See INDUSTRIAL REVOLUTION.

Chaucerian Stanza See RHYME ROYAL.

Chiaroscuro Contrasting light and shade. Originally applied to painting, the term is used in the criticism of various literary forms involving the contrast of light and darkness, as in much of Hawthorne's and Nabokov's fiction and in Faulkner's *Light in August*. Thomas Pynchon's *Gravity's Rainbow* involves complex interplay of black and white. *Chiaroscuro* is patently important in FILM NOIR.

Chiasmus A pattern in which the second part is balanced against the first but with the parts reversed, as in Coleridge's line, "Flowers are lovely, love is flowerlike," or Pope's "Works without show, and without pomp presides." In general, any elements subject to arrangement can take on this chiastic or mirror-image design (X-shaped, like the Greek letter *chi*). Such phrases as "Firestone snow-tire" and "moonstruck mushroom" display phonemic *chiasmus*. A similar effect may be audible in Joyce's "Rain has fallen all the day" and Auden's "Read the *New Yorker* and take short views." There is *chiasmus* at the end of Milton's "Lycidas": "fresh Woods, and Pastures new." Keats's line "Out went the taper as she hurried in" comprises two clauses with syntactic *chiasmus*: adverb, verb, subject; subject, verb, adverb—with a nice play between "out" and "in." Less elaborately, Whitman's "I Hear America Singing" begins, "I HEAR America singing, the varied carols I hear." *Chiasmus* is sometimes combined with *ellipses*, as in these passages from Pope and Hardy:

> And has not Colley still his lord and whore?
> His butchers Henley? his freemasons Moore?
>
> . . . .
>
> I left no calling for this idle trade,
> No duty broke, no father disobeyed.
>
> . . . .
>
> The land's sharp features seemed to be
>   The Century's corpse outleant
> His crypt the cloudy canopy,
>   The wind his death-lament.

Chicago Critics A group of critics, associated with the University of Chicago, who in 1952 published *Critics and Criticism*; also used to mean the followers of the group. The *Chicago Critics* developed theories about the history of criticism and about the practical criticism of literary texts. As historians, they were pluralists, attempting to value critical systems in terms of their assumptions about literature and their contributions to our understanding of literature. As critics, they are Neo-Aristotelian, being concerned with the practical criticism of individual works of literature, emphasizing the principles that govern their construction and tending to see literary texts in broadly defined generic classifications. Among the *Chicago Critics* are Ronald S. Crane, Elder Olson, Richard McKeon, Wayne Booth, Norman Maclean, W. Rea Keast, and Austin M. Wright. See CRITICISM, TYPES OF.

[Reference: R. S. Crane, ed., *Critics and Criticism* (1952).]

Chivalric Romance MEDIEVAL ROMANCE reflecting the customs and ideals of chivalry. See ARTHURIAN LEGEND, COURTLY LOVE.

Chivalry in English Literature The system of manners and morals known as *chivalry*, a product of the feudal system of the Middle Ages, was presented in medieval romance in a highly idealized form amounting almost to a religious faith for the upper classes, and it has furnished colorful subject matter for much later literature. The medieval knight, seen in the light of literary idealization (in reality, the typical medieval knight had many unlovely characteristics), has been portrayed not only by the many writers of medieval romance, but by such later poets as Chaucer, with his "parfit, gentle knight" and Spenser, who fills *The Faerie Queene* with a procession of courteous and heroic Guyons, Scudamores, and Calidores. Knights whose high oaths bind them to fidelity to God and king, truth to their ladyloves, and ready service for all damsels in distress or other victims of unjust tyrants, cruel giants, or fiendish monsters, have become commonplaces of romantic literature.

Chivalric knights figure importantly in such HISTORICAL NOVELS as Scott's *Ivanhoe* and find lofty, sympathetic treatment in Tennyson's *Idylls of the King*. King Arthur, speaking in Tennyson's *Guinevere*, expresses well the ideals of chivalric knighthood:

> I made them lay their hands in mine and swear
> To reverence the King, as if he were
> Their conscience, and their conscience as their King,
> To break the heathen and uphold the Christ,
> To ride abroad redressing human wrongs,
> To speak no slander, no, nor listen to it,
> To honor his own word as if his God's,
> To lead sweet lives in purest chastity,
> To love one maiden only, cleave to her,
> And worship her by years of noble deeds,
> Until they won her.

A more faithful picture may be found in Malory's *Le Morte Darthur*, where the glamour of knighthood, with all the effort to idealize Lancelot and Arthur and find in the "good old days" a perfect pattern for later times, is not allowed to obscure some of the less pleasing actualities of medieval knighthood. So glorious a thing as *chivalry* has not, of course, gone unnoticed by the satirists. The early seventeenth century produced not only the immortal *Don Quixote* in Spain but Beaumont and Fletcher's dramatic burlesque *The Knight of the Burning Pestle* in England, while modern America has brought forth the broadly comic *A Connecticut Yankee in King Arthur's Court* (Mark Twain) as well as the more subtly mocking *Galahad* (John Erskine) and "Childe Roland, etc." (Elder Olson). See ARTHURIAN LEGEND.

[References: Larry D. Benson and John Leyerle, eds., *Chivalric Literature* (1980); Diane Bornstein, *Mirrors of Courtesy* (1975); Lee C. Ramsey, *Chivalric Romances: Popular Literature in Medieval England* (1983).]

Choliambus The most important variety of SCAZON because it has to do with the IAMBIC rhythm that is the most important in English. There are subtle refinements in the use of this device by the ancients; in English all that matters is that the last FOOT in a prevalently iambic line is not an iamb, ANAPEST, AMPHIBRACH, or SPONDEE, but a TROCHEE or DACTYL. In the commonest form, the last foot of a line that is basically iambic tetrameter or pentameter is supplanted by a trochee. Such double frustration of the ear's expectation can be deeply unsettling. There are instances in Marlowe's *Doctor Faustus* ("I think my master means to die shortly"), Tennyson's "Lucretius" ("Strikes through the wood, sets all the tops quivering"), and Stevens's "Sunday Morning" ("Elations when the forest blooms; gusty"). Among Eliot's poems, *choliambus* occurs in both the last line of "Gerontion" ("Thoughts of a dry brain in a dry season") and the first of *The Waste Land* ("April is the cruelest month, breeding"). *Choliambus* differs radically from the common feminine line-ending, which means that the final iamb is replaced by an amphibrach (or is simply augmented by one or more unaccented syllables). See SCAZON.

Choral Character A character in a play or a novel who stands aside from the action and comments on it or speaks about it as a communal voice. See CHORUS.

Choriambus A FOOT in which two accented syllables flank two unaccented syllables: ´˘˘´. This FOOT is sometimes used in a verse form called *choriambics*, in which the line consists of a TROCHEE, three *choriambics*, and an IAMBUS. Swinburne used the form, as did Rupert Brooke, whose line: "Í hăve | ténd ĕd aňd lóved | yéar ŭpŏn yéar, | Í ĭn thĕ sól | ĭ túde" illustrates the *choriambic* line.

Choree Obsolete equivalent of TROCHEE; now preserved only in CHORIAMBUS (*choree* + iambus).

Choreopoem A work that combines dance and poetry so that each complements the other in a highly dramatic way. The term was coined by Ntozake Shange, whose *for colored girls who have considered suicide/ when the rainbow is enuf* is subtitled "a choreopoem."

Chorography Writing that has to do with the specific natural features of a particular place, sometimes accompanied by maps and other illustrations. A good example is Michael Drayton's *Polyolbion* (1612–1622), a county-by-county description of England.

Chorus In ancient Greece, the groups of dancers and singers who participated in religious festivals and dramatic performances. Also the songs sung by the *chorus*. At first the choral songs made up the bulk of the play, the spoken monologue and dialogue being interpolated. Later, however, the *chorus* became subordinate, offering inter-act comments. Finally, it became a mere lyric used to take up the time between acts. In ELIZABETHAN DRAMA the role of the *chorus* was often taken by a single actor, who recited PROLOGUE and EPILOGUE and gave inter-act comments that linked the acts and foreshadowed coming events. So in Sackville and Norton's *Gorboduc*, the first English TRAGEDY, the *chorus* consists of a few stanzas accompanied by a dumb show that foreshadows the coming action. In Kyd's *Spanish Tragedy* the part of the *chorus* is played by a ghost and the figure Revenge. Shakespeare sometimes employed the *chorus*, as in *Pericles*, in which the old poet Gower, accompanied by a dumb show, provides prologue and inter-act comment, and in *King Henry the Fifth*, in which the *chorus* comments on the action, explains changes of scene, and (in a thoroughly traditional convention of choric behavior) begs for the indulgence of the spectators. Sometimes, within the play proper, one of the characters, such as the Fool in *King Lear*, is said to play a "*chorus*-like" role when he or she comments on the action.

Although no longer common, the *chorus* is still used occasionally by modern playwrights, notably T. S. Eliot in *Murder in the Cathedral*. Sometimes a *chorus*-character—one whose role in the drama is to comment on the action—is used; such a character is Seth Beckwith in O'Neill's *Mourning Becomes Electra*. Novelists, too, have used the *chorus*, sometimes as a group of characters who comment on action, sometimes as a single character. Both Scott and Hardy used *choruses* of rustics. The group of goodwives in the first scene of Hawthorne's *The Scarlet Letter* serves the function of a *chorus*. The CONFIDANTE of the Henry James novel is a *chorus*-character. In music, a *chorus* may be a composition in at least four parts written for a larger group of singers, and the term is also applied to the singers of such choral compositions. It is also applied to a REFRAIN.

Chrestomathy A collection of choice passages to be used in the study of a language or a literature and, thus, a kind of anthology. When the term is used today, it may signify a volume of selected passages or stories by a single author; *chrestomathy* was used in this sense by H. L. Mencken, whose adoption of a word so pretentious must have been in jest.

Christianity, Established in England The bishops of London and York are said to have attended a church council in Gaul as early as A.D. 314. After the lapse into barbarism and paganism that followed the Germanic invasions of the fifth century, *Christianity* was reintroduced directly from Rome by St. Augustine of Canterbury, who landed in Kent in A.D. 597.

The establishment of *Christianity* in England profoundly affected literature, because the Church was for centuries the chief sponsor of learning. The pagan literature that survived from early Germanic times passed through the medium of Christian authors and copyists, who gave a Christian coloring to the writings that they did not wholly reject. For centuries most writings owed both their inspiration and direction to a Christian spirit. The Christianization of the great body of Arthurian romances in the thirteenth century is an outstanding example of the dominance of *Christianity* over medieval literary activity.

Chronicle A name of certain forms of historical writing. *Chronicles* differ from ANNALS in their concern with larger aspects of history. Though there were prototypes in Hebrew, Greek, Latin, and French, the comprehensive medieval *chronicles* in English and their Renaissance successors matter most to the student of English literature. The *Anglo-Saxon Chronicle*, begun under King Alfred late in the ninth century and carried on by various writers in a number of monasteries, has been called the "first great book in English prose." The record begins with 60 B.C. and closes with 1154 (Peterborough version). Alfred and his helpers revised older minor *chronicles* and records and wrote firsthand accounts of their own times. The work as a whole is a sort of historical miscellany, sometimes sketchy in detail and detached in attitude, at other times lively, partisan, and detailed. An important Old English poem preserved through its inclusion in the *Anglo-Saxon Chronicle* is the spirited *Battle of Brunanburh*. A famous Latin prose *chronicle* is Geoffrey of Monmouth's *History of the Kings of Britain* (c. 1135), which records not only legendary British history but also romantic accounts of King Arthur. The earliest important verse *chronicle* in Middle English is Layamon's *Brut* (c. 1205), based on Wace's French poetic version of Geoffrey. A long poem composed in an imaginative and often dramatic vein, it exhibits a picturesque style sometimes reminiscent of Old English poetry.

Later Middle English *chronicles* include those of Robert of Gloucester (late thirteenth century), Robert Manning of Brunne (1338), Andrew of Wyntoun (*Original Chronicle of Scotland*, early fifteenth century), John Hardyng (late fifteenth century), and John Capgrave (fifteenth century). With the rise of the Tudor dynasty came a wave of patriotism, one result of which was the production in the sixteenth century of many *chronicles*—some in Latin prose, some in English verse; some mere abstracts, some voluminous; some new compositions, some retellings of older ones. Some of the more important *chronicles* of Elizabeth's time, besides the famous *Mirror for Magistrates*, are Richard Grafton's (1563), John Stowe's (1565, 1580, 1592), and Ralph Holinshed's (1578). Not only are portions of this mass of *chronicle*-writing themselves of genuine literary value, full of anecdote and description, but some of them were important as sources for Shakespeare and other dramatists.

Later writers have used the term in titles: Sir Walter Scott's *Chronicles of the Canongate*, Anthony Trollope's *The Last Chronicle of Barset*, Hugh Walpole's *Herries Chronicle*, and John Cheever's *The Wapshot Chronicle*. A set of historical novels by Gore Vidal have been called his American Chronicles or Chronicles of Empire.

Chronicle Play A type of drama flourishing in the latter part of Elizabeth's reign, which drew its English historical materials from the sixteenth-century CHRONICLES, such as Holinshed's, and stressed the patriotism of the times. It enjoyed increasing popularity with the outburst of nationalistic feeling following the defeat of the Spanish Armada (1588) and served as a medium for teaching English history to the uneducated. The structure of the earlier *chronicle plays* was very loose, unity consisting mainly in the inclusion of the events of a single king's reign. The number of characters was large. The plays featured pageantry (coronations, funerals) and other spectacular elements, such as battles on the stage. The serious action was often relieved by comic scenes or subplots, as in Shakespeare's famous "Falstaff plays" (*King Henry the Fourth*, I, II; *King Henry the Fifth*). The tendency to merge with ROMANTIC COMEDIES appeared as early as Greene's *James IV* (c. 1590); in Shakespeare's *Cymbeline* (c. 1610) the chronicle material is completely subordinated to the demands of romantic comedy. Shakespeare's *Richard III* (c. 1593) exemplifies the tendency of the *chronicle play* to develop into TRAGEDY of character, a movement that culminates in such plays as *King Lear* (1605) and *Macbeth* (1606). The term HISTORY PLAY is sometimes applied to a restricted group of *chronicle plays* such as Shakespeare's *King Henry the Fifth*, which are unified but are neither COMEDY nor TRAGEDY. The earliest true *chronicle play* is perhaps *The Famous Victories of Henry V* (c. 1586). Peele's *Edward I* (1590–91) and Marlowe's *Edward II* (1592) are among the best pre-Shakespearean *chronicle plays*.

Chronique scandaleuse A body of scandalous gossip, usually informal and unofficial but sometimes achieving written form, as in William Byrd's *Secret Diary* and Truman Capote's *Answered Prayers*. Into the twenty-first century, such writing flourished in *Vanity Fair* magazine, especially in the work of Dominick Dunne.

Chronogram A procedure for inscribing a date, in Roman numerals, in a text using the Roman alphabet. In some examples, only initial letters are counted; in others, all qualifying letters (e.g., C, D, I, L, V, X) are counted, either in order or reassembled. The letters to be counted may be capitalized or otherwise distinguished, as in "LorD haVe MerCIe Vpon Vs," representing 1666 (50 + 500 + 5 + 1000 + 100 + 1 + 5 + 5).

Chronography In general, writing about events in the past, arranged in temporal order. More specifically, writing in which a main subject is time itself or a specific time of day, a certain day, a month, a season, or a year.

Chronological Primitivism The belief that, on the whole, the lives and actions of human beings were more admirable and desirable at an earlier stage of history than at present. See PRIMITIVISM.

Chronology The temporal design of a work. A story told from beginning to end has a linear *chronology*. Commonly, with action begun IN MEDIAS RES and many FLASHBACKS, *chronology* can become complicated.

Chronotope The general quality of the time-space world in literary works (literally, the word combines roots meaning "time" and "place"). In a given work, the prevailing *chronotope* may be definite or indefinite; time can be elongated or compressed; space can be cramped or vast; change in time and space can be gradual or abrupt; settings can be urban or rural, by day or by night.

[Reference: Mikhail Bakhtin, *The Dialogic Imagination* (tr. 1981).]

Ciceronian Style A highly ornamental style, modeled after Cicero, the Roman orator, who was noted for his prose rhythms, his cadenced periodic sentences, and his use of balance and antithesis. The *Ciceronian style* is particularly rich in its use of figures of speech. It was very popular with the writers of the English Renaissance (see PURIST), and Samuel Johnson in the eighteenth century and Thomas Babington Macaulay in the nineteenth are outstanding practitioners of *Ciceronian style*. It should be compared with the SENECAN STYLE.

"Ciceronians" A group of Latin stylists in the Renaissance who would not use any word that could not be found in Cicero's writings. See PURIST.

Cinéma Vérité A method of filmmaking that relies on portable equipment and small camera crews. It has been used primarily in making documentary films because the camera can go almost anywhere and capture unstaged action, even when the filmmaker is involved in the action too. The method has been effectively used for regular films also. Because a measure of selection, perspective, judgment, and editing cannot be avoided, the "verity" of *cinéma vérité* is relative and metaphoric.

Cinéaste A word coined in France in the 1920s for a cinema enthusiast.

Cinquain Originally applied to a medieval five-line stanza of varying meter and rhyme scheme, *cinquain* is now often used for any five-line stanza. More precisely, however, it is applied to the five-lined stanza used by Adelaide Crapsey, consisting of five unrhymed lines of, respectively, two, four, six, eight, and two syllables. More recent *cinquains* have been written by Roy Fuller.

Circumlocution Roundabout or evasive speech or writing, in which many words are used where a few would have served. It is a form of PERIPHRASIS.

City Comedy A type of drama flourishing around 1558–1642. Most of them are satires set in the London of the playwright's day with low-life characters involved in various crimes and misdeeds. The *city comedy* characteristically avoids any hint of romance, patriotism, or the supernatural. Some of the writings of Ben Jonson and John Marston are *city comedies*, as are many by Thomas Middleton, such as *A Mad World, My Masters* and *A Chaste Maid in Cheapside.*

[Reference: Brian Gibbons, *Jacobean City Comedy: A Study of Satiric Plays by Jonson, Marston and Middleton*, 2nd ed. (1980).]

Cladistic Analysis In biology, a "clade" is a group of organisms that have evolved from a common ancestor, and "cladistics" is the study of lines of evolutionary descent. Adapted to textual studies, *cladistic analysis* studies such items as manuscripts or printed materials to determine their relation in time, determining whether two similar specimens are derived from a common precursor or else derived one from the other or both from some other source.

Claque Mercenary persons employed to applaud a work or performance.

Classic (noun) In the singular, *classic* is usually applied to a piece of literature that by common consent has achieved a recognized superior status in literary history; also an author of similar standing. Thus, *Paradise Lost* is a *classic* in English literature. Given the connection with "class," a *classic* may be strictly considered as the defining member of a class of whatever sort. Anything may be a *classic*: a shirt, a batting stance, an utterance. General Sherman's celebrated telegram to the 1868 Republican Convention—"If nominated I will not run, if elected I will not serve"—is a *classic* of brevity, as well as the *classic* statement of a politician refusing an offer or overture, so that we still speak of a "Sherman-like" statement. The plural is used in the same sense, as in the phrase "the study of English *classics*"; it is also used collectively to designate the literary productions of Greece and Rome during the period called "*classical* antiquity."

[References: Frank Kermode, *The Classic: Literary Images of Permanence and Change* (1975); Murray Krieger, *The Classic Vision: The Retreat from Extremity in Modern Literature* (1971).]

Classic, Classical (adjectives) Used in senses parallel with those given under CLASSIC (noun); hence, of recognized excellence or belonging to established tradition, as a *classical* piece of music or "a *classic* pronouncement"; used specifically to designate the literature or culture of Greece and Rome or later literature that partakes of its qualities. "*Classical* literature" may mean Greek and Roman literature, or literature that has gained a lasting recognition, or literature that exhibits the qualities of classicism. The adjective has acquired a bewildering array of meanings. In scientific parlance, "*classical* mechanics" means physics before the acceptance of quantum mechanics and theories of relativity. Pathologists speak of "*classic* symptoms" and lawyers of "*classic* cases." When a sporting tournament can be called a "first annual Virginia Slims *classic*," the concept has lost most of its meaning and life.

Classical Tragedy This term may refer to the TRAGEDY of the ancient Greeks and Romans, as Sophocles' *Antigone*; or to tragedies with Greek or Roman subjects, as Shakespeare's *Coriolanus*; or to modern tragedies modeled on Greek or Roman tragedy or written under the influence of the critical doctrines of classicism. The earliest extant English tragedy, Sackville and Norton's *Gorboduc* (acted 1562), is sometimes called *classical* because it is written in the manner of the SENECAN TRAGEDIES. Ben Jonson's tragedies *Catiline* and *Sejanus* not only are based on Roman themes but are *classical* in their conscious effort to apply most of the "rules" of tragic composition derived from Aristotle and Horace. In spite of the fragmentariness of Aristotle and the occasional disorder of Horace, the rules derived from them favor unity, sobriety, order, wholeness, and balance. In the Restoration period John Dryden, under the influence of the French *classical tragedies* of Racine, advocated classical rules and applied them in part to his *All for Love*, which contrasts with Shakespeare's romantic treatment of the same story in *Antony and Cleopatra*. Joseph Addison's *Cato* has been referred to as "the triumph of classical tragedy." See CLASSICISM, TRAGEDY, SENECAN TRAGEDY, UNITIES, ROMANTIC TRAGEDY, NEOCLASSIC PERIOD.

Classicism As a critical term, a body of doctrine thought to be derived from or to reflect the qualities of ancient Greek and Roman culture, particularly in literature, philosophy, art, or CRITICISM. *Classicism* stands for certain definite ideas and attitudes, mainly drawn from the critical utterances of the Greeks and Romans or developed through an imitation of ancient art and literature. These include restraint, restricted scope, dominance of reason, sense of form, unity of design and aim, clarity, simplicity, balance, attention to structure and logical organization, chasteness in style, severity of outline, moderation, self-control, intellectualism, decorum, respect for tradition, imitation, conservatism, maturity, and good sense. The Greeks were notable for their clarity of thought that found articulation in lucid designs and that placed a premium on communication *among* people rather than self expression *by* a person. Unity was a dominating idea in the minds of the Greeks, and they characteristically constructed buildings around central ideas, expending great effort in making the structures symmetrical, logical, balanced, harmonious, and shapely. They had a marked sense of appropriateness or decorum and in structure, style, and subject worked with what was fitting and dignified. Restraint of the passions, emphasis on the common or general attributes of people and states, and a dispassionate objectivity made them the natural foes of enthusiasm, of uniquely personal states and emotions of peevish idiosyncrasy, and of excessive subjectivity. Although not all Greek and Roman writers displayed all these characteristics, some combination of such qualities is what is usually implied by *classicism*.

In English literature *classicism* has been an important force, often an issue since Renaissance times. The humanists became conscious advocates of CLASSICAL doctrine, and even such an essentially romantic artist as Spenser fell strongly under its influence, not only drawing freely on classical materials but definitely espousing classical doctrines and endeavoring to imitate such classical masters as Virgil and Homer. Sir Philip Sidney, though he wrote PASTORAL ROMANCES, speaks mainly as a classicist in his critical essay, *The Defence of Poesie*. Ben Jonson stands as the stoutest Renaissance advocate of *classicism*, both in dramatic criticism and in his influence on English poetry. Milton has been said to show a perfect balance of ROMANTICISM and *classicism*. The classical attitude, largely under French inspiration, triumphed in the RESTORATION and AUGUSTAN AGES, and John Dryden, Joseph Addison, and Alexander Pope, together with Samuel Johnson of the next generation, stand as exemplars of the classical (or neoclassic) spirit in literature and criticism. Though nineteenth-century literature was largely romantic (or in its later phases realistic), the vitality of the classical attitude is shown by the critical writings of such thinkers as Cardinal Newman, Matthew Arnold, and Walter Pater. In the twentieth century there has been a strong revival of classical attitudes in the literary practice and the critical principles of such writers as T. E. Hulme, Wyndham Lewis, T. S. Eliot, and Ezra Pound, and a good deal of the most distinguished poetry and criticism today is redolent of *classicism*. The austere sentiment for order that animated the criticism of Irving Babbitt and Paul Elmer More in the first third of the twentieth century persisted in the "reactionary" thought of Allen Tate and still endures in the criticism of Hugh Kenner, Guy Davenport, and others. See HUMANISM, NEOCLASSICISM, CLASSICAL, ROMANTICISM, REALISM, NEW CRITICISM.

[Reference: W. J. Bate, *From Classic to Romantic* (1961; orig. publ. 1946).]

Clerihew A form of LIGHT VERSE invented by and named for Edmund Clerihew Bentley (1875–1956), who also wrote DETECTIVE fiction. In its proper form, the *clerihew* concerns an actual person, whose name makes up the first line of a quatrain with a strict *aabb* rhyme scheme but no regularity of rhythm or meter. Bentley himself wrote dozens, and some of the best later examples were the work of W. H. Auden. Here are two contemporary *clerihews*:

> Cesare Borgia
> Would probably have preferred the way things were done
>   in Georgia
> Before the Emancipation
> Proclamation.
>
> Henry James
> Came up with some pretty ridiculous names,
> E.g., "Caspar
> Good-wood."

Cliché From the French word for a stereotype plate; a block for printing. Hence, any expression so often used that its freshness and clarity have worn off is called a *cliché*, a stereotyped form. A *cliché* probably begins as an arrestingly colorful expression, possibly in a literary work, but heedless repetition soon dulls the original brightness. Because the user pays no mind to the real meanings of the words, *cliché* diction often devolves into mixed metaphor: "The new policy is just the tip of the iceberg, but it has already bred verbal pyrotechnics that throw a wet blanket over the in-depth brainstorming of seminal issues."

Cliffhanger A work issued in installments that end at a point of great suspense, as when a character is hanging onto the edge of a cliff (as literally happens in Hardy's *A Pair of Blue Eyes*). Movie serials of the 1930s and 1940s were classic *cliffhangers*. A number of novels have been titled *Cliffhanger*, which was also the title of a 1993 movie about mountain climbing and crime.

Climax A rhetorical term for a rising order of importance in the ideas expressed. Such an arrangement is called climactic, and the item of greatest importance is called the *climax*. Earlier, the term meant such an arrangement of succeeding clauses that the last important word in one is repeated as the first important word in the next, each succeeding clause rising in intensity or importance.

In large compositions—the essay, the short story, the drama, or the novel—the *climax* is the point of highest interest, whereat the reader makes the greatest emotional response. In DRAMATIC STRUCTURE *climax* designates the turning point in the action, the crisis at which the rising action reverses and becomes the falling action. In Freytag's five-part view of dramatic structure, the *climax* is the third part or third ACT. Both narrative fiction and drama have tended to move the *climax*, in the sense of turning action and of highest response as well, nearer the end of the work and thus have produced structures less orderly than those that follow FREYTAG'S PYRAMID. In speaking of dramatic structure, *climax* is synonymous with CRISIS. However, crisis is used exclusively in the sense of structure, whereas *climax* is used as a synonym for crisis *and* as a description of the intensity of interest in the reader or spectator. In this latter sense *climax* sometimes occurs at points other than the crisis. See CRISIS, DRAMATIC STRUCTURE.

Clinamen A trope, meaning a "swerving away," latterly adopted in Harold Bloom's criticism to describe the inaugural gesture of a typical "strong" post-Enlightenment lyric.

Cloak and Dagger A type of novel or a play that deals with espionage or intrigue. The novels of John Buchan, Ian Fleming, and Helen MacInnes can properly be so designated; the espionage novels of Graham Greene and John Le Carré perhaps cannot, because they lack the requisite romantic aura. Compare with CLOAK AND SWORD.

Cloak and Sword The term comes from the Spanish *comedia de capa y espada*, a dramatic type of which the ingredients were gallant cavaliers, lovely ladies, elegance, adventure, and intrigue. In English it refers to swashbuckling plays or novels characterized by much action and presenting gallant heroes (often occupied in some attractive but outlawed activity, such as piracy, gambling, or theft) in love with fair ladies, with glamorous color thrown over all. Settings and characters are often, although not necessarily, Mediterranean; the manners are courtly and gracious; the plots are full of intrigue and twists and turns, with plenty of surprises and narrow escapes. The plays of Lope de Vega, Alexandre Dumas's *The Three Musketeers*, Rafael Sabatini's *Scaramouche*, and immense numbers of popular movies, television programs, and best-selling novels are examples (as well as testimony to the continuing appeal of the type). *Cloak and sword* romances were very popular in America between 1890 and 1915.

Closed Couplet Two successive lines rhyming *aa* and containing a grammatically complete, independent statement. It is "closed" in the sense that its meaning is complete within the two lines and does not depend on what precedes or follows for its grammatical structure or thought. Almost all instances in English are iambic tetrameter or pentameter, as in these *closed couplets* by Blake and Pope:

A dog starved at his Master's Gate
Predicts the ruin of the State.

Avoid extremes, and shun the fault of such
Who still are pleas'd too little or too much.

Closet Drama A play (usually in verse) designed to be read rather than acted. Notable examples are Seneca's tragedies, Milton's *Samson Agonistes*, Shelley's *The Cenci*, and Browning's *Pippa Passes*. Giving the term a broader meaning, some writers include in it such dramatic poems as Swinburne's *Atalanta in Calydon* and other products of the effort to write a literary drama by imitating the style of an earlier age, such as Greek drama. Such poetic dramas as Tennyson's *Becket* and Browning's *Strafford* are sometimes called *closet dramas* because, though meant to be acted, they are more successful as literature than as acted drama. In England the nineteenth century was noted for the production of *closet drama*, perhaps because the actual stage was so monopolized by BURLESQUE, MELODRAMA, OPERETTA, and such light forms that serious writers were stimulated either to attempt worthier dramas for the contemporary stage or at least to preserve the tradition of literary drama by imitating earlier masterpieces. Charles Lamb declared that all of Shakespeare's tragedies ought to be regarded as *closet dramas* because they were inevitably debased in production. A note preceding Stephane Mallarmé's *Igitur* says, "This Story is addressed to the Intelligence of the reader which stages things itself." See DRAMATIC POETRY, POETIC DRAMA, PASTICHE.

Closure The principle that structured things do not just stop, they come to an end with a sense of conclusion, completeness, wholeness, integrity, finality, and termination. *Closure* applies to small matters, such as syllables (wherein rhyme is an example of *closure*) and to ever larger structures, such as words, phrases, clauses, sentences, all the way up to whole works. The serious literary study of *closure* can be dated from the mid-1960s, with the appearance of pioneering works by Frank Kermode and Barbara Herrnstein Smith.

[References: Frank Kermode, *The Sense of an Ending: Studies in the Theory of Fiction*, (2000; orig. publ. 1966); David Richter, *Fable's End: Completeness and Closure in Rhetorical Fiction* (1974); Barbara Herrnstein Smith, *Poetic Closure: A Study of How Poems End* (1968); Mariana Torgovnick, *Closure in the Novel* (1981).]

Clothbound (also **Cloth**) Specifically, applied to a book bound in thick paper wrappers covered in cloth, usually cotton; generally used of anything not a paperback.

Clown A comic character originally with a marked rustic quality, much like the hick, bumpkin, or yokel. The nameless "Clown" in *Othello* is merely a servant who makes jokes, mostly lewd puns. Later, in performances that call for a high degree of skill, such as the circus and the rodeo, the *clown* emerged as a character whose ineptitude parodies the virtuosity of the central personages. Nowadays *clowns* are associated with a certain outlandish style of costume and makeup.

Cock-and-Bull Story A long, rambling, somewhat vague and unlikely STORY, a meandering TALL TALE. The term is very old, probably of folk origin. In *The Anatomy of Melancholy*, Robert Burton writes of those whose "whole delight is . . . to talk of a cock and bull over a pot." *Tristram Shandy* ends with Parson Yorick's statement that it has all been a *cock-and-bull story*. Nowadays, the suggestion of rambling has been taken over by the "shaggy dog" story, and the *cock-and-bull story*, because of the connotation of "bull," has come to mean an account that is bogus or hypocritical.

Cockney School A derogatory title applied by *Blackwood's Magazine* to a group of nineteenth-century writers including Hazlitt, Leigh Hunt, and Keats, because of their alleged poor taste in such matters as DICTION and RHYME. The offending rhymes included *name-time* and *vista-sister*, which, the suggestion was, could rhyme only to a cockney ear. One sentence from the denunciation in *Blackwood's Magazine* will illustrate the whole spirit of the attack: "They [the "cockney" writers] are by far the vilest vermin that ever dared to creep upon the hem of the majestic garment of the English muse." The attack reflected the Tory belief that those of "low" breeding would inevitably embrace cockney politics and produce cockney verse. The famous attack on Keats (August 1818) associates his "bad" verse with his radical political friends and his "lowly" beginnings as an apothecary's apprentice.

Coda A conclusion. The *coda* of a work usually restates or summarizes or integrates the preceding themes or movements. Marilyn Hacker has written a sonnet sequence entitled "Coda." The term is also applied to a TAIL-PIECE added to a CAUDATE SONNET and the last element of a SYLLABLE.

Code Generally, an assigned or established meaning for some arbitrary symbol, such as the conventional *codes*, official or unofficial, by which a simple red light means "stop," "the port (left) side of a ship," or "prostitution." More formally, in LINGUISTICS, a "prearranged set of rules for converting messages from one sign system into another" (Hartmann and Stork). According to a model proposed by Roman Jakobson, the *code* or general verbal language is one of six components of an act of communication (the other five being the speaker or originator, the addressee, the message, the contact, and the environment of reference). Roland Barthes' *S/Z* offers a set of *codes* involved in the disentanglement of a literary text: the "proairetic" (for PLOT sequences), the "hermeneutic" (for interpreting and solving mysteries), the "semic" (for STEREOTYPES of character and conduct), and the "referential" (for culturally shaped information). It is common for a developed *code* to provide its users with a paradigm of units (such as a vocabulary) along with syntactical rules for their arrangement. *Codes* are sometimes distinguished from ciphers, which are used to transform a text or a signal into a state intelligible only to those possessing the "key" to the decipherment or decryption.

[References: Roland Barthes, *S/Z* (tr. 1975); Jonathan Culler, *Roland Barthes* (1983); R. R. K. Hartmann and F. C. Stork, eds., *Dictionary of Language and Linguistics* (1972).]

Codex A manuscript book, particularly of biblical or CLASSICAL writing. There are more than 1,200 biblical manuscripts (dating from the fourth to the sixteenth century) that exist as *codices*. Originally manuscripts were written on rolls of papyrus or parchment, but as early as the first century manuscripts were being assembled into book form, or *codices*.

Codicology The study of the relations among manuscripts, especially when considered as physical objects without regard to content.

Coffee Table Book Such large expensive handsome nonfiction volumes, usually with many illustrations and appealing dustjackets, were once called "grand piano books," since they are too big for an ordinary shelf and lend themselves to display. Publishers have taken advantage of the name: a *Coffee Table Book of Astrology* appeared in 1962.

Cognate Descended from a common ancestor: applied to languages (as Greek, Latin, and English qualify as *cognate* languages in the Indo-European family) as well as to words (as *odous*, *dens*, and *tooth* in the same languages).

Coherence A principle demanding that the parts of any composition be so arranged that the meaning of the whole may be immediately clear and intelligible. Words, phrases, clauses within a sentence and sentences, paragraphs, and chapters in larger pieces of writing are the units that, by their progressive and logical arrangement, make for *coherence* or, contrariwise, by illogical arrangement, result in incoherence. Literature has no need, however, of unilateral *coherence* in all its particulars. Occasional incoherence—or even unsuitable *coherence*—may perfectly register uncertainty, anxiety, terror, confusion, illness, or other common states.

Coincidence The coinciding of events so that the movement of a PLOT is determined or significantly altered without a sense of necessity or causal relationship among the events. If two characters by accident happen to be in the same place with results that are important to one or both, it is called *coincidence*. In CLASSICAL TRAGEDY such occurrences were considered the working out of Fate, and the same concept of human lives being drastically affected by seemingly accidental events is used in novels and dramas that are deterministic, such as Thomas Hardy's novels and Eugene O'Neill's dramas. In comedy and particularly in FARCE, *coincidence* is very common. It is also used widely today in the THEATER OF THE ABSURD, the ANTINOVEL, and the ANTIREALISTIC novel, in which the occurrence of fortuitous conjunctions of characters with grave consequences reflects the "motiveless malignity" of a hostile or indifferent universe. Because any element in literature is a contrivance, the work can seem either arbitrary or governed by necessity. The devices of rhythm, foreshadowing, and artful arrangement make what may seem improbable (such as *coincidence*) probable and can make the probable seem inevitable by the confluence of acoustic, grammatical, and thematic rhythms.

Coined Words Words consciously manufactured, as opposed to those entering the language as a result of some more usual process of language development. Many words that were originally *coined words* (such as *telephone*, *airplane*, and *Kodak*) have become accepted terms. Constantly occurring examples of such words are those coined by commercial firms on the lookout for catchiness and enduring appeal; some of these are more or less arbitrary (such as "Kodak"), others are formed on some principle of imitation or combination (such as the words ending in "co," which stands for "company," as in "Nabisco," "Texaco," "Sunoco"). Some *coinages*—such as "zipper" and "cellophane"—lose their proprietary lineaments and take their place in the language at large. The coining of words is a rare and strange practice, but it can be entertaining (as in "palimony") and it has an honored place in literature. Swift, Horace Walpole, Poe, and Lewis Carroll indulged in coining; "blurb" and "spoof" began as happy coinages; James Joyce did so much coining that *Finnegans Wake* can be viewed as a one-man mint. See ACRONYM.

Collaboration The working together of two or more people in the composition of a literary work. Beaumont and Fletcher are a famous instance of *collaboration* in English literature.

Collage In the pictorial arts the technique by which materials not usually associated with one another, such as newspaper clippings, labels, cloth, wood, bottle tops, or theater tickets, are assembled and pasted together on a single surface. By analogy, *collage* is applied in literature to works incorporating quotations, allusions, foreign expressions, and nonverbal elements. James Joyce, T. S. Eliot, and Ezra Pound use the device extensively, as do writers of the ANTINOVEL. The closing section of Eliot's *The Waste Land* is an example of the use of *collage*. See PASTICHE, MONTAGE.

Collate To compare in detail two or more texts, versions, STATES, EDITIONS, IMPRESSIONS, or printings to determine and record the points of agreement and disagreement; also to verify the order of the sheets or SIGNATURES of a book before binding.

Collective Unconscious A term from Jungian psychology, used in archetypal criticism to refer to inherited ideas or concepts that persist as a so-called racial memory in each individual's unconscious mind and thus produce on the unconscious level attitudes and responses over which the individual has no control. See ARCHETYPE, JUNGIAN CRITICISM, MYTH.

[Reference: C. G. Jung, *The Collective Unconscious in Literature* (tr. 1967).]

Colliteration (or **Coliteration**) A name suggested for the effect, similar to ALLITERATION, of beginning accented syllables with similar consonants. Blake's line "And blights with plagues the marriage hearse" displays no outright alliteration but draws some emphasis from the repetition of various bilabial articulations, *b* (voiced), *p* (unvoiced), and *m* (voiced nasal). Much the same effect is produced in Hardy's line "Blisses about my pilgrimage as pain," although that line contains some outright alliteration.

Colloquialism An expression used in informal conversation but not accepted universally in formal speech or writing. It may differ from more formal language in pronunciation, grammar, vocabulary, syntax, imagery, or connotation. As in the case of slang, a colloquial expression eventually may be accepted as "standard" usage. The sensitive employment of *colloquialism* can ventilate a text refreshingly. For all his reputation for stuffiness and elaboration, Henry James was a master of *colloquialism*, including the use of slang, contractions, and lively conversational rhythms. See DIALECTS.

Colloquy (or **Colloquium**) A conversation, especially a formal discussion or a conference; used in this sense occasionally in literary titles, as Erasmus's *Colloquies*. See DIALOGUE.

Colonial Period in American Literature, 1607–1765 From the founding of the colony at Jamestown, which began the *Colonial Period* in America, until the Stamp Act in 1765 finally forced the colonists to see themselves as separate from their motherland, the writing produced in America was generally utilitarian, polemical, or religious. Three major figures emerged in this period: Edward Taylor, whose religious poetry, written at the close of the seventeenth century and the beginning of the eighteenth, did not see publication until 1937; Jonathan Edwards, whose religious and philosophical treatises have not been surpassed by an American; and Benjamin Franklin, whose rephrasings of the teachings of the ENLIGHTENMENT are the stylistic epitome of the period.

That belles-lettres should not have flourished is hardly surprising. Whether PURITANS of the North or Royalists of the South, the colonists were uniformly engaged throughout the period in possessing the land and making it fruitful. Wilderness, Indians, and disease were common foes that demanded strict attention. Wealth, government, progress, and political rights absorbed the attention of the Americans of the later *Colonial Period*. The seventeenth century was the age of travel and personal records, DIARIES, historical and descriptive accounts, sermons, and a little verse—largely instructive, such as Wigglesworth's *The Day of Doom*, or religious, such as the *Bay Psalm Book* and the numerous funeral elegies. Only Anne Bradstreet, "The Tenth Muse Lately Sprung Up in America," raised a poetic voice to be joined by that of Taylor.

In the eighteenth century the dangers of early colonization were over, but the colonial attitude persisted. Religious controversy was prevalent. Newspapers and ALMANACS flourished. Jonathan Edwards both in the pulpit and in his writing demonstrated his greatness as a thinker and a teacher. Benjamin Franklin created what was perhaps the first fully realized and widely popular American fictional character in Richard Saunders of *Poor Richard's Almanac*. William Byrd wrote with CAVALIER grace and urbanity about life in Virginia and North Carolina. But little important verse and no native drama emerged. As the period in which Americans had thought and acted like colonials drew to a close in the 1760s, a vast amount of writing had been done in America, some of it of a high quality, but very little that did not self-consciously take English authors as models and even less that could merit the term *belletristic*. See the section on "Colonial Period in American Literature" in *Outline of Literary History*.

Colophon A publisher's symbol or device formerly placed at the end of a book but now more generally used on the title page or elsewhere near the beginning. The function is to identify the publisher. *Colophons* have incorporated one or more of these items: title and author of book, the printer, the date and place of manufacture. The earliest known use of *colophons* was in the fifteenth century, when they were likely to be complete paragraphs wherein the author addressed the reader in a spirit of reverence—now that the reader had finished reading the author's work. Sir Thomas Malory, for example, closes *Le Morte Darthur* with the statement that it "was ended in the ix yere of the reygne of Kyng Edward the fourth" and asks that his readers "praye for me whyle I am on lyue that God sende me good delyuerance, and whan I am deed I praye you all praye for my soule." The term is also applied to any device, including the words "The End" or "Finis," that marks the conclusion of a printed work.

Ne in penam non paruam imprudenter incurras o bibliopola audiſſi
me ſcias obtentum eſſe ab Illuſtriſſimo & Sapientiſſimo M li principe
reſcriptum ne curtiana conſilia ad decimū vſq3 annū. aut imprimi poſ
ſint, aut alibi impreſſa importari venalia in eius diſtrictum ſub pena
indignationis ceſaree. & cris in eo contenta. Itaq3 ne ignarus erres te
admonitum eſſe voluit Joannes vinzalius, Vale.

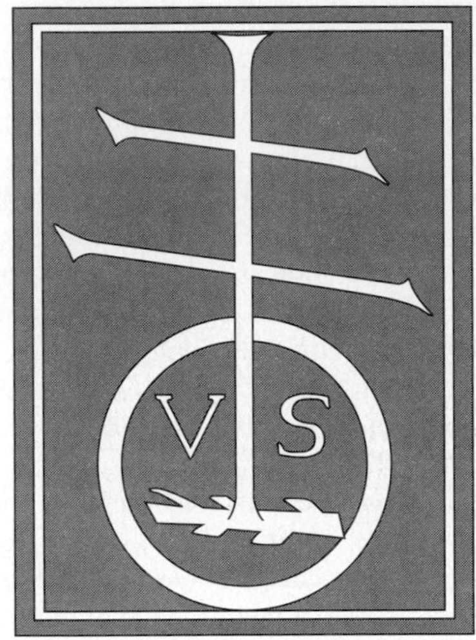

Franciscus Curtius. Consilia. Milan : U. Seinzenzeler, 1496

From Alfred W. Pollard, *An Essay on Colophons* (Chicago, 1905).

Colorhythmic With a docked or truncated rhythm.

Column One of two or more vertical sections of printed material that lie side by side on a page. Most modern newspapers have six columns. In a more literary sense, a feature article that appears periodically in a newspaper or a magazine and is written by a single author. It may be comic, literary, religious, recreational, instructive, polemical, or gossipy. Although a *column* can be serious and solemn, as Walter Lippmann's were, it is the closest modern approximation to the eighteenth-century periodical ESSAY. During the first half of the twentieth century, the syndicated *column* enjoyed great popularity and was a powerful creator and creature of taste and fashion. Two of the best-known American columnists—and exemplars of the use of initials in BYLINES—were Bert Leston Taylor ("B. L. T.") and Franklin P. Adams ("F. P. A.").

Come-All-Ye A type of song, usually anonymous, with "come all ye" at the beginning or in a refrain or moralizing conclusion. An example is "The Factory Girl's Come-All-Ye" from Maine:

Come all ye Lewiston fact'ry girls,
I want you to understand,

I'm a-going to leave this factory,
And return to my native land.
Sing dum de whickerty, dum de way.

Comedic An adjective recently used to make a neutral reference to comedy without the possible ambiguity of "comic," which can mean both "pertaining to comedy" and "laughable."

Comedietta A short or slight comedy. It was mostly a nineteenth-century form, but George Bernard Shaw wrote three: *The Inca of Perusalem: An Almost Historical Comedietta* (1916), *Village Wooing: Comedietta For Two Voices* (1933), and the incomplete *Why She Would Not (1950).*

Comedy In medieval times the word *comedy* was applied to nondramatic literary works marked by a happy ending and a less exalted style than that in TRAGEDY. Dante's *Divine Comedy*, for example, was named a *comedy* by its author because of its "prosperous, pleasant, and desirable" conclusion and because it was written not in Latin but in the vernacular. Compared with tragedy, *comedy* is a lighter form of DRAMA that aims primarily to amuse. It differs from FARCE and BURLESQUE by having a more sustained PLOT, weightier and subtler DIALOGUE, more lifelike CHARACTERS, and less boisterous behavior. The borderline, however, between *comedy* and other dramatic forms cannot be sharply defined, as there is much overlapping, and different "kinds" are frequently combined. Even the difference between *comedy* and tragedy tends to disappear in their more idealistic forms. HIGH COMEDY and LOW COMEDY may be further apart than are tragedy and some serious *comedy*. Psychologists have shown the close relation between laughter and tears, and *comedy* and tragedy alike sprang, both in ancient Greece and in medieval Europe, from diverging treatments of ceremonial performances. Typically, both *comedy* and tragedy begin with some disturbance of equilibrium and end with some establishment or restoration of order.

Comedy, striving to provoke smiles and laughter, uses both wit and humor. In general, the comic effect arises from a recognition of some incongruity of speech, action, or character. The incongruity may be verbal, as with a play on words; or bodily, as when stilts are used; or satirical, as when the effect depends on the beholder's ability to perceive the discrepancy between fact and pretense exhibited by a braggart. The range of appeal here is wide, varying from the crudest effects of obscene LOW COMEDY to the subtlest and most idealistic reactions aroused by some HIGH COMEDY. Viewed in another sense, *comedy* may be considered to deal with people in their human state, restrained and often made ridiculous by their limitations, faults, bodily functions, and animal nature. In contrast, tragedy may be considered to deal with people in their ideal or godlike state. *Comedy* has always regarded human beings more realistically than tragedy and drawn its laughter or satire from the spectacle of individual or collective human weakness or failure; hence its tendency to contrast appearance and reality, to deflate pretense, and to mock excess. English *comedy* developed from native dramatic forms growing out of the religious drama, the MORALITY PLAYS and INTERLUDES, and possibly folk games and plays and the performances of wandering entertainers, such as dancers and jugglers. In the RENAISSANCE the rediscovery of Latin *comedy* and the effort to apply the rules of classical CRITICISM to DRAMA profoundly affected English *comedy*. Foreign influences also have at times been important, as the French influence on

Restoration *comedy* or the Italian on Jacobean PASTORAL DRAMA. The more ambitious *comedy* of the earlier Elizabethans was ROMANTIC, whereas the *comedy* of the seventeenth century, both Jacobean and Restoration, was prevailingly REALISTIC (though the Fletcherian TRAGICOMEDY flourished early in the century). SENTIMENTAL COMEDY was dominant in the eighteenth century but was opposed late in the period by a revival of the realistic COMEDY OF MANNERS. In the early nineteenth century such light forms as BURLESQUE and OPERETTA were popular, serious *comedy* again appearing late in the century. Some of the more prominent authors of English theatrical *comedy* are: John Lyly, Robert Greene, George Peele, William Shakespeare, Ben Jonson, George Chapman, Thomas Middleton, Thomas Heywood, John Fletcher, Philip Massinger (Elizabethans and Jacobeans); Sir George Etheredge, William Congreve, and Thomas Shadwell (Restoration); Richard Steele, Richard B. Sheridan, Oliver Goldsmith (eighteenth century); Oscar Wilde, G. B. Shaw, J. M. Barrie, Philip Barry, Noël Coward, Neil Simon, and Woody Allen (late nineteenth and twentieth centuries).

The nomenclature employed in describing different kinds of *comedy* being somewhat confused, it is impossible in this handbook to include all the terms. An effort has been made to include the most important, however. See HIGH COMEDY, LOW COMEDY, REALISTIC COMEDY, ROMANTIC COMEDY, COURT COMEDY, TRAGICOMEDY, SENTIMENTAL COMEDY, COMEDY OF MANNERS, COMEDY OF MORALS, INTERLUDE, TRAGEDY, DRAMA, WIT AND HUMOR.

Comedy of Humours The special type of REALISTIC COMEDY that was developed in the closing years of the sixteenth century by Ben Jonson and George Chapman and that derives its comic interest largely from the exhibition of CHARACTERS whose conduct is controlled by one characteristic or HUMOUR. Some single psychophysiological humour or exaggerated trait of character gave the important figures in the ACTION a definite bias of disposition and supplied the chief motive for their actions. Thus, in Jonson's *Every Man in His Humour* (acted 1598), which made this type of PLAY popular, all the words and acts of Kitely are controlled by an overpowering suspicion that his wife is unfaithful; George Downright, a country squire, must be "frank" above all things; the country gull in town determines his every decision by his desire to "catch on" to the manners of the city gallant. In his "Induction" to *Every Man out of His Humour* (1599) Jonson explains his character-formula thus:

> Some one peculiar quality
> Doth so possess a man, that it doth draw
> All his affects, his spirits, and his powers,
> In their confluctions, all to run one way.

The *comedy of humours* owes something to earlier vernacular comedy but more to a desire to imitate the classical comedy of Plautus and Terence and to combat the vogue of ROMANTIC COMEDY. Its satiric purpose and realistic method are emphasized and lead later into more serious character studies, as in Jonson's *The Alchemist*. It affected Shakespeare's art to some degree—the "humourous" man appearing now and again in his plays (Leontes in *The Winter's Tale* is a good example)—and most of Shakespeare's tragic heroes are such because they allow some one trait of character (such as jealousy or fastidiousness) to be overdeveloped and thus to upset the balance necessary to a poised, well-rounded personality. The *comedy of humours*, closely related to the contemporary COMEDY OF MANNERS, influenced the comedy of the Restoration period. See COMEDY OF MANNERS.

Comedy of Intrigue A comedy in which the manipulation of the action by one or more characters to their own ends is of more importance than the characters themselves are. Another name for COMEDY OF SITUATION.

Comedy of Manners A term designating the realistic, often satirical, comedy of the Restoration, as practiced by Congreve and others. It is also used for the revival, in modified form, of this COMEDY a hundred years later by Goldsmith and Sheridan, as well as for another revival late in the nineteenth century. Likewise, the REALISTIC COMEDY of Elizabethan and Jacobean times is sometimes called *comedy of manners*. In the stricter sense of the term, the type concerns the manners and conventions of an artificial, highly sophisticated society. The stylized fashions and manners of this group dominate the surface and determine the pace and tone of this sort of comedy. Characters are more likely to be types than individuals. Plot, though often involving a clever handling of situation and intrigue, is less important than atmosphere, dialogue, and satire. The dialogue is witty and finished, sometimes brilliant. The appeal is more intellectual than imaginative.

SATIRE is directed in the main against the follies and deficiencies of typical characters, such as fops, would-be wits, jealous husbands, coxcombs, and others who fail somehow to conform to the conventional attitudes and manners of elegant society. A distinguishing characteristic of the *comedy of manners* is its emphasis on an illicit love duel, involving at least one pair of witty and often amoral lovers. This prevalence of the "love game" is explained partly by the manners of the time and partly by the special satirical purpose of the comedy itself. In its satire, realism, and employment of "humours" the *comedy of manners* was indebted to Elizabethan and Jacobean COMEDY. It owed something, as well, to the French *comedy of manners* as practiced by Molière. The reaction against the questionable morality of the plays and a growing sentimentalism brought about the downfall of this type of comedy near the close of the seventeenth century, and it was largely supplanted through most of the eighteenth century by SENTIMENTAL COMEDY. Purged of its objectionable features, however, the *comedy of manners* was revived by Goldsmith and Sheridan late in the eighteenth century and in a somewhat new and brighter garb by Oscar Wilde late in the nineteenth century. The *comedy of manners* has been popular in the twentieth century in the works of such playwrights as Noël Coward, Somerset Maugham, and Philip Barry. A few typical *comedies of manners* are: Wycherley, *The Plain Dealer* (1674); Etheredge, *The Man of Mode* (1676); Congreve, *The Way of the World* (1700); Goldsmith, *She Stoops to Conquer* (1773); Sheridan, *The Rivals* (1775) and *The School for Scandal* (1777); Wilde, *The Importance of Being Earnest* (1895); Maugham, *The Circle* (1921); Coward, *Private Lives* (1931); and Barry, *The Philadelphia Story* (1939). For a couple of decades, roughly from 1930 to 1950, adaptations of the *comedy of manners* constituted a popular film genre. See HIGH COMEDY, REALISTIC COMEDY, COMEDY OF HUMOURS.

[References: David L. Hirst, *Comedy of Manners* (1979); Kenneth Muir, *The Comedy of Manners* (1970).]

Comedy of Morals A term applied to comedy that uses ridicule to correct abuses, hence a form of dramatic satire, aimed at the moral state of a people or a special class of people. Molière's *Tartuffe* (1664) is often considered a *comedy of morals*.

Comedy of Situation A comedy concentrating chiefly on ingenuity of plot rather than on character interest; COMEDY OF INTRIGUE. Background is less important than ridiculous and incongruous situations, a heaping up of mistakes, plots within plots, disguises, mistaken identity, unexpected meetings, close calls. A capital example is Shakespeare's *The Comedy of Errors*, a play in which the possibilities for confusion are multiplied by the use of twin brothers who have twins as servants. In each case the twins look so much alike that at times they doubt their own identity. A comedy of this sort sometimes approaches farce. Ben Jonson's *Epicoene* and Middleton's *A Trick to Catch the Old One* are later Elizabethan *comedies of situation* or intrigue. A modern example is Shaw's *You Never Can Tell*. The phrase *comedy of situation* is sometimes used also to refer merely to an incident, such as Falstaff 's description of his fight with the robbers in Shakespeare's *King Henry the Fourth*, Part I. See FARCE-COMEDY.

Comic Book A book of cartoons collected in strips or panels and telling unified stories about characters or groups of characters. Originally designed as humorous, *comic books* became increasingly subtle and serious after 1935, eventually reaching the stage of the GRAPHIC NOVEL

Comic Opera An OPERETTA, or comedy opera, stressing spectacle and music but employing spoken dialogue. An early example is Sheridan's *The Duenna* (1775). The best-known *comic operas* are those of Gilbert and Sullivan, such as *The Mikado*, produced in London in the 1870s and 1880s. See BALLAD-OPERA.

Comic Relief A humorous SCENE, incident, or speech in the course of a serious fiction or drama, introduced, it is sometimes thought, to provide relief from emotional intensity and, by contrast, to heighten the seriousness of the story. The original sense, related to "elevate," implies any sort of contrast, as that between high and low or raised and flat in a so-called relief map. The later sense of "easing" may not always apply to *comic relief*, because it can have the nearly immediate effect of deepening tragic pain with scarcely a moment's relaxation. Notable examples are the drunken porter scene in *Macbeth* (see De Quincey's essay, "On the Knocking at the Gate in *Macbeth*"), the gravedigger scene in *Hamlet*, and Mercutio's personality in *Romeo and Juliet*. Although not a portion of Aristotle's formula for a TRAGEDY, *comic relief* has been almost universally employed by English playwrights.

Comitatus The Latin name for the band of military adherents and dependents around a king, hero, or other leader, to whom they are bound by mutual ties of fidelity and allegiance. Originally a warrior group, the *comitatus* was transformed, in the late Middle Ages, into a court of supporters. The concept of fellowship makes the *comitatus* an important element in early Germanic culture (as recorded in Tacitus's *Germania*) and its literature, including *Beowulf*.

Commedia dell'Arte Improvised comedy; a form of Italian LOW COMEDY dating from very early times, in which the actors, who usually performed conventional or stock parts, such as the "pantaloon" (Venetian merchant), improvised their dialogue, though a plot or scenario was provided. A "harlequin" interrupted the action at times with low buffoonery. A parallel or later form of the *commedia dell'arte* was the masked comedy, in which conventional figures (usually in masks) spoke particular dialects (as the Pulcinella, the rogue from Naples). There is some evidence that the *commedia dell'arte* colored English LOW COMEDY from early times, but its chief influence on the English stage came in the eighteenth century in connection with the development of such spectacle forms as the PANTOMIME. The *commedia dell'arte* also influenced the theatrical practice of Shakespeare and Molière.

Commentary Scholarly remarks specifically concerning details of substance or text, usually matters of information and not of judgment. Infrequently used for creative works; the subtitle of W. H. Auden's *The Sea and the Mirror* is *A Commentary on Shakespeare's* The Tempest.

Commission An arrangement whereby an artist produces a work, which in most cases deals with a certain subject, is in a certain form or style, or suits a certain occasion or performing group. *Commissions* are less common in literature than in music and the graphic arts.

Common Measure See COMMON METER.

Common Meter A stanza of four lines, the first and third being iambic tetrameter (eight syllables) and the second and fourth iambic trimeter (six syllables), rhymed *abab* or *abcb*. Isaac Watts wrote many such quatrains:

> There is a land of pure delight
> Where saints immortal reign;
> Infinite day excludes the night,
> And pleasures banish pain.

It is designated in hymnals by the abbreviation *C.M.* Although exceptions abound, the most usual rhyme scheme for the BALLAD type of quatrain is *abcb*, and that of *common meter* is *abab*. See SHORT MEASURE.

Commonplace Book A classified collection of quotations or arguments prepared for reference purposes. Thus, a reader interested in moral philosophy might collect thoughts and quotations under such heads as truth, virtue, or friendship. *Commonplace books* were used by authors of essays, theological arguments, and other serious treatises. The *Commonplace Book* of John Milton is still in existence. The term is also sometimes applied to private collections of favorite pieces of literature such as the poetical miscellanies of Elizabethan times. It is in this sense that W. H. Auden's *A Certain World* is a *commonplace book*. Many BLOGS qualify as well.

Commonwealth (or **Puritan**) **Interregnum** The period between the execution of Charles I in 1649 and the restoration of the monarchy under Charles II in 1660, during which England was ruled by Parliament under the control of the Puritan leader Oliver Cromwell, whose death in 1658 marked the beginning of the end of the Commonwealth. Milton was Latin Secretary in the Commonwealth government. Although the theaters were closed in 1642, dramatic performances continued more or less openly, but the only significant new drama was Davenant's *The Siege of Rhodes* (1656), a spectacle play heralding the heroic drama soon to come in the Restoration. It was an age of major prose works: Milton's political PAMPHLETS, Hobbes's *Leviathan* (1651), Taylor's *Holy Dying* and *Holy Living* (1650, 1651), Walton's *The Compleat Angler* (1653), and works by Sir Thomas Browne and Thomas Fuller. In poetry Vaughan, Waller, Cowley,

Davenant, and Marvell flourished. By the end of the *Commonwealth Interregnum*, Dryden's poetic career was under way. He and Marvell, both of whose best works were to come later, shared with Milton the honor of being the greatest poets of a troubled time, although they wrote little poetry during it. According to some accounts, the Protectorate is limited to a period between 1653 and 1659 inside the limits of the *Commonwealth Interregnum*.

Communication Theory (or **Information Theory**) Thought that treats artworks as part of more general schemes of behavior, which is provisionally identified as a kind of communication of information, and which (according to models adapted from electronics) involves messages transmitted via signal channels invariably disturbed by a certain amount of noise, distortion, and interference.

[Reference: Anthony Wilden, *System and Structure: Essays in Communication and Exchange* (1972).]

Companion A reference work intended to help the reader of a certain text, set of texts, or field of study. A *companion* usually covers more ground than a DICTIONARY but is less comprehensive than an ENCYCLOPEDIA.

Companion Piece A work designed to accompany another. Tom Stoppard's *Dogg's Hamlet, Cahoot's Macbeth* consists of two distinct short plays, quite different as to style and tone, but both have to do with Shakespeare and can be performed as a DOUBLE BILL. The author's preface says, "The comma that divides *Dogg's Hamlet, Cahoot's Macbeth* also serves to unite two plays which have common elements: the first is hardly a play at all without the second, which cannot be performed without the first." Accordingly, they are *companion pieces*.

Companion Poems Poems designed to complement each other. Each is complete by itself, but each is enriched and broadened when viewed with its *companion poem*. Milton wrote complementary *companion poems*, not only in the obvious set-piece pairing of "L'Allegro" and "Il Penseroso" but also in the much larger orbit of *Paradise Lost* and *Paradise Regained*. Robert Browning was fond of *companion poems* and may be said to have specialized therein: "Johannes Agricola in Meditation" and "Porphyria's Lover" are *companion poems*, as are "The Italian in England" and "The Englishman in Italy," "Home-Thoughts, from Abroad" and "Home-Thoughts, from the Sea," "Meeting at Night" and "Parting at Morning," "Fra Lippo Lippi" and "Andrea del Sarto," "Love in a Life" and "Life in a Love," "Before" and "After," "One Way of Love" and "Another Way of Love," "Natural Magic" and "Magical Nature," and "The Cardinal and the Dog" and "The Pope and the Net." The poems constituting Eliot's *Four Quartets*, with their matching titles and general structural parallels and resemblances, qualify as *companion poems*.

Comparative Literature The study of literatures of different languages, nations, and periods. In the Middle Ages the literatures of Western Europe were generally considered to be parts of a unified whole, mostly because they were frequently written in a common language, Latin. In the nineteenth century, concurrently with the beginnings of the comparative study of religion and mythology, various European scholars began to develop theories and methods for the comparative study of the literatures of different languages and nationalities. Among these scholars were Villemain, Ampère,

Baldensperger, Sainte-Beuve, Taine, Brunetière, and Brandes. Several different approaches to the examination of *comparative literature* have developed: the study of popular forms, such as legends, myths, and epics; the study of literary genres and forms—what Brunetière called the *évolution des genres;* the study of sources, particularly those that different literatures have in common; the study of mutual influences among authors and movements; and the study of aesthetic and critical theories and methods. *Comparative literature* is now a major field of literary study.

[References: Robert J. Clements, *Comparative Literature as Academic Discipline: a Statement of Principles, Praxis, Standards* (1978); Henry Gifford, *Comparative Literature* (1969); Ulrich Werner Weisstein, *Comparative Literature and Literary Theory* (tr. 1973).]

Compendium A brief condensation of a longer work or of a whole field of knowledge. A *compendium* is a systematic presentation of essentials. It differs from an ABRIDGMENT in that it does not attempt to present the general characteristics of the work or works from which its data are drawn. Indeed, it most often is used to present a concise and well-organized summary of data on a specific subject drawn from many sources, no single one of which is imitated in tone or organization.

Compensation A means of making up for omissions in a line; a form of SUBSTITUTION. Such omissions are usually unstressed syllables; the customary means of compensating for their absence is the pause, which has the effect of a rest in music, as Tennyson's lines illustrate:

Break, break, break
On thy cold grey stones, O Sea!

These lines may be read with three stressed syllables each, and metrically they are approximately equivalent, despite there being only three syllables in the first but seven in the second. The marked pauses following each word of the first line compensate for the unstressed syllables that have been omitted. This phenomenon, which may seem sophisticated, can be seen at work in lines as simple as "Óne, twó, / Búcklĕ yŏur shóe." See SUBSTITUTION.

Complaint A lyric poem, common in the Middle Ages and the Renaissance, in which the poet (1) laments the unresponsiveness of his mistress, as in Surrey's "A Complaint by Night of the Lover Not Beloved"; (2) bemoans his unhappy lot and seeks to remedy it, as in "The Complaint of Chaucer to his Empty Purse"; or (3) regrets the sorry state of the world, as in Spenser's *Complaints*. In a *complaint*, which usually takes the form of a monologue, the poet commonly explains his sad mood, describes the causes of it, discusses possible remedies, or appeals to some lady or divinity for help from his distress. Ezra Pound's Canto XXXVI is a studied "compleynt," and Samuel Beckett, in some youthful poems, revived the Provençal *complaint* form called *Enueg* for some poems of his own. The BLUES may be seen as a modern counterpart of the *complaint*.

Complication That part of a PLOT in which the entanglement caused by the CONFLICT of opposing forces is developed. It is the tying of the knot to be untied in the RESOLUTION. In the five-part idea of DRAMATIC STRUCTURE, it is synonymous with RISING ACTION. The second act of a five-act tragedy has been called "the act of *complication*."

Composition in Depth A term in FILM CRITICISM that describes a method by which everything in the field of vision of the camera, from immediate foreground to deep background, is kept in focus. This method is in contrast to ANALYTIC EDITING and to montage, in that the camera remains in a relatively fixed position and the action unfolds before it. *Composition in depth* is often called DEEP FOCUS. An early and distinguished example is Orson Welles's *Citizen Kane*.

Compositor A person who sets type by hand or machine and carries out other chores in printing. "*Compositor's* errors" or "compositorial errors" include the use of a wrong font or the arrangement of pages out of order.

Compound Rhyme Rhyme between primary and secondary stressed syllables, as in such pairs as "childhood" / "wildwood" and (an example from a poem by Philip Larkin) "airborne" / "careworn." Other examples are "wear rags" and "bear bags" (Shakespeare, *King Lear*, 2.4.45), "gainsay me / play thee" (Lodge's *Rosalynde*), "tell me" / "befell thee" (Donne's "Go, and Catch a Falling Star"), "bobtailed" / "hobnailed" (Dame Edith Sitwell), and "bootlace" / "suitcase" (Paul McCartney). Slightly longer words, such as "castigate" and "masticate" qualify as well.

Comprobation (also ***Comprobatio***) Seldom-seen rhetorical term for proving or approving; also for flattering an audience by approving their choice of speaker, topic, or venue.

Comstockery The overzealous and prudish censorship of literature and the other arts because of their supposed immorality. The term is derived from Anthony Comstock, a nineteenth- and early-twentieth-century American Social Reformer, crusader against vice, and relentless censor of suspect books and pictures.

Concatenation A name sometimes applied to CHAIN VERSE.

Conceit Originally the term, cognate and almost synonymous with "concept" or "conception," implied something conceived in the mind. Its later application to a type of poetic metaphor retains the original sense, in that *conceit* implies ingenuity whether applied to the Petrarchan conventions of the Elizabethan period or the elaborate analogies of the writers of metaphysical verse.

The term designates fanciful notion, usually expressed through an elaborate analogy and pointing to a striking parallel between ostensibly dissimilar things. A *conceit* may be a brief metaphor, but it also may form the framework of an entire poem. In English there are two basic kinds of *conceit*: the PETRARCHAN CONCEIT, most often found in love poems, in which the subject is compared extensively and elaborately to some object, such as a rose, a ship, a garden; and the METAPHYSICAL CONCEIT, in which complex, startling, paradoxical, and highly intellectual analogies abound. Modern *conceits* turn up in protracted analogies, such as those in Pound's "Portrait d'une Femme" ("Your mind and you are our Sargasso Sea") and Frost's single-sentence sonnet that begins, "She is as in a field a silken tent."

In the eighteenth and nineteenth centuries the term took on a derogatory sense, the *conceit* being considered strained, arbitrary, affected, and false. Samuel Johnson was particularly devastating on the metaphysical conceit. Today the term is more nearly neutral, being used to describe the unhappy overreaches of poets as well as their striking and effective comparisons. In contemporary verse the *conceit* is again a respected vehicle for the expression of witty perceptions and telling analogies. In the past century the *conceit* has figured less in British poetry than in the work of a number of Americans, such as Pound and Frost, mentioned previously, as well as Dickinson, Eliot, Ransom, and Allen Tate. It is rare in prose, but instances have been identified in the Jacobean sermons of John Donne and Lancelot Andrewes. See METAPHYSICAL CONCEIT, PETRARCHAN CONCEIT, CONTROLLING IMAGE, METAPHYSICAL POETRY, BAROQUE, GONGORISM, MARINISM.

[Reference: K. K. Ruthven, *The Conceit* (1969).]

Concordance An alphabetical index of most or all of the words in a text or in the works of an author. Today *concordances* are usually produced by computers.

Concrete Having the quality of the physical, tangible, actual, real, particular; opposed to "abstract."

Concrete Poetry Poetry that exploits the graphic, visual aspect of writing; a specialized application of what Aristotle called *opsis* ("spectacle") and Pound "phanopoeia." A *concrete poem* is one that is also a work of graphic art; the painter Paul Klee produced some early examples. The contemporary American ANAGRAM "Seascape" shows the way in which such poetry can take advantage of the visible shapes of letters and words to make a picture.

```
oceanoceanocean
oceancanoeocean
oceanoceanocean
```

[References: Mary Ellen Solt, *Concrete Poetry: A World View* (19691970); Emmett Williams, ed., *An Anthology of Concrete Poetry* (1967).]

Concrete Universal A critical term used to designate the idea that a work of art expresses the universal through the concrete and the particular. The quarrel between the universal and the particular in literature is at least as old as Aristotle, who located poetry between the universals of philosophy and the particulars of history. The writers in periods of classicism and neoclassicism tend to stress the universal; those in periods of romanticism and realism the particular. Yet, if literature is "knowledge brought to the heart," it must talk ultimately of universals but express them dramatically in concrete terms in particular instances. See ARCHETYPE, ALLEGORY.

[Reference: W. K. Wimsatt, *The Verbal Icon* (1954).]

Condensation A shortened form of a longer work but one that attempts to retain its salient characteristics, including style. *Condensation* is very much like ABRIDGMENT in basic meaning; however, it is usually applied to a shortened version of a work of fiction, whereas the application of abridgment is broader.

"Condition of England" Works From about the middle of the nineteenth century, many of the most serious writers in England addressed grave problems of society, culture, class, and education. Thomas Carlyle's *Past and Present* (1843) was an early examination of the lives of urban workers, a theme soon elaborated in Friedrich Engels's *The Condition of the Working Class in England* (1845), which appeared in the same year as Benjamin Disraeli's *Sybil: Or the Two Nations*, which has been called a *Condition of England* novel. Henry Mayhew's *London Labour and the London Poor* (1851) furnished thousands of detailed examples of unspeakable poverty, ignorance, crime, and suffering. General conditions received further attention—in nonfiction, novels, and plays—from Elizabeth Gaskell, John Ruskin, William Morris, G. B. Shaw, H. G. Wells, and John Galsworthy, so that critics began to speak of "Condition-of-England" novels. In 1909 C. F. G. Masterman published a study called *The Condition of England*. Much of the work of George Orwell, whether fiction or nonfiction, belongs in this category. Later, a group of David Hare's works—*Racing Demon*, *Murmuring Judges*, and *The Absence of War*—were called his "Condition-of-England Plays."

Conduplication Any doubling or repetition.

Confession A form of AUTOBIOGRAPHY that deals with customarily hidden or highly private matters. The *confession* usually has a theoretical or intellectual emphasis in which religion, politics, art, or some such ideological interest is important. One distinctive aspect of the *confession* is the way in which it gives an outward intellectualized account of intensely personal inward experiences. Sir Thomas Browne's *Religio Medici* and John Bunyan's *Grace Abounding* were seventeenth-century English *confessions*. Jean-Jacques Rousseau gave it a modern form and popularity with his *Confessions* in the eighteenth century. Thomas De Quincey's *Confessions of an English Opium Eater* and Alfred de Musset's *Confessions d'un enfant du siècle* are nineteenth-century examples. Elements of *confession* turn up in Eliot's *Four Quartets*, Pound's *Pisan Cantos*, and later, at a pitch that approaches amiable caricature, in Norman Mailer's *Armies of the Night*. In a somewhat narrower sense, the privileged credibility of the so-called deathbed *confession* informs Browning's "The Bishop Orders His Tomb at Saint Praxed's Church."

The term *confession* is often applied to fictional works that place an emphasis on the introspective view of a character in the process of developing attitudes toward life, religion, or art. In this sense the APPRENTICESHIP NOVEL, the BILDUNGSROMAN, and the KÜNSTLERROMAN are all *confessions*.

Confessional Poetry A term applied to the work of a group of contemporary poets whose poetry features a public and sometimes painful display of private, personal matters. In *confessional poetry* the poet often seems to address the audience directly, without the intervention of a PERSONA. Some confessional elements appear in poetry of the 1930s, such as that of Stephen Spender and C. Day Lewis. Notable examples of such poets are Theodore Roethke, Allen Ginsberg, Sylvia Plath, Anne Sexton, Robert Lowell, and John Berryman. [Reference: Robert S. Philips, *The Confessional Poets* (1973).]

Confidant (feminine, Confidante) A character who takes little part in the action but is close to the PROTAGONIST and receives the confidences and intimate thoughts of the protagonist. The use of the *confidant* permits the revelation of the thoughts and intentions of the protagonist without the use of asides or soliloquies or the point of view of an omniscient author. Well-known *confidants* are Horatio in *Hamlet*, Dr. Watson in the Sherlock Holmes stories, and Maria Gostrey in James's *The Ambassadors*. James referred to Maria Gostrey and similar *confidantes* as FICELLES, who function primarily as a means of allowing central characters to comment on their own experience. See CHORUS.

Conflict The struggle that grows out of the interplay of two opposing forces. *Conflict* provides interest, suspense, and tension. At least one of the opposing forces is customarily a person. This person, usually the PROTAGONIST, may be involved in *conflicts* of four different kinds: (1) a struggle against nature, as in Jack London's "To Build a Fire"; (2) a struggle against another person, usually the ANTAGONIST, as in Stevenson's *Treasure Island* and most melodrama; (3) a struggle against society, as in the novels of Dickens and George Eliot; or (4) a struggle for mastery by two elements within the person, as in the Restoration heroic drama or in *Macbeth*. A fifth possible kind of *conflict* is often cited, the struggle against Fate or destiny; however, except where the gods themselves actively appear, such a struggle is realized through the action of one or more of the four basic *conflicts*. Seldom do we find a simple, single *conflict*, but rather a complex one partaking of two or even all of the preceding elements. For example, the basic *conflict* in *Hamlet* may be interpreted as a struggle within Hamlet himself, but it is certainly also a struggle against his uncle as antagonist and, if the Freudian interpretations of motive are accepted, even a struggle against nature and destiny. Dreiser's *Sister Carrie* records a girl's struggle against society, as represented by the city, and yet it is a struggle against her animal nature and even partly with herself.

Even so seemingly simple a story as London's "To Build a Fire," in which the protagonist battles the cold unsuccessfully, is also the record of an inner *conflict*. *Conflict* implies not only the struggle of a protagonist against someone or something, but also the existence of some motivation for the *conflict* or some goal to be achieved thereby. *Conflict* is the raw material out of which plot is constructed. In the terminology associated with Greek drama, the *conflict*, in the form of an extended debate, was called the AGON. Our terms "protagonist" and "antagonist" are derived from the roles these characters play in the *conflict*. See PLOT, MOTIVATION, PROTAGONIST, ANTAGONIST, DRAMATIC STRUCTURE.

Connecticut Wits See HARTFORD WITS.

Connotation The emotional implications and associations that words may carry, as distinguished from their denotative meanings. *Connotations* may be (1) private and personal, the result of individual experience, (2) group (national, linguistic, racial), or (3) general or universal, held by all or most people. *Connotation* depends on usage in a particular linguistic community and climate. A purely private and personal *connotation* cannot be communicated; the *connotation* must be shared to be intelligible to others. See DENOTATION.

Consonance The relation between words in which the final consonants in the stressed syllables agree but the vowels that precede them differ, as "add-read," "mill-ball," and "torn-burn." In view of the vagaries attending the ways in which vowels are pronounced and spelled, most so-called EYE RHYMES (such as "word" and "lord," or "blood," "food," and "good") are instances of *consonance*, as are the hymnals' rhymes between "river" and "ever" or "heaven" and "given." Shelley seems uncommonly fond of *consonance*, as in several terminations in "Ode to the West Wind" ("even," "Heaven," "striven"; "tone," "one"; "fierce," "universe"; "Wind," "behind"). Emily

Dickinson was another devotee, and in her RIDDLE poem beginning "I like to see it lap the Miles" all of the rhyming positions are superseded by *consonance* ("up" "step"; "peer," "pare"; "while," "hill"; and "Star," "door").

Consonant A sound or letter representing the sound made by using various physical features of the mouth and nose. The ONSET and CODA of a syllable are *consonants*.

Conspectus A survey, summary, or outline. An article by Northrop Frye is entitled "A Conspectus of Dramatic Genres."

Constructivism A movement, originating in the Russian theater around 1920, that used mechanical constructions as a means of expression. Huntly Carter suggested a distinction between *constructivism*, employing "symbols or emblems of the world without us," and EXPRESSIONISM, employing "symbols or emblems of the world within us."

[Reference: Huntly Carter, *The New Theatre and Cinema of Soviet Russia* (1925).]

Conte French for TALE, *conte* is used in several and sometimes conflicting senses. In its original sense it referred to a short tale of adventure. It came in the nineteenth century, particularly in France, to be used for SHORT STORIES of tightly constructed PLOT and great concision, such as those by Maupassant. In this sense it designates a work shorter and more concise than a NOUVELLE. However, in England the term is sometimes used for a work longer than a short story and shorter than a novel. This usage is flatly contradictory to the modern French usage. In most cases the reader must consider both the nation and the period to which *conte* is assigned to determine whether it refers to a tale of marvelous adventures, a tightly knit short story, or a NOVELLA.

Context Matter that surrounds a word or text in question. The idea of *context* is normally invoked as a way of determining meaning. Polonius's advice "To thine own self be true," for example, may mean something in isolation, but in the *context* of the character's longer speech the clause is ironic, since it does not agree with other fatherly advice in the same speech. In turn, the meaning of the whole speech is a function of its place in the *context* of an episode, scene, act, and play. Politicians often complain that remarks, taken out of *context*, are given a distorted meaning.

Continuity The principle in film that determines how smoothly one shot follows another. Finite elements include costume, scenery, lighting, editing, and other concerns that contribute to the unity of action in a scene that may have been filmed over a long period of time.

Contrapuntal The adjective of *counterpoint*, a musical term. It is derived from the Latin phase *punctus contra punctum*, meaning "point against point." In music the term refers to the combination of parts or voices, each independently significant and rendered simultaneously or in close sequence with others to form a complex but coherent texture. By analogy *contrapuntal* is applied to literary works in which elements are played against each other by being presented simultaneously or in very close sequence, often creating the effect of MONTAGE or in film of ANALYTIC EDITING. In *Vanity Fair*, for example, the fortunes of Amelia and Becky are in *contrapuntal* relation to each other, one improving as the other deteriorates. An interesting experiment in *contrapuntal* construction is Aldous Huxley's *Point Counter Point*.

Contrast A rhetorical device by which one element (idea or object) is thrown into opposition to another for the sake of emphasis or clarity. The effect of the device is to make both contrasted ideas clearer than either would have been if described by itself. The principle of *contrast*, however, is useful for purposes other than to make definitions or to secure clarity. Skillfully used by an artist, *contrast* may become, like colors to the painter or chords to the musician, a means of arousing emotional impressions of deep artistic significance.

Controlling Image An IMAGE or METAPHOR that runs throughout and determines the form or nature of a literary work. Frost's sonnet "The Silken Tent" involves the *controlling image* that the title indicates; the *controlling image* of the following poem by Edward Taylor is the making of cloth:

Make me, O Lord, thy Spinning Wheele compleat;
Thy Holy Worde my Distaff make for mee.
Make mine Affections thy Swift Flyers neate,
And make my Soule thy holy Spoole to bee.
My Conversation make to be thy Reele,
And reele the yarn thereon spun of thy Wheele.
Make me thy Loome then, knit therein this Twine:
And make thy Holy Spirit, Lord, winde quills:
Then weave the Web thyselfe. The yarn is fine.
Thine Ordinances make my Fulling Mills.
Then dy the same in Heavenly Colours Choice,
All pinkt with Varnish't Flowers of Paradise.
Then cloath therewith mine Understanding, Will,
Affections, Judgment, Conscience, Memory;
My Words and Actions, that their shine may fill
My wayes with glory and thee glorify.
Then mine apparell shall display before yee
That I am Cloathed in Holy robes for glory.

See FUNDAMENTAL IMAGE, CONCEIT, METAPHYSICAL CONCEIT, IMAGE.

Convention A literary *convention* is any device or style or subject matter which has become, in its time and by reason of its habitual usage, a recognized means of literary expression, an accepted element in technique. The use of alliterative verse among the Anglo-Saxons and of the HEROIC COUPLET in the time of Dryden or Pope are *conventions* in this sense. The personified virtues of the MORALITY PLAYS, the braggart soldier of the Elizabethan stage, and the fainting heroine of sentimental fiction are examples of conventional STOCK CHARACTERS. Features that later become *conventions* usually arise from the freshness of appeal, acquire a pleasing familiarity at the hands of good writers, and eventually, through excessive or unskillful use, become distasteful and fall into disuse. Sometimes, however, discarded *conventions* are revived when apparently dead, as when the French poet Villon revived successfully the BALLADE. Poetic imagery tends to become conventional, as when a "code" of EPITHETS, adjectives, METAPHORS, and SIMILES came to be regarded by the Augustans as "poetic." Every medium of literary expression has its necessary *conventions*, that is, its accepted techniques for expressing its materials. The drama has such *conventions* as the SOLILOQUY, in which a character speaks his or her thoughts but is not overheard by others on the stage, and the invisible FOURTH WALL through which the audience watches the action on a BOX SET. The novel and the short story employ the *convention* that action recorded in the past tense is assumed to be unresolved at the time of reading. There are also *conventions* of subject matter; today, for example, frank treatment of sexual matters has become so conventional that it is almost obligatory in fiction. Although *conventions* can be trite and even painful when overdone, it should be recognized that they are also essential to the necessary communication between author and audience. See TRADITION, STOCK CHARACTERS, MOTIF, DRAMATIC CONVENTIONS.

Conversation Piece (or **Conversation Poem**) Some of Horace's works are called *sermones*, which does not mean "sermon" in the modern homiletic sense but rather "discourse" or "conversation" with an addressee and some element of serious satire. Although rather relaxed and informal, the *conversation poem* develops only among cultivated writers in periods of marked refinement. Coleridge, who omitted satire, perfected the form in such personal works as "The Nightingale: A Conversation Poem; written in April 1798," "The Eolian Harp," "This Lime-Tree Bower My Prison," and "Frost at Midnight." The typical example represents only one side of a conversation, which may be with an interlocutor who is absent or asleep. The form is not strictly defined, but most are in blank verse. Among modern writers, Robert Frost and W. H. Auden, openly imitating Horace, have produced *conversation poems* with more bite but less intensity than Coleridge's.

Coprology Filth, literal or figurative. Greek *koprológos* means "dung-gatherer." A. C. Swinburne once wrote, "All English readers, I trust, will agree with me that Coprology should be left to Frenchmen."

Copy Material, either in manuscript or printed form, that is to be set in type or duplicated by some other printing process. The term is used in the singular without an article, as "When can you supply *copy* for the printer?" *Copy* that has been set and that bears printers' and editors' markings is called "foul."

Copy Text That particular text of a work used by a textual scholar as the basic text against which to compare various EDITIONS, IMPRESSIONS, and ISSUES in an effort to arrive at the closest possible approximation of the author's original intent. If the author's manuscript exists, it is usually used as the *copy text*; if no manuscript exists, the first printed edition set directly from the author's manuscript is usually the *copy text*, although works that have undergone major revision by the author between editions present complex problems.

Copyright The exclusive legal right to publish or reproduce for sale works of literature and art. A *copyright* is designed to protect an author, artist, or publisher from having others make and sell copies of works without permission. Books, articles, plays, musical compositions, pictures, films, recordings, and other forms of art can be protected by *copyright*. A *copyright* protects the unique form or mode of expression; subject matter and ideas cannot be copyrighted.

The right to reproduce works is protected for the author or publisher in the United States by a Copyright Act, passed in 1976, which became effective on January 1, 1978. This Act gives *copyright* protection for the life of the author plus fifty years. It extends the *copyright* protection for existing published works to seventy-five years. Such rights had been protected by an Act of 1909, which had given protection for twenty-eight years, renewable once, making a maximum protection of fifty-six years. In England the Copyright Act of 1911 protects a work for the author's life plus fifty years. The International Copyright Convention of 1891 is an agreement dealing with international aspects of *copyright* protection, but it is generally considered inadequate.

Coronach A song of lamentation; a funeral DIRGE. A Gaelic word reflecting a custom in Ireland (where "keening" is the common term) and in the Scottish Highlands. The word means a "wailing together," and a typical *coronach* was sung by women. In one of his novels Sir Walter Scott says, "Their wives and daughters came, clapping their hands, and crying the coronach, and shrieking." In *The Lady of the Lake* (stanza 16 of canto 3) appears a *coronach* of Scott's composition:

He is gone on the mountain,
He is lost to the forest,
Like a summer-dried fountain,
When our need was the sorest. . . .

Corpus Christi Plays Medieval religious plays based on the Bible and performed by town guilds on movable wagons, or PAGEANTS, as a part of the procession on Corpus Christi day (the first Thursday after Trinity Sunday). See MYSTERY PLAYS.

Correlative Verses Verses that take the form of abbreviated sentences having a linear correlative relationship. Ben Jonson's "Celebration of Charis" asks a series of questions about seven things that are white, soft, or sweet, and then concludes, "O so white! O so soft! O so sweet is she!" Another example is from Milton's *Paradise Lost*:

Air, water, earth
By fowl, fish, beast, was flown, was swum, was walked.

These lines constitute three correlative sentences: "Air by fowl was flown. Water by fish was swum. Earth by beast was walked." Another example is these lines from the *Greek Anthology*:

You [wine] are boldness, youth, strength, wealth, country
To the shy, the old, the weak, the poor, the foreign.

These lines constitute five correlative statements, beginning: "You, wine, are boldness to the shy, youth to the old," and so on. *Correlative verses* were frequent in classical Greek and Latin poetry and in medieval and Renaissance writing. They can become bewildering. Ophelia's great lament on Hamlet's ostensible madness ("Oh, what a noble mind is here o'erthrown!") continues with a conspicuously disturbed *correlative* line: "The courtier's, soldier's, scholar's, eye, tongue, sword . . . quite, quite down!"

Correption Shortening or reduction of a syllable. Both "break" and "fast" undergo *correption* when combined into "breakfast."

Corrigenda Plural of *corrigendum*, an item to be corrected. A list of *corrigenda* may be appended to a text after publication.

Cothurnus The BUSKIN, a thick-soled, laced boot worn by actors in Greek TRAGEDY.

Counterplayers Characters who plot against the hero or heroine, e.g., Claudius, Polonius, Laertes, and their associates in *Hamlet*. See ANTAGONIST.

Counterplot A secondary plot that contrasts with the principal plot of the work; a SUBPLOT.

Counterpoint Rhythm A term used by Gerard Manley Hopkins to describe the superimposing of a different rhythm on one already established. According to Hopkins we hear the new rhythm but still remember the old, so that two rhythms run concurrently in our minds. Milton was, Hopkins asserted, the great master of *counterpoint rhythm*, and the choruses of *Samson Agonistes* were excellent examples of it. These lines, which follow speeches in regular iambic pentameter, are examples (the mind is hearing the pentameter behind them):

> Just are the ways of God,
> And justifiable to Men;
> Unless there be who think not God at all.

However, Karl Shapiro feels that such poetry "flows by the count of ear and no more scans . . . than Hebrew." Certainly *counterpoint rhythm* is sufficiently subjective to defy precise analysis. Hopkins applied the term to conspicuous instances of rhythmic substitution, as in his line "Generations have trod, have trod, have trod," in which the first word furnishes two TROCHEES in *counterpoint* to the iambs that the prevailing rhythm leads the ear to anticipate.

Counting-Out Rhyme or Song A formulaic CHANT used to determine who is to be excluded from or included in an activity; largely but not exclusively a children's concern. The most familiar begin "One potato, two potato" and "Eenie, meenie, mynie, moe."

Country House Poem A type of poem, flourishing in the seventeenth century, that used an actual country house, usually the seat of an important family, as the center of a meditation on life and society. The best-known examples are Ben Jonson's "To Penshurst" and Andrew Marvell's "Upon Appleton House."

[Reference: Alastair Fowler, *The Country House Poem: A Cabinet of Seventeenth-Century Poems and Related Items* (1994).]

Country Song A poem related to country life, customarily having to do with young love. Anthologies sometimes use the general title *country song* for such pieces as "It Was a Lover and His Lass" from Shakespeare's *As You Like It*. Thomas Hardy's *Time's Laughingstocks* (1909) includes seventeen poems in a group called "A Set of Country Songs," and one of Elinor Wylie's last poems is called "Country Song."

Coup de Théâtre A surprising and usually unmotivated stroke in a drama that produces a sensational effect; by extension, anything designed solely for effect.

Couplet Two consecutive lines of VERSE with END RHYMES. Formally, the *couplet* is a two-line stanza with both grammatical structure and idea complete within itself, but the form has gone through numerous adaptations, the most famous being heroic verse. In French literature *couplet* is sometimes used in the sense of STANZA. It is customary but not essential that the length of each line be the same. *Couplets* are usually written in octosyllabic and decasyllabic lines. Shakespeare always ends his sonnets with a *couplet*, and often he will use a *couplet* to signal the end of a scene that is otherwise in prose or BLANK VERSE, as at the end of act 2 of *Hamlet*:

I'll have grounds
More relative than this. The play's the thing
Wherein I'll catch the conscience of the King.

See CLOSED COUPLET, HEROIC VERSE.

Court Comedy Comedy written to be performed at a royal court. *Love's Labour's Lost* is a *court comedy* belonging to Shakespeare's early period. Before Shakespeare, the Elizabethan *court comedy* had been developed to a high degree of effectiveness by John Lyly in such plays as *Endimion* and *Alexander and Campaspe*. Characteristics include: artificial plot; little action; much use of mythology; pageantry; elaborate costuming and scenery; prominence of music, especially songs; lightness of tone; numerous and often balanced characters (arranged in contrasting pairs); style marked by wit, grace, verbal cleverness, quaint imagery; puns; prose dialogue; witty and saucy pages; eccentric characters such as braggarts, witches, and alchemists; much farcical action; and allegorical meanings sometimes in characters and action. Though some of these traits of the Lylian *court comedy* dropped out later, *court comedy* in the seventeenth century retained many of them and was operatic in tone and spectacular in presentation. See MASQUE.

Courtesy Books A class of books that, flourishing in late Renaissance times, dealt with the training of the "courtly" person. Often in dialogue form, the *courtesy book* discussed such questions as the qualities of a gentleman or court lady, the etiquette of courtly love, the education of the future courtier or prince, and the duties of a state counsellor. The *courtesy book* originated in Italy, the most famous example being Castiglione's *Il Cortegiano*, "The Courtier" (1528), which exerted great influence on English writers, especially after its translation into English by Sir Thomas Hoby in 1561. The earliest English *courtesy book* is Sir Thomas Elyot's *Book Named the Governour* (1531). Somewhat similar to the *courtesy books*, but not to be confused with them, were the numerous ETIQUETTE BOOKS written not to explain the character of noble or royal persons but to deal with the problems of conduct confronting citizens as well as "gentlefolk." One of the best is *Galateo* by the Italian Della Casa. Early English examples of this type are *The Babees Book* and *The Boke of Curtasye* (1450).

Many books of the seventeenth century carried on the tradition: Henry Peacham's *Compleat Gentleman*, 1622 (courtly); Richard Brathwait's *The English Gentleman*, 1630 (Puritan); and Francis Osborne's *Advice to a Son*, 1658 (a precursor of Lord Chesterfield's Letters). By extension, *courtesy book* can be applied to a poem like Spenser's *The Faerie Queene*, because one of its objects is to portray the moral virtues. A similar extension has applied the term to Franklin's *Autobiography*, written to instruct Franklin's son in the ways of the world.

Courtly Love A philosophy of love and a code of lovemaking that flourished in chivalric times, first in France and later in other countries, especially in England. Exact origins cannot be traced, but fashions set by the Provençal TROUBADOURS and ideas drawn from the Orient and especially from Ovid were probably the chief sources. The conditions of feudal society and the veneration of the Virgin Mary, both of which tended to give a new dignity and independence to women, also affected it. According to the theory of *courtly love*, falling in love is accompanied by great emotional disturbances; the bewildered lover exhibits such "symptoms" as pallor, trembling, loss of appetite, sleeplessness, sighing, and weeping. He agonizes over his condition and indulges in endless self-questioning and reflections on the nature of love and his own wretched state. His condition improves when he is accepted, and he is inspired by his love to great deeds. He and his lady pledge each other to secrecy, and they must remain faithful in spite of all obstacles. In what is now considered a parody, Andreas Capellanus late in the twelfth century wrote a treatise that summarized prevailing notions of *courtly love* through imaginary conversations and through his thirty-one "rules." According to the strictest code, true love was held to be impossible in the married state. Hence, some authorities distinguish between true *courtly love*, as it is illustrated in the story of Lancelot and Guinevere in Chrétien's "The Knight of the Cart," and Ovidian love. *Courtly love* ideas abound in medieval romance and are perhaps not unconnected with the Petrarchan and Platonic love doctrines found in Elizabethan sonnet sequences. The system of *courtly love* largely controls the behavior of the characters in Chaucer's *Troilus and Criseyde*. See COURTS OF LOVE.

[References: Peter Allen, *The Art of Love: Amatory Fiction from Ovid to the Romance of the Rose* (1992); Catherine Bates, *The Rhetoric of Courtship in Elizabethan Language and Literature* (1992); J. D. Burnley, *Courtliness and Literature in Medieval England* (1998); C. S. Lewis, *The Allegory of Love* (1936); James J. Paxson and Cynthia A. Gravlee, eds., *Desiring Discourse: The Literature of Love, Ovid Through Chaucer* (1998).]

"Courtly Makers" The first "makars" were fifteenth-century Scottish Chaucerians. Sometimes applied to any court poet, "*courtly makers*" more accurately refers to court poets of the reign of Henry VIII who introduced the "new poetry" from Italy and France into England. "*Maker*" meant "poet." The work was experimental but imitative, based on forms developed in Italy. The "*courtly makers*" were most successful in translations and in songs. Henry VIII himself was credited with the authorship of words and music of several graceful songs. The introduction of the SONNET into English is due to the efforts of the two most important poets of the group, Sir Thomas Wyatt and the Earl of Surrey. BLANK VERSE was introduced by Surrey. Most of the work of other *courtly makers* has perished, for their ideas of "gentlemanly" conduct did not encourage them to publish. Manuscript collections were made for private libraries, however; such a collection, now known as *Tottel's Miscellany*, published in 1557, exerted a powerful influence on Elizabethan poetry.

Courts of Love Tribunals for settling questions involved in the system of COURTLY LOVE. The judge, a court lady or Venus herself, would hear debate on such questions as: "Can a lover love two ladies at once?" "Are lovers or married couples more affectionate?" Though it was once believed that such courts were actually held in high society in chivalric times, modern scholarship is inclined to regard the *courts of love* as primarily a literary convention. The term *court of love* is also sometimes extended to include allegorical and processional pageants such as the Masque of Cupid passage in Spenser's *The Faerie Queene* (book 3, cantos 11–12).

Covenant Theology A seventeenth-century modification of the doctrines of CALVINISM, particularly important in New England. For divine decrees as a basis for election, it substitutes the idea of a contractual relationship between God and the human race. *Covenant theology* held that God promised Adam and his posterity eternal life in exchange for absolute obedience. When Adam broke this covenant, he incurred punishment as a legal responsibility for himself and his posterity. However, God made another covenant with Abraham, promising human beings the ability to struggle toward perfection. During The Great Awakening Jonathan Edwards attacked the *Covenant theology* and urged a return to Calvinism. See AWAKENING, THE GREAT.

Cover (1) The outer protective wrapper on a book or magazine. (2) Also *cover* version: In popular music, a recording of material already recorded by another.

Cover Story Magazine material related to the pictures or other matter on the cover; normally the most important piece in the issue.

Cowith (Welsh **Cywydd**) A Welsh form featuring COUPLETS joined by ANISOBARIC rhyming.

Cowleyan Ode A form of the irregular ode used by Abraham Cowley in the seventeenth century. See ODE, IRREGULAR ODE.

Cratylism From Plato's *Cratylus*, which considers whether names are arbitrary or necessary. *Cratylism* holds that there is a necessary, essential, mimetic connection between SIGNIFIER and SIGNIFIED. See ANALOGISM VERSUS ANOMALISM, HERMETICISM, HERMOGENISM, ORPHISM.

[Reference: Derek Attridge, *Peculiar Language: Literature as Difference from the Renaissance to James Joyce* (1988).]

Credit Line In illustrated periodicals, the notice under a photograph that tells the name of the photographer or service.

Credits A list of names of persons and institutions that contributed to the making of a film or other production. Mostly devoted to the technical crew, some *credits* extend to legal and financial services, vehicles, and catering.

Crisis The point at which the opposing forces that create the conflict interlock in the decisive action on which a plot will turn. *Crisis* is applied to the episode or incident wherein the situation of the PROTAGONIST is certain either to improve or worsen. Because *crisis* is essentially a structural element of plot rather than an index of the emotional response that an event may produce in a reader or spectator, as CLIMAX is, the *crisis* and the climax do not always occur together. See PLOT, CONFLICT, DRAMATIC STRUCTURE.

Critic One who estimates and passes judgment on the nature, value, and quality of artistic works. The term is used for a great variety of persons ranging from the writers of brief reviews in the popular press to expounders of philosophic principles that define the nature and function of art. A *critic* may employ many different types of criticism and support many different theories. According to an old-fashioned distinction, *critics* publish their findings in REVIEWS, scholars theirs in JOURNALS. See CRITICISM; CRITICISM, TYPES OF.

Critical Realism A term applied to realistic fiction in the late nineteenth and early twentieth centuries, particularly in America. The MUCKRAKERS belong to the school of *critical realism*. Vernon L. Parrington gave the term currency in his posthumously published (1930) third volume of *Main Currents in American Thought*, which he called *The Beginnings of Critical Realism in America*, where he uses the term to refer to the tendency of writers and intellectuals in the period between 1875 and 1920 to apply the methods of realistic fiction to the criticism of society and the examination of social issues.

Criticism The analysis, study, and evaluation of individual works of art, as well as the formulation of general principles for the examination of such works. From the earliest days of literary history, *criticism* has been a major aspect of literary theory and practice.

M. H. Abrams, in *The Mirror and the Lamp*, has pointed out that all critical theories, whatever their language, discriminate four elements in "the total situation of a work of art," and he discriminates among both the kinds of *criticism* and the history of critical theory and practice in terms of the dominance of one of these elements. They are: (1) the *work*, that is, the thing made by the maker; (2) the *artist*; (3) the *universe*, that is, the nature that is imitated, if art is viewed as imitation, the materials of the real world or the world of ideal entities out of which the work may be thought to take its subject; and (4) the *audience* to whom the work is addressed. To view art basically in terms of the *universe*, in terms of what is imitated, is to follow the MIMETIC THEORY. To view art basically in terms of its effect on the *audience* is to use the PRAGMATIC THEORY. To view art basically in terms of the *artist*, that is, as expressive of the maker, is to employ the EXPRESSIVE THEORY. And to view art basically in its own terms, seeing the *work* as a self-contained entity, is to exemplify the OBJECTIVE THEORY. (These categories are themselves the material of critical debate, and some schools of thought assert that the artwork is not a finite product but rather an indefinite process. For others, the work per se simply has no existence; the so-called work has to be something perceived—and partly created or completed—by the active HERMENEUTIC participation of many audiences. Still others deny that independent texts or works exist in any mode of being that permits discussion; all that exists is a network of complex relations among texts. For others, the production of art is not a creative act of invention but an impersonal catalytic assembling of conventional elements.)

A backward glance over the history of *criticism* in the light of Abrams's formulations is revealing. The MIMETIC THEORY is characteristic of the classical age, with Aristotle as its great expounder. Horace, however, introduced the idea of instruction with pleasure—*utile et dulce*—and the effect on the audience was central to his view of art. From Horace through most of the eighteenth century, the PRAGMATIC THEORY was dominant, although the neoclassic critics revived a serious interest in IMITATION. Indeed, as Abrams asserts, "the pragmatic view, broadly conceived, has been the principal aesthetic attitude of the Western world." *Criticism* through the eighteenth century was securely confident of the imitative nature of art. With ROMANTICISM came the expressive theory, in a sense the most characteristic of the romantic attitudes. When Wordsworth calls poetry "the spontaneous overflow of powerful feeling," the *artist*—construed as a person of extraordinary feeling, emotion, and sensibility—has moved to the center. Now the poet's imagination is a new force in the world and a source of unique knowledge, and expression is the true function of art. Beginning in the nineteenth century and becoming dominant in the twentieth has been the notion of the "poem *per se* . . . written solely for the poem's sake," as Poe expressed it. Here form and structure, patterns of imagery and symbols, become the center of the critic's concern, for the *work* of art is viewed as a separate cosmos. However, increasing interest in psychology has kept the contemporary critic also aware of the fact that the *audience* functions in the work of art.

The first important critical treatise, the *Poetics* of Aristotle (fourth century B.C.), has proved to be the most influential. This Greek philosopher defined poetry as an idealized representation of human action, and TRAGEDY as a serious, dramatic representation or imitation of some magnitude, arousing pity and fear wherewith to accomplish a CATHARSIS of such emotions; tragedies ought to have unity and completeness of plot, with beginning, middle, and end. The *Poetics* also treats the element of character in tragedy and the relation of tragedy to epic. Aristotle's treatise on the Homeric epic has not survived. The great attention given by the ancients to RHETORIC is also important critically, though developed largely because of the interest in oratory. The great influence of the *Poetics* began in the Renaissance.

Another important Greek document is the treatise of Longinus, *On the Sublime* (date uncertain, perhaps third century after Christ). Very different from the *Poetics* of Aristotle, this work acclaims sublimity, height, and imagination in a style that is itself enthusiastic and eloquent. Longinus finds the sources of the SUBLIME in great conceptions, noble passions, and elevated diction.

The foremost Latin critic was Horace, whose *Art of Poetry* (known variously as *Ars Poetica*, *De Arte Poetica*, and *Epistle to the Pisos*), written as an informal epistle in verse, has exercised considerable influence. It discusses types of poetry and of character, stresses the importance of Greek models, emphasizes decorum, and advises the poet to write for both entertainment and instruction. Many of Horace's phrases have entered the language of *criticism*, such as *ut pictura poesis*, "poetry, like painting"; *limae labor*, "the labor of the file" (i.e., revision); *aut prodesse aut delectare*, "either to profit or to please"; *purpureus pannus*, "purple patch"; and *in medias res*, "in the midst of things." Other ancient critics include Plato, Dionysius of Halicarnassus, Plutarch, and Lucian among the Greeks; and Cicero, the Senecas, Petronius, Quintilian, and Macrobius among the Latin writers. The art of rhetoric constituted an integral part of this literary *criticism*.

In the Middle Ages most *criticism* dealt with Latin versification, rhetoric, and grammar. The ecclesiastical theologians who dominated intellectual life regarded literature as a servant of theology and philosophy, so that interest in imaginative literature as such declined. The rhetoricians dealt in detail with technical matters of vital interest to the creative writer: FIGURATIVE LANGUAGE, organization, beginnings, endings, development (amplification, condensation), and style—especially the adaptation of style to type of composition. The influence of such teachings on the early work of Chaucer has been shown in detail.

The teachings of St. Augustine (d. 430) contributed to the distrust of literature on moral and religious grounds, a distrust that persisted through the Middle Ages into modern times. His attack on imaginative writing produced replies that anticipate later critical attitudes and arguments, including the arguments that the literary and the moral points of view should not be confused and that the ancients should be followed. Isidore of Seville (sixth and seventh centuries) listed the types and kinds of literature (based on biblical forms). At the end of the medieval period a great critic appeared in the Italian poet Dante, whose *De Vulgari Eloquentia* (early fourteenth century) discusses the problems of vernacular literature and reflects classical ideas on decorum, imitation, and the nature of the poet. He discusses diction, sentence structure, style, versification, and dialects. Petrarch and Boccaccio, Italian writers of the fourteenth century, produced critical works that belong in part to the medieval period and in part to the Renaissance, which they helped to usher in. Boccaccio's defense of poetry in Books 14 and 15 of his *Genealogia Decorum Gentilium* is particularly important to students of later *criticism*.

The Renaissance reacted against the theological interpretation of poetry, which it attempted to justify as an independent art, along lines suggested by humanistic ideals. In Italy, Vida, Robortelli, Daniello, Minturno, Giraldi Cinthio, J. C. Scaliger, Castelvetro, and others were concerned with such topics as: poetry as a form of philosophy and an imitation of life; the doctrine of verisimilitude; pleasurable instruction as the object of poetry; the theory of drama, especially tragedy—the tragic hero and the unities were much debated; and the theory of the epic poem. The causes for the growth of classicism have been assigned to HUMANISM, Aristotelianism, and RATIONALISM—with Platonism, medievalism, and nationalism acting as romantic forces. These tendencies toward classicism actuated Italian *criticism* of the sixteenth century and French *criticism* of the seventeenth. The first French critical works were rhetorical and metrical, the most important being Sibilet's *Art of Poetry* (1548); but the first highly significant French *criticism* centered on the *Pléiade*, a group interested in refining the French language and literature by imitations of the classics, Ronsard being its most famous writer and Du Bellay being the author of its manifesto, his epochal *Defence and Illustration of the French Language* (1549). Among the prominent seventeenth-century French critics were Malherbe, who reacted strongly against the *Pléiade*; Chapelain; Corneille; Saint-Évremond; d'Aubignac; Rapin; Le Bossu; and Boileau, whose influence was especially powerful. These writers illustrate the course of French *criticism* in the direction of classicism, a rational crystallizing of poetic theory, and a codification of the principles of structure.

In Renaissance England the earliest critical utterances concerned rhetoric and diction, as in the "prefaces" of the printer Caxton (late fifteenth century) and the rhetorics of Leonard Cox (c. 1530) and Thomas Wilson (1553). As early as Sir Thomas Elyot's *Book Named the Governour* (1531), the claims of English as a vehicle for literature were being urged against the extreme humanist opposition to the vernacular as crude and transitory. The development of a native literature stimulated discussions of how best to build up the English vocabulary; the extreme humanists and INKHORNISTS, who favored the adoption of heavy Latin and Greek words, were opposed by those who stressed a native lexicon (see PURISTS). Much attention was given to decorum and imitation. The first technical treatise on English versification was Gascoigne's *Certain Notes of Instruction* (1575). Verse devices already developed in English, including rhyme, were perfected in the face of a critical sentiment for such classical forms as the unrhymed hexameter. Practice ran ahead of theory in this matter, as may be seen by comparing the creative practice of Sidney and Campion with their critical condemnation of rhyme. Campion's essay, *Observations in the Art of English Poesie* (1602), was effectively answered by Samuel Daniel's *A Defence of Rime*. Similarly, Shakespearean romantic tragedy developed in spite of the prevailing critical insistence on the unities. A lively critical issue centered on the defense of literature in the face of the Puritan attack based on moral grounds, a movement aimed at the drama in particular, as in Stephen Gosson's *The School of Abuse* (1579). Many of these critical questions were treated in Sidney's *Defence of Poesie* (pub. 1595), the most significant piece of *criticism* of the period. Sidney stressed the vatic or prophetic function of the poet, exalted poetry above philosophy and history, answered the objections to poetic art, examined the types of poetry, and assigned praise and blame among the writers of the preceding generation on the basis of their conformity to classical principles as expressed by the Italian critics. Important critical ideas came from Francis Bacon (*Advancement of Learning*, 1605) and Ben Jonson in *Timber: or Discoveries*. Jonson, a man of vast learning and uncommon common sense, shows a definite tendency toward the NEOCLASSICISM that was to become the center of English *criticism* for more than a century.

The next master critic was John Dryden, with his numerous prefaces and essays, the best known being the *Essay of Dramatick Poesie* (1668). This treatise, written in dialogue form, fairly presents the claims of "ANCIENTS AND MODERNS," of French and English dramatists; rhyme, tragicomedy, and the unities receive consideration; the influence of Corneille is apparent; and much PRACTICAL CRITICISM and dramatic expression keep the *Essay* from being entirely theoretical. In his *Preface to the Fables* (1700) Dryden gives a noteworthy estimate of the genius of Chaucer.

Alexander Pope was not merely the leading poet of his generation but also its most significant critic, with the prefaces to his translation of Homer, his edition of Shakespeare, and his *Essay on Criticism* (1711)—one of the best pieces of verse *criticism* in the language. Here Pope set forth the neoclassic principles of following nature and the ancients, outlined the causes of bad *criticism*, described the good critic, and concluded with a short history of *criticism*. Joseph Addison's critical papers in the *Spectator* (1711–1712) on tragedy, wit, ballads, *Paradise Lost*, and the imagination were designed for a popular audience, but they influenced formal *criticism* and aesthetic theory. The neoclassical critics in general devoted themselves to such topics as reason, correctness, wit, taste, genres, rules, imitation, the classics, imagination, emotion, and enthusiasm. As the sway of authority weakened, the historical point of view gained in acceptance; TEXTUAL CRITICISM became more scientific. Samuel Johnson was the major defender of the older order; his large body of *criticism* is in his periodical essays, the preface to his edition of Shakespeare, and his *Lives of the Poets*.

Joseph Warton (*Essay on the Genius and Writings of Pope*, 1756, 1782) refused Pope the highest rank among poets because of insufficient emotion and imagination; Thomas Warton (*Observations on The Faerie Queene of Spenser*, 1754) emphasized the emotional quality of the poet; Young (*Conjectures on Original Composition*, 1759) spoke in favor of independence and against the imitation of other writers; Hurd (*Letters on Chivalry and Romance*, 1762) justified GOTHIC manners and design, Spenser's poetry, and the Italian poets, and attacked some of the main tenets of the AUGUSTANS. The romantic impulse was growing.

The volume by Wordsworth and Coleridge titled *Lyrical Ballads* (1798) is frequently cited as formally ushering in the romantic movement. For the second edition (1800) Wordsworth wrote a preface that acted as a manifesto for the new school and set forth his own critical creed. His object was to "choose incidents and situations from common life," to write in the "language really used by men." Wordsworth was reacting to what he considered the artificial poetic practice of the preceding era; he condemned the use of personification and poetic diction. There could be "no essential difference between the language of prose and metrical composition." Wordsworth defined the poet as a "man speaking to men" and poetry as "the spontaneous overflow of powerful feelings," which originates in emotion "recollected in tranquillity."

In the *Biographia Literaria* (1817) Coleridge explained the division of labor in the *Lyrical Ballads*: his own endeavors "should be directed to persons and characters supernatural, or at least romantic; yet so as to transfer from our inward nature a human interest and a semblance of truth sufficient to procure for these shadows of imagination that willing suspension of disbelief for the moment, which constitutes poetic faith"; whereas Wordsworth was "to propose to himself as his object, to give the charm of novelty to things of every day, and to excite a feeling analogous to the supernatural, by awakening the mind's attention to the . . . loveliness and the wonders of the world before us." Coleridge disagreed with Wordsworth's statements about the principles of meter and poetic diction: genuinely rustic life is not favorable to the formation of intelligible diction; poetry is essentially ideal and generic; the language of Milton is as much that of real life as is that of the cottager; art strives to give pleasure through beauty. Coleridge's discussion of the imagination and the fancy has had wide influence. English romanticism found some sources in the philosophy, aesthetics, and literature of German romanticism.

Shelley's *Defence of Poetry* (1821) is an impassioned apologia reminiscent of Renaissance treatises. Other critics of this period are: Blake, Newman, Carlyle, De Quincey, Lamb, Hazlitt, Hunt, Landor, Hallam, and Macaulay. The Whig *Edinburgh Review* and the Tory *Quarterly Review* voiced fundamentally conservative opinions and dominated periodical *criticism*.

Matthew Arnold, the leading English critic of the second half of the nineteenth century, thought of poetry as a "criticism of life" and of *criticism* itself as the effort to "know the best that is known and thought in the world and by in its turn making this known, to create a current of true and fresh ideas." Form, order, and measure constituted the classical qualities that Arnold admired. Seeking to judge literature by high standards, he used specimens (or TOUCHSTONES) as well as his own sensitive taste in forming judgments. (However, not all of Arnold's specimens are uniformly appropriate.) "The grand style," he said, "arises in poetry, when a noble nature, poetically gifted, treats with simplicity or with severity a serious subject." The greatness of a poet "lies in his powerful and beautiful application of ideas to life." Three of his better-known critical essays are *The Function of Criticism* (1865), *The Study of Poetry* (1888), and *On Translating Homer* (1861).

In the later nineteenth century romanticism remained strong, but REALISM and IMPRESSIONISM were gaining ground. The expansion of natural science helped the progress of realistic and naturalistic *criticism* (see NATURALISM). Historical *criticism*, the attempt to understand a work in the light of "race, momentum, and milieu," in the process of development for at least two centuries, at last crystallized in the writings of the Frenchmen Saint-Beuve and Taine. Impressionism, growing out of romanticism, obtained an eloquent advocate in Walter Pater. Victorian critics discussed such topics as the function of art and literature, the role of morality, the place of the imagination, the problems of style, the province of the novel, and the theory of the comic. As *criticism* tended away from the application of standards toward the use of impressionistic methods, German influence yielded ground to the French. Significant contributions were made by Thackeray on the English humorists; John Stuart Mill on the nature of poetry; Pater on style and on hedonism in art; and George Meredith on the comic spirit.

Criticism in America, besides reflecting, sometimes tardily, European attitudes, has been concerned with questions peculiar to a literature growing out of a transplanted culture. To what extent is American literature derivative and imitative? How can American literature develop a purely American spirit? What is this spirit? What is the effect of Puritan ethics on American literature? How has the frontier affected it?

Early-nineteenth-century *criticism*, as evidenced by the earlier numbers of the *North American Review* (estab. 1815), was conservative and neoclassic. Pope and the Scottish school reigned. Later, the romantic attitude triumphed, and Byron, Scott, Wordsworth, and eventually Shelley, Keats, Coleridge, Carlyle, and Tennyson were exalted. The earlier writer-critics were in the main romantic: Poe, Lowell, and Emerson. Poe, however, stressed workmanship, technique, structure, reason, and the divorce of art and morality. He enunciated independent theories of the LYRIC and the short story. Emerson believed art should serve moral ends and asserted that all American literature was derivative but should not be so. J. R. Lowell is first impressionistic and romantic, at times professedly realistic, and eventually classical and ethical after his revolt against sentimentalism. After the Civil War a strong critical movement toward realism found two powerful exponents, William Dean Howells and Henry James. Interested almost exclusively in fiction, they advanced a theory that the fidelity of the *work* to the *universe*, defined in a materialistic or psychological-social sense, was the object of art. Realism was defined by Howells as "nothing more and nothing less than the truthful treatment of material." Yet there were aspects of the PRAGMATIC THEORY here, for he saw a moral obligation resting on the *artist* in terms of the *effects* of the works on the *audience*. At the close of the century, under the influence of the French, particularly Zola, a group of American novelists proposed a theory that was frankly MIMETIC; this is the application of scientific method, even of quasi-scientific law, to enhance the seriousness and increase the depth of the portraying of the actual by the artist. The theory is NATURALISM, and Frank Norris was its most vocal expounder as the century ended. However, Henry James, in critical essays already written and in the prefaces prepared for the collected edition of his novels in the first decade of the twentieth century, was to make the most significant formulation of critical principles about fiction that an American has produced. James and Poe emerge from nineteenth-century America as the most powerful and original American critics of that age. Although he conspicuously lacked James's wit, urbanity, common sense, and good manners, Poe was undeniably a prodigious genius whose example foreshadowed James's fastidious craftsmanship, attention to detail, and devotion to logic and symmetry. Poe has also been credited with inventing or improving the SHORT STORY, SCIENCE FICTION, DETECTIVE FICTION, the symbolist poem, the NEW CRITICISM, and a potently iconoclastic style of critical combat later to be adopted by Mencken, Pound, Eliot, and Yvor Winters. Whatever may be the just apportionment of credit, Poe and James together created a vivid and practical critical spirit that suffused the thought and practice of their contemporaries (as in Mark Twain's hilarious bill of complaint against "Fenimore Cooper's Literary Offenses") and all of their important successors.

In England and America the first decade of the twentieth century saw a continuation of the concern with realism and naturalism, but little serious critical examination of them. Impressionism and "appreciation," led in England by Walter Pater and his followers and in America by James Huneker, ruled the day. In the second decade a group of Americans, under the leadership of Van Wyck Brooks, attacked the cultural failures of America and began the search for a "usable past," a search that was to occupy men such as Randolph Bourne, Lewis Mumford, and Bernard De Voto down to the 1950s and that saw in 1927–1930 in Vernon L. Parrington's *Main Currents in American Thought* one of the major documents in critical scholarship. At the same time in England two young Americans, Ezra Pound and T. S. Eliot, were learning with T. E. Hulme to distrust romantic expressionism and to turn to FORMALISM and OBJECTIVITY. Whatever their ideology, Pound and Eliot, especially between 1920 and 1935, eloquently synthesized the most vital thought of their seniors (particularly Henry James, F. H. Bradley, Henri Bergson, Irving Babbitt, and Paul Elmer More) and espoused the cause of their most influential contemporaries (particularly James Joyce, Virginia Woolf, Wyndham Lewis, W. C. Williams, Marianne Moore, and Ford Madox Ford). In the 1920s the impact of the new psychologies was deeply felt in England, particularly in the work of I. A. Richards, whose reaction against impressionism expressed itself in efforts to make an exact science of the examination of how literature produced psychological states in its readers. He was followed by Herbert Read and William Empson. In America, Freudian psychology was applied to literary problems, but the strong movement was the NEW HUMANISM, which, under the leadership of Babbitt and More, formulated a critical position resting on the traditional moral and critical standards of the humanists.

In the 1930s, as a partial aftermath of the financial collapse, came a wave of critics espousing Marxist ideas—a specialized form of pragmatic theory—in both England and America. The major English Marxist was Christopher Caudwell. Although no Americans approached him in excellence, critics such as Granville Hicks and V. F. Calverton urged the reading of literature in the light of radical social views. During the 1930s in America, reacting both against the New Humanists and the Marxist critics came a group, drawn largely from the AGRARIANS, who vigorously embraced an objective theory of art. Led by John Crowe Ransom, who gave them a name and something resembling a credo in his book *The New Criticism*, these essentially conservative and antiromantic writers—Allen Tate, Robert Penn Warren, Donald Davidson, Yvor Winters, and later Cleanth Brooks—started from the position of T. S. Eliot and Ezra Pound and quickly formed themselves into a powerful force in the formal criticism of literature. At the same time a similar group, though much less organized, was practicing a stringent and aesthetically centered criticism in England, among them Eliot himself, F. R. Leavis, and Cyril Connolly. In both England and America, the theories of Carl Jung about the racial unconscious (see ARCHETYPE) have received vigorous expression by such writers as Maud Bodkin in England and Francis Fergusson in America. At about the same time, during the 1930s, Edmund Wilson emerged as a critic of eclectic taste, catholic learning, and trenchant style. Gertrude Stein delivered her Lectures in America that established her as a critical personage of rare insight, scope, and force. R. G. Collingwood, with an intellectual pedigree traceable to John Ruskin and William Morris in England and Benedetto Croce in Italy, combined the expressive and pragmatic approaches in a brilliant application of critical procedures that located art as a psychosomatic transaction in persons who live by an interlocking series of perceptions, intuitions, and expressions. Centered in Chicago and often called the CHICAGO CRITICS, a group of neo-Aristotelians led by Ronald Crane, Richard McKeon, Norman Maclean, and Elder Olson formulated a kind of formal criticism based on Aristotle's principles. From this group have come Wayne Booth's *The Rhetoric of Fiction*, a major critical effort to come to grips with fiction, and the profound critical studies of Austin M. Wright who, like Crane and Booth, has concentrated on fiction.

The method of Husserl, commonly known as PHENOMENOLOGY, has become a widely used method for critics who lean toward EXISTENTIALISM, such as J. Hillis Miller (at the beginning of his career) and Paul Brodtkorb. Another lively concept is STRUCTURALISM, a method of analysis inspired by structural linguistics and structural anthropology. In the pioneering linguistic science of the Swiss Ferdinand de Saussure (1857–1913), language is treated as a system of signifying and signified elements that are related arbitrarily, without "motivation" or causal association. In this complex network of relations, meaning is generated by binary distinctions with no extrinsic reference or positive terms. The -s suffix in English, for example, has no particular meaning except as a convenient means of distinguishing contrasted forms: singular and plural nouns, plural and singular verbs, as well as nominative and possessive nouns. The *-s* that makes a singular noun plural makes a plural verb singular in the third person and present tense. Such a system of analysis, refined by many complications, was subsequently applied to signs not strictly linguistic, such as patterns of kinship and the logic of myth, by the anthropologist Claude Lévi-Strauss. In time, certain thinkers were able to extend the structuralist manner to psychoanalysis (Jacques Lacan), to fashion (Roland Barthes), and to anything, including an artwork, that can be considered as having a structure like that of a Saussurean language. The character of Jay Gatsby in Fitzgerald's novel, say, is not defined as a function of Fitzgerald's personality or American history or any moral dictum (such as "Crime does not pay") but rather as an entity determined and animated by a web of essentially binary relations: Jay Gatsby and James Gatz, Gatsby and Tom, Gatsby and Daisy, Gatsby and Myrtle, Gatsby and Wilson, Gatsby and Carraway, and so on, all adding up to a massive self-standing structure radiant with dramatic meanings potentiated by the linkage between extreme charisma and extreme bureaucracy.

Such scrutiny of structure has been succeeded by "deconstructionist criticism"—exemplified by the markedly creative Jacques Derrida—in which ever more presuppositions of truth and reference come into question. DECONSTRUCTION begins at a point at which the work or text seems to differ from itself and so to undo, dismantle, or deconstruct its own premises. Gatsby, say, as the title of the novel invites the reader to ask, is both great and not great, at one and the same time, and this contradiction or APORIA calls into question the hierarchical presupposition implied in the binary contrast of "great" and "small." It has become the habit of deconstruction to deconstruct everything, including itself, but always—and in an increasing number of disciplines beyond literature and literary theory—in the interest of questioning previously unquestioned postulates of order. The hierarchies in question are such pairs as nature–culture, presence–absence, man–woman, and work–play, with the first term in each pair understood as the privileged one. As a spirit, outlook, or general approach to thinking—and in spite of charges of negativism and nihilism—deconstruction in most of its various modes has been abundantly productive of new readings. See CRITICISM, TYPES OF.

[References: M. H. Abrams, *The Mirror and the Lamp* (1953); Walter J. Bate, ed., *Criticism: The Major Texts*, enl. ed. (1948, 1970); M. C. Beardsley, *Aesthetics from Classical Greece to the Present* (1966); Art Berman, *From the New Criticism to Deconstruction: The Reception of Structuralism and Post-Structuralism* (1988); R. S. Crane, *Critical and Historical Principles of Literary History* (1967, 1971); Jonathan Culler, *Structuralist Poetics: Structuralism, Linguistics and the Study of Literature* (1975); David Daiches, *Critical Approaches to Literature* (1956); Terry Eagleton, *Literary Theory: An Introduction*, 2nd ed. (1996; orig. 1983); Northrop Frye, *Anatomy of Criticism* (1957); Ann Jefferson and David Robey, eds., *Modern Literary Theory: A Comparative Introduction*, 2nd ed. (1983, 1986; orig. 1982); Frank Lentricchia, *After the New Criticism* (1980); J. H. Smith and E. W. Parks, eds., *The Great*

Critics, 3rd ed. (1951); René Wellek, *A History of Modern Criticism,* 4 vols. (1955–65); René Wellek and Austin Warren, *Theory of Literature*, 2nd ed., 3rd rev. ed. (1965; 1956; orig. 1949); W. K. Wimsatt and Cleanth Brooks, *Literary Criticism: A Short History* (1957).]

Criticism, Types of Criticism has been applied since the seventeenth century to the description, justification, analysis, or judgment of art. Of the many ways in which criticism may be classified, some of more common are given here, as supplementary to M. H. Abrams's discrimination among the major critical theories as MIMETIC, PRAGMATIC, EXPRESSIVE, and OBJECTIVE. One common dichotomy is ARISTOTELIAN versus PLATONIC. Aristotelian implies a judicial, logical, formal criticism that tends to find values either within a work itself or inseparably linked to the work; and Platonic implies a moralistic, utilitarian view, whereby the values of a work reside in its usefulness for ulterior purposes. Such a view of Platonic criticism is narrow and in part inaccurate, but those who hold it point to the exclusion of the poet from Plato's *Republic*. Essentially what is meant by the Aristotelian–Platonic dichotomy is an intrinsic–extrinsic separation.

A separation between relativistic and absolutist criticism is also often made, with the relativistic critic employing any system that will aid in elucidating a work, whereas the absolutist critic holds that there is only one proper procedure or set of principles. The relativistic position may be aligned with philosophies called dualism or pluralism (the latter embraced by R. S. Crane), whereas the absolutist position matches the philosophy known as monism (of which Crane accused Cleanth Brooks).

There is also an obvious division between THEORETICAL CRITICISM and PRACTICAL CRITICISM (sometimes called "applied" criticism), which concentrates on particular works. Criticism may also be classified according to its purpose. The principal purposes are: (1) to justify or explain the critic's own work (Dryden, Wordsworth, Henry James); (2) to defend imaginative art in a world that finds its value questionable (Sidney, Shelley, the New Criticism); (3) to prescribe rules for writers and to legislate taste for the audience (Pope, Boileau, some Marxists); (4) to interpret works to readers who might otherwise fail to understand or appreciate them (Matthew Arnold, Edmund Wilson); (5) to judge works by clearly defined standards of evaluation (Samuel Johnson, T. S. Eliot); (6) to discover and apply the principles that describe the foundations of good art (Addison, Coleridge, R. G. Collingwood, I. A. Richards).

Criticism is also often divided into the following types: (1) IMPRESSIONISTIC, which emphasizes how the work of art affects the critic; (2) HISTORICAL, which examines the work against its historical surroundings and the facts of its author's life and times; (3) TEXTUAL, which attempts to reconstruct the original manuscript or textual version of the work; (4) FORMAL, which examines the work in terms of the characteristics of the type or genre to which it belongs; (5) JUDICIAL, which judges the work by certain standards; (6) ANALYTICAL, which attempts to get at the nature of the work as an object in itself through the detailed analysis of its parts and their organization; (7) MORAL, which evaluates the work in relation to human life; (8) MYTHIC, which explores the nature and significance of the archetypes and archetypal patterns in the work; (9) STRUCTURAL, which studies literature as a quasi-linguistic structure whose meanings are made possible through codes or systems of convention; and (10) PHENOMENOLOGICAL, which makes an existential analysis of the worlds created in the consciousness by art. Many other adjectives attach themselves to criticism: idealistic, academic, philological (meaning some emphasis on historical linguistics), technical (meaning, for literature, concentration on diction, grammar, prosody, and graphic effects), establishmentarian, and so forth. These widely differing classification systems for criticism are not mutually exclusive, and there are certainly others. These will serve, however, to indicate that critics have employed a great variety of strategies.

Critique A critical examination of a work of art with a view to determining its nature and assessing its value according to some established standards. A critique is rather more serious and judicious than a REVIEW.

Cross-alliteration ALLITERATION of two separate consonants or clusters the *ch*ill of a *sh*ock" ("The Beast in the Jungle"). See CYNGHANEDD.

Cross-Compound Rhyme Rhyme between the first syllable of one word and the second of another, and vice versa, as in "jughead" and "bedbug." Wallace Stevens used "Lascar" and "Carcass" in the same line.

Cross-cutting A term used in FILM CRITICISM to describe repeated movements within a connected sequence from one subject to another. It suggests simultaneous or parallel actions. First used extensively by D. W. Griffith in 1915 in *Birth of a Nation, cross-cutting* is a staple method for suspense and chase films.

Crossed Rhyme A term applied to couplets, usually hexameter or longer, in the words preceding the CAESURA rhyme, as in Swinburne's lines:

> Thou has conquered, O pale Galilean; the world has grown grey
>   from thy breath;
> We have drunken of things Lethean, and fed on the fullness of
>   death.

Such a couplet tends to break into four short lines rhyming *abab*. The term is also-sometimes applied to quatrains with an *abab* rhyme pattern. See also LEONINE RHYME.

Crotchet Obsolete typographical term for square brackets.

Crown of Sonnets Seven SONNETS interlinked by having the last line of the first form the first line of the second, the last line of the second form the first line of the third, and so forth, with the last line of the last sonnet repeating the first line of the first. Donne's "La Corona" is an example.

Cruelty, Theater of A concept, originated in the 1930s by Antonin Artaud, whereby the theater becomes a ceremonial act of magic purgation. Artaud meant a theater that could demonstrate human beings' inescapable enslavement to things and to circumstance. He hoped to raise (or return) the theater to a level of religious ceremony. In so doing he subordinated words to action, gesture, and sound in order to overwhelm the spectator and liberate instinctual preoccupations with crime, cruelty, and eroticism. It is called the *theater of the cruel* because it employs all means of shock to make the spectator aware of—and even participate in—the fundamental cruelty of life. Artaud delivered several manifestos and projected plays based on Bluebeard and the Marquis de Sade, but he did not complete them. His theories, however, and the *theater of cruelty* appear importantly in the work of several contemporary playwrights, among them

Peter Brook, Jean-Louis Barrault, Roger Blin, and Jean Genet. The most widely successful example of the *theater of cruelty* is Peter Weiss's *The Persecution and Assassination of Jean-Paul Marat as Performed by Inmates of the Asylum of Charenton under the Direction of the Marquis de Sade*, commonly known as *Marat/Sade*. See ABSURD, THEATER OF THE.

Crux A point of decision in textual editing. There is a *crux* in Shakespeare's *Hamlet* (1, 2, 129): A word printed as "sallied" in the Quarto of 1604–05 makes little sense and is customarily emended so that the line reads either "O that this too too sullied flesh would melt" or "O that this too too solid flesh would melt."

Cryptarithm A sophisticated puzzle in which letters of the alphabet are assigned a numerical value such that a spelled-out formula (normally addition) is true of both the words and the numbers. A specialized form is the "zero-sum game":

ZERO)		2391
ZERO)	=	2391
ZERO)		2391
NONE)		7173

This was a trivial pastime of negligible literary interest until the American poet George Starbuck used it seriously. Two other examples:

NIHIL	ZILCH
NIHIL	ZILCH
ZILCH	NIL
	NIL
	NAUGHT

Cubist Poetry Poetry that attempts to do in verse what cubist painters do on canvas; that is, take the elements of an experience, fragment them (creating what Picasso calls "destructions"), and then to rearrange them in a meaningful new synthesis (Picasso's "sum of destructions"). Some of the writings of Gertrude Stein, E. E. Cummings, Kenneth Rexroth, and John Ashbery could be classified as *cubist*, especially if the conventional sequential arrangement of words and other elements is superseded by something like a simultaneous graphic display.

Cue In performance, a signal—such as a word or sound effect—that it is time for something else to happen. Entrances, exits, sound effects, and lighting changes often depend on *cues*.

Cultural Primitivism The belief that nature (in the sense of what exists undisturbed by human artifice) is preferable and fundamentally better than any aspect of human CULTURE (any area of human activity where, by art or craft, people have modified or ordered nature). It is a belief that distrusts artifice, logic, social and political organizations, rules, and conventions. See PRIMITIVISM, CHRONOLOGICAL PRIMITIVISM.

Culture In a state of nature, humankind survives by directly struggling with the environment; in time, the elements of that struggle—practices, habits, customs, beliefs, traditions—become institutions, the body of which is known as *culture*. Because *culture* changes from place to place and from time to time, we speak variously of English *culture*, Elizabethan *culture*, Victorian *culture*, working-class *culture*, and so forth. For literary purposes, we may speak of a work as both a creature and a creator of *culture*; we may study Elizabethan *culture* through Shakespeare's plays, and vice versa. Drama and fiction tend to be popular accounts of cultural and social problems in the first place, so they are the most interesting subjects for cultural analysis; and certain sorts of work—such as those explicitly designed to praise or blame in an overtly social context—yield the best results to such analysis. A cultural approach to literature assumes beforehand that a work exists most interestingly as part of a social context.

[Reference: Stephen Greenblatt, "Culture," in *Critical Terms for Literary Study*, eds. Frank Lentricchia and Thomas McLaughlin, 2nd ed. (1995; orig. 1990).]

Curse An INVOCATION that calls on a supernatural being to visit evil on someone. In this sense it is a MALEDICTION; or, if a formal and solemn IMPRECATION, an ANATHEMA. *Curse* is also used for the effects of the invocation of great evil, as in Hawthorne's *The House of the Seven Gables*, in which the *curse* put on the Pyncheon family by Matthew Maule darkens the history of succeeding generations. See ARA.

Curtain A piece of heavy material that screens the stage from the audience and by being raised or opened and lowered or closed marks the beginning and end of an ACT or SCENE. The *curtain* came into use in the early seventeenth century along with the development of the PROSCENIUM arch. By metonymic extension, *curtain* is used for a line, speech, or situation just before the *curtain* falls. The endings of parts of a drama are sometimes called *curtains*, as in the expression "quick *curtain*" for a sudden conclusion to a scene, or "strong *curtain*" for a powerful conclusion, or "*curtain* speech" for a final speech. The term "*curtain* speech" also applies to a talk given in front of the *curtain* after a performance.

Curtain Call An act of homage by an audience who, by sustained applause, call for performers to reappear on stage one or more times after the curtain has fallen.

Curtain Line The last line before a curtain falls ending a scene, act, or whole drama—typically dramatic in effect.

Curtain Raiser A short play—either one-act or a SKIT—presented prior to the principal dramatic production on a program. By analogy, the term *curtain raiser* is applied to any preliminary event.

Curtal Sonnet Gerard Manley Hopkins's name for a SONNET that has been curtailed. The challenge, according to Hopkins, was to shorten the OCTAVE to a SESTET while preserving the numerical ratio of the first subdivision to the second. Since 8:6::6:4.5, a *curtal sonnet* is divided into parts consisting of six lines and four and a half lines. The octave is shortened to a sestet and rhymes *abcabc*. The sestet is shortened to an augmented quatrain and rhymes either *dbcd* or *dcbd*. A half-line rhyming *c* ends the poem. Hopkins' "Pied Beauty" is the most famous example. There is a *curtal sonnet* by the contemporary American poet R. S. Gwynn.

Cut In film, a switch from one image to another. The *cut* is the most common transitional device in filmmaking. The noun form *cut* is also applied to an uninterrupted sequence. As a verb, *cut* describes the terminating of a scene or an image preparatory to presenting another. See CROSS-CUTTING.

Cutline In newspapers, a detailed caption under a photograph that has no accompanying story.

Cyberpunk Science fiction in the mode popular after 1975, with elements from cybernetics, robotics, and advanced computing, on the one hand, and punk rock culture on the other. Both components involve violence, velocity, brightness, flatness, and a blurring of boundaries between human beings and machines. Philip K. Dick's writings, subsequently turned into such movies as *Blade Runner* and *Total Recall*, were precursors; and some novels by Davis Grubb and Thomas Pynchon partake of some of the style associated with *cyberpunk*. The defining works of *cyberpunk*, however, remain the novels in William Gibson's Cyberspace trilogy: *Neuromancer*, *Count Zero*, and *Mona Lisa Overdrive* (1984–1988).

Cybertext Texts of sorts other than conventional linear narratives experienced by means of prose fiction, movies, and television. The notion of *cybertext* concerns the study of digital literature in many forms: hypertext fiction, computer games, and collaborative interactive texts available on the Internet.

[References: Espen J. Aarseth, *Cybertext: Perspectives on Ergodic Literature* (1997); Michael Joyce, *Of Two Minds: Hypertext Pedagogy and Poetics* (1994–1995); Ilana Snyder, *Hypertext: The Electronic Labyrinth* (1997).]

Cycle A term, originally meaning "circle," applied to a collection of poems or ROMANCES centering on some outstanding event or character. Cyclic narratives are traditional accumulations given literary form by a succession of authors rather than by a single writer. "Cyclic" was first applied to a series of epics supplementing Homer's account of the Trojan War and written by a group of late Greek poets known as the Cyclic Poets. Other examples of cyclic narrative are the Charlemagne epics and Arthurian romances, such as the "Cycle of Lancelot." The religious MEDIEVAL DRAMA presents a cyclic treatment of biblical THEMES. Any set of related works—such as Wagner's *Ring* music dramas or T. S. Eliot's *Four Quartets*—is sometimes called a *cycle*.

Cyclic Drama The great cycles of medieval religious drama. See MYSTERY PLAY.

Cyclopedia (or Cyclopaedia) Same as ENCYCLOPEDIA.

Cynghanedd Originally a medieval Welsh term covering a wide and sophisticated range of verse devices, the term was revived in the late nineteenth century by Gerard Manley Hopkins to refer to various harmonious patterns of interlaced multiple ALLITERATION (see CROSS-ALLITERATION). Simpler sorts of alliteration are linear and unilateral—as in the common American lunch-counter order "A *c*up of *c*offee and a *p*iece of *p*ie" or Keats's deliberately archaistic line "A shielded scutcheon *b*lushed with *b*lood of *q*ueens and *k*ings." Interlacing alliteration, however, in such patterns as *xyyx* and *xyxy* (much the commonest), produces a quadratically ornate effect, such as sometimes occurs in vernacular phrases ("*t*em*p*est in a *t*ea*p*ot," "*p*ar*tr*idge in a *p*ear *tr*ee") and the biblical collocation of *s*words-*p*loughshares and *s*pears-*p*runing-hooks. There is conspicuous and complex *cynghanedd* in Wyatt's "*s*trange *f*ashion of *f*or*s*aking" and in Macbeth's description of life as a "*t*ale / *T*old by an idiot, *f*ull of *s*ound and *f*ury, / *S*igni*f*ying nothing" and in Wordsworth's noble tribute to Milton: ". . . and yet thy *h*eart / The *l*ow*l*iest *d*uties on *h*erself *d*id *l*ay." One of Richard Crashaw's poems includes the sequence "*st*udied *f*ate *st*and *f*orth. As noted, instances of *cynghanedd* turn up in the vernacular and in prose (as in the phrase "*t*ooth*p*aste and *t*oilet *p*aper" in Thomas Heggen's *Mister Roberts*, Faulkner's vivid evocation of a hog's gait as a "*t*winkling *p*ur*p*oseful *p*orcine *t*rot," and Evelyn Waugh's "callously wicked . . . wantonly cruel" and "the mud of Flanders and the flies of Mesopotamia" in *Brideshead Revisited*), but the most distinguished, varied, and engaging employment remains that in almost all of Hopkins's mature poems. The most salient such use is in the sonnet beginning "As *k*ing*f*ishers *c*atch *f*ire, *dr*agon*fl*ies *dr*aw *fl*ame" and the end of "God's Grandeur": "Because the Holy Ghost over the bent/World *b*roods with *w*arm *br*east and with ah! *br*ight *w*ings." The device can be heard in "*s*ad *h*eart" and "*s*ick for *h*ome" in one line of Keats's "Ode to a Nightingale"; in William Barnes's "Ellen Brine ov Allenburn"; in "*g*uidon *fl*ags *fl*utter *g*ayly" in Whitman's "Cavalry Crossing a Ford."; and in "*H*eaded with *fl*int, or *h*ardened with *fl*ame's breath" in C. M. Doughty's *The Titans*. In *transition* magazine (number 26) Keidrych Rhys published a piece called "Cynghanedd Cymry" with such lines as "*B*y *c*oarse *b*eards of *c*urse-*b*ards."

Cynicism Doubt of the generally accepted standards or of the innate goodness of human action. In literature the term characterizes writers or movements distinguished by dissatisfaction. Any highly individualistic writer, scornful of accepted social standards and ideals, can be called cynical. Almost every literature has had its schools of cynics. Samuel Butler's *The Way of All Flesh* and W. Somerset Maugham's *Of Human Bondage* are examples of the cynical NOVEL. The THEATER OF THE ABSURD, the THEATER OF CRUELTY, and many ANTIREALISTIC NOVELS reflect *cynicism*.

Menhart Roman 1939. Designed by Oldrich Menhart.

Dactyl A FOOT consisting of one accented syllable followed by two unaccented, as in *mannikin*.

Dadaism A movement in Europe during and just after the First World War, which ignored a logical relationship between idea and statement, argued for absolute freedom, and delivered itself of numerous provocative manifestoes. It was founded in Zurich in 1916 by Tristan Tzara (who then went to Paris) with the ostensibly destructive intent of demolishing art and philosophy, intending to replace them with conscious madness as a protest against the insanity of the war. Similar movements sprang up in Germany, the Netherlands, Italy, Russia, and Spain. About 1924 the movement developed into SURREALISM. In certain respects it seems to have been a forerunner of the ANTIREALISTIC NOVEL, the THEATER OF THE ABSURD, and the NEW YORK SCHOOL.

[References: C. W. E. Bigsby, *Dada and Surrealism* (1972); Mary Ann Caws, *The Poetry of Dada and Surrealism* (1970); Alan Young, *Dada and After: Extremist Modernism and English Literature* (1981).]

Dagger A dagger-shaped device [†] used in printing for marginal references, cross-references, and other purposes. In some places, the symbol marks the names of the dead. Also called "long cross," obelisk, obelus.

Dandyism A literary style used by the English and French DECADENT writers of the last quarter of the nineteenth century. The term is derived from *dandy*: one who gives exaggeratedly fastidious attention to dress and appearance. *Dandyism* is marked by excessively refined emotion and preciosity of language. One or another species of *dandyism* has been associated with the life or work of Byron, Poe, Disraeli, Wilde, Wallace Stevens, James Merrill, and Tom Wolfe, as well as a long succession of French writers from Baudelaire to the present. A somewhat more subtle and profound ideology than superficial emphasis on the sartorial may suggest, thoroughgoing *dandyism* reflects a preference for culture over nature, city over country, manner over matter, surface over substance, and art over life.

Darwinism Thought affected by the research and theories of Charles Darwin (1809–1882), especially *The Origin of Species* (1859), which advances the idea of the evolution of biological species by a process of selection (natural, sexual, and domestic) in a struggle for existence that usually comes down to the survival of the fittest and the death of the less fit. The thinking is clearly important in biology itself and can be extended to social science (in the form of social *Darwinism*) and even to philosophy. John Dewey observed in 1909 that the very idea that species, instead of being eternal and immutable, have traceable origins, is itself influential in philosophy; in 1914, however, Ludwig Wittgenstein remarked that the Darwinian hypothesis had no more to do with philosophy than any other hypothesis in the natural sciences. The work of the American poet Robinson Jeffers owes much to *Darwinism*.

Dateline In newspapers, a line that tells where and when the story was written.

Daybook An earlier name for DIARY or JOURNAL; also a book listing activities for a day.

Daytime Drama See SOAP OPERA.

Dead Metaphor A figure of speech used so long that it is taken in its denotative sense only, without the conscious comparison to a physical object it once conveyed. For example, in "The keystone of his system is the belief in an omnipotent God," "keystone"—literally an actual stone in an arch—functions as a *dead metaphor*. Many abstract terms are *dead metaphors*. Their presence prompted Emerson to call language "fossil poetry." By historical association that may devolve into sentimentality or superstition, an age-old etymologizing habit tries to trace every abstraction to some primordial physical entity. Most Latinate abstractions seem to be *dead metaphors*, as in the connection between "inspiration" and a Latin verb meaning "to breathe into."

Dead Sea Scrolls About 800 documents written between the first century B.C. and about A.D. 70, discovered in 1947 (and later) in caves near the Dead Sea on the border of Israel and Jordan. The principal finds were in caves on or near the site of the Qumran religious community. The scrolls, stored in jars, contain material of all sorts, including horoscopes and calendars, along with portions of every book of the Bible except Esther. These manuscripts, almost a thousand years older than any previously known versions of the Bible, have been of great importance to students of religion and history. Full-length scrolls have been published, but controversy still attends the handling of thousands of fragments from 600 unpublished documents. Their provenance and meaning remain unclear, and disagreements have been theological, political, and academic. The scrolls contain a treasury of information about Essenism, pre-Rabbinic Judaism, and early Christianity, in particular the accounts of a messianic figure known as the Teacher of Righteousness and his antagonist the Wicked Priest. Controversy of many sorts, from bureaucratic and bibliographic to political and theological, has attended the *Dead Sea Scrolls* from the time of their discovery into the twenty-first century.

[References: John J. Collins, *Apocalypticism in the Dead Sea Scrolls* (1997); Hershel Shanks, *The Mystery and Meaning of the Dead Sea Scrolls* (1998); Edmund Wilson, *The Dead Sea Scrolls, 1947–1969* (1969).]

Débat A type of composition, usually in verse, highly popular in the Middle Ages, in which two contestants, frequently ALLEGORICAL, debate a topic and refer it to a judge. The *débat* may reflect the influence of the "pastoral contest" in Theocritus and Virgil. It was particularly popular in France, where the subjects ranged over most human interests, such as theology, morality, politics, COURTLY LOVE, and social questions. In

England the *débat* tended to be religious and moralistic. The best English example is *The Owl and the Nightingale* (c. 12th century).

Decadence A term denoting the decline that commonly marks the end of a great period. *Decadent* qualities include self-consciousness, restless curiosity, oversubtilizing refinement, confusion of GENRES, eccentricity, and often moral perversity. In English drama, the period following Shakespeare was marked by such *decadent* qualities as a relaxing of critical standards, a breaking down of types (comedy and tragedy merging), a lowered moral tone, sensationalism, overemphasis on some single interest (such as plot construction or "prettiness" of style), a decreased seriousness of purpose, and a loss of poetic power. The "silver age" of Latin literature (reign of Trajan), including such writers as Tacitus, Juvenal and Martial (satirists), Lucan, and the Plinys, is called *decadent* in relation to the preceding "golden age" of Augustus made illustrious by Virgil, Horace, Ovid, and Livy. In the last half of the nineteenth century and the early years of the twentieth, *decadence* found a special expression in the work of a group called the DECADENTS. Nowadays the term is used to describe a period or a work of art in which a deteriorating purpose or loss of adequate subject matter is combined with an increasing skill and even hypertrophied virtuosity of technique to produce an exaggerated sensationalism. Some feel that many contemporary art forms, particularly novels and films, are *decadent*, but some such term has been invoked for centuries by conservatives when confronted with any novelty or departure from petrified norms. Some art is indeed genuinely *decadent* and pernicious, but art called *decadent* (including the poetry of Wordsworth and Eliot) is likely to become in time the least *decadent* sort of orthodoxy.

[Reference: Richard Gilman, *Decadence: The Strange Life of an Epithet* (1979).]

Decadents A group of late-nineteenth- and early-twentieth-century writers, principally in France but also in England and America, who held that art was superior to nature and that the finest beauty was that of dying or decaying things. In both their lives and their art, they attacked the moral and social standards of their time. In France the group included Verlaine, Rimbaud, Baudelaire, Huysmans, and Villiers de l'Isle-Adam. In England the *decadents* included Oscar Wilde, Ernest Dowson, Aubrey Beardsley, and Frank Harris. In America the sentiment is best represented by Edgar Saltus, although there are *decadent* qualities in Stephen Crane. See DANDYISM.

De Casibus Latin, concerning the falls (from greatness). John Lydgate translated Boccaccio's *De Casibus Virorum Illustrium* as *Falls of Princes* (1494). Chaucer's "Monk's Tale" belongs to the tradition. In 1974, when a friend suggested the writing of a *de casibus* poem on the resignation of the president of the United States, a poet commented, "De casibus ain't what dey used to be."

Decasyllabic A line composed of ten syllables. Iambic and trochaic pentameter lines are *decasyllabic*.

Deconstruction A widespread philosophical and critical movement that owes its name and energy to the precepts and examples of Jacques Derrida, whose works have been available in English translation since the 1960s. Precursors of the movement include Ernst Cassirer (especially his distinctions between the concept of the thing and the concept of relation, set forth as early as 1910); modern phenomenological philosophers (Husserl and Heidegger foremost among them); Ferdinand de Saussure and his scientific LINGUISTICS (based on closed systems of arbitrarily connected signifiers and signifieds with no absolute, substantial, or motivated reference and no positive extrinsic terms); a number of Nietzschean revisionists, chiefly in France; Kenneth Burke, with his "logological" emphasis on a rhetoric of relations over a logic of substances, and the example of many artists in many fields, particularly James Joyce in *Finnegans Wake*. One important doctrine leading to *deconstruction* is Saussure's conclusion that "in language there are only differences. Even more important: a difference generally implies positive terms between which the difference is set up, but in language there are only differences *without positive terms*." As the linguistic model is extended to describe other systems, concepts of thing, substance, event, and absolute recede, to be superseded by concepts of relation, ratio, construct, and relativity, all covered by Derrida's stimulating coinage "DIFFÉRANCE," which includes difference, differing, deferring, deference, and deferral. Once one realizes that what seems to be an event is really a construct of a quasi-linguistic system, then one is in a position to undo the construct or to recognize that the construct, by its very nature, has already undone, dismantled, or deconstructed itself—with far-reaching implications. *Deconstruction* affords a perspective from which any number of modern movements can be seen as parts of a generalized shift from a logocentric metaphysic of presence to a new recognition of the play of differences among relations. (The most widely acknowledged text to discuss this theory is Jacques Derrida's essay "Structure, Sign, and Play in the Discourse of the Human Sciences," originally contributed to an international symposium on structuralism held at the Johns Hopkins University in 1966.)

There is something deconstructive about what Darwin did to the biological hierarchies of present–past and human–animal; what Freud did to the psychological hierarchies of adult–child, reason–dream, conscious–unconscious, and several others; what Schönberg did to the sentiments of the diatonic scale, which privileged the tonic and dominant over other notes in a scale; what Picasso (who called his art "a sum of destructions") did to hierarchies of perspective and orientation in painting; and much else. One recent effect of *deconstruction* has been the undoing of the old-order creation-criticism, so that a number of academic critics, including Harold Bloom and Geoffrey Hartman, have been producing critical texts that are, in effect if not in explicit form, PROSE POEMS.

[References: Jonathan Culler, *On Deconstruction; Theory and Criticism after Structuralism* (1982), and *Structuralist Poetics: Structuralism, Linguistics, and the Study of Literature* (1975); Paul de Man, *Allegories of Reading: Figural Language in Rousseau, Nietzsche, Rilke, and Proust* (1979), and *Blindness and Insight: Essays in the Rhetoric of Contemporary Criticism*, 2nd ed., rev. (1983; orig. 1971); Jacques Derrida, *Of Grammatology* (tr. 1976), and *Writing and Différance* (tr. 1978); Judith Fetterley, *The Resisting Reader: A Feminist Approach to American Fiction* (1978); Barbara Johnson, *The Critical Différance: Essays in the Contemporary Rhetoric of Reading* (1980); Christopher Norris, *Deconstruction, Theory and Practice*, rev. ed (1991; orig. 1982); Michael Ryan, *Marxism and Deconstruction* (1982).]

Decorum A term loosely describing what is proper to a character, subject, or setting. By classical standards, the unity and harmony of a work could be maintained by the observance of DRAMATIC PROPRIETY. Style should suit the speaker, the occasion, and the subject. Renaissance authors were careful to have kings speak in a "high" style (such as majestic blank verse), old men in grave style, clowns in prose, and shepherds in a "rustic" style. Puttenham (1589) cites the lack of *decorum* in the case of the English translator of Virgil who said that Aeneas was fain to "trudge" out of Troy (a beggar might "trudge," but not a great hero). Beginning in the Renaissance, the type to which a character belonged was regarded as an important determinant of his or her qualities; age, rank, and status were often held as fundamental. But on the use of *decorum* in the *Iliad* Pope said: "The speeches are to be considered as they flow from the characters, being perfect or defective as they agree or disagree with the manners of those who utter them. As there is more variety of characters in the *Iliad*, so there is of speeches, than in any other poem," and "Homer is in nothing more excellent than in that distinction of characters which he maintains through his whole poem. What Andromache here says can be spoken properly by none but Andromache." *Decorum* has often been considered the controlling critical idea of Horace's poetic doctrine and of the NEOCLASSIC PERIOD in England.

Deduction The process of deductive reasoning (see A PRIORI), which moves from general principles to individual cases.

Deep Focus In FILM, a method by which objects both near and far away are simultaneously in focus. It is widely used in realistic filmmaking. Same as COMPOSITION IN DEPTH.

Deep Image IMAGES from the subconscious, dreams, hallucinations, or fantasies are called *deep images* by certain writers, among them Robert Bly. The deep, underground, or subterranean image, as the terms suggest, argues with IMAGIST fervor for the image in general as the central motivation in a poem and for a specific sort of image in particular: not merely an ornament or conceit but a figure conforming to Freud's notion that dream language puts image and quantity in the places of idea and quality. Any palpable image can take on "deep" characteristics, depending on the setting and situation, but it seems likely that the unconscious deals in tokens such as the explicit images in Bly's "When the Dumb Speak":

> Then the images appear:
> Images of death,
> Images of the body shaken in the grave,
> And the graves filled with seawater;
> Fires in the sea,
> The ships smoldering like bodies,
> Images of wasted life. . . .

Defamiliarization Englishing of Russian *ostranenie*, used by Viktor Šklovskij and other Russian Formalists to indicate a property of great art, which, instead of representing an outside reality by transparent means, is directed at the human means of perceiving and communicating information. Because our senses are forever falling into rigid habits and empty routines, we need art periodically to wake us up by making the familiar suddenly seem strange—and the process of estrangement is *defamiliarization*, by which a painting or sonata can make us realize and exclaim that we have eyes and ears, and by which literature can make us realize that we speak a language with physical features that we can question and enjoy. Art does not strive in the least for VERISIMILITUDE but keeps BARING THE DEVICE to remind us that it *is* art, an invaluable adjunct to our feeble senses.

[Reference: Fredric Jameson, *The Prison-House of Language: A Critical Account of Structuralism and Russian Formalism* (1972).]

Defense An argument defending something from charges or attacks. Poetry seems to need defending more than most institutions, going back to Thomas Lodge's *Defence of Poetry* (in full, *A Reply to Stephen Gosson's* School of Abuse *in Defence of Poetry, Music, and Stage Plays—1579*) and Sir Philip Sidney's *Defence of Poesie* (1595). Percy Bysshe Shelley wrote a *Defence of Poetry* in 1819, and, a century later than Shelley, Benedetto Croce delivered a lecture called "The Defence of Poetry, Variations on the Theme of Shelley" (1933).

Definition A brief explanation of the meaning of a term. Logical *definitions* consist of two elements: (1) the general class (*genus*) to which the object belongs and (2) the specific ways (*differentiae*) in which the object differs from others in the same class. For the sake of efficiency, it is best to locate an object in a relatively small class: one would ordinarily define "ant" as a kind of insect, say, and not merely as a kind of creature or entity. To define a receiver as "that which receives" is to waste time in circular *definition*. Likewise, reciprocating identifications do little toward defining or explaining. Consider: "A typhoon is a hurricane in the eastern hemisphere, and a hurricane is a typhoon in the western hemisphere." It is possible, however, to provide a reasonably effective *definition* simply by giving an apt synonym, example, summary, or paraphrase.

Definition Poem An Elizabethan mode defined by Louis Martz as "a rapid sequence of analogies." Sidney produced notable examples, such as "Come sleep, O sleep, the certain knot of peace, / The baiting place of wit, the balm of woe, / The poor man's wealth, the prisoner's release. . . ." St. Robert Southwell's "Christ's Bloody Sweat" is an example of the *definition poem* and CORRELATIVE VERSE as well: "Fat soil, full spring, sweet olive, grape of bliss / That yields, that streams, that powers, that dost distill, / Untill'd, undrawn, unstamp'd, untouch'd of press, / Dear fruit, clear brooks, fair oil, sweet wine at will." Later examples turn up in the poetry of George Herbert ("Sunday") and Henry Vaughan ("Son-days," imitating Herbert).

Definitive Edition An EDITION claiming to have final or permanent authority. It is sometimes a final text or revision, which the author wishes to be considered the accepted version, such as the 1891–1892 edition of *Leaves of Grass*, of which Whitman said, "As there are now several editions of L. of G., different texts and different dates, I wish to say that I prefer and recommend this present one, complete, for future printing. . . ." The term is also applied to editions determined by scrupulous application of rigorous principles of textual editing, such as those produced under the aegis of the CENTER FOR SCHOLARLY EDITIONS of the Modern Language Association of America.

Deictic A word—usually a pronoun, adjective, or adverb—that refers to another part of a discourse and not outward to a world or context. "Here I am," at the beginning of T. S. Eliot's "Gerontion," contains two *deictics*, "here" and "I," which would normally be explained elsewhere. *Deictics* are customarily prepared for: "A man came into a room; *his* face was pale"; if not prepared for, a *deictic* has the effect of involving the reader in the discourse in MEDIAS RES, as in the first sentence of Charlotte Brontë's *Jane*

Eyre: "There was no possibility of taking a walk that day." Often combined with the LYRIC PRESENT.

Deipnosophist A gourmet, someone wise in the ways of dining; best known from Atheneus's second-century fifteen-book *Deipnosophists*, in which a group eat together and discuss food, literature, and much else.

Deism The religion of those who believe in a God who rules the world by established laws but not in the divinity of Christ or the inspiration of the Bible; "natural" religion, based on reason and a study of NATURE as opposed to "revealed" religion. *Deism* absorbed something from Arianism (opposition to the doctrine of the Trinity) and Arminianism (which stressed moral conduct as a sign of religion and opposed the doctrine of election; see CALVINISM). The notion that the deists believed in an "absentee" God, who, having created the world and set in motion machinery for its operation, took no further interest, is not applicable to all eighteenth-century deists, some of whom even believed in God's pardoning of the sins of the repentant.

The English deists believed: (1) The Bible is not the inspired word of God; it is good so far as it reflects "natural" religion and bad so far as it contains "additions" made by superstitious or designing persons. (2) Certain Christian theological doctrines are the product of superstition or the invention of priests and must be rejected; for example, the deity of Christ, the doctrine of the Trinity, and the theory of the atonement for sins. (3) God is perfect, is the creator and governor of the universe, and works not capriciously but through unchangeable laws (hence "miracles" are rejected as impossible). (4) Human beings are free agents, whose minds work as they themselves choose; even God cannot control their thoughts. (5) Because human beings are rational creatures like God, they are capable of understanding the laws of the universe; and, as God is perfect, so can human beings become perfect through the process of education. (6) Practical religion consists in achieving virtue through the rational guidance of conduct (as exemplified in the scheme for developing certain moral virtues recorded by Franklin in his *Autobiography*).

Deixis The general presence of use of DEICTICS. *Deixis* is the property of discourse that locates an utterance in time, place, and internal reference. Verb tense, indicating time, is an element of *deixis*.

Della Cruscans A late-eighteenth-century group of poets, including Robert Merry, Hannah Cowley, and Hester Thrale. Merry, having belonged to the Della Crusca academy in Florence, used "Della Crusca" as a pen name. The group enjoyed short-lived success between 1785 and 1790, until the affectations of their writing provoked two mordant satires by William Gifford, *The Baviad* in 1791 and *The Maeviad* in 1795. The *Della Cruscans* were also wittily mocked in Robert Southey's "Amatory Poems of Abel Shufflebottom."

Demotic Style A term applied by Northrop Frye to a style shaped by the diction, rhythms, syntax, and associations of ordinary speech. It is differentiated from the HIERATIC STYLE, which uses various conventions and ornaments to create a consciously elevated literary expression.

Demotion (also called **Suppression**) The reduction of STRESS on a syllable caused by the rhythmic environment. *Demotion* usually involves monosyllables of which the stress depends on context, as in the first line of William Blake's "London"—"I wander thro' each charter'd street." "I" and "each" are potentially important monosyllables that could receive stress—"Í wándĕr thró' éach chártĕr'd stréet"—but, because of the percussive influence of the iambic rhythm, they may be demoted, thus: "Ĭ wándĕr thró' ĕach chártĕr'd stréet." Likewise, an established pattern of anapests can effect the *demotion* of a stressed syllable, as when one recites a phrase like "thĕ níght bĕfŏre Chrístmăs" so that the normally iambic "before" is sounded as two weak syllables.

Demy Printing paper measuring $17^1/_2$ by $22^1/_2$ inches.

Denotation The basic meaning of a word, independent of its emotional coloration or associations. See CONNOTATION.

Dénouement Literally, "unknotting." The final unraveling of a plot; the solution of a mystery; an explanation or outcome. *Dénouement* implies an ingenious untying of the knot of an intrigue, involving not only a satisfactory outcome of the main situation but an explanation of all the secrets and misunderstandings connected with the plot complication. *Dénouement* may be applied to both tragedy and comedy, though the common term for a tragic *dénouement* is CATASTROPHE. The final scene of Shakespeare's *Cymbeline* is a striking example of how clever and involved a dramatic *dénouement* may be: exposure of villain, clearing up of mistaken identities and disguises, reuniting of father and children, and reuniting of husband and wife. *Dénouement* is sometimes used as a synonym for FALLING ACTION.

Description One of the four chief types of composition (see ARGUMENTATION, EXPOSITION, and NARRATION) that has as its purpose the picturing of a scene or setting. Though sometimes used for its own sake (as in Poe's *Landor's Cottage*), it more often is subordinated to one of the other types of writing, especially to narration, with which it most frequently goes hand in hand.

Detective Story A story in which a crime, usually a murder—the identity of the perpetrator unknown—is solved by a detective through a logical assembling and interpretation of palpable evidence, known as clues. This definition is the accepted one for the true *detective story*, although in practice much variation occurs. If the variations are too great, however—such as the absence of the detective, a knowledge from the beginning of the identity of the criminal, or the absence of reasoning from clues—the story falls into the looser category of MYSTERY STORY. The specific form *detective story* had its origin in "The Murders in the Rue Morgue" by Edgar Allan Poe (1841). In this and other tales, Poe effectively established every one of the basic conventions of the *detective story*. Generally, American *detective stories* have had greater sensationalism and action than the English, which have usually placed a premium on tightness of plot and grace of style. Wilkie Collins's *The Woman in White* (1860) is a distinguished early example of English *detective* fiction.

The greatest of *detective story* writers was Sir Arthur Conan Doyle, whose Sherlock Holmes stories seem to have established a character, a room, a habit, a few gestures, and a group of phrases in the enduring heritage of English-speaking readers. "S. S. Van Dine" (Willard Huntington Wright) carried ingenious plotting to a very high level in

America in the 1920s in his Philo Vance stories, a course in which he was ably followed by the authors of the Ellery Queen novels. The introduction of brutal realism coupled with a poetic and highly idiomatic style in the *detective stories* of Dashiell Hammett in the 1930s had resulted in distinguished work by Raymond Chandler and Ross MacDonald. In England the ingenuity of Agatha Christie and John Dickson Carr (also "Carter Dickson"), the skill and grace of Dorothy Sayers, and the urbanity of the New Zealander Ngaio Marsh made significant contributions to the form.

The distinguished English poet C. Day Lewis, under the pen name "Nicholas Blake," wrote an entertaining series of *detective* novels with a hero supposedly based on Day Lewis's friend, W. H. Auden. The Americans who wrote as "Emma Lathen" and "Amanda Cross" produced distinguished *detective stories* in the tradition of the NOVEL OF MANNERS. All of these practitioners have made it a point of honor to observe the fundamental rule of the *detective story* (and the rule that most clearly distinguishes it from the MYSTERY STORY): that the clues contributing to a logical solution be fairly presented to the reader at the same time that the detective receives them and that the detective deduce the answer from a logical reading of these clues. From its beginning, the *detective story* has had the potential for touching deep regions of psychology and philosophy; these tendencies have been exploited by such serious thinkers as Jorge Luis Borges and Umberto Eco. See MYSTERY STORY.

[References: Jacques Barzun and W. H. Taylor, *A Catalogue of Crime*, rev. ed. (1989; orig. 1971); Julian Symons, *Mortal Consequences: A History from the Detective Story to the Crime Novel* (1972).]

Determinacy The property of being so defined and circumscribed that objective perception and interpretation are possible without a serious possibility of difference. Increasingly, from the NEW CRITICISM onward, both text and interpretation seem to be forfeiting more and more *determinacy*. See INDETERMINACY.

Determinism The belief that all ostensible acts of the will are actually the result of causes that determine them. When used to describe a doctrine in a literary work, *determinism* has a wide range of philosophical possibilities, and the potential determining forces are many. In classical literature it may be fate or necessity. In writing produced by Christians of Calvinistic leanings it may be the predestined will of God (see CALVINISM). In naturalistic literature it may be the action of scientific law (see NATURALISM). In Marxist writing it may be the inevitable operation of economic forces. In the orthodox Freudian scheme of *determinism*, every detail of daily life, including such seemingly negligible matters as slips of the tongue and pen, is the traceable result of latent psychic mechanisms, so that casual forgetting becomes an episode of suppression or repression, and apparently random choices are far from random. In all these cases characters illustrate *determinism* because their actions are controlled from without rather than being the products of free will. One function of many literary devices, such as rhythmic repetition and rhyme, is to introduce new dimensions of determination and *determinism* in arrays otherwise governed only by whim, guesswork, serendipity, or mere possibility.

Deus* (or *Dea) ex Machina The employment of some unexpected and improbable incident to make things turn out right. In the ancient Greek theater, when gods appeared, they were lowered from the "machine" or structure above the stage. Such abrupt but timely appearance of a god, when used to extricate characters from a situation so perplexing that the solution seemed beyond mortal powers, was referred to in Latin as the *deus ex machina* ("god from the machine"). The term now characterizes any device whereby an author solves a difficult situation by a forced invention.

Deuteragonist The role second in importance to the PROTAGONIST in Greek drama. Historically, Aeschylus added a second actor to the traditional religious ceremonials, thus making drama possible; this second actor was called the *deuteragonist*. The term is sometimes applied to a character who serves as a FOIL to the leading character.

Dial, The A periodical published in Boston from 1840 to 1844 as the organ of the New England transcendentalists. Margaret Fuller was its first editor (1840–42) and Emerson the second (1842–44). Among the most famous contributors were Fuller, Alcott, Emerson, Lowell, Thoreau, and Jones Very.

In 1860 another organ of TRANSCENDENTALISM named *The Dial* appeared briefly in Cincinnati, edited by Moncure Conway and with contributions by Emerson, Alcott, and Howells. From 1880 to 1929, a distinguished literary periodical was published under the name *The Dial*, first in Chicago and after 1916 in New York. Until 1916 it was a conservative literary review. From 1916 to 1920, under the editorship of Conrad Aiken, Randolph Bourne, and Van Wyck Brooks, it was a radical journal of opinion and criticism, publishing such writers as Dewey, Veblen, Laski, and Beard. After 1920 it became the most distinguished literary monthly in America, noted for its reproductions of modern graphic art and for its advocacy of modern movements. It published such writers as Thomas Mann, T. S. Eliot, and James Stephens. Marianne Moore was editor from 1926 until publication ceased in 1929.

Dialectic In the broadest sense, simply the art of ARGUMENTATION or debate, but the term is customarily used in one of its more restricted senses. In classical literature it refers to the tradition of continuing debate or discussion of eternally unresolved issues, such as "beauty versus truth" or "the individual versus the state." Plato's *Dialogues* exemplify this kind of *dialectic*. In philosophy *dialectic* is applied to a systematic analysis of a problem or idea. The most frequent system is that of Hegel, a modification of which Marx employed, in which the material at issue is analyzed in terms of thesis, antithesis, and synthesis (see HEGELIANISM).

In criticism the term is often applied to the ideas, logic, or reasoning that gives structure to certain works, such as Aldous Huxley's *Point Counter Point* or Sartre's novels. W. B. Yeats exploited the *dialectic* structure inherent in the rhyme scheme of *OTTAVA RIMA* (*abababcc*) to create a number of potently dramatic poems, such as "Among School Children," in which the driving energy is generated by dialectical oppositions (walking and dancing, youth and age, man and woman, sacred and secular, labor and play, Plato and Aristotle, past and present, nature and culture) and resolutions. Similarly, T. S. Eliot's *Four Quartets* draw their forcible drama from oppositions and resolutions involving time and eternity, action and suffering, purgatory and paradise.

Dialects When the speech of two groups or of two persons representing two groups both speaking the same "language" exhibits very marked differences, the groups or persons are said to speak different *dialects*. (A personal version of a language is sometimes called an "idiolect.") If the differences are very slight, they may be said to represent "subdialects" rather than *dialects*. If the differences are so great that speakers cannot understand one another, they speak different languages. The chief cause of the development of *dialects* is isolation or separation. Natural barriers such as mountain ranges and social barriers caused by hostility tend to keep groups from frequent contact with one another, with the resultant development of differences in speech, leading toward the formation of *dialects* or even languages. Likewise among neighboring groups, the *dialect* of one group commonly becomes dominant, as did West Saxon in early England. The Teutonic tribes that came to England in the fifth century spoke separate *dialects* of West Germanic. In Old English times (fifth to eleventh centuries) there were four main *dialects*: (1) Northumbrian (north of the Humber River) and (2) Mercian (between the Thames and the Humber), both being subdialects of the original Anglian *dialect*; (3) the Kentish (southeastern England), based on the language of the Jutes; and (4) the Saxon (southern England). In Middle English times the old *dialects* appear under different names and with new subdialects. Northumbrian is called Northern; Saxon and Kentish are called Southern; the Northern English spoken in Scotland becomes Lowland Scottish; Mercian becomes Midland, broken into two main subdialects of West Midland and East Midland. The latter was destined to become the immediate parent of modern English. Layamon's *Brut* and *The Owl and the Nightingale* are in the Southern *dialect*; *Cursor Mundi* and *Sir Tristrem* are in Northern; the *Ormulum* is early Midland, and *Havelok the Dane*, *Piers Plowman*, and the poetry of Chaucer are in later Midland. Though the literary language in modern times has been standardized, it must not be supposed that *dialects* no longer exist, especially in oral speech. Skeat lists nine modern *dialects* in Scotland; in England proper he finds three groups of Northern, ten groups of Midland, five groups of Eastern, two groups of Western, and ten groups of Southern. As a result of the work on the *Linguistic Atlas of the United States* (see AMERICAN LANGUAGE), much more accurate records of remaining regional and local differences of speech were made. There are social *dialects* as well as regional.

Dialogism According to Mikhail Bakhtin, a feature of certain literature (in Dostoyevsky more than Tolstoy, say) that permits the polyphonic interplay of many different voices rather than allowing a single monologic voice to dominate.

[Reference: Mikhail Bakhtin, *The Dialogic Imagination* (tr. 1981).]

Dialogue Conversation of two or more people. *Dialogue*, sometimes used in general expository and philosophical writing, embodies certain values: (1) It advances the action and is not mere ornament. (2) It is consistent with the character of the speakers. (3) It gives the *impression* of naturalness without being a *verbatim* record of what may have been said, because fiction is concerned with "the semblance of reality," not with reality itself. (4) It presents the interplay of ideas and personalities among the people conversing; it sets forth a conversational give and take—not simply a series of remarks of alternating speakers. (5) It varies according to the various speakers participating. (6) It serves to give relief from passages essentially descriptive or expository.

The *dialogue* is also a specialized literary composition in which two or more characters debate or reason about an idea or a proposition. There are many notable examples in the world's literature, the best known being the *Dialogues* of Plato. Others include Lucian's *Dialogues of the Dead*, Dryden's *Essay of Dramatick Poesie*, Landor's *Imaginary Conversations*, Oscar Wilde's "The Critic as Artist," and scattered modern examples by Paul Valéry, T. S. Eliot, Elder Olson, and Hugh Kenner.

Diary A day-by-day CHRONICLE of events, a JOURNAL. Usually a personal and more or less intimate record kept by an individual. Not avowedly intended for publication—although many diarists have certainly kept a possible audience in mind—most *diaries*, when published, have appeared posthumously. The most famous *diary* in English is that of Samuel Pepys, which detail events between January 1, 1660, and May 29, 1669. Other important English *diaries* are those of John Evelyn, Bulstrode Whitelock, George Fox, Jonathan Swift, John Wesley, Fanny Burney, and Evelyn Waugh.

Noted American Diarists include Samuel Sewall, Sarah K. Knight, and William Byrd. Anaïs Nin's prodigious diary, edited in seven substantial volumes covering the period from 1931 to 1974, combines gossip and philosophy with a richly detailed record of encounters with interesting personages, including Henry Miller and Gore Vidal. As a literary device, as in Lockwood's outer narrative in *Wuthering Heights*, the *diary* furnishes a resilient format and the engaging illusion of privileged access to confidential materials.

The *diary* has, in late years, become a conscious literary form used by travelers, statesmen, and politicians as a convenient method of presenting the run of daily events in which they have had a hand. See AUTOBIOGRAPHY, BIOGRAPHY.

Diastich A mode of composition in which a writer chooses a key and a text in order to produce a new text. Given a key of "genesis" and a text of the King James version of Genesis, say, one would locate (1) the first word of which "g" is the first letter, then (2) the next word of which "e" is the second letter, then (3) the next of which "n" is the third, and so on. The new text would be something like this: "God hEaven laNd appEar grasS yieldIng seasonS." The technique has been used mostly by Jackson Mac Low.

Diastole The lengthening of a syllable naturally short.

Diasyrm, Diasyrmus A rhetorical disparaging, of another or of oneself, as in Richard III's lengthy descanting on his own deformities:

> But I, that am not shaped for sportive tricks
> Nor made to court an amorous looking-glass;
> I, that am rudely stamped, and want love's majesty
> To strut before a wanton ambling nymph;
> I, that am curtailed of this fair proportion,
> Cheated of feature by dissembling Nature,
> Deformed, unfinished, sent before my time
> Into this breathing world, scarce half made up,
> And that so lamely and unfashionable
> That dogs bark at me as I halt by them. . . .

Diatribe Writing or discourse characterized by bitter invective or abusive argument; a HARANGUE. Originally it was a treatment in dialogue of a limited philosophical proposition in a simple, lively, conversational tone. Popular with the Stoic and Cynic philosophers, it became noted for the abusiveness of the speakers, a fact which led to the present-day meaning.

Dibrach A term applied in Greek and Latin prosody to a foot consisting of two short or unstressed syllables. It is another name for the PYRRHIC.

Dicatalectic Doubly CATALECTIC: lacking a syllable in the middle and at the end. This happens commonly in the third and sixth feet of the second line of the elegiac couplet in classical languages.

Dict A saying or maxim. Used as a deliberate archaism in Charles Reade's *The Cloister and the Hearth* (1860) and thereafter hardly at all.

Dictamen A formal pronouncement or dictate. Used humorously in Ben Jonson's "Celebration of Charis in Ten Lyric Pieces," one section of which is called "Her Man Described by Her Own Dictamen."

Diction The use of words on oral or written discourse. Diction includes vocabulary, which generally means words one at a time, and syntax, which generally means word order.

Dictionaries At different times during their five hundred years of development, English *dictionaries* have emphasized different elements and have passed through an evolution as great as any of our literary forms or tools. In their modern form *dictionaries* arrange their words alphabetically, give explanations of the meanings, the derivations, the pronunciations, illustrative quotations, along with idioms, synonyms, and antonyms. Sometimes, however, the "*dictionary*" is restricted to word lists of special significance, such as *dictionaries* of law or medicine.

English LEXICOGRAPHY began with attempts to define Latin words by giving English equivalents. The *Promptorium Parvulorum* (1440) of Galfridus Grammaticus, a Dominican monk of Norfolk, printed by Pynson in 1499 was an early example. Which publication deserves to be called the first English *dictionary* is difficult to say because the evolution was so gradual that the conception of what constituted a good wordbook differed from year to year. Vizetelly gives credit to Richard Huloet's *Abecedarium* (1552) as the first *dictionary*; some believe that the first person to succeed in defining all words in good usage in English was Nathaniel Bailey, whose major work was not published until 1721; *The Dictionary of Syr T. Eliot, Knyght* (1538) appears to have been the first work to establish the term "*dictionary*."

The early wordbooks started off listing simply the "hard words" that people might not be expected to know; the classification was sometimes alphabetical, sometimes by subject matter. Later lexicographers regarded themselves as guardians of national speech and listed only those words dignified enough to be of "good usage"; the function of these compilers was to standardize and stabilize the national language. Illustrative of this point of view were the collections of such scholarly academies as those of Italy and France; and, indeed, Samuel Johnson, an academy in himself, first held and later abandoned this same sort of ideal. Archbishop Trench, a British scholar, declared roundly in 1857 that a proper *dictionary* was really an "inventory of language," including colloquial uses as well as literary uses, and Trench's insistence on the philological attitude for the lexicographer probably did much to develop the modern wordbook "on historical principles."

Some of the titles important in the evolution of the *dictionary* are:

- John Florio (1598), *A Worlde of Wordes*.
- Robert Cawdrey (1604) (who used English words only), *A Table Alphabeticall Contyning and Teaching the True Writing and Understanding of Hard Usuall English Wordes*.
- Randle Cotgrave (1611), *A Bundle of Words*.
- John Bullokar (1616), *An English Expositor*.
- Henry Cockeram (1623), *The English Dictionarie* (in which "idiote" was defined as "an unlearned asse").
- Thomas Blount (1656), *Glossographia*.
- Edward Phillips (1658), *A New World in Words*.
- Nathaniel Bailey (1721), *Universal Etymological English Dictionary*.
- Samuel Johnson (1755), *Dictionary of the English Language* (in which 50,000 words were explained. The most ambitious volume published up to that time. The personal element injected into definitions gives us such famous explanations as that for *oats*: "a grain which in England is generally given to horses, but in Scotland supports the people," and, further, that *Whig* was "the name of a faction" whereas *Tory* signified "one who adhered to the antient constitution of the state and the apostolical hierarchy of the Church of England, opposed to a Whig").
- Thomas Sheridan (1780), *Complete Dictionary of the English Language* (which gave special emphasis to pronunciation).
- Samuel Johnson (1798?) *A School Dictionary*. The first American *dictionary*. This Johnson was not related to the earlier Samuel. This *dictionary* simplified some of the English spellings and began the use of phonetic marks as aids to pronunciation.
- Noah Webster (1828), *American Dictionary;* the most famous name in American lexicography.
- Joseph Emerson Worcester (1846), *Universal and Critical Dictionary of the English Language*.

In 1884 the great work *A New English Dictionary on Historical Principles* was begun in England. Edited by James A. H. Murray, Henry Bradley, and W. A. Craigie, this dictionary is more commonly called the *New English Dictionary* or the *Oxford English Dictionary*, and it is often referred to as the *OED* or *O.E.D.* It was completed in 1928 and augmented by a supplementary thirteenth volume in 1933. Beginning forty years later, additional supplements, gathered in four large volumes, were issued to correct errors and bring the work up to date. A standard feature of *Notes and Queries* for more than a century now has been the offering of suggestions for earlier citations and variant meanings, so that use of the first edition of the *OED* called for consulting the main dictionary, one or two supplements, and *Notes and Queries*. The earlier volumes, largely covering the first part of the alphabet, tended to be more subject to error than did the later. Despite these difficulties, the *OED* is easily the greatest of all English *dictionaries* in the fullness of its illustrative examples and in its elaborate analysis of the meanings and etymologies. The citations are drawn from English writings ranging in date from the earliest writings to the contemporary. It is particularly valuable for its dated quotations of actual sentences showing the meanings of a word at various periods. In 1989, the second edition of the *OED* was published; it incorporates the contents of the first edition and the four-volume supplement, plus some 5,000 new words and meanings. Now the *OED* is a twenty-volume work in 22,000 pages with definitions of more than 500,000 words. Even as the new edition was being published in 1989, thousands of notes for changes were on file, so that the *Oxford English Dictionary Additions Series* was begun; before being discontinued, it ran to three volumes "containing new entries which have been prepared for the Third Edition." During the 1990s the *OED* was marketed in CD-ROM form, eventually in three versions with different formats and search properties. It has also taken advantage of the World Wide Web to gather data.

The chief American dictionary, based on current usage, is the third edition of *Webster's New International Dictionary*. See LEXICOGRAPHY.

Didactic Novel Although the term is often applied to any novel plainly designed to teach a lesson, such as the Horatio Alger books, it is properly used as a synonym for the EDUCATION NOVEL, an eighteenth-century form presenting an ideal education for the young.

Didactic Poetry Poetry that is intended primarily to teach a lesson. The distinction between *didactic poetry* and nondidactic poetry is difficult to make and always involves a subjective judgment of the work's purpose. For example, Bryant's "To a Waterfowl" is obviously concerned with an ethical or religious idea; yet it is not generally considered *didactic*, perhaps because most readers sense that the idea of a protective Providence is dramatically appropriate to the physical and emotional situation—that the poet is communicating not the idea itself but his feelings about the idea. On the other hand, Pope's *Essay on Criticism* is an emphatic instance of *didactic poetry*.

Among modern writers, Robert Frost was probably the most cunning in exploiting many readers' conditioned craving for something *didactic*. His "Mending Wall" dramatizes a cynical cliché ("Good fences make good neighbors") that resembles a maxim in *Poor Richard's Almanac*. "Provide, Provide" has a moral exemplar (a "witch who came . . . / To wash the steps with pail and rag"), a percussive rhythm and easily remembered rhyme scheme, and second-person injunctions ("Die early and avoid the fate"). But very few of Frost's poems are genuinely didactic. See DIDACTICISM.

Didacticism Instructiveness in a work, one purpose of which is to give guidance, particularly in moral, ethical, or religious matters. Because all art exists to communicate something—an idea, a teaching, a precept, an emotion, an attitude, a fact, an autobiographical incident, a sensation—the question of *didacticism* in a literary work appears to be one of the author's actual or ostensible purpose. If, of Horace's dual functions of the artist, instruction is selected as the primary goal, then the purpose of the work is didactic. A work is didactic if it would have as its ultimate effect a meaning or a result outside itself. In a sense those who divide criticism into PLATONIC and ARISTOTELIAN are dividing the purposes of literary art into didactic and nondidactic. From this definition it is obvious that *didacticism* is an acceptable aspect of literature, at least up to a certain point, despite the fact that the term usually carries a derogatory meaning in criticism. The principle in *didactic* art is basically that the subject, tone, and form are determined and shaped by considerations, temporary and local, that lie beyond or outside the precinct of art proper. The projected lesson may be simply intellectual, as in such mnemonic rhymes as "*I* before *e* / Except after *c*" and "Thirty days hath September . . ." or simultaneously intellectual and moral, as in the nursery rhyme

"One, two, / Buckle your shoe . . ." wherein the odd-numbered lines teach counting and the even-numbered inculcate tidiness ("shut the door," "pick up sticks," "lay them straight," and so forth).

Allegorical and satiric poetry, such as Dante's *Comedy* and Pope's *The Dunciad*, certainly have some intellectual and moral didactic dimensions. Sententious characters in a mimetic work may be developed by didactic means, such as the outsized fabric of fatherly advice delivered by Polonius in *Hamlet*. In this remarkable twenty-five-line speech, the point is not whether "Neither a borrower or a lender be," say, is intellectually true, morally good, or philosophically wise, but whether it advances our understanding of Polonius's character. Apart from the truth or wisdom of what the maxims may urge, the speech is inconsistent, long-winded, cliché-ridden, and inappropriate to the situation (Polonius has come to make Laertes hurry up). The speech shows Polonius to be forgetful, foolish, hypocritical, but touchingly solicitous as a father.

The objection to *didacticism* results from a feeling that, if carried too far or borne too self-righteously, it will subvert the object of literature to lesser and ignoble purposes. Among those who make didactic demands of literature are the practitioners of MORAL CRITICISM, Marxists, those who measure literature by sociological standards, and those who insist that literature be relevant. The most bitter foes of *didacticism* have probably been the NEW CRITICS, who do not declare poetry to be meaningless but who declare its significant meaning to be intrinsic.

Diectasis Lengthening a word by the interpolation of a syllable, as when "Shakespearean" becomes "Shakespeherian" (T. S. Eliot, *The Waste Land*).

Diegesis A statement, description, or narration without explanation, conclusion, or judgment; an obsolescent theological term recently resurrected by critical theorists.

[Reference: Roland Barthes, *The Responsibility of Forms: Critical Essays on Music, Art, and Representation* (tr. 1985).]

Dieresis A pause in a line of verse falls at the end of a FOOT; now usually called CAESURA.

Différance A virtually untranslatable French NEOLOGISM introduced by Jacques Derrida to combine various denotations and connotations of *difference, differing, deferring*, and *deferral*—with particular reference to Ferdinand de Saussure's celebrated concept that "in language there are only differences *without positive terms*." For the SIGNIFIER and SIGNIFIED to exist and operate, it is inescapably necessary for them to differ between themselves; if they did not differ, they would not be related except by a species of identity or redundancy, neither of which would permit signification. Because they must differ, there is, and always has been, a space or gap between them that constitutes a trace of absence such that any construct has already begun to dismantle or deconstruct itself. Derrida has explained *différance* as "a structure and a movement that cannot be conceived on the basis of the opposition presence/absence. *Différance* is the systematic play of differences, of traces of differences, of the spacing by which elements relate to one another. This spacing is the production, simultaneously active and passive (the *a* of *différance* indicates this indecision as regards activity and passivity, that which cannot yet be governed and organized by that opposition), of intervals without which the 'full' terms could not signify, could not function."

[References: Jonathan Culler, *On Deconstruction: Theory and Criticism After Structuralism* (1982); Jacques Derrida, *Positions* (1981); Irene E. Harvey, *Derrida and the Economy of Différance* (1986).]

Difficulty Formerly considered an incidental feature of certain sophisticated pieces of writing, especially a good deal of poetry and prose in the seventeenth century, and now widely regarded as a general feature of all reading to an extent. Like AMBIGUITY and obscurity, *difficulty* contributes to suspense and even to surprise. Conceivably, some *difficulty* of access may create involvement and engagement on the reader's part. George Steiner has suggested a classification of *difficulty* into four categories: contingent, modal, tactical, and ontological.

[Reference: George Steiner, *On Difficulty; and Other Essays* (1978).]

Digest A systematic arrangement of condensed materials on some specific subject, so that it summarizes the information on that subject. By extension, *digest* is often applied to a journal that publishes condensations or abridgments of material previously published elsewhere, such as *Reader's Digest*.

Digression The insertion of material often not closely related to the subject in a work. In a well-knit plot, a *digression* violates unity. In the FAMILIAR ESSAY it is a standard device, and it was sometimes used in the epic. The device was particularly popular in seventeenth- and eighteenth-century English writing, notable examples being the several in Swift's *Tale of a Tub* (including "A Digression in Praise of Digressions") and those in Sterne's *Tristram Shandy*. If a *digression* is lengthy and formal, it is sometimes called an EXCURSUS. Nowadays, in such works as Thomas Pynchon's novels, the protracted comic *digression* has become virtually as important and extensive as the main body of the work itself.

Dime Novel A cheaply printed, paperbound TALE of adventure or detection, originally selling for about ten cents; an American equivalent of the British PENNY DREADFUL. They were SHORT NOVELS, dealing with the American Revolution, the Civil War, the frontier, lurid crime and spectacular detection, and sometimes exemplary actions for moral instruction of the young. The first *dime novel* was *Malaeska: The Indian Wife of the White Hunter* by Anne Stephens (1860). It sold more than 300,000 copies in one year. During the Civil War *dime novels* were popular with the troops, and afterward they continued to be popular until the 1890s, when boys' stories, such as the Frank Merriwell and the Rover Boys series, and the PULP MAGAZINES began to replace them. At the height of their popularity, they were at least ostensibly written by men such as Ned Buntline, Colonel Prentiss Ingraham, and W. F. "Buffalo Bill" Cody about their own adventures. The two most popular series were the "Deadwood Dick" stories of the frontier by Edward L. Wheeler and the "Nick Carter" detective stories by various writers. The firm of Street and Smith published more than a thousand Nick Carter *dime novels*. Present-day counterparts are some of the cheaper and more sensational "paperback originals." One of the popular series of these paperbacks today is, significantly, the Nick Carter books. See PENNY DREADFUL.

[References: Albert Johannsen, *The House of Beadle and Adams and Its Dime and Nickel Novels: The Story of a Vanished Literature*, 3 vols. (1950–1962); Edmund Pearson, *Dime Novels; or, Following an Old Trail in Popular Literature* (1929).]

Dimeter A line of verse consisting of two feet.

Diminishing Age in English Literature, 1940–1965 The coming of the Second World War in 1939 profoundly changed British life. A beleaguered nation struggling desperately for survival devoted most of its energies for six years to defeating its military enemies. Then, with many of its finest young people dead, its major cities in shambles, and its economy greatly weakened, it had to spend another decade reestablishing itself. Certain ceremonial and traditional events, such as the coronation of Elizabeth II in 1952, seemed to have as much beneficial influence as public events did in the reassertion of the sense of nation and tradition. Also, during the cold war, the defection of intelligence officer Philby and others to the Russians and the discovery that he had been a double agent had a depressing symbolic value for the English. Greatly weakened foreign influence and major internal economic and political problems made England during this period a "diminished thing."

Perhaps the most challenging experimental writer of the period was Samuel Beckett, in both the novel and drama. As a satirist and social commentator, George Orwell wrote brilliantly in such novels as *1984* and in essays. Joyce Cary continued the realistic tradition in fiction, as Graham Greene produced philosophical novels in the tradition of Conrad. Lawrence Durrell, C. P. Snow, and Anthony Powell embarked on long, ambitious series of novels. Stephen Spender and W. H. Auden continued as the leading poetic voices, to be joined by Dylan Thomas during his brief, intense career. Sir John Betjeman, Louis MacNeice, and Philip Larkin were important poets of the time. Christopher Fry joined T. S. Eliot in an effort to revive verse drama. Sean O'Casey continued the strength of the Irish theater, and John Osborne initiated the drama of the "ANGRY YOUNG MEN." F. R. Leavis was the most respected critical voice and *Encounter* the best critical journal. It was a time of literary effort and respectable activity, but it clearly lacked the dominating literary voices needed to make a superlative age. Significantly, toward the end of this period, the greatest aesthetic energy showed in films, television, and the popular songs of the Rolling Stones and the Beatles.

Diminishing Metaphor A type of METAPHOR that uses a deliberate discrepancy of connotation between TENOR and VEHICLE. Its special quality lies in its use of a pejorative vehicle in reference to a tenor of value and desirability. The function seems thus to lie in forcing on the reader an intellectual reaction. Kenneth Koch's "To You" begins, "I love you as a sheriff searches for a walnut / That will solve a murder case unsolved for years. . . ."

Dimoric Containing two MORAE, the equivalent of two short syllables.

Dinner Theatre An establishment, popular in the United States since about 1960, in which a meal is served, after which a play or other show is performed. Typically, the dinner is a buffet, and the diners remain at tables during the performance.

Dionysian A term used by Friedrich Nietzsche for the spirit in Greek tragedy associated with Dionysus, the god of wine. It refers to states of the ecstatic, orgiastic, or irrational. Nietzsche associates it with lunar-nocturnal creative and imaginative power and contrasts it with the critical and rational qualities represented by the solar-diurnal APOLLONIAN.

Dip An unstressed syllable in ALLITERATIVE VERSE; contrasted with LIFT.

Dipody (or Dipodic Verse) In classical prosody, a measure consisting of two metrical feet, usually slightly different. The meter of dialogue in Greek tragedy is three IAMBIC *dipodies*, or twelve syllables. According to some regulations, the foot in Greek prosody must contain no fractions. Since the short syllable is construed as half the length of a long syllable, SPONDEES, DACTYLS, and ANAPESTS come out even $(1 + 1, 1 + \frac{1}{2} + \frac{1}{2}, \frac{1}{2} + \frac{1}{2} + 1)$, but iambs and TROCHEES do not $(\frac{1}{2} + 1, 1 + \frac{1}{2})$. Accordingly, the iambic foot consists of two iambs $(\frac{1}{2} + 1 + \frac{1}{2} + 1)$.

In a looser sense, applied to varied qualitative scansion, *dipody* recognizes more than one level of stress on accented syllables. Much verse in nursery rhymes and ballads is *dipodic*. In these cases the term refers to succeeding feet with strong stress in one and a weaker stress in the other, such feet functioning as a metrical unit, a measure, as in this line from Eliot's *The Waste Land*:

Ànd ă cláttĕr ànd ă cháttĕr fròm wĭthín

which may look like HEADLESS iambic verse with uneven stress but is actually *dipodic verse*, rather like the measure favored by Rudyard Kipling. *Dipodic verse* lends itself easily to SYNCOPATION.

Direct Camera A style of objective, essentially nonnarrative, nonstaged filmmaking used in producing documentary films since the early 1960s. Like CINÉMA VÉRITÉ, it uses light, highly mobile equipment.

Director In theater and film, the individual in charge of the artistic organization of the staging or filming, as distinct from the strictly technical or financial aspects of the operation. In AUTEUR THEORY, the *director* is regarded as the author of the film; the same usage is not normally applied to theater, opera, or other sorts of direction.

Dirge A wailing song sung at a funeral or in commemoration of death; a short lyric of lamentation. See CORONACH, ELEGY, MONODY, PASTORAL ELEGY, THRENODY.

Discordia Concors A term used by Samuel Johnson for "a combination of dissimilar images or discovery of occult resemblances in things apparently unlike" in METAPHYSICAL POETRY. He derived the term by inverting Horace's phrase *concordia discors*, "harmony in discord."

Discourse Mode or category of expression. In grammar, we speak of *discourse* as direct or indirect:

- Direct: She said, "I am sleepy."
- Indirect: She said that she was sleepy.

There is also "free indirect *discourse*," which takes the form of a summary: "She explained her condition. She was sleepy and wanted to go to bed as soon as possible. But many duties remained."

Also used more specifically to mean "discussion," as in Descartes' *Discourse on Method*. In modern critical discussion (itself a *discourse*), *discourse* refers to ways of speaking that are bound by ideological, professional, political, cultural, or sociological communities. *Discourse* is used to refer not just to the special vocabulary of a particular science or social practice ("the *discourse* of medicine," the *discourse* of imperialism") but also to the way in which the use of language in a particular domain helps to constitute the objects it refers to (as medicine defines various conditions and constitutes them as social realities).

Discovery The revelation of a fact previously unknown, knowledge of which now results in the turning of action. See DRAMATIC STRUCTURE.

Disguisings In medieval times (and in some places into the twentieth century) a species of game or spectacle with a procession of masked figures. *Disguisings* were usually of a popular or folk character. See MASQUE.

Disinterestedness An ideal quality of objectivity and impartiality unpolluted by illegitimate self-interest or by conflict of interest. The term was promoted by Kant, Keats, Hazlitt, and Arnold. (To be uninterested is not to care; to be *disinterested* is to care but on an impartial basis with no self-interest.)

Displacement In Freudian analysis of dreams and other expressions, one of the devices for coping with a challenging problem. A desire to kill someone, for example, can undergo displacement and become a desire to insult that person. The process is related to the operations of symbolization and metonymical structures. In a somewhat different application, *displacement* refers to a process whereby critical issues are removed from one arena of analysis to another. Edward Said's *Orientalism*, for instance, argues that the West frequently uses the East to displace issues of sexism, racism, and social violence onto Eastern cultures and avoid thereby an analysis of these issues in Western cultures.

Dissemination In a special application made popular by Jacques Derrida, *dissemination* is exploited in such a way as to take advantage of (1) its historical root in Latin *semen* ("seed") and (2) a fancied relation to Greek *sēma* ("sign")—all as a way of suggesting that meaning in language is variously scattered, seeded, unseeded, signed, and unsigned.

Dissertation A formal exposition written to clarify some scholarly problem. *Dissertation* is sometimes used interchangeably with THESIS, but the usual practice, at least in American academic circles, is to reserve *dissertation* for the more elaborate projects written "in partial fulfillment of the requirements for the doctor's degree" and to limit the use of thesis to smaller enterprises submitted for the bachelor's or master's degree. Both thesis and *dissertation* are commonly used off college campuses simply to signify careful, thoughtful discussions, in writing or speech, on almost any serious problem. In literature the term has been used lightly, as in Lamb's "A Dissertation on Roast Pig" and formally as in Bolingbroke's *Dissertation on Parties* or in Newton's *dissertations*; here the term implies learned formality.

Dissociation of Sensibility A term given wide currency by T. S. Eliot (in his essay of 1921, "The Metaphysical Poets") to describe a disjunction of thought and feeling in the writers of the seventeenth and later centuries. Earlier writers, and particularly John Donne, had had "direct sensuous apprehension of thought." To them a thought was an experience and thus affected their sensibility. For these writers, mind and feeling so functioned together that they possessed "a mechanism of sensibility which could devour any kind of experience." In the seventeenth century, says Eliot, a *dissociation of sensibility* set in, fostered by Milton and Dryden, who performed a part of the total poetic function so well that the rest of it appeared not to exist and, in their imitators, did not exist. In the eighteenth and nineteenth centuries, as language grew in refinement and subtlety, feeling tended to become cruder. The result was poets who thought but neither felt their thoughts nor fused thought and feeling in their poetry or, in other words, poets who suffered from a *dissociation of sensibility*. Eliot seems to have drawn the idea of *dissociation* from his study of French thinkers, particularly Remy de Gourmont and Lucien Lévy-Bruhl. The latter considered primitive people to be "prelogical" creatures with no sense of a difference between past and present, life and death, nature and culture, self and other, so that the acquisition of civilization and logical thought represents a surrender of a "participatory" mentality and, in effect, a *dissociation of sensibility*. This *dissociation*, however, takes place some millennia earlier than the seventeenth century that Eliot located as the setting of the *dissociation* that engaged his attention and provoked his attack. Critics since Eliot's original formulation of his diagnosis have found him to be vague and historically inaccurate—there being plenty of dissociated sensibilities before the seventeenth century and plenty of marvelously unified sensibilities afterward, including Byron's and Eliot's—but the general emphasis on the harmony of thought and feeling remains useful in the study of Donne, Marvell, and others.

Dissolve (noun) In film, a transition between shots, with one shot fading away while another shot fades in.

Dissonance Harsh and inharmonious sounds, a marked breaking of the music of poetry, which may be intentional, as it often is in Robert Browning and Hardy.

Distance The degree of dispassionateness with which reader or audience can view the people, places, and events in a literary work; or the degree of disinterest that the author displays toward his or her characters and actions. Its use as a verb has found currency in such phrases as "distancing device." See AESTHETIC DISTANCE, DISINTERESTEDNESS, ALIENATION EFFECT.

Distich A COUPLET. Any two consecutive lines in similar form. An epigram or maxim completely expressed in couplet form, as in Pope's couplet:

> Hope springs eternal in the human breast;
> Man never is, but always to be, blest.

Distributed Stress A term used for a situation in metrics wherein each of two syllables takes, or shares, the stress. Also called HOVERING STRESS or RESOLVED STRESS. The following lines from Walt Whitman's "Tears" show *distributed stress* in "swift steps" and "night storm":

> Ŏ stórm, ĕmbódĭed, rísĭng, căréerĭng wĭth swíft stéps ălóng thĕ béach!
>
> Ŏ wíld ănd dísmăl níght-stórm wĭth wínd—Ŏ bélchĭng ănd déspĕrăte!

Dithyramb Literary expression characterized by wild, excited, passionate language. Its lyric power relates it most nearly to verse though its unordered sequence and development, its seemingly improvised quality, often give it the form of prose. *Dithyrambic* verse, as it is usually called, was probably meant originally to be accompanied by music and was historically associated with Greek ceremonial worship of Dionysus. It formed the model for the choral element in Greek verse, later developing into the finer quality we know in Greek tragedy. Rather rare in English, *dithyrambic* verse is most closely related to the ODE; it finds its best expression in Dryden's *Alexander's Feast*. By extension the term is applied to any wild chant or song or to particularly extravagant prose.

Ditty A SONG; a REFRAIN. The term is used for any short, simple, popular melody. The term is also used, in the sense of theme, to refer to any short, apt saying or idea running through a composition. In Shakespeare, *ditty* often means the words or theme of a song as distinct from the music; in *As You Like It* (5, 3, 36) Touchstone says of a song, "Truly, young gentlemen, though there was no great matter in the ditty, yet the note was very untuneable"; and in *The Tempest* (1, 2, 406) Ferdinand, after hearing Ariel's song, says, "The ditty does remember my drowned father."

Divine Afflatus Poetic inspiration, particularly the exalted state immediately preceding creative composition, when the poet is felt to be receiving inspiration directly from a divine source. The doctrine of divine inspiration was advocated by Plato. Although the phrase and doctrine have been used in a serious and sincere sense by such a poet as Shelley, the term is often used now contemptuously.

Dizain A verse of ten lines.

Doctrinaire An adjective applied to one whose attitude is controlled by preconception and who disregards other points of view as well as practical considerations. This view is likely to be theoretical, dogmatic, narrow, and one-sided, as compared with practical and broad-minded. Criticism such as Samuel Johnson's may be *doctrinaire* because it is controlled by a limited code of critical doctrines. Literature itself may be called *doctrinaire* when written, like some of Carlyle's books, to demonstrate such a doctrine as "hero-worship" or the "gospel of work"; or like a novel of William Godwin's, to preach a social doctrine. Politically, the word was applied to the constitutional royalists in France after 1815. See DIDACTICISM.

Document Anything written or printed. The technical aspect of a book, for example, treats it as only a *document*, and from this perspective the first edition of *Paradise Lost* is on a par with a telephone directory or a speeding ticket.

Documentary Film (also **Documentary**) Sometimes called "actualities" in the early twentieth century, *documentaries* began during the 1920s, with the leadership and vision of John Grierson, whose *Drifters* (1929) concerned herring fishing fleets. Grierson is given credit for applying *documentary* to film in 1925. The *documentary* avoids actors, studios, stories, special effects, and other aspects of filmed fiction.

Documentary Novel A form of fiction in which there is an elaborate piling up of factual data, frequently including such materials as newspaper articles, popular songs, legal reports, and trial transcripts. The term was used by F. O. Matthiessen to characterize the massive amount of factual detail used in the novels of Theodore Dreiser. *Documentary novels* are usually written by naturalistic novelists such as Émile Zola, Dreiser, John Dos Passos, and James T. Farrell. After the Second World War, the tradition was carried on by Norman Mailer.

Doggerel Rude verse. Any poorly executed attempt at poetry. Characteristic of *doggerel* are monotony of rhyme and rhythm, cheap sentiment and trivial, trite subject matter. Some *doggerel* does, however, because of certain humorous and burlesque qualities, become amusing and earn a place on one of the lower shelves of literature. Samuel Johnson's parody of Percy's "Hermit of Warkworth" is an example:

As with my hat upon my head
I walk'd along the Strand,
I there did meet another man
With his hat in his hand.

Dogme 95 A film-making collective established in Denmark in 1995 under the leadership of Lars Von Trier and Thomas Vinterberg and devoted to revolutionary principles that subvert the dominance of fiction, illusion, and gimmickry. Their "Vow of Chastity" lists ten rules, including: shooting on location without imported props or sets; a handheld camera; natural light; and no identification of the director.

Dolce Stil Nuovo The "sweet new style" (called so in Dante's *Purgatory*) that flourished among lyric poets in certain Romance languages during the thirteenth century with a premium on lucidity and complex musicality. This style, which contributed to Dante's adoption of the Tuscan vernacular and *TERZA RIMA* for his *Comedy*, was the chief precursor and exemplar of modern rhymed verse in Indo-European languages.

Dolichurus A line of dactylic hexameter with a redundant syllable in the last foot. The word means "long-tailed."

Dolly Shot In film, a shot made while the camera is mounted on a dolly, which is a wheeled vehicle that permits movement over considerable distances, so that something can be filmed while in motion. Same as TRACKING SHOT.

Domesday Book Equivalent of "Doomsday Book," in which "dome" or "doom" means "judgment, assessment"; the record of a survey made in 1086, including population figures and details of area, use, ownership, and value of lands in England.

Domestic Tragedy Tragedy dealing with the domestic life of commonplace people. The English stage at various periods has produced tragedies based on the lives not of high-ranking historical personages but of everyday contemporary people. Running contrary to prevailing conceptions of tragedy, *domestic tragedy* was long in winning critical recognition. In Elizabethan and Jacobean times were produced such powerful *domestic tragedies* as the anonymous *Arden of Feversham* (late sixteenth century),

Thomas Heywood's *A Woman Killed with Kindness* (acted 1603), and the anonymous *Yorkshire Tragedy* (1608). This early Elizabethan *domestic tragedy* specialized in murder stories taken from contemporary bourgeois life. Although the characters are far from commonplace, it is possible to consider Shakespeare's *Othello* as something of a domestic tragedy. In the eighteenth century domestic tragedy reappeared, tinged this time with the sentimentalism of the age, as in George Lillo's *The London Merchant* (1731) and Edward Moore's *The Gamester* (1753), in which the tragic hero is a gambler who, falsely accused of murder, takes poison and dies just after hearing that a large amount of money has been left to him. The eighteenth-century *domestic tragedy* was crowded out by other forms, though the idea was taken over by foreign playwrights and later in the nineteenth century reintroduced from abroad, especially under the influence of Ibsen, since whose time the old conception of tragedy as possible only with heroes of high rank has given way to plays that present fate at work among the ordinary. John Masefield's *Tragedy of Nan* (1909) is an early-twentieth-century example of the form. O'Neill's *Desire Under the Elms*, Miller's *The Death of a Salesman* and *All My Sons*, and Williams's *Cat on a Hot Tin Roof* are all examples of *domestic tragedy*.

Donnée Literally, "the given." The term, introduced by Henry James, is based on an analogy to a problem in geometry in which certain data are given, out of which one works out the meaning or solution. A frequent phrase of James's in his prefaces about the *donnée*—"something might be made of that"—is illuminating. The *donnée* can be setting, characters, situation, or idea. In any case, it is the raw material with which the artist starts. That London, say, is a city of a certain size and sort is a *donnée* of much literature, and it would be fatuous to make it into a humble hamlet or to suppose it an arctic or equatorial environment, except in SCIENCE FICTION. William Faulkner uses the homely metaphor of the lumber in the carpenter's shop for the same idea as *donnée*.

Doppelgänger German, "double goer." A mysterious double; a common figure in literature. Poe's "William Wilson"and Conrad's *The Secret Sharer* are stories of people haunted by the image of a double. Wilde's *The Picture of Dorian Gray* is a variation on the theme.

Doric The *Doric* dialect in ancient Greece was thought of as lacking in refinement, and *Doric* architecture was marked by simplicity and strength rather than by beauty of detail. So a rustic of "broad" dialect may be referred to as *Doric*, and many simple idyllic pieces of literature as Tennyson's *Dora* or Wordsworth's *Michael* may be said to exhibit *Doric* qualities. It is often applied to PASTORALS. Perhaps the best single synonym is "simple." See ATTIC, with which *Doric* was and is in conscious contrast.

Double Bill Two plays or other works staged on a single program. Some combinations are arbitrary, others are deliberate, as in *double bills* by Tom Stoppard: *Dogg's Hamlet*, *Cahoot's Macbeth* and *Dirty Linen* with *New Found Land*.

Double Dactyls A form of light verse consisting of two stanzas, each having four lines of two dactyls. It was promoted by Anthony Hecht and John Hollander in the collection *Jiggery-Pokery*. The rules are complex. The first line must be a jingle, such as "Jiggery-pokery." The second line must be a name. The last lines of each stanza must rhyme, and the second stanza must have one line that is a single word. The most dazzling example of diplodactylic virtuosity is George Starbuck's "Monarch of the Sea," in which the required name is *four* dactyls ("Admiral Samuel/Eliot Morison") and the second stanza contains two successive one-word lines ("Historiography's/ Disciplinarian").

Double Dagger Symbol [‡] used in printing for marginal references, footnotes, and other such forms of annotation.

Double Elephant A paper size measuring 40 × 26½ inches. The original volume of John James Audubon's *Birds of America* (1827–38) was a *double elephant* FOLIO.

Double Entendre A statement that is deliberately ambiguous, one of whose possible meanings is risqué or suggestive of some impropriety. In *Romeo and Juliet*, Mercutio executes a notable *double entendre* when he tells the Nurse (who has asked about the time of day), "'Tis no less, I tell ye; for the bawdy hand of the dial is now upon the prick of noon." The *entendre* is *double* here because a dial does have a "hand" and the circumference is marked with "pricks"; by adding "bawdy" to his statement, Mercutio explicitly doubles the meanings of "hand" and "prick" and brings out the still-current vulgar sense of the latter. Later in the same scene, Mercutio sings a song that involves puns on "hair," "hare," "hoar,"and "whore"; these are not *double entendres*. A pun is understood to mean a play on different words that happen to sound alike; a *double entendre* has to do with a single word that happens to have more than one meaning. Both pun and *double entendre* differ from AMBIGUITY, which refers to a multiplicity of meanings, all of which may be decent. Ambiguity may lead to some confusion—as in "He helped the old man across the street"—and even to undecidable contradiction—as in "He is not in the hospital because he is sick."

Double entendre is bad French—the proper French for "double meaning" is *double entente*—but *double entendre* has been used since Dryden as an English term applied to ambiguities in which one of the meanings is indecent. It should not be italicized in normal usage.

Double Part In the theater, the "doubling" of roles that permits one performer to play two or more roles. Some plays are so written that a minor figure who appears early and another who appears late can be portrayed by one player. It is thought that both Cordelia and the Fool in *King Lear* may have been played by the same boy actor. In T. S. Eliot's "Little Gidding," the poet tells of an encounter with a "familiar compound ghost":

> So I assumed a double part, and cried
> And heard another's voice cry: "What! are *you* here?"
> Although we were not. I was still the same,
> Knowing myself yet being someone other. . . .

Double Rhyme FEMININE RHYME; that is, rhyme in which the similar stressed syllables are followed by identical unstressed syllables. "Stream" and "beam" are rhymes; "streaming" and "beaming" are *double rhymes*. ("Double" is a misnomer, because in either case the rhyme is a single phenomenon involving stressed syllables. Genuine doubleness of rhyme, as between "wildwood" and "childhood," is called COMPOUND RHYME.)

Douzain A verse of twelve lines.

Down REFRAIN or BURDEN, especially of a song.

Drab C. S. Lewis's term, subsequently widely adopted, for late-medieval and early-Renaissance English literature, especially the poetry of the early sixteenth century.

[Reference: C. S. Lewis, *English Literature in the Sixteenth Century* (1954).]

Drama Aristotle called *drama* "imitated human action." But because his meaning of imitation is in doubt, the phrase is not as simple as it seems. J. M. Manly saw three necessary elements in *drama*: (1) a story (2) told in action (3) by actors who impersonate the characters. This admits such forms as PANTOMIME, but many believe that spoken dialogue must be present.

Drama arose from religious ceremonial. Greek comedy developed from those phases of the DIONYSIAN rites that dealt with the theme of fertility. Greek tragedy came from the Dionysian rites dealing with life and death; and MEDIEVAL DRAMA arose out of rites commemorating the birth and the resurrection of Christ. These three origins seem independent of one another. The word *comedy* is based on a word meaning "revel," and early Greek comedy preserved in the actors' costumes evidences of the ancient phallic ceremonies. Comedy developed away from this primitive display of sex interest in the direction of greater decorum and seriousness, though the OLD COMEDY was gross in character. SATIRE became an element of comedy as early as the sixth century B.C.

Menander (342–291 B.C.) is a representative of the NEW COMEDY—a more conventionalized form that was imitated by the great Roman writers of comedy, Plautus and Terence, through whose plays classical comedy was transmitted to the Elizabethan dramatists.

The word *tragedy* seems to mean a "goat-song" and may reflect Dionysian death and resurrection ceremonies in which the goat was the sacrificial animal. The dithyrambic CHANT used in these festivals, perhaps the starting point of tragedy, developed into the ceremonial song. The song then became a primitive DUOLOGUE between a leader and a CHORUS, developed narrative elements, and reached a stage in which it told some story. Two leaders appeared instead of one, and the chorus receded somewhat into the background. The great Greek authors of tragedies were Aeschylus (525–456 B.C.), Sophocles (496–406 B.C.), and Euripides (480–406 B.C.). Modeled on these were the Latin CLOSET DRAMAS of Seneca (4? B.C.–A.D. 65), which exercised a profound influence on Renaissance tragedy (see SENECAN TRAGEDY).

The decline of Rome witnessed the disappearance of acted classical *drama*. The MIME survived for an uncertain period and perhaps aided in preserving the tradition of acting through wandering entertainers (see JONGLEUR, MINSTREL). Likewise, dramatic ceremonies and customs, some of them perhaps related to the ancient Dionysian rites themselves, played an uncertain part in keeping alive in medieval times a sort of substratum of dramatic consciousness. Scholars are virtually agreed, however, that the great institution of medieval *drama* in Western Europe, leading as it did to modern *drama*, was a new form that developed around the ninth century from the ritual of the Christian church. The dramatic forms resulting from this development, MYSTERY or CYCLIC PLAYS, MIRACLE PLAYS, MORALITIES, flourishing especially in the fourteenth and fifteenth centuries, lived on into the Renaissance.

The new interests of the Renaissance included TRANSLATIONS and IMITATIONS of classical *drama*, partly through the medium of SCHOOL PLAYS, partly through the work of university-trained professionals engaged in supplying *dramas* for the public stage, the court, or such institutions as the INNS OF COURT, and partly through the influence of classical dramatic criticism, much of which reached England through Italian scholars. Thus, a revived knowledge of ancient *drama* united with the native dramatic traditions developed from medieval forms and techniques to produce in the later years of the sixteenth century the prodigiously robust phenomenon known as ELIZABETHAN DRAMA, with its patriotic CHRONICLE PLAYS, TRAGEDIES OF BLOOD, COURT COMEDIES, ROMANTIC COMEDIES, PASTORAL DRAMA, satirical plays, and realistic presentations of London life. These were written by a group of gifted, versatile dramatists, led by Shakespeare. English *drama* demonstrated DECADENT tendencies in Jacobean and Caroline times, and in 1642 the Puritans closed the theaters.

The efforts of Ben Jonson in Elizabethan times to insist on the observance of classical rules bore late fruit when, in RESTORATION times, under the added influence of French *drama* and theory, English *drama* was revived under court auspices. The heroic play and the new COMEDY OF MANNERS flourished, followed in the eighteenth century first by SENTIMENTAL COMEDY and DOMESTIC TRAGEDIES and in the latter part of the century by a chastened comedy of manners under Goldsmith and Sheridan.

MELODRAMA and SPECTACLE reigned through the early nineteenth century, efforts to produce an actable literary *drama* proving futile. The later nineteenth century witnessed an important revival of serious *drama*, with a tendency, however, away from the established traditions of poetic tragedy and comedy in favor of shorter plays stressing ideas or problems and depending much on dialogue.

In America, theatrical performances occurred early in the eighteenth century in Boston, New York, and Charleston, South Carolina, though no *drama* was written by an American until about the middle of the century, when important professional troupes also appeared. The imitative early *drama* was dependent on English originals or models. The Revolutionary War produced some political plays. The first native tragedy was Thomas Godfrey's *Prince of Parthia* (acted in 1767), and the first comedy professionally produced was Royall Tyler's *The Contrast* (1787). The early nineteenth century witnessed a growing interest in the theater, William Dunlap and John Howard Payne ("Home, Sweet Home") being prolific playwrights. Increased use was made of American themes. In the middle of the century George Henry Boker produced notable ROMANTIC TRAGEDIES in verse, and literary *drama* received some attention. American dramatic art advanced in the period following the Civil War with such writers as Bronson Howard, though it was restricted greatly by commercial theatrical management. The early twentieth century produced several dramatists of note (William Vaughn Moody, Percy MacKaye, Josephine Peabody) and witnessed the growth of the LITTLE THEATER MOVEMENT.

There has been a robust rebirth of dramatic interest and experimentation in the twentieth century both in Great Britain and in the United States. In the Irish Theatre, under the leadership of people such as Lady Gregory and Douglas Hyde, a vital *drama* emerged, with original and powerful plays from the likes of W. B. Yeats, J. M. Synge, Padraic Colum, and Sean O'Casey (see CELTIC RENAISSANCE). In England the influence of Ibsen (also important on the Irish playwrights) made itself strongly felt in the PROBLEM PLAYS and domestic tragedies of Henry Arthur Jones and Arthur Wing Pinero, in the witty and highly intellectual *drama* of G. B. Shaw, and in the realism of John Galsworthy. Somerset Maugham, Noël Coward, and James Barrie were active producers of comedy; John Masefield gave expression to the tragic vision in a long series of plays. T. S. Eliot and Christopher Fry revived and enriched verse *drama*. Also important is John Osborne, the leader of England's "ANGRY YOUNG

MEN" (*Look Back in Anger*), and the absurdist playwrights Harold Pinter and Tom Stoppard.

The twentieth century saw the development of a serious American *drama*. Early in the century REALISM, which had had its first important American dramatic representation in J. A. Herne's *Margaret Fleming* in 1890, was followed, sometimes far off, by MacKaye and Moody. But it remained for the craftsmanship, experimentation, and imagination of Eugene O'Neill to give a truly American expression to the tragic view of experience. Thornton Wilder, Philip Barry, Lillian Hellman, Sidney Howard, Robert Sherwood, Tennessee Williams, Arthur Miller, and Edward Albee have given America a serious *drama* for the first time in its history. Barry, S. N. Behrman, George Kaufman, John van Druten, Neil Simon, and Woody Allen have practiced the comic craft with skill. Maxwell Anderson revived the verse play successfully, and Rodgers and Hammerstein gave the MUSICAL COMEDY unexpected depth and beauty in *Oklahoma!* and other musicals. Later, beginning in the 1970s, Stephen Sondheim continued this enrichment, deepening and dignifying musical theater. In some ways, the most important voice in the musical theater since about 1975 has been Andrew Lloyd-Webber. Details of dramatic history are given throughout the *Outline of Literary History*. See also COMEDY, DRAMATIC STRUCTURE, PLOT, TRAGEDY.

[References: B. H. Clark, *European Theories of the Drama*, rev. ed. (1965; orig. 1929, reprinted 1965), and *A Study of Modern Drama*, rev. ed. (1938); John Gassner and Edward Quinn, eds., *The Reader's Encyclopedia of World Drama* (1969); Richard Gilman, *The Making of Modern Drama: A Story of Bochner, Pirandello, Brecht, Handke* (1974); H. D. F. Kitto, *Form and Meaning in Drama* (1956); A. H. Quinn, *History of the American Drama*, 3 vols. (1927, reprinted 1980).]

Dramatic Conventions Devices that are employed as substitutions for reality in the drama and that the audience accepts as real although they know them to be false. One approaching a drama must, in the first place, accept the fact of impersonation or representation. The actors on the stage must be taken as the persons of the story (though this acceptance by no means precludes a degree of detachment sufficient to enable the spectator to appraise the art of the actor). The stage must be regarded as the actual scene or geographical setting of the action. The intervals between acts or scenes must be expanded or contracted imaginatively to conform to the needs of the story. Moreover, one must accept special conventions, not inherent in drama as such but no less integral because of their traditional use, such as the SOLILOQUY, the ASIDE, the fact that ordinary people are made spontaneously to speak in highly poetic language and that actors speak more loudly than would be natural, pitching their voices to reach the most distant auditor. Similarly, one must be prepared at times to accept costuming that is conventional or symbolic rather than realistic. By a convention almost too obvious to mention, stage characters speak in our own language, even though everyone recognizes that the Romans in *Julius Caesar* could never have spoken Elizabethan English. In the Elizabethan theater the spectator had to picture the platform imaginatively as in a number of different places; in the modern theater the spectator must accept the idea of the invisible FOURTH WALL through which he or she views interior actions. All means of getting inside the minds of characters—and they are many—are conventions (even if only within the single play; see O'Neill's *Strange Interlude*) that are successful exactly to the extent that the audience is willing to believe them. Even the CURTAIN that opens and closes the drama is in its way as pure a convention as the chorus of a Greek tragedy.

Dramatic Irony The words or acts of a character may carry a meaning unperceived by the character but understood by the audience. Usually, the character's own interests are involved in a way that he or she cannot understand. The IRONY resides in the contrast between the meaning intended by the speaker and the different significance seen by others. The term is occasionally applied also to nondramatic narrative and is sometimes extended to include any situation (such as mistaken identity) in which some of the actors on the stage or some of the characters in a story are blind to facts known to the spectator or reader. So understood, *dramatic irony* is responsible for much of the interest in fiction and drama because the reader or spectator enjoys being in on the secret. For an example see TRAGIC IRONY.

Dramatic Monologue A poem that reveals "a soul in action" through the speech of one character in a dramatic situation. The character is speaking to an identifiable but silent listener at a dramatic moment in the speaker's life. The circumstances surrounding the conversation, one side of which we "hear" as the *dramatic monologue*, are made clear by implication, and an insight into the character of the speaker may result. Although quite an old form, the *dramatic monologue* was brought to a very high level by Robert Browning, who is often credited with its creation (although scores of speeches in Dante's *Comedy* and especially in the *Inferno* amount to posthumous *dramatic monologues*). Tennyson used the form on occasion, and modern poets have found it congenial, as witness the work of Robert Frost, Allen Tate, and T. S. Eliot. The name *dramatic monologue* was not used by the nineteenth-century masters of the form and, furthermore, there are important differences among the *dramatic monologue* (best exemplified by Browning's "My Last Duchess"), the SOLILOQUY (Browning's "Soliloquy of the Spanish Cloister"), and the EPISTLE (Browning's "Cleon" and "An Epistle"), although all three involve a single sustained utterance, typically by a character about whom the reader knows something beforehand. Most of the successful poems of this category are spoken not by newly created three-dimensional figures but by historical personages (such as Fra Lippo Lippi and Lucretius), characters from myth, legend, or literature (such as a duke, a bishop, Caliban, and a *gerontion*, or "little old man"). Some early-twentieth-century poems by Eliot and Conrad Aiken seem to belong among *dramatic monologues*, but in some cases (Eliot's "The Love Song of J. Alfred Prufrock" and "Gerontion," for example) the utterance is not patently delivered in a charged dramatic situation to a readily identifiable interlocutor, so that the poems may be related less to the fully formed *dramatic monologue* than to the INTERIOR MONOLOGUE or some type of MEDITATIVE POETRY.

[Reference: Alan Sinfield, *Dramatic Monologue* (1977).]

Dramatic Poetry A term that, logically, should be restricted to poetry employing dramatic form or some element of dramatic technique. The DRAMATIC MONOLOGUE is an example. The dramatic quality may result from the use of dialogue, monologue, vigorous diction, blank verse, or the stressing of tense situation and emotional conflict. Because of the presence of dramatic elements in the poems to be included in the volume *Bells and Pomegranates*, No. 3 (1842), Browning used the phrase "Dramatic Lyrics" as a subtitle. However, the phrase *dramatic poetry* is indefinite enough to include compositions that, like Shakespeare's *The Tempest*, may be more properly classed as POETIC DRAMA, or that, like Browning's *Pippa Passes*, are more commonly called CLOSET DRAMAS. But the question quickly becomes otiose; as one of the speakers in Eliot's "A Dialogue on Dramatic Poetry" asks, ". . . What great poetry is not dramatic? . . . Who is more dramatic than Homer or Dante?"

Dramatic Propriety The principle that a statement or an action within any dramatic situation is to be judged not in terms of its correspondence to standards external to the dramatic situation but in terms of appropriateness to its context. Cleanth Brooks argues, for example, that the statement "Beauty is truth, truth beauty" in Keats's "Ode on a Grecian Urn" is a dramatic statement appropriate to the urn that may utter it and has, therefore, "precisely the same status" as "Ripeness is all" in *King Lear*. We properly ask not whether it is an abstract truth but whether it is in character for the speaker and proper to the dramatic context.

Dramatic Structure The ancients compared the PLOT of a drama to the tying and untying of a knot. The principle of dramatic conflict, though not mentioned as such in Aristotle's definition of drama, is implied in this figure. The technical structure of a serious play is determined by the necessities of developing this dramatic conflict. Thus, a well-built tragedy will commonly show the following divisions, each representing a phase of the dramatic conflict: introduction, rising action, climax or crisis (turning point), falling action, and catastrophe. The relation of these parts is sometimes represented graphically by the figure of a pyramid, called FREYTAG'S PYRAMID, the rising slope suggesting the rising action or tying of the knot, the falling slope the falling action or resolution, the apex representing the climax.

The introduction (or EXPOSITION) creates the tone, gives the setting, introduces the characters, and supplies other facts necessary to the understanding of the play, such as events in the story supposed to have taken place before the part of the action included in the play, since a play, like an epic, is likely to plunge IN MEDIAS RES, "into the midst of things." In *Hamlet*, the bleak midnight scene on the castle platform, with the appearance of the ghost, sets the keynote of the tragedy, while the conversation of the watchers, especially the words of Horatio, supply antecedent facts, such as the quarrel between the dead King Hamlet and the King of Norway. The ancients called this part the PROTASIS. The rising action (or complication) is set in motion by the EXCITING FORCE (in *Hamlet* the ghost's revelation to Hamlet of the murder) and continues through successive stages of conflict between the hero and the counterplayers up to the climax or turning point (in *Hamlet* the hesitating failure of the hero to kill Claudius at prayer). The ancients called this part the EPITASIS.

The falling action stresses the activity of the forces opposing the hero and, although some suspense must be maintained, the trend must lead logically to the disaster with which the tragedy is to close. The falling action, called by the ancients the CATASTASIS, is often set in movement by a single event called the tragic force, closely related to the climax and bearing the same relation to the falling action as the exciting force does to the rising action. In *Macbeth* the tragic force is the escape of Fleance after the murder of Banquo. In *Hamlet* it is the "blind" stabbing of Polonius, which sends Hamlet away from the court just as he appears about to succeed in his plans. The latter part of the falling action is sometimes marked by an event that delays the catastrophe and seems to offer a way of escape for the hero (the apparent reconciliation of Hamlet and Laertes). This is the "moment of final suspense" and aids in maintaining interest. The falling action, usually shorter than the rising action, is often attended by some lowering of interest (as in the case of the long conversation between Malcolm and Macduff in *Macbeth*), because new forces must be introduced and an apparently inevitable end made to seem temporarily uncertain. RELIEF SCENES are often resorted to in the falling action, partly to mark time, partly to provide emotional relaxation for the audience. The famous scene of the gravediggers in *Hamlet* is an example of how a relief scene may be justified through its inherent dramatic interest and through its relation to the serious action (see COMIC RELIEF).

The CATASTROPHE, marking the tragic fall, usually the death, of the hero (and often of his opponents as well) comes as an unavoidable outgrowth of the action. It satisfies not so much by a gratification of the emotional sympathies of the spectator as by its logical conformity and by a final presentation of the nobility of the succumbing hero. A "glimpse of restored order" often follows the catastrophe proper in a Shakespearean tragedy, as when Hamlet gives his dying vote to Fortinbras as the new king. This five-part *dramatic structure* Freytag believed to be reflected in a five-act structure for tragedy. However, the imposing of a rigorous five-act structure on Elizabethan tragedy is questionable, because relatively few plays fall readily into a neat pattern. This structure based on the analogy of the tying and untying of a knot is applicable to comedy, the novel, and the short story, with the adjustment of the use of the broader term *dénouement* for catastrophe in works that are not tragic. See ACT, CATASTROPHE, and DÉNOUEMENT.

During the nineteenth century, conventional structure gave way to a newer technique. First, comedy, under the influence of French bourgeois comedy, the "well-made play" of Eugène Scribe and others, developed a set of technical conventions all its own; and as a result of the movement led by Ibsen, serious drama cast off the restrictions of the five-act tragedy and freed itself from conventional formality. By the end of the century the traditional five-act structure was to be found only in poetic or consciously archaic tragedy, of which the connection with the stage was artificial and generally unsuccessful. However, the fundamental elements of *dramatic structure* given here remained demonstrably present, though in modified form, in these newer types of plays. The fundamental *dramatic structure* seems impervious to basic change. See TRAGEDY, CONFLICT, ACT, CATASTROPHE, CLIMAX, CRISIS, PLOT.

Dramatis Personae The characters in a drama, a novel, or a poem. The term is also applied to a listing of the characters in the program of a play, at the beginning of the printed version of a play, or sometimes at the beginning of a novel. Such a list often contains brief characterizations of the persons of the work and notations about their relationships.

Dramatism A system for analyzing literature developed by Kenneth Burke. It assumes that literature is a form of action—"Somebody is always doing something to somebody else." Burke sees literature as fundamentally related in structure to the sentence patterns of Indo-European languages: that is, subject ("somebody"), verb ("is doing"), object ("something"), indirect object ("to somebody else"). Hence, Burke names his major works on literary analysis a "grammar" and a "rhetoric." His system can be applied to all literary genres. Any literary work contains, he asserts, five elements, which he uses in special senses: act (what happened?), scene (where?), agent (who did it?), agency (how?) and purpose (why?). Simple though such a scheme seems when so outlined, it becomes extremely complex in Burke's hands, for he combines, in finding the answers, most systems of human knowledge.

Drame A form of play between tragedy and comedy developed by the French in the eighteenth century and later introduced into England, where it is often called a "*drama*." It is a serious play, of which the modern PROBLEM PLAY is an example.

Drawing Room Comedy A form of the COMEDY OF MANNERS that deals with high society. It is called a *drawing room comedy* because it is usually a well-made play with its actions centered indoors, often literally in a drawing room.

Dream Allegory (or Vision) The dream was a conventional narrative frame that was widely used in the Middle Ages and is still employed on occasion. The narrator falls asleep and while sleeping dreams a dream that is the actual story told in the dream frame. In the Middle Ages the device was used for allegory. Among the major *dream allegories* are: *The Romance of the Rose*; Dante's *Comedy*; Chaucer's *The Book of the Duchess* and *The House of Fame*; *The Pearl*; and *The Vision of Piers Plowman*. The *dream allegory* forms the narrative frame for Bunyan's *Pilgrim's Progress*, Keats's *The Fall of Hyperion*, and (by adaptation to something like SCIENCE FICTION) Edward Bellamy's *Looking Backward*. See ALLEGORY, FRAMEWORK-STORY.

Dream Book A book that either records one's dreams or offers general interpretations of dreams, sometimes related to prophecy or gambling.

Dream Song A lyric mode brought to a high level of achievement by John Berryman (1914–1972) in an ambitious project ultimately called *The Dream Songs*, a book containing hundreds of the poems, most of which consist of three six-lined stanzas. As in a dream or nightmare, identities fluctuate and boundaries dissolve, and a great deal of almost manic energy is released.

But there were *dream songs* before Berryman was born. Gerhard Wendland produced a *Traumlied* ("dreamsong" in German), and the same term has been applied to the Prize Song in Wagner's *Die Meistersinger.* Eugene Lee-Hamilton (1845–1907) wrote a poem called " Noon's Dream-Song ," and Eleanor Farjeon's first book was called *Dream-Songs for the Beloved* (1911). At about the same time, Farjeon's contemporary Lady Sybil Myra Caroline Primrose Grant published a book called *Dream Songs*. In 1924 T. S. Eliot published "Three Dream Songs," but the set was broken up and the parts renamed, one becoming a section of "The Hollow Men."

Dresser A theater worker whose job includes taking care of costumes and helping performers with changes of clothing and makeup.

Droll A short dramatic piece (also known as "drollery" or "droll humor") cultivated on the COMMONWEALTH INTERREGNUM stage in England as a substitute for full-length or serious plays that were not permitted by the government. A *droll* was likely to be a "short, racy, comic" scene selected from some popular play (as a Launcelot Gobbo scene from *The Merchant of Venice*) and completed by dancing somewhat in the manner of the earlier JIG.

Dróttkvætt A measure commonly used in skaldic poems of the Middle Ages and still found in Icelandic poetry. The eight-lined stanzas with variable rhythm and three stresses per line employ ALLITERATION and INTERNAL RHYME. A close approximation in modern poetry comes in "The Masque" of W. H. Auden's *The Age of Anxiety*:

> Hushed is the lake of hawks
> Bright with our excitement,

And all the sky of skulls
Glows with scarlet roses;
The melter of men and salt
Admires the drinker of iron:
Bold banners of meaning
Blaze o'er the host of days.

The devices alternate: alliteration in the odd-numbered lines, internal rhyme in the even-numbered.

Druid Among the ancient Celts, one in the highest rank of those in charge of religion, government, and literature. A philosophical poet.

Dualism A doctrine (opposed to monism) that recognizes the possibility of the coexistence of antithetical or complementary principles. In monistic schemes, mind is reducible to matter (as in behaviorism), or matter is reducible to mind (as in mysticism); in *dualism*, mind and matter both exist.

Dub A type of poetry, originating in Jamaica around 1975, with words improvised to a background of recorded music. What began as extemporaneous performance subsequently led to works written down and published.

Dubbing In film, recording dialogue in a sound studio and adding it after a scene is shot.

Dubia Items of uncertain or disputed authorship or status. Dame Helen Gardner's edition of *John Donne: The Elegies and the Songs and Sonnets* includes *dubia* in an appendix.

Dumb Show A pantomimic performance used in a play. The term is applied particularly to such specimens of silent acting as appeared in ELIZABETHAN DRAMA. The *dumb show* provided a spectacular element and was often accompanied by music. Sometimes it employed allegorical figures such as those in the MORALITY PLAY and the MASQUE. Sometimes it foreshadowed coming events or provided comment like that of the CHORUS. Sometimes it appeared as PROLOGUE or between acts, and sometimes it was an integral part of the action, being performed by the characters of the play proper. Whatever its origin, it seems to have appeared first in the third quarter of the sixteenth century in the Senecan plays (see SENECAN TRAGEDY). It continued in use well into the seventeenth century. More than fifty extant Elizabethan plays contain *dumb shows*. That in Shakespeare's *Hamlet* (3, 2) is unusual in that it is preliminary to a show that is itself a "play within a play." Other well-known Elizabethan plays containing *dumb shows* are Sackville and Norton's *Gorboduc* (1562), Robert Greene's *James the Fourth* (1591), John Marston's *Malcontent* (1604), John Webster's *Duchess of Malfi* (1614), and Thomas Middleton's *The Changeling* (1623). See DISGUISINGS, PAGEANT, PANTOMIME.

[References: J. W. Cunliffe, *Early English Classical Tragedies* (1912); Dieter Mehl, *The Elizabethan Dumb Show: The History of a Dramatic Convention* (tr. 1966).]

Duodecimo A book size, designating SIGNATURES that result from sheets folded to twelve leaves or twenty-four pages. Its abbreviation is 12mo. See BOOK SIZES.

Duologue A scene or a short play with two actors; a dramatic performance limited to two speakers.

Duple Meter A line consisting of two syllables.

Dynamic Character A character who develops or changes as a result of the actions of the plot. See CHARACTERIZATION.

Dysphemism The opposite of EUPHEMISM. If one starts with a more or less neutral word like "die," for example, then a euphemism would be "pass away" and a *dysphemism* would be "croak."

Dystopia Literally, "bad place." The term is applied to accounts of imaginary worlds, usually in the future, in which present tendencies are carried out to their intensely unpleasant culminations. Literature of *dystopia* flourished in many forms during the twentieth century, in fiction (E. Zamyatin's *We*, George Orwell's *1984*, Aldous Huxley's *Brave New World*, Ray Bradbury's *Fahrenheit 451*, Anthony Burgess's *A Clockwork Orange*, Margaret Atwood's *The Handmaid's Tale*, Thomas Pynchon's *Vineland*, Ursula K. Le Guin's *The Dispossessed*, and several novels by H. G. Wells and Philip K. Dick), drama (Edward Bond's *Lear*, Bertolt Brecht's *The Rise and Fall of the City of Mahagonny*, Karel Căpek's *R.U.R.*, Václav Havel's *The Memorandum*, Craig Raine's *"1953": A Version of Racine's Andromaque*), and film (Fritz Lang's *Metropolis*, Jean-Luc Godard's *Alphaville*, George Lucas's *THX 1138*, Ridley Scott's *Blade Runner*, Terry Gilliam's *Brazil*). See UTOPIA.

[Reference: M. Keith Booker, *Dystopian Literature: A Theory and Research Guide* (1994).]

Goudy Text 1928. Designed by Frederic Goudy. The typeface was first cast as Goudy Black.

Early Tudor Age, 1500–1557 During the early years of the sixteenth century, the ideals of the Renaissance were rapidly replacing those of the Middle Ages. The Reformation of the English church and the revival of learning known as HUMANISM modified English life and thought substantially. It was a time of literary experimentation and of borrowings from French and Italian writings. Wyatt and Surrey imported the ITALIAN SONNET, *TERZA RIMA*, and *OTTAVA RIMA*, and Surrey first used BLANK VERSE, while Barclay and Skelton continued the older satiric tradition. Sir Thomas Elyot and Sir Thomas More were the major prose writers, and the translators and the chroniclers were adding to knowledge and to prose style alike. The late medieval drama was still dominant, with the MYSTERY PLAYS, MORALITIES, and INTERLUDES in great vogue, although SCHOOLPLAYS were beginning to introduce new elements, notably in *Ralph Roister Doister*, the first "regular" English comedy. Perhaps the single most important book, from a literary point of view, was *Tottel's Miscellany* (1557), a collection of the "new poetry" that paved the way for the Elizabethans. See Renaissance, *Outline of Literary History*.

Early Victorian Age, 1832–1870 This period was a time of the gradual tempering of the romantic impulse and the steady growth of REALISM in English letters. Even if the romantic spirit remained powerful, the enactment or realization of it suffered a falling off, and many critics have come to regard this period as one of heightened or even pathological romanticism of spirit. It bears to ROMANTICISM much the same relation that the Age of Johnson bears to the NEOCLASSIC PERIOD—it is an age in which the seeds of the new movement were being sown, but one that was still predominantly of the old. In poetry, the voices of the major romantics had been stilled by death, except for that of Wordsworth, and there emerged a new poetry more keenly aware of social issues and more marked by doubts and uncertainties resulting from the pains of the INDUSTRIAL REVOLUTION and the advances in scientific thought. The chief writers of this poetry were Tennyson, Browning, Arnold, and the young Swinburne. In the novel, Dickens, Thackeray, the Brontë sisters, and Trollope flourished. In the essay, Carlyle, Newman, Ruskin, Arnold, and De Quincey did outstanding work. See Victorian, *Outline of Literary History*.

Echelon One of a group of lines printed stepwise across and down a page. The printing of poetry in *echelon* (in French, *en échelon*) is particularly common in modern Russian poetry and certain modern American writers, such as William

Carlos Williams and Richard Howard. Here is an example from Williams's "The Ivy Crown":

> Daffodil time
>   is past. This is
>   summer, summer!
> the heart says,
>   and not even the full of it.

Echo A complex, subtle, and multifarious acoustic phenomenon involving a faint but perceptible REPETITION inside a work ("aged thrush" *echoes* "ancient pulse" in both sound and meaning in Hardy's "The Darkling Thrush") or between works (the "low damp ground" in Eliot's *The Waste Land* may *echo* the "old camp ground" of the sentimental tenting song). *Echo* sometimes means any recollection of something earlier, not necessarily just the sound. [Reference: John Hollander, *The Figure of Echo: A Mode of Allusion in Milton and After* (1981).]

Echo Verse Poetry in which the closing syllables of one line are repeated, as by an echo, in the following line—and usually making up that line—with a different meaning and thus forming a reply or a comment, as in Barnaby Barnes's lines:

> Echo! What shall I do to my Nymph when I go to behold her?
>   Hold her!

There are *echo* poems in Sidney's *Old Arcadia* and William Percy's *Sonnets to the Fairest Coelia*, and the fashion is ridiculed in Samuel Butler's *Hudibras* (1, 3, 190). Much later and somewhat more seriously, Gerard Manley Hopkins exploited the device in "The Leaden Echo and the Golden Echo." The device is as old as the *Greek Anthology*. It flourished in the sixteenth and seventeenth centuries, most often as a device in pastoral poetry and drama. Hardy's "The Elf-Echo Answers," characteristically bleak, begins

> How much shall I love her?
> For life, or not long?
>   "Not long."

A contemporary example is Fred Chappell's "Narcissus and Echo," which has an added complexity: the right-hand echo words can be read vertically:

> Shall the water not remember   *Ember*
> my hand's slow gesture, tracing above   *of*
> its mirror my half-imaginary   *airy*
> portrait? My only belonging   *longing;*
>   is my beauty. . . .

In Sidney's echoic eclogues, the repetition takes many forms: perfect *echo* (love/love), punning *echo* (woman/woe-man), partial *echo* (desire/ire), and rhyming *echo* (joys/toys). Robert Creeley is one of the modern poets most devoted to the figure, having written a number of poems with some form of *echo* in their titles. One of those called "Echo" seems to concern an ancient myth as well as its acoustic manifestation:

> Broken heart, you
> timeless wonder.
>
> What a small
> place to be.
>
> True, true
> to life, to life.

Eclipsis Omission of material that may be necessary for full clarity. "A friend in need is a friend indeed," for example, has been so compressed that the meaning is somewhat eclipsed. The saying means "A friend *when one is* in need is a friend indeed," but the statement could just as well mean "A friend *who is* in need is a friend indeed."

Eclogue *Eclogue* in Greek meant "selection" and was applied to various kinds of poems. From its application to Virgil's pastoral poems, however, *eclogue* came to have its present restricted meaning of a formal pastoral poem following the traditional technique derived from the idylls of Theocritus (third century B.C.). Conventional *eclogue* types include: (1) the singing match; (2) the rustic DIALOGUE: two "rude swains" engage in banter; (3) the dirge or lament for a dead shepherd (see PASTORAL ELEGY); (4) the love-lay: a shepherd may sing a song of courtship, or a shepherd or shepherdess may complain of disappointment in love; (5) the EULOGY. In the Renaissance, following Mantuan's Latin *eclogues* (fifteenth century), the *eclogue* was used for veiled satire, particularly against the corruptions of the "pastors" of the clergy and against political factions. The earliest and most famous collection of conventional *eclogues* in English is Spenser's *The Shepheardes Calender* (1579), with one *eclogue* for each month. By the eighteenth century a distinction was made between *eclogue* and pastoral, the term *eclogue* being used to describe the form and pastoral the content. Hence, *eclogue* came to mean a DRAMATIC POEM, with little action or characterization but much sentiment expressed in dialogue or soliloquy, and *eclogues* set in towns became possible. *The Age of Anxiety*, by the twentieth-century poet W. H. Auden, is subtitled *A Baroque Eclogue*.

Ecphonema, Ecphonesis An outcry or exclamation, sometimes indicated by "oh" or "ah," along with an exclamation point.

Edinburgh Review A quarterly journal of criticism founded in 1802 by Francis Jeffrey, Sydney Smith, and Henry Brougham. They determined a vigorous, outspoken policy, which not only made a successful publication but also stirred up the whole English-reading world. Among the contributors to the *Review* were some of the most brilliant writers of the time, including the editors themselves and such worthies as Walter Scott, Henry Hallam, and Francis Horner. The motto—*Judex damnatur, cum nocens absolvitur,* "the judge is condemned when the guilty man is acquitted"—indicates clearly the rigorous policy of the founders, who were predominantly Whig in attitude. After seven years of being browbeaten, the Tories started a rival journal, the QUARTERLY

REVIEW (1809). The two publications rode literary and political prejudices hard and enlivened British criticism.

One of the abhorrences of the *Edinburgh Review* was the LAKE SCHOOL of writers, particularly Southey and Wordsworth. An article by Henry Brougham called "Hours of Idleness" provoked Byron's famous satire, *English Bards and Scotch Reviewers*. Later contributors included Macaulay, Carlyle, Hazlitt, and Arnold. The *Edinburgh Review* ceased publication in 1929.

Ectasis Making a short syllable long.

Editing The preparation of manuscript for the compositor and printer. The term is also applied to the establishment of texts and to the preparation of annotated editions. (See BIBLIOGRAPHY.) In filmmaking, *editing* is the establishment of the sequence of a film by selecting and splicing together the various shots into a final form.

Edition The entire number of bound copies of a book printed at any time or times from a single typesetting or from plates or other modes of reproduction made from a single typesetting. The copies made from one continuous operation at one time are called a PRINTING or an IMPRESSION. Thus, there may be several printings or impressions in an *edition*. As applied to old books, however, *edition* and impression are practically synonymous, because of the practice of "distributing" type (taking it apart) after a printing. The term "issue" is applied to a set of copies distinguishable from other copies of that *edition* by variations in printed matter. *Edition* is also applied to a set of copies differing in some way other than in printed matter from others of the same text, as "the illustrated *edition*," "the ten-volume *edition*," or a special form of an author's work, as "the centennial *edition* of Emerson," or an especially edited work, as "Merritt Hughes's *edition* of *Paradise Lost*." The first *edition* of this handbook came out in1936; the fifth *edition* (1986) was called the "Fiftieth Anniversary Edition."

[Reference: Philip Gaskell, *A New Introduction to Bibliography* (1972).]

Editorial A short essay in a newspaper or magazine. The purpose of the *editorial* is usually to express the opinion of the editor or editorial office. Also an occasional feature of radio and television.

Education Novel A form of novel developed in the late eighteenth century, presenting in fictional form a plan for the education of a young person into a desirable citizen and a morally and intellectually self-reliant individual. Among its significant forerunners were the Elizabethan COURTESY BOOKS. Rousseau's *Émile* (1762) was the model for most *education novels*. The form was immensely popular in England in the last third of the eighteenth century, examples being Henry Brooke's *Fool of Quality*, Thomas Day's *Sanford and Merton*, Elizabeth Inchbald's *Simple Story*, and Maria Edgeworth's serialized *Parent's Assistant*. The *education novel* was also attractive to American novelists between 1790 and 1820, notably the Reverend Enos Hitchcock. In one sense the *education novel* is a forerunner of the APPRENTICESHIP NOVEL or BILDUNGSROMAN, but such a work is broader in scope, deeper in characterization, and more interested in the development of a philosophy of life. The term ERZIEHUNGSROMAN, literally "novel of education," is also more like the apprenticeship novel than the *education novel* in its eighteenth-century sense.

Edwardian Age The period between the death of Victoria in 1901 and the beginning of the First World War in 1914, so-called after Edward VII, who ruled from 1901 to 1910. It was marked by a strong reaction in thought, conduct, and art to the stiff propriety and conservatism of the Victorian Age. The typical attitude of the Edwardians was critical and questioning. There was a growing distrust of authority in religion, morality, and art, a basic doubt of the conventional "virtues," and a deep-felt need to examine existing institutions.

The CELTIC RENAISSANCE in Ireland awakened the dramatic talents of Lady Gregory, Douglas Hyde, Lennox Robinson, J. M. Synge, and W. B. Yeats; the intellectual drama of G. B. Shaw continued the Ibsen influence; James Barrie and Lord Dunsany kept romance and whimsy alive on the stage. In England John Galsworthy was producing social plays. In poetry it was an age of endings and beginnings. Victorianism lingered on in the verses of the LAUREATE, Alfred Austin (succeeded in 1913 by Robert Bridges), and in the work of Alfred Noyes and Rudyard Kipling. W. B. Yeats flourished; Masefield's first volumes appeared; and Hardy published a number of volumes of poetry, including *The Dynasts*.

But it was predominantly an age of prose. REALISM and NATURALISM advanced steadily. In the novels of Arnold Bennett were detailed pictures of the grim commonplace; in those of Galsworthy the beginnings of the saga of the middle classes. H. G. Wells launched his novelistic criticisms of society; Kipling recorded the march of empire; Ford Madox Ford began to flourish in criticism, journalism, and fiction. But the greatest writers of prose in the British Isles in the *Edwardian Age* were James Joyce, whose *Dubliners* appeared in 1914, and Joseph Conrad, who published distinguished work, including *Youth* and *Nostromo*. Other works of distinction or promise included Butler's *The Way of All Flesh*, Hudson's *Green Mansions*, Stephens's *Crock of Gold*, and Barrie's *The Admirable Crichton*. English writing was moving away from its older orientations: in the *Edwardian Age* the best dramatist was an Irishman, Shaw; the best poet an Irishman, Yeats; the best novelist an expatriated Pole, Conrad; and the figure with greatest promise for the future an Irishman, Joyce.

[References: Samuel Hynes, *Edwardian Occasions: Essay on English Writing in the Early Twentieth Century* (1972), and *The Edwardian Turn of Mind* (1968).]

Effate (also **Effatum,** plural **Effata**) Obsolete word meaning a DICTUM or MAXIM. In 1685 Robert Boyle referred to "The Effatum, That Nature abhors a Vacuum."

Effect Totality of impression or emotional impact. "The tale of *effect*" was a term used to describe GOTHIC and horror stories of the type published in *Blackwood's Magazine* in the first half of the nineteenth century. Poe considered the primary objective of the SHORT STORY to be the achieving of a unified *effect*. The *effect* striven for may be horror, mystery, beauty, or whatever the writer's mood dictates, but once the *effect* is decided, everything in the story must work toward this controlling purpose. One paragraph in Poe's CRITICISM of Hawthorne's *Twice-Told Tales* stands out as the best explanation of this principle:

> A skillful literary artist has constructed a tale. If wise, he has not fashioned his thought to accommodate his incidents; but having conceived, with deliberate care, a certain unique or single *effect* to be wrought out, he then invents such incidents—he then combines such events as may best aid him in establishing his preconceived *effect*. If his very initial sentence tend not to

> be outbringing of this *effect*, then he has failed in his first step. In the whole composition there should be no word written, of which the tendency, direct or indirect, is not to the one pre-established design. And by such means, with such care and skill, a picture is at length painted which leaves in the mind of him who contemplates it with a kindred art, a sense of the fullest satisfaction.

To study *effect* is to put less emphasis on an author's supposed intention, and it is altogether possible for literature to produce *effects* not intended or even contemplated by the author. See AFFECTIVE FALLACY, INTENTIONAL FALLACY.

Eiron A basic comic character in Greek drama. The *eiron*—typically a swindler, trickster, hypocrite, or picaresque rogue—pretends to ignorance in order to trick others. The opposite of the ALAZON, who pretends to more knowledge than he or she has. The term is sometimes applied to figures in tragedy who deceive through feigned ignorance; Hamlet is an example. IRONY—saying the opposite of what is meant—is the characteristic rhetorical device of the *eiron* (from whom it gets its name).

Eisteddfod A Welsh festival of poetry and song, dating back many centuries. Now annual and more or less official, the *eisteddfod* has been important in maintaining communication among writers.

Ekphrasis (also **Ecphrasis**) Sometimes used in reference to the representation of an artwork of any kind in a literary work, such as a poem or string quartet inside a novel, but usually restricted to the representation of a visual or graphic work inside a literary work. The graphic work may be a painting, statue, tapestry, window, shield, urn, or other such potentially representational artifact. In some cases, such as Robert Browning's "Fra Lippo Lippi" or Yeats's "Leda and the Swan," a real graphic work is involved; in other cases—sometimes called "notional *ekphrasis*"—the work is imaginary, like the shield of Achilles described in the *Iliad* (XVIII) and Auden's "The Shield of Achilles."

[References: James A. W. Heffernan, *Museum of Words: The Poetics of Ekphrasis from Homer to Ashbery* (1993); John Hollander, *The Gazer's Spirit: Poems Speaking to Silent Works of Art* (1995); Grant F. Scott, *The Sculpted Word: Keats, Ekphrasis, and the Visual Arts* (1994).]

Elaboration A rhetorical method for developing a theme or picture in such a way as to give the reader a completed impression. This may be done in various ways, such as: repetition of the statement or idea, a change of words and phrases, or supplying of additional details. *Elaboration* is also used as a critical term characterizing a literary, rhetorical style that is ornate. See AMPLIFICATION.

Electra Complex In psychoanalysis, an obsessive attachment of a daughter to her father and, thus, the female counterpart of the OEDIPUS COMPLEX. It gets its name from Electra, in Greek legend, a daughter of Agamemnon and Clytemnestra, who with her brother Orestes avenged the death of their father by killing their mother and her lover, Aegisthus.

Elegiac In classical prosody, the type of DISTICH employed for lamenting or commemorating the dead; it consists of a line of DACTYLIC HEXAMETER followed by one of PENTAMETER. (The pentameter line is actually the remains of a hexameter with syllables removed in the third and sixth feet.) The ancient poets used *elegiacs* not only for THRENODIES but also for songs of war and love. The *elegiac* meter has been popular in Germany but rarely used in England and America, except by Longfellow and Edmund Wilson. Coleridge's translation of Schiller's distich will serve as an example:

> In the hexameter rises the fountain's silvery column,
> In the pentameter aye falling in melody back.

A set of "Leonine Elegiacs" can be found among Tennyson's earliest poems. *Elegiac* as an adjective describes poetry expressing sorrow or lamentation (as in *elegiac* strains).

Elegiac Stanza The IAMBIC PENTAMETER QUATRAIN, rhyming *abab*. The name comes from Thomas Gray's "Elegy Written in a Country Churchyard," which is in this stanza. Although such a quatrain, rhyming *abab* and called the HEROIC QUATRAIN, was a stanza of long standing before Gray used it, in the last half of the eighteenth and the nineteenth centuries it was usually employed, after Gray's example, in expressing sorrow or lamentation.

Elegy A sustained and formal poem setting forth meditations on death or another solemn theme. The meditation often is occasioned by the death of a particular person, but it may be a generalized observation or the expression of a solemn mood. Common to both Latin and Greek literatures, the *elegy* originally signified almost any type of meditation, whether the reflective element concerned death, love, or war, or merely the presentation of information. In classical writing the *elegy* was more distinguishable by its use of the elegiac meter than by subject matter. The Elizabethans used the term for love poems, particularly complaints. Up through the end of the seventeenth century, *elegy* could mean both a love poem and a poem of mourning. Thereafter, the poem of mourning became virtually the only meaning. Notable English *elegies* include the Old English poem "The Wanderer," *The Pearl*, Chaucer's *Book of the Duchess*, Donne's "Elegies," Gray's "Elegy Written in a Country Churchyard," Tennyson's *In Memoriam*,Whitman's "When Lilacs Last in the Dooryard Bloom'd," and John Berryman's "Formal Elegy." These poems indicate the variety of method, mood, and subject encompassed by *elegy*. A specialized form of *elegy*, popular with English poets, is the PASTORAL ELEGY, of which Milton's "Lycidas" is an outstanding example.

Elements In early cosmologies, the fundamental constituents, or *elements*, of the universe were earth, air, fire, and water. Each was considered to have certain characteristics: earth was cold and dry; air, hot and moist; fire, hot and dry; and water, cold and moist. The HUMOURS of the body were closely allied to the four *elements*. The organization of T. S. Eliot's *Four Quartets* follows the scheme of *elements* somewhat: "East Coker" is a poem of the earth, "The Dry Salvages," of water, and "Little Gidding," of fire. The term *elements* is also applied to the bread and wine in the Eucharist. See HUMOURS.

Elephant A size of paper measuring 28 × 23 inches.

Elision The omission of part of a word. *Elision* is most often accomplished by the omission of a final vowel preceding an initial vowel, as "th'orient" for "the orient," but it also occurs between syllables of a single word, as "ne'er" for "never." John Donne favored *elision* uncommonly; it occurs twice in these three lines from one of his sonnets:

> Divorce me, untie or break that knot again;
> Take me to You, imprison me, for I,
> Except You enthrall me, never shall be free. . . .

Elizabethan Age The segment of the Renaissance during the reign of Elizabeth I (1558–1603). The term is sometimes extended to include the JACOBEAN AGE (1603–1625). This age of great nationalistic expansion, commercial growth, and religious controversy saw the development of English drama to its highest level, a great outburst of lyric poetry, and a new interest in criticism. Sidney, Spenser, Marlowe, and Shakespeare flourished; and Bacon, Jonson, and Donne first stepped forward. It has justly been called the "Golden Age of English Literature." For details, see RENAISSANCE and "Elizabethan Age" in *Outline of Literary History*.

Elizabethan Drama This phrase indicates the body of English drama produced in the century preceding the closing of the theaters in 1642, although it is sometimes employed in a narrower sense for the later years of Elizabeth's reign and the few years following it. Thus, Shakespeare is an Elizabethan dramatist, although more than a third of his active career lies in the reign of James I. Modern English drama not only came into being in the Elizabethan Age but developed so rapidly and brilliantly that the Elizabethan era is the golden age of English drama.

Lack of adequate records makes it difficult to trace the steps by which *Elizabethan drama* developed, though the chief elements contributing to it can be listed. From medieval drama came the tradition of acting and certain conventions approved by the populace, including some buffoonery. From the MORALITY PLAYS and the INTERLUDES came comic elements. With this medieval heritage was combined the classical tradition of drama, partly drawn from a study of the Roman dramatists, Seneca (tragedy) and Plautus and Terence (comedy), and partly from humanistic criticism based on Aristotle. This classical influence appeared first in the SCHOOL PLAYS. Later it affected the drama written under the auspices of the royal court and of the INNS OF COURT. Eventually it influenced the plays of the university-trained playwrights connected with the public stage. The modern theater arose with *Elizabethan drama* (see PUBLIC THEATERS, PRIVATE THEATERS). For types of *Elizabethan drama* and names of dramatists see *Outline of Literary History* and TRAGEDY, ROMANTIC TRAGEDY, CLASSICAL TRAGEDY, TRAGEDY OF BLOOD, COMEDY, COMEDY OF HUMOURS, COURT COMEDY, REALISTIC COMEDY, CHRONICLE PLAY, MASQUE.

Elizabethan Literature Literature produced in England during the Elizabethan Age; that is, 1558–1603, although the meaning is often extended to include the JACOBEAN AGE, which ended in 1625. See ELIZABETHAN AGE.

Elizabethan Miscellanies Poetical anthologies compiled in the Elizabethan Age. See POETICAL MISCELLANIES.

Elizabethan Theaters See PUBLIC THEATERS, PRIVATE THEATERS.

Ellipsis (or Ellipse) The omission of one or more words that, while essential to a grammatic structure, are easily supplied. In the following quotation from Thomas Hardy's "The Darkling Thrush," the first clause contains the "seemed to be" that is omitted by *ellipsis* in the second and third:

> The land's sharp features seemed to be
> The century's corpse outleant,
> His crypt the cloudy canopy,
> The wind his death-lament.

(Note that the inversion in the middle clause complicates the effect.)

Emblem In general, a device of some sort in graphic form that stands for some specific or general meaning. In the Middle Ages and Renaissance, *emblem* came to mean a specific device that typically included a graphic representation of conventional symbols, a MOTTO (often in a foreign language), and an elaboration of the meaning.

Emblem Books An "emblem" consisted of a motto expressing a moral idea and accompanied by a picture and a short poem. The picture (originally itself the "emblem") was symbolic. A collection of emblems was known as an *emblem book*. Emblems and

Emblemata. 129

Vino prudentiam augeri.

EMBLEMA XXIII.

HAEC Bacchus pater, & Pallas communiter ambo
Templa tenent, ſoboles vtraque vera Iouis.
Hæc caput, ille femur ſoluit: huic vſus oliui
Debitus, inuenit primus at ille merum.
Iunguntur meritò: quòd ſi qui abſtemius odit
Vina, Deæ nullum ſentiet auxilium.

COMMENTARII.

I. EIDEM baſi inſiſtunt Bacchus & Pallas: ille nudus, hederis coronatus, pateram tenens; hæc galeata, ſcuto & haſta armata, & capite Gorgonis in pectore munita.

II. *Qui Dij veteribus habiti.* PRO Dijs fuiſſe veteribus habitos, qui ſibi beneficijs humanum genus deuinxiſſent, notius eſt ex M. Tullij libris De nat. Deor. Lactantio & Euſeb. quàm vt confirmare ſit neceſſe. Tantum obiter admonebo, quoſdam Deos ijſdem olim templis & aris fuiſſe cultos, vt Cererem & Neptunum, quòd abſq; ſale cibi penè omnes inſipidi ſint, refert Plutarch. Sympoſ. 4. Vt Herculem & Muſas, quia Euandrum literas docuit Hercules, idem teſtis eſt in quæſtion. Rom. Sic deniq; Mercurium iuxta Venerem ſtatuere, vt oſtenderent, matrimonii voluptatem maximè orationis indigere, itemque Suadam & Gratias, vt innue- *Dij multi ijſdē aris poſiti.*

I rent.

From Andrea Alciati, *Emblematum Liber* (16th century). Photo courtesy of Professor William Barker/University of King's College.

emblem books, which owed their appeal partly to the newly developed art of engraving, were very popular in all Western European languages in the fifteenth, sixteenth, and seventeenth centuries. Examples of emblems are: the motto *Divesque miserque*, "both rich and poor," illustrated by a picture of King Midas sitting at a table where everything was gold and by a verse or "posie" explaining how Midas, though rich, could not eat his gold; *Parler peu et venir au poinct*, "speak little and come to the point," illustrated by a quatrain and a picture of a man shooting at a target with a crossbow. Several of Spenser's poems, such as *The Shepheardes Calender* and *Muiopotmos*, show the influence of emblems. Shakespeare seems to have made much use of emblem literature, as in the casket scene in *The Merchant of Venice*. Francis Quarles is the author of an interesting seventeenth-century *emblem book*.

Emendation A change made in a literary text by an editor for removing error or supplying a supposed correct reading that has been obscured or lost through textual inaccuracy or tampering. Probably the most celebrated *emendation* is Lewis Theobald's change of "a table of green fields" (*King Henry the Fifth*, 2, 3) to "a babbled of green fields."

Empathy The act of identifying ourselves with an object and participating in its physical and emotional sensations, even to the point of making our own physical responses, as, standing before a statue of a discus thrower, we flex our muscles to hurl the discus. It is to be contrasted with "sympathy" through which we have a fellow-feeling for someone, for *empathy* implies an "involuntary projection of ourselves" into something or someone else. Some see in *empathy* the key to the nature and meaning of art. The term is a translation of Hermann Lotze's *Einfühlung*—"feeling into"—and it entered our critical vocabulary in the twentieth century. Now loosely synonymous with "sympathy."

Emphasis A principle dictating that important elements be given important positions and adequate development. The more important positions are, naturally, at the beginning and end. But *emphasis* may also be secured (1) by repetition; (2) by the development of important ideas through supplying plenty of detail; (3) by the allotment of more space to the more important ideas; (4) by contrast, which focuses the reader's attention; (5) by selection of details so chosen that subjects related to the main idea are included and irrelevant material excluded; (6) by climactic arrangement; and (7) by mechanical devices such as capitalization, italics, symbols, and different colors of ink.

Empiricism In philosophy the drawing of rules of practice not from theory but from experience. Hence, an empirical method is sometimes equivalent to an "experimental" method or scientific knowledge. In medicine, however, an "empiric" usually means a quack.

Enallage The substitution of one grammatical form for another, as past for present tense, singular for plural, noun for verb. It is a very common figure, as in "toe the line" or "boot the ball." A famous example is Shakespeare's "But me no buts" (*Richard II*). The poetry of Gerard Manley Hopkins furnishes many kinetic instances: preposition for conjunction, adverb for preposition, objective for nominative, and—particularly—verb for noun ("the achieve of, the mastery of the thing") and vice versa ("the just man justices").

Enantiomorph An object that is a mirror image of another. Applied to words, acoustic *enantiomorphs* would be pairs like "loop" / "pool." But they do not look like mirror images: the class of written *enantiomorphs* is reserved for pairs like capitalized "MAT" / "TAM."

Enchiridion A HANDBOOK, MANUAL, or *VADE MECUM*.

Enclosed Rhyme A term applied to the rhyme pattern of the *IN MEMORIAM* STANZA: *abba*.

Encomium In Greek literature a composition in praise of a living person, object, or event, but not a god, delivered before a special audience. Originally a choral hymn in celebration of a hero at the conclusion of the Olympic games, then a eulogy of the host at a banquet, and finally any eulogy, the *encomium* was apparently first used by Simonides of Ceos and later by Pindar. Encomiastic verse, often in the form of the ode, has been written by many English poets, including Donne, Milton, Dryden, Gray, Wordsworth, and Auden. The Latin title of Erasmus's *Praise of Folly* is *Encomium Moriae* (possibly a pun on Sir Thomas More's name).

Encyclopedia (or **Encyclopaedia**) An inclusive compendium of information. The term comes from the Greek words for "circle" and "instruction." The original "circle of instruction" embraced the SEVEN LIBERAL ARTS. The word was first used in English in Sir Thomas Elyot's *The Book Named the Governor* (1531). There are three major types of *encyclopedias*: comprehensive, taking all knowledge for their province, such as the *Encyclopaedia Britannica* (first edition in 1771); those universal in scope but limited in coverage, such as the *Columbia Encyclopedia*; and those limited to special subjects or interests, such as the *Encyclopaedia of the Social Sciences* or the *Catholic Encyclopaedia*. *L'Encyclopédie* (thirty-five volumes, 1751–1776) was directed by Jean le Rond d'Alembert and Denis Diderot; the contributors included Montesquieu, Rousseau, and Voltaire.

End Rhyme Rhyme at the ends of lines in a poem. The most common kind of rhyme.

End-stopped Lines Lines in which both the grammatical structure and the sense reach completion at the end. The absence of ENJAMBMENT, or RUN-ON LINES. As in Pope's

> All are but parts of one stupendous whole,
> Whose body Nature is, and God the soul.

Here is an example of *end-stopped* blank verse, from Antony's funeral oration (*Julius Caesar* 3, 2):

> He was my friend, faithful and just to me;
> But Brutus says he was ambitious,
> And Brutus is an honorable man.
> He hath brought many captives home to Rome,
> Whose ransoms did the general coffers fill.

Did this in Caesar seem ambitious?
When that the poor have cried, Caesar hath wept;
Ambition should be made of sterner stuff.
Yet Brutus says he was ambitious;
And Brutus is an honorable man.

En face A manner of printing two texts on facing pages. Most often, *en face* translations will present the original on the left-hand page and the translation on the right.

English Language The *English language* developed from the West Germanic dialects spoken by the Angles, Saxons, and other Teutonic tribes who participated in the invasion and occupation of England in the fifth and sixth centuries, a movement that resulted in the virtual obliteration of the earlier Celtic and Roman cultures. The word *English* applied to the language reflects the fact that Anglo-Saxon literature first flourished in the North and was written in the Anglican DIALECTS (hence *Englisc*, "English") spoken in Northumbria and Mercia. Later, under King Alfred, the West Saxon region became the cultural center. The word *Englisc* was still employed as its name, however, and the earlier Anglian literature was copied in West Saxon, now commonly referred to as Old English, or "Anglo- Saxon." As a language West Saxon was very different from modern English. It had grammatical gender, declensions, conjugations, tense forms, and case endings. Nouns, pronouns, and verbs possessed inflectional systems. In addition, the four great dialects of the OLD ENGLISH PERIOD (Northumbrian, Mercian, West Saxon, Kentish) differed among themselves in pronunciation and vocabulary. The first writing was in RUNES, which were displaced later by the Roman alphabet used by the Christian missionaries. Specimens of Old English have survived from as early as the eighth century, but most of the existing manuscripts are in West Saxon of the tenth and eleventh centuries. Though a few Latin and fewer Celtic words were added to the vocabulary in Old English times, most of the words were Germanic, consisting of words used by the Angles and Saxons, augmented by the introduction of Danish and Norse words as the result of later invasions.

The changes that have made modern English look like a different language from Old English come from the operation of certain tendencies in language development, such as the progressive simplification of the grammar. Like some other Indo-European languages, English has moved from an early stage of synthetic-suffixal word formation to a later stage of analytic-prefixal word formation; prepositional phrases, for example, do the work once done by inflected nouns. The greatest change took place in the earlier part of the MIDDLE ENGLISH PERIOD (c. 1100–c. 1500). The leveling of inflections and other simplifying forces, already under way in late Old English times, were accelerated by the results of the Norman Conquest, which dethroned English as the literary language, in favor of the French of the newcomers (see ANGLO-FRENCH and ANGLO-NORMAN). Left to the everyday use of the native population, English changed rapidly in the direction of modern English. By late Middle English times (fourteenth century) the process of simplification had gone so far that in Chaucer's time many of the old inflections were either lost or weakened to a final *-e*, often unpronounced. The introduction of French words enriched the English vocabulary. In the fourteenth and fifteenth centuries a significant step toward the development of a standardized, uniform language came with the new prominence given the London dialect (southeast Midland), which thus became the basis for modern English. This development arose chiefly from the growing importance of London commercially and politically, the influence of the writings of Chaucer and his followers, the adoption of English instead of French in the courts and schools (fourteenth century), and the employment of this dialect by Caxton, the first English printer (late fifteenth century).

Modern English (c. 1500 on) has been marked by an enormous expansion in vocabulary, the new words being drawn from many sources, chiefly Latin and French. Because French is itself based on Latin, English has acquired many doublets, such as "strict" and "strait," permitting further developments in shades of meaning. Other such pairs are "fragile" and "frail" and "regal" and "royal." In special vocabularies, such as that of the church or the law, we have quite a few so-called doublets with one Romance word and one Germanic word both meaning approximately the same ("lord and master," "to have and to hold"). An examination of a dictionary will show the preponderance of foreign over native English words, though the latter include the more frequently used everyday words such as "man," "wife," "child," "go," "hold," "day," "bed," "sorrow," "hand." English prose style is greatly affected by the nature of the vocabulary, particularly as between native words and those derived from Latin, either directly or via French. The native words in general give an effect of simplicity and strength, whereas the Latin or Romance words impart smoothness and make possible fine distinctions in meaning. Germanic words generally consist of a few long and varied syllables, Latinate words of many short and uniform syllables; compare the valences of "happiness" and "felicity" or "sisterhood" and "sorority." Modern English has also drawn freely on many other sources for new words. Greek, for example, has been turned to for scientific terms, new words being formed from Greek root meanings and affixes. In grammar the simplification has been retarded in modern times by such conservative forces as grammars, dictionaries, printers, and schoolteachers.

Today only a quarter of the common words in English come from Old English, yet those that determine the nature of the language—articles, pronouns, and connecting words—are mostly of Old English origin. What inflectional endings remain for pronouns, adjectives, and adverbs are Old English, as are our verb forms. We have retained much of the Germanic word order, the Germanic tendency to associate ACCENT and loudness and to stress the first syllable of nouns. We have borrowed three-fourths of our words but fitted them into an English frame. The result is that English remains basically a Germanic tongue, which perpetually renews itself at the fountain of the world's languages.

[References: A. C. Baugh, *A History of the English Language*, 4th ed. (1993; orig. 1935); Otto Jespersen, *Growth and Structure of the English Language*, 10th ed. (1982; orig. 1905); Thomas Pyles and John Algeo, *The Origins and Development of the English Language*, 4th ed. (1993; orig. 1964); B. M. H. Strang, *A History of English* (1970).]

English Literature, Periods of The division of literary history into periods offers a limited but convenient approach. Hence most literary histories and anthologies are arranged by periods. In the case of English literature, there are almost as many arrangements as there are books on the subject. Such lack of uniformity arises chiefly from two facts. Periods merge into one another because the supplanting of one literary attitude by another is gradual. Thus, the earlier romanticists are contemporary with the later neoclassicists, just as the neoclassical attitude existed in the very heyday of Elizabethan romanticism. Dates given in any scheme, therefore, must be regarded as approximate and suggestive only, even when they reflect some definite fact, as 1660 (the Restoration of the Stuarts) and 1798 (the publication of *Lyrical Ballads*). And the names of periods may be chosen on very different principles: one is naming a period for its greatest or most representative author (Age of Chaucer, Age of Spenser, etc.); another is to coin an adjective from the name of the ruler or the ruling dynasty (such as Tudor); or pure chronology or names of centuries may be preferred (Fifteenth-Century Literature, Eighteenth-Century Literature, etc.); or descriptive titles designed to indicate prevailing attitudes or dominant fashions or "schools" of literature may be used (Neoclassicism, Romanticism, Age of Reason). Logically, some single principle should control in any given scheme, but such consistency is seldom found. The table that follows gives the scheme used in this book. Sketches of the periods listed in this table appear throughout this handbook, and briefer descriptions of the subdivisions of periods (here called ages uniformly) are also given in the handbook. The *Outline of Literary History* gives details of general and literary history.

PERIODS OF ENGLISH LITERATURE

428–1100	OLD ENGLISH PERIOD	
1100–1350	ANGLO-NORMAN PERIOD	
1350–1500	MIDDLE ENGLISH PERIOD	
1500–1660	RENAISSANCE PERIOD	
	1500–1557	EARLY TUDOR AGE
	1558–1603	ELIZABETHAN AGE
	1603–1625	JACOBEAN AGE
	1625–1642	CAROLINE AGE
	1649–1660	COMMONWEALTH INTERREGNUM
1660–1798	NEOCLASSIC PERIOD	
	1660–1700	RESTORATION AGE
	1700–1750	AUGUSTAN AGE
	1750–1798	AGE OF JOHNSON
1798–1870	ROMANTIC PERIOD	
	1798–1832	AGE OF THE ROMANTIC MOVEMENT
	1832–1870	EARLY VICTORIAN AGE
1870–1914	REALISTIC PERIOD	
	1870–1901	LATE VICTORIAN AGE
	1901–1914	EDWARDIAN AGE
1914–1965	MODERN OR MODERNIST PERIOD	
1965–	POST-MODERNIST OR CONTEMPORARY PERIOD	

English Sonnet A SONNET consisting of three quatrains followed by a couplet, rhyming *abab cdcd efef gg*. Often called the Shakespearean sonnet, Shakespeare being by far its most distinguished practitioner.

Englyn A venerable Welsh pattern of verse, usually a quatrain with complex rules governing alliteration and rhyme. The form has been mentioned in passing from time to time by Robert Graves and W. H. Auden, for example. In James Joyce's *Ulysses*(1922), a dog is said to have written a poem: "The metrical system of the canine original . . . recalls the intricate alliterative and isosyllabic rules of the Welsh englyn."

Enjambment (***Enjambement***) The continuation of the sense and grammatical construction of a line on to the next verse or couplet. *Enjambment* occurs in run-on lines and offers contrast to END-STOPPED LINES. The first and second lines from Milton given below, carried over to the second and third, illustrate:

Or if Sion hill
Delight thee more, and Siloa's brook, that flow'd
Fast by the oracle of God. . . .

Enlightenment A philosophical movement of the eighteenth century, particularly in France but effectively over much of Europe and America. The *Enlightenment* celebrated reason, the scientific method, and human beings' ability to perfect themselves and their society. It grew out of a number of seventeenth-century intellectual attainments: the discoveries of Sir Isaac Newton, the RATIONALISM of Descartes and Pierre Bayle, and the EMPIRICISM of Francis Bacon and John Locke. The major champions of its beliefs were the *philosophes*, who made a critical examination of previously accepted institutions and beliefs from the viewpoint of reason and with confidence in natural laws and universal order. The *philosophes* agreed on faith in human rationality and the existence of discoverable and universally valid principles governing human beings, nature, and society. They opposed intolerance, restraint, spiritual authority, and revealed religion. They were deists (see DEISM) and political theorists who considered the state a proper instrument of progress. The *Encyclopédie* of Denis Diderot epitomized the doctrines of the *Enlightenment*. Among the leading French figures in the *Enlightenment* were Montesquieu, Voltaire, Buffon, and Turgot. In England, Addison, Steele, Swift, Pope, Gibbon, Hume, Adam Smith, and Bentham responded to elements of *Enlightenment* thought; as did Moses Mendelssohn, Lessing, Herder, and Kant in Germany. In America, Franklin, Paine, and Jefferson were profoundly influenced by *Enlightenment* principles. The *Enlightenment* was the intellectual ferment out of which the French Revolution came, and it gave philosophical shape to the American Revolution and the two basic documents of the United States, the Declaration of Independence and the Constitution. See AGE OF JOHNSON, AGE OF REASON, DEISM.

Ennead Any set of nine. Porphyry's collection of Plotinus' works comprises six *enneads*, each containing nine books.

Enthymeme A SYLLOGISM informally stated and omitting either the major or the minor premise. The omitted premise is to be understood. Example: "Children should be seen and not heard. Be quiet, John." Here the minor premise—that John is a child—is left to the ingenuity of the reader. The order can be changed with no change in the operation of the figure: "Be quiet, John. Children should be seen and not heard."

Entr'acte An entertainment, often musical, in the interlude between the acts of a play.

Entrance The act of coming on stage. "Making an *entrance*" is doing so vividly.

Entry In an old usage, a PREFACE. Also a theatrical ENTRANCE. Usually applied to an individual item listed or entered in a record, diary, or catalog, as in "the entry for July 4."

Entwicklungsroman A German term for a type of BILDUNGSROMAN that emphasizes the development of the principal character. In English and American criticism the minute differences in such terms as *Entwicklungsroman* and ERZIEHUNGSROMAN are infrequently encountered.

Enumerative Bibliography A listing of works of a particular country, author, printer, or type, or on a particular subject.

Envelope A line or group of lines enclosing a body of verse, giving a sense of structure and closure. Sometimes a complete stanza may be repeated to form an *envelope*, as in Keats's "The Mermaid Tavern." Whitman frequently used the device as an organizational principle. The *In Memoriam* stanza is called an *envelope* stanza because the rhymes of the first and last lines enclose the middle lines, as in:

> We have but faith: we cannot know,
>   For knowledge is of things we see;
>   And yet we trust it comes from thee,
> A beam in darkness: let it grow.

Envoy (also **envoi**) A conventionalized stanza appearing at the close of certain kinds of poems; particularly associated with the French *BALLADE*. The *envoy* (1) is usually addressed to a prince, patron, or other person of importance; (2) repeats the refrain line used throughout the ballade; (3) consists normally of four lines; and (4) usually rhymes *bcbc*. An *envoy* comes as a shorter stanza at the end of the CHANT ROYAL and the SESTINA. At times, the *envoy* serves merely as a conventional summary and conclusion; at other times, however, as in the free-verse "*Envoi*" that closes Ezra Pound's *Hugh Selwyn Mauberley*, an *envoy* functions as a "sending" or "dispatching" poem. This usage tallies with the common diplomatic meaning of *envoy*, "one who is sent." An earlier English form of the plural, *invoyes*, meant "a list of things sent" and became the modern "invoice," which has been used in contemporary poetry for a certain kind of poem that is a "sending" and, by a punning analogy with INSCAPE and INSTRESS, contains an inner voice.

Epanalepsis The repetition at the end of a clause of a word or phrase that occurred at its beginning, as in Shakespeare's lines from *King John* (2, 1):

> Blood hath bought blood, and blows have answer'd blows:
> Strength match'd with strength, and power confronted power.

The device is used extensively by Milton and Whitman.

Epanaphora Repetition of words at the beginnings of lines or sentences; commonly called ANAPHORA.

Epanodos The repetition of the same word or phrase at the beginning and middle, or at the middle and end, of a sentence, as in *Ezekiel*, 35:6—"I will prepare thee unto blood, and blood shall pursue thee: sith thou hast not hated blood, even blood shall pursue thee." Also used for the reiteration of two or more things so as to make distinctions among them, as in "Mary and Elizabeth both spoke; Mary quietly but Elizabeth in harsh and angry tones." *Epanodos* is sometimes applied to progressive repetition, such as that in Touchstone's speech in *As You Like It* (3, 2): "Why, if thou never wast at court, thou never saw'st good manners; if thou never saw'st good manners, then thy manners must be wicked; and wickedness is sin, and sin is damnation." *Epanodos* is also applied to return to the main subject after a DIGRESSION.

Epenthesis The insertion of a sound or letter in a word, as when "family" is pronounced "fambly."

Ephemera Printed matter not intended to endure more than a short time. Some such things are of aesthetic interest as specimens of craft and taste, even if they have no long-term importance. There are collections of advertisements, streetcar tickets, and leaflets of every sort; about the time most people throw them out, they become collectible.

Epic A long narrative poem in elevated style presenting characters of high position in adventures forming an organic whole through their relation to a central heroic figure and through their development of episodes important to the history of a nation or race. According to one theory, the first *epics* took shape from the scattered work of various unknown poets, and through gradual accretion these episodes were molded into a sequence. This theory has largely given way to the belief that, although the materials may have developed in this way, the *epic* itself is the product of a single genius. *Epics* without certain authorship are called FOLK EPICS, whether one believes in a folk or a single-authorship theory of origins.

Most *epics* share certain characteristics: (1) The hero is of imposing stature, of national or international importance, and of great historical or legendary significance. (2) The setting is vast, covering great nations, the world, or the universe. (3) The action consists of deeds of great valor or requiring superhuman courage. (4) Supernatural forces—gods, angels, and demons—interest themselves in the action. (5) A style of sustained elevation is used. (6) The poet retains a measure of objectivity. To these general characteristics (some of which are omitted from particular *epics*) should be added a list of common devices employed by most *epic* poets: The poet opens by stating the theme, invoking a MUSE, and beginning the narrative IN MEDIAS RES—in the middle of things—giving the necessary exposition later; the poet includes catalogs of warriors, ships, armies; there are extended formal speeches by the main characters; and the poet makes frequent use of the EPIC SIMILE.

A few of the more important folk epics are: Homer's *Iliad and Odyssey*, the Old English *Beowulf*, the East Indian *Mahabharata*, the Spanish *Cid*, the Finnish *Kalevala*, the French *Song of Roland*, and the German *Nibelungenlied*. Some of the best-known ART EPICS are Virgil's *Aeneid*, Dante's *Divine Comedy* (although it lacks many of the distinctive characteristics of the *epic*), Tasso's *Jerusalem Delivered*, Milton's *Paradise Lost*. American poets in the late eighteenth and early nineteenth centuries struggled to produce a good *epic* on the American adventure, but without success. Longfellow's *Hiawatha* is an attempt at a Native American *epic*. Whitman's *Leaves of Grass*, considered as the autobiography of a generic American, is sometimes called an American *epic*, as are Stephen Vincent Benét's *John Brown's Body*, Ezra Pound's *Cantos*, and Hart Crane's *The Bridge*.

In the Middle Ages there was a great mass of literature verging on the *epic* in form and purpose though not answering strictly to the conventional formula. These are variously referred to as *epic* and as ROMANCE. Spenser's *The Faerie Queene* is the supreme example.

Epicede, Epicedium A funeral ODE. A group of Donne's poems are titled "Epicedes and Obsequies upon the Deaths of Sundry Persons."

Epic Formula The conventions of structure employed by most epic poets, such as the statement of theme, the invocation to the Muse, beginning IN MEDIAS RES, catalogs of warriors, extended formal speeches, and similar devices.

Epic Question The request or question addressed to the Muse at the beginning of an epic; the answer constitutes the narrative of the work.

Epic Simile An elaborated comparison. The *epic simile* differs from an ordinary simile in being more involved and ornate, in a conscious imitation of the Homeric manner. The VEHICLE is developed into an independent aesthetic object, an IMAGE that for the moment upstages the TENOR with which it is compared. The following is from *Paradise Lost*.

Angel Forms, who lay entranced
Thick as autumnal leaves that strow the brooks
In Vallombrosa, where the Etrurian shades
High over-arched embower; or scattered sedge
Afloat, when with fierce winds Orion armed
Hath vexed the Red-Sea coast, whose waves o'erthrew
Busiris and his Memphian chivalry,
While with perfidious hatred they pursued
The sojourners of Goshen, who beheld
From the safe shore their floating carcasses
And broken chariot-wheels.

Such a protracted comparison seems, on the one hand, to lead away from the subject, while at the same time making a vivid argument about the multitude of "Angel Forms" now rhetorically reduced in dignity to mere vegetation helplessly acted on by a more powerful force. The *epic simile* is also called the HOMERIC SIMILE.

Epicureanism A philosophy similar to that of the Greek Epicurus, who saw philosophy as the art of making life happy, with pleasure the highest goal, and pain and emotional disturbance the greatest evils. But Epicurus was not a simple hedonist (see HEDONISM); for him pleasure came not primarily from sensual delights but from serenity. Thus, intellectual processes were, he held, superior to bodily pleasures. He rejected the belief in an afterlife and the influence of the gods in human affairs, strongly asserted human freedom, and accepted the atomic theory of Democritus. In his social code Epicurus emphasized honesty, prudence, and justice, but chiefly as means through which one encounters the least trouble from society. The Epicurean, therefore, seeks not wine, women, and song but serenity of spirit. "Epicurean" is often but erroneously considered synonymous with hedonistic.

Epideictic Poetry Poetry written for special occasions, primarily for the pleasure and edification of its audience. Aristotle divided rhetoric into deliberative (to persuade), forensic (to condemn or praise actions), and *epideictic* (to demonstrate in ceremonial praise). Classical poetry grew increasingly *epideictic*, particularly in its DECADENT period. Common types of *epideictic poetry* are the ENCOMIUM and the EPITHALAMIUM.

Epigone A less distinguished follower or imitator of a work, author, or movement. The term comes from the Epigonoi (the sons of the Seven against Thebes) who imitated their fathers by themselves unsuccessfully attacking Thebes. Thus, "Thyrsis," by Matthew Arnold, might be called an *epigone* of the great English PASTORAL ELEGY tradition, or the HISTORICAL NOVELS of G. P. R. James might be called *epigones* of Sir Walter Scott's Waverly Novels.

Epigram A pithy saying. An *epigram* is often antithetical, as "Man proposes but God disposes," or La Rochefoucauld's "Only those deserving of scorn are apprehensive of it." The early *epigram* was characterized by compression, balance, and polish. Examples of the ancient *epigram* may be found in the *Greek Anthology* and in the work of Martial (A.D. 40–104), who supplied models for Ben Jonson, the greatest writer of *epigrams* in English. Martial had used the *epigram* for various purposes: eulogy, friendship, compliment, epitaphs, philosophic reflection, JEUX D'ESPRIT, and SATIRE. Although numerous *epigrams* were written by sixteenth-century English writers, notably John Heywood, they did not conform closely to the classical type. With the revolt against Elizabethan romanticism just before 1600, the classical *epigram* was cultivated, chiefly for satire. Many collections were published between 1596 and 1616, including a famous one of Sir John Harington (1615). Jonson wrote not only satirical *epigrams* but epistles, verses of compliment, epitaphs, and reflective verses. An *epigram* of this period typically consisted of two parts, an introduction stating the occasion or setting the tone and a conclusion sharply and tersely giving the point. In the eighteenth century the spirit, though not the form, of the *epigram* continued. Many of Pope's couplets are *epigrams* when separated from their context. Coleridge, too, indulged in the *epigram* on occasion, but Walter Savage Landor was its greatest and most persistent user after Jonson. In the twentieth century a number of poets kept up the tradition of *epigrams* telling and witty: Robert Frost, Ezra Pound, Howard Nemerov, Richard Wilbur, X. J. Kennedy, J. V. Cunningham, Jonathan Williams, John Hollander, and Roy A. Blount, Jr.

Epigraph An inscription on stone or on a statue or a coin. In literature an *epigraph* is a quotation on the title page of a book or a motto heading a section of a work.

Epigraphy (1) Inscriptions collectively; (2) the study of inscriptions, defined as any symbol impressed in any way on stone, metal, wood, and so forth. Because the material on which these matters are inscribed is uncommonly durable, *epigraphy* can study symbols of prodigious antiquity and primitiveness. Linguistic forms—and even misspellings—can be invaluable in the reconstruction of the early stages of a language. In many cases, nothing remains of an extinct language except a few inscriptions.

Epilogue A concluding statement. Sometimes used in the sense of PERORATION but more generally applied to the final remarks of an actor addressed to the audience. An *epilogue* is opposed to a PROLOGUE, which introduces a play. Puck, in *A Midsummer Night's Dream*, recites an *epilogue* that is characteristic of Renaissance plays in that it solicits the goodwill of the audience and courteous treatment by critics. As the use of *epilogues* became more general, respected poets were paid to contribute *epilogues* to plays much as forewords written by prominent authors are now sometimes paid for by publishers. *Epilogues* were a part of major dramatic efforts in the late seventeenth and eighteenth centuries, disappearing from common use about the middle of the nineteenth. They are now rare.

Epimyth, Epimythium The SENTENTIA or moral statement placed at the end of a FABLE.

Epinicion A choral ODE commemorating a victory in the national Games of ancient Greece. The best remembered poets writing such poems are Simonides and Pindar.

Epiphany Literally, a manifestation or showing-forth, usually of some divine being. The Christian festival of *Epiphany* commemorates the manifestation of Christ to the Gentiles in the form of the Magi. It is celebrated on Twelfth Night, January 6. *Epiphany* was given currency as a critical term by James Joyce, who used it to designate an event in which the essential nature of something—a person, a situation, an object—was suddenly perceived. It is thus an intuitive grasp of reality achieved in a quick flash of recognition in which something, usually simple and commonplace, is seen in a new light, and, as Joyce says, "its soul, its whatness leaps to us from the vestment of its appearance." This sudden insight is the *epiphany*. The term is also used for a literary composition that presents such *epiphanies*, so that we say that the stories that make up Joyce's *Dubliners* are *epiphanies*.

Epiphonema A brief summary of an argument, often a quotation or MAXIM, appended as a MORAL.

Epirrhema A feature of the comedy of Aristophanes: a satiric speech on affairs of the day.

Episode An incident presented as one continuous action. Though having a unity within itself, the *episode* in any composition is usually accompanied by other *episodes* woven together to create a total work. In Greek drama, an *episode* referred to that part of a tragedy presented between two choruses. More narrowly, the term is sometimes used for an incident injected into a piece of fiction simply to illuminate character or to create background without advancing the action. Installments of radio and television daytime dramas are routinely called *episodes*.

Episodic Structure A term applied to writing that consists of little more than a series of incidents, with the episodes succeeding each other, with no particularly logical arrangement or complication. Travel books naturally fall into *episodic structure*. The term is applied also to long narratives that may contain complicated plots, such as the Italian ROMANTIC EPIC, if the action is made leisurely by the use of numerous episodes employed to develop character or plot. The METRICAL ROMANCE and the PICARESQUE NOVEL are said to have *episodic structure*.

Epistle An *epistle* is any LETTER, but the term is usually limited to formal compositions written to a distant individual or group. The most familiar use of the term, of course, is to characterize certain books of the New Testament. The *epistle* differs from the letter in that it is a conscious literary form rather than a spontaneous, chatty, private composition. Ordinarily the *epistle* is associated with scriptural writing of the past, but this is by no means a necessary restriction. It is regularly applied to a formal letter of dedication traditionally called "*epistle* dedicatory." Pope used it to describe formal letters in verse.

Epistolary Literature Literature, usually prose fiction, entirely or partly written as letters. Arthur Hugh Clough's "Amours de Voyage" (1849) could be described as an epistolary NOVELLA in verse. The American poets William Stafford and Marvin Bell published a book called *Segues: A Correspondence in Poetry* (1983). Ted Hughes's last work was *Birthday Letters* (1998), a book of poems about his marriage to Sylvia Plath.

Epistolary Novel A novel in which the narrative is carried forward by LETTERS written by one or more of the characters. It has the merit of giving the author an opportunity to present the feelings and reactions without the intrusion of the author; it further gives a sense of immediacy, because the letters are usually written in the thick of the action. The *epistolary novel* also enables the author to present multiple POINTS OF VIEW on the same event. It is also a device for creating VERISIMILITUDE, the author merely serving as "editor" for the correspondence.

Samuel Richardson's *Pamela* (1740) is frequently considered the first English *epistolary novel*, although the use of letters to tell stories and to give racy gossip and instruction goes back in England at least as far as some primitive examples from the mid-sixteenth century and Nicholas Breton's *A Poste with a Packet of Mad Letters* (1602) and includes such other precursors as Aphra Behn's *Love Letters Between a Nobleman and His Sister* (1682). Richardson's *Clarissa Harlowe* (1748) is certainly the greatest, as it is the most extended, of *epistolary novels*. The form was popular in the eighteenth century, particularly for the SENTIMENTAL NOVEL. Other notable examples are Smollett's *Humphrey Clinker* (1771) and Fanny Burney's *Evelina* (1778), as well as the first draft of Jane Austen's *Sense and Sensibility*. Goethe's *The Sorrows of Young Werther* (1774), Choderlos de Laclos's *Dangerous Liaisons* (1782), and A. W. Kinglake's *Eŏthen* are *epistolary*.

The epistolary method has not often been successfully used in the nineteenth and twentieth centuries, although the use of letters within novels has been common. J. P. Marquand's *The Late George Apley*, John O'Hara's *Pal Joey*, John Barth's *Letters*, and Alice Walker's *The Color Purple* are modern instances of epistolary fiction.

[References: Godfrey Frank Singer, *The Epistolary Novel* (1963); Natascha Würzbach, ed., *The Novel in Letters* (1969).]

Epistrophe A rhetorical term applied to the repetition of the closing word or phrase at the end of several clauses, as in Sidney's "And all the night he did nothing but weep Philoclea, sigh Philoclea, and cry out Philoclea" (*The New Arcadia*).

Epitaph An inscription used to mark burial places. Commemorative verses or lines appearing on tombs or written as if intended for such use. Since the days of early Egyptian records, *epitaphs* have had a long and interesting history, and, although they have changed as to purpose and form, they show less development than most literary types. The information usually incorporated in such memorials includes the name of the deceased, the dates of birth and death, age, profession (if a dignified one), together with some pious motto. Many prominent writers—notably Jonson, Milton, Pope, and Auden—have left *epitaphs* they wrote in tribute to the dead. Early *epitaphs* were usually serious and dignified—because they appeared chiefly on the tombs of the great—but more recently they have, either consciously or unconsciously, taken on humorous qualities. One of the most famous inscriptions is that marking Shakespeare's burial place:

Good frend, for Jesus sake forbeare
To digg the dust encloased here;
Bleste be ye man yt spares thes stones,
And curst be he yt moves my bones,—

but this is as much a CURSE as an *epitaph*. "O rare Ben Jonson"—which may be a serious pun on *orare* (pray for)—and "*Exit* Burbage" are two examples of effective *epitaphs*. A famous French inscription is from Père Lachaise in Paris:

Ci-gît ma femme: ah! que c'est bien
Pour son repos, et pour le mien!

The *epitaph* "On the Countess Dowager of Pembroke," once attributed to Ben Jonson but now credited to William Browne, deserves quotation:

Underneath this sable hearse
Lies the subject of all verse:
Sidney's sister, Pembroke's mother.
Death, ere thou hast slain another,
Fair and learned and good as she,
Time shall throw a dart at thee.

Epitasis The RISING ACTION of a drama. See DRAMATIC STRUCTURE.

Epithalamium (or **Epithalamion**) A poem written to celebrate a wedding. Many ancient poets (Pindar, Sappho, Theocritus, and Catullus) as well as modern poets (the French Ronsard and the English Spenser) have cultivated the form. Perhaps Spenser's *Epithalamion* (1595), written to celebrate his own marriage, is the finest English example. The successive stanzas treat such topics as: invocation to the muses to help praise his bride; awakening of the bride by music; decking of the bridal path with flowers; adorning of the bride by nymphs; assembling of the guests; description of the physical and spiritual beauty of the bride; the bride at the altar; the marriage feast; welcoming the night; asking the blessing of Diana, Juno, and the stars. Any number of later works, from Coleridge's *Rime of the Ancient Mariner* to Salinger's "Raise High the Roof Beam, Carpenters," exploit various engaging features of the tradition of the *epithalamium*.

Epithet Strictly, an adjective used to point out a characteristic of a person or thing, as Goldsmith's "noisy mansions" (for schoolhouses), but sometimes applied to a noun or noun phrase used for a similar purpose, as Shakespeare's "the trumpet of the dawn" (for the cock). Memorable *epithets* are often figurative, as Keats's "snarling trumpets" and Milton's "laboring clouds." Classical literature is mocked in Milton's *Paradise Regained*:

> Remove their swelling Epithets thick laid
> As varnish on a Harlot's cheek, the rest,
> Thin sown with aught of profit or delight,
> Will far be found unworthy to compare
> With *Sion's* songs. . . .

The HOMERIC EPITHET, often a compound adjective, as "all-seeing" Jove, "swiftfooted" Achilles, "blue-eyed" Athena, "rosy-fingered" dawn, depends on aptness combined with familiarity rather than on freshness or variety. It is almost a formulaic part of a name. Because *epithets* often play a prominent part in the name-calling that characterizes invective or personal SATIRE, some have the mistaken notion that an *epithet* is always uncomplimentary.

A TRANSFERRED EPITHET is an adjective used to limit grammatically a noun that it does not logically modify, though the relation is so close that the meaning is left clear, as Shakespeare's "dusty death," or Milton's "blind mouths." The same device turns up in such common terms as "foreign policy" and "abnormal psychology": the policy itself is not foreign but rather domestic—one state's policy with respect to foreign states; the psychology itself is not abnormal but rather normal—the psychological study of abnormality.

Epitome A summary or ABRIDGMENT. A "miniature representation" of a subject. Thus, the Magna Charta has been called the *epitome* of the rights of English people, and Ruskin referred to St. Mark's as an *epitome* of the changes of Venetian architecture through a period of nine centuries.

Epitrite In classical prosody, a foot consisting of one short and three long syllables; in the "first *epitrite*" the short syllable comes first, second in the second, and so forth.

Epitrope A rhetorical submission (either genuine or ironic) to an opponent.

Epizeuxis Empathic repetition.

Epode One of the three stanza forms in the PINDARIC ODE. The others are STROPHE and ANTISTROPHE.

Eponym The name of a person so commonly associated with some widely recognized attribute that the name comes to stand for the attribute, as Helen for beauty, Croesus for wealth, Machiavelli for duplicity, or Caesar for dictator. *Eponym* also means the name of some historical or legendary personage, such as Hellen, Romulus, Israel, or Bolívar, whose name has been bestowed on a place or people (Hellas, Rome, Israel, Bolivia). Some *eponyms* are clearly traceable, such as those of Constantinople and Leningrad; others, such as the hero called Dardanus in the prehistory of the Dardans, are more obscure. Sometimes names that become applied to general entities—such as "bloomers" and "boycott"—are also called *eponyms*.

Epopee Epic poetry in general or (more rarely) a particular EPIC.

Epyllion A NARRATIVE POEM usually presenting an episode from the heroic past and resembling an EPIC but much briefer and more limited. Matthew Arnold's *Sohrab and Rustum* and Tennyson's *Idylls of the King* are *epyllions*.

Equivalence In METRICS, a kind of SUBSTITUTION, in which a FOOT equal to the one expected but different from it is used. In quantitative verse, one long syllable was considered the *equivalent* of two short syllables, and thus a SPONDEE (two long syllables) could be substituted for an ANAPEST (two shorts and a long) or for a DACTYL (a long and two shorts). See SUBSTITUTION, COMPENSATION.

Equivoque A kind of PUN in which language is so used that it has two different but appropriate meanings. If the *equivoque* is used with the intention to deceive, the result is equivocation, as in "Nothing is too good for him," which sounds like a compliment but is intended as a condemnation.

Erastianism The doctrine that the civil authority has dominance over the church in all matters. It is attributed to Thomas Erastus, a sixteenth-century Swiss theologian, who insisted that the civil authority and not the church should act in all punitive measures, but who did not intend to give the state authority in ecclesiastical matters, although the doctrine named for him came to mean such civil dominance over spiritual matters. *Erastianism* became an issue in England during the OXFORD MOVEMENT controversies. The Public Worship Act of 1874 attempted to "put down Ritualism" as it had developed under the Oxford Movement. The Act was vigorously and successfully resisted by Pusey and his followers as an instance of *Erastianism*.

Erethism An exaggerated degree of mental or emotional excitement; a term occasionally applied to highly passionate writers such as Percy Shelley and Hart Crane.

Ergodic Literature Espen J. Aarseth, borrowing a term from physics and statistics (involving roots meaning "work" and "path"), applies "ergodic" to "open, dynamic texts in which the reader must perform specific actions to generate a literary sequence, which may vary for every reading." Such texts include video games and interactive or collaborative works, especially if electronically preserved.

[Reference: Espen J. Aarseth, *Cybertext: Perspectives on Ergodic Literature* (1997).]

Erotema (also **Erotesis**) Obsolete term meaning RHETORICAL QUESTION.

Erotic Literature (or **Erotica**) A type of writing characterized by treatment of sexual love in more or less explicit detail. Although the inclusive term "the literature of love" includes the *erotic*, writings customarily labeled "love story" or "love poetry" usually avoid the specific sexual details and words ordinarily associated with *erotic literature*. On the other hand, *erotic literature* need not include PORNOGRAPHY, which employs sexual material as an end in itself. In *erotic literature* the sexual element is a portion of the aesthetic, thematic, or moral aspect of the work; that is, it contributes to some other objective than titillation or sexual arousal. Erotic elements may be used aesthetically, as in Ovid's *Ars Amatoria* or Spenser's *Epithalamion*; thematically, as in Indian scriptures or D. H. Lawrence's *Lady Chatterley's Lover*; or metaphorically, as in the Song of Songs. In the medieval FABLIAUX, erotic materials were put to comic use, sometimes with great skill, as in Chaucer's "Miller's Tale." Love and its sexual expression are among the permanent central issues of literature, and they are present to some degree in much of the world's great writing.

Errata Plural of *erratum*, a mistake. A list of printing errors, often appended to a text after publication.

Erziehungsroman The novel of upbringing or education. Strictly speaking, *Erziehungsroman* and BILDUNGSROMAN are synonymous, but in customary usage Bildungsroman is the more general, including the *Erziehungsroman*, the ENTWICKLUNGSROMAN, and the KÜNSTLERROMAN. These fine distinctions, except for KÜNSTLERROMAN, tend to be lost in English and American criticism.

Escape Literature Writing whose clear intention is to amuse and beguile by offering readers a strong world, exciting adventures, or puzzling mysteries. It aims at no higher purpose than amusement. Adventure stories, DETECTIVE STORIES, tales of FANTASY, and many humorous stories are frankly *escape literature*, and they exist for no other purpose than to translate readers for a time from the care-ridden actual world to an entrancing world of the imagination. Longfellow, in "The Day Is Done," defined the effect of *escape literature*:

Come, read to me some poem,
Some simple and heartfelt lay,
That shall soothe this restless feeling,
And banish the thoughts of day.
And the night shall be filled with music.
And the cares that infest the day
Shall fold their tents, like the Arabs,
And as silently steal away.

Esemplastic A term applied by Coleridge to the quality in the IMAGINATION that enables it to shape disparate things into a unified whole. The word means "molding into a unity." In *Look Homeward, Angel*, Thomas Wolfe uses the word "esymplastic"— an instance of creative misspelling.

Esperanto An artificial speech constructed from roots common to the chief European languages and designed for universal use. *Esperanto* was devised by Dr. L. L. Zamenhof, a Russian, and took its name from Zamenhof's pseudonym, "Dr. Esperanto," used in signing his first pamphlet on the subject in 1887. The grammar is so simple as to be clear after a few minutes' study, the spelling is strictly phonetic, the language is euphonious and adaptable, and pronunciation is easy because the accent always falls on the penult. However, *Esperanto* gives no promise of becoming a universal tongue.

Essay A moderately brief prose discussion of a restricted topic. Classifying the *essay* has eluded human skill. A basic and very useful division can, however, be made: formal and informal. The *informal essay* includes aphoristic *essays* such as Bacon's, PERIODICAL ESSAYS such as Addison's, and PERSONAL ESSAYS such as Lamb's. Qualities that make an *essay* informal include: the personal element, humor, graceful style, rambling structure, unconventionality or novelty, freedom from stiffness and affectation, incomplete or tentative treatment of topic. Qualities of the *formal essay* include: serious purpose, dignity, logical organization, length. The term may include both short discussions, expository or argumentative (such as the serious magazine article), and longer treatises (such as the chapters in Carlyle's *Heroes and Hero-Worship*). However, a sharp distinction between even formal and informal *essays* cannot be maintained at all times. In the following sketch the informal essay will be given chief consideration, because it falls better into the realm of literature.

The French philosopher Montaigne collected pithy sayings— MAXIMS, APHORISMS, ADAGES, APOTHEGMS, PROVERBS—along with ANECDOTES and quotations from his reading. He developed the habit of recording also the results of self-analysis and became attracted by the idea that he was himself representative of human beings in general. He published his first collection of such writings in two volumes in 1580 under the title *Essais*—the first use of the word for short prose discussions. The word means "attempts," and by its use Montaigne indicated that his discussions were tentative. By adding the personal element to the aphoristic *leçon morale*, Montaigne created the modern *essay*. "Myself," he said, "am the groundwork of my book." Mainly philosophical and ethical, the *essays* cover a wide range of topics, such as "Of Idleness," "Of Liars," "Of Ready and Slow Speech," "Of Smells and Odors," "Of Cannibals," "Of Sleeping," and "Upon Some Verses of Virgil."

When Francis Bacon published in 1597 his first collection of aphoristic *essays*, he borrowed his title, *Essays*, from Montaigne's book— and became the first English "essayist." The ten *essays* initially published were short and consisted chiefly of a collection of maxims on a given subject. The book was very popular, and enlarged editions were issued in 1612 and 1625. The later *essays* are longer, more personal, and developed by a wealth of illustration and quotation. The "aphoristic" quality of Bacon's style is seen in such typical quotations as these: "The errors of young men are the ruin of business," and "He that hath a wife and children hath given hostages to fortune." Bacon's *essays*, like the Renaissance COURTESY BOOKS, had for their chief purpose the giving of useful advice to those who wished to get on in practical life.

After Bacon the seventeenth century contributed little to the development of the informal *essay*. There was, however, much prose writing closely related to the informal and formal *essay*. The chapters of Sir Thomas Browne's *Religio Medici* (1642) in their style as well as their tendency toward self-revelation and moralizing suggest the informal *essay*. So do the miscellaneous sketches in Ben Jonson's *Timber, or Discoveries Made upon Men and Matter* (1640). Dryden's *Essay of Dramatick Poesie* (1668) is an example of a critical *essay* in dialogue form. Milton's *Areopagitica*, in form an argumentative address, is a masterly example of a formal *essay*. Related to *essay* writing are such long prose treatises as Robert Burton's *Anatomy of Melancholy* (1621), Locke's *Essay Concerning Human Understanding* (1690), and Izaak Walton's *Compleat Angler* (1653).

The formal EPISTLE as a vehicle for writing much like the informal *essay* appeared in James Howell's *Epistolae Ho-Elianae: Familiar Letters* (1650). The seventeenth century also saw the development in English of the CHARACTER, a brief sketch of a quality or personality type. It became popular and exerted an appreciable influence on the periodical *essay* of the eighteenth century, partly, to be sure, through the work of a French writer of characters, La Bruyère, who had combined the character with the *essay*.

The second great step in the history of the informal *essay* came in the early eighteenth century with the creation by Steele and Addison of the periodical *essay*. In 1691 Dunton's *Athenian Gazette*, a new type of PERIODICAL, had appeared, small in format and designed to entertain as well as instruct. A feature of Daniel Defoe's *A Weekly Review of Affairs in France* (1704) had been a department called "Advice from the Scandalous Club," gossipy in character. From this germ Richard Steele developed the new *essay* in his *Tatler* (1709–1711). The purpose was "to recommend truth, innocence, honor, virtue, as the chief ornaments of life." Joseph Addison and Steele later launched the informal daily *Spectator* (1711–1712; 1714). The new *essay* was affected not only by its periodical form, which prescribed the length, but by the spirit of the times. Renaissance individualism was giving way to a centering of interest in society, and the moral reaction from the excesses of the Restoration made timely the effort of the essayists to reform manners, refine tastes, and provide topics for discussion at the popular coffeehouses of London.

As compared with earlier *essays*, the periodical *essay* is briefer, less aphoristic, less intimate and introspective, less individualistic, less "learned," and more informal, making more use of HUMOR and SATIRE and embracing a wider range of topics. It appeals to the middle classes as well as to the cultivated, but the city reader seems always to have been in the authors' minds. Addison referred to two types of *Spectator* papers: "serious essays" on such well-worn topics as death, marriage, education, and friendship; and "occasional papers," dealing with the "folly, extravagance, and caprice of the present age." The latter class especially aided in fixing as a tradition of the informal *essay* that informality, whimsicality, humor, and grace that appear in scores of *essays* on such topics as fashion, dueling, witchcraft, coffee houses, and family portraits. The type developed much machinery, such as fictitious characters, clubs, and imaginary correspondents.

The popularity of the form led to many imitations, such as the *Guardian*, the *Female Tatler*, and the *Whisperer*, and such writers as Swift, Pope, and Berkeley contributed *essays*. Later in the century Samuel Johnson (in the *Rambler*, 1750–1752, and the *Idler* papers, 1758–1760), Lord Chesterfield, Horace Walpole, and Oliver Goldsmith appeared as accomplished informal essayists. Goldsmith's *Letters from a Citizen of the World* (1760–1761) are noted examples of the form. After Goldsmith the *essay* declined as a literary form.

A revival of interest in the writing of both formal and informal *essays* accompanied the romantic movement. The informal type responded to the impulses of the time. The production of the personal *essay* was stimulated by the development of a new type of periodical: *Blackwood's Magazine* (1817) and the *London Magazine* (1820), which provided a market for the *essays* of Lamb, Hazlitt, Hunt, De Quincey, and others. Lamb's *Essay of Elia* (begun in 1820) exhibited an intimate style, an autobiographical interest, an easy humor and sentiment, an urbanity and refined literary taste. Freed from the space restrictions of the *Tatler* type and encouraged by a public eager for "original" work, these writers modified the Addisonian *essay* by making it more personal, longer, and more varied. Late in the century a successor to Lamb appeared in Robert Louis Stevenson, for whose whimsical humor, nimble imagination, and buoyant style, the personal *essay* formed an ideal medium. Later writers of the informal essay in England are A. C. Benson, G. K. Chesterton, E. V. Lucas, George Orwell, Malcolm Muggeridge, Laurie Lee, Kingsley Amis, and Clive James.

The formal *essay* of the early nineteenth century was largely the result of the appearance of the critical magazine, especially the *Edinburgh Review* (1802), the *Quarterly Review* (1809), and the *Westminster Review* (1824). Book reviews in the form of long critical *essays* were written by Francis Jeffrey, Macaulay, De Quincey, Scott, Carlyle, and later by George Eliot, Matthew Arnold, and many others. The separate chapters in the books of such writers as Thomas Carlyle, John Ruskin, Walter Pater, T. H. Huxley, Matthew Arnold, J. S. Mill, and Cardinal Newman are essaylike.

Though there is some reflection of *essay* literature in such early American writers as Cotton Mather, Jonathan Edwards, Franklin, Jefferson, Hamilton, and such itinerants as Tom Paine and J. H. St. John de Crèvecoeur, the first really great literary essayist in America is Washington Irving, whose *Sketch-Book* (1820) contains *essays* of the Addisonian type. Some of Thoreau's works (e.g., *Walden*) exhibited characteristics of the informal *essay*, and Oliver Wendell Holmes in *The Autocrat of the Breakfast Table* (1857) wrote informal, humorous *essays*. Ralph Waldo Emerson, fired with transcendental idealism, became the best known of all American essayists. Edgar Allan Poe produced important critical *essays*. Later able essayists, formal or informal, include W. D. Howells and Mark Twain. More recent names are those of Henry Van Dyke, Paul Elmer More, H. L. Mencken, Christopher Morley, James Thurber, E. B. White, Gore Vidal, Rachel Carson, James Baldwin, Joan Didion, Susan Sontag, and L. E. Sissman.

The formal *essay*, instead of crystallizing into a set literary type, has tended to become diversified in form, spirit, and length. At one extreme it is represented by the brief, serious magazine article and at the other by scientific or philosophical treatises, which are books rather than *essays*. The technique of the formal *essay* is now practically identical with that of all factual or theoretical prose in which literary effect is secondary. The informal *essay*, on the other hand, beginning in aphoristic and moralistic writing, animated by the injection of the personal, broadened and lightened by a free treatment of human manners, controlled somewhat by the limitations of periodical publication, has developed into a recognizable genre, the first purpose of which is to entertain. As such, the form has aided in giving something of a Gallic grace to other forms of prose, notably letter writing. But, valuable though its contributions to prose writing have been and respected as it is today as a genre, the informal *essay* has had few skillful or serious practitioners in the twentieth century. After the Second World War, the frontier between fiction and journalism became a robust environment for essayists such as Alice Walker, John Hersey, Norman Mailer, William F. Buckley, Jr., John McPhee, Roy A. Blount, Jr., Tom Wolfe, and Hunter S. Thompson, Jr.

Essentialism A philosophical position, opposed by EXISTENTIALISM, holding that the business of philosophy is to seek out and express real essences of things.

Establishing Shot The opening shot of a film sequence, usually with a substantial distance between the camera and the scene, so that characters and actions are visibly placed in context. It is usually followed by the camera's moving in closer.

Estates From the Middle Ages until about 1800, European politics recognized three so-called *estates*: the first was the clergy (Lords Spiritual); the second the nobility (Lords Temporal); the third the bourgeoisie (Commons). In time, a fourth estate was jocularly added (Lords Journalistic).

Ethos The character of the speaker or writer as reflected in speech or writing; the quality or set of emotions that a speaker or writer enacts in order to affect an audience. Aristotle divided the elements of persuasion into the devices of rhetoric and the value of the speaker's character. The *ethos* of a composition may also be considered the image of its maker that it projects. For Aristotle the image of a persuasive speaker should be that of a person of intelligence, rectitude, and goodwill. Quintilian distinguished between pathos, which he used for violent emotions, and *ethos*, which he used for the calmer emotions. In Renaissance criticism, *ethos* was often used simply to mean CHARACTER. In Aristotle's *Poetics*, *ethos* (moral character) ranks after *mythos* (PLOT) among the qualitative parts of a literary work.

Etiquette Books (Renaissance) Books of instruction in manners, conduct, and the art of governing for young princes and noblemen. See COURTESY BOOKS.

Euchologion A prayer book or book of ritual, especially in the Greek Church.

Euhemerism A Sicilian Greek named Euhemerus of around the fourth century B.C. has given his name to a practice of explaining myths as the exaggeration of human stories, so that gods are understood to be deified heroes and kings. *Euhemerism* is also applied to any practical or common-sense reading of a far-fetched story. Actaeon, say, devoured by his own hounds because of some offense to Artemis, is interpreted to be a person bankrupted ("eaten up") by a fanatical devotion to hunting. The account in Genesis of Lot's wife becoming a pillar of salt is euhemerized into an explanation of some peculiar salt formations, such as those on Jebel Usdum.

Eulogy A dignified, formal speech or writing, praising a person or a thing. See ENCOMIUM.

Euphemism A device in which indirectness replaces directness of statement, usually in an effort to avoid offensiveness.

To say "at liberty" instead of "out of work," "senior citizens" instead of "old people," "in the family way" instead of "pregnant," "anti-Semite" instead of "Jew-hater," and "pass away" instead of "die" is to practice *euphemism* of one sort or another. It is possible for *euphemism* to signal false delicacy, insincerity, hypocrisy, sentimentality, or excessive modesty; *euphemism* may also mean a decent respect for the feelings of others. There can also be a measure of irony in *euphemism*, as when a novel about desertion in wartime is called *A Farewell to Arms*.

Euphony Pleasing sounds. Opposite of CACOPHONY, the subjective impression of unpleasantness of sound. It has been difficult to establish that sounds as such can be either pleasing or unpleasing in isolation from meaning: It is conceivable that "South Dakota" or "free refills" may impress certain partisans as beautiful sounds. In some cases, the relative difficulty of certain articulations in a given language may constitute cacophony, whereas relative ease makes for *euphony*; but these responses remain relative and subjective. Some hearers find *euphony* even in "Schenectady" and "sphygmomanometer." Generously allowing for subjective interpretation, we can suppose that unvoiced consonants are more abrupt (*p*, *t*, *k*, *f*, *s*), voiced consonants are relatively softer (*b*, *d*, *g*, *v*, *z*), and simple vowels nicely varied between front and back, high and low are relatively more pleasing than diphthongs and monotones. A persistent legend of folk-linguistics claims that "cellar door" has been found to be the most euphonious phrase in English.

Euphuism An affected style that flourished late in the sixteenth century in England, especially in court circles. It took its name from *Euphues* (1578, 1580) by John Lyly. Its chief characteristics are: balanced construction, often antithetical and combined with alliteration; excessive use of the rhetorical question; and a heaping up of similes, illustrations, and examples, especially those drawn from the mythology and "unnatural natural history" about the fabulous qualities of animals and plants. Following are some typical passages from *Euphues*: "Be sober but not too sullen; be valiant but not too venturous"; "For as the finest ruby staineth the color of the rest that be in place, or as the sun dimmeth the moon, so this gallant girl more fair than fortunate and yet more fortunate than faithful," etc.; "Do we not commonly see that in painted pots is hidden the deadliest poison? that in the greenest grass is the greatest serpent? in the clearest water the ugliest toad?"; "Being incensed against the one as most pernicious and enflamed with the other as most precious." Lyly did not invent *euphuism*; rather he wittily combined and popularized elements that others had developed. Important forerunners of Lyly in England were Lord Berners, in his translation of Froissart's *Chronicle* (1523, 1525); Sir Thomas North's translation (1557) of *The Dial of Princes* by Guevara (whose Spanish itself was highly colored); and George Pettie in his *A Petite Palace of Pettie his Pleasure* (1576). One of Pettie's sentences, for example, reads: "Nay, there was never bloody tiger that did so terribly tear the little lamb, as this tyrant did furiously fare with the fair Philomela."

The chief vogue of *euphuism* was in the 1580s. Courtiers cultivated it for social conversation, and such writers as Robert Greene and Thomas Lodge used it in their novels (as *Menaphon* and *Rosalynde*). Sir Philip Sidney reacted against it and was followed by many others. Shakespeare both employed it and ridiculed it in *Love's Labour's Lost*. In a justly famous scene between Falstaff and Prince Hal, Shakespeare mocks the euphuistic style (*Henry IV*, Part I, 2, 4).

Though the extravagance and artificiality of *euphuism* make it seem ludicrous today, it actually played a powerful and beneficial role in the development of English prose. It established the idea that prose (formerly heavy and Latinized) might be written with imagination and fancy, and its emphasis on short clauses and sentences and on balanced construction aided in imparting clarity. These virtues of clearness, lightness, and pleasant ornamentation remained as a permanent contribution after a better taste had eliminated the vices of extravagant artificiality.

Eutopia A good place. The Greek roots of this word are unambiguous. Sir Thomas More used both *Eutopia* and UTOPIA in his *Utopia* (1516), but the latter, which sounds like the former, seems to mean "no place." Some consider the words synonyms, others consider one a mistake for the other, while yet others regard them as opposites. It is to More's credit that his inventiveness has given the world two words that have occupied its attention for almost 500 years and inspired others to create "cacotopia" (Jeremy Bentham) and "dystopia" (John Stuart Mill).

Examen A detailed study. John Dryden's *Of Dramatick Poesy: An Essay* includes an *examen* of Ben Jonson's *Epicene, or The Silent Woman*.

Exciting Force The force that starts the conflict of opposing interests and sets in motion the RISING ACTION of a play. Example: the witches' prophecy to Macbeth, which stirs him to schemes for making himself king. See DRAMATIC STRUCTURE.

Excursus A formal, lengthy DIGRESSION.

Exegesis An explanation and interpretation of a text. It is applied to the detailed study of the Bible. When used in reference to a literary text, it usually implies a close analysis and is equivalent to EXPLICATION DE TEXTE.

Exemplum (plural, ***Exempla***) A moralized tale. Just as modern preachers often make use of illustrations, so medieval preachers made extensive use of tales, anecdotes, and incidents, both historical and legendary, to point morals or illustrate doctrines. Often highly artificial and to a modern reader incredible, these "examples" seem to have appealed strongly to medieval congregations because of their concreteness, narrative, and human interest, as well as their moral implications. An important collection was Jacques de Vitry's *Exempla* (early thirteenth century). At times sermons degenerated into series of anecdotes, sometimes even humorous in character. Dante in thirteenth-century Italy and Wycliffe in fourteenth-century England protested against this tendency, and Wycliffe, as part of his reform program, omitted *exempla* from his own sermons. The influence of *exempla* and example-books on medieval literature was great, as may be illustrated from several of Chaucer's poems. The "Nun's Priest's Tale," for example, uses *exempla*, as when Chanticleer tells Pertelot anecdotes to prove that dreams have a meaning. The "Pardoner's Tale" is itself an *exemplum* to show how Avarice leads to an evil end.

Exequy, Exequies Formally, a funeral rite. From the title of Bishop Henry King's poem on the death of his wife, "An Exequy to His Matchless Never To Be Forgotten Friend," *exequy* has been taken to mean "funeral ode."

Exergasia, Exargasia A single point made over and over in different ways, something established and reestablished; a repetition of one idea in various forms, as in "false, fake, phony, fraud" or "nothing, nought, nada, nichts, zilch, zip."

Exergue Originally a small space on a coin, medal, or other such artifact. The *exergue* is set apart for a minor inscription. The term is also used for a set of EPIGRAPH-like quotations near the beginning of Jacques Derrida's *Of Grammatology* (tr. 1976).

Existential Criticism A school of criticism, led by Jean-Paul Sartre, that questions the legitimacy of traditional questions and examines a literary work in terms of the ways in which it explores the *existential* questions and in terms of its *existential* impact on the reader. See EXISTENTIALISM.

Existentialism A group of attitudes (current in philosophical, religious, and artistic thought during and after the Second World War) that emphasizes existence rather than essence and sees the inadequacy of human reason to explain the enigma of the universe as the basic philosophical question. The term is so broadly and loosely used that an exact definition is not possible. In its modern expression it had its beginning in the writings of the nineteenth-century Danish theologian, Søren Kierkegaard. The German philosopher Martin Heidegger is important in its formulation, and the French novelist-philosopher Jean-Paul Sartre did the most to give it form and popularity. *Existentialism* has found art and literature to be unusually effective methods of expression; in the novels of Franz Kafka, Dostoyevski, Camus, and Simone de Beauvoir, and in the plays and novels of Sartre and Samuel Beckett, and the plays of Eugène Ionesco, it found its most persuasive media. Basically, the existentialist assumes that existence precedes essence, that the significant fact is that we and things in general exist, but that these things have no meaning for us except as we can create meaning through acting upon them. Sartre claims that the fundamental truth of *existentialism* is in Descartes' formula, "I think; therefore, I exist." The existential philosophy is concerned with the personal commitment of this unique existing individual in the human situation. It attempts to codify the irrational aspect of human nature, to objectify nonbeing or nothingness and see it as a universal source of fear, to distrust concepts, and to emphasize experiential concreteness. The existentialist's point of departure is human beings' immediate awareness of their situation.

A part of this is a sense of meaninglessness in the outer world; this meaninglessness produces discomfort, anxiety, loneliness in the face of limitations, and desire to invest experience with meaning by acting upon the world, although efforts to act in a meaningless, "absurd" world lead to anguish, greater loneliness, and despair. Human beings are totally free but also wholly responsible for what they make of themselves. This freedom and responsibility are the sources for their most intense anxiety. Such a philosophical attitude can result in nihilism and hopelessness, as, indeed, it has with many of the literary existentialists. Patently, however, purely nihilistic art is a practical impossibility, any creative act constituting a gesture of at least some small affirmation.

The existential view can assert the possibility of improvement. Most pessimistic systems find the source of their despair in the fixed imperfection of human nature or of the human context; the existentialist, however, denies all absolute principles and holds that human nature is fixed only in that we have agreed to recognize certain human attributes; it is, therefore, subject to change if human beings can agree on other attributes or even to change by a single person if the person acts authentically in contradiction to the accepted principles. Hence, for the existentialist, the possibilities of altering human nature and society are unlimited, but, at the same time, human beings can hope for aid in making such alterations only from within themselves.

In contradistinction to this essentially atheistic *existentialism*, there has also developed a sizable body of Christian existential thought, represented by Karl Jaspers, Jacques Maritain, Nicolas Berdyaev, Martin Buber, Paul Tillich, and others.

Exordium The first of the seven parts of a classical ORATION. By extension, *exordium* is now applied to the introductory portion of a composition or a discourse. Edgar Allan Poe, for example, opens his section of critical notices in *Graham's Magazine* for January 1842 with an "*Exordium*" that sets forth his critical principles.

Exornation Obsolete term for rhetorical embellishment.

Exoticism A spirit of adherence to foreign or exotic elements, especially in setting. In some cases, only the setting is exotic, so that certain general values are asserted. The opening of Joseph Conrad's *Heart of Darkness*, set in England at the end of the nineteenth century, argues that England was once exotic to the Romans, "one of the dark places of the world."

[Reference: Roger Celestin, *From Cannibals to Radicals: Figures and Limits of Exoticism* (1996).]

Expatriate A term applied to those who leave their native lands and reside elsewhere. The move is usually voluntary, unlike that of some exiles. A number of American writers have been *expatriates*. Among them are Henry James and T. S. Eliot, who became British subjects, Ezra Pound, Henry Miller, James Jones, Richard Wright, and James Baldwin. The most celebrated American group of *expatriates* were those who lived in Paris following the First World War, including Gertrude Stein, Ernest Hemingway, Malcolm Cowley, and Louis Bromfield. Other noted *expatriates* are the Polish writer Joseph Conrad, who lived much of his mature life in England; the Irish writer James Joyce, who lived for a long time on the Continent; and the Russian-born Vladimir Nabokov, who lived in France, Germany, the United States, and Switzerland.

Expedition (also ***Expeditio***) The rhetorical device of expeditiously disposing of many secondary points and arguments so that one may concentrate forcibly on a main idea.

Expletive An interjection to lend emphasis to a sentence or, in verse especially, the use of a superfluous word (some form of the verb "to do," for example) to make for rhythm. Profanity is another form of *expletive*.

Explication de texte A method, which originated in the teaching of literature in France, involving the painstaking analysis of the meanings, relationships, and ambiguities of the words, images, and other small units that make up a literary work. It is one of the tools of NEW CRITICISM and of certain later scholars, such as Hugh Kenner.

Expolition (also **Expolitio**) A rhetorical polishing by many ornamental devices.

Exposition One of the four chief types of composition, the others being ARGUMENTATION, DESCRIPTION, and NARRATION. Its purpose is to explain something. *Exposition* may exist apart from the other types of composition, but frequently two or more of the types are blended. The following are some of the methods used in *exposition* (they may be used singly or in various combinations): identification, definition, classification, illustration, comparison, and analysis.

In drama the *exposition* is the introductory material that creates the tone, gives the setting, introduces the characters, and supplies other facts necessary to understanding.

Expressionism A movement affecting painting and literature, which followed and went beyond IMPRESSIONISM in its efforts to "objectify inner experience." Fundamentally it means the yielding up of the realistic and naturalistic method of VERISIMILITUDE in order to use external objects not as representational but as transmitters of the internal impressions and moods. In painting, for instance, "childhood" might be shown, not through a conventional representational picture of children at play or at school, but by seemingly unarticulated and exaggerated physical details that suggest "childhood" or convey the impression that the artist has of the concept "child."

Expressionism was strongest in the theater in the 1920s, and its entry into other literary forms was probably through the stage. *Expressionism* had its origin in the German theater in the early years of the century. It was a response to several different forces: the growing mass and mechanism of society, with its tendency to depress the value of the arts, made artists seek new ways of making art forms valuable instruments; at the same time, scientists, notably Freud, laid bare the phantasms in the human unconscious and offered artists a challenge to record them accurately; meanwhile, Marxism had instructed even non-Marxist artists that the individual was being lost in a mass society; to these pressures came the example of Strindberg, whose plays *The Dance of Death* (1901) and *A Dream Play* (1902) employ extensive nonrealistic devices. The German dramatists Frank Wedekind and Ernst Toller and the Czech Karel Čapek (the author of the nightmarish fantasy of the future, *R. U. R.*—the source, by the way, of the coinage *robot*) were the major figures in European expressionistic drama, which flourished in the 1920s. It was marked by unreal atmosphere, nightmarish action, distortion and oversimplification, the de-emphasis of the individual (characters were likely to be called the "Father" or the "Bank Clerk"), antirealistic settings, and staccato, telegraphic dialogue. The expressionistic drama strongly influenced Pirandello and Lorca. For American students it is most important in its impact on Eugene O'Neill, whose *Emperor Jones* attempts to project by symbolic scenes and sound effects the racial memories of a modern African American. Elmer Rice's *The Adding Machine*, which uses moving stages and other nonrealistic devices to express the mechanical world seen by one cog named Mr. Zero, is almost equally noted. Elements of *expressionism* can be seen in some plays of Thornton Wilder, Arthur Miller, and Tennessee Williams.

In the novel the presentation of the objective outer world as it expresses itself in the impressions or moods of a character is a widely used device. The most famous extended example is Joyce's *Finnegans Wake*, although the *expressionistic* intent and method are often apparent in works using STREAM OF CONSCIOUSNESS, as witness the "Circe" episode in Joyce's *Ulysses*. Probably the most complete transfer of the quality of *expressionistic* drama to the novel, however, is to be found in the works of Franz Kafka. The ANTIREALISTIC NOVEL is also a genre in the expressionistic tradition. More recent novelists, such as Kurt Vonnegut, Jr., Thomas Pynchon, Joseph Heller, and Ken Kesey, can also be included in the expressionistic tradition.

The revolt against realism, the distortion of the objects of the outer world, and the violent dislocation of time sequence and spatial logic in an effort accurately but not representationally to show the world as it appears to a troubled mind can be found in modern poetry, particularly that of T. S. Eliot, whose *The Waste Land* is the classic of the movement. The work of some of THE LANGUAGE POETS may be read as the verbal counterpart of abstract *expressionism* in painting, which retains the gestures of expressionist art but subdues the overt subject matter.

Expressive Theory of Criticism M. H. Abrams's term that designates a theory that holds the object of art to be the expression of the artist's emotions, impressions, or beliefs; an essential doctrine of romantic critics.

Extravaganza A fantastic, extravagant, or irregular composition. It is most commonly applied to dramatic compositions such as those of J. R. Planché, the creator of the dramatic *extravaganza*. Planché himself defined it as a "whimsical treatment of a poetical subject as distinguished from the broad caricature of a tragedy or serious opera, which was correctly described as burlesque." The subject was often a FAIRY TALE. The presentation was elaborate and included dancing and music. An example is Planché's *Sleeping Beauty* (acted 1840). A later use of *extravaganza*, still current, is to designate any extraordinarily spectacular production. *Extravaganza* is also applied to musical compositions, especially musical caricatures. In literature the term is occasionally used to characterize such rollicking or unrestrained work as Butler's *Hudibras*, a caricature of the English Puritans.

Eye Dialect The misspelling of a word to suggest dialect, even though the common pronunciation of the word is what the speaker said. In the sentence "Ah cain't kum raht naow," "kum" is an *eye dialect* spelling. The other words in the sentence are all pronounced by the speaker in nonstandard ways; "kum" could have been spelled "come" with the same resulting sound. *Eye dialect* is sometimes used for comic effect and is sometimes called comic misspelling. At the beginning and end of *Huckleberry Finn* we are told by Huck of unsuccessful attempts to "sivilize" him. Presumably the word is pronounced the same as "civilize."

Eye Rhyme RHYME that appears correct from the spelling but is not so from the pronunciation, as "watch" and "match" or "love" and "move." Both these examples, displaying the notorious vagaries of vowels in English spelling, are cases of CONSONANCE. Other *eye rhymes*—"imply" and "simply," "Venus" and "menus," "laughter" and "daughter"—scarcely qualify as any sort of rhyme, even so-called HALF RHYME or SLANT RHYME. Ezra Pound's *Hugh Selwyn Mauberley* wittily exploits a thematically significant *eye rhyme* between "mistress" and "distress," in which the only rhymes exist between the stressed syllable of one word with the unstressed of the other.

Fraktur Early German. A general-use typeface based on the Fraktur style of Spire Gothic.

Fable A brief tale told to point a moral. The characters are frequently animals, but people and inanimate objects are sometimes central. By far the most famous *fables* are those accredited to Aesop, a Greek slave living about 600 B.C.; but almost equally popular are those of La Fontaine, a seventeenth-century Frenchman, because of their distinctive humor, wit, and satire. Other important fabulists are Gay (England), Lessing (Germany), and Krylov (Russia). A *fable* in which the characters are animals is called a BEAST FABLE, a form popular in almost every period of literary history, usually as a satiric device to point out human follies. The beast fable continues to be vigorous in such diverse works as Kipling's *Just So Stories*, Joel Chandler Harris's Uncle Remus stories, and George Orwell's *Animal Farm*. T. S. Eliot's *Old Possum's Book of Practical Cats* and its incarnation on the musical stage (*Cats*) can be understood as a set of *fables*; much work in animated cartoons and puppetry—from Walt Disney's inescapable mice and ducks to Jim Henson's Muppets—likewise fall into the category of *fable*. Many critics, particularly in the NEOCLASSIC PERIOD, have used *fable* to equal PLOT (because the Latin equivalent of Greek *mythos* is *fabula*).

Fabliau (plural, ***Fabliaux***) A humorous tale popular in medieval France. The conventional verse form of the *fabliau* was the eight-syllable couplet. *Fabliaux* were stories of various types, but one point was uppermost—humorous, sly satire. These stories, often bawdy, dealt familiarly with the clergy, ridiculed womanhood, and were pitched in a key that made them readily understandable to anybody. The form was also present in English literature, Chaucer especially leaving examples of *fabliaux* in the tales of the Miller, Reeve, Merchant, and Shipman. Although *fabliaux* may have ostensible "morals" appended, they lack the serious intention of the fable, and they differ from the fable too in always having human characters and in always maintaining a realistic tone and manner. Wallace Stevens titled one of his poems "Fabliau of Florida," but the poem is not a *fabliau*.

Fade (noun) In film, a change from bright to dark (fade out) or dark to light (fade in).

Fairy Tale A story relating mysterious pranks and adventures of spirits who manifest themselves in the form of diminutive human beings. These spirits possess supernatural wisdom and foresight, a mischievous temperament, the power to regulate the affairs of human beings for good or evil, and the capacity to change their shape. *Fairy tales* as such—though they had existed in varying forms before—became popular toward the close of the seventeenth century. Some of the great source-collections are the *Contes de ma Mère l'Oye* of Perrault (French) and those of the Grimm brothers in German and of Keightley and Croker in English. Hans Christian Andersen, of Denmark, is probably the most famous writer of original *fairy tales*. English writers of original *fairy tales* include Ruskin, Kingsley, Wilde, and Kipling.

Falling Action The second half or RESOLUTION of a dramatic plot. It follows the climax, beginning often with a tragic force, exhibits the failing fortunes of the hero (in tragedy) and the successful efforts of the COUNTERPLAYERS, and culminates in the CATASTROPHE. See DRAMATIC STRUCTURE.

Falling Rhythm A FOOT in which the first syllable is accented, as in a TROCHEE or DACTYL. Coleridge's lines on the poetic feet illustrate it:

Trochee is in falling double,
Dactyl is falling, like—Tripoli.

Thomas Hardy's "The Voice" is one of the few English poems that uses both of the chief *falling rhythms*—dactyls and trochees.

False Friend A word that people wrongly think they know the meaning of. Most often applied to foreign words that may be cognate or similar to native words but have divergent meaning, as with French *magasin* that means "store" and not "magazine" or German *Weib* that means "woman" and not "wife." Sometimes the result of such misunderstanding can be comic. In Chapter 3 of Thackeray's *Vanity Fair*, Rebecca Sharp, already pained by some spicy curry, is offered a pepper:

> "Try a chili with it, Miss Sharp," said Joseph, really interested. "A chili," said Rebecca, gasping. "Oh yes!" She thought a chili was something cool, as its name imported, and was served with some. "How fresh and green they look," she said, and put one into her mouth. It was hotter than the curry; flesh and blood could bear it no longer.

Familiar Essay The more personal, intimate type of INFORMAL ESSAY. It deals lightly, often humorously, with personal experiences, opinions, and prejudices, stressing especially the unusual or novel, and having to do with the varied aspects of everyday life. Goldsmith, Lamb, and Stevenson were particularly successful in the form. See ESSAY.

Fancy In English literature *fancy* and IMAGINATION were synonyms until the nineteenth century, although John Dryden had assigned a comprehensive role to imagination and had limited *fancy* to language and variations of a thought and Joshua Reynolds had associated imagination with genius and *fancy* with taste. The term *fancy* is now used almost exclusively in the Coleridgean opposition of imagination and *fancy*, in which *fancy* is mechanic, logical, "the aggregative and associative power," "a mode of Memory emancipated from the order of time and space." Imagination is, on the other hand, organic and creative. For Coleridge *fancy* is a distinct and inferior faculty, dependent on the primary imagination and confined to manipulating phenomenal materials but incapable of creating materials.

Fantastic Sometimes "the *fantastic*" is a synonym for FANTASY. Sometimes, however, the *fantastic* is distinguished from fantasy (which can be whimsical and thin) and from SCIENCE FICTION by its reliance on the imagination for the realization of inward states of mind. Thomas Pynchon's *Gravity's Rainbow* can be called *fantastic*, but it is not a fantasy based on vapid imaginings.

[Reference: Tzvetan Todorov, *The Fantastic: A Structural Approach to a Literary Genre* (1975; orig. 1973).]

Fantastic Poets A term applied by Milton to the school of metaphysical poets. See METAPHYSICAL POETRY.

Fantasy Though sometimes used as an equivalent of FANCY and even of IMAGINATION, *fantasy* usually designates a conscious breaking free from reality. The term is applied to a work that takes place in a nonexistent and unreal world, such as fairyland, or concerns incredible and unreal characters, as in Maeterlinck's *The Blue Bird*, or relies on scientific principles not yet discovered or contrary to present experience, as in some SCIENCE FICTION and UTOPIAN fiction. *Fantasy* may be employed merely for whimsical delight, or it may be the medium for serious comment on reality. The most sustained examples of *fantasy*, combining both intentions, in recent literature are the novels of James Branch Cabell laid in the mythical kingdom of Poictesme. The Brontë children created a *fantasy* world called Gondal, which they equipped with a geography, history, and even newspapers. Austin Tappan Wright's *Islandia* is an enormous fictional record of an imaginary world. J. R. R. Tolkien's trilogy *The Lord of the Rings* is currently proving the still-strong appeal of *fantasy*.

Fanzine A magazine addressed to fans of a certain performer, group, cult, movement, period, or style.

Farce The word developed from Late Latin *farsus*, connected with a verb meaning "to stuff." Thus, an expansion or amplification in the church liturgy was called a *farse*. Later, in France, *farce* meant any sort of extemporaneous addition in a play, especially jokes or gags, the clownish actors speaking "more than was set down" for them. In the late seventeenth century *farce* was used in England to mean any short humorous play, as distinguished from regular five-act comedy. The development in these plays of elements of low comedy is responsible for the modern meaning of *farce*: a dramatic piece intended to excite laughter and depending less on plot and character than on improbable situations, the humor arising from gross incongruities, coarse wit, or horseplay. *Farce* merges into comedy, and the same play (e.g., Shakespeare's *The Taming of the Shrew*) may be called by some a *farce*, by others a comedy. James Townley's *High Life Below Stairs* (1759) has been termed the "best farce" of the eighteenth century. There are elements of *farce* in Oscar Wilde's *The Importance of Being Earnest*, though not so much in his other comic plays (see FARCE-COMEDY). Brandon Thomas's *Charley's Aunt* (1892), dealing with the extravagant results of a female impersonation, is the best known American *farce*, although *farce* is the stock-in-trade of film and television comedy. See FARCE-COMEDY.

Farce-Comedy A term sometimes applied to comedies that rely for their interest chiefly on farcical devices (see FARCE, LOW COMEDY) but that contain some truly comic elements elevating them above most farce. Shakespeare's *The Taming of the Shrew* and

The Merry Wives of Windsor are called *farce-comedies* by some. One writer distinguishes between the *farce-comedy* of Aristophanes (loose structure, variety of appeal, operatic quality) and that of Plautus (careful structure, intrigue, broad humor). More recently, *farce-comedy* has been detected in Oscar Wilde's plays—especially *The Importance of Being Earnest*—and in many subsequent presentations, such as movies with W. C. Fields, the Marx Brothers, Woody Allen, and Richard Pryor, as well as such television productions as "The Honeymooners."

[Reference: R. M. Smith, ed., *Types of Farce-Comedy* (1928).]

Fatalism The theory that certain events must occur in the future regardless of what our present actions or choices may be. Strictly speaking, *fatalism* removes ethical concerns from human actions, for fate indifferently assigns each person to the predetermined course of events. The Greeks held to the idea of the allotment, by the Moirai, to each individual at birth of a certain quantity of misfortune which he or she must endure. The Romans saw their gods, the Parcae, spinning human destiny. In Islamic belief everything is ruled by an inexorable fate, called Kismet. It is important to distinguish between fate and chance. If fate is conceived as acting, any event, however independent of the actions or merits of an individual, is the result of an impersonal force predetermining it and everything else that happens. If chance is believed to be operative, the event is accidental rather than part of a design, the working of coincidence rather than of fate. Although *fatalism* often coincides with a belief in predestination, as in Calvinism or Islamic belief, it does not necessarily entail the existence of a purposive agent through whose decree the necessary events occur; it merely asserts that these necessary events are inevitable.

Fates, The The Greeks and Romans believed that *the Fates* controlled the birth, life, and death of all human beings. The Romans called them the Parcae, the Greeks the Moirai. They were three sisters who controlled the thread of life. Clotho held the distaff; Lachesis spun the thread; and Atropos cut the thread to end life.

Feature A piece of journalism that is neither news nor fiction but an account of something of general interest. Also the main item in a movie program, which may also include short subjects.

Federalist Age in American Literature The period between the formation of the national government and the "Second Revolution" of Jacksonian Democracy. Called the *Federalist Age* because of the dominance of the Federalist Party, the period extends from 1790 to 1830. Internationally, the United States emerged as a world force through the War of 1812. Internally, it was an "Era of Good Feeling," with the sectional and social issues that were later to plague the nation just beginning to be felt. It was an age of rapid literary development. Poetry moved from the imitative neoclassicism of Barlow and Dwight, through the limited romanticism of Freneau, to the first notable American achievements in verse in the work of Bryant. The novel, first practiced in America in 1789, saw good work by Charles Brockden Brown and H. H. Brackenridge and the establishment of a distinctively American romance with Cooper's Leatherstocking Tales. Irving in his burlesque "Knickerbocker's" *History of New York* and in his essays and tales found an international audience.

The *North American Review*, founded in 1815, was a thriving quarterly. In the decade 1800–1810, Hawthorne, Simms, Whittier, Longfellow, Poe, and Holmes were born; and 1819 was an *annus mirabilis*, being the birth year of Lowell, Melville, and Whitman. By 1830 the neoclassic, restrained, aristocratic Federalist that America had been had given way to a romantic, exuberant, democratic young giant that was flexing its muscles and was beginning effectively to express itself in art as well as action. See *Outline of Literary History* and REVOLUTIONARY AND EARLY NATIONAL PERIOD IN AMERICAN LITERATURE.

Feminine Ending An extrametrical unstressed syllable added to the end of a line in IAMBIC or ANAPESTIC rhythm. This variation, which may give a sense of movement and irregularity, is commonly used in BLANK VERSE. The most famous soliloquy in English begins with four lines that all have *feminine endings*:

> To be, or not to be—that is the question:
> Whether 'tis nobler in the mind to suffer
> The slings and arrows of outrageous fortune
> Or to take arms against a sea of troubles
> And by opposing end them. . . .

Feminine Rhyme A rhyme in which the rhyming stressed syllables are followed by an undifferentiated identical unstressed syllable, as *waken* and *forsaken*. Also called DOUBLE RHYME. In Chaucer, the *feminine rhyme* was very common because of the frequency of the final *-e* in Middle English. The phenomenon may be random, in which case *feminine rhymes* will almost always be in the minority, or there may be some patterned arrangement. In the latter case—as in Shakespeare's "Oh Mistress Mine," Longfellow's "Snowflakes," and Browning's "Soliloquy of the Spanish Cloister"—the normal tendency is for *feminine rhymes* to precede masculine. The opposite effect, masculine before *feminine rhymes*, as in E. A. Robinson's "Miniver Cheevy," seems syncopated, ironic, and even unsettling. Such alternation is clearly humorous in the first four lines of "Yankee Doodle" (ending "town," "pony," "cap," "macaroni"); the effect is more problematic in the corresponding lines of "The Star-Spangled Banner," which is said to be based on a drinking song. The lines end "light," "gleaming," "fight," "streaming."

Feminist Criticism Growing out of the women's movement following the Second World War—two of whose founding works, Simone de Beauvoir's *The Second Sex* and Kate Millett's *Sexual Politics*, included sustained analyses of the representation of women in literature—*feminist criticism* has pursued what Elaine Showalter calls "feminist critique" (analysis of the works of male authors, especially in the depiction of women and their relation to women readers) on the one hand and "gynocriticism" (the study of women's writing) on the other. In addition to recovering neglected works by women authors through the ages and creating a canon of women's writing, *feminist criticism* has become a wide-ranging exploration of the construction of gender and identity, the role of women in culture and society, and the possibilities of women's creative expression.

[References: Sandra M. Gilbert and Susan Gubar, *The Madwoman in the Attic: The Woman Writer and the Nineteenth-century Literary Imagination*, 2nd ed. (2000; orig. 1979) and (eds.) *The Norton Anthology of Literature by Women: The Tradition in*

English (with separate *Classroom Guide*) (1985); Ellen Moers, *Literary Women* (1976); Toril Moi, *Sexual/Textual Politics: Feminist Literary Theory* (1985); Elaine Showalter, *A Literature of Their Own: British Women Novelists from Brontë to Lessing*, new rev. ed. (1982; orig. 1977) and (ed.) *The New Feminist Criticism: Essays on Women, Literature, and Theory* (1985).]

La Femme Inspiratrice A type of real person or literary character: the woman who inspires an artist. Real women placed in the category include the wives of Thomas Hardy, William Butler Yeats, James Joyce, D. H. Lawrence, T. S. Eliot, and Robert Lowell. Fictional instances may be found in Thomas Mann's *Doctor Faustus*, Boris Pasternak's *Doctor Zhivago*, and John Fowles's *Mantissa*. A divine version is approached in Graves's *The White Goddess*.

Festschrift (plural, ***Festschriften***) From the German for celebration and writing. A volume of miscellaneous learned essays by the students, colleagues, or admirers of a scholar and presented on some special occasion, such as retirement or birthday.

Feudalism The system of social and political organization that prevailed in Western Europe during much of the medieval period. Every landholder was merely the tenant of some greater landlord. Thus, the barons or powerful prelates were the tenants of the king; the lesser lords, knights, and churchmen were tenants of the barons and prelates; and the serfs and "villeins" were tenants of the lesser nobles. In practice—as the whole system was based on force—the relations were more complicated: even kings sometimes owed allegiance to a great churchman or baron.

As rent, the various groups paid to their immediate superiors "service," which might consist of visible property or of military aid. Socially, there were two sharply defined classes: the workers (villeins or free renters; serfs or bondmen) and the "prayers and fighters" (knights, upper clergy, lords). *Feudalism* broke down in the fifteenth century. The ideals of chivalry grew partly out of *feudalism* and powerfully affected the character of much medieval and Renaissance literature, notably the romances and romantic epics. The feudal social order is pictured in Chaucer's *Canterbury Tales*, and its evils are set forth in the *Vision of Piers Plowman* (fourteenth century).

Ficelle Literally, one of the strings by means of which marionettes are controlled. The term is used by Henry James for CONFIDANTE, a means by which a self-effacing author conveys necessary information.

Fiction Narrative writing drawn from the imagination rather than from history or fact. The term is most frequently associated with NOVELS and SHORT STORIES, though drama and narrative poetry are also forms of *fiction*. Sometimes authors weave fictional episodes around historical characters, epochs, and settings and thus make "historical *fiction*." Sometimes authors use imaginative elaborations of incidents and qualities of a real person, resulting in a type of writing popular in recent years, the "fictional biography." Sometimes the actual events of the author's life are presented under the guise of imaginative creations, resulting in "autobiographical *fiction*." Sometimes actual persons and events are presented under the guise of *fiction*, resulting in the ROMAN À CLEF. "*Fiction*" is now often used to describe any literary construction or "making"—any of the ways in which writing seeks to impose order on the flux of thought or experience, as in "the poetics of fiction." See also FORMALISM (RUSSIAN), NARRATOLOGY.

[References: Wayne Booth, *The Rhetoric of Fiction*, 2nd ed. (1983; orig. 1961); Northrop Frye, *Anatomy of Criticism* (1957); Käte Hamburger, *The Logic of Literature*, 2nd rev. ed. (1993; orig. tr. 1973); Frank Kermode, *The Sense of an Ending*, new ed. (2000; orig. 1967); J. Hillis Miller, *Fiction and Repetition: Seven English Novels* (1982); Sheldon Sacks, *Fiction and the Shape of Belief* (1964); Robert Scholes and Robert Kellogg, *The Nature of Narrative* (1966); Mark Spilka, ed., *Towards a Poetics of Fiction* (1977).]

Field Day The Field Day Theater Company, founded in Northern Ireland in 1980 by Brian Friel and Stephen Rea, who were later joined by Seamus Heaney, Tom Paulin, David Hammond, and Seamus Deane. At first the company concentrated on an annual production that toured Northern Ireland and the Republic of Ireland; later the group added publishing to its enterprises and has generated or is planning to generate pamphlets and anthologies.

[Reference: Mitchell Wayne Harris, *Field Day Theatre Company and the Mythic Revision of Ireland* (1985).]

Figurative Language Intentional departure from the normal order, construction, or meaning of words. *Figurative language* embodies one or more FIGURES OF SPEECH.

Figure Poem A poem written so that its printed shape suggests its subject matter. See CARMEN FIGURATUM.

Figures of Speech The various uses of language that depart from customary construction, order, or significance. *Figures of speech* are of two major kinds: rhetorical figures, which are departures from customary usage to achieve special effects without a change in the radical meaning of the words; and TROPES, which involve basic changes in the meaning of words. "*Figures of speech*" is sometimes synonymous with rhetorical figures, and "figures of thought" is synonymous with tropes; but *figures of speech* and figures of thought in this distinction have undergone so many changes and direct reversals of meaning from the classical rhetoricians to the present that their use in this way results in confusion.

It makes sense to use *figures of speech* as the generic term and to use rhetorical figures and tropes as the subgenera. It is possible to distinguish figures of thought, *figures of speech*, and figures of sound. In Cassius's line early in Shakespeare's *Julius Caesar*—"Rome, thou hast lost the breed of noble bloods"—we see all three sorts of figure. The APOSTROPHE "Rome" (Cassius is really talking to Brutus) is one of the rhetorical figures. The SYNECDOCHE "blood" (using one component of the organism conventionally to represent human quality in the abstract) is a trope. The pentameter, the iambic rhythm, and the emphatic REPETITION of certain sounds (*b* and *l* in particular) are figures of sound.

Filidh (plural, ***fili***) Early Irish professional poets. See IRISH LITERATURE.

Film Literally, a sheet or roll of transparent material coated with a light-sensitive emulsion for making photographs or moving pictures. By extension, a motion picture made or preserved on such material is itself called a *film*. The term is applied to an individual motion picture, to motion pictures as an art form, as in FILM CRITICISM, and to the industry engaged in making motion pictures. In America *film* has largely replaced the term "cinema," which was once widely used.

Film Criticism The analysis and evaluation of films by applying to them various standards, theories, and aesthetic beliefs, such as AUTEUR THEORY and FORMATIVE THEORY.

Film noir Nino Frank's name for a type of American crime film that flourished between 1940 and 1960. More a matter of style than of subject, *film noir* is distinguished by a serious, somber, even gloomy tone; fast pace; complex texture; exaggerated CHIAROSCURO; unusual angles and perspectives; VOICE-OVER narration; frequent FLASHBACKS; settings mostly urban, interior, nocturnal; and a moral postulate whereby evil and corruption are not limited to bad individuals but pollute all of society, especially those at the top. *Film noir* owed much to American fiction of the 1920s and 1930s, especially the range from Hemingway and Faulkner through the hard-boiled crime writers like Dashiell Hammett, Raymond Chandler, and James M. Cain. According to Spencer Selby, *film noir* embraces such generic categories as crime drama, gangster film, mystery, suspense thriller, and psychological melodrama, with such common subgenres as POLICIER, DETECTIVE, prison, heist, fight, and newspaper films. The leading studios producing such films were United Artists, RKO, Warner Brothers, and Columbia; the best-known directors were Fritz Lang, Alfred Hitchcock, Lewis Allen, John Farrow, John Huston, and Orson Welles.

Although most films in the category are black-and-white American crime stories, there are many off-genre specimens that, without satisfying all the criteria, still seem to belong. Selby suggests such headings as WESTERN (*Blood on the Moon* and *The Gunfighter*), COMEDY (*Beat the Devil*), Problem Picture (*The Lost Weekend*), Espionage Thriller (*Cloak and Dagger*), SCIENCE FICTION (*Invasion of the Body Snatchers*), and Adventure (*The Treasure of Sierra Madre*). Welles's *Macbeth* is classified among Miscellaneous Dramas and Oddities; and there is also room for the paradoxical Color Films Noir (such as Hitchcock's *Vertigo*) and Black and White Postnoirs (such as Thompson's *Cape Fear* and Brooks's *In Cold Blood*).

[Reference: Spencer Selby, *Dark City: The Film Noir* (1984).]

Fin de Siècle "End of the century," a phrase applied mostly to the last ten years of the nineteenth century, but not much to the end of the twentieth. The 1890s were a transition in which artists were consciously abandoning old ideas and attempting to discover new techniques. One writer (Holbrook Jackson) has noted three main characteristics of the decade in art and literature: DECADENCE, exemplified in Oscar Wilde and Aubrey Beardsley; REALISM or "sense of fact," represented by Gissing, Shaw, and George Moore; and radical or revolutionary social aspirations, marked by numerous new movements (including the New Woman) and by a general sense of emancipation from the traditional order. When the term *fin de siècle* is used about a literary work, it usually is in the sense of decadence or preciosity.

Final Suspense, Moment of A term for the ray of hope sometimes appearing just before the catastrophe of a tragedy. Thus, Macbeth's continued faith that he cannot be hurt by any man born of woman keeps a spectator in some suspense as to the apparently inevitable tragic ending. See DRAMATIC STRUCTURE.

First Rejection A stipulation in some book contracts giving a publisher the right to consider the author's next work along with the right to reject it before another publisher sees it.

Five Points See CALVINISM.

Fixed Forms A name sometimes given to definite patterns of line and stanza. Although forms such as the SONNET, the SPENSERIAN STANZA, and RHYME ROYAL are "fixed" in this general sense, the term usually refers to a specific group of stanzaic patterns that originated in France. See FRENCH FORMS.

Flag A slip of paper or other device by which a copy editor or proofreader marks the place on a manuscript where there is a query or correction. A typical flag addressed to an author might read: "Au: do you mean 'casual' or 'causal'?" In newspaper layout, the *flag* is the graphic element on the front page that tells what the newspaper is called; also "nameplate."

Flashback A device by which a work presents material that occurred prior to the opening scene of the work. Various methods may be used, among them recollections of characters, narration by the characters, dream sequences, and reveries. Notable examples in the theater occur in Elmer Rice's *Dream Girl* and Arthur Miller's *Death of a Salesman*. Maugham used the *flashback* skillfully and effectively in *Cakes and Ale*, and it is employed consistently in the novels of John P. Marquand. Commonly enough, as in John O'Hara's novel *Ten North Frederick* and the film version thereof, a work may begin with a funeral or other such terminal event and then go back to show what passed before, so that a large part of the work is technically one protracted *flashback*. See EXPOSITION.

Flat Character E. M. Forster's term for a CHARACTER constructed around a single idea or quality, such as the HUMOURS characters of the seventeenth-century stage. A *flat character* is immediately recognizable and can usually be represented by a single sentence, as "I never will desert Mr. Micawber," which, Forster asserts, *is* Mrs. Micawber and is *all* she is. See ROUND CHARACTER.

Fleshly School of Poetry, The A critical essay in the *Contemporary Review*, October 1871, signed "Thomas Maitland," a pseudonym for Robert W. Buchanan. The critic takes to task Swinburne, Morris, and Rossetti, though most of the article is couched as a review of Rossetti's poems, and Rossetti himself draws most of the fire. Buchanan accuses the three of being in league to praise one another's work and refers to them as the "Mutual Admiration School." The following passage makes clear the general tone of Buchanan's criticism:

> The fleshly gentlemen have bound themselves by solemn league and covenant to extol fleshliness as the distinct and supreme end of poetic and pictorial art, to aver that poetic expression is greater than poetic thought, and by inference that the body is greater than the soul, and sound superior to sense; and that the poet, properly to develop his poetic faculty, must be an intellectual hermaphrodite. . . .

Rossetti replied with "The Stealthy School of Criticism," in *The Athenaeum* (December 16, 1871). The episode resurfaces in Ezra Pound's *Hugh Selwyn Mauberley* (1920):

> Gladstone was still respected,
> When John Ruskin produced
> "King's Treasuries"; Swinburne
> And Rossetti still abused.
>
> Foetid Buchanan lifted up his voice. . . .

Floater Generally used for a minor mistake; sometimes applied to a metaphor gone astray, such as "I wouldn't kiss you with a ten-foot pole."

Flyting An extended and vigorous verbal exchange. In Old English poetry it was a boasting match between warriors before combat. Similar contests ornament Greek, Arabic, Celtic, Italian, and Provençal literature. It is typical of the cycles of Charlemagne. However, it has been from the sixteenth century to the present a marked characteristic of Scottish writing, where it is an exchange of personal abuse or ridicule in verse between two characters in a poem or between two poets. In a *flyting* the poets attack each other in scurrilous verse, filled with vigorous and vulgar invective and profanity. *The Flyting of Dunbar and Kennedie* is an effervescent example from sixteenth-century Scotland.

Foil Literally, a "leaf" of bright metal placed under a jewel to increase its brilliance. In literature the term is applied to any person who through contrast underscores the distinctive characteristics of another. Thus, Laertes, Fortinbras, and even the Players—all of whom are willing and able to take action with less reason than Hamlet has—serve as *foils* to Hamlet.

Folio A standard-size sheet of paper folded in half. The term is also used to describe a volume made up of *folio* sheets—that is, whose SIGNATURES result from sheets folded to two leaves or four pages. It is the largest regular BOOK SIZE. Shakespeare's plays were first assembled in a *folio* edition in 1623, and the term *folio* is used to designate any of the early collections of Shakespeare's works. Hence it takes on a special meaning, referring in this case to content rather than size. The word is also used by editors and printers to refer to page numbers.

Folk Ballad An anonymous ballad transmitted orally and usually existing in many variants. In America *folk ballad* is often associated with the folk songs of the Appalachian mountains, of the western plains, and of mills and factories. See BALLAD and FOLK SONG.

Folk Drama In its stricter and older sense, as usually employed by folklorists, the term means dramatic activities of the folk—the unsophisticated treatment of folk themes by the folk themselves, particularly activities connected with popular festivals and religious rites. Medieval *folk drama* took such forms as the sword dance, the St. George play, and the mummers' play. The medieval religious drama, though based on scriptural materials and a religion with a fully developed theology, is by some regarded as a form of *folk drama*, and the "folk" character of such twentieth-century plays as Marc Connelly's *Green Pastures* is commonly recognized.

The religious drama of the Middle Ages, however, is usually treated as a special form, not as *folk drama*. Another sense in which *folk drama* is being employed, especially in America, includes plays that, even though written by sophisticated and consciously artistic playwrights, reflect the customs, language, attitudes, and environmental difficulties of the folk. These plays are commonly performed, not by the folk themselves, but by amateur or professional actors. They tend to be realistic, close to the soil, and sympathetically human. The plays of J. M. Synge, Lady Gregory, and other authors of the CELTIC RENAISSANCE and the American plays by Paul Green and others published in the several volumes of *Carolina Folk-Plays* are examples. Early in his career, Thomas Wolfe wrote such a play and acted in it.

Folk Epic An epic of unknown authorship, assumed to be the product of communal composition. See ART EPIC.

Folklore A term first used by W. J. Thoms in the middle nineteenth century as a substitute for "popular antiquities." The definition adopted by the Folklore Society of London about 1890 is: "The comparison and identification of the survivals of archaic beliefs, customs, and traditions in modern ages." Alexander H. Krappe, in *The Science of Folklore* (1930) affirms that *folklore* "limits itself to a study of the unrecorded traditions of the people as they appear in popular fiction, custom and belief, magic and ritual," and he regards it as the function of *folklore* to reconstruct the "spiritual history" of the human race. Some forms of *folklore* (for example, superstitions and proverbs) belong also to the life of modern peoples, literate as well as illiterate, and may therefore be transmitted by written record as well as by word of mouth. *Folklore* includes myths, legends, stories, riddles, proverbs, nursery rhymes, charms, spells, omens, beliefs of all sorts, popular ballads, cowboy songs, plant lore, animal lore, and customs dealing with birth, initiation, courtship, marriage, medicine, work, amusements, and death. A FOLKTALE may be retold by an author writing for a highly cultivated audience and later in a changed form again be taken over by the folk.

Literature is full of elements taken over from *folklore*, and some knowledge of the conventions of *folklore* can aid the understanding of great literature. The acceptance of the rather childish love-test in *King Lear* may rest on the fact that the motif was an already familiar one in *folklore*. The effects of such works as Coleridge's *Christabel*, Keats's *Eve of St. Agnes*, or Hardy's *The Return of the Native* depend on the recognition of popular beliefs, and some familiarity with fairy lore is necessary if one is to appreciate fully the quality of James Stephens's *The Crock of Gold*. The MEDIEVAL ROMANCE *Sir Gawain and the Green Knight*, written for a cultivated audience, centers on the folk formula of the challenging of a mortal by a supernatural being to a beheading contest: the binding force of the covenant between Gawain and the Green Knight is explained by primitive attitudes rather than by rational rules of conduct. Shakespeare's *Hamlet* is a retelling of an old, popular tale of the "exile-and-return" formula and may have its origins, as Francis Fergusson has suggested, in a series of religious rituals.

[References: Jan Harold Brunvand, *The Study of American Folklore: An Introduction*, 4th ed. (1998; orig. 1968); Richard M. Dorson, ed., *Folklore and Folklife: An Introduction* (1972), and *Handbook of American Folklore* (1983); A. H. Krappe, *Science of Folklore* (1930, reprinted 1974).]

Folk Song A song of unknown authorship preserved and transmitted orally. It is generally believed to be the expression of a whole community. *Folk songs* are very old and appear in all cultures, although they flourish best in illiterate or preliterate communities. See BALLAD and FOLK BALLAD.

Folktale A short narrative handed down through oral tradition, with various tellers and groups modifying it, so that it acquires cumulative authorship. Most *folktales* eventually move from oral tradition to written form. Noted collections of such *tales* from oral tradition have been made, among them Jakob and Wilhelm Grimm's collection of *Märchen*, which resulted from their interviews with German peasants who retold stories handed down in their families over generations. *The Thousand and One Nights, or Arabian Nights' Entertainments* derives from Persian and Egyptian *folktales*. In America a famous example is Joel Chandler Harris's Uncle Remus stories, a collection of transplanted African *folktales* told by plantation slaves. The frontier has been an active source for American *folktales* dealing with characters such as Paul Bunyan, John Henry, and Mike Fink. The range of *folktales* goes from MYTH through LEGENDS, FABLES, TALL TALES, GHOST STORIES, and humorous anecdotes to FAIRY TALES. On occasion, a character or a story that had a clear literary origin becomes by various means folk property and functions as a *folktale*. Rip Van Winkle, created by Washington Irving, and Uncle Tom, from Harriet Beecher Stowe's *Uncle Tom's Cabin*, are examples.

[References: Richard M. Dorson, *America in Legend: Folklore From the Colonial Period to the Present* (1974–1973); Stith Thompson, *The Folktale* (1946).]

Font A set of type distinguished as to TYPEFACE and size. Originally limited to mechanical typography, *font* has recently been extended to electronic printing. *Fonts* often bear names that honor printers, designers, publishers, publications, and cities. Walt Whitman, who had worked as a printer and set some of the type for the first edition of *Leaves of Grass*, wrote "A Font of Type," which includes the names of the typefaces most in use in the 1880s:

> This latent mine—these unlaunch'd voices—passionate powers,
> Wrath, argument, or praise, or comic leer, or prayer devout,
> (Not nonpareil, brevier, bourgeois, long primer merely,)
> These ocean waves arousable to fury and to death,
> Or sooth'd to ease and sheeny sun and sleep,
> Within the pallid slivers slumbering.

Foolscap A size of printing paper, with dimensions varying through history: $16^1/_4 \times 13$, 12×15, $12^1/_2 \times 16$, $17 \times 13^1/_2$.

Foot The unit of rhythm in verse, whether quantitative or accentual-syllabic. The names by which the various *feet* are known in English are borrowings from classical antiquity, which had only QUANTITATIVE VERSE. The result has been substantial confusion. Prosodists consider the fundamental character of regular verse in Middle English and Modern English to be a rhythm consisting of units of accented and unaccented syllables, arranged in patterns called *feet*. The line of verse usually consists of a definite number of specific *feet*. The most common are:

- IAMB: ˘´, as in "rĕtúrn"
- TROCHEE: ´˘ as in "dóublĕ"
- ANAPEST: ˘˘´, as in "cŏntrăvéne"
- DACTYL: ´˘˘, as in "mérrĭlў"
- SPONDEE: ´´, as in "fóotbáll"

The PYRRHIC: ˘˘, is usually included, although a few prosodists deny it a place in English verse, believing that an accented syllable must also be present in a *foot*. In any event, it is virtually inconceivable that a whole poem could be written in the pyrrhic rhythm, if, indeed, it be a rhythm at all. Other *feet* than these are sporadically used in English, most of them of classical origin:

- AMPHIBRACH: ˘´˘, as in "ărrángemĕnt"
- AMPHIMACER: ´˘´, as in "áltĭtúde"
- ANTIBACCHIUS: ´´˘, as in "hígh móuntăin"
- BACCHIUS: ˘´´, as in "ăbóvebóard"
- CHORIAMBUS: ´˘˘´, as in "yéar ŭpŏn yéar"
- PAEON:´˘˘˘, as in "végĕtăblĕ," although the accent may occupy any one of the four syllabic positions.

See METER, SCANSION.

Footnote Material added to a text to provide additional information or documentation. Common in scholarly writing, *footnotes* turn up in a few literary works, such as fiction by John O'Hara and J. D. Salinger. With type often smaller than the main text, some such notes are placed at the foot of the page, others at the end of a chapter or book, in which case they may be called "endnotes."
[Reference: Anthony Grafton, *The Footnote: A Curious History* (1997).]

Foregrounding The effect, in any art, of giving emphatic but unaccustomed prominence to something. Verse ordinarily foregrounds a regular rhythm in language not found in speech or prose. Once a verse idiom becomes established, the prevailing rhythm recedes into the "background" so that a different rhythm will be foregrounded. In Hopkins's line "Generations have trod, have trod, have trod," the double trochee "generations" is foregrounded against the prevailing background of iambs. Our notions of *foregrounding* owe much to Russian Formalism. See BARING THE DEVICE.

Foreshadowing The presentation of material in a work in such a way that later events are prepared for. *Foreshadowing* can result from the establishment of a mood or atmosphere, as in the opening of Conrad's *Heart of Darkness* or the first act of *Hamlet*. It can result from an event that adumbrates the later action, as does the scene with the witches at the beginning of *Macbeth*. It can result from the appearance of physical objects or facts, as the clues do in a detective story, or from the revelation of a fundamental and decisive character trait, as in the opening chapter of Edith Wharton's *The House of Mirth*. In all cases, the purpose of *foreshadowing* is to prepare the reader or viewer for action to come.

Foreword A short preliminary statement that explains some aspect of the work to follow. *Foreword* is virtually synonymous with PREFACE or INTRODUCTION. To strict constructionists, *prefaces* are written by authors, *forewords* by someone else. Both count as parts of front matter, whereas an introduction is part of the text proper.

Forgeries, Literary Plagiarists offer as their own what someone else has written. Literary forgers offer as the genuine writing of another what they have themselves composed. Their motive may be to supply authority for some religious or political doctrine or scheme, or it may be to cater to some prevailing literary demand (as when spurious ballads were composed in the eighteenth century in response to a romantic fad) or it may be, as Bacon would say, "for the love of the lie itself." *Literary forgeries* seem to flourish in all countries and ages. A book of nearly three hundred pages by J. A. Farrer details many famous *literary forgeries*, yet, as Andrew Lang says, several additional volumes would be needed to make the account of known forgeries complete.

The Greek statesman Solon inserted forged verses in the revered *Iliad* to further his political purposes. A forged "diary" of a supposed soldier in the Trojan War, Dares the Phrygian, actually composed by some Roman about the fourth century after Christ, turned the sympathy of European peoples from the Greeks to the Trojans and supplied an account of the war that for more than a thousand years was accepted as more authentic than Homer's. In addition it supplied the kernel for what developed into one of the most famous love stories of all time, that of Troilus and Cressida. A famous Italian scholar, Carlo Sigonio, about 1582 composed what pretended to be the lost *Consolatio* of Cicero. The imitation was so clever that, although there was always some doubt, it was not until two hundred years later that the facts were discovered.

In English literary history an example is afforded by Thomas Chatterton (1752–1770), the "boy poet," who wrote faked pieces supposed to have been written by a fifteenth-century priest. Chatterton's imitation of medieval English was so convincing and his actual poetic gifts were so great that his efforts attracted wide attention before his suicide at the age of eighteen. About the same time came another famous case of an effort to supply the current romantic interest in the medieval and the primitive with supposedly ancient pieces of literature, James Macpherson's "Ossianic" poems (1760–1765). Macpherson seems to have made some use of genuine Celtic tradition but in the main to have composed himself the epic *Fingal*, which he claimed had been written in the third century by Ossian, son of Fingal. Macpherson's public was sharply divided between those who accepted this "discovery" as genuine and those who, like Samuel Johnson, denounced it as an imposture. The episode is referred to as the OSSIANIC CONTROVERSY. (An incidental byproduct of that enterprise has been the popularity, especially in the American South, of the place-name "Selma," for which the only source is in Macpherson.)

Just as it is not easy for editors and publishers to detect all plagiarized writing presented to them, so it is difficult for them to avoid being exploited by literary forgers, who sometimes mix the authentic and the spurious so cleverly that not only the editors and publishers, but the general public and professional critics, are deceived. And this is as true of the twentieth century as of the eighteenth. The most celebrated recent case is Clifford Irving's spurious autobiography of Howard Hughes that fooled (for a while) a number of readers and publishers.

Another kind of *literary forgery* results from the manufacture of spurious EDITIONS of works. The works themselves are authentic—they were actually written by the authors to whom they are ascribed—but the editions are not authentic. Such *forgery* is directed toward the bibliophile rather than the literary scholar, although such editions produce bibliographical difficulties. Thomas Wise, for example, created a number of bogus first editions of nineteenth-century English works.

[References: Denis Dutton, ed., *The Forger's Art: Forgery and the Philosophy of Art* (1983); Wilfred Partington, *Forging Ahead* (1939, rev. ed. 1946).]

Form A term designating the organization of the elementary parts of a work of art in relation to its total effect. Verse *form* refers to the organization of rhythmic units. Stanza *form* refers to the organization of lines in groups. The *form* of the ideas refers to the organization or structure of thought in the work.

Some approaches distinguish *form* from content, *form* being the pattern that gives expression to the content. A similar distinction is often made between "conventional" *form* and organic *form*. This is the difference between what Coleridge called "mechanic" *form* and *form* that "is innate; it shapes, as it develops, itself from within, and the fullness of its development is one and the same with the perfection of its outward form." Another way of expressing this difference is to think of "conventional" *form* as representing an ideal pattern or shape that precedes the content and meaning of the work and of organic *form* as representing a pattern or shape that develops as it is because of the content and meaning of the work. "Conventional" *form* presupposes certain characteristics of organization or pattern. Organic *form* asserts that each poem has, as Herbert Read has said, "its own inherent laws, originating with its very invention and fusing in one vital unity both structure and content."

Form is also loosely used for the common attributes that distinguish one genre from another. In this sense *form* becomes an abstract term describing not one work but the commonly held qualities of many. This abstract *form* in neoclassic periods tends to become a set of rules to be followed. See STRUCTURE.

Formal Criticism Criticism that examines a work in terms of the type or GENRE to which it belongs. See CRITICISM, TYPES OF.

Formal Essay A serious, dignified, orderly ESSAY.

Formal Satire One of the two major categories of SATIRE; the other is INDIRECT SATIRE. In *formal* (or direct) *satire*, the persona speaks in the first person either directly to the reader or to the ADVERSARIUS.

Formalism (or **Formalist Criticism**) A term applied to CRITICISM that emphasizes the form of the artwork, with "form" variously construed to mean generic form, type, verbal form, grammatical and syntactical form, rhetorical form, or verse form. It is applied to NEW CRITICS, CHICAGO CRITICS, and students of prosody, such as Paul Fussell (in view of his *Theory of Prosody in Eighteenth-Century England* and *Poetic Meter and Poetic Form*). In most cases the name is applied to the species of study that this handbook categorizes as the OBJECTIVE THEORY OF ART. One can usefully distinguish "containing form" from "shaping form" (as does Northrop Frye in *Anatomy of Criticism*, 1957), but, beyond that, the whole form-formal-*formalism* family is beset by problems of reference. With a clearly tangible object of culture, such as a cup, we can use Aristotle's echelon of four "causes"—final, formal, material, and efficient—and say that the size and shape are the formal cause, which some efficient cause (a cupmaker, say) imposes on some material cause (such as wood or clay) to serve some final cause, such as holding liquids. With artworks, however, it is difficult to specify what the form is, because plot may be the form that contains the characters, the characters the form that contains the thoughts and feelings, the thoughts and feelings the form that shapes the diction, the diction the form that shapes the acoustic effects, and so on.

Formalism (Russian) A lively and important multidisciplinary school that flourished around 1920. Influenced by Husserlian PHENOMENOLOGY and Saussurean linguistics, Russian Formalists emphasized form over content, "device" over message, and strangeness over familiarity. Because everyday language is sentenced to fall into banality and automatic flatness, it is the function of literary language by its unusual "literariness" to break up predictable patterns—of sound, grammar, plot—by means of conspicuous DEFAMILIARIZATION (*ostranenie*) that restores freshness and vitality to language. The most important members of the school—who resisted being called a school and even being classified as Formalists—were Viktor Šklovskij, Roman Jakobson, Boris Èjchenbaum, Lev Jakubinskij, Vladimir Propp, Boris Tomaševskij, Jurij Tynjanov, Grigorij Vinokur, and Viktor Žirmunskij. Much of Mikhail Bakhtin's earlier work, in the 1920s and 1930s, was devised as an extension or refutation of his Formalist compatriots.

[References: Victor Erlich, *Russian Formalism: History—Doctrine*, 3rd ed. (1969, 1965); Fredric Jameson, *The Prison-House of Language: A Critical Account of Structuralism and Russian Formalism* (1972); Peter Steiner, *Russian Formalism: A Metapoetics* (1984).]

Format The physical makeup of a printed work or an electronic document, including page size, typeface, margins, paper, and binding. *Format* has been extended to include the structure of a wide variety of things; one may speak, for example, of the *format* of a debate.

Formative Theory A form of FILM CRITICISM that, looking on the actual world as the raw material with which the creative imagination works, emphasizes how various techniques are employed to manipulate that material, using it not as statement in itself but as a means by which statements are made. It is broadly but not exclusively related to EXPRESSIONISM.

Forme (also **Form**) A collection of metal type set up in a frame or chase and used for printing at a single IMPRESSION.

Formula A hackneyed sequence of events characteristic of some popular forms of writing. Low-budget motion pictures with similar plots are said to follow a *formula*. In television dramatic series *formula* is almost always present and easily recognizable. Many detective stories and western stories are written to *formula*.

Formulaic A term applied to work that relies excessively on set patterns of plot, character, sentiment, and language—as though written to a FORMULA. A good deal of nonfiction—travel books, for example—tends to be *formulaic*. Any traveler, it seems, must get into amusing scrapes caused by misunderstanding of a foreign language (tourists in Germany may seek help in finding a "gift shop," unaware that *Gift* in German means "poison," and there are *formulaic* witticisms involving travelers being offered a *lei* in Hawaii).

Fortis A strongly articulated consonant, opposite of LENIS.

Fortisparsison In Welsh prosody, a foreign diphthong followed by a consonant cluster such as *dr* or *gr*. *Fortisparsison* is a species of ALIENISPARSISON.

Foul Copy Manuscript that, having already been used for typesetting, bears printer's marks, editor's queries, and frequently spike holes, ink stains, and fingerprints (and occasionally authors' execrations against editors).

Foul Proof Marked printer's proof from which corrections have been made. See FOUL COPY.

Foundationalism A general philosophical position that argues or assumes the existence of a fixed foundation for ideas, beliefs, and procedures; akin to ESSENTIALISM and opposed to EXISTENTIALISM and RELATIVISM.

[References: Stephen Crook, *Modernist Radicalism and Its Aftermath: Foundationalism and Anti-Foundationalism in Radical Social Theory* (1991); Stewart Shapiro, *Foundations Without Foundationalism: A Case for Second-Order Logic* (1991).]

Four Ages A scheme of great antiquity, dividing history into a line or cycle of ages, conventionally associated with gold, silver, brass, and iron. The scheme appears in Hindu and Roman cosmologies, in Giambattista Vico's fourfold vision of the world (more or less preserved in the structure of Joyce's *Finnegans Wake*), in a wittily rearranged order (iron, gold, silver, brass) in Thomas Love Peacock's "The Four Ages of Poetry," and in Northrop Frye's *Anatomy of Criticism* (in the form of a cycle of MYTH, ROMANCE, MIMESIS, IRONY).

Four Master Tropes Kenneth Burke's designation for METAPHOR, METONYMY, SYNECDOCHE, and IRONY. Burke claims to be concerned with the tropes "not with their purely figurative usage, but with their role in the discovery and description of 'the truth.'" According to Burke, the "literal" or "realistic" applications of the tropes go by different names, and he aligns metaphor with perspective, metonymy with reduction, synecdoche with representation, and irony with DIALECTIC.

[Reference: Kenneth Burke, *A Grammar of Motives* (1945).]

Four Senses of Interpretation The levels traditionally used in interpreting scriptural and allegorical materials: the literal, the allegorical, the moral, and the anagogical. See ANAGOGE.

Fourteeners A verse form consisting of fourteen syllables arranged in IAMBS. Its commonest employment is in couplets of iambic HEPTAMETER. George Chapman in the 1590s translated the *Iliad* in this meter.

Fourth Wall The invisible wall of a room through which the audience conventionally witnesses what occurs on a stage imagined as a room with four walls and a ceiling, the *fourth wall* being presented as just behind the CURTAIN. One of the most striking uses of the *fourth wall* was in a scene of William Gillette's *Sherlock Holmes*, when Holmes, sealed in a room, taps the walls and continues tapping the *fourth wall* while the sound effects of the tapping continue without interruption. See BOX SET.

Fractal A word that is a part of another word, significant only when there is some possible meaning in the containment. For example, it may be important that "Dick" is a *fractal* of "Dickens," because Dickens's *David Copperfield* includes a character named "Mr. Dick." Likewise, it is significant that "books" is a *fractal* of "brooks," because a thematic point about one's including of the other is made in *As You Like It* ("books in the running brooks").

Framework-Story A story inside a *framework*, a story inside a story. Perhaps the best-known examples are found in the Book of Job, the *Arabian Nights*, the *Decameron*, and the *Canterbury Tales*. Chaucer, for example, introduces in his Prologue a group making a pilgrimage. This general setting may be thought of as the *framework*; the stories that the various pilgrims tell along the way are *framework-stories*. The extent to which the *framework* becomes an actual plot within which other plots are inserted varies greatly. In the *Decameron* the tellers of the tales assemble and talk, and there is no plot in the *framework*. In the *Canterbury Tales* there is a plot in the *framework*, although it is very limited. In a work like *Moby-Dick*, in which the narrator participates in an action within which the story of Ahab's quest for the whale occurs, both *framework* and *framework-story* are inextricably mixed. *Frankenstein* is a frame-tale, because the story of Victor Frankenstein and his monster-creature is included in Robert Walton's account of his northward explorations, related in letters to his sister. What most readers think of as the real story of *Wuthering Heights* is the account of Heathcliff, but that is included inside the first-person account of the "outer" or "frame" narrator, Lockwood. A half century later, Joseph Conrad was fond of a similar form of framing, which led in some cases to three or four degrees of quotation as the nameless narrator tells what a storytelling character (Marlow, say) tells about what other characters say, and so forth. The *framework* was particularly popular around the turn of the twentieth century with such writers as Kipling, in "The Man Who Would Be King"; Joel Chandler Harris, in the Uncle Remus stories; Mark Twain, in "Jim Baker's Blue Jay Yarn"; and Henry James, in *The Turn of the Screw*, in which the story does not return to the frame situation at the end, with the result that the unclosed frame leaves unanswered questions.

Franco-Norman A term for material written in England shortly after the Conquest by Normans or persons of Norman descent using the Norman dialect of French. See ANGLO-NORMAN (language).

Frankfurt School The broadly Marxist group of social theorists identified with Frankfurt, including Theodor Adorno, Max Horkheimer, Jürgen Habermas, and Herbert Marcuse. Their concentration has been on economics, politics, and sociology, but their studies have been influential also in shaping concepts of language and literature as sociocultural reflexes.

Free Verse Ezra Pound once quoted T. S. Eliot as saying, "No *vers* is *libre* for the man who wants to do a good job." Because *vers libre* equals "free verse," the same maxim applies. It certainly may be the case that no verse is free if it uses a common language, because every human language is an overweening system of regulation and bondage that no speaker can escape without landing in unintelligibility.

Even so, verse may be relatively free, especially if we take pains in specifying what it is free *of*. It seems that the quantitative or alliterative verse of the ancients—speakers of Sanskrit, Greek, Latin, and all Old Germanic languages—was already so lax in its requirements that nobody thought of trying to emancipate verse. Once, however, rhymed verse in ACCENTUAL-SYLLABIC qualitative measures was established, the noose must have felt a bit too tight, for poets began looking for some relief. Surrey's innovation of BLANK VERSE (unrhymed iambic pentameter) in the mid-sixteenth century offered a measure of freedom in one dimension. By the eighteenth century, a few farseeing poets could manage without rhyme, meter, or regular rhythm, and Christopher Smart and William Blake could write a verse qualifying for the term *free*. Several poets of the nineteenth century continued the tradition; among them Thoreau, Emerson, and Whitman were foremost. In much of the newer *free verse*, from the mid-nineteenth century onward, the old shackles of rhyme were thrown off but, in some cases, new chains (such as Whitman's reliance on PARALLELISM and ANAPHORA) quickly took their place. Even today, very little of published verse is truly *free* in every respect.

[References: Charles O. Hartman, *Free Verse: an Essay on Prosody* (1980); Graham Hough, *Free Verse* (1958); Walter Sutton, *American Free Verse; the Modern Revolution in Poetry* (1973).]

French Forms (Sometimes referred to as the FIXED FORMS.) A name for certain prescribed patterns that originated in France largely during the time of the TROUBADOURS. The more usual are: *BALLADE*, CHANT ROYAL, RONDEAU, RONDEL, SESTINA, TRIOLET, and VILLANELLE.

Freudian Criticism Criticism based on psychological speculations and discoveries by Sigmund Freud and his disciples. In Freud's system the great source of psychic energy is in the unconscious, which influences every action but through forces and means not subject to recall or understanding by normal processes. The mind has three major areas of activity: the id, which is in the unconscious and is a reservoir of impulses, working for the gratification of its instincts (primarily sexual) through the pleasure principle; the superego, which is an internal censor bringing social pressures to bear on the id; and the ego, which is the part of the id that is modified by contact with the social world. The ego, which is consciousness, must always mediate among the demands of social pressure or reality, the libidinal demands for satisfaction arising from the id, and the claims of the superego. A mature ego conforms to the reality principle, i.e., the denial of immediate pleasure to avoid painful consequences or to make gratification possible later. Furthermore, the ego has various defense mechanisms, in addition to repression and sublimation, with which to protect itself against the demands of the id. In a rare expression of optimism, Freud once said, "Where id was, ego shall be."

Although Freud himself was most interested in the pathological aspects of psychoanalysis, the schema of the human mind that he unfolded has had incalculable influence. The emphasis on the unconscious with its hidden springs of motivation, the drama of the eternal conflict of id, ego, and superego, and the plot situations inherent in relationships such as those in the OEDIPUS COMPLEX—all have been grist for the creative mind as well as instruments for the critical faculty. Biographers have tried to unlock the mysteries of creative personalities, as Marie Bonaparte did in *The Life and Works of Edgar Allan Poe*. Critics have seen character relationships in literary works in new lights, as Ernest Jones did in *Hamlet and Oedipus*. Imaginative overviews of literary history colored by psychoanalytical assumptions have been taken, as Leslie Fiedler did in *Love and Death in the American Novel*.

More recently, criticism has benefited from the reinterpretation of Freud in linguistic terms, stressing the formative role of linguistic mechanisms in the creation and functioning of the psyche. But misapplications of Freudian thought have brought about a lively reaction.

[Reference: Louis Breger, *Freud: Darkness in the Midst of Vision* (2000); Lesley Chamberlain, *The Secret Artist: A Close Reading of Sigmund Freud* (2000); Frederick Crews, ed., *The Memory Wars: Freud's Legacy in Dispute* (1995), *Psychoanalysis and Literary Process* (1970), *Unauthorized Freud: Doubters Confront a Legend* (1998); F. J. Hoffman, *Freudianism and the Literary Mind*, 2nd ed. (1957); Kaja Silverman, *The Subject of Semiotics* (1983); Meredith Skura, *The Literary Use of the Psychoanalytic Process* (1981).]

Freytag's Pyramid A diagram of the structure of a five-act tragedy, given by Gustav Freytag in *Technik des Dramas* (1863):

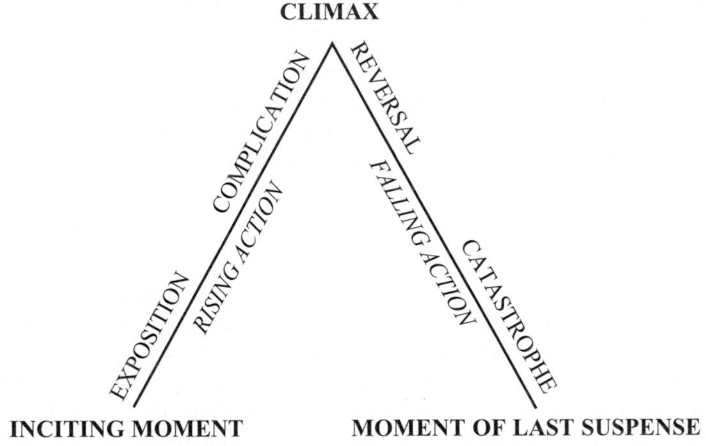

This pyramid has been widely accepted as a heuristic means of getting at the structure of many kinds of fiction in addition to drama. See appropriate entries for the terms on the pyramid, PLOT, and DRAMATIC STRUCTURE.

Frisket In older presses, a hinged metal frame outfitted with tapes or paper strips that keep a sheet in position during printing.

Frontier Literature Writing about the American frontier and frontier life. Up to 1890, when all the free lands had generally been claimed, one aspect of American history was the steady westward movement of the frontier. Cooper, for example, could write of the frontier as being in New York State; Brackenridge in *Modern Chivalry* saw the wilds of Pennsylvania as the outer edge of cultivation; Simms in his border romances could see Georgia and Alabama as untamed wildernesses. Horace Greeley, when he enjoined young men to "go west," was probably thinking about Pittsburgh. Mark Twain in *Roughing It* could picture a primitive West. The extent to which this westward-moving frontier colored and shaped American thought and life and the extent to which its passing marked a sharp turn in the character of the American experience are matters of debate. But, whatever one may think of Frederick Turner's thesis that the frontier has been the dominant influence in American history, there is little question that frontiers have consistently found literary expression in a robust, humorous, often crude body of songs, tales, and books that have been marked by a realistic view of life, sanguine contemplation of violence, and immense gusto. Much of the writing of this frontier was subliterary, confined to oral tradition and to newspapers, but it kept constantly alive in America a hearty humor and a healthy realism, even in the face of the GENTEEL TRADITION. Important writers in the frontier tradition have been T. B. Thorpe, Timothy Flint, Augustus Baldwin Longstreet, Joseph Glover Baldwin, Artemus Ward, Caroline Kirkland, Joseph Kirkland, Jane Tompkins, Bret Harte, Mark Twain, and Hamlin Garland. Some of Larry McMurtry's novels—*Leaving Cheyenne*; *Horseman, Pass By*; *The Last Picture Show*; *Lonesome Dove*—qualify as the contemporary counterpart of *frontier literature*.

[References: William Humphrey, *Ah, Wilderness!: The Frontier in American Literature* (1977); Howard Mumford Jones, *The Frontier in American Fiction* (1956); Annette Kolodny, *The Land Before Her* (1984).]

Fu A technical term in the Briggsian school of FILM CRITICISM; appropriated from the Chinese "kung fu," the Briggsian application of *fu* means mindless violence. The term seldom appears alone; instead, it is a suffix appended to the instrument or perpetrator of the violence, as in "firehose *fu*," "chainsaw *fu*," or "bimbo *fu*."

Fugitives, The A group associated with Vanderbilt University which in the 1920s published the magazine *The Fugitive*. Members of the group later came to be known as *The Fugitive*-Agrarians. See AGRARIANS.

Fundamental Image A controlling figure around which a work is organized. When the controlling figure is a metaphor, it is called a CONTROLLING IMAGE, a device often used in metaphysical verse. *Fundamental image* is used to designate the simpler, nonmetaphorical use of some important aspect or feature of an object being described or discussed. This reduction of the complex whole to one main feature or unifying principle simplifies and focuses the description in such a way as to make for clearness. The famous description of the battle of Waterloo, in which Victor Hugo employed the outline of the letter *A* is illustrative of the position of the various armies, is a notable example of the clarifying value of the *fundamental image*. A more recent example is the passage in T. S. Eliot's "Burnt Norton" beginning "Here is a place of disaffection," which seems general and even rather vague until one associates the tone and details with the Gloucester Road underground station.

Fused Rhyme A curious phenomenon, scarcely found anywhere in English outside a few poems by Gerard Manley Hopkins, in which a *rhyme* sound is begun at the end of a line but not completed until the beginning of the next. Here are three instances from Hopkins's "The Wreck of the Deutschland":

> leeward . . . drew her / Dead . . . endured.
> rest of them . . . unconfessed of them . . . breast of the / Maiden
> door / Drowned . . . Reward . . . Lord.

"Leeward" and "endured" rhyme normally with each other but with "drew her / Dead" only by means of fusion that creates a sound unit out of "drew her / D" and so forth; similarly with "door / D" and "breast of the / M."

Fustian A coarse, cotton cloth, usually dyed some dark color to resemble velveteen. By extension, it is used as a derogatory term for overblown diction. Thomas Heywood, in *Faire Maid of the Exchange*, speaks of "Some scurvy quaint collection of *fustian* phrases, and uplandish words."

Egyptian. This typeface was based on original Egyptian typefaces of the early nineteenth century and was recut by Monotype Corp. Ltd., England, under the same name.

Gaelic Movement A movement that began late in the nineteenth century, especially as embodied in the Gaelic League, founded by Douglas Hyde in 1893, and devoted to the preservation of the Gaelic language, which had been gradually giving way to English since the seventeenth century and had not been permitted in the new schools established in the middle of the nineteenth century. The *Gaelic Movement* attempted to foster a new native IRISH LITERATURE. Hyde himself wrote plays in Gaelic. The movement was overshadowed by the IRISH LITERARY MOVEMENT, which encouraged the use of English in creating a new Irish literature exploiting Irish materials. See CELTIC RENAISSANCE.

Galliambic The River Gallos in Phrygia gave its name to the Galli, eunuch priests of Cybele, who in turn gave their name to *galliambics*, or lines in the *galliambic* measure. In quantitative terms, the *galliambic* line consists of four four-syllabled feet; in qualitative terms, these feet would be:

1. pyrrhic + trochee
2. trochee + spondee
3. pyrrhic + trochee
4. pyrrhic + pyrrhic, or pyrrhic + iamb.

Supposedly, as used by Catullus in his "Attis" poem, the rhythm resembled that of the chant of the priests. *Galliambics* have rarely been attempted in English, but the few experiments are noteworthy. George Meredith's "Phaethon" and Tennyson's "Boädicéa" adapt the measure to English; here is the beginning of the latter:

While about the shore of Mona those Neronian legionaries
Burnt and broke the grove and altar of the Druid and Druidess,
Far in the East Boädicéa, standing loftily charioted,
Mad and maddening all that heard her in her fierce volubility,
Girt by half the tribes of Britain, near the colony Cámulodúne,
Yell'd and shriek'd between her daughters o'er a wild confederacy.

The latest poet to attempt a qualitative approximation of *galliambics* is John Frederick Nims in "Niagara" (1990):

> Eyes can't leave the livid seething, its reiterative *Memento!*
> Reading, in this bubble-chamber, stuff of the world as effervescence,
> Reading every life as half-life, reading in form the one prognosis. . . .

Gallicism Diction characteristic of the French language, or a custom or turn of thought suggestive of the French people. The term is applied to any borrowing from the French, especially one in which the borrower stops short of using the French correctly. Although *Gallicisms* have obviously enriched and enlivened the language, they often become forms of affectation. Words such as "morale" and "mystique," which look and sound French, have acquired senses in English that are different and even remote from their French meaning. The French sense of psychological *moment* (meaning "momentum") wandered into English as a "moment" of time (expanded by Ezra Pound into a title, "The Psychological Hour"). The almost meaningless "rationale," which is Latin and strictly ought to be pronounced as four syllables (two trochees), has become a three-syllabled amphimacer as though it were French; it is not. The use of this latter pronunciation of "rationale" meaning nothing more than "reason" is one sort of *Gallicism*.

Gasconade Because Gascons were considered inveterate boasters, *gasconade* came to mean bravado or boastful talk.

Gathering A group of leaves in a book cut from a single sheet after it has been folded. A FOLIO makes a *gathering* of two leaves or four pages, a QUARTO one of four leaves or eight pages (see BOOK SIZES). A *gathering* is often called a SIGNATURE. Modern printers use *gathering* to mean the process by which signatures or *gatherings* are assembled to make a book; they rarely use it in the sense of signature.

Gematria Assigning numerical values to letters and thereby computing totals for words. Such procedures originate in certain styles of interpreting Hebrew scripture but carry on in other alphabets. Donne's "A Valediction of My Name, in the Window" has to do with the physical appearance of "Jo: Donne" scratched in glass and the calculation of the numerical values of his name as seven and thirty-six.

Gemination Any twinning, doubling, duplication, or repetition. In rhetoric, *gemination* is the repetition of a word or phrase for emphasis, as in "no, no." In general, *gemination* involves the doubling of a single consonant sound or of a letter.

Generative Metrics A theory employing the methods of transformational-generative linguistics. This theory sees a number of positions in a line rather than a number of feet. The line "When I consider how my light is spent" is said to have ten positions. The STRESSES on positions are those that result from the assignment of stress in transformational-generative linguistics rather than how the line is read aloud, if the two differ. Stress maximum—that is stress relatively greater than that in positions on either side of it—normally does not fall on a weak position. In an iambic line the odd positions are usually considered weak, the even strong. However, certain phrasal stress situations in transformational-generative linguistics can result in stress maximum falling on odd positions. So far, *generative metrics* has been applied primarily to iambic lines in an attempt to do for "metricality" what transformational-generative linguistics does for "grammaticality."

[Reference: Morris Halle and S. J. Keyser, *English Stress: Its Form, Its Growth, and Its Role in Verse* (1971).]

Genethliacon A birthday ODE.

Geneva School A group of critics, including Georges Poulet, Marcel Raymond, Albert Béguin, and the early J. Hillis Miller, who see a literary work as a series of existential expressions of the author's individual consciousness. Although they vary in method and emphasis—Poulet, for example, seeing the author's consciousness displayed in temporal and spatial coordinates and Miller in the expression of an immanent reality—the group is consistent in placing the highest value on individual consciousness and in seeing literature as the expression of that consciousness revealed in the act of reading. See also PHENOMENOLOGY.

Genre Used to designate the types or categories into which literary works are grouped according to form, technique, or, sometimes, subject matter. The French term means "kind," "genus," or "type." The traditional *genres* include tragedy, comedy, epic, lyric, and pastoral. Today a division of literature into *genres* would also include novel, short story, essay, television play, and motion picture scenario.

Genre classification implies that there are groups of formal or technical characteristics among works of the same generic kind regardless of time or place of composition, author, or subject matter; and that these characteristics, when they define a particular group of works, are of basic significance in talking about literary art. Prior to the Romantic age in England, there was a tendency to assume that literary kinds had an ideal existence and obeyed laws of kind, these laws being criteria by which works could be judged. In the Romantic Age, *genre* distinctions were often looked upon merely as restatements of conventions and were suspect. Critics today frequently regard *genre* distinctions as useful descriptive devices but rather arbitrary ones. *Genre* boundaries have been much subject to flux and blur in recent times, and it is almost the rule that a successful work will combine *genres* in some original way. The long-running *Dallas* on television, for example, combined elements of the WESTERN and the soap opera. There has also been a proliferation of hyphenated hybrids such as the prose poem, the nonfiction novel, and the television movie.

In painting, *genre* is applied to works that depict ordinary, everyday life in realistic terms. The term is sometimes extended to work that deals with commonplace or homely situations in subdued tones. Whittier's *Snow-Bound* is sometimes called "a *genre* study."

[Reference: Rosalie L. Colie, *The Resources of Kind: Genre-Theory in the Renaissance* (ed. Barbara Lewalski) (1973).]

Genre Criticism That type of CRITICISM dedicated to defining GENRES and tracing their histories and interactions. It is particularly useful in understanding how a work came to be at a given time and why some problematical works have been ignored or misunderstood on account of some confusion of their category. *Moby-Dick*, say, which is classifiable as an anatomy, cannot be fully understood or enjoyed if it is approached as a novel of adventure or education. See CHICAGO CRITICS; STRUCTURALISM.

A term also applied to the method of FILM CRITICISM that analyzes and evaluates a film in terms of the particular genre to which it belongs, such as Western, detective, gangster, or romantic comedy. The GENRE film critic usually employs one of two distinct approaches. In the first genre is seen as a model of a kind of statement, as an archetype. In the second the genre is seen as employing a group of conventions whose uses in a particular film are evaluated.

[References: Northrop Frye, *Anatomy of Criticism* (1957).]

Genteel Comedy Addison's term for such early eighteenth-century comedy as Cibber's *The Careless Husband*. It was a continuation of the Restoration COMEDY OF MANNERS, adapted to the genteel manners of the age of Anne. Compared with Restoration comedy, the moral tone was higher, the motives more artificial, and the wit less brilliant.

Genteel Tradition A tradition of conventional correctness in American writing in the late nineteenth and early twentieth centuries. It was largely associated with New England. Both REALISM and NATURALISM were reactions against the *genteel tradition*. Among its leading figures were R. H. Stoddard, Bayard Taylor, E. C. Stedman, T. B. Aldrich, and E. R. Sill. See BRAHMINS.

Georgian Used for two distinct periods in English literary history. In the first it pertains to the reigns of the first four Georges (1714–1830). The Romantic poets have been called "*Georgians*" in this sense. A group including Thomas Lovell Beddoes, W. M. Praed, and Thomas Hood are sometimes styled the "second *Georgian* school." From 1912 to 1922 there appeared five anthologies entitled *Georgian Poetry*, *Georgian* here referring to the reign of George V (1910–1936). These volumes, according to their editor, E. H. Marsh, reflect a belief that English poetry was "once again putting on new strength and beauty." W. W. Gibson, Rupert Brooke, John Masefield, and Walter de la Mare are representative of the poets included. The term is also applied to the GEORGIAN AGE, between the beginning of the First World War and the beginning of the Second.

Georgian Age in English Literature, 1914–1940 The *Georgian Age in English Literature* begins with the First World War. It is named for George V, although he reigned from 1910 to 1936. The war effected a fundamental change in English life and thought, a true start of a new age, marked by a long and bitter struggle for national survival, by a flowering of aesthetic talent and experiment in the 1920s, and by the harshness of the Great Depression in the 1930s. In 1940 England had become once more an embattled fortress, destined to suffer six years of harsh attack and the destruction of much of its finest talent.

It was a rich period for the novel. The Edwardians Galsworthy, Wells, Bennett, and Conrad continued to do fine work, and in the 1920s experimental fiction was triumphantly developed by Dorothy Richardson, Virginia Woolf, and James Joyce. In the 1930s Aldous Huxley, Evelyn Waugh, and Graham Greene joined Maugham and Lawrence in producing fiction that constituted a serious commentary on social and moral values. The theater was marked by the social drama of Galsworthy, Jones, and Pinero, and the plays of ideas of Shaw. Maugham and Coward practiced the COMEDY OF MANNERS with distinction. Although Thomas Hardy turned seventy-four in 1914, he was still producing extraordinarily powerful poetry, especially that in the volume *Satires of Circumstance* (1914). Hundreds of other poems followed in the years before Hardy's death, at eighty-seven, in early 1928. Throughout the *Georgian Age* Yeats was a major poetic voice, as was T. S. Eliot, whose *The Waste Land* was the most important single poetic publication. The posthumous publication of the poetry of Gerard Manley Hopkins in 1918 added significantly to the new poetry. T. E. Hulme, Wyndham Lewis, I. A. Richards, T. S. Eliot, and William Empson created an informed, basically anti-Romantic, analytical criticism. Modernism found its doctrines and its voice and did much of its best work during the *Georgian Age*.

It was a time of national troubles, of major war, of deep depression, and of declining empire, yet the literary expression of the age was vital, fresh, and varied. By the coming of the Second World War, the chief literary figures were turning inward, but they still showed little of the diminishment that was to come.

Georgic A poem ostensibly about farming and the practical aspects of rustic life; so called from Virgil's *Georgics*.

Gest An old word occasionally found in English, especially in literary titles from the medieval period, meaning a tale of war or adventure, as the *Gest Historiale of the Destruction of Troy* (fourteenth century). The word is probably borrowed from the more common word in Old French, *geste*, as in the *CHANSON DE GESTE*. The corresponding Latin word appears in a somewhat similar sense in the title of a collection of Latin stories written about 1250, the *Gesta Romanorum*, "deeds of the Romans."

Gestalt A configuration such that the whole possesses properties not derivable from its parts or their simple sum. The term comes from *Gestalt* psychology. Some critics, among them Herbert J. Muller, see in it a concept that allows concrete experience to precede logical analysis. Leonard Meyer has systemically applied *Gestalt* principles to the study of music, which, given its emphasis on purely formal and physical qualities, seems amenable to such analysis. The *Gestalt* critic sees all the elements of any work of art or literature as being variables with values that depend on their position in the "configuration" and on its total effect. A variable element like rain, say, seems more or less neutral until it becomes part of some *Gestalt*—physical and symbolic—and means one thing (positive) in Eliot's *The Waste Land* and quite another thing (negative) in Hemingway's *A Farewell to Arms* and in Edith Sitwell's "Still Falls the Rain."

Ghazal (or **Ghasel**) A flexible lyric form, usually in a small number of couplets with or without rhyme, first employed in various Middle Eastern literatures and later enjoying a vogue among German romanticists and just recently among American poets. It has been suggested that Tennyson's "Now Sleeps the Crimson Petal" satisfies many of the formal and thematic requirements of the *ghazal*. William Barnes's "Woak Hill" and "In the Spring" resemble Tennyson's poem. Barnes's "The Knoll" consists of ten couplets of anapestic pentameter; in each couplet the first line has an unrhymed FEMININE ENDING, and the second ends with "knoll." Barnes's pupil and friend, Thomas Hardy, wrote a couple of poems ("My Cicely" and "A Mother Mourns") that resemble such *ghazal*-like experiments, except that Hardy's quatrains end with a consistent rhyming line, whereas the earlier poets used repetition, possibly with INTERNAL RHYME.

Ghost (1) Or "ghost word": a word created by a misprint or a misreading. "Syllabus," for example, seems to have begun as a misreading of "sittybas" as "syllabos." Webster's *Second International Dictionary* (1934) seems to list "Dord" as a synonym for "density"; the text should have been "D or d," indicating that the capital or lowercase letter is used as an abbreviation. (2) Or "ghost signature": a mirror-image impression of a signature in ink, created by folding the paper over or by applying another piece of paper. (3) In bibliography, an item that finds its way onto a list without actually existing. Such a *ghost* may be bred by an error (as between "Gay" and "Gray") or by a premature announcement in a publisher's advertisement of forthcoming titles, not all of which come forth. (4) Same as GHOSTWRITER.

Ghost Story A story that involves a ghost or similar spirit. In some, the ghost is overtly labeled as such; in others, such as Henry James's *The Turn of the Screw*, there is more mystery and doubt.

Ghostwriter One who does journalistic writing to be published under the name of another. People who are much in the public eye but who are also either unskilled or uninterested in writing often allow their names to be attached to material written by journalists employed for the purpose. *Ghostwriting* is more frequently used in the preparation of newspaper and magazine articles than in the writing of books, although it is by no means unknown in book publishing.

Gift Books Miscellaneous collections of literary materials published annually in book form for purchase as gifts. They were popular in England and America in the nineteenth century. Their value in American literary history has been great. See ANNUALS.

Gigantism A tendency toward morbid exaggeration or other distortion. The term literally has to do with magnitude, as in certain writers' practice of piling up item after item in epic inventories (like many passages in Walt Whitman's poetry); figuratively—as when Robert Lowell mentioned "the gigantism of the sonnet"—the term refers to a spirit of aggrandizement and hyperbole that is as prevalent in sonnets as in epics.

Glance In the seventeenth century, an allusive satirical jest.

Glee A poem written as though to be sung by a group. Sir Walter Scott's *Woodstock, or the Cavalier: A Tale of the Year 1651* includes "Glee for King Charles." A musical composition for unaccompanied solo male voices, usually a setting of a light or patriotic poem. Subsequently, with the development of *glee* clubs in the English-speaking world, the term came to mean choral settings for male, female, or mixed voices, accompanied or unaccompanied.

Gleeman A musical entertainer among the Anglo-Saxons. *Gleemen* were usually traveling professionals who recited poetry composed by others, though some of them were original poets. They were sometimes attached to kings' courts but occupied a less dignified and permanent position than the SCOP. In the main, the SCOP composed and the *gleeman* sang or recited the scop's compositions to the accompaniment of the harp or other instrument. Some use the term loosely for any kind of medieval composer or reciter.

Gloss An explanation. A difficult word in a text might be explained by a marginal or interlinear word or phrase, usually in a more familiar language. Thus, Greek manuscripts were *glossed* by Latin copyists who gave the readers the Latin word or phrase equivalent to the difficult one in Greek. Similar bilingual *glosses* were inserted in medieval manuscripts by scribes who would explain Latin words by native, vernacular words. Some of the earliest examples of written Irish, for example, are found in the margins and between the lines of Latin manuscripts written in the early Middle Ages. Extended explanatory and interpretive comment on medieval scriptural texts were called *glosses*. They have been used extensively in interpreting medieval literature in recent years. Later the word came to have a still broader use in "E. K.'s" "*Gloss*" to Spenser's *The Shepheardes Calender* (1579), which undertakes not only to explain the author's purpose and to comment on the degree of his success, but also to supply notes explaining difficult words and phrases and giving miscellaneous learned comments. The marginal *gloss* that Coleridge supplied in 1817 for his earlier *Rime of the Ancient Mariner* is more than a summary of the story; it amounts to a different version of the story, with Coleridge using the form both self-consciously and ironically. Among modern writers, Paul Valéry and James Joyce made occasional use of marginal glosses, as have Thomas Hardy, Hart Crane, and James Dickey. The word is sometimes used in a derogatory sense, as when to *gloss* a passage means to misinterpret it and "to *gloss* over" is used in the sense of "explain away." Glossaries developed from the habit of collecting *glosses* into lists.

Glossary A list, usually alphabetical, of terms needing explanation. *Glossaries* are seldom very detailed.

Glossator A writer of GLOSSES, especially those dealing with the law.

Glyconic A classical quantitative measure of three or four feet, sometimes simplified to the pattern TROCHEE-trochee-trochee-DACTYL, but with plenty of room for variation. Also the name of a four-lined stanza.

Gnomic Aphoristic, moralistic, sententious, from *gnome*, a Greek poem that expressed a general truth. The "*Gnomic* Poets" (sixth century B.C.) arranged their wise sayings in a series of maxims; hence, the term *gnomic* was applied to poetry that dealt in a sententious way with ethical questions, such as the wisdom poetry of the Bible, the Latin *sententiae*, the *Elder Edda*, and the *gnomic* verses in Old English. Although more properly applied to a style of poetry, as to some of the verse of Francis Quarles, the prose style of Bacon's early essays is also called *gnomic* when marked by the use of APHORISMS.

Gnosticism The beliefs of various cults in late pre-Christian and early Christian times. The *Gnostics* thought that human beings had an immediate knowledge of spiritual truth that was available to them through faith alone. The *Gnostics* claimed mystic and esoteric religious insights, placed great emphasis on transcendent human knowledge, and believed that all matter is evil. They incorporated some Christian beliefs into their system. The *Gnostics* believed that the world is ruled by evil archons, one of whom was the Jehovah of the Old Testament, who held the spirit of humanity captive. Jesus Christ was interpreted as a special power (an aeon) sent from the heavens to restore to human beings the lost knowledge of their divine nature and powers. Various cults of *Gnostics* incorporated elements of many religions in this syncretic movement, which later merged with MANICHAEISM. *Gnosticism* was the great heresy against which many of the early formal doctrinal statements of the church were formulated.

Golden Line Usually refers to a PENTAMETER line with the pattern adjective-noun-adjective-noun, as in William Morris's "The idle singer of an empty day" and T. S. Eliot's "The vanished power of the usual reign."

Goliardic Verse Lilting Latin verse, usually satiric, composed by university students and wandering scholars in Germany, France, and England in the twelfth and thirteenth centuries. *Goliardic verse* celebrated wine, women, and song; was often licentious; and was marked by irreverent attacks on church and clergy. Its dominant theme was CARPE DIEM. Its name comes from a legendary bishop and archpoet, Golias. Another of the *Goliardic* poets was Walter Map, to whom more verses have been attributed than he could possibly have written.

Gongorism A highly affected style taking its name from the Spanish poet Luis de Gongóra y Argote (1561–1627), whose writings exhibited stylistic extravagances, such as the introduction of new words, innovations in grammar, BOMBAST, PUNS, PARADOXES, CONCEITS, and obscurity. It has some of the qualities of EUPHUISM. See MARINISM.

Gossip A staple of human culture from the beginning, *gossip* is the unofficial exchange of information and opinions having to do with the private conduct of others. We customarily say that *gossip* is repeated, that *gossip* spreads, passed from one person to another until the original personnel and activities are quite transformed. The ROMAN À CLEF in particular tends toward *gossip*, as is certainly the case with Somerset Maugham's *Cakes and Ale* and Truman Capote's *Answered Prayers*.

Gossip Column A recurrent feature in a periodical, devoted to scraps, hints, and guesses about private lives of public persons and the scandals of the day.

Gothic Though the Goths were a single Germanic tribe of ancient and medieval times, the meaning of *Gothic* was broadened to mean Teutonic or Germanic and, later, "medieval" in general. In architecture, *Gothic*, though it may mean any style not classic, is more specifically applied to the style that succeeded the Romanesque in Western Europe, flourishing from the twelfth century to the sixteenth. It is marked by the pointed arch and vault, vertical effects (suggesting aspiration), stained windows (mystery), slender spires, flying buttresses, intricate traceries, wealth and variety of detail, and flexibility of spirit. Applied to literature, the term was used by the eighteenth-century neoclassicists as synonymous with "barbaric." Addison said that artists who were unable to achieve the classic graces of simplicity, dignity, and unity resorted to the use of foreign ornaments, "all the extravagances of an irregular fancy." The romanticists of the next generation, however, looked with favor on the *Gothic*; to them it suggested whatever was medieval, natural, primitive, wild, free, authentic, romantic. Indeed, they praised such writers as Shakespeare and Spenser because of their *Gothic* elements—variety, richness, mystery, aspiration. Later vigorous celebrators of the *Gothic* were Ruskin, Pater, and Henry Adams. The comic books and movies devoted to Batman emphasize pointed arches and vertical movement in dark spaces. The 1989 movie ends in a *Gothic* cathedral in the aptly named *Gotham* City. Joyce Carol Oates called Cormac McCarthy's *Blood Meridian* a "Gothic western." See GOTHIC NOVEL.

Gothic Novel A novel in which magic, mystery, and chivalry are the chief characteristics. Horrors abound: One may expect a suit of armor suddenly to come to life among ghosts, clanking chains, and charnel houses. Although anticipations of the *Gothic novel* appear in Smollett (especially in *Ferdinand Count Fathom*, 1753), Horace Walpole was the real originator, his famous *Castle of Otranto* (1764) being the first. Its setting is a medieval castle with long underground passages, trap doors, dark stairways, and mysterious rooms whose doors slam unexpectedly. William Beckford's *Vathek, an Arabian Tale* (1786) added the element of Oriental luxury and magnificence to the species. Anne Radcliffe's five romances (1789–1797), especially *The Mysteries of Udolpho*, added to the popularity of the form. Her emphasis on setting and story rather than on character became conventional, as did the types of characters she employed. Succeeding writers who produced Gothic romances include: Matthew ("Monk") Lewis, William Godwin, and Mary Wollstonecraft Shelley, whose *Frankenstein* is a striking performance in the tradition. The form spread to practically every European literature, being especially popular in Germany. In America the type was cultivated early by Charles Brockden Brown. The *Gothic novels* not only are of interest in themselves but have exerted a significant influence on other forms. This influence made itself felt in the poetry of the Romantic Period, as in Coleridge's *Christabel* and *Kubla Khan*, Wordsworth's *Guilt and Sorrow*, Byron's *Giaour*, and Keats's *Eve of St. Agnes*. Some of the romances were dramatized, and dramas not based on romances, such as Byron's *Manfred* and Morton's *Speed the Plough*, have *Gothic* elements. The novels of Scott, Charlotte Brontë, and others, as well as the mystery and horror type of short story exploited by Poe and his successors, contain materials and devices traceable to the *Gothic novel*. The term is today often applied to works, such as Daphne du Maurier's *Rebecca*, that lack the Gothic setting or the medieval atmosphere but that attempt to create the same atmosphere of brooding and unknown terror as the true *Gothic novel*. It is also applied to a host of currently popular tales of "damsels in distress" in strange and terrifying locales—a type ridiculed as early as Jane Austen's *Northanger Abbey*. A century later, the great Danish writer "Isak Dinesen" (pseudonym of Karen Christence Dinesen, Baroness Blixen-Finecke) used "Gothic" in titles to indicate simultaneously a literal setting in northern Europe and a fantastic spirit combining horror, crime, romance, and realism.

[References: Brendan Hennessy, *The Gothic Novel* (1978); Ann B. Tracy, *The Gothic Novel, 1790–1830: Plot Summaries and Index to Motifs* (1981).]

Götterdämmerung A German word meaning "the twilight of the gods." It is the title of the last of Richard Wagner's music dramas in *The Ring of the Nibelung*. In English the word is used to describe a massive collapse and destruction with great violence and disorder.

Graces, The In Greek myth, the three sister goddesses who confer grace, beauty, charm, and joy on human beings and nature. They are Aglaia (splendor or elevation), Euphrosyne (mirth), and Thalia (abundance).

Grammatology The science of writing, especially of systems of graphic representation of language. Rare in English (except in the subtitle of the first edition of I. J. Gelb's *A Study of Writing*, 1952), the term was revived and expanded by Jacques Derrida in *Of Grammatology* (tr. 1976), in which *grammatology* takes on philosophical depth and complexity beyond the relatively simple considerations of whether a given mark represents a sound, an idea, or a combination of both.

Grand Style, The A concept traceable back as far as classical antiquity (Longinus) and coming forward to theorists of the eighteenth and nineteenth centuries (Edmund Burke and Matthew Arnold), involving a host of lofty elements; nobility of character, sublimity of conception, dignified simplicity or severity of utterance, and grandeur of scope.

Graphic Novel A story, most often FANTASY or SCIENCE FICTION, presented in the format of a COMIC BOOK. After about 1975 graphic novels became increasing serious and subtle, and some were as well-produced as standard books and magazines. Related to MANGA, which began as a specifically Japanese adaptation of such a style.

Graustark A fictional country that seems to be a small and minor Central European monarchy that has held on to some feudal ways. The concepts of *Graustark* and all things *Graustarkian* come from a prodigiously successful set of light romance novels by the American George Barr McCutcheon (1866–1928): *Graustark: The Story of a Love Behind a Throne* (1901), *Beverly of Graustark* (1904), *The Prince of Graustark* (1914), *East of the Setting Sun: A Story of Graustark* (1924). The model for *Graustark* could be the kingdom of Ruritania in Anthony Hope's *The Prisoner of Zenda* (1894) and *Rupert of Hentzau* (1898). The *Graustark* stories, some of which became hit silent movies for such stars as Norma Talmadge and Marion Davies, involve comic contrasts between Europe and America, past and present, women and men, royal and common.

"Graveyard School" A group of eighteenth-century poets who wrote long poems on death and immortality. The "graveyard" poetry was related to early stages of the English romantic movement. The poets so called tried to get the atmosphere of pleasing gloom by efforts to call up not only the horrors of death but the very "odor of the charnel house." A forerunner was Thomas Parnell, whose "Night-Piece on Death" (1722) not only anticipates Gray's famous "Elegy Written in a Country Churchyard" (1751)—the most famous poem produced by the group—but whose "long palls, drawn hearses, cover'd steeds, and plumes of black" show an approach to the phraseology of Robert Blair's "The Grave" (1743), one of the most typical poems of the movement, and of the "Night-Thoughts" (1745) of Edward Young. Although the *Graveyard School* was philosophically contemplating immortality, the lasting effect of their poetry, with the exception of a few such pieces as Gray's "Elegy," has been one element in the Gothic aspect of romanticism. In America the poetry of the *Graveyard School* was reflected in Philip Freneau's "The House of Night" (1779) and most famously in William Cullen Bryant's "Thanatopsis" (1817).

Gravisparsison In Welsh prosody, the effect produced by a foreign diphthong followed by such consonant clusters as *rs*; a category of *alienisparsison*.

Great Awakening, The See AWAKENING, THE GREAT.

Great Chain of Being The belief that everything partakes of a hierarchical system, extending upward from inanimate matter to things that have life but do not reason, to the rational human being (whom Pope called "a creature in a middle state"), to angels, and finally to God. Each thing in nature occupies its proper place. The idea of the universe as a hierarchical system found expression in Plato's *Timaeus* and *The Republic*, but the figure of the *chain* is probably from Milton's lines ". . . hanging in a golden chain / This pendant world." The concept was powerful and widespread in the seventeenth and eighteenth centuries. Pope gave it clear expression in *Essay on Man*:

> Vast chain of being! which from God began,
> Natures aethereal, human, angel, man,
> Beast, bird, fish, insect, what no eye can see,
> No glass can reach; from Infinite to thee,
> From thee to nothing.—On superior pow'rs
> Were we to press, inferior might on ours;
> Or in the whole creation leave a void,
> Where, one step broken, the great scale's destroy'd:
> From Nature's chain whatever link you strike,
> Tenth, or ten thousandth, breaks the chain alike.

A more optimistic concept of upward progression was expressed by Emerson:

> Striving to be man, the worm
> Mounts through all the spires of form.

[Reference: A. O. Lovejoy, *The Great Chain of Being: A Study in the History of an Idea* (1936, reprinted 1964).]

Great Vowel Shift A massive change in the sounding of many long vowels in English (and only in English) between 1350 and 1550. Informally speaking, the letter "a," which had represented the sound of "ah," after the shift came to represent "ay"; the letter "e," which had represented the sound of "ay," came represent "ee"; and the letter "i," which had represented the sound of "ee," came to represent "eye." This is a gross summary of a few long vowels, but it omits many details, anomalies, and subtleties.

Greek Romance A work of prose fiction such as those produced between A.D. 100 and 300 by the *Erōtoici Graeci*. The best known of these exciting novels are the anonymous *Apollonius of Tyre*, Heliodorus' *Aethiopica*, and Longus' *Daphnis and Chloe*. The stories often involve the adventures and ordeals of high-born lovers who are separated and finally rejoined. The appearance of Thomas Underdown's *Ethiopian History* (a translation of a Latin translation of Heliodorus) around 1570 started a fad for *Greek romances* in England. Sidney's *Arcadia* was an adaptation of the fashion, the Shakespeare's *Pericles* owes its plot to *Apollonius of Tyre*.

Green-Room An area in a theater where performers and other functionaries may gather when not carrying out their duties.

Grimm's Law In 1822 Jakob Grimm formulated a principle that describes a complex of relations among consonants in Indo-European languages. The table below summarizes a sampling of these shifts as heard in Latin and English:

Latin		English	Example
p	→	f	*pater/father*
t	→	th	*tu/thou*
k	→	h	*cor/heart*
b	→	p	*bursa/purse*
d	→	t	*dens/tooth*
g	→	k	*genus/kind*

Grotesque A term applied to a decorative art in sculpture, painting, and architecture, characterized by fantastic representations of human and animal forms often combined into formal distortions of the natural to the point of absurdity, ugliness, or caricature. It was so named after the ancient paintings and decorations found in the underground chambers (*grotte*) of Roman ruins. By extension, *grotesque* is applied to anything having the qualities of *grotesque* art: bizarre, incongruous, ugly, unnatural, fantastic, abnormal. Poe called one of his collections *Tales of the Grotesque and Arabesque* (1840), suggesting a fairly precise distinction between the spirits of Christian northern Europe and Muslim western Asia.

Modern critics use "the *grotesque*" to refer to special types of writing, to kinds of characters, and to subject matters. The interest in the *grotesque* is usually considered an outgrowth of interest in the irrational, distrust of any cosmic order, and frustration at humankind's lot in the universe. In this sense, *grotesque* is the merging of the comic and tragic, resulting from our loss of faith in the moral universe essential to tragedy and in a rational social order essential to comedy. Where nineteenth-century critics like Walter Bagehot saw the *grotesque* as a deplorable variation from the normal, Thomas Mann sees it as the "most genuine style" for the modern world and the "only guise in which the sublime may appear" now. Jorge Luis Borges echoed Mann's sentiment. Flannery O'Connor seems to mean the same thing when she calls the *grotesque* character "man forced to meet the extremes of his own nature."

Although German writers have practiced the *grotesque* with distinction, notably Mann and Günter Grass, William Van O'Connor seems to have been on target when he called the *grotesque* an American genre. Sherwood Anderson subtitled his *Winesburg, Ohio* "The Book of the Grotesque," and defined a *grotesque* character as a person who "took one of the [many] truths to himself, called it his truth, and tried to live by it." Such a person, Anderson asserted, "became a grotesque and the truth he embraced a falsehood." Whenever fictional characters appear who are either physically or spiritually deformed and perform abnormal actions, the work can be called *grotesque*. It may be used for allegorical statement, as Flannery O'Connor uses it. It may exist for comic purposes, as it does in the work of Eudora Welty. It may be the expression of a deep moral seriousness, as it is in the works of William Faulkner. It may make a comment on human beings as animals, in works like Frank Norris's *McTeague* and *Vandover and the Brute*. It may partake of satire, as in Nathanael West's novels. It may be a basis for social commentary, as it is in the works of Erskine Caldwell. Clearly, the *grotesque* suits the spirit of the modern age.

[References: Arthur Clayborough, *The Grotesque in English Literature* (1965); Willard Farnham, *The Shakespearean Grotesque* (1971); Geoffrey Galt Harpham, *On the Grotesque* (1982); W. J. Kayser, *The Grotesque in Art and Literature* (tr. 1968); Neil Rhodes, *Elizabethan Grotesque* (1980); Philip Thomson, *The Grotesque* (1972).]

Grub Street Because some hacks lived in Grub Street in London (now Milton Street), *Grub Street*, since the eighteenth century, has meant either the "tribe" of poor writers living there or the qualities that characterized them. *Grub Street* poets were bitterly attacked by Pope, and Grub Street has been used contemptuously by Samuel Johnson, Byron, and others to suggest trash.

Grundy, Mrs. A character from Thomas Morton's play *Speed the Plough*, who does not actually appear but of whose judgments everyone in the play is very much afraid. The question "What will *Mrs. Grundy* say?" points to her symbolic value as a ridiculously strict upholder of social conventions. She reappears, anagrammatized, as the feared goddess Ydgrun in Samuel Butler's *Erewhon* (1871).

Gutter In a newspaper, the space that runs between COLUMNS.

Cloister Old Style 1913. Based on a typeface cut by Nicolas Jenson in 1470. Redesigned by M. F. Benton.

Habbie A component of the names of STANZAS used in Scottish poetry. Robert Sempill's "The Life and Death of Habbie Simpson," about a piper, uses a six-lined stanza that Allan Ramsay later named "standard Habbie." The rhyme scheme is *aaabab*, with TETRAMETER in the *a*-lines and DIMETER in the *b*-lines. FEMININE RHYMES are common. Robert Burns used such a stanza in many of his best-known poems, including "To a Mouse" and "To a Louse"; the latter ends:

O wad some Pow'r the giftie gie us
To see oursels as others see us!
It wad frae monie a blunder free us
An' foolish notion:
What airs in dress an' gait wad lea'e us,
And ev'n Devotion!

See BURNS STANZA.

Hagiography Writing about saints. By extension, a BIOGRAPHY that praises the virtues of its subject. Continuing certain habits of biography derived from classical antiquity (Plutarch and Suetonius) and the New Testament—as well as legal requirements of evidence for canonization—*hagiography* developed conventions (such as miracles and martyrdom) that have continued to influence literature, especially drama, as recently as Shaw's *Saint Joan*, Gertrude Stein's *Four Saints in Three Acts*, Eliot's *Murder in the Cathedral*, and, it can be argued, J. D. Salinger's stories about Seymour Glass.

Haiku A form of Japanese poetry that gives—usually in three lines of five, seven, and five syllables—a clear picture designed to arouse a distinct emotion and suggest a specific spiritual insight. Unlike *senryu*, which is also in seventeen syllables but has a lighter mood, *haiku* poetry is deeply serious and also profoundly conventional. Every season, element, bird, flower, insect, and so forth comes equipped with a large set of associations that the *haiku* exploits. Approximations of the spirit of *haiku* have been found in many Western writers—Wordsworth, Thoreau, Pound, Bly, Snyder—usually in short poems but also in short passages of prose; and attempts have been made to produce translations of original *haiku* (the best by R. H. Blyth and the Greek master George Seferis), but the spirit as well as the form tend to get lost. For one thing, the Japanese syllable is uncommonly short and uniform, typically consisting of one simple consonant followed by one simple vowel (as in "sayonara") with no marked stress on any syllable. Because an English syllable can contain as many as seven or eight separate sounds (as in "strengths"), seventeen English syllables will probably consume more time than seventeen Japanese syllables, so that someone who writes seventeen English syllables under the impression that they constitute a *haiku* is probably wrong. A closer formal approximation in English would be eleven syllables arranged in a symmetrical pattern of three, five, three. (The Japanese are not fussy about the seventeen: Some *haiku* run somewhat longer, and nobody objects.)

[Reference: R. H. Blyth, *A History of Haiku*, 2 vols. (1963–64).]

Half Rhyme Imperfect rhyme, usually the result of CONSONANCE.

Hamartia The error, frailty, mistaken judgment, or misstep through which the fortunes of the hero of a TRAGEDY are reversed. Aristotle asserts that this hero should be a person "who is not eminently good or just, yet whose misfortune is brought about by some error or frailty." This error is not necessarily a flaw in character, although *hamartia* is often inaccurately called the tragic flaw. Aristotle sees a movement from happiness to misery as essential to tragedy, and he says, "It is their characters that give men their quality, but their doings that make them happy or the opposite." Hence *hamartia* can be an unwitting, even a necessary, misstep in doing rather than an error in character. *Hamartia* may be the result of bad judgment, bad character, ignorance, inherited weakness, accident, or any of many other possible causes. It must, however, express itself through a definite action or failure to act.

Handbook Originally and literally, a book small enough to be held in the hand, corresponding to Greek *enchiridion* and Latin *manual*, both of which have to do with the hand. Although *handboc* can be found in Old English documents, the modern word is deliberately modeled on German *Handbuch*; in 1838 a grammarian called using *handbook* for *manual* a "tasteless innovation." In the nineteenth century, many *handbooks* had to do with touring, but since then the word has come to mean any handy collection of useful information.

Hapax Legomenon Literally, from the Greek, "something said only once." A word or grammatical form that occurs only once, either because of genuine uniqueness or because all other occurrences have been lost. Several instances turn up in classical and medieval texts, and there are some *hapax legomena* in Shakespeare, Swift, Hardy, and T. S. Eliot. The "Moby" in *Moby-Dick* seems to be something of a *hapax legomenon*.

Haplography Writing something once when it should be written twice. Sometimes a random accident, sometimes caused by an awkward situation, such as "the author of *Of Human Bondage*" or "the situation in *In the Penal Colony*." A line from John Crowe Ransom's "Captain Carpenter"—"And took the red, red vitals of his heart"—appeared in a standard anthology as "And took the red vitals of his heart."

Haplology The utterance of one syllable or word instead of two that might seem called for. Latin *idololatria* became *idolatria* (English "idolatry"). Modern "pacifist" and "feminist" may have evolved from earlier "pacificist" and "femininist" by this procedure. Something that hovers, say, would be a "hoverer," but that word is transformed by *haplology* into "hover," as in the title of Gerard Manley Hopkins's "The Windhover." However, the noun "hover" may derive from the rare verb form "hove," meaning "hover."

Harangue A vehement speech designed to arouse strong emotions. Antony's speech over Caesar's body, in Shakespeare's *Julius Caesar*, is a well-known example. Today the term is applied to any form of rabble-rousing address.

Hardback Since about 1950, informal term for anything not a PAPERBACK; CLOTHBOUND.

Hardy Stanza Although maybe not invented by Thomas Hardy, a certain stanza was adapted and perfected by him in ways that make it his own. The eight lines follow this pattern:

1.	TETRAMETER	*a*
2.	DIMETER (repeats end of first line)	*a′*
3.	tetrameter	*a*
4.	TRIMETER	*b*
5.	tetrameter	*c*
6.	tetrameter	*c*
7.	tetrameter	*c*
8.	trimeter	*b*

The stanza, with its BALLAD-like mixture of four-stress and three-stress lines and plangent echo effect in the second line, recalls certain Renaissance lyrics. The *Hardy stanza* is in early poems ("Tess's Lament" and "A Trampwoman's Tragedy") as well as the very late "He Never Expected Much." Variants are found in "In a Wood," "Song of the Soldiers' Wives and Sweethearts," "The Ghost of the Past," and "Summer Schemes."

Harlem Renaissance The first major, self-conscious literary movement of African American writers, although there had been much black writing in America earlier. Immediately after the First World War, as a result of a massive migration to northern cities, a group of young, talented writers congregated in Harlem and made it their cultural and intellectual capital. The artistic and literary of New York considered a visit to the Cotton Club, where Duke Ellington played, a necessary journey. DuBose Heyward and Julia Peterkin, Southern novelists, gave in *Porgy* and *Scarlet Sister Mary* immensely popular pictures of poor African Americans; however, the motive force of the *Harlem Renaissance* was not this fashionable position among intellectual whites but the accumulation in Harlem of an impressive group who created the true power of the *Renaissance*. They were Langston Hughes, poet, novelist, and playwright; Jean Toomer, author of the distinguished collection of poetry and poetic prose, *Cane*; the poets Countee Cullen and Claude McKay; the novelists Eric Waldron and Zora Neale Hurston; and the poet and novelist Arna Bontemps, who was to become the historian of the movement. The *Harlem Renaissance* was the first intellectual and artistic movement that brought African America to the attention of the entire nation. The defining event of the *Harlem Renaissance* was the publication in 1925 of *The New Negro: An Interpretation*, an anthology edited by Alain Locke.

[References: Arna Bontemps, ed., *The Harlem Renaissance Remembered* (1972); Nathan Irvin Huggins, *Harlem Renaissance* (1971); Margaret Perry, *The Harlem Renaissance: an Annotated Bibliography and Commentary* (1982).]

Harlequinade A play featuring a "harlequin" or buffoon. See COMMEDIA DELL'ARTE.

Hartford Wits A group of Connecticut writers, active around the period of the American Revolution. The most prominent were Joel Barlow, Timothy Dwight, and John Trumbull. They were conservative in their models, following Addison and Pope, the two literary gods of their century. Some of their best-known works are Trumbull's *M'Fingal*, Timothy Dwight's *Conquest of Canaan* (an epic in eleven books mingling Christian and Revolutionary history), and Barlow's *Columbiad*, planned as another American epic, a ten-book recitation of the coming glories of America as revealed to Columbus in prison. Also known as the Connecticut Wits.

Head The top of a sheet, leaf, or page. Also material printed at the *head* with titles, topics, and so forth.

Headless Line A line from which an unstressed syllable has been dropped at the beginning. See CATALEXIS.

Headline In newspapers and some other printed documents, material printed in relatively large type that tells what a story is about. Also the top line on a theatrical or advertising BILL with the name of the featured performer or other such material. Sometimes, especially with material printed in two or more COLUMNS, accompanied by a STRAP-LINE above or a TAG-LINE below the main *headline*.

<u>Local News</u>

MAYOR RE-ELECTED

"I promise reform."

TYPICAL FORMATTING:
STRAP-LINE (UPPER LEFT), HEADLINE (CENTER), TAG-LINE (LOWER RIGHT)

Headliner A performer or other personage whose name is listed as part of a HEADLINE on a BILL; the STAR attraction.

Headnote Material in the form of a note placed at the head of page; the physical opposite of a footnote and usually without numbers, asterisks, or other symbols. Some *headnotes* are in smaller type than the text they introduce.

Head Rhyme See ALLITERATION.

Heaping Figure The heaping up of EPITHETS, as in the description of the Citizen in James Joyce's *Ulysses*: "a broadshouldered deepchested stronglimbed frankeyed redhaired freely freckled shaggybearded widemouthed largenosed longheaded deepvoiced barekneed brawnyhanded hairylegged ruddyfaced sinewyarmed hero."

Hebraism The attitude that subordinates all other ideals to those of obedient conduct and ethical purpose. It is opposed to the Hellenistic conception of life that subordinates everything to the intellect. *Hebraism* and HELLENISM have each taken on a special and limited significance—neither of which does full justice to the genius of the two peoples—as the result of critical discussion of the question of conduct and wisdom in living. The most notable discussion of the two conflicting ideals is found in Matthew Arnold's *Culture and Anarchy*:

> We may regard this energy driving at practice, this paramount sense of the obligation of duty, self-control, and work, this earnestness in going manfully with the best light we have, as one force. And we may regard the intelligence driving at those ideas which are, after all, the basis of right practice, the ardent sense for all the new and changing combinations of them which man's development brings with it, the indomitable impulse to know and adjust them perfectly, as another force. . . . The governing idea of Hellenism is *spontaneity of consciousness;* that of Hebraism, *strictness of conscience.*

Hedge Club An informal group of transcendentalists living in or near Boston, headed by Frederick Henry Hedge. See TRANSCENDENTAL CLUB.

Hedonism A doctrine that pleasure is the chief good of human beings. It takes two forms; in one, following the doctrines of the Cyrenaic school of philosophy, founded by Aristippus in the fifth century B.C., the chief good is held to be the gratification of the sensual instincts. In the other, following Epicurus, the absence of pain rather than the gratification of pleasurable impulses is held to be the source of happiness. Today *hedonism* is generally associated with sensual gratification; its motto might be "Eat, drink, and be merry, for tomorrow we may die" (see CARPE DIEM). See EPICUREAN.

Hegelianism The system devised by G. W. F. Hegel in the early nineteenth century, its basic assumption being that what is real is rational, so that a logical relation exists among all things. Anything less than a totality of rational relationships represents distortions of reality. History is the process by which reason realizes itself in human affairs. Dialectic reasoning is a process by which all things pass through ascending stages, moving from thesis to antithesis to synthesis, the synthesis then becoming a new thesis. Such reasoning is the method by which human beings can understand history and the development of consciousness and freedom. Hegel's ideas influenced many British and American writers in the nineteenth century. As modified by Karl Marx, they continue to exert great influence.

Hellenism The Greek spirit, which manifests itself in the celebration of the intellect and of beauty. See HEBRAISM.

Hemistich A half-line. See STICH.

Hendecasyllabic Verse A line of eleven syllables, frequent in Greek and Latin poetry and a standard line in Italian. Its English users have been relatively few, the chief among them being Tennyson. The SAPPHIC stanza requires hendecasyllables in three of its four lines.

Hendiadys A FIGURE OF SPEECH in which an idea is expressed by giving two components as though they were independent and connecting them with a coordinating conjunction rather than subordinating one part to the other. "Try and do better" instead of

"Try to do better" is an example. The *hendiadys* was common in classical writing and continues to turn up in modern languages in certain cases in which "and" or some other coordinating conjunction joins words (such as *Sturm und Drang*, "sound and fury," "fun and games") not exactly on the same level. Early in *Paradise Lost*, Milton refers to Satan's war "Against the Throne and Monarchy of God"—clearly a *hendiadys*. A similar sort of "SLEIGHT OF 'AND'" yields Dylan Thomas's phrase "five and country senses." Arguably, Gray's ". . . and leaves the world to darkness and to me" constitutes a *hendiadys*.

Heptameter A line consisting of seven feet.

Heptastich A seven-lined stanza.

Heresy of Paraphrase, The When Robert Frost remarked that poetry is what is lost in translation, he was suggesting much the same point that critics make when they call paraphrase heretical. A work of art means what it means in the terms in which it delivers that meaning, so that paraphrase, summary, abridgment, expansion, or translation is bound to miss the point, usually by understating the complexity and misconstruing the uniqueness of the original statement.

[Reference: Cleanth Brooks, *The Well Wrought Urn: Studies in the Structure of Poetry* (1947).]

Hermeneutic Circle The notion that a reader cannot fully understand any part of a text until the whole is understood, while the whole cannot be understood until all the parts are understood. Presumably, one reads piecemeal, provisionally modifying the sense of the whole as one accrues experience of the parts, and one accrues experience of the parts—including the understanding that they *are* parts—in accordance with the ever-changing experience of the whole that the parts have been constituting. You cannot interpret what a given part of *King Lear* means, let us say, until you know what the totality of the play means; and you cannot know what the totality means until you know what the parts mean. W. Wolfgang Holdheim has extended such a philosophy of reading to include "the insight that human perception and understanding always proceed from foreknowledge of a (however dimly apprehended) totality that is gradually modified and clarified in a mutual approximation of the one and the multitude, the comprehensive and the subordinate, the whole and its parts."

[Reference: W. Wolfgang Holdheim, *The Hermeneutic Mode* (1984).]

Hermeneutics A term once limited to the interpretation of religious texts, particularly the allegorical, but now a synonym for theory of interpretation—including the theory that a work of art considered as a work of art cannot (according to T. S. Eliot) be interpreted, because there is nothing to interpret. Since the time when Eliot's dismissal was possible—and in spite of it—*hermeneutics* has become an important part of theory, with a background in modern linguistics and philosophy; nowadays, *hermeneutics* refers to the theory of perception and understanding, along with the premises, procedures, methods, and limitations of interpretation.

[References: Hans-Georg Gadamer, *Truth and Method*, 2nd rev. ed. (1989; orig. 1960, tr. 1982); E. D. Hirsch, *Validity in Interpretation* (1967); W. Wolfgang Holdheim, *The Hermeneutic Mode* (1984); R. E. Palmer, *Hermeneutics: Interpretation in Schleiermacher, Dilthey, and Gadamer* (1969).]

Hermeticism Defined by Gerald L. Bruns as "the idea of the 'pure expressiveness' of literary speech, in which a writer's use of language deviates sufficiently from the structures of ordinary discourse to displace or arrest the function of signification."

[Reference: Gerald L. Bruns, *Modern Poetry and the Idea of Language: A Critical and Historical Study* (1974).]

Hermogenism The sentiment, associated with Hermogenes in Plato's *Cratylus*, that there is no essential, organic, or mimetic connection between SIGNIFIER and SIGNIFIED; there may be a formal or structural connection. No dog, for example, has ever said "bow wow," but whatever a dog does say rhymes, as do "bow" and "wow"; and rhyme is a structural relation. *Hermogenism* holds that all words are arbitrary. The notion has been espoused by some linguists since about 1875, but the idea goes back to the Greeks of classical antiquity (see ANALOGISM VERSUS ANOMALISM) and can even be found in Juliet's assertion, "That which we call a rose / By any other name would smell as sweet."

[Reference: Derek Attridge, *Peculiar Language: Literature as Difference from the Renaissance to James Joyce* (1988).]

Hero or **Heroine** The central character (masculine or feminine) in a work. The character who is the focus of interest. See PROTAGONIST.

Heroic Couplet Iambic pentameter lines rhymed in pairs. A favorite measure of Chaucer—*The Legend of Good Women* is an instance—this verse form did not come into its greatest popularity, however, until the middle of the seventeenth century (with Waller and Denham), after which time it was long the dominant mode for the poetic drama. The distinction of having made first use of the *heroic couplet* in dramatic composition is variously given to Orrery's *Henry V*, in which it was used throughout, and Etheredge's *The Comical Revenge*, in which it was employed for most passages of dramatic action. Both plays date from 1664. Davenant had as early as 1656 made some use of the *heroic couplet* in *Siege of Rhodes*. The form became best known with Dryden, who used it in such plays as *Tyrannick Love*, *The Conquest of Granada*, and *Aureng-Zebe*. With Pope the *heroic couplet* became so important and fixed a form—for various purposes—that its influence dominated English verse for decades, until the romanticists dispelled the tradition in their demand for a new freedom. An example of the *heroic couplet* from Pope is:

> But when to mischief mortals bend their will,
> How soon they find fit instruments of ill!

In the Neoclassic Period, the *heroic couplet* was usually made up of a rhymed pair of END-STOPPED LINES. The use of CAESURAS and a highly symmetrical grammatical structure made the *heroic couplet* a form well adapted to epigrammatic expression and to balanced sentences marked by symmetry and antithesis. The inherent DECORUM of the *heroic couplet* makes it an answerable medium for (1) the exposition of ideas of order and (2) the showing-up of rogues and hypocrites who embody disorder and discrepancy. In the Romantic Age, poets like Keats, in *Endymion*, retained rhymed pairs of iambic pentameter lines but abandoned the other restrictions of the *heroic couplet*, although Byron used and defended Pope's sort of *couplet*. George Crabbe (1754–1832) continued writing *heroic couplets* well into the nineteenth century, such as these at the end of *The Borough* (Letter XXII, "The Poor of the Borough: Peter Grimes"):

> But here he ceased and gazed
> On all around, affrighted and amazed;
> And still he tried to speak, and looked in dread
> Of frightened females gathering round his bed;
> Then dropped exhausted and appeared at rest,
> Till the strong foe the vital powers possessed
> Then with an inward, broken voice he cried,
> "Again they come," and muttered as he died.

Only a few decades later, Browning's "My Last Duchess" was to demonstrate forcibly how subtle one could be with couplets of iambic pentameter that are not so conspicuously end-stopped as the usual *heroic couplets*:

> Sir, 'twas not
> Her husband's presence only, called that spot
> Of joy into the Duchess' cheek: perhaps
> Frà Pandolf chanced to say "Her mantle laps
> Over my lady's wrist too much," or "Paint
> Must never hope to reproduce the faint
> Half-flush that dies along her throat": such stuff
> Was courtesy, she thought, and cause enough
> For calling up that spot of joy. . . .

Heroic Drama A type of TRAGEDY and TRAGICOMEDY developed in England during the Restoration, characterized by excessive spectacle, violent conflicts among the main characters, bombastic dialogue, and epic personages. The heroic play was usually set in a distant land such as Mexico, Morocco, or India. Its hero is constantly torn between his passion and his honor. If he is able to satisfy the demands of both love and duty, the play ends happily for hero and heroine and unhappily for the villain and villainess. The heroine is always a paragon, often torn between loyalty to her villain-father and love for the hero. The villain is usually a tyrant and usurper with an overweening passion for power or else with a base love for a virtuous woman. The villainess is the dark, violently passionate rival of the heroine. The hero's rival in love is sometimes the villain and sometimes the hero's best friend. All speak in HYPERBOLE. The writers of heroic plays commonly, though not always, used HEROIC COUPLETS. The action was grand, often revolving around the conquest of some empire. The scenery was elaborate. The influences that produced the *heroic drama* were the romantic plays of the Jacobeans, especially those of Beaumont and Fletcher; the development of opera in England; and the French court romances by Scudéry and La Calprenède, some of which were brought to England by the court of Charles II. Though elements of the heroic play appear in Davenant's *Siege of Rhodes* (1656), the Earl of Orrery wrote perhaps the first full-fledged *heroic drama*, *The General* (1664). Dryden, however, is its greatest exponent, his *Conquest of Granada* typifying all that is best and worst in the species. Although the faults of the type were recognized early, the most brilliant attack being *The Rehearsal* (1671), a satirical play by George Villiers, Duke of Buckingham, and others, *heroic drama* flourished until about 1680, and its extravagances affected eighteenth-century tragedy.

Heroic Line IAMBIC PENTAMETER is called the *heroic line* because it is often used in EPIC or heroic poetry. In classical literature the *heroic line* was DACTYLIC HEXAMETER; in French it was the ALEXANDRINE.

Heroic Quatrain Four lines of IAMBIC PENTAMETER (or, much more rarely, TETRAMETER) rhyming *abab*, a component of the SHAKESPEAREAN SONNET, used as a stanza by Dryden and others, but brought to such perfection in Gray's "Elegy Written in a Country Churchyard" that little employment remained for it afterward except in a rather grim TRAVESTY in the third part of T. S. Eliot's *The Waste Land* and in ironic elegies by John Crowe Ransom and heroic experiments by Hart Crane. In recent years the most notable use of the *heroic quatrain* has been in "Bridge for the Living" by Philip Larkin.

Heroic Stanza Another name for the HEROIC QUATRAIN.

Heroic Verse Poetry composed in HEROIC COUPLETS.

Heterodyne A term borrowed from electronics to describe a piece of verse in which the lexical units and rhythmic units do not coincide, as in the first line of Tennyson's "Ulysses"—"It little profits that an idle king"—broken down thus into iambic feet: It lit | tle pro | fits that | an id | le king (one and a half words, two halves, a half and a whole, one and a half, a half and a whole). The effect is relatively unsettled, as against the HOMODYNE coincidence in the last line, "To strive, to seek, to find, and not to yield," where every rhythmic unit is also a lexical unit, with the effect of relative resolution and strength.

Heteroglossia "Different tongues" or "different speech"; a term introduced by Mikhail Bakhtin to designate the presence of more than one voice in a given narrative or other work.

Heteromerous Rhyme A fairly rare species of multiple rhyme (also called "mosaic") in which, typically, one word is forced into a rhyme with two or more words. Being somewhat strained and exotic, most rhymes of this sort tend to be outlandish and comic, as in Byron's *Don Juan*:

> But—Oh! ye lords of ladies intellectual,
> Inform us truly, have they not hen-pecked you all?

Some serious uses have been made of *heteromerous rhyme*, notably by Robert Browning, Hardy, Hopkins, Kipling, Yeats, and Eliot. Hopkins once pluckily rhymed "I am and" with "diamond." In "The Wreck of the Deutschland," Hopkins combines *heteromerous* rhyme with FUSED RHYME, when "Providence" rhymes with "of it and / S[tartle]. . . ."

Heteronym A word spelled the same as another but pronounced and defined differently, such as "does" (present-tense singular verb) and "does" (plural noun). *Heteronym* was also used by the important Portuguese poet Fernando Pessoa (1888–1935) for certain PERSONAS or alter egos that he invented. These—including Alberto Caeiro, Ricardo Reis, Ivaro de Campos, and dozens of others—not only were names attached to various creative and critical works but also had complex personalities and biographies of their own, including interactions among some of them. It is as though Charles Lutwidge Dodgson used "Lewis Carroll" as a pseudonym for some of his works and then went on to outfit Carroll with a whole life radically different from Dodgson's. Pessoa claimed to have "created a nonexistent coterie." "The mental origin of my heteronyms," he said, "lies in my relentless, organic tendency to depersonalization and simulation."

Heterostrophic Having two different metrical systems, as with Thomas Hardy's "The Voice," which has three stanzas of DACTYLIC TETRAMETER and one TROCHAIC QUATRAIN with lines of TRIMETER, trimeter, TETRAMETER, and DIMETER.

Hexameter A line of six feet. In Latin or Greek, in which the *hexameter* was the conventional medium for epic and didactic poetry, the term was definitely restricted to a set pattern: six feet, the first four of which were DACTYLS or SPONDEES, the fifth almost always a dactyl (though sometimes a spondee, in which case the verse is called spondaic), the sixth a spondee or TROCHEE. True *hexameters* of the classical sort are scarce in English because of the supposed rarity of spondees. However, poets writing in English, notably Longfellow in *Evangeline* and *The Courtship of Miles Standish*, have variously adapted the classical form to the exigencies of our language and have left us *hexameters* much less strictly patterned than the classical. See ALEXANDRINE, ELEGIACS.

Hexapla (also **Hexaple**) A sixfold text arranged in parallel columns to permit detailed comparison of versions. Origen made a *hexapla* of versions of the Old Testament (Septuagint, Aquila, Theodotion, Symmachus, and texts found at Jericho and Nicopolis).

Hexastich A stanza of six lines.

Hiatus A pause or break between two vowel sounds not separated by a consonant. It is the opposite of ELISION, which prompts the sliding over of one of the vowels, whereas a *hiatus* occurs only in a break between two words when the final vowel of the first and the initial vowel of the second are each sounded. In logic *hiatus* signifies the omission of one of the logical steps in a process of reasoning.

Hieratic Style Literally "priestly," *hieratic* was applied to a highly conventionalized style of ancient Egyptian writing. It is used by Northrop Frye to designate a self-consciously formal and elaborate style, in contrast to the DEMOTIC.

Hieronymy The idea of sacred names and naming, more recently applied to any special name (or proper noun) for persons, places, gods, days, months, and so forth. According to one critical program, poetry is distinguished by the foregrounded presence of *hieronymy* and its antithetical complement, ONOMATOPOEIA. Eliot's *The Waste Land*, for example, begins with the hieronymic "April" and ends with a reference to the onomatopoeic "DA" (thunder in Sanskrit).

High Comedy Pure or serious comedy, as contrasted with LOW COMEDY. *High comedy* appeals to the intellect and arouses thoughtful laughter by exhibiting the inconsistencies and incongruities of human nature and by displaying the follies of social manners. The purpose is not consciously didactic or ethical, though serious purpose is often implicit in the satire that is frequent in *high comedy*. Emotion, especially sentimentality, is avoided. If people make themselves ridiculous by their vanity or ineffective by their stupid conduct or blind adherence to tradition, *high comedy* laughs at them. But, as George Meredith suggests in *The Idea of Comedy*, care must be taken that the laughter be not derisive but intellectual. Although *high comedy* actually offers plenty of superficial laughter that the average playgoer or reader can enjoy, its higher enjoyment demands detachment. "Life is a comedy to him who thinks." But the term *high comedy* is used in various senses. In neoclassic times a criterion was its appeal to and reflection of a higher social class and its observance of decorum, as illustrated in Etheredge and Congreve. In a broader sense it is applied to some of Shakespeare's plays, such as *As You Like It*, and to the comedies of G. B. Shaw.

Higher Criticism A term applied to certain aspects of the study of biblical texts in the nineteenth century. The *higher criticism* seeks to determine the authorship, date, place of origin, circumstances of composition, author's purpose and intended meaning, and the historical credibility of the various books of the Bible. It was called the *higher criticism* in contrast to technical or "lower criticism," which concerns the establishment of the text itself. The *higher criticism* is important in literary study not only for its method but also for its impact on religious thought.

Historical Criticism Criticism that approaches work in terms of the social, cultural, and historical context in which it was produced. The historical critic attempts to recreate the meaning and values of the work for its own time; the critic's objective is not to elucidate the meaning of the work for the present so much as it is to lead the reader into a responsive awareness of the meaning the work had for its own age.

Historical Fiction Fiction whose setting is in some time other than that in which it is written. Arguably, *historical fiction* can be any in which the temporal setting is of paramount importance, so that a contemporary work, set in "the present" can be *historical*, and so can a work of SCIENCE FICTION, set in the future.

Historical Novel A novel that reconstructs a past age. The classic formula for the *historical novel*, as expressed by Scott in his numerous prefaces and introductions to the Waverly Novels, calls for an age when two cultures are in conflict; into this cultural conflict are introduced fictional personages who participate in actual events and move among actual personages. *Ivanhoe*, with its disinherited Saxon hero in a Norman world, is a striking example.

Two tendencies to depart from the formula should be noted: One is the costume romance, in which history is merely a background for adventurous or sexual exploits; the other is the novel of the character, in which the setting and the age are secondary to the representation of characters; *The Scarlet Letter* exemplifies the latter.

Although historians have found adumbrations of the *historical novel* in many forms and works, it seems to have required the development of a serious view of history before a serious *historical novel* could develop. Such a view came in the eighteenth century, and writers began to attempt works that would correspond to the ideals of the *historical novel*, but it remained for Scott in *Waverly* in 1814 to establish the form. Among his noted successors have been Thackeray, Dumas, Hugo, Tolstoi, Cooper, and Bulwer-Lytton. More recently, *historical novels* have been attempted by Robert Graves, Gore Vidal, John Barth, Erica Jong, Norman Mailer, E. L. Doctorow, William Kennedy, and Thomas Pynchon. David Stacton (1925–1968) wrote distinguished *historical novels* about fourteenth-century Japan, the Thirty Years' War, the Bonapartes, King Ludwig II of Bavaria, and the American political scene around 1940.

[References: G. Lukács, *The Historical Novel* (tr. 1965); Nicholas Rance, *The Historical Novel and Popular Politics in Nineteenth-Century England* (1975).]

Historicism A set of concepts about works of literature and their relationships to the social and cultural contexts in which they were produced. Although HISTORICAL CRITICISM and scholarly pursuits such as literary history are frequently elements in it, the primary concern of *historicism* is methodological and systematic. It strives to establish relationships among the historical context in which the work was produced, the work as an imaginative artifact, the reception of the work in its own world, and the significance of the work for the reader today.

There are four broad concepts of *historicism*. The metaphysical or ideal concept, following Hegel, interprets the work in terms of a transcendental continuity of historical process. The naturalistic or positivistic concept sees the work as a sociological key to contemporary social meanings and values, as did Ste.-Beuve and Taine. The nationalistic sees the work as an expression of ideals framed by national boundaries, as do workers in the field of American Studies. The fourth and most frequent form of *historicism* is aesthetic. For it the work has unique value as a created artifact, shaped to some important degree by the forces of its time, but in its uniqueness also helping to shape its time; having a meaning appropriate to its own world and understandable fully only in terms of its own age. There are many views on these issues, but all of them are concerned with the complex problems resulting from a work's being a discrete and timeless aesthetic object that, to be understood fully, must be seen also as a product of historical forces. See NEW HISTORICISM, THE.

History Play Strictly speaking, any drama whose time setting is in some period earlier than that in which it is written. It is most widely used, however, as a synonym for CHRONICLE PLAY.

Hoax An act of mischievous trickery designed to expose folly. A literary hoax may involve a fabrication (a work, a person, or a whole school) that is presented, often to a periodical or publisher, as genuine. During War World I, the American poets Witter Bynner and Arthur Davison Ficke invented the Spectra movement, with Anne Knish and Emmanuel Morgan as the leading Spectrist poets. In 1943 (again during wartime), the Australian poets James McAuley and Harold Stewart concocted the person and works of Ernest Lalor (Ern) Malley. Some of the poems were published and even prosecuted for obscenity. In 1996 the journal *Social+Text* published a long article called "Transgressing the Boundaries: Towards a Transformative Hermeneutics of Quantum Gravity" by the physicist Allan Sokal, who used his own name to perpetrate a serious and most effective hoax designed to call attention to the limitations of many academic pursuits, including philosophy, literary theory, psychoanalysis, and culture studies.

[References: Michael Heyward, *The Ern Malley Affair* (1993); Yves Jeanneret, *L'affaire Sokal ou la querelle des impostures* (1998); William Jay Smith, *The Spectra Hoax* (1961).]

Hobson-Jobson The process of transforming something foreign into a more familiar native article, as when a child (reported in a poem by Lorine Niedecker) converts the German *Tannenbaum* in a Christmas song into something more familiar: "atomic bomb." By a similar process, Spanish *Cayo Hueso* becomes "Key West" and French *les trois sauvages* becomes "the dry salvages." Accuracy of translation seems to mean less than accommodation to native sounds, since "west" has no semantic relation to *hueso* ("bone") and "the dry salvages"—three rocks in the water—are usually not dry or connected to salvage. The Purgatoire River becomes the Picketwire by the process of *Hobson-Jobson*. In Tennessee Williams's *The Glass Menagerie*, "pleurosis" becomes "Blue Roses" by the same process that converts "Raymond" into "Rain Man."

Hollywood Novel A novel set in Hollywood itself or else about the film industry at large. Such novels typically involve much ironic contrast between appearance and reality and between the claims of art and those of profit. Among the best known are F. Scott Fitzgerald's *The Love of the Last Tycoon*, Nathanael West's *The Day of the Locust*, Christopher Isherwood's *Prater Violet*, Budd Schulberg's *What Makes Sammy Run?* and Elmore Leonard's *Get Shorty*.

Holograph Something completely handwritten by the author. *Holographs* of important literary works not only have very high value for the bibliophile and the collector but may be useful in determining something of the author's intention.

Holy Grail The cup from which Christ is said to have drunk at the Last Supper and which was used to catch his blood at the Crucifixion. It became the center of a tradition of Christian mysticism and eventually was linked with Arthurian ROMANCE as an object of search. The *grail* as it appears in early Arthurian literature (Chrétien's *Perceval*) is perhaps of pagan origin, a sort of magic object not now to be traced with assurance. In the poems of Robert de Boron (c. 1200) it appears as a mystic symbol and is connected with Christian tradition (having been brought to England by Joseph of Arimathea). In the Vulgate romances, two great cycles are devoted to the *grail*: the first or History dealing with the Joseph tradition, the second or Quest dealing with the search for it by Arthurian knights. Perceval, the first hero of the quest, because he was not a pure knight, and Lancelot, because he was disqualified by his love for Guinevere, gave place to Galahad, the wholly pure knight, conceived as Lancelot's son and Perceval's kinsman. The pious quest for the *grail*, no less than the sinful love of Lancelot and Guinevere, helped bring about the eventual downfall of the Round Table fellowship. *Grail* lore continues into the modern age, appearing in Eliot's *The Waste Land*, Frost's "Directive," and even in the films *Indiana Jones and the Last Crusade* and *The Fisher King*. See ARTHURIAN LEGEND.

Homeoarchy The occurrence of the same or similar unstressed syllables preceding rhyming stressed syllables, as in "indeed" rhymed with "in need." If "deny" and "reply" are used in a rhyming situation, the rhyme proper is between the stressed syllables "-ny" and "-ply," while the preceding unstressed syllables "de-" and "re-" are related by *homeoarchy*. Two lines of Hopkins's "Inversnaid" end with the rhyming words "bereft" and "be left," in which there is perfect rhyme between the stressed syllables "-reft" and "left" and *homeoarchy* in the unstressed "be-" and "be." Consider the video rental store request: "Be kind—rewind."

Homeoteleuton Sameness or similarity of endings of consecutive words or words near each other, often considered unsettling or graceless but sometimes unavoidable, as in adjacent adverbs ("relatively easily"), verbal forms ("emerging meaning becoming fashionable"), accidental sameness of affixes ("truly holy family"), or, rarely, echoic names (Lyndon Johnson, Dudley Bradley, Charlton Heston, Edward Woodward). Most instances of *homeoteleuton* have to do with unstressed syllables, so it can usually be distinguished from proper rhyme. In John Crowe Ransom's "Bells for John Whiteside's Daughter," "window" and "shadow" are placed in a rhyming position, but the only significant relation between them is *homeoteleuton*, because they share the same unstressed syllable (*-dow*) and their stressed syllables have nothing in common (*win*- and *sha*-).

Homeric Indicative of or resembling the work of the Greek epic poet Homer (c. 8th century B.C.), author of *The Iliad* and *The Odyssey*; hence possessing grandeur and imposing magnitude, having heroic dimensions. *Homeric* events, for example, are events that are large, world-shaking, and of great importance.

Homeric Epithet An adjectival phrase so often repeated in connection with a person or thing that it almost becomes a part of the name, as in "swift-footed Achilles." See EPITHET.

Homeric Simile See EPIC SIMILE.

Homily A form of oral religious instruction given by a minister to a church congregation. The *homily* is sometimes distinguished from the sermon, which is usually on a theme drawn from a scriptural text. A *homily* usually gives practical moral counsel rather than discussion of doctrine. Old English literature contains *homilies* by Aelfric and Wulfstan.

Hommage A tribute or act of homage by one artist to another. Robert Lowell's "Ezra Pound" quotes Pound dismissing "an abomination, Possum's hommage to Milton"—referring to T. S. Eliot's tribute in an essay called "Milton II."

Homodyne A word borrowed from electronics for the situation in a passage of verse when lexical and rhythmic units coincide, as in the last line of Tennyson's "Ulysses": "To strive, to seek, to find, and not to yield." See HETERODYNE.

Homostrophic Consisting of structurally identical strophes; hence made up of stanzas of the same pattern. A HORATIAN ODE is *homostrophic*.

Horatian Ode Horace applied the term *ode* to informal poems written in a single stanzaic form, in contrast to the STROPHE, ANTISTROPHE, and EPODE of the PINDARIC ODE. Notable examples are Marvell's "Horatian Ode upon Cromwell's Return from Ireland," and Keats's "Ode on a Grecian Urn." See ODE.

Horae A book of offices for the CANONICAL HOURS.

Horary (also **Horarium**) (1) Same as HORAE. (2) An hour-by-hour record, account, narrative; also a schedule.

Horatian Satire Satire in which the voice is indulgent, tolerant, amused, and witty. The speaker holds up to gentle ridicule the absurdities and follies of human beings, aiming at producing in the reader not the anger of a Juvenal (see JUVENALIAN SATIRE) but a wry smile. Much of Pope's satire is *Horatian*, as is that common to the COMEDY OF MANNERS or novels like those of John P. Marquand and LIGHT VERSE like that of W. H. Auden.

Hornbook A kind of primer common in England from the sixteenth to the eighteenth centuries. On a sheet of vellum or paper were printed the alphabet, the Lord's Prayer, and a list of Roman numerals. The sheet was mounted on wood and covered (for protection) by transparent horn. Its most famous use in literature is in *The Gull's Hornbook* by Thomas Dekker, a satirical "primer" of instructions for the young innocent of early-seventeenth-century London.

Hornpipe An obsolete wind instrument, a dance to its music (usually by one person), or the music for such a dance. All three uses are associated with sailors' merriment. One of C. Day Lewis's poems is titled "Hornpipe."

House Style The general writing and printing style belonging to a publisher, printer, or periodical; spelling and punctuation are distinguishing features of a *house style*.

Hovering Stress (or **Accent**) A term for the effect that results from two adjacent syllables sharing the ICTUS, so that the stress appears to hover over both syllables. It is also called distributed stress and resolved stress. It appears often in the work of Gerard Manley Hopkins and is sometimes considered a metrical device used by Whitman. See DISTRIBUTED STRESS for an example.

Howler A small error that begins in innocence or ignorance and ends in folly and potential embarrassment. In the 1855 Preface to *Leaves of Grass* and in three later editions of the poem "By Blue Ontario's Shore," Walt Whitman wrote "semitic muscle" when he meant "seminal muscle." Near the end of Browning's *Pippa Passes*, Pippa sings:

> But at night, brother Howlet, far over the woods,
> Toll the world to thy chantry;
> Sing to the bats' sleek sisterhoods
> Full complines with gallantry:
> Then, owls and bats, cowls and twats,
> Monks and nuns, in a cloister's moods,
> Adjourn to the oak-stump pantry!

The *OED* notes that Browning's erroneous use of "twat" was perpetrated "under the impression that it denoted some part of a nun's attire." (Browning was presumably misled by a scurrilous verse from 1660—"They talk't of his having a Cardinalls Hat, / They'd send him as soon an Old Nuns Twat." Maybe Browning associated the word with French *le toit*, "roof," believing it to suggest a gable-shaped wimple.) Hardy's "The Caged Goldfinch" appeared in *Moments of Vision* with three stanzas; in later publications, however, the last stanza was omitted:

True, a woman was found drowned the day ensuing
And some at times averred
The grave to be her false one's, who when wooing
Gave her the bird.

Hubris Overweening pride or insolence that results in the misfortune of the protagonist of a tragedy. *Hubris* leads the protagonist to break a moral law, attempt vainly to transcend normal limitations, or ignore a divine warning with calamitous results.

Hudibrastic Verse The OCTOSYLLABIC couplet as adapted by Samuel Butler in his MOCK HEROIC poem, *Hudibras*, published in three parts between 1663 and 1678. Butler satirized the PURITANS. *Hudibras* was conspicuous for HUMOR, BURLESQUE elements, MOCK EPIC form, and wealth of satiric epigram. The meter is iambic tetrameter in rhyming couplets. It is filled with outrageous rhymes that are often double and even triple. The term today characterizes verse following Butler's general manner and particularly his rhymes. Here is a passage about astrologers:

They'll find in the physiognomies
O' the planets all men's destinies;
Like him that took the doctor's bill
And swallowed it instead o' the pill;
Cast the nativity o' the question,
And from positions to be guessed on,
As sure as if they knew the moment
Of native's birth, tell what will come on't.

Humanism Broadly, any attitude that tends to exalt the human element, as opposed to the supernatural, divine elements—or as opposed to the grosser, animal elements. In a more specific sense, *humanism* suggests a devotion to those studies supposed to promote human culture most effectively—in particular, those dealing with the life, thought, language, and literature of ancient Greece and Rome. In literary history the most important use of the term is to designate the revival of classical culture that accompanied the Renaissance. Renaissance humanists found in the classics a justification to exalt human nature and build a new and highly idealistic gospel of progress. Also they found it necessary to break sharply with medieval attitudes that had subordinated one aspect of human nature by exalting the divine. The Renaissance humanists agreed with the ancients in asserting the dignity of human beings and the importance of the present life, as against those medieval thinkers who considered the present life useful chiefly as a preparation for a future life.

Renaissance *humanism* developed in the fourteenth and fifteenth centuries in Italy and spread to other Continental countries and finally to England, where efforts to develop humanistic activities culminated successfully late in the fifteenth century with the introduction of the study of Greek at Oxford (see OXFORD REFORMERS). Early humanists—in particular the so-called Christian Humanists—in England devoted themselves to mastering Greek and Latin and to applying their new methods to theology, statecraft, education, criticism, and literature. Unlike some Continental humanists, the English group, though they reacted against medieval asceticism and SCHOLASTICISM and attacked abuses in the Church, retained their faith in Christianity. Indeed, they believed that the best of classical culture could be fused with Christianity. The efforts of such humanists as Dean John Colet and Erasmus to reform church conditions and theology through education and an appeal to reason were checked by the success of the more radical Lutheran movement.

A later phase of humanistic activity was its interest in literary criticism, through which it affected powerfully the practice of Renaissance authors. Ideas drawn from Aristotle and Horace encouraged the production of a vernacular literature that imitated the classics. Although this led to some unsuccessful efforts to restrict the English vocabulary and to repress native verse forms in favor of classical forms, in general humanistic criticism exerted a wholesome effect on literature by lending it dignity (as in the epic and tragedy) and grace (as in the Jonsonian lyric). The texture of Renaissance literature, too, was greatly enriched by the familiarity with classical mythology, history, and literature. Sidney's *Defence of Poesie* is generally taken as the first major document in English criticism, and the establishment of the classical attitude through the influence of Jonson and others was itself a fruit of Renaissance *humanism*. One phase of the reaction against ROMANTICISM in the nineteenth century was a revival of *humanism*, as exemplified in Matthew Arnold.

More recently, certain public figures (called "pulpit bullies" by detractors) have taken to using "secular humanism" as a label for any ideology not meeting their standards of spiritual correctness. See HUMANISM, THE NEW.

[References: Frederick B. Artz, *Renaissance Humanism, 1300–1550* (1966); Douglas Bush, *The Renaissance and English Humanism* (1939).]

Humanism, The New A movement called *The New Humanism* took place in America between 1910 and 1930, inspired somewhat by the humanist position of Matthew Arnold. Its leaders were Irving Babbitt, Paul Elmer More, and Norman Foerster. *The New Humanism* was a protest against the philosophies and psychologies of "our professedly scientific time." No complete codification of the tenets of the New Humanists can be made, but the following summary, based on Foerster's *American Criticism*, suggests their general doctrines: (1) that assumptions are unavoidable, (2) that the essential quality of experience is not natural but ethical, (3) that there is a sharp dualism between human beings and nature, and (4) that human will is free.

The movement failed to achieve a large following outside academic circles. After 1930 it fell before attacks from sociological critics and advocates of the NEW CRITICISM (Allen Tate most articulately).

Humor A term used in English since the early eighteenth century to denote one of the two major types of writing (*humor* and wit) whose purpose is to evoke laughter. It is derived from the physiological theory of HUMOURS, and it was used to designate a peculiar disposition that led to a person's readily perceiving the ridiculous, the ludicrous, and the comical and effectively giving expression to this perception. In the eighteenth century it was used to name a comical mode that was sympathetic, tolerant, and warmly aware of the depths of human nature, as opposed to the intellectual, satiric, intolerant quality associated with wit. However, it is impossible to discuss *humor* separately; see WIT AND HUMOR.

Humours (or **Humors**) In an old theory of physiology the four chief liquids of the human body—blood, phlegm, yellow bile, and black bile—were called *humours*. They were closely allied with the four ELEMENTS. Thus, blood, like *air*, was hot and moist; yellow bile, like *fire*, was hot and dry; phlegm, like *water*, was cold and moist; black bile, like *earth*, was cold and dry. Both physical diseases and mental and moral dispositions ("temperaments") were caused by the condition of the *humours*. Disease resulted from the dominance of some element within a single *humour* or from a lack of balance or proportion among the *humours* themselves. The *humours* gave off vapors that ascended to the brain. An individual's personal characteristics, physical, mental, and moral, were explained by his or her "temperament" or the state of the person's *humours*. The perfect temperament resulted when no one *humour* dominated. The sanguine person, with a dominance of blood, was beneficent, joyful, amorous. The choleric person was easily angered, impatient, obstinate, vengeful. The phlegmatic person was dull, pale, cowardly. The melancholic person was gluttonous, backward, unenterprising, thoughtful, sentimental, affected. A disordered state of the *humours* produced more exaggerated characteristics. These facts explain how the word *humour* in Elizabethan times came to mean "disposition," then "mood," or "characteristic peculiarity," later specialized to "folly," or "affectation." Shylock in Shakespeare's *The Merchant of Venice* says,

> You'll ask me why I rather choose to have
> A weight of carrion flesh than to receive
> Three thousand ducats. I'll not answer that,
> But say it is my humour.

By 1600 it was common to use *humour* as a means of classifying characters. The influence on Elizabethan literature of the doctrines based on *humours* was very great, and familiarity with them is an aid in understanding such characters as Horatio, Hamlet, and Jacques in Shakespeare. Many passages often taken as figurative may have had a literal meaning to the Elizabethans, as "my liver melts." See COMEDY OF HUMOURS.

Hymn A poem expressing religious emotion and generally intended to be sung by a chorus. Originally the term referred to almost any song of praise, whether of gods or famous people. The early Christian churches developed many famous *hymn* writers, and the importance of *hymns* during the Middle Ages can hardly be exaggerated, because they gave people a new verse form as well as a means of emotional expression. In medieval usage *hymn* was restricted to settings in which the same music was repeated for successive strophes. The twelfth and thirteenth centuries saw the greatest development of Latin *hymns*, some in rhymed qualitative verse, some in unrhymed qualitative verse, and some in prose (*hymns* of this period include *Dies Irae*). The wide use of *hymns* helped to destroy certain literary conventions of the past and exerted an important influence on the versification of English and German poetry as well as that of the Romance languages. Some famous *hymn* writers of England are Charles and John Wesley, Isaac Watts, John Newton, Cowper, Keble, Toplady, and Newman; of America, Whittier, Holmes, Longfellow, P. P. Bliss, and Phillips Brooks. Thomas Hardy wrote two poems based on Latin hymns: "Sine Prole" with the epigraph "Medieval Latin Sequence-Meter" and "Genetrix Laesa" with the epigraph "Measure of a Sarum Sequence"; it is possible that Hardy had in mind some Latin sequences by Adam of St. Victor. There are secular hymns by some writers, including Shelley and Ammons. See ANTHEM, TROPE.

Hymnal Stanza See COMMON MEASURE.

Hymnody (or **Hymnology**) The formal study of hymns, including the words and the music, as well as details of performance, conventions, traditions, and aesthetic interactions.

Hypallage A FIGURE OF SPEECH in which an EPITHET is moved from the proximate to the less proximate of a group of nouns. Virgil writes of "the trumpet's Tuscan blare" when the normal order would be "the Tuscan trumpet's blare."

Hyperbaton A FIGURE OF SPEECH in which normal sentence order is transposed or rearranged in a major way, as illustrated by these lines from Book II of Milton's *Paradise Lost*:

> Which when *Beëlzebub* perceiv'd, than whom
> *Satan* except, none higher sat, with grave
> Aspect he rose. . . .

See ANASTROPHE.

Hyperbole Exaggeration. The figure may be used to heighten effect, or it may be used for humor. Macbeth is using *hyperbole* here:

> No; this my hand will rather
> The multitudinous seas incarnadine,
> Making the green one red.

Hypercatalectic (or **Hypermetrical**) A line with an extra syllable at the end. Many of Chaucer's lines are *hypercatalectic* when the terminal *-e*'s at the ends of lines are pronounced, such as these:

> Short was his gowne, with sleeves long and wyde.
> Wel koude he sitte on hors and faire ryde.

Hypergraphia An irresistible or uncontrollable compulsion to write; the reverse of WRITER'S BLOCK.

Hypermeter A line with an extra syllable, most often because of a FEMININE ENDING.

Hypermonosyllable Used in Robert Bridges's *Milton's Prosody* for a word like "power" when scanned as a monosyllable. Bridges observed that such words count as two syllables in Milton's earlier poetry and as one in his later, the two sometimes distinguished as "power" and "pow'r." One line in a poem by Gerard Manley Hopkins—usually printed "What hours, O what black hoürs we have spent"—can be scanned as iambic pentameter only if the first "hours" is counted as one syllable (a *hypermonosyllable*) and the second as two.

Hypertext Defined in 1965 by T. H. Nelson, the coiner of the term, as "a body of written or pictorial material interconnected in such a complex way that it could not conveniently be presented or represented on paper."

Hyperthesis TRANSPOSITION or METATHESIS of a sound or syllable, as when "realtor" becomes "relator."

Hypheresis (also **Hyphæresis**) The omission of a letter or syllable in the body of a word, as when "grandmother" and "grandfather" (or, by some accounts, "godmother" and "godfather") become "gammer" and "gaffer."

Hypocorism, Hypochorisma Pet names, usually for children, but also shown in locutions such as Ezra Pound's "Tommy Jeff" for "Thomas Jefferson."

Hypolemniscus A mark like the division symbol ÷ minus the upper dot, formerly used for ANNOTATIONS and GLOSSES, especially in biblical commentary.

Hypotaxis Arrangement of clauses, phrases, or words in dependent or subordinate relationships. The phrase *hypotactic style* refers to writing that uses subordination to reflect logical, causal, temporal, or spatial relations. Occasionally, *hypotaxis* refers to the use of a subordinate clause in a place where one might normally expect a coordinate. Instead of the coordination of " 'Twas the night before Christmas, and all through the house . . ." for example, Clement Moore actually wrote ". . . when all through the house." In any event, PARATAXIS is a feature of ordinary speaking—especially the naive, simple, rustic, or juvenile—and *hypotaxis* of writing. One might say aloud, "I tried but I failed" (parataxis); one would probably write, "Although I tried, I failed" (*hypotaxis*).

Hypotyposis Vivid description, especially when used for rhetorical or dramatic effect. Preachers may use evocations of the pains of hell, for example, in a sermon designed to frighten the wicked. Some of Yeats's poems begin with instances of *hypotyposis*:

> Now as at all times I can see in the mind's eye,
> In their stiff, painted clothes, the pale unsatisfied ones
> Appear and disappear in the blue depth of the sky. . . .
> . . . .
> I have met them at close of day
> Coming with vivid faces
> From counter or desk among grey
> Eighteenth-century houses.

Hypozeugma The combination of a single subject with several predicates.

Hypozeuxis The paralleling of a number of clauses, each with a subject and predicate.

Hysteron Proteron "Latter before": a FIGURE OF SPEECH in which what should logically come last comes first. Dogberry's speech in *Much Ado About Nothing* is an example: "Masters, it is proved already that you are little better than false knaves, and it will go near to be thought so shortly." Some say, "It is vain to want to have your cake and eat it too," but that is not so vain; it is vain to want to eat your cake and have it too. Children saying "Trick or treat" at Hallowe'en really mean "Treat or trick." These are common examples of *hysteron proteron*.

Castellar 1957. Designed by John Peters.

Iamb (or **Iambus**) A FOOT consisting of an unaccented syllable and an accented (˘ ´). The most common rhythm in English verse for many centuries.

Icon In the Eastern churches, a stylized representation of a sacred personage. In modern critical usage, *icon* has come to mean a SIGN that goes beyond arbitrary reference—in which there is no necessary resemblance between the sign and that which is referred to (the signified)—and resembles, in form or shape or nature, that which it signifies. "Cuckoo"—to take a low-level example—refers to the sound made by a certain bird and also to the bird itself; although "cuckoo" does not equal the sound, it does bear a measure of acoustic resemblance and so can be called an "*icon*" and not just an arbitrary sign. At a higher level of "iconicity" than the simple resemblance between two sounds, the sign "cuckoo" refers to the source or maker of the sound and not just the sound itself; this process is a kind of metonymy, by which the bird's call is made to stand for the bird itself. At more sophisticated levels of representation and presentation, a verbal or aesthetic *icon* states a case and also embodies or enacts the case.

[References: Jonathan Culler, *Structuralist Poetics: Structuralism, Linguistics and the Study of Literature* (1975); C. W. Morris, *Signs, Language, and Behavior* (1946); W. K. Wimsatt, *The Verbal Icon: Studies in the Meaning of Poetry* (1954).]

Ictus The stress that falls on a syllable; *ictus* does not refer to the stressed syllable but to the stress itself.

Identical Rhyme A phenomenon, also called redundant rhyme or *rime riche*, in which a syllable both begins and ends in the same way as a rhyming syllable, without being the same word. If two lines end with "rain" (as in Eliot's "Gerontion"), that is simple repetition. If, however, "rain" occurs in a rhyming position with "rein" or "reign," that is *identical rhyme*. Tennyson at one time began "The Lotos-Eaters" with a rhyme between "strand" and "land" but later changed it to the "lazy no rhyme" of "land" and "land"—which is technically a repetition and not an *identical rhyme*. One of John Peale Bishop's sonnets is composed entirely of *identical rhymes*. That is virtually unique in English, but such patterns are relatively common in French, which relies on *identical rhymes* much more than English does. One of Mallarmé's sonnets has these rhyming words: *temps, s'extenue, nue* (noun), *tends, meditants, avenue, nue* (adjective), *contents, sure, morsure, amant, touffe, diamant, etouffe*. This quatrain by Emily Dickinson shows both simple repetition and *identical rhyme*:

All men for Honor hardest work
But are not known to earn—
Paid after they have ceased to work
In Infamy or Urn—

See RHYME.

Ideology A comprehensive notion that includes generalities pertaining to formal and informal thought, philosophy, cultural presuppositions, and the realms studied by social science. In literary applications, one could try to separate and isolate artworks from ideological considerations—and such isolation has been tried by a number of critical schools—but that gesture in itself has ideological implications, just as the axiom that a work of art should be approached on its own terms or in itself as an aesthetic object may yield what Marx ridiculed as "commodity fetishism." Critics since the Second World War have been learning that *ideology* cannot be marginalized or trivialized, nor can it be eliminated from consideration of artworks. With such a lesson taken to heart, most critics try to include in their studies both an awareness of the *ideology* surrounding a work and an admission that they themselves are working from an ideological base.

Idiom A use of words peculiar to a given language; an expression that cannot be translated literally. "To carry out" literally means to carry something out (of a room perhaps), but idiomatically it means to see that something is done, as "to carry out a command." *Idioms* in a language usually arise from a peculiarity that is syntactical or structural—as in a common but untranslatable phrase such as "How do you do?"—or from the obscuring of a meaning in a metaphor (as in the preceding example). The adjectives "brief" and "short" mean much the same, but their adverbial forms, by a quirk of *idiom*, are different; compare "I'll be there shortly" and "I'll be there briefly."

Idiotism A departure from linguistic norms, peculiar to a single speaker, dialect, or period. Although linking verbs ought to be followed by nominative forms, we permit the *idiotism* "woe is me" because "me" preserves an archaic dative form that corresponds to "*mir*" in the German "*Weh ist mir*."

Idyll (or **Idyl**) A term describing one or another of the poetic genres that are short and possess marked descriptive, narrative, and pastoral qualities. In this sense, Whittier's "Maud Muller" might be called an *idyll*, and the subtitle of his *Snow-Bound* is *A Winter Idyl*. Pastoral and descriptive elements are usually the first requisites of the *idyll*, although the pastoral is usually presented in a conscious literary manner. The point of view of the *idyll* is that of a civilized and artificial society glancing from a drawing room window over green meadows, or of the weekend farm viewed through a picture window. Historically, the term goes back to the *idylls* of Theocritus, who wrote short pieces depicting rustic life in Sicily to please the civilized Alexandrians. It has also been applied to long descriptive and narrative poems, particularly Tennyson's *Idylls of the King*. Both Southey and Tennyson wrote poems called "English Idylls." Celia Thaxter is known for *Idyls and Pastorals*, and Charles Kingsley wrote *Prose Idylls*.

Idyllium Archaic or affected equivalent of IDYLL.

Illocutionary Act A speech act that is discharged in the act of speaking, as in such transactions as pronouncing, declaring, proclaiming, telling, promising, nominating, warning, asking, requesting, betting, and moving (in the parliamentary sense), especially in the first person and present tense.

[Reference: J. L. Austin, *How to Do Things with Words*, 2nd ed., 1975.]

Image Originally a sculptured, cast, or modeled representation of a person; even in its most sophisticated critical usage, this fundamental meaning is still present, in that an *image* is a literal and concrete representation of a sensory experience or of an object that can be known by one or more of the senses. As I. A. Richards pointed out, it represents a sensation by being a "relict" of an already known sensation. The *image* is a distinctive element of the language of art by which experience in its richness and complexity is communicated, as opposed to the simplifying and conceptualizing processes of science and philosophy. The *image* is, therefore, a portion of the essence of the meaning of the literary work, not just decoration.

Images may be either literal or figurative, a literal *image* being one that involves no necessary change or extension in the obvious meaning of the words, one in which the words call up a sensory representation of the literal object or sensation; and a figurative *image* being one that involves a "turn" on the literal meaning of the words. An example of a collection of literal *images* may be seen in Coleridge's "Kubla Khan":

In Xanadu did Kubla Khan
A stately pleasure-dome decree:
Where Alph, the sacred river, ran
Through caverns measureless to man
  Down to a sunless sea.

The opening lines of a Wordsworth sonnet show both literal and figurative *images*:

It is a beauteous evening, calm and free;
The holy time is quiet as a Nun
Breathless with adoration; the broad sun
Is sinking down in its tranquillity.

The two middle lines are highly figurative, whereas the first and fourth are literal, although there are figurative "turns" present by implication in "free" and "tranquillity."

The qualities usually found in images are particularity, concreteness, and an appeal to sensuous experience or memory—an appeal that seems to work best through specifically visual *images*.

[Reference: Don Cameron Allen, *Image and Meaning: Metaphoric Traditions in Renaissance Poetry*, 2nd ed. (1968).]

Imagery *Imagery* in its literal sense means the collection of IMAGES in a literary work. In another sense it is synonymous with TROPE or FIGURE OF SPEECH. Here the trope designates a special usage of words in which there is a change in their basic meanings.

Patterns of *imagery*, often without the conscious knowledge of author or reader, are sometimes taken to be keys to a deeper meaning of a work. A few critics tend to see the "image pattern" as indeed being the basic meaning of the work and a better key to its interpretation than the explicit statements of the author or the more obvious events of plot or action. One notable contribution of the New Critics was their awareness of the importance of the relationships among images to the meaning of lyric poetry. Such patterning is important in fiction, as well, contrasting images of light and dark being among the most conspicuous.

Imagination The theories of poetry advanced in the early nineteenth century by Wordsworth, Coleridge, and others led to many efforts to distinguish between *imagination* and FANCY. The word *imagination* had passed through three stages of meaning. In Renaissance times it was opposed to reason and regarded as the means for attaining poetical and religious conceptions. Bacon cited it as one of the three faculties of the rational soul: "History has reference to the memory, poetry to the *imagination*, and philosophy to the reason"; and Shakespeare says the poet is "of *imagination* all compact." In the Neoclassic Period it was the faculty by which images were called up, especially visual images (see Addison's *The Pleasures of the Imagination*), and was related to the "imitation of nature." Because of its tendency to transcend the testimony of the senses, the poet who might draw on *imagination* must subject it to the check of reason. Later in the eighteenth century the *imagination*, opposed to reason, was conceived as such a vivid imaging process that it affected the passions and formed "a world of beauty of its own," a poetical illusion that served to produce immediate pleasure.

Romantic critics conceived the *imagination* as a unifying of the mental powers that enabled the poet to see such inner relationships as the identity of truth and beauty. So Wordsworth says that poets

> Have each his own peculiar faculty,
> Heaven's gift, a sense that fits him to perceive
> Objects unseen before . . .
> An insight that in some sort he possesses, . . .
> Proceeding from a source of untaught things.

This conception of *imagination* necessitated a distinction with fancy. Coleridge (*Biographia Literaria*) especially stressed, though he never fully explained, the difference. He called *imagination* the "shaping and modifying" power, fancy the "aggregative and associative" power. The former "struggles to idealize and to unify," whereas the latter is merely "a mode of memory emancipated from the order of time and space." To illustrate the distinction Coleridge remarked that Milton had a highly imaginative mind, Cowley a very fanciful one. Leslie Stephen summarized the distinction, "Fancy deals with the superficial resemblances, and *imagination* with the deeper truths that underlie them."

Although *imagination* is usually viewed as a "shaping" and ordering power, the function of which is to give art its special authority, the assumption is almost always present that the "new" creation shaped by the *imagination* is a new form of reality, not a fantasy or a fanciful project. When Shakespeare writes

> As imagination bodies forth
> The forms of things unknown, the poet's pen
> Turns them to shapes and gives to airy nothing
> A local habitation and a name,

his reference is genuinely to imagination, not to fancy.

[References: R. L. Brett, *Fancy and Imagination* (1969); Denis Donoghue, *The Sovereign Ghost: Studies in Imagination* (1976); Richard Kearney, *The Wake of Imagination: Toward a Postmodern Culture* (1988); J. L. Lowes, *The Road to Xanadu: A Study in the Ways of the Imagination* (rev. ed. 1964, 1955; orig. 1927); I. A. Richards, *Coleridge on Imagination*, 2nd ed. (1960, 1950; orig. 1934); Jean Paul Sartre, *Imagination: A Psychological Critique* (tr. 1962).]

Imagists A group of poets active in England and America between 1909 and 1918. Their name came from the French title *Des Imagistes*, given to the first anthology of their work (1914), this, in turn, having been borrowed from a critical term that had been applied to some French precursors of the movement. The most conspicuous figures of the movement were Ezra Pound, Hilda Doolittle ("H. D."), and F. S. Flint, who collectively formulated a set of principles as to treatment, diction, and rhyme. The image, according to Pound, presented "an intellectual and emotional complex in an instant of time"—with the intellectual component borne by visual images, the emotional by auditory. According to Amy Lowell's *Tendencies in Modern American Poetry* (1917), the major objectives of the movement were: (1) to use the language of common speech but to employ always the exact word—not the nearly exact; (2) to avoid the cliché; (3) to create new rhythms as the expressions of a new mood; (4) to allow absolute freedom in the choice of subject; (5) to present an image (that is, to be concrete, firm, definite in their pictures—harsh in outline); (6) to strive always for concentration, which, they were convinced, was the very essence of poetry; (7) to suggest rather than to offer complete statements. Pound soon dismissed Lowell's crusading as "Amygism," but her labors did help somewhat. As early as 1914, Pound moved from *imagism* to VORTICISM, the more kinetic movement, and eventually let the coinage PHANOPOEIA supersede both image and *imagism*.

[References: John T. Gage, *In the Arresting Eye: The Rhetoric of Imagism* (1981); Glenn Hughes, *Imagism and the Imagists: A Study in Modern Poetry* (1931); W. C. Pratt, *The Imagist Poem* (1963).]

Imitation The concept of art as *imitation* has its origin with classical critics. Aristotle said at the beginning of his *Poetics* that all arts are modes of *imitation*, and he defines a tragedy as an *imitation* of an action of a certain sort. Aristotle seems to be defending art against Plato's charge that it is twice removed from truth or reality. On the other hand, the Greek and Roman schools of rhetoric used the *imitation* of literary models as an accepted form of composition. Both views of *imitation* have persisted in English literary history.

According to Aristotle, all the productive arts work by imitating, and what they particularly imitate is form. The Aristotelian concept of *imitation*—that art *imitates* nature—was pervasively present in English critical thought until the end of the eighteenth century. This *imitation* came to be regarded as a realistic portrayal of life, a reproduction of natural objects and actions. Moreover, admiration of the success with which the classic writers had followed nature bolstered the rhetorical theory of following in their footsteps. Critics in the Renaissance and the Neoclassic Period accepted *imitation* in the sense of copying models in the various types of poetry. They did not believe that *imitation* should replace genius, but an adherence to established models was considered a safe method of avoiding literary vices and attaining virtues. *Imitation* as a copying of other writers was discussed and employed in all degrees of dependence, from the most inspired and dignified to the most servile.

In the Romantic Period, the MIMETIC THEORY OF ART gave way to the EXPRESSIVE THEORY, and the meaning of Aristotle's term *imitation* underwent serious change. NATURE then became the creative principle of the universe, and Aristotelian *imitation* was considered to be "creating according to a true idea," and a work of art was "an idealized representation of human life—of character, emotion, action—under forms manifest to sense." One can imitate *natura naturans* ("nature naturing") by creating works in a vital, organic, energetic way; or *natura naturata* ("nature natured") by creating works that are symmetrical and orderly.

With the rise of REALISM and NATURALISM, a renewed emphasis on the accurate portrayal of the palpable actual returned, although the term *imitation* was not often used. Today there is some interest in the implications of the depth psychologies for the theory of *imitation*.

[References: S. H. Butcher, *Aristotle's Theory of Poetry and Fine Art*, 4th ed. (1951; orig. 1911); R. S. Crane, ed., *Critics and Criticism* (1952).]

Immutation Obsolete equivalent of "mutation," occasionally used for HYPALLAGE.

Imperial A name formerly used for a size of printing paper approximately 22 × 32 inches.

Implied Author A term applied, particularly by Wayne C. Booth, to the sense of a human agency presenting the materials of a literary work to the reader. The concept of the *implied author* is similar to Aristotle's concept of the ETHOS of a piece of oratory, in that the ethos is the image of the speaker projected by the speech as a whole. Booth regards an *implied author*, always present, as a created, idealized version of the real author; it is important, however, to discriminate between the real and the *implied author*, who remains always a creation, figment, or PERSONA, even when bearing the same name as the real author (a phenomenon that turns up in novels by Somerset Maugham and Christopher Isherwood).

[Reference: Wayne Booth, *The Rhetoric of Fiction*, 2nd ed. (1983).]

Implied Reader A hypothetical reader, defined by Wolfgang Iser as one who "embodies all those predispositions necessary for a literary work to exercise its effect—predispositions laid down, not by an empirical outside reality, but by the text itself. Consequently, the implied reader as a concept has his roots firmly planted in the structure of the text; he is a construct and in no way to be identified with any real reader."

[References: Stanley Fish, *Surprised by Sin: The Reader in Paradise Lost*, 2nd ed. (1998; orig. 1967) and *Self-Consuming Artifacts: The Experience of Seventeenth-Century Artifacts* (1972); Wolfgang Iser, *The Act of Reading: A Theory of Aesthetic Response* (tr. 1978) and *The Implied Reader: Patterns of Communication in Prose Fiction from Bunyan to Beckett* (tr. 1974).]

Imprecation A CURSE; a MALEDICTION.

Impression All the copies of a book printed at one time or without removing the type or plates from the press; a PRINTING.

Impressionism A highly personal manner of writing in which the author presents materials as they appear to an individual temperament at a precise moment and from a particular vantage point rather than as they are presumed to be in actuality. The term is borrowed from painting. About the middle of the nineteenth century the French painters Manet, Monet, Degas, Renoir, and others revolted against the conventional academic doctrines and held that it was more important to retain the impressions that an object makes on the artist than to present the appearance of that object by precise detail and careful, realistic finish. Their special concern was with the use of light on their canvases. They suggested the chief features of an object with a few strokes; they were more interested in atmosphere than in perspective or outline. "Instead of painting a tree," says Lewis Mumford, the impressionist "painted the effect of a tree." The movement had its counterpart in literature, writers accepting the same conviction that the personal attitudes and moods of the writer were legitimate elements in depicting character, setting, or action. The literary impressionist holds that the registration of such elements as these through the fleeting impression of a moment is more significant artistically than a photographic presentation. The object of the impressionist, then, is to present material not as it is to the objective observer but as it is *seen* or *felt* to be by the impressionist or a character in a single moment. The impressionistic writer employs highly selective details, the "brush strokes" of sense-data that can suggest impressions. In poetry *impressionism* was an important aspect of the work of the imagists; in fiction it is present in the works of such writers as Henry James, Oscar Wilde, Joseph Conrad, Ford Madox Ford, James Joyce, Dorothy Richardson, and Virginia Woolf and in the "Camera Eye" sections of Dos Passos's *U.S.A.*

[References: Maria Elisabeth Kronegger, *Literary Impressionism* (1973); H. Peter Stowell, *Literary Impressionism: James and Chekhov* (1980).]

Impressionistic Criticism Criticism that attempts to communicate what the critic subjectively feels in the presence of a work of art. Anatole France called *impressionistic criticism* "the adventures of a sensitive soul among masterpieces."

Imprimatur An official license to print a work; usually the sign of approval of the Roman Catholic church. The term is also used ironically to refer to the approval of an autocratic critic self-appointed as custodian of public morality or taste. *Imprimatur* literally means "Let it be printed."

Improvisation A work or performance that is done on the spur of the moment, without conscious preparation or preliminary drafts or rehearsals. It is unlikely that pure *improvisation* is possible, but a sizable margin remains for relatively unpremeditated work. Music especially values skill at *improvisation*; many concerti include a cadenza that can be the performer's own *improvisation*. A. R. Ammons called some of his poems "improvisations."

Incantation A formulaic use of language, usually spoken or chanted, either to create intense emotional effects or to produce magical results. The witches' chants in *Macbeth* are well-known examples, as is Ariel's song "Full fathom five" in *The Tempest*.

Incident A single event or occurrence, the smallest unit of action. An *incident* is usually connected to, or dependent on, something else that is larger and of which it is a subordinate part. When *incidents* are arranged in some kind of logical pattern, they begin to be elements of plot. See PLOT.

Inciting Moment The name used by Freytag for the event or force that sets in motion the RISING ACTION of a play. It is also called the EXCITING FORCE. See FREYTAG'S PYRAMID.

Incremental Repetition A form of iteration frequently found in the BALLAD. This kind of repetition is not that of a refrain but the repeating of phrases and lines in such a way that their meaning is enhanced either by their appearing in changed contexts or by minor successive changes in the repeated portion of the ballad. A common form of *incremental repetition* occurs in the question-and-answer pattern in the ballad. These two stanzas from "Child Waters" illustrate *incremental repetition*:

There were four and twenty ladies
  Were playing at the ball,
And Ellen, she was the fairest lady,
  Must bring his steed to the stall.

There were four and twenty ladies
  Was a playing at the chess,
And Ellen, she was the fairest lady,
  Must bring his horse to grass.

A complex instance of *incremental repetition* occurs in the "Nevermore" at the end of each stanza of Poe's "The Raven," where the meaning of the word changes as the poem progresses.

[Reference: Louise Pound, *Poetic Origins and the Ballad* (1921, reprinted 1962).]

Incunabulum A term applied to any book printed in the last part of the fifteenth century (before 1501). Since the first printed books resembled in size, form, and appearance the medieval manuscript, which had been developed to a high degree of artistic perfection, *incunabula* are commonly large and ornate. They are prized by modern collectors. From a historical and literary viewpoint, they are valuable as reflecting the intellectual and literary interests of the late fifteenth century. The number of existing *incunabula* is large, including about 360 printed in England. Among famous English *incunabula* are Caxton's edition of Chaucer's *Canterbury Tales* and *Le Morte Darthur* of Malory. (Latin *incunabulum* means "swaddling clothes.")

Indeterminacy The concept that the meaning or reference of a text is ultimately undecidable; sometimes applied to all human discourse, sometimes limited to certain realms bounded by semantic, psychological, or cultural constraints, and sometimes limited (as by Marjorie Perloff) to certain modern movements in the arts. The general notion supposes that no final or determinate appeal is possible outside a given system of signs.

[References: Charles Altieri, *Act and Quality: A Theory of Literary Meaning and Humanistic Understanding* (1981); Geoffrey H. Hartman, *Saving the Text: Literature / Derrida / Philosophy* (1981); Marjorie Perloff, *The Poetics of Indeterminacy: Rimbaud to Cage* (1981).]

Index At one time, *index* meant TABLE OF CONTENTS. Since the eighteenth century, however, *index* has meant a systematic list of items in a book, volume, or series, along with some indication of location. Some *indexes* are general, listing major and minor topics; others are more specific, as in the Metrical Index of a hymnal, an Index of Names, an Index of Places, and so forth.

Index Expurgatorius A list of passages that are to be expurgated from books that may be read by members of the Roman Catholic church.

Index Librorum Prohibitorum A list of prohibited books; a list of titles of works—forbidden by church authority to be read by Roman Catholics, pending revision or deletion of some parts. Enumerations of forbidden books go back as far as the Muratorian Canon (about A.D. 170) and a list promulgated by Pope Innocent I in 405; the Gelasian Decree of 496 is sometimes mentioned as the first *Index Librorum Prohibitorum*, but it was 1559 before a list of forbidden books carried the name "*Index*." Subsequently there were many revisions, and Pope Leo XIII sponsored the issuance of a new *Index* (1900) that went through several editions, the last coming in 1948. A good deal of sentiment against the *Index* emerged during Vatican Council II, and in 1966 it was announced by Cardinal Ottaviani that there would be no further editions.

Indirect Satire Whereas FORMAL SATIRE is cast in the form of direct address, the satiric voice being the instrument by which ridicule is expressed, *indirect satire* is in narrative or dramatic form, and the characters who speak and act are themselves the objects of the satire in which they appear.

Induction (1) An old word for *introduction*. This term was sometimes used in the sixteenth century to denote a framework introduction (see FRAMEWORK-STORY). Thus, Sackville's "Induction" to a portion of *The Mirror for Magistrates* tells how the poet was led by Sorrow into a region of Hell where dwelt the shades of the historical figures whose lives are the subject of the *Mirror*. In the book proper each "shade" relates his own sad tale; the *induction* supplies the framework much as the famous "Prologue" supplies the framework for the stories making up Chaucer's *Canterbury Tales*. In *The Taming of the Shrew* Shakespeare employs an *induction* in which a drunken tinker is persuaded that he is a lord, for whose amusement is performed a play—*The Taming of the Shrew* itself. (2) Inductive reasoning (see A POSTERIORI), which proceeds from individual cases to general principles.

Industrial Revolution The social-political-economic struggle that characterized life in England for a hundred years or more, most intensely in the last quarter of the eighteenth and first quarter of the nineteenth centuries. Invention, scientific discovery, and changing economic, political, and social ideas all contributed to the furor. By 1760 blast furnaces had begun to manufacture iron; the textile industry grew apace with the invention of the spinning jenny and the power loom (1785). James Watt made even greater strides possible through his perfection of the steam engine. Roads, canals, and railroads increased transportation facilities. Agriculture was nearly abandoned; by 1826 not a third of the former population was left on the farms. Hundreds of thousands wandered through the country, many dying, impoverished and diseased. The sweatshop was born; master artisans found their trade taken from them by the machine. Home work gave way to factory work. Industry and commerce flourished in cities, which grew rapidly. The villages were all but deserted. A middle-class capitalistic group developed almost overnight and progressed at the expense of men, women, and children, whom they overworked in their mills.

Writers of the period concerned themselves with these problems. Crabbe in such pieces as *The Village* and *The Borough* set forth pictures of the conditions; Kingsley in such novels as *Yeast* and *Alton Locke* and Gaskell in *Mary Barton, a Tale of Manchester Life* presented the struggles and unfairness of the times. Dickens turned his attention to the relief of the poor. Ruskin and Carlyle sought to point the way to reform; Arnold in his essays condemned a Philistine England that measured greatness by wealth and numbers. Mill (*Principles of Political Economy*), Bentham (*Radical Reform*), Owen (*New View of Society*), and Malthus (*Principles of Political Economy*) attacked the problems of the time from the viewpoint of the new social sciences.

Influence A term used in literary history for the impact that a writer, work, school, or whole foreign or early culture has on an individual writer or work. Early in the twentieth century the tracing of *influence* was a major activity of literary historians. Despite much good work, however, the *influence* tracing was often far-fetched, and the method generally fell into disrepute. Today a revisionist approach, founded on a Freudian construction of certain TROPES, appears in Harold Bloom's *The Anxiety of Influence*.

Bloom's thesis is that *influence* involves a misprision or misreading—sometimes quite remarkable—of a previous writer as an unconscious strategy of creating room for a writer's present activity, so that every poem is a misinterpretation of a hypothetical parent poem. A related approach—less psychologistic and more typological and acoustic—is illustrated by John Hollander's *Vision and Resonance* and *The Figure of Echo*.

[Reference: Harold Bloom, *The Anxiety of Influence*, 2nd ed. (1997; orig. 1973).]

Informal Essay See ESSAY.

Ingemination Old term for repetition of a word or phrase.

Inkhorn A term at least 450 years old for needlessly learned, pedantic, and affected language, especially the use of foreign words.

Inkhornists A group in the Renaissance who favored the introduction of heavy Latin and Greek words into the standard English vocabulary. See PURIST.

In medias res A term from Horace, literally meaning "in the midst of things." It is applied to the literary technique of opening a story in the middle of the action and then supplying information about the beginning of the action through flashbacks and other devices for exposition. The term *in medias res* is usually applied to the EPIC, where such an opening is one of the conventions.

***In Memoriam* Stanza** A quatrain of IAMBIC TETRAMETER rhyming *abba*. A few earlier poets, such as Ben Jonson, used such a stanza occasionally, but it remained for Tennyson to invest the form with singular dignity and variety. As an added constraint in Tennyson's *In Memoriam*, all the rhymes are masculine, and all the constituent lyrics have at least three stanzas.

Inns of Court The four voluntary, unchartered societies or legal guilds in London that have the privilege of admitting persons to the bar. They take their names from the buildings they occupy—the Inner Temple, the Middle Temple, Lincoln's Inn, and

Gray's Inn—which they have been in since the fourteenth century. Though the origin of these societies is lost in the medieval inns of law, it is clear that in late medieval times they became great law schools and so continued for centuries: Today they are little more than lawyers' clubs, though they do exert considerable influence in guarding admissions to the bar. The *Inns of Court* were cultural institutions in the sixteenth and seventeenth centuries, with substantial libraries. Regular drama, as well as MASQUES and INTERLUDES, was nurtured by the *Inns*. Shakespeare's *Comedy of Errors* was acted before the fellows of Gray's Inn during the Christmas season of 1594. The *Inns*, like the universities, saw much playwriting and amateur acting on the part of "gentlemen" who would scorn connection with the early public theaters. Many English authors have received their education, in whole or in part, in the *Inns of Court*. Chaucer may have belonged to one; Sir Thomas More was a Lincoln's Inn product; George Gascoigne and Francis Bacon were admitted to law practice from Gray's Inn; Thomas Shadwell and Nicholas Rowe were members of the Inner Temple. A vivid description of life in the *Inns* appears in Thackeray's *Pendennis*.

Inscape A term used by Gerard Manley Hopkins to refer to the "individually distinctive" inner structure or nature of a thing; hence the essence of a natural object, which, being perceived through a moment of illumination—an EPIPHANY—reveals the unity of all creation. *Inscape* is the inward quality of objects and events, as they are perceived by the joined observation and introspection of a poet, who in turn embodies them in unique poetic forms. One of Hopkins's poems says, "Each mortal thing does one thing and the same"; it forcibly "selves"—a verb coined by Hopkins in a typical gesture to catch the unique *inscape* of the universal activity. See INSTRESS.

Inscription An older sense has to do with symbols cut or scratched into a hard surface, such as stone, wood, shell, or metal. A narrower use concerns the way some works have of inserting themselves into other works, as Joyce's *Ulysses* is inscribed within Homer's *Odyssey* or Mann's *Doktor Faustus* is inscribed within the whole dossier of Faust legends, including works by Marlowe and Goethe. Yet another sense has to do with the foregrounded presence of a written text inside the written text of a literary work, as when Hardy's Jude inscribes "Thither" on the signpost for Christminster.

Instress A term used by Gerard Manley Hopkins to refer to the force, ultimately divine, that creates the INSCAPE of an object or an event and impresses that distinctive inner structure of the object on the mind of the beholder, who can perceive it and embody it in a work of art.

Intended Reader That imaginable intellect for whom a given work was designed. One can proceed from the nature of the work to construct or reconstruct the reader, beginning with the stipulation that the reader be able to understand the language in which the work is written. In some works the *intended reader* is included as a fiction or part of the fiction, sometimes called "dear reader" or "gentle reader."

Intentional Fallacy The judging of the meaning of success or a work of art by the author's expressed or ostensible intention in producing it. The term was introduced by W. K. Wimsatt and M. C. Beardsley to insist that "the poem is not the critic's own and not the author's. . . . What is said about the poem [by the author] is subject to the same scrutiny as any statement in linguistics or in the general science of psychology or morals." The *intentional fallacy*, like the AFFECTIVE FALLACY, is an error particularly when viewed from an OBJECTIVE THEORY OF ART, for holders of the objective theory tend—at least in their extreme statements—to see the work of art as AUTOTELIC. Wimsatt and Beardsley say, "The author must be admitted as a witness to the meaning of his work." But they would subject the authors' testimony to rigorous scrutiny in the light of the work itself. Insofar as the artist is competent and articulate, and insofar as the work may be construed as the objective realization of some subjective state that we can recognize as common, no specific intention can be recovered or reconstructed from anything in a well-executed work, which will be, in effect, "nearly anonymous" (in John Crowe Ransom's phrase). See also AFFECTIVE FALLACY, AUTOTELIC, HISTORICAL CRITICISM, INTERTEXTUALITY.

[Reference: W. K. Wimsatt and M. C. Beardsley, *The Verbal Icon: Studies in the Meaning of Poetry* (1954).]

Intergeneric Prose Prose that belongs between or among genres; it may combine prose and poetry (as in some of the works of J. P. Donleavy and Nelson Algren), or it may cross the boundary between fiction and history (as in Dos Passos's *U.S.A.* and E. L. Doctorow's *Ragtime*).

Interior Monologue One of the techniques for presenting the STREAM OF CONSCIOUSNESS of a character. Recording the internal emotional experience of the character, it reaches downward to the nonverbalized level, where images must be used to represent sensations or emotions. It assumes the unrestricted and uncensored portrayal of the totality of interior experience. It gives, therefore, the appearance of being illogical and associational. There are two distinct forms of *interior monologue*: direct, in which the author seems not to exist and the interior self of the character is given directly, as though the reader were overhearing an articulation of the stream of thought and feeling flowing through the character's mind; and indirect, in which the author serves as selector, presenter, guide, and commentator. The Molly Bloom section at the close of Joyce's *Ulysses* is the best-known example of direct *interior monologue* in English; the novels of Virginia Woolf illustrate the indirect. It is generally agreed that Édouard Dujardin, in *Les Lauriers sont coupés* (1887), was the first to use the *interior monologue* extensively.

Some of Robert Browning's poems may be taken as *interior monologues*: "Johannes Agricola in Meditation" and "Soliloquy of the Spanish Cloister" are instances. Some of Eliot's poems—"The Love Song of J. Alfred Prufrock" and "Gerontion," for example—may be read in much the same way.

Interlaced Rhyme CROSSED RHYME.

Interlocking Rhyme A rhyme pattern in which one line in a rhyming unit carries forward the rhyme for the next unit. An example is *TERZA RIMA*, in which the middle line in each three-line unit establishes the rhyme for the first and third lines of the succeeding three-line unit. Robert Frost extended this sort of practice to the quatrain in "Stopping by Woods on a Snowy Evening." *Terza rima* goes *aba bcb cdc ded* and so forth. Frost's poem rhymes *aaba bbcb ccdc dddD* (with the last line repeated).

Interlude A kind of drama, developed in late-fifteenth- and early-sixteenth-century England, that played an important part in the secularization of the drama and in the evolution of REALISTIC COMEDY. The word may mean a play brief enough to be presented in the interval of a dramatic performance, entertainment, or feast (for example, Medwall's *Fulgens and Lucres*, 1497), or it may mean a PLAY or dialogue between two persons. Some *interludes* imitate French farce and do not exhibit symbolic technique and didactic purpose, whereas others appear to have developed from the MORALITY PLAY, and still others from the Latin SCHOOL PLAYS: the two latter types are likely to be moralistic. The *interlude* was understood in Tudor times to mean a short play exhibited by professionals at the meals of the great and on other occasions where, later, MASQUES would be fashionable. The essential qualities are brevity and wit. Some writers regard such an episode as that of the sheep-stealing Mak in the Towneley *Second Shepherd's Play* as an *interlude*. The chief developers of the *interlude* were John Heywood and John Rastell, the first English dramatists, so far as known, to recognize that a play might be justified by its ability to amuse. Heywood's *interludes* were produced in the 1520s and 1530s, the most famous being *The Four P's* (the Palmer, the Pardoner, the Pothecary, and the Pedlar, who engage in a sort of lying contest managed as a satire against women) and *The Merry Play of John John the Husband, Tyb His Wife, and Sir John the Priest* (in which the priest and Tyb hoodwink the husband). Rastell's *interludes* include *The Nature of the Four Elements, The Field of the Cloth of Gold*, and *Gentilness and Nobility*. Homely details and realistic treatment are significant features of the *interludes*, which still followed the allegorical pattern of the MORALITY and yet represented growth toward the individual and particular.

Internal Rhyme Rhyme that occurs at some place before the last syllables in a line. In the opening line of Eliot's "Gerontion"—"Here I am, an old man in a dry month"—there is *internal rhyme* between "an" and "man" and between "I" and "dry." There are two instances of proximate *internal rhyme* in these lines by Dickinson:

It dropped so low—in my Regard—
I heard it hit the Ground. . . .

International Novel A novel in which one important spring of conflict is national difference, especially among characters who must travel. Many of Scott's historical novels involve such conflict, but the most brilliant exploitation of the mode has been in the novels of Henry James, such as *The American* and *The Golden Bowl*. Many of the novels of Maugham, Lawrence, Huxley, Hemingway, Fitzgerald, and Kingsley and Martin Amis have to do with international themes.

Interpolation In editing, we can sometimes interpolate an item in a series by some process of deduction or induction. If a damaged text reads, "A man had —— sons, and their names were James and Charles," we can interpolate "two" in the blank space. With verse, *interpolations* may be suggested by patterns of rhythm, meter, and rhyme.

Interpretation, Fourfold Method The levels employed in biblical interpretation in the Middle Ages and the Renaissance. In our time, a similar method has been advanced by Northrop Frye. See FOUR SENSES OF INTERPRETATION.

Interpretive Community A term used by Stanley Fish to distinguish readers sharing the same fundamental strategy of reading and interpreting. The "correctness" of an interpretation is relative to the conventions and assumptions of an *interpretive community*. One community might assume that reconstruction of the meaning for original readers was the only proper procedure; another might insist on the necessity for readers to transform the text by various codes.

[Reference: Stanley Fish, *Is There a Text in This Class?: The Authority of Interpretive Communities* (1980).]

Intertextuality A term created by Julia Kristeva, who said, "Every text builds itself as a mosaic of quotations, every text is absorption and transformation of another text" (tr. Jeanine Parisier Plottel). Eliot's *The Waste Land*, for example, makes a point of foregrouding self-reflexive elements of repetition and annotation as well as intertextual elements of quotation, allusion, echo, parody, and revision. Hawthorne's *The Scarlet Letter*, by its very title, presents itself as a comment on another text: the single color-coded letter that Hester Prynne is sentenced to wear.

[Reference: Jeanine Parisier Plottel, Hannah Charney, eds., "Introduction," *Intertextuality: New Perspectives in Criticism, New York Literary Forum*, vol. 2 (1978).]

Interview A critical feature that has come into popularity since the Second World War. The format is customarily question-and-answer, although sometimes the discussion is more informal. Most interviews require at least two persons, but James Dickey has written so-called self-interviews. Probably the most distinguished interviews in English have been those appearing for many years in the *Paris Review* and collected in the *Writers at Work* series.

Intrigue Comedy A comedy in which the major interest is in complications resulting from scheming by one or more characters. See COMEDY OF SITUATION.

Introduction The opening of a piece of writing. All compositions have three parts: beginning, middle, and end. On this basis the *introduction* is the beginning of the beginning. Sometimes the term is applied to an explanatory essay at the beginning of a book.

Intrusive Narrator An omniscient narrator who freely and frequently interrupts a narrative to explain, interpret, or qualify, sometimes in the form of essays. An *intrusive narrator* must be accepted as authoritative unless strong clues point to an ironic intention. Fielding in *Tom Jones*, Tolstoi in *War and Peace*, and George Eliot in *Adam Bede* (particularly Chapter 17) are good examples.

[Reference: Wayne Booth, *The Rhetoric of Fiction*, 2nd ed. (1983).]

Invective Harsh, abusive language directed against a person or cause. Vituperative writing. The *Letters* of Junius and the open letter written by Stevenson in defense of Father Damien have qualities of *invective*.

Invention In this present-day sense the term implies original creative power of an independent sort. But the use of the term by early English critics often is colored by an older meaning and by the implications of the theory of imitation. In Latin rhetoric *inventio* meant the "finding" of material and was applied, for example, to an orator's preliminary "working up" of his case. According to the Aristotelian doctrine of imitation, authors did not create their materials "out of nothing"; they found them in nature. A critic influenced by these conceptions would not think of *invention* in its narrower, modern sense. Yet the idea of originality, of using "new" devices, and of avoiding the trite expression appears in the use of the term in England as early as Renaissance times. As the term was used somewhat loosely for several centuries, it is not possible to give a single definition explaining all the passages in which the term appears in writings of the sixteenth, seventeenth, and eighteenth centuries. In the Romantic Period and since, *invention*, in the sense of the discovery or creation of an original or organizing principle, has been replaced by IMAGINATION. We commonly speak of an interplay between convention and *invention*. If poets devise a new stanza—as Hardy, Yeats, Auden, and Larkin have done—they have adhered to convention in using a stanza at all but have displayed *invention* in the creation of something new.

Inversion The placing of a sentence element out of its normal position. Probably the most offensive common use of *inversion* is the placing of the adjective after the noun in such expressions as "house beautiful" or "lady fair." Of the several varieties of *inversion*, the commonest are noun-adjective, object-verb, and adverb-auxiliary. The last sort is made possible by the peculiar structure of verb forms in Germanic languages, whereby a fairly neutral clause such as "I have never seen such a mess" gains a measure of emphasis in the inverted form "Never have I seen such a mess." Once in a while, as in "Jerk though he may be," even conjunctions can be dramatically relocated.

The device is often happily employed in poetry. Where the writer of prose might say: "I once saw a vision of a damsel with a dulcimer," Coleridge writes:

A damsel with a dulcimer
In a vision once I saw.

Investigative Journalism Journalism that turns from the reporting and analysis of the news of the day to dig more deeply into a particular event or issue. Gaston Leroux (1868–1927), trained as a lawyer, was a pioneer of *investigative journalism* in France in the late nineteenth century (although his fame rests on different basis: *The Phantom of the Opera*). Journalists have long been in the business of investigating, but *investigative journalism* has evolved to a position of importance since about 1960, particularly in the work of Seymour Hersh, Joe McGinniss, Robert Woodward, and Carl Bernstein.

Invocation An address to a deity for aid. In classical literature, convention demanded an opening address to the Muses, requesting their assistance in the writing. Epics, particularly, were likely to begin in this way. Milton, in *Paradise Lost*, accepts the tradition, but instead of invoking a traditional Muse, he addresses the

Heavenly Muse, that, on the secret top
Of Oreb, or of Sinai, didst inspire
That shepherd who first taught the chosen seed
In the beginning how the heavens and earth
Rose out of Chaos. . . .

Ionic A classical FOOT with two long and two short syllables. It is used by Horace in his *Odes*. When it is occasionally attempted in English, stressed syllables are used for the long ones and unstressed for the short. This "greater" *Ionic* foot is rarer in English than the "lesser," which amounts to a PYRRHIC followed by a SPONDEE. Something of the sort may turn up as a variation in a generally iambic poem, as in Tennyson's line "On the bald street breaks the blank day." In songs, which permit some license in shortening and lengthening syllables, we may occasionally hear a "lesser" *Ionic* effect in lines such as "In the evening by the moonlight."

Ipse Dixit Any dogmatic statement. Literally the Latin means: "He himself or she herself has said." Hence the term is used to characterize any edict or brief statement emphatically uttered, but unsupported by proof.

Irish Bull See BULL.

Irish Literary Movement, Irish Literary Revival, Irish Renaissance Variant terms for the movement that encouraged the production of Anglo-Irish literature. See CELTIC RENAISSANCE.

Irish Literature The early literature of Ireland is greater in bulk, earlier in date, and more striking in character than any other preserved vernacular Western European literature. It has furnished a storehouse of literary materials for later writers, especially those of the early ROMANTIC PERIOD and of the CELTIC RENAISSANCE as well as a clue to the origins of ARTHURIAN LEGEND. The development of this extensive native literature, as well as the remarkable flourishing of Latin learning in Ireland in the early Middle Ages, is due in part to the fact that the Teutonic invasions, which destroyed Roman power in the fifth century, failed to reach Ireland, which became a refuge for European scholars and for several centuries the chief center of Christian culture in Western Europe. The Irish clerics, too, seem to have been unusually tolerant of native pagan culture and therefore aided in preserving a great mass of native, often primitive, legendary and literary materials of interest to the student of folklore and linguistics.

Although poetry in Irish was written in very early times, definite metrical forms that employed alliteration and rhyme having been developed as early as the seventh century, the bulk of early *Irish literature* is in prose. The early Irish epics are distinguished from most other early epic literature by their use of prose (though the Irish prose epics frequently include poetic paraphrases or commentaries—"rhetorics"—scattered throughout). The basic stories of the chief epic cycle reflect a state of culture prevailing about the time of Christ. Orally preserved from generation to generation for centuries, they seem to have been written down as early as the seventh and eighth centuries. These early copies of the old stories were largely destroyed and scattered as a result of the Norse invasion (eighth and ninth centuries), the stories being imperfectly recovered and again recorded in manuscripts by antiquarians of the tenth and later centuries. Two large manuscripts of the twelfth century containing these retellings of ancient story are still in existence, the *Book of the Dun Cow* (before 1106) and the *Book of Leinster* (before 1160).

The early SAGA literature is divided into three great cycles: the "mythological," based on early Celtic myths and historical legends concerning population groups or "invasions"; the Ulster Cycle, or "Red Branch," of which Cuchulain is the hero; and the Fenian Cycle, concerned mostly with the exploits of Finn mac Cool. The Ulster Cycle was more aristocratic than the Fenian and is preserved in greater volume in the early manuscripts. The chief story is the *Táin bó Cuailgne*, "The Cattle Raid of Cooley," the greatest of the early Irish epics. Other important stories of this cycle are *The Feast of Bricriu* (containing a beheading game like that in *Sir Gawain and the Green Knight*), *The Wooing of Etaine* (a fairy mistress story), and *The Exile of the Sons of Usnech* (the Deirdre story). The Fenian stories, perhaps later in origin than the Ulster tales, have shown greater vitality in oral tradition, many of them still being current among the Gaelic peasants of Ireland and Scotland. They were used by James Macpherson in the eighteenth century. (See FORGERIES, LITERARY.) Early Irish professional poets (*fili*) or storytellers were ranked partly by the extent of their repertory of tales, the highest class being able to recite no less than 350 separate stories. These stories were divided into numerous classes or types, such as cattle raids, wooings, battles, deaths, elopements, feasts, exiles, destructions, slaughters, adventures, voyages, and visions.

In addition to the saga literature, there has been preserved (partly in Latin) a vast amount of historical, legal, and religious literature, the latter including a great many saints' lives as well as hymns, martyrologies, and one of the earliest examples of medieval biographical writing, Adamnan's "The Life of Saint Columba" (before A.D. 700). The traditional literary technique of the native Irish writers was much altered after the spread of English power and culture in Ireland in the seventeenth century, and the decline in the employment of the Irish language since that time has been accompanied by a lessening of literary activity. In modern times the versatile writer Brendan Behan was best known for plays in English prose but could write respectable poems in the Irish language as well. For "revivals" of Gaelic literature and culture see CELTIC RENAISSANCE, CELTIC REVIVAL, GAELIC MOVEMENT.

[References: Myles Dillon, *Early Irish Literature* (1948); Robin Flower, *The Irish Tradition* (1947); Patrick Rafroidi, *Irish Literature in English: The Romantic Period*, 2 vols. (1980).]

Irony A broad term referring to the recognition of a reality different from appearance. Verbal *irony* is a FIGURE OF SPEECH in which the actual intent is expressed in words that carry the opposite meaning. We may say, "I could care less" while meaning "I couldn't care less." *Irony* is likely to be confused with SARCASM, but it differs from sarcasm in that it is usually less harsh. Its presence may be marked by a sort of grim humor and "unemotional detachment," a coolness in expression at a time when one's emotions appear to be really heated. Characteristically, it speaks words of praise to imply blame and words of blame to imply praise. In a popular song, a farmer says to the wife who has abandoned him, "You picked a fine time to leave me, Lucille." At a certain depth of *irony*, saying what you do not mean gives way to being unable to say what you mean, as in Prufrock's outburst, "It is impossible to say just what I mean!" (which, ironically, seems to be just what he means). The effectiveness of *irony* is the impression it gives of restraint. The ironist writes with tongue in cheek; for this reason *irony* is more easily detected in speech than in writing, because the voice can, through its intonation, easily warn the listener of a double significance. One of the most famous ironic remarks in literature is Job's "No doubt but ye are the people, and wisdom shall die with you." Antony's insistence, in his oration over the dead Caesar, that "Brutus is an honorable man" bears a similar ironic stamp. Goldsmith, Austen, and Thackeray, in one novel or another, make frequent use of irony. Swift is an archironist. His "Modest Proposal" for saving a starving Ireland, by suggesting that the Irish sell their babies to the English landlords to be eaten, is perhaps the most savagely sustained ironic writing in literature. Pope used *irony* brilliantly in poetry. The novels of Hardy and James are elaborate artistic expressions of the ironic spirit, for *irony* applies not only to statement but also to event, situation, and structure. One of Hardy's volumes of short stories is called *Life's Little Ironies*, and even the "little" is ironic. In drama, *irony* has a special meaning, referring to knowledge held by the audience but hidden from the characters.

In tragic irony, characters use words that mean one thing to them but have foreboding, different meaning to those who understand the situation better. In contemporary criticism *irony* is used to describe a poet's "recognition of incongruities" and his or her controlled acceptance of them. Recent criticism, prompted particularly by Frye's *Anatomy of Criticism*, has concentrated on many sorts of *irony* as the typical habit of the EIRON, who does not and cannot speak directly. Other critics important in the analysis of *irony* are Kenneth Burke, Wayne Booth, and Harold Bloom.

[References: Wayne Booth, *A Rhetoric of Irony* (1974); Northrop Frye, *Anatomy of Criticism* (1957); Norman Knox, *The Word Irony in Its Context*, 1500–1755 (1961); G. G. Sedgewick, *Of Irony, Especially in Drama* (1948).]

Irregular Ode An ODE that does not follow either the pattern of STROPHE, ANTISTROPHE, and EPODE of the PINDARIC ODE or the repetition of stanzas of the HORATIAN ODE but freely alters its stanzaic forms both in number and in length. It was introduced by Abraham Cowley in the seventeenth century. Wordsworth's "Ode: Intimations of Immortality from Recollections of Early Childhood" and Coleridge's "Dejection: An Ode" are noted examples. It is sometimes called the "pseudo-Pindaric ode."

Isobaric A meteorological term having to do with equal weight or atmospheric pressure, also used for syllables that bear the same level of stress. A majority of the rhymes in English verse are between syllables that are stressed equally. See ANISOBARIC.

Isorhythmic In quantitative prosody, applied to feet that have equal duration in both halves. Since the short syllable was reckoned at half the duration of the long, an *isorhythmic* foot would have to consist of two long syllables (SPONDEE) or one long and two short (AMPHIBRACH, DACTYL, ANAPEST).

Isotype Acronym for "International system of typographic picture education," a picture language devised by O. Neurath (1882–1945) for the display of statistical information.

Issue A distinct set of copies of an EDITION of a book. An *issue* is distinguishable from other copies or sets of copies of the edition by variations in the printed matter. A PRINTING may contain more than one *issue* if variations in the printed matter occur during the printing.

Italian Sonnet A sonnet divided into an OCTAVE rhyming *abbaabba* and a SESTET rhyming *cdecde*. That is the classic form, which asserts the avoidance of rhyme in couplets in the sestet and a limiting of the overall number of rhymes to five. Ideally, the sense of the lines falls into groups different from the rhyme groups, thus: *ab-ba-ab-bacde- cde*, so that nowhere do we encounter a pat couplet. The least objectionable departures are the *abbaacca* octave and the *cdcdcd* sestet. Also called PETRARCHAN SONNET.

J

Baskerville 1915. Based on a typeface cut by John Baskerville, c. 1750, it is now in general use. This is a redesigned version by M. F. Benton.

Jacobean Age That portion of the RENAISSANCE during the reign of James I (1603–1625). Early Jacobean literature was a rich flowering of the Elizabethan, and late Jacobean writing showed the attitudes characteristic of the CAROLINE AGE. During the *Jacobean Age* the breach between Puritan and Cavalier widened, and there was a robust growth of REALISM in art and CYNICISM in thought. It is the greatest period for the English drama; Shakespeare wrote his greatest tragedies and his tragicomedies; Jonson flourished, producing classical tragedy, realistic comedy, and MASQUES; and Beaumont and Fletcher, Webster, Chapman, Middleton, and Massinger were at their peaks. In poetry, Shakespeare's *Sonnets* appeared, Drayton published his *Poems*, and Donne published his metaphysical verse. In prose, the *Jacobean Age* saw the publication of the King James translation of the Bible, Bacon's major work, Donne's and Andrewes's sermons, Burton's *Anatomy of Melancholy*, the character essays, and Dekker's realistic "novels." See RENAISSANCE and *Outline of Literary History*.

Jargon Confused speech, resulting particularly from the mingling of several languages or dialects. The term is also used to refer to any strange language that sounds uncouth to us; in this sense outlandish speech. Sometimes *jargon* means simply nonsense or gibberish. *Jargon*, like cant, also signifies the special language of a group or profession, such as legal *jargon*, pedagogic *jargon*, thieves' *jargon*.

Jeremiad A work that foretells destruction because of the evil of a group. It takes its name from Jeremiah, whose prophecy opens with the Lord saying, "Out of the north an evil shall break forth upon all the inhabitants of the land . . . who have forsaken me, and have burned incense unto other gods, and worshiped the works of their own hands" (Jeremiah 1:14, 16). The term is also used for severe expressions of grief and complaint, similar to Jeremiah's *Lamentations*, an expression of his deep sorrow over the capture of Jerusalem.

[Reference: Sacvan Bercovitch, *The American Jeremiad* (1978).]

Jest Books Collections of humorous, witty, or satirical anecdotes and jokes that had some vogue in Europe in the sixteenth and succeeding centuries. The "jests" in these miscellanies owe something to the Latin *facetia*, the medieval FABLIAU and EXEMPLUM, the epigram, the proverb, and the adage. They are usually short and often end with a "moral." Coarseness, ribaldry, realism, satire, and cynicism often characterize the witty turns. The material in the *jest books* probably is similar in character to the stock-in-trade of the medieval MINSTRELS, the printing press making possible the dissemination of such matter in book form. Women, friars, cuckolds, Welshmen, courtiers, tradesmen, foreigners, military officers, doctors, students, travelers, and many other classes are butts of the wit or victims of practical jokes. The earliest English *jest book* is *A Hundred Merry Tales* (c. 1526). Another famous one was *The Gest of Skoggan* (c. 1565), which illustrates a tendency of *jest books* to be "biographical" in making the jokes cluster about a single person. There were in the seventeenth and eighteenth centuries *jest books* on Ben Jonson. One famous court jester, Archie Armstrong, published his own *jest book*, *A Banquet of Jests and Merry Tales* (1630), divided into "Court Jests," "Camp Jests," "College Jests," "City Jests," and "Country Jests."

Jesuits Members of the Society of Jesus, a Catholic religious order founded by Saint Ignatius Loyola in 1534. In contrast with the ascetic orders, the *Jesuits* were conceived as a band of spiritual soldiers who were expected to engage actively in affairs. The discipline is strict, the individual having no rights as such but vowing to serve God through the Society. The members are bound by personal vows of poverty, chastity, and obedience. The head of the Order, called the "General," lives in Rome and is subject to the Pope. The *Jesuits*, famous as schoolmasters, have raised the educational as well as spiritual standards of the clergy. The letters of *Jesuit* missionaries in America give important pictures of early life in the colonies. Although political activities were technically forbidden, the objectives of the Order actually led the *Jesuits* into political intrigue, and this fact has led to much criticism of the Order, which is often accused of duplicity and casuistry, a charge perpetuated unjustly in the use of "Jesuitical" as derogatory. English poetry has been enriched by the work of some *Jesuits*, notably Saint Robert Southwell (1561–1595), whose *Saint Peter's Complaint* and short poems such as "The Burning Babe" anticipate both the seriousness of Milton and the conceits of Donne, and another *Jesuit*, Gerard Manley Hopkins (1844–1889), whose poems demonstrate an intensity of feeling and a mastery of experimental devices. It is probable that Hopkins's rigorous training as a *Jesuit* contributed much to his linguistic and verbal sensitivity and to his philosophical breadth and subtlety. The ideas of praise and glory that saturate Hopkins's poems seem related to the Jesuits' mottoes: *Ad majorem Dei gloriam* (to the greater glory of God) and *Laus Deo Semper* (praise to God always).

Jeu d'esprit A witty playing with words, a clever sally. Much of Thomas Hood's verse, for example, may be said to be marked by a happy *jeu d'esprit*. The term is also applied to brief, clever pieces of writing, such as Benjamin Franklin's "bagatelles."

Jewish American Literature A field of study that has emerged since about 1935 and concentrated on the work of Jewish writers living in America. Although some poets (such as Karl Shapiro, Allen Ginsberg, and more recently Irving Feldman) have been studied in this setting, most of the critical attention has gone to playwrights (such as Arthur Miller) and, preeminently, to fiction writers (such as J. D. Salinger, Norman Mailer, Saul Bellow, Mark Harris, Philip Roth, and Bernard Malamud—some of whom raise the question of what constitutes "Jewishness"). Studies have been made of linguistic, social, cultural, religious, political, and historical backgrounds; and some attention has been paid to the importance of certain continental precursors (Proust and Kafka, for example) and certain recurrent themes or problems (violence, generational strife, guilt, political loyalty).

Jig A nonliterary farcical dramatic performance, the words being sung to the accompaniment of dancing. It was popular on the Elizabethan stage, often being used as an afterpiece. "He's for a *jig*, or a tale of bawdry," Hamlet says of Polonius. *Jig* was also used around 1700 for a song-and-dance number serving as a theatrical finale. C. Day Lewis wrote a poem called "Jig." See DROLL.

Jingle A versicle, or short verse or sentence, set to catchy music and used to sell something. The heyday of the *jingle* was during the flourishing of radio, around 1930–1950. The effect of *jingle* in a different sense, implying short lines, percussive rhymes, and unevolved rhythm, temporarily entertaining but eventually disagreeable, was found by Emerson in the poems of Poe and Tennyson. Also applied to RHYME and other acoustic devices in general.

Johnson's Circle (also **Doctor Johnson's Circle**) A name often applied to a literary group whose leader was Samuel Johnson, but better known as THE LITERARY CLUB.

Jongleur Medieval French entertainer of times, similar to the Saxon GLEEMAN and the MINSTREL.

Journal (1) A form of autobiographical writing including a day-by-day account of events and a record of personal impressions. It is usually less intimate than a DIARY and more obviously chronological than an autobiography. (2) The term is also applied to any PERIODICAL that contains news or deals with matters of current interest in any particular sphere, as *The Journal of Southern History*. As a point of etiquette, some learned and literary periodicals prefer "journal" to "magazine," the latter being considered less dignified and more miscellaneous.

Judicial Criticism See CRITICISM, TYPES OF.

Jungian Criticism Criticism based on the psychology of Carl Jung, a Swiss psychiatrist and the founder of analytical psychology. His postulate of two dimensions in the unconscious—the personal, consisting of repressed events in the individual's life, and the archetypal, which is a part of the collective unconscious—has been widely employed, particularly by those interested in myth criticism. Jung also contributed the valuable concepts of the *animus* and the *anima* as components of character. Jung himself remarked that his thought was more useful in approaching popular and even vulgar art—such as the writings of H. Rider Haggard (*King Solomon's Mines*) than in approaching canonical or "high" art. See ARCHETYPE, MYTH.

[Reference: Bettina L. Knapp, *A Jungian Approach to Literature* (1984).]

Juvenalian Satire FORMAL SATIRE in which the speaker attacks vice and error with contempt and indignation. It is so called because it is like the dignified satires of Juvenal. Samuel Johnson's "The Vanity of Human Wishes" is a well-known example. *Juvenalian satire* in its realism and its harshness is in strong contrast to HORATIAN SATIRE, the other principal type of formal satire.

Juvenilia Works produced in an author's youth and usually marked by immaturity. Dryden's poem "Upon the Death of Lord Hastings," written when he was eighteen, Pope's *Pastorals*, written when he was sixteen, and Lord Byron's *Hours of Idleness*, written when he was eighteen, are examples, as is Poe's volume *Tamerlane and Other Poems*, published when he was eighteen.

K

Augustea Roman 1951. Designed by Allesandro Butti and Aldo Novarese.

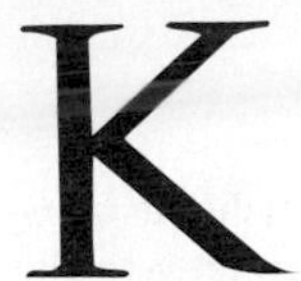

Kabbalah (also **Cabala, Caballa, Kaballa**) According to certain post-biblical Hebrew accounts, the oral tradition transmitted from Moses to the Rabbis of the Mishnah and the Talmud. Around 1200, applied to an elaborate tradition of the mystical interpretation of the Old Testament.

[References: Harold Bloom, *Kabbalah and Criticism* (1975); David Rosenberg, *Dreams of Being Eaten Alive: The Literary Core of the Kabbalah* (2000).]

Kabuki The most popular form of theater in Japan since the mid-seventeenth century. *Kabuki* is an eclectic form using stories, scenes, dances, and music, some more than a thousand years old. It is a dance and musical theater, with elaborate sets. The actors, all of whom are skilled dancers and acrobats, are men, but some portray women. The plays themselves, which function primarily as vehicles for spectacle, fall into several categories: EPIC plays of the heroic period in Japanese history; "common-people's plays," tending toward naturalistic tragedy; FARCES; and dance plays. All are marked by extreme FORMALISM and theatricality. See NOH PLAYS.

Kailyard School A name given to a group of Scottish writers whose work dealt idealistically with village life in Scotland. DIALECT was an important element. J. M. Barrie and "Ian Maclaren" are two of the best-known members of the school, which was popular toward the close of the nineteenth century. *Kailyard* means "cabbage garden."

Katauta A Japanese verse form that lays out a question and answer in three lines consisting of one line of five syllables and two lines of seven syllables.

Keats Ode Stanza A STANZA developed by John Keats (1795–1821) for some of the ODES that he wrote toward the end of his life. The stanza contains ten or eleven lines, mostly PENTAMETER, with a rhyme scheme that exploits the benefits of both the ENGLISH and the ITALIAN SONNET while avoiding the drawbacks of an unwieldy fourteen-line unit. The rhyme scheme through the first seven lines is consistently *ababcde*; thereafter the final lines may be *cde, dce, ced, dcce*, or *cdde*. "Ode to a Nightingale" is *ababcdecde* throughout, with TRIMETER in the eighth line (the other odes are pentameter throughout); "Ode on a Grecian Urn" and "Ode on Indolence" rhyme *ababcdedce*, *ababcdeced*, or *ababcdecde*; "Ode on Melancholy" rhymes either *ababcdecde* or *ababcdecde*. The stanza in "To Autumn" is eleven lines long, rhymed either *ababcdedcce* or *ababcdecdde*. Matthew Arnold (1822–1888) adapted the stanza for two of his greatest poems, "The Scholar Gipsy" and "Thyrsis," both of which use a stanza rhymed *abcbcadeed*, with trimeter in the sixth line. A century later, in "The Whitsun Weddings," Philip Larkin (1922–1985) employed a stanza rhyming *ababcdecde* with DIMETER in the second line, a pattern followed scrupulously in Gavin Ewart's PARODY, "The Larkin Automatic Car Wash."

Keen An Irish funeral song. In Fitzgerald's *This Side of Paradise*, when Amory Blaine is leaving for war, Monsignor Darcy tells him in a letter, "I have written a keen for you . . ." and attaches a poem called "A Lament for a Foster Son, and He Going to the War Against the King of Foreign." A poem in Paul Muldoon's *Mules* is titled "Keen."

Kenning A figurative phrase used in Old Germanic languages as a synonym for a simple noun. *Kennings* are often picturesque metaphorical compounds. Specimen *kennings* from *Beowulf* are "the bent-necked wood," "the ringed prow," "the foamy-necked," "the sea-wood," and the "sea-farer" for *ship*; "the swan-road" and "the whale-road" for the *sea*; the "leavings of the file" for the *sword*; the "twilight-spoiler" for the *dragon*; the "storm of swords" for *battle*; and the "peace-bringer among nations" for the *queen*. "Widow-maker" has a pedigree going back to 1595 as a *kenning* for anything or anyone that kills men. G. M. Hopkins refers to "the widow-making unchilding unfathering deeps," and Kipling calls the sea "the old grey Widow-maker." To say "red badge of courage" for *wound* may be a species of ironic *kenning*. Bodies of water seem to challenge poets to find new names to call them, as witness the "undried sea, / Houses for fishes" in Auden's "The Wanderer" and the "whaleroad" in Robert Lowell's "The Quaker Graveyard in Nantucket."

Kenosis Literally, an emptying, an evacuation; theologically, the deed or process by which Christ took on humble human form, surrendering divinity. Some translations (though not the King James) render Philippians II. 7 to say that Christ "emptied himself, taking the form of a servant, being born in the likeness of men" In some of Harold Bloom's criticism, *kenosis* is treated as a TROPE, presumably a turn from a high level to a lower.

Kill Fee Money paid to an author in compensation for material that has been requested or commissioned but not used (that is, the material has been killed).

Kind A term used in the Neoclassic Period for GENRE or literary type. It implies an assumption that genres have an objective, absolute existence analogous to the "*kinds*" or species of the natural world and that they obey "the laws of *kind*."

Kit-Cat Club A club believed to have existed in London between 1703 and 1733, founded by Whigs and dedicated in part to ensuring a Protestant succession to the throne. Among its members were Addison, Steele, Congreve, Vanbrugh, and Marlborough. It met at the "Cat and Fiddle" pastry shop, kept by one Christopher Cat, from whom it seems to have taken its name. Sometimes it met in a room with a very low ceiling at the home of the publisher Jacob Tonson. When Sir Godfrey Kneller painted the portraits of the members to hang in this room, he was forced to use small canvases, 36 by 28 inches, dimensions later called *kit-cat* size.

Kitsch From the German for "gaudy trash"; shallow, flashy art designed to have popular appeal and commercial success. At the beginning of the twenty-first century, categories had become so uncertain that *kitsch* began to merge with serious and durable art.

[References: Matei Calinescu, *Faces of Modernity: Avant-Garde, Decadence, Kitsch* (1977); Tomáš Kulka, *Kitsch and Art* (1996); "On Kitsch: A Symposium," *Salmagundi: A Quarterly of the Humanities and Social Sciences*, No. 85–86 (Winter– Spring 1990).]

Knickerbocker Group A group writing in and about New York during the first half of the nineteenth century. The name was made famous by Washington Irving in "Knickerbocker's" *History of New York*. The heyday of the group was the first third of the century, although it was represented in the *Knickerbocker Magazine* (1833–1865); the remnants of the *Knickerbocker* school were pilloried in Poe's *The Literati of New York City*. Journalism, editorship, the frontier, poetry, novels, songs, and, in the case of Bryant at least, translation from the classics, were what claimed the attention of these writers. Their association was one of geography and chance rather than of close organization. Some members of the school were: Washington Irving, James Fenimore Cooper, William Cullen Bryant, Joseph Rodman Drake, Fitz-Greene Halleck, John Howard Payne, and Samuel Woodworth.

Koine The language spoken throughout the ancient Greek world; colloquial Attic with numerous supplements from other dialects and other languages. The language of the New Testament. A second sense of *koine* is any such local dialect that becomes the official language of a larger area.

Koran (also **Quran**) A Muslim collection of scriptural writings. The text is believed to have been revealed to Muhammad from time to time over a period of years and, after many changes and much editing, took shape in an official transcription after Muhammad's death in 632. The book, the sacred scripture of millions, presents—in addition to matters of theology—moral teaching, liturgical directions, and advice on religious conduct and ceremonials. The speaker is usually God.

Künstlerroman A form of the APPRENTICESHIP NOVEL in which the protagonist is an artist struggling from childhood to maturity toward an understanding of his or her creative mission. The most famous in English is James Joyce's *A Portrait of the Artist as a Young Man*.

Kyrielle A rare French form, usually composed of short rhymed COUPLETS with a word or larger verbal group repeated as a REFRAIN.

American Uncial c. 1953. Designed by Victor Hammer at Klingspor Typefoundry, Germany.

Laconism Brevity of speech, in the supposed manner of the ancient Lacedemonians. Also a laconic speech or pithy sentence.

Lai A song or short narrative poem. See LAY.

Lake Poets and Lake School Coleridge, Wordsworth, and Southey—three poets who at the beginning of the nineteenth century were living in the Lake District (Cumbria). The pejorative "lakers" is credited to the *Edinburgh Review*, which for several years behaved contemptuously toward the poets. Although there was no "school" in the sense of the three all working for common objectives. Coleridge and Wordsworth had certain convictions in common and on occasion worked together.

Lament A poem expressing grief, usually more intense and more personal than in a COMPLAINT. *Deor's Lament*, an early Anglo-Saxon poem, for instance, presents the plaintive regret of the SCOP at his changed status after a rival has usurped his place in the esteem of a patron. The separate "tragedies" in such collections as the sixteenth-century *Mirror for Magistrates*, in which the ghosts of dead worthies tell the stories of their fall from fortune, were called *laments* in the Renaissance, an example being Sackville's "Lament" for the Duke of Buckingham.

Lampoon Writing that ridicules and satirizes a person in a bitter, scurrilous manner, in verse or prose. Lampooning became a dangerous sport and fell into disuse with the development of the libel laws. The word endured awhile in the humor magazine called the *Harvard Lampoon*, later the *National Lampoon*, which augmented its magazine with film production. See EPIGRAM.

Language Poets, The A term applied (often in the form L=A=N=G=U=A=G=E) around 1980 to a group of American poets whose work shows radical suspicion, skepticism, or cynicism about the efficacy of written language to record, register, represent, communicate, or express anything much beyond its own intramural apparatus.

[References: Bruce Andrews and Charles Bernstein, eds., *The L=A=N=G=U=A=G=E Book* (1984); Jerome J. McGann, *Social Values and Poetic Acts: A Historical Judgement of Literary Work* (1988); Douglas Messerli, ed., *"Language" Poetries: An Anthology* (1987).]

Late Victorian Age, 1870–1901 The period between 1870 and the death of Queen Victoria saw the full flowering of the movement toward REALISM, which had begun as early as the 1830s but had been subordinated to the dominant ROMANTICISM of the first half of Victoria's reign. George Eliot and Hardy carried the realistic novel to new heights. Spencer, Huxley, Newman, Arnold, and Morris, in the essay, argued the meaning of the new science, religion, and society. The drama, which had been sleeping for more than a century, awoke under the impact of Ibsen and the CELTIC RENAISSANCE. Stevenson, W. H. Hudson, and Kipling revived romantic fiction. Wilde, following the lead of Pater, advanced the doctrine of "ART FOR ART'S SAKE." The tendency to look with critical eyes on human beings, society, and God, to ask pragmatic questions, and to seek utilitarian answers—a tendency that had begun in the second quarter of the century—had become the dominant mode of thought and writing by the time that Queen Victoria died. A remarkable amount of abidingly popular literature was also produced during this period: Robert Louis Stevenson's *Treasure Island* and *Doctor Jekyll and Mister Hyde*, Conan Doyle's Sherlock Holmes stories, Bram Stoker's *Dracula*, Gilbert and Sullivan's operettas, Kipling's *The Jungle Book* series, and much else. For many readers in the twenty-first century, the idea of what constitutes literature was formed in the late nineteenth century. See REALISTIC PERIOD IN ENGLISH LITERATURE and *Outline of Literary History*.

Laugh Track A recording of audience laughter; the *laugh track* can be replayed later, either accompanying a live performance or mixed with another recording.

Laureate One honored by a crown of laurel, symbolizing distinctive achievement. The term has come to be most frequently used in POET LAUREATE. It is also applied to the recipient of other major honors, as a Nobel *laureate*.

Lay (or ***Lai***) A song or short narrative poem. The word has been applied to several different forms in French and English literature. The earliest existing French *lais*, composed in the twelfth century, were based on earlier songs or verse tales sung by Breton minstrels on themes from Celtic legend; hence the term "Breton *lay*." Though some of the early French *lais* were lyric, most were narrative, like those of Marie de France, who wrote at the court of the English King Henry II about 1175. A few of her *lais* are related to ARTHURIAN LEGEND. The prevailing verse form of early *lais* was the eight-syllable line rhyming in couplets. Later *lais* developed more complicated forms. The word *lay* was applied to English poems written in the fourteenth century in imitation of the Breton *lays*. Though a few followed the couplet form, more used the popular TAIL-RHYME STANZA, although any short narrative poem similar to the French *lai* might be called a "Breton *lay*" in English. Themes from various sources were employed, including classical, Oriental, and Celtic. Some of the best known are the *Lay of Launfal*, *Sir Orfeo*, *Sir Gowther*, and Chaucer's *Franklin's Tale*.

Since the sixteenth century, *lay* has been used in English as synonymous with SONG. In the early nineteenth century, *lay* sometimes meant a short historical BALLAD, as Scott's *Lay of the Last Minstrel* and Macaulay's *Lays of Ancient Rome*. (*Lais* as used by François Villon for the title of the poems now known as *Petit Testament* [1456] is a different word, corresponding to modern French *legs*, "bequest" or "legacy.")

Leading (rhymes with "sledding") The space between lines of type in a newspaper or other such publication.

Legend A narrative or tradition handed down from the past; distinguished from a myth by having more of historical truth and perhaps less of the supernatural. *Legends* often indicate the lore of a people and thus serve as at least partial expressions of a national spirit. Saints' *legends* are narratives of the lives of the early church heroes. *Legend* is also used for any brief explanatory comment or code accompanying paintings, graphs, charts, maps, or photographs.

Legitimate Theater The presentation of regular plays, depending entirely on acting, on a stage before an audience, using living actors. It has distinguished what are commonly called "stage plays" from films, television, vaudeville, puppet shows, ballets, and musical comedy. The term derives from the English PATENT THEATERS to which the presentation of drama in the traditional sense was restricted from 1660 to 1843.

Leitmotif (also **Leitmotiv, Leitmotive**) In art, a recurrent repetition of some word, phrase, situation, or idea, such as tends to unify a work through its power to recall earlier occurrences. The phrases "A stone, a leaf, an unfound door" and "Ghost, come back again" in Thomas Wolfe's *Look Homeward, Angel* are examples of the *leitmotif*. In a subtler way, "rain" in *A Farewell to Arms* functions as a *leitmotif*. The term has long been associated with Richard Wagner, who seems to have preferred "Hauptmotiv." See MOTIF.

Leitwortstil "Key word style," a concept that has been evolving in the study of Hebrew poetry, in which certain words and phrases are isolated for interpretation; such key words tend to involve concrete matters such as seeing that can be elevated to higher levels such as Vision.

[References: Martin Buber, *On the Bible: Eighteen Studies*, ed. N. N. Glatzer (1968); Jo Milgrom, *The Binding of Isaac: The Akedah, a Primary Symbol in Jewish Thought and Art* (1988).]

Lemma Variously used to mean a THEME or ARGUMENT, especially when employed as a TITLE, MOTTO, or CAPTION.

Lemniscus A symbol (÷) used in antiquity for GLOSSES and ANNOTATIONS.

Lenis A consonant with relatively gentle articulation, opposed to FORTIS.

Leonine Rhyme The internal rhyming of the last stressed syllable before the CAESURA with the last stressed syllable of the line. Ordinarily, *Leonine rhyme* is restricted to pentameters and hexameters, but less rigidly the term is applied to verses such as the "Stabat Mater" of the church. The expression is said to be derived from the name of a writer of the Middle Ages, Leoninus, canon of St. Victor in Paris, who wrote elegiac lines containing such internal rhyme. Some interpolated Latin verses in Langland's *Piers Plowman* rhyme in *Leonine* fashion:

> Sum Rex, sum Princeps neutrum fortasse deinceps—
> O qui iura regis Christi specialia regis,
> Hoc quod agas melius iustus es, esto pius.

In his youth, Tennyson wrote some "Leonine Elegiacs." An example of *Leonine rhyme* is italicized in the following: "There's a whisper down the *field* where the year has shot her *yield*" (Kipling, "Envoy").

Letter Used in some derogatory phrases to mean the sounds repeated in ALLITERATION: "affect the *letter*," "hunt the *letter*," "lick the *letter*" and so forth.

Letterpress Used to distinguish the text of a book from the illustrative matter. This use of the term may have derived from the fact that, in older printing, the *letterpress* printed directly from type instead of from the plates, woodcuts, or blocks used for illustrations. The term is also employed to refer to the typography of a work or to printing in a general sense. Among book manufacturers, *letterpress* refers to the process of printing by direct contact of the sheet to the inked raised surfaces of type, cuts, or those kinds of plates that duplicate raised type. *Letterpress* is then used in distinction to offset, gravure, and images printed by such methods as xerography or cathode-ray scanner-printing.

Letters A general name for literature (see BELLES-LETTRES); more specifically, notes and epistles. A great body of informal literature is preserved through collections of actual *letters*. The correspondence of such figures as Lord Byron, Jane and Thomas Carlyle, Lord Chesterfield, Charles Dickens, Edward FitzGerald, William Hazlitt, Charles Lamb, Mary Wortley Montagu, Thomas Gray, Horace Walpole, Sydney Smith, Ezra Pound, and Robert Louis Stevenson—to mention a few of the notable letter writers—constitutes a pleasant byway in the realm of literature. *Letters*, in this sense, are distinguished from epistles in that they present personal and natural relationships among friends. Numerous modern poets have written poems in the form of the *letter*; examples are Pound's "The River-Merchant's Wife: A Letter" and "Exile's Letter," W. H. Auden's long funny "Letter to Lord Byron," and later poems by Richard Hugo, John Wain, and Jim Harrison.

Yet another sense has to do with the constituents of the alphabet, figuratively employed to mean "literal" (as in "letter of the law").

Level A metaphor that relates to our sense of the relative dignity, complexity, and rarity of something. We speak of the *level* of one's vocabulary as high, plain, or low; we also speak of *levels* of meaning—surface or deep.

Lettrine A decorated initial letter, usually larger than the rest of the text. This rare word, originally French, was used by James Joyce in connection with work by his daughter, Lucia.

Lexeme A minimal lexical unit: an item of vocabulary, such as a word or stem, independent of grammatical function.

Lexicography The making of DICTIONARIES or LEXICONS. The most ancient dictionary extant is said to be a Greek lexicon called *Homeric Words*, prepared by Apollonius the Sophist in the reign of Augustus (27 B.C.–A.D. 14). *Lexicography* developed slowly from the mere explanation of hard words by means of simpler ones in the same language, to the preparation of elaborate lists, alphabetically arranged, with derivations, pronunciations, spellings, illustrative quotations, and meanings, either in the same or other languages. In the late nineteenth century, Gustave Flaubert produced a *Dictionary of Received Ideas* (of which the modern counterpart would include such entries as "Sweden—High suicide rate") and Ambrose Bierce a satirical *Devil's Dictionary* ("Egotist" is defined as "A person of low taste, more interested in himself than in me").

Lexicon A word list or wordbook; a vocabulary; a standard term for dictionary. See LEXICOGRAPHY.

Libretto The text or book, containing the story, tale, or plot of an opera or of any long musical composition—a cantata, for instance. It is the diminutive of the Italian *libro*, a book.

Life and Letters A type of biography popular in the nineteenth century. Thomas Moore's *Letters and Journals of Lord Byron, with Notices of His Life* (1833) and Elizabeth Gaskell's *Life of Charlotte Brontë* (1857) belong in this category. The usual modern approach is to produce separate volumes of biography and correspondence.

Lift A stressed syllable in ALLITERATIVE VERSE; opposed to DIP or SINKING.

Light Ending A FEMININE ENDING.

Light Opera A form of opera that lacks the passion, dignity, and seriousness of grand opera. It is unlike comic opera in that spoken dialogue is not commonly employed. An example is M. W. Balfe's *The Bohemian Girl* (1843).

Light Verse Humorous, comic, witty poems. There are many varieties: PARODY, LIMERICK, OCCASIONAL VERSE, EPIGRAMS, VERS DE SOCIÉTÉ, CLERIHEWS, NONSENSE VERSE. Grace and ease of expression, fancifulness and will to delight, charming but mordant wit, and frequently some serious or satiric intent are characteristic of a kind of poetry that has been practiced with grace and honor by Aristophanes, Chaucer, Skelton, Shakespeare, Jonson, the CAVALIER LYRICISTS, Milton, Swift, Pope, Goethe, Byron, Edward Lear, Lewis Carroll, Hardy, W. S. Gilbert, T. S. Eliot, Dorothy Parker, Phyllis McGinley, Christopher Morley, Helen Bevington, Ogden Nash, Gavin Ewart, Kingsley Amis, X. J. Kennedy, George Starbuck, John Updike, John Hollander, and Roy A. Blount, Jr.

Limerick A form of light verse that follows a definite pattern: five anapestic lines of which the first, second, and fifth, consisting of three feet, rhyme; and the third and fourth lines, consisting of two feet, rhyme. Sometimes a *limerick* is written in four lines, but when so composed, its third line bears an INTERNAL RHYME and might easily be considered two lines. Some of his holograph-illustrated texts suggest that Edward Lear thought of the form as two, three, or four lines—in some cases, his contributions are indistinguishable from couplets of POULTER'S MEASURE with internal rhyme and anapestic rhythm. There seem to be associations among the *limerick*, poulter's measure, and the SHORT MEASURE of the hymnals. (*Limericks* can be sung to the tune of "Blest Be the Tie That Binds.") *Limericks* have been written by the most distinguished modern poets, including Robert Frost and W. H. Auden, as well as by hundreds of humble, anonymous vernacular writers whose output has been gathered in prodigious collections by Gershon Legman. The genesis of the *limerick* is not definitely known. Some NURSERY RHYMES come close to the format:

Hickory, dickory, dock,
The mouse ran up the clock.
    The clock struck one,
    And down he run,
Hickory, dickory, dock.

Robert Herrick's "The Nightpiece, To Julia" (mid-seventeenth century) conforms even better:

Let not the dark thee cumber;
What though the moon does slumber?
    The stars of the night
    Will lend thee their light,
Like tapers clear without number.

Though originally a kind of epigrammatic song, passed around orally, *limericks* increased the range of their subject matter to encompass every possible theme, nothing being sacred to their humor. They were chiefly concerned, however, with the manners, morals, and peculiarities of imaginary people. An important early appearance in print was in 1820, when *Anecdotes and Adventures of Fifteen Young Ladies* and *The History of Sixteen Wonderful Old Women* were published, but they reached the peak of their vogue when Edward Lear published his *Book of Nonsense* in 1846.

Liminality The state of being on a threshold in space or time. The Latin *limen* ("threshold") figures in "eliminate," "preliminary," and "subliminal." The anthropologists Arnold Van Gennep and Victor Turner have used the concept of the "liminal" to study social habits and customs that ritualize certain "passages" in life marked as the crossing of a threshold, so that a threshold is a place where many social meanings congregate. A wedding or graduation ceremony, say, is a threshold in time, with systematic changes of clothing, name, and carriage. Thomas Hardy's "The Darkling Thrush" is a poem of many thresholds (and has been called "multiliminal"), set at the end of a day, a month, a year, and a century (that is, the evening of December 31, 1900) when the author is sixty years old, with also a liminal setting in space (a gate). Literal *liminality* is seen in works with thresholds, windows, sills, edges, borders, and passages. In quite a few modern works, the seashore functions as a powerfully charged threshold: Arnold's "Dover Beach," Eliot's "The Love Song of J. Alfred Prufrock" and "The Dry Salvages," Stevens's "The Idea of Order at Key West," Crane's "Cape Hatteras," Frost's "Kitty Hawk," and Ammons's "Corsons Inlet." In at least three of those, the threshold in space is paralleled by a threshold in time betokened by a full moon.

Limited Edition An EDITION of a book or other printed matter limited to a fixed number, often with special paper, type, and binding, sometimes numbered and signed.

Line A fundamental conceptual unit, normally realized as a single spoken or written sequence of elements and possibly zoned by various sorts of punctuation, meter, rhyme, and other devices. Necessarily, prose is printed in conventional *lines*, but the *lines* are seldom distinguished by demarcation. A *line* of poetry conventionally equates a spatial measure with a temporal, but the two arrays need not be closely linked. Some poems, including the Old English poems in the Exeter Book and other manuscript sources, can be written out as prose; two paragraphs printed as ordinary prose in Fitzgerald's *This Side of Paradise* turn out, on inspection, to be SPENSERIAN STANZAS. As a rule, however, poems look like poems.

Linguistics The scientific study of language. It is concerned with the description, comparison, or history of languages. *Linguistics* studies phonology (speech sounds), morphology (the history of word forms), semantics (the meaning of words), and syntax (the relationships among elementary components of larger units). Although once considered a division of philology, *linguistics* is today an independent and highly complex science. The theories of Saussure have been particularly influential in other disciplines; the structural anthropology of Lévi-Strauss and the neo-Freudian psychiatry of Lacan have both been guided by the concept that myth and the unconscious are structured "like a language." See PHILOLOGY.

[References: Leonard Bloomfield, *Language* (1933, reprinted 1965); Noam Chomsky, *Chomsky: Selected Readings* (1971); David Crystal, *Linguistics* (1971); Victoria Fromkin and Robert Rodman, *An Introduction to Language*, 6th ed. (1998; orig. 1974, 1983); Roman Jakobson, *Main Trends in the Science of Language* (1973); Winfred P. Lehmann, *Language: An Introduction* (1983); Ferdinand de Saussure, *Course in General Linguistics* (1916) (posthumous); Benjamin Lee Whorf, *Language, Thought, and Reality* (1956).]

Linguistics and Literary Criticism This connection is as old as linguistics and criticism themselves, but it reached one high point of importance in the nineteenth century (with the Grimms' philological examination of both language and folklore) and another after the Second World War when the techniques of structural linguistics were extended to individual texts and to literature as a whole. Any realm that can be understood in some way as a system of SIGNS can be studied as though it were a language, subject to the common linguistic rules of differentiation, closure, variation, transformation, and the weakness or absence of reference and signification outside the system of the language itself. See DECONSTRUCTION; PHILOLOGY; STRUCTURALISM.

Linked Rhyme Another name for FUSED RHYME.

Link Sonnet An English SONNET in which the three quatrains are linked by repeating the second rhyme of one quatrain as the first rhyme of the succeeding quatrain. The SPENSERIAN SONNET, rhyming *abab bcbc cdcd ee* is a *link sonnet*.

Lipogram A kind of writing in which words containing certain letters of the alphabet are not used; the challenge is greater if the letter is a vowel. In 1995, Gilbert Adair published a translation of Georges Perec's detective novel *A Void*, the text of which, in French or English, contains no letter *e*. The story concerns the disappearance of a character named "A. Vowl."

Lipography The omission of a letter or syllable in writing.

Litany A ritualistic form of supplication commonly used in the Catholic church. A series of petitions often chanted by a choir in procession. The form is sometimes adopted by writers for poetic expression. John Ashbery has written a long poem called "Litany."

Literal Accurate to the letter; without embellishment. Thus, in the first sense, the word is used, as in a "literal translation," to signify fidelity in presenting the exact meaning of the original—a translation that preserves the usual meaning of the text and allows no freedom of expression or imagination to the translator—quite different from PARAPHRASE. The ideal implicit in "word-for-word" translation is unattainable, even at an elementary level. What is one word in Latin, say, may take many words to be translated into English; some common words in English, such as many prepositions and any article, simply do not exist in Latin. Attempts to transfer the lexical units and syntactic arrangement of one language to another may yield nonsense. In the second sense of "without embellishment," the term is frequently used to distinguish language that is matter of fact from language that is given to much use of figures of speech. *Literal* language is the opposite of FIGURATIVE.

Literary Ballad A ballad composed by an author, as opposed to the anonymous FOLK BALLAD.

Literary Club, The (also **Doctor Johnson's Circle**) A club formed in London in 1764 at the suggestion of Sir Joshua Reynolds, the painter, and with the cooperation of Samuel Johnson. Among the charter members were Edmund Burke and Oliver Goldsmith. Famous men admitted to membership during Johnson's lifetime included Bishop Percy (ballad collector), David Garrick (actor), Edward Gibbon (historian), Adam Smith (economist), and James Boswell (Johnson's biographer). Their meetings fostered free and spirited discussion of books and writers, classic and contemporary, Johnson frequently dominating the conversation. Johnson became a sort of literary dictator, and the Club itself exercised a formidable power: Whole editions of a book were sold off in one day by its sanction. Though commonly thought of only in connection with late-eighteenth-century literature, the Club has continued in existence, its later membership including fifteen prime ministers and such authors as Scott, Macaulay, Hallam, and Tennyson.

Literary Epic A long narrative poem by a poet self-consciously employing the epic formula. Also called the ART EPIC.

Literation Representing dialect sounds or words by letters, as in this line from Tennyson's "Northern Farmer: Old Style": "What atta stannin' theer fur, an' doesn bring ma the aäle?"

Literatus A literary person; see LITTERATEUR.

Litotes A form of UNDERSTATEMENT in which a thing is affirmed by stating the negative of its opposite. To say "She was not unmindful" when one means that "She gave careful attention" is to employ *litotes*. Although a common device in ironic expression, *litotes* was also one of the characteristic figures of speech of Old English poetry. In Tennyson's "Ulysses," the heroic speaker resorts to *litotes* several times, with an effect of stoic restraint and (this is still the crafty warrior) subtlety: "little profits" for "profits not at all," "not least" for "great," "not to fail" for "succeed splendidly," and "not unbecoming" for "thoroughly appropriate." Many today express the idea "good" by saying "not bad."

Litterateur A literary person. Although the term means one who is engaged in literary work or who has adopted literature as a profession, in practical usage it has—like "literatus"—a connotation of the dilettante.

Little Magazine A literary JOURNAL of small circulation, limited capital, and usually quite a short life, dedicated to the fostering of avant-garde aesthetic ideas and to publishing experimental writing. Notable early examples were *The Yellow Book* (1894–1897) and *The Savoy* (1896), which gave expression to the English revolt against Victorian ideas, ideals, and materialism. Early American *little magazines* were *The Lark* (1895–1897) and *The Chap-Book* (1894–1898), but the most influential of all such American journals has been *Poetry: A Magazine of Verse*, founded in 1912 and still in existence.

A heyday of the *little magazine* came between the First World War and the Depression of the thirties. In England, in the United States, and particularly in Paris, a generation of artists in revolt against their culture and its standards found in the *little magazine* an outlet for their ideas. *The Little Review* (1914–1929), *The Seven Arts* (1916–1917), *The Fugitive* (1922–1925), *The Dial* (after its move to New York in 1916 and to its end in 1929), *Hound and Horn* (1927–1934), *Secession* (1922–1924), *transition* (1927–1938), *Broom* (1921–1924), and *The Double Dealer* (1921–1925) were among the best of hundreds of such publications.

In the Depression young writers tended to desert advanced aesthetic positions for radical social postures, and the *little magazines* were in large measure casualties. After the Second World War, the equivalent of the *little magazine* was frequently a joint student–faculty production operating under a grant from a university.

Beginning in the late 1960s, however, a new *little magazine* movement got vigorously underway, as a result partly of the UNDERGROUND PRESS, partly of the anti-establishmentarian new avant-garde. Although most of these *little magazines* are too numerous to count and too new and untried to evaluate, there are several that have lasted long enough to achieve distinction; we can mention a series superintended by Robert Bly (*The Fifties, The Sixties, The Seventies*), Cid Corman's *Origin*, and—liveliest and most uncompromising of all—George Hitchcock's *kayak*, which endured pluckily from the late 1960s to the middle 1980s.

Thousands of pages of bad experimental writing have been published in the *little magazines*, but such deficits are more than offset by the fact that James Joyce, T. S. Eliot, Sherwood Anderson, Ernest Hemingway, William Faulkner, Wallace Stevens, Ezra Pound, Hart Crane, E. E. Cummings, Edmund Wilson, the New Critics, Gertrude Stein, Thornton Wilder, John Crowe Ransom, and Allen Tate, among many others, found in the pages of the *little magazines* their first sympathetic publication. Their present-day counterparts are publishing in today's *little magazines*.

[Reference: Elliott Anderson and Mary Kinzie, *The Little Magazine in America: A Documentary History* (1978).]

Little Theater Movement A term applied to a succession of efforts to encourage the writing and production of significant plays, as opposed to productions designed primarily for box-office success. The movement was originated by André Antoine in Paris in 1887. There gathered about Antoine, himself a gifted actor, a group of young authors, whose plays he produced at the *Théâtre Libre* before a select audience. His attempts to advance the cause of good drama included also the introduction of foreign plays by such writers as Tolstoi, Ibsen, Hauptmann, Björnson, Strindberg, and Turgenev. His experiment aided in the development of French dramatists and influenced the founding of two other French *little theaters*: Lugné-Poë's *Théâtre de l'Oeuvre* (1893) and Jacques Copeau's *Vieux Colombier* (1913). In Germany the *Frei Bühne* was established in 1899, followed by a rapid development of native talent.

In England the movement began with the opening of the Independent Theatre (1891). Shaw, Jones, Pinero, Barrie, Granville-Barker, and Galsworthy were to some degree products of the movement. In Ireland the Irish Literary Theatre (1899) attempted to encourage Irish writers and the use of Irish themes; William Boyle, Lennox Robinson, J. M. Synge, Lady Gregory, and William Butler Yeats wrote for the Abbey players (see ABBEY THEATRE). The *little theater movement* began in America in 1906 and 1907 when three groups were organized in Chicago: the New Theatre, the Robertson Players, and the Hull House Theatre. From 1911 to 1912 came additional establishments: the Little Theatre of Maurice Browne (Chicago), Mrs. Lyman Gale's Toy Theatre (Boston), and the Festival Players of the Henry Street Settlement, the Provincetown Players, and the Washington Square Players (New York) whose members formed the Theatre Guild, which operated with spectacular success and by 1925 could build its own million-dollar playhouse.

A splinter from the Guild formed the Group Theatre, which produced plays by such writers as Paul Green and Clifford Odets. Despite these professional successes, however, the *little theater movement* in America remained essentially local and amateur, spread over thousands of groups in towns and cities across the country. It sometimes had a strong university flavor, coming largely from the work of George P. Baker at Harvard and later at Yale and Frederich H. Koch at the University of North Carolina. The *little theater movement* established a flexible theater for serious writing and acting, brought the drama to thousands who might never otherwise have seen it, and developed such talent as Eugene O'Neill, Paul Green, Philip Barry, and Thornton Wilder.

An outgrowth of the *little theater movement* came in 1936 with the establishment of the Federal Theater Project, which annually employed 1,300 theater workers and in its three years of existence produced more than 1,200 plays. Its purpose was to supplement the commercial stage with serious and experimental drama at low prices.

[References: Alexander Dean, *Little Theater Organization and Management, for Community, University, and School* (1926); Constance d'Arcy Mackay, *The Little Theater in the United States* (1917).]

Liturgical Drama A name for the early phase of medieval religious drama when the MYSTERY PLAYS were performed as part or extension of the liturgical service of the church. In their earliest form, in Latin, they were operatic in character, the lines being chanted or sung rather than spoken. *Liturgical drama* is also sometimes used for the mystery plays developed from the liturgy.

Loan Word A word that passes in its native form from one language to another without being translated. *Kindergarten*, for example, retains its German form in English. See also CALQUE.

Local Color Writing Writing that exploits the speech, dress, mannerisms, habits of thought, and topography peculiar to a certain region, primarily for the portrayal of the life of a geographical setting. About 1880 this interest became dominant in American literature; a "local color movement" developed for various sections. Bret Harte, Mark Twain, and Joaquin Miller wrote of the West; George Washington Cable, Lafcadio Hearn, Mary Noailles Murfree, and Joel Chandler Harris of the South; Sarah Orne Jewett and Mary E. Wilkins Freeman of New England.

Local color writing was marked by dialect, eccentric characters, and sentimentalized pathos or whimsical humor. A subdivision of REALISM, *local color writing* lacked the basic seriousness of true realism; largely, it was content to be entertainingly informative about the surface of special regions. It emphasized verisimilitude of detail without being much concerned about truth to the larger aspects of life. Although local color novels were written, the bulk of the work done in the movement was in the sketch and the short story, aimed at the newly developing mass-circulation magazine audience. See REGIONALISM.

Locale The physical setting of some action. It denotes geographical and scenic qualities rather than the less tangible aspects of setting.

Locus Classicus That place or passage invariably cited as the "classic example" of a principle or type. Antony's speech beginning "Friends, Romans, countrymen" in Shakespeare's *Julius Caesar* is the *locus classicus* of the funeral oration, just as Hamlet's "To be, or not to be" is the *locus classicus* of the SOLILOQUY.

Locus Communis A commonplace.

Locus Desperatus A desperately corrupt or unintelligible place in a text transmitted by manuscript.

Locution A term applied to a word or a group of words that constitutes a meaning group. It is also applied to a style of speech or verbal expression, particularly when it involves some peculiarity of idiom or manner.

Locutionary Act The usual act of saying something, with a verb that represents, describes, or narrates phenomena beyond itself. In an illocutionary act, the verb represents an action discharged in the utterance of the verb, such as "proclaim." Finally, in a perlocutionary act, the verb represents the effect of the illocutionary act, such as "scare."

[Reference: J. L. Austin, *How to Do Things with Words*, 2nd ed. (1975).]

Logaoedic In classical prosody a line composed of anapests and iambs or of dactyls and trochees. The term also designates any mixed rhythm.

Logatom A meaningless syllable arbitrarily formed on the pattern of consonant-vowel-consonant, for testing telephone systems.

Logical Positivism A philosophical movement that primarily emphasizes empirical sensory observation as the means of evaluating claims about matters of fact. It uses rigorous methods of logical analysis to clarify the meaning of statements. Among its major advocates are Rudolf Carnap, A. J. Ayer, and Ludwig Wittgenstein.

Logion (plural, **Logia**) A saying attributed to a religious teacher, usually sayings attributed to Jesus but not preserved in the canonical Gospels; also for sayings in general, as in the *Logia* and *Acta* of Buddha: words and deeds.

Logo (earlier, **Logotype**) Originally, a single piece of type that represented a whole word. The most familiar example is the ampersand: &. Not all modern printed versions preserve the history, but the symbol began centuries ago as a way of writing Latin *et* ("and") in one gesture, as though

e + t → &

—later stylized. Now *logo* means any symbol, emblem, or device.

Logocentrism A key term in DECONSTRUCTION; it argues that there is a persistent but morbid centering of Logos (meaning thought, truth, law, reason, logic, word, and the Word) in Western thought since Plato. Putting Logos at the center of discourse gives it an unquestioned status of priority and privilege—a maneuver sometimes extended to a privileging of the male order in the form of "phallogocentrism." Jonathan Culler, following Jacques Derrida, defines *logocentrism* as "the orientation of philosophy toward an order of meaning . . . conceived as existing in itself, as foundation." *Logocentrism* is the fundamental error of mistaking what is an arbitrary and artificial construct for a verifiable event.

[Reference: Jonathan Culler, *On Deconstruction: Theory and Criticism After Structuralism* (1982).]

Logogriph A word puzzle in which a clue is a SYNONYM of a word to be guessed, along with ANAGRAMS. "Yellow fish," for example, might lead to "amber bream."

Logopoeia A term coined by Ezra Pound to identify one way in which poetry charges language with meaning. MELOPOEIA has to do with the ear, PHANOPOEIA with the eye, and LOGOPOEIA with the mind and emotions—an exploitation of denotation, connotation, overtones, undertones, irony, ambiguity, and etymology.

Lollards The name for the followers of John Wycliffe, who inspired a popular religious reform movement in England late in the fourteenth century. Lollardism sprang from the clash of two ideals—that of worldly aims, upheld by the rulers of church and state, and that of self-sacrificing religion, separated from worldly interests, upheld by the humbler elements among the clergy and the laity. Although Wycliffe himself died in 1384 after sponsoring and aiding in the translation of parts of the Bible into English, the movement continued to gain strength. In 1395 the *Lollards* presented to Parliament a petition demanding reform in the church. Although it was not successful, its terms stand as early expressions of the attitude that triumphed with the Reformation in the sixteenth century. It denounced the riches of the clergy, asked that war be declared unchristian, and expressed disbelief in such doctrines and practices as transubstantiation, image-worship, and pilgrimages. Though suppressed early in the fifteenth century, Lollardism lived on secretly and later flared up in time to furnish a strong native impetus to the Lutheran Reformation in England early in the sixteenth century. This survival of Lollardism helps explain the fact that the English Reformation in its early stages was a popular movement rather than a scholarly one. Some Lollards were burned as heretics. Early Lollardism is reflected in *Piers Plowman's Crede* (1394). Chaucer's country parson, sympathetically described in the "General Prologue" to the *Canterbury Tales*, was accused by the Host of being a "Loller."

Long Measure A stanza of four lines of IAMBIC TETRAMETER rhyming either *abab* or *abcb*.

Long Song A composition printed on long sheets of paper and peddled by street sellers. Such things were popular in the middle of the nineteenth century. The sheets were wide enough to accommodate three columns—"three songs abreast," according to one

From Henry Mayhew, *London Labour and the London Poor* (1861–62). Kodansha Ltd.

seller—and the paper was about a yard long, so that the purchaser would get "three yards of song" for a penny.

Loose Sentence A sentence grammatically complete before the end; the opposite of PERIODIC SENTENCE. A complex *loose sentence* consists of an independent clause followed by a dependent clause. Most of the complex sentences we use are *loose* (the term implies no fault in structure), the periodic sentence being usually reserved for emphasis, drama, and variety. *Loose sentences* with too many dependent clauses become limp. "Although I just ate, I'm still hungry" is periodic; "I'm still hungry, although I just ate" is *loose*.

Lord of Misrule (also **Abbot, King, Monk,** or **Master of Misrule**) Around the beginning of the sixteenth century, an official appointed to preside over Christmas revels at court and in some academic communities. Sir Walter Scott's novel *The Abbot* (1820) refers to "the venerable Father Howleglas, the learned Monk of Misrule, and the Right Reverend Abbot of Unreason."

Lost Generation A group of American writers, born around 1900, who served in the First World War and reacted against certain tendencies of older writers in the 1920s. Although many of them spent much of their time in Paris, others lived and worked in New York, and some remained in the Middle West and the South. They were very active in the publication of LITTLE MAGAZINES. The term "*Lost Generation*" came from Gertrude Stein's remark to a mechanic (or vice versa) that "You are all a lost generation." Ernest Hemingway used it as one epigraph of *The Sun Also Rises*, whose hero, the emasculated Jake Barnes, is often considered the archetype of the generation. Hemingway subsequently hinted that he had wanted his novel to counter the Stein epigraph, not confirm or illustrate it, but his case seems disingenuous.

Low Comedy *Low comedy* has been called "elemental comedy," in that it lacks seriousness of purpose or subtlety of manner and has little intellectual appeal. Some features are: quarreling, fighting, noisy singing, boisterous conduct in general, boasting, burlesque, trickery, buffoonery, clownishness, drunkenness, coarse jesting, wordplay, and scolding. In English dramatic history *low comedy* appears first as an incidental expansion of the action, often originated by the actors themselves, who speak "more than is set down for them." Thus, in medieval religious drama Noah's stubborn wife has to be taken into the ark by force, or Pilate or Herod engages in uncalled-for ranting. In the MORALITY PLAYS, *low comedy* became much more pronounced, with the antics of the VICE and other horseplay. In Elizabethan drama such elements persisted, in spite of their violation of DECORUM, because the public demanded them; but playwrights such as Shakespeare frequently made them serve serious dramatic purposes (such as relief, marking passage of time, echoing main action). A few of the many examples of *low comedy* in Shakespeare are: the porter scene in *Macbeth*, Launcelot Gobbo and old Gobbo in *The Merchant of Venice*, the Audrey-William lovemaking scene in *As You Like It*, and the Trinculo-Stephano-Caliban scene in *The Tempest*. The famous Falstaff scenes in *King Henry the Fourth* are examples of how Shakespeare could lift *low comedy* into pure comedy by stressing the human elements of character and by infusing an intellectual content into what might otherwise be buffoonery. *Low comedy* is not a recognized special type of play as is the COMEDY OF HUMOURS, for example, but may be found either alone or combined with various sorts of both comedy and tragedy.

Luddites English workmen of the late eighteenth and early nineteenth centuries who sabotaged textile machinery that was taking away their jobs. The term connotes opposition to progress.

Luminism A movement in painting, especially since about 1875, in which the art concentrates on the effect of light. The term has also been applied to some of the works of the poet-painter A. R. Ammons, especially the volume called *The Snow Poems*.

Lunulae Plural of *lunula*, "little moon," or crescent. Erasmus's coinage for round parentheses.

Lyric A brief subjective poem strongly marked by imagination, melody, and emotion, and creating a single, unified impression. The early Greeks distinguished between *lyric* and choric poetry: *lyric* was the expression of the emotion of a single singer accompanied by a lyre. This distinction has now disappeared, though the conception of the *lyric* as individual and personal emotion still holds and is one basis for discriminating between the *lyric* and other poetic forms. No longer primarily designed to be sung to an accompaniment, the *lyric* nevertheless is essentially melodic, because the melody may be secured by a variety of means. Subjectivity, too, is an important element of a form that is the individual expression of personal emotion imaginatively phrased. It partakes, in certain high examples, of the quality of ecstasy.

The history of the *lyric* in English starts almost with the beginnings of our literature. *Deor's Lament* is essentially lyrical. Later the introduction of Latin hymns and the NORMAN CONQUEST brought in French and Italian elements. By about 1280 we have in "Sumer is icumen in" what would pass the strictest test for lyrical expression. By 1310 a manuscript collection was made that, in addition to South European forms, presented some forty English *lyrics*. Before 1400 Chaucer had written a fair body of *lyrics*, particularly modeled on FRENCH FORMS. The TROUBADOUR of France so awakened interest in lyrical forms as to make them common to the various European literatures, and Petrarch gave currency to the SONNET. Sir Thomas Wyatt and the Earl of Surrey in England popularized these Italian lyrical forms, particularly the sonnet, and by the time of Tottel's *Miscellany* (1557) the body of English *lyrics* was large and creditable. In Elizabethan England the *lyric* burst into full bloom in the work of such poets as Sidney, Spenser, Daniel, and Shakespeare. Songs, madrigals, airs became numerous. Jonson and Herrick carried the tradition further. To seventeenth-century England Cowley introduced the IRREGULAR ODE (a *lyric* form), and later Dryden adopted the form. Milton was a great *lyric* poet. The romantic revival brought English literature some of its noblest poetry in the odes of Gray, Collins, Wordsworth, and Coleridge. Burns and Blake raised the *lyric* to new power. Coleridge and Wordsworth made it the vehicle of romanticism. Scott, Byron, Shelley, and Keats molded the form to new perfection. Tom Moore wrote the lovely "Believe Me, If All Those Endearing Young Charms," which is still sung today. Bryant, Whittier, Longfellow, and Poe gave it expression in America. Victorian poets spoke through it frequently. Tennyson, the Rossettis, William Morris, Swinburne—England's greatest poets of the period—were also some of the greatest lyricists. And in modern England and America the *lyric*—in its various types—is still the most frequently used poetic expression. The tradition has endured into the twenty-first century, from Hardy and Yeats through Auden and Dylan Thomas to Larkin and Geoffrey Hill in England and Louise Glück and W. S. Merwin in the United States.

The *lyric* is perhaps the most broadly inclusive of all the various types of verse. In a sense it could be argued to be not so much a form as a manner of writing. Subjectivity, imagination, melody, emotion—these qualities have been preserved fairly well. But, as the *lyric* spirit has flourished, the manner has been confined in various ways with the result that we have, within the *lyric* type, numerous subclassifications. HYMNS, SONNETS, SONGS, BALLADS, ODES, ELEGIES, VERS DE SOCIÉTÉ, the whole host of French forms, BALLADE, RONDEL, RONDEAU—all these are varieties of lyrical expression classified according to differing form, matter, and mood.

[References: Maurice Bowra, *Mediaeval Love-Song* (1961); Chaviva Hošek and Patricia Parker, *Lyric Poetry: Beyond New Criticism* (1985); C. Day Lewis, *The Lyric Impulse* (1965); W. R. Johnson, *The Idea of Lyric: Lyric Modes in Ancient and Modern Poetry* (1982); Jerome Mazzaro, *Transformations in the Renaissance English Lyric* (1970); W. E. Rogers, *The Three Genres and the Interpretation of Lyric* (1983); Helen Vendler, *The Music of What Happens* (1988).]

Lyric Present A term suggested by George T. Wright to designate the use of the simple present tense ("I walk") in a place where a normal speaker would use the progressive ("I am walking"). English does not normally use the simple present form of the verb for simple present actions; Wright observes that such a statement as Yeats's "I walk through the long schoolroom, questioning" occurs almost exclusively in lyric poems—hence *lyric present* tense.

Lyrical Drama A term used for a dramatic poem (see DRAMATIC POETRY) in which the form of drama is used to express lyric themes (author's own emotions or ideas of life) instead of relying on a story as the basis of the action. Newman's "The Dream of Gerontius" is an example.

Lyrical Novel A species of novel in which conventional narration is subordinated to the presentation of inner thoughts, feelings, and moods. According to Ralph Freedman, the *lyrical novel* transforms "the materials of fiction (such as characters, plots, or scenes) into patterns of imagery. . . . In this strangely alienated, yet somehow essential genre, the direct portrayal of awareness becomes the outer frontier where novel and poem meet."

[Reference: Ralph Freedman, *The Lyrical Novel: Studies in Hermann Hesse, André Gide, and Virginia Woolf* (1963).]

Comstock 1860. Designed by Barnhart Brothers & Spindler, which is now the American Type Founders Company.

Mabinogion A collection of old Welsh tales translated by Lady Charlotte Guest from the *Red Book of Hergest*, a manuscript from the thirteenth or fourteenth century containing tales composed centuries earlier. Only four of these tales, *Pwyll, Prince of Dyved; Branwen, Daughter of Llyr; Manawyddan, Son of Llyr;* and *Math, Son of Mathonwy* (the so-called four branches), are in the strict sense of the word included in the term *mabinogion*. Modern authorities explain *mabinogion* as the plural of *mabinogi*, "a collection of tales every young poet should know." For a classification of the contents of the *Mabinogion* and for the possible relation of the tales to Arthurian romances, see WELSH LITERATURE.

Macabre Originally, in *danse macabre* or Dance of Death, the obscure word relates to both subject and style, a gruesome combination of farce and tragedy. There are *macabre* elements in Jacobean tragedies (especially those of Webster) and the work of T. L. Beddoes and Edgar Allan Poe. Ezra Pound called Beddoes "prince of morticians."

Macaronic (1) Words related to "macaroni" and "macaroon" bore two distinct pejorative meanings during the seventeenth and eighteenth centuries: "a blockhead" (in Donne and Addison and in the definition of "macaroon" in Johnson's *Dictionary:* "a coarse, rude, low fellow," a meaning also implicit in John Hall-Stevenson's BURLESQUE *Makarony Fables*, the style of which matches Johnson's description of "*macaronick* poetry, in which the language is purposely corrupted"); also, a little later in the eighteenth century, "a dandy," probably the sense intended in "Yankee Doodle." (2) *Macaronic* also concerns writing that combines two or more languages. As a device of humor, *macaronic* sometimes includes putting inflections from one language onto stems from another, as in "muchibus thankibus" or "summa cum difficulte." Not all *macaronic* writing is comic. Recent scholarship has concentrated on English-Latin *macaronic* sermons between 1350 and 1450.

[Reference: Siegfried Wenzel, *Macaronic Sermons: Bilingualism and Preaching in Late-Medieval England* (1994).]

Macaronic Verse A type of verse that mingles two or more languages. More especially it refers to poems incorporating modern words (given Latin or Greek endings) with Latin or Greek. The origin of this often nonsensical entertainment is credited to Tisi degli Odassi, who interspersed Latin with Italian in *Carmen Maccaronicum* (1488). A Benedictine monk, Teofilo Folengo (1491–1544), wrote a mock heroic called

Liber Macaronicus (1520). Verse of the sort was soon written in France and other European countries; the best example in English is said to be the *Polemo-Middinia*, credited to William Drummond of Hawthornden. The following, by "E.C.B.," will be self-explanatory:

> Cane carmen sixpence, pera plena rye,
> De multis atris avibus coctis in a pie:
> Simul hæc apert' est, cantat omnis grex.
> Nonne permirabile, quod vidit ille rex?

Macaronic verse was not always nonsense; its intent was frequently that of serious satire. The term is sometimes applied to any verse having two languages, such as many parts of *Piers Plowman* and William Dunbar's "Lament for the Makaris" (c. 1508), with its Latin refrain, "*Timor mortis conturbat me*." Serious use of a macaronic technique may be found in Eliot's *The Waste Land* and Pound's *Cantos*.

Macédoine A collection of verbal items, such as sentences, gathered to illustrate some point of grammar but not making logical sense. For example, Mitchell and Robinson furnish a *Macédoine* that may help one remember the alphabetic designations and the rhythmic patterns of the six types of half-line detected by Sievers in Old English poetry:

A.	Anna Angry	(falling-falling)
B.	And Byrhtnoth bold	(rising rising)
C.	In keen conflict	(clashing)
Da.	Ding down strongly	(falling by stages)
Db.	Deal death to all	(broken fall)
E.	Each one with edge.	(fall and rise)

[Reference: Bruce Mitchell and Fred C. Robinson, *A Guide to Old English*, 5th ed. (1992; orig. 1964).]

MacGuffin A term, originated by Angus MacPhail but most often associated with Alfred Hitchcock, for any pretext in itself not very important or relevant but necessary to get a plot moving. Donald Spoto says, "In the case of *The 39 Steps*, the MacGuffin is a secret formula. . . . But it is to *prevent* the secret from being known—rather than to reveal it—that the adventure-chase is precipitated; thus the formula, which at first seems crucial, is immediately reduced in significance." Maybe the dying word "Rosebud" that motivates much of the surface action in Orson Welles's *Citizen Kane* turns out to have been something of a *MacGuffin*. The "Conclusion" of T. S. Eliot's *The Use of Poetry and the Use of Criticism* (1933) suggests that meaning itself can function as a *MacGuffin:* "The chief use of the 'meaning' of a poem, in the ordinary sense, may be (for here again I am speaking of some kinds of poetry and not all) to satisfy one habit of the reader, to keep his mind diverted and quiet, while the poem does its work upon him: much as the imaginary burglar is always provided with a bit of nice meat for the house-dog."

The word has established itself as part of the language, appearing in the titles of a film (Joe Camp's *The Double McGuffin* [sic], 1979) and a novel (Stanley Elkin's *The MacGuffin*, 1991, about a man's nagging sense of being trapped in a Hitchcock-style plot of suspicion, persecution, and betrayal).

[Reference: Donald Spoto, *The Dark Side of Genius: The Life of Alfred Hitchcock* (1983).]

Machinery In the Neoclassical Period, the term *machinery* was applied, in Pope's words, "to signify that part which the deities, angels or demons are made to act in a poem." It was derived from the mechanical means used by Greek dramatists to introduce a god on the stage (see DEUS EX MACHINA). It was extended from this use in tragedy to epic, where it refers to supernatural beings who participate in the action. Thus, *machinery* is applied to the being introduced by the machine rather than to the machine itself.

Macron The name of the symbol (-) used to indicate a long syllable in QUANTITATIVE VERSE.

Macrosegment A continuous unit of speech between two pauses or junctures, with a single intonation.

Mad Song A verse supposedly spoken or sung by an insane person. Distinguished by repetition, nonsense, incoherence, and morbid or bawdy wordplay. Shakespearean characters who are mad or feigning madness—such as Ophelia in *Hamlet* and Edgar in *King Lear*—often sing *mad songs*. Thomas D'Urfey's "I'le Sail upon the Dog-Star" from *New Songs Sung in the Fool's Preferment* (1688) is an insanely boastful *mad song*. A number of "Tom O'Bedlam's Songs" were published in the seventeenth century. A poem in Blake's *Poetical Sketches* (1783) is titled "Mad Song," a name that would also suit "Twinkle, twinkle, little bat," the Mad Hatter's song in Chapter 7 of *Alice's Adventures in Wonderland* (1865). Both Elinor Wylie and Denise Levertov wrote poems titled "Mad Song." James Wright's "A Mad Fight Song for William S. Carpenter, 1966" combines the connotations of the traditional *mad song* with the "fight song" sung at pep rallies before football games at American schools. Peter Maxwell Davies's *Eight Songs for a Mad King* (1969) with "text by Randolph Stow and George III" is a complex example.

Madrigal A short lyric, usually dealing with love or a pastoral theme and designed for—or at least suitable for—a musical setting. In the Elizabethan Age the term was used for a kind of song sung without accompaniment by five or six voices with intricate interweaving of words and melody. The Italian *madrigal* usually consisted of six to thirteen lines based on three rhymes. Today the term is used quite loosely. Shakespeare's "Take, O, take those lips away" from *Measure for Measure* is a *madrigal*, as is "The Nightingale" in Gilbert and Sullivan's *HMS Pinafore*. A modern example is "Have Yourself a Merry Little Christmas," written by Hugh Martin and Ralph Blane for the film *Meet Me in St. Louis*.

Magazine A term applied to any of several kinds of PERIODICAL miscellanies containing various kinds of material by several authors. *Magazine* is sometimes reserved for the more informal sort of periodical, distinguished from JOURNAL.

Maggot A fanciful piece of whimsy, sometimes perverse or morbid. Seventeenth-century usage put "maggot in the brain" where modern usage puts "worm in the head." Samuel Wesley's *Maggots; or Poems on Several Subjects* was published in 1685. *Maggot*, commonly used by sixteenth- and seventeenth-century composers in titles of instrumental dances, has been revived in *Miss Donnithorne's Maggot* (1974), a theater piece by Peter Maxwell Davies to a text by Randolph Stow, who called the work "a slur on the reputation of an unfortunate lady." (The real-life Eliza Emily Donnithorne was one of the models for Miss Havisham in Dickens's *Great Expectations*.) The Prologue of John Fowles's *A Maggot* (1985) combines and extends the meanings of the word: "A maggot is the larval stage of a winged creature; as is the written text, at least in the writer's hope. But an older though now obsolete sense of the word is that of whim or quirk. By extension it was sometimes used in the late seventeenth and early eighteenth century of dance-tunes and airs that otherwise had no special title. . . . This fictional maggot was written very much for the same reason as those old musical ones of the period in which it is set; out of obsession with a theme. . . . What follows may seem like a historical novel; but it is not. It is maggot." Some of Dylan Thomas's poems use *maggot* suggestively.

Magic Realism (or **Magical Realism**) An international tendency in the graphic and literary arts, especially painting and prose fiction. The frame or surface of the work may be conventionally realistic, but contrasting elements—such as the supernatural, myth, dream, fantasy—invade the realism and change the whole basis of the art. *Magical realism* in literature enjoyed popularity in many parts of the world just after World War II, with such influential exemplars as Jorge Luis Borges and Gabriel García Márquez in South America, Günter Grass in Germany, and Italo Calvino and Umberto Eco in Italy. Among those writing in English, quite a few novelists show some affinity with *magical realism:* John Fowles, John Barth, Thomas Pynchon, Emma Tennant, Don DeLillo, and Salman Rushdie.

Magnum Opus A great work, a masterpiece. Formerly the term was used in all seriousness, but nowadays it often connotes IRONY or SARCASM.

Majuscule Old typographical name for a large letter, especially a capital.

Make-rhyme A word or phrase used merely for the sake of rhyme.

Malapropism An inappropriateness of speech resulting from the use of one word for another, which resembles it. The term is derived from a character, Mrs. Malaprop, in Sheridan's *The Rivals*, who was constantly giving vent to such expressions as the following: "as headstrong as an allegory on the banks of the Nile," "a progeny of learning," "illiterate him, I say, quite from your memory." The Nurse in *Romeo and Juliet* says "confidence" for "conference," and the *malapropism* prompts Benvolio to say, "She will indite [for "invite"] him to some supper." In *The Innocents Abroad* by Mark Twain, a versifier (based on Bloodgood Haviland Cutter) styles himself "the poet lariat."

Instances can be found in Smollett and much dialect writing; the most notable modern instance is in the works of James Joyce, as when Molly Bloom in *Ulysses* speaks of "the preserved seats" in a theater. The vernacular indulges occasionally in *malapropism*, as when someone says, "Mind your own beeswax."

Malediction A CURSE. The famous "Cursed be he that moves my bones" used as an epitaph for Shakespeare is an example.

Manga Since about 1950, a style of COMIC BOOK or GRAPHIC NOVEL, originally Japanese, typically presenting in book form a story of FANTASY, SCIENCE FICTION, or ROMANCE, with drawings in panels or strips; the action is violent and extreme, and the drawing is detailed and eccentric. The figures, whether human, monstrous, or otherwise, tend to have extraordinarily large eyes and exaggerated anatomies. Related to ANIME.

From *xxxHOLiC*, volume 2 (Del Ray–Random House, 2004). Rischgitz/Hulton Archive/Getty Images.

Manichaeism, Manicheism, or **Manichaeanism** A religion founded about A.D. 250 by a Persian, Mani (or Manes). *Manichaeism* sees God and Satan as coeval and engaged in an eternal struggle. The forces of light do endless battle against those of darkness. This cosmic struggle also takes place in individuals. Our bodies, like all material substance, are evil and belong to Satan, but they are also infused with a modicum of godly light, and the struggle between the material and the godly continues as long as body and soul are united. The elect succeed in freeing the light from the evil of darkness. Through metempsychosis the unelect may progress upward toward election. Such beliefs led to a very ascetic way of life for the true believers. Mani borrowed from the Gnostics, various Oriental religions, including the Zoroastrian, and Christianity. His teachings were popular through the fifth century but since the sixth century have been considered a major source of heresy in most religions. See GNOSTICISM.

Mannerism A highly affected style that was fashionable in the graphic arts around the turn of the sixteenth century, roughly contemporary with GONGORISM and MARINISM in literature. It resembles both in specializing in exaggeration, distortion, and eccentricity. In a looser sense, *mannerism* is applied to any artwork in which manner eclipses matter.

Manners When used in the sense of defining various literary genres, *manners* refers to prevailing modes of social conduct of a specific class at a definite period of time. It involves, in addition to the accepted rules of polite behavior for that class, its system of values and mores, as reflections of moral attitudes. See COMEDY OF MANNERS, NOVEL OF MANNERS.

Manual A HANDBOOK: a book offering information and guidance on any subject, nowadays in the form of an "owner's *manual*," "operating *manual*," or "technical *manual*" for appliances and other such articles.

Manuscript, Medieval The art of manuscript making was highly developed in the Middle Ages; the finer existing "illuminated" manuscripts and early printed books modeled on them show an artistry equal to that of the best examples of modern bookmaking.

Because there was no mechanical means for multiplying copies, a prodigious amount of skilled labor was required for the production of each manuscript. Parchment was first employed, the finest kind being vellum (made from calfskin), though paper came into use in the later Middle Ages. The actual writing was done chiefly in the monasteries, first by ordinary monks and later by professional scribes. The process of making a book included (1) the copying of the text by the scribe on separate sheets, (2) the inspection by the corrector, (3) the insertion of the capital letters, rubrics, and other colored decorative matter by the rubricator and illuminator, (4) the binding by a binder who arranged the sheets (usually by folding a group of four sheets once to make a "quire" of eight leaves, or sixteen pages) and completed the binding by the use of wooden boards, leather, and velvet. The result was a substantial "manuscript" in form much like a modern book of large size but far sturdier. The illuminator did his work with great care. Favorite colors were gold, blue, and red (the origin of "rubric" is a Latin word for "red") though green, purple, and yellow were also used. In spite of losses from fire, war, robbery, and neglect, thousands of *medieval manuscripts* still exist, carefully preserved in numerous libraries. Early printed books (see INCUNABULUM) were modeled on the manuscript. In England, many *medieval manuscripts* were destroyed as a result of the dissolution of the monasteries during the Protestant Reformation.

Map Poem A poem that gives the impression of having been written while the poet was studying a map. Such poems are in the same category as chorographic and topographical works, such as Michael Drayton's *Polyolbion*, Thomas Babington Macaulay's "The Armada" (telling how the news of the spotting of the Spanish Armada was passed all the way from Cornwall in the south to Scotland in the north), and Robert Browning's "How They Brought the Good News from Ghent to Aix" (a substantial horseback journey in Belgium), Archibald MacLeish's "You, Andrew Marvell," Stephen Vincent Benét's "American Names," and a passage in A. R. Ammons's *Sphere*. Milton's "Lycidas" partakes of the tradition, surveying the west coast of Britain from the Hebrides to Cornwall.

Märchen German FAIRY TALES. They may be simple folktales of the sort collected by Wilhelm and Jakob Grimm, known as *Volksmärchen*, or they may be short allegories laid in a fantastic realm of the sort written in the nineteenth century by Goethe, Novalis, Tieck, and E. T. A. Hoffmann, known as *Kunstmärchen* (art tales).

Marginalia Marginal material, literal or figurative. First used in English by Samuel Taylor Coleridge, adapting a Latin plural adjective, now applied to anything written in the margins of a work (or as though in the margins). In some cases such *marginalia* make valuable critical comments, as Coleridge's do, or have value in reconstructing the reader's life and mind, as *marginalia* by Herman Melville have. The term is also sometimes used for brief critical OBITER DICTA, as in Edgar Allan Poe's *Marginalia*.

[References: H. J. Jackson, *Marginalia: Readers Writing in Books* (2001); Barbara Herrnstein Smith, *On the Margins of Discourse: The Relation of Literature to Language* (1978).]

Marinism An affected style practiced by the Italian poet Giambattista Marino (1569–1625) and his followers. It is the manifestation of a general tendency toward a strained, flamboyant, or shocking style during the later Renaissance, in some respects analogous to the BAROQUE in art. A typical conceit of Marino is his calling stars "blazing half-dimes of the celestial mint." Another aspect of *Marinism* was its "effeminate voluptuousness." Some English Metaphysical poets were influenced by Marino. See EUPHUISM, CONCEIT, GONGORISM.

[Reference: J. B. Fletcher, *Literature of the Italian Renaissance* (1934, reprinted 1964).]

Marprelate Controversy In the 1580s the Puritan opposition to the bishops of the established church in England, whose power was greatly strengthened by state support, expressed itself in outspoken pamphlets. Some of the authors were severely punished—one executed—and in 1585 censorship was made more rigid by a provision limiting printing rights to London and the two universities. In defiance, the Puritan party in 1588 began issuing a series of violent attacks on the episcopacy, printed surreptitiously and signed by the pen name "Martin Marprelate." The attacks were answered with corresponding scurrility by conservatives, including Robert Greene, John Lyly, and Thomas Nash. The authorship of the Marprelate pamphlets has never been definitely established, but, whoever the author or authors, the exchange supplied interesting examples of spirited prose satire. The controversy was suppressed by the death in prison of one alleged author and the execution in 1593 of two others.

Martian School (or **Martians**) Craig Raine's second book of poems, *A Martian Sends a Postcard Home* (1979), prompted James Fenton to label a school of British poets born in the 1940s as *Martians*, that is, as poets who struggle to see the world afresh, as might a visitor from Mars. The title poem of Raine's volume begins, "Caxtons are mechanical birds with many wings. . . ." Eventually, Fenton conceded that his original reference to "the Martian School," of which Raine and Christopher Reid were "leading members," may have been, at least in part, a flippancy that gained critical status.

Marxist Criticism Criticism based on the doctrines of Karl Marx, Friedrich Engels, and their disciples. Marxism assumes the independent reality of matter and its priority over mind (dialectical materialism). It teaches a theory of value based on labor, the economic determination of all social actions and institutions, the class struggle as the basic pattern in history, the inevitable seizure of power through the revolution of the proletariat, the dictatorship of that proletariat, and the ultimate establishment of a classless society. In one sense Marxism is an interpretation of history and a prophecy of an evolutionary process in which revolution is not necessary. In another sense, that taken by the Communists, Marxism must be revolutionary. The principal Marxist doctrines were set forth in *The Communist Manifesto*, by Marx and Engels (1848), and *Das Kapital*, by Marx (1867). The impact of Marxism on historical theory has been pervasive, and in this sense it has permeated much modern thought, even that of the anti-Marxist. Marxism has had notable influence on fiction, particularly that of radical sociological leanings, and on sociologically inclined literary criticism. It was a strong influence on the writing done in America in the 1930s, and to some extent on English writing of the same period. Even after the collapse of the Soviet Union in 1989, Marxist thought continued to shape literary criticism. Leading Marxist critics have been Georg Lukács, Walter Benjamin, Raymond Williams, Louis Althusser, Antonio Gramsci, Fredric Jameson, and Terry Eagleton.

Masculine Ending A line of verse that ends on a stressed syllable, as does any regular iambic line. Compare with FEMININE ENDING.

Masculine Rhyme Rhyme that falls on the stressed, concluding syllables of the rhyme words. *Masculine rhyme* accounts for a majority of rhymes in English. "Mount" and "fount" make a *masculine rhyme*, "mountain" and "fountain" a feminine.

Masked Comedy A name applied to COMMEDIA DELL'ARTE because all the actors except the two playing the romantic lovers wore masks.

Masorah The body of critical commentary on the texts of Hebrew Scriptures, compiled at least a thousand years ago by Jewish scholars known as Masoretes.

Masque In medieval Europe there existed, partly as survivals or adaptations of ancient pagan seasonal ceremonies, species of games or SPECTACLES characterized by a procession of masked figures. In these DISGUISINGS or MUMMINGS, a procession of masquers would go through the streets, enter house after house, silently dance, play at dice with the citizens or with each other, and pass on. Adopted by the aristocracy, these games, modified by characteristics borrowed from civic pageants, chivalric customs, sword-dances, and the RELIGIOUS DRAMA, developed into elaborate spectacles, which evolved into the entertainments known as *masques*. The famous Epiphany spectacle of 1512, given by and participated in by Henry VIII, is sometimes referred to as the first English *masque*.

The chief development of the *masque* came in the latter part of Elizabeth I's reign and, especially, in the reigns of James I and Charles I, and reached its climax under such poets as Daniel, Beaumont, Middleton, and Jonson. The greatest development was due to the genius of Jonson and Inigo Jones, court architect and deviser of stage MACHINERY. The "essential" *masque*, as distinguished from the "literary" *masque* (for example, Milton's *Comus*), makes an appeal to the eye and the ear, with a succession of rapidly changing scenes and TABLEAUX crowded with beautiful figures. Gods, monsters, heroes, fauns, satyrs, fairies, and witches were presented to the eye, while music charmed the ear.

Masques became increasingly expensive, with exorbitant amounts being spent on costumes, scenery, and properties and for professional musicians, dancers, and actors. In the *masque* proper, which was the arrival and dancing of masked figures, the actors were amateurs drawn from the court society. With the development by Jonson of the ANTIMASQUE, the dramatic and literary qualities increased. Mythological and PASTORAL elements were emphasized, Jonson maintaining (against Daniel and Jones) that the *masque* should be based on some poetic idea and that the action should be significant as well as spectacular, so that Milton's *Comus* (1634), one of the best-known *masques*, represents a development of what was originally little but spectacle. The *masque* commonly was a feature of some celebration, such as a wedding or coronation, served as a formal preliminary entertainment to a court ball, and was frequently employed at the entertainments in the INNS OF COURT. Spenser incorporates *masque*-like episodes in *The Faerie Queene*. The effect on the popular drama itself was probably great, because some dramatists wrote for both the court and the London stage. Peele's *Arraignment of Paris* is a pastoral play much like a *masque*. Many of Shakespeare's plays show the influence; the betrothal *masque* in *The Tempest* is an example. *As You Like It* has been called a mere "series of tableaux and groupings," *masque*-like in the deficiency of serious action, in the prominence of music, and in the spectacular appearance of Hymen as a DEUS EX MACHINA at the end. The glorious era of the *masque* ended with the triumph of the Puritan Revolution (1642).

Late in his career, Robert Frost wrote "A Masque of Reason" and "A Masque of Mercy," BLANK VERSE dramas.

[References: Angus Fletcher, *The Transcendental Masque: An Essay on Milton's Comus* (1971); Sarah P. Sutherland, *Masques in Jacobean Tragedy* (1983).]

Masthead In certain periodicals, a box near the top of the first page or the editorial page or elsewhere that gives the names and titles of important officers and other information, such as date of founding, names of founders, and mottoes.

Matin A morning song, as of birds. The plural *matins* refers to the first of the seven CANONICAL HOURS in the Catholic church at which prescribed prayers are sung.

Maxim A concise statement, usually drawn from experience and inculcating some practical advice; an ADAGE. Hoyle's "When in doubt, win the trick" is a *maxim* in bridge. See APHORISM, AXIOM, PROVERB.

Meaning It is possible to distinguish four different aspects of *meaning*. As given by I. A. Richards, they are (1) sense, the denotative message that one is trying to communicate; (2) feeling, one's attitude toward this sense; (3) tone, one's attitude toward the audience; and (4) intention, the effect one consciously or unconsciously intends through what is said, how one feels about it, and the attitude one takes toward the audience. In another way, *meaning* can be seen as of two kinds: DENOTATION and CONNOTATION. For a literary work there are also four possible kinds of *meaning:* the literal, the allegorical, the tropological or moral, and the anagogical or spiritual. See FOUR SENSES OF INTERPRETATION.

Measure Frequently a synonym for METER, *measure* is more strictly either a metrical grouping, such as a foot, or a period of time. In musical theories of prosody a *measure* is usually the time sequence beginning with an accented syllable and running to the next accented syllable. In hymnody, *measure* refers to STANZA, as in COMMON MEASURE and LONG MEASURE.

Medieval Drama A term that includes all drama in the Middle Ages, though religious drama and its allied forms are usually meant. Medieval religious drama grew out of the liturgical services of the church. As early as the tenth century, perhaps in northern France, TROPES or musical elaborations of the church services, particularly of the Easter Mass, developed into genuine drama when the Latin lines telling the story of the Resurrection, instead of being sung antiphonally by the two parts of the choir, were sung or spoken by priests who impersonated the two angels and the three Marys in the scene at the tomb of Christ.

Such dramatic tropes later became detached, and *medieval drama* was born. That such performances appeared early in England is shown by the existence of the *Concordia Regularis* (c. 975), a complete set of stage directions supplied by the Bishop of Winchester. The conscious dramatic intent is shown in the first few lines of the *Concordia:* "While the third lesson is being changed, let four brethren vest themselves. Let one of these, vested in an alb, enter as though to take part in the service, and let him approach the sepulchre without attracting attention and sit there quietly with a palm in his hands . . . and let them all . . . stepping delicately as those who seek something, approach the sepulchre" (Chambers's translation).

It was not long until the performances were transferred from the church to the outdoors; Latin gave way to the native language; and eventually the performances became secularized when the town authorities, utilizing the trade guilds as dramatic companies, took charge of the production. Eventually great CYCLES developed in which the whole plan of salvation was dramatically set forth (see MYSTERY PLAY). Plays employing the same technique as the scriptural plays but based on the lives of saints, especially miracles performed by saints including the Virgin Mary (MIRACLE PLAYS, or SAINTS' PLAYS), also developed about A.D. 1100. Much later (c. 1400) the MORALITY PLAY (dramatization of a moral allegory) became popular and with the somewhat similar play known as an INTERLUDE became an immediate precursor of Elizabethan drama. There was also a considerable body of folk drama in the late Middle Ages, performed out of doors on festival days: Robin Hood plays, sword-dance plays, MUMMINGS, and DISGUISINGS.

The cycle drama (mystery plays) and the moralities became so secularized that the church disapproved. The stressing of comic features such as the shrewish behavior of Noah's wife or the addition of comic scenes not demanded by the serious action, such as the sheep-stealing in the Towneley *Second Shepherd's Play*, led definitely toward Elizabethan comedy. As Felix E. Schelling remarks, it was "in the ruins and debris of the miracle play and morality that Elizabethan drama struck its deepest roots."

Medievalism A spirit of sympathy for the Middle Ages along with a desire to preserve or revive certain qualities of medieval life. Traces can be found as early as Spenser and throughout the seventeenth and eighteenth centuries, with their more or less amateur interest in antiquities. It was nineteenth-century romanticism, however, that sponsored the most robust flourishing of *medievalism*, the development of which was aided by increasingly accurate scholarship, along with a growing respect for the Roman Catholic unity of pre-Reformation Europe. One or more elements of *medievalism* can be found in Scott, Byron, Keats, Tennyson, the Pre-Raphaelites, Ruskin, Morris, Poe, Henry Adams, Newman, Hardy, Hopkins, and such more recent figures as E. A. Robinson, C. M. Doughty, T. E. Lawrence, J. R. R. Tolkien, C. S. Lewis, Charles Williams, David Jones, and a host of writers of fantasy and science fiction. Mark Twain was the chief enemy of *medievalism* in the late nineteenth century. He attacked it indirectly (by using *Walter Scott* as the name of a wrecked steamboat in *Huckleberry Finn*) and directly throughout *A Connecticut Yankee in King Arthur's Court*.

Medieval Romance A tale of adventure in which knights, kings, or distressed ladies, motivated by love, religious faith, or the mere desire for adventure, are the chief figures. The *medieval romance* appears in Old French literature of the twelfth century, supplanting the older CHANSON DE GESTE, an epic form. The epic reflects a heroic age, whereas the *romance* reflects a chivalric; the epic has weight and solidity, whereas the *romance* exhibits mystery and fantasy; the tragic seriousness of the epic is not matched in the lighter-hearted *romance;* the epic observes narrative UNITY, whereas the STRUCTURE of the *romance* is loose; love, usually absent or of minor interest in the epic, is supreme in the *romances;* the epic uses the dramatic method of having the characters speak for themselves, whereas the reader of a *romance* remains conscious of a narrator. The *romances* became extremely popular in Western Europe, occupying a place comparable with that of the novel in modern literature. The earliest *romances* were in verse (hence the term METRICAL ROMANCES), but prose was also employed later. The materials for the early French *romances* were drawn chiefly from the Charlemagne dossier or *chansons de geste* ("Matter of France"), ancient history and literature ("Matter of Rome the Great"), and Celtic lore, especially Arthurian material ("Matter of Britain").

Romances were produced in English as early as the thirteenth century. They flourished in the fourteenth century and continued through the fifteenth and sixteenth centuries, though the disfavor of Renaissance humanists caused them to lose standing, and Renaissance versions as well as versions appearing in seventeenth- and eighteenth-century CHAPBOOKS are frequently degenerate forms, written for the middle and lower classes. Middle English *romances* may be grouped on the basis of their subject matter. The "Matter of England" includes stories based on Germanic (including English) tradition and embraces *King Horn* (c. 1275), *Richard Lionheart* (1350), *Beves of Hampton* (c. 1300), *Havelock the Dane* (before 1300), *Guy of Warwick* (c. 1300), and *Athelston* (c. 1350). Important *romances* of the French group are *Sir Ferumbras* (c. 1375), *Otuel* (c. 1300), and *Huon of Bordeaux* (thirteenth century). The "Matter of Antiquity" includes various legends of Alexander the Great, legends of Thebes, and legends of Troy (including Chaucer's famous *Troilus and Criseyde*). The "Matter of Britain" includes the important Arthurian literature and is represented by such classics as the fourteenth-century metrical romance *Sir Gawain and the Green Knight* and the fifteenth-century prose *Le Morte Darthur* of Malory. The Arthurian *romances* developing around the legend of King Arthur (see ARTHURIAN LEGEND) had eventually developed into great cycles of stories in Old French literature, some of the heroes of which, such as Tristram and Lancelot, did not belong to the original Arthurian legend. They were greatly elaborated in the bulky thirteenth-century French prose *romances* ("VULGATE ROMANCES"), which became sources for such English treatments as Malory's. A fifth group might include *romances* of miscellaneous origin, especially Oriental. Examples are *Amis and Amiloun* (before 1300), *Floris and Blanchefleur* (c. 1250), *Sir Isumbras* (1350–1400), and *Ipomedon* (twelfth century).

The MIDDLE ENGLISH *romances*, which are in verse, usually show less artistry, less attention to psychological treatment, less sophistication, more credulity and use of the GROTESQUE (such as Richard's eating of the lion's heart), and a higher moral tone than the French.

The *medieval romance* follows the structure of the quest. Usually, the protagonist sets out on a journey to accomplish some goal—rescue a maiden, seek the HOLY GRAIL. He encounters numerous adventures, many of them unrelated to his original quest except that they impede him.

Meditation A work, usually religious or philosophical, in which serious subjects are handled in a reflective, contemplative, meditative manner; the tradition was mocked by Swift in a short work called "A Meditation upon a Broom-Stick" (1710).

Meditative Poetry A term for certain kinds of METAPHYSICAL POETRY of the sixteenth and seventeenth centuries that yoke religious meditation with Renaissance poetic techniques. "The Practical Methode of Meditation" (1614), by the Jesuit Edward Dawson, describes the religious practice in an approach much like Ignatius Loyola's *Spiritual Exercises*. Most *meditative poetry* deals with memorable moments of self-knowledge and of union with some transcendent reality. Louis L. Martz, while acknowledging that a precise definition is impossible, suggests that its "central meditative action consists of an interior drama, in which a man projects a self upon a mental stage, and there comes to understand that self in the light of a divine presence." Often such poems were written as part of the author's preparation for religious ceremonies, such as the American Edward Taylor's

Preparatory Meditations before My Approach to the Lord's Supper. Among notable writers of *meditative poetry* were Saint Robert Southwell (1561–1595), John Donne (1572–1631), George Herbert (1593–1633), Richard Crashaw (c. 1612–1649), Henry Vaughan (1621–1692), and Thomas Traherne (1637–1674). The tradition may be said to continue through Tennyson's *In Memoriam* and into the twentieth century in Eliot's *Four Quartets* and Geoffrey Hill's *Lachrimae*.

[References: Louis Martz, (ed.) *The Meditative Poem: An Anthology of Seventeenth-Century Verse* (1963), and *The Poetry of Meditation*; *a Study in English Religious Literature of the Seventeenth Century* (1954, rev. ed. 1962).]

Meiosis Intentional UNDERSTATEMENT for humorous or satiric effect. See LITOTES, IRONY.

Melic Poetry Poetry written to be accompanied by the lyre or flute. It was to this poetry that the Alexandrians applied the term LYRIC, the designation by which it is generally known. *Melic poetry* flourished in Greece between the seventh and the fifth centuries B.C. Among its greatest poets were Sappho, Anacreon, and Pindar.

Meliorism A name applied to the belief—widely held in the nineteenth century—that society has an innate tendency toward improvement and that that tendency can be furthered by conscious human effort. At the conclusion of *Middlemarch* George Eliot expresses the idea clearly: ". . . the growing good of the world is partly dependent on unhistoric arts; and that things are not so ill with you and me as they might have been, is half owing to the number who lived faithfully a hidden life, and rest in unvisited tombs." Thomas Hardy believed in what he called—maybe in jest—an evolutionary *meliorism*, although his confidence in its operation or its rate was much smaller than George Eliot's. His "Apology" in *Late Lyrics and Earlier*, says, "Whether the human and kindred animal races survive till exhaustion or destruction of the globe . . . pain to all upon it, tongued or dumb, shall be kept down to a minimum by loving-kindness, operating through scientific knowledge, and actuated by the modicum of free will conjecturally possessed by organic life when the necessitating forces . . . happen to be in equilibrium, which may or may not be often."

Melodrama A work, usually a play, based on a romantic plot and developed sensationally, with little regard for motivation and with an excessive appeal to the emotions of the audience. The object is to keep the audience thrilled by the arousal of strong feelings of pity, horror, or joy. Poetic justice is superficially secured, the characters (either very good or very bad) being rewarded or punished according to their deeds. Though typically a *melodrama* has a happy ending, tragedies that use much of the same technique are sometimes referred to as melodramatic.

The term literally means "a play with music," and at one time it was applied to the opera in a broad sense. In strict musical usage, *melodrama* is confined to works in which a text is spoken, recited, or chanted with a musical commentary that does not qualify as an actual setting of the text. Richard Strauss's *Enoch Arden* (to Tennyson's poem) and Ralph Vaughan Williams's *An Oxford Elegy* are examples. *Melodrama* came into widespread use in England in the nineteenth century as a device to circumvent the Licensing Act, which restricted "legitimate" plays to the PATENT THEATERS but which allowed musical entertainments in other theaters. The use of songs, recitative, and incidental music disguised the dramatic nature of popular stage pieces, and they came to be known as *melodramas*. The first English *melodrama* is believed to have been Thomas

Holcroft's *A Tale of Mystery* (1802). These *melodramas* usually exhibited the deplorable characteristics already listed, and finally the term by extension was applied to these characteristics independent of the presence or absence of music. T. S. Eliot's *Sweeney Agonistes* is subtitled *An Aristophanic Melodrama*.

[Reference: Robert B. Heilman, *Tragedy and Melodrama* (1968).]

Melologue A musical composition in which some words are sung and others recited.

Melopoeia A Greek term renovated by Ezra Pound, who used it for the whole articulatory-acoustic-auditory range of poetry.

Memoir A form of autobiographical writing dealing usually with the recollections of one who has been a part of or has witnessed significant events. *Memoirs* differ from AUTOBIOGRAPHY proper in that they are usually concerned with personalities and actions other than those of the writer, whereas autobiography stresses the inner and private life of its subject. Because "autobiography" did not come into widespread use until well into the nineteenth century, some works that we now call "autobiography" (such as Benjamin Franklin's) were called something else, usually *memoirs*, by their authors.

Mendose Spuriously, falsely, erroneously; a notation sometimes found in glosses.

Menippean Satire A form of SATIRE originally developed by the Greek cynic Menippus and transmitted by his disciples Lucian and Varro. Varro in turn influenced Petronius and Apuleius. *Menippean satire* deals more with mental attitudes than with fully realized characters. It uses plot freely and loosely to present the world in sharply controlled intellectual patterns. In its shorter forms *Menippean satire* is a DIALOGUE or a COLLOQUY, with its interest in the conflict of ideas. In longer works the Menippean satirist piles up vast accumulations of fact and presents this erudition through some intellectual organizing principle. Robert Burton's *Anatomy of Melancholy* is an outstanding example of *Menippean satire*. Other works that may be so classified include *Gulliver's Travels*, by Swift; *Imaginary Conversations*, by Landor; Peacock's novels; *Alice in Wonderland*, by Lewis Carroll; *Noctes Ambrosianae*, by Christopher North; *Tristram Shandy*, by Laurence Sterne; and the whaling material in *Moby-Dick*, by Melville. A recent work that is an almost perfect example of *Menippean satire* is *Giles Goatboy*, by John Barth. Thomas Pynchon's novels—*V., The Crying of Lot 49, Gravity's Rainbow*, and *Vineland*—display many Menippean elements, including masses of fantastic learning and patches of verse mixed in with prose. Such works are sometimes referred to by the term ANATOMY rather than *Menippean satire*. The current use of *Menippean satire* to define a GENRE was made popular by Northrop Frye in his *Anatomy of Criticism* and by Mikhail Bakhtin, especially in his studies of Rabelais.

Merism Generally, a repetition of parts; specifically, the use of a pair of opposites to mean a whole, as when "the long and the short of it" means "the whole story." Biblical poetry employs merism freely, as when Psalm 95 expresses the totality of God's power by saying "In his hand are the deep places of the earth: the strength of the hills is also his."

Mesostich (or **Mesostic**) An ACROSTIC in which the middle letters form a word. John Cage has composed a *mesostic* using various source texts and the key word "performance," along with rules about pauses (indicated by isolated apostrophes) and the inclusion of surrounding text ("wing words"):

com**P**osition is
is ask**E**d
fo**R**th through us
Filled with
right t**O** one
my pictu**R**e isn't vivid enough for
te**M**po only
A '
suggesti**N**g a vast and undeveloped nature '
Communist
it us**E**s

Meta- A prefix often applied by contemporary critics to various literary terms, forming such words as METACRITICISM and METAFICTION. The basic meaning is "beyond, above, of a higher logical type." When it is added to form a new noun from the name of a discipline or process, it designates a new but related discipline or process that deals logically and critically with the nature, structure, logic, or behavior of the original discipline or process. For example, "metatheory" is a theory that investigates, analyzes, or describes theory itself. Probably the most widely accepted use of the prefix is in "metalinguistics," because one common function of language is to talk about language, as in "'I' is a pronoun," in which treatment of the word as such changes its grammatical person from first to third. It is likely that any system of SIGNS comes equipped with a built-in mechanism of metasystemic metasigns, which permit the establishment and clarification of contact, code, and rule.

Metacriticism A process or method whose primary subject is the critical examination of the nomenclature, premises, principles, or structure of CRITICISM itself. For example, if a writer asserts that *War and Peace* is a better novel than *Nicholas Nickleby*, we get a work of criticism. If another sets out to explore the bases on which the judgment that one novel is better than another can be made, we get a piece of *metacriticism*. The metacritic criticizes criticism, and the metacritic's major efforts are devoted to the analysis of meaning and the logical appraisal of critical reasoning. In one sense then, *metacriticism* is simply a synonym for THEORETICAL CRITICISM when it is distinguished from PRACTICAL CRITICISM. However, as it is currently used, it always implies an intellectual rigor and a logical concern with underlying principles.

Metafiction A work of fiction, a major concern of which is the nature of fiction itself. John Fowles's *The French Lieutenant's Woman* is a *metafiction*, as are many modern works, even as far back as Henry James, Joseph Conrad, and Marcel Proust. By now, virtually any serious fiction—that, say, of Samuel Beckett, J. D. Salinger, John Barth, Donald Barthelme, Ken Kesey, B. S. Thomas, Robert Coover, Kurt Vonnegut, Jr., and Norman Mailer—contains, as one of its structural and thematic dimensions, a testing of fiction itself.

Metalepsis A complex figure, also called TRANSUMPTION, dismissed by classical and Renaissance critics (Quintilian, Puttenham) as affected and farfetched but during the 1970s and 1980s given newly sympathetic attention by some sensitive critics (Angus Fletcher, Harold Bloom, John Hollander). Definitions vary and even diverge, but the point of *metalepsis* seems to be the adding of one trope or figure to another, along with such extreme compression that the literal sense of the statement is eclipsed or reduced to anomaly or nonsense.

The figure crops up in rhetorical situations of maximal drama and interest. We can say discursively, for example, that the sisters Helen and Clytemnestra had much to do with causing the Trojan War and certain events in its aftermath, such as the murder of Agamemnon. The many parts and steps of this complex process are transumed in the very powerful *metaleptic* figure in Marlowe's *Doctor Faustus:* "Was this the face that launched a thousand ships / And burnt the topless towers of Ilium?" In two lines, Marlowe compounds a dozen figures, including question, metonymy, metaphor, hyperbole, and paradox (fortified by an elementary reference to water and fire, a deletion of all fully human elements, and emphatic alliteration and megaphonic IAMBS with very short short syllables and very long long ones).

Then, in Yeats's "Leda and the Swan," the same topic is enlarged to embrace the event that led to the birth of Helen and Clytemnestra: the rape of Leda by Zeus in the form of a swan. Yeats's *metalepsis* here transumes even more than does Marlowe's:

A shudder in the loins engenders there
The broken wall, the burning roof and tower
And Agamemnon dead.

Now, the process of orgasm, conception, gestation, and birth, that leads by and by, after forty years or so, to the killing of Agamemnon by Clytemnestra is collapsed into a figure that reduces to a paradoxical "Shudder . . . engenders . . . Agamemnon dead" instead of the logical "shudder . . . engenders . . . Clytemnestra" (who caused the death of Agamemnon).

Metanalysis Reinterpretation or misconstruction of the division between words or other units, as when "a nadder" becomes "an adder" (the process also possibly at work in the history of "apron," "orange," "newt," "the nonce," and some others).

Metanoia A rhetorical figure whereby a speaker retracts or corrects something said, as in Yeats's "Easter 1916": "What is it but nightfall? / No, no, not night but death."

Metaphor An ANALOGY identifying one object with another and ascribing to the first object one or more of the qualities of the second. I. A. Richards's distinction between the TENOR and the VEHICLE of a *metaphor* may be useful. The tenor is the idea being expressed or the subject of the comparison; the vehicle is the image by which this idea is conveyed or the subject communicated. When Shakespeare writes:

That time of year thou mayst in me behold
When yellow leaves, or none, or few, do hang

Upon those boughs which shake against the cold,
Bare ruined choirs where late the sweet birds sang—

the tenor is old age, the vehicle is the season of late fall or early winter, conveyed through a group of images unusually rich in implications. The tenor and vehicle taken together constitute the figure, trope, or "turn" in meaning that the *metaphor* conveys. At one extreme, the vehicle may be merely a means of decorating the tenor; at the other extreme, the tenor may be merely an excuse for having the vehicle. ALLEGORY, for example, may be thought of as an elaborate *metaphor* in which the tenor is never expressed, although it is implied. In the simplest kinds of *metaphors* there is an obvious direct resemblance objectively existing between tenor and vehicle, and in some *metaphors*, particularly those that lend themselves to elaborate CONCEITS, the relation between tenor and vehicle is in the mind of the maker of the *metaphor*, rather than in specific qualities of vehicle or tenor.

Aristotle praised the *metaphor* as "the greatest thing by far" for poets—a sentiment seconded by Ezra Pound, who endorsed Aristotle's calling apt *metaphor* "the hallmark of genius"—and saw it as the product of their insight, which permitted them to find the similarities in seemingly dissimilar things. It ought to be noted that Aristotle's attention to the art of finding resemblances resembles the lineaments of his doctrine of formal MIMESIS; art in a way is a *metaphor* for nature. Modern criticism follows Aristotle in placing a similarly high premium on poets' abilities to make *metaphors*, and ANALYTICAL CRITICISM tends to find almost as much rich suggestiveness in the differences between the things compared as it does in the recognition of surprising but unsuspected similarities. Cleanth Brooks uses the term "functional *metaphor*" to describe the way in which the *metaphor* is able to have "referential" and "emotive" characteristics and to go beyond them and become a direct means in itself of representing a truth incommunicable by any other means. Clearly, when a *metaphor* performs this function, it is behaving as a SYMBOL.

Metaphors may be simple, that is, may occur in the single isolated comparison, or a large *metaphor* may function as the controlling image of a whole work (see Edward Taylor's poem quoted in the article on CONTROLLING IMAGE), or a series of vehicles may all be associated with a single tenor, as in Hamlet's "To be or not to be" soliloquy. In this last kind of case, however, unless the images can harmoniously build the tenor without impressing the reader with a sense of their incongruity, the possibility of a MIXED FIGURE is imminent.

According to a fairly ingenuous notion of language, abstractions can be treated only in terms that are not abstract, presumably because the primitive mind cannot handle abstractions. But no evidence establishes the existence of any such limitations. To presume that any human being has to have a grasp of physical "pulling away" (*abs* + *trahere*) before being able to grasp an abstract "abstraction" is little more than bigotry. Even so, mentally negotiable systems of SIGNS do resemble metaphoric displacements and substitutions enough for Emerson to assert, "Every word was once a poem. . . . Language is fossil poetry." See IMAGE, TROPE, FIGURE OF SPEECH, CONTROLLING IMAGE, ALLEGORY, METAPHYSICAL CONCEIT, METONYMY.

[References: Christine Brooke-Rose, *A Grammar of Metaphor* (1958, reprinted 1970); Terence Hawkes, *Metaphor* (1972); L. C. Knights and Basil Cottle, eds., *Metaphor and Symbol* (1960); Paul Ricoeur, *The Rule of Metaphor* (tr. 1977); Sheldon Sacks, ed., *On Metaphor* (1979); Philip Wheelwright, *Metaphor and Reality* (1962, reprinted 1968).]

Metaphysical Conceit An ingenious kind of CONCEIT widely used by the Metaphysical poets, who explored all areas of knowledge to find, in the startlingly esoteric or the shockingly commonplace, telling and unusual ANALOGIES for their ideas. The use of such unusual conceits as CONTROLLING IMAGES is a hallmark of the writers of METAPHYSICAL POETRY. The *metaphysical conceit* often exploits verbal logic to the point of the GROTESQUE, and it sometimes achieves such extravagant turns on meaning that it becomes absurd, as when Richard Crashaw writes of Mary Magdalene's eyes as

> Two walking baths; two weeping motions,
> Portable and compendious oceans.

But when a *metaphysical conceit* strikes from our minds the same spark of recognition that the poet experienced, so that it gives us a perception of a real but previously unsuspected similarity that is enlightening, it speaks to both our minds and our emotions with force, as in Donne's "The Flea" or his comparison of the union of himself with his lover in the figure of a drafter's compass in "A Valediction Forbidding Mourning" or in Taylor's "Huswifery" (quoted in the article on CONTROLLING IMAGE). Something of the vigor and audacity of the *metaphysical conceit* can be seen in modern poems, such as that by Pound beginning "Your mind and you are our Sargasso Sea" and that by Frost beginning "She is as in a field a silken tent."

Metaphysical Poetry Although sometimes used in the broad sense of philosophical poetry, the term is commonly applied to the work of the seventeenth-century writers called the "Metaphysical Poets." They formed a school in the sense of employing similar methods and of revolting against the conventions of Elizabethan love poetry, in particular the PETRARCHAN CONCEIT. Their tendency toward psychological analysis of the emotions of love and religion, their penchant for the novel and the shocking, their use of the METAPHYSICAL CONCEIT, and the extremes to which they sometimes carried their techniques resulted frequently in obscurity, roughness, and strain—faults that gave them a bad reputation in the Neoclassic Period. However, there has been a modern revival of interest in their work and admiration for their accomplishments. In the tidal vicissitudes of fashion, Donne's reputation, very high indeed from 1912 to 1972, may now be ebbing somewhat. The term *metaphysical* was applied to Donne in derogation of his excessive use of philosophy by Dryden in 1693, but its present use to designate a special poetic manner originated with Samuel Johnson's description of *metaphysical poetry* in his "Life of Cowley."

The characteristics of the best *metaphysical poetry* are logical elements in a technique intended to express honestly, if unconventionally, the poet's sense of life's complexities. The poetry is intellectual, analytical, psychological, disillusioning, bold; absorbed in thoughts of death, physical love, religious devotion. The diction is relatively simple and may echo common speech. The imagery is drawn from the commonplace or the remote, actual life or erudite sources, the figure itself often being elaborated with self-conscious ingenuity. The form is frequently that of an argument. The Metaphysical poets wrote elaborately but usually with a high regard for form and the intricacies of meter and rhyme. Yet the verse is often intentionally rough; Ben Jonson thought Donne "deserved hanging" for not observing accent. The roughness may be explained in part by the dominance of eccentric thought over strict form, in part by the fact that irregularity suits the seriousness and perplexity of life, with the realistic method, with the spirit of revolt, and with the sense of an argument expressed in speech rather than song.

Eighteenth- and nineteenth-century critics usually found the result unpleasing. Samuel Johnson called *metaphysical poetry* DISCORDIA CONCORS, inverting Horace's phrase *concordia discors*, "harmony in discord." *Discordia concors* described, he said, "a combination of dissimilar images or discovery of occult resemblances in things apparently unlike." No exact list of Metaphysical poets can be drawn up. Donne was the acknowledged leader. Crashaw and Cowley have been called the most typically *metaphysical*. Some were Protestant religious mystics, such as George Herbert (as well as his brother, Lord Herbert of Cherbury), Vaughan, and Traherne; some Catholic, such as Crashaw; some were CAVALIER LYRICISTS, such as Carew and Lovelace; some were satirists, such as Donne and Cleveland; one was an American clergyman, Edward Taylor. T. S. Eliot, John Crowe Ransom, Allen Tate, and John Hollander are modern poets affected by the metaphysical influence. Among those even younger, the same influence may be detected in some of the works of Charles Tomlinson, Richard Wilbur, W. D. Snodgrass, Geoffrey Hill, Alan Williamson, and Jorie Graham.

If the results of the metaphysical manner are not always happy, if the unexpected details and surprising figures are not always integrated imaginatively and emotionally, it ought to be remembered that these poets were attempting a more difficult task than confronts the complacent writer of conventional verse. Their failures appear most strikingly in their fantastic conceits. When they succeed—as they often do—their poetry, arising out of a sense of incongruity and confusion, is hauntingly real in a perplexing world.

[References: T. S. Eliot, *Selected Essays*, 3rd ed. (1972); H. J. C. Grierson, ed., *Metaphysical Lyrics and Poems of the Seventeenth Century*, 2nd ed. (1995; orig. 1921, reprinted 1959); George Williamson, *The Donne Tradition* (1930, reprinted 1958).]

Metaplasm The movement of any element in a piece of language from its customary place. *Metaplasm* applies to written letters and spoken sounds as well as to words and larger units. *Metaplasm* has also been used as a general term for almost any alteration of words or patterns, including APOCOPE, SYNCOPE, synaloepha (merging a final vowel with the initial vowel of the succeeding word, as in "they're" for "they are"), prosthesis (adding at the beginning of a word), epenthesis (adding in the middle), PARAGOGE, APHAERESIS, and METATHESIS.

[Reference: O. B. Hardison, Jr., *Prosody and Purpose in the English Renaissance* (1989).]

Metastasis A rapid transition from one point to another, sometimes for the sake of deception.

Metathesis The interchange of position between sounds in a word. Many modern English words have undergone *metathesis;* an example is the word "curly," which in Chaucer was "crulle." It is not unusual in the United States to hear "pretty" and "perspiration" sounded as though they were spelled "perty" and "prespiration." Likewise, "nuclear" and "realtor" are sounded "nucular" and "relator" by some speakers. When *metathesis* occurs between words, the result is a SPOONERISM, whereby "loving shepherd" is changed to "shoving leopard."

Meter The recurrence in poetry of a rhythmic pattern, or the RHYTHM established by the regular occurrence of similar units of sound. The four basic kinds of rhythmic patterns are: (1) QUANTITATIVE, in which the rhythm is established by patterns of long and short syllables; this is the classical *meter;* (2) accentual, in which the occurrence of a syllable marked by STRESS or ACCENT determines the basic unit regardless of the number of unstressed or unaccented syllables surrounding the stressed syllable; OLD ENGLISH VERSIFICATION employs this kind of *meter*, as does SPRUNG RHYTHM; (3) syllabic, in which the number of syllables in a line is fixed, although the accent varies; much Romance and Japanese versification employs this *meter;* and (4) ACCENTUAL-SYLLABIC, in which both the number of syllables and the number of accents are fixed or nearly fixed; when the term *meter* is used in English, it often refers to accentual-syllabic rhythm.

The rhythmic unit within the line is called a FOOT. In English ACCENTUAL-SYLLABIC VERSE, the standard feet are: IAMBIC (˘ ´), TROCHAIC (´ ˘), ANAPESTIC (˘ ˘ ´), DACTYLLIC (´ ˘ ˘), SPONDAIC (´ ´), and PYRRHIC (˘ ˘), although others sometimes occur. The number of feet in a line forms another means of describing the *meter*. The following are the standard English *meters:* MONOMETER, one foot; DIMETER, two; TRIMETER, three; TETRAMETER, four; PENTAMETER, five; HEXAMETER, six, also called the ALEXANDRINE; HEPTAMETER, seven, also called the "FOURTEENER" when the feet are iambic.

Metonymy The substitution of the name of an object closely associated with a word for the word itself. We commonly speak of the monarch as "the crown," an object closely associated with royalty thus being made to stand for it. So, too, in the book of Genesis we read, "In the sweat of thy face shalt thou eat bread," in which sweat represents that with which it is closely associated, hard labor. Recent critics, led by Roman Jakobson, have come to consider *metonymy*, which involves a continuous association from whole to part, radically different from METAPHOR, which involves a discontinuous analogy between two wholes. According to Jakobson, neurological research into common forms of aphasia confirms his hypothesis about the functions of speech and the structure of the brain, both of which involve a process of selecting and combining units according to rules of continuity and discontinuity, association and analogy, paradigm and syntax, all subsumable under categories of *metonymy* and metaphor. The distinction promises important implications for the differences between prose and poetry, say, or between two sorts of poetry. Frost's, for example, may be classified as radically metonymic, so that his poem called "New Hampshire" concerns the state of New Hampshire as a metonymic figure representing the whole United States of America. Eliot's, on the other hand, is radically metaphoric, so that *his* "New Hampshire" has virtually nothing to do with the state except as a local metaphor for the human soul. See HYPALLAGE, SYNECDOCHE.

Metrical Accent The accent called for by the rhythm pattern in poetry.

Metrical Romance A romantic TALE in verse. The term applies both to such medieval verse romances as *Sir Gawain and the Green Knight* and to the verse romances by Sir Walter Scott (*The Lady of the Lake, Marmion*) and Lord Byron (*The Bride of Abydos, The Giaour*). The latter kind reflects the tendencies of romanticism in its freedom of technique and its preference for remote settings (the past in Scott, the Near East in Byron) as well as in its sentimental qualities. See MEDIEVAL ROMANCE.

Metrics The study of the patterns of rhythm in poetry.

Middle English English as spoken and written between the NORMAN CONQUEST and the Modern English period beginning at the Renaissance. The dates commonly given are 1100 to 1500, though both are approximate, because the Norman Conquest came in

1066 and some writings earlier than 1500 (such as Malory's *Le Morte Darthur*) may properly be called "Modern" English. See ENGLISH LANGUAGE.

Middle English Period The period in English literature between the replacement of French by MIDDLE ENGLISH as the language of court and the early appearances of definitely Modern English writings, roughly between 1350 and 1500. The Age of Chaucer (1340–1400) was marked by political and religious unrest, the Black Death (1348–1350), the Peasants' Revolt (1381), and the rise of the LOLLARDS. The fifteenth century was torn by the Wars of the Roses. There was a steadily increasing nationalistic spirit in England, and early traces of HUMANISM began to appear.

The great CYCLES of MYSTERY PLAYS flourished. Toward the end of the period the MORALITY came into existence, and the last years of the fifteenth century saw the arrival of the INTERLUDE. In prose it was the period of Wycliffe's sermons and his translation of the Bible, of Mandeville's *Travels*, of the medieval CHRONICLES, of prose ROMANCES, and, supremely, of Malory's *Le Morte Darthur*. ROMANCES, both prose and metrical, continued to be popular, with *Sir Gawain and the Green Knight* as the finest example.

The period between 1350 and 1400 was a rich poetic age: It saw the first major English poet, Chaucer, as well as such poetry as *The Pearl, The Vision of Piers Plowman*, and Gower's *Confessio Amantis*. There was a revival of ALLITERATIVE VERSE, although the accentual-syllabic meters eventually prevailed. The fifteenth century was a weak poetic age; its poetry consisted chiefly of Chaucerian imitations, and only Hoccleve, Skelton, and James I of Scotland gave it any distinction. With the establishment of the Tudor dynasty in 1485, however, England once more had internal peace, possessed a language close to Modern English, and had a powerful dramatic tradition. The glories of the Renaissance were just over the horizon. See MIDDLE ENGLISH PERIOD in *Outline of Literary History*.

[References: George Kane, *Middle English Literature* (1951); W. L. Renwick and H. Orton, *The Beginnings of English Literature to Skelton*, 3rd ed. (1966); David M. Zesmer, *Guide to English Literature from Beowulf through Chaucer and Medieval Drama* (1961).]

Midrash Hebrew, "explanation." Rabbinical notes and commentaries on the Scriptures, composed between 800 and 2,500 years ago.

Miles Gloriosus The braggart soldier, a STOCK CHARACTER in COMEDY. The type appeared in Greek comedy as the ALAZON, was stressed by the Roman playwrights (Terence's Thraso in *Eunuchus* and Plautus's *Miles Glorious*), and adopted by RENAISSANCE dramatists. An early example is Ralph Roister Doister. Examples in Elizabethan drama are Captain Bobadil in Jonson's *Every Man in His Humour*, Quintiliano in Chapman's *May Day*, and Shakespeare's Sir John Falstaff (*King Henry the Fourth*, Parts I and II), Don Adriano de Armado (*Love's Labour's Lost*), Parolles (*All's Well*), and Ancient Pistol (*King Henry the Fifth*). Although the treatments differ in different examples, the *miles gloriosus* is likely to be cowardly, parasitical, bragging, and subject to victimization by practical jokers. The aptly named Miles Standish is something of a *miles gloriosus* in Longfellow's *Courtship* poem. Saint Joan in Shaw's play is a combination of two virtually antithetical and mutually exclusive types: *miles gloriosus* (she is a soldier and she even cusses, though unwittingly) and *ingenue* (she is a virgin and dies while still a teenager); she is also a bumpkin, a visionary, and a proper saint. George C. Scott's film portrayal of *Patton* was a lively study of the contradictions and complexities of a modern *miles gloriosus*. The figure is familiar nowadays in almost any book about war, such as Joseph Heller's *Catch-22;* in cartoons such as Major Hoople ("Our Boarding House") and "Beetle Bailey"; and in television characters such as Jackie Gleason's "Ralph Kramden" (who wears a uniform) and Dan Rowan's "Bull Wright."

Milieu The general environment in which a work is produced. Much literary history and criticism in the nineteenth and early twentieth centuries made the *milieu* a major factor. Hippolyte Taine's influential *Histoire de la litterature anglaise* (1864), for example, made race, momentum, and *milieu* the essentials to literary interpretation.

Miltonic Sonnet A variation made by Milton on the ITALIAN SONNET, in which the rhyme scheme is kept but the "turn" between the octave and the sestet is eliminated.

Mime A form of popular comedy developed by the ancients (fifth century B.C. in southern Italy), with dancing, imitative gestures, and witty dialogue. It finally degenerated into sensual displays, and the performers sank to a low social level. The Christian church disapproved, and the performances were largely driven from the public stage. They were kept alive, however, by wandering entertainers. In England, the exhibitions seem to have consisted generally of low forms of buffoonery. The *mime* aided in preserving the comic spirit in drama, its influence possibly being apparent in the medieval MYSTERY PLAY and the Renaissance INTERLUDE—perhaps also the Renaissance "DUMB SHOW" and through it the modern PANTOMIME. Many elements of VAUDEVILLE are in direct line of descent from the *mime*. The *mime* is not regarded as a true link between ancient classical drama and modern drama, except as it aided in keeping alive the acting profession in the Middle Ages. Samuel Beckett's *Act Without Words* is a modern counterpart of the *mime* play.

Mimesis The Greek for IMITATION, often used specifically to indicate Aristotle's theory of imitation. *Mimesis* in a narrower sense has been used by Northrop Frye to designate works that imitate characters on a human level (as distinct from the superhuman levels of myth and romance as well as the subhuman level of irony).

[References: Erich Auerbach, *Mimesis: The Representation of Reality in Western Literature* (tr. 1953); Northrop Frye, *Anatomy of Criticism* (1957).]

Mimetic Theory of Art A theory emphasizing the actuality imitated in the artwork. See CRITICISM.

Minimalism A modern movement in politics, economics, and all the arts, especially noticeable in architecture (Mies van der Rohe: "Less is more") and music (for example, the works of Anton Webern). In literature, one can see *minimalist* tendencies in Samuel Beckett's late works: brevity, economy, modesty. Among poets, Robert Creeley and A. R. Ammons have been called *minimalists*.

Minnesinger "Singer of love," a medieval German lyric poet whose art was perhaps inspired by that of the TROUBADOUR. Though the German poets reflect the system known as COURTLY LOVE, their poetry in general is more elevated than that of the troubadours. They flourished in the twelfth and thirteenth centuries. Walther von der Vogelweide is regarded as the greatest of them.

Minor Plot A subordinate action of complication running through a work of fiction or drama. See SUBPLOT.

Minstrel A musical entertainer or traveling poet of the later Middle Ages who carried on the tradition of the earlier GLEEMAN and JONGLEUR. *Minstrels* flourished especially in the late thirteenth and the fourteenth centuries. The typical *minstrel* was a gifted wandering entertainer, skilled with the harp and tabor, singing songs, reciting romances, and carrying news from place to place. Love lyrics, ballads, legends, and romances were so composed and disseminated. The *minstrels* were at once the actors, journalists, poets, and orchestras of their time. The *Lay of Havelok the Dane* is a good example of the "minstrel ROMANCE." Flourishing in Chaucer's day, minstrelsy declined in the fifteenth century and died out after the introduction of printing. In their enthusiasm for untutored genius and for medievalism in general, the poets and novelists of the Romantic Period, such as Beattie and Scott, imparted an idealized meaning to *minstrel*, as they did to BARD.

Minstrel Show A form of VAUDEVILLE very popular in America in the last half of the nineteenth century and the early years of the twentieth. In the *minstrel show* white men with blackened faces—"in blackface"—impersonated stereotypical characters in song and dance routines and in exchanges between a white "straight man" (compare with the satiric ADVERSARIUS) and the blackface characters, who usually won in the battle of wits. The straight man was called "Mr. Interlocutor"; he exchanged repartee with the "end men," "Mr. Tambo," who played a tambourine, and "Mr. Bones," who played bone castanets. The blackface *minstrel show* had its beginning in 1830 when T. D. Rice began to "dance Jim Crow." Christy's Minstrels, which began in 1842 and later featured songs by Stephen Foster, developed the form of the *minstrel show*, which became immensely popular. In John Berryman's *The Dream Songs* there is a character named Mr. Bones, who is partly a *minstrel-show* figure and partly the central character's skeleton.

Minuscule Old typographical name for a small letter, especially lowercase.

Miracle Play Although this term is used by many authorities in a broad sense that includes the scriptural CYCLIC DRAMA (see MYSTERY PLAY), it is restricted by others to its early sense of a nonscriptural PLAY based on the legend of a saint or on a miracle performed by a saint or sacred object (such as the sacramental bread). However common *miracle plays* in this stricter sense may have been, very few have been preserved. It is known that a play of St. Catherine, probably in Latin or ANGLO-NORMAN, was performed at Dunstable about A.D. 1100. At this time *miracle plays* on St. Nicholas were being produced in France. A play called *Dux Moraud* (thirteenth or fourteenth century), in English, may have been a *miracle play* in which the Virgin Mary supplied the DEUS EX MACHINA. Other extant English plays that are either *miracle plays* or of very similar character are the *Play of the Sacrament* (late fifteenth century), the *Conversion of St. Paul*, and *Saint Mary Magdalene* (c. 1500). See MYSTERY PLAY.

Miscellany A group of diverse items. In literature a *miscellany* is a book that collects compositions by several authors, usually on a variety of topics. The first such *miscellany* in English was the collection of poems by Wyatt, Surrey, and others, published by Richard Tottel in 1557 as *Songs and Sonnets*, commonly known as *Tottel's*

Miscellany (see COURTLY MAKERS). Nearly twenty poetical *miscellanies* appeared within the next half-century, usually with highly figurative or alliterative titles and varying greatly in quality. Some are posthumous publications of COMMONPLACE BOOKS such as the *Paradise of Dainty Devices* of Richard Edwards (1576), a popular collection of serious poems. Some *miscellanies* have a specialized character, such as the *Handful of Pleasant Delights* (1584), a collection of BALLADS. Some of the later ones, such as *England's Parnassus* (1600), are collections not of complete poems but of poetical quotations. One, *The Passionate Pilgrim* (1599), was published as Shakespeare's and does contain some of Shakespeare's verse. Frequently, the *miscellany* was made up of poems selected from other *miscellanies* or from manuscript sources. Much of the verse is anonymous, some is falsely ascribed, and some indicates authorship by initials not now understandable. New poems were frequently printed along with old, and old ones sometimes appear in variant forms. The *miscellanies* reflect the great poetical activity of the time, particularly of the years preceding the appearance of Spenser, Sidney, and other major figures. They reflect, too, the metrical experiments of this earlier period. The poems in *A Gorgeous Gallery of Gallant Interventions* (1584), for example, make free use of ALLITERATION and varied metrical forms. Such poet-dramatists as Shakespeare borrowed lyrics from the earlier *miscellanies* and lived to see their own verse appear in the later. Aside from *Tottel's*, particularly important *miscellanies* are *The Phoenix Nest* (1593) and England's *Helicon* (1600).

The practice of publishing poetical *miscellanies* thus begun in the sixteenth century has continued to the present. Arthur E. Case's *Bibliography of English Poetical Miscellanies, 1521–1750* lists several hundred titles.

Mise en Abyme In heraldry the representation of a small shield on a big shield (escutcheon) is called *en abyme*. More generally, placement *en abyme* has to do with any occasion when a small text is imprinted on or contained in a bigger text that replicates. Fairly often, a film will contain another film, which serves as a commentary of sorts on the outer story. Emeric Pressburger's *The Red Shoes* (1948), for example, contains a performance of the ballet *The Red Shoes*. Nathanael West's *The Day of the Locust* includes *The Burning of Los Angeles*, a surrealist painting by the character Tod Hackett. At the end, the novel and painting seem to merge. As one critic has observed, not only does *Hamlet* contain a play-within-the-play, it contains a *Hamlet*-within-*Hamlet*. An inner text placed *en abyme* has a way of making the surrounding outer text seem relatively lifelike, especially if the artificiality of the inner text is emphasized (as is the case with the inner television news program *en abyme* on the outer Mary Tyler Moore television program, or the inner soap opera included in the outer text of *Twin Peaks*).

[Reference: Lucien Dällenbach, *Le Récit Speculaire: Essai sur la Mise en Abyme*, (1977, translated as *The Mirror in the Text*, 1989).]

Mise en Scène The stage setting of a play, including scenery, properties, and the general arrangement of the piece. Modern drama relies far more on *mise en scène* for its effects than did earlier drama. Indeed, the lack of scenery has been given as a partial explanation of the high literary quality of Elizabethan drama, the playwright being forced to rely on language for descriptive effects; whereas the increased dependence on scenery is said to be one of the reasons for the decreased attention to purely literary devices on the modern stage.

In film criticism *mise en scène* refers to the entire part of the filmmaking process that takes place on the set, as opposed to effects produced by other means, such as MONTAGE. It includes direction, actors, costumes, setting, lighting—everything that makes a scene.

Mishnah (also **Mishna**) The collection of legal principles and decisions that form the basis of the *Talmud*.

Misreading A reading—or reading in general—that makes a mistake in perception or interpretation. A man arrested for fishing in a forbidden place may plead that he understood the sign "FINE FOR FISHING" to mean that it was a fine place for fishing, not that one would be fined for fishing there. Since about 1970, Harold Bloom has been arguing that any reading must be imperfect and may be deliberately distorted, so that critics can productively study the dynamics of misprision, misconstruction, misinterpretation, and *misreading*. Bloom has been particularly interested in how later poets misread their precursors.

Mixed Figures The incongruous mingling of one FIGURE OF SPEECH with another immediately following. A notable example is the sentence of Castlereagh: "And now, sir, I must embark into the feature on which this question chiefly hinges." Here, obviously, the sentence begins with a nautical figure ("embark") but closes with a mechanical ("hinges"). The effect is grotesque. Lloyd George reportedly said, "I smell a rat. I see it floating in the air. I shall nip it in the bud." Mixed imagery, however, is sometimes deliberately used by writers with great effectiveness when the differing figures contribute cumulatively to a single referent, which is increasingly illuminated as they pile up. It is important, however, that the cumulative effect of the various images not be one of bizarre incongruity. The line "Some heart once pregnant with celestial fire" (Gray's "Elegy Written in a Country Churchyard") mixes the METONYMY of "heart" with three metaphors ("pregnant," "celestial," "fire") in such a way that some readers may be confused.

Mock Drama A term applied to plays whose purpose is to ridicule the theater of their time. Henry Fielding's *The Tragedy of Tragedies; or, The Life and Death of Tom Thumb the Great* (1731) held up to boisterous ridicule the conventions of the HEROIC DRAMA, as the Duke of Buckingham's *The Rehearsal* (1671) had done sixty years earlier. Oscar Wilde, in *The Importance of Being Earnest* (1895), produced a parody of the WELL-MADE PLAY and the sentimental comedy popular in his time and mocked, as well, his fellow playwrights for their failure to acknowledge the hypocrisy and self-deception of their age. There is an element of *mock drama* in many of the plays of Harold Pinter, Tom Stoppard, and David Mamet.

Mock Epic (or **Mock Heroic**) Terms for a literary form that burlesques the epic by treating a trivial subject in the "grand style" or uses the epic formulas to make a trivial subject ridiculous by ludricrously overstating it. Usually, the characteristics of the classical epic are employed, particularly the INVOCATION to a deity; the formal statement of theme; the division into books and cantos; the grandiose speeches (challenges, defiances, boastings) of the heroes; descriptions of warriors (especially their dress and equipment), battles, and games; the use of the HOMERIC SIMILE; and the involvement of supernatural machinery (gods directing or participating in the action). When the mock poem is much shorter than a true epic, some prefer to call it *mock heroic*, a term also applied to poems that mock romances rather than epics. In ordinary usage, however, the terms are interchangeable. Chaucer's *Nun's Priest's Tale* is partly *mock heroic* in character, as is Spenser's finely wrought *Muiopotmos*, "The Fate of the Butterfly," which imitates the opening of the *Aeneid* and employs elevated style for trivial subject matter. Swift's *Battle of the Books* is an example of a satirical *mock epic* in prose. Pope's *The Rape of the Lock* is perhaps the finest *mock heroic* poem in English, satirizing in polished verse the trivialities of polite society. The cutting of a lady's lock by a gallant is the central act of heroic behavior, a card game is described in military terms, and such airy spirits as the sylphs hover over the scene to aid their favorite heroine. A brilliantly executed *mock epic* has a manifold effect: to ridicule trivial or silly conduct; to mock the pretensions and absurdities of epic proper; to bestow an affectionate measure of elevation on low or foolish characters; and to bestow a humanizing, deflating, or debunking measure of lowering on elevated characters.

Mockumentary A mock documentary, in which a work of fiction borrows the techniques of DOCUMENTARY. The best known writer of such projects has been Christopher Guest, who sometimes also directs and appears in the picture. His projects include *This Is Spinal Tap* (1984), *Best in Show* (2000), and *A Mighty Wind* (2003).

Mode A term for broad categories of treatment of material, such as romance, comedy, tragedy, or satire. In this usage *mode* is broader than GENRE. Northrop Frye sees ROMANCE, COMEDY, TRAGEDY, and IRONY as *modes* of increasing complexity.

Model A earlier work that serves as a verbal SOURCE without necessarily providing any deeper thematic resonances. According to Grover Smith, for example, the second part of Eliot's *The Waste Land* ("The Chair she sat in, like a burnished throne . . .") owes a double debt to Shakespeare: to *Antony and Cleopatra*, which is the verbal *model* and, more significantly, to many passages in the second act of *Cymbeline*, which is a SOURCE.

[Reference: Grover Smith, *The Waste Land* (1983).]

Modern For much of its history, "*modern*" has meant something bad. In a general sense it means having to do with recent times and the present day, but we shall deal with it here in a narrow sense more or less synonymous with that of "modernist." It is not so much a chronological designation as one suggestive of a loosely defined congeries of characteristics. Much twentieth-century literature is not "*modern*" in the common sense, as much that is contemporary is not. *Modern* refers to a group of characteristics, and not all of them appear in any one writer who merits the designation *modern*.

In a broad sense *modern* is applied to writing marked by a strong and conscious break with tradition. It employs a distinctive kind of imagination that insists on having its general frame of reference within itself. It thus practices the solipsism of which Allen Tate accused the modern mind: It believes that we create the world in the act of perceiving it. *Modern* implies a historical discontinuity, a sense of alienation, loss, and despair. It rejects not only history but also the society of whose fabrication history is a record. It rejects traditional values and assumptions, and it rejects equally the rhetoric by which they were sanctioned and communicated. It elevates the individual and the inward over the social and the outward, and it prefers the unconscious to the self-conscious. The psychologies of Freud and Jung have been seminal in the *modern* movement in literature. In many respects it is a reaction against REALISM and NATURALISM and the scientific postulates on which they rest. Although by no means can all *modern* writers be termed philosophical existentialists, EXISTENTIALISM has created a schema within which much of the *modern* temper can see a reflection of its attitudes and assumptions. The *modern* revels in a dense and often unordered actuality as opposed to the practical and systematic, and in exploring that actuality as it exists in the mind of the writer it has been richly experimental. What has been distinctively worthwhile in the literature of this century has come, in considerable part, from this *modern* temper.

[References: Carlos Baker, *The Echoing Green: Romanticism, Modernism, and the Phenomena of Transference in Poetry* (1984); Carol T. Christ, *Victorian and Modern Poetics* (1984); Peter Faulkner, *Modernism* (1977); Irving Howe, ed., *The Idea of the Modern in Literature and the Arts* (1967); Monroe K. Spears, *Dionysus and the City: Modernism in Twentieth-Century Poetry* (1970).]

Modernist Period in English Literature The *Modernist Period* in England may be considered to begin with the First World War in 1914, to be marked by the strenuousness of that experience and by the flowering of talent and experiment that came during the boom of the twenties and that fell away during the ordeal of the economic depression in the thirties. The catastrophic years of the Second World War, which made England an embattled fortress, profoundly and negatively marked everything British, and it was followed by a period of uncertainty, a sadly diminished age. By 1965, which to all purposes marked an end to the *Modernist Period*, the uncertainty was giving way to anger and protest.

In the early years of the *Modernist Period*, the novelists of the EDWARDIAN AGE continued as major figures, with Galsworthy, Wells, Bennett, Forster, and Conrad dominating the scene, joined before the 'teens were over by Ford Madox Ford and Somerset Maugham. A new fiction, centered in the experimental examination of the inner self, was coming into being in the works of such writers as Dorothy Richardson and Virginia Woolf. It reached its peak in the publication in 1922 of James Joyce's *Ulysses*, a book perhaps as influential as any prose work by a British writer in the past century. In highly differing ways D. H. Lawrence, Aldous Huxley, and Evelyn Waugh protested against the nature of modern society; and the maliciously witty novel, as Huxley and Waugh wrote it in the twenties and thirties, was typical of the attitude of the age and is probably as truly representative of the English novel in the contemporary period as is the NOVEL exploring the private self through the STREAM OF CONSCIOUSNESS. In the thirties and forties, Joyce Cary and Graham Greene produced a more traditional FICTION of great effectiveness. Throughout the period English writers have practiced the short story with distinction; notable examples being Katherine Mansfield and Somerset Maugham, working in the tradition of Chekhov.

The theater saw the social plays of Galsworthy, Jones, and Pinero, the play of ideas of Shaw, and the COMEDY OF MANNERS of Maugham—all well-established in the EDWARDIAN AGE—continue and be joined by Noël Coward's comedy, the proletarian drama of Sean O'Casey, the serious verse plays of T. S. Eliot and Christopher Fry, and the high artistry of Terence Rattigan.

Perhaps the greatest changes in literature, however, came in poetry and criticism. In 1914 Bridges was POET LAUREATE; he was succeeded in 1930 by John Masefield, who died in 1967. Wilfred Owen was a powerful poetic voice, but his career ended with an untimely death in the First World War. Through the period Yeats continued poetic creation, steadily modifying his style and subjects to his late form. At the time of his death in 1939 he probably shared with T. S. Eliot the distinction of being the most influential poet in the British Isles. Yet Eliot's *The Waste Land*, although its author was American, was the most important single poetic publication in England in the period. (One striking feature of *The Waste Land* is its specificity as to geography in the "City" part of London, along with its global scope, which includes even Australia and the South Pole while omitting—as if deliberately—virtually any reference to the United States.) In the work of Yeats and Eliot, of W. H. Auden, Edith Sitwell, and Gerard Manley Hopkins (whose poems were posthumously published in 1918) a new poetry emphatically emerged. The death at thirty-nine of Dylan Thomas in 1953 silenced a powerful lyric voice that had already produced fine poetry and gave promise of doing even finer work. T. S. Eliot and I. A. Richards, along with T. E. Hulme, Wyndham Lewis, Herbert Read, R. G. Collingwood, F. R. Leavis, Cyril Connolly, William Empson, and others created an informed, essentially anti-Romantic ANALYTICAL CRITICISM, concentrating on the work of art itself.

Between 1914 and 1965, modernism gained a powerful ascendancy, and, disparate as many of the writers and movements of the period were, they seem, in hindsight, to have shared most of the fundamental assumptions embraced in the term MODERN. But, however much the literary movement in the *Modernist Period* seems to enjoy unified history, Great Britain was in the process of national and cultural diminution, for England in the twentieth century has watched her political and military supremacy gradually dissipate, and since the Second World War she has found herself somewhat reduced in the international scene and torn by internal economic and political troubles. Her writers during these turbulent and unhappy years turned inward for their subject matter and expressed bitter and often despairing cynicism. Her major literary figures in the *Modernist Period*, as they were in the Edwardian Age, were often non-English. Her chief poets were Irish, American, and Welsh; her most influential novelists, Polish and Irish; her principal dramatists, Irish and American. See *Outline of Literary History*.

Modulation In music a change in key in or between passages. In poetry a variation in the metrical pattern by the substitution of a foot that differs from the basic rhythm of the poem or by the addition or deletion of unstressed syllables. Hardy's "The Voice" may be said to modulate from a largely dactylic rhythm in its first three stanzas to a largely trochaic rhythm in the fourth. Gerard Manley Hopkins's "Inversnaid" modulates from SPONDEES to ANAPESTS.

Monodrama The term *monodrama* is used in three senses, all related to its basic meaning of a dramatic situation in which a single person speaks. At its simplest level a *monodrama* is a DRAMATIC MONOLOGUE. It is more often applied to a series of extended dramatic monologues in various meters and stanzas that tell a connected story. The standard example is Tennyson's *Maud*, which the poet called a *monodrama*. The term is also applied to theatrical presentations that feature only one actor.

Monody A DIRGE or LAMENT in which a single mourner expresses grief, for example, Arnold's *Thyrsis, A Monody*. See DIRGE, ELEGY, THRENODY.

Monoglot Using only one language.

Monograph A rather indefinite term for a piece of scholarly writing, usually on a relatively limited topic. *Monographs* may be published as separate volumes, alone, or as part of a series, but their size normally falls between that of an article and that of a full-length book.

Monolingual Same as MONOGLOT. In 1999, Jacques Derrida published a book called *Monolingualism of the Other; or, The Prosthesis of Origin*.

Monologism Mikhail Bakhtin's term for the tendency of some works (Tolstoi's more than Dostoevski's, for example) to be the utterance of a single, consistent voice, with no interruption or dialogic play.

Monologue A composition giving the discourse of one speaker. By convention, a *monologue* represents what someone would speak aloud in a situation with listeners, although they do not speak; the *monologue* therefore differs somewhat from the SOLILOQUY, which represents what someone is thinking inwardly, without listeners. See DRAMATIC MONOLOGUE, INTERIOR MONOLOGUE, MONODRAMA.

Monometer A line of verse consisting of one FOOT.

Monorhyme A poem that uses only one rhyme. Even short examples are uncommon: Browning's "Home-Thoughts, from the Sea" is seven lines, Frost's "The Hardship of Accounting" five. Longer examples are rarer yet: Browning's "Through the Metidja to Abd-el-Kadr" is a forty-line poem on one rhyme sound, but, because of a recurring refrain, there are only twenty-six different rhyme words; C. Day Lewis's "A Rune for Anthony John" is an eighteen-line *monorhyme*; Hardy's "The Respectable Burgher," thirty-five lines on one rhyme sound with thirty-five different rhyme words, seems to have established a record, at least among poems with any claim to seriousness. Gavin Ewart's "The Owl Writes a Detective Story," forty-one lines long, has the same rhyme throughout, but the poem repeats a few rhyming words, so that Hardy's record stands.

Monosemy The state of having only one meaning; opposite of POLYSEMY.

Monostich A poem consisting of one line. A recent instance is A. R. Ammons's "Coward."

Monostrophic A term used by Milton for the form of the choruses in *Samson Agonistes*. These choruses are continuous, each consisting of a single sustained STROPHE not subdivided into such quantitative parts as the traditional strophe, antistrophe, and epode.

Montage French for "mounting" or "editing." The director Sergei Eisenstein believed that by juxtaposing contrasting shots properly one can create a meaning different from that actually recorded in any of the shots, and he developed a method of rhythmic pacing of shots. In American filmmaking *montage*, sometimes called "dynamic cutting," refers to the deliberate and stylized rapid transition from shot to shot to produce a particular effect.

In twentieth-century experimental fiction a similar device, borrowed from film, is used to establish a scene or an atmosphere by a series of brief pictures or impressions following one another quickly without apparent order. The "Newsreels" in Dos

Passos's *U.S.A.* and the "choruses" in Mailer's *The Naked and the Dead* are examples of *montages*. The device is sometimes used in the INTERIOR MONOLOGUE.

Mood In a literary work the *mood* is the emotional-intellectual attitude of the author toward the subject. A group of poems about death may range from a *mood* of noble defiance in Donne's "Death, Be Not Proud," to pathos in Frost's "Out, Out—," to irony in Housman's "To an Athlete Dying Young," to morbidly joyous acceptance in Whitman's "When Lilacs Last in the Dooryard Bloom'd."

If a distinction exists between *mood* and TONE, it will be the fairly subtle one between mood as the attitude of the author toward the subject and tone as the attitude of the author toward the audience. In cases in which the writer uses ostensible "authors" within the work, *mood* and tone can be quite distinct, as in Irving's use of Diedrich Knickerbocker. Byron, in canto III of *Don Juan*, has "a poet" (presumably Southey) write a poem beginning "The isles of Greece, the isles of Greece!" which seems solemn, brave, and freedom-loving in *mood*; yet the tone of Byron (not the *mood* of the imaginary "poet") is mocking and satiric.

Mora, Morae Terms used to designate duration in QUANTITATIVE VERSE, the *mora* being the duration of a short syllable and the *morae* being that of a long syllable.

Moral Criticism Criticism that judges art according to ethical principles. See CRITICISM, TYPES OF.

Morality (or **Morality Play**) A kind of poetic drama that developed in the late fourteenth century, distinguished from the religious drama proper, such as the MYSTERY PLAY, by being a dramatized ALLEGORY in which abstractions (such as Mercy, Conscience, Perseverance, and Shame) appear in personified form and struggle for a human soul. The central figure may represent humanity in general, as in *Everyman* (c. 1500). The limited-scope *morality* deals with a single problem applicable to a certain person. Thus, Skelton's *Magnificence*, possibly written as advice to Henry VII, concerns the dangers of uncontrolled expenditures. *Morality plays* can be classified as religious (*Everyman*), doctrinal (John Bale's *King Johan*), didactic-pedagogical (*Wyt and Science*), or political (*Magnificence*). By the sixteenth century some of the *morality plays* had admitted so much realistic and farcical material that they began to establish a tradition of English comedy and contributed much to the INTERLUDE. Such comic figures as the VICE and the Devil were especially well-developed and influenced later comedy. Though morality themes were widely employed in the drama of the sixteenth century, the *morality play*s as such lost their popularity in Elizabethan times.

Morpheme A minimal meaningful linguistic unit. The word *dismemberings*, for example, contains four *morphemes: dis, member, ing*, and *s* (variously understood as base forms, affixes, and inflections.).

Morphology A word coined by Goethe for the study of forms at any level. Brooks Adams and Leo Frobenius studied culture-morphology (*Kulturmorphologie*); Vladimir Propp wrote a book called *Morphology of the Folktale*. Linguistic *morphology* is the study of MORPHEMES.

Mosaic Another name for HETEROMEROUS RHYME. *Mosaic* is also applied to compositions consisting of quotations from one or more authors. See CENTO.

Mot French for "word." Sometimes *bon mot*, "good word." A brief, apt saying.

Motif (or **Motive**) A simple element that serves as a basis for expanded narrative; or, less strictly, a conventional situation, device, interest, or incident. The carrying off of a mortal queen by a fairy lover is a *motif* around which full stories were built in MEDIEVAL ROMANCE. In the BALLAD called *The Elfin Knight*, the "fairy music" *motif* appears when the sound of the knight's horn causes the maiden to fall in love with the unseen hero. In music and art the term is used in various other senses, as for a recurring melodic phrase, a prevailing idea or design, or a subject for detailed sculptural treatment. In literature, recurrent images, words, objects, phrases, or actions that tend to unify the work are called *motives*. Nabokov's *Lolita*, for example, is saturated by a light-dark *motif* that is found in the names of the protagonist and antagonist (Humbert Humbert and Clare Quilty); patterns of day and night, blonde and brunette, summer and winter, north and south, white and black; and the game of chess. See LEITMOTIF.

Motivation The reasons, justifications, and explanations for the action of a character. *Motivation* results from a combination of the character's moral nature with the circumstances in which the character is placed. *Motivation* helps to determine what the character does, says, and feels or fails to feel. When *motivation* is persuasively presented, one accepts the action as convincing; when the *motivation* is inadequate, the action may seem arbitrary, facile, or contrived.

Mot juste French for "apt or proper word." A notion associated with Gustave Flaubert's principle of realistic prose employing lucid, correct words and not some platitude or approximation.

Motto A short expression, sometimes only a word or two, often in a foreign language, expressing the ideal spirit of a person, family, company, or nation. *Motto* is also used for EPIGRAPH.

Motto Theme Originally a musical term for a theme that recurs, sometimes transformed, throughout a composition, as in Beethoven's Fifth Symphony, Tchaikovsky's Fourth and Fifth Symphonies, and Elgar's First Symphony; akin to Wagner's LEITMOTIV, Berlioz's *idée fixe*, and Liszt's "metamorphosis of themes."

Movement The term for new development or direction in literary activity or interest, as the OXFORD MOVEMENT, the FREE-VERSE movement. Occasionally, in a work with a title drawn from music, such as T. S. Eliot's *Four Quartets*, the sections are called *movements*.

Movement, The A rather short-lived focus of British literary activity in the mid-1950s, expressed mostly in poetry and prose fiction, with emphases on normality, regularity, practicality, stoicism, traditionalism, and solid middle-class virtues rather than flamboyant heroics in substance or style. The vague label was first applied by J. D. Scott in 1954 to a group of younger writers just then emerging into prominence: Kingsley

Amis in fiction, light verse, and criticism; Philip Larkin in poetry; John Wain in a few poems and many novels; and Donald Davie in criticism and poetry.

Muckrakers A group of American writers who between 1902 and 1911 worked to expose the dishonest methods and unscrupulous motives in big business and in city, state, and national government. A group of magazines—*The Arena, Everybody's, McClure's*, the *Independent, Collier's*, and the *Cosmopolitan*—led the movement, publishing the writings of the leading *muckrakers*—Ida Tarbell, Lincoln Steffens, T. W. Lawson, Mark Sullivan, and Samuel H. Adams. Upton Sinclair's novel *The Jungle* and some of the novels of Winston Churchill and D. G. Phillips are *muckraking* books. The term, which comes from a character in Bunyan's *Pilgrim's Progress* who is so busy raking up muck that he does not see a celestial crown held over him, was applied derogatorily to this group by Theodore Roosevelt. The more substantial work of these journalists, along with a spirit of reform in the atmosphere of their age, led to many practical improvements in life, such as the Pure Food and Drug legislation of 1905.

Mummerset (also **Mummersetshire**) An imaginary rustic county in the West of England, and its dialect, invented by actors. The name seems to combine the sounds and associations of "Somerset" and MUMMER.

Mummery A simple dramatic performance usually presented by players masked or disguised. A farcical presentation; a sort of PANTOMIME. See MASQUE.

Mummings Masked folk processions, dancing, and plays. See MASQUE.

Muses Nine goddesses represented as presiding over the various departments of art and science. They are the daughters of Zeus and Mnemosyne (memory). In literature, their traditional significance is that of inspiring and helping poets. The conventional names and areas of interest are: Calliope (epic), Clio (history), Erato (lyrics and love poetry), Euterpe (music), Melpomene (tragedy), Polyhymnia (sacred choric poetry), Terpischore (choral dance and song), Thalia (comedy), and Urania (astronomy).

Musical Comedy A combination of music with comic drama. Though much use is made of music, both vocal and orchestral, the dialogue is spoken, not sung. Satirical kidding of current figures and interests is frequent. The comic effects are sometimes farcical. Closely related, especially in its earlier forms, to BURLESQUE and VAUDEVILLE, *musical comedy* developed in the early twentieth century into one of the most popular of all dramatic forms. Its heyday was between 1920 and 1950. Some, such as *Oklahoma!* and *South Pacific*, were more than simple comedies with music, and later, when Stephen Sondheim flourished, the form took on quite a serious coloration. Kurt Weill and Bertolt Brecht collaborated in the 1920s and 1930s on works—most brilliantly in *The Threepenny Opera*—that converted the musical theater into a telling instrument of satire and propaganda.

Mystery Play A medieval play based on biblical history; a scriptural play. *Mystery plays* originated in the liturgy of the church and developed from LITURGICAL DRAMAS into the great CYCLIC PLAYS, performed outdoors and eventually on movable pageants. They were the most important forms of the MEDIEVAL DRAMA of Western Europe and flourished in England from the late Middle Ages until well into the Renaissance. They seem to have developed around three nuclei, which presented the whole scheme of salvation: (1) Old Testament plays dealing with such events as the Creation, the fall of Adam and Eve, the death of Abel, and the sacrifice of Isaac, and the Prophet plays, which prepared for (2) the New Testament plays dealing with the birth of Christ—the Annunciation, the birth, the visit of the wise men, the shepherds, and the visit to the temple; and (3) the Death and Resurrection plays—entry into Jerusalem, the betrayal of Judas, trial and crucifixion, lamentation of Mary, sepulchre scenes, the resurrection, appearances to disciples, Pentecost, and sometimes the Day of Judgment. *Mystery plays* were often known as CORPUS CHRISTI PLAYS because of the habit of performing the plays on PAGEANTS connected with the Corpus Christi processional. The great cycles whose texts have been preserved are the York, Chester, Coventry, and Wakefield (or "Towneley"). They differ in length and in the list of plays or scenes included as well as in literary and dramatic value, the Towneley plays being especially important in dramatic development.

After the PLAYS became secularized, they were performed by trade guilds, sometimes on fixed stages or stations (the crowds moving from station to station), sometimes on movable pageants.

The word *mystery* was first applied to these plays in the eighteenth century, on the analogy of the French *mystère*, a scriptural play; medieval writers were more likely to refer to the plays as Corpus Christi plays, "Whitsuntide plays," and "pageants," and possibly as MIRACLE PLAYS, the term preferred by many modern authorities. It has been conjectured that *mystery* is related not only to Latin *mysterium* ("secret rite") but also to *ministerium* ("work," "occupation"), the latter sense pertaining to the guilds that were involved in the staging of the plays, so that *mystery play* may basically mean "guild play." (It is thought that the Latin *ministerium* in Vulgar Latin or Late Latin became shortened to *misterium*, which was confused or at least associated with *mysterium; misterium* eventually yielded the French *métier*, "trade or occupation.")

Mystery Story (or **Novel**) A term used to designate a work in which mystery or terror plays a controlling part. It is applied to such various types of fiction as the DETECTIVE STORY, the GOTHIC NOVEL, the story of strange or frightening adventure, the suspense novel, the tale of espionage, and the tale of crime; often called just *mysteries*.

Mysticism The theory that a knowledge of God or immediate reality is attainable by a human faculty that transcends intellect and logic. W. T. Stace finds in all mystical experiences five common characteristics: (1) a sense of objectivity or reality, (2) a sense of peace or blessedness, (3) a feeling of holiness, sacredness, or divinity, (4) a paradoxical quality, and (5) an ineffabiltity. There are two broad types of *mysticism:* in one, God is seen as transcendent, outside the human soul, and union with Him is achieved through a series of steps or stages; in the other, God is immanent, dwelling within the soul and to be discovered by penetrating deeper into the inner self. The terminology of *mysticism*, because it is forced to be figurative, is often obscure. A conventional statement of the Christian mystic's progress on the path to God is as follows: The soul undergoes a purification (the purgative way), which leads to a sense of illumination in the love of God (the illuminative way), and after a period the soul enters into a union with God (the unitive way), and progresses into a final ecstatic state of perfect knowledge of God (the spiritual marriage), during some period of which there comes a time of alienation and loss in which the soul cannot find God at all (the soul's dark night).

Aspects of *mysticism* and the mystical experience are common in literature, although to call any single writer—with a few exceptions such as Richard Rolle of Hampole and William Blake—a mystic is to invite a challenge. Clearly, however, there are mystical elements in the work of Crashaw, George Herbert, Bunyan, Cowper, Wordsworth, Coleridge, Shelley, Carlyle, the New England transcendentalists, Whitman, I. B. Singer, and T. S. Eliot. To survey the works of so heterodox a group of writers is to realize that *mysticism* refers to a wide spectrum of experience and is a means of perceiving reality or absolute truth in many different forms and in many different patterns of religious belief. During the first half of the twentieth century, prevailing critical sentiments favored clarity and precision, and numerous influential writers—including Irving Babbitt, T. E. Hulme, Wyndham Lewis, and Ezra Pound—expressed doubt or suspicion when it came to the claims of *mysticism*. But there has been something of a reaction, and many of the most important critics—including Northrop Frye, Harold Bloom, Mircea Eliade, and Helen Vendler—have found ways of judging and appreciating the mystical dimensions in Blake, Emerson, Whitman, D. H. Lawrence, and Eliot.

Myth An anonymous story that presents supernatural episodes as a means of interpreting natural events. *Myth* makes concrete and particular a special perception of human beings or a cosmic view. *Myth* is the absence of anomaly—at least from one perspective. From another, staked out by Émile Durkheim's school of sociology, *myth* represents a projection of social patterns upward onto a superhuman level that sanctions and stabilizes the secular ideology. *Myths* differ from legends by comprising less of historical background and more of the supernatural; they differ from the fable in that they are less concerned with moral didacticism and are the product of a racial group rather than the creation of an individual. Every literature has its mythology, the most familiar to English readers being the Greek, Roman, and Norse. But the mythology of all groups takes shape around certain common themes: They all attempt to explain creation, divinity, and religion; to probe the meaning of existence and death; to account for natural phenomena; and to chronicle the adventures of cultural heroes. They also have a startlingly similar group of motifs, characters, and actions, as a number of students of *myth* and religion, particularly Sir James Frazer, Georges Dumézil, Claude Lévi-Strauss, and Joseph Campbell, have pointed out. Although there was a time when *myth* was a virtual synonym for error, notably in the Neoclassic Period, the tendency today is to see *myths* as dramatic or narrative embodiments of a people's perception of the deepest truths. Various modern writers have insisted on the necessity of *myth* as a material with which the artist works, and in varying ways and degrees have appropriated the old *myths* or created new ones as necessary substances to give order and a frame of meaning to their personal perceptions and images; notable among such "myth-makers" have been Blake, Thackeray, Shaw, Hart Crane, Gary Snyder, and Stephen King.

Since the introduction of Jung's concept of the "racial unconscious" (see ARCHETYPE) and of Ernst Cassirer's theories of language and *myth*, critics have found in *myth* a useful device for examining literature. There is a type of imagination, Philip Wheelwright argues, that can properly be called "the Archetypal Imagination, which sees the particular object as embodying and adumbrating suggestions of universality." The possessors of such imagination arrange their works in archetypal patterns and present us with narratives that stir us as "something at once familiar and strange." They thus give concrete expression to something deep and primitive in us all. Those critics—and they are many—who approach literature as *myth* see in it vestiges of primordial ritual and ceremony; the repository of racial memories; a structure of unconsciously held value systems; an expression of the general beliefs of a race, social class, or nation; or a unique embodiment of ideology. One significant difference should be noted, however; *myth* in its traditional sense is an anonymous, nonliterary, essentially religious formulation of the cosmic view of a people who approach its formulations not as representations of truth but as truth itself; *myth* in the sophisticated literary sense in which it is currently used is the intelligible and often self-conscious use of such primitive methods to express something deeply felt by the individual artist that will, it is hoped, prove to have universal responses. It has been suggested—by C. G. Jung among others—that sophisticated works of literary art, which may be shaped by a strong individual subjectivity, are of less use in the discovery of *myths* than rather vulgar, unsophisticated works such as popular novels and even comic strips. The mythopoeic writer attempts to return to the role of the prophet-seer, by creating a *myth* that strikes resonances in the minds of readers and speaks with something of the authority of the old *myths*.

[References: Albert Cook, *Myth and Language* (1980); Mircea Eliade, *Myth and Reality* (tr. 1963); Northrop Frye, *Anatomy of Criticism* (1957); William Righter, *Myth and Literature* (1975); K. K. Ruthven, *Myth* (1976).]

Mythical Method A phrase used in 1923 by T. S. Eliot to describe the structure of Joyce's *Ulysses*, which sustains a "continuous parallel" between the ten-year verse epic of Homer's *Odyssey* and a one-day prose narrative (with much technical innovation) of contemporaneity. A method already used by Yeats (as in "No Second Troy" and elsewhere) and Shaw (as in *Pygmalion*) in different moods and with different effects. Eliot likened Joyce's work to a scientific discovery, which others could take advantage of (as he himself had taken advantage of Joyce's methods as early as 1919, when he borrowed a passage from *Ulysses* before the novel appeared in book form).

Mythic Criticism Criticism that explores the nature and significance of the ARCHETYPES and archetypal patterns in a work of art. See MYTH; JUNGIAN CRITICISM; ARCHETYPE; CRITICISM, TYPES OF.

Mythopoeia Myth-making, construed as either an individual function of a single artist or a collective spirit.

Mythopoetics A term applied to criticism that places an emphasis on MYTH and ARCHETYPE.

Delphian Open Title 1930. Designed by R. H. Middleton.

Naïve and Sentimental A distinction laid out in the essay "On Naïve and Sentimental Poetry" (1795) by Johann Christoph Friedrich von Schiller (1759–1805), arguing that poets are either naïve (like Homer, Shakespeare, Cervantes, and Goethe: original, pure, authentic, directly in touch with nature) or sentimental (derivative, civilized, removed from nature). The opposition has persisted, turning up in John le Carré's novel *The Naïve and Sentimental Lover* (1971) and John Adams's *Naïve and Sentimental Music* (1997–98).

Naïve Narrator (or **Hero**) An ingenuous character who is the ostensible author (often the oral narrator) of a narrative, the implications of which are plainer to the reader than they are to the narrator. The *naïve narrator* can be a device for IRONY, either gentle or savage, or it can be a device for PATHOS, as it frequently is when a child narrates, with innocence, events with tragic or horrible implications. The *naïve narrator* is used a great deal by Sherwood Anderson in such short stories as "I'm a Fool" and "The Egg"; Swift employs the device in "A Modest Proposal" with savage effectiveness; Mark Twain's *Adventures of Huckleberry Finn* and Ring Lardner's "Haircut" are other well-known examples of the use of the *naïve narrator*. William Faulker made memorable use of various sorts of *naïve narrator* in *The Sound and the Fury* and *As I Lay Dying*. A similar approach can be seen in J. D. Salinger's *The Catcher in the Rye* and Ken Kesey's *One Flew Over the Cuckoo's Nest*. Ernest Hemingway used a *naïve narrator* for most of his earlier novels and stories.

Narration One of the four types of composition (see ARGUMENTATION, DESCRIPTION, and EXPOSITION); its purpose is to recount events. Although *narration* may exist by itself, it is likely to incorporate considerable description. There are two forms: *simple narrative*, which recites events chronologically, as in a newspaper account; and NARRATIVE with plot, which is less often chronological and more often arranged according to a principle determined by the nature of the plot and the type of story intended. It is conventionally said that *narration* deals with time, DESCRIPTION with space.

[References: Wayne Booth, *The Rhetoric of Fiction*, 2nd ed. (1983); E. M. Forster, *Aspects of the Novel* (1927); Robert Scholes and Robert Kellogg, *The Nature of Narrative* (1966); Meir Sternberg, *Expositional Modes and Temporal Ordering in Fiction* (1978).]

Narrative An account of events; anything that is narrated. See NARRATION.

Narrative Essay An INFORMAL ESSAY in narrative form. It differs from a SHORT STORY not only in its simpler structure but especially in its essay-like intent, the story being a means of developing an idea rather than an end in itself. Addison's *Vision of Mirzah* is an example. See ESSAY.

Narrative Hook Any device at the opening of a work to capture the interest of readers and make them continue reading. The *narrative hook* may be an exciting incident, an unusual statement, or a beginning IN MEDIAS RES.

Narrative Poem A poem that tells a story. EPICS, BALLADS, and METRICAL ROMANCES are among the many kinds of *narrative poems*.

Narratology The sophisticated analysis of the relations among a story—conceived in simple terms—and all the other elements involved in the telling thereof. Some narratological questions include the possibility of a "straight" or neutral quasi-historical telling; the presence and function of a NARRATOR with a PERSONA, voice, and style; the importance of verb tense and pronoun person in establishing the connections among story, teller, and audience; the different CODES and levels of discourse; the possible variations in amount of outward and inward knowledge involved in the act of NARRATION; and the relation between the real author, the IMPLIED AUTHOR, and the narrating voice or voices. *Narratology* has commanded the respect and attention of some of the acutest contemporary critics, including Paul Ricoeur and J. Hillis Miller.

[References: Frank Kermode, *The Art of Telling* (1983); Wallace Martin, *Recent Theories of Narrative* (1986); Gerald Prince, *Dictionary of Narratology* (1987).]

Narrator Anyone who recounts a NARRATIVE. In fiction the term is used for the ostensible author or teller of a STORY. In fiction presented in the first person, the "I" who tells the story is the *narrator*; the *narrator* may be in any of various relations to the events described, ranging from being their center (the PROTAGONIST) through various degrees of importance (minor characters) to being merely a witness. In fiction told from an OMNISCIENT POINT OF VIEW, the author acts self-consciously as *narrator*, recounting the story and freely commenting on it. A *narrator* is always present, at least by implication, in any work, even a story in which a SELF-EFFACING AUTHOR relates events with apparent objectivity. A *narrator* may be reliable or unreliable. If the *narrator* is reliable, the reader accepts without serious question the statements of fact and judgment. If the *narrator* is unreliable, the reader questions or seeks to qualify the statements of fact and judgment. See NAIVE NARRATOR, UNRELIABLE NARRATOR, POINT OF VIEW, PANORAMIC METHOD.

Native American Literature Literature by Native Americans is older than any other on the continent, including such anonymous tribal records as the *Walam Olum* of the Leni-Lenape. By the beginning of the twenty-first century, an impressive body of writing in all genres was being produced by such Native Americans as Sherman Alexie, Russell Means, John Rollin Ridge, Scott Momaday, Roberta Hill Whiteman, Leslie Marmon Silko, and Louise Erdrich.

[Reference: Andrew Wiget, *Native American Literature* (1985).]

Naturalism A term best reserved for a literary movement in the late nineteenth and early twentieth centuries.

In its simplest sense *naturalism* is the application of principles of scientific determinism to literature. It draws its name from its basic assumption that everything real exists in NATURE, conceived as the world of objects, actions, and forces that yield their secrets to objective scientific inquiry. The naturalistic view of human beings is that of animals in the natural world, responding to environmental forces and internal stresses and drives, none of which they can control or understand. It tends to differ from REALISM in the organization of materials, selecting not the commonplace but the representative and so arranging the work that its structure reveals the pattern of ideas—in this case, scientific theory—which forms the author's view of life.

Naturalism is a response to the revolution in thought that science has produced. From Newton it gains a sense of mechanistic determinism; from Darwin (the greatest single force operative on it) it gains a sense of biological determinism and the inclusive metaphor of competitive jungle that it has used perhaps more often than any other; from Marx it gains a view of history as a battleground of economic and social forces; from Freud it gains a view of the determinism of the inner and subconscious self. In the most influential statement ever made of the theory of *naturalism*, Émile Zola's *Le roman expérimental*, the ideal of the naturalist is stated as the selection of truthful instances subjected to laboratory conditions in a novel, where the hypotheses of the author about the nature and operation of the forces that work on human beings can be put to the test. Zola's term *expérimental*, usually translated "experimental," is better understood as "empirical" or "experiential."

Naturalism shapes the work of George Eliot and Thomas Hardy, but American novelists have been generally more receptive to its theories. Frank Norris (1870–1902) wrote naturalistic novels in conscious imitation of Zola and made an American critical defense of the school, *The Responsibilities of the Novelist*. Stephen Crane (1871–1900) used the devices of IMPRESSIONISM in producing naturalistic novels. Jack London (1876–1916) wrote naturalistic novels with Nietzchean supermen (and superdogs) as protagonists. But the greatest American naturalistic novelist—after Zola perhaps the greatest of all—was Theodore Dreiser (1871–1945), whose *An American Tragedy* is an archetypal example. In some of his plays, Eugene O'Neill employed *naturalism* with distinction. James T. Farrell, John O'Hara, and James Jones, among others, kept the school alive in America.

Naturalistic works tend to emphasize either a biological or a socioeconomic determinism. Occasionally, as in the works of Thomas Hardy, human beings are seen as the victims of destiny or fate. But, whichever view is taken, the naturalist strives to be objective in the presentation of material; amoral in the view of the struggle in which human animals find themselves, neither condemning nor praising human beings for actions beyond their control; pessimistic about human capabilities—life, the naturalists seem to feel, is a vicious trap; frank in the portrayal of human beings as animals driven by fundamental urges—fear, hunger, and sex.

[References: Donald Pizer, *Realism and Naturalism in Nineteenth-Century American Literature*, rev. ed. (1984; orig. 1976, 1966), and *Twentieth-Century Literary Naturalism* (1982); Émile Zola, *Le roman expérimental* (tr. 1964 as *The Naturalist Novel*, ed. Maxwell Geismar).]

Naturalistic and Symbolistic Period in American Literature The period between 1900 and 1930 in America is sharply divided by the First World War, the part before the war being dominated by NATURALISM, and the part after by a growing international awareness, a sensitivity to European literary models, and a steadily developing SYMBOLISM in literature. The first decade of the twentieth century saw the flourishing of the muckraking magazine exposé and the corresponding novel. During this decade Henry James carried American realism probably to its greatest height in *The Ambassadors, The Wings of the Dove*, and *The Golden Bowl*. Frank Norris, Theodore Dreiser, and Jack London were producing crude but powerful examples of the naturalistic novel, and Edwin Arlington Robinson had launched the career that was to flower into distinction and popularity.

The second decade saw the virtual birth of modern American poetry, with the founding of *Poetry* magazine in Chicago in 1912 by Harriet Monroe, the emergence of the IMAGISTS, and the beginning of the careers of Frost, Pound, Doolittle, Eliot, Stevens, and W. C. Williams. The realistic novel continued in the works of W. D. Howells, Willa Cather, and Edith Wharton. As the decade ended, the plays of Eugene O'Neill gave promise of a theatrical revival to match the growing LITTLE THEATER MOVEMENT. Prior to the twentieth century, American criticism had been sporadic and uncertain, but the work of W. C. Brownell, James Huneker, Joel Spingarn, and a group of young critics demanding a "usable past"—among them, Randolph Bourne and Van Wyck Brooks—joined with the developing artistic concern of the AVANT-GARDE groups and the LITTLE MAGAZINES to produce an increasingly sensitive body of critical work.

The First World War produced a major dislocation of a number of talented writers, most of them born between 1895 and 1902, who came early in contact with European culture and emerged from the war disillusioned with American idealism and crassness. This postwar generation, considering itself self-consciously as a "LOST GENERATION," set about a repudiation of American culture in three ways: One group, largely from the East, went back to Europe and there published little magazines, waited on Gertrude Stein, took part in DADAISM, and formulated a polished and *symbolistic* style—among them were F. Scott Fitzgerald, Ernest Hemingway, Edmund Wilson, E. E. Cummings, Malcolm Cowley, and Sherwood Anderson; another group, largely from the Middle West, came east and in Cambridge, New Haven, and Greenwich Village produced satire aimed at the standardized mediocrity of the American village—among them were Ring Lardner and Sinclair Lewis; and another group, largely Southern, repudiated the meaningless mechanism of capitalistic America by looking backward to a past that had tradition and order—these were the poets and critics who published *The Fugitive* in Nashville and were AGRARIANS, and others who contributed to such magazines as the *Double Dealer* in New Orleans. Out of this last group came the modern Southern novel and much of the NEW CRITICISM; the group included John Crowe Ransom, Allen Tate, Robert Penn Warren, Cleanth Brooks, and William Faulkner.

All of these groups—expatriates, revolters against the village, and seekers of a tradition of order—sought standards different from those of the traditional American writer, and they found them in the methods of the French symbolists, in the work of Joyce and Proust, in the complex intellectual poetry of the seventeenth-century Metaphysicals, and in the kind of experimentation that the little magazines fostered. By the end of the period a group of academic critics, the New Humanists, were formulating a doctrine of life and art that repudiated the contemporary artist, and in the late fall of 1929 the collapse of the stock market, signaling the beginning of the Great Depression, marked an effective end to a period in which most of the seeds of contemporary American writing had been sown. See *Outline of Literary History*.

Nature A. O. Lovejoy found as many as sixty different meanings for "*nature*" in its normative functions. Both neoclassicists and romanticists would "follow *Nature*"; but the former drew from the term ideas of order, regularity, and universality, both in external and in human *nature*, whereas the latter found in *nature* the justification for their enthusiasm for wildness in external *nature* and for individualism in human *nature*. Other contradictory senses may be noted: the term *nature* might mean, on the one hand, human *nature* (typical human behavior) or, on the other hand, whatever is antithetical to human *nature* and human works—what has not been spoiled by human beings. In certain formulaic sets of antitheses, *nature* is opposed to nurture or to culture.

The neoclassic view of *nature* led to reverence for rules based on proven models. Opposed to this was the romantic tendency to regard the primitive as "natural"—a conception that justified the disregard of rules and the exaltation of individual freedom. Among some neoclassic writers the words "reason" and "nature" were closely allied, because both were related to the idea of "order" (John Dennis said that *nature* was order in the visible world, whereas reason was order in the invisible realm). The distinction between *nature* and WIT (in one of its senses) was not always clear, because both provided tests of excellence, as indicated in Pope's *Essay on Criticism*:

True Wit is Nature to advantage dressed,
What oft was thought, but ne'er so well expressed.

Nature as "external nature"—such objects as mountains, trees, rivers, flowers, and birds—has supplied a large part of the imaginative substance of literature. Writers make the following different uses of external *nature*: (1) They express childlike delight in the open-air world; (2) they use *nature* as the background to human action or emotion; (3) they see *nature* through historic coloring; (4) they make *nature* sympathize with their own feelings; (5) they dwell on the infinite side of *nature*; (6) they give description of *nature* for its own sake; (7) they interpret *nature* with imaginative sympathy; (8) they use *nature* as a symbol of the spirit.

The comparatively small amount of Anglo-Saxon literature remaining reflects some love of *nature*, a power for picturesque description—as in the Riddles and such poems as the *Wife's Complaint* and the *Husband's Message*—and especially a sense of mystery and awe in the presence of *nature*, as in *Beowulf*. The *nature* here seems to be partly a disagreeable and even hostile force—winters, oceans, beasts, long nights. Late medieval literature—Chaucer and the ROMANCES—was apt to present *nature* in idyllic, conventionalized forms, a pleasant garden or "bower" on a spring morning. In the Renaissance there was sometimes a genuine, subjective response to natural surroundings, as in some of Surrey's poems, though often the treatment was conventional in character, as in the PASTORALS and the sonnets.

The eighteenth century brought the great conflict between NEOCLASSICISM and ROMANTICISM, and nowhere were the issues sharper than in the treatment of external *nature*. In their zeal to follow "correct" models and to favor urban over rural life, neoclassicists found little room for recording intimate observations of *nature*. For the wilder aspects of *nature* they expressed abhorrence. Winter was "the deformed wrong side of the year," whereas mountains were a positive blemish on the landscape and the ocean was a dangerous, wearying waste of waters. The writers who adumbrated the coming change, such as Lady Winchilsea, John Dyer, and James Thomson (especially *The Seasons*, 1726–1730), were giving voice to the new enthusiasm for *nature* while neoclassicism was at its height, and the movement grew with Gray, Collins, Cowper, and others until readers a little later were ready to respond to the values of the homelier aspects of *nature*—even mice and lice—as sung by Robert Burns.

With Wordsworth came a new complexity, as the poet seemed both closer to *nature* and alienated therefrom. Wordsworth often seems to be turning to *nature*—registered as "the earth" as opposed to "the world" of culture—in the hope of finding a realm comparable with his spiritual needs. In some poems Wordsworth seems to find what he is looking for; in others, however, he seems to discover that *nature* is "other" rather than "self." Coleridge, too, gave climactic expression to the romantic enthusiasm for the wilder *nature* that the neoclassicists could not tolerate. Observe the sharp contrast between the following passages, the first from Pope, and the second from Coleridge:

Here hills and vales, the woodland and its plain,
Here earth and water seem to strive again;
Not chaos-like together crushed and bruised,
But, as the world, harmoniously confused:
Where order in variety we see,
And where, though all things differ, all agree.
(*Windsor Forest*)

But oh! that deep romantic chasm which slanted
Down the green hill athwart a cedarn cover!
A savage place! as holy and enchanted
As e'er beneath a waning moon was haunted
By woman wailing for her demon lover!
(*Kubla Khan*)

The acceptance of Darwinism since 1859 has colored and modified the view of *nature*, and Wordworth's gentle instructor in beauty can become "nature red in tooth and claw" in Tennyson's *In Memoriam*, although that is not his persistent attitude. With the development of naturalism, a view of *nature* as a raw and primitive jungle where the struggle for survival relentlessly continues came into being, with *nature* viewed as a scientific fact, devoid of philosophical meaning. However, in its calmer moments, it still can minister to the human spirit, as can be seen in Hemingway's "Big Two-Hearted River" or the fishing scenes in *The Sun Also Rises* or in Faulkner's "The Bear." *Nature* is for contemporary writers what it has always been for writers, not an objective fact, but the "world's body" through which they speak in concrete terms their perceptions of themselves and the world. Emerson's *nature*, in his essay *Nature*, exists for five uses: as commodity, beauty, language, discipline, and finally, ideal symbol.

[Reference: George Economou, *The Goddess Natura in Medieval Literature* (1972).]

Near Rhyme The repetition in accented syllables of the final consonant sound without the correspondence of the preceding vowel sound, as in "grope" and "cup," "restored" and "word," "drunkard" and "conquered." *Near rhyme* of this sort is CONSONANCE rhyme. Complementarily, the repetition of vowel sound without exact correspondence of succeeding consonants amounts to *near rhyme* that is called ASSONANCE rhyme, as between "enough" and "love." Here, as with "face" and "ways," the consonant components tend to be the unvoiced and voiced forms of the same basic articulation—or, as with "dame" and "lane," identical articulation (voiced-nasal) of neighboring sounds. It is also called HALF RHYME, SLANT RHYME, and OBLIQUE RHYME.

Negative Capability A celebrated phrase put forward in a letter (December 1817) by John Keats to account for "what quality went to form a Man of Achievement especially in Literature & which Shakespeare possessed so enormously—I mean *Negative Capability*, that is when man is capable of being in uncertainties, Mysteries, doubts, without any irritable reaching after fact & reason. . . ." As a counterexample, Keats mentioned Coleridge, who "would let go by a fine isolated verisimilitude caught from the Penetralium of mystery, from being incapable of remaining content with half knowledge."

Nekuia A work having to do with the land of the dead, especially a visit by a living person. Book XI of Homer's *Odyssey* and Book VI of Virgil's *Aeneid* are examples; all of Dante's *Commedia* is a *nekuia*. Ezra Pound's Canto I, a version of Book XI of the *Odyssey*, establishes the *nekuia* as a good inauguration for a poem.

Nemesis The Greek goddess of retributive justice or vengeance. The term *nemesis* is applied to the divine retribution, when an evil act brings about its own punishment. The term is also applied to both agent and act of merited punishment. It thus often becomes synonymous with fate, although a sense of justice is often associated with the term.

Neoclassicism The term for the classicism that dominated English literature in the RESTORATION AGE and in the eighteenth century. It draws its name from its finding of models in CLASSICAL literature and contemporary French neoclassical writings. It was in part a reaction against the enthusiasm that had blazed in the RENAISSANCE. Against the Renaissance idea of limitless human potentiality was opposed a view of humankind as limited, dualistic, imperfect; on the intensity of human responses were imposed a reverence for order and a delight in reason and rules; the burgeoning of IMAGINATION into new and strange worlds was countered by a distrust of innovation and invention: On expanding individualism was imposed a view that saw people most significantly in their generic qualities; on the enthusiasm of MYSTICISM was imposed the restrained good sense of DEISM. Artistic ideals prized order, concentration, economy, utility, logic, restrained emotion, accuracy, correctness, good taste, and DECORUM.

A sense of symmetry, a delight in design, and a view of art as centered in humanity, and the belief that literature should be judged according to its service to humanity (see PRAGMATIC THEORY OF ART) resulted in the seeking of proportion, unity, harmony, and grace in literary expressions that aimed to delight, instruct, and correct human beings, primarily as social animals. It was the great age of the ESSAY, of the LETTER and EPISTLE, of SATIRE, of moral instruction, of PARODY, and of BURLESQUE. The play of mind mattered more than the play of feeling, with the result that a polite, urbane, witty, intellectual art developed.

Poetic diction and imagery tended to become conventional, with detail subordinated to design. The appeal to the intellect resulted in a fondness for wit and the production of satire in both prose and verse. A tendency to realism marked the presentation of life with stress on the generic qualities of men and women. Literature exalted form and avoided obscurity and mystery. It imitated (see IMITATION) the classics and cultivated such classical forms and types as satire and the ODE. The earlier English authors whose works were produced in a benighted age either were ignored or were admired more for their genius than for their art. Didactic literature flourished. Though BLANK VERSE and the SPENSERIAN STANZA were cultivated somewhat, rhymed couplets were the favorite form of verse. Poetic technique as developed by Pope has become a permanent heritage. In the twentieth century there was a strong neoclassical tendency, growing out of a reaction against ROMANTICISM and out of distrust of the potentialities of human beings, together with a new respect for the place of intellect in life and art. Writers such as T. E. Hulme, T. S. Eliot, Ezra Pound, Wyndham Lewis, Irving Babbitt, Mark Van Doren, Edith Sitwell, Hugh Kenner, Louis Zukofsky, Guy Davenport, Richard Wilbur, W. H. Auden, and the New Critics are on many issues at one with *neoclassicism*.

Neoclassic Period The period in English literature between the return of the Stuarts to the English throne in 1660 and the publication of *Lyrical Ballads* by Wordsworth and Coleridge in 1798. It includes the RESTORATION AGE (1660–1700), the AUGUSTAN AGE (1700–1750), and the AGE OF JOHNSON (1750–1798).

In the Restoration Age England underwent a strong reaction against the Puritanism of the COMMONWEALTH INTERREGNUM; its already strong interest in scientific investigation and philosophical thought increased; and neoclassicism, with particularly strong French influences, developed steadily. The HEROIC COUPLET became a major verse form; the ode was a widely used genre; and poetry usually served didactic or satiric purposes. In prose, despite the tendency toward utilitarian goals, the "modern" style was developing, notably in Dryden's work. In drama the reopening of the theaters and the establishment of the PATENT THEATERS led to the development of the HEROIC DRAMA in couplets and the COMEDY OF MANNERS in prose. Milton, Bunyan, and Dryden were the principal writers of the period, with *Paradise Lost* and *Pilgrim's Progress* being its major achievements in literature. Dryden's accomplishments, although none quite reached the individual heights of Milton or Bunyan, were signally fine and pointed forward toward the Augustan Age. Otway, Wycherley, and Congreve enriched the stage, and the prose of Locke found its way into a permanent place in English thought.

In the Augustan Age, classical ideals of taste, polish, common sense, and reason were more important than emotion and imagination. DEISM was advancing, and the rule of reason resulted in a literature that was realistic, satirical, moral, correct, and affected strongly by politics. Poetry sparkled with the polished couplets of Pope. The MOCK EPIC and the verse essay were common forms. In the work of James Thomson was to be found a growing concern with nature and science and, in the "GRAVEYARD SCHOOL," a sentimental melancholy.

On the stage the heroic drama was replaced by the DOMESTIC TRAGEDY of such writers as Lillo and imitations of CLASSICAL TRAGEDY such as Addison's *Cato*. SENTIMENTAL COMEDY replaced the less "moral" COMEDY OF MANNERS, and the Licensing Act of 1737 imposed a stifling political censorship on the English theater.

It was a great age of prose. The essay PERIODICAL was adumbrated in JOURNALS such as Defoe's *Review, The Tatler*, and *The Spectator*, which had a profound influence on English prose style and were followed by a host of imitators. The audacious prose satires of Swift were among the glories of the age. The prose fiction of Defoe and the early novels of Richardson, Fielding, and Smollett had all appeared before the mid-century mark.

The AGE OF JOHNSON was a period of transition that was still dominated by the critical energies and the prose vigor of a prodigious representative of the passing tradition, Samuel Johnson. The developing interest in human freedom, the widening range of intellectual interests and human sympathies, the developing appreciation of external nature and the country life, the evolving cult of the primitive—all joined with such political events as the American and the French revolutions and such religious movements as the rise of Methodism to establish the bedrock on which English romanticism was to rest. In poetry Gray, Cowper, Smart, Burns, and Crabbe were active. An interest in folk literature and popular BALLADS developed. In the drama Goldsmith and Sheridan returned laughter to the stage with the comedy of manners, although sentimental comedy still flourished. Shakespeare—often in a laundered form—was immensely popular on the stage; and BURLESQUE, the PANTOMIME, and the MELODRAMA—forms that freed the drama (although at a high price) from the sharp restrictions of the PATENT THEATERS—developed. In prose the novel advanced steadily. Sterne and Mackenzie developed the NOVEL OF SENSIBILITY; Horace Walpole, Anne Radcliffe, and Clara Reeves the GOTHIC NOVEL. By the end of the century Brooke and Godwin were producing novels of political and philosophical propaganda.

In the Age of Johnson the greatest literary figures were Johnson himself, as poet, critic, novelist, essayist, journalist, and lexicographer—a superlative embodiment of neoclassic ideals—and Robert Burns, as poet of the common people, the Scottish soil, and the romantic soul—a precursor of the coming Romantic Period. By 1798, Wordsworth, Coleridge, and Blake had already launched their careers; Johnson and Burns were dead; and Shelley, Byron, and Keats had been born. See the *Outline of Literary History*, AUGUSTAN, RESTORATION AGE, and the AGE OF JOHNSON.

Neologism (or **Neology**) A new word introduced into a language, especially for enhancing style. There was much conscious use of *neologisms*, mostly from Greek and Latin, in the Renaissance, partly as a result of a definite critical attitude toward the enrichment of the native English vocabulary. But the practice is not confined to any one period. Many *neologisms* employed by authors or by stylistic "schools" (see EUPHUISM, GONGORISM) have not gained a permanent foothold in the vocabulary. The current of English is constantly fed by a steady stream of new words, some of them eventually cliché (as the oversupply of "gate"-suffix scandals after Watergate), some entertaining (such as "palimony" or Kenneth Tynan's invention to describe both bland and grandiose: "blandiose"). See COINED WORDS.

Neoplatonism A philosophical system that originated in Alexandria in the third century, with elements of PLATONISM mixed with Oriental beliefs and with some aspects of Christianity. Its leading representative was Plotinus.

New Comedy Greek COMEDY of the fourth and third centuries B.C. After the decline of Greece and the rise of Macedonia, the OLD COMEDY, of which Aristophanes was the greatest creator, was replaced by a COMEDY OF MANNERS, featuring STOCK CHARACTERS and conventional plots. The locale was usually a street, the characters young lovers, courtesans, parsimonious elders, and scheming servants. The best writers of the *New Comedy* were Menander, Philemon, and Diphilus. The *New Comedy* had a powerful influence on the Roman comedies of Plautus and Terence, and through them on much subsequent comedy.

New Criticism In a strict sense the term applies to the criticism practiced by John Crowe Ransom, Allen Tate, R. P. Blackmur, Robert Penn Warren, and Cleanth Brooks; it is derived from Ransom's book *The New Criticism* (1941), which discusses a movement in America in the 1930s that paralleled movements in England led by critics such as T. S. Eliot, I. A. Richards, and William Empson. Generally, however, the term is applied to the whole body of criticism that concentrates on the work of art as an object in itself; finds in it a special kind of language opposed to—or at least different from— the languages of science or philosophy; and subjects it to close analysis. The New Critics constitute one school in modern criticism that employs the OBJECTIVE THEORY OF ART. The movement has varied sources; among them are I. A. Richard's *The Principles of Literary Criticism* (1924), Laura (Riding) Jackson's criticism that appeared in the late 1920s, William Empson's *Seven Types of Ambiguity* (1930), the work of Remy de Gourmont, the anti-romanticism of T. E. Hulme, the French *explication de texte*, the concepts of order and tradition of the southern AGRARIANS, and the work of Ezra Pound and T. S. Eliot.

Not even the group to which the term can be applied in its strictest sense has formed a school subscribing to a fixed dogma; when to this group are added others such as Yvor Winters and Kenneth Burke, it can be seen that the *New Criticism* is really a cluster of attitudes toward literature rather than an organized critical system. The primary concern of these critics has been to discover the intrinsic worth of literature.

The *New Criticism* has been primarily a protest against certain conventional and traditional ways of viewing life and art. The New Critics were originally protesting against THE NEW HUMANISM of Babbitt and More; and their protest took the form of an insistence that the morality and value of a work of art are functions of its inner qualities and that literature cannot be evaluated in general terms or terms not directly related to the work itself. Their concern has been with IMAGE, SYMBOL, and MEANING. This aspect of the *New Criticism* has led to attacks by critics interested in GENRE or FORM who assert that the New Critics reduce literature to a linguistic or symbolic monism that makes the significant discrimination among types impossible. In actual practice the *New Criticism* has most often been applied, and has worked best when applied, to the LYRIC; it has been less successful when applied to extended prose works of fiction or drama. See CRITICISM, TYPES OF; INTENTIONAL FALLACY; AFFECTIVE FALLACY; EXPLICATION DE TEXTE; AUTOTELIC.

[References: Cleanth Brooks, *The Well Wrought Urn; Studies in the Structure of Poetry* (1947); R. S. Crane, ed., *Critics and Criticism* (1952); Frank Lentricchia, *After the New Criticism* (1980); John Crowe Ransom, *The New Criticism* (1941).]

New Formalism (or **Neoformalism**) This term first emerged around 1980 to cover a movement in verse writing that had been going on all along, so that one cannot locate a precise moment in history when some Old Formalism gave up the ghost or *New Formalism* was born and christened. *New Formalism* chiefly concerns the production of verse with recognizable rhythms, meters, rhymes, stanza patterns, structures, and rhetorical strategies—all associated with a group of poets born between about 1915 and 1940: Howard Nemerov, Anthony Hecht, Richard Wilbur, John Hollander, X. J. Kennedy, J. V. Cunningham, Robert Pinsky, and several others.

[Reference: Wyatt Prunty, *"Fallen from the Symboled World": Precedents for the New Formalism* (1990).]

Newgate A prison of unsavory reputation in London, dating from the twelfth century to 1902, when it was demolished. Until 1868 executions held outside *Newgate* attracted large crowds. The *Newgate Calendar* (begun 1773) was a biographical record of the most notorious criminals there confined. A popular work of the sixteenth century is sometimes titled "The Ballad which Anne Askew Made and Sang when She Was in Newgate." (At one time the "Spies and Thrillers" column in the *New York Times Book*

Review was written by "Newgate Callendar.") Stories dealing with London crime and criminals are often referred to as *Newgate* novels and tales. Gay's *Beggar's Opera* has been called a "Newgate pastoral."

New Historicism The *New Historicism* resembled old historicism in treating literature in a certain way—not as a self-standing transcendent entity capable of analysis on its own terms but rather as a part of history and, furthermore, as an expression or representation of forces on history. Older historicism tended to push literature back into linguistic history, so that Chaucer, say, is read as an example of certain formal traditions. The *New Historicism* tends to be social, economic, and political, and it views literary works (particularly Renaissance dramas and Victorian novels) as instruments for the displaying and enforcing of doctrines about conduct, etiquette, and law. In a dynamic circle, the literature tells us something about the surrounding ideology (for example, primogeniture, rights of women, slavery, or royal succession), and the study of ideology tells us something about the embedded literary works. We can, for example, read *The Tempest* as an index of Jacobean concern for exploration of new lands, and vice versa. Stephen Greenblatt, perhaps the most influential practitioner of the *New Historicism*, has written in this vein: "Near the end of his career Shakespeare decided to take advantage of his contemporaries' lively interest in New World exploration. His play *The Tempest* contains many details drawn from the writings of adventurers and colonists. . . . The play reiterates the arguments that Europeans made about the legitimacy and civilizing force of their presence in the newly discovered lands. . . ."

[References: Stephen Greenblatt, "Culture," in *Critical Terms for Literary Study*, eds. Frank Lentricchia and Thomas McLaughlin (1990); Jean E. Howard, "The New Historicism in Renaissance Studies," *English Literary Renaissance* 16 (1986) 13–43; D. G. Myers, "The New Historicism in Literary Studies," *Academic Questions* (Winter 1988–89) 27–36.]

New Humanism, The An American critical school in the first third of the twentieth century that emphasized the moral qualities of literature. See HUMANISM, THE NEW.

New Journalism, The A species of writing that owes something to the example of H. L. Mencken, John Dos Passos, and Ernest Hemingway (especially his *Death in the Afternoon*) and even reaches back as far as Daniel Defoe for precursors. As it emerged after the Second World War, the *New Journalism* was founded on conventional journalistic or historical coverage of events or phenomena but gave up the traditional impersonality and invisibility of the journalist as such and offered instead a subjective style and voice that openly admit the personal presence and involvement of a human witness. The most vocal and visible practitioners have been Tom Wolfe, Norman Mailer, Hunter S. Thompson, Joan Didion, Mark Harris, John McPhee, and Truman Capote. Many of these writers also work as producers of ordinary fiction, and to their ostensibly journalistic chores they take along a number of imaginative devices— including INTERIOR MONOLOGUE, FLASHBACKS, shifts of focus from documentation to philosophy, and the invention of imaginary characters.

New Novel A term, literally from the French *nouveau roman*, often applied to the ANTINOVEL.

New York School A group of American poets who flourished between 1950 and 1970, distinguished by urbanity, wit, learning, spontaneity, and exuberance. Led by Frank O'Hara (1926–1966), these poets exploited certain interests and sympathies: the culture of France, modern painting (SURREALISM and abstract expressionism in particular), jazz, Hollywood movies, and city life. Besides O'Hara, the chief members of the group are John Ashbery (born 1927), Kenneth Koch (1925–2002), and James Schuyler (1923–1991).

[Reference: David Lehman, *The Last Avant-Garde: The Making of the New York School of Poets* (1998).]

Nihil obstat Latin for "nothing obstructs," used in the Roman Catholic church to grant permission to publish a book. See IMPRIMATUR.

Nine Worthies, The Late medieval and early Renaissance literature reflects the widespread tradition of the heroes known as the "*nine worthies.*" Caxton's preface to Mallory's *Le Morte Darthur* lists them in the conventional three groups: Hector, Alexander, Julius Caesar (pre-Christian pagans); Joshua, David, Judas Maccabeus (pre-Christian Jews); Arthur, Charlemagne, Godfrey of Boulogne (Christians). They are impersonated in the BURLESQUE play incorporated in Shakespeare's *Love's Labour's Lost.*

Nobel Prize The Swedish chemist and engineer Alfred Bernhard Nobel (1833–1896) willed the income from practically his entire estate for the establishment of annual prizes in literature and other fields. Originally, the literature prize was to go to the person who had produced *during the year* the most eminent piece of work in the field of *idealistic* literature; in practice, however, the prize rewards a recipient's total career, and some of the literature is not notably idealistic. Even so, the Nobel Prize is the highest honor in the literary world. Many great writers have received it, and many just as great have not. The 2004 prize was reported to carry an award of about $1.2 million.

Noble Savage The idea that primitive human beings are naturally good and that whatever evil they develop is the product of the corrupting action of civilization. Montaigne's essay "Of Cannibals" (1580) stated the basic concept. Dryden, in *The Conquest of Granada* (1671), has a character say:

> I am as free as nature first made man,
> Ere the base laws of servitude began
> When wild in wood the noble savage ran.

Aphra Behn's *Oroonoko: or, The Royal Slave* (1688) portrayed a *noble savage* in chains. But the greatest impulse toward the doctrine of a natural nobility came from Rousseau's *Émile* (1762): "Everything is well when it comes fresh from the hands of the Maker; everything degenerates in the hands of Man." The idea was used extensively by Chateaubriand, and it became a commonplace of romanticism. The continuing popularity of Kipling's *The Jungle Book* and Edgar Rice Burroughs's Tarzan (who is also the literally noble Lord Greystoke) is testimony to the durability of the idea. See PRIMITIVISM.

Nocturne A work expressing moods appropriate to evening or nighttime. Also called a SERENADE.

Noh (or **Nō**) **Plays** The most important form of Japanese drama, *noh* literally means "highly skilled or accomplished." The *noh plays* are harmonious combinations of dance, poetry, music, mime, and acting. There are 240 *noh plays* in the standard repertory, all written between 1300 and 1600. *Noh plays* were originally a part of the religious ritual of the Japanese feudal aristocracy, and they continue that tradition. They are short, one or two acts, and are usually presented at a festival in programs consisting of one each of the five types of *noh plays*: (1) a play of praise for a god, adorned with dancing, (2) a play about a warrior hero from the epic period in Japanese history, (3) a play in which a male actor impersonates a woman, (4) a play of great violence, sensationalism, and often of ghosts and supernatural beings, and (5) a solemn play of warlike dancing, which ends with a grateful recognition of the occasion of the festival. These plays, aimed at creating serene contemplation of beauty and a sense of religious sublimity, are performed on stylized sets, with lavish, symbolic costuming. Elevated speech is in verse and common speech in prose. Their performance techniques, settings, costuming, and acting styles represent a tradition stretching back to the fourteenth century. They thus constitute one of the oldest continuous aesthetic traditions in the world. Among modern Western writers, W. B. Yeats and Ezra Pound exploited certain features of *noh* drama. See KABUKI plays.

[References: Donald Keene, ed., *Twenty Plays of the Nō Theatre* (1970); Ezra Pound, ed., *Certain Noble Plays of Japan* (1916, reprinted 1971); L. C. Pronko, *Guide to Japanese Drama*, 2nd ed. (1984; orig. 1973).]

Noir An adjective taken over from the phrase FILM NOIR to apply to any work, especially one involving crime, that is notably dark, brooding, cynical, complex, and pessimistic. (A recurrent parodic character on *Prairie Home Companion* is named Guy Noir.) The television series *Twin Peaks* was called a "soap *noir*."

Nom de plume (or **pen name**) A name adopted by a writer for professional use or to disguise his or her true identity. For example, William Sydney Porter assumed the pen name "O. Henry"; and Amandine Aurore Lucie Dupin, Baroness Dudevant, almost unknown by her real name, was famous as the French novelist, George Sand. In certain traditions, notably the Japanese and the French, the pen name is more the rule than the exception. Some fastidious scholars insist that pen names should always be cited in their full form with quotation marks; this practice applies especially to those like "Mark Twain" and "Scholem Aleichem" that are really phrases and not a first name plus a last name. Strictly construed, a *nom de plume* is the name an author writes under, and it may be close to the legal name. "Walt Whitman" and "X. J. Kennedy" thus are *noms de plume* for writers actually named Walter Whitman and Joseph Kennedy. See PSEUDONYM.

Nominalism A philosophical doctrine, first advanced by Roscellinus (twelfth century) and revived by William of Ockham (fourteenth century), that holds that abstract concepts, general terms, and universals have no objective referents but exist only as names. This doctrine, which leads toward materialism and empiricism in its insistence that only particular things exist, has been popular in the nineteenth and twentieth centuries.

[Reference: Umberto Eco, *The Name of the Rose* (1983).]

Nonce Word In earlier forms of a language, a word for which there is a single recorded occurrence. There are a number of *nonce words* in Old English writing. In modern times a *nonce word*—originally "an once word"—is one invented by an author for a particular usage or special meaning.

Nonfiction Novel A classification offered by Truman Capote for his *In Cold Blood*, in which a historical event (a multiple murder in Kansas) is described in a way that exploits some of the devices of fiction, including a nonlinear time sequence and access to inner states of mind and feeling not commonly present in historical writing. Later used by Norman Mailer (in *Armies of the Night* and other books) and John McPhee (in *Levels of the Game* and *The Deltoid Pumpkin Seed*), the form is indebted to such earlier writers as "Isak Dinesen" (especially *Out of Africa*) and Ernest Hemingway (*Green Hills of Africa)*. Mark Harris *(Drumlin Woodchuck: Saul Bellow)* has argued that there is no such thing as a prose poem or a *nonfiction novel*; others have suggested that hyphenated forms of behavior, such as the TV-movie and the prayer-breakfast, do justice to neither of their components.

Nonsense Verse A variety of LIGHT VERSE entertaining because of its strong rhythmic quality and lack of logic, *nonsense verse* is often characterized by the presence of coined nonsense words, NONCE WORDS ("frabjous day"), and a mingling of words from various languages (MACARONIC VERSE). LIMERICKS are a popular *nonsense verse* form. Edward Lear and Lewis Carroll built large reputations through writing *nonsense verse*. Calling such things "nonsense" amounts to either hyperbole or a misnomer, because genuinely nonsensical writing is unintelligible.

Norman Conquest The conquest of England by the Normans following the victory of William I in 1066 at the Battle of Senlac (Hastings). It affected English literature and the English language drastically by the introduction of Norman-French culture and the French language. It was followed by three centuries of readjustment, out of which modern England was to come. See ANGLO-NORMAN (LANGUAGE), ANGLO-NORMAN PERIOD, ENGLISH LANGUAGE, MIDDLE ENGLISH, MIDDLE ENGLISH PERIOD.

Nostos A work describing a return, especially a homecoming. The preeminent example is Homer's *Odyssey*. Milton's *Paradise Regained*, the last word of which is "returned," may be read as a *nostos*.

Note A markedly short piece of writing that makes a single point. A. C. Swinburne entitled a book *A Note on Charlotte Brontë*. The term is also used for an item of explanatory apparatus (such as Eliot's "Notes" to *The Waste Land)* or for pieces supposedly—and maybe by understatement—informal and incomplete, such as Eliot's *Notes towards the Definition of Culture*, Stevens's *Notes toward a Supreme Fiction*, and Baldwin's *Notes of a Native Son*.

Notice (1) A brief REVIEW. (2) Formerly, a longer piece of informative writing, as in Thomas Moore's *Letters and Journals of Lord Byron with Notices of His Life* (1833).

Nouvelle A SHORT NOVEL or NOVELETTE; a work of fiction of intermediate length between the SHORT STORY and the NOVEL. Henry James used the French term *nouvelle* for short novel.

Novel *Novel* is used in its broadest sense to designate any extended fictional narrative almost always in prose. In practice, however, its use is customarily restricted to narratives in which the representation of character occurs either in a static condition or in the process of development as the result of events or actions (see CHARACTERIZATION). Often the term implies that some organizing principle—PLOT, THEME, or idea—should be present in a narrative that is called a *novel*. The term *novel* is an English counterpart of the Italian NOVELLA, a short, compact, broadly realistic tale popular in the medieval period and best represented by those in the *Decameron*. In most European countries the word *roman* is used rather than *novel*, thus linking the *novel* with the older ROMANCE, of which, in a sense, the *novel* is an extension. The conflict between the imaginative recreation of experience implied in *roman* and the realistic representation of the soiled world of common people implied in *novel* has been present in the form from its beginning, and it accounted for a distinction often made in the eighteenth and nineteenth centuries between the romance and the *novel*, in which the romance was the tale of the long ago, the far away, or the imaginatively improbable; whereas the *novel* was bound by the facts of the actual world and the laws of probability.

The *novel* may concentrate on character, almost to the exclusion of plot. It may amount to no more than a series of incidents, as the PICARESQUE NOVEL tends to be. It may be solidly plotted, with a structure as firm and sure as that of a tragedy. It may attempt to present the details of life with a scientist's detached and objective completeness, as in NATURALISM; or it may try by image and verbal modification to reproduce the unconscious flow of the emotions, as in the STREAM-OF-CONSCIOUSNESS NOVEL.

It may be episodic, loose in structure, epic in proportion—what is called "panoramic"—or it may be as tightly knit as a WELL-MADE PLAY, bringing its material forward in dramatic orderliness—what is called "scenic."

The English *novel* is essentially an eighteenth-century product. However, without the richness of earlier literary activity, the *novel* could not have matured. The narrative interest developed in the stories of Charlemagne and Arthur, the various romantic CYCLES, the FABLIAUX; the descriptive values and appreciation of nature found in the pastorals; the historical interest of DIARIES and JOURNALS; the enthusiasm for character portrayal developed in SKETCHES and BIOGRAPHIES; the use of suspense in tales and MEDIEVAL ROMANCES—all these had to be familiar and understood before writers could evolve the *novel*, which draws certain elements from many preceding literary types.

In the second century B.C., Aristides wrote a series of tales of his home town, Miletus. The collection was called *Milesiaka*; it is not extant today, though it may have been the beginning of the modern *novel*. Six centuries later Heliodorus, a Syrian, wrote *Aethiopica*—a love story at least somewhat true to life. *Daphnis and Chloë* (Greek), attributed to Longus of the third century, can be strictly called a *novel*. In Latin there were various works, such as the *Golden Ass* of Apuleius, a translation from the Greek, and the so-called *Satyricon* of Petronius, which presented the life and customs of the time of Nero.

The NOVELLA of Italy is one of the early literary forms to which the modern *novel* is indebted both for its narrative form and for its name. The appearance of *Cento Novelle Antiche* just before the opening of the fourteenth century gave great vogue to the form. These novelle (or novellas) were stories of scandalous love, chivalry, mythology, and morals, of the type best known to modern English readers through the stories of

Boccaccio's *Decameron* (c. 1348). Loose women, unscrupulous priests, rough peasants, and high-born nobles formed the central figures of most of these.

From Spain came at least two works that were major influences on the development of the *novel*: the *Lazarillo de Tormes* of 1554 and Cervantes's *Don Quixote* of 1605 (see PICARESQUE NOVEL).

France, like Italy, produced novelle. In 1535 appeared the *Gargantua* of Rabelais, which, although not a *novel*, nevertheless has sustained narrative interest. Honoré d'Urfé's *Astrée* (1610) has more definitely the qualities we demand in a *novel* today, and in the middle of the seventeenth century Madeleine de Scudéry (1607–1701) wrote romances that might pass muster in the twentieth century. The romantic qualities of Scudéry called forth a realistic reaction by Scarron, who wrote *Roman Comique*. Some literary historians assign to Marguerite Pioche de la Vergne the honor of having created the first full-blown French *novels* in her *Princesse de Montpensier* (1662) and *Princesse de Cléves* (1678).

English writers of the eighteenth century had as a background the experience of continental Europe. In addition to these beginnings, the English novelists had native parallels of their own—the Arthurian materials, the *Euphues* of Lyly (1579), the *Arcadia* of Sir Philip Sidney (1580–1581), the narrative interest in Lodge's *Rosalynde* (1590), the picaresque element in Nash's *The Unfortunate Traveler* (1594), the narrative chronicle of Aphra Behn's *Oroonoko* (1688), the extended narrative of moral significance in John Bunyan's *Pilgrim's Progress* (1678–1684), and the CHARACTER element present in the *Spectator* papers of Addison and Steele. Defoe, in *Robinson Crusoe* (1719) and *Moll Flanders* (1722), using very loose narrative structures, and Swift, in *Gulliver's Travels* (1726), using satiric ALLEGORY, had brought VERISIMILITUDE to the chronicling of human life.

With these narrative qualities already rooted in various types of English and European writing, the ground was fertile, tilled, and seeded when Samuel Richardson, in 1740, issued *Pamela; or, Virtue Rewarded*, the first English book that practically all readers are willing to call a fully realized *novel*. Richardson's three *novels, Pamela, Clarissa Harlow* (1747–1748), and *Sir Charles Grandison* (1753) are EPISTOLARY. After Richardson's success with *Pamela*, other significant *novels* came rapidly. Henry Fielding began *Joseph Andrews* (1742) as a satire on *Pamela*—Joseph is supposedly Pamela's brother, whose problem with his employer is the mirror image of hers—but Fielding soon forgot his ironical intent and told a vigorous story of his own. In 1748 Smollett published *Roderick Random*; in 1749 came Fielding's greatest novel, *Tom Jones*, important for its development of plot and its realistic interpretation of English life; in 1751 both Smollett and Fielding repeated, the former with *Peregrine Pickle* and the latter with *Amelia*. Defoe, Richardson, Fielding, and Smollett stand at the source of the English *novel*. The succeeding years brought other *novels* and novelists, but the first real impetus to long fiction was given by them. Sterne wrote *Tristram Shandy* (1760–1767), a work that broke, even so early, the narrative form of the *novel* and, applying Locke's psychological theories, undertook the exploration of the inner self. Horace Walpole made much of GOTHIC mysteries in his *Castle of Otranto* (1764). Two years later Oliver Goldsmith published the *Vicar of Wakefield*. Then came such works as Fanny Burney's NOVEL OF MANNERS, *Evelina* (1778), and Anne Radcliffe's Gothic *novel, Mysteries of Udolpho* (1794).

The nineteenth century saw the flowering of the English *novel* as an instrument portraying middle-class society. Jane Austen produced NOVELS OF MANNERS, and Scott created the HISTORICAL NOVEL and carried it to a high point in the first quarter of the century. The great Victorian novelists—Dickens, Thackeray, and Trollope—created vast fictional worlds loaded with an abundance of social types and arranged in intricate melodramatic plots. In Thomas Hardy and George Eliot the last half of the century found writers who, in differing degrees, applied some of the tenets of NATURALISM.

In the twentieth century the English *novel* probed more and more deeply into the human mind. Virginia Woolf, Dorothy Richardson, and James Joyce, writing STREAM-OF-CONSCIOUSNESS NOVELS, greatly expanded and deepened the subject matter of the *novel* and modified the techniques of fiction so that this new subject matter may be dealt with. This century has been marked, too, by a growing concern over critical and technical issues in fiction.

For fifty years after Richardson published *Pamela*, no *novels* were written in America, although *Pamela* appeared in an American edition within two years of its English publication. The first *novel* written by an American and published in America, *The Power of Sympathy*, a moralistic tale of seduction, by William Hill Brown, did not appear until 1789. Charles Brockden Brown was the first important American novelist. Brown, who wrote chiefly in the Gothic manner, was the author of four readable tales: *Wieland* (1798), *Arthur Mervyn* (1799), *Ormond* (1799), and *Edgar Huntly* (1799). Some twenty years later James Fenimore Cooper published *The Spy* (1821), *The Pioneers* (1823), and *The Pilot* (1823). In addition to *The Pioneers*, his Leatherstocking series included *The Deerslayer* (1841), *The Last of the Mohicans* (1826), *The Pathfinder* (1840), and *The Prairie* (1827). By 1850, when Hawthorne's *The Scarlet Letter* appeared, the American *novel* had come into its full powers, a fact made abundantly clear by the publication in 1851 of Herman Melville's *Moby-Dick*. In the last half of the nineteenth century, REALISM, articulated as a theory by William Dean Howells and well-exemplified in his work and made the basis of a highly self-conscious art by Henry James, dominated the American *novel*. This control gave way in the early years of the twentieth century to the naturalism of Norris and Dreiser. After the First World War, a group of talented young novelists introduced a number of ideas drawn from French realists and symbolists into American fiction and produced a new, vital, but essentially romantic *novel* with strong naturalistic overtones. Foremost among them were F. Scott Fitzgerald, Ernest Hemingway, and William Faulkner. Today the American *novel* is a varied form practiced with self-conscious skill by a number of novelists and read by large audiences more earnestly than any other serious literary form. John Updike's work is both serious and popular; Thomas Pynchon (b. 1937), who seems to be a sort of logarithm of Hawthorne, Poe, and Melville, has written five *novels* of prodigious scope and great brilliance, and he has enjoyed a measure of commercial success at the same time.

In this handbook special forms of the *novel* are discussed in separate entries, broadly classified by subject matter. They are DETECTIVE NOVEL, PSYCHOLOGICAL NOVEL, SOCIOLOGICAL NOVEL, SENTIMENTAL NOVEL, PROPAGANDA NOVEL, HISTORICAL NOVEL, NOVEL OF MANNERS, NOVEL OF CHARACTER, NOVEL OF INCIDENT, NOVEL OF THE SOIL, PICARESQUE NOVEL, GOTHIC NOVEL, APPRENTICESHIP NOVEL, STREAM-OF-CONSCIOUSNESS NOVEL, PROBLEM NOVEL, EPISTOLARY NOVEL, and KÜNSTLERROMAN. The principal modes are defined in this handbook under general terms such as REALISM, ROMANTICISM, IMPRESSIONISM, EXPRESSIONISM, NATURALISM, and NEOCLASSICISM.

Novelette A work of prose fiction of intermediate length, longer than a SHORT STORY and shorter than a NOVEL. In general, the *novelette* displays the compact structure of the short story with the greater development of character, theme, and action of the NOVEL.

Melville's *Billy Budd*, Stevenson's *Dr. Jekyll and Mr. Hyde*, James's *The Turn of the Screw*, Conrad's *Heart of Darkness*, and William Styron's *The Long March* are examples. See SHORT NOVEL.

Novelization The conversion of a screenplay or a television play into novel form, usually to capitalize on its popularity.

Novella A tale or short story. The term is particularly applied to the early tales of Italian and French writers—such as the *Decameron* of Boccaccio and the *Heptameron* of Marguerite of Valois. The form interests students of English literature for two reasons: (1) Many of these early *novelle* were used by English writers as sources for their own work, and (2) it was from this form that the NOVEL developed. *Novella* is also a term borrowed from the German and applied to the kind of short novel that developed in Germany in the nineteenth century.

Novel of Character A NOVEL that emphasizes character rather than exciting episode, as in the NOVEL OF INCIDENT, or unity of plot.

Novel of Incident A term for a NOVEL in which episodic action dominates, and plot and character are subordinate. The structure is loose; emphasis is on thrilling incident rather than on characterization or suspense. Defoe's *Robinson Crusoe* is such a *novel of incident*. Here the shipwreck, the meeting with Friday, the clash with visiting natives, and other incidents follow each other chronologically, but they are more or less independent of one another. Dumas's *Three Musketeers* is also a *novel of incident*, though with a plot more developed than in Defoe's story.

Novel of Manners A NOVEL dominated by social customs, manners, conventions, and habits of a definite social class. In the true *novel of manners* the mores of a specific group, described in detail and with great accuracy, become powerful controls over characters. The *novel of manners* is often, although by no means always, satiric; it is always realistic, however. The HISTORICAL NOVEL could be called the "*novel of manners* laid in the past." The novels of Jane Austen, Edith Wharton, and John P. Marquand are *novels of manners*. Some critics consider the works of Edward Higgins and Elmore Leonard *novels of manners*, even though the manners in question belong to low-life characters.

Novel of Sensibility A NOVEL in which the characters have a heightened emotional response to events, producing in the reader a similar response. Sterne's *Tristram Shandy* is a major example; Mackenzie's *Man of Feeling* carries the idea of intensity of character response beyond the limits of reason. See SENTIMENTAL NOVEL.

Novel of the Soil A special kind of REGIONALISM in the NOVEL, in which the lives of people struggling for existence in remote rural sections are starkly portrayed. Examples are Ellen Glasgow's *Barren Ground*, O. E. Rölvaag's *Giants in the Earth*, and Elizabeth Madox Roberts's *Time of Man*. Pearl S. Buck's *The Good Earth* may fit into this category. The term *novel of the soil* refers primarily to matter rather than to manner; however, the term is usually restricted to portrayals in the manner of REALISM or NATURALISM.

Nucleus The heart of a syllable; almost always a vowel. A paradigmatic syllable consists of a *nucleus* necessarily, and possibly an ONSET (consonant matter) before and a CODA (consonant matter) after.

Numbers A term, now just about obsolete, meaning "measured language" or regular verse in general. Pope, confessing to have been a poet virtually since infancy, says, "I lisped in numbers." Longfellow's "A Psalm of Life" begins, "Tell me not, in mournful numbers. . . ." Borrowing a term from mathematics, Kenneth Rexroth titled one of his books of poetry *Natural Numbers*.

Nursery Rhyme Brief verses, often anonymous and traditional, with percussive rhythm and frequent, heavy rhyme, written for young children. The first important collection of *nursery rhymes* in English was made in the eighteenth century by "Mother Goose," whose actual identity has long been a matter of dispute. *Nursery rhymes* include songs, counting-out games, narratives, nonsense verse, and rhymes that seem to have links with English political history.

Fournier le Jeune 1913. Based on a typeface cut by Pierre Simon Fournier, c. 1746. Recut by Fonderie Deberny Peignot, Paris.

O. P., o.p. In stage directions and elsewhere: "opposite the prompt (or prompter) side": stage left in Britain, stage right in the United States. P. G. Wodehouse's *My Man Jeeves* (1919) includes this description: "Lady Malvern was a hearty . . . female . . . measuring about six feet from the O.P. to the Prompt Side."

Obiter dicta Things said "by the way"; incidental remarks. Though legal in origin, the term is sometimes used in literary association.

Objective Correlative T. S. Eliot's term for a pattern of objects, actions, or events, or a situation that can serve effectively to awaken in the reader an emotional response without being a direct statement of that subjective emotion. It is a means of communicating feeling. Eliot calls the *objective correlative* "the only way of expressing emotion in the form of art" and defines it as "a set of objects, a situation, a chain of events which shall be the formula of that *particular* emotion, such that when the external facts, which must terminate in sensory experience, are given, the emotion is immediately evoked." Eliot's argument—to the effect that *Hamlet* is an "artistic failure"—is that Shakespeare's tragedy lacks an adequate *objective correlative* for Hamlet's state of mind. The term was used by Washington Allston in a lecture on art as early as 1850 to describe the process by which the external world produces pleasurable emotion, but Eliot gave it new meaning and made of it a new term.

Objective Theory of Art A term applied by M. H. Abrams to the view that holds the literary work to be most significant as an object in itself, independent of the facts of its composition, the actuality it imitates, its author's stated intention, or the effect it produces on its audience. See CRITICISM and AUTOTELIC.

Objectivism A term used by various philosophies to stress the reality or value of the objective world, the need for some sort of objectivity, or the importance of the status of an artwork as a physical object. The term has been appropriated by writers as divergent as William Carlos Williams, Louis Zukofsky, and Ayn Rand.

Objectivity A quality in an artwork of impersonality and freedom from the expression of personal sentiments, attitudes, or emotions by the author.

Obligatory Scene An episode of which the circumstances are so strongly foreseen that the writer is obliged to deliver the SCENE. *Obligatory scene* is the equivalent of the French SCÈNE À FAIRE.

Oblique Rhyme Approximate but not true RHYME; *oblique rhyme* is another term for NEAR RHYME, HALF RHYME, and SLANT RHYME.

Occasional Verse Poetry written for some particular occasion. Although the term can include VERS DE SOCIÉTÉ, it usually designates writing more serious and more dignified. POETS LAUREATE are called on to produce *occasional verse* in the discharge of their responsibilities. Love poems of a highly personal nature and addressed to a specific person can be called *occasional*. Among notable examples of *occasional verse* are Spenser's "Epithalamion," celebrating his marriage; Dryden's "Astraea Redux," celebrating the return to the throne of Charles II; Marvell's "Horatian Ode upon Cromwell's Return from Ireland"; Milton's "Lycidas," on the death of Edward King; and Whitman's "When Lilacs Last in the Dooryard Bloom'd," commemorating the death of Lincoln. Many later poems, including Yeats's "September 1913" and "Easter 1916" and Auden's "September 1, 1939," are *occasional*. The official Laureate poems in C. Day Lewis's *Complete Poems* are grouped under the title *"Vers d'Occasion."*

Occultatio Rhetorical term for emphasizing something by seeming to pass over it.

Occupatio Device somewhat like *OCCULTATIO*, especially when one says "Not to mention . . ." or "To say nothing of . . ." and then goes ahead and talks about something.

Ockham's (or **Occam's**) **Razor** The principle of parsimony, attributed to William of Ockham (1285–1349), one of the most famous of the Franciscan thinkers of the late Middle Ages, and resembling another British-born Franciscan, Johannes Duns Scotus. The famous "Razor" is customarily stated as *Entia non sunt multiplicanda praeter necessitatem*: "Entities should not be multiplied beyond necessity."

Octameter A LINE of eight FEET. *Octameter* is fairly rare in English VERSE. Of the rhythm and meter of "The Raven," Edgar Allan Poe said, "The former is trochaic—the latter is octameter acatalectic, alternating with heptameter catalectic repeated in the refrain of the fifth verse, and terminating with tetrameter catalectic." These lines from Tennyson's "Locksley Hall" illustrate HEADLESS iambic *octameter*:

> In the spring a fuller crimson comes upon the robin's breast;
> In the spring the wanton lapwing gets himself another crest.

Octapla (also **Octaples**) "Eightfolds": eight versions of something in parallel columns; almost always applied to ancient texts or translations of Scripture.

Octastich A group of eight lines of verse.

Octave An eight-line STANZA. The chief use of the term, however, is to denote the first eight-line division of the ITALIAN SONNET as separate from the last six-line division, the SESTET. In this sense it is a synonym for OCTET. In the strict sonnet usage the *octave* rhymes *abbaabba*, serves to state a position resolved in the sestet, and comes to such a complete close at the end of the eighth line as to be marked by a full stop.

Octavo A BOOK SIZE designating a book whose SIGNATURE results from sheets folded to eight leaves or sixteen pages.

Octet A group of eight lines of verse; an OCTASTICH. Sometimes used as a synonym for OCTAVE, the first eight lines of an ITALIAN SONNET.

Octosyllabic Verse Poetry in lines of eight syllables; however, the term is customarily applied to TETRAMETER verse in iambic or trochaic feet. It is used in many stanzaic FORMS, including LONG MEASURE and the *IN MEMORIAM* STANZA, but it most frequently appears in the octosyllabic couplet. Although it lends itself to what Byron called a "fatal facility," it has been used vividly and memorably by Herrick, Vaughan, Marvell, and Blake.

Ode A single, unified strain of exalted lyrical verse, directed to a single purpose, and dealing with one theme. The term connotes certain qualities of both manner and form. The *ode* is elaborate, dignified, and imaginative. In form the *ode* is more complicated than most LYRIC types. One useful distinction of form is the division into STROPHE, ANTISTROPHE, and EPODE. Originally a Greek form used in dramatic poetry, the *ode* was choral. Accompanied by music, the chorus of singers moved up one side during the strophe and down the other during the antistrophe and stood in place during the epode, a pattern that emphasized the rise and fall of emotion.

In English there are three types of *odes*: the PINDARIC (regular), the HORATIAN or homostrophic, and the IRREGULAR. The PINDARIC is characterized by the three-strophe division: the strophe and the antistrophe alike in form, the epode different. The meter and line length may vary within any one strophe of the *ode*, but when the movement is repeated, the metrical scheme for corresponding divisions should be similar though accompanied by new rhymes. It is not essential that strophe, antistrophe, and epode alternate regularly, because the epode may be used at the end or inconsistently between the strophe and the antistrophe (Collins's "Ode to Liberty"). The second type of *ode*, the HORATIAN or homostrophic, consists of only one stanza type, which may be almost infinitely varied within its pattern (Coleridge's "Ode to France"). The IRREGULAR *ode* is credited to Cowley, who seems to have thought he was writing Pindaric odes. Freedom within the strophe is characteristic, but the strophes are rules unto themselves, and all claim to stanza pattern may be discarded. The length of the lines may vary, the number of lines per strophe may fluctuate widely, the rhyme pattern need not be maintained, and the metrical movement will quicken and slacken with the mood and emotional intensity. Much more flexible than the two other types, the irregular *ode* affords greatest freedom of expression and greatest license as well. In English these three types are well represented in the following: Gray's "The Bard," an example of the strict PINDARIC; Collins's "Ode to Evening," an example of the HORATIAN; and Wordsworth's "Ode: Intimations of Immortality," an example of the IRREGULAR.

For his *odes*, Keats devised a number of regular or irregular stanzas, the basic being ten iambic lines mostly pentameter with a rhyme scheme combining the HEROIC QUATRAIN (or first quatrain of an ENGLISH SONNET) and the SESTET of an ITALIAN SONNET: *ababcdecde*. In contemporary poetry the public nature, solemn diction, and stately gravity of the *ode* have on occasion been effectively used for ironic overtones, as in Allen Tate's "Ode to the Confederate Dead."

[References: John Heath-Stubbs, *The Ode* (1969); Carol Maddison, *Apollo and the Nine: A History of the Ode* (1960).]

Odelet A little ODE.

Oedipus Complex In psychoanalysis, a libidinal feeling that develops in a child, especially a male child, between the ages of three and six, for the parent of the opposite sex. This attachment is generally accompanied by hostility to the parent of the child's own sex. The *Oedipus complex* is named for the ancient Theban hero who unwittingly slew his father and married his mother. See ELECTRA COMPLEX, with which it is in contrast.

[Reference: André Green, *The Tragic Effect: The Oedipus Complex in Tragedy* (tr. 1979).]

Off-Broadway Associated with an area of New York other than the theaters within a few blocks of Broadway and Times Square in Manhattan. "Broadway" connotes conventional plays expensively mounted at high prices; *Off-Broadway* connotes the experimental. The geographic setting of most *Off-Broadway* theaters is downtown Manhattan and other parts of New York. One also hears of "Off-Off-Broadway" and so forth.

Old Comedy Greek COMEDY of the fifth century B.C. performed at festivals of Dionysus. *Old Comedy* blended religious ceremony, satire, wit, and buffoonery. Farcical and bawdy, it contained much social satire, laughing harshly at most religious, political, military, and intellectual institutions and issues of its day, and containing LAMPOONS of individuals. It used STOCK CHARACTERS: the ALAZON, the EIRON, the sly dissembler, the entertaining clown, and the foil, along with a CHORUS costumed as animals.

The greatest writer of the *Old Comedy* was Aristophanes. Probably the most energetic modern counterpart is Eliot's fragmentary *Sweeney Agonistes*, subtitled *An Aristophanic Melodrama*.

Old English (Language) That Germanic dialect spoken in the British Isles between the ANGLO-SAXON invasions in the fifth century and the NORMAN CONQUEST in the eleventh. See ENGLISH LANGUAGE.

Old English Period The period between the invasion of England by the Teutonic tribes of Angles, Saxons, and Jutes, beginning around 428, and the establishment of the Norman rule around 1100, following the triumphant Conquest by the Norman French under William the Conqueror. Saxon monarchies were established in Sussex, Wessex, and Essex in the fifth and sixth centuries; Anglian monarchies in Northumbria, East Anglia, and Mercia in the sixth and seventh centuries. Christianity was introduced early and gradually won out over the pagan culture. It was an age of intertribal conflict and, in the ninth century, of struggles with the invading Danes. The greatest ruler of the period was Alfred, who, in the ninth century, effected a unification of the Teutonic groups. Still, even after a thousand years, Alfred remains the only English ruler to be styled "the Great."

Learning and culture flourished in the monasteries, with Whitby the cradle of English poetry in the North and Winchester of English prose in the South. Although much writing throughout the period was in Latin, Christian monks began writing in the vernacular that we call OLD ENGLISH around 700. In the earliest part of the period the poetry was centered on the life of the Germanic tribes and was basically pagan, although Christian elements were incorporated early. The best of the surviving poems are the great epic *Beowulf* (c. 700), "The Seafarer," "Widsith," and "Deor's Lament." Early poetry of a more emphatically Christian nature included Caedmon's "Song"; biblical PARAPHRASES such as *Genesis, Exodus, Daniel, Judith*; religious narratives such as the *Christ, Elene, Andreas*; and the allegorical *Phoenix* (translated from Latin). Literature first flourished in Northumbria, but in the reign of Alfred the Great (871–899) West Saxon became the literary medium. Under Alfred, much Latin literature was translated into English prose, such as Pope Gregory's *Pastoral Care*, Boethius's *Consolation of Philosophy*, and Bede's *Ecclesiastical History*; and the *Anglo-Saxon Chronicle* was revised and expanded. A second prose revival took place in the HOMILIES of Aelfric and Wulfstan (tenth and eleventh centuries), works noted for their rich style, reflecting Latin models. Late examples of Anglo-Saxon verse are the "Battle of Maldon" and the "Battle of Brunanburgh," heroic poems. The NORMAN CONQUEST (1066) put an end to serious literary work in the OLD ENGLISH LANGUAGE. See *Outline of Literary History*.

[References: Stanley B. Greenfield, *A Critical History of Old English Literature* (1965); F. M. Stenton, *Anglo-Saxon England*, 3rd ed. (1971); C. L. Wrenn, *A Study of Old English Literature* (1967); David M. Zesmer, *Guide to English Literature from Beowulf through Chaucer and Medieval Drama* (1961).]

Old English Versification The metrical system employed by poets before 1100. It is accentual, consisting of equal numbers of accented syllables per line with a varying number of unaccented syllables. The normal Old English line fell into two HEMISTICHS, having two accented syllables each and separated by a CAESURA. The accents are grammatical: They fall on syllables that would normally carry stress. The hemistichs are bound by ALLITERATION, one or both the accented syllables of the first alliterating with the first accented syllable of the second or, much more rarely, with the second accented syllable. Variants were the rare "short line," which contains only two stressed syllables and no caesura, the stressed syllables being bound by alliteration; and the HYPERMETRICAL line in which three or more stressed syllables may appear in each hemistich. Some modern poets have attempted to use the measure: Ezra Pound in his Canto I ("Bore sheep aboard her and our bodies also") rather loosely; W. H. Auden throughout his long poem *The Age of Anxiety* much more strictly; and Richard Wilbur, W. S. Merwin, and Fred Chappell occasionally.

[References: A. J. Bliss, *The Metre of Beowulf* (1958); John C. Pope, *The Rhythm of Beowulf*, rev. ed. (1966, orig. 1942); Eduard Sievers, *An Old English Grammar*, 3rd ed. (tr. 1903).]

Ollave (also **Ollamh, Ollam, Ollav**) Among the early Irish, a person of wisdom and learning; a poet sometimes ranking below DRUID but above BARD.

***Omar Khayyám* Stanza** See RUBÁIYÁT STANZA.

Omnibus (Latin dative plural, "for all.") A volume of selected works, usually by one author but sometimes by several, on one subject. The works are usually reprinted from earlier volumes.

Omniscient Point of View The POINT OF VIEW in a work of fiction in which the narrator is capable of knowing, seeing, and telling all. It is characterized by freedom in shifting from the exterior world to the inner selves of a number of characters, a freedom in movement in both time and place, and a freedom of the narrator to comment on the meaning of actions.

One-Act Play A form of drama that has come into its own since about 1890. Before that date *one-act plays* had been used chiefly on VAUDEVILLE programs and as CURTAIN RAISERS in the LEGITIMATE THEATER. Special attention to the *one-act play* came with the LITTLE THEATER MOVEMENT and the practice of staging a group of them for an evening's entertainment. That the form was adopted by playwrights of high ability (J. M. Barrie, A. W. Pinero, Gerhart Hauptmann, G. B. Shaw) furthered its development. A widening circle of authors has produced *one-act plays* in the twentieth century, including John Masefield, Lord Dunsany, Lady Gregory, J. M. Synge, John Galsworthy, A. A. Milne, Betty Smith, Eugene O'Neill, Paul Green, Thornton Wilder, Noël Coward, Tennessee Williams, Arthur Miller, Edward Albee, and Tom Stoppard.

Onomatopoeia Words that by their sound suggest their meaning: "hiss," "buzz," "whirr," "sizzle." However, *onomatopoeia* becomes a much subtler device when, in an effort to suit sound to sense, the poet creates verses that themselves carry their meaning in their sounds. A notable example appears in *The Princess* by Tennyson:

> The moan of doves in immemorial elms,
> And murmuring of innumerable bees.

The rhythm, the succession of sounds, and the effect of rhymes all contribute to the effect by which a poem as a pattern of sounds echoes the sense that its words denote. Such devices fall into several subdivisions. The "Gr-r-r" in Browning's "Soliloquy of the Spanish Cloister" comes close to being a direct transcription of noise and is not actually a word (it is not in any dictionary). Some *onomatopoeic* forms represent a sound, like "coo," while others, like "cuckoo," refer to the thing that makes the sound. Some forms are not recognizably mimetic or echoic and must be classified as merely formulaic or conventional *onomatopoeia*. No dog ever uttered a sound resembling "bow-wow," and yet we use that word to mean both the sound and the creature. By a sort of sentimental or associative bonding, most people feel that words somehow "sound like" what they mean or connote. But "soft," say, with its three unvoiced consonants, is hardly a soft sound, and "hard," with no unvoiced consonants, is hardly hard. Mallarmé complained that the French for "day" (*jour*) sounds dark, whereas "night" (*nuit*) sounds bright. "Big" is a relatively small syllable, "small" relatively big. One needs, therefore, to exercise caution in the search for relations between sound and sense. The great Swiss linguist Saussure argued convincingly that there is no such relation, even in exclamations or *onomatopoeia*, except according to conventions that are completely arbitrary and, as he said, "unmotivated." It remains possible for *onomatopoeia* to retain or suggest the *form* of a sound without really echoing its *substance*. A dog, for instance, may not say "bow-wow," but whatever it does say rhymes, as do "bow" and "wow." The cuckoo may not say "cuckoo," but whatever it does say is repetitive and reduplicative, as is "cuckoo." Although now discredited, the old sentimental-associative case was well argued by Pope in *An Essay on Criticism*:

> 'Tis not enough no harshness gives offense,
> The sound must seem an echo to the sense:
> Soft is the strain when Zephyr gently blows,
> And the smooth stream in smoother numbers flows:
> But when loud surges lash the sounding shore,
> The hoarse, rough verse should like the torrent roar:
> When Ajax strives some rock's vast weight to throw,
> The line too labors, and the words move slow.

Tennyson's "murmuring of innumerable bees" has been prized as an example of apt *onomatopoeia*, but John Crowe Ransom responded that sound and sense are mutually irrelevant, that Tennyson's line means what it means because of the discursive significance of the words and that one could completely change the meaning of the line without changing the sound very much: "murdering of innumerable beeves." The sentiment favoring answerable or significant *onomatopoeia* remains robust, however, and it has been observed by recent existentialist-phenomenological critics that poetry percussively directs our attention to sound as such, with all its powers and mysteries, and the heart of many sophisticated poems seems situated in a region of *onomatopoeia* made significant—as, say, Eliot's *The Waste Land* ends with a fable of interpreting a single onomatopoeic Sanskrit syllable: "DA." See HIERONYMY.

Onset One of the three components of a SYLLABLE. The *onset*, which is optional, consists of one or more consonants and comes before the NUCLEUS (vowel), which in turn comes before the optional CODA (consonant matter again).

Open Couplet A couplet in which the second line is not complete but depends on succeeding material for completion. Browning uses the *open couplet* in "My Last Duchess" with such virtuosity that many readers fail to notice the presence of rhyme:

> That's my last Duchess painted on the wall,
> Looking as if she were alive. I call
> That piece a wonder, now. . . .

Consider also the beginning of Browning's "Rudel to the Lady of Tripoli":

> I know a Mount, the gracious Sun perceives
> First, when he visits, last, too, when he leaves
> The world; and, vainly favored, it repays
> The day-long glory of his steadfast gaze
> By no change of its large calm form of snow.

See ENJAMBEMENT, RUN-ON LINES.

Open-Endedness With increased awareness of closure as a structural element, some recent critics have become simultaneously aware of the possibility of *open-endedness*, by which a work need not be tied up tidily at the end with a terminal final cadence and a caption reading END. A work can stop, as Ezra Pound's "Near Perigord" does, without concluding or closing:

She who could never live save through one person,
She who could never speak save to one person,
And all the rest of her a shifting change,
A broken bundle of mirrors . . . !

Pound and his friend William Carlos Williams specialized in open-ended poems. Another open-ended work is Joyce's *Finnegans Wake*, which stops in mid-sentence with a suspended

the

not followed by a period. John Updike said that he wanted *Rabbit Redux* to end on an"open note."

Opera Though the primary interest in *opera* is musical, it has exerted influence on English literary history. *Opera* is musical DRAMA in which the dialogue instead of being spoken is sung, to the accompaniment of instrumental music, now almost always an orchestra. A play in which incidental music is stressed may be called "operatic," but is not true *opera* if the dialogue is spoken. Greek drama contained dialogue sung to the accompaniment of the lyre or flute and is therefore a precursor of modern *opera*, which developed in Italy as a result of amateur efforts to recapture the quality of the musical effects of Greek tragedy by means of musical recitation instrumentally accompanied. The form was at first a MONODY, as in Jacopo Peri's *Euridice* (1600), the first public production in the new style. From these beginnings the important form now known as grand *opera* developed. Italian *opera* reached England soon after 1700, but before this date certain definite advances in the direction of *opera* had taken place. To some degree an outgrowth of the Renaissance MASQUE, Sir William Davenant's *Siege of Rhodes* (1656) was a musical entertainment, written in rhyme and designed to be sung in recitative and aria. The attention to scenery as well as the SONGS and orchestral accompaniment suggest later English *opera*. During the Restoration Age operatic versions of some of Shakespeare's plays (*The Tempest, Macbeth*) were called "dramatic *operas*," but the dialogue was spoken. About 1689 Henry Purcell and Nahum Tate brought out *Dido and Aeneas*, with the dialogue in recitative. Early in the eighteenth century Italian *operas* were translated and sung by English singers. Later, bilingual *operas* appeared, in which Italian singers sang part of the dialogue in Italian and English singers sang the rest in English. The first Italian *opera* sung in Italian in England was *Almahide* (1710), which established the success of the form in England. George Frederick Handel came to England and produced *Rinaldo* in 1711. He exerted a powerful influence for many years thereafter. From the first, efforts to employ Italian singers met with disfavor, as evidenced by Addison's satire and by John Gay's famous BURLESQUE *opera, The Beggar's Opera* (1728). The success of *opera* and various forms of burlesque *opera* at this time probably had much to do with the tendency toward lyrical and spectacular elements on the stage, which the presence of the PATENT THEATERS encouraged in the eighteenth and nineteenth centuries. For later literature in English, the *operas* of Mozart and Wagner proved to be most influential, particularly for George Bernard Shaw, who wrote a book on Wagner and appropriated certain operatic devices and effects in *Man and Superman* and other plays; and for W. H. Auden, who wrote translations and also an occasional *libretto*.

Three Wagner music dramas (the term he favored over "operas") figure in Eliot's *The Waste Land* (*Tristan, Parsifal*, and The *Ring*). The most useful English writers from the viewpoint of opera composers have been Shakespeare and Scott, whose *Bride of Lammermoor* has been transformed into opera more than once.

Opéra bouffe A French term for a very light form of COMIC OPERA developed from VAUDEVILLE music and said to be the ancestor of the comic operas of Gilbert and Sullivan.

Operetta A COMIC OPERA, with music, songs, and spectacular effects but with the dialogue spoken.

Opsis Aristotle's term for the SPECTACLE as an element in drama—the least important, coming sixth in order after *mythos, ethos, dianoia, lexis*, and *melos*. Nowadays the term is used for both spectacle as what an audience sees and the visual or graphic aspect of what a reader sees on a page.

Opuscule (often in Latin form **opusculum**, plural, **opuscula**) A small work. In 1860 Robert Gordon Latham published *Opuscula: Essays, Chiefly Philological and Ethnographical*. Wallace Stevens's "Study of Two Pears" begins, "Opusculum paedagogum."

Oral Transmission The transmission of material by word of mouth and memory. Materials such as the FOLK EPIC, the BALLAD, FOLKLORE, PROVERBS, and many songs that originated among illiterate, semiliterate, or preliterate people were presented aloud to their audiences and transmitted by memory rather than in writing. Such materials use many formulaic expressions, pronounced rhythms, refrains, and other devices to aid memory. Materials preserved through *oral transmission* have usually undergone many changes and often exist in several versions. Some established practices of written literature, and of verse most particularly, still bear the traces of their oral origins among persons of marginal literacy. Various levels of repetition, for example, are hardly needed with a written text.

[References: A. B. Lord, *The Singer of Tales*, 2nd ed. (2000; orig. 1960, reprinted 1968); Walter J. Ong, *Orality and Literacy: The Technologizing of the Word* (1982).]

Oration A formal speech delivered in an impassioned manner. Although a major cultural interest in classical times and even up to a few decades ago, the *oration* has lost its popular appeal and is now heard but rarely in legislative halls, the courtroom, the church. The classical *oration* has seven parts: (1) the entrance, or EXORDIUM, to catch the audience's attention; (2) the NARRATION, to set forth the facts; (3) the EXPOSITION or DEFINITION; (4) the proposition, to clarify the points at issue and state exactly what is to be proved; (5) the confirmation, to set forth the arguments for and against and to advance proof; (6) the confutation or refutation, to refute the opponent's arguments; and (7) the conclusion or EPILOGUE, to sum up.

Organic Form A notion of the structure of a literary work as growing from its conception in the thought, feeling, and personality of the writer, rather than being shaped arbitrarily and mechanically in a preconceived mold. A work grows like a living organism, its parts inseparable and indivisible, the whole greater than the sum of its parts. The concept was advanced by Coleridge, most vigorously in his defense of Shakespeare against the charge of formlessness: "No work of true genius dare want its appropriate form; neither indeed is there any danger of this. As it must not, so neither can it, be lawless! For it is even this that constitutes its genius—the power of acting creatively under laws of its own origination. The true ground of the mistake [about Shakespeare's formlessness] lies in the confounding of mechanical regularity with organic form. The form is mechanic, when on any given material we impress a predetermined form, not necessarily arising out of the properties of the material;—as when to a mass of wet clay we give whatever shape we wish it to retain when hardened.

The *organic form*, on the other hand, is innate; it shapes, as it develops, itself from within, and the fulness of its development is one and the same with the perfection of its outward form. "Such as the life is, such is the form." This concept has been pervasive for the past 150 years. The symbol most frequently used for such a work has been that of a plant, as having a *form* and a growth uniquely true to its individual nature. Cleanth Brooks's statement that "The parts of a poem are related as are the parts of a growing plant" is a representative example. As R. G. Collingwood argued, something produced by a mechanical, technical operation can be analyzed according to principles of form and matter, end and means, cause and effect; such artifacts can be mass-produced, and their modular parts or components may be detached and interchanged. None of this applies to art proper, because it is not mechanical but vital and organic. Discussing differences among description, dialogue, and incident, Henry James, in "The Art of Fiction," makes the case for organic unity: "People often talk of these things as if they had a kind of internecine distinctness, instead of melting into each other at every breath, and being intimately associated parts of one general effort of expression." More recent critics (for example, Paul de Man in *Blindness and Insight*) have been suspicious or skeptical of the notion of organic form as a metaphor seeking to treat linguistic artifact as if it were a living object and not language at all.

Orientalism A general or specific quality of thought or expression associated with the Orient, the East, or Asia; in some older instances "the Orient" includes Israel and Greece. Although occasionally neutral and sometimes positive, ideas of the Oriental have often been condescending and contemptuous. This *Orientalism* has been painted by Edward Said as "a way of coming to terms with the Orient that is based on the Orient's special place in European Western Experience. The Orient is not only adjacent to Europe; it is also the place of Europe's greatest and richest and oldest colonies, the source of its civilizations and languages, its cultural contestant, and one of its deepest and most recurring images of the Other."

[Reference: Edward Said, *Orientalism* (1979).]

Ornamentalism The quality of being ornamental, usually with the disparaging implication of mere ornament as inferior to substance.

Orphism Defined by Gerald L. Bruns as "the idea of poetic speech as the ground of all signification—as an expressive movement which 'objectifies' a world for man . . . or which establishes the world within the horizon of human knowing and so makes signification possible."

[Reference: Gerald L. Bruns, *Modern Poetry and the Idea of Language: A Critical and Historical Study* (1974).]

Ossianic Controversy See FORGERIES, LITERARY.

Ottava rima A stanza consisting of eight IAMBIC PENTAMETER (or HENDECASYLLABIC) lines rhyming *abababcc*. Boccaccio is credited with originating the stanza, which was much used by Tasso and Ariosto. Some English poets using *ottava rima* are Wyatt (the earliest in English), Spenser, Milton, Keats, Byron, Longfellow, Browning, and Yeats (notably in fifteen of his greatest later poems). Contemporary poets using the stanza include Kenneth Koch and Clive James. The couplet of the stanza, like that at the end of a SHAKESPEAREAN SONNET, is often used for a pithy summary, a reversal, a sudden concentration of information, or (as in the example from Byron) surprise and deflation. The following is from Byron's *Don Juan*:

> But words are things, and a small drop of ink
> Falling like dew, upon a thought, produces
> That which makes thousands, perhaps millions, think;
> 'Tis strange, the shortest letter which man uses
> Instead of speech, may form a lasting link
> Of ages; to what straits old Time reduces
> Frail man, when paper—even a rag like this,
> Survives himself, his tomb, and all that's his!

Outride A term Gerard Manley Hopkins applied to a SLACK SYLLABLE—that is, an unstressed syllable—added to a FOOT. An *outride* does not change the basic scansion of a line, for, in Hopkins's system, only the stressed syllables determine the scansion. There may be as many as three *outrides* attached to a foot—that is, following a stressed syllable.

Outsider Art Art produced by persons on the outside of every official or unofficial arena of production. These are the songs that nobody will sing, the poems that no magazine will publish—at the time. In most cases, *outsider art* remains on the outside; it is just no good. Once in a great while, however, what is one age's *outsider art* becomes the officially canonized art of a succeeding generation, to whom the peculiar status of certain honored classics (poems by Dickinson and Hopkins, for example) must remain baffling.

Overstatement General or specific exaggeration; HYPERBOLE.

Overweighting In the scansion of ALLITERATIVE VERSE in Old Germanic languages, overweighting describes the situation when the four accented syllables in a line are joined by one or more syllables with substantial secondary accent, normal in compounds.

Ownership Box In newspapers and other periodicals, the area set aside for the names of persons in management, subscription information, the postal service identification number, and other such information, required by the U.S. Postal Service to be printed somewhere in the first five pages of a publication.

Oxford Movement Also known as the "Tractarian Movement" and the "Anglo-Catholic Revival." During the first third of the nineteenth century the English Church had become lax about ancient doctrines, discipline, ritual, and the upkeep of church edifices. In 1833 a reform movement got under way at Oxford following a sermon on "national apostasy" by John Keble. The leader was John Henry Newman, who wrote the first of the ninety papers (*Tracts for the Times*, 1833–1841) in which the ideas of the group were advocated. Other leaders were R. H. Froude, Isaac Williams, Hugh James Rose (Cambridge), and E. B. Pusey. The reformers aimed primarily at combating liberalism and skepticism and regaining the dignity, beauty, purity, and zeal of earlier times. They hoped also to protect the Church from the encroachment of the State, as threatened by the Whig Reform Bill of 1832 and other measures aimed at reducing both the revenues and the authority of the Church.

The sponsors of the movement undertook to prove the divine origin of the Church and the historical continuity of the early Church with the Church of England. This led them to an espousal of doctrines that some regarded as Roman Catholic, and after the publication of Newman's final tract in 1841 a storm of criticism arose. Newman lost his position at Oxford, became a layman, and finally (1845) joined the Roman Catholic church, eventually to become Cardinal. When Charles Kingsley attacked his sincerity, Newman replied with the famous *Apologia pro Vita Sua* (1864), a full statement of his spiritual and mental history. Though some of Newman's followers also became Roman Catholics, the main movement, led now by Pusey, continued, though in its later stages it became less controversial and theoretical and more practical, furthering the establishment of guilds, the improvement of church music, the revival of the ritual, and the building and beautifying of church buildings. The movement attracted the attention of various literary men, with Carlyle heaping disdain on it and Arnold attacking it. The sponsors of the movement wrote a number of PROGAGANDA NOVELS, such as Newman's *Loss and Gain* and Charlotte M. Yonge's *The Heir of Redclyffe*.

The Episcopal Church in the United States reflects much of the reform doctrine of the Tractarians.

Oxford Reformers A term applied to a group of humanist scholars whose association began at Oxford in the early Renaissance, particularly John Colet, Sir Thomas More, and the Dutch scholar Erasmus. Though Erasmus, who had come to Oxford to study Greek, was the most famous of the group and More the best loved, Colet seems to have been the real leader. The group was interested in effecting certain reforms in Church and State based on humanist ideas. Moral training and reform were to be accomplished through reason rather than emotion. Humanity should be uplifted through education and the improvement of individual character. The Church should be purged of corrupt practices. The group advocated the historical method in the study of the Bible and opposed medieval SCHOLASTICISM and asceticism. More recorded his dream of a perfect human society in *Utopia* (1516); Colet, when dean of St. Paul's, founded with his own funds the St. Paul's school for boys, where new methods of instruction were developed and sons of commoners might be admitted; Erasmus outlined his ideals in his *Education of a Christian Prince*. Although keenly interested in purging the Church of the evils that Luther a few years later rebelled against, the *Oxford Reformers* were unwilling to follow either Luther or Henry VIII in breaking with Rome, and they died good Catholics, though disappointed idealists.

Oxymoron A self-contradictory combination of words or smaller verbal units; usually noun-noun, adjective-adjective, adjective-noun, adverb-adverb, or adverb-verb. "*Oxymoron*" itself is an *oxymoron*, from the Greek meaning "sharp-dull." Others are "bittersweet," "jumbo shrimp," "guest host," "pianoforte," and "chiaroscuro." Politics seems to favor *oxymoron*, as in a self-designated "conservative Christian anarchist" (Henry Adams), "Tory anarchist" (George Orwell), or "left conservative" (Norman Mailer). The Latin maxim *Festina lente* ("Hurry slowly") is an *oxymoron*. The second half of George Herbert's "Bitter-Sweet" seems to be an exercise in *oxymoron*:

I will complain, yet praise;
I will bewail, approve;
And all my sour-sweet days
I will lament and love.

An exaggerated employment of *oxymoron* is seen in Romeo's speech early in *Romeo and Juliet*:

Why, then, O brawling love! O loving hate!
O anything, of nothing first create!
O heavy lightness! serious vanity!
Misshapen chaos of well-seeming forms!
Feather of lead, bright smoke, cold fire, sick health!
Still-waking sleep, that is not what it is!

Oxytone Having an acute accent on the final syllable.

Prisma 1931. Designed by Rudolf Koch at the Klingspor Typefoundry, now defunct. The design has been continued by D. Stempel AG, Germany.

P.M. An abbreviation found occasionally in hymnals, variously indicating PARTICULAR, PECULIAR, or PROPER METER or measure. All three can mean, among other possibilities, a meter peculiar or proper to one particular hymn or to a musical setting of unmetered PROSE.

P.S. Stage direction for "prompt side" (or "prompter side"), stage left in Britain, stage right in the United States.

Paean A song of praise or joy. Originally restricted to ODES sung by a Greek chorus in honor of Apollo, the term was later broadened to include praise of other deities. Homer indicates, too, that *paeans* were frequently sung on military occasions: before an attack, after a victory, when a fleet set sail. The word now means any song of joy or expression of praise.

Paeon A FOOT consisting of one long or stressed syllable and three short or unstressed syllables. *Paeons* are named according to which of the four syllables is long or stressed, a "first *paeon*" being ´˘˘˘, a "second" ˘´˘˘, a "third" ˘˘´˘, and a "fourth" ˘˘˘´. Although not common in English, this essentially classic foot does occasionally appear. Gerard Manley Hopkins argued that all the feet of SPRUNG RHYTHM began with a stressed syllable followed by any number of unstressed: a stressed syllable followed by one unstressed is a TROCHEE, followed by two is a DACTYL, and followed by three is a first *paeon*.

Paganism Belief or conduct different from that contained in a prevailing religion; in the English-speaking world, *paganism* often means "not Christian." Charges of *paganism* are brought against writers—such as Byron, Baudelaire, Rimbaud, William Carlos Williams, Ezra Pound, D. H. Lawrence, Karen Blixen, and Henry Miller—whose works or lives oppose what a majority accept. Williams wrote an autobiographical novel titled *Voyage to Pagany*, about an American in Europe.

Pageant Used in three senses: (1) a scaffold or stage on which dramas were performed in the Middle Ages; (2) plays performed on such stages; and (3) modern dramatic spectacles designed to celebrate some historical event. The medieval *pageant*, constructed on wheels for processions, as in celebrating Corpus Christi day, was used by a particular guild for the production of a particular play. Thus, the *pageant* of the fishermen, designed to present the play of Noah, would represent the Ark.

Though the modern *pageant* is an outgrowth of an ancient tradition that includes religious festivals and Roman triumphs, its recent development makes it essentially a twentieth- century form. It is usually an outdoor exhibition consisting of scenes presented with recitation (prologues, etc.), ordinarily with dialogue, with historical costumes, often with music, the whole designed to commemorate some event that appeals to the loyalties of the populace. Sometimes the *pageant* is a processional, with a series of floats, bands, and dignitaries, though it is sometimes presented in an outdoor theater, such as an athletic stadium. In America *pageants*—also called outdoor dramas—with actors, dramatic scenes, dances, and songs have become widespread for the celebration of historical events of special local interest. *The Lost Colony*, by Paul Green—which has run for the summer months every year since 1937, at Manteo, North Carolina, the historical scene of much of its action—is the best known of these *pageants.*

Page-Turner Vernacular term for a book, usually a novel, that, because of fast pace and engrossing suspense, is irresistibly readable.

Paleography The study of old forms of handwriting, important in textual studies for establishing texts and deciding authorship.

Palilogy (or **Palillogy**) Deliberate repetition of words, as in Lincoln's "Gettysburg Address": "that government of the people, by the people, for the people, shall not perish from the earth."

Palimbacchius An ANTIBACCHIUS: two long or strong syllables followed by one short or weak.

Palimpsest A writing surface, whether of vellum, papyrus, or other material, that has been used more than once for manuscript purposes. Before the invention of paper, the scarcity of writing material made such substances very valuable, and the vellum surfaces were often scraped or rubbed and the papyrus surfaces washed. With material so used a second time it frequently happened that the earlier script either was not completely erased or that, with age, it showed through the new. In this way many documents of very early periods have been preserved for posterity. In one instance, a Syriac text of St. Chrysostom of perhaps the tenth century was found to be superimposed on a sixth-century grammatical work in Latin, which again had covered some fifth-century Latin records. Modern technology makes it possible to recover many of the original texts. Because almost any piece of language has been used already over and over again, both Ezra Pound and Hilda Doolittle have used *palimpsest* metaphorically to suggest the many layers and tissues of meaning in any text.

Palindrome Writing that reads the same from left to right and from right to left, such as the word "civic" or the statement fancifully attributed to Napoleon, "Able was I ere I saw Elba." "Et tu, Brute" is almost a *palindrome*. A near-palindromic mirror-image pattern of consonants occurs in Dickinson's line "His notice sudden is." Keats, Poe, and Bridges all used "dim" and "mid" near each other in poems. On the acoustic or graphic level, *palindrome* is a species of CHIASMUS.

Palinode A piece of writing recanting or retracting a previous writing, particularly such a recanting, in verse, of an earlier ode.

Pamphlet A short piece, usually on a current topic, issued as a separate publication. A *pamphlet* has fewer pages than a book, is always unbound, and may or may not have paper covers. Most *pamphlets* are polemical tracts of only transitory value.

Pan (from PANORAMA or PANORAMIC) In film-making: (1) Strictly, a horizontal camera move on a stationary vertical axis, from right to left or left to right. (2) Loosely, any horizontal camera move. (3) More loosely yet, any camera movie (as in "pan up" or "pan down").

Panegyric A formal composition lauding a person for an achievement; a EULOGY. Roman *panegyrics* were usually presented in praise of a living person, thing, or achievement. In Greek they were often reserved for praise of the dead. This was a popular form of oratory among fulsome speakers who praised living emperors. Two famous *panegyrics* are that of Gorgias, the *Olympiacus*, in praise of those who established the festivals, and that of Pliny the Younger praising Trajan. The term now often bears a derogatory connotation. See ENCOMIUM.

Panorama Originally, a device (invented in the late eighteenth century) for showing a large graphic representation of a whole landscape or other scene. In time, the word has been applied to any wide or complete view of a subject, such as *A Panorama of the Napoleonic Wars* or *A Panorama of the Indo-European Languages*. Sometimes used to describe a literary technique that presents such a view.

Panoramic Method A term for that POINT OF VIEW in which an author presents material by EXPOSITION rather than in SCENES, giving actions and conversations in summary rather than in detail. In film, it refers to scenes photographed at some distance or by moving the camera ("panning") over a series of connected distant objects. It is similar to DEEP FOCUS or COMPOSITION IN DEPTH.

Pantheism A philosophic-religious attitude that finds the spirit of God manifest in all things and that holds that whereas all things speak the glory of God it is equally true that the glory of God is made up of all things. Finite objects are at once both God and the manifestation of God. The term is impossible to define exactly since it is so personal a conviction as to be differently interpreted by different philosophers, but for its literary significance it is clearly enough described as an ardent faith in nature as both the revelation of deity and deity itself. The word was first used in 1705 by the deist John Toland who called himself a pantheist (from *pan* meaning "all" and *theos* meaning "deity"). The pantheistic attitude, however, is much older than the eighteenth century, since it pervades the primitive thought of Egypt and India, was common in Greece long before the time of Christ, was taken up by the Neoplatonists of the Middle Ages, and has played an important role in Christian and Hebraic doctrine. Spinoza is, from the philosophical point of view, the great spokesman of *pantheism*, as Goethe is the great poet of the idea. In literature *pantheism* finds frequent expression. Wordsworth in England and Emerson in America may be selected from many in giving typical expression to the pantheistic conception. The following line from Wordsworth's *Lines Composed a Few Miles Above Tintern Abbey* express the idea clearly:

. . . a sense sublime
Of something far more deeply interfused,
Whose dwelling is the light of setting suns,
And the round ocean and the living air,
And the blue sky, and in the mind of man:
A motion and a spirit, that impels
All thinking things, all objects of all thought,
And rolls through all things.

Pantisocracy A Utopian community in which all are equal and all rule. The word was first used by Robert Southey in the 1790s, and he and Coleridge entertained dreams of establishing a *pantisocratic* community on the banks of the Susquehanna. In *Don Juan* (3:93) Byron cracked, "All are not moralists like Southey, when / He prated to the world of 'Panti-socrasy.' "

Pantomime In its broad sense the term means silent acting; the form of dramatic activity in which silent motion, gesture, expression, and costume express emotional states or narrative situations. Ritual dances may be pantomimic. Partly pantomimic was the Roman MIME and completely so the English DUMB SHOW. In English stage history, *pantomime* usually means the spectacular dramatic form that flourished from the early years of the eighteenth century. Though "*pantomime* proper" (no speaking) is said to have been introduced by a dancing master in 1702 at the Drury Lane Theatre, the usual form of *pantomime*, as sponsored at Lincoln's Inn Fields theater by John Rich some years later, was more varied. There was usually a serious legendary story told through dancing and songs. In these stories moved the figures of the COMMEDIA DELL'ARTE, burlesquing the action in silent movement. A background of the most spectacular description, the lavish use of "machinery," and many changes of scene made the *pantomime* visually exciting. The *pantomime* flourished in the eighteenth and nineteenth centuries. English *pantomimes* (sometimes with a girl as the "leading boy," and including dance, song, and SLAPSTICK) have been common in this century and are often built around such traditional themes as Humpty-Dumpty, Dick Whittington and his cat, and Cinderella. In film, particularly in the days of silent motion pictures, *pantomime* acting was a major way of storytelling. Charlie Chaplin, Harpo Marx, and Buster Keaton were notable *pantomime* actors; something of the art has persisted into the "age of sound," as, say, in some of Red Skelton's and Jackie Gleason's television routines.

Pantoum The *pantoum* may consist of any number of four-lined stanzas, but in any case the second and fourth lines of one stanza must reappear as the first and third lines of the following stanza. The stanzas are quatrains rhyming *abab*. In the final stanza the first and third lines of the first stanza recur in reverse order, the poem thus ending with the same line with which it began. The *pantoum* was actually taken over from the Malaysian by Victor Hugo and other French poets. Excellent examples have been produced by the contemporary poets John Ashbery ("Hotel Lautréamont") and Robert Morgan ("Audubon's Flute").

Paperback A book with a paper or other softback or cover, a format that gained in popularity around 1900 and has continued. Some books are published first in a CLOTHBOUND or hardback form and then later in *paperback*; some are published in both formats simultaneously; some only in one or the other. Publishers tend to favor the hardback first, because it is more profitable.

Parabasis In Greek OLD COMEDY, a long address to the audience by the chorus speaking for the author. It usually consisted of witty remarks on contemporary affairs, frequently with overt personal references. It was not directly related to the plot of the comedy itself.

Parable An illustrative story teaching a lesson. A true *parable* parallels, detail for detail, the situation that calls forth the *parable* for illustration. A *parable* is, in this sense, an ALLEGORY. In Christian countries the most famous *parables* are those told by Christ, the best known of which is that of the Prodigal Son.

Paradiastole (1) Distinguishing two meanings of the same word, as in "I am responsible for the oversight in this case, if 'oversight' means 'supervision' but not if 'oversight' means 'mistake.'" (2) Euphemistic replacement of a negative word with something more pleasant.

Paradox A statement that although seemingly contradictory or absurd may actually be well founded or true. As we approach the conceptual limits of discourse—as commonly happens in philosophy and theology—language seems to rely increasingly on *paradox.* Incarnation, Immaculate Conception, Virgin Birth, and the Holy Trinity all involve some elements of *paradox*, as do many of St. Paul's utterances, particularly in 2 Corinthians ("For when I am weak, then I am strong"). *Paradox* teases the mind and tests the limits of language; it can be a potent device. Religious poems by Southwell, Donne, Hopkins, and T. S. Eliot show a conspicuous degree of *paradox*, also discoverable in such OXYMORONS as "soft hardness" in Henry James's *The American* and "happy sadness" in Frost's "The Wind and the Rain." Richard Bentley's statement that there are "none so credulous as infidels" is an illustration, as is "less is more" in Robert Browning's "Andrea del Sarto." *Paradox* is a common element in epigrammatic writing, as the work of G. K. Chesterton or Oscar Wilde shows. The presence of *paradox* in poetry became a serious concern of some of the New Critics, notably Cleanth Brooks, who sees *paradox* as a fundamental element of poetic language. In Brooks's celebrated formulation, the language of science necessarily relies on the principles of noncontradiction, leaving a countervailing principle of contradiction, registered somehow as a *paradox*, to be the necessary language of poetry.

[Reference: Cleanth Brooks, *The Well Wrought Urn; Studies in the Structure of Poetry* (1947).]

Paragoge The addition of an extra letter, syllable, or sound at the end of a word, as in "dearie" for "dear." Such extra syllables are frequently added for the sake of the meter in nursery rhymes and ballads, as in these lines from "The Baffled Knight":

> Quoth he, "Shall you and I, lady,
>   Among the grass lie down a?
> And I will have a special care
>   Of rumpling of your gown a."

Paragoge still turns up in the vernacular, as in the locutions spelled "drownded" and "oncet" (for "drowned" and "once").

Paragram Generally, a word that resembles another and is used in its place for the sake of EUPHEMISM, APOTROPAIC deformation, insult, avoidance of libel, or some other purpose. "Gad," "gosh," and "golly," for example, are *paragrams* of "God." Specifically, *paragram* refers to an alteration of a name, as when the insulting "Moloch" or "Molech" (from Hebrew *mōlek*) replaces the Canaanite *Melek* ("king"). In Chapter 1 of *The Great Gatsby* (1925), Tom Buchanan asks, "Have you read 'The Rise of the Colored Empires' by this man Goddard?" "Goddard," a *paragram* of "Stoddard," clearly refers to Lothrop Stoddard, author of *The Rising Tide of Color Against White-World-Supremacy* (1920). One cannot be sure whether the replacement has been effected by Buchanan, by Carraway the narrator, by Fitzgerald the author, or by Scribners, who published Stoddard's book as well as Fitzgerald's. The name of Ezra Pound's invented poetaster "Alfred Venison" is obviously a *paragram* of "Alfred Tennyson." Similarly, the "Colonel C. E. Florence, who preferred to become a private soldier again" in Chapter 18 of *Lady Chatterley's Lover* represents Colonel T. E. Lawrence—with added interest because the author of the novel is also named "Lawrence" (the two were not related). In modern works that parallel older legends or myths, names may work as *paragrams*: "John Tanner" (for "Juan Tenorio") in Shaw's *Man and Superman*, "Ezra Mannon" (for "Agamemnon") in O'Neill's *Mourning Becomes Electra*, "Urfe" (for "Orpheus") in Fowles's *The Magus*, and "Nick Noxin" for Dick Nixon in John Seelye's *Dirty Tricks*.

Paraleipsis, Paralepsis, Paralipsis Pretending to say nothing about something one goes on to say quite a bit about, as in phrases beginning in the manner of "to say nothing of his reputation as the drug dealers' favorite lawyer for seven years running." Similar to *OCCUPATIO*.

Paralipomena (plural of **Paralipomenon**) Something omitted from a text but later included in an APPENDIX or elsewhere. The plural form is sometimes applied to the Old Testament Book of Chronicles, supposed to contain materials omitted from the Books of Kings. Also used in such other texts as Novalis's *Heinrich von Ofterdingen* and philosophical works by Schopenhauer.

Parallelism Such an arrangement that one element of equal importance with another is similarly developed and phrased. The principle of *parallelism* dictates that coordinate ideas should have coordinate presentation. Within a sentence, for instance, where several elements of equal importance are to be expressed, if one element is cast in a relative clause the others should be expressed in relative clauses. Conversely, of course, the principle of *parallelism* demands that unequal elements should *not* be expressed in similar constructions. Practiced writers are not likely to attempt, for example, the comparison of positive and negative statements, of inverted and uninverted constructions, of dependent and independent clauses. And, for an example of simple *parallelism*, the sentence immediately preceding may serve. Some departures from *parallelism* may qualify as "SLEIGHT OF 'AND,'" but most are just signs of carelessness, as when someone says, "I don't like to fish or swimming." But a deliberate violation of *parallelism* can be highly dramatic. Consider the couplet in Housman's "Hell Gate" in which coordinating conjunctions (POLYSYNDETON) create the expectation of a parallel group of active verbs but abruptly end with a linking verb:

> Then the sentry turned his head,
> Looked, and knew me, and was Ned.

Parallelism is characteristic of Hebrew poetry, being notably present in the Psalms, as in:

The Heavens declare the glory of God;
And the firmament sheweth his handiwork.

Paralogism A piece of faulty reasoning. "Scorpions have eight legs. Two horses have eight legs. Ergo, two horses are a scorpion."

Paraphrase A restatement of an idea in such a way as to retain the meaning while changing the diction and form. A *paraphrase* is often an amplification of the original for the purpose of clarity, though the term is also used for any rather general restatement of an expression or passage. Thus, one might speak of a *paraphrase* from the French, meaning a loose statement of the idea rather than an exact translation, or of a *paraphrase* of a poem, indicating a prose explanation of a difficult passage. In some contemporary criticism the paraphrasing of works of literary art is frowned on, and the followers of the NEW CRITICISM condemn what they call the "heresy of *paraphrase*," a term suggesting their stand that the essential nature of a poem is incommunicable in terms other than its own.

Pararhyme An acoustic effect, practiced by Wilfred Owen, W. H. Auden, Keith Douglas, and others, whereby the place of rhyme is taken by a combination of ALLITERATION and CONSONANCE RHYME. In ordinary rhyme, such syllables as "skip" and "lip" have different ONSETS (*sk* and *l*) but share a NUCLEUS and CODA (*ip*). In *pararhyme*, such syllables as "skip" and "scoop" have different nuclei but share an onset and coda.

Parasynthesis Derivation from a stem-word in such a way as not to affect accent. Such a process can be heard in the formation of "neighborhood" from "neighbor" or "workmanship" from "workman," where the accent remains on the first syllable; in some procedures involving Greek or Latin, however, as when "photography" is formed from "photograph" or "denotation" is formed from "denote," the accent shifts (by a process called "synthesis").

Parataxis An arrangement of sentences, clauses, phrases, or words in coordinate rather than subordinate constructions, often without connectives, as in Julius Caesar's "Veni, vidi, vici" ("I came, I saw, I conquered"), or with coordinate conjunctions, as in Hemingway's or Whitman's extensive use of "and" as a connective. Thus, POLYSYNDETON (especially in the form "and . . . and . . . and . . .") often accompanies *parataxis*. As a rule *parataxis* is found more in speech than in writing and more in juvenile or uncultivated utterance than in the mature of sophisticated. See HYPOTAXIS.

Paregmenon The same as POLYPTOTON: the use of two different words derived from the same root, as in this passage from Frost's "Directive": "Your destination and your destiny's / A brook. . . ."

Parembole (also **Paremptosis**) A PARENTHESIS involving relevant material, with the supposition that parenthesis itself involves the irrelevant.

Paremia (also **Paroemia, Parimia**) A PROVERB or ADAGE.

Parenthesis An explanatory remark inside a statement and frequently separated from it by parentheses ( ). However, any comment that is an interruption of the immediate subject is spoken of as a *parenthesis*, whether it be a word, phrase, clause, sentence, or paragraph. Commas and dashes are substituted for the *parenthesis* marks when the interruption is not so abrupt as to demand the ( ). Brackets [ ] are used for parenthetical material more remote from the subject of the sentence than *parentheses* will control and also to enclose material injected or interpolated by some editorial hand. Modern novelists, interested in accurately reporting the fluid and unstable nature of thought and feeling, frequently employ *parentheses*, although often without formal punctuation. Joyce and Faulkner are noted examples. Others, anxious to qualify and define precise shades of meaning find the extensive use of parenthetical material helpful, as does Henry James. J. D. Salinger's later fiction makes ample and varied use of the device; in a stroke of typographical wit, Buddy Glass, the narrator of "Seymour: An Introduction," concludes a very long sentence addressed to the reader, "I privately say to you, old friend (unto you, really, I'm afraid), please accept from me this unpretentious bouquet of very early-blooming parentheses: (((( ))))."

Parergon Something done in addition to one's ordinary business; used sometimes (as in texts of Schopenhauer and Derrida) for supplementary parts of a text. Richard Strauss composed a *Parergon zur Symphonia Domestica*, for piano (left-hand) and orchestra, based on material from his earlier *Symphonia Domestica*.

Parison PARALLELISM of syntax, manifest as an even balance of the components of a sentence: "One drinks too much and sees snakes, another eats too little and sees God."

Parnassians A group of nineteenth-century French poets, so called from their journal *Parnasse contemporain*. Influenced by Gautier's doctrine of ART FOR ART'S SAKE, they were in reaction against the prevailing romanticism of the first half of the century. The *Parnassians* wrote impersonal poetry with great objective clarity and precision of detail. They had a strong preoccupation with form and reintroduced the FRENCH FORMS. Their leader was Leconte de Lisle; among the other *Parnassians* were René Sully-Prudhomme, Albert Glatigny, François Coppée, and Théodore de Banville. In the 1870s they influenced some English poets, including A. C. Swinburne, particularly in the use of the FRENCH FORMS. The influence continued in some of the poetry of Ezra Pound and T. S. Eliot, particularly in their poems in quatrains between 1915 and 1920.

Parnassus A Greek mountain famed as the haunt of Apollo and the MUSES. The word has also been used as a title for a collection or anthology of poetry, such as *England's Parnassus* (1600). Now the name of distinguished quarterly subtitled "Poetry in Review."

Parodos In ancient Greek drama, the ODES sung by the CHORUS when they first enter.

Parody A composition imitating another, usually serious, piece. It is designed to ridicule a work or its style or author. When the *parody* is directed against an author or style, it is likely to fall simply into barbed witticisms. When the subject matter of the original composition is parodied, however, it may prove to be a valuable indirect criticism or it may even imply a flattering tribute to the original writer. Often a *parody* is more powerful in its influence on affairs of current importance—politics, for instance—than an original composition. The *parody* is in literature what the caricature and the cartoon are in art. Known as a potent instrument of satire and ridicule even as far back as Aristophanes, *parody* has made a definite place for itself in literature and has become a popular type of literary composition. *Parody* makes fun of some familiar style, typically by keeping the style more or less constant while markedly lowering or debasing the subject. Thus Dickinson's:

> The Soul selects her own Society—
> Then—shuts the Door—

has been parodied:

> The Soul selects her own Sorority—
> Then—shuts the Dorm—

(Note that the craft of *parody* prizes minimal tampering.) The opposite strategy—keeping a subject more or less constant while lowering or debasing style—generates BURLESQUE or TRAVESTY.

Paræmia (also **Paremia, Parimia**) A PROVERB, PARABLE, or ADAGE. From this word are formed also *parœmiographer* ("writer of proverbs") and *parœmiography* ("writing of proverbs").

Paræmiac (also **Paroemiac**) In ancient prosody, the line of CATALECTIC ANAPESTIC DIMETER at the end of a system of anapests.

Paromæon ALLITERATION; beginning two or more words or syllables with the same letter or sound.

Paronomasia PUN.

Paroxytone Having an acute accent on the next-to-last syllable.

Parrhesia (also **Parresia, Parisia, Parrhesy**) Frankness of speech, sometimes licentious.

Partheniad A work honoring a virgin (in practice, Queen Elizabeth I).

Participatory Journalism Originated by Paul Gallico and perfected by George Plimpton, a type of journalism in which journalists participate in the activity about which they are writing, producing reports from the inside. Plimpton wrote thus about football, golf, trapeze gymnastics, movie acting, and playing in a symphony orchestra.

Particular Meter or **Particular Measure** A designation in some hymnals for a metrical or syllabic pattern used in one hymn; also used for an expanded stanza, with a QUATRAIN becoming a six-lined unit. COMMON METER (syllabically 8.6.8.6) yields common *particular meter* (8.8.6.8.8.6); likewise short *particular meter* (6.6.8.6.6.8) and long *particular meter* (8.8.8.8.8.8).

Part Title A title given to a subsidiary part of a work, such as those in T. S. Eliot's *The Waste Land* and Edward Albee's *Who's Afraid of Virginia Woolf?*

Pasquinade A SATIRE or LAMPOON hung up in a public place. The term is derived from Pasquilla or Pasquino, the name of a mutilated statue exhumed in Rome in 1501, which was saluted on St. Mark's Day by having satirical Latin verses hung on it. Such verses were called *pasquinades*, and the term was later extended to any lampoon displayed in a public place.

Passional (also **Passionale, Passionary**) A book that describes the sufferings of saints.

Passion Play A drama that portrays a portion of the life of a god. The plays in the MYSTERY PLAY CYCLES that dealt with the life of Christ were *Passion Plays*. The term is now customarily restricted to plays dealing with the last days, trial, crucifixion, and resurrection of Christ. ("Passion" here means "suffering.") Such a *Passion Play* has been presented at Oberammergau, in Upper Bavaria, every tenth year since the 1630s.

Pastiche A French word for a PARODY or literary imitation. Perhaps for humorous or satirical purposes, perhaps as a mere literary exercise or *JEU D'ESPRIT*, perhaps in all seriousness (as in some CLOSET DRAMAS), a writer imitates the style or technique of some recognized writer or work. Amy Lowell's *A Critical Fable* (1922) might be called a *pastiche*, because it is written in the manner of James Russell Lowell's *A Fable for Critics*. In art a picture is called a *pastiche* when it manages to catch something of a master's peculiar style. In music *pastiche* is applied to a medley or assembly of various pieces into a single work. The term is also applied to literary patchworks formed by piecing together extracts from various works by one or several authors.

[References: Ingeborg Hoesterey, *Pastiche: Cultural Memory in Art, Film, and Literature* (2001).]

Pastoral A poem treating of shepherds and rustic life, after the Latin for "shepherd," *pastor*. The *pastoral* began in the third century B.C. when Theocritus included poetic sketches of rural life in his *Idylls*. The Greek *pastorals* existed in three forms: the dialogue or singing-match, usually between two shepherds, often called the ECLOGUE because of the number of singing-matches in Virgil's "Selections"; the MONOLOGUE, often the PLAINT of a lovesick or forlorn lover or a poem praising some personage; and the ELEGY or LAMENT for a dead friend. The *pastoral* became a highly conventionalized form, the poet (Virgil is an example) writing of friends and acquaintances as though they were poetic shepherds. The "shepherds" of the *pastoral* often speak in courtly language and appear in dress more appropriate to the drawing room than to rocky hills. Between 1550 and 1750 many such conventionalized *pastorals* were written in England. In modern use the term often means any poem of rural people and setting (Louis Untermeyer, for instance, called Robert Frost a "*pastoral*" poet). Robert Langbaum classifies *Out of Africa* by "Isak Dinesen" as *pastoral*. Because this classification is based on subject matter and manner rather than on form, we often use the term in association with other poetic types; we thus have *pastoral* lyrics, elegies, dramas, or even epics. Milton's "Lycidas," Shelley's "Adonais," and Arnold's "Thyrsis" are examples of English *pastorals*, as is Spenser's *The Shepheardes Calender*. Although the term can be construed broadly enough to include, say, Whitman's "When Lilacs Last in the Dooryard Bloom'd," its application is usually limited to poems that somehow adhere to the literal sense of *"pastoral"* and include "shepherds," however farfetched. Often, in Judeo-Christian environments, the *pastoral* will include some recollection of the imagery of the Psalms.

Many modern critics employ a highly sophisticated concept of the *pastoral* advanced by William Empson. In this specialized usage the *pastoral* is considered a device for INVERSION, a means of "putting the complex into the simple"—of expressing complex ideas through simple personages, for example. In Empson's scheme, *pastoral* is opposed to heroic. Empson, using a specialized definition, finds *pastoral* elements in such widely differing works as the proletarian novel (whose hero undergoes an inversion of function) and *Alice in Wonderland*. See IDYLL, BUCOLIC, ECLOGUE, PASTORAL DRAMA, PASTORAL ELEGY.

[References: William Empson, *Some Versions of Pastoral* (1935, 1974); Frank Kermode, *English Pastoral Poetry* (1952); Harold E. Toliver, *Pastoral Forms and Attitudes* (1971).]

Pastoral Drama The PASTORAL conventions so popular at times in poetry (as the ECLOGUE) and in the PASTORAL ROMANCE are reflected also in a form of drama occasionally cultivated by English dramatists. The type developed in Italy in the sixteenth century and was affected by the PASTORAL ROMANCE. Tasso's *Aminta* and Guarini's *Il Pastor Fido* (1590) were models for English Renaissance pastoral plays by Samuel Daniel, John Fletcher, and Ben Jonson. The best is Fletcher's *The Faithful Shepherdess* (acted 1608–1609). Some of Shakespeare's ROMANTIC COMEDIES, such as *As You Like It*, were affected by the pastoral influences and are sometimes called pastoral plays. The eighteenth-century stage saw some translations and imitations of Italian *pastoral drama*.

Pastoral Elegy A poem employing conventional PASTORAL imagery, written in dignified, serious language, and taking as its theme the expression of grief at the loss of a friend or important person. The form represents a combining of the pastoral eclogue and the elegy. The conventional divisions, as evidenced in Milton's "Lycidas," are: the invocation of the MUSE, an expression of grief, a procession of mourners, a digression (on the church), and, finally, a consolation in which the poet submits to the inevitable and declares that everything has turned out for the best. Other conventions include: appearance of the poet as shepherd, praise of the dead, the PATHETIC FALLACY, flower symbolism, invective against death, reversal of the ordinary processes of nature a result of the death, bewilderment caused by grief, and declaration of belief in some form of immortality. Moschus's lament for Bion (second century B.C.), the November eclogue of Spenser's *The Shepheardes Calender*, and Shelley's "Adonais" are examples of the form. In many such elegies, "shepherd" becomes a conventional code word for "poet," and those for whom Milton, Shelley, and Arnold wrote their elegies were poets (King, Keats, and Clough). Accordingly, almost any poet's elegy for another poet—such as W. H. Auden's for W. B. Yeats—will display some pastoral elements.

Pastoral Romance A prose narrative, usually long and complicated in plot, in which the characters bear PASTORAL names and in which pastoral conventions dominate. It often contains interspersed songs. Though the Greek *Daphnis and Chloë* of Longus (third century) is classed as a *pastoral romance*, the form was reborn in the Renaissance with Boccaccio's *Ameto* (1342). Montemayor's *Diana Enamorada* (c. 1559) is an important Spanish *pastoral romance*. Typical English examples are Sir Philip Sidney's *Arcadia* (1580–1581) and Thomas Lodge's *Rosalynde* (1590), which was the source of

Shakespeare's *As You Like It*. Elements of *pastoral romance* persist in Thomas Hardy's *Far from the Madding Crowd*, which includes a literal shepherd called Gabriel Oak and a few interspersed songs. See ECLOGUE, PASTORAL.

Pastourelle A medieval DIALOGUE poem in which a shepherdess is wooed by a man of higher social rank. In the Latin *pastoralia*, a scholar does the courting; in the French and English, a poet, knight, or clerk. Sometimes the suit is successful, but often a father or brother happens along and ends the wooing. In the English forms the poet asks permission to accompany the maid to the fields; she refuses and threatens to call her mother. The *pastourelle* possibly developed from popular wooing games and wooing songs, though one of Theocritus's IDYLLS is much like the medieval *pastourelle*. The form seems to have influenced the pastoral dialogue-lyrics of the Elizabethans and may have figured in the development of early romantic drama in England. Robert Frost's "The Subverted Flower" may be read as a shocking, realistic inversion of the lineaments of the *pastourelle.*

Patent Theaters The removal of the ban against theatrical performances in England in 1660 resulted in much rival activity among groups seeking to operate playhouses. Sir William Davenant and Thomas Killigrew secured from Charles II a "patent" granting them the privilege of censorship of plays and the right to organize two companies and erect two theaters that should have a monopoly. Though opposed by the jealous master of the revels, Sir Henry Herbert, and by some of the independent managers, Davenant and Killigrew succeeded in enforcing their rights. Davenant's "Duke of York's Company" occupied in 1661 a new theater in Lincoln's Inn Fields and later one at Dorset Garden. Killigrew's company, the "King's Company," erected the Theatre Royal, the first of a famous succession of houses on this spot, all known as Drury Lane since 1663. The theaters used by these two favored companies are known as *patent theaters*. The companies united in 1682, but in 1695 Thomas Betterton led a rebellious group of actors to a second theater in Lincoln's Inn Fields. After a generation of confusion, Parliament passed a licensing act in 1737, reaffirming the patent rights and establishing the monopoly of Drury Lane and Covent Garden (erected 1732). Despite strenuous efforts of rival managers, this act remained in force until 1843, when it was repealed and the patents revoked.

Pathetic Fallacy A phrase coined by Ruskin to denote the tendency to credit nature with human emotions. In a larger sense the *pathetic fallacy* is any false emotionalism resulting in a too impassioned description of nature. It is the carrying over to inanimate objects of the moods and passions of a human being. This crediting of nature with human qualities is a device often used by poets. A frequently occurring expression of the imagination, it becomes a fault when it is overdone to the point of absurdity, in which case it approaches the CONCEIT. The following passage from Ruskin (*Modern Painters*, vol. 3, part 4, chap. 12) discusses the *pathetic fallacy*:

> They rowed her in across the rolling foam—
> The cruel, crawling foam.

> The foam is not cruel, neither does it crawl. The state of mind which attributes to it these characters of a living creature is one in which the reason is unhinged by grief. All violent feelings have the same effect. They produce in

> us a falseness in all our impressions of external things, which I would generally characterize as the "pathetic fallacy."

The fallacy may be in the mind of a character who is upset or unhinged, so that an author who shows such a state of mind is not guilty of fallacious logic or technique. Indeed, no one can get through a day without saying something like "happy birthday" that could be classified as a *pathetic fallacy* on the grounds that a day is incapable of feeling happiness.

Pathos From the Greek root for feeling, *pathos* is the quality in art and literature that stimulates pity, tenderness, or sorrow. Although in its strict meaning it is closely associated with the pity that tragedy is supposed to evoke, in common usage it describes an acquiescent or relatively helpless suffering or the sorrow occasioned by unmerited grief, as opposed to the stoic grandeur and awful justice of the tragic hero. In this distinction, Hamlet is a tragic figure and Ophelia a pathetic one; Lear's fate is tragic, Cordelia's pathetic. See BATHOS.

Patronage Until well into the nineteenth century, many authors survived because of *patronage* from a wealthy benefactor. Given the conditions of performance and publication, a writer generally could not make a living simply by income from the work alone. Patrons are important in the lives of authors from Chaucer to Wordsworth—even in the life of Samuel Johnson, although he said that a patron is "a wretch who supports with insolence and is paid with flattery." The last major author to benefit substantially from an individual patron was probably James Joyce, supported by a gift from Harriet Shaw Weaver.

Patter The special or secret language of thieves, beggars, and low-life types in general; the spiel delivered by a street-seller or carnival barker; rapid speech associated with a comedian, magician, or other performer.

Patter Song Most often a comic solo of rapidly spoken words with only sketchy musical accompaniment. Found in operas by Mozart and Rossini, ubiquitous in the operettas of Gilbert and Sullivan. Some of the speeches in T. S. Eliot's *Sweeney Agonistes* are *patter songs*.

Pattern Poem Another name for CARMEN FIGURATUM or FIGURE POEM.

Peculiar Meter or Measure Occasionally applied to a meter peculiar to one hymn, or not conforming to any named meter.

Pedantry A display of learning for its own sake. The term is often used in critical reproach when style is marked by big words, quotations, foreign phrases, allusions, and such. Holofernes in Shakespeare's *Love's Labour's Lost* can hardly open his lips without giving expression to *pedantry:*

> Most barbarous intimation! yet a kind of insinuation, as it were, *in via*, in way, of explication; *facere*, as it were, replication, or rather, *ostentare*, to show, as it were, his inclination,—after his undressed, unpolished, uneducated, unpruned, untrained, or rather, unlettered, or, ratherest, unconfirmed fashion—to insert again my *haud credo* for a deer.

Pegasus The winged horse of Grecian fable said to have sprung from Medusa's body at her death. *Pegasus* is associated with the inspiration of poetry (though in modern times in a somewhat jocular vein) because he is supposed by one blow of his hoof to have caused Hippocrene, the inspiring fountain of the MUSES, to flow from Mount Helicon. As a symbol of poetic inspiration, poets have sometimes invoked the aid of *Pegasus* instead of the Muses.

Pejorative A locution or word-form designed to belittle or ridicule someone or something, such as "so-called" and "self-styled" (applied, say, to a leader who fails to lead); sometimes a denigrating suffix, as in "poetaster," "criticoid," or "fashionista."

Pelagianism A doctrine asserting the original innocence of human beings and their capacity to achieve moral and spiritual power through their own unaided efforts. Although it was attacked by St. Augustine and officially declared a heresy early in the fifth century, unofficial items of Pelagian thought—and particularly the denial of original sin—have persisted to the present. Randall Jarrell found the sentiment in the poetry of William Carlos Williams; in *After Strange Gods: A Primer of Modern Heresy*, T. S. Eliot found fault with both D. H. Lawrence and Ezra Pound because of their failure to accept the orthodox (anti-Pelagian) position on original sin. Walt Whitman, who denied that any such thing as sin or evil ever existed, can be seen an adherent of *Pelagianism*.

P.E.N. Abbreviation for International Association of Poets, Playwrights, Editors, Essayists, and Novelists.

Penny Dreadful A cheaply produced paperbound novel or novelette of mystery, adventure, or violence popular in the late nineteenth and early twentieth centuries in England; equivalent of the American DIME NOVEL.

Pentameter A line of verse of five FEET. Serious verse in English since the time of Chaucer—epic, drama, meditative, narrative—and many conventional forms—*TERZA RIMA*, HEROIC QUATRAIN, RHYME ROYAL, *OTTAVA RIMA*, the SPENSERIAN STANZA, and the SONNET—have made *pentameter* the staple measure. See SCANSION.

Pentastich A poem or a stanza of five lines; a QUINTET; a CINQUAIN.

Perfluency A Welsh measure of two lines consisting of ten syllables followed by nine syllables, with rhyme between the seventh syllable of the first and the ninth of the second.

Pericope In general, any short section of a text. Specifically, a section consisting of STROPHE and ANTISTROPHE.

Periergy Labored bombastic style fussing too much over details, as in Shakespeare's *Hamlet* (2:2) when Polonius says,

> Mad let us grant him then, and now remains
> That we find out the cause of this effect—
> Or rather say, the cause of this defect,
> For this effect defective comes by cause.

Period A complete sentence, especially when containing more than one clause.

Periodical Any publication that appears at regular intervals; it includes such publications as JOURNALS, MAGAZINES, and REVIEWS but customarily not newspapers.

Periodical Essay An ESSAY written for publication in a PERIODICAL. The most notable were written for *The Tatler* and *The Spectator*, but the form was very popular through most of the eighteenth century.

Periodic Sentence A sentence not grammatically complete before its end; the opposite of a LOOSE SENTENCE. The *periodic sentence* is effective when it is designed to arouse interest and curiosity, to hold an idea in suspense before its final revelation. Periodicity is accomplished by the use of parallel phrases or clauses at the opening, by the use of dependent clauses preceding the independent clause, and by the use of such correlatives as *neither . . . nor, not only . . . but also*, and *both . . . and*. The first stanza of Longfellow's "Snowflakes" is a maximally *periodic sentence*, beginning with a succession of adverbial phrases and not grammatically complete until the very last word, which is the subject:

Out of the bosom of the Air,
  Out of the cloud-folds of her garments shaken,
Over the woodlands brown and bare,
  Over the harvest-fields forsaken,
    Silent, and soft, and slow,
    Descends the snow.

Period of Modernism and Consolidation in American Literature, 1930–1960 The year 1930 was a turning point in American social history as well as the beginning of the period in literary history that lasted to 1960. In October 1929 the stock-market crash heralded the end of the prosperous twenties, and by the end of 1930 the impact of the Depression was being felt throughout American life and thought. As the Depression intensified, the social and economic revolution called the New Deal occurred, and a steadily increasing concern with social or sociological issues occupied the serious writer. Shortly after the Depression began, the expatriate group that had in Paris made a religion of art came back to America and joined the radical movements that earned the thirties the name of "The Red Decade."

Hemingway's career had been launched in the twenties, and his work in the thirties added little to his stature; but Faulkner was to produce in the first half of the decade the largest single body of his best work. Dos Passos wrote his trilogy, *U.S.A.*; and James T. Farrell, Thomas Wolfe, Henry Miller, and John Steinbeck did their best work. In the meantime, the poets who had in the twenties produced *The Fugitive* magazine in Nashville reacted strongly against the radical political thought and the sociological literary orientations of their world; they expressed their politico-economic reaction through the principles of AGRARIANISM and their rejection of sociological concerns in the artist through the formulation of the NEW CRITICISM. Edwin Arlington Robinson, Robert Frost, T. S. Eliot, Edna St. Vincent Millay, and Carl Sandburg continued their dominant position in poetry, and E. E. Cummings, Robinson Jeffers, and William Carlos Williams raised newer strong poetic voices. Maxwell Anderson, Eugene O'Neill, Clifford Odets, and Thornton Wilder dominated the stage. Gertrude Stein cannot be tidily classified, but her influence was certainly felt in American drama, fiction, poetry, criticism, opera, autobiography, and even folklore.

The coming of the Second World War put an end to the radicalism of the thirties. The war and its aftermath resulted in an age of conformity and conservatism, bolstered by a burgeoning economy. American life in the forties and the fifties was marked by a tendency toward conformity, traditionalism, and reverence for artistic form and restraint, although there was marked informality in social conduct and freedom of subject matter in art.

The postwar drama revealed the strong new talents of Arthur Miller and Tennessee Williams, while Thornton Wilder was doing his most mature work and Eugene O'Neill was at the end of his career dramatizing powerfully the tragic lineaments of his own experience. Both poetry and criticism tended to retreat to the critical quarterlies, where each operated with a high level of technical skill but without great distinction or vitality. The major figures in the novel were still Hemingway and Faulkner, both of whom received the NOBEL PRIZE. Despite a small output (one short novel and scarcely more than a dozen stories, some fairly long), J. D. Salinger became one of the best and most important American fiction writers. To the vernacular humor of Ring Lardner's writing, Salinger added the grace, sophistication, and depth of Fitzgerald's along with elements of Jewish and Oriental culture, the symbolist poetry of Rilke and Eliot, and the idiom of show business. Ralph Ellison's *Invisible Man* made high art of the African American man's situation. In James Jones, Norman Mailer, and a group of other young neonaturalists, a strong, frank, and rather unkempt kind of fiction appeared. But the remark that, perhaps, best characterizes the literature of America from the Second World War to 1960 is that most of its major works and its major literary events were produced by writers whose careers had been firmly established in the twenties and the thirties and who had done their best work then. The chaos of a hot war and the constraint of a cold one conspired to produce a literature either of conformity or of confusion. See *Outline of Literary History*.

Period of the Confessional Self in American Literature, 1960– The 1960s marked a time of uncertainty, revolt, and cynicism in America and a strong turning inward of many American writers. One of the most important events of the decade was American involvement in the war in Vietnam and Cambodia. The most unpopular war in the history of the United States, it ignited a massive revolt of the young against war and against many aspects of the so-called establishment. Higher education was marked by widespread student revolt and by sporadic violence. Adding to the disillusionment of the nation was the gradual uncovering of the Watergate scandal, a disclosure that drove Richard Nixon to resign the presidency in 1974. American withdrawal from Vietnam, a slackening of the cold war, and a renewal of communication with China substantially reduced intensity of feeling about foreign policy, but in the 1970s severe energy shortages and major environmental problems continued to raise serious questions about capitalism and technology. The struggle for the civil rights of minorities in the 1960s was a rallying point for many, but by the 1970s that struggle appeared to be well on the way to being won.

The result of these varying forces was a tendency for imaginative writers to find their chief values in the self rather than in society and to see the proper realm of art to be introspection and confession rather than the creation of imaginary worlds. The rebellion of the late sixties found political expression in new LITTLE MAGAZINES, along with a remarkable freedom of language and the gesture as public act. The poetry of many of the older poets tended toward strict forms and academic tidiness. A younger group, including Anne Sexton, Sylvia Plath, and a number of African American poets, practiced an intensely personal poetry of a marked confessional quality. They were joined by older writers such as Theodore Roethke, John Berryman, and most notably Robert Lowell. The novelists of the sixties who gave the greatest promise of substantial work were William Styron, Saul Bellow, Bernard Malamud, John Updike, and Norman Mailer. John Barth and Thomas Pynchon produced works of great experimental ingenuity. The Southern writers, who had dominated the 1930s, 1940s, and 1950s were largely dead or silent, and a group of Jewish writers—Bellow, Malamud, Philip Roth, Mark Harris, and Mailer—came closest to being their successors as a group. Edward Albee, writing a skillful kind of absurdist drama, joined with Tennessee Williams to dominate the American stage, as television made increasing inroads on both film and legitimate drama. Criticism, under the influence of European theoreticians, such as the structuralists, the deconstructionists, and the phenomenologists, seemed increasingly to regard literary expression as a complex linguistic strategy.

By 1990, American writers appeared to be committed to a private, largely asocial exploration of the self and toward experiments in form. The emergence of a generation of writers born after 1940 and even after 1950—including the critics Edward Mendelson and Jonathan Culler and the poets James Tate, Louise Glück, Alan Williamson, Robert Morgan, Everette Maddox, Kathleen Norris, and Albert Goldbarth—promised a continuation of varied and vigorous accomplishment in American literature. See *Outline of Literary History* and POSTMODERNIST PERIOD IN ENGLISH LITERATURE.

Periods of English and American Literary History See ENGLISH LITERATURE, AMERICAN LITERATURE, and *Outline of Literary History*.

Period Style A term recently employed by David Perkins for literary manners, especially in poetry, that distinguish a given period. After some time has elapsed, it is possible to distinguish a *period style* of the 1930s or 1960s, say—an affair of rhetoric, diction, or versification. One point of the "Oxen of the Sun" chapter in Joyce's *Ulysses* is that one *period style* follows another in the manner of developmental stages in a human embryo.

Peripety (or **Peripeteia**) The reversal of fortune for a protagonist—possibly either a fall, as in a tragedy, or a success, as in a comedy. See DRAMATIC STRUCTURE.

Periphrasis An indirect, abstract, roundabout method of stating ideas; the application of the old conviction that "the longest way 'round is the shortest way home." Used with restraint, *periphrasis* may be a successful device, but the danger is that it will be overdone, resulting in mere Polonius-like verbosity. Some people, anxious to seem cultivated, never say they want a drink; they are "desirous of obtaining a beverage." Fowler cites as an objectionable use of *periphrasis* (for "No news is good news") the periphrastic circumlocution, "The absence of intelligence is an indication of satisfactory developments." Authors frequently use the form to secure humorous effects; for example, Shenstone refers to pins as "the cure of rents and separations dire, and chasms enormous." In T. S. Eliot's "East Coker," after a lyric passage, the poet comments, "That was a way of putting it—not very satisfactory: / A periphrastic study in a worn-out poetical fashion." See ANTONOMASIA.

Perissology REDUNDANCY, as in "Rio Grande River" (*rio* means "river"), "Mount Fujiyama" (*yama* means "mountain"), "La Brea Tar Pits" (*la brea* means "tar pits").

Perissosyllabic Having one or more redundant syllables.

Perlocutionary Act A speech act in which the utterance is defined by its effect, as in frightening, soothing, or persuading.

[Reference: J. L. Austin, *How to Do Things with Words*, 2nd ed. (1975).]

Peroration The conclusion of an ORATION in which the discussion is summed up; a recapitulation of the major points of any speech.

Persistence of Vision The physiological phenomenon that makes motion pictures possible. An image is retained on the retina of the eye for a very brief time after the object creating the image has disappeared. When another image only slightly changed is seen before the first image fades, the illusion of motion is created. Because of the *persistence of vision*, a film, which consists of a series of individual photographs of objects in successive states of motion, when projected rapidly and sequentially on a screen, creates the illusion of motion. The term *persistence of vision* is applied to this physiological phenomenon, which Ingmar Bergman has called a "defect." See PHI PHENOMENON.

Persona Literally, a mask. The term is widely used to refer to a "second self" created by an author and through whom the narrative is told. The *persona* may be a narrator, as in *Huckleberry Finn*, and the debate about the freedom that the use of Huck Finn gave Mark Twain as a mask through whom he could speak things he dared not utter in his own person is instructive about the function of the *persona*. The *persona* can be not a character but "an implied author"; that is, a voice not directly the author's but created by the author and through which the author speaks. All fiction is in some sense a story told by someone; all self-consciously artistic fiction is told by someone created by the author and who serves, therefore, as a *persona*. The term is also used in biography to describe the public self that some writers presented to the world and behind which they worked. In this sense "Papa Hemingway" was a *persona* behind which Ernest Hemingway hid. *Persona* takes on special coloration in Jungian psychology; and there is always the sense in which everybody presents a prepared "mask" to the world.

Personal Essay A kind of informal essay, with an intimate style, autobiographical content or interest, and an urbane conversational manner. See ESSAY.

Personation John Hollander has described Richard Howard's art of "*personation* having exemplary persons, actual or fictional but usually quite dead, return from the grave to tell us what they had never said before." Hollander's usage here resembles Thomas Hardy's appropriation of "personative" for some of his own poems.

Personification A figure that endows animals, ideas, abstractions, and inanimate objects with human form; the representing of imaginary creatures or things as having human personalities, intelligence, and emotions; also an impersonation in drama of one character or person, whether real or fictitious, by another person. Keats's representation of the Grecian urn as the

> Sylvan historian, who canst thus express
> A flowery tale more sweetly than our rhyme . . .

is an obvious *personification*, as are his earlier references to the urn as an "unravished bride of quietness" and as a "foster child of silence and slow time." *Personification* is called PROSOPOPOEIA, specifically when the personified figure speaks, as Wisdom does in the Book of Proverbs. See ALLEGORY.

Personism A term coined by Frank O'Hara (1926–1966) for his own sort of poetry. He seems to have been serious but in no way solemn, and he did not offer a definition. To judge from his strongest poems as examples of *personism*, however, one could say that the emphasis is on persons and personalities and the informal communications within and between them—shapely, elegant, spontaneous, sophisticated, urbane. O'Hara, for whom "the Enemy," according to Marjorie Perloff, was "the Great Insight or the Mythic-Symbolic Analogue," ridiculed philosophy, abstraction, emotional "identification" in the place of living "recognition," and what conventionally passes for a kind of aesthetically posed "personality or intimacy." "The poem," according to O'Hara's description of *personism*, "is at last between two persons instead of two pages."

Perspectivism The theory that perception and knowledge are conditioned by the peculiar perspective of the perceiver. René Wellek and Austin Warren situate *perspectivism* between the extremes of ABSOLUTISM and RELATIVISM and describe *perspectivism* as "a process of getting to know the object from different points of view which may be defined and criticized in their turn."

[Reference: René Wellek and Austin Warren, *Theory of Literature*, 3rd rev. ed. (1965; orig. 1949).]

Persuasion The type of composition intended to convince others of the wisdom of a certain line of action. *Persuasion* is calculated to arouse to some action. A common form of *persuasion* is the ORATION.

Pes (plural, **Pedes**) A name for each of the two quatrains forming the first part of a sonnet.

Petitio Principii (also ***Petitio Quæsiti***) BEGGING THE QUESTION.

Petrarchan Conceit The kind of CONCEIT used by Petrarch in his love sonnets and widely imitated or ridiculed by Renaissance English sonneteers. It rests on exaggerated comparisons expressing the beauty, cruelty, and charm of the beloved and the suffering of the forlorn lover. Hyperbolic analogies to ships at sea, marble tombs, wars, and alarums are used; OXYMORON is common. Shakespeare in Sonnet 130, which begins,

> My mistress' eyes are nothing like the sun;
> Coral is far more red than her lips' red:
> If snow be white, why then her breasts are dun;
> If hairs be wires, black wires grow on her head—

satirizes the Petrarchan conventions while giving a reasonably accurate catalog of some of the more common.

Petrarchan Sonnet The ITALIAN SONNET.

Phaleucian (also **Phalaecean**) A classical quantitative measure, usually with the pattern SPONDEE, DACTYL, and three TROCHEES. Sidney experimented with the form in his *Arcadia*.

Phanopoeia A word that Ezra Pound began using after "*imagism*" was vitiated by misuse and turned by Amy Lowell into "Amygism." *Phanopoeia*, like Aristotle's *opsis*, has to do with the power of language to cast visual images onto the mind or imagination. One of its roots also appears in *epiphany*, an outward and visible showing-forth of an inward and invisible meaning.

Pheme Defined by C. S. Peirce as "a Sign which is equivalent to a grammatical sentence, whether it be Interrogative, Imperative, or Assertory. . . . Such a Sign is intended to have some sort of compulsive effect on the interpreter of it."

[Reference: J. L. Austin, *How to Do Things with Words*, 2nd ed. (1975).]

Phememe Leonard Bloomfield's term for the smallest linguistic unit.

[References: J. L. Austin, *How to Do Things with Words*, 2nd ed. (1975); Leonard Bloomfield, *Language* (1933).]

Phenomenology A philosophical system that provides the basis for a contemporary school of criticism. *Phenomenology* is a method that inspects the data of consciousness without presuppositions about epistemology or ontology. (Epistemology is the theory of the nature of knowledge, ontology that of the nature of being.) To the phenomenologist, any object, although it has existence in time and space, achieves meaning or intelligibility only through the active use of a consciousness in which the object registers. Hence *phenomenology* finds reality not in a noumenal realm—in cause or material being—but in the psychical realm of awareness, to which it applies exhaustive analysis and description. Edmund Husserl, the founder of *phenomenology*, saw it as a psychology that distinctly separated the physical from the psychical and concentrated its attention on the psychical. To accomplish the analysis of the object as it registers in the consciousness, the phenomenologist suspends all presuppositions, inferences, or judgments about the object outside the consciousness.

Phenomenology as such has scarcely mattered in the creation of literature, unless one considers the sentence from Husserl's *Ideas*— "The natural wakeful life of our Ego is a perceiving"—that turns up in Eliot's fragmentary "Triumphal March." When phenomenological philosophy is applied to literary criticism, the result is a form of EXISTENTIAL CRITICISM, such as that practiced by the GENEVA SCHOOL. Phenomenological criticism sees the work of art as an aesthetic object, existing only in the consciousness of the perceiver; an aesthetic object does not have existence in a material universe of temporal and spatial coordinates but only in the coordinates of pure consciousness. Phenomenological critics, of whom Gaston Bachelard, Roman Ingarden, Mikel Dufrenne, and Georges Poulet are chief, tend to see imagination as essentially free of perception and thus an expression of freedom. They tend to have little interest in the ontology of the aesthetic object—a major concern of the NEW CRITICISM—and instead to value highly the affective aspects of works of art. They tend to see the experience of reading as an aesthetic meditation or intuitive communication between the aesthetic object and the reader. Frequently, the phenomenological critic examines the corpus of an author's work to seek out the intentions behind the creation of the autonomous aesthetic objects. In this sense, phenomenological criticism, when applied to film, becomes like the AUTEUR THEORY. Phenomenological criticism thus becomes the description of the way in which the consciousness becomes aware of a work of art.

[References: Gaston Bachelard, *The Poetics of Reverie* (tr. 1969); Robert Detweiler, *Story, Sign, and Self: Phenomenology and Structuralism as Literary Critical Methods* (1978); Hans-Georg Gadamer, *Philosophic Hermeneutics* (tr. 1976); Vernon W. Gras, ed., *European Literary Theory and Practice: From Existential Phenomenology to Structuralism* (1973); Robert R. Magliola, *Phenomenology and Literature: An Introduction* (1977); José Ortega y Gasset, *Phenomenology and Art* (tr. 1975).]

Pherecratean (also **Pherecratian, Pherecratic**) In classical prosody, a variable three-foot quantitative line, most often SPONDEE-DACTYL-spondee or spondee-dactyl-TROCHEE.

Philippic Any bitter speech or HARANGUE. The term comes from the twelve orations of Demosthenes berating Philip II of Macedon as an enemy of Greece.

Philistinism The worship of material and mechanical prosperity and the disregard of culture, beauty, and spirit. The term, originally German, was made popular in English by Matthew Arnold's use of it in "Sweetness and Light," the first chapter of *Culture and Anarchy*. Arnold wrote:

> If it were not for this purging effect wrought upon our minds by culture, the whole world, the future as well as the present, would inevitably belong to the Philistines. The people who believe most that our greatness and welfare are proved by our being very rich, and who most give their lives and thoughts to becoming rich, are just the very people whom we call Philistines. Culture says: "Consider these people, then, their way of life, their habits, their manners, the very tones of their voices; look at them attentively; observe the literature they read, the things which give them pleasure, the words which come forth out of their mouths, the thoughts which make the furniture of their minds; would any amount of wealth be worth having with the condition that one was to become just like these people by having it?"

Philology In its general sense *philology* means the scientific study of both language and literature. Thus, there are philological clubs and journals devoted to linguistic and literary research. *Philology* was at one time used in a narrower sense to mean the scientific and historical study of language. Today, however, the systematic study of language by scientific principles is usually called LINGUISTICS, with *philology* confined to the historical study of language.

Phi Phenomenon (or **Effect**) The psychological perception of motion resulting from PERSISTENCE OF VISION, called the *phi phenomenon* by the GESTALT psychologists. It is the psychological basis of FILM.

Phone Any single unique articulation of a speech sound, minutely different from every other *phone*.

Phoneme In LINGUISTICS, the smallest potentially significant unit of articulated sound in a language.

Phonestheme (also **Phonaestheme**) Unit or units of sound with a specific semantic meaning, either inherently or sentimentally. Certain meanings can be adduced for *sl* from the series *slick-slip-slide-slime-slope* and so forth. Whether such meanings precede the formation of words or follow inductively from one's gaining of a vocabulary, the possibility of such kinship between sound and meaning is robustly exploited by ALLITERATION and RHYME.

Phonetics The study of the production of speech sounds; the study of sounds as physical objects or events.

Phonology The general study of phonemics, the nature and history of the sound system of a language. *Phonology* studies the meaningful units of sound in a linguistic system.

Phosphorists A group of Romantic Swedish poets associated with the magazine *Fosforos* ("Phosphorus") at the beginning of the nineteenth century. The best known was Per Daniel Amadeus Atterbom (1790–1855).

Physiocrats A school of political economists founded by François Quesnay in eighteenth-century France, guided by belief in government according to an inherent natural order, in the soil as the sole source of wealth, and in the security of property and freedom of economy.

Pica A printer's measurement that is roughly 1/6 of an inch. In most newspapers related items have a *pica* of space between them and unrelated items have 1.5 *picas*. GUTTERS are usually one *pica* wide.

Picaresque Novel A chronicle, usually autobiographical, presenting the life story of a rascal of low degree engaged in menial tasks and making his living more through his wits than his industry. The *picaresque novel* tends to be episodic and structureless. The *picaro*, or central figure, through various pranks and predicaments and by his associations with people of varying degree, affords the author an opportunity for SATIRE of the social classes. Romantic in the sense of being an ADVENTURE STORY, the *picaresque novel* nevertheless is strongly marked by realism in petty detail and by uninhibited expression.

As far back as the *Satyricon*, Petronius at the court of Nero recognized the possibilities of the rogue. In the Middle Ages the fables continued the manner, though they transferred roguery from people to animals. Reynard is a typical picaroon. It was not until the sixteenth century that this rogue literature crystallized into a definite type. A novel called *La Vida de Lazarillo de Tormes y de sus fortunas y adversidades*, probably dating from 1554, was one of the most-read books of the century. Cervantes took up the manner in *Don Quixote*. Soon French imitators sprang up; Le Sage's *Gil Blas* (1715) was the most popular. So definitely was the form fixed as Spanish that the French writers—Le Sage among them—gave their characters Spanish names and placed their episodes in Spain.

In 1594 appeared *The Unfortunate Traveller: or, The Life of Jack Wilton* by Thomas Nash—the first significant *picaresque novel* in English. With Daniel Defoe in the eighteenth century the type became important in English literature. His *Moll Flanders* presents the life record of a female picaroon. Fielding in *Jonathan Wild* and Smollett in *Ferdinand, Count Fathom* lent dignity to the type.

Seven chief qualities distinguish the *picaresque novel.* (1) It chronicles a part or the whole of the life of a rogue. It is likely to be in the first person. (2) The chief figure is drawn from a low social level, is of loose character, and, if employed at all, does menial work. (3) The novel presents a series of episodes only slightly connected. (4) Progress and development of character do not take place. The central figure starts as a picaro and ends as a picaro, manifesting the same qualities throughout. When change occurs, as it sometimes does, it is external, brought about by the picaro's falling heir to a fortune or by marrying money. (5) The method is realistic. Although the story may be romantic in itself, it is presented with a plainness of language and a vividness of detail such as only the realist is permitted. (6) Thrown in with people from every class and often from different parts of the world, the picaro serves them intimately in some lowly capacity and learns all their foibles and frailties. The *picaresque novel* may in this way be made to satirize social castes, national types, or ethnic peculiarities. (7) The hero usually stops just short of being an actual criminal. The line between crime and petty rascality is hazy, but somehow the picaro always manages to draw it. Carefree, amoral perhaps, the picaro avoids actual crime and turns from one peccadillo to disappear down the road in search of another.

Pictorialism Pictorial style, extended from painting to the other arts insofar as they are capable of representing or depicting; usually patronizing or pejorative.

Picturesque A word applied to certain kinds of writing by analogy to a type of painting that grew out of the effort to find a middle ground between the SUBLIME and the beautiful as defined by Edmund Burke's essay "Of the Sublime and the Beautiful" (1756). The *picturesque* was a regulative principle that allowed the painter to organize nature into what Pope called a "wild civility" rather than a series of sublime elements. William Gilpin codified the *picturesque* in his series of illustrated tours in the 1790s and established a group of conventions for nineteenth-century painters. Among its features were irregularity of line, roughness and ruggedness of texture, contrasts of light and shadow, and intricacy. Typical objects in a *picturesque* painting were fractured rocks, blighted or twisted trees, winding streams, and ruins. The *picturesque* painter usually sought a prospect view for landscapes. American painters of the Hudson River School were noted for their use of the *picturesque*. It was also widely used in the description of landscapes in fiction. James Fenimore Cooper's and Washington Irving's use of the *picturesque* method in their writing has been frequently noted.

Pièce bien faite See WELL-MADE PLAY, the English equivalent of the French term.

Pindaric Ode The regular ODE, characterized by a division into units containing three parts—the STROPHE and ANTISTROPHE, alike in form, and the EPODE, different from the other two.

Pindarism Generally, following the practice of Pindar; specifically, lapsing into exaggerated enthusiasm, in a manner associated with Pindar. In 1713 Sir Richard Steele referred to "a sort of madness which the Athenians call the Pindarism," and in 1867 Matthew Arnold equated *Pindarism* with "a sort of intoxication of style."

Pirated Edition An unauthorized edition of a work, usually stolen from one country and produced for sale in another. It represents an infringement of copyright through illegal publication. The term is most often applied to the period before the establishment of modern international copyright conventions, when the use without permission or payment of literary works copyrighted in another country was a common practice. An edition of an outdated collection of Robert Frost's poetry was issued by the Buccaneer Press.

Pit The part of a theater on the main floor, normally behind the STALLS. Also the audience members occupying this area.

Pitch A potentially significant quality of articulated sound, determined by relative frequency, intensity, and volume; its importance varies from language to language and, in some, is an element of prosody.

Pithanology Beguiling speech, usually in the company of a specious argument. (Saint Paul uses the Greek *pithanología* in Colossians 2:4.)

Plagiarism Literary theft. A writer who steals the detailed plot of some obscure, forgotten story and uses it as new in a story of his or her own is a plagiarist. *Plagiarism* is more noticeable when it involves a stealing of language than when substance only is borrowed. From flagrant exhibitions of stealing both thought and language, *plagiarism* shades off into such less serious actions as unconscious borrowing, borrowing of minor elements, and mere imitation. In fact, the critical doctrine of imitation, as understood in the Renaissance, often led to what would nowadays be called *plagiarism*. Thus, Spenser's free borrowings from other romantic epics in composing his *Faerie Queene* were by him regarded as virtues, because he was following a predecessor in the same type of writing. A modern dramatist could not with impunity borrow plots from other dramas and from old stories in the way Shakespeare did. With *plagiarism* compare literary FORGERIES, its converse, where authors pretend that another has written what has actually been written by the authors themselves.

It is difficult to prove the borrowing of an idea and easy to demonstrate the stealing of a passage. Hence, as a legal term, *plagiarism* has very sharp limits and is considered to be a clearly demonstrable use of material plainly taken from another without credit. One may accommodate quotation, reference, allusion, echo, imitation, derivation, revision, parody, pastiche, and even larceny, but many of these devices of transmission and tribute were considered *plagiarism* by Poe, and he made its detection and punishment a stock-in-trade of his reviews. G. T. Wright began a poem on student plagiarism "Whose words these are I think I know. . . ."

Plainsong A term derived from the Latin *cantus plānus*, even or level singing. *Plainsong,* which resulted from the singing or chanting of nonmetrical materials, has the free rhythm of ordinary speech. After the sixth century, it was known as the Gregorian chant.

Plain Style The simplest of the three classical types of style; the others are the high and the middle. *Plain style* is free, natural, untrammeled by contrived cadences. *Plain style* was much prized by the American Puritan preachers. *Plain style*, sometimes called "low style," is one of the DEMOTIC STYLES.

Plaint Verse expressing grief or tribulation; a LAMENT. See COMPLAINT.

Planh Provençal equivalent of "plaint," used by Pound in the title of a translation.

Platea In medieval drama, the area before a raised stage, providing additional space for performing and for seating of the audience; the *platea* developed into the PIT and STALLS of the modern theater.

Platen A wooden or metal plate in a printing press designed to press the paper against the inked type. In a typewriter, the cylindrical roller against which the paper is held.

Platonic Criticism A type of criticism that finds the values of a work of art in its extrinsic rather than its intrinsic qualities, in its usefulness for ulterior nonartistic purposes. The term is used in opposition to ARISTOTELIAN CRITICISM.

Platonism The idealistic doctrines of Plato, because of their concern with the aspirations of the human spirit and tendency to exalt mind over matter, have appealed to certain English authors, particularly the poets of the Renaissance and of the Romantic Period. Plato himself declined to "codify" his philosophical views and perhaps altered them much during his own life. He left expressions of them in his great *Dialogues*, in which various personages (such as Socrates, Alcibiades, and Aristophanes) discuss problems, particularly those involving the universe and our relation to it, the nature of love and beauty, the constitution of the human soul, the relation of beauty to virtue. Unlike Aristotelian philosophy, which tends to be systematic, formal, scientific, logical, and critical, occupying itself chiefly with the visible universe, the natural world, and secular humanity, *Platonism* is flexible and interested in the unseen world. Plato founded his famous "Academy" in 380 B.C., where he taught students attracted from far and near (including Aristotle himself). Later followers, now known as Neoplatonists, modified Plato's teachings. It is difficult to distinguish the purely Platonic elements from elements added by later Platonists. Among the Neoplatonists were two groups of special importance: (1) The Alexandrian school; this group, especially Plotinus (third century), stressed the mystical elements and amalgamated them with many ideas drawn from other sources. Their NEOPLATONISM was in fact a sort of religion, which, though itself supplanted by Christianity, supplied medieval Christian thinkers (including Boethius and St. Augustine) with ideas. (2) The Neoplatonists of the Italian Renaissance; under the leadership of Marsilio Ficino (1433–1499), who ran the Platonic Academy at Florence and who translated and explained Plato, a highly complex and mystical system developed, one of the aims of which was the fusing of Platonic philosophy and Christian doctrine. This particular kind of Neoplatonism kindled the imagination of such poets as Sidney and Spenser.

Important Platonic doctrines found in English literature include: (1) The doctrine of ideas (or "forms"). True reality is found not in the mutable realm of sense but in the higher, spiritual realm of the ideal and the universal. Here exist the "ideas" or images or patterns of which material objects are only transitory symbols or expressions. As Yeats put it: "Plato thought nature but a spume that plays / Upon a ghostly paradigm of things. . . ." (2) The doctrine of recollection, which implies the preexistence and immortality of the soul, which passes through a series of incarnations. Most of what the soul has seen and learned in "heaven" it forgets when imprisoned in the body, but it has some power of "recalling" ideas and images; hence human knowledge. (3) The doctrine of love. There are two kinds of love and beauty, a lower and a higher. The soul or lover of beauty in its quest for perfect beauty ascends gradually from the sensual, through a process of idealization, to the spiritual and thereby develops all the virtues both of thought and of action. Beauty and virtue become identified.

Representative English poems embodying Platonic ideas include: Spenser's "Hymn in Honor of Beauty," Shelley's "Hymn to Intellectual Beauty," and Wordsworth's "Ode: Intimations of Immortality."

Play A literary composition of any length, ordinarily written to be performed by actors who impersonate the characters, speak the dialogue, and enact the appropriate actions. A *play* usually, but not always, assumes that this enactment will be on a stage before an audience.

Player A performer in a play; a somewhat commoner term than *actor* in Shakespeare's time, the word is now seldom used.

Play-poem The genre into which Virginia Woolf placed her novel *The Waves* (1931).

Pléiade A term originally applied to an ancient group of seven authors (named after the constellation of the Pleiades) and to several later groups, the most important of which was the collection of critics and poets that flourished in France in the second half of the sixteenth century. The leading figures were Ronsard, Du Bellay, and Desportes. Their poetic manifesto is Du Bellay's *Défense et Illustration de la Langue Française* (1549), which shows an interest in developing a new vernacular literature following the types cultivated by classical writers. The popular and the medieval were to be avoided, except that certain medieval courtly pieces were to be rewritten. The native language was to be enriched by coining words, by borrowing from the Greek and Latin, and by restoring lost native words, so that a literary language might be produced that would foster a new French literature comparable with the classical. The influence of the group was important for Elizabethan poets, notably Spenser, and the more or less mythical AREOPAGUS has been regarded as an English counterpart of the *Pléiade,* because Sidney and his group were engaged in the effort to refine the English language and to found a new national literature based on humanistic ideals.

Pleonasm The use of superfluous syllables or words. *Pleonasm* may consist of needless repetition or of the addition of unnecessary words. For example, in the sentence, "He walked the entire distance to the station on foot," "the entire distance" and "on foot" are pleonastic. *Pleonasm* may be employed occasionally for emphasis, and in such instances its use may be legitimate. Many common locutions qualify as *pleonasm:* "focal point" for "focus," "third-down situation" for "third down," "is supportive of" for "supports," and so forth. See TAUTOLOGY.

Pleophony Duplication of a vowel that harmonizes with that in the preceding syllable.

Ploce A kind of repetition whereby different forms and senses of a word are "woven" through an utterance, as in Blake's ". . . And mark in every face I meet / Marks of weakness, marks of woe": the first "mark" is a verb; the second and third are nouns. "Boys will be boys" employs a general and a specific meaning of "boy." Also found in cognate objects, such as "sleep the sleep," "say your say," "mail the mail," "nail the nail," and "He died the death of a salesman"; or cognate subjects, such as "The small rain down can rain."

Plot Although an indispensable part of all fiction and drama, *plot* is a concept about which there has been much disagreement. Aristotle, who assigns it the chief place of honor in writing and calls it "the first principle, and, as it were, the soul of a tragedy," formulated, in his *Poetics*, a very precise definition, which has been the basis for most discussions of *plot*. He called it "the imitation of an action" and also "the arrangement of the incidents." The action imitated should be "a whole"—that is, it should have a beginning, "that which does not itself follow anything by causal necessity, but after which something naturally is or comes to be"; a middle, "that which follows something as some other thing follows it"; and an end, "that which itself follows some other thing, either by necessity, or as a rule, but has nothing following it." A *plot*, Aristotle maintained, should have unity: It should "imitate one action and that a whole, the structural union of the parts being such that, if any one of them is displaced or removed, the whole will be disjointed and disturbed." His test for a sound *plot* was "whether any given event is a case of *propter hoc* or *post hoc*." ("*Propter hoc*" means "on account of this," "*post hoc*" merely "after this." Because effects come after causes and also on account of them, it can be hard to figure out whether a given sequence is logical as well as chronological.)

E. M. Forster made a helpful distinction between STORY and *plot*. A story is "a narrative of events in their time-sequence. A *plot* is also a narrative of events, the emphasis falling on causality." A story arouses only curiosity; a *plot* demands some intelligence and memory. Thus, plotting is the process of converting STORY into *plot*, of changing a chronological arrangement of incidents into a causal and inevitable arrangement. This functioning of some kind of intelligent overview of ACTION, which establishes principles of selection and relationship among EPISODES, makes a *plot*. Clearly there must be more than one episode, the relation among the episodes must be close, and the selection of episodes must constitute a "whole" action.

Many critics, particularly in the nineteenth and twentieth centuries, have quarreled with Aristotle's assigning *plot* the chief place in a dramatic composition, and have insisted that CHARACTER is more important, the *plot* being merely a means by which a structure to display characters is arranged. In some schemes critics speak of a *plot* of action (mythos) in Aristotle's sense but also a *plot* of character (ethos) and a *plot* of thought (dianoia), all involving potentially maximal change. Neo-Aristotelian critics have attempted to extend the meaning of *plot* to make it a function of a number of elements in the work of art. Ronald S. Crane says, "The form of a given plot is a function of the particular correlation among . . . three variables which the completed work is calculated to establish, consistently and progressively, in our minds." These variables are "(1) the general estimate we are induced to form . . . of the moral character and deserts of the hero . . . ; (2) the judgments we are led similarly to make about the nature of the events that actually befall the hero . . . as having either painful or pleasurable consequences for him . . . permanently or temporarily; and (3) the opinions we are made to entertain concerning the degree and kind of his responsibility for what happens to him." In such a definition, although much has been added to the simple idea of a structure of incidents, the basic view of *plot* as a large and controlling frame is still present.

The minimal definition of *plot* is "pattern." Only slightly less simple is "pattern of events." *Plot* is an intellectual formulation about the relations among the incidents and is, therefore, a guiding principle for the author and an ordering control for the reader.

Because the *plot* consists of characters performing actions in incidents that comprise a "single, whole, and complete" action, this relation involves conflict between opposing forces (see CONFLICT for a detailed statement of the types of such struggle available to the writer). Without conflict, *plot* hardly exists. We must have a Claudius flouting a Hamlet, an Iago making an Othello jealous, if we are to have *plot*. These forces may be physical (or external), or they may be spiritual (or internal); but they must in any case afford an opposition. The struggle between the forces, moreover, comes to a head in one incident—the CRISIS—that forms the turning point and usually marks the moment of greatest SUSPENSE. In this climactic episode the RISING ACTION comes to a termination and the FALLING ACTION begins; and as a result of this incident some DÉNOUEMENT or CATASTROPHE is bound to follow.

[Reference: R. S. Crane, ed., *Critics and Criticism* (1952).]

Pluralism A philosophical position that recognizes the possibility of multiple ultimate principles, contrasted with monism. Also, the political theory opposed to monolithic state power; more generally, the toleration of diversity in a society.

Plurisignation A term sometimes used to describe the AMBIGUITY that results from the capacity of words to stimulate several different streams of thought. Richard Wilbur's *The Beautiful Changes*, for example, has a double signification set up by the possibility of reading it as both a noun plus a verb and an adjective plus a noun.

Poem It is generally agreed that a *poem* is a cultural artifact of some sort; beyond that, however, there is little agreement. A *poem* may not be in words at all, and a *poem* can exist without being written down. Even so, it is commonly accepted that most *poems* are literary compositions typically characterized by IMAGINATION, emotion, significant meaning, sense impressions, and concrete language that invites attention to its own physical features (such as sound and appearance on the page). Most *poems* have an orderly arrangement of parts subsumed under some principle of unity, and they seem to have been composed with the dominant purpose of giving aesthetic or emotional pleasure.

Poesie or **Poesy** A variant and synonym of POETRY, current until about 1650 but thereafter picking up connotations of ARCHAISM, preciousness, affectation, and folly.

Poet In the strictest sense, anyone who writes poetry; a maker of verses. However, the term *poet*, in its possible original meaning of "maker," is applied to certain qualities held in unusual degree by a writer without reference to a particular type of composition; these qualities include imaginative power, flexible and effective expressiveness, a special sensitivity to experience, and a sense of appropriateness, grace, and energy in the use of language. By further extension, the term is sometimes used for an artist in fields other than writing whose work has the qualities of imagination, spontaneity, and lyricism, as in the phrase "a *poet* of the violin." (In some languages—German and Japanese, for instance—the standard word for *poet* is reserved for special honorific uses. In Japan, you may say, "I am a writer [*shi-jin*]," but to say, "I am a poet [*hai-jin*]" is bad manners.)

Poetaster An incompetent poet.

Poète Maudit The doomed or damned poet; a figure coming out of France in the second half of the nineteenth century. Typically brilliant, moody, morbid, consumptive, alcoholic, self-destructive, sometimes even self-destroyed: once a serious term (for the likes of Poe and Baudelaire) but now largely a CLICHÉ.

Poetical Miscellanies See MISCELLANY.

Poetic Diction Language chosen for a supposedly inherent poetic quality. At one time, writers in England sought a special language for poetry different from common speech. Some dictionaries label entries "poetical" if the item (such as "yestreen" for "yesterday evening") is thought to exist only in poetry. Spenser sought in ARCHAISMS, for example, the materials out of which to fashion a diction properly poetic; the Augustan poets subjected poetic language to the test of decorum and evolved a special vocabulary. The Romantic poets, led by Wordsworth, denied the essential difference between the proper language of poetry and that of everyday speech. The tendency in our own time is to allow the poet the widest possible range of vocabulary and to use a consciously *poetic diction* only for ironic effect. Amateurs may think they are writing poetry if they distort their normal diction and say "upon," "beneath," and "about" instead of "on," "under," and "around." The same class of writers indulge in syntactic INVERSIONS, sometimes for the sake of a rhyme but sometimes for their own sake. Beginners tend to replace the diction of regular speech with an uncommon employment of the LYRIC PRESENT tense and DEIXIS. Elder Olson has argued that the only genuinely *poetic diction* is appropriate diction.

Poetic Drama In the strictest sense, poetic plays written to be acted, distinguished from DRAMATIC POETRY and CLOSET DRAMA, although some writers treat the terms as synonymous.

Poetic Justice Loosely, that ideal judgment that rewards virtue and punishes vice. (The term was first used by Thomas Rymer 300 years ago.)

Aristotle announced that "the mere spectacle of a virtuous man brought from prosperity to adversity moves neither pity nor fear; it merely shocks us." Suffering as an end in itself is intolerable dramatically. Hamlet dead with poison, Desdemona smothered, Juliet dead—all these placed before us on the stage unmotivated, unexplained, constitute not tragedy but sheer pain. Such scenes would be exhibitions of fate over which the characters had no control and for which they were not responsible; they would be mere accidents and have no claim to *poetic justice*. But, in a higher, more dramatic sense, *poetic justice* may be said to have been attained, because in the way in which Shakespeare wrote the plays, the actions moved logically, thoughtfully, consistently to some such CATASTROPHES as those that awaited these three tragic characters. *Poetic justice*, then, in this higher sense, is something greater than the mere rewarding of virtue and the punishing of vice; it is the logical and motivated outcome of the given conditions and terms of the tragic plan. *Poetic justice* may be considered as fulfilled when the outcome, however dangerous to virtue, however it may reward vice, is the logical and necessary result of the action and principles of the major characters as they have been presented by the dramatist. In common parlance we use "*poetic justice*" to describe an apt symmetry of fortune, as when a hangman is hanged.

Poetic License The privilege, sometimes claimed by poets, of departing from normal order, diction, rhyme, or pronunciation. The idea of a measure of *license* goes back at least as far as Quintilian, and the Elizabethan writer George Gascoigne granted that some distortions and deviations may be justified "*per licentiam Poeticam*"; in the seventeenth century Dryden described such *license* as the liberty taken by all poets in all ages to liberate their work from the strictness and severity of prose.

Poetics A system or body of theory about poetry; the principles and rules of poetic composition. The term is used in two forms, *poetic* and *poetics*, with *poetics* the more common. The classic example is Aristotle's *Poetics*, the first paragraph of which indicates that its purpose is to treat of "poetry in itself and of its various kinds, noting the essential quality of each; to inquire into the structure of the plot as requisite to a good poem; into the number and nature of the parts of which a poem is composed; and similarly into whatever else falls within the same inquiry." The term is often used today as equivalent to "aesthetic principles" governing the nature of any literary form. Thus, critics sometimes speak of a "*poetics* of fiction." In a large sense, justified by its supposed etymology, a *poetics* is the science of any mimetic activity that produces a product, whether a set of sonnets or a set of dentures.

Poet Laureate Medieval universities had a custom of crowning with laurel a student who was admitted to an academic degree, such as the bachelor of arts. (The "laurel" root is still evident in "baccalaureate.") Later, *poet laureate* was used as a special degree conferred by a university in recognition of skill in Latin grammar and versification. There was also the medieval custom of bestowing a laurel crown on a poet, Petrarch being so honored in 1341. Independent of these customs and usages was the ancient practice of rulers, in cultivated and barbarous nations alike, of maintaining court poets to celebrate the virtues of the royal family and sing the praises of military exploits. Court poets of this type included the SCOP among the Anglo-Saxons, the SKALD among the Scandinavians, the FILIDH among the Irish, and the higher ranks of BARDS among the Welsh.

The modern office of *Poet Laureate* in England resulted from the application of the academic term *poet laureate* to the traditional court poet. It was established in the seventeenth century, though there were interesting anticipations earlier. Henri d'Avranches, for example, was official *versifactor regis* for Henry III. At the courts of Henry VII and Henry VIII, an academic *poet laureate* named Bernardus Andreas of Toulouse was officially recognized as *Poet Laureate*, wrote Latin odes for his masters, and received a pension. The tradition was not carried on after his death. The first officially appointed *Poet Laureate* was John Dryden, though Skelton, Spenser, Daniel, Drayton, Ben Jonson, and William Davenant are often included in the list, the latter two with strong justification. Jonson received a pension and a grant of wine, and was an official writer of MASQUES for James I and Charles I; his contemporaries called him "the *Poet Laureate*." After Jonson's death in 1637, Davenant was hailed as Jonson's successor and at the Restoration (1660) was informally recognized as *Poet Laureate*, though he seems not to have received any official designation. On Davenant's death, however, Dryden received (1670) an official appointment and thus was the first whose designation is recorded. After the Revolution Dryden was displaced, and in 1689 Thomas Shadwell was appointed *Poet Laureate*. Successive laureates were Nahum Tate (1692–1715), Nicholas Rowe (1715–1718), Laurence Eusden (1718–1730), Colley Cibber (1730–1757), William Whitehead (1757–1785), Thomas Warton (1785–1790), Henry

James Pye (1790–1813), Robert Southey (1813–1843), William Wordsworth (1843–1850), Alfred Tennyson (1850–1892), Alfred Austin (1896–1913), Robert Bridges (1913–1930), John Masefield (1930–1967), Cecil Day Lewis (1968–1972), Sir John Betjeman (1973–1984), Ted Hughes (1984–1998), and Andrew Motion (1999–).

The early, primary duty of the laureate was to render professional service to the royal family and the court. The practice of composing odes for special occasions developed in the seventeenth century and became obligatory on the laureate in the eighteenth century. Each year such an ode was sung at a formal court reception held to wish the monarch a happy New Year. This custom lapsed during the illness of George III and was abolished in Southey's time. Sometimes the laureate has served as a "poet-defender" of the monarch in personal and political as well as national disputes (for example, Dryden). Later the more appropriate custom of expecting a poem in times of national stress or strong patriotic feeling developed, though since Southey the writing of verse for special occasions has not been obligatory. Two of the best-known laureate poems are Tennyson's "Ode," written to be sung at the funeral of the Duke of Wellington, and his "Charge of the Light Brigade."

The perfunctory character of the laureate's duties often prevented the appointment of the best living poets, though since Wordsworth's time the appointment has with occasional exception been regarded as a recognition of poetic distinction. Gray, Scott, and Samuel Rogers declined appointments as *Poet Laureate*. Beginning with the appointment of Andrew Motion to the Laureateship in 1999, the term is limited to ten years, with an annual stipend of £5,000.

The title was established in the United States in 1985, the appointee serving for a renewable one-year term. Up through 2004, the *Poets Laureate* of the United States had been Robert Penn Warren, Richard Wilbur, Howard Nemerov, Mark Strand, Joseph Brodsky, Mona Van Duyn, Rita Dove, Robert Hass, Robert Pinsky, Billy Collins, Louise Glück, and Ted Kooser.

Poetry A term applied to the many forms in which human beings have given rhythmic expression to their most intense perceptions of the world, themselves, and the relation of the two. *Poetry* is imaginative, a quality Shakespeare described in *A Midsummer Night's Dream*:

> . . . imagination bodies forth
> The forms of things unknown, the poet's pen
> Turns them to shapes and gives to airy nothing
> A local habitation and a name.
> Such tricks hath strong imagination,
> That, if it would but apprehend some joy,
> It comprehends some bringer of that joy.

Poetry has *significance;* it adds to our store of knowledge or experience. This is what Matthew Arnold meant when he wrote of it as a "criticism of life"; what Watts-Dunton meant when he called it an "artistic expression of the human mind." The existence of an idea, a significance, a meaning, an attitude, or a feeling distinguishes *poetry* from DOGGEREL. However, the fact that *poetry* is concerned with meaning does not make it didactic. Great didactic poetry exists, but it is not great because it is didactic.

The first characteristic of *poetry*, from the standpoint of form, is RHYTHM. True, good prose has a more or less conscious rhythm, but the rhythm of *poetry* is marked by a regularity far surpassing that of prose. In fact, one of the chief rewards of reading *poetry* is the satisfaction that comes from finding "variety in uniformity," a shifting of rhythms that, nevertheless, return to the basic pattern. The ear recognizes the existence of recurring accents at stated intervals and recognizes, too, variations from these patterns. Whatever the pattern, there is, even in FREE VERSE, a recurrence more regular than in prose. Frequently RHYME affords an obvious difference by which one may distinguish *poetry* from prose. INVERSION is rather more justified in *poetry* than in prose. Because most *poetry* is relatively short, it is likely to be characterized by compactness, intense UNITY, and a climactic order. A vital element of *poetry* is its *concreteness. Poetry* insists on the specific, the concrete, and the bodily. The point may be made more obvious by citing Shakespeare:

Our revels now are ended. These our actors,
As I foretold you, were all spirits, and
Are melted into air, into thin air:
And, like the baseless fabric of this vision,
The cloud-capp'd towers, the gorgeous palaces,
The solemn temples, the great globe itself,
Yea, all which it inherit, shall dissolve,
And, like this insubstantial pageant faded,
Leave not a rack behind. We are such stuff
As dreams are made on; and our little life
Is rounded with a sleep.

Here almost every line presents a concrete image. The lines are alive with specific language. In a passage on the imagination Shakespeare has written imaginatively.

To Milton the language of *poetry* was "simple, sensuous, and impassioned." Because one function of *poetry* is to present images concretely, it is the responsibility of the poet to select language that succeeds in making those images concrete. Modern *poetry* tends to dispense with the special vocabulary that was once thought of as the language of *poetry* (see POETIC DICTION). *Poetry* is not fundamentally a kind of language or a kind of use of language. With *poetry*, the chief purpose is *to please*. The various senses of sight, sound, and color may be appealed to, the various emotions of love, fear, and appreciation of beauty may be called forth, but, whatever the immediate appeal, the ultimate effect of *poetry* is the giving of pleasure.

The art of poetic composition has undergone a long process of change. From its original collective interest it has become intensely individualistic; from the ceremonial recounting of tribal and group movements it has become the vehicle for drama, history, and personal emotion. It is, however, still common today to classify *poetry* into three great type-divisions: EPIC, DRAMATIC, and LYRIC. These three types are, in turn, broken into further classifications. Further subdivisions have been made on the basis of mood and purpose, such as the PASTORAL and DIDACTIC POETRY. Most of these types and manners are discussed in their own entries in this handbook.

Poikilomorphism "Variable form." Applied to rare cases of verse form that preserves RHYTHM, METER, and STANZA length but varies RHYME SCHEME from stanza to stanza. Thomas Hardy's "Shut Out That Moon" comprises four six-lined stanzas rhyming *abcbdb abcbab ababcb ababab*. Robert Frost's "In a Disused Graveyard" consists of four quatrains, in iambic tetrameter, each in a different rhyme scheme: *abba, aaaa, aabb, abab*—quite a tour de force. W. H. Auden's "Leap Before You Look" rhymes *abab bbaa baab abba aabb baba*, in effect turning itself inside out.

Point Printer's measurement of the size of TYPE, with roughly 72 *points* to an inch, twelve *points* to a PICA.

Point of Attack A term for the moment in the work at which the main action of the plot begins. *Point of attack* may, but does not necessarily, coincide with the actual beginnings of the story being told. It can come just before the CATASTROPHE, with the antecedent events and situations being presented through various kinds of EXPOSITION as the plot advances to its conclusion.

Point of View The vantage point from which an author presents a story. If the author serves as a seemingly all-knowing maker, the *point of view* is called OMNISCIENT. At the other extreme, a character in the story—major, minor, or marginal—may tell the story as he or she experienced it. Such a character is usually called a first-person narrator; if the character does not comprehend the implications of what is told, the character is called a NAIVE NARRATOR. The author may tell the story in the third person and yet present it as it is seen and understood by a single character, restricting information to what that character sees, hears, feels, and thinks; such a *point of view* is said to be limited. The author may employ such a *point of view* and restrict the presentation to the interior responses of the *point of view* character, resulting in the INTERIOR MONOLOGUE. The author may present material by a process of narrative EXPOSITION, in which actions and conversations are presented in summary rather than in detail; this method is called PANORAMIC. On the other hand, the author may present actions and conversations in detail, as they occur, and more or less objectively—without authorial comment; such a method is usually called SCENIC. If the author never speaks in his or her own person and does not obviously intrude, the author is said to be SELF-EFFACING. In extended works, authors frequently employ several methods. Since the flourishing of Joseph Conrad and Henry James, both of whom wrote technique-centered prefaces, *point of view* has often been considered the technical aspect of fiction that leads the critic most readily into the problems and the meanings of a work. Since about the middle of the nineteenth century, a particular sort of novel, defined by its artistic management of *point of view*, has become a favorite: a charismatic but mysterious hero (Heathcliff, Ahab, Holmes, Kurtz, Gatsby, Leverkühn, Willy Stark, McMurphy, Seymour Glass) is presented by a bureaucratic but sympathetic narrator (Lockwood, Ishmael, Watson, Marlow, Carraway, Zeitblom, Jack Burden, Bromden, Buddy Glass).

[Reference: Wayne Booth, *The Rhetoric of Fiction*, 2nd ed. (1983).]

Point of View Shot (also P. O. V. SHOT) A film shot that shows a scene as viewed by a character; also called SUBJECTIVE CAMERA.

Polemic A vigorously argumentative work, setting forth its author's attitudes on a highly controversial subject. Milton's *Areopagitica* is the best-known English example. *The American Crisis*, by Thomas Paine, is a series of American *polemics*.

Policier A police film or one based on a ROMAN NOIR; sometimes construed as a variety of FILM NOIR.

Political Novel A novel that deals with significant aspects of political life and in which those aspects are essential ingredients of the work. Such works as Henry Adams's *Democracy*, Joyce Cary's *Chester Nimmo* trilogy, C. P. Snow's *Strangers and*

Brothers series, and John Dos Passos's *District of Columbia* trilogy are *political novels*. Fletcher Kneble, Gore Vidal, Ward Just, and Jeffrey Archer are continuing the tradition.

Polyhyphenation The use of more than a usual number of hyphens. Oddly versatile, the simple-seeming hyphen can make one word out of two or more, and two or more out of one. An example of *polyhyphenation* is the coinage "dapple-dawn-drawn" in Hopkins's "The Windhover." (This may be an editor's emendation of Hopkins's original "dappledawndrawn.")

Polyptoton The repetition in close proximity of words that have the same roots. *Polyptoton* may involve the use of the same word but in a different grammatical case; more commonly, there is a basic difference in the words, although they share common roots. Shakespeare gives three examples in two lines of *Troilus and Cressida* (1, 1):

> The Greeks are strong and skilful in their strength,
> Fierce to their skill, and to their fierceness valiant.

Polyptoton is present in "strong-strength," "skilful-skill," and "fierce-fierceness." Consider also Landor's line "I strove with none, for none was worth my strife." See PLOCE.

Polysyndeton The use of more conjunctions than is normal. Milton's Satan, for example:

> . . . pursues his way,
> And swims, or sinks, or wades, or creeps, or flies.

The opposite is ASYNDETON. See PARATAXIS.

Pooter The model of a thoroughly ordinary person, first presented as Charles Pooter in George and Weedon Grossmith's *Diary of a Nobody* (1892).

Popular Ballad A traditional BALLAD of unknown authorship, transmitted orally.

Popular Culture The phenomenon of what people really but unofficially do and say; also the academic study thereof. Presumably, once it becomes the subject of objective classification and analysis, a piece of slang or music loses much of its vitality. Even so, *popular culture* has emerged since about 1960 as a serious and legitimate precinct of aesthetic and anthropological study. (For instance, one can perceive the persistence and metamorphosis of certain figures or motives from Shakespeare's *The Tempest* in the television series "Fantasy Island" and elsewhere.)

Popular Etymology (also **Folk Etymology**) A process that explains a word by tracing it to some fanciful origins or components and then maybe altering the pronunciation or spelling to reflect the imagined etymology. Thus, the ancient Greeks explained "Amazon" as derived from *amazós* "without breast," imagining that such warriors removed a breast to facilitate handling a bow. Such etymologizing installs "corn" in "acorn," "rose" in "tuberose," "fish" in "crayfish," and "house" in "penthouse"; it assimilates "admiral" to "admire" and explains "Welsh rabbit" as a "rare bit." None of these associations can be justified technically.

Popular Literature Writing in one of the commercially viable modes, especially prose fiction. This literature is valued on a strictly quantitative basis—number of copies sold. It is both creature and creator of popular taste, and it may be a more reliable index of what the majority of people really have on their minds. James Hilton and James Michener, for example, are seldom taken very seriously as writers of prose fiction, but their works have had a much greater influence on many more people than have the works of canonical, serious writers. Hilton added some words to the language, at least in the short term ("Mr. Chips" and "Shangri La"). Retrospectively, we can sometimes recognize that a Shakespeare or a Dickens was conforming to the demands of the *popular literature* of an earlier time.

Pornography Writing designed to arouse sexual lust. To such a definition is usually added: "and without major serious or aesthetic intention." The issue is highly subjective and varies greatly from individual to individual, and it varies even more from one age or nation to another. There have been pornographic elements in the literatures of every age and every language—for example, Aristophanes's *Lysistrata*, the *Satyricon* of Petronius, or Boccaccio's *Decameron*—but the first significant work of English *pornography* was John Cleland's *Memoirs of a Woman of Pleasure; or, the Life of Fanny Hill* (1749). More recent centuries have witnessed many ostensibly pornographic books, some of which, though initially banned, have come to be recognized as masterpieces. Notable among such works are James Joyce's *Ulysses* (1922), D. H. Lawrence's *Lady Chatterley's Lover* (1928), Henry Miller's *Tropic of Cancer* (1934) and *Tropic of Capricorn* (1939), and Nabokov's *Lolita* (1955). In addition to being a moral and aesthetic issue for the individual, *pornography* is also a legal problem for the state. The most important of the American legal decisions was made by Judge John Woolsey in 1933, which lifted the ban on *Ulysses*. The action rested on a view of the book as a whole, on the author's intention, and on the reaction of a normal reader. One workable definition of *pornography* is: that which deals explicitly with sex in a way that contemporary society judges to be prurient in intention, without major redeeming elements. Recently, some have tried to discriminate between so-called hard-core and soft-core *pornography*, the former having no art or redeeming purpose whatever; but the distinction seems to have little critical and no legal validity. We seem doomed to have to cope with inconsistent standards inconsistently applied: one set of rules (loose) for books, another (middling) for film, yet another (strict) for radio and television, with the Internet in a state of flux.

[Reference: David O. Frantz, *Festum Voluptatis: A Study of Renaissance Erotica* (1989).]

Portmanteau Words Words formed by telescoping two words into one, as the making of "squarson" (attributed to Bishop Wilberforce) from "squire" and "parson," "smog" from "smoke" and "fog," "motel" from "motor car" and "hotel," "brunch" from "breakfast" and "lunch," "meld" from "melt" and "weld," and "muppet" from "marionette" and "puppet." More recent examples are Paul Harvey's "palimony" and Kenneth Tynan's "blandiose." "*Portmanteau words*" was a name given by Lewis Carroll to such inventions, which he used in *Through the Looking Glass*. An example occurs in his famous "Jabberwocky" poem where, for instance, he made "slithy" from "lithe" and "slimy." In his preface to *The Hunting of the Snark* Carroll explained the system by which such words were made: "For instance, take the two words 'fuming' and 'furious.' Make up your mind that you will say both words, but leave it unsettled which you will say first. Now open your mouth and speak. If your thoughts incline ever so little towards 'fuming' you will say 'fuming-furious'; if they turn by even a hair's breadth toward 'furious,' you will say 'furious-fuming'; but if you have that rarest of gifts, a perfectly balanced mind, you will say 'frumious.'" James Joyce in *Ulysses* and particularly in *Finnegans Wake* employs many *portmanteau words*. Linguists use the term *blend* for these words, which have gained a considerable foothold in English over the past century. One explanation is the rise of the constricted newspaper headline that squeezes "Chicago White Sox" into "Chisox."

Positivism A philosophy that denies validity to speculation or metaphysical questions, maintaining that the proper goal of knowledge is the description and not the explanation of phenomena. Although its history stretches back as far as Berkeley and Hume, the doctrine was most emphatically formulated in the nineteenth century by Auguste Comte, who coined the term *positivism*. In the twentieth century *positivism* developed into LOGICAL POSITIVISM, a form of empiricism that introduced the methods of mathematics and experimental science into philosophy. Logical positivism developed in the first quarter of the twentieth century. The leader in its articulation was Wittgenstein, who defined the object of *positivism* as the logical clarification of thought. *Positivism* has permeated much of modern thought, and, although its influence on literature is indirect, it has been pervasive and powerful.

Postil A marginal note, usually on a Biblical text or commentary.

Postmodern Around 1900 the Roman Catholic church condemned a good many doctrines and practices, ancient *and* modern, under the capacious umbrella of "modernism," and right away, as early as 1914, in spite of the appearance of nonsense in the term, theologians began speaking of "postmodernism" by careless analogy with "postimpressionism." "*Postmodern*" has been applied to much contemporary writing, particularly with reference to the use of experimental forms. The fundamental philosophical assumptions of modernism, its tendency toward historical discontinuity, alienation, asocial individualism, solipsism, and EXISTENTIALISM continue to permeate contemporary writing, perhaps in a heightened sense. But the tendencies of the modernist to construct intricate forms, to interweave symbols elaborately, to create works of art that, however much they oppose some established present order, create within themselves an ordered universe, have given way since the 1960s to a denial of order, to the presentation of highly fragmented universes in the created world of art, and to critical theories that are forms of PHENOMENOLOGY. Myth has given way to the experiencing of aesthetic surfaces. Traditional forms, such as the novel, have given way to denials of those forms, such as the ANTINOVEL. The typical protagonist has become not a hero but an ANTIHERO. Writers such as Robbe-Grillet, Fowles, Pynchon, Barthelme, and Pinter are called *postmodern* in that they carry modernist assumptions about the world into the very realm of art itself.

[References: Donald Allen and George F. Butterick, eds., *The Postmoderns: The New American Poetry Revised* (1982); Ihab Hassan, *The Dismemberment of Orpheus: Toward a Postmodern Literature*, 2nd ed. (1982); Linda Hutcheon, *A Poetics of Postmodernism* (1989); Jean François Lyotard, *The Postmodern Condition* (tr. 1984);

Jerome Mazzaro, *Postmodern American Poetry* (1980); Martin Pops, *Home Remedies* (1984); Manfred Putz and Peter Freese, eds., *Postmodernism in American Literature: A Critical Anthology* (1984).]

Postmodernist Period in English Literature, 1965– Little changed during the 1960s in the national life of England; what had been characteristic in the 1950s continued and was accentuated. The Empire continued to shrink to an island realm. Struggles in Ireland between Catholics and Protestants intensified and demanded more and more of the attention of the English. A kind of spiritual malaise seemed to envelop many of the English people, a malaise sharply defined by Margaret Drabble in her novel *The Ice Age* (1977).

In literature it was a time of continuance and completion. Graham Greene, Kingsley Amis, and Lawrence Durrell continued to produce work typical of their younger days. Doris Lessing completed the *Children of Violence* series. C. P. Snow brought his ambitious *Strangers and Brothers* series to a conclusion, and Anthony Powell completed *A Dance to the Music of Time*. The most challenging new novelistic talents were John Fowles, Margaret Drabble, and Martin Amis, serious although very different experimenters in form. The death of Cecil Day Lewis in 1972 vacated the poet laureateship, which was filled by Sir John Betjeman. When Betjeman died in 1984, Ted Hughes took his place. Hughes died in 1998; Andrew Motion succeeded him as laureate. For much of the period, the strongest poet was Philip Larkin, who explicitly aligned himself with the native tradition of Thomas Hardy. Of the newer playwrights, John Osborne, Harold Pinter, and Tom Stoppard showed the most vitality and talent.

As England entered the twenty-first century, it seemed to be groping for position and definition in a diminished world, both of social and political reality and of art. See *Outline of Literary History* and PERIOD OF THE CONFESSIONAL SELF IN AMERICAN LITERATURE.

Poststructuralism A term loosely applied to an array of critical and intellectual movements, including DECONSTRUCTION and radical forms of psychoanalytic, feminist, and revisionist Marxist thinking, which are deemed to lie "beyond" STRUCTURALISM. The heyday of structuralism was between 1945 and 1970. However deeply it differed from other schools of thought, it agreed that aesthetic texts possessed a kind of objective existence that permitted one to approach them in a determinate way and to expect determinate results. Structuralism tended to locate value—always relative—inside a text (such as the greatness of Gatsby as a function of inner structures in Fitzgerald's novel) instead of locating value—possibly everlasting—in some realm outside a text (such as an "AMERICAN DREAM" that relates to figments and real people alike). Whether meaning is construed as intrinsic or extrinsic, it could be determined.

From about 1970 on, however, the assurance of structuralism gave way before encroachments from later styles of thought, including DECONSTRUCTION and READER RESPONSE CRITICISM, both of which called into question the objective reliability of the supposed text, along with the acts of writing and reading *per se*. With powerfully persuasive cases being made by influential theorists—including Michel Foucault, Wolfgang Iser, Paul de Man, Harold Bloom, Stanley Fish, J. Hillis Miller, and, preeminently, Jacques Derrida—much of the enterprise of criticism, reading, and writing was rethought and put, for the time being, on a sounder philosophical footing. According to the usual protocols of *poststructuralism*, it turned out that exemplary texts—from the

Old Testament to today's crossword puzzle—already include the seeds of their own deconstruction.

Perhaps the most definitive quality of *poststructuralism* is the questioning of the distinction between language and metalanguage, which renders problematic the idea of a science of literature or of culture. For poststructuralists, the language in which analysis is conducted is to be regarded as continuous with, rather than distinct from, the phenomena being analyzed. Hence it becomes important to ask in what way a discussion of metaphor is itself worked by metaphor, or to psychoanalyze the language of psychoanalysis. Jacques Lacan's assertion that "there is no metalanguage" (paralleled by Derrida) means that any metalanguage is more language, inextricably entangled with the forces and structures it seeks to analyze.

Posy (Posie) Sometimes used in the sense of "a collection of flowers" to indicate an ANTHOLOGY. The term also signifies a MOTTO, usually in verse, inscribed on a ring. When the "mouse-trap" play begins and the prologue has been spoken, Hamlet asks Ophelia: "Is this a prologue, or the posy of a ring?"

Potboiler Something written solely for money. It is writing that will "keep the pot boiling."

Poulter's Measure A couplet, now rarely used, with a first line in IAMBIC HEXAMETER and a second line in iambic HEPTAMETER. It seems to be an adaptation of SHORT MEASURE. *Poulter's measure* reduces short measure's four lines to two and eliminates one of the rhymes. The term is said to have originated from a custom of the London poulters of giving customers twelve eggs in their first dozen and fourteen in the second (presumably, like a "baker's dozen" of thirteen, to make up for breakage). Wyatt, Surrey, Sidney, Nicholas Grimald, Barnabe Googe, and Arthur Brooke are some of the poets who have used this form. The opening lines of Brooke's *Romeus and Juliet* afford an example:

> There is beyond the Alps, a town of ancient fame,
> Whose bright renown yet shineth clear, Verona men it name;
> Built in a happy time, built on a fertile soil,
> Maintained by the heavenly fates, and by the townish toil.

After enjoying a vogue around 1575, when it was one of the most popular verse forms in England, *poulter's measure* faded out, although faint lineaments may survive in short measure (especially if it rhymes *abcb*) and even in the LIMERICK, which has the same basic meter although a different rhythm, rhyme scheme, and lineation.

P.O.V. Shot Same as POINT OF VIEW SHOT.

Practical Criticism Criticism in which aesthetic principles are applied to specific works; often called "applied criticism," the term is used in opposition to THEORETICAL CRITICISM. See CRITICISM, TYPES OF.

Praeoccupatio (also **Preoccupatio**) The Latin counterpart of PROCATALEPSIS, the anticipation and answering of objections or questions.

Pragmatic Theory of Art A theory of art, according to M. H. Abrams, in which the major interest is in the effect that the art object produces in its audience. See CRITICISM.

Pragmatism A term, first used by C. S. Peirce in 1878, describing a doctrine that determines value through the test of consequences or utility. (Eventually, believing that the force of his original coinage had been drained by overuse and misuse, Peirce took to saying "pragmaticism" instead.) Its principal exponents were William James and John Dewey, through whose work and influence it made itself pervasively felt in America. The pragmatist insists that no questions are significant unless the results of answering them in one way rather than another have practical consequences. In William James's words: "The 'whole meaning' of a conception expresses itself in practical consequences, consequences either in the shape of conduct to be recommended, or in that of experience to be expected, if the conception be true." The pragmatists' world is pluralistic, attentive to context, relativistic about truth and value, devoid of metaphysical concerns except as they have practical consequences. On the other hand, it places a high premium on conduct and ethical concerns. In literature *pragmatism* found its most vigorous expression in the realism that developed in America after 1870. (Henry James, who was a friend of Peirce's when both were young, once drolly claimed to have been "unconsciously pragmatizing" all along.)

Preamble An introduction. In formal sets of "resolutions" there is usually a *preamble* giving the occasion for the resolutions. The *preamble* is introduced by one or more statements beginning with "Whereas" and is followed by the resolutions proper, each article of which is introduced by "Therefore."

Précis An ABSTRACT or EPITOME of the essential facts or statements of a work, retaining the order of the original.

Precursor The forerunner, the earlier strong poet with whom the belated poet must struggle in a deliberate act of misprision and misreading. The term was given a new emphasis by Harold Bloom.

Predestination The belief that God or Fate has foreordained all things. See CALVINISM and FATALISM.

Preface A statement at the beginning of a book or article—and separate from it—which states the purpose of the work, makes necessary acknowledgments, and, in general, informs the reader of such facts as the author thinks pertinent. Some writers, notably Dryden, Shaw, and Henry James, have written *prefaces* that are really extended essays. Some whole books are called *prefaces*, as with C. S. Lewis's *A Preface to "Paradise Lost."*

Prefix An element placed at the beginning of a word or word-group, sometimes remaining a separate word (as the "to" as an infinitive prefix in English), more often joined to the basic word (as in "reform").

Prelude A short poem, introductory in character, prefixed to a long poem or to a section of a long poem. J. R. Lowell's *The Vision of Sir Launfal* contains *preludes* of the latter sort. Rarely, as in the case of Wordsworth's famous *Prelude*, a poem so entitled may itself be lengthy, although Wordsworth's *Prelude* was written as an introduction to a much longer but incomplete work. (*The Prelude* is the title given to the poem by Wordsworth's wife after his death.) Some so-called *preludes*, such as some early poems by Eliot and Aiken, are not *preludes* to anything, strictly speaking, but may capture something of the spirit of similarly nonprelusive *preludes* in the music of Chopin and Debussy.

Prequel A SEQUEL that is set at an earlier time than the work it follows. There is precedent in Cooper's Leatherstocking novels, but the practice did not seem to need a name until the last quarter of the twentieth century, when popular films bred many generations of offspring. Some of Part Two of *The Godfather*, for example, provided earlier background material for Part One, so that the whole could later be re-edited into a chronological sequence. *Missing in Action II* and *Psycho IV* were both subtitled *The Beginning.*

Pre-Raphaelitism The Pre-Raphaelite movement began with the establishment in 1848 of the Pre-Raphaelite Brotherhood by Dante Gabriel Rossetti, Holman Hunt, John Everett Millais, and others as a protest against the prevailing conventional methods of painting. The Pre-Raphaelites wished to regain the spirit of simple devotion and adherence to nature that they found in Italian religious art before Raphael. (Although Raphael's particular responsibility for any radical change is unclear—the point seems to be rather to suggest a time, before 1500 or so, rather than a practice.) Ruskin asserted that *Pre-Raphaelitism* had but one principle, that of absolute uncompromising truth in all that it did, truth attained by elaborating everything, down to the most minute detail, from nature and from nature only. This meant the rejection of all conventions designed to heighten effects artificially. Several of the group were both painters and poets, and the effect of the cult was felt in English literature. Rossetti's "Blessed Damozel," printed in 1850 in one of the four issues of *The Germ*, the organ of the group, is a narrative poem with pictorial qualities. Characteristics of Pre-Raphaelite poetry are: pictorial elements, symbolism, sensuousness, a tendency to metrical experimentation, attention to minute detail, and an interest in the medieval and the supernatural. Certain critics, who deemed sensuousness the dominant characteristic of their poetry, called the Pre-Raphaelites the "FLESHLY SCHOOL." The chief literary products of the movement were Rossetti's translation of Dante, sonnets, and BALLAD-like verse; Christina Rossetti's lyrics; and the poems of William Morris, such as "The Earthly Paradise" and "The Defense of Guinevere." Morris's practical application of medieval artisanship to business effected a change in taste in home decoration.

Preterition In rhetoric, explicitly passing over something, either to call attention to it (as in "I shall pass over his worldwide financial interests that have earned him millions") or to slight it (as in "I shall say nothing of his earnest claims to the name of philanthropist").

Priamel A derivative of *praeambulum* for a verse form, popular among ancient Greeks and sixteenth-century Germans, in which a number of parallel statements serve as a preamble to a climactic conclusion.

Priapic In the prosody of classical antiquity, a meter consisting of a catalectic GLYCONIC and a PHERECRATEAN, associated with poems to Priapus.

Primitivism The doctrine that supposedly primitive peoples, because they had remained closer to nature and had been less subject to the influences of society, were nobler than civilized peoples. The idea flourished in the eighteenth century and was an important element in the romantic movement. A few steps in the development of the *primitivistic* doctrine may be suggested. The rationalistic philosopher, the third Earl of Shaftesbury (fl. c. 1710), in his effort to show that God had revealed himself completely in nature—and that nature was therefore perfect—reasoned that primitive peoples were close to God and therefore essentially moral. Human beings are by nature prone to do good: Their evil comes from self-imposed limitations of their freedom. Accounts of savage peoples by writers of travel books added impetus to the movement, as did the fanciful researches into an origin of language by such men as Lord Monboddo (*The Origin and Progress of Language*, 1773–1792). The movement was advanced by the writings of Rousseau, particularly his belief that human beings were potentially perfect and that their faults were due to the vicious effect of conventional society.

One aspect of *primitivism* significant in English literature was its doctrine that the best poetry should be natural or instinctive, which resulted in a search for a perfect "untutored" poet. Among the many savages brought by the primitivists to England in their search for the perfect natural human being, the enthusiasts searched for evidence of poetic genius. The "inspired peasant" was sought for, too, among the unlettered, and many were feted by high society until their fame wore out: Henry Jones, the poetical bricklayer; Stephen Duck, the "thresher-poet"; James Woodhouse, the poetical shoemaker; and Ann Yearsley, the poetical milk-woman, who signed her poems "Lactilla" and was sponsored by the BLUESTOCKINGS. Gray's *The Bard* (1757) and James Beattie's *The Minstrel* (1771–1774) reflect such a doctrine of primitive genius. For a time the forged "Ossian" poems of James Macpherson (see FORGERIES, LITERARY) seemed an answer to the romantic prayer for the discovery in Britain of a primitive epic poem. When Robert Burns appeared, the search for the peasant poet seemed over, and the Scottish bard was received with enthusiasm.

All England did not go primitivistic. The movement was attacked by such conservatives as Samuel Johnson and Edmund Burke. The idea of the "NOBLE SAVAGE" produced the idealized American Indian, as in Cooper's novels, and American life was exploited as ideal because it was primitive, as in Crèvecoeur's *Letters from an American Farmer*. Elements of *primitivism*, related to the idea of natural goodness, appear throughout American writing in the nineteenth century.

A common and useful distinction is made between cultural primitivism and chronological primitivism, cultural being used for the *primitivism* that prefers the natural to the artificial, the uninhibited to the controlled, the simple and primitive to that on which people have worked, nature to art; and chronological being used for the *primitivism* that looks backward to a "Golden Age" and sees our present sad state as the product of what culture and society have done to them. If this distinction is made—and the terms are not mutually exclusive—it becomes apparent that many of the political doctrines of the American founding fathers were influenced by chronological primitivism, whereas cultural primitivism has been a powerful, although silent, force in American realism. Any number of nineteenth-century intellectual movements—the Grimms' FOLKLORE and PHILOLOGY, Darwin's developmental-historical biology, Freud's psychoanalysis (stimulated in part by Darwin's *The Descent of Man*), medievalism, scientific ethnography and anthropology—contributed to the flourishing of *primitivism* in the arts, from Longfellow's *The Song of Hiawatha* to Wagner's music dramas. Frazer's monumental *The Golden Bough* stimulated interest in myth and folklore, so that what seemed to be experimental, sophisticated art in the vanguard of human enterprise turned out to receive a sanction of antiquity and primordiality from the pervasive spirit of *primitivism*. Many influential artists born during the 1880s—Pablo Picasso, James Joyce, Igor Stravinsky, D. H. Lawrence, Ezra Pound, Béla Bartók, T. S. Eliot—moved forward technically while (and by) moving backward culturally. Few movements or general sentiments can match the decisive importance of *primitivism* in modern art and thought.

Print The general condition of being printed. "In print" and "out of print" have to do with whether or not an item is still available from a publisher.

Printing The copies of a publication printed at the same time; IMPRESSION. See EDITION.

Printing, Introduction into American Colonies Although the Spaniards had brought printing presses to Mexico and elsewhere much earlier, the real beginning of printing in America dates from 1639, when, according to Governor Winthrop's *Diary*, a printing house was begun by Stephen Daye. The first document printed was *The Freeman's Oath*, the next an almanac, and the third the famous *Bay Psalm Book* (1640), the earliest surviving American book. William Bradford was printing in Philadelphia as early as 1683. Later he moved to New York and became the government printer. The introduction of printing into Virginia was opposed by Governor Berkeley, and a printing establishment was suppressed in 1682, though printing was reintroduced not long thereafter.

Printing, Introduction into England The circumstances of the invention and development of printing in Western Europe (the Chinese and Japanese had a form of printing centuries before) are so obscure that it is impossible to assign the invention to any country, person, or exact date. It is fairly certain that the most important development of the art took place in Mainz, Germany, during the 1440s and 1450s. The earliest existing book that can be dated is an "Indulgence" (Mainz, 1454); the most famous existing early book is the Gutenberg Bible (Mainz, 1456). On the authority of fifteenth-century writers, Johann Gutenberg of Mainz is commonly given credit for the invention.

From Mainz the art spread to other countries, reaching England in 1476, when William Caxton set up his famous press at Westminster. Caxton had learned printing on the Continent, and at Bruges, probably in 1475, had brought out the first book printed in English, the *Recuyell of the Historyes of Troye*. The first printed books in England were probably PAMPHLETS, some in Latin, but the first dated English book printed in England was Caxton's *Dicts or Sayings of the Philosophers* (1477). Before his death Caxton had printed about a hundred separate books and had done much to direct the public taste in reading. He specialized in translations, poetry, and romances, two of his most important books being his edition of Chaucer's *Canterbury Tales* (1483) and his publication of Malory's *Le Morte Darthur* (1485). Other early presses in England include one at Oxford (1478) and one at St. Albans (1479), both devoted chiefly to learned works. Caxton himself was succeeded by his assistant, Wynkyn de Worde, a printer without literary talent but important because he published, during his long career, about eight hundred books, some of them of literary interest. An important contemporary printer was Richard Pynson (fl. 1490–1530).

Private Theaters The term *private theater* came along about 1596, when the Blackfriars theater was so described by its sponsors, who were seeking privileges not granted to the PUBLIC THEATERS. The *private theaters*, though they charged more and attracted a higher class of spectator than did their "public" rivals, were open to all classes. They differed from the public theaters in being indoor institutions, artificially lighted, smaller, and typically rectangular. In origin, they were connected with companies of child actors and continued to be used chiefly, but not exclusively, by such companies. These companies performed at various times at the Blackfriars, St. Paul's, the INNS OF COURT, and the Court. Shakespeare's company in the early seventeenth century controlled both the Blackfriars, the chief *private theater*, and the Globe, the chief public theater. The *private theaters* gained importance in the seventeenth century, when the Court was fostering elaborate exhibitions (see MASQUE) and encouraging drama with spectacular features, and it is from them rather than from the public theaters that the playhouses of the Restoration and later times directly descended.

Problem Novel A narrative that derives its chief interest from working out some central problem. The term is sometimes applied to those novels written for a deliberate purpose or thesis, which are better called PROPAGANDA NOVELS. Because human character is the subject matter surest to interest readers and because humankind is constantly confronted by the problems of life and conduct, it follows that the *problem novel*—when it is thought of as a story *with* a purpose rather than *for* a purpose—is fairly common. The REALISTIC NOVEL, centered as it is in social setting, has often employed social issues as the cruxes of its plots. This matter of illustrating a problem by showing people confronted thereby is at the core of the *problem novel*.

Problem Play Like the PROBLEM NOVEL, its analogue in nondramatic fiction, this term is used both in a broad sense to cover all serious drama in which problems of human life are presented as such, for example, Shakespeare's *King Lear*, and in a more specialized sense to designate the modern "drama of ideas," as exemplified in the plays of Ibsen, Shaw, Galsworthy, and many others. It is most commonly used in the latter sense, and here it means the representation in dramatic form of a general social problem or issue, shown as it is confronted by the protagonist.

Procatalepsis The device of anticipating and answering an opponent's objection or question. "I know you will wonder how much this will cost. This will cost you nothing at all."

Proceleusmatic A FOOT consisting of four short syllables.

Procephalic Having an extra syllable at the beginning; applied to the first foot of a DACTYLIC HEXAMETER.

Proem A brief introduction; a PREFACE or PREAMBLE.

Profile An essay that combines a biographical sketch and a character study of a contemporary figure. The type of essay and the term *profile* come from *The New Yorker* magazine, which has been publishing such sketches and calling them "*Profiles*" for many years.

Program A theatrical term for the schedule of a single planned entertainment; also the printed pamphlet thereof.

Program Notes Material included in a program, such as information about works being performed and summaries of the careers of the performers.

Progress The belief that in many ways human history shows a pattern of improvement over the past is often called "the idea of *progress*." In some cases, this idea is almost made into a system under which *progress*—that is, the improvement of human and social conditions—is inevitable with the passage of time. In its naive statements it can be a childishly optimistic doctrine. When held by serious and thoughtful people, as it often has been, the idea of *progress* is a strong antidote to the doctrine of CHRONOLOGICAL PRIMITIVISM. It has often been said that American romanticism in the nineteenth century rested upon the doctrine of natural goodness (CULTURAL PRIMITIVISM) and the idea of *progress*. See PRIMITIVISM.

Progymnasma A preparatory or preliminary exercise.

Projective Verse A kind of free verse that regards meter and form as artificial, and in which the poet "projects" a voice primarily through the content and the propulsive quality of breathing, which alone determines the line. *Projective verse* is also called "breath verse" because of this primary role of breathing in determining the line structure. Projectivists deny that form creates meaning and are actively in revolt against formalist doctrines. Charles Olson was the chief theoretician of the projectivists. The influence of "projectivism" reaches back to William Carlos Williams and forward to a large number of poets born after 1920, including Denise Levertov, Ed Dorn, Imamu Amiri Baraka, and Gerard Malanga.

[References: Paul Christensen, *Charles Olson: Call Him Ishmael* (1979); Charles Olson, *Projective Verse* (1959); Sherman Paul, *Olson's Push: Origin, Black Mountain, and Recent American Poetry* (1978).]

Prolegomenon A PREFACE. The heading *prolegomena* (plural) may be given to the introductory section of a book containing observations. Occasionally, a whole book will be called "*prolegomenon*" or "*prolegomena*," suggesting a sustained study or set of studies preliminary to further work, as in Jane Harrison's *Prolegomena to the Study of Greek Religion*. Thomas Carlyle wrote, "Johnson's own writings . . . for some future generation may be valuable chiefly as Prolegomena and expository Scholia to this Johnsoniad of Boswell."

Prolepsis An anticipating; the type of anachronism in which an event is pictured as taking place before it could have done so, the treating of a future event as if past. Rhetorically, the word may be applied to a preliminary statement or summary that is to be followed by a detailed treatment. In argumentation *prolepsis* may mean the device of anticipating and answering an opponent's argument before the opponent has an opportunity to introduce it, thus detracting from its effectiveness if later employed. In *The White Goddess* Robert Graves applies *prolepsis* to trances in which one is given a glimpse of the future.

Prologue An introduction most frequently associated with drama and especially common in England in the plays of the Restoration and the eighteenth century. In the plays of ancient Greece a speaker announced, before the beginning of the play proper, such salient facts as the audience should know to understand the play itself. In Latin drama the same custom prevailed, Plautus having left some of the most sophisticated *prologues* in dramatic literature. Dramatists in France and England followed the classical tradition, from the time of the MIRACLE and MYSTERY PLAYS (which used *prologues* of a "moral" nature) well into modern times. *Prologues* were frequently written by the author of a play and delivered by one of the chief actors; in the eighteenth century, however, it was common practice for writers of established reputations, such as Pope, Johnson, and Garrick, to write *prologues* for plays by their friends and acquaintances. Sometimes, as in the play within the play in *Hamlet*, the actor who spoke the *prologue* was himself called "the *prologue*." The first part of Shakespeare's *King Henry the Fourth* opens with an explanatory speech, not formally a *prologue*, which serves the function of a real *prologue*. Part two of the same play opens with a *prologue* called an INDUCTION.

Prolusion One of many words meaning a prefatory piece of writing; also a preliminary exercise, as in those of Milton's called "Oratorical Performances (Prolusions)" (or *Prolusiones*).

Promotion The assignment of stress to an unstressed syllable, usually as the result of patterns of rhythm and rhyme. In many cases, a change of vowel quality also occurs. *Promotion* is most often encountered when a word of three or more syllables, ending as a DACTYL, occurs at the end of a rhymed IAMBIC line, as in the familiar

My country 'tis of thee,
Sweet land of liberty. . . .

The last word is normally stressed as a dactyl ("líbĕrtў") but, by promotion, picks up courtesy stress on the final syllable ("líbĕrtý") along with a change of the final vowel to make a rhyme with "thee." As a rule, the fully stressed syllable (such as "thee") comes before the promoted syllable (as in "liberty") to guide the pronunciation of the newly stressed syllable.

Promptbook (also **Prompt Script, Prompt-Copy**) The text of a play used by a PROMPTER, often with changes and notes of considerable interest.

Prompter One whose job is to assist players by staying just offstage at a desk in the wings or a *prompter's* box at the front of the stage. The *prompter* follows the play scrupulously, gives words or lines to actors suffering lapses of memory, and otherwise assists in production.

Prompt Side (abbreviated **P. S.** or **p. s.**) The side of the stage where the PROMPTER remains, stage left in Britain, stage right in the U.S. "Prompt-center" is the place on the stage between the *prompt-side* and center stage.

Promythium Complement of EPIMYTHIUM. A moral tag put before a FABLE.

Propaganda Material propagated for the purpose of advocating a political or ideological position; also the mechanism for such *propaganda*. Earlier, in European use, *propaganda* carried a positive or neutral sense of "distributing information" or "advertising"; since about 1930, however, the connotations have become increasingly negative.

[References: Toby Clark, *Art and Propaganda in the Twentieth Century: The Political Image in the Age of Mass Culture* (1997); Jane DeRose Evans, *The Art of Persuasion: Political Propaganda from Aeneas to Brutus* (1992); George H. Szanto, *Theater and Propaganda* (1978).]

Propaganda Novel A novel dealing with a special social, political, economic, or moral issue or problem and possibly advocating a doctrinaire solution. If the propagandistic purpose dominates the work so as to dwarf or eclipse all other elements, such as plot and character, then the novel belongs to the realm of the didactic and probably cannot be understood or appreciated for its own sake as a work of art. It may be good propaganda and bad literature at the same time. William Godwin's *Things as They Are: or The Adventures of Caleb Williams* (1794) is an early example. See PROBLEM NOVEL.

Proparalepsis The addition of a syllable to the end of a word, as in "dampen" from "damp."

Proparoxytone Having an acute accent on the antepenultimate syllable, that is, that before the next-to-last.

Proper Meter (or **Proper Measure**) (abbreviated **P.M.**) In some hymnals, a notation that a hymn has a meter proper only to itself; sometimes used of prose texts.

Propriety In the general sense, conformity to accepted standards of taste or conduct. The term is used in literary criticism in the special sense of correspondence to the demands of the situation within the particular work of art. Dramatic *propriety* is a very good example of this literary usage.

Prosa, Prose For a while during the late Middle Ages and early Renaissance, the honorific "VERSE" was reserved for poetry in the classical style: quantitatively scanned and unrhymed (see QUANTITATIVE VERSE). Other kinds of writing, even that using qualitative scansion and RHYME (see ACCENTUAL-SYLLABIC VERSE), were disdainfully classified as *prose*; and "in prose" meant "in rhymed accentual verse." *Prosa* or *prose* was also applied to a musical SEQUENCE, distinguished from a HYMN (in which the musical setting was repeated for each STROPHE). In a *prose* or sequence, the music was varied strophe by strophe.

Prosaics Formed by analogy with POETICS: the systematic study of the principles of PROSE. A book on Mikhail Bakhtin by G. S. Morson and Caryl Emerson is called *Creation of a Prosaics*.

Prosaist A writer of prose (sometimes neutral, sometimes with the added sense of "prosaic" or "unpoetical").

Proscenium That part of the stage in a modern theater that lies between the orchestra and the curtain. In the ancient theater the *proscenium* extended from the orchestra to the background, and the term is sometimes used, even nowadays, merely as a synonym for the stage itself. The arch over the front of the stage from which the CURTAIN hangs and which, together with the curtain, separates the stage from the audience is called the *proscenium arch*. In a BOX SET it forms the FOURTH WALL of the stage-as-room.

Prose In its broadest sense the term is applied to all forms of written or spoken expression not having a regular rhythmic pattern. *Prose* is most often meant to designate a consciously shaped writing, not merely a listing of ideas or a catalog of objects. And, although good *prose* is like verse in having a rhythm, it is unlike verse in that this rhythm is not to be scanned by normal metrical schemes or marked by such devices of reiteration as FREE VERSE exploits. But a clear line between *prose* and POETRY is difficult to draw. Some of the qualities of *prose* are: (1) It is without sustained rhythmic regularity; (2) it has some logical grammatical order, and its ideas are connectedly stated rather than merely listed; (3) it is characterized by style; (4) it will achieve variety of expression through varied diction.

Prose in all literatures has developed more slowly than verse. English *prose* is usually said to find its beginnings in the work of Alfred, whose *Handbook* (887) is sometimes cited as the earliest specimen of finished English *prose*. Other names significant in the development of English *prose* are Thomas Usk, John Wycliffe, Malory, Caxton, Roger Ascham, Holinshed, Lyly, Ralegh, Donne, Jeremy Taylor, Milton, Dryden, Addison, Mark Twain, and Hemingway. For many centuries English *prose* had to compete with Latin for recognition, and for many more years Latin forms and syntax shaped its style. The single book that did the most to mold present English *prose* style was the King James Version of the Bible.

In another use of the term, medieval hymn sequences are sometimes called *proses*. See PROSA.

[References: Robert Adolphe, *The Rise of Modern Prose Style* (1968); George Williamson, *The Senecan Amble: A Study in Prose Form from Bacon to Collier* (1951).]

Prose Poem A POEM printed as PROSE, with both margins justified. Edgar Allan Poe used "prose-poem" in 1842; in 1850 Charles Kingsley praised "That great prose poem, the single epic of modern days, Thomas Carlyle's *French Revolution*."

Largely a modern phenomenon, the *prose poem* can be found in the works of Baudelaire, Rimbaud, and Valéry in France and, derivatively, in Eliot's "Hysteria" (around 1915). Despite some doubts about the possibility of such a hyphenated transgeneric form, the *prose poem* has persisted; John Ashbery's *Three Poems* is a whole book consisting of three long pieces of prose. The point seems to be that a writing in prose, even the most prosaic, is a poem if the author says so. Mark Harris has argued, polemically if not rationally, that neither the *prose poem* nor the "nonfiction novel" really exists. It may be that *prose poem* is a graphic or print category determined, finally, by how a piece is laid out in print. A poem that is printed in the format of prose is a *prose poem*. If it is labeled as such by a title or other indicator, then the attitude of most readers will probably be affected, so that they read with something of the exaggerated care and attention to detail usually reserved for poetry.

Prose Rhythm The recurrence of stress and emphasis at irregular intervals, affording a pleasurable rise and fall. *Prose rhythm* is distinguished from the rhythm of verse in that it never for long falls into a recognizable pattern, for if it does it becomes verse rather than prose. The greater freedom of *prose rhythm*, as compared with verse, springs from its wider choice in the placing of stress. The normal accent of words first determines the rhythmic emphasis. But this is augmented by the secondary accents (in such words as òbsĕrvātĭon and èlĕméntărȳ) and increased again by the tendency of the reader to emphasize certain words importantly placed or rendered significant because of their meaning. (See RHETORICAL ACCENT.) As far as various kinds of lexical and acoustic rhythm are concerned, the rhythm of prose is essentially indistinguishable from that of poetry. Indeed, there are passages in the prose of Dickens, Melville, Hemingway, and Wolfe that can be scanned as more or less regular verse. Distinguishable *prose rhythm* probably occurs only at the levels of SYNTAX and concept.

Prosody The principles of VERSIFICATION, particularly as they refer to RHYME, METER, RHYTHM, and STANZA.

Prosonomasia Calling someone by a punning nickname, such as "G. Gordon Giddy."

Prosopopoeia Another name for PERSONIFICATION. In *prosopopoeia*, the personified abstraction is capable of speech and often does speak, as, for example, in the first chapter of Proverbs:

> Wisdom cries aloud in the street;
>   in the markets she raises her voice;
> on the top of the walls she cries out;
>   at the entrance of the city gates she speaks:
> "How long, O simple ones, will you love being simple?
> How long will scoffers delight in their scoffing
>   and fools hate knowledge? . . ."

Protagonist The chief character in a work. The word was originally applied to the "first" actor in early Greek drama. The actor was added to the CHORUS and was its leader; hence, the continuing meaning of *protagonist* as the "first" or chief player. In Greek drama an AGON is a contest. The *protagonist* and the ANTAGONIST, the second most important character, are the contestants. In Shakespeare's *Hamlet*, Hamlet is himself the *protagonist*, as his fortunes are the chief interest of the play. King Claudius and Laertes are his ANTAGONISTS. The sentence "The protagonists of Christopher Marlowe's tragedies are usually the super-personality type" illustrates a normal use of the word.

Protasis A classical term for the introductory act or the exposition of a drama. See DRAMATIC STRUCTURE.

Prothalamion From the Greek, "before the bridal chamber." The term was coined by Edmund Spenser as the title of a poem celebrating the double weddings of Lady Elizabeth and Lady Katherine Somerset. Spenser devised the term by analogy with EPITHALAMION.

Prothesis The addition of a syllable at the beginning of a word, as in Keats's line, "The owl for all his feathers was a-cold."

Prototype A first form or original instance of a thing, or model or pattern for later form or examples. Thus, the periodical essay of the eighteenth century as written by Addison or Steele may be called the *prototype* of the familiar essay as written by Lamb or Stevenson, the later form being developed from the earlier. Or the VICE of the morality plays may be regarded as the *prototype* of the clown of Elizabethan Drama.

Proverb A saying that briefly and memorably expresses some recognized truth about life; originally preserved by oral tradition, though it may be transmitted in written literature as well. *Proverbs* may owe their appeal to metaphor ("Still waters run deep"); antithesis ("Man proposes, God disposes"); a play on words ("Forewarned, forearmed"); rhyme ("A friend in need is a friend indeed"); or alliteration or parallelism. Some are epigrammatic. Because the true *proverb* is old, its language is sometimes archaic. Words, meanings, idioms, or grammatical constructions not now common may be used. A misunderstanding of the original meaning may result. Thus, in "Time and tide wait for no man" *tide* is probably the old word for "season." In "The exception proves the rule," the "proves" ought to retain its old meaning of "tests" or "challenges"; exceptions do not establish rules, certainly, except in a *proverb* that has achieved currency. "Good fences make good neighbors," from Robert Frost's "Mending Wall," is one of the rare *proverbs* that has a traceable source in literature and a named author.

Provincialism A word, phrase, or manner of expression peculiar to a special region and not commonly used outside that region, therefore, not fashionable or sophisticated. The term is applied not only to language but to customs, dress, and other characteristics of a special region.

Pruning Poem A poem in which succeeding rhyme words have initial sounds or letters pared away. A notable example is George Herbert's "Paradise":

What open force, or hidden *charm*
Can blast my fruit, or bring me *harm*
While the inclosure is thine *arm?*

A variation of the *pruning poem* is the "diminishing" or "vanishing" poem like Alan Ansen's sestina "A Fit of Something Against Something," which begins with a strophe of long lines ending "be," "austere," "order," "undergone," "master," and "sestina"; each succeeding strophe has ever-shorter lines; the poem ends with six words in three lines:

Sestina order,
Austere master,
BE GONE!!!

Psalm A lyrical composition of praise. Most frequently the term is applied to the sacred lyrics in the Book of Psalms ascribed to David. The contemporary American W. S. Merwin has written some distinguished poems called *psalms*.

[Reference: Robert Alter, *The Art of Biblical Poetry* (1985).]

Pseudomorph A mineralogical term adapted for a literary work with a title that belongs to a form different from that of the work itself. Dickens's *A Christmas Carol,* for example, has parts called "staves" but is really a work of prose fiction, not a carol.

Pound's "Villanelle: The Psychological Hour" is not a VILLANELLE at all. Poems titled "Sonnet" by Williams Carlos Williams and John Ashbery do not fit the fourteen-lined format expected of the SONNET, but that designation has been flexible in the past.

Pseudonym A false name sometimes assumed by writers and others. See *NOM DE PLUME*, PUTATIVE AUTHOR, ALLONYM.

Pseudo-Shakespearean Plays Plays attributed to Shakespeare at one time but now not accepted as his by the best authorities. Some, such as *Locrine*, were printed during Shakespeare's lifetime with his initials or name on the title page; others, such as *The Birth of Merlin*, were so printed after Shakespeare's death. Another group, including *Mucedorus*, consists of plays labeled as Shakespeare's in the copies of them found in the library of Charles II. Many others, including *Sir Thomas More* (the manuscript copy of which is thought by some experts to be partly in Shakespeare's hand) and *Arden of Feversham*, have been assigned to Shakespeare by editors, booksellers, or critics chiefly on the basis of literary or technical qualities. A collection of *pseudo-Shakespearean plays* has been printed by Tucker Brooke in his *Shakespeare Apocrypha*. Some plays dubiously assigned to Shakespeare, such as *Cardenio*, have not survived.

Psychoanalytical Criticism The emphasis in criticism on the values of symbols and language that, often unconsciously, explain meanings or unconscious intention. The term is also often applied to the examination of the motives and actions of characters, as in Ernest Jones's *Hamlet and Oedipus*. Most *psychoanalytical criticism* employs the doctrines of Sigmund Freud. In *Jacques Lacan and the Adventure of Insight* (1987), Shoshana Felman traces psychoanalytical approaches to Edgar Allan Poe from J. W. Krutch and Marie Bonaparte to Jacques Lacan, demonstrating significant development in the field. See FREUDIAN CRITICISM.

Psychological Novel Prose fiction that places unusual emphasis on interior CHARACTERIZATION and on the motives, circumstances, and internal action that spring from, and develop, external action. The *psychological novel*, not content to state what happens, goes on to explain the *why* of this action. In this type of writing, characterization is more than usually important. Chaucer's *Troilus and Criseyde* can be regarded as a *psychological novel* in verse. *Hamlet* is a psychological drama, but so are most of Shakespeare's better plays. The *psychological novel* is, as one critic has said, an interpretation of "the invisible life." The term was first importantly applied to a group of novelists in the middle of the nineteenth century, of whom Elizabeth Gaskell, George Eliot, and George Meredith were the chief. Gaskell stated that "all deeds however hidden and long passed by have their external consequences"—thus giving expression to an attitude long realized and felt if not always deliberately expressed. Thackeray and Dickens, too, were interested enough in motives and mental states to be classified, in a looser sense, with the forerunners of the *psychological novel*. Hardy and Conrad were also interested in the picturing of interior motive and psychological effect. Henry James, with his intense concern for the psychological life of his characters and with his development of a novelistic technique centered in the representation of the effect produced in the inner self by external forces, may be said to have created the modern *psychological novel*.

By the twenty-first century, with the advance of psychology and psychiatry, the term has come into popular use. The modern *psychological novel* may at one extreme record the inner experience of characters as reported by an author, as James tends to do, or at the other extreme utilize the INTERIOR MONOLOGUE to articulate the nonverbalized and subconscious life of a character, as in some of the work of James Joyce and William Faulkner.

Public Theaters The English playhouse developed in the Elizabethan Age in response to the increased interest in the drama. In earlier times plays had been produced on PAGEANTS and in such indoor rooms as guild halls and the halls of great houses, schools, INNS OF COURT, and inn-yards, which were square or rectangular courts enclosed by the inner porches or balconies of the inn building. At one end would be erected a temporary stage connected with rooms of the inn. The spectators might stand in the open court ("groundlings") or get seats on the surrounding balconies. In the meantime, the need for a place for bear- or bull-baiting spectacles and acrobatic performances had been met in the development of a sort of ring or amphitheater. Out of the physical features of the inn-yard (surrounding galleries or boxes, open central space or pit, stage extending into pit) and the bear garden (circular form of building), evolved the plan of the first *public theater*. The front stage was open to the sky, the rear stage covered by a ceiling. Above this ceiling was a room for the machinery needed in lowering persons and objects to the stage below, or raising them from it. There was an "inner" stage at the rear, provided with a CURTAIN and connected with a balcony above, also curtained. The rear stage was used chiefly for special settings such as a forest or bedroom, whereas the bare outer stage was used for street scenes, battles, and the like. The scenery and the costumes of the actors were largely conventional and symbolic, though certainly very realistic at times.

The first *public theater* in London was the Theatre, built in 1576 by James Burbage in Shoreditch. It was followed in 1577 by the Curtain in the same neighborhood. About ten years later Henslowe built the Rose on the Bankside, and in this locality appeared also the Swan (1594). In 1599 the Theatre was torn down and re-erected on the Bankside as the Globe, the most important of the *public theaters*. The Globe was used and controlled by the company to which Shakespeare belonged. Henslowe built the Fortune in 1600, the Red Bull appeared soon after in St. John's Street, and the Hope in 1614 near the Rose and the new Globe. See PRIVATE THEATERS.

Pultizer Prizes Annual prizes for journalism, literature, and music, awarded annually since 1917 by the School of Journalism and the Board of Trustees of Columbia University. The prizes are supported by a bequest from Joseph Pulitzer. An Advisory Board selects work published or produced in the United States during the preceding year and recommends recipients to the Board of Trustees, who make the awards. Eight prizes are awarded for various kinds of meritorious service rendered by newspapers, and one prize is awarded for a musical composition. Six awards are given for books: novel, play, American history, biography or autobiography, verse, and general nonfiction. Listings of the *Pulitzer Prizes* for fiction, poetry, and drama are given in the Appendices.

Pull Quote In newspapers, a quotation pulled from a story and increased in size as an enticement to the reader.

Pulp Magazines Magazines printed on rough pulp paper, cheaply produced, with lurid illustrations and gaudy covers, and featuring tales of love, crime, and adventure. Popular in the first half of the twentieth century, particularly in the 1920s and 1930s, the *pulp magazines* were the successors to the DIME NOVELS. Pulp magazines were given new life and dignity by Quentin Tarentino's film *Pulp Fiction* (1994), with literal and figurative senses of *pulp*.

Pun A play on words based on the similarity of sound between two words with different meanings. An example is Thomas Hood's: "They went and told the sexton and the sexton tolled the bell." The *pun* is a humble thing, and many find it trifling or irritating. Even so, *puns* are found in the most sublime scriptures (as with Aramaic *qalmâ*, "gnat," and *gamlâ*, "camel," in Matthew 23.24) and throughout Shakespeare's works (drawing the contempt of critics as diverse as Samuel Johnson and Thomas Wolfe—see QUIBBLE). From its earlier low or marginal status, the *pun* has steadily risen in dignity, to the point of being a main structural principle of Joyce's *Ulysses* and *Finnegans Wake*. Most *puns* are exotic, parochial, and short-lived; some, however, such as those involving "son" and "sun" and "I" and "eye," are important staples of English literature.

[Reference: Jonathan Culler, ed., *On Puns: The Foundation of Letters* (1988).]

Punchline The line in a joke—normally the last—containing the point of it all. Philip Roth's novel *Portnoy's Complaint* ends with what is labeled a *punchline*, as though the entire work were a protracted joke.

Pure Poetry Poetry supposedly free from conceptualized statement or moral preachment; or those portions of a poem remaining after such materials as can be paraphrased adequately in prose are removed. The term was first used by Baudelaire in an essay on Poe. For many critics Poe's theory and practice of poetry are archetypically pure; George Moore said that Poe's poems "are almost free from thought." Wallace Stevens is often cited as a modern poet who practiced an art close to that of *pure poetry*. Moore classified as "pure" such poems as are "born of admiration of the only permanent world, the world of things." Moore's rather quaint anthology came out in 1925; twenty years later, Robert Penn Warren published his essay "Pure and Impure Poetry," a subtler argument than Moore's.

[References: George Moore, ed., *Anthology of Pure Poetry* (1925); Robert Penn Warren, *Selected Essays* (1958).]

Purist One who habitually stresses correctness in language, particularly in minor points of grammar, pronunciation, and style. Although the term is commonly used in deprecation or reproach, it is difficult to draw the line between the *purist* and one who takes a commendable interest in achieving accuracy and precision. Some have been technical or scientific *purists*. H. G. Wells once wrote a story about a fat man who wanted to lose weight, but when he did lose weight, he floated up into the air, "gravityless." What he really wanted to lose, it seems, is *mass*.

A related use of the word is its application to a person who feels that the purity of a language can be preserved by the exclusion of foreign words and of words not used by the best stylists. Thus, the so-called Ciceronians of the Renaissance, a group of Latin stylists who would not use any Latin word that could not be found in Cicero's writings, have been called *purists*, as have the English scholars of the sixteenth century and later who insisted on a pure English diction "unmixed and unmangled with borrowing of other tongues." The famous schoolmasters Sir John Cheke and Roger Ascham and the rhetorician Thomas Wilson were leaders in this movement. The struggle between these *purists* and their INKHORNIST opponents is sometimes referred to as the "purist-improver" controversy.

Later movements toward purism included: the unsuccessful effort in the seventeenth century to establish (on the model of the French Academy) a British Academy to regulate language; eighteenth-century efforts at standardization through the establishment of some definite linguistic authority (opposed by Samuel Johnson); and efforts to stress the Anglo-Saxon elements in the vocabulary and to check the importation of foreign words (noteworthy is Edna St. Vincent Millay's long poem, *The King's Henchman,* that employs only words of Anglo-Saxon derivation). In both prose and poetry Charles M. Doughty strove to regain a measure of what he regarded as purity of diction, and the results are still readable. There has been a Society for Pure English well into our own day; and a number of important writers—Morris, Barnes, Hardy, Hopkins, and Bridges, for example—have been involved in a *purist* sentiment of linguistic nationalism of the same sort that prompted Beethoven to abandon for a while the alien "piano" and adopt in its stead the good Germanic "Hammerklavier." Some of the effects of this sentiment have to be called salubrious—as in Hopkins's preference for the potent native "windhover" over the colorless "kestrel"; but Modern English is so mixed and has long been so hospitable to so-called LOAN WORDS that the effort to replace "omnibus" with "folkswain," say, or to place spelling on a "rational" basis (one of George Bernard Shaw's hobbyhorses) seems utterly vain. Another species of *purist* emphasizes purity of diction on the basis of fidelity to historical roots (saying, for instance, "oblivious *of*" instead of "oblivious *to*"), and it may be conceded that that effort has more respectable results in clarity and economy than the *purist*'s longing for a supposedly native vocabulary.

Puritanism A movement that developed in England about the middle of the sixteenth century and later spread its influence into the New England colonies in America. Although it died politically with the return of Charles II to London in 1660, *Puritanism* left its impress and many of its attitudes on the habits and thought of the people, especially those of America. As a term, *Puritan* was, in Elizabeth's reign, applied in derision to those who wished to purify the Church of England. The spirit behind *Puritanism* was an outgrowth of CALVINISM.

In principle the Puritans objected to certain forms of the Established Church: for instance, to the wearing of the surplice and to government by the prelates; and they demanded the right to partake of the communion in a sitting posture. Their Millenary Petition (1603) requested a reform of the church courts, a doing away with superstitious customs, a discarding of the use of APOCRYPHAL books of the Bible, a serious observance of the Sabbath, and various ecclesiastical reforms. At first *Puritanism* in England was not directly affiliated with Presbyterianism, but later on it allied itself with that movement. Thomas Cartwright, the first important exponent of *Puritanism,* most emphatically hated the Church of England.

The conception of the Puritans popularly held today, however, is unfair to the general temper of the early sponsors of the movement. These early English Puritans were not long-faced reformers, teetotalers, or haters of art and music. They were often patrons of art and lovers of music, fencing, and dancing. They were intelligent, disciplined, plainly dressed citizens who held to simplicity and to democratic principles. But under the persecution of Charles and the double-dealing of Laud they were harried into bitterness.

Puritanism was a logical aftermath of the Renaissance, the Reformation, the establishment of the Church of England, and the growth of Presbyterianism. Through all these movements one sees emerging the right of individuals to political and religious independence. The reading of the Bible had become general. The Catholic church had lost power in England, but there were still thousands of Catholics who wanted their old power restored. Political power for the commoners lay with Presbyterianism, a religious movement based on the political control of presbyters drawn from the people. Catholicism and even the Church of England were far too reminiscent of autocracy and of divine right to rule. James I had promised that if necessary he would "harry the Puritans out of the land." Charles I and Laud fought popular rights and suppressed Parliament. From 1642 to 1646 there raged civil war, from which rose to power a new Puritan leader, Oliver Cromwell. In 1649 Charles was beheaded. The Puritan Commonwealth was established, to end when, on May 25, 1660, Charles II landed at Dover.

Some of the "Brownists," a group of Puritans who had earlier left England for seclusion in Holland, came to America in the *Mayflower*, wishing to set up a new theocracy. "I shall call that my country where I may most glorify God and enjoy the presence of my dearest friends," said young Winthrop. In one year as many as three thousand rebels left England for the Colonies; in ten years there were twenty thousand English in America. Many of these newcomers were people of education, intelligence, family position, and culture. What now seems a movement toward conservatism, a threat against freedom of speech, art, and individualism, was at that time essentially a radical movement with leanings that have even been characterized as communistic.

In America a dozen or more writers attained positions in literature largely because they happened to stand at the source of the stream. Such theologians as John Cotton, Thomas Hooker, John Eliot, Cotton Mather; such historians as William Bradford, John Winthrop, Thomas Hutchinson, and Samuel Sewall; and such poets as Anne Bradstreet, Michael Wigglesworth, and Edward Taylor derive importance from their work and their historical position. The *Bay Psalm Book* (1640) became almost the book of a people.

With the Scotch-Irish settlements of the Middle Atlantic and Southern colonies came another and a stronger strain of *Puritanism*, that of the Presbyterians. And as the restless and the discontented, North and South, moved westward into the beckoning frontier they carried with them the Bible, a simple and fundamentally Puritan faith, and the stern impulse to independence and freedom. An extreme form of the Reformation sensibility, *Puritanism* exaggerated those Protestant traits—especially industry and frugality—which, according to Max Weber and others, contributed to the rise of capitalism.

[References: Sacvan Bercovitch, *The American Jeremiad* (1978), (ed.) *The American Puritan Imagination* (1974), and *The Puritan Origins of the American Self* (1975); Alan Simpson, *Puritanism in Old and New England* (1955); Page Smith, *As a City upon a Hill* (1966).]

"Purple Patch" A piece of notably fine writing. Now and then authors in a strongly emotional passage will give free play to most of the stylistic tricks in their bag. They will write prose intensely colorful and more than usually rhythmic. When there is an unusual piling up of these devices in such a way as to suggest a self-conscious literary effort, the section is spoken of as a *purple patch*—a colorful passage standing out from the writing around it. (The expression comes from Horace, for whom purple dye was much rarer—hence more conspicuous—than it is for us.) Although sometimes used in a nonevaluative, descriptive sense, the term is more often employed derogatorily.

Puseyism The later OXFORD MOVEMENT, so-called for one of the leaders, Edward B. Pusey.

Pushkin Stanza The stanza used by Alexander Pushkin in his VERSE-NOVEL *Eugene Onegin:* fourteen TETRAMETER lines rhyming *abab ccdd effe gg*.

Putative Author The fictional author of a work, supposedly written by someone other than its actual author. Lemuel Gulliver is the *putative author* of his *Travels*, not Jonathan Swift; Tristram Shandy is the *putative author* of his *Life and Opinions*, not Laurence Sterne. The writer using a *putative author* creates a character who writes the book. Washington Irving merely hid his name when he signed the *Sketch Book* as "Geoffrey Crayon," but he created a *putative author* who wrote and signed Diedrich Knickerbocker's *History of New York*.

Pyramidal Line A line in which there is a symmetrical distribution of syllables-per-word, as in

> Of Man's First Disobedience, and the Fruit . . .
> That's my last duchess painted on the wall . . .
> Build thee more stately mansions, O my soul . . .
> The moon, the little silver cloud, and she . . .
> Do not go gentle into that good night . . . .
> I knew a woman, lovely in her bones . . . .

Pyrrhic A FOOT of two unaccented syllables (˘˘) . As an occasional phenomenon, the *pyrrhic* foot is unavoidable in English, with its large population of unstressed syllables and combinations of slight prepositions and articles; but it is virtually inconceivable that a whole poem could be written in the foot. *Pyrrhic* feet occur most often as variants in iambic verse; it is not unusual to find one or two *pyrrhics* in most lines of blank verse read with normal emphasis; here are some lines from Shakespeare's *Julius Caesar*:

> Thĕ év|ĭl thăt | mén dó | líves áf|tĕr thém;
> Thĕ góod | ĭs óft | ĭntér|rĕd wĭth | thĕir bónes.
> Só lét | ĭt bé | wĭth Cáe|săr. Thĕ nób|lĕ Brútŭs
> Hăth tóld | yóu Cáe|săr wăs | ămbí|tĭóus.
> Ĭf ĭt | wĕre só, | ĭt wăs | ă gríe|vŏus fáult,
> Aňd gríe|vŏuslÿ | hăth Cáe|săr án|swĕred ít.

Rosart 1759. Designed by J. F. Rosart. This typeface was the prototype for tooled roman capitals.

Quadrivium In the medieval university curriculum, the four subjects leading to the Master of Arts (Magister Artium) degree: arithmetic, music, geometry, and astronomy. See SEVEN LIBERAL ARTS, TRIVIUM.

Qualitative Versification Versification based on patterns of accented and unaccented syllables. Most European languages since about 1350, including English, have followed some model of *qualitative versification*.

Quantitative Versification Versification in patterns based on QUANTITY, that is, relative duration of sound. Classical poetry in Sanskrit, Greek, and Latin was *quantitative*, whereas English poetry has been qualitative or ACCENTUAL-SYLLABIC. However, a number of English poets have experimented with *quantitative verse* forms, among them Campion, Sidney, Spenser, Coleridge, Tennyson, Longfellow, Lanier, Pound, Auden, and Nims. Special (and quite elastic) rules have been devised for the calculation of long and short syllables in a language distinguished by the extreme variability of its syllables.

Quantity In classical prosody, *quantity*, the fundamental rhythmic unit, is the relative length of time required to utter a syllable. In Greek and Latin a syllable was considered long if it contained either a long vowel or a short vowel followed by two consonants; otherwise, it was considered short, except for a few vowels and syllables that varied between these limits and were called common. A long syllable was roughly the equivalent of two short syllables. Although duration is unquestionably a property of English versification, the chief rhythmic pattern of English is ACCENTUAL-SYLLABIC.

Quarterly Review A British Tory critical journal founded in 1809. See *EDINBURGH REVIEW*.

Quaternion A literary work with four as a basic part of its structure. *Quaternion* usually implies several interlocking sets of fours. Floyd Stovall, for example, calls "The Bells," by Poe, a *quaternion* because it consists of four parts, describes four bells made of four metals, and represents four stages of life. Wagner's four-drama *Der Ring des Nibelungen* was answered by Nietzsche's four-part *Also Sprach Zarathustra*. Eliot's *Four Quartets,* the title of which suggests a double *quaternion*, has four main sections based, none too programmatically, on the four elements along with the seasons and directions. Whether any quadratic or fourfold work—*Paradise Regained*, Blake's "London," *The Testament of Beauty, Finnegans Wake*, or Ashbery's *Shadow Train*, say—ought to be called a *quaternion* depends on whether the quantitative structure is markedly foregrounded.

Quarto A BOOK SIZE designating a book whose SIGNATURES result from sheets folded to four leaves (eight pages).

Quatorzain A stanza of fourteen lines. The term is usually reserved for fourteen-line poems not conforming to one or another of the SONNET patterns.

Quatrain A stanza of four lines. The possible rhyme schemes vary from an unrhymed *quatrain* to almost any arrangement of one-rhyme, two-rhyme, or three-rhyme lines. Perhaps the most common form is the *abab* sequence; other popular rhyme patterns are *aabb; abba; aaba; abcb*. Robert Frost's "In a Disused Graveyard" consists of four *quatrains*, in IAMBIC TETRAMETER, each in a different rhyme scheme: *abba, aaaa, aabb, abab*—quite a *tour de force*.W. H. Auden's "Leap Before You Look" rhymes *abab bbaa baab abba aabb baba*, in effect turning itself inside out.

Queer Theory Warren Hedges has suggested that "Identity-based gay and Lesbian criticism" around 1988 gave way to *Queer Theory*, the main difference being that the former "assumes that representations are a function of sexual identities" while the latter "assumes that sexual identities are a function of representations." "Queer theorists," according to Hedges, "read texts with a great degree of specificity, attending to what characters take pleasure in, how this is tied to historically specific circumstances, and the representational dynamics and dilemmas in which characters find themselves enmeshed." Ideally, scrutiny of "what characters want and do"—often involving play on many senses of "queer" (adjective, noun, verb) and "query"—is independent of preconceptions about identity, sexuality, and authenticity. The growth of *Queer Theory* is attested to by such titles as *Queering the Pitch: The New Gay and Lesbian Musicology* (1994) and *Que(e)rying Religion: A Critical Anthology* (1997).

[References: Lisa Duggan, *Sex Wars: Essays on Sexual Dissent and American Politics* (1995); Jonathan Goldberg, ed., *Queering the Renaissance* (1994).]

Question The grammatical form of asking; interrogation. Whether the answer is known beforehand or not, the *question* seems to be an inherently interesting and exciting form of utterance. Marlowe's most famous lines are a *question*: "Was this the face that launched a thousand ships / And burnt the topless towers of Ilium?" Likewise, Francis Scott Key's most famous lines ask, "Oh, say, can you see . . . ?" It is a peculiarly powerful way of ending a poem, such as Keats's "Ode to a Nightingale" and many of Yeats's poems. Blake's "The Tyger" is nothing but *questions*. See RHETORICAL QUESTION.

Quibble Earlier, a PUN. Nowadays a verbal device for evading the point at issue, as when debaters engage in *quibbles* over the interpretation of a term. Low as it may be, the *quibble* inspired Samuel Johnson's loftiest rhetoric and most sublime display of humor:

> A quibble is to Shakespeare what luminous vapors are to the traveler: he follows it at all adventures; it is sure to lead him out of his way, and sure to engulf him in the mire. It has some malignant power over his mind, and its

fascinations are irresistible. Whatever be the dignity or profundity of his disquisitions, whether he be enlarging knowledge or exalting affection, whether he be amusing attention with incidents, or enchaining it in suspense, let but a quibble spring up before him, and he leaves his work unfinished. A quibble is the golden apple for which he will always turn aside from his career or stoop from his elevation. A quibble, poor and barren as it is, gave him such delight that he was content to purchase it by the sacrifice of reason, propriety, and truth. A quibble was to him the fatal Cleopatra for which he lost the world, and was content to lose it.

Quintain (or **Quintet**) A stanza of five lines.

Quip A retort or sarcastic jest; hence any witty saying. George Herbert wrote a poem called "The Quip," in which the speaker, jeered at by "the merry world" (Beauty, Money, Glory, Wit, and Conversation), responds only with the oblique REFRAIN, "*But thou shalt answer, Lord, for me*." The last stanza assigns to the Lord the pleasure of answering the jeers with a *quip*:

Yet when the hour of thy design
To answer these fine things shall come;
Speak not at large; say, I am thine:
And then they have their answer home.

Walbaum Reissued 1919. Originally cut by Justin E. Walbaum in the early nineteenth century.

Rack Focus In film-making, a change of focus in the middle of shooting, with the effect of shifting attention from one thing to another.

Rahmengeschichte (or ***Rahmenerzählung***) German, "FRAMEWORK-STORY."

Raissoneur A character who is the level-headed personification of reason. This character, usually not closely connected to the central action, is present for any of three duties: (1) to serve as a standard against which the actions of others may be measured, (2) to articulate the questions in the audience's mind, as the chorus did in Greek drama, and (3) to utter judgments on the characters and their actions, thus serving as an author-surrogate. The *raisonneur*, a very common character in the WELL-MADE PLAY of the nineteenth century, functions somewhat like the CONFIDANT in a novel.

Rann In Irish literature, a piece of verse, usually a STANZA or, specifically, a QUATRAIN. W. B. Yeats's "To Ireland in the Coming Times" salutes those "Who sang to sweeten Ireland's wrong, / Ballad and story, rann and song."

Rap Earlier, informal conversation. Margaret Mead and James Baldwin published a collaborative *Rap on Race*. Later, beginning in New York City in the 1980s, *rap* was the name for a style of performance that usually involved improvised rhymed verse sung or chanted to recorded instrumental music. Most *rap* performers take on colorful PSEUDONYMS. The verse tends to be in rhymed lines of DIMETER or TETRAMETER:

You said I was a jerk
Because I wouldn't go to work.
You said I was a fool
Because I wouldn't go to school.
You said I was an oaf
Because all I did was loaf,
Standing on the street,
Staring at my feet.

Rare Books A category in libraries and the book trade for items relatively scarce. The scale moves in increasing rarity from *rare* through RARIORA (comparative) to RARISSIMA (superlative).

Rariora Very rare books. Literally, *rariora* ought to include "rarer" books; see RARISSIMA.

Rarissima (also **Rarissime**) Extremely rare books.

Ratiocination A process of reasoning from data to conclusions. The term was given literary significance by Poe, who wrote several ratiocinative tales, among them "The Murders in the Rue Morgue," "The Gold Bug," "The Purloined Letter," and "The Mystery of Marie Rogêt." *Ratiocination*, as a literary term, signifies a type of writing that solves, through logical processes, some sort of enigma. It was once applied to the DETECTIVE STORY.

Rationalism This term embraces related systems of thought that rely on reason rather than sense-perceptions, revelation, tradition, or authority. In England the rationalist attitude, especially in the eighteenth century, profoundly affected religion and literature. The early humanists (see OXFORD REFORMERS) had insisted on the control of reason, but their teachings had little effect on prevailing religious thought until reinforced by the scientific thinking of the seventeenth century. By the end of the century the theologians were generally agreed that the most vital religious doctrines were deducible from reason or nature. The more conservative ("supernatural rationalists") insisted on the importance of revelation, rejected by the more radical "deists" (see DEISM). The former group included Isaac Newton and John Locke. The "natural religion" arising from *rationalism* stressed reason as a guide and good conduct as an effect. For some of the effects of *rationalism* on literature, see DEISM, PRIMITIVISM, ROMANTICISM, SENTIMENTALISM, NEOCLASSICISM, HUMANISM.

Rationalize A verb used to indicate a rather specious form of *ex parte* reasoning. An author is said "to *rationalize*" when, once having accepted a position or a belief, through some intuitive process or through some prejudice, the author tries to justify his or her stand by some process of the mind. That is, writing is said to *rationalize* when the author reasons insincerely and with intellectual sophistry to justify a position prompted by emotions rather than by reason.

Reaction Shot In film-making, a shot of someone looking off screen or listening without speaking.

Reader (1) A proof-reader. (2) An employee of a journal, publisher, or theater who screens works submitted for publication. (3) An instructional book with passages for reading, such as Henry Sweet's *An Anglo-Saxon Reader: In Prose and Verse* (1876).

Reader-Response Criticism This kind of criticism suggests that a piece of writing scarcely exists except as a text designed to be read; indeed, scarcely exists until somebody reads it. The *reader-response* approach does not so much analyze a reader's responding apparatus as scrutinize those features of the text that shape and guide a reader's reading. A work that generates and then discharges, seemingly in itself, the terms of its own understanding has been called "self-consuming" by Stanley Fish. From charges of excessive RELATIVISM, subjectivism, and IMPRESSIONISM, *reader response criticism* escapes by recourse to a concept of a hypothetical reader different from any real reader—a hypothetical construct of norms and expectations that can be derived or projected or extrapolated from the work and that may even be said to inhere in the work. This hypothetical reader becomes, in effect, a part of the fiction itself. Wolfgang Iser has analyzed many types: contemporary, fictitious, hypothetical, ideal, implied, intended, and informed readers, along with Michael Riffaterre's "super-reader." (See IMPLIED READER.) Once such a reader is situated in a text, then the immediate drawbacks of the AFFECTIVE FALLACY can be forestalled.

[References: Wayne Booth, *Critical Understanding: The Powers and Limits of Pluralism* (1979); Stanley Fish, *Is There a Text in This Class?: The Authority of Interpretive Communities* (1980); Wolfgang Iser, *The Act of Reading: A Theory of Aesthetic Response* (tr. 1978), and *The Implied Reader: Patterns of Communication in Prose Fiction from Bunyan to Beckett* (tr. 1974).]

Realism *Realism* is, in the broadest literary sense, fidelity to actuality in its representation; a term loosely synonymous with VERISIMILITUDE; and in this sense it has been a significant element in almost every school of writing. To give it more precise definition, however, one may limit it to the movement in the nineteenth century that was centered in the novel and dominant in France, England, and America from roughly midcentury to the closing decade, when it was replaced by NATURALISM. In this sense *realism* defines a literary method and a particular range of subject matter. Along one axis *realism* opposes idealism; along another it opposes NOMINALISM. Confusingly, the latter kind of *realism*, asserting that only ideas are "real," seems idealistic; whereas nominalism, asserting that ideas are only names, would seem to be what most people probably mean by "realistic."

Generally, realists are believers in PRAGMATISM, and the truth they seek to find and express is a relativistic or pluralistic truth, associated with discernible consequences and verifiable by experience. Generally, too, realists are believers in democracy, and the materials they elect to describe are the common, the average, the everyday. Furthermore, *realism* can be thought of as the ultimate of middle-class art, and it finds its subjects in bourgeois life and manners. Where romanticists transcend the immediate to find the ideal, and naturalists plumb the actual or superficial to find the scientific laws that control its actions, realists center their attention to a remarkable degree on the immediate, the here and now, the specific action, and the verifiable consequence. (See NATURALISM.) Realists espouse what is essentially a MIMETIC THEORY OF ART, concentrating on the thing imitated and asking for something close to a one-to-one correspondence between the representation and the subject. Furthermore, realists are unusually interested in the effect of their work on the audience and its life (in this respect they tend toward a PRAGMATIC THEORY OF ART).

Realists eschew the traditional patterns of the novel. Life, they feel, lacks symmetry and plot; fiction truthfully reflecting life should, therefore, avoid symmetry and plot. Fiction should concern itself with ethical issues and—because selection is a necessary part of any art—select with a view to presenting these issues accurately. Furthermore, the democratic attitudes of realists tended to make them value the individual very highly and to praise characterization as the center of the novel. In Henry James, perhaps the greatest of the realists, a tendency to explore the inner selves of characters confronted with complex ethical choices earned for him the titles "father of the psychological novel" and "biographer of fine consciences."

The surface details, common actions, and minor catastrophes of middle-class society constituted the chief subject matter of the movement. Most of the realists avoided situations with tragic or cataclysmic implications. Their tone was often comic, frequently satiric, seldom grim or somber.

Although aspects of realism appeared early in the English novel, for they are certainly present in Defoe, Richardson, Fielding, Smollett, Austin, Trollope, Thackeray, and Dickens, the realistic movement found its effective origins in France with Balzac, in England with George Eliot, and in America with Howells and Mark Twain. Writers such as Arnold Bennett, John Galsworthy, and H. G. Wells in England, and Henry James, Edith Wharton, Ellen Glasgow, Sinclair Lewis, John O'Hara, John P. Marquand, and Louis Auchincloss in America kept the realistic tradition alive. (The concept of "social *realism*" or "socialist *realism*" that was once a staple of MARXIST CRITICISM seems to have receded, although *realism* itself remains important in the work of such Marxist thinkers as Georg Lukács.)

[References: Erich Auerbach, *Mimesis: The Representation of Reality in Western Literature* (tr. 1953); George J. Becker, *Documents of Modern Literary Realism* (1963); Harry Levin, *The Gates of Horn: A Study of Five French Realists* (1963); G. Lukács, *Studies in European Realism: A Sociological Survey of the Writing of Balzac, Stendhal, Zola, Tolstoy, Gorki, and Others* (tr. 1964); Donald Pizer, *Realism and Naturalism in Nineteenth-Century American Fiction*, rev. ed. (1960; 1984); R. Stang, *The Theory of the Novel in England, 1850–1870* (1961; 1959); Ian Watt, *The Rise of the Novel* (1957); René Wellek, *Concepts of Criticism* (1963).]

Realistic Comedy Any comedy employing the methods of REALISM but particularly that developed by Jonson, Chapman, Middleton, and other Elizabethan and Jacobean dramatists. It is opposed to the ROMANTIC COMEDY of the Elizabethans. It reflects the general reaction in the late 1590s against extravagance as well as an effort to produce an English comedy like the CLASSICAL. This *realistic comedy* deals with London life, is strongly satirical and sometimes cynical, is interested in both individuals and types, and rests on observation of life. The appeal is intellectual and the texture coarse. This comedy became especially popular in the reign of James I. The COMEDY OF HUMOURS was a special form representing the first stage of the development of important *realistic comedy*. Jonson's *The Alchemist* and Middleton's *A Trick to Catch the Old One* are typical *realistic comedies*. Though in the main Shakespeare represents the tradition of romantic comedy, some of his plays, including the comic subplot of the *King Henry the Fourth* plays, are realistic. The Restoration COMEDY OF MANNERS, though chiefly a new growth, owes something to this earlier form, and one Restoration dramatist (Shadwell) actually wrote comedy of the Jonsonian type.

Realistic Novel A type of novel that emphasizes truthful representation of the actual.

Realistic Period in American Literature, 1865–1900 In the period following the Civil War, modern America was born and grew to a lusty although not always happy or attractive adolescence. The Civil War had been, at least in part, a struggle between agrarian democracy and industrial-capitalist democracy, and the result of the Northern victory was the triumphant emergence of industrialism, which was to yield material advances but was also to bring difficulties: severe labor disputes and economic depression. Capitalism was to produce a group of powerful and ruthless "robber barons"; its application to politics, particularly in the rapidly developing cities, begot "bossism" and a species of political corruption known by Lincoln Steffens's phrase, "the shame of cities." Great advances were made in communications and transportation: The Atlantic cable was laid in 1866; the transcontinental railroad was completed in 1869; the telephone was invented in 1876; and the automobile was being manufactured by the 1890s. By the last two decades of the century many thoughtful people had begun to declare that somehow the promise of America had been lost—they often said "betrayed"—and that drastic changes were needed. The Populist party, the Grange, and the socialism of the American intellectual all reflected a disillusionment never before so widespread. Intellectually, average Americans were living in a new world, although they did not always realize it. The impact of Darwin, Marx, Comte, Spencer, and others advancing a scientific view sharply at variance with the older religious view was cutting from beneath thoughtful Americans—even while they vehemently denied it—their old certainty about perfectibility and progress. The passing of the physical frontier around 1890 removed from their society a natural safety valve that had acted to protect them against the malcontents and the restless in their world; now they must absorb them and adjust to the fact of their presence; no longer could they seek virgin land. The rapid growth of education and the rise of the mass-circulation magazine, paying its way by advertising, created an enormous audience for authors, and the passage in 1891 of the International Copyright Act protected foreign authors from piracy in America and, by the same token, protected the native literary product.

In poetry the field appeared to be held by a group of sentimental imitators of the English romantics—Stedman, Stoddard, Hovey, Aldrich—but three new and authentic poetic voices were raised in the period: Whitman's, Lanier's, and Dickinson's. Toward the close of the century Stephen Crane used a haunting but strident voice in sparse experimental verse that was close to that of the IMAGISTS to come, and Edwin Arlington Robinson published his first volume in a somber tone of stoic irony. A word may be added here to suggest the popularity of the versifier James Whitcomb Riley. No one claims profundity or complexity for Riley's verse, but it was wholesomely patriotic and charming, and it had not only warmth but also a marked degree of technical finish and originality (Riley wrote the first American VILLANELLE). His influence on Ezra Pound's idea of American speech can be traced, and something ought to be recorded in praise of the poet whose "Little Orphant Annie" inspired a comic strip of prodigious longevity, an important Broadway musical comedy, and the Raggedy Ann doll.

On the stage the older melodramatic habits held, and the STAR SYSTEM that subordinated play and players to a name actor continued to fill the American theater with spectacle but little meaning. American drama felt only slight impacts of the new European PROBLEM PLAYS before the end of the century.

In fiction, however, the new turbulence and the growing skepticism and disillusionment found an effective voice. The developing mass audience was served by LOCAL COLOR WRITING and the HISTORICAL NOVEL, which had a great upsurge of popularity as the century ended. But in the work of Mark Twain, William Dean Howells, and Henry James, the greatest contributions of the age were made. In the works of these and of lesser writers—largely from the Midwest—realism dominated the scene. William James's PRAGMATISM not only expressed the mood of the period but also shaped its literary expression, an expression that became increasingly critical of American life. By the 1890s a cynical application of Darwinism to social structures, together with an acceptance of Nietzsche's doctrine of the superman and of Émile Zola's concept of the experimental novel, resulted in a NATURALISM different from anything America had known. The publication of Theodore Dreiser's *Sister Carrie* in 1900 told, more clearly than any historical document could have done, that a new America had grown from the travail of the post–Civil War period. See REALISM, *Outline of Literary History*.

Realistic Period in English Literature, 1870–1914 In the latter portion of the reign of Queen Victoria and during the reign of Edward VII, the reaction to ROMANTICISM reached its peak in full-fledged REALISM, and by the beginning of the First World War the reaction had itself begun to come under attack.

The last three decades of the nineteenth century saw the parliamentary contests between Gladstone and Disraeli, the rise of British imperialism, and a growth in British cosmopolitanism. Intellectuals began to feel the impact of the scientific revolution that distinguished nineteenth-century thought. Newton's mechanics, Darwin's evolution, Marx's view of history, Comte's view of society, Taine's view of literature—each in its way chipped away at the complacency and optimism of the early years of Victoria's rule. Foreign writers began to be read—Zola, Balzac, Flaubert, Maupassant, Sudermann, Ibsen, Tolstoi, Chekhov, Turgenev, Whitman. By the turn of the century a reaction to Victorian earnestness was being expressed, notably in the work of DECADENTS Oscar Wilde and Ernest Dowson. A revolt against Victorian standards marked the early years of the twentieth century. Politically, the protest of Carlyle and Ruskin gave way to a full embracing of Fabian socialism in William Morris and George Bernard Shaw. The imperial adventure of the Boer War (1899–1902) was hailed by many as a proper extension of the Empire, but at the same time it raised grave doubts.

In poetry the voices of the great Victorians, Tennyson and Browning, were still heard, but a new poetry, interested in FRENCH FORMS and lacking in moral earnestness, was present in Swinburne and the DECADENTS. Hardy, Kipling, Yeats, and Bridges were to do distinguished work before the beginning of the First World War. Gerard Manley Hopkins wrote all of his extraordinary poetry during the 1870s and 1880s, but most of it was not published until 1918, nearly thirty years after his death.

In drama the French stage and Ibsen combined to offer examples of REALISM. The LITTLE THEATER MOVEMENT began in England in the 1890s, about the same time that the CELTIC RENAISSANCE was enlivening the Irish stage. The PROBLEM PLAY established itself in the works of A. W. Pinero, H. A. Jones, and John Galsworthy. In the last decades of the century Wilde's genius and the LIGHT OPERAS of Gilbert and Sullivan brightened the English theater, while the comedy and philosophy of G. B. Shaw's plays enlightened most of the period. Under the impact of realism the British stage abandoned Shakespeare for a life of its own.

In the ESSAY, Arnold, Huxley, Spencer, and Pater explored a variety of topics with earnestness and force, but it was in the novel that the age found its profoundest expression. A few writers such as Blackmore, Kipling, and Stevenson continued a romantic vein, but George Eliot, Thomas Hardy, George Meredith, George Gissing, Joseph Conrad, John Galsworthy, Arnold Bennett, H. G. Wells, and Samuel Butler established a realistic mode for the novel potent enough to make it the stronghold against which the SYMBOLISTS of the next age launched their attacks. See REALISM, EDWARDIAN AGE, LATE VICTORIAN AGE, *Outline of Literary History*.

Realist Theory In film criticism, a theory that sees the primary value of film in its ability to record the phenomenal world around it. In contrast to FORMATIVE THEORY, which emphasizes artistic aspects of film, the *realist theory* advocates close correspondence between film and the literal world.

Rebus A text in which ordinary verbal symbols are supplemented by pictures and other devices to suggest a total meaning. The common "IOU" may be a kind of *rebus*, because the letters of the alphabet do not all function in their usual way: the letter *I* means the pronoun "I," but the letters *O* and *U* just mean their sounds, which play on the words "owe" and "you." The street sign

PED
XING

has an element of the *rebus*, because the letter X functions, not as a letter or a sound but as a shape, meaning "cross." Here is a *rebus* that is the registered trademark of an apparel chain:

In another variety, a sixteenth-century Italian painting shows the letters "CI" inscribed in a small crescent moon, that is, "CI" inside "LUNA," which amounts to "Lucina," the name of a woman and also of the Roman goddess of childbirth.

Rebuttal A term borrowed from debating procedure and signifying a rejoinder or reply to an argument, particularly a final summing up of answers to the arguments of the opposition.

Recalcitrance Used by Austin M. Wright for certain challengingly resistant features of a text. In Wright's "critical fiction" *Recalcitrance, Faulkner, and the Professors* (1990), a character argues that "a successful novel is a device calculated to give the reader the impression of discovering unity while at the same time preventing final verification of this." The operation of various forces of prevention, such as discontinuity and disruption, is collectively called *recalcitrance*.

Recantation A PALINODE, a formal repudiation of something written earlier. *The Canterbury Tales* ends with a *recantation* of Chaucer's "enditynges of worldly vanitees . . . and many a song and many a lecherous lay. . . ." After his "A Hymn to the Name and Honour of the Admirable St. Theresa," Richard Crashaw placed a *recantation* called "An Apology for the Foregoing Hymn, having been writ when the Author was yet among the Protestants."

Recension A text that incorporates the best readings taken by critical editing from several sources. The word means "survey," so that a *recension* is a critical text established through a survey of all surviving sources. It has been most often applied to texts of materials existing in manuscript sources, such as biblical texts. In this sense *The New English Bible* may be called a *recension*.

Reception Theory The historical application of READER-RESPONSE CRITICISM. It assumes that a work has no determinate meaning and so needs to be approached via a present reader's informed response and by an examination of the history of the reception of the work through time.

[Reference: Hans Robert Jauss, *Aesthetic Experience and Literary Hermeneutics* (1982).]

Recessive Accent When the rhythmical pattern of a poem forces the stress to fall on the first syllable of a word normally accented on the second syllable, it is called *recessive accent*, as in this line from *Love's Labour's Lost*:

Thĕ éxtrēme párts ŏf tíme ĕxtrémelў fórms.

In current speech a normally IAMBIC word such as "entire" may become a TROCHEE or SPONDEE, for some speakers if not all, in a phrase such as "the entire world."

Recitative In musical performance, especially opera and oratorio, the delivery of words in the tempo of speech but in musical tones.

Recognition A *recognition* plot is one in which the principal REVERSAL or PERIPETY results from someone's acquisition of knowledge previously withheld but which, now known, works a decisive change. In *Oedipus Rex*, considered by Aristotle the finest example of a *recognition* plot, the king, seeking the one whose crime has brought on the national calamity, at last discovers that he himself has killed his father and married his mother. In James's *The Ambassadors*, Lambert Strether discovers the true nature of the liaison between Chad and Madame de Vionnet, with the result that his whole course of action is changed. A *recognition* plot may result in either tragedy or comedy. A DETECTIVE STORY, for instance, is sometimes said to have a *recognition* plot used as an end in itself, in that the entire purpose is to have the detective come into knowledge ("whodunit") not possessed at the beginning of the story. The part of a work in which the *recognition* occurs is called a recognition scene. See DRAMATIC STRUCTURE, ANAGNORISIS.

Reconverging Metaphor This is the third step in a complex process whereby (1) words start off with literal meanings, such as "concrete" and "steps" meaning just that; (2) those words acquire figurative meanings, as when "concrete" means "practical" and "steps" means "parts of a process"; the same words, in combination, have both a literal and a figurative meaning, as when someone says "concrete steps," which could mean literally "steps made of concrete" and figuratively "practical parts of a process."

Recto In paper made with a distinguishable front and back side, *recto* is the front. In a book, *recto* is the right-hand page. See VERSO.

Redaction A revision or editing of a manuscript. Sometimes the term implies a DIGEST of a longer work or a new version of an older piece of writing. Malory's *Le Morte Darthur* is a *redaction* of many of the Arthurian stories. Recently, *redaction* suggests a process of removing sensitive material from a document released to the public.

Redende Name German, "speaking name"; a name that is significant. Outside literature we sometimes encounter tailors named Taylor and dentists named Payne; each is a *Redende Name* in one sense or another. Inside literature such names are ubiquitous. *Vanity Fair* includes a sharp woman named Sharp, a corrupt nobleman named Steyne, a repulsive baronet named Pitt Crawley, and an auctioneer called Hammerdown. *The Beggar's Opera* includes a receiver of stolen goods named Peachum and a prison warden named Lockit. Readers of *The Golden Bowl* have been at a loss when it comes to a character named Fanny Assingham. Arthur Miller's Willy Loman is a low man.

Redondilla A Spanish measure, usually in octosyllabic couplets or quatrains with various rhyme schemes; used in Ezra Pound's early "Redondillas."

Reductio ad absurdum A "reducing to absurdity" to show the falsity of an argument or position. One might say, for instance that the more sleep one gets the healthier one is, and then, by the logical *reductio ad absurdum* process, someone would be sure to point out that, on such a premise, one who has sleeping sickness and sleeps for months on end is really in the best of health. The term also refers to a type of reductive-deductive SYLLOGISM:

- *Major premise:* Either A or B is true.
- *Minor premise:* A is not true.
- *Conclusion:* B is true.

The particular *reductio* here comes in the minor premise, where one alternative is reduced to falseness or "absurdity."

Redundant Characterized by superfluous words. *Redundant* is applied to a style marked by verbiage, an excess of repetition, or PLEONASM. The use of repetition and pleonasm may, on occasion, be justified for emphasis, but "redundancy" is usually applied to unjustified repetition. Polonius is shown to be a doddering old man through redundancies:

> Madam, I swear I use no art at all.
> That he is mad, 'tis true; 'tis true 'tis pity;
> And pity 'tis 'tis true; a foolish figure;
> But farewell it, for I will use no art.
> Mad let us grant him, then; and now remains
> That we find out the cause of this effect,
> Or rather say, the cause of this defect,
> For this effect defective comes by cause;
> Thus it remains and the remainder thus.

A couplet in Pope's "The Rape of the Lock" exploits the comic possibilities of multiple redundancy:

> Or alum styptics with contracting power
> Shrink his thin essence like a riveled flower—

in which "alum" or "styptics" alone would suffice and "with contracting power" is completely unnecessary, because that is what "alum" connotes and "styptics" denotes anyway. *Redundant* is also used to mean IDENTICAL RHYME, as in that between "cell" and "sell."

Reduplication (1) The rhetorical repetition of a word or phrase, as in "But two months dead, nay, not so much, not two" (*Hamlet*, 1.2). (2) The repetition of all or part of a syllable, sometimes for a diminutive ("Mimi," "Fifi") or nickname ("Namby Pamby"), sometimes for a grammatical function (as in the formation of certain perfect-tense forms in Indo-European languages, such as Latin *dedi*, "I have given").

Redux An element in titles of works having to do, seriously or ironically, with a restoration or return, as in William Gager's *Ulysses Redux*, Dryden's *Astraea Redux*, Trollope's *Phineas Redux*, and Updike's *Rabbit Redux*.

Reference A direct indication of a topic or work. *Reference* differs from ALLUSION, which is indirect. A *reference* book is something that one can refer to for information.

Reform Bill of 1832 This important liberal enactment of the English Parliament was proposed in 1830 and passed in 1832 with the support of King William IV and the Whig party over the strong opposition of Wellington. The measure denied parliamentary representation to 56 "rotten" boroughs, provided representation for 156 new communities, and extended the voting power to include large numbers of the middle classes; it did not, however, give the franchise to the laborers. It was the beginning of a series of reform measures that followed during the next decade, including the suppression of slavery in the British colonies (1833), the curbing of commercial monopoly, a lessening of pauperism, a liberalization of the marriage laws, and great expansion of public education. These events stimulated the idealism of many of the authors of the time, some of whom were agitators for reform, and affected profoundly the spirit of literature. Carlyle and Ruskin in their lectures and essays; Dickens, Disraeli, Gaskell, Kingsley, and George Eliot in their novels; and Hood, Tennyson, and Elizabeth Barrett Browning in their poems reflect the new aspirations. The Reform Bill of 1867, passed by the Conservatives under pressures from the Liberals, further extended the franchise. By this stage, however, many observers became skeptical. To these reforms toward "completed Democracy," Carlyle responded with the polemical *Shooting Niagara: And After?* Democratic representation was carried still further by the Reform Bill of 1884, extending suffrage to nearly all men. In 1918 suffrage was extended to all men and to women over thirty, and in 1928 to all persons over twenty-one. See CHARTISM, INDUSTRIAL REVOLUTION.

Refrain One or more words repeated at intervals in a poem, usually at the end of a stanza. The most regular is the use of the same line at the close of each stanza (as is common in the BALLAD). Another, less regular form is that in which the *refrain* recurs somewhat erratically throughout the stanza—sometimes in one place, sometimes in another. Again a *refrain* may be used with a slight variation in wording at each recurrence, though here it approaches the REPETEND. Still another variety of the *refrain* is the use of language that, by its mere repetition at the close of stanzas presenting different ideas and moods, seems to take on a different significance on each appearance—as in Poe's "Nevermore" and William Morris's "Two red roses across the moon." In later work, apart from popular songs and folklore, the *refrain* appears in some of the poems of W. B. Yeats and Thomas Hardy.

Reggae A style of music, song, and performance that became popular in the 1970s, beginning in Jamaica and spreading through the Caribbean. The music is strongly accented on the second and fourth beat, and the words follow a similar pattern, usually rhymed COUPLETS of IAMBIC TETRAMETER; the subjects are religion and politics.

Regionalism Fidelity to a particular geographical area; the representation of its habits, speech, manners, history, folklore, or beliefs. A test of *regionalism* is that the action and personages of such a work cannot be moved, without major loss or distortion, to any other geographical setting. Thomas Hardy, in his portrayal of life in Wessex, wrote regional novels. The LOCAL COLOR WRITING in America in the last third of the nineteenth century was a form of regionalism. Arnold Bennett's novels of the Five Towns are markedly regional, as is Margaret Drabble's treatment of the same region.

The recent literature of the American South has been largely regional. In the twentieth century a concept of *regionalism* rather more complex than that of its nineteenth-century counterpart has developed, partly as the result of the work of cultural anthropologists and sociologists (notably Howard W. Odum), and has expressed itself in literature through the conscious seeking out, in the local and the particular, of those aspects of character and destiny common to all people. In this respect the work of Willa Cather, Ellen Glasgow, William Faulkner, and Robert Penn Warren stands out.

Reification The treatment of abstractions as concrete things. The representation of ideas as though they had concrete form. "Truth is a deep well," "Love is a many splendored thing," "Thoughts sink into the sea of forgetfulness"—each of these statements represents *reification*. Byron's "She walks in beauty" gives a kind of physical reality to beauty. MARXIST CRITICISM has given *reification* an additional meaning that has to do with the translation of abstract concepts into the form of material things; such a transformation includes the reduction of people and ideas into marketable commodities.

Relativism The denial of the validity of principles that are everlasting, ubiquitous, changeless, and absolute. A contextual *relativism* would claim that the meaning of some such symbol as whiteness is relative to its immediate context—Melville's *Moby-Dick* or Frost's "Design," for example—and cannot be referred to some absolute extrinsic standard. Similarly, cultural *relativism* would claim that any artifact or convention has meaning only in a way *relative* to its immediate cultural context. Looking at color symbolism again, for example, we can notice that brides wear white in some societies, whereas, in others, white is worn only by widows; or, say, the same yellow that Americans sentimentally associate with cowardice connotes courage in many parts of Asia. A kind of critical-historical *relativism* can even claim that literature as an institution has no permanent role or significance but fluctuates—in function, structure, status, and so forth—from place to place and time to time.

Relief Scene That part of a tragedy, usually as a part of the FALLING ACTION, whose purpose is to provide temporary emotional relaxation for the audience. There is also a sense of "*relief*" that means simple "contrast" without relaxation—quite the contrary. See DRAMATIC STRUCTURE.

Religious Drama A term applied to the drama of the Middle Ages, when its relation to the church and to religious subject matter was very great. See MEDIEVAL DRAMA.

Relique An old spelling of "relic." The most famous use of the term is in the title of Bishop Percy's collection of old ballads: *Reliques of Ancient English Poetry* (1765).

Reliteralization The process of returning a metaphorical expression to its literal meaning. "To catch one's death," for example, usually means "to contract a cold so severe that it seems fatal." Geoffrey Hill, however, describes Saint Sebastian, as he is being killed by arrows, so that "he catches his death"—literally. James Dickey says that a suburban lawnmower is "resting on its laurels"—literally—adapting a metaphorical expression that usually means "taking advantage of an honored status in order to relax."

Renaissance This word, meaning "rebirth," is commonly applied to the period of transition from the medieval to the modern world in Western Europe. Special students of the movement are inclined to trace the impulse back to the earlier *Renaissance* of the twelfth and thirteenth centuries and to date the full realization of *Renaissance* forces as late as the eighteenth century. In the usual sense of the word, however, *Renaissance* suggests the fourteenth, fifteenth, sixteenth, and early seventeenth centuries, the dates differing for different countries (the English *Renaissance*, for example, flourishing a full century behind the Italian *Renaissance*). The break from medievalism was gradual, some *Renaissance* attitudes going back into the heart of the medieval period and some medieval traits persisting through the *Renaissance*.

The *Renaissance* resulted from new forces arising within the old order, with attempts to effect some kind of adjustment between traditional allegiances and modern demands. So it was an age of compromise, a chief aspect of which was an endeavor to harmonize a newly interpreted Christian tradition with an ardently admired and in part a newly discovered tradition of pagan classical culture.

The new humanistic learning (see HUMANISM) that resulted from the rediscovery of classical literature is frequently taken as the beginning of the *Renaissance* on its intellectual side, because it was to the treasures of classical culture and to the authority of classical writers that the people of the *Renaissance* turned for inspiration. *Renaissance* people had caught from their glimpses of classical culture a vision of human life quite at odds with the attitudes of feudalism. The Hellenistic spirit had taught them that human beings were glorious creatures capable of individual development in the direction of perfection in a world that was theirs to interrogate, explore, and enjoy.

The individualism implied in this view of life exerted a strong influence on English *Renaissance* life and literature, as did many other facts and forces, such as: the Protestant Reformation, itself in part an aspect of the *Renaissance* in Germany; the introduction of printing, leading to a commercial market for literature; the great economic and political changes fostering the rise of democracy, the spirit of nationalism, an ambitious commercialism, and opportunities for individuals to rise economically and politically; the revitalized university life; the courtly encouragement and PATRONAGE of literature; the new geography (discovery of America) and astronomy (Copernicus, Galileo); and the growing "new science," which regarded human beings and nature as the results of natural and demonstrable law rather than a mysterious group of entities subject to occult powers.

The period in English literature generally called the *Renaissance* is usually considered to have begun a little before 1500 and to have lasted until the COMMONWEALTH INTERREGNUM (1649–1660). It consisted of the EARLY TUDOR AGE (c. 1500–1557), the ELIZABETHAN AGE (1558–1603), the JACOBEAN AGE (1603–1625), and the CAROLINE AGE (1625–1642). In the early period, English authors felt the impact of classical learning and of foreign literatures, together with some release from church authority. The New World was transforming England into a trading nation no longer at the periphery of the world but at its crossroads. During the reign of Elizabeth, England became a world power; its drama and its poetry attained great heights in the work of such writers as Spenser, Sidney, Marlowe, and Shakespeare. By the time that James came to the throne, a reaction was beginning to set in, expressed through a growing cynicism, a classical dissatisfaction with the extravagance and unbounded enthusiasm of the sixteenth century, a tendency toward melancholy and decadence. At the same time, as though in reaction to this reaction, there was a flourishing of BAROQUE elements in literature. As the conflict of Puritan and Cavalier grew in intensity, these elements grew also. And by the time Charles lost his head, the PURITANISM that was itself a major outgrowth of the intense individualism of the *Renaissance* had spelled an end to most of its literary greatness. Yet Cromwell had as Latin Secretary the last of the great English *Renaissance* figures, John Milton, who was to produce his greatest work in the hostile world of the Restoration. For details, see EARLY TUDOR AGE, ELIZABETHAN AGE, JACOBEAN AGE, CAROLINE AGE, HUMANISM, ELIZABETHAN DRAMA, *Outline of Literary History*.

Rendering A term made popular by Henry James to describe the presentation of an action rather than reporting of it; the use of the SCENIC METHOD as opposed to exposition or summary; a direct representation of details, images, actions, and speech.

Repartee A "comeback"; a quick, ingenious response or rejoinder; a retort aptly twisted; conversation made up of brilliant witticisms; loosely, any clever reply; also anyone's facility and aptness in such ready wit. The term is borrowed from fencing. Sydney Smith, Charles Lamb, Oscar Wilde, and Dorothy Parker are famous for their *repartee*. An instance of *repartee* may be cited from an Oxford account of "Beau" Nash and John Wesley meeting on a narrow pavement. Nash was brusque. "I never make way for a fool," he said. "Don't you? I always do," responded Wesley, stepping to one side.

Repeat An old name for REFRAIN.

Repetend A device marked by full or partial repetition of a word, phrase, or clause more or less frequently throughout a stanza or poem. *Repetend* differs from REFRAIN in that the refrain usually appears at predetermined places within the poem, whereas the chief merit of the *repetend* is the surprise it brings through its irregular appearance. A further difference lies in the fact that the *repetend* only partially repeats, whereas the refrain usually repeats in its entirety a whole line or combination of lines. Both Coleridge and Poe make frequent use of the *repetend*. In this example from Poe's "Ulalume" the *repetends* are italicized:

The skies *they were* ashen *and* sober:
   The leaves they were crisped *and sere—*
   The leaves they were withering *and sere;*
It was night in the lonesome October
   Of my most immemorial year;
It was hard *by the* dim lake *of Auber,*
   In the misty mid region *of Weir—*
It was down *by the* dank tarn *of Auber,*
In the ghoul-haunted woodland *of Weir*.

Repetition Reiteration of a word, sound, phrase, or idea. *Repetition* is favored by orators. The use in verse of the REPETEND or REFRAIN makes *repetition* more obvious than is usual in prose. One of the most notable examples is Poe's "The Bells." *Repetition* is present in rhyme, in meter, and in stanza forms. It appears to be an inescapable element of poetry. Whitman, for example, who eschews *repetition* in the form of rhyme, meter, or stanza, employs it widely in his elaborate verbal and grammatical parallelism and ANAPHORA. *Repetition* at the verbal level precludes the registration of significant *repetition* at a lower (acoustic) level, so that we do not usually claim that a repeated word is an instance of ALLITERATION, nor does a word rhyme with itself; a *repetition* of a word, even in a rhyming position, does not qualify even as IDENTICAL RHYME.

Since Freud's essay "Beyond the Pleasure Principle" (1920), *repetition* has been recognized as an important element in narratives.

Report Song, Reporting Poem A verse including a degree of repetition or ECHO, as in Nicholas Breton's "A Report Song" (1600) in TRIPLETS that begins with such lines as "Shall we go dance the hay, the hay?" and "Shall we go learn to woo, to woo?"

Requiem A chant embodying a prayer for the repose of the dead; a dirge; a solemn mass beginning as in *Requiem aeternam dona eis, Domine* ("Give eternal rest to them, O Lord"). The following is an example from Matthew Arnold's "Requiescat":

> Strew on her roses, roses
>   And never a spray of yew!
> In quiet she reposes;
>   Ah, would that I did too!

More recently the word has been broadened to mean almost anything sad: Faulkner's *Requiem for a Nun*, Serling's *Requiem for a Heavyweight*, Corso's "Spontaneous Requiem for the American Indian," for example.

Resolution The events following the CLIMAX. See FALLING ACTION (for which it is a synonym), PLOT, DRAMATIC STRUCTURE.

Resolved Stress The same as HOVERING STRESS and DISTRIBUTED STRESS.

Rest A pause or silence that, as in music, is counted as a prosodic element. In some of Shakespeare's "short" lines, the situation suggests that a dramatic silence may fill out the pentameter, as when Seyton reports, "The Queen, my lord, is dead" [*rest* for four syllables] and Macbeth says, "She should have died hereafter" [*rest* for three syllables]. Because the printing of Shakespeare's plays cannot be trusted, we may consider a later example. In a draft of a poem, Gerard Manley Hopkins wrote a characteristic line of IAMBIC PENTAMETER with a feminine ending: "Keeps grace, and that keeps all his goings graces." In revising, Hopkins added a colon after "grace" and eliminated the "and": "Keeps grace: that keeps all his goings graces" [*rest* of one syllable before "that"].

Restoration Age The restoration of the Stuarts in 1660 has given a name to a literary period embracing the latter part of the seventeenth century. The fashionable literature of the time reflects the reaction against PURITANISM, the receptiveness to French influence, and the dominance of classical points of view. The revival of the drama, under new influences and theories, is an especially interesting feature of the *Restoration Age*. The COMEDY OF MANNERS was developed by such writers as Etheredge, Wycherly, and Congreve; the HEROIC DRAMA by such as Dryden, Howard, and Otway. Dryden was the greatest poet of the whole period, although no one equaled Milton, whose greatest works came in the 1660s and 1670s. John Locke, Sir William Temple, and Samuel Pepys were, in their differing ways, the major prose writers after John Bunyan. See NEOCLASSIC PERIOD, *Outline of Literary History*.

Restraint A critical term applied to writing that holds in decent check the emotional elements of a given situation. Great literature, fiction and poetry especially, makes frequent use of emotion but distinguishes itself from tawdry writing in that the emotional qualities of the situation are held in reserve. Psychologically it is true that one attributes greater strength and force of character to the person who gives the impression of holding something back than to a person who pours forth all his or her feelings and sensibilities—or to an outburst in spite of previously demonstrated *restraint*, as with Lear on the heath. In fact, it is often *restraint* in emotional situations that marks the work of great artists.

Résumé In general, a SUMMARY of a work or collection of material. Specifically, since about 1960, a biographical summary of one's career; a curriculum vitae (c.v.).

Revenge Tragedy A form of tragedy made popular on the Elizabethan stage by Thomas Kyd, whose *Spanish Tragedy* is an early example of the type. It is largely SENECAN in its inspiration and technique. The theme is the revenge of a father for a son or vice versa, the revenge being directed by the ghost of the murdered man, as in *Hamlet*. Other traits often found in *revenge tragedies* include the hesitation of the hero, the use of either real or pretended insanity, suicide, intrigue, an able scheming villain, philosophic SOLILOQUIES, and the sensational use of horrors (murders on the stage, exhibition of dead bodies, and so forth). Examples are Shakespeare's *Titus Andronicus* and *Hamlet*, Marston's *Antonio's Revenge*, and Tourneur's *Atheist's Tragedy*. In the management of the dynamics of revenge, we encounter (1) the offense, which can be maximized by the multiplication of injuries and the adding of insult; (2) the antagonist, most effectively some really formidable (but still vulnerable) person or force; (3) clarification of strategy and marshaling of resources; (4) a series of delays, obstacles, diversions, mistakes, reservations, and so forth—anything to retard the momentum; (5) some unforeseen development that almost thwarts the scheme, but not quite; and finally (6) the showdown, with the revenge carried out in some answerable style. See TRAGEDY OF BLOOD.

Reverdie A song celebrating the reappearance of spring. T. S. Eliot's *The Waste Land* (1922) varies the theme ironically, but William Carlos Williams's *Spring and All* (1923) restores the positive sense to the *reverdie*.

Reversal The change in fortune for a protagonist. See PERIPETY, DRAMATIC STRUCTURE.

Review A notice of a current work or performance. One can distinguish between a *review* and other sorts of serious CRITICISM: The *review* gives readers an idea of the work under consideration. The CRITIC, on the other hand, usually writes about works of some established standing. The boundary line between the two forms is very uncertain in actual practice, however. For example, Poe's *review* of Hawthorne's *Twice-Told Tales* fits almost perfectly the description given here and yet is one of the major critical documents in American literary history.

Review is also used in the titles of PERIODICALS to indicate the presence in the journal both of critical articles and of articles on current affairs; for example, the *North American Review*, the *Saturday Review*, the *Edinburgh Review*, the *Sewanee Review*. At one time it was said that periodicals called *reviews* were for criticism, those called JOURNALS were for scholarship; but such distinctions have faded.

Review Copy A copy of a work sent to a journal or reviewer, possibly an ordinary copy, possibly an advance copy or even bound galleys.

Revival Bringing back an old work for new performance; also such a work itself, as in "The current production of *Annie Get Your Gun* is a revival."

Revolutionary Age in American Literature, 1765–1790 Between the Stamp Act in 1765 and the formation of the Federal government in 1789, American writers were mostly engaged in nonbelletristic pursuits. Poetry was largely neoclassical, with the influence of Pope dominating, although strains of early romanticism, notably those associated with the GRAVEYARD SCHOOL and with a renewed appreciation of wild nature, were felt. Trumbull, Freneau, Hopkinson, Dwight, and Barlow produced patriotic works in varied forms, often BURLESQUE and satiric. The first play written by an American and acted in America, Godfrey's *The Prince of Parthia*, was performed in 1767, and the stage grew to be an increasing influence on American art outside of New England. It was particularly important in Philadelphia and New York, and after 1773 it was a significant aspect of Southern life through the theater at Charleston. Much of the prose was polemical, such as that of Thomas Paine, Samuel Adams, and Hamilton and Madison (*The Federalist* papers). The first American novel, *The Power of Sympathy* by William Hill Brown, was published in 1789. But the two major prose writers of the period were Franklin, with his memoirs (later called his *Autobiography*), and Jefferson, whose Declaration of Independence is one of the most influential pieces of writing in human history. See REVOLUTIONARY AND EARLY NATIONAL PERIOD IN AMERICAN LITERATURE, *Outline of Literary History*.

Revolutionary and Early National Period in American Literature, 1765–1830 This period, ending with the "second revolution" represented by the ascendancy of Jacksonian democracy, was the time of the establishment of the new nation. It saw the first strong reaction to British rule in the response to the Stamp Act in 1765, the First Continental Congress in 1774, the beginnings of armed rebellion in 1775, the Declaration of Independence in 1776, the surrender of Cornwallis in 1781, the Constitutional Convention in 1787, the establishment of a Federal government in 1789, the founding of the Library of Congress in 1800, and in 1812–1814 a second war with England. In 1820 the Missouri Compromise, following by twelve years the abolition of the importing of slaves, inaugurated a pattern of political compromise; in 1823 America asserted its dominance in the New World through the Monroe Doctrine. In 1829 Andrew Jackson, the seventh president, brought backwoods egalitarianism to triumph over the conservative federalism that had dominated the early life of the country.

It was a time of literary beginnings as well. There are two relatively distinct ages, that of the Revolution, 1765–1790, and that of the Federalists, 1790–1830. During this time the faint and imitative voices of the Revolutionary poets—Brackenridge, Freneau, and Hopkinson—and the HARTFORD WITS gave way before the calm strength of Bryant's verses. By 1827 Poe had published *Tamerlane*. In 1767 Thomas Godfrey's

Prince of Parthia, the first American play to be acted, was performed, and American playwriting was established, although it was to be highly imitative of English drama and largely lacking in literary value throughout the period. In 1789 the first American novel, *The Power of Sympathy* by William Hill Brown, was published. Charles Brockden Brown, the first American novelist of marked ability, flourished briefly between 1798 and 1801; his *Wieland* (1798) was a distinguished piece of American GOTHIC. Before 1830 the career of James Fenimore Cooper, America's first major novelist, was well launched; his first significant novel, *The Spy*, appeared in 1821, and the first of the Leatherstocking Tales in 1823. Washington Irving, writing with urbane wit and Addisonian grace, became the first truly successful American prose writer, gaining international fame, particularly for "Knickerbocker's" *History* (1809) and *The Sketch Book* (1820). The first major American magazine that was to have a long history, the *North American Review*, was established in 1815.

In 1830 America was a young nation, fully established, rawboned, robust, and self-confident, but possessed of a great internal problem, slavery, which was just beginning to put the Federal Union to a serious test. Those who were to produce the important literary works of the nation's first major artistic period had already been born, and many were already at work. See FEDERALIST AGE IN AMERICAN LITERATURE, REVOLUTIONARY AGE IN AMERICAN LITERATURE, *Outline of Literary History*.

Revue A light, plotless musical entertainment consisting of a variety of songs, dances, choruses, and skits. Satiric comment on contemporary affairs is a characteristic element, as is spectacular display in scenery and costume.

Rhapsody A selection from epic poetry sung by a rhapsodist—that is, a wandering MINSTREL or court poet of ancient Greece. Originally, the rhapsodist got his name from the "stitching together" of the work of various poets with the rhapsodist's own poetry, but by 500 B.C. the term *rhapsodist* was applied to professional reciters of epic poetry, principally the *Iliad* and the *Odyssey*. The term has come to be applied to highly emotional utterance. It has also been occasionally applied to a literary miscellany or a disconnected series of works. According to Louis Martz, the poem of Henry Vaughan's called "A Rhapsody" plays on all of the usual senses of the word. The effusiveness and incoherence of the poem are attributable to its being a drinking song in the form of a mock heroic. In the next century, Swift produced "On Poetry: A Rapsody," a lively burlesque almost 500 lines long. Eliot's "Rhapsody on Windy Night" is hardly rhapsodic in any usual sense, so the title may be taken as ironic.

Rheme (also **Rhema**) (adjective **Rhetic**) The part of an utterance or proposition expressing a single idea.

Rhetoric The art of PERSUASION. It has to do with the presentation of ideas in clear, persuasive language. *Rhetoric* has had a long career in ancient and modern schools. The founder of *rhetoric* is believed to have been Corax of Syracuse, who in the fifth century B.C. stipulated fundamental principles for public argument and laid down five divisions for a speech: proem, narrative, argument, remarks, and peroration. Aristotle wrote a *rhetoric* about 320 B.C.; Quintilian's *Institutio Oratoria* (about A.D. 90) later served as the background for study at Oxford and Cambridge; Longinus wrote an *Art of Rhetoric* (about A.D. 260), and Aphthonius (about A.D. 380) gave the subject a code and organization that have persisted. According to the Aristotelian conception *rhetoric* was a manner of effectively organizing material for the presentation of truth, for an appeal to the intellect; and it was distinct from poetry, a manner of composition presenting ideas emotionally and imaginatively. At one time the sophists and others so exalted *rhetoric* that it threatened to become little more than a system whereby, rightly or wrongly, a point was carried. It was, as Isocrates once noted, "the art of making great matters small, and small things great." This tendency has given the suggestion of emptiness that we associate today with "rhetorical." Along with grammar and logic, *rhetoric* made up the TRIVIUM of medieval academic study. Some later classical students of *rhetoric*, following Aristotle's lead, subdivided *rhetoric* into the "deliberative" (having to do with debate and deliberation of public action), the "forensic" (from "forum"—having to do with legal decisions of guilt and innocence), and the "epideictic" (having to do with formal praise). During the Middle Ages *rhetoric* was continued as a serious study through its place in the trivium, and elaborate rhetorical systems kept alive an interest in the forms of expression. In England the RENAISSANCE brought little that was new to *rhetoric*, though such books as Sir Thomas Wilson's *The Arte of Rhetorique* (1553) and George (or Richard) Puttenham's *Arte of English Poesie* (1589) did much to popularize the best practice of the classical writers. In modern education *rhetoric* continues as a phase of study in courses in composition and persists in debating and oratorical contests. In CRITICISM the study of the devices of PERSUASION has again become important. The great number of rhetorical terms included in this handbook shows, perhaps as clearly as any other testimony, the basic importance of rhetorical principles in their relation to literature. Since the end of the Second World War, some of the most influential literary critics have subjected *rhetoric* to a searching examination and have restored to it a dignity it has not enjoyed since classical antiquity. In Kenneth Burke's criticism, for example, *rhetoric* is much more than a simple trick of ornamentation designed to persuade; *rhetoric* becomes in a way the whole underpinning of literature. Later critics, such as Northrop Frye and Harold Bloom, could refine the means of reading underlying cultural and psychological meanings in various TROPES; in this species of analysis of rhetorical moments such as jokes and slips of the tongue or pen, Freud led the way. At the same time, *rhetoric* was given new depths and new definitions by such world-class critics as Roland Barthes, Paul de Man, Jacques Derrida, and Tzvetan Todorov.

[References: George Kennedy, *Classical Rhetoric and Its Christian and Secular Tradition from Ancient to Modern Times*, 2nd ed. (1999; orig. 1980); Ronald Schleifer, *Rhetoric and Death: The Language of Modernism and Postmodern Discourse Theory* (1990).]

Rhetorical Accent The accent determined by the meaning or intention of the sentence; used in metrics in opposition to METRICAL ACCENT, in which only the prosodic pattern of the line determines the placement of stress. Although articles and prepositions are normally unaccented, special circumstances may dictate a departure: "She's laughing *at* you, not *with* you." "Are you *the* Otis Sistrunk?"

Rhetorical Criticism CRITICISM that emphasizes communication between author and reader. *Rhetorical criticism* analyzes the elements employed in a literary work to impose on the reader the author's view of the meaning, both denotative and connotative, of the work. *Rhetorical criticism* examines the devices that an author uses to persuade the reader to make a proper interpretation of a work. See HERMENEUTICS; READER-RESPONSE CRITICISM.

Rhetorical Question A question propounded for its rhetorical effect and not requiring a reply or intended to induce a reply. The principle supporting the use of the *rhetorical question* is that, because its answer is obvious and usually the only one possible, a deeper impression will be made by raising the question than by the speaker's making a direct statement. Pope's lines from "The Rape of the Lock" illustrate the use of *rhetorical questions* for MOCK HEROIC effect:

Was it for this you took such constant care
The bodkin, comb, and essence to prepare?
For this your locks in paper durance bound?
For this with tort'ring irons wreath'd around?
For this with fillets strain'd your tender head,
And bravely bore the double loads of lead?
Gods! shall the ravisher display your hair,
While the fops envy, and the ladies stare!

Much the same language animates W. B. Yeats's "September 1913":

Was it for this the wild geese spread
The grey wing upon every tide;
For this that all that blood was shed,
For this Edward Fitzgerald died,
And Robert Emmet and Wolfe Tone,
All that delirium of the brave?

Most *rhetorical questions* generate strongly negative answers. We may once in a while register an emphatic "yes" by asking a *rhetorical question*: "Is the Pope a Catholic?" Usually, however, when we ask "Who knows?" and "Who cares?" with a special intonation, we mean "Nobody knows" and "Nobody cares." Often, the negative element is built into the question: "Aren't we all patriots?" Many of W. B. Yeats's poems contain questions. Not all are *rhetorical*: those at the end of "The Second Coming" and "Leda and the Swan" are not. On the other hand, his "No Second Troy" consists of nothing but *rhetorical questions*.

Rhopalic A sequence that "thickens" as it moves toward its end, with each word a syllable longer than the preceding one, as in this line by Ausonius:

Spes deus aeternae stationis conciliator.

The term also applied to a stanza in which each line is a foot longer than the preceding, as in Crashaw's "Wishes To His (Supposed) Mistress":

Who ere shee bee,
That not impossible shee
That shall command my heart and mee. . . .

The sequence need not be a strict matter of one-two-three; any pattern of increase or decrease may be *rhopalic*. The beginning of Antony's "Friends, Romans, countrymen" speech in *Julius Caesar* and the title of Ezra Pound's *Hugh Selwyn Mauberley* are clear examples of the simpler kind of pattern. *Rhopalic* patterning is also evident in Frost's "Drink and be whole again beyond confusion" and Milton's

> I did but prompt the age to quit their clogs
> By the known rules of ancient liberty. . . .

A similar design occurs in prose, as well, as in the passages "life, liberty, and the pursuit of happiness" and "our lives, our fortunes, and our sacred honor" in the Declaration of Independence. Fitzgerald's *The Great Gatsby* includes this allusive discussion of Gatsby: "He was a son of God . . . and he must be about His Father's business, the service of a vast, vulgar, and meretricious beauty."

Rhyme Identity of terminal sound between accented syllables, usually occupying corresponding positions in two or more lines of verse. The correspondence of sound is based on the vowels and succeeding consonants of the accented syllables, which must, for a true *rhyme*, be preceded by different consonants. That is, "fan" and "ran" constitute a true *rhyme* because the vowel and succeeding consonant sounds ("an") are the same but the preceding consonant sounds are different.

The recurrence of *rhyme* at regular intervals helps to establish the form of a STANZA. *Rhyme* serves to unify and distinguish divisions of a poem, because it is likely that the *rhyme* sounds followed in one stanza—the Spenserian for instance—will be changed when the next stanza is started, although the RHYME SCHEME remains the same. This principle gives unity to one stanza and marks it off as separate from the next, affording a sense of movement.

The types of *rhyme* are classified according to two schemes: (1) the position of the *rhymes* in the line, and (2) the number of syllables involved.

On the basis of position, we have: (1) END RHYME, much the most common type, which occurs at the end of the line; (2) INTERNAL RHYME (sometimes called LEONINE RHYME), which occurs at some place after the beginning and before the end of the line; and (3) BEGINNING RHYME, which occurs in the first syllable (or syllables). On the basis of the number of syllables presenting similarity of sound, we have: (1) MASCULINE RHYME, in which the correspondence of sound is restricted to the final accented syllable as in "fan" and "ran." This type of *rhyme* is generally more forcible, more vigorous than those following; (2) FEMININE RHYME—also called DOUBLE RHYME—in which the rhyming stressed syllable is followed by an undifferentiated unstressed syllable exactly matching another such unstressed syllable in the other *rhyme* words (note that FEMININE RHYME, as between "fountain" and "mountain," differs considerably from COMPOUND RHYME, as between "childhood" and "wildwood," in which there is *rhyme* between both pairs of components); and (3) TRIPLE RHYME, in which the rhyming stressed syllable is followed by two undifferentiated unstressed syllables, as in "glorious" and "victorious." Triple rhyme has been used for serious work—such as Thomas Hood's "Bridge of Sighs" and Thomas Hardy's "The Voice"—but usually it is reserved for humorous, satirical verse, for the sort of use Byron made of it in his satiric poems and Ogden Nash in his comic verse. Certain conventions about *rhyme* persist. These are: (1) A true *rhyme* is based on the correspondence of sound in *accented* syllables as opposed to unaccented syllables. "Stating" and "mating" thus make a true *rhyme*, and, for the same reason, "rating" and "forming" do not make a *rhyme*, because the correspondence is between unaccented syllables. If there is unequal accent on rhyming syllables, as between "afraid" and "decade," the *rhyme* is sometimes called ANISOBARIC or "ironic" because of its subtlety and slight dissonance; this kind of *rhyme* occurs often in Pound's *Hugh Selwyn Mauberley* and in much of Laura (Riding) Jackson's poetry. (2) For a true *rhyme* all syllables *following* the accented syllable must be identical; "fascinate" and "deracinating" would not be true *rhyme*, because of the difference between the last syllables. (3) The repetition of the same vowel sounds in different *rhymes* that occur near each other should ordinarily be avoided. For instance, "stone" and "bone" are good *rhymes* as are "home" and "tome," but a quatrain composed of those four *rhymes* would usually be considered poor because of the repetition of the same vowel sound throughout followed by nasalized consonants. (4) There should not be too great a separation between *rhyme* sounds, because such separation will result in a loss of effect. A *rhyme* occurring in the first line and the sixth line, for instance, places a strain on the reader's attention. Such strain can be useful in achieving certain unifying effects. In Eliot's largely unrhymed "Gerontion," two passages ten lines apart end "Titians" and "ambitions," with a touch of surprise and refreshment. The *rhyme* between "gates" and "straits," almost seventy lines apart in the same poem, may add a bit to a motif of narrow or blocked passages, because the rhyming words have similar meanings. (5) It is permissible for a *rhyme* to fall on an unaccented syllable. If a word of three or more syllables with a dactylic ending is placed in a rhyming position, then the second unstressed syllable is given a courtesy PROMOTION to accented status with some alteration of vowel quality and quantity. "Liberty," say, is normally a dactyl—a stressed syllable followed by two unstressed—but, if the word is put into a rhyming position (as in "My country, 'tis of thee, / Sweet land of liberty"), then the third syllable is promoted, lengthened, and modified as to vowel quality. Note that the normal rhyme word "thee" precedes the promoted word, to guide the ear. (Marvell and Blake so promote "eternity" and "symmetry" that they *rhyme* with "lie" and "eye.") If the promoted rhyme word precedes the normal (as in the *rhyme* between "rarity" and "me" at the end of Browning's "My Last Duchess"), then the effect is slightly unusual and adds emphasis to the second rhyme word. Promotion can also yield an IDENTICAL RHYME, which does not constitute true *rhyme* (as when Shakespeare puts "memory" and "masonry" in a rhyming position). "Full" *rhyme* occurs between stressed syllables with more or less equal accent; "ironic" *rhyme* between stressed syllables with detectably unequal accent ("good" and "childhood," say); "promotion" when courtesy stress is given to the last syllable of a dactyl; the very rare attempt to squeeze a *rhyme* out of inflexibly unstressed syllables (as between "water" and "number") is HOMEOTELEUTON, which is the repetition of the same or similar unstressed syllables (as in John Crowe Ransom's "Bells for John Whiteside's Daughter," which places "window" and "shadow" in a rhyming position). (6) Syllables that are spelled differently but have the same pronunciation (such as "rite" and "right") (called IDENTICAL RHYME or *RIME RICHE*) do not make fully acceptable rhymes.

What constitutes a *rhyme* changes as pronunciation changes, and sometimes between nations or sections of nations. "Clerk" rhymes with "jerk" in the United States and with "bark" in Britain.

Rhyme and the importance it enjoys in modern versification are comparatively modern developments. Ancient Sanskrit, Greek, and Latin poetry was not rhymed; our earliest English verse (*Beowulf* is an example) was not based on *rhyme*. Historians sometimes credit the development of *rhyme* to ceremonials within the Catholic church and suggest that the priests made use of *rhyme* as a device to aid the worshipers in their singing and memorizing of the ritualistic procedure. *Dies Irae* is an example of one of the earliest rhymed songs of the church. Because even so-called Late Latin remained a markedly synthetic-suffixal language, loading the end of virtually every noun, verb, and adjective with one or more weakly accented syllables of inflection, most of these church songs were either unrhymed (as is "Adeste Fideles" in Latin and in the English translation) or else rhymed on syllables once or twice removed from the ends of words. It seems that *rhyme* as a common feature of poetry does not and maybe cannot emerge until a language can furnish a large number of usable words that have a stressed syllable at or very near the end—until, that is, a synthetic-suffixal language loosens up in the direction of becoming analytic-prefixal.

Among contemporary poets a tendency to use imperfect *rhymes*, substituting ASSONANCE, CONSONANCE, and DISSONANCE for true *rhymes*, is widespread; and many present-day poets take interesting liberties with the traditional "rules" for *rhyme* cited in this article. Among the names given such variations are SLANT RHYME, NEAR RHYME, OBLIQUE RHYME, off-rhyme, pararhyme. See ASSONANCE, CONSONANCE, DISSONANCE.

Rhyme Royal (or **Rime Royal**) A seven-lined IAMBIC PENTAMETER STANZA rhyming *ababbcc*, sometimes with an ALEXANDRINE (hexameter) seventh line. The name has been said to derive from its employment by the Scottish King James I; but, because Chaucer and other predecessors of James had used *rhyme royal* extensively, it must be attributed to James, if at all, as an honor in recognition of the fact that a king wrote verse rather than that he originated the pattern. Chaucer used *rhyme royal* in the *Parlement of Foules*, the "Man of Law's Tale," the "Clerk's Tale," and *Troilus and Criseyde*. Some other poets who have written in *rhyme royal* are Lydgate, Hoccleve, Dunbar, Skelton, Wyatt, Shakespeare, Milton, Wordsworth, Morris, and W. H. Auden. John Masefield wrote both *The Widow in the Bye Street* and *Dauber* in *rhyme royal*. The last stanza of Shakespeare's *Rape of Lucrece* is a good example:

> When they had sworn to this advised doom,
> They did conclude to bear dead Lucrece thence;
> To show her bleeding body thorough Rome,
> And so to publish Tarquin's foul offence:
> Which being done with speedy diligence,
> The Romans plausibly did give consent
> To Tarquin's everlasting banishment.

An idea of the pleasingly various tonalities available in *rhyme royal* can be had by comparing Auden's *Letter to Lord Byron* and "The Shield of Achilles" (in part) with Wordsworth's "Resolution and Independence." *Rhyme royal* enjoys the unique distinction of being the only stanza used by all three poets customarily called the greatest in English—Chaucer, Shakespeare, and Milton—as well as by Wordsworth and Auden.

Rhyme Scheme The pattern in which RHYME sounds occur in a stanza. *Rhyme schemes*, for the purpose of analysis, are usually presented by the assignment of the same letter of the alphabet to each similar sound in a stanza. Thus, the pattern of the SPENSERIAN STANZA is *ababbcbcc*. Sometimes capital letters or "prime" marks are used to indicate REPETITIONS. See RONDEL.

Rhythm The passage of regular or approximately equivalent time intervals between definite events or the recurrence of specific sounds or kinds of sound. Human beings have a seemingly basic need for such recurrence, or for the effect produced by it, as laboratory experiments in psychology have demonstrated and as one can see for oneself by watching a crew of workers digging or hammering.

In both prose and poetry the presence of rhythmic patterns lends both pleasure and heightened emotional response, for it establishes a pattern of expectations and it rewards the listener or reader with the pleasure of a series of fulfillments of expectation. In poetry three different elements may function in a pattern of regular occurrence: quantity, accent, and number of syllables. In English poetry the rhythmic pattern is most often established by a combination of accent and number of syllables. This pattern lends itself to certain kinds of basic rhythmic analysis in English VERSIFICATION. The *rhythm* may be rising—that is, beginning with unstressed and ending with stressed syllables, as in IAMBS and ANAPESTS; or falling—that is, beginning with stressed and ending with unstressed syllables, as in TROCHEES and DACTYLS.

In prose, despite the absence of the formal regularity of pattern here described for verse, cadence is usually present; in impassioned prose it often establishes definite patterns of rhythmic recurrence.

Riddle The modern *riddle* has its more dignified ancestor in the *riddles* of ancient and medieval literature. Based on Latin prototypes, *riddles* became an important type of the vernacular literatures of Western Europe, including Old English. The *Exeter Book* (eleventh century) contains an interesting collection of nearly a hundred Old English *riddles* of unknown authorship. The interpretation of the *riddles* is sometimes obvious, sometimes obscure; but the descriptive power is often high, and the imagery is fresh and picturesque. The new moon is a young Viking sailing the skies; the falcon wears the bloom of trees on her breast; the swan is a wandering spirit dressed in a "noiseless robe." The swan, the falcon, the helmet, the horn, the hen, the onion, beer, the Bible manuscript, the storm-spirit, and many other objects connected with war, seamanship, nature, religion, and everyday life describe themselves by descriptive EPITHET, characteristic act, apt METAPHOR, and end with a "Tell me what I'm called." These *riddles* contain some of the best existing evidence of the use of external nature in the period and have been termed the most secular of all existing Old English literature. *Riddles* persist among serious poets: see Dickinson's "A Narrow Fellow" and Frost's "Three Guesses."

[References: Paull F. Baum (tr.), *Anglo-Saxon Riddles of the Exeter Book* (1963); Archer Taylor, *English Riddles from Oral Tradition* (1951).]

Riding Rhyme The HEROIC COUPLET, sometimes with run-on lines but without CAESURAS.

Rime Couée A TAIL-RHYME STANZA, one in which two lines, usually in tetrameter, are followed by a short line, usually in trimeter, two successive short lines rhyming—as, for example, *aabccb*, where the *a* and *c* lines are tetrameter and the *b* trimeter.

Rime retournée The relation between such syllables as "pal" and "lap," also called AMPHISBAENIC or BOUSTROPHEDON rhyme.

Rime Riche Words with identical sounds but different meanings, as "stair" and "stare" or "well" (adjective) and "well" (noun). See IDENTICAL RHYME.

Rising Action The part of a dramatic PLOT that has to do with the COMPLICATION of the action. It begins with the EXCITING FORCE, gains in interest and power as the opposing groups come into CONFLICT (the hero usually being in the ascendancy), and proceeds to the CLIMAX. See DRAMATIC STRUCTURE.

Rising Rhythm A foot in which the last syllable is accented; thus, in English the IAMB and the ANAPEST. Coleridge illustrates *rising rhythm* in these lines:

> Ĭámbĭcs márch frŏm shórt tŏ lóng.
> Wĭth ă léap ănd ă bóund thĕ swĭft Ánăpĕsts thróng.

Robinsonade (also **Robinsonnade**) A term coined by J. G. Schnabel in 1731 for a work similar to *Robinson Crusoe*, with a shipwreck on a desert island followed by adventures of survival. The ANANYM "Nosnibor" as the name of a character in Samuel Butler's *Erewhon* (1872) hints at elements of the *Robinsonade*. The mode continues through J. M. Barrie's play *The Admirable Crichton* (1902), which is the ancestor of *Gilligan's Island*. (*Lost in Space* is another instance from television and movies.) H. de Vere Stacpoole's *The Blue Lagoon* (1908) added an erotic dimension later exploited in movies. William Golding's *Lord of the Flies* (1954) provides a melodramatic permutation. The American poet Weldon Kees wrote a series of poems about a man named Robinson (the "Robinson Poems").

Rock and Roll (or **Rock**) The alliterative combination "rollrock" occurs in a nineteenth-century poem by Gerard Manley Hopkins, and the phrase *rock and roll* (evidently with veiled sexual implications) was current in the American vernacular well before "Rock and Roll" was used in a song title in 1934. It was not until the 1950s, however, that the broad style of music became popular and spread beyond the confines of popular song to other realms as well, including opera (The Who composed a rock opera called *Tommy*). The movement grew and spread rapidly, soon embracing performers of all races and many nations. Although music remains the heart of *rock and roll*, the pervasive sentiment and spirit have reached literature as well in many manifestations. Some respected poets—such as Ed Sanders and Jim Carroll—are also respected singers and songwriters.

Rocking Rhythm A FOOT in which a stressed syllable falls between two unstressed syllables; an AMPHIBRACH. *Rocking rhythm* is illustrated in this line from Swinburne:

> Thĕ séarch, ănd | thĕ sóught, ănd | thĕ séekĕr, | —thĕ
> sóul ănd | thĕ bódy | thăt ís.

Rococo In the history of European architecture the *rococo* period follows the BAROQUE and precedes the NEOCLASSIC, embracing most of the eighteenth century. The style arose in France, flourished on the Continent, but made little headway in England. It was marked by a wealth of decorative detail suggestive of grace, intimacy, and playfulness. The fashion spread to furniture. It avoided grandiose effects. Because the style was often regarded in England as decadent, the term *rococo* has been employed in a derogatory sense to suggest the overdecorative and is not infrequently confused with the BAROQUE (also unfavorably interpreted). In its older sense Swinburne uses the term as the title of one of his love lyrics—one in which the lover implores his three-day mistress not to forget their ardent but brief love.

[References: Helmut Hatzfeld, *The Rococo: Eroticism, Wit, and Elegance in European Literature* (1972); George Hitchcock, *The Rococo Eye* (1970).]

Rodomontade Bragging or blustering. Falstaff's famous description of his bold fight with the highwaymen is an example of *rodomontade*, as is his boastful, "There live not three good men unhanged in England, and one of them is fat and grows old. . . ." So called after the braggart Moorish king Rodomonte in Ariosto's *Orlando Furioso*. See MILES GLORIOSUS.

Roman à Clef A novel in which actual persons are presented under the guise of fiction. (Like the "Schlüssel" in SCHLÜSSELROMAN, the "clef" here means "key," in the sense of a program of true identities.) Notable examples have been Madeleine de Scudéry's *Clélie*, Thomas Love Peacock's *Nightmare Abbey*, Hawthorne's *The Blithedale Romance*, Somerset Maugham's *Cakes and Ale*, Aldous Huxley's *Point Counter Point*, Ernest Hemingway's *The Sun Also Rises*, Truman Capote's *Answered Prayers*, Carrie Fisher's *Postcards from the Edge*, and almost any of Jack Kerouac's novels.

Roman à Thèse French: a THESIS NOVEL, one intended to establish and illustrate a social doctrine.

Romance Languages proximately derived from Latin are called *Romance* languages. The first Old French *romances* were translated from Latin, and this fact may have helped to fix the name *romance* on them. (See MEDIEVAL ROMANCE.) In Renaissance criticism ROMANTIC EPICS, such as *The Faerie Queene*, were called *romances*. The term *romance* has had special meanings as a kind of fiction since the early years of the novel. In his preface to *Incognita* (1692) William Congreve made a distinction between NOVEL and *romance* as works of long fiction, and in 1785 Clara Reeve in *The Progress of Romance* declared, "The Novel is a picture of real life and manners, and of the times in which it was written. The Romance in lofty and elevated language, describes what has never happened nor is likely to." This distinction has resulted in two distinct uses of *romance*. In common usage, it refers to works with extravagant characters, remote and exotic places, highly exciting and heroic events, passionate love, or mysterious or supernatural experiences. In another and more sophisticated sense, *romance* refers to works relatively free of the more restrictive aspects of realistic verisimilitude. As Hawthorne expressed it in the preface to *The House of the Seven Gables*, the *romance* "sins unpardonably, so far as it may swerve aside from the truth of the human heart"; yet it has, he insisted, "a right to present that truth under circumstances, to a great extent, of the writer's own choosing or creation." In America particularly, the *romance* has proved to be a serious, flexible, and successful medium for the exploration of philosophical ideas and attitudes, ranging through such differing works as Hawthorne's *The Scarlet Letter*, Melville's *Moby-Dick*, Fitzgerald's *The Great Gatsby*, Faulkner's *Absalom, Absalom!*, and Warren's *World Enough and Time*. According to Northrop Frye's very useful scheme of modes, *romance* occupies the zone between MYTH and MIMESIS; in this special application *romance* has to do with characters whose powers exceed those of normal human beings but fall short of those of gods.

[References: Northrop Frye, *Anatomy of Criticism* (1957); E. C. Pettet, *Shakespeare and the Romance Tradition* (1949).]

Roman de Geste Same as *CHANSON DE GESTE*.

Romanesque A term sometimes used to characterize writing that is fanciful or fabulous. It is more rarely used to denote the presence of a romance quality in a work.

Roman-Fleuve "River novel": a substantial, slow-moving NOVEL that typically chronicles the lives of several generations; sometimes a set or sequence of novels.

Roman Noir A thriller, a NOVEL in the dark mode of FILM NOIR, involving crime, detection, punishment, and corruption in high places.

Romantic Comedy A comedy in which serious love is the chief concern and source of interest, especially the type of comedy developed on the early Elizabethan stage by such writers as Robert Greene and Shakespeare. Greene's *James the Fourth*, which represents the *romantic comedy* as Shakespeare found it, is supposed to have influenced Shakespeare in his *Two Gentlemen of Verona*. A few years later Shakespeare perfected the type in such plays as *The Merchant of Venice* and *As You Like It*. Characteristics commonly found include: love as chief motive; much out-of-door action; an idealized heroine (who usually masks as a man); love subjected to great difficulties; poetic justice often violated; balancing of characters; easy reconciliations; and happy ending. Shakespeare's last group of plays, the TRAGICOMEDIES or "serene romances" (such as *Winter's Tale* and *Cymbeline*), are in some sense a modification of the earlier *romantic comedy*.

[Reference: Peter G. Phialas, *Shakespeare's Romantic Comedies* (1966).]

Romantic Criticism A term sometimes used for the ideas that developed late in the eighteenth and early in the nineteenth centuries as a part of the triumph of ROMANTICISM. *Romantic criticism* was inspired in part by the necessity of "answering" conservatives such as Francis Jeffrey, Sydney Smith, and William Gifford. The artificial character of Pope's imagery was attacked by W. L. Bowles, who in turn was answered by Lord Byron and others. New theories about the genius of Shakespeare were espoused by Coleridge and others: instead of being regarded as a wild, irregular genius, who succeeded in spite of his violation of the laws of composition, his art was studied on the assumption that it succeeded because it followed laws of its own organism, which were more authentic than artificial formal rules. (See ORGANIC FORM.) The *romantic criticism* of Shakespeare thus led to the view that Shakespeare, like nature, was infallible. "If we do not understand him, it is our fault or the fault of copyists or typographers" (Coleridge). Another aspect of *romantic criticism* was Wordsworth's theory of poetry as calling for simple themes drawn from humble life expressed in the language of ordinary life—a sharp reaction from the conventions of neoclassic poetry. In general the romantic critic saw art as an expression of the artist (the EXPRESSIVE THEORY OF CRITICISM), valued it as a living organism, and sought its highest expressions among simple people, primitive cultures, and aspects of the world unsullied by artifice or by commerce. See PRIMITIVISM, ROMANTICISM.

Romantic Epic A type of long narrative poem developed by Italian Renaissance poets (late fifteenth and sixteenth centuries) by combining the MEDIEVAL ROMANCE with the classical EPIC. Such poets as Pulci, Boiardo, and Ariosto produced *romantic epics* that were like medieval romances in stressing the love element, in their complicated loose structure, in the profusion of characters and episodes, and in freedom of verse form. Yet they were like the Virgilian epic in their use of a formal invocation, statement of theme, set speeches, formal descriptions, use of epic SIMILES, supernatural MACHINERY, and division into books. Later Tasso (*Jerusalem Delivered*, 1581) infused moral instruction and religious propaganda into the type. ALLEGORY was also employed in the Italian *romantic epics*. The literary critics of the time were divided in their attitudes toward the new type of epic, the conservatives strongly opposing it because of its departure from classical standards. The form proved generally popular with readers, however, and when Edmund Spenser came to write his ambitious English epic, he modeled his poem largely on the *romantic epics* of Ariosto (*Orlando Furioso*, 1516) and Tasso. Thus, *The Faerie Queene*, epic in its high patriotic purpose and in much of its technique, romantic in its chivalric atmosphere and Arthurian setting, became, by following the general method of Ariosto and Tasso, the great example in English literature of a *romantic epic*.

Romanticism A movement of the eighteenth and nineteenth centuries that marked the reaction in literature, philosophy, art, religion, and politics from the NEOCLASSICISM and formal orthodoxy of the preceding period. *Romanticism* arose so gradually and exhibited so many phases that a satisfactory definition is not possible. The aspect most stressed in France is reflected in Victor Hugo's phrase "liberalism in literature," meaning especially the freeing of the artist and writer from restraints and rules and suggesting that phase of individualism marked by the encouragement of revolutionary political ideas. The poet Heine noted the chief aspect of German *romanticism* in calling it the revival of medievalism in art, letters, and life. Walter Pater thought the addition of strangeness to beauty (the neoclassicists having insisted on order in beauty) constituted the romantic temper. An interesting schematic explanation calls *romanticism* the predominance of IMAGINATION over reason and formal rules (classicism) and over the sense of fact or the actual (REALISM), a formula that recalls Hazlitt's statement (1816) that the classic beauty of a Greek temple resided chiefly in its actual form and its obvious CONNOTATIONS, whereas the "romantic" beauty of a GOTHIC building or ruin arose from associated ideas that the imagination was stimulated to conjure up. The term is used in many senses, a recent favorite being that which sees in the romantic mood a psychological desire to escape from unpleasant realities.

Perhaps more useful to the student than definitions will be a list of romantic characteristics, though *romanticism* was not a clearly conceived system. Among the aspects of the romantic movement in England may be listed: SENSIBILITY; PRIMITIVISM; love of NATURE; sympathetic interest in the past, especially the medieval; MYSTICISM; individualism; ROMANTIC CRITICISM; and a reaction against whatever characterized NEOCLASSICISM. Among the specific characteristics embraced by these general attitudes are: the abandonment of the HEROIC COUPLET in favor of BLANK VERSE, the SONNET, the SPENSERIAN STANZA, and many experimental verse forms; the dropping of the conventional poetic diction in favor of fresher language and bolder figures; the idealization of rural life (Goldsmith); enthusiasm for the wild, irregular, or GROTESQUE in nature and art; unrestrained imagination; enthusiasm for the uncivilized or "natural"; interest in human rights (Burns, Byron); sympathy with animal life (Cowper); sentimental melancholy (Gray); emotional psychology in fiction (Richardson); collection and imitation of popular ballads (Percy, Scott); interest in ancient Celtic and Scandinavian mythology and literature (see CELTIC REVIVAL); and renewed interest in Spenser, Shakespeare, and Milton. Typical literary forms include the lyric, especially the love lyric, the reflective lyric, the nature lyric, and the lyric of morbid melancholy (see GRAVEYARD SCHOOL); the SENTIMENTAL NOVEL; the METRICAL ROMANCE; the SENTIMENTAL COMEDY; the BALLAD; the PROBLEM NOVEL; the HISTORICAL NOVEL; the GOTHIC romance; the sonnet; and the critical essay (see ROMANTIC CRITICISM).

Although the romantic movement in English literature had its beginnings or anticipations in the earlier eighteenth century (Shaftesbury, Thomson, Dyer, Lady Winchilsea), it was not until the middle of the century that its characteristics became prominent and self-conscious (Blair, Akenside, Joseph and Thomas Warton, Gray, Richardson, Sterne, Walpole, Goldsmith, and somewhat later Cowper, Burns, and Blake), and its complete triumph was reserved for the early years of the nineteenth century (Wordsworth, Coleridge, Scott, Southey, Byron, the Shelleys, Keats, Jane Austen). A little later in the nineteenth century came the great ROMANTIC PERIOD IN AMERICAN LITERATURE (Bryant, Emerson, Lowell, Thoreau, Whittier, Hawthorne, Melville, Poe, Whitman, Dickinson, Holmes).

The last third of the nineteenth century witnessed a more sober mood than prevailed earlier in the century, and, although the late nineteenth century and the early twentieth century, in both England and America, have been marked by a sharp reaction against the romantic, especially the sentimental spirit in literature, much late Victorian literature was romantic, and the vitality of *romanticism* is evidenced by the volume of romantic writing still being produced.

By way of caution it may be said that such descriptions of *romanticism* as this one probably overstress the distinction between *romanticism* and CLASSICISM or NEOCLASSICISM and cannot hope to resolve the confusion over what "romantic" means which, A. O. Lovejoy asserted, has "for a century been the scandal" of literary history and criticism. Some writers have even urged the abandoning of the terms *romantic* and *classic*. Several have noted that Homer's *Odyssey*, for example, is cited by some as the very essence of the *romantic*, by others as a true exemplar of classicism. Even if the term *romantic* were always employed in the same sense and its characteristic could be safely and comprehensively enumerated, it would still be true that one could not use a single characteristic, such as the love of wild scenery, as a key for classifying as romantic any single poem or poet.

Yet *romanticism* does have a fairly definite meaning. The term designates a literary and philosophical theory that tends to see the individual at the center of all life, and it places the individual, therefore, at the center of art, making literature valuable as an expression of unique feelings and particular attitudes (the EXPRESSIVE THEORY OF CRITICISM) and valuing its fidelity in portraying experiences, however fragmentary and incomplete, more than it values adherence to completeness, unity, or the demands of genre. Although *romanticism* tends at times to regard nature as alien, it more often sees in nature a revelation of Truth, the "living garment of God," and a more suitable subject for art than those aspects of the world sullied by artifice. *Romanticism* seeks to find the Absolute, the Ideal, by transcending the actual, whereas REALISM finds its values in the actual and NATURALISM in the scientific laws that undergird the actual.

[References: M. H. Abrams, *The Mirror and the Lamp* (1953); Irving Babbitt, *Rousseau and Romanticism* (1919, reprinted 1947); Harold Bloom, ed., *Romanticism and Consciousness: Essays in Criticism* (1970); Douglas Bush, *Mythology and the*

Romantic Tradition in English Poetry (1937); Paul de Man, *The Rhetoric of Romanticism* (1976); Morris Eaves and Michael Fischer, eds., *Romanticism and Contemporary Criticism* (1986); Northrop Frye, ed., *Romanticism Reconsidered* (1963); J. B. Halstead, *Romanticism* (1969); Geoffrey Hartman, *Wordsworth's Poetry, 1787–1814* (1971); T. E. Hulme, *Speculations*, ed. Herbert Read (1924, reprinted 1954); Frank Kermode, *The Romantic Image* (1957); A. O. Lovejoy, *Essays in the History of Ideas* (1944); Logan Pearsall Smith, *Words and Idioms*, 5th ed. (1943); René Wellek, *Concepts of Criticism* (1963).]

Romantic Novel A type of novel marked by strong interest in action, with episodes often based on love, adventure, and combat. The term "*romantic*" owes its origin to the early type of story embraced by the ROMANCE of medieval times, but with the march of time other elements have been added. The FABLIAU and the NOVELLA, particularly, have contributed qualities. A romance, in its modern meaning, signifies that type of novel more concerned with action than with character; more properly fictional than legendary because it is woven so largely from the imagination; read more as a means of escape from existence than of engagement with the actualities of life. The writers of modern romance are too numerous to mention: Sir Walter Scott's name may be allowed to represent the long list of romancers in English and American literature. In another sense *romantic novel* is used interchangeably with romance, as a form relatively free of the demands of the actual and thus able to reflect imaginative truth.

Romantic Period in American Literature, 1830–1865 The period between the "second revolution" of the Jacksonian Era and the close of the Civil War in America saw the testing of a nation and its development by ordeal. It was an age of great westward expansion, of the increasing gravity of the slavery question, of an intensification of the spirit of embattled sectionalism in the South, and of a powerful impulse to reform in the North. Its culminating act was the trial by arms of the opposing views in a civil war, whose conclusion certified the fact of a united nation dedicated to the concepts of industry and capitalism and philosophically committed to egalitarianism. In a sense it may be said that the three decades following the inauguration of President Andrew Jackson in 1829 put to the test his views of democracy and saw emerge from the test a secure union committed to essentially Jacksonian principles.

In literature it was America's first great creative period, a full flowering of the romantic impulse on American soil. Surviving from the FEDERALIST AGE were its three major literary figures: Bryant, Irving, and Cooper. Emerging as new writers of strength and creative power were the novelists Hawthorne, Simms, Melville, and Harriet Beecher Stowe; the poets Poe, Whittier, Holmes, Longfellow, Lowell, Dickinson, and Whitman; the essayists Thoreau, Emerson, and Holmes; the critics Poe, Lowell, and Simms. The South, moving toward a concept of Southern independence, advanced three distinguished periodicals, the *Southern Review*, the *Southern Literary Messenger*, and the *Southern Quarterly Review*. In the North the *Knickerbocker Magazine* and the *Democratic Review* joined the continuing arbiter of Northern taste, the *North American Review*, and then were followed by *Harper's Magazine* (1850) and the *Atlantic Monthly* (1857). Between 1830 and 1855 the GIFT BOOKS and ANNUALS proved to be remunerative markets for essays and tales.

The poetry was predominantly romantic in spirit and form. Moral qualities were significantly present in the verse of Emerson, Bryant, Longfellow, Whittier, Holmes, Lowell, and Thoreau. The sectional issues were debated in poetry by Whittier and Lowell speaking for abolition, and Timrod, Hayne, and Simms speaking for the South. Poe formulated his theories of poetry and in some fifty lyrics practiced a symbolist verse that was to be, despite the charge of triviality by such contemporaries as Emerson, the strongest single poetic influence emerging from pre–Civil War America, particularly in its impact on European poetry. Lowell wrote satiric verse in DIALECT. Whitman, beginning with the 1855 edition of *Leaves of Grass*, was the ultimate expression of a poetry organic in form and romantic in spirit, united to a concept of democracy that was pervasively egalitarian.

In essays and in lectures the New England transcendentalists—Emerson, Thoreau, Fuller, and Alcott—carried the expression of philosophic and religious ideas to a high level. In critical essays, Lowell wrote with distinction, Simms with skill, and Poe with genius. Until 1850 the novel continued to follow the path of Scott, with Cooper and Simms as its major producers. In the 1850s, however, emerged the powerful symbolic novels of Hawthorne and Melville and the effective PROPAGANDA NOVEL of Harriet Beecher Stowe. Poe, Hawthorne, and Simms practiced the writing of short stories throughout the period, taking up where Irving had left off in the development of the form. Humorous writing by A. B. Longstreet, George W. Harris, Artemus Ward, Josh Billings, and the early Mark Twain was establishing a basis for a realistic literature in the vernacular, but it failed in this period to receive the critical attention that was to come its way later.

In the drama the STAR SYSTEM, the imitation of English SPECTACLE drama, and ROMANTIC TRAGEDY modeled on Shakespeare were dominant. Although N. P. Willis and R. M. Bird were successful, only George Henry Boker, with *Francesca da Rimini*, displayed any distinctive literary talent in the theater. *Uncle Tom's Cabin* and *Rip Van Winkle* began stage careers that were to be phenomenally successful.

At the end of the Civil War a new nation had been born, and it was to demand and receive a new literature less idealistic and more practical, less exalted and more earthy, less consciously artistic and more honest than that produced in the age when the American dream had glowed with greatest intensity and American writers had made a great literary period by capturing on their pages the enthusiasm and the optimism of that dream. See *Outline of Literary History*.

Romantic Period in English Literature, 1798–1870 In the period between the publication of *Lyrical Ballads* (1798) and the death of Dickens, English literature was dominated by ROMANTICISM. One common way of designating literary periods in English history is to call the AGE OF THE ROMANTIC MOVEMENT (1798–1832) the *Romantic Period* and to lump together the time between the death of Scott in 1832 and the end of the century as the VICTORIAN AGE, because Queen Victoria reigned through much of it. However, the romantic impulse, which flowered with such spectacular force in 1798, remained the dominant literary impulse well into the 1860s; hence the divisions employed here.

The *Romantic Period* came into being during the Napoleonic Wars and flourished during the painful economic dislocations that followed. It saw union with Ireland; it witnessed the suffering attendant on the INDUSTRIAL REVOLUTION; it was torn by CHARTISM and the great debates centering on the REFORM BILL; it developed a sensitive humanitarianism out of witnessing the suffering of the masses; it both espoused and despised the doctrine of UTILITARIANISM. An industrial England was being born in pain and suffering. The throes of developing democracy, the ugliness of the sudden growth of cities, the prevalence of human pain, the blatant presence of the profit motive—all helped to characterize what was in many respects "the best of times . . . the worst of times."

In the first half of the period a philosophical romanticism based on value in the individual, on the romantic view of nature, and on an organic concept of art dominated the English literary mind. There was some skepticism and cynicism, expressed in the form of abusive parody and satire, but optimism was the spirit of the times, although it was often an optimism closely associated with the impulse to revolt and with radical political reform. In the second half of the period, the EARLY VICTORIAN AGE, the impact of the Industrial Revolution was more deeply felt and the implications of the new science for philosophy and religion began to be obvious. The romantic philosophy still held, and the spirit of romanticism permeated literature and much of life; but it found itself seriously in conflict with much of the world around it, and out of that conflict came a literature of doubt and questioning. If, for example, the attitudes of Coleridge and Shelley are compared with those of Carlyle—all three clearly romantics—the extent to which the romanticism of the earlier period was being qualified by the conditions of industrial England and was being used to test those conditions becomes clearer.

In poetry the *Romantic Period* heard the voices of Wordsworth, Coleridge, Shelley, Keats, Byron, Tennyson, Arnold, the Pre-Raphaelites, and Browning. It was a great age for the novel, producing Godwin, Scott, Austen, the Brontës, Thackeray, Dickens, Trollope, and the early George Eliot. A period of serious critical and social debate in prose, it produced Carlyle, Ruskin, Macaulay, Arnold, Pater, Mill, and Newman. In the informal essay it produced Lamb, Hazlitt, Hunt, and De Quincey. Only in the drama, bound by the PATENT THEATERS and a blind idolatry of Shakespeare and hampered by the STAR SYSTEM, did the *Romantic Period* fail to produce work of true distinction; it was virtually the weakest period in the English stage since Elizabeth I ascended the throne. For the literary history of the period, see AGE OF THE ROMANTIC MOVEMENT, EARLY VICTORIAN AGE, *Outline of Literary History*. See also ROMANTICISM.

Romantic Tragedy Nonclassical tragedy. The term is used for such modern tragedy as does not conform to the traditions or aims of CLASSICAL TRAGEDY. It differs from the latter in its greater freedom of technique, wider scope of theme and treatment, greater emphasis on character (as compared with emphasis on plot), looser structure, freer employment of imagination, greater variety of style, and readiness to admit humorous and even grotesque elements. Elizabethan tragedy—Shakespeare's, for example—is largely romantic.

Romany The language of the gypsies. It belongs to the Indian branch of the Indo-Iranian languages, blended with words from various European languages and spoken in many dialects. A gypsy, or anything pertaining to the gypsies. *Romany* ways and manners were much written about by George Borrow.

Rondeau A set French verse pattern, artificial but very popular with many English poets. The *rondeau* consists characteristically of fifteen lines, the ninth and fifteenth being a short REFRAIN. Only two rhymes (exclusive of the refrain) are allowed, the rhyme scheme running *aabba aabc aabbac*. The *c*-rhyme here represents the refrain, a group of words, usually the first half of the line, from the opening. The form divides itself into three stanzas with the refrain at the end of the second and third stanzas. The lines most frequently consist of eight syllables. There is also a form of the *rondeau* consisting of twelve lines, ten using two rhymes plus refrains, rhyming *abba abc abbac*. Another, known as the *rondeau redoublé*, consists of six quatrains rhyming *abab*, with the first four lines forming in succession the last lines of the second, third, fourth, and fifth quatrains. Leigh Hunt's poem familiarly known as "Jenny Kissed Me" was actually titled "Rondeau," but it is only eight lines long and the opening words are repeated only once. John McCrae's "In Flanders Field" and Paul Lawrence Dunbar's "We Wear the Mask" are notable *rondeaux*. Marilyn Hacker's "Rondeau After a Transatlantic Telephone Call" (1980) comes close to satisfying the technical requirements.

Rondel A French verse form, a variant of the RONDEAU, to which it is related historically. It consists of fourteen or thirteen lines (depending on whether the two-lined REFRAIN is kept at the close or simply one line). The most usual rhyme scheme is *ab*baab*ab*abba*ab* (the italics here represent lines used as a refrain and repeated in their entirety). As in the other FRENCH FORMS, repetition of rhyme words is not allowed. The *rondel* differs from the rondeau in the number of lines and the use of complete (rather than partial) lines for the refrain. Chaucer sometimes used the *rondel* as a stanza and not as a poem in itself; in his examples unity is achieved by the use of recurring lines or rhyme sounds.

Rondelet (also **Rondlet, Roundlet**) A rare seven-lined song stanza, construed as half of a fourteen-lined RONDEL, employing only two rhymes, as in an *abaabba* pattern.

Rough Cut In film-making, the edited material, between the stages of being a mere assembly and a fine cut.

Round A song for at least three voices, in which each singer begins a line or a phrase behind the preceding one but repeats what the preceding one is singing. Sometimes called a CATCH.

Round Character A term used by E. M. Forster for a character sufficiently complex to be able to surprise the reader without losing credibility. A *round character*, Forster says, "has the incalculability of life about it." See CHARACTERIZATION, FLAT CHARACTER.

Roundel A variation of the RONDEAU, generally attributed to Swinburne, who wrote "A Century of Roundels." The *roundel* is characterized by its eleven-lined form and the presence, in the fourth and eleventh lines, of a REFRAIN taken, as in the rondeau, from the first part of the first line. The rhyme scheme (using *c* to indicate the refrain) is *abacbababac. Roundel* is also Chaucer's spelling for RONDEL.

Roundelay A modification of the RONDEL. The *roundelay* is a simple poem of about fourteen lines in which part of one line frequently recurs as a REFRAIN. The term may also mean the musical setting of a rondeau so that it may be sung or chanted as an accompaniment for a folk dance.

Roundheads During the English Civil War the members of the Puritan or Parliamentarian party. See CAVALIER LYRICISTS.

Rubáiyát The plural of the Arabic word for QUATRAIN; hence a collection of four-lined stanzas. The best-known use of the word in English is in Edward FitzGerald's translation of the *The Rubáiyát of Omar Khayyám*.

Rubáiyát Stanza The stanza that FitzGerald used for his translation of *The Rubáiyát of Omar Khayyám*: a quatrain of iambic pentameter rhyming *aaba*.

Rubric From the Latin for "red." A title, description, direction, or other element independent but explanatory of the text. The term derives from the fact that the directions for religious services in liturgical books were printed in red to distinguish them from the text proper. Now used for any heading, label, or category.

Run Theatrical usage going back to the eighteenth century: an uninterrupted period of holding the stage.

Rune A character in the alphabet developed about the second or third century by the Germanic tribes in Europe. A *boc* (modern "book") was a runic tablet of beech wood. Later, *runes* were carved on stones, drinking horns, weapons, and ornaments. In very early times *rune* developed the special meaning of a character, sign, or written formula with magical power. *Runes* were used for charms, healing formulas, and incantations. Likewise, a *rune* came to mean any secret means of communication. Thus, the Anglo-Saxon poet Cynewulf signed some of his poems by placing in their text, in runic characters, a sequence of words whereof the first letters spelled his name. Runic writing was very common in Anglo-Saxon England until it was gradually crowded out by the Latin alphabet used by the Christian missionaries. Emerson used the word in the sense of "any song, poem, or verse." Poems involving *runes* have been written by Rudyard Kipling, Rolfe Humphries, C. Day Lewis, and Muriel Rukeyser.

Running Generally applied to smoothly running verse. Sometimes restricted to the trochaic rhythm. Gerard Manley Hopkins used *running* rhythm for ordinary English meter, distinct from SPRUNG RHYTHM.

Run-on Lines The carrying over of grammatical structure from one line to the next. The opposite of END-STOPPED LINES. See ENJAMBEMENT.

Rushes In film-making, the working material, unedited, which is reviewed to check for quality and completeness. Also called "dailies."

S

Garamond 1914. Designed by M. F. Benton and Thomas Cleland. This typeface was based on an original cut by Claude Garamont, c. 1531.

Saga In a strict sense, applied to Icelandic and Norse stories of the medieval period giving accounts of heroic adventure, especially of members of certain important families. The earlier Icelandic *sagas*, like the early Irish epics and romances, were in prose. There were also mythological *sagas*. The term came to be used for a historical legend developed until it was accepted as true—a form lying between authentic history and intentional fiction. The meaning is not confined to Scandinavian pieces, and the commonest meaning now for *saga* is a narrative having the characteristics of the Icelandic *sagas;* hence, any traditional tale of heroic achievement or adventure. The best example of the true *saga* is that of Grettir the Strong. Others are included in the famous *Heimskringla*, from which Longfellow drew material for his *Saga of King Olaf*. John Galsworthy has used the term in the title of his series of novels, *The Forsyte Saga*.

[References: Theodore M. Andersson, *The Icelandic Family Saga: An Analytic Reading* (1967); Carol J. Clover, *The Medieval Saga* (1982); M. I. Steblin-Kamenskij, *The Saga Mind* (tr. 1973); Hreinsson, Vidar, ed., *The Complete Sagas of Icelanders*, 5 vols. (1997).]

Saints' Lives Eulogistic accounts of the miraculous experiences of the saints; a kind of religious BIOGRAPHY extremely popular in the medieval world. See HAGIOGRAPHY.

[References: G. H. Gerould, *Saints' Legends* (1916); Charles Williams Jones, *Saints' Lives and Chronicles in Early England* (1947).]

Saint's Play A medieval play based on the legend of a saint. See MIRACLE PLAY.

Samizdat An underground system of publication and distribution used in the former Soviet Union to print, copy, and circulate literature that was out of favor, such as Alexander Solzhenitsyn's *The First Circle*. Those taking part in these activities were called *samizdatchiki* (singular *samizdatchik*).

Sapphic A stanzaic pattern deriving its name from the Greek poet Sappho, who wrote love lyrics of great beauty about 600 B.C. The pattern consists of three lines of eleven syllables each (¯ ˘ ˘ | ¯ ¯ | ¯ ˘ ˘ | ¯ ˘ | ¯ ˘) and a fourth of five syllables (¯ ˘ ˘ | ¯ ˘). The pattern has been occasionally tried in English. From about the middle of the sixteenth century, English poets have been attracted to the form, scanned either quantitatively or qualitatively. They include Sir Philip Sidney, Richard Stanyhurst, Fulke Greville, Mary Herbert (Countess of Pembroke), Thomas Campion, Thomas Lodge, Isaac Watts, and E. E. Cummings. Swinburne, Hardy, and Pound are generally conceded to have been the most successful modern writers of *sapphics*. The following by Swinburne is given qualitative scansion:

Thēn tŏ | mē sō | lŷĭng ă | wāke ă | vīsĭon
Cāme wĭth | ōut slēep | ōvĕr thĕ | sēas ănd | tōuched mĕ,
Sōftlў | tōuched mīne | ēyelĭds ănd | līps: ănd | Ī tŏo,
Fūll ŏf thĕ | vīsĭon.

Here are the opening stanzas of Hardy's "The Temporary the All" and Pound's "Apparuit":

Change and chancefulness in my flowering youthtime,
Set me sun by sun near to one unchosen;
Wrought us fellowlike, and despite divergence,
Fused us in friendship.
. . . .
Golden rose the house, in the portal I saw
thee, a marvel, carven in subtle stuff, a
portent. Life died down in the lamp and flickered,
caught at the wonder.

Sarcasm A caustic and bitter expression of strong disapproval. *Sarcasm* is personal, jeering, intended to hurt. See IRONY.

Satanic School A phrase used by Southey in the preface to his *Vision of Judgment* (1821) to designate the members of the literary group made up of Byron, Shelley, Hunt, and others, whose irregular lives and radical ideas—defiantly flaunted in their writings—suggested the term. They were contrasted with the "pious" group of the LAKE SCHOOL—Wordsworth, Coleridge, and Southey. More recent writers who have attacked conventional morality sometimes have been spoken of as belonging to the *Satanic School*.

Satanism The worship of Satan, possibly a survival of heathen fertility cults. In the twelfth century it gained strength through a secret rebellion against the Church. At its center is the Black Mass, a parody of the Christian Mass, with a nude woman on the altar, with the Host sometimes being the ashes and blood of murdered children. It was revived during the reign of Louis XIV in France and again in the 1890s, when it attracted some literary attention. Interest in witchcraft and *Satanism*, or at least their literary expression, seems to be increasing.

Satire A work or manner that blends a censorious attitude with humor and wit for improving human institutions or humanity. Satirists attempt through laughter not so much to tear down as to inspire a remodeling. If attackers simply abuse, they are writing invective; if they are personal and splenetic, they are writing SARCASM; if they are sad and morose over the state of society, they are writing IRONY or a JEREMIAD. As a rule modern *satire* spares the individual and follows Addison's self-imposed rule: to "pass over a single foe to charge whole armies." Most often, *satire* deals less with great sinners and criminals than with the general run of fools, knaves, ninnies, oafs, codgers, and frauds. Indeed, a good deal of enduring *satire* has to do with literature and the literary life itself.

Satire existed in classical antiquity (Aristophanes, Juvenal, Horace, Martial, and Petronius). Through the Middle Ages *satire* persisted in the FABLIAU and BEAST EPIC. In Spain the PICARESQUE NOVEL developed a strong element of *satire;* in France Molière and Le Sage handled the manner deftly, and Voltaire later established himself as an archsatirist. In England, from the time of Gascoigne (*Steel Glass*, 1576) and Lodge (*A Fig for Momus*, 1595), writers condemned vice and folly (Hall, Nash, Donne, Jonson). By the time of Charles I, however, interest in *satire* had declined, only to revive with the struggle between Cavaliers and Puritans. At the hands of Dryden, the HEROIC COUPLET, already the favorite form with most English satirists, developed into the finest satiric form. The eighteenth century in England became a period of *satire*; poetry, drama, essays, and criticism all took on the satirical manner at the hands of such writers as Dryden, Swift, Addison, Steele, Pope, and Fielding. In the nineteenth century Byron and Thackeray were sharp satirists.

Early American *satire* naturally followed the English in style. Before the Revolution, American *satire* dealt chiefly with the political struggle. Of the HARTFORD WITS, Trumbull produced *M'Fingal*, a Hudibrastic *satire* on Tories. Hopkinson amusingly attacked the British in his "Battle of the Kegs" (1778). Freneau (*The British Prison Ship*) wrote the strongest Revolutionary *satire*. Shortly after the Revolution, the *Anarchiad*, by Trumbull, Barlow, Humphreys, and Hopkins, and *Modern Chivalry* (fiction), by Brackenridge, attacked domestic political difficulties and the crudities of our frontier. Irving's good-humored *satire* in *The Sketch Book* and "Knickerbocker's" *History*, Holmes's society verse, Lowell's dialect poems (*Biglow Papers*), and Mark Twain's prose represent the general trend of American satire up to the twentieth century. In the twentieth century such British writers as G. B. Shaw, Noël Coward, Evelyn Waugh, and Aldous Huxley maintained the satiric spirit in the face of the gravity of NATURALISM and the earnestness of SYMBOLISM. In America, Eugene O'Neill (on occasion), Edith Wharton, Sinclair Lewis, George Kaufman and Moss Hart, John P. Marquand, and Joseph Heller commented satirically on human beings and their institutions.

Satire is of two major types: *formal* (or direct) *satire*, in which the satiric voice speaks, usually in the first person, either directly to the reader or to a character in the *satire*, called the ADVERSARIUS; and *indirect satire*, in which the *satire* is expressed through a narrative and the characters who are the butt are ridiculed by what they themselves say and do. Much of great literary *satire* is indirect; one of the principal forms of indirect satire is the MENIPPEAN.

Formal satire is fundamentally of two types, named for its distinguished classical practitioners: *Horatian* is gentle, urbane, smiling; it aims to correct by broadly sympathetic laughter; *Juvenalian* is biting, bitter, angry; it points with contempt and indignation to the corruption of human beings and institutions. Addison is a *Horatian* satirist, Swift a *Juvenalian*.

For centuries the word *satire*, which literally means "a dish filled with mixed fruits," was reserved for long poems, such as the pseudo-Homeric *Battle of the Frogs and Mice*, the poems of Juvenal and Horace, Langland's *The Vision of Piers Plowman*, Chaucer's "Nun's Priest's Tale," Butler's *Hudibras*, Pope's "The Rape of the Lock," and Lowell's *A Fable for Critics*. Almost from its origins, however, the drama has been suited to the satiric spirit, and from Aristophanes to Shaw and Noël Coward, it has commented with penetrating irony on human foibles. There was a notable concentration of its attention on Horatian *satire* in the COMEDY OF MANNERS of the RESTORATION

AGE. But it has been in the fictional narrative, particularly the novel, that *satire* has found its chief modern vehicle. Cervantes, Rabelais, Voltaire, Swift, Fielding, Jane Austen, Thackeray, Mark Twain, Edith Wharton, Sinclair Lewis, Aldous Huxley, Evelyn Waugh, John P. Marquand, Joseph Heller, and Thomas Pynchon all have made extended fictional narratives the vehicles for a wide-ranging and powerfully effective satiric treatment of human beings and institutions.

Founded in England in 1841, *Punch* maintained a high level of comic *satire* until closing in 1992. After being re-launched in 1996, the magazine finally ceased publication in 2002. In America, *The New Yorker* has demonstrated since 1925 the continuing appeal of sophisticated Horatian *satire*. The motion pictures, the plastic and graphic arts, and the newspaper comic strip and political cartoon have all been instruments of satiric comment on human affairs. The playwright and wit George S. Kaufman is supposed to have said that "Satire is what closes on Saturday night"—a remark that gave the title in 1975 to NBC's *Saturday Night*, later *Saturday Night Live*, a long-running television *satire*.

[References: R. C. Elliott, *The Power of Satire: Magic, Ritual, Art* (1960); John Heath-Stubbs, *The Verse Satire* (1969); Alvin Kernan, *The Cankered Muse: Satire of the English Renaissance* (1959); Ronald Paulson, *Satire and the Novel in Eighteenth-Century England* (1967); John Peter, *Complaint and Satire in Early English Literature* (1956); James Sutherland, *English Satire* (1958).]

Saturday Club A club of literary and scientific people in and around Cambridge and Boston in the mid-nineteenth century who came together chiefly for social intercourse and good conversation, at irregular intervals. Some of the more famous members were Emerson, Longfellow, Agassiz, Prescott, Whittier, and Holmes; among the frequent visitors were Hawthorne, Motley, and Sumner. Holmes paid tribute to the organization in verse (*At the Saturday Club*), and Dr. E. W. Emerson wrote an official history.

Satyr Play The fourth and final play in the bill of tragedies in Greek drama: so called because the CHORUS was made up of horse-tailed goat-men called satyrs. The *satyr play* was intended to bring COMIC RELIEF after the three tragedies that preceded it. It had the structure of a tragedy and subject matter from serious mythology but was grotesquely comic in manner. Euripides's *Cyclops* is the only surviving *satyr play*. It has been conjectured that Euripides's *Alcestis* may belong to the type, and a few lineaments survive in that play's modern avatar, Eliot's *The Cocktail Party*. Thornton Wilder wrote a modern *satyr play, The Drunken Sisters*. Since Igor Stravinsky's *Oedipus Rex* is too short to make up a whole program, it has been suggested that the same composer's *Mavra* follow it "as *satyr play*." W. H. Auden applied "miniature *satyr play*" to the intermezzo called "The Judgment of Calliope" in *The Bassarids*. The American composer Harry Partch's *Plectra and Percussion Dances* is subtitled *Satyr-Play Music for Dance Theater*.

Saussurean Linguistics An influential theory derived from the work of the Swiss linguist Ferdinand de Saussure (1857–1913). Saussure tried to put linguistics on a scientific footing by emphasizing the priority of the abstract underlying system of language (*la langue*) over particular mutable manifestations thereof in actual speech (*la parole*), along with the priority of timeless or simultaneous phenomena considered synchronically over historical or successive phenomena considered diachronically. He defined the linguistic SIGN as a combination of a SIGNIFIER and a SIGNIFIED and insisted that the essential nature of the sign is an arbitrary and conventional relation that does not reach out, back, or down to any substance, entity, or absolute outside language. Saussure's emphasis on synchronic systems—instead of diachronic so-called organisms somehow evolving continuously—has had far-reaching effects in linguistic and literary study, anthropology, psychiatry, and historiography. Because signifier and signified are radically discontinuous, and because the system of language is similarly discontinuous from any world conceived of as its environment, a staggering range of concepts have to be modified. We are enjoined to take care in thinking about etymology as important; "noon" and "November," say, both contain an element that historically means "nine," but noon is not the ninth hour and November is not the ninth month: these signs are arbitrary and can function perfectly as long as the community of speakers can agree on the meaning of "noon" and "November." (In his thinking about arbitrariness and discontinuousness, Saussure admitted a debt to the earlier American linguist William Dwight Whitney and to the school of German Neogrammarians; he could almost as well have seen a kinship with Stéphane Mallarmé.)

Because of Saussure, critics have revised their ideas of everything from ONOMATOPOEIA to MIMESIS and expression. More recently, the Saussurean concept of language as a system of differences without positive terms has been centrally important in both STRUCTURALISM and DECONSTRUCTION.

[References: Jonathan Culler, *Ferdinand de Saussure*, rev. ed. (1986; orig. 1976), *On Deconstruction: Theory and Criticism after Structuralism* (1982), and *Structuralist Poetics: Structuralism, Linguistics, and the Study of Literature* (1975); Ferdinand de Saussure, *Course in General Linguistics* (1983, tr. 1959).]

Saying A proverb (especially as "old *saying*") or a much-repeated remark supposedly said by someone.

Scald Variant spelling for SKALD, an early Scandinavian poet.

Scandal Sheet See TABLOID.

Scansion A system for describing conventional rhythms by dividing lines into FEET, indicating the locations of binomial ACCENTS, and counting the syllables. Three methods for the *scansion* of English VERSE exist: the traditional graphic one; the musical, employing musical notations; and the acoustic, developed by linguists using complex machines. However, only the graphic is readily comprehensible without much specialized knowledge. The graphic method is a written means of indicating the mechanical elements of rhythmical effects. The METER, once the scanning has been performed, is named according to the number of feet employed in a line. In English the major feet, explained elsewhere, are IAMB (˘ ´), TROCHEE (´ ˘), ANAPEST (˘ ˘ ´), DACTYL (´ ˘ ˘), SPONDEE (´ ´), and PYRRHIC (˘ ˘). A verse of one foot is called MONOMETER; two, DIMETER; three, TRIMETER; four, TETRAMETER; five, PENTAMETER; six, HEXAMETER; seven, HEPTAMETER; eight, OCTAMETER. Thus, a verse consisting of two trochaic feet is called trochaic dimeter; of five iambic, iambic pentameter; of six dactylic, dactylic hexameter.

The *scansion* of this stanza from Keats's *The Eve of St. Agnes* (when the lines are treated mechanically and the accents emphasized in reading) shows the following:

> Ănd stíll | shĕ slépt | ăn áz | ŭre-líd | dĕd sléep |
> Ĭn blánch | ĕd lín | ĕn, smóoth | ănd láv | ĕndéred, |
> Whĭle hé | frŏm fórth | thĕ clós | ĕt bróught | ă héap |

Ŏf cán | dĭed áp | plĕ, quínce, | ănd plúm, | ănd góurd; |
Wīth jél | lĭes sóoth | ĕr thán | thĕ créam | y cúrd, |
Aňd lú | cĕnt sýr | ŏps, tínct | wĭth cín | nămón; |
Mánnă | ănd dátes, | ĭn ár | gŏsý | trănsférred |
Frŏm Féz; | ănd spíc | ĕd dáin | tĭes, év | ĕry óne |
Frŏm sílk | ĕn Sám | ăr cánd | tŏ cé | dăred Léb | ă nón. |

Such a marking discloses that the rhythm is predominantly composed of one unaccented syllable followed by an accented, called an iambic foot. Next we discover that characteristically there are five feet to the line; such a line is called pentameter. We are now, as the result of our scanning, prepared to state that the measure of *The Eve of St. Agnes* can be summed up as iambic pentameter. As our stanza is scanned, there are only two obvious exceptions to this pattern: (1) the first foot of the seventh line consists of an accented syllable preceding an unaccented (a TROCHEE) and (2) the ninth line consists of six feet (a hexameter or an ALEXANDRINE). (One further possible exception is suggested by uncertainty as to the scanning of "argosy," which in normal pronunciation is a DACTYL; the final syllable may, however, receive courtesy stress of the sort called PROMOTION; see RHYME.) So, finally, we have found that our STANZA consists of eight IAMBIC PENTAMETER LINES with a ninth that is an ALEXANDRINE—a pattern called the SPENSERIAN STANZA. *Scansion* usually includes the rhyme scheme. We would say of the stanza that it rhymes *ababbcbcc*. Because, however, the rhyme scheme in the case of the SPENSERIAN STANZA is always the same, it would be redundant to say that Keats's lines make up a Spenserian stanza rhyming *ababbcbcc*.

This binary mechanical system of *scansion*, which is generally employed for English poetry, was borrowed from classical QUANTITATIVE VERSE and does not always fit readily on the English ACCENTUAL-SYLLABIC rhythmic pattern. It cannot be applied easily to SPRUNG RHYTHM or to FREE VERSE. An additional caveat is in order: the failure of a piece of English poetry to fit readily into a regular *scansion* pattern does not necessarily indicate ineptness; it may mean that the poem is constructed on rhythmic patterns that do not readily lend themselves to such analysis. The art of rhythm in any poem shows as much in apt departure from patterning as in apt adherence.

[References: Paul Fussell, *Poetic Meter and Poetic Form*, rev. ed. (1979); John Hollander, *Rhyme's Reason*, new enl. ed. (1989; orig. 1981); George Saintsbury, *Manual of English Prosody* (1930).]

Scat A vocal style developed during the 1920s, with a singer improvising patterns of repetitive nonsense syllables that suggest the sound of a musical instrument. Louis Armstrong was among the first and greatest of *scat* singers. A. R. Ammons punningly entitled a poem "Scat Scan."

Scazon Another name for the CHOLIAMB; sometimes choliamb is limited to the deliberate reversal of an IAMB. This rare and delicate effect occurs at the end of a line when a TROCHEE or DACTYL takes the place of the iamb or ANAPEST that the ear has been conditioned to expect. It can be refreshing, surprising, and even shocking. Consider the line "that the wind came out of the cloud, chilling" in Poe's "Annabel Lee," wherein the trochaic "chilling" supplants the RISING RHYTHM established by the rest of the poem. Line 186 of Tennyson's "Lucretius" shows the same effect, with a dactyl supplanting an iamb at the end: "Strikes through the wood, sets all the tops quivering." There is a dramatic reversal at the end of one line in Wallace Stevens's "Sunday Morning": "Elations when the forest blooms; gusty." There is a double *scazon* at the end of the first line of John Crowe Ransom's "Bells for John Whiteside's Daughter": "There was such speed in her little body." The American poet John Frederick Nims has accomplished a similar *doubling* of the reversal in the last two feet of the first line of his "Love Poem": "My clumsiest dear, whose hands shipwreck vases." A line of Philip Larkin's—"That how we live measures our own nature"—ends with three *scazons*. That may be the outside limit, beyond which a line is just transformed into trochees (as in the line in *King Lear*, "Never, never, never, never, never").

Scenario An outline giving the sequence of actions making up the plot and the appearances of the principal characters. The plot of a drama is itself sometimes called the *scenario*. The form of a play written as the basis of a film is also called a *scenario*. Recently, *scenario* has acquired the meaning of a provisional acting-out of possible situations, as in the jargon phrase "worst-case *scenario*."

Scène à faire A scene in a play so thoroughly prepared for that the author is obliged to provide it. See OBLIGATORY SCENE.

Scenes (of a **Drama**) The division of an ACT into *scenes* is somewhat less systematic than the division of the play itself into acts, for there is incomplete agreement about what constitutes a *scene*. Sometimes the entrances and exits of important personages determine the beginning and ending of *scenes*, as in French drama. In some plays a *scene* is a logical unit. Many English dramatists regard the clearing of the stage as the sign of a change of *scene*. Some authorities, however, think that not all stage-clearings or entrances and exits really indicate a new *scene*. Theoretically, a well-managed *scene* should have a structure comparable to that of a play itself, with the five logical parts (see DRAMATIC STRUCTURE). The plays of Shakespeare seldom conform to this requirement, though some of the *scenes* can be analyzed successfully on this basis, and we ought to remember that our divisions into *scenes* of these plays were not made by Shakespeare himself. The most important principle in *scene*-construction, perhaps, is that of climactic arrangement. There may be long *scenes* and short *scenes*, transitional *scenes*, expository *scenes*, development *scenes*, climactic *scenes*, relief *scenes*, messenger *scenes*, MONOLOGUE *scenes*, DIALOGUE *scenes*, ensemble *scenes*, forest *scenes*, battle *scenes*, balcony *scenes*, street *scenes*, garden or orchard *scenes*, court *scenes*, banquet-hall *scenes*, nude *scenes*, and chamber *scenes*. In some plays not nominally divided into acts, the main parts or sections may be called *scenes* (as in O'Neill's *The Hairy Ape* and *The Emperor Jones*), a practice that suggests, perhaps, that the dramatic action or activity implicit in "act" is subordinate to the static or symbolic display suggested by the neutral *scene*.

In film-making, a *scene* is a single shot, but the word is often applied to a sequence of several shots.

Scenic Method In a novel that can be called dramatic, that is, presenting its actions as they are imagined to occur rather than summarizing them in narrative exposition, there is a tendency for the author to construct the story in a sequence of self-explanatory scenes, similar in many respects to those of the drama. This tendency in novels using the SELF-EFFACING AUTHOR is sufficiently marked for the technique to be called the *scenic method*. The construction of a typical chapter of a Henry James novel illustrates the *scenic method:* such a chapter (it may be selected almost at random from

The Portrait of a Lady) will usually open with a detailed description of setting and of the interior state of the character through whom the action is being presented (Isabel Archer, say); then, when everything has been well prepared for, the action and conversation are presented directly and in great detail, rising to a CLIMAX on which the curtain figuratively falls at the abrupt ending. See POINT OF VIEW.

Schema A fancy word for "outline," applied nowadays to the elaborate *schemata* (Greek plural) that Joyce gave out to diagram *Ulysses*.

Scheme In RHETORIC an unusual arrangement of words in which their literal sense is not modified. See TROPE.

Schlüsselroman German for a "NOVEL with a key." See the more frequent term *ROMAN À CLEF*.

Scholasticism The name is said to have come from the title *doctor scholasticus* applied to a teacher in the religious schools established in the ninth and tenth centuries. Although such doctors were supposed to teach all of the SEVEN LIBERAL ARTS, they became chiefly professors of logic. As developed later, *scholasticism* became a complicated system that relied on logic to reconcile Christianity with reason. Using methods derived from Aristotle, *scholasticism* undertook the solution of a number of difficult philosophical and theological problems.

Scholastic reasoning as applied by different thinkers led to diverging views. The "first era" of *scholasticism* (twelfth century) marked the break from the freer reasoning of the earlier ("patristic") theologians and includes Abelard, Bernard of Clairvaux, and Anselm, "father of *scholasticism*." The second era (thirteenth century) was the flourishing, marked by the dominance of Aristotelian influence, and includes the two great Schoolmen Thomas Aquinas and Duns Scotus, heads of opposing groups known as "Thomists" and "Scotists." The third era (especially fifteenth century) marked the decline of *scholasticism*, when it became largely occupied with trivialities. This lost vitality made it an easy victim of the intellectualism of the RENAISSANCE, and *scholasticism* lost its dominance by the early sixteenth century. Indeed, the great Erasmus, typical of Renaissance humanists, at first an adherent of the scholastic method, is said to have been persuaded to forsake it by the English scholar John Colet. *Scholasticism* employed the deductive method of reasoning, and its overthrow prepared the way for the inductive method, advocated by Francis Bacon, which has led to the achievements of modern science. The positive effect of scholastic thinking on all medieval literature and thinking was incalculable in extent, and its insistence on reasoning has had a wholesome effect on succeeding thought and writing.

[References: Étienne Gilson, *The Spirit of Thomism* (1964); Jacques Maritain, *Art and Scholasticism, and the Frontiers of Poetry* (tr. 1930, reprinted 1962); Erwin Panofsky, *Gothic Architecture and Scholasticism* (1951).]

Scholiast One who provided the SCHOLIA on medieval manuscripts, particularly copies of Greek and Latin texts needing explanation.

Scholium (plural, **Scholia**) (1) An explanatory note or comment. Thomas Carlyle wrote, "Johnson's own writings . . . for some future generation may be valuable chiefly as Prolegomena and expository Scholia to this Johnsoniad of Boswell." (2) A trite saying.

Schoolmen Medieval philosophers who followed the method of SCHOLASTICISM. Called "hair-splitters" by Francis Bacon.

School of Donne Another name for the Metaphysical poets. In the preface to *For Lancelot Andrewes* (1928), T. S. Eliot announced that he had in preparation three small books, including one to be called *The School of Donne*. No such book ever appeared, but in 1961 A. Alvarez, with Eliot's permission, used the title for his own study of the Metaphysicals.

School of Night A group of Elizabethan dramatists, poets, and scholars, with, perhaps, some of the nobility. Its leader was Sir Walter Ralegh, and its members included Christopher Marlowe, George Chapman, and the mathematician Thomas Harriot. They studied the natural sciences, philosophy, and religion, and were suspected of being atheists. Shakespeare seems to condemn them in *Love's Labour's Lost* in the lines:

> . . . Black is the badge of hell,
> The hue of dungeons and the School of Night.

[References: Arthur Acheson, *Shakespeare and the Rival Poet* (1903); Muriel C. Bradbrook, *The School of Night: A Study in the Literary Relationships of Raleigh* (1936).]

School of Spenser A name given to a group of seventeenth-century poets who showed the influence of Edmund Spenser. Chief among them were Giles and Phineas Fletcher, William Browne, George Wither, William Drummond of Hawthornden, and Sir John Davies. The school is marked by sensuousness, melody, personifications, pictorial quality, interest in narrative, medievalism (especially in use of ALLEGORY), ARCHAISMS, modified or genuine SPENSERIAN STANZA, pastoralism, and moral earnestness. The art and outlook of the school led in the direction of Milton, whom they influenced. They thus form a link between Spenser and Milton, the two great Puritan poets of the English RENAISSANCE.

School Plays One of the most important traditions contributing to the development of ELIZABETHAN DRAMA was the practice of writing and performing plays at schools. Little is known of the history, extent, or character of dramatic activities in universities before the Renaissance, though there is some evidence that student plays existed throughout the late Middle Ages. Records of *school plays* from the fifteenth century possibly refer to such medieval forms as DISGUISINGS (see MASQUE). The interest in Latin drama aroused by the Italian Renaissance (Petrarch wrote a Terentian comedy about 1331) led to translations and imitations of Plautus and Terence in other countries, such as Germany and Holland (where *school plays* in the "Prodigal Son" formula flourished), and eventually England (early sixteenth century). Boys in grammar schools (St. Paul's, Eton) acted in both classical and original plays in the 1520s. By 1560 both Latin and English plays were produced at Eton, and in Spenser's time (1560s) boys at the Merchant Taylors' School performed plays annually before the queen. Nicholas Udall's *Ralph Roister Doister*, written for performance by the boys of Westminster School, is regarded as the first regular English comedy.

Of greater significance was the practice, common in the sixteenth century, of writing and performing plays at the universities. Plays by Terence were acted in Cambridge as early as 1510. In 1546 at Trinity College, Cambridge, refusal of a student to take part in a play was punishable by expulsion. Though the primary purpose of the plays was educational, entertainment for its own sake was more and more recognized, and the use of English became more and more common. When Queen Elizabeth visited Cambridge in 1564 and Oxford in 1566, she was entertained with a series of plays of various types, foreshadowing later forms on the Elizabethan stage. The earliest extant university play in English is *Gammer Gurton's Needle* (written c. 1560). Some university pieces were connected with later Elizabethan plays, such as Thomas Legge's SENECAN TRAGEDY on Richard III, which may have contributed features to Shakespeare's play. The plays were usually performed at night by costumed actors in the college hall before a restricted audience. The UNIVERSITY WITS left the universities at a time when academic plays were flourishing and went to London to play important roles during the formative period of ELIZABETHAN DRAMA.

Science Fiction A form of fantasy in which scientific facts, assumptions, or hypotheses form the basis, by logical extrapolation, of adventures in the future, on other planets, in other dimensions in time or space, or under new variants of scientific law. Conceivably, if the element of time (either past or future) is conspicuously important, then some *science fiction* may qualify as HISTORICAL FICTION. The first edition of this handbook (1936), by the way, does not mention *science fiction*; in the decades since, however, the mode has spread in popularity, gained in seriousness and dignity, and come up in the world, both in writing and in film, boosted, probably, by impressive advances in science and engineering and by quantum improvements in special effects. *Science fiction* has been honored by a number of influential critics, such as J. O. Bailey, Kingsley Amis, and Susan Sontag. Many distinguished writers, including Ray Bradbury, Kurt Vonnegut, Jr., Calder Willingham, Doris Lessing, Davis Grubb, and Thomas Pynchon, have either written *science fiction* outright or employed many of its devices and conventions in works not belonging to the genre. Many readers—and many critics and scholars as well—have come to appreciate *science fiction* in itself and in its potential relations to fantasy, utopia, folklore, and medievalism. See FANTASY.

[References: Kingsley Amis, *New Maps of Hell: A Survey of Science Fiction* (1960); J. O. Bailey, *Pioneers through Space and Time: Trends and Patterns in Scientific and Utopian Fiction* (1947, reprinted 1972); H. Bruce Franklin, *Future Perfect: American Science Fiction of the Nineteenth Century* (1966, rev. ed. 1978); Ursula K. Le Guin, *The Language of the Night: Essays on Fantasy and Science Fiction*, rev. ed. (1989; orig. 1979); Walter E. Meyers, *Aliens and Linguists: Language Study and Science Fiction* (1980); Darko Suvin, *Metamorphoses of Science Fiction: On the Poetics and History of a Literary Genre* (1979); Colin Wilson, *Science Fiction as Existentialism* (1978).]

Scop An Anglo-Saxon court poet. Though the *scop* probably traveled from court to court like the GLEEMAN, he occupied a position of importance in the king's retinue comparable to that of the Welsh BARD and the Irish FILIDH. He was a composer as well as a reciter, and his themes were drawn chiefly from the heroic traditions of the early Germanic peoples, though later he employed biblical themes, and he was probably expected to eulogize the family that employed him.

Scoptic Characterized by jeering and mockery, usually applied to SATIRE. As a noun, *scoptic* refers to a piece of satirical writing.

Scottish Chaucerians Poets of fifteenth- and sixteenth-century Scotland who wrote in imitation of Chaucer. They included Robert Henryson, William Dunbar, Gavin Douglas, and James I (*The Kingis Quair*).

Scottish Literature The main stream of the literature of Scotland is a part of English literary history. The fact of political independence in early times and the use of the Scots language or Scottish dialect of English by many writers, however, warrants special notice. John Barbour's *Bruce* (1375), a sort of Scottish national epic, is often taken as the beginning of *Scottish literature*. In the fifteenth and sixteenth centuries there flourished a school of SCOTTISH CHAUCERIANS. Somewhat later appeared Sir David Lyndsay's *Satire of the Three Estates*, an ambitious MORALITY PLAY reportedly acted in 1540. Early Scotland is noted, too, for popular BALLADS, some of which probably belong to the fifteenth and sixteenth centuries, though most seem to have been composed a century or more later. The controversial prose, on religious and political topics, of the famous John Knox (sixteenth century) encouraged the use of English by Scottish writers. Among the poets, Alexander Montgomerie (c. 1545–c. 1610) is sometimes called the last of the native Scottish "makers." By the seventeenth century the Scottish dialect as a literary vehicle was rare.

A migration of Scottish professional and business people to London in the seventeenth and eighteenth centuries makes a separation of Scottish and English literature increasingly difficult. In poetry the works of James Thomson (*The Seasons*) and Robert Blair (*The Grave*) are noteworthy in English literary history, as are such prose pieces as Adam Smith's *Wealth of Nations* and David Hume's *Enquiry Concerning Human Understanding*. At the very end of the century appeared Robert Burns, whose use of native dialect (following a tradition set by Allan Ramsay and others) found an immediate response in the literary circles of Edinburgh.

Though much conscious feeling for native tradition appears in some nineteenth-century Scottish writers (such as Sir Walter Scott) and though the native dialects have been employed by such writers of regional literature as J. M. Barrie (see KAILYARD SCHOOL), in general literary writers of Scottish birth (for example, Carlyle, Stevenson) have been regarded, since 1800, as English. One notable achievement in English literary history was the establishment in Scotland in the early nineteenth century of literary and critical magazines, among them the *Edinburgh Review* (1802). The best-known modern Scottish writer has been C. M. Grieve ("Hugh MacDiarmid").

[References: Alan Bold, *Modern Scottish Literature* (1983); Maurice Lindsay, *History of Scottish Literature* (1977); Trevor Royle, *The Macmillan Companion to Scottish Literature* (1983).]

Scribal Error An error made by a SCRIBE in the copying of a manuscript. The commonest involve spelling and translation. It is possible that the modern word *syllabus* came about because of a *scribal error* in copying *sittybas*, a Latin version of a Greek word.

Scribe Anyone who writes, specifically a copyist of manuscripts of classical or medieval texts.

Scriblerus Club A club organized in London in 1714 by Jonathan Swift to satirize literary incompetence. Among its members were Pope, Arbuthnot, Bolingbroke, Gay, and Congreve. It expressed its opinions of the false taste of the age, particularly in learning, through the satiric fragment, *The Memoirs of the Extraordinary Life, Works, and Discoveries of Martinus Scriblerus*, written in large part by Arbuthnot.

Scriptural Drama Plays based on the Old and New Testaments, produced first by churches and then by town guilds in the Middle Ages. See MYSTERY PLAY.

Scythism, Scythianism A movement in Russian culture from 1910 on, favoring the PRIMITIVISM associated with Russia's ancient Asiatic past over the sophistication of modern western Europe. The ancient Scythians have been claimed as ancestors by some modern Russians. The most important manifestations of *Scythism* have been in such music as Stravinsky's *The Rite of Spring* and Prokofiev's *Scythian Suite*.

Secondary Stress A stress that is medial in weight (or force) between a full (primary) stress and an unstressed syllable. It usually occurs in polysyllabic words but is sometimes the result of the cadence and sense of a line. In the word élĕmèntăry the third syllable carries a stress, indicated by the mark ˋ, lighter than that on the first syllable. However, in the scansion of English verse, the rhythmic pattern is formed of stressed and unstressed syllables, and those with *secondary stress* are conventionally resolved into one or the other. In actual practice, however, *secondary stress* creates effective variations within basically regular lines. See DIPODY.

Self-effacing Author When OBJECTIVITY is so used in the narrative POINT OF VIEW that the author ostensibly ceases to exist and seems to become merely an impersonal and nonevaluating medium through whom the story is witnessed, the author is said to be *self-effacing*. The *self-effacing author* is a typical device in the SCENIC METHOD.

Semantics The study of meaning; sometimes limited to linguistic meaning (see LINGUISTICS); and sometimes used to discriminate between surface and substance.

Semiotics The study of the rules that enable social phenomena, considered as SIGNS, to have meaning. Hence, in literary criticism, *semiotics* is the analysis of literature in terms of language, conventions, and modes of discourse.

If there is a causal relation between form and meaning, as in "That wound was made by a bullet," the form is called an index and the relation between form and meaning can be studied by an appropriate branch of science and not by *semiotics*. A common sort of index, in this sense, is the symptom, which is a part of an affliction used in the diagnosis of the whole. That is, the disease is the cause and the symptoms are the effects. If the relationship is one of resemblance, as in "This photograph is of John Banks," the form is called an icon, to be analyzed by philosophical theories of representation and not by *semiotics*. If there is a relation between the object and its respondent, as between the Cross and a believing Christian, or if the relation between form and meaning is the "unmotivated" or arbitrary product of convention, the form is a sign and can be analyzed by *semiotics*.

When *semiotics* is used in literary criticism, it deals not with the simple relation between sign and significance, but with literary conventions, such as those of prosody, genre, or received interpretations of literary devices at particular times. It studies how these conventions create meanings unique to such literary expression. If a prose statement is converted into verse, although it may still literally say the same thing, its meaning undergoes change through the effect of the conventions of versification used in making the conversion; *semiotics* would attempt to concentrate on those conventions. In practice, *semiotics* often appears to emphasize the extent to which works of art are about the making of works of art. With an increase in anxious skepticism and linguistic sophistication, a reader may grow morbidly aware of the limitations of any system of signs, so that a work of art may be dismissed, ignored, or attacked as a mere fiction with no relevance. Modern writing in particular seems to have become self-conscious of its precarious, contingent situation about which both reader and writer entertain doubts. Joseph Conrad, for example, often seems not to be telling a story directly but rather to be telling a story about telling a story (so doing the thing, as Henry James observed, that it takes the most doing); Tennessee Williams seems, in *The Glass Menagerie*, not to be presenting a play directly but rather to be dramatizing one process by which a playwright arrives at the position of being able to write a play. But, paradoxically, the very presence of an uncertain author-surrogate such as Conrad's Marlow or Williams's Tom Wingfield seems to disarm our skepticism so that we may regard the work as realistic after all. In scrutinizing these devices, we may be helped by *semiotics*.

[References: Jonathan Culler, *The Pursuit of Signs—Semiotics, Literature, Deconstruction* (1981); Umberto Eco, *A Theory of Semiotics* (1976); Julia Kristeva, *Revolution in Poetic Language* (tr. 1984); Robert Scholes, *Semiotics and Interpretation* (1982); Wendy Steiner, ed., *The Sign in Music and Literature* (1981).]

Senecan Style The anti-Ciceronian style of the late sixteenth and seventeenth centuries. It is abrupt and uneven, giving the effect of unadorned factual statement. Its chief characteristic is the so-called exploded period, a series of independent statements set down in simple sentences or clauses and tied together, if at all, by coordinating conjunctions. It tends to be jagged and excited. It is sometimes called ATTIC. See CICERONIAN STYLE.

[Reference: George Williamson, *The Senecan Amble: A Study in Prose Form from Bacon to Collier* (1951).]

Senecan Tragedy The nine Latin tragedies attributed to the Stoic philosopher Seneca (first century) were modeled largely on the Greek tragedies of Euripides (but written to be recited rather than acted); they exerted a great influence on Renaissance playwrights, who thought them intended for actual performance. In general the plays are marked by: (1) conventional five-act division (a formal design that we seem to owe to Seneca); (2) the use of a CHORUS (for comment rather than participation in the action) and such STOCK CHARACTERS as a ghost, a cruel tyrant, the faithful male servant, and the female CONFIDANTE; (3) the presentation of action (especially the horrors) through long reports recited by messengers as a substitute for stage action; (4) the employment of sensational themes drawn from Greek mythology, involving "blood and lust" material connected with unnatural crimes, such as cannibalism, incest, infanticide, and often motivated by revenge and leading to retribution; (5) a highly rhetorical style marked by HYPERBOLE, exaggerated comparisons, APHORISMS, EPIGRAMS, and the sharp line-for-line dialogue known as STICHOMYTHIA; and (6) the lack of careful characterization but much use of introspection and SOLILOQUY.

Renaissance HUMANISM stimulated interest in the *Senecan tragedies*, and they were translated and imitated in early court and school DRAMA in Italy, France, and England. The first English tragedy, Sackville and Norton's *Gorboduc* (acted 1562), was an imitation of Seneca, as were such later INNS-OF-COURT plays as *Jocasta* (acted 1566), *Tancred and Gismund* (acted 1568), and *The Misfortunes of Arthur* (1588), some of which were influenced by Italian Senecan plays rather than by the Latin plays themselves. After 1588, two groups of English *Senecan tragedies* are to be distinguished. The Countess of Pembroke and playwrights under her influence produced "true" Senecan plays modeled on the French *Senecan tragedies* of Robert Garnier. In this group are Kyd's translation of Garnier's *Cornélie*, Daniel's *The Tragedy of Cleopatra* and *Philotas* (1605), and Fulke Greville's original plays, *Mustapha*, for example, based on Senecan models.

The second and far more important group begins with the plays produced by Marlowe and Kyd for the popular stage. These combined native English tragic tradition with a modified Senecan technique and led directly toward the typical ELIZABETHAN TRAGEDY. Kyd's *Spanish Tragedy*, for example, though reflecting such Senecan traits as sensationalism, bombast, and the use of the chorus and the ghost, departed from the Senecan method in placing the murders and horrors on the stage, in response to popular Elizabethan taste and in defiance of Horace's dictum that good taste demanded the handling of such matters offstage. The fashion so inaugurated led to a long line of tragedies, the greatest of which is Shakespeare's *Hamlet*. The importance of the Latin Senecan plays in the evolution of English tragedy is very great, for they called attention to drama not only as an exposition of events or as an allegory of life but also as a field for the study of human emotion. Their rhetoric aroused interest in the drama as literature, and their reflective style encouraged an effort to elevate tragedy into the realm of philosophy. Two of T. S. Eliot's most important essays are "Seneca in Elizabethan Translation" and "Shakespeare and the Stoicism of Seneca" (both 1927). Grover Smith and Hugh Kenner are among the critics who have pointed out the importance of Seneca (directly from the Latin or indirectly through the Elizabethans) in Eliot's poetry and drama. See REVENGE TRAGEDY, TRAGEDY OF BLOOD.

[References: H. B. Charlton, *The Senecan Tradition in Renaissance Tragedy* (1921, 1946); T. S. Eliot, *Selected Essays*, 3rd ed. (1951, reprinted 1972; orig. 1932).]

Senryu Named for the poet Karai Senryu (1718–1790), the *senryu* has the same form as the HAIKU—seventeen syllables arranged in lines of five, seven, and five syllables—but a different spirit, relying on humor or satire rather than conventions related to certain seasons.

Sensibility A term for a reliance on feelings as guides to truth and not on reason and law. It is connected with such eighteenth-century attitudes as PRIMITIVISM, SENTIMENTALISM, the NATURE movement, and other aspects of ROMANTICISM. The high value that the eighteenth century put on *sensibility* was a reaction against the STOICISM of the seventeenth century and the theories advanced by Hobbes and others that human beings were motivated primarily by self-interest. Benevolence, resting on the ability to sympathize to a marked degree with the joys and the sorrows of one's fellows, was asserted by many, notably the third Earl of Shaftesbury, as an innate human characteristic. From this position to the idea of the virtue of the sympathetic tear was a short distance soon traveled. This extreme *sensibility* expressed itself in SENTIMENTAL COMEDY and in the SENTIMENTAL NOVEL.

Nowadays the term *sensibility* is used in a different sense, to designate innate sensitivity to sensory experience, out of which the poet fashions his or her art. It is most common in the phrase "DISSOCIATION OF SENSIBILITY," by which T. S. Eliot designates the disunion of feeling and thought that presumably occurred in English poetry with Dryden and Milton.

Sensual and Sensuous *Sensuous* is a critical term characterizing writing that plays fully on the various senses of the reader. The term is not to be confused with *sensual*, which is now generally used in an unfavorable sense and implies writing that is fleshly or carnal, in which the author displays the voluptuous. *Sensuous*, then, denotes writing that makes a restrained use of the various senses; *sensual* denotes writing that approaches unrestrained abandonment to one sense—the passion of physical love. Through the careful use of images that appeal to the senses, such as Keats makes in *The Eve of St. Agnes*, writing may be said to be made *sensuous*, a quality that Milton stipulated as characterizing good poetry in his famous estimate of poetry as "simple, sensuous, and passionate." The writing of Ernest Hemingway, with its use of physical images and its attempt to "rub the fact on the exposed nerve end," is markedly *sensuous*, though only occasionally *sensual*. In a quite different style, Thomas Wolfe's writing, evoking sharp sensory response—especially to smells and tastes—is also *sensuous*.

Sentence A rhetorical term formerly in use in the sense of MAXIM (Latin *sententia*), usually applied to quoted "wise sayings." In old writings, too, the student may come on the use of *sentence* for *sense, gist*, or *theme*, as when Chanticleer in Chaucer's "Nun's Priest's Tale" tell Pertelot (trickily) that the *sentence* of the Latin phrase is such and such. Chaucer describes the speech of his taciturn Clerk as "short and quyk and ful of hy sentence" (the last four words echoed five centuries later by J. Alfred Prufrock).

Sententia A Latin term for a short, pithy statement of general truth. See APHORISM, MAXIM, SENTENCE.

Sentimental Comedy Just as the COMEDY OF MANNERS reflected in its immorality the reaction of the Restoration from the severity of the Puritan code on the Commonwealth period, so the comedy that displaced it, known as *sentimental comedy*, or "reformed comedy," sprang up in the early years of the eighteenth century in response to a growing reaction against the tone of Restoration plays. Signs of this reaction appeared soon after the dethronement of James II (1688) and found influential expression in Jeremy Collier's famous *Short View of the Immorality and Profaneness of the English Stage* (1698), which charged that plays as a whole "rewarded debauchery," "ridiculed virtue and learning," and were "disserviceable to probity and religion." Although Colley Cibber's *Love's Last Shift* (1696) shows transitional anticipations of the new reformed comedy, Richard Steele is generally regarded as the founder of the type. His *The Funeral* (1701), *The Lying Lover* (1703), and *The Tender Husband* (1705) reflect the development of the form, and his *The Conscious Lovers* (1722) is the classic example of the fully developed type.

Because of the violence of its reaction, *sentimental comedy* became very weak dramatically, lacking humor, reality, spice, and lightness of touch. The characters were either so good or so bad that they became caricatures, and plots were violently handled so that virtue would triumph. The dramatists resorted shamelessly to sentimental emotion in their effort to interest and move the spectators. The hero in *The Conscious Lovers* ("conscious" in the sense of "conscientious") is perfectly moral; he has no bad habits; he is indifferent to "sordid lucre" and superior to all ordinary passions. His conversations with the heroine Indiana, whom he loves but who agrees with him that he must marry Lucinda to please his parents, are travesties. Where the comedy of manners of the preceding age had sacrificed moral tone in its effort to amuse, the *sentimental comedy* sacrificed dramatic reality in its effort to instruct through an appeal to the heart. The domestic trials of middle-class couples are usually portrayed: Their private woes are exhibited with much emotional stress intended to arouse the spectator's pity and suspense in advance of the approaching melodramatic happy ending.

This comedy held the boards for more than a half century. Hugh Kelly's *False Delicacy* (1768), first acted shortly before the appearance of Goldsmith's *Good Natured Man* (brought out in protest against *sentimental comedies*), and Richard Cumberland's *The West Indian* (1771) illustrate the complete development of the type. Though weakened by the attacks and dramatic creations of Goldsmith and Sheridan, who revived in a somewhat chastened form the old comedy of manners, plays of the sentimental type lived on until after the middle of the nineteenth century, though no longer dominant. The DOMESTIC TRAGEDY of a sentimental sort developed by Nicholas Rowe (1674–1718) and George Lillo (1693–1739) shows many of the same characteristics as the comedy with which it coexisted. Both forms have the same fundamentals as those of MELODRAMA.

Sentimentalism The term is used in two senses: (1) an overindulgence in emotion, especially the conscious effort to induce emotion in order to enjoy it; (2) an optimistic overemphasis of the goodness of humanity (SENSIBILITY), representing in part a reaction against Calvinism, which regarded human nature as depraved. In the first sense given above *sentimentalism* is found in MELODRAMA, in the fainting heroines of sentimental fiction, in the melancholic verse of the GRAVEYARD SCHOOL, in humanitarian literature, and in such modern phenomena as film and legal and political oratory. In the second sense it appears in SENTIMENTAL COMEDY, sentimental fiction, and primitivistic poetry. Both types of *sentimentalism* figured largely in the literature of the romantic movement. Writers reflecting the eighteenth-century *sentimentalism* include Richard Steele (*The Conscious Lovers*); Joseph Warton (*The Enthusiast*); William Collins and Thomas Gray in their poetry; Laurence Sterne (*A Sentimental Journey*); Oliver Goldsmith (*The Deserted Village*); and Henry Mackenzie (*The Man of Feeling*). The neoclassicists themselves, though opposed fundamentally to *sentimentalism*, sometimes exhibit it, as when Addison avers that he resorts to Westminster Abbey for the purpose of enjoying the emotions called up by the sombre surroundings. In a broad sense *sentimentalism* may be said to result whenever a reader or an audience is asked to experience an emotional response in excess of that merited by the occasion or one that has not been adequately prepared for.

[References: L. I. Bredvold, *The Natural History of Sensibility* (1962); Arthur Sherbo, *English Sentimental Drama* (1957).]

Sentimentality The effort to induce an emotional response disproportionate to the situation, and thus to substitute heightened and generally unthinking feeling for normal ethical and intellectual judgment. See SENTIMENTALISM.

Sentimental Novel The SENTIMENTALISM of the eighteenth century was reflected not only in the SENTIMENTAL COMEDY and the DOMESTIC TRAGEDY but in the early novels as well. Richardson's *Pamela, or Virtue Rewarded* (1740) was the beginning of the vogue; and although the rival REALISTIC NOVEL sprang up in protest (for example, Fielding's *Tom Jones*), the *sentimental novel* (also called NOVEL OF SENSIBILITY) continued to be popular for many years. One of the best of the type is Goldsmith's *The Vicar of Wakefield* (1766), and one of the most extravagant is Henry Mackenzie's *The Man of Feeling* (1771). Laurence Sterne's *Tristram Shandy* (1760–1767) is another example of the type.

Septenary See FOURTEENERS.

Septet A STANZA of seven lines. One form of the *septet* is the RHYME ROYAL stanza.

Septuagint A Greek version of the Old Testament begun in the third century before Christ. Still in use in the Greek church, it is the version from which New Testament writers quote. Its name (meaning "Seventy") comes from an old but discredited story that it was prepared by seventy or seventy-two Jewish scholars at the request of Ptolemy Philadelphus (309–246 B.C.).

Sequel A literary work that continues from another. A *sequel* may in fact be written before rather than after the work whose narrative it follows; whether a work is a *sequel* to another depends on the setting of the works and not on the order of their being written. For example, Cooper's *The Last of the Mohicans*, written in 1826, is technically the *sequel* to *The Deerslayer*, not written until 1841.

Sequelula A little sequel. The only familiar example is a PARODY of Thomas Hardy: Max Beerbohm's "A Sequelula to 'The Dynasts'" (1912). Possibly the odd word itself makes fun of Hardy's diction.

Serenade A composition written as though intended to be sung out of doors at night under a window and in praise of a loved one. Bayard Taylor's "Bedouin Song" was once very popular.

Serial The publication of a work—usually of prose fiction—in periodical installments. *Serial* publication was the rule around the middle of the nineteenth century, with novels published month-by-month in magazines before being issued in book form. In some cases the work was finished before serialization began, but many writers, including Dickens, composed their installments (ordinarily of a few chapters) as the *serial* was being published. The conditions of *serial* publication often have a discernible effect on the shape of the eventual novel, because it was the practice—still persisting in television and film *serials*—to end an installment at a moment of suspense or surprise (a "CLIFFHANGER"). Some newspapers and magazines continue the practice, and Norman Mailer experimented with *serial* composition and publication of his novel *An American Dream*, but there has been a great falling off from the heyday of *serial* writing.

Series Generally, items arranged in a row with some sort of coherence. According to Sally M. Gall and M. L. Rosenthal, a "linked *series*" of poems presents more of design than a mere miscellany but less than a fully sustained sequence. *Series* is also used for a group of works centering on a single character or set in a single place or time, as when we speak of Lucy Maud Montgomery's "Anne of Green Gables Series" or, more familiarly, "Anne Series."

Serpentine Verse A line of poetry that begins and ends with the same word.

Sesquipedalian Literally, "a foot and a half"; used for a style unduly and pretentiously polysyllabic. The word itself is an example.

Sestet The second, six-line division of an ITALIAN SONNET. Following the eight-line division (OCTAVE), the *sestet* usually makes specific a general statement that has been presented in the octave or indicates the personal emotion of the author in a situation that the octave has developed. The preferred rhyme scheme is the *cdecde* (following the *abbaabba* of the OCTAVE), and the next best is *cdcdcd* or any other that (1) avoids the pat rhymed couplet and (2) uses not more than a total of five rhymes for the poem as a whole. Technically, any six-lined poem or stanza is a *sestet*.

Sestina One of the most difficult and complex of verse forms. The *sestina* consists of six six-lined stanzas and a three-lined ENVOY. The first *sestina* is thought to be in Provençal: "Lo ferm voler qu'el cor m'intra" by Arnaut Daniel. This form is usually unrhymed, the effect of rhyme being taken over by a fixed pattern of end-words. These end-words in each stanza must be the same, though arranged in a different sequence each time. If we take 1–2–3–4–5–6 to represent the end-words of the first stanza, then the first line of the second stanza must end with 6 (the last end-word used in the preceding stanza), the second with 1, the third with 5, the fourth with 2, the fifth with 4, the sixth with 3—and so to the next stanza. The order of the first three stanzas, for instance, would be: 1–2–3–4–5–6; 6–1–5–2–4–3; 3–6–4–1–2–5. The three-line conclusion must use as end-words 5–3–1, these being the final end-words, in the same sequence, of the sixth stanza. But the poet must exercise even greater ingenuity than all this, because buried in each line of the envoy must appear the other three end-words, 2–4–6. Thus, so highly artificial a pattern affords a form that, for most poets, can never prove anything more than a prosodic exercise. Yet it has been practiced with success in English by Sidney, Swinburne, Kipling, Auden, Nims, Ashbery, and Merrill. (A variant, with rhymes instead of repetitions, is in Eliot's "The Dry Salvages.") The strictest construction of the rule requires complete and unvarying repetition of end-words, but some license is granted in the use of identicals. In James Merrill's very clever "Tomorrows," for instance, the original set of end-words consists of "one," "two," "three," "four," "five," and "six," in that order. Later lines end with "won" and "someone"; "to," "Timbuctoo," "tu," "into," and "too"; "for," "fore," and "before"; "belief I've"; "Sikhs" and "classics." See discussion of Alan Ansen's "vanishing" *sestina* under PRUNING POEM.

[Reference: J. F. Nims, *A Local Habitation: Essays on Poetry* (1985).]

Set The physical equipment of a stage, including furniture, properties, lighting, and backdrops.

Set Piece A work of any conventional kind, designed to impress. In some uses, a performer or contestant must execute both *set pieces* and optional pieces; in literature the counterpart would be a formulaic study with little room for originality, innovation, or improvisation. In some juvenile exercises—like Milton's PROLUSIONS on topics such as the case "That Sportive Exercises Are Occasionally Not Adverse to Philosophic Studies"—one cannot escape the impression of the rather arid *set piece*.

Setting The background against which action takes place. The elements making up a *setting* are: (1) the geographical location, its topography, scenery, and such physical arrangements as the location of the windows and doors in a room; (2) the occupations and daily manner of living of the characters; (3) the time or period in which the action takes place, for example, epoch in history or season of the year; and (4) the general environment of the characters, for example, religious, mental, moral, social, and emotional conditions. When *setting* dominates, or when a work is written largely to present the manners and customs of a locality, the result is LOCAL COLOR WRITING or REGIONALISM. The term is also often applied to the stage *setting* of a play. See MISE EN SCÈNE.

Seven Cardinal Virtues In medieval theology the *seven cardinal virtues* were faith, hope, and love (drawn from biblical teaching) along with prudence, justice, fortitude, and temperance (adapted from the four cardinal virtues of the Greeks and called the natural virtues).

Seven Deadly Sins Those sins, which, according to medieval theology, entailed spiritual death and could be atoned for only by perfect penitence: pride, envy, wrath, sloth, avarice, gluttony, and lust. Dante treats all seven as arising from imperfect love—pride, envy, and wrath resulting from perverted love; sloth from defective love; avarice, gluttony, and lust from excessive love. Pride was the most heinous of the sins because it led to treachery and disloyalty, as in the case of Satan. Innumerable didactic and theological works on the *seven deadly sins* appeared in the Middle Ages. The conception permeated the literature of medieval and Renaissance times, its influence not only appearing in the ideas implicit in many literary works but often controlling the very structure, as in Dante's *Purgatorio*, in which the "visions" are built around the seven sins. A few examples of the idea in English literature are: Chaucer's "Parson's Tale" in the *Canterbury Tales*, Langland's *The Vision of Piers Plowman*, Gower's *Confessio Amantis*, and Spenser's *The Faerie Queene* (book 1, canto 4).

Seven Liberal Arts The seven subjects studied in the medieval university. The three studies pursued during the four-year course leading to the Bachelor of Arts degree were known as the trivium. They were grammar (Latin), logic, and rhetoric (especially public speaking). The four branches following in the three-year course leading to the Master of Arts degree were arithmetic, music, geometry, and astronomy (the quadrivium).

Sextain A STANZA or STROPHE of six lines. Poems so titled by William Drummond of Hawthornden rhyme *ababcc*.

Sfumato An Italian word meaning "smoked" that refers to a quality of smokily obscuring details in a painting; later applied to film and television productions with a similar quality: vapory, foggy, soft-focus, dark or dim.

Shakespeare, Early Editions of About half of Shakespeare's plays were printed separately during his lifetime in QUARTO editions, presumably without the author's consent in most cases. Shakespeare was a shareholder in the company that acted his plays, and companies owning acting rights often objected to efforts to sell their plays in printed form while the plays were in their current repertoire. Though there may have been an imperfect effort in 1619, three years after the dramatist's death, to get together a collection of Shakespeare's plays, the first edition is the famous First Folio (1623) prepared by Shakespeare's friends, the actors John Heminge and Henry Condell. For several reasons the texts in the First Folio vary greatly in accuracy. Some follow quarto texts closely, others vary in both length and readings, and there are a good many mistakes—for example, the printing of one word for another similar in sound or spelling—so that in many places we cannot be sure what Shakespeare wrote. There is also reason for thinking that the folio both omits plays that Shakespeare wrote, at least in part (as *Pericles*), and includes some that he possibly had little to do with (see PSEUDO-SHAKESPEAREAN PLAYS). This situation has created problems that have concerned later editors. The Second Folio appeared in 1632 and a third in 1663, the third being reissued in 1664 with *Pericles* and six "spurious" plays added. The fourth was printed in 1685. These late folios were only slightly edited.

The first real editor of Shakespeare was Nicholas Rowe. In his editions (1709 and 1714) Rowe made some corrections in the text, modernized the punctuation and spelling, supplied lists of characters, made act and scene divisions for most of the plays (this had been partly done in the folios), and added stage directions. In 1725 Alexander Pope undertook to make an authoritative edition. In fact, however, he did some mischievous tampering with Rowe's text, and he omitted the seven plays not in the First Folio. Pope's work was followed by a careful edition by Lewis Theobald (1733), who had before exposed some of Pope's mistakes and made some ingenious emendations. In retaliation Pope made Theobald the chief dunce in the revised edition of his *Dunciad*. In 1765 appeared the famous edition of Samuel Johnson, whose preface and notes have critical value.

Edward Capell (1768) made the first serious effort to prepare a scientific text based on all the early editions, including quartos. In 1773 appeared the Johnson-Steevens VARIORUM EDITION; this reappeared in 1785 with revisions by Isaac Reed. In 1790 was printed an edition by the important scholar Edward Malone, whose still more extensive "third variorum" edition, published after Malone's death by James Boswell (the younger), came in 1821. Many editions have appeared since. Most of the plays were edited separately in the *New Variorum Shakespeare* (beginning in 1871), by Henry Howard Furness (father and son), which undertakes to give a complete abstract of all earlier efforts to establish a text.

Shakespearean Sonnet The ENGLISH SONNET, rhyming *abab cdcd efef gg*, so called because Shakespeare was its most distinguished practitioner.

Shanty A sailor's working SONG. See CHANTEY.

Shaped Verse A poem so constructed that its printed form suggests its subject matter. See CARMEN FIGURATUM.

Short Couplet An octasyllabic couplet; two rhyming lines of iambic or trochaic tetrameter.

Short Measure (or **Meter**) A stanza widely used for hymns, consisting of four lines rhyming either *abab* or *abcb*. It usually has the first, second, and fourth lines in IAMBIC TRIMETER and the third in iambic TETRAMETER. "Blessed Be the Tie That Binds" is perhaps the best known hymn in *short measure*. It has been observed that a single basic metrical pattern runs through *short measure*, POULTER'S MEASURE, the LIMERICK, and certain NURSERY RHYMES (such as "Hickory Dickory Dock"). A passage of doggerel in Shakespeare's *King Lear* (3.4.112ff.) looks a lot like *short measure:*

> Swithold footed thrice the 'old;
> He met the nightmare, and her nine fold;
> Bid her alight
> And her troth plight,
> And aroint thee, witch, aroint thee!

W. S. Gilbert's "Poor Wand'ring One" (*The Pirates of Penzance*) is a *short measure* lyric, as are several of Emily Dickinson's poems: "A Bird came down the Walk," "The Heart asks Pleasure—first," "Ample make this Bed," "The Bustle in a House," and "There's a certain Slant of light." Thomas Hardy (ten years younger than Dickinson) used *short measure* in "'I Look into My Glass'" and "The Man He Killed." See COMMON METER.

Short Novel A work of an intermediate length between the SHORT STORY and the NOVEL, roughly between 15,000 and 50,000 words. Where the short story is usually content to reveal a character through an action, to be what Joyce called an EPIPHANY, the *short novel* is concerned with character development. Where the novel in its concern with character development employs a broad canvas, a number of characters, and frequently a long time span, the *short novel* concentrates on a limited cast of characters, a relatively short time span, and a single chain of events. Thus, it is an artistic attempt to combine the compression of the short story with the development of the novel. Although no one has ever formulated a wholly satisfactory definition of the *short novel*, it has had a distinctive history. Henry James, who did distinguished work in the form, called it "our ideal, the beautiful and blest *nouvelle*." Other writers who have found it an attractive form in which to work include: Sterne, Melville, Tolstoi, Conrad, Thomas Mann, Kafka, Camus, Gide, Moravia, Wharton, Wolfe, Steinbeck, Faulkner, Woolf, Cather, Fitzgerald, and John O'Hara.

Short-Short Story A brief short story, usually no more than 2,000 words, sometimes with a surprise ending. Its best-known practitioner was O. Henry.

Short Story Egyptian papyri dating from 4000 B.C. reveal how the sons of Cheops regaled their father with narrative. Some three hundred years before the birth of Christ, we had such Old Testament stories as those of Jonah and of Ruth. Christ spoke in parables. A hair-raising werewolf story is embedded in Petronius's *Satyricon*. In the Middle Ages the impulse to storytelling manifested itself in fables and epics about beasts and in the MEDIEVAL ROMANCE. In England, about 1250, some two hundred well-known tales were collected in the *Gesta Romanorum*. In the middle of the fourteenth century Boccaccio assembled the hundred tales in *The Decameron*. In the same century Chaucer wrote his framework collection, *The Canterbury Tales*. In the eighteenth century came the modern novel, growing out of the PICARESQUE NOVEL of the sixteenth and seventeenth centuries. The eighteenth century also saw the development of the INFORMAL ESSAY, which frequently derived some of its interest from such episodes and sketches as Addison uses in the "Sir Roger de Coverley papers" or "The Vision of Mirzah." In France in the second half of the eighteenth century, Denis Diderot made important contributions to the development of the *short story*. In the nineteenth century came Scott, Irving, Hawthorne, Poe, Mérimée and Balzac, Gautier and Musset,

Maupassant, Chekhov, and E. T. A. Hoffman. With these writers the *short story* as a distinct genre came into being. Some of these writers consciously formulated the *short story* as an art form. This development flowered with such speed and force in America that the modern *short story* is often called an American art form, with only minor exaggeration.

In the mid-nineteenth century, under the impulse of Poe's persuasive statement in his 1842 review of Hawthorne's *Twice-Told Tales*, critics postulated a definite structure and technique for the *short story*. To this was added, around the end of the century, the tight "surprise-ending story" of O. Henry, and the *short story* came to be thought of as corresponding to a formula, a pattern that was much repeated in the popular *short story*. After the turn of the century, however, the impact of REALISM and NATURALISM joined with the example of Chekhov's SLICE OF LIFE stories to force open the formula, and such masters of the form as Somerset Maugham and Katherine Mansfield in England and Sherwood Anderson, F. Scott Fitzgerald, Ernest Hemingway, and, most recently, Raymond Carver in America developed the *short story* to a dominant form of literary expression in the twentieth century.

A *short story* is a relatively brief fictional NARRATIVE in PROSE. It may range in length from the SHORT-SHORT STORY of 500 words up to the "long-short story" of 12,000 to 15,000 words. It may be distinguished from the SKETCH and the TALE in that it has a definite formal development, a firmness in construction. It finds its unity in many things other than plot—although it often finds it there—in effect, theme, character, tone, mood, and style. It may be distinguished from the NOVEL in that it tends to reveal character through actions, the purpose of the story being accomplished when the reader comes to know what the true nature of a character is. The novel tends, on the other hand, to show character developing as a result of actions.

However natural and formless the *short story* may sometimes give the impression of being, a distinguishing characteristic of the genre is that it is consciously *made* and reveals itself to be the result of conscious, skilled work. Furthermore, however slight the *short story* may appear, it consists of more than a mere record of an incident or an ANECDOTE. It has a beginning, a middle, and an end; it possesses at least the rudiments of plot.

Short Title A shortened form of a title. In quite a few cases, a *short title* is much more familiar and convenient than what an author originally called a work. Thus, we seldom speak of *The Life of Timon of Athens, Alice's Adventures in Wonderland*, or *An Essay in Aid of a Grammar of Assent. Huckleberry Finn* serves as a respectable *short title* in place of *The Adventures of Huckleberry Finn*. Such usages as *Huck Finn* and "Prufrock," however, are better called "nicknames," which some may consider in bad taste.

Short-Title Catalogue Of several such catalogues, the best known is that compiled in 1926 by A. W. Pollard and G. R. Redgrave: *A Short-Title Catalogue of Books Printed in England, Scotland, and Ireland and of English Books Printed Abroad 1475–1640*, offered as "a catalogue of the books of which its compilers have been able to locate copies, not a bibliography of books known or believed to have been produced." A second edition, begun by W. A. Jackson and F. S. Ferguson and completed by Katharine F. Pantzer, came out in 1991 in three volumes. Donald Wing's three-volume *Short-Title Catalogue of Books Printed in England . . . and British America 1641–1700* was published between 1945 and 1951.

Shot A unit of film-making, measured as a continuous running of the camera.

Showing versus Telling An empirical concept, unsophisticated but still useful, that emphasizes the superiority of dramatization, demonstration, enactment, and embodiment over mere telling. In *To Have and Have Not*, for example, Hemingway could have told us something rather abstract—"Shots were fired"—but he chose instead to make us see and hear: "The first thing a pane of glass went and the bullet smashed into a row of bottles on the show-case wall to the right. I heard the gun going and, bop, bop, bop, there were bottles smashing all along the wall." See DIEGESIS, MIMESIS.

Sidebar In a newspaper or magazine, material that accompanies a main story, often printed to the side in a box, to explain an aspect or detail.

Sigla (plural of **Siglum**) A letter or other written character used as a shorthand designation for versions of a text. For example, the phrase "mastry in the Arts" in Jonson's "An Execration upon Vulcan" may carry a textual note such as this:

> mastry] mistery Q mystery D

—wherein "Q" and "D" are *sigla*. The note means that the place of "mastry" in the definitive text is taken by "mistery" in Text Q (a quarto published in 1640) and by "mystery" in Text D (a duodecimo volume also published in 1640). James Joyce used emblematic *sigla*—such as Δ for "Anna Livia Plurabelle"—while *Finnegans Wake* was being written.

Sigmatism The marked use of the sibilant ("hissing") sounds represented by *s, z, sh, zh*, and so forth. Five of the six lines of Robert Herrick's "Upon Julia's Clothes" contain sibilants, as though to echo the sound of silk. Edgar Allan Poe's "Valley of Unrest" has twenty-seven lines each with its sibilants, the whole somehow planned to give an effect of unease:

> Now ea*ch* vi*s*itor *sh*all confe*ss*
> The *s*ad valley'*s* re*s*tle*ss*ne*ss*.
> Nothing there i*s* motionle*ss*—
> Nothing *s*ave the air*s* that brood
> Over the magic *s*olitude.

Tennyson tried to avoid excessive use of sibilants and is credited with calling his efforts "kicking the geese out of the boat."

Sign A radically important problem in SEMIOTICS and SAUSSUREAN LINGUISTICS with a great deal of influence on criticism. The ideal "linguistic *sign*," according to Saussure, is made up of two elements, a signifier (such as a sound-image) and a signified (such as a mental concept), and the relation between the two is arbitrary, conventional, and "unmotivated"—that is, no property of the signifier, as substance or entity, qualifies it to be a signifier. In certain systems of thought, a pure *sign* is arbitrary and variable from context to context; the letter "H" means certain things in English and something else in the Greek alphabet (*eta:* the long *e*) and something else in the Russian alphabet (*n*). A *sign* called an ICON is said to resemble the signified, as a portrait resembles its subject or a blueprint resembles the layout of a building. A *sign* called an index or symptom is a part of what it signifies or is closely associated with it as part-and-whole or cause-and-effect—as a high temperature may be a symptom or *sign* of a disease. Systems of *signs* can also be perceived in chains: a high temperature is a *sign* of fever, fever a *sign* of illness, illness a *sign* of exposure to contagion, contagion a *sign* of unwholesome living conditions, and so forth. METAPHOR and METONYMY have been classified as two sorts of signifying operation—the former by resemblance, the latter by participation; both are obviously important for literature. ALLEGORY, likewise, is a process of serial signification, in which words signify a journey, say, and the journey signifies life (as when we call a birthday a "milestone").

[Reference: Jonathan Culler, *The Pursuit of Signs: Semiotics, Literature, Deconstruction* (1981).]

Signature (in printing) A letter or figure placed at the foot of the first page of each GATHERING of a book, such a gathering consisting of the pages resulting from a sheet folded to page size; hence, the term *signature* is also applied to the gathering itself or to the sheet after it is folded and ready to be gathered. In early printing the *signature* was often placed on the first, third, fifth, and seventh pages of an OCTAVO gathering (sixteen pages). See BOOK SIZE.

Signifier and Signified In SAUSSUREAN LINGUISTICS, the two elements of a piece of language—the *signifier* being the relatively concrete and the *signified* the relatively abstract. In some situations, there are chains of *signifiers:* the written "road" signifies the spoken "road," which in turn signifies the idea of "road," which, in turn, in an ANALOGY or ALLEGORY, can signify life.

Silent Correction If an editor changes a text by correcting an indisputably obvious error with no indication that a change has been made, that correction is called "silent."

Silver-Fork School A name applied in derision to a group of nineteenth-century English novelists who emphasized gentility and etiquette. Among the members of the *Silver-Fork School* were Frances Trollope, Theodore Hook, Lady Blessington, Lady Caroline Lamb, and Benjamin Disraeli.

Simile A figure in which a similarity between two objects is directly expressed, as in Milton's "A dungeon horrible, on all sides round. / As one great furnace flamed. . . ." Here the comparison between the dungeon (Hell) and the great furnace is directly expressed in the *as*. Most *similes* are introduced by *as* or *like* or even by such a word as "compare," "liken," or "resemble." In the preceding illustration, the similarity between Hell and a furnace is based on the great heat of the two. A *simile* is generally the comparison of two things essentially unlike, on the basis of a resemblance in one aspect. It is, however, no *simile* to say, "My house is like your house," although, of course, comparison does exist. Another way of expressing it is to say that in a *simile* both TENOR and VEHICLE are clearly expressed and are joined by some overt indicator of resemblance such as "like" or "as." See METAPHOR, EPIC SIMILE.

Simpsonian Rhyme In 1943 Percy Simpson published an article entitled "The Rhyming of Stressed with Unstressed Syllables," whereupon C. S. Lewis (following the practice of naming diseases for their discoverers), in *English Literature in the Sixteenth Century*, used *Simpsonian* for such ANISOBARIC rhymes as that between "Cupid" and "did."

Simultaneism (also **Simultanism**) A French poetic movement led by Henri-Martin Barzun (father of Jacques Barzun), seeking simultaneity of images and sounds.

Situation A term for (1) a given group of circumstances in which characters find themselves or (2) the given conditions under which a story opens before the plot proper actually begins. Thus, to use *Hamlet* for illustration, the question might be asked, in the first sense, what the proper line of action was for Hamlet when he found himself in the *situation* brought about by the fact that Laertes had challenged him to a duel. In the second, and more technical, sense the *situation* consists of those events that had taken place before the play opened: the murder of Hamlet's father, the incestuous acts of his mother, the sorry condition of the state.

Situation Comedy (Sitcom) A term used in television and elsewhere to refer to a general sort of comedy, normally in a continuing series, involving scrapes, jams, and mild predicaments besetting a group of STOCK CHARACTERS.

Sixain A STANZA or STROPHE of six lines.

Skald, Scald An ancient Scandinavian poet, especially of the Viking period, corresponding roughly to the Anglo-Saxon SCOP. (The word *skald* may be related to *scold.*)

Skel Line (short for **Skeleton Line**) A short (usually one line) caption to a newspaper photograph that is accompanied by a story.

Skeltonic Verse ("Skeltonics" or "Skeltoniads") A rollicking form of verse employed by the English poet John Skelton (c. 1460–1529) consisting of short lines rhymed in groups of varying length, designed to suggest unconventionality and lack of dignity. Skelton considered such verse a fitting vehicle for his "poetry of revolt." *Skeltonic verse* is akin to DOGGEREL. Something of its spirit and characteristics, though not its full variety, may be found in the following passage from *The Tunnynge of Elynoure Rummynge:*

But to make up my tale,
She brueth noppy ale,
And maketh thereof sale
To travellers, to tinkers,
To sweaters, to swinkers,
And all good ale-drinkers,
That will nothing spare
But dryncke till they stare
And bring themselves bare,
With now away the mare
And let us slay Care,
As wise as an hare.

Skelton himself was at odds with the humanists of his day, and much of his poetry is satirical. In his desire to shock, to be novel, and to write in a form as defiant as his satire, he plays with this peculiar verse in a fashion that irritated his more formal contemporaries. *Skeltonic verse* has analogues in French and Italian; it derives from a form of medieval Latin verse associated with the unruly side of university life that was particularly distasteful to Skelton's learned humanistic contemporaries. *Skeltonic verse* is also called TUMBLING VERSE.

Sketch A brief composition presenting a single scene, character, or incident. It lacks plot and deep characterization. Originally used in the sense of an artist's *sketch* as preliminary groundwork for more developed work, it is now often employed for a finished product of simple proportions, as a character *sketch* or a VAUDEVILLE *sketch*.

Skit A short dramatic SKETCH or a brief, self-contained comic or BURLESQUE scene, usually presented as a part of a REVUE or on a television or radio program.

Slack Syllable (or **Slack**) An unstressed syllable.

Slam A mode of informal public performance and competition by poets. Poetry *slams*, first introduced in Chicago around 1990, quickly spread throughout the United States. A typical *slam*, usually in a saloon or other such setting, involves a number of persons reading their own poems to an audience that is encouraged to respond vocally while a number of judges hold up Olympic-style scorecards. Local winners may go on to regional and national competitions.

Slang A vernacular speech, not accepted as suitable for highly formal usage, though much used in conversation. The aptness of *slang* is usually based on humor, exaggeration, onomatopoeic effect, or a combination of these qualities. Frequently, too, *slang* develops as a shortcut. There are, as well, the special terms used in professions or trades, in sports, in localities, among groups possessing any common interest, including the underworld. Collections of *slang* date from the sixteenth century, but there is plenty of evidence showing that *slang* developed much earlier. François Villon, for instance, introduced much rogue's *argot* in his verses of the fifteenth century. *Slang* terms ultimately pass in one of three directions: (1) they die out and are lost unless their vividness is such that (2) they continue as *slang* over a long period, in which case (3) they frequently become accepted as standard. "Skidoo" in the sense of "go away" is an instance of the first; "guy" meaning "a man" is an instance of the second; and "banter" in the sense of "ridicule" is an example of the third. The thoroughly respectable English "salary" may have come from Roman soldiers' *slang* meaning "salt-money" or "just salt" (much as current *slang* calls money "dough" or "bread").

[References: H. L. Mencken, *The American Language*, 3 vols. and *Supplements*, 4th ed. (1963; 1919–1948); Eric Partridge, *A Dictionary of Slang and Unconventional English*, 8th ed. (1985), and *Slang, Today and Yesterday*, 4th ed. (1970).]

Slant Rhyme NEAR RHYME; usually the substitution of ASSONANCE or CONSONANCE for true rhyme. *Slant rhyme* is also called OBLIQUE RHYME, off-rhyme, and pararhyme.

Slapstick Low comedy involving physical action, practical jokes, and such actions as pie-throwing and pratfalls. The name is taken from a paddle consisting of two flat pieces of wood so attached to a handle (and maybe spring-loaded) that it makes a racket when a painless blow is struck with it.

Slave Narratives In the period between 1830 and 1860, as a part of the abolition movement in America, a number of autobiographical accounts of slavery by escaped slaves were published. The best of these *slave narratives* was *A Narrative of the Life of Frederick Douglass: An American Slave* (1845).

Sleight of "and" A general term that indicates those tropes—such as HENDIADYS, SYLLEPSIS, and ZEUGMA—that involve "and" or another coordinating conjunction.

Slice of Life A term used to describe the unselective and nonevaluative presentation of a segment of life, such as was considered an objective of the naturalists. *Slice of life* is the English translation of the French *tranche de vie*, applied to the work of Zola and the French naturalists.

Slick Magazine A magazine printed on coated—slick—paper, illustrated lavishly, and carrying extensive advertising. The term was applied in the 1920s, 1930s, and 1940s to general-circulation magazines with broad popular appeal, such as the *Saturday Evening Post* and the *American Magazine*. Although the name is taken from the kind of paper on which the magazine is printed, its use is restricted to general-purpose, mass-circulation publications. Many magazines printed on coated paper but addressed to specialized audiences are anything but *slick magazines*, as *The New Yorker, House Beautiful*, and the *National Geographic* illustrate.

Slot Man A newspaper's chief sub-editor, often the news editor.

Soap Opera, Soap Daily daytime drama series broadcast on radio and television. The early examples on radio in the 1930s, designed for a housebound audience, were often sponsored by laundry soaps and other such products; one show was even called "Oxydol's Own Ma Perkins." A few, like *The Guiding Light*, survived the transition from radio to television, but the most durable examples on television date from the 1950s. The typical *soap opera* is set in a small town, most of the action occurs indoors, and there is a good deal of conversation. The stories, which grow extremely complex, involve interactions between men and women, parents and children, rich and poor, domestic and foreign, with extended families encompassing three or more generations. By the 1970s a number of weekly prime-time television *soaps* emerged, no longer confined to daytime schedules and audiences. The most durable, such as *Dallas, Dynasty,* and *Sisters*, adhered to established melodramatic formulas with passion, intrigue, violence, villainy, suspense, and surprise aplenty. After 1985, a new style of prime-time *soap*, led by *Beverly Hills 90210* and *Melrose Place*, appealing to a younger audience, began to dominate the field. By the beginning of the twenty-first century, there were cable channels running nothing but *soaps* of one sort or another.

Society Verse Light, sophisticated verse. See *VERS DE SOCIÉTÉ*, OCCASIONAL VERSE, and LIGHT VERSE.

Sociological Criticism Study of literature that emphasizes either of two aspects of writing: (1) the conditions of production, including schools, magazines, publishers, and fashions; or (2) the applicability of a given work—fiction especially—in studying the dynamics of a given society. In some situations, the study of myth can be sociological, as in the way Émile Durkheim and Georges Dumézil approach myth as the projection of social principles (such as caste or patriarchy) onto a supernatural plane. There have also been adaptions of Max Weber's sociological theories, especially those having to do with the rise of capitalism, Protestantism, and the interaction of charisma and bureaucracy.

Sociological Novel A form of the PROBLEM NOVEL that concentrates on the nature, function, and effect of the society in which characters live. Usually, the *sociological novel* presents a thesis as a resolution to a social problem, but it is by no means always a PROPAGANDA NOVEL. The serious examination of social issues grew important with the INDUSTRIAL REVOLUTION and scrutinized the condition of laborers and their families. The result was such novels as Dickens's *Hard Times*, Kingsley's *Yeast*, and Gaskell's *Mary Barton*. George Eliot in *Middlemarch* subjected an entire provincial town to sociological examination. Stowe's *Uncle Tom's Cabin* explored the conditions and the social status of blacks, a theme that was to prove of enduring interest as a social problem through such works as G. W. Cable's *The Grandissimes* and the novels of Richard Wright and Ralph Ellison. The MUCKRAKERS at the turn of the century produced a number of *sociological novels*, the most successful being Upton Sinclair's *The Jungle*. John Steinbeck, John Dos Passos, Erskine Caldwell, and James T. Farrell all wrote novels whose central issues were sociological.

Sock The low-heeled slipper conventionally worn by the comic actor on the ancient stage, hence (figuratively) comedy itself. See BUSKIN.

Socratic The "*Socratic* method" in argument or explanation is the use of the question-and-answer formula employed by Socrates in Plato's *Dialogues*. Socrates would feign ignorance and then proceed to develop his points by the question-and-answer device. The method of assuming ignorance for the sake of taking advantage of an opponent in debate is known as "*Socratic* IRONY."

Solecism A violation of prescriptive grammatical rules. "He don't" and "between you and I" are *solecisms*. Loosely, any error in diction, grammar, or propriety is called a *solecism*. Some, however, reserve the term *solecism* for errors in grammar and idiom alone, distinguished from CATACHRESIS. Some practices classified as wrong today have not always been so (Chaucer, for example, freely indulged in double negatives); practices now regarded as wrong (the use of "loan" as a verb, for example) may gain in acceptance. Besides, a resourceful writer may use *solecism* with fine effect. Gerard Manley Hopkins uses an objective pronoun in a position calling for a nominative, as in "What I do is me" and "My taste was me." These *solecisms* have the effect of surprise and of colloquial ease (for, indeed, most speakers of English have long said things like "It's me").

Soliloquy A speech delivered while the speaker is alone (*solus*), calculated to inform the audience of what is passing in the character's mind. Hamlet's famous "To be, or not to be" is an obvious example. Browning's "Soliloquy of the Spanish Cloister" is indeed a *soliloquy;* "Porphyria's Lover" and "Johannes Agricola in Meditation" may be *soliloquies*, although the titles make no explicit statement. See also ASIDE, MONOLOGUE.

Solution A term sometimes employed in place of CATASTROPHE or DÉNOUEMENT. It is used in the sense that a *solution* is presented for the complication that was developed in the plot. See DRAMATIC STRUCTURE.

Song A lyric poem adapted to musical expression. *Song* lyrics are usually short, simple, sensuous, emotional—perhaps the most spontaneous lyric form. *Songs* have been of every type and subject. There have been working *songs*, dance *songs*, love *songs*, war *songs*, play *songs*, drinking *songs*, and *songs* for festivals, church gatherings, and political meetings, as well as a host of others. Perhaps the period in English literature richest in *songs* was the Elizabethan, when Shakespeare gave us such *song* poems as "Who is Sylvia?" and Jonson, "Drink to Me Only with Thine Eyes." The so-called popular *song* is ubiquitous and influential nowadays. *"Song"* has, furthermore, long been applied to works that cannot really be sung in the usual sense: Longfellow's *Song of Hiawatha* and Whitman's *Song of Myself* are not literally singable, nor are Eliot's "The Love-Song of J. Alfred Prufrock" and the poems called DREAM SONGS that Eliot and John Berryman wrote.

Sonnet A poem almost invariably of fourteen lines and following one of several set rhyme schemes. The two basic *sonnet* types are the ITALIAN or PETRARCHAN and the ENGLISH or SHAKESPEAREAN. The Italian form is distinguished by its division into the OCTAVE and the SESTET: the octave rhyming *abbaabba* and the sestet *cdecde, cdcdcd*, or *cdedce*. The octave presents a narrative, states a proposition, or raises a question; the sestet drives home the narrative by making an abstract comment, applies the proposition, or solves the problem. The octave–sestet division is not always kept; the rhyme scheme is often varied, but within the limitation that no Italian *sonnet* properly allows more than five rhymes or rhymed couplets in the sestet. Iambic pentameter is usual. Certain poets have, however, experimented with other meters.

In the ENGLISH or SHAKESPEAREAN *sonnet*, four divisions are used: three quatrains (each with a rhyme scheme of its own, usually rhyming alternate lines) and a rhymed concluding couplet. The typical rhyme scheme is *abab cdcd efef gg*. The SPENSERIAN SONNET complicates the Shakespearean form, linking rhymes among the quatrains: *abab bcbc cdcd ee*. (Note how the rhyme scheme resembles that of the SPENSERIAN STANZA.)

The *sonnet* developed in Italy, probably in the thirteenth century. Petrarch, in the fourteenth century, raised it to its greatest Italian perfection and gave it, for English readers at least, his name. The form was introduced into England by Thomas Wyatt, who translated Petrarchan sonnets and left more than thirty of his own compositions in English. Surrey, an associate, shares with Wyatt the credit for introducing the form to England and is important as an early modifier of the Italian sonnet. Gradually, the Italian *sonnet* pattern was changed, and, because Shakespeare attained fame for the greatest poems of this modified type, his name has often been given to the English form. Among the most famous sonneteers in England have been Sidney, Shakespeare, Milton, Wordsworth, Keats, D. G. Rossetti, Meredith, Auden, and Geoffrey Hill. Longfellow, Robinson, Frost, Cummings, and Berryman are generally credited with writing some of the best *sonnets* in America.

Certain poets following the example of Petrarch have written a series of *sonnets* linked to one another and dealing with a single, although sometimes generalized, subject. Such series are called SONNET SEQUENCES. Some of the most famous in English literature are Shakespeare's *Sonnets*, Sidney's *Astrophil and Stella*, Spenser's *Amoretti,* Rossetti's *House of Life*, Elizabeth Barrett Browning's *Sonnets from the Portuguese*, and Meredith's *Modern Love*. John Berryman, Allen Tate, W. H. Auden, and Marilyn

Hacker have done distinguished work in the *sonnet* sequence in this century. In the last decade of his life, Robert Lowell wrote scores of fourteen-lined poems that, without rhyming or adhering to any very strict pattern of rhythm, manage to preserve the appearance of sonnets, along with something of their spirit, passion, and personal focus.

Sonnet Cycle (or **Sequence**) A connected group of SONNETS.

"Sons of Ben" Poets of the reign of Charles I who were admirers and imitators of the lyric poetry of Ben Jonson; more commonly called the "TRIBE OF BEN."

Sorrow Song A LAMENT, particularly a song expressing the sorrows of African and African American people.

Sotadic (or **Sotadean**) A classical quantitative line consisting of three greater IONIC feet followed by a SPONDEE (essentially spondee-PYRRHIC, spondee-pyrrhic, spondee), used occasionally for humorous or satirical verse. *Sotadic* is also used for PALINDROME. (Named for Sotades of Maroneia who flourished around 300 B.C., notorious for bad manners and scurrilous attacks on sacred subjects; supposedly condemned to death by Ptolemy II.)

Sound-Over In film-making the technique by which dialogue or other sound begun at the end of one scene is completed at the beginning of the next, usually by the same person or object but sometimes by a different person or object. It is thus a sound bridge between scenes. The term should not be confused with VOICE-OVER.

Soundtrack The audio component of a film or video recording, especially when marketed separately. *Soundtrack* sometimes means selections only from a musical score.

Source The person, manuscript, or book from which something is derived. If such a person, manuscript, or book represents a direct and immediate acquaintance with the information, the *source* is called "primary." If the person, book, or manuscript represents an indirect acquaintance, the *source* is called "secondary." *Source* also designates the origin of works, ideas, or forms. Lodge's *Rosalynde* is a *source* for Shakepeare's *As You Like It*, because the dramatist took his plot in part from the prose IDYLL. At one time, up to about 1930, much academic scholarship was devoted to *Quellenforschung:* research into *sources* and analogues. J. L. Lowes's study of Coleridge, *The Road to Xanadu*, remains a classic of *source*-study. Grover Smith's *T. S. Eliot's Poetry and Plays: A Study in Sources and Meaning* has been a valued companion for decades. Some of the less-inspired labors in such research have been dismissed as "*source*-hunting" and even caricatured as the activity of "carrion-eaters." Although the NEW CRITICISM and other schools of thought have drawn attention away from extrinsic genealogy, the study of *sources* remains an important area of scholarship. See MODEL.

Spasmodic School A phrase applied by W. E. Aytoun in 1854 to a group of contemporary English poets. Their verse (influenced by Shelley and Byron) reflected discontent and unrest, and their style was marked by jerkiness and strained emphasis. In his poem "America" (1855) Sydney Dobell in addressing "Columbia" refers to the typical early English progenitor of Americans as "thy satchelled ancestor." Belonging to the group were Dobell, Alexander Smith, P. J. Bailey, George Gilfillan, and others. The general *spasmodic* tendency is said also to appear in the early verse of Robert Browning and Elizabeth Barrett Browning, and in Tennyson's *Maud*.

Spatial Form A term applied by Joseph Frank to forms of twentieth-century writing in which various means combine to suspend or abolish the customary temporal structure of literature and to substitute virtual space for time as the controlling dimension. Joyce's *Ulysses* and Eliot's *The Waste Land* are examples of spatial form in this sense.

[Reference: Joseph Frank, *The Widening Gyre: Crisis and Mastery in Modern Literature* (1963).]

Spatialism A French movement that emphasized time, form, and energy; typical poems avoided rhyme and favored plain diction and strong rhythms.

Spectacle A display that is large, lavish, unusual, and striking, usually employed as much for its own effect as for its role in a work. During the nineteenth century, under the influences of the large PATENT THEATERS and the STAR SYSTEM, drama relied to an unusual extent on *spectacle. Spectacle* often occurs in the novel; the huge ball on the eve of Waterloo in Thackeray's *Vanity Fair* is an example. *Spectacle* is frequent in film, its greatest exponent and exploiter probably being the director Cecil B. DeMille. *Spectacle* is also our counterpart of what Aristotle called OPSIS.

Speculum Latin for "mirror"; an important concept in medieval and Renaissance literature, representing reflection and portraiture for the sake of MIMESIS and also for purposes of instruction. The idea is found in titles (*Mirror for Magistrates*, mid-sixteenth century) and in metaphors, as when Ophelia says that Hamlet has been "The glass of fashion and the mould of form" (meaning a model) or when, soon after, Hamlet tells the players that the purpose of their art is "to hold, as 'twere, the mirror up to nature."

Speech Act Theory A recent development in the philosophy of language according to which we can divide utterances into the "constative" (that have to do with describing some state of affairs and can be judged as true or false) and the "performative" (that, in the act of being uttered, perform what they utter or say and are not subject to judgment as to truth or falsity, as when one says "I promise" and performs the *speech act* of promising simultaneously). The theory also divides speech acts into the "locutionary" (the act of uttering), the "illocutionary" (the act of carrying out some performative function, such as warning), and the "perlocutionary" (the act of achieving some ulterior rhetorical purpose, such as persuading).

[References: J. L. Austin, *How to Do Things with Words*, 2nd ed. (1975); John Searle, *Speech Acts: An Essay in the Philosophy of Language* (1969).]

Spell A kind of charm or incantation designed to influence the behavior of a person, force, or thing.

Spenserian Sonnet A SONNET of the ENGLISH type in that it has three quatrains and a couplet but features quatrains joined by the use of linking rhymes: *abab bcbc cdcd ee*. It was used by Spenser in his sonnet sequence, *Amoretti*. The only competent modern instances are Thomas Hardy's "Her Reproach" and Richard Wilbur's "Praise in Summer."

Spenserian Stanza A stanza of nine iambic lines, the first eight in pentameter and the ninth in hexameter. The rhyme scheme is *ababbcbcc*. The name honors Edmund Spenser, who created the pattern for *The Faerie Queene*, from which an early stanza provides an example:

A Gentle Knight was pricking on the plaine,
  Y-cladd in mightie armes and silver shielde,
  Wherein old dints of deepe wounds did remaine,
  The cruell markes of many a bloudy fielde;
  Yet armes till that time did he never wield:
  His angry steede did chide his foming bitt,
  As much disdayning to the curbe to yield:
  Full jolly knight he seemd, and faire did sitt,
As one for knightly giusts and fierce encounters fitt.

This stanza is notable for three qualities: (1) the "tying-in" of the three rhymes promotes unity and tightness, somewhat relieved by the shifting variety of rhyme (two *a,* four *b*, three *c*) with the sense so distributed that pentameter couplets containing a complete thought are avoided; (2) the ALEXANDRINE at the close adds dignity; and (3) at the same time, it affords an opportunity for summary and epigrammatic expression. (C. S. Lewis has suggested that the fifth line of the *Spenserian stanza* is crucial because it completes the first *couplet*, acoustically if not grammatically). Poets other than Spenser have made notable use of the form. Burns used the *Spenserian stanza* in *The Cotter's Saturday Night*, Shelley in *The Revolt of Islam* and *Adonais*, Keats in *The Eve of St. Agnes*, and Byron in *Childe Harold*. A part of Tennyson's "The Lotos-Eaters" is written in the *Spenserian stanza*. More recently, however, it has fallen into disuse; except for two stanzas printed as paragraphs of prose in Fitzgerald's *This Side of Paradise,* it is hard to find modern examples of any distinction.

Spin A rhetorical disposition applied to a statement or situation to shape its reception and interpretation. Usually applied to politics but also available for any cirsumstance in which rhetoric applies. One speaks of "putting a favorable (or positive) spin" on something.

Spondee A foot composed of two accented syllables (´ ´). The ideal form is rare in English, because most of our polysyllabic words carry one primary accent. *Spondees* in our poetry are usually composed of two monosyllabic words, as *all joy*. Poe in writing of the subject found only three or four instances (one of which was *football*) in English where real *spondees* occurred in a single word. Untermeyer finds a longer list (really compounds composed of monosyllabic words) and cites *heartbreak, childhood, bright-eyed, bookcase, wineglass*, and *Mayday*. In Milton's line

Silence, ye troubled waves, and thou deep, peace!

"deep, peace" is a good spondaic foot. Despite the paucity of perfect *spondees*, English contains thousands of usable approximations involving pairs of syllables with some degree of stress. The *spondee*, like its converse, the PYRRHIC, cannot seriously be used as the only foot in a poem, but most poets have been able to vary predominantly iambic poetry with *spondees* and other feet for substitution. Here are two lines with *spondees* and other feet but no iambs, even though the lines come from iambic poems:

Hót sún, | cóol fíre, | témpĕred wĭth | swéet áir
(*Peele*)
Oň thĕ | báld stréet | bréaks thĕ | blánk dáy
(*Tennyson*)

Spoof A light satirical PARODY of a work, style, or genre.

Spoken Word Movement A movement begun on the West Coast of America late in the twentieth century that stresses poetry as an oral art involving public performance.

Spoonerism An accidental interchange of sounds, usually the initial consonants, in two or more words, such as *bl*ushing *cr*ow for *cr*ushing *bl*ow or well-*b*oiled icicle for well-oiled *b*icycle. The term owes its name to Dr. W. A. Spooner, of New College, Oxford, who was supposedly prone to such transpositions. Research suggests that Spooner's affliction (or gift) has been much exaggerated, but the folklore has been abundant and amusing. He is supposed to have told a lazy student, "You've hissed all your mystery lectures and tasted two whole worms."

Sporting Novel A piece of prose fiction, usually comic, having to do with sporting activities, especially fox-hunting. By far the most familiar books of the type are those by John Smith Surtees, including *Jorrocks's Jaunts and Jollities, Mr. Sponge's Sporting Tour*, and *Mr. Facey Romford's Hounds*.

Sprung Rhythm A term coined by Gerard Manley Hopkins for rhythm based on the number of stressed syllables in a line without regard to the number of unstressed syllables. *Sprung rhythm* may be said to designate verse that contains feet of varying numbers of syllables, with the first syllable accented in each case. The feet possible are the monosyllabic (a single stressed syllable), the TROCHEE, the DACTYL, and the first PAEON: ´ | ´ ˘ | ´ ˘ ˘ | ´ ˘ ˘ ˘. The obvious result of a line composed of such varying feet is irregularity. The SCANSION of such poetry is, as W. B. Yeats noted, difficult because "it may not be certain at first glance where the stress falls." The following lines from Hopkins's "The Starlight Night" indicate both the effect of *sprung rhythm* and the difficulty of scanning it:

Lóok ăt thĕ | stárs! | lóok, lŏok | úp ăt thĕ | skíes!
Ŏ| lóok ăt call thĕ | fíre- | fólk | síttĭng ĭn thĕ | áir!
Thĕ | bríght | bórŏughs, thĕ | círclĕ- | cítădĕls | thére! |
Dówn ĭn | dím wŏods thĕ | díămŏnd | délves! thĕ | élves'-ĕyes!

(Note that a foot may continue to the beginning of the next line.) These lines are pretty clearly PENTAMETER but of an indeterminable type of foot.

Hopkins said that he used *sprung rhythm* because "it is nearest to the rhythm of prose, that is the native and natural rhythm of speech," and he cited as earlier users the author of *Piers Plowman*, the choruses in Milton's *Samson Agonistes*, and old nursery rhymes. Both "One, two" and "Buckle your shoe" have two stresses, but the first contains only two syllables; the second contains four. See PROSE RHYTHM, OLD ENGLISH VERSIFICATION.

Spuria Collective plural for such spurious items as forgeries and fakes.

Square Poem A poem with a certain number of syllables per line and the same number of lines in a stanza, such as the Epilogue to "December" in Edmund Spenser's *The Shepheardes Calender*, which is twelve lines with twelve syllables each. Donald Hall has written nine-lined stanzas with nine syllables per line, John Hollander thirteen-lined stanzas with thirteen-syllables per line.

Squib A short satirical piece; a LAMPOON.

Stage The physical area, normally a raised platform—on which theatrical performances take place. As METONYMY, *stage* also means the life of the theater. *Stage* directions are customarily worded from the perspective of someone standing on a *stage* facing the audience: "stage right" and "stage left" are to the right and left of that position; "downstage" is in the direction of the audience, "upstage" away from the audience.

Stage Directions Material that an author, editor, prompter, performer, or other person adds to a text to indicate movement, attitude, manner, style, or quality of a speech, character, or action. Some of the simplest and oldest are "enter," "exit" or "exeunt," and "aside." During the nineteenth century, others came into fashion, such as adverbs ("angrily") or protracted descriptions of characters and settings. George Bernard Shaw is notorious for sometimes inserting small discursive essays in the place of *stage directions*. Almost all *stage directions* occur in the texts of plays meant for theatrical production, but some occur also in nondramatic poems and novels. Melville's *Moby-Dick*, for example, makes extensive use of quasi-theatrical exposition, including *stage directions* (one chapter is even given a title that is itself a *stage direction:* "Enter Ahab; to him, Stubb").

Since the late nineteenth century, standard *stage directions* have assumed a layout from the viewpoint of a performer on a sloping platform facing the audience:

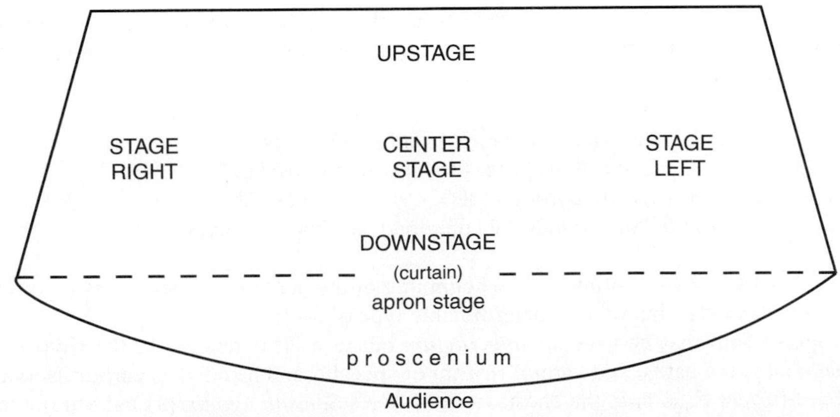

Stalls Seats in front of the PIT in a theater or other such establishment. Orchestra seats.

Standby A performer ready to take the place of a regular performer in case of emergency; such people may be used less often than ordinary UNDERSTUDIES.

Stanza A recurrent grouping of two or more verse lines in terms of length, metrical form, and, often, rhyme scheme. However, the division into *stanzas* is sometimes made according to *thought* as well as form, in which case the *stanza* is a unit like a prose paragraph. STROPHE is another term used for *stanza*, but one should avoid VERSE in this sense, because the word has so many other meanings. For convenience, *stanza* is limited to units that are regular, rhymed, and recurrent; other subdivisions are called STROPHES.

Star A performer of superlative talent, charisma, or interest; also, the featured performer or role.

Star System Usually the emphasis on the presence of STARS as the chief determinant in producing and promoting works.

State Just as an EDITION (all the copies made from a setting of type) may comprise more than one IMPRESSION or PRINTING (all the copies made at one given time), an impression may comprise more than one *state* (all the copies in exactly the same condition, with no accidental or deliberate changes).

Stationers' Company and Stationers' Register Originally, a stationer was a publisher and bookseller. The *Stationers' Company* was granted a royal charter in 1557, and, without special permission, no one else could print anything for sale. Every member was required to enter the names of forthcoming books in the *Stationers' Register*.

Static Character A character who changes little if at all. Things happen to *static characters* without modifying their interior selves. See CHARACTERIZATION.

Stave A STANZA, particularly of a song.

Stave-Rime (from German *Stabreim*) ALLITERATION in general or an alliterating word.

Stereotype The metal duplication of a printing surface, cast from a mold made of the surface, usually by wet paper pulp. A *stereotype* plate enables the original surface to be exactly duplicated many times. *Stereotype* has come to mean anything that repeats or duplicates something else without variation; hence, something that lacks individualizing characteristics. The term is applied to oversimplified mental pictures or judgments. Note that *stereotype*, like CLICHÉ and "rubber-stamp" (meaning perfunctory or bureaucratic treatment), comes from the idiom of printing.

[Reference: Marshall McLuhan, *From Cliché to Archetype* (1970).]

Stich A word or stem meaning "line," as in HEMISTICH or DISTICH.

Stichomythia A form of REPARTEE developed in classical drama and often employed by Elizabethan writers, especially those imitating the SENECAN TRAGEDIES. It is a sort of line-for-line verbal fencing match in which the principals retort sharply to each other in lines that echo and vary the opponent's words. Antithesis is freely used. A few lines from Hamlet's interview with his mother in the scene in which Polonius is killed will serve as an instance of *stichomythia:*

Hamlet: Now, mother, what's the matter?
Queen: Hamlet, thou hast thy father much offended.
Hamlet: Mother, you have my father much offended.
Queen: Come, come, you answer with an idle tongue.
Hamlet: Go, go, you question with a wicked tongue.

A more sustained example is found in the interview between King Richard and the Queen in *Richard III* (4, 4).

Stock In the theater, a stock company is a group—writers, performers, technicians—who work together in a single theater.

Stock Characters Conventional character types. Thus, a boisterous character known as the Vice came to be expected in a MORALITY PLAY. The Elizabethan REVENGE TRAGEDY commonly employed, among other *stock characters*, a high-thinking vengeance-seeking hero (Hamlet), the ghost of a murdered father or son, and a scheming murderer-villain (Claudius). In Elizabethan dramatic tradition in general, one may expect such stock figures as a disguised romantic heroine (Portia), a melancholy man (Jaques), a loquacious old counsellor (Polonius), a female servant-CONFIDANTE (Nerissa), a court fool (Feste), a witty clownish servant (Launcelot Gobbo). In fairy tales the cruel stepmother and prince charming are examples. Every type of literature tends to develop *stock characters* whose nature readers do well to recognize so that they can distinguish between the individual characteristics and the conventional traits drawn from the tradition of the *stock character*. A feature of modern art is its tendency to take *stock characters* from the past, move them from the periphery to the center of attention, and reveal new complexities. Shaw's St. Joan begins as a standard ingenue, for example. Eliot's "Gerontion" is a *gerontion*—the word itself is the name of a favorite *stock character* of Greek (and later) comedy: the geezer, codger, "little old man."

Stock Situation A situation recurring frequently in a literary form, whether it be a general plot situation, such as boy-meets-girl or rags-to-riches, or a recurrent detail, much as mixed identity or birthmarks that betray kinship. However, certain fundamental situations, such as the search for a father, death and rebirth, the Oedipus attachment, and the loss of Paradise are more nearly archetypal patterns than *stock situations*, because they seem to register recurrent views of life and its meaning. See ARCHETYPE.

Stoffgeschichte German equivalent of THEMATICS.

Stoicism The philosophy of the Stoics, a group of Greek philosophers, founded by Zeno late in the fourth century B.C. *Stoicism* exalts endurance and self-sufficiency. Virtue consists in living in conformity to the laws of nature. Endurance lies in the recognition that what is experienced comes by necessity and therefore must be endured. Self-sufficiency resides in extreme self-control, which restrains all feelings, whether pleasurable or painful. *Stoicism* was the most attractive of the Greek philosophies to the

Roman world, and its great influence in English literature comes through three Roman writers: Cicero, Epictetus, and Marcus Aurelius. There is also a strain of *Stoicism* in Seneca. There have been notable instances of the use of Stoic philosophy in English literature from the "Knight's Tale" in *The Canterbury Tales* to Addison's *Cato*—perhaps the most complete statement of the Stoic position in our language—to Ernest Hemingway's ideal of courage, defined as "grace under pressure."

[Reference: Duane J. MacMillan, ed., *The Stoic Strain in American Literature: Essays in Honour of Marston LaFrance* (1979).]

Storm and Stress An eighteenth-century German movement. See STURM UND DRANG.

Stornello (plural, ***Stornelli***) In Italy, a short lyric, sometimes improvised.

Story Any account of actions in a time sequence; any NARRATIVE of events in a sequential arrangement. The one merit of *story* is its ability to make us want to know what happened next; other merits may be gained through what is done to *story* and not through *story* alone.

Story is thus the basis of all literature that is narrative or dramatic, for *story* is the collection of things that happen in the work. It is thus a common element (E. M. Forster would insist the only common element) among novels, romances, short stories, dramas, films, epic poems, narrative poems, allegories, parables, sketches, and all other forms with any basis in a sequence of events. *Story* may be regarded as raw material, and the forms differ significantly in how and why they use *story* in the shaping of the work. *Story*, in this sense, is not PLOT but is an ingredient thereof. Plot takes a *story*, selects its materials in terms not of time but of causality; gives it a beginning, a middle, and an end; and makes it serve to elucidate character, express an idea, or incite to an action.

Straight Man In a MINSTREL SHOW or other performance in which comic or satiric dialogue occurs, the *straight man* is the character who asks the seemingly serious questions or makes the grave comment that triggers the comic or satiric retort. He often plays the same role as that of the ADVERSARIUS in FORMAL SATIRE.

Stranger One quotation from the Middle Ages suggests that a certain STANZA was called "strangere," but nothing is known about it.

Strap, Strap-line A line or two of material added above a HEADLINE, usually with pieces printed in two or more COLUMNS. The typical formatting is: Strap-line, upper left; Headline, center; and Tag-line, lower right.

Local News

MAYOR RE-ELECTED

"I promise reform."

Stream of Consciousness The total range of awareness and emotive-mental response of an individual, from the lowest prespeech level to the highest fully articulated level of rational thought. The assumption is that in the mind of an individual at a given moment a *stream of consciousness* (the phrase originated in this sense with Alexander Bain in 1855 and was given currency later by William James) is a mixture of all the levels of awareness, an unending flow of sensations, thoughts, memories, associations, and reflections; if the exact content of the mind ("consciousness") is to be described at any moment, then these varied, disjointed, and illogical elements must find expression in a flow of words, images, and ideas similar to the unorganized flow of the mind. However, because consciousness is neither a stream nor a thing given to verbal articulation, the *stream-of-consciousness* technique has become as artificial and convention-bound as any other literary technique, although it may give the impression or illusion of preserving a lifelike resemblance to real consciousness. Joyce's approximation involved the removal of customary signals, such as quotation marks, hyphens in compounds, and chapter numbers and titles. By moving the written text closer to the realm of speech, which is normally unpunctuated, Joyce gave the impression, in effect, of moving his discourse from the outer world of the reading eye to the inner world of the listening ear.

[References: Dorrit Cohn, *Transparent Minds: Narrative Modes for Presenting Consciousness in Fiction* (1978); Melvin Friedman, *Stream of Consciousness: A Study in Literary Method* (1955); Robert Humphrey, *Stream of Consciousness in the Modern Novel* (1954).]

Stream-of-Consciousness Novel The type of novel taking as its subject matter the flow of the STREAM OF CONSCIOUSNESS of one or more of its characters. The *stream-of-consciousness novel* uses varied techniques to represent this consciousness. In general, most PSYCHOLOGICAL NOVELS report the flow of conscious and ordered intelligence, as in the work of Henry James, or the flow of memory activated by association, as in the work of Marcel Proust; but the *stream-of-consciousness novel* tends to concentrate its attention chiefly on the nonverbalized level, in which the IMAGE must express the unarticulated response without the logic of grammar. However differing the techniques employed, the writers of the *stream-of-consciousness novel* seem to share certain common assumptions: (1) that the significant existence of human beings is to be found in their mental–emotional processes and not in the outside world, (2) that this mental–emotional life is disjointed and illogical, and (3) that a pattern of free psychological association rather than of logical relation determines the shifting sequence of thought and feeling.

Attempts to concentrate the subject matter of fiction on the inner consciousness are not new by any means. The earliest impressive example seems to be Laurence Sterne's *Tristram Shandy* (1759–1767), with its motto from Epictetus: "It is not actions, but opinions about actions, which disturb men," and with its application of Locke's psychological theories of association and duration to the functioning of the mind. Yet Sterne, although he freed the sequence of thought from the rigors of logical organization, did not get below the speech level in his portrait of Tristram's consciousness. Henry James, too, remained on a consciously articulated level. In a major sense the present-day *stream-of-consciousness novel* is a product of Freudian psychology with its structure of subliminal levels, although a precursor appeared in *Les lauriers sont coupés*, by Édouard Dujardin, 1888, in which the INTERIOR MONOLOGUE was used for the first time in the modern sense. Other important users of the interior monologue to create reports on the stream of consciousness have been Dorothy Richardson, Virginia Woolf, James Joyce, Thomas Wolfe, and William Faulkner.

Street Ballad A form of FOLK BALLAD that flourished during much of the sixteenth and seventeenth centuries. Printed as BROADSHEETS or BROADSIDES, often in BLACK LETTER with woodcut illustrations, these were sung or recited while being peddled in public places. *Street ballads* often reported the more sensational news of the day.

[Reference: Natascha Würzbach, *The Rise of the English Street Ballad, 1550–1650* (tr. 1990).]

Stress The emphasis given a spoken syllable. There is debate as to whether *stress* equals ACCENT or whether *stress* should be used for metrical emphasis, with accent reserved for emphasis that is determined by the meaning of the sentence (see RHETORICAL ACCENT). In this handbook, *stress* and accent both mean the articulatory vocal emphasis placed on a syllable or potentially there.

Stromatic Mixed, like a patchwork quilt. Clement of Alexandria wrote a MISCELLANY called *Stromateis* ("Patchwork Quilts").

Strong Curtain A powerful conclusion to an act or a play. See CURTAIN.

Strophe A STANZA. In the PINDARIC ODE (see ODE) the *strophe* signifies particularly the first stanza, and every subsequent third stanza—that is, the fourth, seventh, and so forth. To avoid fuzziness, some writers limit STANZA to regular, recurrent, and usually rhymed subdivisions of a poem, leaving *strophe* to cover irregular and unrhymed subdivisions.

Structuralism An intellectual movement utilizing the methods of structural linguistics and structural anthropology. Where linguists, such as Ferdinand de Saussure, study the underlying system of language rather than concrete speech events, and where anthropologists, such as Claude Lévi-Strauss, examine cultural phenomena in terms of the underlying formal systems of which they are manifestations, structuralist literary critics, such as Roland Barthes, seek not explication of unique texts but an account of the modes of literary discourse and their operation. The border separating such study of the structures of literature from SEMIOTICS, the study of signs, is nebulous and frequently crossed. What is really *structural* about Saussure's linguistic science is its insistence on the decisive importance of structures and relations, along with the insignificance of substances as such. No matter what we may superstitiously or sentimentally feel, a given articulatory-acoustic entity or substance, such as the usual sound of *k* or *n*, say, has absolutely no inherent meaning by itself. It acquires meaning only as part of a complex set of differential structural relations. Neither the dot nor the dash in Morse code has any absolutely defined duration or inherent meaning. A beginner's transmitted dot may be longer than an expert's dash. All that matters—as far as meaning is concerned—is the structural relation *between* dot and dash. How short is the dot? Shorter than the dash. How long is the dash? Longer than the dot. Such procedures can be applied likewise to any other system of arbitrary and conventional signs. (These systems are said to comprise such units as graphemes, phonemes, lexemes, sememes, mythologems, and so forth.)

There are two basic types of *structuralism*. One concentrates its study on the patterns formed by linguistic elements in a work in order to find which ones unify the text and throw certain elements in relief. The more common type, which has close affinities to semiotics, sees literary conventions as a system of CODES that contribute to and convey meaning. The special interest here is on the organization and function of distinctively literary elements, on how meaning is conveyed rather than what meaning is conveyed, on how a literary device or even GENRE functions rather than how it imitates an external reality or expresses an internal feeling. *Structuralism* has been employed most frequently in the analysis of prose fiction, but there is a growing body of work applying structuralist principles to poetry.

Although primarily a European and particularly a Francophone movement reaching its first flowering in the 1960s, *structuralism* represented at one time a growing interest among American critics. As a revolt against literary history and biographical criticism, it is a return to the text, but unlike the NEW CRITICISM it seeks to see the text in terms of a methodological model. See PHENOMENOLOGY.

[References: Jonathan Culler, *Structuralist Poetics: Structuralism, Linguistics, and the Study of Literature* (1975); Jacques Ehrmann, ed., *Structuralism* (1970; 1966); Terence Hawkes, *Structuralism and Semiotics* (1977); Michael Lane, ed., *Structuralism* (1970); Jean Piaget, *Structuralism* (tr. 1970); Robert Scholes, *Structuralism in Literature: An Introduction* (1974); John Sturrock, ed., *Structuralism and Since: From Lévi-Strauss to Derrida* (1979).]

Structure The planned framework of a piece of literature. Though such external matters as kind of language used (French or English, prose or verse, or kind of verse, or type of sentence) are sometimes referred to as "structural" features, the term usually is applied to the general plan or outline. Thus, the scheme of topics (as revealed in a topical outline) determines the *structure* of a FORMAL ESSAY. The logical division of the action of a drama (see DRAMATIC STRUCTURE) and also the mechanical division into acts and scenes are matters of *structure*. In a narrative the plot itself is the structural element. Groups of stories may be set in a larger structural plan (see FRAMEWORK-STORY) such as the pilgrimage in Chaucer's *Canterbury Tales*. The *structure* of an ITALIAN SONNET suggests first its division into OCTAVE and SESTET, and more minutely the internal plan of each of these two parts. A PINDARIC ODE follows a special structural plan that determines not only the development of the theme but also the sequence of parts. Often authors advertise their *structure* as a means of securing clarity (as in some college textbooks), whereas at other times their artistic purpose leads them to conceal the *structure* (as in narratives) or subordinate it altogether (as in some INFORMAL ESSAYS). In fiction the *structure* is generally regarded today as the most reliable as well as the most revealing key to the meaning of the work. In the contemporary criticism of poetry, too, *structure* is used to define not only verse form and formal arrangement but also the sequences of images and ideas that convey meaning. The elementary basis of *structure* seems to be binary or binomial, a matter of contrastive relations that are differential, without positive or absolute terms. A perfected work of good art is a conspicuous example of foregrounded *structure* with many levels and sorts of organization (graphic, acoustic, grammatical, semantic, thematic, and so forth). A shapely work of art has both an endoskeleton and an exoskeleton: inward and outward *structures*. An entity inside a work of art generates its meaning and power within the well-marked limits of the work. Hamlet, for example, means whatever he means inside the play as a complex function of many binary relations (with Horatio, Polonius, Laertes, Ophelia, Claudius, Gertrude, and so forth). Outside the play, as a portrait of a legendary Danish prince named Amlotha or as a self-portrait of Shakespeare or as an incarnation of an ill-resolved Oedipal fixation, Hamlet has no determinate meaning because those relations lack both *structure* and substance. See STRUCTURALISM.

Sturm und Drang **(Storm and Stress)** A movement in Germany during the last quarter of the eighteenth century. The name comes from the title of a drama, *Sturm und Drang* (1776) by Klinger, although Goethe's *Götz von Berlichingen* was probably the most significant literary production of the group. Goethe's novel *The Sorrows of Young Werther* reflects the *Sturm und Drang* attitude, as does *Schiller's Die Räuber* (1781). The real founder and pioneer of the movement was Herder (1744–1803). Other participants were Lenz, Klinger, and Friedrich Müller. The drama was much used, and the dramatists were greatly influenced by Shakespeare and his supposed freedom from classical standards. The *Sturm und Drang* movement was a revolt from the conventions and tenets of French classicism. The writing, imbued with a strong nationalistic and folk element, was characterized by fervor, enthusiasm, restlessness, the portrayal of great passion, and a reliance on emotional experiences and spiritual struggles.

Style *Style* combines two elements: the idea to be expressed and the individuality of the author. From the point of view of *style* it is impossible to change the diction to say exactly the same thing; for what the reader receives from a statement is not only what is said, but also certain CONNOTATIONS that affect the consciousness. Just as no two personalities are alike, no two *styles* are exactly alike. It has been observed that even infants have individual *styles*. Even in so limited a medium as Morse code, each sender has a *style*, called a "fist."

A mere recital of some categories may suggest the infinite range of manners the word *style* covers: We speak, for instance, of journalistic, scientific, or literary *styles*; we call the manners of other writers abstract or concrete, rhythmic or pedestrian, sincere or artificial, dignified or comic, original or imitative, dull or vivid, low or plain or high. But, if we are actually to estimate a *style*, we need more delicate tests than these; we need terms so scrupulous in their sensitiveness as to distinguish the work of each writer from that of all other writers, because, as has been said, no two *styles* are exactly comparable.

A study of *styles* for the purpose of analysis will include, in addition to the infinity of personal detail suggested above, such general qualities as: DICTION, sentence structure and variety, IMAGERY, RHYTHM, REPETITION, COHERENCE, emphasis, and arrangement of ideas. There is a growing interest in the study of *style* and language in fiction. See PHENOMENOLOGY, SEMIOTICS, STRUCTURALISM.

[References: M. W. Croll, *Style, Rhetoric, and Rhythm*, ed. J. Max Patrick et al. (1966); D. C. Freeman, ed., *Linguistics and Literary Style* (1970); Northrop Frye, *The Well-Tempered Critic* (1963); Graham Hough, *Style and Stylistics* (1969).]

Stylistics The formal and objective study of style. It concentrates on the choices available to a writer, chiefly: vocabulary (familiar or not, plain or fancy, and so forth); SYNTAX (HYPOTAXIS versus PARATAXIS, loose versus periodic, and so forth); level and texture of DICTION; and acoustic and graphic effects.

Subject Bibliography A list of books, articles, manuscripts, or other forms of writing, either complete or selected, on any of various principles, or some specific subject. See BIBLIOGRAPHY.

Subjective A term for something expressive in a personal manner of inward convictions, beliefs, dreams, or ideals. *Subjective* writing is opposed to objective, which is impersonal, concrete, and concerned largely with narrative, analysis, or description of exteriors. One might, for instance, speak of the *subjective* element in Shakespeare's sonnets and the objective qualities of *The Rape of Lucrece;* the first may tell of Shakespeare's reflective spirit; the second retells an old Roman story.

Another way of seeing the distinction is to associate *subjective* with the seer of an object and objective with the object seen. If the emphasis is on the response of the reporter, the work is *subjective;* if it is on the object reported, the work is objective. *Subjective* may be used in two distinct senses, just as the PERSONA has two possible distinct connections with the author. *Subjective*, in one sense, may refer to the presence in the work of events and emotions that are autobiographical (the persona speaks the author's personal responses, as the character Eugene Gant speaks Thomas Wolfe's). In the other sense, *subjective* may refer to the recounting of an emotional response by a persona who is a dramatically realized character, assumed to be feeling emotions peculiar to the dramatic situation and not necessarily those of the author, as Ishmael speaks dramatically rather than autobiographically in Melville's *Moby-Dick*. By present-day critical standards the first kind of subjectivity is suspect, the second admirable. See OBJECTIVITY, NEGATIVE CAPABILITY, OBJECTIVE CORRELATIVE, AESTHETIC DISTANCE.

Subjective Camera In a film, camera work from the point of view of a character; also called POINT OF VIEW SHOT; a fairly rare device.

Subjectivity The quality of originating and existing in the mind of a perceiving subject and not necessarily corresponding to any object outside that mind. Sometimes the phrase "subjective impressionism" is used for judgments that are based on nothing but personal and emotional considerations, with no effort to achieve OBJECTIVITY.

Sublime Characterized by nobility and grandeur, impressive, exalted, raised above ordinary human qualities—these were asserted to be the essential qualities of great art in the treatise *On the Sublime* by Longinus (A.D. 50). Longinus regarded the *sublime* as a thing of spirit, a spark leaping from writer to reader, rather than a product of technique. He lists five sources of the *sublime*, the first two of which—great thoughts and noble feelings—are gifts of nature, and the last three of which—lofty figures of speech, diction, and arrangement—are products of art.

Edmund Burke in 1756 wrote *A Philosophical Inquiry into the Origin of our Ideas of the Sublime and the Beautiful*. Kant followed Burke's line of thinking, in his *Critique of Judgment* (1790), which links beauty with the finite and the *sublime* with the infinite. Burke's doctrine powerfully influenced eighteenth- and nineteenth-century writers. He believed that a painful idea creates a *sublime* passion and thus concentrates the mind on that single facet of experience and produces a momentary suspension of rational activity, uncertainty, and self-consciousness. If the pain producing this effect is imaginary rather than real, a great aesthetic object is achieved. Thus, mountains, storms, ruins, and castles are appropriate subjects to produce the *sublime*. Burke's theory underlies the poetry of the GRAVEYARD SCHOOL and the GOTHIC NOVEL. Edgar Allan Poe's theory that the death of a beautiful woman is the most poetic of subjects is an instance of such thinking. Among contemporary critics, Elder Olson seems the most sympathetic to Longinus. Olson has carefully analyzed *On the Sublime* and even reconstructed some of its missing parts. A good deal of Olson's monograph on the poetry of Dylan Thomas amounts to an application of Longinian criticism to a challenging body of poetry. Note, by the way, that *Peri Hypsous*, or *Hupsous*, the Greek title given to Longinus's treatise, is burlesqued in Pope's *Peri Bathous: Or, Martinus Scriblerus, His Treatise on the Art of Sinking on Poetry*. See PICTURESQUE.

[References: Harold Bloom, *Poetry and Repression: Revisionism from Blake to Stevens* (1976); W. J. Hipple, *The Beautiful, the Sublime, and the Picturesque in Eighteenth-Century British Aesthetic Theory* (1957).]

Subplot A subordinate or minor story in a piece of fiction. This secondary plot interest, if skillfully handled, has a direct relation to the main plot, contributing to it in interest and in complication. Some writers have carried the intricacies and surprises of plot relations so far as to create not only one but sometimes three or more *subplots*. The characteristic difference, it has been observed, between the fiction of France, Italy—the Romance countries in general—and that of the Anglo-Saxons is that the Romance authors are generally satisfied with simple, unified plot relations, whereas northern writers are more given to an intricate series of *subplots*. There are said to be seventy-five characters in Dickens's *Our Mutual Friend* and sixty in Thackeray's *Vanity Fair*. When so many people are introduced, their relation to the chief characters of the main plot must shade off into quite subordinate *subplots*. As an instance of *subplot* in Shakespeare, we may cite the Laertes–Hamlet struggle (as subordinate to the Claudius–Hamlet major plot). Writers use *subplots* of at least two different degrees: first, those directly related to, and giving impetus and action to, the main plot; and second, those more or less extraneous, on hand frankly as a secondary story to give zest and relief.

Substantive Distinguished from ACCIDENTAL: applied to the actual words and meanings of a text.

Substitution A term for the use of one kind of foot in place of that normally demanded by the pattern of a verse, as a trochee for an iamb, or a dactyl or anapest for a trochee or iamb. Once a rhythmic pattern is established or realized, the need for variety and surprise dictates plentiful *substitution*, particularly in the early part of a line. The iamb, much the commonest foot in English, is the one most often displaced by *substitution*, usually by a trochee, spondee, pyrrhic, or anapest. When an iambic line has a so-called feminine ending, we could say that an amphibrach (˘´˘) has been substituted for the final iamb (˘´). Because a whole poem using the spondee or pyrrhic is virtually impossible, those feet almost always function as *substitutions*. Here, tentatively scanned, are two opening lines from poems more or less in blank verse, although, because of thoroughgoing *substitution*, the prevailing form is obscured:

Márў | sát mús | ĭng ŏn | thĕ lámp- | fláme ăt | thĕ táblĕ
(*Frost*)
Hére Í | ám, ăn | óld mán | ĭn ă | drý mónth
(*Eliot*)

Poststructuralist theory, or deconstruction, employs another sense of *substitution. Substitution* (and displacement) occurs in any process of signification. Rather than a stable center of a structure, Jacques Derrida posits that such a center is always already a *substitution* for a center. See COMPENSATION.

Subtitle A secondary title, usually an elaboration or explanation of the title proper. *Subtitles* have been fairly common in literature since the Renaissance, and from time to time they seem to enjoy quite a vogue. For some centuries "or" was used to indicate *subtitles*, along with an unregulated sprinkling of periods, colons, semicolons, and commas. If a standard format could be settled on, its punctuation would probably follow the model of Goldsmith's "An Essay on the Theatre; or, a Comparison Between Laughing and Sentimental Comedy" or Aphra Behn's "The Dumb Virgin; or, The Force of Imagination"; but variations are plentiful. *Twelfth Night, or What You Will* seems to be the only Shakespearean play equipped with a full *subtitle*, although *All Is True* is sometimes given as the *subtitle* (or alternate or alternative title) of *The Famous History of the Life of King Henry the Eighth*. Since the seventeenth century, what might be called the "formal" *subtitle*, specifying the form of the work, has been popular. In 1667 Milton published *Paradise Lost. A Poem Written in Ten Books* and then, in 1674, *Paradise Lost. A Poem in Twelve Books*. Occasionally, we encounter multiple *subtitles;* one of Dryden's works is called "Alexander's Feast; or the Power of Musique. An Ode, in Honour of St. Cecilia's Day." Successive versions or editions of a work may undergo changes of title and *subtitle;* Fielding's *Tom Thumb: A Tragedy* (1730) appeared later in a revised form with the title *The Tragedy of Tragedies; or the Life and Death of Tom Thumb the Great* (and two further *subtitles*) (1731). Thackeray gave *Vanity Fair* two different *subtitles:* first *Pen and Pencil Sketches of English Society*, then later *A Novel Without a Hero*. In our age the "or" has all but vanished (Nabokov's *Ada, or Ardor* being one droll exception), and "formal" *subtitles* for imaginative works have been waning somewhat, although we ought to pay attention to provocative suggestions in such works as Chekhov's *The Cherry Orchard: A Comedy in Four Acts* or Fitzgerald's *The Love of the Last Tycoon: A Western*. Even as imaginative writers were disembarking from the *subtitle* bandwagon, however, scholars were crowding on. From about 1930 many perfunctory academic works adopted a formulaic sort of title that soon devolved into cliché: typically a dramatic adjective (such as "broken" or "angry") and a more or less concrete noun (such as "weapon"), or else two vivid nouns ("wound" and "bow," say), and then, after a portentous colon, a thoroughly bland explanatory *subtitle*. Caricaturists enjoyed a field day, concocting titles such as *The Wing and the Prayer: Optical Allusions in the Poetry of George Herbert*. See TITLE.

[Reference: Atom Egoyan and Ian Balfour, *Subtitles: On the Foreignness of Film* (2004).]

Successive Patterning A relatively simple arrangement of items by succession, as in a rhyme scheme of *aabb* and so forth; distinguished from alternation (*abab*) and CHIASMUS (*abba*).

Summa A COMPENDIUM, often with the word *Summa* in its title. The best known are the *Summa Totius Philosophiae* and the *Summa Contra Gentiles* by Saint Thomas Aquinas.

Supernumerary (Super) A member of a troupe or stock company with a subordinate job in a production, such as being a member of a crowd, with no speaking or singing, sometimes not even paid.

Superscription A heading, address, or EPIGRAPH written before or above a text. Some of the Psalms in the Old Testament are preceded by *superscriptions*, such as "To the choirmaster: with stringed instruments. A Psalm of David." D. G. Rossetti's sonnet *The House of Life* is entitled "A Superscription," as though written above an allegorical picture.

Supertitle See SUR-TITLE.

Suppression See DEMOTION.

Surprise Ending An ending of a movie, play, or other such relatively short work such that the audience are given a development they did not expect or foresee.

Surrealism A movement in art emphasizing the expression of the imagination as realized in dreams and presented without conscious control. It developed in France under the leadership of André Breton, whose *Manifeste du surréalisme* appeared in 1924. *Surrealism* is often regarded as an outgrowth of DADA, although it has discernible roots reaching back to Baudelaire and Rimbaud, and it demonstrates the marked influence of Freud. As a literary movement it has flourished most robustly in Spain, France, and Latin America. As a movement in graphic art it has had many followers, among them Salvador Dali, Joan Miró, Marcel Duchamp, René Magritte, and Max Ernst. What seems genuinely "superreal" or "surreal" about *surrealism*, whether in graphic or literary art, is its habit of lucidly juxtaposing scarcely compatible tokens of potentially symbolic concrete objects (so that music, which does not ordinarily represent the concrete, cannot be *surrealistic*).

Literary *surrealism* finally reached the United States after the Second World War and became an important feature in the work of Robert Lowell and many younger poets: Philip Lamantia, John Ashbery, Frank O'Hara, Kenneth Koch, Michael Benedikt, Robert Bly, James Wright, James Tate, Bill Knott, Kathleen Norris, Charles Simic, and others. To a lesser extent, some surrealist features are found in modern American fiction, from Nathanael West's *The Dream Life of Balso Snell* to Bob Dylan's *Tarantula*.

[References: Savone Sarane Alexandrian, *Surrealist Art* (1970); Ferdinand Alguié, *The Philosophy of Surrealism* (1969); C. W. E. Bigsby, *Dada and Surrealism* (1972); J. H. Matthews, *An Introduction to Surrealism* (1965); Maurice Nadeau, *The History of Surrealism* (tr. 1968); Patrick Waldberg, *Surrealism* (1965).]

Surrogate A person or a thing substituted for, or speaking for, another. If an author creates a character—such as the RAISONNEUR of the WELL-MADE PLAY—who embodies the ideals of the author or who utters speeches expressing the author's opinions, such a character is said to be an author-*surrogate*.

Sur-Title (also **Surtitle, Supertitle**) Words and other such material projected on a surface above the stage of a play or an opera or other musical performance, most often consisting of a translation.

Suspense Anticipation as to the outcome of events, particularly as they affect a character for whom one has sympathy. *Suspense* is a major device for securing and maintaining interest. It may be either of two major types: in one, the outcome is uncertain and the *suspense* resides in the question of who or what or how; in the other, the outcome is inevitable from foregoing events (see DRAMATIC IRONY) and the *suspense* resides in the audience's anxious or frightened anticipation, in the question of when. It has been argued that, on a verbal level, the function of ambiguity is to create *suspense,* which is also a possible effect of rhyme.

Suspension of Disbelief The willingness to withhold questions about truth, accuracy, or probability in a work. This willingness to suspend doubt makes possible the temporary acceptance of an author's imaginative world. The phrase comes from

Coleridge's *Biographia Literaria*, which describes "that willing suspension of disbelief for the moment, which constitutes poetic faith." See BELIEF, PROBLEM OF.

"Sweetness and Light" A phrase given great popularity by Matthew Arnold, who used it as the title of the first chapter of *Culture and Anarchy* (1869). Arnold borrowed it from Swift's *The Battle of the Books*, where Swift, in recounting the apologue of the Spider and the Bee, summarizes the argument relating to the superiority of ancient over modern authors (see ANCIENTS AND MODERNS, QUARREL OF THE) thus: "Instead of dirt and poison we have rather chosen to fill our hives with honey and wax, thus furnishing mankind with the two noblest of things, which are sweetness and light." These two "noblest of things," as Arnold uses the term, are *beauty* and *intelligence*—and it is to these that "*sweetness and light*" refer.

Syllabic Verse Verse in which the measure is determined by the number of syllables in the line. The naming of lines in *syllabic verse* is by the use of numerical prefixes added to *syllabic*, as *monosyllabic* for one syllable, *trisyllabic* for three, *hendecasyllabic* for eleven, and so forth. In English—and in the Germanic, Slavic, and Celtic languages in general—the syllable is a highly variable phenomenon, ranging from a single simple unstressed neutral vowel of short duration (as at the end of "comma") all the way to amalgams of as many as six or seven sounds (as in "traipsed" and "strengths"); accordingly, the syllable as such makes an unstable and presumably uninteresting unit. The situation is different in Chinese, Japanese, and many Romance languages, which tend toward marked uniformity of syllable (a simple consonant followed by a simple vowel, say) along with a leveling of stress. If a language abounds in such words as *ditalini* and *sayonara*, then the syllable, being relatively uniform and stable, becomes a viable unit for measure, as indeed it has been in Italian and Japanese. Handicaps notwithstanding, a few modern poets have written interesting *syllabic verse* in English; among the best are poems by Marianne Moore, Kenneth Rexroth, W. H. Auden, and John Hollander.

Syllabism Paul Fussell's term for a "theory of the poetic line which takes the number of syllables in the line to be its primary structural basis." *Syllabism*, espoused in various forms by such conservative writers as Edward Bysshe, Henry Pemberton, and Samuel Johnson, saw poetry as governed by strict rules that determined the number of syllables, pattern of accents, and placement of caesura. Tending to argue that English verse before 1600 was all flawed by barbarisms and lawlessness, such critics routinely favored Edmund Waller as the poet who established harmonious regularity in English and John Dryden as the one who brought such regularity to perfection.

[Reference: Paul Fussell, *Theory of Prosody in Eighteenth-Century England* (1954).]

Syllable A linguistic sound produced in a single effort of articulation. The ideal syllable can be diagrammed

(X) O (X)
1 2 3

with (1) as the ONSET (one, two, or three consonants), (2) the NUCLEUS (vowel or vowels), and (3) the CODA (one, two, three, or four consonants). Each *syllable* has a nucleus; onset and coda are not necessarily present.

Syllabus An outline of the major heads of a book, course, argument, or program. *Syllabus* (the offspring of a SCRIBAL ERROR or an uncouth misreading of a Latin text) does not differ significantly (except as an elegant substitution) from *outline* or *schedule*, the preferable terms.

Syllepsis A grammatically correct construction in which one word is placed in the same grammatical relationship to two words but in quite different senses, as *stain* is linked in different senses to *honor* and *brocade* in Pope's line, "Or stain her honor, or her new brocade." Most instances of *syllepsis* involve a word that can take an object and can have both a concrete and an abstract meaning, or else a literal and a metaphorical meaning. The two kinds of word that fit this category are prepositions and transitive verbs. *Syllepsis* occurs when one of these object-taking words takes two or more objects that are on different levels. "Stain," say, is a transitive verb capable of taking both a concrete object ("brocade") and an abstract ("honor"). By putting "honor" first and "brocade" second, Pope adds ANTICLIMAX to *syllepsis*, because the step from abstract to concrete is downward. See SLEIGHT OF "AND," ZEUGMA.

Syllogism A formula for presenting an argument logically. The *syllogism* affords a method of demonstrating logic through analysis. In its simplest form, it consists of three divisions: a major premise; a minor premise, and a conclusion.

- *Major premise:* All public libraries should serve the people.
- *Minor premise:* This is a public library.
- *Conclusion:* Therefore, this library should serve the people.

There are, it is to be noticed, three terms as well as three divisions to the *syllogism*. In the major premise "should serve the people" is the "major term"; in the minor premise "this (library)" is the "minor term"; and the term appearing in both the major and the minor premise, "public library," is called the "middle term." This kind of deductive or categorical *syllogism* always takes the form of three statements: A certain class has a certain quality; a given entity belongs to that class; that entity has that quality. Accordingly, the minor premise and the conclusion share a subject, and the major premise and the conclusion share a predicate. Note, as well, that the REDUCTIO AD ABSURDUM is another kind of *syllogism*.

Symbol A *symbol* is something that is itself and also stands for something else; as the letters *a p p l e* form a word that stands for a particular objective reality; or as a flag is a piece of colored cloth that stands for a country. All language is symbolic in this sense, and many of the objects that we use in daily life are also.

In a literary sense a *symbol* combines a literal and sensuous quality with an abstract or suggestive aspect. It is advisable to distinguish *symbol* from IMAGE, ALLEGORY, and METAPHOR. If we consider an image to have a concrete referent in the objective world and to function as image when it powerfully evokes that referent, then a *symbol* is like an image in doing the same thing but different from it in going beyond the evoking of the objective referent by making that referent suggest a meaning beyond itself; in other words, a *symbol* is an image that evokes an objective, concrete reality and prompts that reality to suggest another level of meaning. The *symbol* evokes an object that suggests the meaning. As Coleridge said, "It partakes of the reality which it renders intelligible." In allegory the objective referent evoked is without value until it is translated into the fixed meaning that it has in its own particular structure of ideas, whereas a *symbol* includes permanent objective value, independent of the meanings that it may suggest. In "The Rhetoric of Temporality," Paul de Man argues that "Whereas the symbol postulates the possibility of an identity or identification, allegory designates primarily a distance in relation to its own origin, and, renouncing the nostalgia and the desire to coincide, it establishes its language in the void of this temporal difference." A metaphor evokes an object in order to illustrate an idea or demonstrate a quality, whereas a *symbol* embodies the idea or the quality. As W. M. Urban said, "The metaphor becomes a symbol when by means of it we embody an ideal content not otherwise expressible."

Literary *symbols* are of two broad types: One includes those embodying universal suggestions of meaning, as flowing water suggests time and eternity, a voyage suggests life. Such *symbols* are used widely (and sometimes unconsciously) in literature. The other type of *symbol* acquires its suggestiveness not from qualities inherent in itself but from the way in which it is used in a given work. Thus, in *Moby-Dick* the voyage, the land, the ocean are objects pregnant with meanings that seem almost independent of Melville's use of them in his story; on the other hand, the white whale is invested with meaning—and differing meanings for different crew members—through the handling of materials in the novel. The very title of *The Scarlet Letter* points to a double *symbol:* a color-coded letter of the alphabet; the work eventually develops into a testing and critique of *symbols*, and the meanings of "A" multiply. Thomas Pynchon's *V.* continues much the same line of testing an alphabetical symbol. Similarly, in Hemingway's *A Farewell to Arms*, rain, which is a mildly annoying meteorological phenomenon in the opening chapter, is converted into a *symbol* of death through the uses to which it is put in the book. The meaning of practically any general *symbol* is thus partly a function of its environment.

Symbolism In its broad sense *symbolism* is the use of one object to represent or suggest another; or, in literature, the serious and extensive use of SYMBOLS. Recently, the word has taken on a pejorative connotation of mere rhetoric without reality, surface without substance, speciousness and tokenism, all smoke and no fire, all hat and no cattle. In America in the middle of the nineteenth century, *symbolism* of the sort typical of romanticism was the dominant literary mode. In this movement the details of the natural world and the actions of people were used to suggest ideas. Romantic *symbolism* was the fundamental practice of the transcendentalists. Emerson, the chief exponent of the movement, declared that "Particular natural facts are symbols of particular spiritual facts" and that "Nature is the symbol of spirit," and Henry David Thoreau made life itself a symbolic action in *Walden*. The symbolic method was present in the POETRY of these two and also in that of Walt Whitman. *Symbolism* was a distinctive feature of the novels of Hawthorne—notably *The Scarlet Letter* and *The Marble Faun*—and of Melville, whose *Moby-Dick* is probably the most original work of symbolic art in American literature.

Symbolism is also the name of a movement that originated in France in the last half of the nineteenth century, strongly influenced British writing around the turn of the twentieth century, and has been a dominant force in much British and American literature ever since. This *symbolism* sees the immediate, unique, and personal emotional response as the proper subject of art, and its full expression as the ultimate aim of art. Because the emotions experienced by a poet in a given moment are unique to that person and that moment and are finally both fleeting and incommunicable, the poet is reduced to the use of a complex and highly private kind of symbolization in an effort to give expression to an evanescent and ineffable feeling. The result is a kind of writing consisting of what Edmund Wilson has called "a medley of metaphor" in which symbols lacking apparent logical relation are put together in a pattern, one of whose characteristics is an indefiniteness as great as the indefiniteness of experience itself and another of whose characteristics is the conscious effort to use words for their evocative musical effect, without much attention to precise meaning. As Baudelaire, one of the principal forerunners of the movement, said, human beings live in a "forest of symbols," which results from the fact that the materiality and individuality of the physical world dissolve into the "dark and confused unity" of the unseen world. In this process SYNAESTHESIA takes place. Baudelaire and the later Symbolists, particularly Mallarmé and Valéry, were deeply influenced by Poe's theory and poetic practice. Other important French writers in the movement were Rimbaud, Verlaine, Laforgue, Gourmont, and Claudel, as well as Maeterlinck in the drama and Huysmans in the novel. The Irish writers of this century, particularly Yeats in poetry, Synge in the drama, and Joyce in the novel, have been notably responsive to the movement. In Germany, Rilke and Stefan George were great Symbolist poets. In America, the Imagist poets reflected the movement, as did Eugene O'Neill in the drama. Through its pervasive influence on T. S. Eliot, *symbolism* has affected much of the best British and American poetry in our time. One of the most evocative passages of *symbolist* poetry is that beginning "Garlic and sapphires in the mud" in Eliot's "Burnt Norton."

[References: Maurice Bowra, *The Heritage of Symbolism* (1943); C. K. Ogden and I. A. Richards, *The Meaning of Meaning: A Study of the Influence of Language upon Thought and of the Science of Symbolism*, 8th ed. (1956); Arthur Symons, *The Symbolist Movement in Literature*, rev. ed. (1919; orig. 1899, reprinted 1958); Philip Wheelwright, *The Burning Fountain: A Study in the Language of Symbolism*, new rev. ed. (1969; orig. 1954), Edmund Wilson, *Axel's Castle: A Study in the Imaginative Literature of 1870–1930* (1931).]

Symploce A figure of speech combining ANAPHORA and EPISTROPHE, resulting in repetition of a word or a phrase at the beginning of successive clauses, along with the repetition of another or the same word or phrase at the end of these successive clauses, as in this example from Sidney's *Arcadia:* "Such was as then the estate of this Duke, as it was no time by direct means to seek her, and such was the estate of his captive will, as he could delay no time in seeking her."

Symposium A Greek word meaning "a drinking together" or banquet. As such convivial meetings were characterized by free conversation, the word later came to mean discussion by different persons of a single topic or a collection of speeches or essays on a given subject. One of Plato's best-known dialogues is *The Symposium*, and later literary uses of the word are much under its influence.

Synaeresis Making two syllables into one, especially by compressing two vowels. Modern English "prose" descends from a sequence running "prouersa-proersa-prorsa-prosa."

Synaesthesia The concurrent response of two or more of the senses to the stimulation of one. The term is applied in literature to the description of one kind of sensation in terms of another—that is, the description of sounds in terms of colors, as a "blue note," of colors in terms of sound, as "loud shirt," of sound in terms of taste, as "how sweet the sound," of colors in terms of temperature, as a "cool green." Poe employed *synaesthesia* often; Baudelaire gave it wide currency through his practice and particularly his sonnet, "*Correspondances*." Rimbaud, in a famous sonnet, more or less systematically assigned colors to the commonest French vowels. *Synaesthesia* is one of the most distinctive characteristics of the poetry of the symbolist movement. Dame Edith Sitwell employed it as a major device.

Synathroesmus A piling up of items, as in the line "Painted emulsion of snow, eggs, yarn, coal, manure" in Hart Crane's "The Wine Menagerie" or the phrase "mactations, immolations, oblations, impetrations" in T. S. Eliot's "Difficulties of a Statesman."

Synchoresis The rhetorical gesture of agreeing or seeming to agree with an opponent. Godfrey Turner's "Synchoresis" summarizes the tactic:

Would you adopt a strong logical attitude,
  Bear this in mind, and, whatever you do,
Always allow your opponent full latitude,
  Whether or not his assumptions be true.
Then, when he manifests feelings of gratitude
  Merely because you've not shut him up flat,
Turn his pet paradox into a platitude,
  With the remark, "Why, *of course*, we know that!"
So, if you'd learn a good logical attitude,
  Keep this infallible maxim in view,
Always to grant your opponent full latitude,
  Whether or not his inductions be true.

Synchysis (also, erroneously, **Synchisis** and **Synchesis**) Confusion, as of words poured out on a page. John Dryden quotes the lines "And be free / Not Heaven it self from thy Impiety" as such an "ill-placing of words."

Syncopation A musical term used for the effect produced by a temporary displacing or shifting of the regular beat. In prosody it is used to describe the effect produced by substitution and also the effect produced when the METRICAL ACCENT and the RHETORICAL ACCENT differ sufficiently to create the effect of two different metrical patterns existing concurrently. In another sense *syncopation* occurs when a stress is forced out of its normal place in a line by the omission of an expected syllable or the inclusion of more syllables than the metrical pattern demands. Gerard Manley Hopkins classified the first two feet of his line "Generations have trod, have trod, have trod" as *syncopation;* a more familiar source of *syncopation* is popular music, with such syncopated DIPODIC lines as "January, February, June or July."

Syncope A cutting short of words through the omission of a letter or a syllable. *Syncope* is distinguished from ELISION in that it is usually confined to the omission of elements (usually vowels) inside a word, whereas elision usually runs two words together by the omission of a final or initial sound. *Ev'ry* for *every* is an example of *syncope*. The greatest use for this omission of sounds is in verse where a desired metrical effect is sought. The "juvescence" in Eliot's "Gerontion" represents a *syncope* of "juvenescence." However, *syncope* has taken place frequently in English simply to shorten words, as *pacificist* has become *pacifist. Syncope* sometimes results when the addition of a suffix creates repetition or reduplication, which some speakers, according to a sentiment built in to Indo-European languages, avoid. "Inimitable" and "educable" may so come about, as may "poulter," "fruiter," and "windhover," and as "narcissism" is becoming "narcism." Many Latin words have undergone *syncope* when passing into other languages, especially if an intervocalic consonant ("between vowels") is involved, as in *magister*, which becomes, variously, "master," "maître," "maestro," and "Meister."

Synecdoche A TROPE in which a part signifies the whole or the whole signifies the part. To be clear, a good *synecdoche* ought to be based on an *important* part of the whole and, usually, the part standing for the whole ought to be directly associated with the subject under discussion. Thus, under the first restriction we say "threads" and "wheels" for "clothes" and "car," and under the second we speak of infantry on the march as *foot* rather than as *hands* just as we use *hands* rather than *foot* for people who work at manual labor. See METONYMY.

Synoeceiosis, Synaeciosis, Syneciosis Associating opposite things, as in OXYMORON and PARADOX.

Synonyms Words with the same or similar meanings. Rarely are two words exact *synonyms*, although it may happen that in a single sentence any one of two or three words may serve. Conventional usage has given most of our words associations, connotations, and idiomatic connections, which make impossible a free substituting of one for another. As one commentator has pointed out, "alter" and "change" seem synonymous, but "He changed his pants" differs markedly from "He altered his pants"; similarly, "brief" and "short" seem to be *synonyms*, until one confronts the difference between "I'll be there shortly" and "I'll be there briefly." The presence of Romance words in English has proved a rich source of *synonyms*, offering a choice between forms; for example, the Romance *assist* for the English *help*. It has been suggested that lawyers, sometimes paid by the word, have developed synonymy into a fine art, never using one word when two will do, often joining a German word with its Romance *synonym,* as in such doublets as "lord and master" and "to have and to hold."

Synopsis A summary of the main points of a composition so made as to show the relation of parts to the whole; an ABSTRACT. A *synopsis* is usually more connected than an outline, because it is likely to be given in complete sentences.

Syntax DICTION consists of vocabulary (words one at a time) and *syntax* (patterns of arrangement). *Syntax* is the rule-governed arrangement of words in sentences. In Frost's lines "Something there is that doesn't love a wall" and "Whose woods these are I think I know," the vocabulary is quite common but the *syntax* is unusual. *Syntax* seems to be that level of language that most distinguishes poetry from prose. It is unlikely that any prose writer or speaker would say, "I will arise and go now, and go to Innisfree, and a small cabin build there, of clay and wattles made."

Systrophe A listing of several properties of something in an elaborate metaphorical catalogue, as in *Macbeth* (2.2.37):

> Sleep that knits up the ravell'd sleave of care,
> The death of each day's life, sore labour's bath,
> Balm of hurt minds, great nature's second course,
> Chief nourisher in life's feast. . . .

George Herbert's "Prayer" (I) is an extended example:

> Prayer the Churches banquet, Angels age,
>   Gods breath in man returning to his birth,
>   The soul in paraphrase, heart in pilgrimage,
> The Christian plummet sounding heav'n and earth. . .

and so on for ten more lines.

Syzygy In classical prosody, a term for two coupled feet serving as a unit. As used by Sidney Lanier and later prosodists, it refers to the use of consonant sounds at the end of one word and at the beginning of another that can be spoken together easily and harmoniously. Both Poe and Lanier were greatly concerned with *syzygy*. More broadly, *syzygy* means the articulation or "yoking together" of terminal and initial consonants, whether euphonious or cacophonous. In this line of Thomas Hardy's, for example, notice the relatively difficult *syzygy* in the passage from one word to the next:

> The land's sharp features seemed to be. . . .

Codex 1956. Designed by Georg Trump.

Table A tabulated list; formerly a CONCORDANCE or INDEX; sometimes used for TABLE OF CONTENTS.

Table of Contents An orderly summary of the contents of a book, usually toward the beginning of the book in the FRONT MATTER, typically providing chapter numbers and titles and page numbers. Occasionally with ANNOTATIONS.

Tableau An interlude in which the actors freeze in position and then resume action as before or hold their positions until the curtain falls. In the nineteenth century many plays ended their acts with *tableaux*, and frequently a play ended with a *tableau*. For the costumed representation of well-known scenes, pictures, or personages, the term *tableau vivant* (living picture) was used. Such *tableaux* are often presented in PAGEANTS or on floats. The identification of the figure represented in a *tableau vivant* was once a social game; an instance is in *The House of Mirth* by Edith Wharton.

Tag (1) An interrogative clause placed after a statement, in the form "It's hot, isn't it?" Also called "tag question," these clauses function less as genuine questions than as confirmation or assertion. (2) A label, nickname, or EPITHET. (3) Brief addition at the end of a piece to give a quick SUMMARY, MORAL, or ornament; sometimes a QUOTATION or CLICHÉ expression. (4) A REFRAIN or other matter at the end of a song or speech.

Tag-line (1) PUNCHLINE. (2) Material placed under a document or illustration; a CAPTION. (3) Matter printed under a HEADLINE so as to amplify, illustrate, or elaborate a main point. Used especially for material in two or more COLUMNS. The typical formatting is: Strap-line, upper left; Headline, center; Tag-line, lower right.

Local News

MAYOR RE-ELECTED

"I promise reform."

Tail-Piece A device placed at the end of a text or major part of a text; see COLOPHON. Also anything put at the end of the work, such as the "Tail-Piece" at the end of C. Day Lewis's "A Country Comet."

Tail-Rhyme Romance A term applied to METRICAL ROMANCES employing the TAIL-RHYME STANZA, especially the large group, including *Amis and Amiloun, Athelston, Horn Childe* (and some twenty others), which employed a tail-rhyme stanza of twelve lines made up of four groups or parts, each with a short "tail" line, such as *aab aab ccb ddb*. A school of MINSTRELS writing *tail-rhyme romances* flourished in East Anglia in the fourteenth century.

Tail-Rhyme Stanza A stanza containing, among longer lines, two or more short lines that rhyme with each other and serve as "tails" to the divisions of the stanza. The form developed in medieval times and is known in French as RIME COUÉE. Chaucer's "Rime of Sir Thopas" in *The Canterbury Tales* is written in a *tail-rhyme stanza*.

Tale A relatively simple narrative. Formerly, no very real distinction was made between the *tale* and the short story. *Tale*, however, has always been a more general term, because short story has been reserved for fictional narratives having a conscious structure and *tale* has been used loosely for any short narrative, either true or fictitious. Some titles of full-length novels seem to suggest understatement—for example, *A Tale of Two Cities*.

Talking Blues A type of BLUES song with a strong narrative dimension (although sometimes employing a REFRAIN and some of the features of the BALLAD). From time to time the singing may become more like ordinary speech, at least for interludes. Woody Guthrie wrote such songs during the 1930s and 1940s, and his son Arlo Guthrie kept up the tradition with "Alice's Restaurant" (1967), which takes on EPIC proportions. At about the same time, Tom Paxton produced the more conventional "Talking Vietnam Pot Luck Blues." In 1980 George Starbuck published his *Talkin' B.A. Blues; the Life and a Couple of Deaths of Ed Teashack; or, How I Discovered B.U., Met God, and Became an International Figure: A Rhyming Fiction in Seven Chapters*.

Tall Tale A kind of humorous tale, common on the American frontier, that uses realistic detail, a literal manner, and common speech to recount extravagantly impossible happenings, usually resulting from the superhuman abilities of a character. The tales about Mike Fink and Davy Crockett are typical frontier *tall tales*. The German *Adventures of Baron Munchausen* is, perhaps, the best-known literary use of the *tall tale*.

Talmud Teaching or instruction; specifically the body of Jewish law pertaining to conduct and ceremony.

Tanka A type of Japanese poetry similar to the HAIKU. It consists of thirty-one syllables, arranged in five lines, each of seven syllables, except the first and third, which are each of five. (Note that the haiku—and SENRYU as well—seems to amount to the first three lines and first seventeen syllables of the *tanka*.)

Tapinosis Belittlement by (1) using a low term such as "union card" for "doctoral degree" or (2) using exaggeration in parts of a description. The clerk in part 3 of T. S. Eliot's *The Waste Land* is described in belittling terms:

> He, the young man carbuncular, arrives,
> A small house agent's clerk, with one bold stare,

One of the low on whom assurance sits
As a silk hat on a Bradford millionaire.

Much of this comes from the style of heroic or romantic poetry. "Carbuncular," for example, a roundabout way of saying "pimply," is especially nasty coming after "young man" rather than before. The exaggerated figure of the silk hat on a vulgar millionaire makes the man's assurance doubly ridiculous; and the whole episode is written in a variant of the HEROIC QUATRAIN, so that both characters are reduced in size, stature, and dignity.

Taste A term for the basis of personal reception of a work of art. Perhaps no critical term remains, despite all efforts, more purely subjective. However, as it is commonly used, it has two distinct meanings: it may refer to the mere condition of liking or disliking, in which case it may be deplored but not debated ("There is no accounting for taste," *"De gustibus non est disputandum"*); on the other hand, it may refer to the ability to discern the beautiful and to appreciate it, in which case *taste* is capable of being cultivated. T. S. Eliot had such a view of *taste* when he saw one function of criticism to be "the correction of taste," and so had Addison when he said that *taste* "discerns the Beauties of an Author with Pleasure, and the Imperfections with Dislike." *Taste* in the first sense is used to describe a purely impressionistic response, as in the criticism of Croce; in the second sense it designates a kind of aesthetic judgment, as it does with Eliot.

[Reference: H. A. Needham, *Taste and Criticism in the Eighteenth Century* (1952).]

Tautology The use of repetitious words. *Tautology* repeats an idea without adding force or clarity. "Devoid," say, means "completely empty," so that "wholly devoid" is a *tautology*.

Technique The sum of working methods or special skills. *Technique* may be applied very broadly, as when one says, "The symbolic journey is a major *technique* in Joyce's *Ulysses*," or very narrowly to refer to the minutiae of method, or in an intermediate sense, as in STREAM-OF-CONSCIOUSNESS *technique*. In all cases, however, *technique* refers to *how* something is done rather than to *what* is done. *Technique*, FORM, STYLE, and "manner" overlap somewhat, with *technique* connoting the literal, mechanical, or procedural parts of execution.

Technopaegnion Greek for "craft-play"; a *jeu d'esprit:* a game or trick that involves a display of wit or cleverness. The Latin poem by Ausonius called "The Technopaegnion" includes a passage in which each line begins and ends with a monosyllable and the word at the end of one line is also at the beginning of the next. The plural *technopaegnia* (or *technopaignia*) is used collectively for playful literary practices.

Techno-Thriller A work of fiction characteristically involving military or paramilitary characters in far-fetched adventures centering on technical equipment: weaponry, computers, space technology, and vehicles. Tom Clancy and Clive Cussler are among the most successful authors of *techno-thrillers*; Ian Fleming's James Bond stories could become PARODIES of the fashion.

T.e.g. Bookseller's abbreviation of "top-edges gilt," referring to the paper on which a book is printed.

Telenovela A NOVEL for television, very popular in Latin America and elsewhere around the world, appealing to viewers of many sorts. Rather like the SOAP OPERA, the *telenovela* is a serialized melodrama with romance and emotional action; unlike the SOAP OPERA, the *telenovelas* are shown six days a week in prime time. They tend to run for about six months.

Telestich An ACROSTIC in which the final letters form a word.

Teleuton Any terminal element, such as the last syllable in a word or the last word in a line of verse. Such forms as the SESTINA call for repeating the *teleuton* words instead of rhyming.

Tendency Adopted from German *Tendenz* as an element in such terms as *tendency* drama or *tendency* novel for a work with an ulterior purpose. In 1855 George Eliot explained that in a *tendency* novel "the characters and incidents are selected with a view to the enforcement of a principle."

Tenor and Vehicle Terms used by I. A. Richards for the two elements of a METAPHOR. The *tenor* is the subject that the *vehicle* illustrates; the *vehicle* is the FIGURE that carries the weight of the comparison. According to Richards's definition, a METAPHOR always involves these two ideas. If it is impossible to distinguish them, we are dealing with a literal statement. If we can distinguish them, even slightly, we are dealing with METAPHOR. Hamlet's question, "What should such fellows as I do crawling between earth and heaven?" is metaphoric. Although Hamlet may literally crawl, there is, as Richards points out, "an unmistakable reference to other things that crawl . . . and this reference is the vehicle as Hamlet . . . is the tenor."

[Reference: I. A. Richards, *The Philosophy of Rhetoric* (1936).]

Tension A term introduced by Allen Tate, meaning the integral unity that results from the successful resolution of the conflicts of abstraction and concreteness, of general and particular, of DENOTATION and CONNOTATION. The term results from removing the prefixes from two terms in logic: *intension*, which refers to the abstract attributes of objects that can properly be named by a word; and *extension*, which refers to the specific object named by the word. Good poetry, Tate asserts, is the "full, organized body of all the extension and intension that we can find in it." This concept was widely used by the New Critics, particularly in their examination of poetry as a pattern of paradox or as a form of irony. See CONCRETE UNIVERSAL.

Tenson (also ***Tenzon***) A verse contest between TROUBADOURS; also a lyric piece composed for such a contest. Ezra Pound titled a poem "Tenzone."

Tercet (also **Terzetta, Terzetto**) A STANZA of three lines, a triplet, in which each line ends with the same rhyme. The term is also used to denote either of the two three-line groups forming the SESTET of the ITALIAN SONNET. A *tercet* of the first type is quoted from Herrick:

> Whenas in silks my Julia goes,
> Then, then, methinks, how sweetly flows
> That liquefaction of her clothes.

The term is also applied to *TERZA RIMA*.

Terminal Rhyme See END RHYME.

Terribilità A quality of artworks, such as Michelangelo's sculptures, such that a figure appears at ease but also shows great tension and strength. In 1974 Stanley Kunitz applied the term to the poetry of Robert Lowell.

Terza rima A three-line STANZA, supposedly devised by Dante (for his *Divine Comedy*) with RHYME SCHEME *aba bcb cdc ded* and so forth. In other words, one rhyme sound is used for the first and third lines of each stanza, and a new rhyme introduced for the second line, this new rhyme, in turn, being used for the first and third lines of the next stanza. A set of such stanzas can close with some variation—a COUPLET or QUATRAIN, say—that will avoid leaving loose ends among the rhymes. Usually in IAMBIC PENTAMETER. The opening of Shelley's *Ode to the West Wind* illustrates it:

> O wild West Wind, thou breath of Autumn's being,
> Thou, from whose unseen presence the leaves dead
> Are driven, like ghosts from an enchanter fleeing,
>
> Yellow, and black, and pale, and hectic red,
> Pestilence-stricken multitudes: O thou,
> Who chariotest to their dark wintry bed. . . .

Terza rima has been popular with English poets, being used by Wyatt, Milton, Shelley, Byron, Yeats, Eliot, Ransom, Auden, and Walcott. The rhyme scheme but not the usual meter was used by Hardy, and the principle of interlocking stanza-to-stanza rhyme appears in Frost's "Stopping by Woods on a Snowy Evening." Shelley, Hardy, Nims, Larkin, Robert Morgan, and Michael McFee have written fourteen-lined poems in *terza rima*, a form sometimes called "*terza rima* sonnet"; Frost's "Acquainted with the Night" is a *terza rima* sonnet with a return to the *a*-rhyme and a repeated line at the end, so that the effects of *terza rima* and the sonnet are abetted by those of the RONDEL.

Terzina A TERCET.

Testament The term may refer to a literary "last will and testament" or to a piece of literature that "bears witness to" or "makes a covenant with" in the biblical sense. The former sort originated with the Romans of the decadent period and was developed by the French in the late medieval and early Renaissance periods. It was especially popular in the fifteenth century and was often characterized by humor, ribaldry, and satire, as in the half-serious, half-ribald *Grand Testament* and *Petit Testament* of François Villon, perhaps the greatest examples of this type. In the popular literature of the first half of the sixteenth century in England, there were many *testaments* of the humorous and satiric sort, such as *Jyl of Breyntford's Testament, Colin Blowbol's Testament*, and Humphrey Powell's popular *Wyll of the Devil* (around 1550). Some literary *testaments*, however, were more serious; for example, the *Testament of Cresseid* by Robert Henryson (1430–1506), a continuation of Chaucer's *Troilus and Criseyde*, picturing Cressida as thoroughly degraded in character and suffering from leprosy. In her poverty-stricken last days she bequeaths her scant belongings to her fellow sufferers.

Another serious *testament* is the love complaint, "The Testament of the Hawthorne" in *Tottel's Miscellany* (1557). Thomas Nashe wrote "Summers [or Summer's] Last Will and Testament" (1592), with puns on the names of Will Summers, court jester of King Henry VIII.

The second type of *testament*, that which "bears witness to," was also developed in the late medieval period. Its best representative in English is perhaps *The Testament of Love* by Thomas Usk (?), written about 1384. This is a long prose treatise in which Divine Love appears in a role similar to that of Philosophy in Boethius's *Consolation of Philosophy*. A modern representative is Robert Bridges's *The Testament of Beauty* (1929).

Tetrabrach (also **Tetrabrachys**) In classical prosody, a foot of four short syllables; PROCELEUSMATIC.

Tetralogy Four works constituting a group. Thus, Shakespeare's CHRONICLE PLAYS *Richard II, Henry IV*, Parts I and II, and *Henry V* constitute a *tetralogy*. Greek drama was presented in *tetralogies*, consisting of three tragedies followed by a SATYR PLAY. Lawrence Durrell's *Alexandria Quartet* is a modern *tetralogy*. In 1990 John Updike published the fourth of his novels about Rabbit Angstrom (*Rabbit at Rest*) and announced that there would be no more. At about the same time, Philip Roth completed his Zuckerman *tetralogy*.

Tetrameter A line consisting of four feet.

Tetrapla A text consisting of four versions or translations of a work, in parallel columns.

Text Traditionally, a *text* is anything isolated for attention, especially a piece of writing. A speaker who improvises "departs from his prepared *text*." *Text* also means a special writing prepared for school use, as a textbook, and some publishers are divided into a trade division and a *text* division. Since about 1960, thanks to the influence of Roland Barthes, *text* has taken on a special meaning distinguished from that of "work." A "work" is a closed, finite product of traditional canonical literature; a "text" is an open process with which one can interact creatively. A single piece can be considered as both work and *text*. Roland Barthes distinguishes between "lisible" and "scriptible" *texts*. The former, as Denis Donoghue comments, "are parsimonious in offering plurality, the latter are lavish in this respect because they are *ourselves writing*, engaged in the play of the world."

Textual Criticism A scholarly activity that attempts to establish the authoritative text of a work. According to Fredson Bowers, the four basic functions of the textual critic are (1) to analyze the characteristics of an extant manuscript, (2) to recover the characteristics of the lost manuscript that served as copy for a printed text, (3) to study the transmission of a printed text, and (4) to present an established and edited text to the public.

[Reference: Jerome J. McGann, *A Critique of Modern Textual Criticism* (1983).]

Textuality The condition of being a TEXT as such and not another kind of work or document. The term is sometimes used metaphorically to refer to the process of understanding an event, object, or phenomenological field as if it were to be read as text—a system of organized and interpretable signs; hence, for example, we can speak of "Wordsworth's textuality of nature."

Texture A term applied to the elements remaining in a literary work after a paraphrase of its argument has been made. Among such elements are details of situation, metaphor, meter, imagery, rhyme—in fact, all elements that are not considered part of the STRUCTURE of the work. The separation of *texture* and structure has been a strategy employed by John Crowe Ransom and some others among the New Critics.

Theater in the Round The presentation of plays on a stage surrounded by the audience. See ARENA STAGE.

Theater of Cruelty See CRUELTY, THEATER OF.

Theater of the Absurd See ABSURD, THEATER OF THE.

Thematics, Thematology The counterpart of German *Stoffgeschichte:* the systematic comparative study of recurrent thematic elements. Such study is founded on the belief (as stated by Theodore Ziolkowski) "that themes, motifs, and images constitute an important link between the literary work and the social, cultural, and historical contexts in which a post-formalist age now again insists on apprehending the work of art." *Thematics* can embrace comparisons among different treatments of a figure like Ulysses, Faust, or Don Juan; of types like the feral child or the *femme fatale;* of images like the tower or the bridge; or of figures like the "fire-rose" in Dante, Lovelace, Crashaw, Novalis, Scott, Ruskin, George MacDonald, Hardy, Yeats, Hedwig Lachmann, T. S. Eliot, Orson Welles, Stephen King, and certain Nintendo games.

[Reference: Theodore Ziolkowski, *Varieties of Literary Thematics* (1983).]

Theme A central idea. In nonfiction prose it may be thought of as the general topic of discussion, the subject of the discourse, the THESIS. In poetry, fiction, and drama it is the abstract concept that is made concrete through representation in person, action, and image. No proper *theme* is simply a subject or an activity. Both *theme* and thesis imply a subject and a predicate of some kind—not just vice in general, say, but some such proposition as "Vice seems more interesting than virtue but turns out to be destructive." "Human wishes" is a topic or subject; the "vanity of human wishes" is a *theme.*

Theoretical Criticism Criticism that attempts to arrive at general principles and to formulate inclusive aesthetic tenets. Anglo-American criticism has been predominantly practical, a matter of detail more than design; but the CHICAGO CRITICS, on their own and in a running debate with several New Critics, returned criticism to a theoretical basis around 1950. Thereafter, *theoretical criticism* gained in scope and influence, stimulated by the example of French intellectual fashions. See CRITICISM, TYPES OF.

Theory Since about 1980, "*theory*" by itself has come to mean a complex of literary, aesthetic, and cultural *theory,* which operates at a high level of abstraction and tends to be theorizing about the problematic nature of language, meaning, art, culture, and history. By definition, *theory* as such is distinct both from an implicit *theory* (a critical principle) and from practice and can be carried on independently. Presumably, a practical piece of interpretation ought to be based on a general *theory* of interpretation.

Thesis An attitude or position on a problem taken by a writer or speaker with the purpose of proving or supporting it. The term is also used for the paper written to support the *thesis*. In academic circles the word has the narrower meaning of a paper expounding some special problem and written as a requirement for a degree. (See DISSERTATION.) *Thesis*, as a term in prosody, was used by the Greeks to refer to stressed syllables; however, later Latin usage applied ARSIS to the stressed and *thesis* to the unstressed syllables. The terms are rarely used today, but when they are, the later Latin usage is almost always intended. See ARSIS.

Thesis Novel A novel that deals with some problems so as to suggest a THESIS, usually in the form of a solution to the problem. Among the types of novels that are called *thesis novels* are SOCIOLOGICAL NOVELS, POLITICAL NOVELS, PROBLEM NOVELS, and PROPAGANDA NOVELS. The French "*roman à thèse*" is sometimes used instead of *thesis novel.*

Thesis Play A drama that presents a social problem and proposes a solution; sometimes known by the French "*pièce à thèse*." See PROBLEM PLAY.

Threnody A song of death, a DIRGE.

Thriller A fast-paced work involving crime, pursuit, suspense, and surprise.

Tilt In film-making, a camera movement up or down on a horizontal axis.

Tipping In Attaching a loose single leaf to a bound leaf by a thin line of adhesive on the inside edge.

Title The chief distinguishing name attached to any written production or performance. Although modern *titles* are usually brief, an older practice produced *titles* that sometimes filled a closely printed page. For bibliographical purposes the entire *title* page, including the author's name and the publication facts, is considered the *title*, and when it is copied, the actual typography and lineation are usually indicated. In most cases we use the *title* that the author gave the work. With some works, however, convention has evolved a *title* different from what the author may have called the work.

Horace's epistle to his friends the Pisos on the art of poetry is called his *Ars Poetica* or *De Arte Poetica*. Benjamin Franklin died some decades before "autobiography" achieved much currency in English, but we conventionally use *Autobiography* as the *title* of the memoirs he wrote on and off in his later years. See SUBTITLE.

Tmesis Literally, a "cutting." A fairly rare verbal figure whereby a word is cut into two parts between which other verbal matter—one word or more—is inserted. American vernacular usage offers the example of "a whole nother thing," in which, by *tmesis*, the word "another" is split into "a" and "nother" with "whole" inserted between. "Enough" and "whatsoever" have received similar treatment. Gerard Manley Hopkins converted "brimful in a flash" into "brim, in a flash, full"; Pound used "consti-damn-tution" in *The Cantos*. *Tmesis* should probably be avoided in ordinary discourse. It has been argued that the English infinitive, although conventionally written as two words, is essentially one word, as the infinitive is a single verbal unit in virtually every other language; so that the so-called split infinitive amounts to *tmesis*.

Tombeau The French for "tomb" or "tombstone" was used by seventeenth-century composers for memorial works; the musical term, revived in the twentieth century, has been used rather more specifically for memorial works by one artist for another, as in Ravel's *Le Tombeau de Couperin*. It was Mallarmé in the late nineteenth century who first used *tombeau* for poetry; among his poems are "Le Tombeau d'Edgar Poe," "Le Tombeau de Charles Baudelaire," and "Tombeau" on Paul Verlaine. Notable such works in English include Surrey's memorial poems on Wyatt, Ben Jonson's poems on Drayton and Shakespeare, Wordsworth's "Extempore Effusion upon the Death of James Hogg," Hardy's "A Singer Asleep" on Swinburne, and several by Auden, such as "At the Grave of Henry James" and "In Memory of W. B. Yeats." Swift wrote a satirical *tombeau* on himself: "Verses on the Death of Dr. Swift, D.S.P.D. Occasioned by Reading a Maxim in Rochefoucault"; the first section in Pound's *Hugh Selwyn Mauberley* is titled "E. P. Ode pour L'Election de Son Sepulchre," which suggests that the verses constitute a sort of *tombeau* for the title character (a poet) or for the author himself (E. P.).

[Reference: Lawrence Lipking, *The Life of the Poet: Beginning and Ending Poetic Careers* (1981).]

Tone (or **Tone Color**) *Tone* has been used, following I. A. Richard's example, for the attitudes toward the subject and toward the audience implied in a literary work. *Tone* may be formal, informal, intimate, solemn, sombre, playful, serious, ironic, condescending, or many another possible attitude.

Tone or *tone color* sometimes designates a musical quality in language that Sidney Lanier discussed in *The Science of English Verse*, which asserts that the sounds of words have qualities equivalent to timbre in music. "When the ear exactly coordinates a series of sounds with primary reference to their tone-color, the result is a conception of (in music, flute-tone as distinct from violin-tone, and the like; in verse, rhyme as opposed to rhyme, vowel varied with vowel, phonetic syzygy, and the like), in general . . . tone-color."

Topographical Poetry A genre established in English by Jonson's "To Penshurst" (1616) and John Denham's *Cooper's Hill* (1642), *topographical poetry* is that in which, according to Samuel Johnson's definition, "the fundamental subject is some particular landscape." It was immensely popular in the seventeenth and eighteenth centuries. Among its practitioners were Thomson, Dyer, and Crabbe. During its ascendancy critics recognized nine categories of *topographical poetry*, such as hills, towns, rivers, caves, and buildings.

Topos Etymologically, a place, surviving in "commonplace." In classical rhetoric, *topos* was a rhetorical commonplace in terms of either structure or the *loci communes* (conventions), or both. E. R. Curtius applied the rhetorical term to frequently used literary situations or subjects in the Middle Ages, such as poets decrying their inability to do justice to their subject, the illustration of a disordered world by having fish in trees or servants ruling masters, the description of ideal gardens, the CARPE DIEM idea, and many others.

Touchstone A term used metaphorically as a critical standard by Matthew Arnold in "The Study of Poetry." A *touchstone* is, literally, a hard black stone once used to test the quality of gold or silver by comparing the streak left on the stone by one of these metals with that made by a standard alloy of the metal. *Touchstones* for Arnold were "lines and expressions of the great masters," which the critic should hold always in mind and apply "as a touchstone to other poetry." They form, he believed, an infallible way of "detecting the presence or absence of high poetic quality . . . in all other poetry which we may place beside them." Arnold adduced three passages from Homer, three from Dante, two from Shakespeare, and three from Milton.

[Reference: J. S. Eells, *The Touchstones of Matthew Arnold* (1955).]

Tour de force A feat of strength and virtuosity. *Tour de force* is used in criticism to refer to works that make outstanding demonstrations of skill. Although some works so called have great literary merit, such as Joyce's *Ulysses*, James's *The Turn of the Screw,* and Faulkner's *The Sound and the Fury, tour de force* more often implies technical virtuosity than literary strength.

Tracking Shot A shot for which the camera, mounted on a dolly, is moved while filming, tracking some action.

Tract A PAMPHLET, usually an argumentative document on some religious or political topic, often distributed free for propaganda purposes. For an example of the use of the term, see OXFORD MOVEMENT.

Tractarianism The religious attitudes and principles of the founders of the OXFORD MOVEMENT, as set forth in the ninety *Tracts for the Times* (1833–1841).

Tradition A body of beliefs handed down from generation to generation. Thus, ballads and folk literature in general as well as superstitions and proverbs are passed on by oral *tradition*. (See ORAL TRANSMISSION.) A set idea may be called a *tradition*, like the idea prevailing throughout the Middle Ages that Homer's account of the Trojan War was to be discredited in favor of certain forged accounts supposedly written by participants in the war. The *tradition* of PASTORAL literature means certain conceptions and techniques carried down, with modifications, from Theocritus (third century B.C.) to ourselves. A traditional element suggests something inherited rather than something invented. In another sense *tradition* may be thought of as an inheritance of a body of conventions that are still alive in the present, as opposed to past conventions that died with their peculiar age.

[References: J. V. Cunningham, *Tradition and Poetic Structure* (1960); Harold Rosenberg, *The Tradition of the New* (1959).]

Traditional Ballad A term sometimes applied to the FOLK BALLAD.

Tragedy A term with many meanings and applications. In drama it refers to a particular kind of play, the definition of which was established by Aristotle's *Poetics*. In narrative, particularly in the Middle Ages, it refers to a body of work recounting the fall of persons of high degree. It concerns in general the effort to exemplify what has called "the tragic sense of life"; that is, the sense that human beings are inevitably doomed, through their own failures or errors or even the ironic action of their virtues, or through the nature of fate, destiny, or the human condition to suffer, fail, and die, and that the measure of a person's life is to be taken by how he or she faces that inevitable failure. The tragic impulse celebrates courage and dignity in the face of defeat and attempts to portray the grandeur of the human spirit.

In drama a *tragedy* recounts a causally related series of events in the life of a person of significance, culminating in an unhappy CATASTROPHE, the whole treated with dignity and seriousness. According to Aristotle, who gave in the *Poetics* a normative definition of *tragedy*, illustrated by the Greek plays, with Sophocle's *Oedipus Rex* as the best example, the purpose of a *tragedy* is to arouse pity and fear and thus to produce in the audience a CATHARSIS of these emotions. Given this purpose, Aristotle says that fear and pity may be aroused by SPECTACLE or by the structure of the PLAY. The latter method is, he insists, the better; hence PLOT is "the soul of a tragedy." Such a plot involves a PROTAGONIST who is better than ordinary people, and this person must be brought from happiness to misery. The question of what constitutes significance for the hero is answered in each age by its concept of significance. In a period of monarchy Shakespeare's protagonists were rulers; in other ages they have been and will be other kinds of persons. In an egalitarian nation, a tragic hero can be the archetypal common citizen—a worker, a police officer, a gangster, a New England farmer, a slave. But to qualify as a tragic protagonist, the hero or heroine must be a person of high character and must face his or her destiny with courage and nobility of spirit. CLASSICAL TRAGEDY and ROMANTIC TRAGEDY both emphasize the significance of a choice made by the protagonist but dictated by the protagonist's HAMARTIA. To insist, however, that *tragedy* be confined to this particular view of the universe is to limit it in unacceptable ways. In the nineteenth century, for example, both Hegel and Nietzsche, in greatly differing ways, evolved definitions of *tragedy* for their philosophical stances. With some *tragedies*, such as that of *Antigone*, we can gain a good deal of insight from Hegel's notion that *tragedy* comes from the dynamic collision of equally justified causes which, at the end of the play, is resolved or "sublated" in Hegel's "eternal justice." In *Fear and Trembling*, Kierkegaard sought to refute Hegel's aesthetic of *tragedy*.

In the Middle Ages the term *tragedy* referred to any narrative recounting how a person of high rank, through ill fortune or vice or error, fell from high estate to low. The *tragedies* in Chaucer's "Monk's Tale," Lydgate's *Fall of Princes*, and the Renaissance collection *The Mirror for Magistrates* are of this sort. In the sixteenth century the influence of classical tragedy, particularly of SENECAN TRAGEDY, combined with elements of the MEDIEVAL DRAMA to produce English *tragedy*. In 1559 came the first translation of a Senecan tragedy, and in 1562 Sackville and Norton's *Gorboduc*, the first regular English *tragedy*, was acted. The genius for the stage that characterized the Elizabethan Age worked on this form to produce the greatest flowering in the drama that England has known. Yet the *tragedy* that emerged was not that of Aristotle's definition, despite the efforts of such writers as Ben Jonson to school it into being so, but plays of a heterogeneous character known as romantic tragedy—plays that tended to ignore the UNITIES, followed medieval tradition in mixing sadness and mirth, and strove to satisfy the spectators with vigorous action and gripping spectacle. Shakespeare worked in the forms of the REVENGE TRAGEDY, the DOMESTIC TRAGEDY, and the CHRONICLE PLAY.

The seventeenth century saw the Elizabethan *tragedy* continued with a growing emphasis on violence and shock during its first half, to be replaced with the HEROIC DRAMA, with its stylized conflict of love and honor, during its second half. Milton's *Samson Agonistes* is a bold experiment involving the use of Hellenic manner for Hebraic matter to yield the lineaments of classic *tragedy*. The eighteenth century saw the development of a drama around middle-class figures, known as domestic *tragedy*, which was serious but superficial. With the emergence of Ibsen in the late nineteenth century came the concept of middle-class *tragedy* growing out of social problems and issues. In the twentieth century, middle-class and laboring-class characters are often portrayed as the victims of social, hereditary, and environmental forces. When they receive their fate with a self-pitying whimper, they can hardly be said to have tragic dimensions. But when, as happens in much modern serious drama, they face their destiny, however evil and unmerited, with courage and dignity, they are probably as truly tragic, *mutatis mutandis*, as Hamlet was to Shakespeare's Londoners.

[References: R. P. Draper, ed., *Tragedy: Developments in Criticism* (1980); T. R. Henn, *The Harvest of Tragedy* (1956); Murray Krieger, *The Tragic Vision: Variations on a Theme in Literary Interpretation* (1968, rev. 1973); Raymond Williams, *Modern Tragedy* (1966, rev. 1979).]

Tragedy of Blood An intensified form of the REVENGE TRAGEDY popular on the Elizabethan stage. It works out the theme of revenge and retribution (borrowed from Seneca) through murder, assassination, mutilation, and carnage. The horrors that in the Latin Senecan plays had been merely described were placed on the stage to satisfy the craving for morbid excitement displayed by an Elizabethan audience brought up on bear-baiting spectacles and public executions. Besides including such revenge plays as Kyd's *Spanish Tragedy* and Shakespeare's *Titus Andronicus* and *Hamlet*, the *tragedy of blood* led to such later "horror" tragedies as Webster's *The Duchess of Malfi* and *The White Devil*. Thomas Pynchon's novel *The Crying of Lot 49* contains a TRAVESTY of this kind of tragedy.

Tragic Flaw The theory that there is a flaw in the tragic hero that causes his or her downfall. The theory has been revised or refuted by criticism that considers the supposed flaw as an integral and even defining part of the protagonist's character. Oedipus's thirst for knowledge and Antigone's devotion to duty are hardly flaws; rather, these qualities are at the heart of their character. It may be better to consider this element as more of an inconsistency or contradiction, a sort of APORIA in character that opens the way for undeserved tragic consequences. See HAMARTIA, for which *tragic flaw* is often loosely used as a synonym.

Tragic Irony That form of DRAMATIC IRONY in which a character uses words that mean one thing to the speaker and another to those better acquainted with the real situation, especially when the character is about to become a tragic victim of fate. Othello's referring to the villain who is about to deceive him as "honest Iago" is an example.

Tragicomedy A play that employs a plot suitable to TRAGEDY but ends happily, like a COMEDY. The action seems to be leading to a tragic CATASTROPHE until an unexpected turn in events, often in the form of a DEUS EX MACHINA, brings about the happy DÉNOUEMENT. In this sense Shakespeare's *The Merchant of Venice* is a *tragicomedy,* though it is also a ROMANTIC COMEDY. If the trick about the shedding of blood were omitted and Shylock allowed to "have his bond," the play might be made into a tragedy; conversely, Shakespeare's *King Lear*, a pure tragedy, was made into a comedy by Nahum Tate for the Restoration stage. In English dramatic history the term *tragicomedy* is usually employed to designate that kind of play, developed by Beaumont and Fletcher about 1610, of which *Philaster* is typical. Fletcher's own definition is useful: "A tragicomedy is not so called in respect of mirth and killing, but in respect it wants deaths, which is enough to make it no tragedy, yet brings some near it, which is enough to make it no comedy, which must be a representation of familiar people, with such kind of trouble as no life be question'd; so that a god is as lawful in this [*tragicomedy*] as in a tragedy, and mean people as in a comedy" (from "To the Reader," *The Faithful Shepherdess*). Some of the characteristics are: complex and improbable plot; unnatural situations; characters of high social class, usually of the nobility; love as the central interest, pure love and gross love often being contrasted; rapid action; contrast of deep villainy and exalted virtue; rescues in the nick of time; penitent villain (as Iachimo in *Cymbeline*); disguises; surprises; jealousy; treachery; intrigue; and enveloping action of war or rebellion. Shakespeare's *Cymbeline* and *The Winter's Tale* are examples. Fletcher's *The Faithful Shepherdess* is a PASTORAL *tragicomedy*. Later seventeenth-century *tragicomedies* are Killigrew's *The Prisoner*, Davenant's *Fair Favorite*, Shadwell's *Royal Shepherdess*, and Dryden's *Secret Love* and *Love Triumphant*. Such plays tended to approach the HEROIC DRAMA. The type practically disappeared in the early eighteenth century, although a number of its characteristics reappear in the MELODRAMA of the nineteenth century and later.

Transcendental Club An informal organization of leading transcendentalists living in and around Boston. After their first meeting in 1836 at the home of George Ripley, they met occasionally at Ralph Waldo Emerson's home in Concord and elsewhere, calling themselves "The Symposium" and the "HEDGE CLUB." Their chief interests were new developments in theology, philosophy, and literature. The movement was closely associated with the growth of the Unitarian spirit in New England. The leading members were Emerson, Convers Francis, Frederick Henry Hedge, Amos Bronson Alcott, Ripley, Margaret Fuller, Nathaniel Hawthorne, Henry D. Thoreau, and William Ellery Channing.

Transcendentalism A reliance on the intuition and the conscience, a form of IDEALISM; a philosophical ROMANTICISM reaching America a generation or two after it developed in Europe. *Transcendentalism*, though based on doctrines of European philosophers (particularly Kant) and sponsored in America chiefly by Emerson after he had absorbed it from Carlyle, Coleridge, Goethe, and others, took on special significance in the United States, where it so dominated the New England authors as to become a literary as well as a philosophic movement. The movement gained its impetus in America in part from meetings of a small group that came together to discuss "new thought." The group seemed to agree that within the nature of human beings there was something that transcended human experience—an intuitive and personal revelation. The movement informally sponsored two important activities: the publication of *The Dial* (1840–1844) and BROOK FARM.

Transcendentalists believed in living close to nature and taught the dignity of manual labor. They strongly felt the need of intellectual companionships and emphasized spiritual living. Every person's relation to God was to be established directly by the individual rather than through a ritualistic church. They held that human beings were divine in their own right, an opinion opposed to the doctrines held by the Puritan Calvinists in New England. Self-trust and self-reliance were to be practiced at all times, because to trust self was really to trust the voice of God speaking intuitively within us. The transcendentalists believed in democracy and individualism. Some extremists went so far as to evolve a system of dietetics and to rule out coffee, wine, and tobacco. Most of the transcendentalists were by nature reformers, though Emerson—the most vocal interpreter of the group—refused to go so far in this direction as, for instance, Bronson Alcott. Most of the reforms were attempts to regenerate the human spirit rather than to prescribe particular movements. The transcendentalists were among the early advocates of the enfranchisement of women.

Ultimately, despite these practical manifestations, *transcendentalism* was an epistemology—a way of knowing—and what tied together the frequently contradictory attitudes of the loosely formed group was the belief that human beings can intuitively transcend the limits of the senses and of logic and directly receive higher truths denied to more mundane methods of knowing.

[References: Paul F. Boller, Jr., *American Transcendentalism, 1830–1860: An Intellectual Inquiry* (1974); O. B. Frothingham, *Transcendentalism in New England* (1876, reprinted 1959); Perry Miller, ed., *The Transcendentalists: An Anthology* (1950); Lindsay Swift, *Brook Farm* (1900, reprinted 1961).]

Transferred Epithet An adjective used to limit a noun that it really does not logically modify. Examples abound in ordinary discourse ("foreign policy" is *domestic* policy, and the "foreign minister" and "foreign office" are not at all foreign) and in literature (Carew's "A Rapture" mentions "Petrarch's learned arms"—an obvious transference). Sometimes, when we want to make a buck fast, we say we want to make a fast buck.

Translation The rendering of a work, originally in one language, into another. At one extreme stands the literal *translation* of the work into the other language, "word for word." "Word for word" is something of a misnomer, because what is one word in one language may amount to a half-dozen in another or may have no counterpart at all. *Translation* cannot take place consistently at the level of the syllable or the word. Even such common elements as number, gender, tense, mood, and aspect cannot be translated on a one-for-one basis. At the other extreme is the ADAPTATION of the work into the other language, an attempt to communicate the spirit of the work by adapting it to the conventions and idioms of the language into which it is being rendered. Each translator must strike some kind of balance between these extremes—which Croce called "faithful ugliness or faithless beauty." Some *translations* have great literary merit in themselves; notably, the King James Version of the Bible, Amyot's Plutarch, Schlegel's Shakespeare, Baudelaire's Poe, and Putnam's Cervantes. Chaucer was a notable translator, as were many later writers: Wyatt, Surrey, Golding, Sir Thomas North, Jonson, Hobbes, Pope, Longfellow, Bayard Taylor, Housman, Pound, Auden, Nims, Bly, Merwin, and Howard—to name but a few.

[References: William Arrowsmith and Roger Shattuck, eds., *The Craft and Context of Translation* (1961); Walter Benjamin, *Illuminations* (tr. 1970); R. A. Brower, ed., *On Translation* (1966); C. H. Conley, *The First English Translators of the Classics* (1927); F. O. Matthiessen, *Translation: An Elizabethan Art* (1931); E. Nida, *Toward a Science of Translating* (1964).]

Transliteration A character-by-character transfer of material from one alphabet or writing system to another. In a late volume, W. H. Auden used *transliteration* for poems that would customarily be called TRANSLATIONS.

Transposition Formerly, TRANSLATION. Any rearrangement of elements, such as letters, sounds, or words, by accident or by design.

Transumption Another name for METALEPSIS.

Transverse Alliteration ALLITERATION in the patterns *abab* or *abba*; successive or chiastic CYNGHANEDD, most common in Old Germanic and Old Celtic poetry but persisting into the poetry of Wagner's *Ring* and a good deal of poetry since (Wallace Stevens, Robert Frost, W. H. Auden, and Dylan Thomas, to name a few).

Transvocalization A rare species of language-to-language writing that attempts to preserve the *sound* of the original while using real words in the new language—not necessarily words that translate the *sense* of the original. Two lines from Plautus's *Rudens—"Pol minime miror, navis si fractast tibi, / scelus te et sceleste parta quae vexit"*—have been rendered by Paul Nixon as "Gad! I don't wonder at all that your ship was wrecked, with a rascal like you and your rascally goods aboard"—a translation of the sense but with nothing of the sound of the Latin preserved. On the other hand, there is a *transvocalization* by Louis Zukofsky that preserves some of the sound but with some sacrifice of particulars of sense: "Pole! minimal mirror! the ship / fractured from your ill-begot goods." The first three words sound rather like Plautus's *"Pol minime miror"* but translate nothing of the words. David Melnick's *Men in Aida transvocalizes* the *Iliad* in a syllable-by-syllable way that keeps almost all the sound and even hits on the sense now and again:

> Men in Aïda, they appeal, eh? A day, O Achilles!
> Allow men in, emery Achaians. All gay ethic, eh?
> Paul asked if tea mousse suck, as Aida, pro, yaps in.

Luis d'Antin Van Rooten's *Mots d'Heures: Gousses, Rames* contains a number of humorous *tranvocalizations*, such as verses beginning "Jacques s'apprête," "Lit-elle messe, moffcte," "Polis poutre catalane," and "Pousse y gâte, pousse y gâte." A Chinese comedian has *transvocalized* "gentleman" into *jiantouman* ("man with a pointed head").

Travesty Writing that by its incongruity of treatment ridicules a subject inherently noble or dignified. The derivation of the word—the same as that of "transvestite"—suggests presenting a subject in a dress intended for another type of subject. *Travesty* may be thought of as the opposite of the MOCK EPIC, because the latter treats a frivolous subject seriously and the *travesty* usually presents a serious subject frivolously. *Don Quixote* is a *travesty* of the MEDIEVAL ROMANCE. In general, PARODY ridicules a style by lowering the subject; *travesty*, BURLESQUE, and CARICATURE ridicule a subject by lowering the style.

Treatise Formerly used of any writing or story, now restricted to a formal treatment of a serious subject.

Treatise Poem Term suggested by C. S. Lewis for an eighteenth-century DIDACTIC poem. "In our Augustan period we find a form which has not yet been named and which is only less dominant than satire. I mean the long Treatise Poem (if I may risk the invention of a name where one is badly needed) as practised by Thompson, Armstrong, Young, Akenside, Cowper, and the like."

[Reference: C. S. Lewis, *The Allegory of Love* (1936).]

Treatment (1) General manner or style in handling a certain subject, as in "Shakespeare's treatment of the assassination of Julius Caesar." (2) In film, a preliminary sketch of a screenplay or adaptation, including technical considerations but not necessarily dialogue.

Triad In classical prosody, a set of three lyric stanzas, the first two (STROPHE and ANTISTROPHE) metrically alike and the third (EPODE) different.

"Tribe of Ben" A contemporary nickname for young poets and dramatists of the seventeenth century who acknowledged "rare Ben Jonson" as their master. Their chief was Robert Herrick, and the group included the CAVALIER LYRICISTS and others of the younger Jacobean writers. Jonson influenced his followers in the direction of classical polish and symmetry, imitation of classical writers and types (as ode, epigram, satire), and classical ideas of criticism. The attitude represented a revolt from the PURITANISM and Italian romanticism represented in Spenser. The poets strove to make the lyric graceful and in general followed the creed: "Live merrily and write good verses." They were also called the "SONS OF BEN."

Tribrach A foot of three short or unstressed syllables. It rarely occurs in English verse. The foot may occur as a SUBSTITUTION for a DACTYL, ANAPEST, AMPHIBRACH, or AMPHIMACER. There may be a *tribrach* or two in Hardy's "The Voice," in which the predominant foot is the dactyl:

Ŏr ĭs ĭt | ónlȳ thĕ | bréeze, ĭn ĭts | lístlĕssnĕss . . .

Trilogy A composition in three substantial parts, each of which is in itself a complete unit. Shakespeare's *King Henry VI* is an example. A *trilogy* usually is written against a large background. O'Neill's *Mourning Becomes Electra* is a dramatic *trilogy;* Faulkner's *The Hamlet, The Town*, and *The Mansion* are called "The Snopes Trilogy."

Trimeter A line of three feet.

Triolet One of the simpler French verse forms. It consists of eight lines, the first two being repeated as the last two, and the first line recurring also as the fourth. There are only two rhymes, and their arrangement is *ab* a*a* ab*ab*. (Italics indicate whole lines that are repeated.) Poets have given meanings to the REFRAIN lines that are different from the meanings that they carried at the opening, as in this example by Austin Dobson:

Rose kissed me today,
   Will she kiss me tomorrow?
Let it be as it may,
Rose kissed me today.
But the pleasure gives way
   To a savor of sorrow;—
Rose kissed me today,—
   Will she kiss me tomorrow?

A serious *triolet* is very hard to write, but Hardy produced more than one.

Triple Meter The use of feet of three syllables; that is, of ANAPESTS, DACTYLS, AMPHIBRACHS, or AMPHIMACERS.

Triple Rhyme Rhyme in which the rhyming stressed syllable is followed by two unstressed, undifferentiated syllables, as in "meticulous" and "ridiculous."

Triplet A sequence of three rhyming lines, sometimes introduced as a variation in the HEROIC COUPLET. With heroic couplets, the *triplet* may be indicated by marginal braces; the third line may be HEXAMETER.

Tristich A STANZA of three lines.

Tritagonist The actor taking the part third in importance in a Greek drama. Sophocles added this third actor to the PROTAGONIST and the DEUTERAGONIST of the Greek plays through Aeschylus. By analogy, the term is sometimes applied to the character of third ranking importance in a play. See PROTAGONIST, DEUTERAGONIST.

Trivium The three studies leading to the bachelor's degree in the medieval universities: grammar, logic, and rhetoric. See QUADRIVIUM, SEVEN LIBERAL ARTS.

Trochee A FOOT consisting of an accented and an unaccented syllable, as in the word *happy. Trochees* are generally unpopular for sustained writing, because they soon degenerate into ROCKING RHYTHM. Long rhymed trochaic poems are extremely rare, because all the rhymes would have to be FEMININE, and such rhymes are relatively few and can be monotonous. Long unrhymed trochaic poems are less rare than the rhymed. Longfellow's *Song of Hiawatha* is in unrhymed trochaic TETRAMETER. (This poem and Longfellow's *Evangeline* and *The Courtship of Miles Standish*—both in DACTYLIC HEXAMETERS—are virtually unique in being long works in a regular unrhymed measure that is *not* BLANK VERSE). Browning's "One Word More" is a 200-line poem in unrhymed *trochaic* PENTAMETER.

Trope In rhetoric a *trope* is a FIGURE OF SPEECH involving a "turn" or change of sense—the use of a word in a sense other than the literal; in this sense figures of comparison (see METAPHOR, SIMILE) as well as ironical expressions are *tropes*. Until recently, *tropes* occupied a subordinate place in literary studies. When the NEW CRITICISM began to regard poetry as a special kind of use of language, however, certain *tropes*—IRONY and PARADOX in particular—began to enjoy an unprecedented measure of prestige. Beginning around 1970, Harold Bloom attempted to align (1) certain *tropes* in a certain order, (2) the parts of a typical post-Enlightenment "strong" poem, and (3) certain Freudian defense mechanisms. Along with Angus Fletcher and John Hollander, Bloom has joined Kenneth Burke in giving "tropology" a new meaning and a new viability much exceeding its early function as a branch of biblical studies.

Another use of the word is important to students of the origin of MEDIEVAL DRAMA. As early as the eighth or ninth century, certain musical additions to the Gregorian ANTIPHONS in the liturgy of the Catholic church were permitted as pleasurable elaborations of the service. At first they were merely prolongations of the melody on a vowel sound, giving rise to *jubila*, the manuscript notation for a *jubilum* being known as a *neuma*, which looked somewhat like shorthand notes. Later, words were added to old *jubila* and new compositions of both words and music added, the texts of which were called *tropes*. These *tropes*, or "amplifications of the liturgical texts," were sometimes in prose, sometimes verse; sometimes purely musical, sometimes requiring dialogue, presented antiphonally by the two parts of the choir. From this dialogue form of the *trope* developed the LITURGICAL DRAMA.

[References: Harold Bloom, *A Map of Misreading* (1975); Kenneth Burke, *A Grammar of Motives* (1945); Francis Fergusson, *Trope and Allegory: Themes Common to Dante and Shakespeare* (1977); Hayden White, *Tropics of Discourse: Essays in Cultural Criticism* (1978).]

Troubadour A name given to the lyric poets and composers of Provence (southern France) in the twelfth and thirteenth centuries. The name comes from a word meaning "to find," suggesting that the *troubadour* was regarded as an inventor and experimenter. *Troubadours* were essentially lyric poets, occupied with love and chivalry. *Troubadour* poetry figured in the development of COURTLY LOVE and influenced the TROUVÈRES of northern France. The earliest *troubadour* of record is William IX of Aquitaine (1071–1127); other famous *troubadours* are Bernard de Ventadour, Bertran de Born, and Arnaut Daniel. Some of the forms invented by them are: the CANSO (love song), *ballada* (dance song), *tenson* (dialogue), PASTOURELLE (pastoral wooing song), and ALBA (dawn song). Varied stanzas were developed, including the SESTINA used later by Dante and others. The SONNET probably developed from *troubadour* stanzaic inventions. The poetry was intended to be sung, sometimes by the *troubadour* himself, sometimes by an apprentice or professional entertainer, such as the JONGLEUR. Influence of the *troubadours* reaches in our time to Ezra Pound's poetry and, through Pound, to T. S. Eliot's and Paul Blackburn's as well.

Trouvère A term applied to poets who flourished in northern France in the twelfth and thirteenth centuries. The *trouvères*, influenced by the art of the TROUBADOURS of southern France, concerned themselves with lyrics of love.

Truncation In metrics the omission of a syllable or syllables at the beginning or end of a line. See CATALEXSIS.

Tudor The royal house that ruled England from 1485 to 1603: Henry VII (1485–1509), Henry VIII (1509–1547), Edward VI (1547–1553), Mary (1553–1558), and Elizabeth I (1558–1603).

Tumbling Verse Another name for SKELTONIC VERSE.

Turpiloquence, Turpiloquium Base, shameful speech.

Twiner A sort of double limerick devised by Walter de la Mare and displayed in his *Stuff and Nonsense* (1927). "The Shubble" is an example and, to a degree, a defense of the form:

> There was an old man said, "I fear
> That life, my dear friends, is a bubble,

Still, with all due respect to a Philistine ear,
A limerick's best when it's double."
When they said, "But the waste
Of time, temper, taste!"
He gulped down his ink with cantankerous haste,
And chopped off his head with a shubble.

Twist A feature of a plot such that something unexpected creates a complication or variation in the story. In "*twists* of fate," for example, POETIC JUSTICE may cause a rebound or reversal in fortune that is the last thing one expected.

Type A group having certain characteristics in common that distinguish them as being members of a definite class. In criticism the term *type* has two distinct usages. In one it refers to a literary genre with definable distinguishing characteristics. In the other it is applied to a character who is a representative of a class or kind of person. Henry James uses it in this sense in "The Art of Fiction" when he says, "She had got her direct personal impression, and she turned out her *type*. She knew what youth was, and what Protestantism; she also had the advantage of having seen what it was to be French, so that she converted these ideas into a concrete image and produced a reality [of French Protestant youth]." A *type* character in this sense differs from a STOCK CHARACTER. The *type* character need not have any qualities borrowed from tradition and may be sharply individualized; a *type* character is one that embodies a substantial number of significant distinguishing characteristics of a group or class. A stock character, on the other hand, is a STEREOTYPE, modeled on other and frequently used characters, but often representing no actual group. F. Scott Fitzgerald once remarked that, if you set out to create an individual, you may create a *type*, but, if you set out to create a *type*, you will create nothing. In creating the individual Jay Gatsby, Fitzgerald seems to have created an abiding *type* as well. *Type* is also sometimes used for SYMBOL, particularly in the religious sense of standing for something that is to come, as in the statement, "The Old Testament sacrificial lamb was a *type* of Christ." This latter sense is the usual meaning of the province of TYPOLOGY. John Hollander's *Types of Shape*—the title and the book alike—illustrates at least four meanings of *type*.

Typology The study of allegorical symbols, especially with the Bible, in which much of the Old Testament is read as a *type* of the revelation to come in the New Testament. Both Jonah and Solomon are *types* of Christ, who offers an interpretation in Matthew 12: "For as Jonah was three days and three nights in the belly of the whale, so will the Son of man be three days and three nights in the heart of the earth."

Clearface 1907. Designed by M. F. Benton.

***Ubi sunt* Formula** A convention much used in verse, rhetorically asking "where are those who were before us?" *(ubi sunt qui ante nos fuerunt?)* The most famous example in English is probably Dante Gabriel Rossetti's "The Ballade of Dead Ladies," a translation of François Villon's *BALLADE*:

But where are the snows of yester-year?

(Villon's "où sont" is the exact counterpart of "*ubi sunt.*") Some variant of *"ubi sunt"* appears in Wordsworth ("Where is it now, the glory and the dream?"), Keats ("Where are the songs of spring?"), and Lamb ("Where are they gone, the old familiar faces?"). In Justin H. McCarthy's poem "I Wonder in What Isle of Bliss," successive stanzas close with "Where are the Gods of Yesterday?" "Where are the Dreams of Yesterday?" "Where are the Girls of Yesterday?" "Where are the Snows of Yesterday?" In Edmund Gosse's "The Ballad of Dead Cities," the three stanzas begin with "Where are the Cities of the plain?" "Where now is Karnak, that great fane . . . ?" "And where is white Shushan, again . . . ?" Each of the stanzas in this poem closes with "Where are the cities of old time?" The formula, especially as transmitted through Villon's ballade, has touched the modern literary imagination powerfully and productively. Edgar Lee Masters's "The Hill" asks, "Where are Elmer, Herman, Bert, Tom and Charley . . . ?" The formula may be said to haunt not only poetry but drama (Tennessee Williams's *The Glass Menagerie*) and fiction (Heller's *Catch-22*) as well.

Uchronia "No time": The counterpart in time or history of UTOPIA, which means "no place." Sometimes applied to DYSTOPIA or ALTERNATIVE HISTORY.

Ultima The last syllable of a word.

Ultima Thule The farthest possible place. Used often in the sense of a remote goal, an ideal and mysterious country. To the ancients *Thule* was one of the northern lands of Europe, most likely one of the Shetland Islands, although Iceland and Norway have been suggested. From the Latin reference to the region as the *ultima* (farthest) *Thule*, the expression has taken on literary significance, conspicuous in Poe's "Dreamland" (in which "ultimate dim Thule" is repeated) and Longfellow's late "Ultima Thule."

Unanimism A movement associated with "Jules Romains" in the first quarter of the twentieth century, emphasizing the collective spirit (unanimity) in society and even in language. The movement owed something of its impetus to Walt Whitman, and it interested Ezra Pound in his youth.

Uncial Descriptive of large, rounded letters such as those used in some Latin and Greek manuscripts from the Middle Ages through the eighteenth century. Modern capitals are descended from these letters.

Uncut Bookseller's term meaning "top and bottom edges not trimmed flush." Often confused with UNOPENED.

Underground Press The mid-1960s saw the beginning of a large number of *underground* publications by numerous groups, some of them clandestine but many associated with universities. Many of these publications were newspapers, but a number were magazines publishing essays, poetry, and fiction, usually of an experimental, AVANT-GARDE, or politically radical sort. The term *underground* is now applied to any avant-garde art that is privately produced and concerned with experiment. There are *underground* films, *underground* art, as well as the *underground press*. Much of the work produced by the *underground press* is in the form of LITTLE MAGAZINES, of which there are now thousands with very limited—and in most cases very local—circulation.

Understudy A member of a theatrical company designated to prepare to take the place of a major performer or other person (such as the stage manager).

Understatement A common FIGURE OF SPEECH in which the literal sense of what is said falls detectably short of (or "under") the magnitude of what is being talked about. When someone says "pretty fair" but means "splendid," that is clear *understatement. Understatement* is particularly noticeable in Old Germanic literature. See LITOTES.

Unintrusive Narrator When a narrator merely describes or reports actions in dramatic scenes, without commentary or personal judgment, the work is being presented through an *unintrusive narrator*. No narrator narrates with complete, dispassionate objectivity; every selection of detail and treatment represents a subjective decision. Even so, a narrator who does not indulge in editorial comments, ASIDES, exclamations, addresses to the characters or the "dear reader," and so forth, may seem relatively *unintrusive*. See NARRATOR, SELF-EFFACING AUTHOR, SCENIC METHOD.

Unitarianism The creed of a sect coming into importance in America about 1820; it discarded the earlier faith in the existence of a Trinity and retained belief in the unity of God, accepting Christ as divine in the same sense that a human being is but not as a member of a divine Trinity. In its more evolved form, this new *Unitarianism* stood for "the fatherhood of God, the brotherhood of man, the leadership of Jesus, salvation by character, and the progress of mankind onward and upward forever." The members joined with the Universalists in 1961 to form the Unitarian Universalist Association.

Unities The principles of DRAMATIC STRUCTURE involving the *unities of action, time*, and *place*. The most important *unity* and the only one enjoined by Aristotle is that of action. He called a tragedy "an imitation of an action that is complete, and whole, and of a certain magnitude"; a whole should have beginning, middle, and end, with the parts related in a clear causal pattern. Inevitability and concentration result from adherence to the *unity of action*, which, Aristotle warned, was not necessarily obtained simply by making one person the subject. Later critics declared that a SUBPLOT tends to destroy *unity* and that tragic and comic elements should not be mixed. Thus, the legitimacy of TRAGICOMEDY was for a long time a matter of dispute; Sidney opposed it and Johnson vindicated it.

The *unity of time* was developed from Aristotle's simple and undogmatic statement concerning tragic usage: "Tragedy endeavors, as far as possible, to confine itself to a single revolution of the sun, or but slightly to exceed this limit." Italian critics of the sixteenth century formulated the doctrine that the action should be limited to one day; many French and English critics of the seventeenth and eighteenth centuries accepted this *unity*, and many dramatists used it. There were different interpretations of the *unity of time*—some favored the natural cycle of twenty-four hours, others the artificial day of twelve hours, and others the several hours that correspond to the actual time of theatrical representation. Seldom does the "represented time" amount to less than the actual elapsed time. A three-hour play will usually represent an *action* longer than three hours, sometimes by many years.

The *unity of place*, limiting the action to one place, was the last to emerge and was not mentioned by Aristotle. It logically followed the requirement of limiting the action to a particular time; as the Renaissance Italian critics developed their theories of VERISIMILITUDE, of making the action of a play approximate that of stage representation, the *unity of place* completed the triad. Some critics were content to have the action confined merely to the same town or city.

The dramatic *unities* have had a long and complicated history. For more than two centuries in England the three *unities* were denounced, defended, and (as in Dryden's *Essay of Dramatic Poesy*) debated. When NEOCLASSICISM gave way to ROMANTICISM, they lost much of their importance.

Many great English plays violate all three *unities*. *Unity of action*, however, is commonly recognized as an important requirement in serious drama, and Shakespeare's greatest tragedies, such as *Hamlet* and *Othello*, show the effects of such *unity*. In two plays, the *Comedy of Errors* and *The Tempest*, Shakespeare observed all three of the *unities*. The concentration and strength that result from efforts at attaining *unity of action, time*, and *place* may be regarded as dramatic virtues.

Modern dramatists are less interested in traditional formulas than in the unity of impression, the singleness of emotional effect. Moreover, in recent years, effective experiments with the minor *unities of time* and *place* have been made. In a play by Patrick Hamilton (later a Hitchcock film) called *Rope*, the elapsed time exactly matches the represented time. Likewise, John Badham's film *Nick of Time* (1995) takes 98 minutes to tell a story that covers 98 minutes. During the 2001–2005 television seasons, a series called *24* attempted to represent the hours of an important day one at a time; that is, each weekly episode spent an hour of real time representing one full hour of the day.

Unity The concept that a work shall have in it some organizing principle to which all its parts are related so that the work is an organic whole. A work with *unity* is cohesive in its parts, complete, self-contained, and integrated. The concept of *unity* in the drama has often been mechanically applied (see UNITIES). In other literary forms it is often considered to reside in a unified action or plot or in characterization. A work may, however, be unified by form, intent, theme, symbolism—in fact, by any means that can so integrate and organize its elements that they have a necessary relation to one another and an essential relation to the whole of which they are parts. For many, *unity* of some sort has been among the highest ideals. Romantic confusion, according to Irving Babbitt, conflicted with classical *unity* of spirit. Henry Adams opposed twentieth-century multiplicity to thirteenth-century *unity*. Both W. B. Yeats and T. S. Eliot saw disunity and chaos as afflictions of the modern age and expressed a longing for a predissociation world, which they located in ancient Rome, medieval Byzantium, or Renaissance Italy and England. Among critics, Poe expounded uncompromising *unity* of EFFECT, and the CHICAGO CRITICS—preeminently R. S. Crane and Austin M. Wright—have concentrated on principles of *unity*.

University Plays Plays produced by undergraduates at Oxford and Cambridge during the Elizabethan Age. See SCHOOL PLAYS.

University Wits A name used for certain young university people who came to London in the late 1580s and undertook careers as professional writers. They played an important part in the development of the great literature, especially the drama, that characterized the latter part of Elizabeth's reign. The most important was Christopher Marlowe. Others were Robert Greene, George Peele, Thomas Lodge, Thomas Nash, and Thomas Kyd. Some authorities include John Lyly, though he was older and perhaps not personally associated with the others. They lived irregular lives, Greene and Marlowe being particularly known as Bohemians. Their literary work, although uneven in quality, much of it being hack work, was varied and influential. They were largely instrumental in freeing tragedy from the artificial restrictions imposed by classical authority, and their cultivation of BLANK VERSE, especially the "mighty line" of Marlowe, paved the way for Shakespeare's masterful use thereof. They devised or developed types of plays later perfected by Shakespeare: the REVENGE TRAGEDY or TRAGEDY OF BLOOD (Kyd), the tragedy built around a great personality (Marlowe), the ROMANTIC COMEDY (Greene and Peele), the CHRONICLE PLAY (Marlowe and others), and the COURT COMEDY (Lyly). Lodge and Greene cultivated the PASTORAL ROMANCE, and Nash wrote the first PICARESQUE NOVEL in English. The group was especially active between 1585 and 1595.

Unopened Bookseller's term meaning "edges still joined at folds."

Unreliable Narrator A NARRATOR who may be in error in his or her understanding or report of things and who thus leaves readers without the guides needed for making judgments. The *unreliable narrator* is most frequently found in works by a SELF-EFFACING AUTHOR. For example, Lambert Strether, the viewpoint character in Henry James's *The Ambassadors*, is often wrong in his conclusions about things, but we must await the outcome of events. In James's *The Turn of the Screw*, the debate over what actually happens is really over the reliability of the Governess's narrative. Huck Finn, in Mark Twain's *Adventures of Huckleberry Finn*, is often uncomprehending about the situations he describes, as are most NAIVE NARRATORS; hence he is *unreliable*. Immature narrators—such as Huckleberry Finn, Quentin Compson in *The Sound and the Fury*, and Holden Caulfield in *The Catcher in the Rye*—may be unreliable on account of their lack of sophistication. Others—such as Benjy in *The Sound and the Fury* and Humbert in *Lolita*—suffer some retardation or derangement that impedes or precludes reliability.

Unvoiced See VOICELESS.

Upstaging A stage movement in which one performer moves *upstage* of another (that is, to the rear of the stage), forcing the latter to turn away from the audience.

Utilitarianism A theory of ethics formulated in England in the eighteenth century by Jeremy Bentham, who believed that the test of ethical concerns was their usefulness to society and who defined utility as "the greatest happiness for the greatest number." The theory was advanced and modified in the nineteenth century by James Mill and his son John Stuart Mill, both of whom wanted to define "happiness" in qualitative rather than quantitative terms, whereas Bentham had equated it with pleasure. It is significant in nineteenth-century thought not only because of the excellence with which John Stuart Mill expounded it but also because it was a central issue for a number of writers, among them Carlyle and Dickens, both of whom attacked the system. It is sometimes called "BENTHAMISM."

Utopia A fiction describing an imaginary ideal world. The term comes from Sir Thomas More's *Utopia*, written in Latin in 1516, describing a perfect political state. The word *utopia* is a pun on the Greek "outopia," meaning "no place," and "eutopia," meaning "good place." The earliest utopian work was Plato's *Republic*. Many utopian fictions have been produced since More's, including Campanella's *Civitas Solis* (1623), Bacon's *New Atlantis* (1627), Harrington's *Oceana* (1656), Samuel Butler's *Erewhon* (1872), Bellamy's *Looking Backward* (1888), William Morris's *News from Nowhere* (1891), and H. G. Wells's *A Modern Utopia* (1905). DYSTOPIA, meaning "bad place," is the term applied to unpleasant imaginary places, such as those in Aldous Huxley's *Brave New World* and George Orwell's *1984*.

[References: Joyce O. Hertzler, *The History of Utopian Thought* (1923); Mark Holloway, *Heavens on Earth: Utopian Communities in America, 1680–1880*, 2nd ed. (1966); Lewis Mumford, *The Story of the Utopias*, rev. ed. (1966).]

Centaur 1914. Private design of Bruce Rogers that was redesigned by Monotype Corp Ltd., England, in 1931. This typeface was based on one cut by Nicolas Jenson in 1470.

Vade mecum An article that one keeps constantly on hand. By association the term has come to mean any book much used, as a handbook. The phrase means "go with me."

Vapours A word commonly used in eighteenth-century literature to account for eccentricity. *Vapours* were exhalations, given off by the stomach or other organs of the body, that rose to the head, causing depression, melancholy, hysteria, and so forth. In 1541 Sir Thomas Elyot wrote that "of humours some are more grosse and cold, some are subtyl and hot and are called vapours." Heroines of eighteenth-century fiction were particularly susceptible. Young, in 1728, produced these lines:

> Sometimes, thro′ pride the sexes change their airs;
> My lord has vapours, and my lady swears.

See HUMOURS.

Variorum Edition An EDITION of an author's work presenting complete variant readings of the possible texts and full notes of critical comments and interpretation. The term is an abbreviation of the Latin *cum notis variorum* ("with notes of various persons"). In English literature the most conspicuous successes in this type of editing are the "New Variorum Shakespeare" edited by Furness and the "Variorum Spenser" edited by Edwin Greenlaw. Lately, *variorum editions* have tended to present various readings rather than commentary by various critics.

Varronian Satire A form of INDIRECT SATIRE, named for the Roman writer Varro. The more common names are MENIPPEAN SATIRE and ANATOMY.

Vatic From the earliest times it was believed that some poets or BARDS were divinely inspired seers who spoke prophetic truth; such poets were called *vates*, of which Sybil was the most famous. Hence, the term *vatic* in reference to poetry means that it is regarded as divinely inspired, prophetic, or oracular. Smart, Blake, Shelley, Whitman, Ginsberg, and Synder have been called *vatic* poets.

Vaudeville An entertainment consisting of successive performances of unrelated songs, dances, sketches, acrobatic feats, juggling, PANTOMIME, puppet shows, animal acts, and varied stunts. The word is derived from *Vaude-Vire*, a village in Normandy, where a famous composer of lively, satirical songs lived in the eighteenth century. From these songs, modified later by pantomime, developed the variety shows known as *vaudeville*. The elements of *vaudeville* are old (see LOW COMEDY, BURLESQUE, FARCE), but the modern *vaudeville* show developed in the eighteenth and nineteenth centuries. These shows became very popular in eighteenth-century England, continued so through the nineteenth century and for about the first half of the twentieth. The name *vaudeville* seems to have become finally attached to the variety show as a result of its development in America, especially in the early years of the twentieth century, when *vaudeville* actors were organized into "circuits" by B. F. Keith and others and when elaborate theaters were devoted to their use. The popularity of *vaudeville* decreased after the advent of talking movie pictures, radio, and television.

Vehicle (1) The immediate subject, as opposed to the ultimate or ulterior intentional subject, of a METAPHOR. The *vehicle* "carries" the meaning of the TENOR. If you call an easy job "a piece of cake," the piece of cake is the *vehicle* and the easiness of the job is the tenor. (2) A work, especially one that serves to display the talents of a performer.

***Venus and Adonis* Stanza** Six lines of IAMBIC PENTAMETER rhyming *ababcc*, named from its use in Shakespeare's poem.

***Verbum Infans* Formula** A conventional paradoxical *topos*, meaning "the unspeaking word," applied to the infant (*infans*, "not speaking") Christ, who incarnates the Word (verbum). The formula, which comes from patristic sources, was used by Lancelot Andrewes in combination with two other paradoxical commonplaces: *Tonans Vagiens* ("thundering-mewling") and *Immensum Parvulum* ("measureless-diminutive"). The paradox recurs in many of T. S. Eliot's poems, as both "Word without a word" and "Word within a word, unable to speak a word."

Verfremdungseffekt German for ALIENATION EFFECT. Of particular importance in the drama, the *Verfremendungseffekt* was advocated by Bertolt Brecht as a means by which performers and audiences alike could avoid undue emotional identification with a work—an identification that needs to be neutralized and controlled if the work is to have its intended intellectual and political influence.

Verisimilitude The semblance of truth. The term indicates the degree to which a work creates the appearance of the truth. In his *Life of Swift*, Scott writes: "Swift possessed the art of verisimilitude." The word was a favorite with Poe, who used it in the sense of presenting details, however far-fetched, in such a way as to give them the impression of truth. An example of *verisimilitude* to support an amazing story is Daniel Defoe's "True Relation of the Apparition of One Mrs. Veal" (1706).

Vers de circonstance One French name for OCCASIONAL VERSE.

Vers de société Brief lyrical verse in a genial, sportive mood and sophisticated in both subject and treatment; LIGHT VERSE. Its characteristics are polish, *savoir faire*, grace, and ease. It usually presents aspects of conventional social relationships. Locker-Lampson in the introduction to *Lyra Elegantiarum* states: "Occasional verse should be short, graceful, refined, and fanciful, not seldom distinguished by chastened sentiment, and often playful. The tone should not be pitched high; it should be terse and idiomatic, and rather in the conversational key. The rhythm should be crisp and sparkling, the rhyme frequent and never forced, while the entire poem should be marked by tasteful moderation, high finish and completeness." Though gaining in favor in recent centuries, such verse was popular in classical literature. The seventeenth and eighteenth centuries in England saw a high development of the type. In the nineteenth century *vers de société* was practiced by Fitz-Greene Halleck and N. P. Willis in the United States and by C. S. Calverley and W. M. Praed in Britain.

[References: Frederick Locker-Lampson, *Lyra Elegantiarum* (1867, rev. ed. 1891); Carolyn Wells, *A Vers de Société Anthology* (1907, reprinted 1976).]

Vers d'Occasion French for OCCASIONAL VERSE. The laureate pieces in C. Day Lewis's *Complete Poems* are grouped under the heading "Vers d'Occasion."

Verse Used in two senses: (1) as a unit of poetry, in which case it has the same significance as STANZA or LINE; and (2) as a name given generally to metrical composition. In the second sense *verse* means rhythmical and, frequently, metrical and rhymed composition, in which case it implies little as to merit, the term POETRY or POEM often being reserved for *verse* of high merit. An inherent suggestion that *verse* is of a lower order than poetry lies in the fact that *verse* is used in association with such terms as SOCIETY VERSE and LIGHT VERSE, which, it is generally conceded, are rarely applied to great poetry.

Verse Drama A drama in verse; not usually applied to dramas from antiquity or earlier periods of modern literature when most dramas (and all tragedies) were in verse. Modern verse dramas, written in a period when most dramas are in prose, are a special category constituting a small portion of the whole body of dramatic works. There are distinguished examples by Thomas Mann (*Fiorenza*, 1905) and T. S. Eliot, all of whose plays are *verse dramas*.

Verse-Novel (or **Novel In Verse**) The name of this rare phenomenon explains itself. Some examples use rhymed stanzas, while others employ BLANK VERSE. The greatest *verse-novel* is Alexander Pushkin's *Eugene Onegin* (1823–31), which uses the fourteen-line PUSHKIN STANZA. Elizabeth Barrett Browning's *Aurora Leigh* (1857), in blank verse, is the best-known *verse-novel* by an English-speaking author. In 1893 Wilfred Scawen Blunt published *Griselda: A Society Novel in Rhymed Verse*. Raymond Roussel's *La Doublure* is a French example. Vikram Seth's *The Golden Gate: A Novel in Verse* (1986) uses the PUSHKIN STANZA not only for its main text but also for Acknowledgments, Dedication, Contents, and "About the Author." Anthony Burgess's *Byrne* (1995) is a *verse-novel* that defends its own stanza:

> He thought he was a kind of living myth
> And hence deserving of ottava rima. . . .

W. S. Merwin's *The Folding Cliffs: A Narrative* (1998) is a poetic account of episodes from Hawaiian history. A recent example of the *verse-novel* is Brad Leithauser's *Darlington's Fall* (2002).

Verse Paragraph A nonstanzaic, continuous verse form, in which the lines are grouped in unequal blocks according to content. The beginning of a *verse paragraph* may be indicated by indentation, as in prose. Poetry written in *paragraphs* is usually either

BLANK VERSE or FREE VERSE. Milton's *Paradise Lost* is in blank verse *paragraphs;* much of Whitman's *Leaves of Grass* is in free verse *paragraphs*. Dryden, Pope, Johnson, Goldsmith, and other virtuosi of the HEROIC COUPLET routinely wrote in *verse paragraphs*.

Verset A VERSE or VERSICLE, especially one of the short verses of a religious scripture.

Versicle (also **versicule, versiculus** [plural **versiculi**]) A short VERSE, VERSET; in liturgical use, a short sentence from the Psalms recited in responsive readings. Also a special symbol—such as *V*, *V*′, or *V̸*—used in religious texts.

Versification The art and practice of writing verse. The term includes all the mechanical elements making up poetic composition: ACCENT, RHYTHM, METER, RHYME, STANZA form, diction, and such aids as ASSONANCE, ONOMATOPOEIA, and ALLITERATION. In a narrower sense *versification* signifies the form of a poem as revealed by SCANSION. The word is also applied to the transformation of prose into verse. Some passages of Shakespeare's *Antony and Cleopatra*, for example, amount to little more than a *versification* of the prose in North's translation of Plutarch.

Version A particular form or variant. One speaks of Tennyson's "*version* of the story of Arthur" but also of "*version* 1 of the OED on CD-ROM."

Vers Libre A nineteenth-century French poetic movement to free poetry from strict rules resulted in cadenced and rhythmic poetry called *vers libre*, which means "free verse." Because language and every other cultural institution are governed by rules of selection and combination, the freedom of *vers libre* is relative and may even be illusory. T. S. Eliot is supposed to have said that "no *vers* is *libre* for the man who wants to do a good job."

Verso In paper made with a distinguishable front and back, *verso* is the back. In a book, *verso* is the left-hand page. See RECTO.

Verticalism A rare nineteenth-century architectural term, roughly the same as "verticality," was revived by Eugene Jolas to designate a mode of aesthetic thought associated with some of the writers who contributed to *transition*, a magazine that, according to Jolas,

> contained elements of gothic, romantic, baroque, mystic, expressionist, Dada, surrealist, and, finally, verticalist modes of thinking. In the last phase it tried to blend these traditions into a cosmic, four-dimensional consciousness. . . . Harking back to Novalis and Jean Paul's symbolism of the flying dream, *verticalism* revolted against the nightmare quality of its predecessors and inaugurated an attempt to liberate the human personality from the possession of nihilism. It stressed the creative urge towards a liturgical renascence by reconstructing the myth of voyage, migration, flight, and particularly ascent, in all its romantic-mystic manifestations. It sought the "marvelous of the skies" in the poetry of aeronautical flight, in the conquest of the law of gravitation, and in an aspiration towards aerial perspectives. It also developed the poetry of cosmic or sidereal flight, tried to sing of the

> stellar spaces, and accentuated the vision of the "third eye." In the poetry of mystic flight it sought a transcendental reality. This new poetry of ascent wanted to express its vision in a language that would make possible a hymnic vocabulary.

Among those subscribing to some of the ideals in Jolas's "Manifesto: The Revolution of the Word" were Kay Boyle and Hart Crane.

Vice A STOCK CHARACTER in the MORALITY PLAY, a tempter both sinister and comic. Most historians of the drama see the *Vice* as a predecessor of the cynical VILLAIN and also of certain Elizabethan comic characters. Shakespeare's Falstaff has many of the qualities of the *Vice*.

Victorian A term used (1) to designate broadly the literature written during the reign of Queen Victoria (1837–1901); and (2) more narrowly, to suggest a certain complacency, hypocrisy, or squeamishness assumed to characterize Victorian attitudes. A certain prudery led to egregious exaggeration in costume, furnishings, architecture, and industrial design. Pride in the growing power of England, optimism born of the new science, the dominance of Puritan ideals tenaciously held by the rising middle class, and the example of a royal court scrupulously adhering to high standards of decency and respectability combined to produce a spirit of moral earnestness linked with self-satisfaction, all of which was protested against at the time and in the generations to follow as hypocritical, false, complacent, narrow, smug, and mean. The cautious manner in which "mid-Victorian" writers in particular were prone to treat such matters as profanity and sex has been especially responsible for the use of "*Victorian*" or "mid-*Victorian*" to indicate false modesty, empty respectability, or callous complacency. Though justified in part, this use of *Victorian* rests in some degree on exaggeration and at best fails to consider that a large part of the literature either did not exhibit such traits or set itself flatly against them. Many-sided and complex, *Victorian* literature reflects both romantically and realistically the great changes that were going on in life and thought. The doubts and hopes raised by the new science, the social problems arising from the new industrial conditions, the conscious resort of literary men and women to foreign sources of inspiration, and the rise of a new middle-class audience and new media of publication are among the forces that colored literature during Victoria's reign. Because there are marked differences between the literature of the early years of Victoria's reign and that of the later years, this handbook treats the early years as a part of the ROMANTIC PERIOD and the later years as a part of the REALISTIC PERIOD. See the *Outline of Literary History*.

Vignette A SKETCH or brief narrative characterized by precision and delicacy. The term is borrowed from that used for unbordered but delicate decorative designs for a book, and it implies writing with comparable grace and economy. It may be a separate whole or a portion of a larger work. The term is also applied to SHORT-SHORT STORIES less than five hundred words in length.

Villain An evil character, potentially or actually guilty of serious crimes; he or she acts in opposition to the HERO. The *villain* is the chief ANTAGONIST in a drama.

Villanelle A fixed nineteen-line form, originally French, employing only two rhymes and repeating two of the lines according to a set pattern. Line 1 is repeated as lines 6, 12, and 18; line 3 as lines 9, 15, and 19. The first and third lines return as a rhymed couplet at the end. The scheme of rhymes and repetitions is *abá aba abá aba abá abaá*. The *villanelle* first appeared in English verse in the second half of the nineteenth century, originally for fairly lighthearted poems. (The earliest American *villanelle* was written by James Whitcomb Riley.) The obsessive repetition that can represent ecstatic affection also works for static preoccupation, as in serious *villanelles* by E. A. Robinson and William Empson. The finest *villanelle* in any language—and one of the greatest modern poems in any form—is Dylan Thomas's "Do Not Go Gentle into That Good Night."

Virelay A French verse form (related to LAI) of which the number of STANZAS and the number of lines to the stanza are unlimited. Each stanza is made up of an indefinite number of TERCETS rhyming *aab* for the first stanza, *bbc* for the second, *ccd* for the third, etc. The *virelay* has never become popular among the English poets, probably because of the monotony of the rhyme scheme.

Virgin Play A medieval nonscriptural play based on SAINTS' LIVES, in which the Virgin Mary takes an active role in performing miracles. See MIRACLE PLAY.

Virgule A slanting or an upright line used in PROSODY to mark off feet, as in the following example from Shelley:

Thĕ sún | ĭs wárm, | thĕ ský | ĭs cléar,
Thĕ wáves | ăre dán | cĭng fást | ănd bríght.

Since the Second World War, the slanting *virgule*, sponsored by Ezra Pound and Charles Olson, has joined the customary punctuation of poems.

Vision In literary use, the experience of seeing something by extraordinary sight, also that which is seen in a mystical *vision*. Typical titles are Langland's *The Vision of William concerning Piers the Plowman*, Addison's *The Vision of Mirza*, Barlow's *The Vision of Columbus* (later revised as *The Columbiad*), Blake's *Visions of the Daughters of Albion*, Southey's *A Vision of Judgment* and Byron's PARODY thereof called *The Vision of Judgment*, and J. R. Lowell's *The Vision of Sir Launfal*. Coleridge's "Kubla Khan" is subtitled "A Vision in a Dream."

Voiced Applied to consonant sounds uttered with vibration of the vocal chords, such as the sounds commonly represented by the letters *b, d, g, v*, and *z*.

Voiced Nasal Applied to VOICED consonant sounds with a nasal component, such as those represented by the letters *m* and *n* and the symbol *ŋ*.

Voiceless (also **Unvoiced**) Applied to consonant sounds uttered without voice. For the VOICED sounds commonly represented by the letters *b, d, g, v*, and *z*, the *voiceless* counterparts are commonly represented by the letters *p, t, k, f*, and *s*.

Voice-Over In film the use of a narrator's or commentator's words when the speaker is not seen by the viewer. The *voice-over* may be a bridge between scenes, a statement of facts needed by the viewer, or a comment on the scene. In special cases the *voice-over* may be in the voice of the character represented in the scene but not a part of the action in the scene. In Olivier's *Hamlet*, for example, we hear Olivier in a *voice-over* speaking the words of soliloquies while we see his motionless, pensive face on the screen. Compare with SOUND-OVER.

Volta The turn in thought—from question to answer, problem to solution—that occurs at the beginning of the SESTET in the ITALIAN SONNET. The *volta* sometimes occurs in the SHAKESPEAREAN SONNET between the twelfth and thirteenth lines. The *volta* is routinely marked at the beginning of line 9 (Italian) or 13 (Shakespearean) by "but," "yet," or "and yet." The design of Hardy's "Hap" is perspicuous:

Line 1 "If . . ."
Line 5 "Then . . ."
Line 9 "But not so . . ."

The distinctive characteristic of the MILTONIC SONNET is the absence of the *volta* in a fixed position, although the form is Italian in rhyme scheme.

Volume Sometimes a synonym for BOOK, occasionally with special reference to poetry, as in "*volume* of verse." Also used for a group of issues of a periodical, usually what is produced in a year, sometimes bound separately. *Volume* also means the physical object that makes up a work, although the work itself may be in more than one *volume*, as a three-*volume* novel.

Vorticism Earlier, a term applied to the binominal epistemology of Descartes. A movement in modern poetry related to the manifestation of certain abstract developments and methods in painting and sculpture. *Vorticism* originated in 1914 with Wyndham Lewis's effort to oppose romantic and vitalist theories with a kind of verbal and visual art based on SPATIAL FORM, clarity, definite outline, and mechanical dynamism. Ezra Pound used the *vorticist* idea in poetry as an extension of imagism, which seemed constrained to work only in short works or limited passages and to lack force. In *vorticism* abstraction frees the artist from the imitation of nature, and the vortex is energy changed by the poet or artist into form, this form being paradoxically both still and moving. Aside from the work of Pound, *vorticism* had limited influence. The practice of *vorticism* in the graphic arts can best be seen in Lewis's paintings and Henri Gaudier-Brzeska's sculpture.

[References: Timothy Materer, *Vortex: Pound, Eliot, and Lewis* (1979); William C. Wees, *Vorticism and the English Avant-Garde* (1972).]

Vox Nihili A worthless or meaningless word.

Vulgaria (also **Vulgar**) (1) Up through the early seventeenth century, a set of words, sentences, or passages in a vernacular to be translated into Latin as an exercise. The best known in English are by John Stanbridge (1508) and Robert Whittinton (1520). (2) *Vulgaria* is also a collective term for items considered vulgar (in the sense of "crude") in a given collection, as in descriptions of "the *vulgaria* in Pepys's library."

Vulgate The word comes from Latin *vulgus*, "crowd," and means "common" or "commonly used." Note two chief uses: (1) the *Vulgate* Bible is the Latin version made by Saint Jerome in the fourth century and is the ancestor of the authorized Bible of the Catholic church; (2) the "*Vulgate* ROMANCES" are the versions of various CYCLES of Arthurian romance written in Old French prose (common or colloquial speech) in the thirteenth century; they were the most widely used forms of these stories, forming the basis of Malory's *Le Morte Darthur* and other later treatments.

Cancelleresca Bastarda 1934. Designed by Jan Van Krimpen and based on fifteenth-century humanistic curve.

Wardour-Street English A style strongly marked by ARCHAISMS; an insincere, artificial expression. Wardour Street, in London, houses many antique dealers selling genuine and imitation antiques. *Wardour-Street English* is a term coined on the analogy of imitation archaisms in writing and imitation antiques in furniture. It was, for instance, applied to William Morris's translation of the *Odyssey*. Such writing persists in commerce and journalism with "ye olde," "yclept," "shoppe," and so forth. Ezra Pound, late in life, dismissed his youthful poetry as *"Wardour-Street."*

War of the Theaters A series of quarrels among certain Elizabethan dramatists (1598–1602). Ben Jonson and John Marston were the chief opponents, though many others, including Dekker certainly and Shakespeare possibly, were concerned. Among the causes were the personal and professional jealousies among some of the playwrights and the competition among the rival theaters and their companies of players. Particularly important was the struggle for supremacy between the stock companies of professionals (see PUBLIC THEATERS) and the companies of boy actors, the "Children of the Chapel"—acting at the Blackfriars—and the "Children of Paul's." The child actors were becoming very popular and were threatening to supersede the "common stages," as Shakespeare termed his fellows and himself in his allusion to the situation in *Hamlet* (2, 2). The details of the affair have not been completely recovered. Some of the plays concerned are: Jonson's *Every Man in his Humour* (1598) and *Cynthia's Revels* (1600), Marston's *Histriomastix* (1599) and *Jack Drum's Entertainment* (1600), Dekker and others' *Patient Grissel* (1600), and Dekker's *Satiromastix* (1601). Shakespeare's connection with the quarrel is inferred from the statement in the university play *The Return from Parnasus* (1601–1602) that Shakespeare had bested Jonson and from the theory that *Troilus and Cressida* reflects the "war." See SCHOOL PLAYS.

Watermark A mark of some kind—words or emblematic designs—placed on paper to identify the manufacturer, style, place of origin, size, and so forth. Names of certain sizes of printing paper, such as "pot" (or "pott") and "FOOLSCAP," originated as names of *watermarks*. As a rule, verbal material will read from left to right when viewed from the front or RECTO side of a sheet. *Watermarks* are important in the study of printing, in dating documents, and in the authentication of paper currency and postage stamps.

Weak Ending A syllable at the end of a line, with METRICAL ACCENT somewhat in excess of normal or rhetorical ACCENT. These lines from Shakespeare's *Antony and*

Cleopatra illustrate *weak ending*, in that "shall" as an auxiliary would not normally be stressed and yet is placed where the meter calls for stress:

> Your scutcheons and your signs of conquest shall
> Hang in what place you please.

In this passage from *The Tempest*, "that" (twice) and "with" make for *weak endings* (usually, as here, a matter of articles, prepositions, and conjunctions):

> Some food we had, and some fresh water, that
> A noble Neapolitan, Gonzalo,
> Out of his charity, who being then appointed
> Master of this design, did give us, with
> Rich garments, linens, stuffs, and necessaries,
> Which since have steaded much. So, of his gentleness,
> Knowing I loved my books, he furnished me
> From mine own library with volumes that
> I prize above my dukedom.

Wellerism Although named for Dickens's characters Sam and Tony Weller, the *Wellerism* is a type of expression much older than Dickens. There are many forms, but the general structure calls for three parts: (1) an utterance, usually conventional, metaphorical, or proverbial; (2) a speaker; (3) a situation. One type gives a literal sense to a figurative expression: "I've got you covered, as the rug said to the floor"—also available as a riddle: "What did the rug say to the floor?" A nearby type involves a PUN: "I'm delighted, as the firefly said when he backed into the fan."

[Reference: Wolfgang Mieder and Stewart A. Kingsbury, *A Dictionary of Wellerisms* (1994).]

Well-Made Novel A novel with a tightly constructed plot, freedom from extraneous incidents or subplots, clear motivation for the actions of its characters, and a sense of economy and inevitability. In a *well-made novel* all the parts are in a strict causal relation to one another. Although such requirements sound mechanical, great novels have been produced that qualify as *well-made*. Jane Austen was remarkably successful with the *well-made novel*, and both Hawthorne's *The Scarlet Letter* and Emily Brontë's *Wuthering Heights* display a clarity and symmetry that deserve to be called *well-made*. The qualities of the *well-made novel*, however, most frequently appear in the SHORT NOVEL.

Well-Made Play Certain PROBLEM PLAYS, COMEDIES OF MANNERS, and FARCES in the nineteenth century, particularly in France (where the equivalent term was PIÈCE BIEN FAITE) but also in England and America. The term describes tight, logical construction, with apparent inevitability. They usually contained these conventions: (1) a plot based on a withheld secret that, being revealed at the climax, produces a favorable reversal for the hero; (2) steadily mounting suspense depending on rising action, exactly timed entrances, mistaken identity, misplaced documents, and a battle of wits between hero and villain; (3) a climax culminating in an OBLIGATORY SCENE (SCÈNE À FAIRE) in which the withheld secret is revealed and the reversal of the hero's fortunes achieved; and (4) a logical DÉNOUEMENT. The chief creators of the *well-made play* were Eugène Scribe and Victorien Sardou. Much French drama of the nineteenth century was influenced by

Scribe and Sardou, and their plays were translated and performed with great success in England and America. The popular British playwrights Bulwer-Lytton, Tom Taylor, and T. W. Robertson wrote *well-made plays*, and Henrik Ibsen directed more than twenty Scribe plays in Norway before he launched his own powerfully influential dramas, which incorporate some characteristics of the *well-made play*.

Welsh Literature Though records are scanty, it is probable that there was much literary activity in Wales from the sixth to the ninth century. In eastern and central Wales there developed the *ENGLYN*, a form of epigrammatic verse possibly derived from Latin literature. The northern district produced the most famous of early Welsh poets, Taliessin and Aneurin (sixth century?) who sang of early warriors, including heroes associated with King Arthur. This literature is probably related to the Irish. The Western cycle deals with very early material, such as myths. Chiefly from this Western literature come the best-known stories of early Welsh authorship, those now collected in the famous *MABINOGION*. The tales were probably collected and written down in the eleventh and twelfth centuries, though the manuscripts date from a few centuries later. The stories fall into five classes. The first is the *Mabinogion* proper, or the "four branches." It includes four stories (belonging to the repertory of the lower orders of BARDS) that preserve primitive tradition: *Pwyll Prince of Dyved, Branwen daughter of Llyr, Manawyddan son of Llyr*, and *Math son of Mathonwy*. The second group includes two tales based on legendary tradition: *Dream of Macsen Wledig* and *Llud and Llefelys*. The third class, old Arthurian folktales current in southwest Wales retold by eleventh- or twelfth-century writers, partly Irish, is represented by *Culhwh and Olwen*. This story may reflect a very early stage of the development of Arthurian lore, before magic and grotesqueness had been displaced by chivalric manners. The fourth class consists of Arthurian stories paralleled in courtly French versions of the twelfth century: *Peredur, Gereint, The Lady of the Fountain* (or *Owein*). The fifth class (sophisticated tales) is represented by *The Dream of Rhonabwy*.

Under Gruffydd ab Cynan (1054–1137) there was a renaissance of Welsh poetry with courtly PATRONAGE—the bardic system was now flourishing. These court poets followed a traditional technique, employing ancient conventions and archaic words so much that a contemporary could hardly understand. With the English conquest (1282) the old poetry declined, and in the fourteenth and fifteenth centuries, known as a golden age, under the leadership of the poet Dafydd ap Gwilym, a contemporary of Chaucer, modern Welsh poetry had its earliest beginnings. The language actually spoken was employed, and love and nature were favored themes. Under the TUDORS the aggressive English influence depressed native Welsh poetry, though the bards remained active until the middle of the seventeenth century. A new school of poets utilizing native folk materials arose, and in the eighteenth century came the CLASSICAL revival under the influence of the English AUGUSTANS. Poetry in the nineteenth century was largely religious.

The development of prose in Wales, as in England, in the sixteenth and seventeenth centuries was fostered by the availability of the printing press and by the vogue of controversial writings, especially those connected with the religious movements of early Protestant times. In the late eighteenth and early nineteenth centuries the liberal movement in politics stimulated further activity in prose, and thereafter *Welsh literature,* both prose and poetry, has been inclined to follow general European movements. Coincident with other phases of the CELTIC RENAISSANCE there was a distinct revival of literary activity in the late nineteenth and early twentieth centuries. Although few modern poets of the first rank are speakers of the Welsh language, several have exploited Welsh devices (such as the CYNGHANEDD throughout Gerard Manley Hopkins's work). Dylan Thomas wrote in English, but a Welsh contour comes through his bardic or VATIC persona and in the gorgeous resonance and complexity of his poetry.

[References: Thomas Parry, *A History of Welsh Literature* (1955); Gwyn Williams, *An Introduction to Welsh Poetry, From the Beginnings to the Sixteenth Century* (1952); Ifor Williams, *The Beginnings of Welsh Poetry*, 2nd ed. (1980; orig. 1972).]

Welsh Triads (*Trioedd Ynys Prydein*) A MISCELLANY, surviving in many versions, of formulaic triadic sayings concerning personages, events, or places in British history, with special emphasis on Welsh materials. "The Three Ardent Lovers of the Island of Britain" is typical:

> Caswallawn the son of Beli for Flur the daughter of Mugnach Gorr,
> and Trystan the son of Talluch for Yseult the wife of March Meirchawn his uncle,
> and Kynon the son of Clydno Eiddin for Morvyth the daughter of Urien.

West End A fashionable part of London west of Charing Cross and Regent Street, including Mayfair; site of many theaters that, with their traditions, conventions, writers, performers, and technical personnel, are collectively known as *the West End*.

Westerns Literature set in the western United States and dealing with the lives of frontier men and women. The West has been a major source for American romance since early in the nineteenth century. Cooper's *The Prairie* (1827) has many of the characteristics of the *Western. Westerns* were staple fare in the DIME NOVELS and the PULP MAGAZINES, and through these popular mass media *Westerns* passed into the consciousness of the American public. *Westerns* are usually written to a very simple FORMULA, in which the characters are conventionalized and the actions so stylized that they often seem like movements in an intricate dance. A few novelists, such as Owen Wister (*The Virginian*, 1902) and Walter van Tilburg Clark (*The Ox-Bow Incident*, 1940), produced fiction of substantial literary worth using these materials, but most *Westerns* have been written by prolific writers such as Zane Grey, Max Brand, Ernest Haycox, W. M. Raine, C. E. Mulford, B. M. Bower, and Louis L'Amour. The *Western* became a stock plot for low-budget films, and since the advent of television, these STEREOTYPE stories have been among the most common fictional fare of the average American. If out of the American experience there has come a representative action that has the characteristics of a myth and expresses the average American's view of the cosmos, it appears to be the *Western*. F. Scott Fitzgerald's unfinished *The Love of the Last Tycoon* is a HOLLYWOOD NOVEL, but it is subtitled "A Western"—a reminder that the narrator of *The Great Gatsby* reflects that he, Gatsby, Tom, Daisy, and Jordan are all "Westerners" of some sort; it is significant that he and Gatsby live in West Egg. The finest recent *Western* writing is to be found in the stories of Norman Maclean (also one of the CHICAGO CRITICS). At the beginning of the twenty-first century, two of the most important writers of *Western* fiction have been Horton Foote and Larry McMurtry. Their fiction has regularly been made into films and television miniseries such as *Tender Mercies, The Trip to Bountiful, Terms of Endearment, The Last Picture Show, Horseman, Pass By* (filmed as *Hud*), *Lonesome Dove*, and *Texasville*. Joyce Carol Oates calls Cormac McCarthy's *Blood Meridian* a "Gothic western."

[References: Thomas J. Lyon, ed., *The Literary West: An Anthology of Western American Literature* (1999).]

Whimsical A general term characterizing writing that is fanciful, odd, eccentric. Whimsy, in a sense now obsolete, was used as "a whimsy in the head, or in the blood," implying a sort of vertigo. *Whimsical* writing, then, is that inspired by a fantastic or fanciful mood. Lamb's essays are often *whimsical* in this sense.

Whitespace Space in a graphic work designed to have the effect of isolating or emphasizing a word or line. In the printing of Frost's "The Death of the Hired Man," for example, certain important lines, such as "*I* can't think Si ever hurt anyone," are set off with lines of *whitespace* before and after. Sometimes, from one printing to the next, *whitespace* in a poem coming at the bottom of a page disappears, with a possible alteration of sense or structure.

Widow In printing, a short line ending a paragraph and appearing at the top of a page or a column. It looks abandoned and alone, and printers (including Updike's Rabbit) try to avoid them.

Wildtrack, Wild Track A SOUNDTRACK originally recorded independently but intended to be later combined with a photographic or video track. The poet John Wain entitled a volume *Wildtrack*.

Wisdom Literature Literature in which literary elements—plot, character, and so forth—are subordinate to the direct formulaic expression of moral wisdom and truth. Clearest in scripture like the Book of Proverbs and the *Bhagavad-Gita* but also present in some form in the writing of Samuel Johnson, John Ruskin, and D. H. Lawrence.

Wit and Humor Although neither originally was concerned with the laughable, both words now find their chief uses in this connection. At present the distinction between them is difficult to draw. One great "wit" in fact made a witticism out of his observation that any person who attempted to distinguish between *wit* and *humor* thereby demonstrated the possession of neither *wit* (in the sense of superior mental powers) nor *humor* (which implies a sense of proportion and self-evaluation that would show one the difficulty of attempting a cold analysis of so fugitive a thing as *humor*). *Humor* is the American spelling of HUMOUR, originally a physiological term that, because of its psychological implications, came to carry the meaning of "eccentric": from this meaning developed the modern implications of the term. *Wit*, originally meaning knowledge, came in the late Middle Ages to signify "intellect," "the seat of consciousness," the inner senses as contrasted with the five outer senses. The serious side of *wit* persists in such words as "witless," "halfwit," "dimwit," and "unwitting." In Renaissance times, though used in various senses, *wit* usually meant "wisdom" or "mental activity." An important critical use developed in the seventeenth century when the term, as applied for example to the Metaphysical poets, meant "fancy," in the sense of inspiration, originality, or imagination—the literary virtues particularly prized at the time. With the coming of neoclassicism, however, the term took on new meanings to reflect new critical attitudes, and for a hundred years many philosophers (including Hobbes, Locke, and Hume) and critics (including Dryden, Addison, Pope, and Johnson) struggled to define *wit*. Hobbes asserted that fancy without judgment or reason could not constitute *wit*, though judgment without fancy could. Pope used the word in both of the contrasting senses of fancy and judgment. Dryden had called *wit* "propriety of thought and words," and Locke thought of it as an agreeable and prompt assemblage of ideas, an ability to see comparisons (similar to Aristotle's placing of a premium on the aptness of a poet's metaphors). Hume stressed the idea that *wit* is what pleases ("good taste" being the criterion). Amid the confusing variety of eighteenth-century uses of the word, this notion of *wit* as a social grace that gives pleasure led to its comparison with *humor*, and before 1800 both words came to be associated with laughter, though the older, serious meaning of *wit* did not die out, as the earlier meanings of *humor* (both the medical meaning of one of the four liquids of the human body and the derived meaning of "individual disposition" or "eccentricity") had done. A modern *wit* is distinguished by quickness and brightness, especially in the use of language.

It is for the most part agreed that *wit* is primarily intellectual, the perception of similarities in seemingly dissimilar things—the "swift play and flash of mind"—and is expressed in skillful phraseology, plays on words, surprising contrasts, paradoxes, epigrams, and so forth, whereas *humor* implies a sympathetic recognition of human values and deals with the foibles and incongruities of human nature, good-naturedly exhibited. Falstaff in Shakespeare's *King Henry the Fourth*, Part I, is an example of a subtle interweaving of *wit* and *humor*. The verbal fencing, the punning, and particularly the sophistical maneuvering whereby Falstaff extricates himself from difficult situations with an apparent saving of face, rest on his *wit*. Between boast and complaint, Falstaff says, "I am not only witty in myself, but the cause that wit is in other men." On the other hand, the easy recognition on the part of the reader not only that Falstaff is bluffing and is cutting a highly ludicrous figure but also that the old rascal is inwardly laughing at himself, that he sees clearly the incongruities of his situation and behavior and knows that his lies will be recognized as such by the Prince, is an element of *humor*.

[References: William Empson, *The Structure of Complex Words* (1951); C. S. Lewis, *Studies in Words*, 2nd ed. (1967; orig. 1961); D. J. Milburn, *The Age of Wit: 1650–1750* (1966); George Williamson, *The Proper Wit of Poetry* (1961).]

Women as Actors Although they appeared on the Italian and French stages during the Renaissance, women were not countenanced on the professional stage in England, where boys were specially trained to act women's parts. Some critics have conjectured that Shakespeare, Webster, and other playwrights of the age gave some of their women characters—Cordelia, Cleopatra, Juliet, the Duchess of Malfi—an extra dimension of personality and brilliance in compensation for the obvious limitations on the boy actors. There were sporadic cases of the appearance of women on the stage in England, as in the case of the French actresses in London in 1629, but they were unfavorably received. The part of Ianthe in Davenant's *Siege of Rhodes* (1656) was played by Catherine Coleman, and the tradition of English actresses is usually dated from this event. However, this piece was more musical and spectacular than dramatic, and Coleman's appearance may have been regarded as justified by the custom of having women (not professional actresses) take parts in masques. With the sudden revival of dramatic activity in 1660, actresses became a permanent feature of the English stage. The influence of the French theater and the lack of a supply of trained boy actors were perhaps chiefly responsible. Boy actors were by no means unknown in feminine roles on the Restoration stage, however. Some women who early gained fame as actresses were Ann Barry, Mary Betterton, Anne Bracegirdle (seventeenth century); and Susannah Cibber, Anne Oldfield, and Sarah Siddons (eighteenth century).

Word Accent The normal stress on syllables. See RHETORICAL ACCENT.

Wrenched Accent An alteration in the customary pronunciation of a word—that is, a shift in WORD ACCENT—to accommodate the demands of METRICAL ACCENT. Christopher Marlowe's "The Passionate Shepherd to His Love" mocks the awkwardness of rustic verse, including a wrenching of accent to achieve rhyme:

The shepherds' swains shall dance and sing
For thy delight each May morning.

"Utah" is a TROCHEE, but these lines by Robert Frost impose a rhyme pattern that transforms the word into an IAMB rather humorously exaggerated:

Something I saw or thought I saw
In the desert at midnight in Utah. . . .

See ACCENT.

Locarno 1922. Designed by Rudolf Koch at Klingspor Typefoundry, Germany.

Xenoglossia (also **Xenoglossy**) The intelligible use of a foreign language that one does not know. Sometimes distinguished from "glossolalia," defined as the uttering of lexically noncommunicative material.

Xenolalia Same as XENOGLOSSIA.

Melior 1952. Designed by Herman Zapf.

Yapp A style of bookbinding in limp leather with overlapping edges or flaps, most often seen in Bibles. Used in such phrases as "*yapped* bindings" and "*yapp* edges."

Yeats Stanza A stanza that W. B. Yeats employed in a few poems, including "A Prayer for My Daughter" and "Byzantium." The stanza has eight lines rhyming *aabbcddc*; the rhythm is IAMBIC, and the meter is PENTAMETER except in lines four, six, and seven, which are shorter (either TETRAMETER or TRIMETER). The same stanza was used by Abraham Cowley in the seventeenth century, but it is not certain if Yeats knew about it.

Yellow Journalism Newspapers and magazines specializing in scandal and sensation. *Yellow journalism* has flourished robustly into the twenty-first century. (The best explanation of the curious nomenclature here has to do with the notorious *New York World*, in which the "Yellow Kid" cartoon appeared.)

Young Man from the Provinces A phrase used by Lionel Trilling for a kind of novel that deals with the experiences of a young provincial in a great city. The last third of Fielding's *Tom Jones* is the story of such a provincial in London, as is Burney's *Evelina*. Other examples are Stendhal's *The Red and the Black*, Balzac's *Lost Illusions*, Dickens's *Great Expectations*, Flaubert's *Sentimental Education*, Fitzgerald's *The Great Gatsby*, and Wolfe's *Of Time and the River*. With a twist—the pernicious forces of the city move to the outermost provinces and corrupt a pure savage—the same pattern appears in Huxley's *Brave New World*.

Libra 1938. Designed by S. H. De Roos.

Zeugma A term used in several ways, all involving a sort of "yoking": (1) as a synonym of SYLLEPSIS: when an object-taking word (preposition or transitive verb) has two or more objects on different levels, such as concrete and abstract, as in Goldsmith's witty sentence, "I had fancied you were gone down to cultivate matrimony and your estate in the country," wherein figurative and literal senses of the transitive "cultivate" are yoked together by "and"; (2) when two different words that sound exactly alike are yoked together, as in "He bolted the door and his dinner," wherein "bolted" is actually two different concrete verbs; (3) a grammatical irregularity that arises when a conjunction yokes together forms that cannot all be reconciled with other material in the sentence, as in "Either you or he was responsible," wherein the "you" cannot be reconciled with the verb "was." In "one or two years ago," the singular "one" does not match the plural "years," but hardly anyone will try to avoid such a *zeugma* by going the long way round with "one year or two years ago." See SLEIGHT OF "AND."

Zohar The major text of Jewish KABBALISM, in the form of an ALLEGORICAL interpretation of the PENTATEUCH.

Zoom Shot In filmmaking the shot resulting from the use of a camera lens with an adjustable focal length, so that the viewer appears to move rapidly closer to or farther from an object.

Outline of Literary History: British and American

British and American literary history has been divided here into relatively arbitrary *periods*, and historical subdivisions within these periods are called *ages*. Treatments of these units are given in the handbook, where brief essays on the *periods* and shorter comment on the *ages* appear.

Beginning with 1607, American items appear in a separate column.

Titles are often abbreviated or modernized. Translated titles appear in quotation marks in the early periods.

Dates of printed books ordinarily indicate first publication. Dates for works written before the era of printing are dates of composition, often approximate.

The following abbreviations and symbols are used:

?	questionable date or statement
*	non-English item
w	written
a	acted
c.	circa, around, about: dating is approximate
fl.	flourishing, or flourished
et seq.	and following
Lat.	Latin
A.S.	Anglo-Saxon
MS	manuscript
estab.	established

? B.C.–A.D. 428 Celtic and Roman Britain

?B.C.–A.D. 82	Celtic Britain.
55, 54 B.C.	Julius Caesar invades Britain.
A.D. 43–410	Roman-Celtic period in Britain: government Roman, population largely Celtic. No literature extant.
43	Invasion of Claudius.
c. 85	Roman power established in Britain.

98	*Tacitus, *Germania* (Lat.): early account of Teutonic ancestors of English.
313	*Christianity established at Rome by Constantine.
410	*Rome sacked by Alaric.
	Roman legions leave Britain.

428–1100 Old English (Anglo-Saxon) Period

c. 428	Germanic tribes begin invasion of Britain.
449	Traditional date (from Gildas and Bede) for Germanic invasion of Britain under Hengist and Horsa.
c. 450–c. 700	Probable period of composition of Old English poems reflecting Continental life: *Beowulf*, epic; *Waldhere*, fragmentary epic of Theodoric saga; *Finnsburg*, fragmentary, related to *Beowulf* background; *Widsith*, lyric, adventures of a wandering poet; *Deor's Lament*, lyric account of poet's troubles; *The Wanderer*, reflective poem on cruelty of fate; *The Seafarer*, reflective, descriptive lyric on sailor's lot in life; *The Wife's Complaint, The Husband's Message*, love poems notable for romantic treatment of nature; *Charms*, miscellaneous incantations reflecting early superstitions, ceremonies, and remedies; formulistic.
c. 500–c. 700	*Christian culture flourishes in Ireland after being almost obliterated on Continent by Teutonic invasion; activity of Irish missionaries in Scotland, Iceland, France, Germany, Switzerland, and Italy aids in rechristianizing Western Europe.
c. 524	*Boethius, "Consolation of Philosophy" (Lat.); translated into English, successively, by King Alfred, Chaucer, and Queen Elizabeth.
563	St. Columba (Irish monk) establishes monastery at Iona, thus preparing for spread of Celtic Christianity in Scotland and northern England.
597	Saint Augustine (the missionary) places Roman Christianity on firm basis in southern England.
600–700	Establishment of powerful Anglo-Saxon kingdoms.
c. 600–c. 800	*Irish saga literature assumes written form.
c. 633	*The Koran; texts recorded; canonical version, 651–52.
640?–709	Aldhelm: famous scholar of Canterbury school—Latin works survive; English poems (probably ballads) lost.
664	Synod of Whitby: triumph of Roman over Celtic Christianity in Britain.
c. 670	Caedmon, *Hymns*, etc.: first English poet known by name.
c. 690	Adamnan, *Life of St. Columba* (Lat.): first biography in Britain.
c. 700	"School of Caedmon" fl.: Genesis, Exodus, Daniel—biblical paraphrases; Judith, apocryphal.
	Beowulf composed in present form: great A.S. epic.
731	Bede (Baeda) the Venerable, "Ecclesiastical History" (Lat.): first history of English people.

750

c. 750–c. 800	Flourishing period of Christian poetry in Northumbria (preserved in later West Saxon versions).
	Cynewulf and his "school": *Christ*, narrative; *Elene, Juliana, Fates of the Apostles, Andreas*, saints' legends. *The Phoenix*, myth interpreted as Christian allegory.

787	First Danish invasion.
c. 800	Nennius (a Welshman), "History of the Britons" (Lat.): first mention of Arthur.

850

c. 850	Danish conquest of England.
871–899	Reign of Alfred the Great. Alfred's translations of Pope Gregory's *Pastoral Care*, Boethius, Orosius, Bede; *Anglo-Saxon Chronicle* revised and continued to 892; West Saxon *Martyrology*; sermons; saints' lives.
c. 875–900	*Probable beginnings of medieval drama. Dramatization of liturgy. First known text an Easter trope, *Quem Quaeritis*, from Swiss monastery of St. Gall.
878	Peace of Wedmore; partial Danish evacuation.
893	Asser, *Life of Alfred the Great:* "first life-record of a layman."
901–1066	Later Old English Period. *Chronicle* continued; poetry, sermons, biblical translations and paraphrases, saints' lives, lyrics.
c. 937	*Battle of Brunanburh:* heroic poem.
c. 950	*Junius* MS written: contains "School of Caedmon" poems.
950–1000	Monastic revival under Dunstan, Aethelwold, and Aelfric.
971	*Blickling Homilies:* colloquial tendencies.
c. 975	St. Aethelwold's *Regularis Concordia:* earliest evidence of dramatic activity in England.
979–1016	Second period of Danish invasions.
c. 991	*Battle of Maldon:* heroic poem.

1000

1000–1200	Transition period, English to Norman French. Decline of A.S. heroic verse; reduced literary activity in English.
c. 1000	A.S. *Gospels* written. Aelfric, *Sermons*.
	Beowulf MS written.
c. 1000–1025	The *Exeter Book:* A.S. MS containing Cynewulf poems.
c. 1000–1100	*Vercelli Book:* A.S. MS containing *Andreas*, etc.
	*Probable period of full development of Christmas and Easter cycles of plays in Western Europe.
1017–1042	Danish kings (Canute to Hardicanute).
1042–1066	Saxon kings restored (Edward the Confessor to Harold II).
1066	Battle of Senlac (Hastings). Norman Conquest.
1066–1154	Norman kings (William I to Stephen).
1086	*Domesday Book:* important English census.
1087–1100	William II: centralization of kingdom.
1096–1099	The First Crusade.

1100–1350 Anglo-Norman Period

1100–1200	*French literature dominating Western Europe.
1100–1135	Reign of Henry I ("Beauclerc").
c. 1100–1250	*Icelandic sagas written: *Grettirsaga, Volsungsaga*, etc.
c. 1100	"Play of St. Catherine" (*a* at Dunstable): first recorded "miracle" or saint's play in England.
	*Earlier tales in Welsh *Mabinogion (w)*.
	*Great period of French poetry begins. *Chanson de Roland:* epic.
c. 1124	Eadmer, *Life of Anselm:* human element in biography.
c. 1125	Henry of Huntingdon and William of Malmesbury: chronicles.
c. 1125–1300	Latin chronicles fl.
1135–1154	Reign of Stephen.
c. 1136	Geoffrey of Monmouth, "History of the Kings of Britain" (Lat. chronicle). First elaborate account of Arthurian court.

1150

1154	End of entries in *A.S. Chronicle* (Peterborough).
1154–1399	Plantagenet kings (Henry II to Richard II).
1154–1189	Reign of Henry II: his court a center of literature and learning—historians, philosophers, theologians, poets.
c. 1170	*Poema Morale*.
c. 1185–1190	*Giraldus Cambrensis, "Itinerary": description of Wales.
1189–1199	Reign of Richard I ("The Lion-Hearted").
c. 1190	Nigel Wireker, *Speculum stultorum* (Lat.), "The Fools' Looking-glass."
1199–1216	Reign of John.

1200

c. 1200	Walter Map fl.: court satirist.
	Orm, *Ormulum:* scriptural poem.
c. 1200–1225	*The Vulgate Romances (expansion of Arthurian romance material in French prose).
c. 1200–1250	*King Horn, Beves of Hampton* (earliest form): English metrical romances using English themes.
c. 1205	Layamon, *Brut*.
1215	Magna Charta.
1216–1272	Reign of Henry III.
c. 1225	*St. Thomas Aquinas born. Died 1274.
c. 1230, c. 1270	**Roman de la Rose* by Guillaume de Lorris and Jean de Meun.

1250

c. 1250	Nicholas of Guilford, *The Owl and the Nightingale*. The "Cuckoo Song" (*Sumer is icumen in*).
c. 1250	**Gesta Romanorum*.
c. 1250–1300	*Sir Tristem, Floris and Blanchefleur:* romances.
1258	Henry III uses English as well as French in proclamation.
1265	*Dante born. Died 1321.
1272–1307	Reign of Edward I.
c. 1294	*Dante, *Vita Nuova*.

1300

1300–1400	English displaces French in speech of upper classes and in schools and law pleadings. Mystery plays now in hands of guilds: more actors, more spectators, outdoor stages, comic elements, "cyclic" development (York plays probably oldest existing cycle).
c. 1300	*Marco Polo, "Travels."
	Cursor Mundi.
c. 1300–1350	*Guy of Warwick, Havelok the Dane, Richard Lionheart, Amis and Amiloun:* romances.
c. 1307–1321	*Dante's *Divina Commedia*.
1304	*Petrarch born. Died 1374.
1307–1327	Reign of Edward II.
1311	Feast of Corpus Christi, established in 1264, was made operative, leading to popularization of cyclic plays at this summer festival and perhaps to use of movable stages or "pageants."
1313	*Boccaccio born. Died 1375.
1314	Battle of Bannockburn.
c. 1320	John Barbour born. Died 1395.
1327–1377	Reign of Edward III.
1328(?)	Chester cycle of plays composed.
1337–1453	The Hundred Years' War.
c. 1340	Geoffrey Chaucer born. Died 1400.
	The Prick of Conscience.
1342	*Boccaccio, *Ameto:* "first pastoral romance."
1346	Battle of Crécy.
1348–1350	The Black Death in England.

1350–1500 Middle English Period

1350–1400	*Sir Eglamour, Morte Arthure, Sir Gawayne and the Green Knight, Athelston, William of Palerne, Sir Ferumbras, Sir Isumbras*, and other romances.
c. 1350	*Petrarch, eclogues (Lat.), printed 1504. "Sonnets to Laura" partly written.
	*Boccaccio, *Decameron*.

1356(?)	"Sir John Mandeville," *Voyage and Travels*.
c. 1360	*The Pearl*.
1362	English language used in court pleadings and in opening Parliament.
c. 1362 *et seq*.	*Piers Plowman*.
c. 1370	Chaucer, *The Book of the Duchess*.
c. 1375	Barbour, *The Bruce*.
	"Paternoster" and "Creed" plays *(a)*: forerunners of morality plays.
1377–1399	Richard II.
c. 1379	Chaucer, *House of Fame*.
c. 1380	Wycliffe and others, translation of Bible into English.
1381	Wat Tyler's rebellion.
c. 1383	Chaucer, *Troilus and Criseyde*.
c. 1385	English replaces French as language of the schools.
	Chaucer, *Legend of Good Women*.
c. 1387	Chaucer, "Prologue" to *Canterbury Tales* (tales themselves written, some earlier, some later).
c. 1388	Usk (?), *The Testament of Love*.
c. 1390	Gower, *Confessio Amantis*.
1394	James I of Scotland born. Died 1437.
1399–1461	House of Lancaster (Henry IV to Henry VI).
1399–1413	Reign of Henry IV.
1400	Death of Chaucer.

1400

1400–1450	Later romances in prose and verse.
1400	*Froissart, *Chronicles*.
1400–1425	Wakefield cycle of plays (MS, c. 1450).
	The Pride of Life (fragmentary): earliest extant morality play.
c. 1405	*Castle of Perseverance*; first complete morality play.
c. 1412	Hoccleve, *The Regiment of Princes (w)*.
1413–1422	Reign of Henry V.
1415	Battle of Agincourt.
c. 1415	Lydgate, *Troy Book*.
1422–1461	Reign of Henry VI.
1422–1509	The *Paston Letters:* family correspondence reflecting social conditions.
c. 1424	Robert Henryson born. Died c. 1506.
c. 1425	Humanists active under patronage of Humphrey, Duke of Gloucester: Lydgate, Pecock, etc.
1437	Death of James I of Scotland.
1440	Galfridus Grammaticus, *Promptorium Parvulorum:* English-Latin word list, beginning of English lexicography.

1450

1450	Jack Cade's rebellion.
c. 1450	"Tiptoft" School of humanists active.
	*Gutenberg press: beginning of modern printing.
	Beginning of Lowland Scots as northern literary dialect.
c. 1450–1525	Scottish poets of Chaucerian school: Henryson, Dunbar, Douglas, and probably King James I of Scotland.
1453	*Fall of Constantinople: end of Eastern Empire.
1455–1485	Wars of the Roses: depressing effect on literary activity.
1456	*The Gutenberg Bible.
c. 1456	William Dunbar born. Died c. 1513.
c. 1460	John Skelton born. Died 1529.
1461–1485	House of York (Edward IV to Richard III).
1461–1483	Reign of Edward IV.
1469	Sir Thomas Malory completes composition of *Le Morte Darthur* (pub. 1485).
1474	Caxton prints (at Bruges) the *Recuyell of the Histories of Troy:* first book printed in English.
c. 1477	Caxton's press set up at Westminster: first printing press in England. *Dictes and Sayings of the Philosophers*, the first dated book (1477) printed in England.
1478	Sir Thomas More born. Died 1535.
1483	Reign of Edward V.
1483–1485	Reign of Richard III.
1485	Caxton publishes Malory's *Le Morte Darthur.*
1485–1603	House of Tudor (Henry VII to Elizabeth I).
1485–1509	Reign of Henry VII.
1490–1520	"Oxford Reformers" (Linacre, Grocyn, Colet, Erasmus, More) active.
1491	Greek taught at Oxford.
1492	*Discovery of America by Columbus.
c. 1497	Medwall, *Fulgens and Lucres (a).*
1499	Erasmus in England.

1500–1660 The Renaissance

	1500–1557 Early Tudor Age
c. 1500	*Everyman.*
1500–1550	Romances: *Valentine and Orson,* Lord Berners's *Arthur of Little Britain, Huon of Bordeaux*, etc.
1503 (?)	Sir Thomas Wyatt born. Died 1542.
c. 1508	Skelton, *Philip Sparrow.*
1509–1547	Reign of Henry VIII.
1509	Barclay, *Ship of Fools.*

	Hawes, *Pastime of Pleasure.*
	*Erasmus, "The Praise of Folly" (Lat.) *(w)*, social satire.
1510	Acting of Terence's comedies becomes an established practice at Oxford and Cambridge.
1515	Roger Ascham born. Died 1568.
1516	More, *Utopia* (Lat.).
c. 1516	*Ariosto, *Orlando Furioso.*
	Skelton, *Magnificence.*
1517	*Luther posts his theses in Wittenberg; leads to Protestant Revolution, 1520 *et seq*.
c. 1517	Henry Howard, Earl of Surrey born. Died 1547.
1519	Rastell, *The Four Elements:* first published interlude. Advocates adequacy of English for literary purposes.
	*Cortez conquers Mexico.
c. 1520	Skelton's poetical satires (*Colin Clout, Why Come Ye Not to Court*, etc.).
1520–1530	Latin plays acted in grammar schools.
1523	Lord Berners's trans. of Froissart's *Chronicles.*

1525

1525	Tyndale, *New Testament:* printed at Worms; first printed English translation of any part of Bible.
1528	*Castiglione, *The Courtier.*
1529	Simon Fish, *Supplication for the Beggars.*
	Fall of Wolsey.
c. 1530	The "New Poetry" movement under way.
c. 1530–1540	Heywood's "Interludes": realistic farce.
1531	Elyot, *The Boke Named the Governour.*
1532	*Machiavelli, *The Prince* (*w* 1513).
	*Rabelais, *Pantagruel.*
1533	Separation of English church from Rome.
	John Leland made "King's Antiquary."
1534	Act of Supremacy: Henry VIII head of Church of England.
1535	Execution of More.
	Coverdale's first complete English Bible.
1536	Execution of Tyndale.
	*Calvin, *Institutes of Christian Religion* (Lat.).
1538	Sir Thomas Elyot, *Dictionarie.*
1539	English Bible (the "Great Bible") published.
1540	Lyndsay, *Satyre of the Three Estaits.*
1542	Death of Wyatt.
	Hall's *Chronicle.*
1542 (?)	George Gascoigne born. Died 1577.

1545	Ascham, *Toxophilus*.
	*Council of Trent.
1547	Execution of Surrey.
1547–1553	Reign of Edward VI.
1549–1552	*Book of Common Prayer*.

1550

c. 1552	Edmund Spenser born. Died 1599.
	Sir Walter Ralegh born. Died 1618.
	Udall, *Ralph Roister Doister* (*w*): first "regular" English comedy.
1553	Wilson, *Arte of Rhetorique*.
1553–1558	Reign of Mary.
1554	Sir Philip Sidney born. Died 1586.
c. 1555	Roper, *Life of Sir Thomas More* (*w*).
	Cavendish, *Life of Cardinal Wolsey* (*w*).
1557	*Songs and Sonnets* ("Tottel's Miscellany"), containing Surrey's trans. of two books of the *Aeneid* in blank verse.
	North's trans. of Guevara's *Dial of Princes*.
	Stationer's Company incorporated.

	1558–1603 Elizabethan Age
1558–1603	Reign of Elizabeth I.
1558	John Knox, *First Blast of the Trumpet against the Monstrous Regiment of Women*.
1558–1575	Translations numerous; classics often translated into English through French versions. Much interest in lyrics.
1559	Elizabethan prayer book.
	The Mirror for Magistrates.
	*Amyot, Plutarch's *Lives* translated into French: basis of North's English version of Plutarch.
	*Minturno, *De Poeta:* Italian critical work.
1559 (?)	George Chapman born. Died 1634.
c. 1560	*Gammer Gurton's Needle* (*w*).
1561	Hoby's translation of Castiglione's *The Courtier*.
	Francis Bacon born. Died 1626.
	*Scaliger, *Poetics:* Italian critical work.
1562	Sackville and Norton, *Gorboduc* (*a*): first English tragedy.
	Samuel Daniel born. Died 1619.
1563	Foxe, *Book of Martyrs* (Lat. original, 1559).
	Sackville's "Induction" (to portion of *Mirror for Magistrates*).
	Michael Drayton born. Died 1631.
c. 1563	Sir Humphrey Gilbert, *Queen Elizabeth's Academy*.

1564	Preston, *Cambises* (*a*).
1564	Christopher Marlowe born. Died 1593.
	William Shakespeare born. Died 1616.
	*Galileo born. Died 1642.
1565–1567	Golding's translation of Ovid's *Metamorphoses*.
1566	Gascoigne's *Supposes* (*a*) and *Jocasta* (*a*).
1566–1567	Painter, *Palace of Pleasure*.
1567	Turberville, *Epitaphs, Epigrams, Songes, and Sonets*.
1570	Ascham, *Schoolmaster*.
c. 1573	John Donne born. Died 1631.
	Ben Jonson born. Died 1637.

1575

1575	Gascoigne, *The Posies:* poems with first English treatise on versification appended.
	Mystery plays still being acted at Chester.
1576	*Paradise of Dainty Devices*.
	The Theatre (first London playhouse) built.
	Gascoigne, *The Steel Glass*.
	George Pettie, *A Petite Palace of Pettie his Pleasure*.
1577–1580	Spenser's early poetry (*w*).
1577	Holinshed, *Chronicles*.
	A Gorgeous Gallery of Gallant Inventions: poetical miscellany.
1577–1580	Drake circumnavigates globe.
1579	Lyly, *Euphues, the Anatomy of Wit*.
	Spenser, *The Shepheardes Calendar* (pub. anonymously).
	Gosson, *School of Abuse:* attack on poetry and the stage.
	North, trans. of Plutarch's *Lives*.
	John Fletcher born. Died 1625.
1580	*Montaigne, *Essays:* beginning of modern "personal" essay.
1580–1600	Elizabethan "novels" popular: Lyly, Greene, Lodge, Sidney, Nash, Deloney. Pastoral poetry popular.
c. 1581	Peele, *Arraignment of Paris* (*a*).
	Sidney, *Defense of Poesie* (*w*) (pub. 1595).
1582	Stanyhurst, trans. of Virgil's *Aeneid* (i–iv) in quantitative verse.
1582–1600	Hakluyt publishes various collections of "voyages"—Renaissance and medieval, notably *Principal Navigations* (1st ed. 1589).
1583	P. Stubbs, *Anatomie of Abuses*.
c. 1583	Lyly, *Alexander and Campaspe* (*a*).
1584	Scot, *Discovery of Witchcraft*.
	Handful of Pleasant Delights: ballad miscellany.
1585–1586	Ralegh fails in effort to colonize Virginia.

1586	Kyd, *The Spanish Tragedy* (*a*).
	Warner, *Albion's England*.
	Camden, *Britannia* (Lat.).
	Death of Sidney.
1586 (?)	Shakespeare comes to London.
1587	Marlowe, *Tamburlaine* (*a*).
	Execution of Mary Queen of Scots.
1588	Defeat of Spanish Armada.
c. 1588	Marlowe, *Doctor Faustus* (*a*).
1588–1589	"Martin Marprelate" papers.
1589	Greene, *Menaphon*.
	Puttenham (?), *The Arte of English Poesie*.

1590

1590	Lodge, *Rosalynde*.
	Sidney, *Arcadia* (*w* c. 1581).
	Spenser, *Faerie Queene*, Books I–III.
c. 1590	Greene (?), *James IV* (*a*).
	Shakespeare begins career as playwright with *The Comedy of Errors*.
1591	Spenser, *Complaints:* includes *Mother Hubberd's Tale*.
	Harington, trans. of Ariosto's *Orlando Furioso*.
	Sidney, *Astrophil and Stella*.
	Robert Herrick born. Died 1674.
1591–1596	Sonnet cycles: Sidney, Daniel, Drayton, Lodge, Spenser, and others.
1592–1593	Shakespeare, *Richard III* (*a*).
1593	Shakespeare, *Venus and Adonis*.
	Phoenix Nest: poetical miscellany.
	Death of Marlowe.
	Izaak Walton born. Died 1683.
	George Herbert born. Died 1633.
1594	Hooker, *Ecclesiastical Polity*, Books I–IV.
	Shakespeare, *Rape of Lucrece*.
	Nash, *The Unfortunate Traveler:* picaresque romance.
1595	Spenser, *Amoretti; Epithalamion*.
	Sidney, *Defence of Poesie* (*w* c. 1581).
	Daniel, *Civil Wars*.
	Lodge, *A Fig for Momus*.
	Donne's poetry circulating in manuscript.
1595	Shakespeare, *A Midsummer Night's Dream* (*a*).
1596	Ralegh, *Discovery of Guiana* (*w*) (pub. 1606).
	Shakespeare, *Romeo and Juliet* (*a*).
	Spenser, *Faerie Queene*, Books IV–VI.

1597	Shakespeare, *Merchant of Venice* (*a*).
	Drayton, *Heroical Epistles*.
	Bacon, *Essays* (1st ed.).
	Hall, *Virgidemiarum*, Vol. I.
	King James (of Scotland), *Demonology:* answers Scot and defends reality of witchcraft.
1597–1600	Shakespeare's Falstaff plays (*a*): *Henry IV*, Parts I, II; *Henry V*; *Merry Wives of Windsor*.
1598	Shakespeare, *Julius Caesar* (*a*).
	Meres, *Palladis Tamia*, "Wit's Treasury."
	Ben Jonson begins career as playwright—*Everyman in His Humour* (*a*).
	Chapman, translation of *Iliad* (seven books in fourteeners).
c. 1598	Deloney, *The Gentle Craft*.
1598–1600	Shakespeare's "joyous comedies": *Much Ado about Nothing; As You Like It; Twelfth Night*.
1599	*The Passionate Pilgrim:* miscellany containing some of Shakespeare's poems.
	Globe theater built: used by Shakespeare's company.
	Death of Spenser.

1600

1600	*England's Helicon:* poetical miscellany.
1601	Shakespeare, *Hamlet* (*a*).
1602	Campion, *Observations in the Art of English Poesie*.
	Founding of the Bodleian Library (Oxford).
c. 1602	Daniel, *Defence of Ryme*.
1602–1604	Shakespeare's "bitter comedies": *Troilus and Cressida, All's Well That Ends Well, Measure for Measure* (*a*).
	1603–1625 Jacobean Age
1603–1688	The Stuarts.
1603–1625	Reign of James I: union of English and Scottish crowns.
1603	T. Heywood, *A Woman Killed with Kindness* (*a*).
	Jonson, *Sejanus* (*a*).
	Florio, translation of Montaigne.
1604	Shakespeare, *Othello* (*a*).
1605	Bacon, *Advancement of Learning*.
	Gunpowder Plot.
	*Cervantes, *Don Quixote*, Part I.
	Sir Thomas Browne born. Died 1682.
	Shakespeare, *Macbeth* (*a*), *King Lear* (*a*).
1606	Jonson, *Volpone* (*a*).
	Sir William Davenant born. Died 1668.

	BRITISH	AMERICAN
		1607–1765 Colonial Period
1607	Shakespeare, *Antony and Cleopatra (a).* Beaumont and Fletcher, *The Knight of the Burning Pestle* (*a*).	Settlement at Jamestown, Virginia.
1608	John Milton born. Died 1674.	Capt. John Smith, *True Relation:* early experiences in Virginia.
1609	Shakespeare, *Sonnets* (*w* earlier). Beaumont and Fletcher, *Philaster* (*a*). Dekker, *Gull's Hornbook.*	Champlain discovers Lake Champlain. Henry Hudson explores Hudson River.

1610

1609–1611	Shakespeare, tragicomedies: *Cymbeline, The Winter's Tale, The Tempest* (*a*).	
1610	Jonson, *Alchemist* (*a*).	Strachey, *True Repertory.*
1611	King James translation of the Bible.	
c. 1611	Shakespeare returns to Stratford.	
1612	Bacon, *Essays* (2d ed.). Donne, First and Second *Anniversaries.* Samuel Butler born. Died 1680.	Capt. John Smith, *A Map of Virginia.* Anne Bradstreet born (in England). Died 1672.
1613	*Purchas His Pilgrimage:* travel literature. Wither, *Abuses Stript and Whipt.*	
1614	Overbury, *Characters.* Ralegh, *History of the World.* Webster, *Duchess of Malfi* (*a*).	
1614–1616	Chapman, *Odyssey* translated.	
1615	Harington, *Epigrams.*	
1616	Deaths of Shakespeare and *Cervantes.	Capt. John Smith, *A Description of New England.*
1618	Ralegh executed. Harvey discovers circulation of the blood. Abraham Cowley born. Died 1667.	
1619	Drayton, *Collected Poems.* Death of Daniel.	First American legislative assembly, at Jamestown. Negro slavery introduced into Virginia.

	BRITISH	AMERICAN
	1620	
1620	Bacon, *Novum Organum* (Lat.).	Pilgrims land at Plymouth. Mayflower Compact (*w*).
1621	Burton, *Anatomy of Melancholy*.	*Mourts's Relation* by Bradford and others: journal.
1622	Donne, *Sermon on Judges* 20:15; (others published later.)	
1623	First Folio edition of Shakespeare's plays.	
1624	George Sandys completes translation of Ovid's *Metamorphoses*.	Capt. John Smith, *General History of Virginia*. Edward Winslow, *Good News out of New England*.
	1625	
	1625–1649 Caroline Age	
1625–1649	Reign of Charles I.	
1625	Bacon, *Essays*, final edition.	Morrell, *Nova Anglia*.
1626	Death of Bacon.	Minuit founds New Amsterdam.
1627	Bacon, *New Atlantis* (Lat.): fragmentary "utopia." Drayton, *Battle of Agincourt*.	Thomas Morton sets up Maypole at Merrymount: reflects opposition to Puritans.
1628	John Bunyan born. Died 1688.	
1629	Ford, *The Broken Heart* (*a*). Milton, *Ode on the Morning of Christ's Nativity* (*w*).	
	1630	
1630	Milton, *On Shakespeare* (*w*).	Massachusetts Bay Colony established at Salem.
1630–1647		Bradford, *History of the Plymouth Plantation* (*w*).
1630–1649		Winthrop, *History of New England* (*w*).
1631	Deaths of Drayton and Donne. John Dryden born. Died 1700.	
1632	Second Folio edition of Shakespeare.	Thomas Hooker, *The Soul's Preparation*.
1633	Herbert, *The Temple*. Donne, *Poems* (first collected edition).	

	BRITISH	AMERICAN
	Phineas Fletcher, *The Purple Island*.	
1633 (?)	Milton's "L'Allegro" and "Il Penseroso" written.	
	Samuel Pepys born. Died 1703.	
	Milton, *Comus* (*a*).	
1634	Davenant, *The Temple of Love*: French Platonic love.	Maryland settled by English. Connecticut Valley settled.
	Death of George Chapman.	
1635	Quarles, *Emblems*.	
1636	*Corneille, *The Cid*.	Roger Williams founds Providence; all sects tolerated.
		Harvard College founded.
1637	Death of Jonson.	Pequót War.
	*Descartes, *Discours sur la Méthode*.	Thomas Morton, *New English Canaan*.
1638	Milton, *Lycidas*.	
1639		First printing press in America set up at Cambridge.
		Increase Mather born. Died 1723.

1640

	BRITISH	AMERICAN
1640	Jonson, *Timber, or Discoveries Made upon Men and Matter*.	*Bay Psalm Book:* first book printed in America.
	Izaak Walton, *Life of Donne*.	
	Aphra Behn born. Died 1689.	
1641		Shepard, *The Sincere Convert*.
1642	Fuller, *Holy State*.	
	Denham, *Cooper's Hill*.	
	Sir Thomas Browne, *Religio Medici*.	
	Sir Isaac Newton born. Died 1727.	
	Civil War. Theaters closed.	
1644	Milton, *Areopagitica, Tractate on Education*, and divorce pamphlets.	Roger Williams, *Bloody Tenent of Persecution*.
		Roger Williams visits Milton; teaches him Dutch.
1645	Howell, *Familiar Letters*.	
	Waller, *Poems*.	
	Founding of Philosophical Society.	

	BRITISH	AMERICAN
c. 1645		Edward Taylor born. Died 1729. *Poems*, posthumously pub. 1939.
1646	Vaughan, *Poems*.	
1647		Nathaniel Ward, *Simple Cobbler of Aggawam*.
1648	Herrick, *Hesperides*.	
	1649–1660 Commonwealth Interregnum	
1649	Execution of Charles I. Lovelace, *Lucasta*.	

1650

	BRITISH	AMERICAN
1650	Davenant, *Gondibert*. Taylor, *Holy Living*.	Anne Bradstreet, *The Tenth Muse, Lately Sprung up in America*.
c. 1650	Many French romances and novels translated into English.	
1650–1728		Flourishing of the "Mather Dynasty."
1651	Milton, *Defence of the English People* (Lat.). Hobbes, *Leviathan*.	*Cambridge Platform* passed by General Court.
1652	"Quaker" Movement culminating.	
1653	Walton, *The Compleat Angler*.	
1654	Boyle, *Parthenissa*.	Capt. Edward Jonson, *Wonder-Working Providence*.
1656	Cowley, *Poems, Davideis, Pindaric Odes*. Davenant, *Siege of Rhodes* (*a*).	Hammond, *Leah and Rachel*, or *The Two Fruitful Sisters, Virginia and Maryland*. Quakers arrive in Massachusetts.
1658	Dryden, *Stanzas on the Death of Cromwell*.	
1659		John Eliot, *The Christian Commonwealth*.

1660–1798 Neoclassical Period

	BRITISH	AMERICAN
	1660–1700 Restoration Age	
1660–1714	Stuarts restored (Charles II to Anne).	
1660–1685	Reign of Charles II.	
1660	Dryden, *Astraea Redux:* welcomes Charles II.	

	BRITISH	AMERICAN
c. 1660	Daniel Defoe born. Died 1731.	
1660–1669	Pepys's *Diary* (*w*) (pub. 1825).	
1660–1700		Verse elegies popular.
1661	Anne Finch, Countess of Winchilsea, born. Died 1720.	
1662	Fuller, *Worthies of England*.	Wigglesworth, *Day of Doom*.
	The Royal Society founded as reorganization of the Philosophical Society.	"Half-Way Covenant": lowers requirements for church membership in Massachusetts.
1663	Butler, *Hudibras*, Part I.	Eliot translates Bible into Indian language.
	Drury Lane Theatre (first called Theatre Royal) built.	Cotton Mather born. Died 1728.
1664	Dryden and Howard, *The Indian Queen* (*a*).	
1665	Dryden, *The Indian Emperor*.	Baptist Church established in Boston.
	Head, *The English Rogue*.	
1666	Bunyan, *Grace Abounding*.	George Alsop, *A Character of the Province of Maryland*.
1667	Jonathan Swift born. Died 1745.	
	Sprat, *History of the Royal Society*.	
	Milton, *Paradise Lost*.	
1668	Sprat, *Life of Cowley:* starts tradition of "discreet" biography.	
	Dryden, *Essay of Dramatic Poesy*.	

1670

1670	Dryden, *Conquest of Granada* (*a*).	Denton, *Brief Description of New York*.
	Dryden made Poet Laureate.	Mason, *Pequót War* (*w*) (pub. 1736).
1671	Milton, *Paradise Regained* and *Samson Agonistes*.	Eliot, *Progress of the Gospel Among the Indians in New England*.
	Villiers (Buckingham) and others, *The Rehearsal* (*a*).	
1672	Joseph Addison born. Died 1719.	Eliot, *The Logick Primer:* "for the use of praying Indians."
	Sir Richard Steele born. Died 1729.	
1673		Increase Mather, *Woe to Drunkards*.
1674	Wycherley, *The Plain-Dealer* (*a*).	
	Deaths of Milton and Herrick.	
1674–1729		Samuel Sewall, *Diary* (*w*).

	BRITISH	AMERICAN
1676	Etheredge, *The Man of Mode.*	
1677		Urian Oakes, *Elegy on Thomas Shepard.*
1678	Bunyan, *Pilgrim's Progress,* Part I.	
	Dryden, *All for Love.*	
	Popish Plot.	

1680

1680		*The Burwell Papers* (*w*).
1681	Dryden, *Absalom and Achitophel.*	
1682	Otway, *Venice Preserved.*	Penn settles Pennsylvania.
	Dryden, *MacFlecknoe.*	La Salle explores Mississippi.
		Mary Rowlandson, *Narrative of the Captivity* (*w*): life among the Indians.
1683		Increase Mather, *Discourse Concerning Comets.*
1684		Increase Mather, *Illustrious Providences.*
1685	John Gay born. Died 1732.	Cotton Mather, *Memorable Providences.*
1685–1688	Reign of James II.	
1687	Sir Isaac Newton, *Principia* (Lat.).	Church of England worship established in Boston.
	Dryden, *The Hind and the Panther.*	
1688	The "Bloodless Revolution."	
	Aphra Behn, *Oroonoko.*	
	Death of Bunyan.	
	Alexander Pope born. Died 1744.	
1689–1702	Reign of William and Mary.	
1689	Lady Mary Wortley Montagu born. Died 1762.	
	Samuel Richardson born. Died 1761.	

1690

1690	Locke, *Essay Concerning the Human Understanding.*	
1691	Dunton, *Athenian Gazette.*	(or earlier) *New England Primer.*
1692	Sir William Temple, *Essays.*	Salem witchcraft executions.

	BRITISH	AMERICAN
		Cotton Mather, *Wonders of the Invisible World.*
1694	Wotton, *Reflections upon Ancient and Modern Learning.*	
1695	Congreve, *Love for Love.*	
1696	Toland, *Christianity not Mysterious.*	
1697	Dryden, *Alexander's Feast.*	
1698	Jeremy Collier, *Short View of the Immorality and Profaneness of the English Stage.*	
1699		Jonathan Dickinson, *God's Protecting Providence.*
	1700–1750 Augustan Age	
1700	Death of Dryden.	Samuel Sewall, *The Selling of Joseph.*
1701	Steele, *The Christian Hero; The Funeral.*	Cotton Mather, *Death Made Easy and Happy.*
1702	*The Daily Courant:* first daily newspaper.	Cotton Mather, *Magnalia Christi Americana.*
	Defoe, *The Shortest Way with the Dissenters.*	Increase Mather, *Ichabod.*
1702–1714	Reign of Anne.	
1703	John Wesley (founder of Methodist Church) born. Died 1791.	Jonathan Edwards born. Died 1758.
	Rowe, *The Fair Penitent.*	
1704	Swift, *Battle of the Books* (*w* c. 1697); *Tale of a Tub.*	First American newspaper, *Boston News Letter.*
		Sarah K. Knight, *Journal of a Journey* (*w*).
1704–1713	Defoe, *The Review.*	Anon., *Questions and Proposals.*
1705	Steele, *The Tender Husband.*	
1706		Benjamin Franklin born. Died 1790.
1707	Henry Fielding born. Died 1754.	
1708		Ebenezer Cook, *Sot-Weed Factor.*
1709	Pope, *Pastorals.*	
	Rowe's edition of Shakespeare.	
	Samuel Johnson born. Died 1784.	
1709–1711	Steele (and Addison), *The Tatler.*	

	BRITISH	AMERICAN
	1710	
1710	Berkeley, *Principles of Human Knowledge*.	Cotton Mather, *Essays to Do Good*.
	First complete performance of Italian opera in England (*Almahide*).	John Wise, *The Churches' Quarrel Espoused*.
	Handel comes to England.	
1710–1713	Swift, *Journal to Stella* (*w*).	
1711	Pope, *Essay on Criticism*.	
	Shaftesbury, *Characteristics of Men*.	
1711–1712	Addison, Steele, etc. *The Spectator*.	
1712, 1714	Pope, *Rape of the Lock*.	
1713	Pope, *Windsor Forest*.	Increase Mather, *A Plain Discourse Showing Who Shall and Who Shall Not Enter Heaven*.
	Addison, *Cato*.	
1714–1901	House of Hanover (George I to Victoria).	
1714–1727	George I.	
1714	Mandeville, *Fable of the Bees*.	
	Spectator revived.	
1715	Pope, trans. *Iliad*, I–IV.	
	Jacobite Revolt.	
1716	Thomas Gray born. Died 1771.	
1717	Horace Walpole born. Died 1797.	William Southeby, *An Anti-Slavery Tract*.
	David Garrick born. Died 1779.	
1719	Watts, *Psalms and Hymns*.	Establishment of *Boston Gazette* and the *American Weekly Mercury* (Phila.).
	Defoe, *Robinson Crusoe*.	
	Death of Addison.	
	1720	
1720	"South Sea Bubble."	Wadsworth, *The Lord's Day Proved to Be the Christian Sabbath*.
		James Franklin establishes the *New England Courant*.
1722	Defoe, *Journal of the Plague Year; Moll Flanders*.	Benjamin Franklin, *Silence Dogood* papers.
	Steele, *The Conscious Lovers* (*a*).	
	Parnell, *Night-Piece on Death*.	
	Christopher Smart born. Died 1771.	

	BRITISH	AMERICAN
1723		Death of Increase Mather.
1724	Swift, *Drapier's Letters*. Ramsay, *The Evergreen:* collection of old Scots poetry.	
1725	Pope's edition of Shakespeare.	Josiah Dwight, *Essay to Silence the Outcry . . . Against Regular Singing*. *New York Gazette* estab.
1725–1775		Nathaniel Ames, *Astronomical Diary and Almanac*.
1726	Thomson, *Winter*. Swift, *Gulliver's Travels*. Dyer, *Grongar Hill*.	
1727		Byles, *Poem on the Death of King George I*.
1727–1760	George II.	
1728	Pope, *Dunciad*. Gay, *Beggar's Opera*. Oliver Goldsmith born. Died 1774.	First newspaper in Maryland estab. Death of Cotton Mather.
1729	Swift, *A Modest Proposal*. Death of Steele. Edmund Burke born. Died 1797.	Byrd, *History of the Dividing Line* (*w*). Death of Edward Taylor.

1730

	BRITISH	AMERICAN
1730	Methodist Society at Oxford. Tindal, *Christianity as Old as the Creation*.	Seccomb, *Father Abbey's Will*. Printing press set up in Charleston, South Carolina.
1731	*Gentleman's Magazine* estab. Lillo, *The London Merchant*. Death of Defoe. William Cowper born. Died 1800.	
1732	Covent Garden Theatre built. Death of Gay.	Byles, *Sermon on the Vileness of the Body*.
1732–1757		Franklin, *Poor Richard's Almanac*.
1733	Pope, *Essay on Man*. Theobald's edition of Shakespeare.	William Byrd, *Journal of a Journey to the Land of Eden* (North Carolina) (*w*). Georgia settled by Oglethorpe. J. P. Zenger begins publication of *New York Weekly Journal*. Edwards conducts his first great revival meetings at Northampton.

	BRITISH	AMERICAN
1735	Pope, *Epistle to Dr. Arbuthnot.*	John and Charles Wesley visit America.
		Zenger found not guilty in libel suit over *Journal;* first important "freedom of the press" suit.
1736	Joseph Butler, *The Analogy of Religion.*	First newspaper in Virginia.
1737	Edward Gibbon born. Died 1794.	
	Theatre Licensing Act.	
1737–1742	Shenstone, *Schoolmistress.*	
1738	Johnson, *London.*	
	Wesley, *Psalms and Hymns.*	
	Bolingbroke, *Letters on the Study of History.*	Whitefield's first preaching tour in America.

1740

1740	Cibber, *Apology for the Life of Colley Cibber.*	
	Richardson, *Pamela.*	
1740–1745		The "Great Awakening" (religious revival).
1741		Edwards, *Sinners in the Hands of an Angry God.*
1742	Fielding, *Joseph Andrews.*	
	Young, *Night Thoughts.*	
1742–1744	Roger North, *Lives of the Norths.*	
1743	Blair, *The Grave.*	Thomas Jefferson born. Died 1826.
1744	Joseph Warton, *The Enthusiast.*	
	Johnson, *Life of Richard Savage.*	
	Death of Pope.	
1745	Death of Swift.	
	Jacobite Rebellion.	
1747	Collins, *Odes.*	Stith, *First Discovery and Settlement of Virginia.*
1748	Thomson, *Castle of Indolence.*	
	Richardson, *Clarissa Harlowe.*	
	Smollett, *Roderick Random.*	
	Hume, *Inquiry Concerning Human Understanding.*	
1749	Fielding, *Tom Jones.*	University of Pennsylvania founded.

	BRITISH	AMERICAN
	Johnson, *The Vanity of Human Wishes.*	
	1750–1798 Age of Johnson	
1750–1752	Johnson, *The Rambler:* periodical essays.	
1751	Gray, "Elegy Written in a Country Churchyard."	Bartram, *Observations on American Plants.*
		Franklin, *Experiments and Observations in Electricity.*
1752	Gregorian Calendar adopted.	Philip Freneau born. Died 1832.
1753	British Museum founded.	
1754	T. Warton, *Observations on the Fairy Queen of Spenser.*	Edwards, *Freedom of the Will.*
1755	Johnson, *Dictionary.*	
1755–1772		Woolman, *Journal* (*w*) (pub. 1774).
1756	J. Warton, *Essay on Pope.*	
	Home, *Douglas.*	
1757	Gray, "The Bard" and "The Progress of Poesy."	Witherspoon, *Serious Inquiry into the Nature and Effects of the Stage.*
	William Blake born. Died 1827.	Edwards, *The Great Christian Doctrine of Original Sin Defended.*
		Death of Edwards.
1758–1760	Johnson, The *Idler* papers.	
1759	Johnson, *Rasselas.*	Winthrop, *Lectures on the Comets.*
	Annual Register established.	
	Robert Burns born. Died 1796.	
	Mary Wollstonecraft born. Died 1797.	

1760

1760–1820	George III.	
1760	Macpherson publishes his Ossianic *Fragments.*	
1760–1761	Goldsmith, *Letters from a Citizen of the World.*	
1760–1767	Sterne, *Tristram Shandy.*	
1761	Churchill, *The Rosciad.*	Otis, *Speeches.*
1762	Macpherson, *Fingal.*	Printing press set up in Georgia.
	Leland, *Longsword.*	

	BRITISH	AMERICAN
1764	Walpole, *Castle of Otranto.*	
	Literary Club established in London (Samuel Johnson and others).	Otis, *Rights of British Colonies.*
	Ann (Ward) Radcliffe born. Died 1823.	
1764–1770	The Chatterton poems (*w*) (pub. 1777).	

1765–1830 Revolutionary and Early National Period

1765–1790 Revolutionary Age

	BRITISH	AMERICAN
1765	Percy, *Reliques of Ancient English Poetry.*	The Stamp Act.
	Invention of steam engine by Watt.	
1766	Goldsmith, *The Vicar of Wakefield.*	Franklin, *Examination before the House of Commons.*
1766–1770	Brooke, *The Fool of Quality.*	
1767		Godfrey, *Prince of Parthia* (*a*): tragedy; first American play to be acted.
1767–1768		Dickinson, *Letters of a Farmer in Pennsylvania.*
1768	Kelly, *False Delicacy* (*a*). Goldsmith, *Good-Natured Man* (*a*).	
	Gray, *Poems.*	
	Sterne, *Sentimental Journey.*	
	Maria Edgeworth born. Died 1849.	
	Spinning machine invented.	
1769		Samuel Adams (and others), *Appeal to the World.*
1769–1772	*Letters of Junius.*	

1770

	BRITISH	AMERICAN
1770	Goldsmith, *Deserted Village.*	
	Burke, *Thoughts on the Present Discontent.*	
	William Wordsworth born. Died 1850.	
1771, 1784, and later		Franklin, *Autobiography* (*w*).
1771	Beattie, *The Minstrel*, Book I.	Charles Brockden Brown born. Died 1810.
	Smollett, *Expedition of Humphry Clinker.*	

	BRITISH	AMERICAN
	Sir Walter Scott born. Died 1832.	
	Death of Smart.	
1772	Samuel Taylor Coleridge born. Died 1834.	Trumbull, *Progress of Dullness*, Part I.
		Freneau, *Rising Glories of America*.
1773	Goldsmith, *She Stoops To Conquer*.	Phillis Wheatley (Peters), *Poems:* poetry written by a young slave girl.
	Steevens's edition of Shakespeare.	First theater in Charleston, South Carolina.
	Lord Monboddo, *Origin and Progress of Language*.	
1774	T. Warton, *History of English Poetry*, Vol. I.	Jefferson, *Summary View of Rights of British America*.
	Chesterfield, *Letters to His Son*.	Rush, *Natural History of Medicine Among Indians of North America*.
	Death of Goldsmith.	First Continental Congress.
	Robert Southey born. Died 1843.	
1775–1783	War with American colonies.	Revolutionary War.
1775	Sheridan, *The Rivals*.	Trumbull, *M'Fingal*, Canto I.
	Burke, *Speech on Conciliation*.	Warren, *The Group*.
	Mason, *Memoirs of the Life and Writings of Thomas Gray*.	Battles of Lexington and Bunker Hill.
	Charles Lamb born. Died 1834.	
	Walter Savage Landor born. Died 1864.	
	Jane Austen born. Died 1817.	
1776	Gibbon, *Decline and Fall of the Roman Empire*.	Paine, *Common Sense*.
	Adam Smith, *Wealth of Nations*.	Brackenridge, *Battle of Bunker's Hill*.
		Jefferson, Declaration of Independence.
1776–1783		Thomas Paine, *The Crisis*.
1777	Sheridan, *School for Scandal* (*a*).	Articles of Confederation.
	Burke, *Letter to the Sheriffs of Bristol*.	Surrender of Burgoyne.
1778	Frances Burney, *Evelina*.	Franklin, *Ephemera*.
	William Hazlitt born. Died 1830.	Freneau, *American Independence*.
		Carver, *Travels*.
1778		Hopkinson, *Battle of the Kegs*.
1779	Johnson, *Lives of the Poets*.	Odell, *The Conflagration*.
	Rev. John Newton and William Cowper, *Olney Hymns*.	Ethan Allen, *Narrative of the Captivity*.
	Hume, *Natural History of Religion*.	John Paul Jones's naval victories.

1780

	BRITISH	AMERICAN
1781	Macklin, *Man of the World.*	Surrender of Cornwallis at Yorktown. Articles of Confederation ratified.
1782	Cowper, *Table Talk.*	Crèvecoeur, *Letters from an American Farmer.* Paine, *Letter to the Abbé Raynal.*
1783	Crabbe, *The Village.* Blair, *Rhetoric.* Ritson, *Collection of English Songs.*	Washington Irving born. Died 1859. England acknowledges American independence.
1783–1785		Noah Webster, *Grammatical Institute of the English Language* (speller, grammar, reader).
1784	Death of Samuel Johnson. Leigh Hunt born. Died 1859.	Franklin, *Information for Those Who Would Remove to America.*
1785	Cowper, *The Task.* Thomas De Quincey born. Died 1859.	Dwight, *Conquest of Canaan:* epic.
1786	Burns, *Poems.* Beckford, *Vathek.*	Freneau, *Poems.*
1786–1787		Trumbull and others, *The Anarchiad.*
1787–1788		Hamilton (and others), *The Federalist.*
1787		Barlow, *Vision of Columbus:* epic. Tyler, *The Contrast* (*a*): first American comedy acted by professionals. Constitutional Convention.
1788	George Gordon, Lord Byron, born. Died 1824.	Markoe, *The Times.* Constitution ratified by eleven states.
1789	Blake, *Songs of Innocence.* Bowles, *Fourteen Sonnets.* *French Revolution begins.	William Hill Brown, *The Power of Sympathy:* first American novel. James Fenimore Cooper born. Died 1851. Federal government established.
		1790–1830 Federalist Age
1790	Burke, *Reflections on the Revolution in France.* Malone's edition of Shakespeare.	Death of Franklin.

	BRITISH	AMERICAN
1791	Boswell, *Life of Johnson.* Erasmus Darwin, *The Botanic Garden.* Susanna Rowson, *Charlotte Temple.*	William Bartram, *Travels Through North and South Carolina.*
1791–1792		Paine, *Rights of Man.*
1792	Wollstonecraft, *Rights of Woman.* Percy Bysshe Shelley born. Died 1822.	
1792–1815		Brackenridge, *Modern Chivalry.*
1793	Wordsworth, *Descriptive Sketches.* Godwin, *Political Justice.* Felicia (Browne) Hemans born. Died 1835. War with France.	Barlow, *Hasty Pudding* (*w*). Imlay, *Emigrants.*
1794	Blake, *Songs of Experience.* Radcliffe, *Mysteries of Udolpho.* Godwin, *Caleb Williams.*	Dwight, *Greenfield Hill.* Dunlap, *Leicester: "The Fatal Legacy"* (*a*). William Cullen Bryant born. Died 1878.
1794–1796		Paine, *Age of Reason.*
1795	John Keats born. Died 1821. Thomas Carlyle born. Died 1881.	Murray, *English Grammar.*
1796	Coleridge, *The Watchman.* Southey, *Joan of Arc.* Colman, *Iron Chest* (*a*). Lewis, *The Monk.* Death of Burns.	Washington, *Farewell Address.* Dennie, *Lay Preacher.*
1797	Wordsworth, *The Borderers* (*w*) (pub. 1842). Death of Mary Wollstonecraft (Godwin). Mary Wollstonecraft Shelley born. Died 1851.	Tyler, *Algerian Captive.*
1797–1798	*The Anti-Jacobin.*	

1798–1870 Romantic Period

1798–1832 Age of the Romantic Movement

	BRITISH	AMERICAN
1798	Wordsworth and Coleridge, *Lyrical Ballads.* Landor, *Gebir.* Malthus, *Essay on Population.*	C. B. Brown, *Alcuin: A Dialogue on the Rights of Women; Wieland.*

	BRITISH	AMERICAN
1799	Campbell, *Pleasures of Hope*.	Brown, *Ormond; Arthur Mervyn*, Part I; *Edgar Huntly*.

1800

	BRITISH	AMERICAN
1800	Coleridge, trans. of Schiller's *Wallenstein*. Maria Edgeworth, *Castle Rackrent*. Wordsworth and Coleridge, *Lyrical Ballads*, 2d. ed., with famous Preface. Thomas Babington Macaulay born. Died 1859.	Weems, *Life of Washington*. Brown, *Arthur Mervyn*, Part II. Library of Congress founded.
1801	Southey, *Thalaba*. John Henry Newman born. Died 1890.	Brown, *Clara Howard; Jane Talbot*.
1802	Scott, *Minstrelsy of the Scottish Border*. *Edinburgh Review* founded.	
1803	Jane Porter, *Thaddeus of Warsaw*. Bulwer-Lytton born. Died 1873.	Wirt, *Letters of a British Spy*. Louisiana Purchase. Ralph Waldo Emerson born. Died 1882.
1804	Benjamin Disraeli, Earl of Beaconsfield, born. Died 1881.	J. Q. Adams, *Letters*. Nathaniel Hawthorne born. Died 1864.
1805	Wordsworth, *Prelude* (*w*) (pub. 1850). Scott, *Lay of the Last Minstrel*.	
1806	Elizabeth Barrett (Browning) born. Died 1861. John Stuart Mill born. Died 1873.	Noah Webster, *Compendious Dictionary of the English Language*. William Gilmore Simms born. Died 1870.
1807	Byron, *Hours of Idleness*. C. and M. Lamb, *Tales from Shakespeare*. Abolition of slave trade.	Barlow, *Columbiad*. Irving and Paulding, *Salmagundi Papers*. Henry Wadsworth Longfellow born. Died 1882. John Greenleaf Whittier born. Died 1892.
1808	Hunt, *The Examiner*. Scott, *Marmion*.	Bryant, *The Embargo*.

	BRITISH	AMERICAN
	Lamb, *Specimens of English Dramatic Poets*.	
1809	Byron, *English Bards and Scotch Reviewers*. Charles Darwin born. Died 1882. Alfred, Lord Tennyson born. Died 1892. First issue of *Quarterly Review*.	Irving, "Knickerbocker's" *History*. Edgar Allan Poe born. Died 1849. Oliver Wendell Holmes born. Died 1894. Abraham Lincoln born. Died 1865. Harriet Beecher Stowe born. Died 1896.

1810

	BRITISH	AMERICAN
1810	Scott, *Lady of the Lake*. Porter, *Scottish Chiefs*. Crabbe, *The Borough*.	
1811	Austen, *Sense and Sensibility*. William Makepeace Thackeray born. Died 1863.	
1812–1815		War with England.
1812	Byron, *Childe Harold*, Cantos I, II. Robert Browning born. Died 1889. Charles Dickens born. Died 1870.	
1813	Byron, *Bride of Abydos*. Austen, *Pride and Prejudice*. Southey made Poet Laureate.	Allston, *Sylphs of the Seasons*.
1814	Scott, *Waverley:* begins vogue of historical novel. Wordsworth, *Excursion*.	
1815	Scott, *Guy Mannering*. Battle of Waterloo. Anthony Trollope born. Died 1882.	Freneau, *Poems on American Affairs*. *North American Review* estab.
1816	Coleridge, *Christabel* (*w* 1797–98 and 1800). Byron, *Prisoner of Chillon*. Shelley, *Alastor*. Peacock, *Headlong Hall*. Charlotte Brontë born. Died 1855.	Pickering, *Vocabulary of Americanisms*.
1817	Mary Shelley, *Frankenstein*. Byron, *Manfred*.	Bryant, "Thanatopsis" (*w* 1811).

	BRITISH	AMERICAN
	Coleridge, *Biographia Literaria*.	Henry David Thoreau born. Died 1862.
	Keats, *Poems*.	
	Blackwood's Magazine estab.	
1818	Keats, *Endymion*.	Payne, *Brutus* (*a* London).
	Scott, *Heart of Midlothian*.	
	Austen, *Northanger Abbey* (*w* c. 1800).	
	Emily Brontë born. Died 1848.	
1819	Byron, *Don Juan*, I, II.	Halleck, *Fanny*.
	Shelley, *The Cenci:* tragedy.	Drake, *The Culprit Fay* (*w*).
	Mary Ann Evans ("George Eliot") born. Died 1880.	James Russell Lowell born. Died 1891.
	Charles Kingsley born. Died 1875.	Herman Melville born. Died 1891.
		Walt Whitman born. Died 1892.
	John Ruskin born. Died 1900.	
1820–1830	George IV.	
1820	Scott, *Ivanhoe*.	Missouri Compromise.
	Shelley, *Prometheus Unbound*.	Irving, *Sketch Book*.
	Keats, *Lamia . . . and other Poems*.	
	Maturin, *Melmoth the Wanderer*.	
	Herbert Spencer born. Died 1903.	
1820–1823	Lamb, *Essays of Elia*.	
1821	Scott, *Kenilworth*.	Bryant, *Poems*.
	Southey, *Vision of Judgment*.	Cooper, *The Spy*.
	Shelley, *Adonais*.	
	De Quincey, *Confessions of an English Opium-Eater*.	
	Byron, *Cain*.	
	Death of Keats.	
1822	Byron, *Vision of Judgment*.	Irving, *Bracebridge Hall*.
	Matthew Arnold born. Died 1888.	
	Death of Shelley.	
1823	Scott, *Quentin Durward*.	Cooper, *Pioneers:* first of Leatherstocking series.
	Carlyle, *Life of Schiller*.	
	Death of Radcliffe.	Francis Parkman born. Died 1893.
1824	Landor, *Imaginary Conversations*, Vol. I.	Irving, *Tales of a Traveler*.
	Death of Byron.	E. Everett, *Progress of Literature in America*.
1825	Macaulay, *Essay on Milton*.	Halleck, *Marco Bozzaris*.

	BRITISH	AMERICAN
	Hazlitt, *Spirit of the Age.* Thomas Henry Huxley born. Died 1895.	Italian opera introduced into America.
1826	Scott, *Woodstock.* Disraeli, *Vivian Gray.*	Cooper, *Last of the Mohicans.* Payne, *Richelieu* (*a*). *The Atlantic Souvenir:* annual "gift book."
1827		Cooper, *The Prairie.* Poe, *Tamerlane.* Willis, *Sketches:* poems.
1827–1838		Audubon, *Birds of America.*
1828	Catholic Emancipation Act. George Meredith born. Died 1909. Dante Gabriel Rossetti born. Died 1882.	Hawthorne, *Fanshawe.* Irving, *Columbus.* Webster, *An American Dictionary.* Hall, *Letters from the West.*
1828–1830	Taylor, *Historic Survey of German Poetry.*	
1829	Jerrold, *Black-ey'd Susan.*	Irving, *Conquest of Granada.* Henry D. Timrod born. Died 1867.
		1830–1865 Romantic Period
1830	Tennyson, *Poems Chiefly Lyrical.* Moore, *Letters and Journals of Lord Byron.* Scott, *Letters on Demonology and Witchcraft.* Christina Rossetti born. Died 1894.	Holmes, *Old Ironsides.* Seba Smith starts the "Jack Downing Letters." *Godey's Lady's Book* founded. Emily Dickinson born. Died 1886.
1830–1833	Lyell, *Principles of Geology.*	
1830–1837	William IV.	
1831	Disraeli, *The Young Duke.* Scott, *Castle Dangerous.*	Poe, *Poems.* Whittier, *Legends of New England.* Garrison founds *The Liberator.* William T. Porter founds *Spirit of the Times.* New England Anti-Slavery Society founded.
	1832–1870 Early Victorian Age	
1832	Reform Bill. C. L. Dodgson ("Lewis Carroll") born. Died 1898. Deaths of Scott and *Goethe.	Poe: five tales appear in *Philadelphia Saturday Courier.* Bryant, *Poems* (2d ed). Simms, *Atalantis.*

	BRITISH	AMERICAN
		Irving, *The Alhambra*. Dunlap, *History of the American Theatre*.
1833	Lamb, *Last Essays of Elia*. Browning, *Pauline*. Newman, *Tracts for the Times* (begun). Surtees, *Jorrocks' Jaunts and Jollities*.	Longfellow, *Outre-Mer* (first numbers). Poe, *Manuscript Found in a Bottle*.
1833–1834	Carlyle, *Sartor Resartus*.	
1833–1841	The Oxford Movement (Tractarians).	
1834	Bulwer-Lytton, *Last Days of Pompeii*. William Morris born. Died 1896. Deaths of Coleridge and Lamb.	Bancroft, *History of the United States*, Vol. I. Crockett, *Autobiography*. *Southern Literary Messenger* estab.
1835	Browning, *Paracelsus*. Death of Felicia Hemans. Samuel Butler born. Died 1902. Alfred Austin born. Died 1913.	Simms, *The Partisan; The Yemassee*. Longstreet, *Georgia Scenes*. S. L. Clemens ("Mark Twain") born. Died 1910.
1836	Dickens, *Pickwick Papers*. Marryat, *Mr. Midshipman Easy*.	Emerson, *Nature*. Holmes, *Poems*. Irving, *Astoria*.
1837–1901	Victoria.	
1837	Dickens, *Oliver Twist*. Browning, *Strafford*. Carlyle, *French Revolution*. Lockhart, *Life of Scott*. Algernon Charles Swinburne born. Died 1909.	Hawthorne, *Twice-Told Tales*. Whittier, *Poems*. Emerson, *The American Scholar*. William Dean Howells born. Died 1920.
1838	Ocean steamships connect England and United States.	Morse demonstrates telegraph apparatus before President Van Buren.
1838–1849	The Chartist Movement for extending the franchise.	
1839	Bulwer-Lytton, *Cardinal Richelieu*. Carlyle, *Chartism*. Walter Pater born. Died 1894.	Longfellow, *Hyperion; Voices of the Night*.

	BRITISH	AMERICAN
	1840	
1840	Browning, *Sordello*. Dickens, *Old Curiosity Shop*. Thomas Hardy born. Died 1928.	Cooper, *Pathfinder*. Dana, *Two Years Before the Mast*. Poe, *Tales of the Grotesque and Arabesque*. Brook Farm estab. *The Dial* estab. (discontinued 1844).
1841	Browning, *Pippa Passes*. Carlyle, *Heroes and Hero-Worship*. Macaulay, *Warren Hastings*. Boucicault, *London Assurance* (*a*).	Cooper, *The Deerslayer*. Emerson, *Essays*. Longfellow, *Ballads and Other Poems*. T. B. Thorpe, "The Big Bear of Arkansas."
1842	Browning, *Dramatic Lyrics*. Tennyson, *Poems*. Dickens, *American Notes*. Macaulay, *Lays of Ancient Rome*. Newman, *Essay on Miracles*.	Longfellow, *Poems on Slavery*. Griswold, *Poets and Poetry of America*. Sidney Lanier born. Died 1881.
1843	Carlyle, *Past and Present*. Dickens, *Christmas Carol*. Ruskin, *Modern Painters*, Vol. I. Wordsworth made Poet Laureate. Repeal of Licensing Act of 1737: end of monopoly of the "patent" theaters in London.	Prescott, *Conquest of Mexico*. Whittier, *Lays of My Home and Other Poems*. Henry James born. Died 1916.
1844	Thackeray, *Barry Lyndon*. Elizabeth Barrett (Browning), *Poems*. Disraeli, *Coningsby*. Robert Bridges born. Died 1930. Gerard Manley Hopkins born. Died 1889.	Emerson, *Essays: Second Series*.
1845	Dickens, *Cricket on the Hearth*. Repeal of Corn Laws.	Poe, *The Raven*. Margaret Fuller (Ossoli), *Woman in the Nineteenth Century*. Johnson J. Hooper, *Some Adventures of Simon Suggs*.
1846	Brontë sisters, *Poems*.	Hawthorne, *Mosses from an Old Manse*. Holmes, *Poems*. Melville, *Typee*.

	BRITISH	AMERICAN
1847	E. Brontë, *Wuthering Heights*. C. Brontë, *Jane Eyre*. Tennyson, *The Princess*.	Emerson, *Poems*. Longfellow, *Evangeline*. Prescott, *Conquest of Peru*.
1847	Hunt, *Men, Women, and Books*.	Agassiz, *Introduction to Natural History*. Melville, *Omoo*.
1847–1848	Thackeray, *Vanity Fair*.	
1848	Mill, *Political Economy*. Macaulay, *History of England*, Vols. I, II. Pre-Raphaelite Brotherhood founded by Rossetti. Death of Emily Brontë.	Lowell, *A Fable for Critics: Biglow Papers*. Bartlett, *Dictionary of Americanisms*.
1849	Ruskin, *Seven Lamps of Architecture*. Bulwer-Lytton, *The Caxtons*. Death of Maria Edgeworth.	Whittier, *Voices of Freedom*. Parkman, *Oregon Trail*. Thoreau, *Week on the Concord and Merrimac Rivers*. Melville, *Mardi*. Sarah Orne Jewett born. Died 1909. Death of Poe.
1849–1850	Dickens, *David Copperfield*.	

1850

1850	E. B. Browning, *Sonnets from the Portuguese*. Thackeray, *Pendennis*. Tennyson, *In Memoriam*. Hunt, *Autobiography: Table Talk*. Kingsley, *Alton Locke*. Death of Wordsworth. Tennyson made Poet Laureate. Robert Louis Stevenson born. Died 1894.	Emerson, *Representative Men*. Hawthorne, *Scarlet Letter*. Irving, *Mahomet*. Whittier, *Songs of Labor*. Poe, *Poetic Principle*. *Harper's Magazine* estab.
1851	Ruskin, *Stones of Venice*. Borrow, *Lavengro*. Death of Mary Wollstonecraft Shelley.	Hawthorne, *House of the Seven Gables*. Melville, *Moby-Dick*. Kate Chopin born. Died 1904.
1852	Thackeray, *Henry Esmond*. Tennyson, *Ode on the Death of the Duke of Wellington*.	Hawthorne, *Blithedale Romance*. Harriet Beecher Stowe, *Uncle Tom's Cabin*.

	BRITISH	AMERICAN
	Lady Augusta Gregory born. Died 1932.	
1853	Thackeray, *English Humorists*. Dickens, *Bleak House*. Gaskell, *Cranford*. Kingsley, *Hypatia*. Arnold, *Poems*. C. Brontë, *Villette*.	
1854	Dickens, *Hard Times*. The Crimean War. Oscar Wilde born. Died 1900.	Thoreau, *Walden*.
1855	Browning, *Men and Women*. Tennyson, *Maud*. Thackeray, *The Newcomes*. Trollope, *The Warden*. Kingsley, *Westward Ho*. Death of Charlotte Brontë.	Whitman, *Leaves of Grass*. Longfellow, *Hiawatha*. Irving, *Life of Washington* (begun, completed 1859). Hayne, *Poems*. Boker, *Francesca da Rimini*.
1856	E. B. Browning, *Aurora Leigh*. George Bernard Shaw born. Died 1950.	Emerson, *English Traits*. Motley, *Rise of the Dutch Republic*.
1857	Trollope, *Barchester Towers*. Dickens, *Little Dorrit*. Joseph Conrad born. Died 1924.	Child, ed., *English and Scottish Popular Ballads*. *Atlantic Monthly* estab. *Dred Scott* decision.
1858	George Eliot, *Scenes of Clerical Life*. Morris, *Defence of Guinevere*.	Holmes, *Autocrat of the Breakfast Table*. Longfellow, *Courtship of Miles Standish*.
1859	Tennyson, *Idylls of the King*. Dickens, *Tale of Two Cities*. Thackeray, *The Virginians*. George Eliot, *Adam Bede*. Meredith, *Ordeal of Richard Feverel*. FitzGerald, trans. *Rubáiyát of Omar Khayyám*. Darwin, *Origin of Species*. John Stuart Mill, *On Liberty*. Deaths of Macaulay, Hunt, DeQuincey. Arthur Conan Doyle born. Died 1930. A. E. Housman born. Died 1936. Francis Thompson born. Died 1907.	Margaret Fuller (Ossoli), *Life Without and Life Within*. Joseph Jefferson, *Rip Van Winkle* (*a*).

	BRITISH	AMERICAN
		1860
1860	George Eliot, *Mill on the Floss.* "Owen Meredith," *Lucile.* Collins, *Woman in White.* James Barrie born. Died 1937.	Emerson, *Conduct of Life.* Hawthorne, *Marble Faun.* Timrod, *Poems.* Marsh, *Lectures on the English Language.*
1860–1863	Thackeray, *Roundabout Papers.*	
1861	George Eliot, *Silas Marner.* Reade, *The Cloister and the Hearth.* Arnold, *On Translating Homer; Thyrsis.*	Holmes, *Elsie Venner.* Lincoln becomes president. Outbreak of Civil War.
1862	Ruskin, *Unto This Last.* Spencer, *First Principles.* Meredith, *Modern Love.*	Browne, *Artemus Ward: His Book.* Battle of Shiloh; *Monitor* and *Merrimac.* Edith Wharton born. Died 1937.
1863	George Eliot, *Romola.* Huxley, *Man's Place in Nature.* Kingsley, *Water Babies.* Death of Thackeray.	Longfellow, *Tales of a Wayside Inn.* Louisa M. Alcott, *Hospital Sketches.* Lincoln, *Gettysburg Address.*
1864	Browning, *Dramatis Personae.* Tennyson, *Enoch Arden.* Newman, *Apologia pro Vita Sua.* *Taine, *History of English Literature.*	Thoreau, *The Maine Woods.* Lowell, *Fireside Travels.* Bryant, *Thirty Poems.*
1865	Arnold, *Essays in Criticism.* Ruskin, *Sesame and Lilies.* Lewis Carroll, *Alice's Adventures in Wonderland.* Robertson, *Caste.* Swinburne, *Atalanta in Calydon.* Dickens, *Our Mutual Friend.* Rudyard Kipling born. Died 1936. William Butler Yeats born. Died 1939.	Whittier, *In War Times.* Thoreau, *Cape Cod.* Lowell, *Commemoration Ode.* Whitman, *Drum Taps.* Whittier, *National Lyrics.* End of Civil War.
		1865–1900 Realistic Peroid
1866	Swinburne, *Poems and Ballads.* Ruskin, *Crown of Wild Olive.* Kingsley, *Hereward the Wake.*	Shaw, *Josh Billings: His Sayings.* Whittier, *Snow-Bound.* Howells, *Venetian Life.*

	BRITISH	AMERICAN
	H. G. Wells born. Died 1946.	Transatlantic cable completed.
1867	Bagehot, *English Constitution.*	Mark Twain, *The Celebrated Jumping Frog of Calaveras County.*
	Darwin, *Animals and Plants Under Domestication.*	George W. Harris, *Sut Lovingood's Yarns.*
	*Karl Marx, *Das Kapital.*	Holmes, *Guardian Angel.*
	Arnold Bennett born. Died 1931.	Lanier, *Tiger Lilies.*
	John Galsworthy born. Died 1933.	Longfellow, translation of Dante.
		Lowell, *Biglow Papers* (2d series).
1868	Collins, *The Moonstone.*	Alcott, *Little Women.*
	Morris, *Earthly Paradise*, Vols. I, II.	Hawthorne, *American Notebooks.*
1869	Trollope, *Phineas Finn.*	Mark Twain, *The Innocents Abroad.*
	Blackmore, *Lorna Doone.*	Whittier, *Among the Hills.*
	Ruskin, *Queen of the Air.*	Transcontinental Railroad completed.
	Arnold, *Culture and Anarchy.*	Edwin Arlington Robinson born. Died 1935.
	Browning, *The Ring and the Book.*	William Vaughn Moody born. Died 1910.
	Suez Canal opened.	

1870–1914 Realistic Period

1870–1901 Late Victorian Age

	BRITISH	AMERICAN
1870	Rossetti, *Poems.*	Lowell, *Among My Books* (1st series).
	Huxley, *Lay Sermons.*	Harte, *Luck of Roaring Camp.*
	Death of Dickens.	Bryant, translation of *Iliad.*
		Frank Norris born. Died 1902.
1871	Darwin, *Descent of Man.*	Eggleston, *Hoosier Schoolmaster.*
	John Millington Synge born. Died 1909.	Whitman, *Democratic Vistas.*
		Howells, *Their Wedding Journey.*
		Theodore Dreiser born. Died 1945.
		Bryant, translation of *Odyssey.*
		Mark Twain, *Roughing It.*
1872	Butler, *Erewhon.*	
	Hardy, *Under the Greenwood Tree.*	
	George Eliot, *Middlemarch.*	
1873	Arnold, *Literature and Dogma.*	Aldrich, *Marjorie Daw.*

	BRITISH	AMERICAN
	Pater, *Studies in the Renaissance.* Newman, *The Idea of a University.* Ford Madox Ford born (originally Ford Hermann Hueffer). Died 1939. Dorothy Richardson born. Died 1957.	Willa Cather born. Died 1937. Ellen Glasgow born. Died 1945.
1874	Hardy, *Far from the Madding Crowd.* John Stuart Mill, *Autobiography.*	Robert Frost born. Died 1963. Amy Lowell born. Died 1925. Gertrude Stein born. Died 1946.
1875	Arnold, *God and the Bible.*	Howells, *A Foregone Conclusion.*
1876	George Eliot, *Daniel Deronda.* Morris, *Sigurd the Volsung.* Tennyson, *Queen Mary* (*a*). Trevelyan, *Life of Macaulay.*	Mark Twain, *Tom Sawyer.* Henry James, *Roderick Hudson.* Sherwood Anderson born. Died 1941. Invention of telephone.
1877		James, *The American.* Lanier, *Poems.*
1878	Stevenson, *An Inland Voyage.* Hardy, *Return of the Native.*	
1879	Meredith, *The Egoist.* Spencer, *Data of Ethics*, Part I of *Principles of Ethics.* Browning, *Dramatic Idylls* (1st series). Bagehot, *Literary Studies.* *Ibsen, *The Doll's House.* E. M. Forster born. Died 1970.	Howells, *The Lady of the Aroostook.* Cable, *Old Creole Days.* Henry George, *Progress and Poverty.* James, *Daisy Miller.* Wallace Stevens born. Died 1955.

1880

1880	Gissing, *Workers in the Dawn.* Sean O'Casey born. Died 1964.	Longfellow, *Ultima Thule.* Harris, *Uncle Remus.* Cable, *The Grandissimes.* Lanier, *Science of English Verse.*
1881	Stevenson, *Virginibus Puerisque.* Rossetti, *Ballads and Sonnets.* Swinburne, *Mary Stuart.* Death of Carlyle.	James, *The Portrait of a Lady; Washington Square.* Cable, *Madame Delphine.*
1882	Swinburne, *Tristram of Lyonesse.*	Mark Twain, *The Prince and the Pauper.*

	BRITISH	AMERICAN
	Stevenson, *Familiar Studies, New Arabian Nights.*	Howells, *A Modern Instance.*
	Froude, *Life of Carlyle.*	Whitman, *Specimen Days.*
	Deaths of Darwin, Rossetti, Trollope.	
	James Joyce born. Died 1941.	
	Virginia Woolf born. Died 1941.	
1883	Schreiner, *The Story of an African Farm.*	Mark Twain, *Life on the Mississippi.*
	Stevenson, *Treasure Island.*	Howe, *Story of a Country Town.*
		William Carlos Williams born. Died 1963.
1884	Tennyson, *Becket.*	Mark Twain, *Huckleberry Finn.*
	Jones, *Saints and Sinners* (*a*).	Jewett, *A Country Doctor.*
		"Charles Egbert Craddock," *In the Tennessee Mountains.*
1885	Hudson, *The Purple Land.*	Howells, *Rise of Silas Lapham.*
	Gilbert and Sullivan, *The Mikado* (*a*).	Sinclair Lewis born. Died 1951.
	Meredith, *Diana of the Crossways.*	Ezra Pound born. Died 1972.
	Ruskin, *Praeterita.*	
	Pater, *Marius the Epicurean.*	
	*Karen Blixen ("Isak Dinesen") born (Danish). Died 1962.	
	D. H. Lawrence born. Died 1930.	
1886	Hardy, *Mayor of Casterbridge.*	Howells, *Indian Summer.*
	Stevenson, *Doctor Jekyll and Mr. Hyde; Kidnapped.*	James, *The Bostonians; Princess Casamassima.*
	Tennyson, *Locksley Hall Sixty Years After.*	Death of Dickinson.
	Kipling, *Departmental Ditties.*	Hilda Doolittle ("H. D.") born. Died 1961.
1887	Lang, *Myth, Ritual, and Religion.*	Page, *In Ole Virginia.*
	Edith Sitwell born. Died 1964.	Freeman, *A Humble Romance.*
		Marianne Moore born. Died 1972.
1888	Kipling, *Plain Tales from the Hills.*	James, *Partial Portraits; Aspern Papers.*
	Ward, *Robert Elsmere.*	Bellamy, *Looking Backward.*
	Katherine Mansfield born. Died 1923.	Howard, *Shenandoah* (*a*).
	Death of Arnold.	T. S. Eliot born. Died 1965.
		Eugene O'Neill born. Died 1953.
		John Crowe Ransom born. Died 1974.

	BRITISH	AMERICAN
1889	Browning, *Asolando*. Stevenson, *Master of Ballantrae*. Pater, *Appreciations*. Barrie, *A Window in Thrums*. Deaths of Browning and Hopkins.	Mark Twain, *A Connecticut Yankee at King Arthur's Court*.

1890

	BRITISH	AMERICAN
1890	Watson, *Wordsworth's Grave*. Bridges, *Shorter Poems*.	Dickinson, *Poems*. James, *Tragic Muse*. William James, *Principles of Psychology*.
1891	Hardy, *Tess of the d'Urbervilles*. Doyle, *Adventures of Sherlock Holmes*. Kipling, *The Light that Failed*. Barrie, *The Little Minister*. Gissing, *New Grub Street*. Independent Theatre opens: start of "Little Theatre" movement in England.	Garland, *Main-Travelled Roads*. Bierce, *Tales of Soldiers and Civilians*. Freeman, *A New England Nun*. Howells, *Criticism and Fiction*. Henry Miller born. Died 1980. International Copyright Act: protecting rights of foreign authors and publishers.
1892	Kipling, *Barrack-Room Ballads*. Zangwill, *Children of the Ghetto*. Wilde, *Lady Windermere's Fan* (*a*). Death of Tennyson. "Rebecca West" (Cecily Isabel Fairfield) born. Died 1983.	Page, *The Old South*. Howard, *Aristocracy* (*a*). Djuna Barnes born. Died 1982.
1893	Thompson, *Poems*.	James, *The Real Thing and Other Tales*.
1894	Shaw, *Mrs. Warren's Profession* (*w*, acted 1902). Pinero, *The Second Mrs. Tanqueray* (*a*).	Crane, *Maggie: A Girl of the Streets*.
1894	Yeats, *Land of Heart's Desire*. Moore, *Esther Waters*. Kipling, *Jungle Book*. Death of Stevenson. Jean Rhys born. Died 1979.	Howells, *A Traveler from Altruria*. Hearn, *Glimpses of Unfamiliar Japan*. Mark Twain, *Pudd'nhead Wilson*.
1895	Wilde, *The Importance of Being Earnest* (*a*). Wells, *The Time Machine*. Conrad, *Almayer's Folly*.	Crane, *The Red Badge of Courage*.

	BRITISH	AMERICAN
	Kipling, *The Brushwood Boy.*	
1896	Housman, *A Shropshire Lad.* Barrie, *Sentimental Tommy.* Hardy, *Jude the Obscure.* Alfred Austin made Poet Laureate.	Robinson, *The Torrent and the Night Before.* Jewett, *Country of the Pointed Firs.* Frederic, *The Damnation of Theron Ware.* John Dos Passos born. Died 1970. F. Scott Fitzgerald born. Died 1940.
1897	Conrad, *The Nigger of the "Narcissus."* Kipling, *Captains Courageous.*	Allen, *The Choir Invisible.* James, *What Maisie Knew; Spoils of Poynton.* William Faulkner born. Died 1962.
1898	Hardy, *Wessex Poems.* Shaw, *Plays Pleasant and Unpleasant.* Wilde, *Ballad of Reading Gaol.* Moore, *Evelyn Innes.* Wells, *The War of the Worlds.*	Page, *Red Rock.* Dunne, *Mr. Dooley in Peace and War.*
1899	Irish Literary Theatre founded in Dublin. Elizabeth Bowen born. Died 1973.	Churchill, *Richard Carvel.* Crane, *War Is Kind.* James, *The Awkward Age.* Markham, *The Man with the Hoe.* Norris, *McTeague.* Hart Crane born. Died 1932. Ernest Hemingway born. Died 1961. *Vladimir Nabokov born (in Russia). Died 1977.
		1900–1930 Naturalistic and Symbolistic Period
1900	Conrad, *Lord Jim.* Hudson, *Nature in Downland.* *Edmond Rostand, *L'Aiglon.* Death of Ruskin. Basil Bunting born. Died 1985. V. S. Pritchett born. Died 1997.	Bacheller, *Eben Holden.* Dreiser, *Sister Carrie.* Dunne, *Mr. Dooley's Philosophy.* Tarkington, *Monsieur Beaucaire.*
1901	Barrie, *Quality Street.* Kipling, *Kim.* Binyon, *Odes.*	Moody, *Poems.* Norris, *The Octopus.* Washington, *Up from Slavery.* James, *The Sacred Fount.*

	BRITISH	AMERICAN
	Death of Victoria.	Zora Neal Hurston born. Died 1960.
		Laura (Riding) Jackson born. Died 1991.
	1901–1914 Edwardian Age	
1901–1910	Reign of Edward VII.	
1902	Bennett, *Anna of the Five Towns.*	Glasgow, *The Battle-Ground.*
	Conrad, *Youth.*	James, *The Wings of the Dove.*
	Masefield, *Saltwater Ballads.*	Wister, *The Virginian.*
	Yeats, *Cathleen ni Houlihan.*	Deaths of Bret Harte and Frank Norris.
	Death of Samuel Butler.	Langston Hughes born. Died 1967.
	Stevie Smith born. Died 1971.	Norman Maclean born. Died 1990.
1903	Conrad, *Typhoon and Other Stories.*	James, *The Ambassadors.*
	Butler, *The Way of All Flesh.*	London, *The Call of the Wild.*
	Kipling, *The Five Nations.*	Norris, *The Pit.*
	Shaw, *Man and Superman.*	
	Evelyn Waugh born. Died 1966.	
1904	Barrie, *Peter Pan.*	Churchill, *The Crossing.*
	Conrad, *Nostromo.*	O. Henry, *Cabbages and Kings.*
	Hardy, *The Dynasts* (first part).	James, *The Golden Bowl.*
	Hudson, *Green Mansions.*	London, *The Sea-Wolf.*
	Kipling, *Traffics and Discoveries.*	Moody, *The Fire-Bringer.*
	Synge, *Riders to the Sea.*	Steffens, *The Shame of Cities.*
	Graham Greene born. Died 1991.	J. T. Farrell born. Died 1979.
	Christopher Isherwood born. Died 1986.	*I. B. Singer born (in Poland). Died 1991.
1905	Anthony Powell born. Died 2000.	Wharton, *The House of Mirth.*
		Lillian Hellman born. Died 1984.
		John O'Hara born. Died 1970.
		Kenneth Rexroth born. Died 1982.
		Robert Penn Warren born. Died 1989.
1906	Conrad, *Mirror of the Sea.*	O. Henry, *The Four Million.*
	Kipling, *Puck of Pook's Hill.*	Sinclair, *The Jungle.*
	Samuel Beckett born. Died 1989.	Beginning of "Little Theater" movement in America.
	Sir John Betjeman born. Died 1984.	Henry Roth born. Died 1995.
1907	Russell ("A.E."), *Deirdre.*	Fitch, *The Truth.*

	BRITISH	AMERICAN
	Synge, *The Playboy of the Western World*. Yeats, *Discoveries*. W. H. Auden born. Died 1973.	Adams, *The Education of Henry Adams*. William James, *Pragmatism*.
1908	Barrie, *What Every Woman Knows*. Bennett, *The Old Wives' Tale*. Wells, *New Worlds for Old*.	O. Henry, *The Voice of the City*. Josephine Jacobson born. Died 2003. Theodore Roethke born. Died 1963. Richard Wright born. Died 1960.
1909	Galsworthy, *Plays*. Kipling, *Actions and Reactions*. Pinero, *Mid-Channel*. Wells, *Ann Veronica; Tono-Bungay*. Deaths of Meredith and Swinburne.	London, *Martin Eden*. Moody, *The Great Divide*. Pound, *Personae*. Stein, *Three Lives*. Eudora Welty born.

1910

	BRITISH	AMERICAN
1910–1936	Reign of George V.	
1910	Bennett, *Clayhanger*. Lord Dunsany, *A Dreamer's Tales*. Galsworthy, *Justice*. Kipling, *Rewards and Fairies*. Noyes, *Collected Poems*.	Robinson, *The Town Down the River*. Sheldon, *The Nigger*. Deaths of William Vaughn Moody and Mark Twain.
1911	Beerbohm, *Zuleika Dobson*. Bennett, *Hilda Lessways*. Masefield, *The Everlasting Mercy*. William Golding born. Died 1993. Brian O'Nolan ("Flann O'Brien") born. Died 1966.	Belasco, *The Return of Peter Grimm*. Dreiser, *Jennie Gerhardt*. Wharton, *Ethan Frome*. Elizabeth Bishop born. Died 1979. Tennessee Williams born. Died 1983.
1912	Bridges, *Poetical Works*. Galsworthy, *The Pigeon*. Monro (ed.), *Georgian Poetry*. Shaw, *Pygmalion*. Stephens, *The Crock of Gold*. Tomlinson, *The Sea and the Jungle*. Lawrence Durrell born. Died 1990. Patrick White born (Australian). Died 1990.	Dreiser, *The Financier*. *Poetry: A Magazine of Verse* founded. Millay, *Renascence*.

	BRITISH	AMERICAN
1913	D. H. Lawrence, *Sons and Lovers.* Masefield, *Dauber.* Robert Bridges made Poet Laureate. Barbara Pym born. Died 1980. Death of Alfred Austin.	Cather, *O Pioneers!* Glasgow, *Virginia.* Lindsay, *General William Booth Enters into Heaven.* Frost, *A Boy's Will.* John Frederick Nims born. Died 1999.

1914–1965 Modernist Period

1914–1940 Georgian Age

	BRITISH	AMERICAN
1914–1918	First World War.	
1914	Sinclair, *The Three Sisters.* Dylan Thomas born. Died 1953.	Frost, *North of Boston.* Lindsay, *The Congo.* Amy Lowell, *Sword Blades and Poppy Seeds.* Stein, *Tender Buttons.* John Berryman born. Died 1972. Ralph Ellison born. Died 1994. Randall Jarrell born. Died 1965.
1915	Conrad, *Victory.* Brooke, *Collected Poems.* Ford, *The Good Soldier.* Galsworthy, *The Freelands.* Maugham, *Of Human Bondage.* D. Richardson, *Pointed Roofs.*	Brooks, *America's Coming of Age.* Cabell, *The Rivet in Grandfather's Neck.* Masters, *Spoon River Anthology.* Saul Bellow born. Died 2005. Arthur Miller born. Died 2005.
1916	W. H. Davies, *Collected Poems.* Joyce, *Portrait of the Artist as a Young Man.* Moore, *The Brook Kerith.* Wells, *Mr. Britling Sees It Through.* David Gascoyne born. Died 2001.	Frost, *Mountain Interval.* Amy Lowell, *Men, Women, and Ghosts.* Robinson, *Man Against the Sky.* Sandburg, *Chicago Poems.* Mark Twain, *The Mysterious Stranger.* Deaths of Henry James and Jack London.
1917	Douglas, *South Wind.* Shaw, *Heartbreak House.* Hodgson, *Poems.* Barrie, *Dear Brutus.*	United States enters war. Garland, *A Son of the Middle Border.* Eliot, *Prufrock.* Pound, first *Cantos* (magazine publication). Robert Lowell born. Died 1977.

	BRITISH	AMERICAN
		Carson McCullers born. Died 1967.
1918	D. H. Lawrence, *New Poems*. Hopkins, *Poems* (first published). Strachey, *Eminent Victorians*.	Cather, *My Ántonia*. Sandburg, *Cornhuskers*. O'Neill, *Moon of the Caribees*. Theatre Guild established.
1919	Conrad, *The Arrow of Gold*. Maugham, *The Moon and Sixpence*. Hardy, *Collected Poems*. Masefield, *Reynard the Fox*. Doris Lessing born. Iris Murdoch born. Died 1999.	S. Anderson, *Winesburg, Ohio*. Cabell, *Jurgen*. Amy Lowell, *Pictures of the Floating World*. Howard Nemerov born. Died 1991. J. D. Salinger born.

1920

	BRITISH	AMERICAN
1920	De la Mare, *Collected Poems*. Mansfield, *Bliss*. Wells, *The Outline of History*.	Eliot, *Poems 1920*. Fitzgerald, *This Side of Paradise*. Lewis, *Main Street*. Millay, *A Few Figs from Thistles*. O'Neill, *Beyond the Horizon; The Emperor Jones*. Robinson, *Lancelot*. Wharton, *The Age of Innocence*. Charles Bukowski born (in Germany). Died 1994. Amy Clampitt born. Died 1994.
1921	De la Mare, *Memoirs of a Midget*. Strachey, *Queen Victoria*. Huxley, *Crome Yellow*. D. H. Lawrence, *Women in Love*. Moore, *Héloise and Abelard*.	S. Anderson, *The Triumph of the Egg*. Dos Passos, *Three Soldiers*. O'Neill, *Anna Christie*. Tarkington, *Alice Adams*. Wylie, *Nets to Catch the Wind*. Mona Van Duyn born. Died 2004. Richard Wilbur born.
1922	Galsworthy, *The Forsyte Saga* (1906–1922). Housman, *Last Poems*. Joyce, *Ulysses*. Mansfield, *The Garden Party*. Woolf, *Jacob's Room*. Philip Larkin born. Died 1985.	Cummings, *The Enormous Room*. Eliot, *The Waste Land*. Lewis, *Babbitt*. O'Neill, *The Hairy Ape*. Jack Kerouac born. Died 1969.
1923	Coppard, *The Black Dog*.	Cather, *A Lost Lady*.

	BRITISH	AMERICAN
	Hardy, *Collected Poems.* Huxley, *Antic Hay.* D. H. Lawrence, *Studies in Classic American Literature.* Shaw, *Saint Joan.* Brendan Behan born. Died 1964. Nadine Gordimer born (South African).	Frost, *New Hampshire.* Rice, *The Adding Machine.* Stevens, *Harmonium.* Williams, *Spring and All.* James Dickey born. Alan Dugan born. Anthony Hecht born. Died 2004. Denise Levertov born (in England). Died 1997. Joseph Heller born. Died 1999.
1924	Ford, *Some Do Not.* Forster, *A Passage to India.* Masefield, *Sard Harker.* O'Casey, *Juno and the Paycock.* Death of Conrad. Robert Bolt born. Died 1995.	M. Anderson (with L. Stallings), *What Price Glory?* Hemingway, *In Our Time.* Jeffers, *Tamar and Other Poems.* Melville, *Billy Budd* (first published). Ransom, *Chills and Fever.*
1925	Galsworthy, *Caravan.* Woolf, *Mrs. Dalloway.* *Gide, *The Counterfeiters.* *Kafka, *The Trial.* Nobel Prize awarded to Shaw.	James Baldwin born. Died 1987. Cather, *The Professor's House.* Cummings, *XLI Poems.* Dos Passos, *Manhattan Transfer.* Dreiser, *An American Tragedy.* Fitzgerald, *The Great Gatsby.* Glasgow, *Barren Ground.* Lewis, *Arrowsmith.* O'Neill, *Desire Under the Elms.* Donald Justice born. Died 2004. Flannery O'Connor born. Died 1964.
1926	Kipling, *Debits and Credits.* D. H. Lawrence, *The Plumed Serpent.* T. E. Lawrence, *Seven Pillars of Wisdom.* Stephens, *Collected Poems.* John Fowles born. Anthony and Peter Shaffer born.	Death of Amy Lowell. Glasgow, *The Romantic Comedians.* Hemingway, *The Sun Also Rises.* O'Neill, *The Great God Brown.* Roberts, *The Time of Man.* A. R. Ammons born. Died 2001. Robert Bly born. Robert Creeley born. Died 2005. Allen Ginsberg born. Died 1997. James Merrill born. Died 1995. Frank O'Hara born. Died 1966.

	BRITISH	AMERICAN
1927	T. E. Lawrence, *Revolt in the Desert.* Tomlinson, *Gallions Reach.* Woolf, *To the Lighthouse.*	Cather, *Death Comes for the Archbishop.* Jeffers, *The Women at Point Sur.* O'Neill, *Marco Millions.* Robinson, *Tristram.* Wilder, *The Bridge of San Luis Rey.* John Ashbery born. W. S. Merwin born.
1928	Ford, *Parade's End* (completed). Huxley, *Point Counter Point.* D. H. Lawrence, *Lady Chatterley's Lover.* Death of Thomas Hardy. David Mercer born. Died 1980.	James Wright born. Died 1980. Benét, *John Brown's Body.* Frost, *West-Running Brook.* MacLeish, *The Hamlet of A. MacLeish.* Laura (Riding) Jackson, *Contemporaries and Snobs; Anarchism Is Not Enough.* Tate, *Mr. Pope and Other Poems.* Maya Angelou born.
1929	Aldington, *Death of a Hero.* Bridges, *The Testament of Beauty.* Galsworthy, *A Modern Comedy.* Graves, *Goodbye to All That.* Woolf, *A Room of One's Own.* Thom Gunn born. Died 2004. John Osborne born. Died 1994.	O. B. Hardison, Jr., born. Died 1990. Connelly, *Green Pastures.* Faulkner, *The Sound and the Fury.* Glasgow, *They Stooped to Folly.* Hemingway, *A Farewell to Arms.* Lewis, *Dodsworth.* Wolfe, *Look Homeward Angel.* John Hollander born. Richard Howard born. Adrienne Rich born.

1930–1960 Period of Conformity and Criticism

	BRITISH	AMERICAN
1930	Bunting, *Redimiculum Matellarum.* Coward, *Private Lives.* Maugham, *Cakes and Ale.* Edith Sitwell, *Collected Poems.* Waugh, *Vile Bodies.* Death of Bridges. Masefield made Poet Laureate.	Eliot, *Ash Wednesday.* M. Anderson, *Elizabeth the Queen.* H. Crane, *The Bridge.* Dos Passos, *The 42nd Parallel.* Porter, *Flowering Judas.* Lewis awarded the Nobel Prize. Gary Snyder born.

	BRITISH	AMERICAN
	*Chinua Achebe born (in Nigeria). John Arden born. Ted Hughes born. Died 1998. Harold Pinter born. *Derek Walcott born (St. Lucia).	Lorraine Hansberry born. Died 1965.
1931	Binyon, *Collected Poems*. Galsworthy, *Maid in Waiting*. Woolf, *The Waves*.	Cather, *Shadows on the Rock*. Faulkner, *Sanctuary*. O'Neill, *Mourning Becomes Electra*. Donald Barthelme born. Died 1989. Toni Morrison born. George Starbuck born. Died 1996.
1932	Auden, *The Orators*. Huxley, *Brave New World*. Shaw, *Pen Portraits*. Galsworthy awarded Nobel Prize. *Athol Fugard born (in South Africa). Geoffrey Hill born. *V. S. Naipaul born (Trinidad). Edna O'Brien born.	Caldwell, *Tobacco Road*. Farrell, *Young Lonigan*. Faulkner, *Light in August*. Dos Passos, *1919*. Glasgow, *The Sheltered Life*. MacLeish, *Conquistador*. Death of Hart Crane. Sylvia Plath born. Died 1963.
1933	Auden, *Dance of Death*. Spender, *Poems*. Woolf, *Flush, a Biography*. Yeats, *Collected Poems*. B. S. Johnson born. Died 1973. Death of Galsworthy.	Caldwell, *God's Little Acre*. Cozzens, *The Last Adam*. MacLeish, *Frescoes for Mr. Rockefeller's City*. Stein, *The Autobiography of Alice B. Toklas*. Susan Sontag born. Died 2004.
1934	Beckett, *More Pricks than Kicks*. Graves, *I, Claudius*. Swinnerton, *Elizabeth*. Waugh, *A Handful of Dust*.	Farrell, *The Young Manhood of Studs Lonigan*. Fitzgerald, *Tender Is the Night*. Miller, *Tropic of Cancer*. O'Hara, *Appointment in Samarra*. *Mark Strand born (Prince Edward Island).
1935	C. Day Lewis, *A Time to Dance*. MacNeice, *Poems*. Spender, *The Destructive Element*. David Lodge born.	M. Anderson, *Winterset*. Eliot, *Murder in the Cathedral*. Farrell, *Judgment Day* (completes the "Studs Lonigan Trilogy"). Stevens, *Ideas of Order*. Wolfe, *Of Time and the River*.

	BRITISH	AMERICAN
1936	Auden, *Look, Stranger*. Housman, *More Poems*. Huxley, *Eyeless in Gaza*. Thomas, *25 Poems*. A. S. (Antonia Susan) Byatt born. Simon Gray born. Edward VIII, 1936.	Ken Kesey born. Died 2001. Barnes, *Nightwood*. Frost, *A Further Range*. Faulkner, *Absalom, Absalom!* Dos Passos, *The Big Money* (completes the "U.S.A. Trilogy"). Mitchell, *Gone with the Wind*. Sandburg, *The People, Yes*. O'Neill awarded the Nobel Prize. June Jordan born. Died 2002.
1936–1952	George VI.	
1937	Maugham, *Theatre*. Woolf, *The Years*. Tom Stoppard born.	Marquand, *The Late George Apley*. Millay, *Conversations at Midnight*. Steinbeck, *Of Mice and Men; The Red Pony*. Stevens, *The Man with the Blue Guitar*. Thomas Pynchon born. Hunter S. Thompson born. Died 2005. Death of Edith Wharton.
1938	Beckett, *Murphy*. Bowen, *The Death of the Heart*. Graves, *Collected Poems*. Hughes, *In Hazard*. Richardson, *Pilgrimage* (12-novel sequence completed). C. Day Lewis, *Overtures to Death*. Caryl Churchill born. Ian Hamilton born. Died 2001.	Hemingway, *The Fifth Column and the First Forty-Nine Stories*. Wilder, *Our Town*. Pearl Buck awarded the Nobel Prize. Joyce Carol Oates born. Death of Wolfe.
	1939–1945 Second World War	
1939	Joyce, *Finnegans Wake*. C. Day Lewis, *A Hope for Poetry*. Greene, *The Power and the Glory*. "Flann O'Brien," *At Swim-Two-Birds*. Thomas, *The World I Breathe*. Death of Yeats.	Taylor, *Poetical Works* (first published). Miller, *Tropic of Capricorn*. Porter, *Pale Horse, Pale Rider*. Steinbeck, *The Grapes of Wrath*. Wolfe, *The Web and the Rock*. Margaret Atwood born (in Canada).

	BRITISH	AMERICAN
	Alan Ayckbourn born. Shelagh Delaney born. Margaret Drabble born. Seamus Heaney born.	Ted Kooser born.
	1940–1965 Diminishing Age	
1940	Auden, *Selected Poems.* Snow, *Strangers and Brothers* (begun; completed in 11 novels, 1970). Yeats, *Last Poems and Plays.*	Faulkner, *The Hamlet.* Hemingway, *For Whom the Bell Tolls.* McCullers, *The Heart Is a Lonely Hunter.* Pound, *Cantos LII–LXXI.* Wolfe, *You Can't Go Home Again.* Wright, *Native Son.* Russell Banks born. Death of Fitzgerald.
1941	Barker, *Selected Poems.* Cary, *Herself Surprised.* De la Mare, *Bells and Grass.* Huxley, *Grey Eminence.* Spender, *Ruins and Visions.* Deaths of Joyce, Woolf, Walpole.	Attack on Pearl Harbor; the United States declares war on Japan. Fitzgerald, *The Last Tycoon.* Glasgow, *In This Our Life.* Jeffers, *Be Angry at the Sun.* McCullers, *Reflections in a Golden Eye; The Ballad of the Sad Café.* Welty, *A Curtain of Green.*
1942	Cary, *To Be a Pilgrim.* Coward, *Blithe Spirit.* Waugh, *Put Out More Flags.*	Cozzens, *The Just and the Unjust.* Faulkner, *Go Down, Moses.* Jarrell, *Blood for a Stranger.* Wilder, *Skin of Our Teeth.* Barry Hannah born. William Matthews born. Died 1997.
1943	Coward, *This Happy Breed.* H. Green, *Caught.*	Dos Passos, *Number One.* Eliot, *Four Quartets.* Warren, *At Heavens' Gate; Selected Poems.* Louise Glück born. Sam Shepard born. James Tate born. Kathy Acker born. Died 1997.

	BRITISH	AMERICAN
1944	Barker, *Eros in Dogma*. Cary, *The Horse's Mouth*. Connolly, *The Unquiet Grave*. Huxley, *Time Must Have a Stop*. Craig Raine born.	R. Lowell, *Land of Unlikeness*. Porter, *The Leaning Tower*. Shapiro, *V-Letter*. Robert Morgan born. Alan Williamson born.
1945	Connolly, *The Condemned Playground*. H. Green, *Loving*. Isherwood, *Prater Violet*. C. Day Lewis, *Short Is the Time*. Waugh, *Brideshead Revisited*.	Frost, *A Masque of Reason*. Jarrell, *Little Friend, Little Friend*. Ransom, *Selected Poems*. T. Williams, *The Glass Menagerie*. Wright, *Black Boy*. Death of Ellen Glasgow. August Wilson born.
1946	H. Green, *Back*. Orwell, *Animal Farm*. Spender, *European Witness*. Thomas, *Deaths and Entrances*.	Jeffers, *Medea*. McCullers, *The Member of the Wedding*. O'Neill, *The Iceman Cometh*. Warren, *All the King's Men*. Welty, *Delta Wedding*. W. C. Williams, *Paterson, I*. Death of Gertrude Stein.
1947	Auden, *The Age of Anxiety*. Barker, *Love Poems*. Spender, *Poems of Dedication*. Salman Rushdie born (in Bombay).	Dreiser, *The Stoic*. Frost, *A Masque of Mercy*. Stevens, *Transport to Summer*. T Williams, *A Streetcar Named Desire*. Cleanth Brooks, *The Well Wrought Urn*. Death of Willa Cather. David Mamet born.
1948	Fry, *The Lady's Not for Burning*. H. Green, *Concluding*. G. Greene, *The Heart of the Matter*. Huxley, *Ape and Essence*. Waugh, *The Loved One*.	Cozzens, *Guard of Honor*. Faulkner, *Intruder in the Dust*. Jarrell, *Losses*. Mailer, *The Naked and the Dead*. Pound, *Pisan Cantos*. David Lehman born.
1949	Cary, *A Fearful Joy*. Orwell, *Nineteen Eighty-Four*. Spender, *The Edge of Being*. Christopher Reid born.	Frank Stafford born. Died 1977. Dos Passos, *The Grand Design* (completes "District of Columbia Trilogy"). Marquand, *Point of No Return*. Miller, *Death of a Salesman*. Welty, *The Golden Apples*.

	BRITISH	AMERICAN
	1950	
1950	Auden, *The Enchafed Flood.* Barker, *The Dead Seagull.* De la Mare, *Inward Companion.* H. Green, *Nothing.* Thomas, *Twenty-six Poems.* Death of Shaw.	Cummings, *XAIPE: Seventy-One Poems.* Eliot, *The Cocktail Party.* Hemingway, *Across the River and Into the Trees.* Stevens, *Auroras of Autumn.* Faulkner awarded the Nobel Prize.
1951	Auden, *Nones.* Beckett, *Molloy.* Fry, *A Sleep of Prisoners.* G. Greene, *The End of the Affair.* Spender, *World Within World.*	Faulkner, *Requiem for a Nun.* Jarrell, *Seven-League Crutches.* Jones, *From Here to Eternity.* R. Lowell, *Mills of the Kavanaughs.* Salinger, *Catcher in the Rye.* Jorie Graham born. Death of Sinclair Lewis.
1952	Elizabeth II, 1952–. Betjeman, *First and Last Loves.* Beckett, *Waiting for Godot.* Cary, *Prisoner of Grace.* H. Green, *Dying.* Thomas, *In Country Sleep.* Andrew Motion born.	Davis, *Winds of Morning.* Hemingway, *The Old Man and the Sea.* O'Connor, *Wise Blood.* Steinbeck, *East of Eden.*
1953	Cary, *Except the Lord.* Waugh, *Love Among the Ruins.* Churchill awarded the Nobel Prize. Death of Thomas.	Baldwin, *Go Tell It on the Mountain.* Roethke, *The Waking.* Warren, *Brother to Dragons.* T. Williams, *Camino Real.* Death of O'Neill.
1954	Barker, *A Vision of Beasts and Gods.* Betjeman, *A Few Late Chrysanthemums.* MacNeice, *Autumn Sequel.* Thomas, *Under Milk Wood.* Amis, *Lucky Jim.*	Eliot, *The Confidential Clerk.* Faulkner, *A Fable.* Jeffers, *Hungerfield and Other Poems.* Hemingway awarded the Nobel Prize.
1955	Auden, *The Shield of Achilles.* Cary, *Not Honour More.* Thomas, *Adventures in the Skin Trade.*	E. Bishop, *North and South—A Cold Spring.* Nabokov, *Lolita.* T. Williams, *Cat on a Hot Tin Roof.*

	BRITISH	AMERICAN
		Pound, *Section: Rock Drill.* Death of Wallace Stevens.
1956	Behan, *The Quare Fellow.* O'Casey, *Mirror in My House.* Osborne, *Look Back in Anger.*	Ginsberg, *Howl.* O'Neill, *A Long Day's Journey into Night.* Wilbur, *Things of This World.*
1957	Edith Sitwell, *Collected Poems.* Hartley, *The Hireling.* Joyce, *Letters.* Osborne, *The Entertainer.* Stevie Smith, *Not Waving But Drowning.* Waugh, *The Ordeal of Gilbert Pinfold.* Death of Dorothy Richardson.	Agee, *A Death in the Family.* Faulkner, *The Town.* Kerouac, *On the Road.* O'Neill, *A Touch of the Poet.* Singer, *Gimpel the Fool.* Warren, *Promises.* Li-Young Lee born.
1958	Achebe, *Things Fall Apart.* Arden, *Live Like Pigs.* Beckett, *Endgame.* Behan, *Borstal Boy; The Hostage.* Delaney, *A Taste of Honey.* C. Day Lewis, *Pegasus and Other Poems.* White, *The Once and Future King.*	Cummings, *95 Poems.* MacLeish, *J.B.* Pound, *Pavannes and Divagations.* W. T. Scott, *The Dark Sister.* Jill McCorkle born.
1959	Arden, *Serjeant Musgrave's Dance.* Cary, *The Captive and the Free.* Golding, *Free Fall.* Sacheverell Sitwell, *Journey to the Ends of Time*, Vol. I.	Eliot, *The Elder Statesman.* Faulkner, *The Mansion.* R. Lowell, *Life Studies.* P. Roth, *Goodbye, Columbus.* Snodgrass, *Heart's Needle.* Hellman, *Toys in the Attic.*
		1960– Period of the Confessional Self
1960	Achebe, *No Longer at Ease.* Bolt, *A Man for All Seasons.* Durrell, *Alexandria Quartet* (completed). Powell, *Casanova's Chinese Restaurant.* Redgrove, *The Collector.*	Jarrell, *The Woman at the Washington Zoo.* Pound, *Thrones.* O'Connor, *The Violent Bear It Away.* Updike, *Rabbit Run.* Deaths of Zora Neal Hurston and Richard Wright.
1961	Hughes, *The Fox in the Attic.* MacNeice, *Solstices.*	Dos Passos, *Midcentury.* Heller, *Catch-22.*

	BRITISH	AMERICAN
	Murdoch, *A Severed Head.* Osborne, *Luther.* Wain, *Weep Before God.*	Salinger, *Franny and Zooey.* Steinbeck, *The Winter of Our Discontent.* Wilbur, *Advice to a Prophet.* Death of Hemingway.
1962	Graves, *New Poems 1962.* C. Day Lewis, *The Gate.* Powell, *The Kindly Ones.* Edith Sitwell, *The Outcasts.* Ustinov, *Photo Finish.* *Death of Karen Blixen ("Isak Dinesen").	Albee, *Who's Afraid of Virginia Woolf?* Ashbery, *The Tennis Court Oath.* Bly, *Silence in the Snowy Fields.* Faulkner, *The Reivers.* Frost, *In the Clearing.* Koch, *Thank You and Other Poems.* Nabokov, *Pale Fire.* P. Roth, *Letting Go.* W. C. Williams, *Pictures from Brueghel.* Porter, *Ship of Fools.* T. Williams, *The Night of the Iguana.* Deaths of Cummings, Faulkner, Jeffers. Steinbeck awarded the Nobel Prize.
1963	Fowles, *The Collector.* G. Greene, *A Sense of Reality.* MacBeth, *The Broken Places.*	Cummings, *73 Poems.* Ginsberg, *Reality Sandwiches.* Jeffers, *The Beginning and the End.* Merwin, *The Moving Target.* Pynchon, *V.* Salinger, *Raise High the Roof Beam, Carpenters.* Simpson, *At the End of the Open Road.* Wright, *The Branch Will Not Break.* Deaths of Frost, Roethke, and W. C. Williams.
1964	Achebe, *Arrow of God.* Larkin, *The Whitsun Weddings.* Powell, *The Valley of Bones.* Thomas, *The Bread of Truth.*	Ammons, *Expressions of Sea Level.* Bellow, *Herzog.* Berryman, *77 Dream Songs.* Hemingway, *A Moveable Feast.*

	BRITISH	AMERICAN
	Deaths of Brendan Behan and Sean O'Casey.	Frank O'Hara, *Lunch Poems.* O'Neill, *More Stately Mansions.* Roethke, *The Far Field.* R. Lowell, *For the Union Dead.* Shapiro, *The Bourgeois Poet.* Death of Flannery O'Connor.
	1965– Postmodernist Period	
1965	C. Day Lewis, *The Room.* Walcott, *The Castaway.* Waugh, *Sword of Honor.*	Albee, *Tiny Alice.* Ammons, *Corsons Inlet; Tape for the Turn of the Year.* Dickey, *Buckdancer's Choice.* Mailer, *American Dream.* O'Connor, *Everything That Rises Must Converge.* Deaths of T. S. Eliot, Jarrell, and Lorraine Hansberry.
1966	Achebe, *A Man of the People.* Bunting, *Briggflatts.* Fowles, *The Magus.* G. Greene, *The Comedians.* MacNeice, *One for the Grave.* West, *The Birds Fall Down.* Death of Waugh.	Albee, *A Delicate Balance.* Barth, *Giles Goat-Boy.* Capote, *In Cold Blood.* Malamud, *The Fixer.* Plath, *Ariel.* Pynchon, *The Crying of Lot 49.* Death of Frank O'Hara.
1967	Isherwood, *A Meeting by the River.* MacDiarmid, *A Lap of Honour.* A. Wilson, *No Laughing Matter.* Death of John Masefield.	Ashbery, *Rivers and Mountains.* Bly, *The Light Around the Body.* Merwin, *The Lice.* Moore, *Complete Poems.* Oates, *them.* Potok, *The Chosen.* Reed, *The Freelance Pallbearers.* P. Roth, *When She Was Good.* Styron, *Confessions of Nat Turner.* Tate, *The Lost Pilot.* Wilder, *The Eighth Day.* Deaths of Hughes and McCullers.
1968	Amis, *I Want It Now.* Barker, *Collected Poems, 1930–1965.* Burgess, *Enderby.*	Beagle, *The Last Unicorn.* G. Brooks, *In the Mecca.* Coover, *The Universal Baseball Association, Inc., J. Henry Waugh, Prop.*

	BRITISH	AMERICAN
	Durrell, *Tunc*. Murdoch, *The Nice and the Good*.	Sackler, *The Great White Hope*. Snyder, *The Back Country*. Wright, *Shall We Gather at the River*. Death of Steinbeck.
1969	Fowles, *The French Lieutenant's Woman*. Lessing, *Children of Violence* (series completed). Heaney, *Door into the Dark*.	Angelou, *I Know Why the Caged Bird Sings*. Berryman, *The Dream Songs*. Cheever, *Bullet Park*. Connell, *Mr. Bridge*. Hollander, *Types of Shape*. Howard, *Untitled Subjects*. R. Lowell, *Notebook 1967–1968*. Nabokov, *Ada*. Pound, *Drafts and Fragments of Cantos CX to CXVII*. Roth, *Portnoy's Complaint*. Death of Kerouac.

1970

	BRITISH	AMERICAN
1970	Hughes, *Crow*. Braine, *Stay with Me Till Morning*. Ian Hamilton, *The Visit*. Death of E. M. Forster.	Ashbery, *The Double Dream of Spring*. Barthelme, *City Life*. Hemingway, *Islands in the Stream*. Bellow, *Mr. Sammler's Planet*. Merwin, *The Carrier of Ladders*. Snyder, *Regarding Wave*. Van Duyn, *To See, To Take*. Welty, *Losing Battles*. Deaths of Dos Passos and O'Hara.
1971	Gray, *Butley*. Forster, *Maurice*. Compton-Burnett, *The First and the Last*. G. Greene, *A Sort of Life*. Hill, *Mercian Hymns*. Rice and Lloyd Webber, *Jesus Christ, Superstar*. Death of Stevie Smith.	Warren, *Meet Me in the Green Glen*. Doctorow, *The Book of Daniel*. Hawkes, *The Blood Oranges*. Updike, *Rabbit Redux*. Wright, *Collected Poems*.
1972	Auden, *Epistle to a Godson*. Drabble, *The Needle's Eye*.	Ammons, *Collected Poems: 1951–1971*.

	BRITISH	AMERICAN
	Lessing, *The Story of a Non-Marrying Man.*	Berryman, *Delusions, Etc.* Buchanan, *Maiden.* Gardner, *The Sunlight Dialogues.* Laura (Riding) Jackson, *The Telling.* Shulman, *Memoirs of an Ex-Prom-Queen.* Schuyler, *The Crystal Lithium.* Singer, *Enemies: A Love Story.* Welty, *The Optimist's Daughter.* Deaths of Berryman and Pound.
1973	Enright, *The Terrible Shears.* G. Greene, *The Honorary Consul.* Murdoch, *The Black Prince.* Shaffer, *Equus.* Thwaite, *Inscriptions.* Deaths of Auden, Elizabeth Bowen, and B. S. Johnson.	Ginsberg, *The Fall of America.* Jong, *Fear of Flying.* Lowell, *The Dolphin.* Pynchon, *Gravity's Rainbow.* Rich, *Diving into the Wreck: Poems 1971–1972.* Wilder, *Theophilus North.*
1974	Auden, *Thank You, Fog.* Durrell, *Monsieur.* Fowles, *The Ebony Tower.* Larkin, *High Windows.*	Ammons, *Sphere.* Baldwin, *If Beale Street Could Talk.* Heller, *Something Happened.* Kinnell, *The Avenue Bearing the Initial of Christ into the New World.* P. Roth, *My Life as a Man.* Stone, *Dog Soldiers.* Thomas, *Down These Mean Streets.*
1975	Ayckbourn, *The Norman Conquests* (trilogy). Gray, *Otherwise Engaged.* Heaney, *North.* Jhabvala, *Heat and Dust.* Lessing, *Memoirs of a Survivor.* Lodge, *Changing Places.* Powell, *Hearing Secret Harmonies* (completes *A Dance to the Music of Time*, begun 1951).	Ashbery, *Self-Portrait in a Convex Mirror.* Bellow, *Humboldt's Gift.* Doctorow, *Ragtime.* Gaddis, *JR.* Rossner, *Looking for Mr. Goodbar.*
1976	Amis, *The Alteration.* Hughes, *A Season of Songs.* Waugh, *Diaries.* White, *A Fringe of Leaves.*	Anaya, *Bless Me, Ultima.* Beattie, *Chilly Scenes of Winter.* Gardner, *October Light.* Guest, *Ordinary People.* Haley, *Roots.*

	BRITISH	AMERICAN
		Kingston, *Notes of a Woman Warrior*. Sexton, *45 Mercy Street*. Vonnegut, *Slapstick*. Walker, *Meridian*. Welch, *Riding the Earthboy Forty*.
1977	Fowles, *Daniel Martin*. McCullough, *The Thorn Birds*. Tolkien, *The Silmarillion*. Drabble, *The Ice Age*.	Cheever, *Falconer*. Didion, *A Book of Common Prayer*. Heinemann, *Close Quarters*. R. Lowell, *Day by Day*. Morrison, *Song of Solomon*. P. Roth, *The Professor of Desire*. Silko, *Ceremony*. Stegner, *The Spectator Bird*. Warren, *A Place to Come To*. Death of Lowell.
1978	Greene, *Human Factor*. White, *Book of Merlyn*.	Harper, *Images of Kin*. Irving, *The World According to Garp*. O'Brien, *Going After Cacciato*. Singer, *Shosha*. Updike, *The Coup*.
1979	Burgess, *Abba Abba*. Churchill, *Cloud Nine*. Hill, *Tenebrae*. Lewis, *Naples '44*. Raine, *A Martian Sends a Postcard Home*. Shaffer, *Amadeus*. Wain, *The Pardoner's Tale*.	Heller, *Good as Gold*. Hill, *Hanta Yo*. Mailer, *The Executioner's Song*. O'Connor, *The Habit of Being: Letters*. Death of J. T. Farrell.

1980

	BRITISH	AMERICAN
1980	Golding, *Rites of Passage*. Hughes, *Moortown*. Rhys, *Smile, Please*. Deaths of David Mercer and Barbara Pym.	Howard, *Misgivings*. Merrill, *Scripts for the Pageant*. Schuyler, *The Morning of the Poem*. Toole, *A Confederacy of Dunces*. Death of Henry Miller.
1981	James, *Charles Charming's Challenges*.	Ammons, *A Coast of Trees*. Barthelme, *Sixty Stories*.

	BRITISH	AMERICAN
	Lessing, *The Sirian Experiments.* Murdoch, *Nuns and Soldiers.* Osborne, *A Better Class of Person.* Rushdie, *Midnight's Children.*	Betts, *Heading West.* Carver, *What We Talk About When We Talk About Love.* Plath, *Collected Poems.* Price, *The Source of Light.* P. Roth, *Zuckerman Unbound.* Stone, *A Flag for Sunrise.* Updike, *Rabbit Is Rich.*
1982	Churchill, *Top Girls.* Coward, *Diaries.* Durrell, *Constance.* Fowles, *Mantissa.* Sillitoe, *Her Victory.*	Barth, *Sabbatical.* Bellow, *The Dean's December.* Harrison, *Selected and New Poems.* Kinnell, *Selected Poems.* Nims, *Selected Poems; The Kiss: A Jambalaya.* Starbuck, *The Argot Merchant Disaster.* Tyler, *Dinner at the Homesick Restaurant.* Walker, *The Color Purple.* Wright, *This Journey.* Death of Rexroth.
1983	Beckett, *Worstward Ho.* Burgess, *The End of the World News.* Coward, *Collected Stories.* Rushdie, *Shame.* Death of "Rebecca West."	Ammons, *Lake Effect Country.* Clampitt, *The Kingfisher.* Creeley, *Collected Poems.* Garrett, *The Succession.* Goldbarth, *Original Light.* Knott, *Becos.* Mailer, *Ancient Evenings.* McMurtry, *The Desert Rose.* Merrill, *The Changing Light at Sandover.* Oliver, *American Primitive.* Ozick, *The Pagan Rabbi and Other Stories.* P. Roth, *The Anatomy Lesson.* Schaeffer, *The Madness of a Seduced Woman.* Song, *Picture Bride.* Williamson, *Presence.* Death of Tennessee Williams.

	BRITISH	AMERICAN
1984	Churchill, *Softcops.* Connolly, *Selected Essays.* Lodge, *Small World.* Powell, *O, How the Wheel Becomes It!* Death of Sir John Betjeman.	Adams, *Superior Women.* Burroughs, *The Place of Dead Roads.* Heller, *God Knows.* Howard, *Lining Up.* Kizer, *Yin.* Matthews, *A Happy Childhood.* Pynchon, *Slow Learner.* Wurlitzer, *Slow Fade.* Death of Lillian Hellman.
1985	Fowles, *A Maggot.* Murdoch, *The Good Apprentice.* Deaths of Basil Bunting and Larkin.	Banks, *Continental Drift.* Carver, *Cathedral.* DeLillo, *White Noise.* Glück, *The Triumph of Achilles.* Harper, *Healing Song for the Inner Ear.* Kennedy, *Cross Ties.* Kooser, *One World at a Time.* Mason, *In Country.* McMurtry, *Lonesome Dove.* P. Roth, *Zuckerman Bound.*
1986	Amis, *The Old Devils.* Cope, *Making Cocoa for Kingsley Amis.* Powell, *The Fisher King.* Death of Christopher Isherwood.	Atwood, *The Handmaid's Tale.* Barthelme, *Paradise.* Creeley, *Memory Gardens.* Erdrich, *The Beet Queen.* Hemingway, *The Garden of Eden* (posthumous). Kooser, *The Blizzard Voices.* Price, *Kate Vaiden.* P. Roth, *The Counterlife.* Schaeffer, *The Injured Party.* Tyler, *The Accidental Tourist.*
1987	Achebe, *Anthills of the Savannah.* Barker, *Collected Poems.* Golding, *Close Quarters.* Heaney, *The Haw Lantern.* Murdoch, *The Book and the Brotherhood.*	Hannah, *Hey Jack!* Heinemann, *Paco's Story.* Kizer, *The Nearness of You.* McCorkle, *Tending to Virginia.* Morgan, *At the Edge of the Orchard Country.* Morrison, *Beloved.* Olds, *The Gold Cell.* Ozick, *The Messiah of Stockholm.*

	BRITISH	AMERICAN
		Simic, *Unending Blues*. Wolfe, *The Bonfire of the Vanities*. Death of Baldwin.
1988	Amis, *Difficulties with Girls*. Davie, *Scorch or Freeze*. Lessing, *The Fifth Child*. O'Brien, *The High Road*. Rushdie, *The Satanic Verses*. Spark, *A Far Cry from Kensington*.	Crews, *The Knockout Artist*. Merwin, *The Rain in the Trees*. Tyler, *Breathing Lessons*. Wilson, *Joe Turner's Come and Gone*.
1989	Armitage, *Zoom*. Brookner, *Lewis Percy*. Drabble, *A Natural Curiosity*. Golding, *Fire Down Below*. Hughes, *Wolfwatching*. Death of Beckett. Murdoch, *The Message to the Planet*.	Banks, *Affliction*. Chappell, *Brighten the Corner Where You Are*. Gurganus, *The Oldest Living Confederate Widow Tells All*. Hannah, *Boomerang*. Pynchon, *Vineland*. Tan, *The Joy Luck Club*. Deaths of D. Barthelme and R. P. Warren.

1990

	BRITISH	AMERICAN
1990	Deaths of Lawrence Durrell and Patrick White.	Morgan, *Sigodlin*. Ozick, *Shawl*. P. Roth, *Deception*. Updike, *Rabbit at Rest*.
1991	Cope, *Serious Concerns*. Drabble, *The Gates of Ivory*. Motion, *Love in a Life*. Death of Graham Greene.	Deaths of O. B. Hardison, Jr., and Norman Maclean. Cruz, *Red Beans*. Gibbons, *A Cure for Dreams*. Morgan, *Green River*. Deaths of Howard Nemerov, I. B. Singer, and Laura (Riding) Jackson.
1992	Amis, *The Russian Girl*. Bennett, *The Madness of King George*. Heaney, *The Gravel Walks*. Hughes, *Rain-Charm for the Duchy*. Clemo, *Approach to Murano*.	Ashbery, *Hotel Lautréamont*. Clampitt, *Westward*. Glück, *The Wild Iris*. Jackson, *First Awakenings*. Sontag, *The Volcano Lover*.

	BRITISH	AMERICAN
1993	Muldoon, *Shining Brow*. Stoppard, *Arcadia*. Deaths of William Golding and Anthony Burgess.	Albee, *Three Tall Women*. Barks, *Gourd Seed*. Death of William Stafford.
1994	Raine, *History: The Home Movie*. Death of John Osborne.	Gaddis, *A Frolic of His Own*. Gunn, *Collected Poems*. Henry Roth, *Mercy of a Rude Stream*. Deaths of Charles Bukowski, Ralph Ellison, and Amy Clampitt.
1995	Nobel Prize awarded to Seamus Heaney. Death of Sir Stephen Spender.	Banks, *Rule of the Bone*. Morgan, *The Truest Pleasure*. Deaths of James Merrill and Henry Roth.
1996	Raine, *Clay: Whereabouts Unknown*. Muldoon, *New Selected Poems*.	Snyder, *Mountains and Rivers Without End*. D. F. Wallace, *Infinite Jest*. Deaths of Joseph Brodsky and George Starbuck.
1997	Churchill, *Blue Heart*. Death of V. S. Pritchett.	Pynchon, *Mason and Dixon*. P. Roth, *American Pastoral*. Deaths of William Burroughs, James Dickey, Allen Ginsberg, Denise Levertov, and William Matthews.
1998	Hare, *The Judas Kiss*. Hughes, *Birthday Letters*. Stoppard, *The Invention of Love*. Death of Ted Hughes.	Banks, *Cloudsplitter*. Morrison, *Paradise*. Tom Wolfe, *A Man in Full*.
1999	Andrew Motion appointed Poet Laureate. Death of Iris Murdoch.	Morgan, *Gap Creek*. Deaths of John Frederick Nims and Joseph Heller.
2000	Craig Raine, *Collected Poems, 1978–1999*. Death of Anthony Powell.	Graham, *Swarm*. P. Roth, *The Human Stain*. Updike, *Gertrude and Claudius*.
2001	Drabble, *The Peppered Moth*. Reid, *Mermaids Explained*. Spark, *Aiding and Abetting*. Deaths of Ian Hamilton and David Gascoyne.	Dugan, *Poems Seven: New and Complete Poems*. Morgan, This Rock. P. Roth, *The Dying Animal*. Simic, *Night Picnic*. Charles Wright, *Negative Blue: Selected Later Poems*.

	BRITISH	AMERICAN
		Deaths of Ammons, Kesey, and Welty.
2002	Byatt, *A Whistling Woman.*	Death of June Jordan.
	Drabble, *The Seven Sisters.*	
2003		Deaths of Alan Dugan and Josephine Jacobsen.
2004	Drabble, *The Red Queen.*	P. Roth, *The Plot Against America.*
	Spark, *The Finishing School.*	T. Wolfe, *I Am Charlotte Simmons.*
	Death of Thom Gunn.	Deaths of Anthony Hecht, Donald Justice, and Mona Van Duyn.
2005		Deaths of Saul Bellow, Arthur Miller, and Hunter S. Thompson.

Appendices

Monetary Terms and Values

We know that in 1360 Geoffrey Chaucer, captured by the French, was ransomed for £60; that William Shakespeare's will left £1000 to his sister Joan and twenty-eight shillings and sixpence (28/6) to several friends "to buy them rings"; that John Milton had to pay £150 for his own upkeep while in jail in 1660 and lost savings of £2000 when the Excise collapsed. We know that Thomas Hobbes, at the time of his death in 1679, left an estate valued under £1000; that Alexander Pope, a century younger than Hobbes, was worth about £6000 when he died in 1744; that Lord Byron, a century younger than Pope, was worth £100,000 when he died in 1824; and that T. S. Eliot, a century younger than Byron, was worth £105,272 when he died in 1965. And we know that characters in literary works are forever going on about livings, incomes, and prices. But we may not know how much those sums are worth in today's money.

The pound has been the basic unit of English money for almost a thousand years. Until 1971, the pound consisted of twenty shillings, and the shilling consisted of twelve pence (pennies). The pound has been long represented by the £ symbol (standing for Latin *libra*, plural *librae*—hence also "lb" for "pound"), while shillings and pence were represented by "*s*." (for *solidus*, *solidi*) and "*d*." (for *denarius*, *denarii*), so that a version of "£.s.d." or "L.s.d." came to mean money in general, as in Thomas Hood's couplet on suicide: "But p'rhaps, of all the felonies de se, / Two-thirds have been through want of *L. s. d.*!" At times a slanting line or *solidus* separated shillings from pence, as "12/6" for "twelve shillings and sixpence." ("Pence" is the standard plural of "penny," although one may hear "pence" as a singular and "pennies" as the plural.) Some of the terms have been streamlined, as "ha'penny" and "ha'pence" for "halfpenny" and "halfpence"; likewise "tuppence," "thruppence," "fippence," and so forth. The following list gives some of the commoner terms from the monetary vocabulary, formal, casual, obsolete, slang, and dialect:

Bar: One pound, often in form of "half a bar," meaning ten shillings.
Berry: One pound.
Bob (plural also "bob"): Also Bobstick: A shilling.
Bord: A shilling.
Brad: A halfpenny. "Brads" means money in general.
Bull: A crown (five shillings).
Clod: A penny.
Couter, Cooter: A sovereign: one pound.
Cracker: A pound note (Australia).
Crown: Five shillings. A half-crown coin, worth two shillings and sixpence, was in use until 1971.
Dibs: Money in general.
Dollar: A crown; five shillings.
Finnip (related to U. S. "fin" for five dollars): A five-pound note.
Fiver: A five-pound note.
Flag: A groat, fourpence.
Florin: Two shillings, a coin used until 1971.
Groat: Fourpence. Any small amount of money.
Guinea: Has meant "twenty-one shillings."

Half-crown: Two shillings and sixpence. A large coin, in use until 1971.
Half-dollar: A half-crown.
Hog: A shilling.
Hole: A shilling.
Iron man: One pound.
Jacks, Jax: Five pounds.
Lill: A five-pound note.
Make: A halfpenny
Mopus: A halfpenny or farthing. "Mopus" and "mopusses" have also meant money in general. Thackeray used "mopus box" for "money box."
Nicker: One pound.
Oncer: One pound.
Posh: A halfpenny; any small coin.
Quid (plural also "quid"): One pound.
Saucepan lid: A one-pound note.
Scuddick: A very small coin.
Sheet: A pound or pound note.
Shilling: After 1971, five new pence.
Single: One pound
Smacker: One pound.
Sovereign: In recent times, a pound.
Sprazer, Spraser, Sprasy: sixpence, a sixpenny coin.
Sterling: A distinction of genuineness, originally referring to the silver penny used by Normans, later meaning genuine and native English money; also money in general
Stiver: A penny or any small coin.
Tanner: A sixpence.
Tosh: Short for "tosheroon"; also loosely for a two-shilling piece; money
Tosheroon: A half-crown
Two ender: A two-shilling piece; a florin.
Win, Wyn: A penny

The following table of relative values is based on materials available from Economic History Services (http://www.eh.net/hmit/ppowerbp/). Used with permission.

£1 as of	in 2002 would have been worth (£)	in 2002 would have been worth ($)
1275	303	515
1300	333	566
1325	259	440
1350	366	622
1375	259	440
1400	341	580
1425	402	683
1450	443	753
1475	468	796
1500	427	726
1525	398	677

Continued

£1 as of	in 2002 would have been worth (£)	in 2002 would have been worth ($)
1550	207	352
1575	157	267
1600	120	204
1625	117	199
1650	75	128
1675	107	182
1700	111	189
1725	104	177
1750	118	201
1775	83	141
1800	44	75
1825	56	95
1850	70	119
1875	57	97
1900	66	112
1925	34	58
1950	21	36
1975	5	9

For example, £1 in 1625 had about the purchasing power of £117 as of 2002, which in turn was worth about $199 at the prevailing exchange rate.

Nobel Prizes for Literature

1901 René F. A. Sully-Prudhomme (1839–1907), French
1902 Theodor Mommsen (1817–1903), German
1903 Bjørnstjerne Bjørnson (1832–1910), Norwegian
1904 Frédéric Mistral (1830–1914), French
José Echegaray (1832–1916), Spanish
1905 Henryk Sienkiewicz (1846–1916), Polish
1906 Giosuè Carducci (1835–1907), Italian
1907 Rudyard Kipling (1865–1936), British
1908 Rudolf C. Eucken (1846–1926), German
1909 Selma Lagerlöf (1858–1940), Swedish
1910 Paul J. L. Heyse (1830–1914), German
1911 Maurice Maeterlinck (1862–1949), Belgian
1912 Gerhart Hauptmann (1862–1946), German
1913 Rabindranath Tagore (1861–1941), Indian
1914 No award
1915 Romain Rolland (1866–1944), French
1916 Verner von Heidenstam (1859–1940), Swedish
1917 Karl A. Gjellerup (1857–1919), Danish
Henrik Pontoppidan (1857–1943), Danish
1918 No award
1919 Carl F. G. Spitteler (1845–1924), Swiss
1920 Knut Hamsun (1859–1952), Norwegian
1921 Anatole France (1844–1924), French
1922 Jacinto Benavente y Martínez (1866–1954), Spanish
1923 William Butler Yeats (1865–1939), Irish
1924 Władysław S. Reymont (1868–1925), Polish
1925 George Bernard Shaw (1856–1950), British (*b.* Ireland)
1926 Grazia Deledda (1871–1936), Italian
1927 Henri Bergson (1859–1941), French
1928 Sigrid Undset (1882–1949), Norwegian (*b.* Denmark)
1929 Thomas Mann (1875–1955), German
1930 Sinclair Lewis (1885–1951), American
1931 Erik A. Karlfeldt (1864–1931), Swedish (awarded posthumously)
1932 John Galsworthy (1867–1933), English
1933 Ivan A. Bunin (1870–1953), French (*b.* Russia)
1934 Luigi Pirandello (1867–1936), Italian
1935 No award
1936 Eugene O'Neill (1888–1953), American
1937 Roger Martin du Gard (1881–1958), French
1938 Pearl S. Buck (1892–1973), American
1939 Frans E. Sillanpää (1888–1964), Finnish
1940 No award
1941 No award
1942 No award
1943 No award

1944 Johannes V. Jensen (1873–1950), Danish
1945 Gabriela Mistral (1889–1957), Chilean
1946 Hermann Hesse (1877–1962), Swiss (*b*. Germany)
1947 André Gide (1869–1951), French
1948 T. S. Eliot (1888–1965), British (*b*. United States)
1949 William Faulkner (1897–1962), American
1950 Bertrand A. W. Russell (1872–1970), British
1951 Pär F. Lagerkvist (1891–1974), Swedish
1952 François Mauriac (1885–1970), French
1953 Sir Winston Churchill (1874–1965), British
1954 Ernest Hemingway (1899–1961), American
1955 Halldór K. Laxness (1902–1998), Icelandic
1956 Juan Ramón Jiménez (1881–1958), Spanish
1957 Albert Camus (1913–1960), French
1958 Boris L. Pasternak (1890–1960), Russian (prize declined)
1959 Salvatore Quasimodo (1901–1968), Italian
1960 Saint-John Perse (1887–1975), French
1961 Ivo Andrić (1892–1975), Yugoslav
1962 John Steinbeck (1902–1968), American
1963 George Seferis (1900–1971), Greek
1964 Jean-Paul Sartre (1905–1980), French (prize declined)
1965 Mikhail A. Sholokhov (1905–1984), Russian
1966 Shmuel J. Agnon (1888–1970), Israeli (*b*. Poland)
Nelly Sachs (1891–1970), Swedish (*b*. Germany)
1967 Miguel Ángel Asturias (1899–1974), Guatemalan
1968 Yasunari Kawabata (1899–1972), Japanese
1969 Samuel Beckett (1906–1989), Anglo-French (*b*. Ireland)
1970 Alexander I. Solzhenitsyn (1918–), Russian
1971 Pablo Neruda (1904–1973), Chilean
1972 Henrich Böll (1917–1985), German
1973 Patrick White (1912–1990), Australian
1974 Eyvind Johnson (1900–1976), Swedish
Harry Edmund Martinson (1904–1978), Swedish
1975 Eugenio Montale (1896–1981), Italian
1976 Saul Bellow (1915–2005), American
1977 Vicente Aleixandre (1898–1984), Spanish
1978 Isaac Bashevis Singer (1904–1991), American (*b*. Poland)
1979 Odysseus Elýtis (1911–1996), Greek
1980 Czesław Miłosz (1911–2004), Polish-American
1981 Elias Canetti (1905–1994), Bulgarian (resident in U. K.)
1982 Gabriel García Márquez (1928–), Colombian
1983 William Golding (1911–1993), British
1984 Jaroslav Seifert (1901–1986), Czech
1985 Claude Simon (1913–), French
1986 Wole Soyinka (1934–), Nigerian
1987 Joseph Brodsky (1940–1996), Russian-American
1988 Naguib Mahfouz (1911–), Egyptian
1989 Camilo José Cela (1916–2002), Spanish
1990 Octavio Paz (1914–1998), Mexican

1991 Nadine Gordimer (1923–), South African
1992 Derek Walcott (1930–), West Indian
1993 Toni Morrison (1931–), American
1994 Kenzaburo Oe (1935–), Japanese
1995 Seamus Heaney (1939–), Northern Irish
1996 Wislawa Szymborska (1923–), Polish
1997 Dario Fo (1926–), Italian
1998 José Saramago (1922–), Portuguese
1999 Günter Grass (1928–), German
2000 Gao Xingjian (1940–), Chinese
2001 V. S. Naipaul (1932–), British–Indian (*b.* Trinidad)
2002 Imre Kertész (1929–), Hungarian
2003 John M. Coetzee (1940–), South African
2004 Elfriede Jelinek (1946–), Austrian

Pulitzer Prizes for Fiction

1917 No award
1918 *His Family*, by Ernest Poole
1919 *The Magnificent Ambersons*, by Booth Tarkington
1920 No award
1921 *The Age of Innocence*, by Edith Wharton
1922 *Alice Adams*, by Booth Tarkington
1923 *One of Ours*, by Willa Cather
1924 *The Able McLaughlins*, by Margaret Wilson
1925 *So Big*, by Edna Ferber
1926 *Arrowsmith*, by Sinclair Lewis (prize declined)
1927 *Early Autumn*, by Louis Bromfield
1928 *The Bridge of San Luis Rey*, by Thornton Wilder
1929 *Scarlet Sister Mary*, by Julia Peterkin
1930 *Laughing Boy*, by Oliver LaFarge
1931 *Years of Grace*, by Margaret Ayer Barnes
1932 *The Good Earth*, by Pearl S. Buck
1933 *The Store*, by T. S. Stribling
1934 *Lamb in His Bosom*, by Caroline Miller
1935 *Now in November*, by Josephine Winslow Johnson
1936 *Honey in the Horn*, by Harold L. Davis
1937 *Gone with the Wind*, by Margaret Mitchell
1938 *The Late George Apley*, by John Phillips Marquand
1939 *The Yearling*, by Marjorie Kinnan Rawlings
1940 *The Grapes of Wrath*, by John Steinbeck
1941 No award
1942 *In This Our Life*, by Ellen Glasgow
1943 *Dragon's Teeth*, by Upton Sinclair
1944 *Journey in the Dark*, by Martin Flavin
1945 *A Bell for Adano*, by John Hersey
1946 No award
1947 *All the King's Men*, by Robert Penn Warren
1948 *Tales of the South Pacific*, by James A. Michener
1949 *Guard of Honor*, by James Gould Cozzens
1950 *The Way West*, by A. B. Guthrie, Jr.
1951 *The Town*, by Conrad Richter
1952 *The Caine Mutiny*, by Herman Wouk
1953 *The Old Man and the Sea*, by Ernest Hemingway
1954 No award
1955 *A Fable*, by William Faulkner
1956 *Andersonville*, by MacKinlay Kantor
1957 No award
1958 *A Death in the Family*, by James Agee
1959 *The Travels of Jaimie McPheeters*, by Robert Lewis Taylor
1960 *Advise and Consent*, by Allen Drury
1961 *To Kill a Mockingbird*, by Harper Lee

1962 *The Edge of Sadness*, by Edwin O'Connor
1963 *The Reivers*, by William Faulkner
1964 No award
1965 *The Keepers of the House*, by Shirley Ann Grau
1966 *Collected Short Stories*, by Katherine Anne Porter
1967 *The Fixer*, by Bernard Malamud
1968 *The Confessions of Nat Turner*, by William Styron
1969 *House Made of Dawn*, by N. Scott Momaday
1970 *Collected Stories*, by Jean Stafford
1971 No award
1972 *Angle of Repose*, by Wallace Stegner
1973 *The Optimist's Daughter*, by Eudora Welty
1974 No award
1975 *The Killer Angels*, by Michael Shaara
1976 *Humboldt's Gift*, by Saul Bellow
1977 No award
1978 *Elbow Room*, by James Alan McPherson
1979 *The Stories*, by John Cheever
1980 *The Executioner's Song*, by Norman Mailer
1981 *A Confederacy of Dunces*, by John Kennedy Toole
1982 *Rabbit Is Rich*, by John Updike
1983 *The Color Purple*, by Alice Walker
1984 *Ironweed*, by William Kennedy
1985 *Foreign Affairs*, by Alison Lurie
1986 *Lonesome Dove*, by Larry McMurtry
1987 *A Summons to Memphis*, by Peter Taylor
1988 *Beloved*, by Toni Morrison
1989 *Breathing Lessons*, by Anne Tyler
1990 *The Mambo King Plays Songs of Love*, by Oscar Hijuelo
1991 *Rabbit at Rest*, by John Updike
1992 *A Thousand Acres*, by Jane Smiley
1993 *A Good Scent from a Strange Mountain*, by Robert Olen Butler
1994 *The Shipping News*, by E. Annie Proulx
1995 *Stone Diaries*, by Carol Shields
1996 *Independence Day*, by Richard Ford
1997 *Martin Dressler*, by Steven Millhauser
1998 *American Pastoral*, by Philip Roth
1999 *The Hours*, by Michael Cunningham
2000 *Interpreter of Maladies*, by Jhumpha Lahiri
2001 *The Amazing Adventures of Kavalier & Clay*, by Michael Chabon
2002 *Empire Falls*, by Richard Russo
2003 *Middlesex*, by Jeffrey Eugenides
2004 *The Known World*, by Edward P. Jones
2005 *Gilead*, by Marilynne Robinson

Pulitzer Prizes for Poetry

Previous to the establishment of this prize in 1922, the following awards had been made from gifts provided by the Poetry Society:

1918 *Love Songs*, by Sara Teasdale
1919 *Old Road to Paradise*, by Margaret Widdemer
1919 *Corn Huskers*, by Carl Sandburg

The Pulitzer Prizes for Poetry follow:
1922 *Collected Poems*, by Edwin Arlington Robinson
1923 *The Ballad of the Harp-Weaver; A Few Figs from Thistles*; eight sonnets in *American Poetry, 1922; A Miscellany*, by Edna St. Vincent Millay
1924 *New Hampshire: A Poem with Notes and Grace Notes*, by Robert Frost
1925 *The Man Who Died Twice*, by Edwin Arlington Robinson
1926 *What's O'Clock*, by Amy Lowell
1927 *Fiddler's Farewell*, by Leonora Speyer
1928 *Tristram*, by Edwin Arlington Robinson
1929 *John Brown's Body*, by Stephen Vincent Benét
1930 *Selected Poems*, by Conrad Aiken
1931 *Collected Poems*, by Robert Frost
1932 *The Flowering Stone*, by George Dillon
1933 *Conquistador*, by Archibald MacLeish
1934 *Collected Verse*, by Robert Hillyer
1935 *Bright Ambush*, by Audrey Wurdemann
1936 *Strange Holiness*, by Robert P. Tristram Coffin
1937 *A Further Range*, by Robert Frost
1938 *Cold Morning Sky*, by Marya Zaturenska
1939 *Selected Poems*, by John Gould Fletcher
1940 *Collected Poems*, by Mark Van Doren
1941 *Sunderland Capture*, by Leonard Bacon
1942 *The Dust Which Is God*, by William Rose Benét
1943 *A Witness Tree*, by Robert Frost
1944 *Western Star*, by Stephen Vincent Benét
1945 *V-Letter and Other Poems*, by Karl Shapiro
1946 No award
1947 *Lord Weary's Castle*, by Robert Lowell
1948 *The Age of Anxiety*, by W. H. Auden
1949 *Terror and Decorum*, by Peter Viereck
1950 *Annie Allen*, by Gwendolyn Brooks
1951 *Complete Poems*, by Carl Sandburg
1952 *Collected Poems*, by Marianne Moore
1953 *Collected Poems 1917–1952*, by Archibald MacLeish
1954 *The Waking*, by Theodore Roethke
1955 *Collected Poems*, by Wallace Stevens
1956 *Poems—North & South*, by Elizabeth Bishop
1957 *Things of This World*, by Richard Wilbur

1958 *Promises: Poems 1954–1956*, by Robert Penn Warren
1959 *Selected Poems 1928–1958*, by Stanley Kunitz
1960 *Heart's Needle*, by W. D. Snodgrass
1961 *Times Three: Selected Verse from Three Decades*, by Phyllis McGinley
1962 *Poems*, by Alan Dugan
1963 *Pictures from Brueghel*, by William Carlos Williams
1964 *At the End of the Open Road*, by Louis Simpson
1965 *77 Dream Songs*, by John Berryman
1966 *Selected Poems*, by Richard Eberhart
1967 *Live or Die*, by Anne Sexton
1968 *The Hard Hours*, by Anthony Hecht
1969 *Of Being Numerous*, by George Oppen
1970 *Untitled Subjects*, by Richard Howard
1971 *The Carrier of Ladders*, by W. S. Merwin
1972 *Collected Poems*, by James Wright
1973 *Up Country*, by Maxine Winokur Kumin
1974 *The Dolphin*, by Robert Lowell
1975 *Turtle Island*, by Gary Snyder
1976 *Self-Portrait in a Convex Mirror*, by John Ashbery
1977 *Divine Comedies: Poems*, by James Merrill
1978 *The Collected Poems*, by Howard Nemerov
1979 *Now and Then: Poems 1976–1978*, by Robert Penn Warren
1980 *Selected Poems*, by Donald Justice
1981 *The Morning of the Poem*, by James Schuyler
1982 *Collected Poems*, by Sylvia Plath
1983 *Selected Poems*, by Galway Kinnell
1984 *American Primitive*, by Mary Oliver
1985 *Yin*, by Carolyn Kizer
1986 *The Flying Change*, by Henry Taylor
1987 *Thomas and Beulah*, by Rita Dove
1988 *Partial Accounts: New and Selected Poems*, by William Meredith
1989 *New and Collected Poems*, by Richard Wilbur
1990 *The World Doesn't End*, by Charles Simic
1991 *Near Changes*, by Mona Van Duyn
1992 *Selected Poems*, by James Tate
1993 *The Wild Iris*, by Louise Glück
1994 *Neon Vernacular*, by Yusef Komunyakaa
1995 *The Simple Truth*, by Philip Levine
1996 *The Dream of the Unified Field*, by Jorie Graham
1997 *Alive Togther: New and Selected Poems*, by Lisel Mueller
1998 *Black Zodiac*, by Charles Wright
1999 *Blizzard of One*, by Mark Strand
2000 *Repair*, by C. K. Williams
2001 *Different Hours*, by Stephen Dunn
2002 *Practical Gods*, by Carl Dennis
2003 *Moy Sand and Gravel*, by Paul Muldoon
2004 *Walking to Martha's Vineyard*, by Franz Wright
2005 *Delight and Shadows*, by Ted Kooser

Pulitzer Prizes for Drama

1917 No award
1918 *Why Marry?* by Jesse Lynch Williams
1919 No award
1920 *Beyond the Horizon*, by Eugene O'Neill
1921 *Miss Lulu Bett*, by Zona Gale
1922 *Anna Christie*, by Eugene O'Neill
1923 *Icebound*, by Owen Davis
1924 *Hell-Bent fer Heaven*, by Hatcher Hughes
1925 *They Knew What They Wanted*, by Sidney Howard
1926 *Craig's Wife*, by George Kelly
1927 *In Abraham's Bosom*, by Paul Green
1928 *Strange Interlude*, by Eugene O'Neill
1929 *Street Scene*, by Elmer L. Rice
1930 *The Green Pastures*, by Marc Connelly
1931 *Alison's House*, by Susan Glaspell
1932 *Of Thee I Sing*, by George S. Kaufman, Morrie Ryskind, and Ira Gershwin, music by George Gershwin
1933 *Both Your Houses*, by Maxwell Anderson
1934 *Men in White*, by Sidney Kingsley
1935 *The Old Maid*, by Zoë Akins
1936 *Idiot's Delight*, by Robert E. Sherwood
1937 *You Can't Take It with You*, by Moss Hart and George S. Kaufman
1938 *Our Town*, by Thornton Wilder
1939 *Abe Lincoln in Illinois*, by Robert E. Sherwood
1940 *The Time of Your Life*, by William Saroyan (prize declined)
1941 *There Shall Be No Night*, by Robert E. Sherwood
1942 No award
1943 *The Skin of Our Teeth*, by Thornton Wilder
1944 No award
1945 *Harvey*, by Mary Chase
1946 *State of the Union*, by Russel Crouse and Howard Lindsay
1947 No award
1948 *A Streetcar Named Desire*, by Tennessee Williams
1949 *Death of a Salesman*, by Arthur Miller
1950 *South Pacific*, by Richard Rodgers, Oscar Hammerstein II, and Joshua Logan
1951 No award
1952 *The Shrike*, by Joseph Kramm
1953 *Picnic*, by William Inge
1954 *The Teahouse of the August Moon*, by John Patrick
1955 *Cat on a Hot Tin Roof*, by Tennessee Williams
1956 *The Diary of Anne Frank*, by Albert Hackett and Frances Goodrich
1957 *Long Day's Journey into Night*, by Eugene O'Neill
1958 *Look Homeward, Angel*, by Ketti Frings
1959 *J. B.*, by Archibald MacLeish

1960 *Fiorello!*, book by Jerome Weidman and George Abbott, music by Jerry Bock, and lyrics by Sheldon Harnick
1961 *All the Way Home*, by Tad Mosel
1962 *How to Succeed in Business Without Really Trying*, by Frank Loesser and Abe Burrows
1963 No award
1964 No award
1965 *The Subject Was Roses*, by Frank D. Gilroy
1966 No award
1967 *A Delicate Balance*, by Edward Albee
1968 No award
1969 *The Great White Hope*, by Howard Sackler
1970 *No Place To Be Somebody*, by Charles Gordone
1971 *The Effect of Gamma Rays on Man-in-the-Moon Marigolds*, by Paul Zindel
1972 No award
1973 *That Championship Season*, by Jason Miller
1974 No award
1975 *Seascape*, by Edward Albee
1976 *A Chorus Line*, by James Kirkwood and Nicholas Dante
1977 *The Shadow Box*, by Michael Cristofer
1978 *The Gin Game*, by Donald L. Coburn
1979 *Buried Child*, by Sam Shepard
1980 *Talley's Folly*, by Lanford Wilson
1981 *Crimes of the Heart*, by Beth Henley
1982 *A Soldier's Play*, by Charles Fuller
1983 *'Night, Mother*, by Marsha Norman
1984 *Glengarry Glen Ross*, by David Mamet
1985 *Sunday in the Park with George*, by Stephen Sondheim and James Lapine
1986 No award
1987 *Fences*, by August Wilson
1988 *Driving Miss Daisy*, by Alfred Uhry
1989 *The Heidi Chronicles*, by Wendy Wasserstein
1990 *The Piano Lesson*, by August Wilson
1991 *Lost in Yonkers*, by Neil Simon
1992 *The Kentucky Cycle*, by Robert Schenkkan
1993 *Angels in America: Millennium Approaches*, by Tony Kushner
1994 *Three Tall Women*, by Edward Albee
1995 *The Young Man from Atlanta*, by Horton Foote
1996 *Rent*, by Jonathan Larson
1997 No award
1998 *How I Learned to Drive*, by Paula Vogel
1999 *Wit*, by Margaret Edson
2000 *Dinner with Friends*, by Donald Margulies
2001 *Proof*, by David Auburn
2002 *Topdog/Underdog*, by Suzan-Lori Parks
2003 *Anna in the Tropics*, by Nilo Cruz
2004 *I Am My Own Wife*, by Doug Wright
2005 *Doubt: A Parable*, by John Patrick Shanley

Index of Proper Names